Codification of Statements on Auditing Standards

(Including Statements on Standards for Attestation Engagements)

Volume 1

> U.S. Auditing Standards – AICPA [AU]

> Attestation Standards [AT]

> Numbers 1 to 121

AS OF JANUARY 2012

10909-344

AICPA®

Reprinted from
AICPA *Professional Standards*
Auditing and Attestation Engagements Parts
(as of January 2012)

1 2 3 4 5 6 7 8 9 0 PrP 1 9 8 7 6 5 4 3 2

ISBN 978-1-93735-023-9

PREFACE

This set, issued by the Auditing Standards Board (ASB), is a codification of Statements on Auditing Standards (SASs) and the related auditing interpretations applicable to the preparation and issuance of audit reports for all nonissuers. Nonissuers are all entities other than issuers as defined by the Sarbanes-Oxley Act, or other entities who are required to be audited by a registered public accounting firm as prescribed by the rules of the Securities and Exchange Commission. Volume 1 contains the codified auditing standards that will be applicable until December 15, 2012, as well as Statements on Standards for Attestation Engagements (SSAEs), and the related attestation interpretations. Volume 2 contains the clarified codified auditing standards (SAS Nos. 122–125), which are effective for audits of financial statements for periods ending on or after December 15, 2012.

SASs are issued by the ASB, the senior technical body of the AICPA designated to issue pronouncements on auditing matters applicable to the preparation and issuance of audit reports for entities that are nonissuers. Rule 202, *Compliance With Standards* (AICPA, *Professional Standards*, ET sec. 202 par. .01), of the AICPA Code of Professional Conduct requires an AICPA member who performs an audit (the auditor) of the financial statements of a nonissuer to comply with standards promulgated by the ASB. An auditor is required to comply with an unconditional requirement in all cases in which the circumstances exist to which the unconditional requirement applies. An auditor is also required to comply with a presumptively mandatory requirement in all cases in which the circumstances exist to which the presumptively mandatory requirement applies; however, in rare circumstances, an auditor may depart from a presumptively mandatory requirement provided the auditor documents his or her justification for the departure and how the alternative procedures performed in the circumstances were sufficient to achieve the objectives of the presumptively mandatory requirement.

Auditing interpretations of SASs are *interpretive publications* pursuant to AU section 150, *Generally Accepted Auditing Standards*. Interpretive publications are recommendations on the application of SASs in specific circumstances, including engagements for entities in specialized industries. Interpretive publications are issued under the authority of the ASB. An auditor should be aware of and consider interpretations applicable to his or her audit. An interpretation is not as authoritative as a pronouncement of the ASB; however, if an auditor does not apply an auditing interpretation, the auditor should be prepared to explain how he or she complied with the SAS provisions addressed by such auditing guidance. The specific terms used to define professional requirements in the SASs are not intended to apply to interpretations because interpretations are not auditing standards. It is the ASB's intention to make conforming changes to the interpretations over the next several years to remove any language that would imply a professional requirement where none exists.

SSAEs are issued by senior technical bodies of the AICPA designated to issue pronouncements on attestation matters. Rule 202 of the AICPA Code of Professional Conduct requires an AICPA member who performs an attest engagement (a practitioner) to comply with such pronouncements. A practitioner is required to comply with an unconditional requirement in all cases in which the circumstances exist to which the unconditional requirement applies. A practitioner is also required to comply with a presumptively mandatory requirement in all cases in which the circumstances exist to which the presumptively mandatory requirement applies; however, in rare circumstances, a practitioner may depart from a presumptively mandatory requirement provided that the practitioner documents his or her justification for the departure and how the alternative procedures performed in the circumstances were sufficient to achieve the objectives of the presumptively mandatory requirement.

Attestation interpretations are recommendations on the application of SSAEs in specific circumstances, including engagements for entities in specialized industries, issued under the authority of AICPA senior technical bodies. An interpretation is not as authoritative as a pronouncement of the ASB; however, if a practitioner does not apply an attestation interpretation, the practitioner should be prepared to explain how he or she complied with the SSAE provisions addressed by such attestation guidance. The specific terms used to define professional requirements in the SSAEs are not intended to apply to interpretations because interpretations are not attestation standards. It is the ASB's intention to make conforming changes to the interpretations over the next several years to remove any language that would imply a professional requirement where none exists.

The Accounting and Review Services Committee and the ASB are the senior technical committees of the AICPA designated to issue enforceable standards under Rule 201, *General Standards*, and Rule 202 of the AICPA's Code of Professional Conduct concerning attest services in their respective areas of responsibility.

AUDITING STANDARDS BOARD
Darrel R. Schubert, Chair
Charles E. Landes, Vice President—
Professional Standards and Services

WHAT'S NEW IN THIS EDITION

See volume 2 for the following Statements on Auditing Standards (SASs):

- No. 122, *Statements on Auditing Standards: Clarification and Recodification*
- No. 123, *Omnibus Statement on Auditing Standards—2011*
- No. 124, *Financial Statements Prepared in Accordance With a Financial Reporting Framework Generally Accepted in Another Country*
- No. 125, *Alert That Restricts the Use of the Auditor's Written Communication*

Section	Change
AU Cross-References to SASs	Revision of parts I–II to better reflect the structure and organization of the U.S. Auditing Standards—AICPA [AU] section and to relocate the Statements on Standards for Attestation Engagements content to the Attestation Standards section.
AU 324	Revisions due to the issuance of Statement on Standards for Attestation Engagements (SSAE) No. 16, *Reporting on Controls at a Service Organization* (AT sec. 801).
AU 328	Revisions due to the issuance of SSAE No. 16.
AU 332	Revisions due to the issuance of SSAE No. 16.
AU 532	Revisions due to the issuance of SSAE No. 16.
AU 550A	Deletion of section due to the effective date of SAS No. 118, *Other Information in Documents Containing Audited Financial Statements*.
AU 9550A	Deletion of section due to the effective date of SAS No. 118.
AU 9551.01–.04	Addition of Interpretation No. 1, "Dating the Auditor's Report on Supplementary Information," of AU section 551, *Supplementary Information in Relation to the Financial Statements as a Whole*.
AU 551A	Deletion of section due to the effective dates of SAS No. 118 and SAS No. 119, *Supplementary Information in Relation to the Financial Statements as a Whole*.
AU 558A	Deletion of section due to the effective date of SAS No. 120, *Required Supplementary Information*.
AU 9558A	Deletion of section due to the effective date of SAS No. 120.
AU 801	Revisions due to the issuance of SSAE No. 16.
AU 801A	Deletion of section due to the issuance of SAS No. 117, *Compliance Audits*.

Section	Change
AU Risk Assessment Standards: SAS No. 104–SAS No. 111	Deletion of section due to the passage of time.
Clarity Project	Deletion of section due to the issuance of SAS No. 122.
AT Cross-References to SSAEs	Addition of new section to the beginning of the Attestation Standards section. The new section contains two tables, "Statements on Standards for Attestation Engagements" and "Sources of Sections in Current Text," which were previously located in the Cross-References to SASs section.
AT 201	Revisions due to the issuance of SSAE No. 16.
AT 501	Revisions due to the issuance of SSAE No. 16.

TABLE OF CONTENTS

HOW THIS VOLUME IS ORGANIZED

This volume is organized into three main sections.

The first section, "Applicability of AICPA Professional Standards and PCAOB Standards," provides guidance about standards applicable to nonissuers and standards applicable to issuers. Information about the Public Company Accounting Oversight Board's (PCAOB's) Interim Standards is included, as well as information about major differences between GAAS and PCAOB Standards.

The next section, "U.S. Auditing Standards," contains the codified auditing standards that will be applicable until December 15, 2012, and the related auditing interpretations.

The final section, "Attestation Standards," contains the codified attestation standards, and the related attestation interpretations.

These sections are described in more detail in the following sections.

U.S. Auditing Standards [AU Sections]

The AU sections include extant standards issued before Statement on Auditing Standards (SAS) No. 122, *Statements on Auditing Standards: Clarification and Recodification*, and will be applicable through December 15, 2012. Superseded portions have been deleted, and all applicable amendments have been included. These standards are arranged as follows:

AU Cross-References to SASs

Introduction

The General Standards

The Standards of Field Work

The First, Second, and Third Standards of Reporting

The Fourth Standard of Reporting

Other Types of Reports

Special Topics

Compliance Auditing

Special Reports of the Committee on Auditing Procedure

Appendixes

Topical Index

The AU Cross-References to SASs is a list of SASs issued through SAS No. 121 and a list of sources of sections in the current text.

The standards are divided into sections, each with its own section number. Each paragraph within a section is decimally numbered.

Auditing interpretations are numbered in the 9000 series with the last three digits indicating the section to which the interpretation relates. Interpretations immediately follow their corresponding section. For example, interpretations related to section 311 are numbered 9311, which directly follows section 311.

There are four appendixes relating to auditing standards as follows:

Appendix A provides the historical background for the SASs.

Appendix B is reserved.

Appendix C is reserved.

Appendix D provides a list of AICPA Audit and Accounting Guides and Statements of Position.

Appendix E provides a schedule of changes in extant SASs since the issuance of SAS No. 1, *Codification of Auditing Standards and Procedures*.

Appendix F provides a list of other auditing publications published by the AICPA that have been reviewed by the AICPA Audit and Attest Standards staff.

The AU topical index uses the keyword method to facilitate reference to the pronouncements. The index is arranged alphabetically by topic and refers the reader to major divisions, sections, and paragraph numbers.

Attestation Standards [AT Sections]

The AT sections include attestation standards issued through Statement on Standards for Attestation Engagements (SSAE) No. 17, *Reporting on Compiled Prospective Financial Statements When the Practitioner's Independence Is Impaired*. Superseded portions have been deleted, and all applicable amendments have been included. These sections are arranged as follows:

AT Cross-References to SSAEs

Defining Professional Requirements in Statements on Standards for Attestation Engagements

SSAE Hierarchy

Attest Engagements

Agreed-Upon Procedures Engagements

Financial Forecasts and Projections

Reporting on Pro Forma Financial Information

An Examination of an Entity's Internal Control Over Financial Reporting That Is Integrated With an Audit of Its Financial Statements

Compliance Attestation

Management's Discussion and Analysis

Reporting on Controls at a Service Organization

Topical Index

The AT Cross-References to SSAEs is a list of all issued SSAEs and a list of sources of sections in the current text.

The standards are divided into sections, each with its own section number. Each paragraph within a section is decimally numbered.

Attestation interpretations are numbered in the 9000 series with the last three digits indicating the section to which the interpretation relates. Interpretations immediately follow their corresponding section. For example, interpretations related to section 101 are numbered 9101, which directly follows section 101.

The AT topical index uses the key word method to facilitate reference to the statements and interpretations. The index is arranged alphabetically by topic with references to section and paragraph numbers.

Part I

Applicability of AICPA Professional Standards and Public Company Accounting Oversight Board Standards

Background

As a result of the passage of the Sarbanes-Oxley Act of 2002 (the act), auditing and related professional practice standards to be used in the performance of and reporting on audits of the financial statements of public companies are now established by the Public Company Accounting Oversight Board (PCAOB). Note that the term *public companies* is a general reference to the entities subject to the securities laws. The act more specifically defines these entities as *issuers*, the definition of which is provided in the section that follows.

Among other significant provisions, the act requires a public accounting firm that prepares or issues, or participates in the preparation or issuance of, any audit report with respect to any issuer to register with the PCAOB. Accordingly, public accounting firms registered with the PCAOB are required to adhere to all PCAOB standards in the audits of issuers. Moreover, the act authorizes the PCAOB to establish auditing and related attestation, quality control, ethics, and independence standards to be used by registered public accounting firms in the preparation and issuance of audit reports for issuers.

Who Is an Issuer?

As provided in Section 2 of the act, the term *issuer* means an issuer (as defined in Section 3 of the Securities Exchange Act of 1934 [15 U.S.C. 78c]), the securities of which are registered under Section 12 of that act (15 U.S.C. 78l) or that is required to file reports pursuant to Section 15(d) [15 U.S.C. 78o(d)], or that files or has filed a registration statement that has not yet become effective under the Securities Act of 1933 (15 U.S.C. 77a et seq.), and that it has not withdrawn.

Accordingly, nonissuers are those entities not subject to the act or the rules of the Securities and Exchange Commission (SEC). For audits of nonissuers, the preparation and issuance of audit reports must be conducted in accordance with the AICPA Code of Professional Conduct (AICPA Code) and the standards promulgated by the AICPA Auditing Standards Board (ASB). Audits of nonissuers remain governed by generally accepted auditing standards (GAAS) and the Statements on Quality Control Standards (SQCS) as issued by the ASB.

Standards Applicable to the Audits of *Nonissuers*

With the formation of the PCAOB, the ASB was reconstituted and its jurisdiction amended to recognize the ASB as the body authorized to promulgate auditing, attestation and quality control standards relating to the preparation and issuance of audit reports for nonissuers.

Failure to follow ASB standards in the audit of a nonissuer would be considered a violation of Rule 201, *General Standards*, and Rule 202, *Compliance With Standards* (ET sec. 201 par. .01 and ET sec. 202 par. .01), of the AICPA Code, or both.

As a caution to readers, pursuant to AU section 150, *Generally Accepted Auditing Standards*, interpretative publications are recommendations on the application of the Statements on Auditing Standards (SASs) in specific circumstances, including engagements for entities in specialized industries. Interpretative publications, which include auditing interpretations, auditing guidance in AICPA Audit and Accounting Guides, and auditing guidance found in Statements of Position (SOPs), are issued under the authority of the ASB. The auditor should identify interpretative publications applicable to his or her audit. If the auditor does not apply the auditing guidance included in an applicable interpretative publication, the auditor should be prepared to explain how he or she complied with the SAS provisions addressed by such auditing guidance.

The ASB continues to issue SASs and interpretative publications that relate to audits of nonissuers and auditors should be alert to those issuances.

Standards Applicable to the Audits of *Issuers*

Rule 3100, *Compliance With Auditing and Related Professional Practice Standards* (AICPA, *PCAOB Standards and Related Rules*, Select Rules of the Board), issued by the PCAOB (see PCAOB Release No. 2003-009, dated June 30, 2003) generally requires all registered public accounting firms to adhere to the PCAOB's standards in connection with the preparation or issuance of any audit report on the financial statements of an issuer. Rule 3100 requires registered public accounting firms and their associated persons to comply with all applicable standards. Accordingly, if the PCAOB's standards do not apply to an engagement or other activity of the firm, Rule 3100, by its own terms, does not apply to that engagement or activity.

Rule 3101, *Certain Terms Used in Auditing and Related Professional Practice Standards* (AICPA, *PCAOB Standards and Related Rules*, Select Rules of the Board), issued by the PCAOB (see PCAOB Release No. 2004-007, dated June 9, 2004) defines the degree of responsibility imposed on the auditor by the use of certain terms in the PCAOB's auditing and related professional practice standards, including the interim standards adopted in Rule 3200T, *Interim Auditing Standards*; Rule 3300T, *Interim Attestation Standards*; Rule 3400T, *Interim Quality Control Standards*; Rule 3500T, *Interim Ethics Standards*; and Rule 3600T, *Interim Independence Standards* (AICPA, *PCAOB Standards and Related Rules*, Select Rules of the Board) (further described in a later section). Effectively, Rule 3101 creates three categories of professional responsibilities:

1. *Unconditional responsibility*. The words *must*, *shall*, and *is required* indicate unconditional responsibilities. The auditor must fulfill responsibilities of this type in all cases in which the circumstances exist to which the requirement applies. Failure to discharge an unconditional responsibility is a violation of the relevant standard and Rule 3100.
2. *Presumptively mandatory responsibility*. The word *should* indicates responsibilities that are presumptively mandatory. The auditor must comply with requirements of this type specified in the PCAOB's standards unless the auditor demonstrates that alternative actions he or she followed in the circumstances were sufficient to achieve the objectives of the standard. Failure to discharge

a presumptively mandatory responsibility is a violation of the relevant standard and Rule 3100 unless the auditor demonstrates that, in the circumstances, compliance with the specified responsibility was not necessary to achieve the objectives of the standard.

3. *Responsibility to consider*. The words *may*, *might*, *could*, and other terms and phrases describe actions and procedures that auditors have a responsibility to consider. Matters described in this fashion require the auditor's attention and understanding. How and whether the auditor implements these matters in the audit will depend on the exercise of professional judgment in the circumstances consistent with the objectives of the standard.

Compliance With Standards Applicable to the Audits of *Issuers*

Any registered public accounting firm or person associated with such a firm that fails to adhere to applicable PCAOB standards in connection with an audit of the financial statements of an issuer may be the subject of a PCAOB disciplinary proceeding in accordance with Section 105 of the act. In addition, the act provides that any violation of the PCAOB's rules is to be treated for all purposes in the same manner as a violation of the Securities Exchange Act of 1934, 15 U.S.C. 78a et seq., or the rules and regulations issued thereunder, and any person violating the PCAOB's rules "shall be subject to the same penalties, and to the same extent, as for a violation of [the Exchange] Act or such rules or regulations."

Rule 201 and Rule 202 require a member who performs auditing and other professional services to comply with standards promulgated by bodies designated by the AICPA Council. The AICPA Council has designated the PCAOB as the body authorized to promulgate auditing and related attestation standards, quality control, ethics, independence and other standards relating to the preparation and issuance of audit reports for issuers.

The AICPA's Professional Ethics Division is able to hold an AICPA member who performs audits of the financial statements of issuers accountable under Rules 201 and 202 of the AICPA Code for complying with PCAOB's auditing and related professional practice standards when performing such audits.

PCAOB's Adoption of Interim Standards

The PCAOB is subject to SEC oversight. As such, rules and standards issued by the PCAOB must be approved by the SEC before they become effective.

Pursuant to PCAOB Release No. 2003-006, dated April 18, 2003, the PCAOB adopted, on an initial, transitional basis, five temporary rules that refer to professional standards of auditing, attestation, quality control, ethics, and independence in existence on that date (known collectively as the Interim Professional Auditing Standards). The SEC granted approval to these rules (see SEC Release No. 33-8222, dated April 25, 2003).

Essentially, the interim standards that the PCAOB adopted were the auditing standards, attestation standards, quality control standards issued by the ASB, certain former AICPA SEC Practice Section (SECPS) membership requirements, certain AICPA ethics and independence rules, and Independence Standards Board (ISB) rules as they existed on April 16, 2003. These interim standards will remain in effect while the PCAOB conducts a review of standards applicable to registered public accounting firms. Based on this review, the PCAOB may modify, repeal, replace, or adopt, in part or in whole, the interim standards. As reiterated in a succeeding paragraph, the PCAOB's interim independence standards are not to be interpreted to supersede the SEC's independence requirements. The PCAOB has also made certain conforming amendments to the interim standards to reflect the adoption of PCAOB standards.

If a provision of a PCAOB standard addresses a subject matter that also is addressed in the interim standards, the affected portion of the interim standard should be considered superseded or effectively amended.

The five rules that comprise the PCAOB's interim standards consist of Rules 3200T, 3300T, 3400T, 3500T, and 3600T, and are described in the paragraphs that follow.

Rule 3200T, *Interim Auditing Standards*, as Amended by PCAOB Release No. 2003-026

Rule 3200T provides that, in connection with the preparation or issuance of any audit report on the financial statements of an issuer, a registered public accounting firm shall comply with GAAS as described in AU section 150, as in existence on April 16, 2003, to the extent not superseded or amended by the PCAOB.

Rule 3300T, *Interim Attestation Standards*, as Amended by PCAOB Release No. 2003-026

Rule 3300T governs the conduct of engagements that (1) are described in the ASB's Statement on Standards for Attestation Engagements (SSAE) No. 10, *Attest Engagements* (AT sec. 101), and (2) relate to the preparation or issuance of audit reports for issuers. Registered public accounting firms involved in such engagements are required to comply with the ASB's SSAEs, and related interpretations and AICPA SOPs, as in existence on April 16, 2003, to the extent not superseded or amended by the PCAOB.

Rule 3400T, *Interim Quality Control Standards*, as Amended by PCAOB Release No. 2003-026

Rule 3400T sets forth minimum quality control standards with which registered public accounting firms must comply, in order to ensure that registered public accounting firms, and their personnel, comply with applicable accounting and auditing (and other professional) standards. Pursuant to Rule 3400T, the PCAOB has provisionally designated the SQCSs (QC sections 20–40) proposed and issued by the ASB and certain former AICPA SECPS [1] membership requirements, as they existed, and as they applied to SECPS members, on April 16, 2003, to the extent not superseded or amended by the PCAOB, as the PCAOB's Interim Quality Control Standards.

Because the PCAOB intends the Interim Quality Control Standards (QC sections 20–40) to preserve existing standards as they applied on April 16, 2003

---

[1] The Center for Audit Quality (CAQ) restructured and expanded the AICPA's Center for Public Company Audit Firms, which was the successor to the Securities and Exchange Commission Practice Section (SECPS). The CAQ, which began operating in January 2007, is an autonomous, nonpartisan, public policy organization affiliated with the AICPA and dedicated to enhancing investor confidence and public trust in the global capital markets by fostering high quality performance by auditors of public entities.

consistent with Section 103(a)(3) of the act, those Interim Quality Control Standards (QC sec. 20–40) adapted from the former AICPA SECPS requirements apply only to those firms that were members of the AICPA's SECPS on April 16, 2003.

Rule 3500T, *Interim Ethics Standards*, as Amended by PCAOB Release No. 2003-026

Rule 3500T sets forth ethical standards for registered public accounting firms and their personnel. Pursuant to Rule 3500T, the PCAOB has provisionally designated Rule 102, *Integrity and Objectivity*, and its interpretations (ET sec. 102 and .191) of the AICPA Code, and interpretations and rulings thereunder, as they existed on April 16, 2003, to the extent not superseded or amended by the PCAOB, as the PCAOB's Interim Ethics Standards.

Rule 3600T, *Interim Independence Standards*, as Amended by PCAOB Release No. 2003-026

Rule 3600T sets forth independence standards for registered public accounting firms and their personnel. Pursuant to Rule 3600T, the PCAOB has provisionally designated Rule 101, *Independence*, and its interpretations (ET sec. 101 and ET sec. 191) of the AICPA Code, and interpretations and rulings thereunder, as they existed on April 16, 2003, to the extent not superseded or amended by the PCAOB, and Standard Nos. 1, 2, and 3, and Interpretation Nos. 99-1, 00-1, and 00-2 of the ISB, to the extent not superseded or amended by the PCAOB, as the PCAOB's Interim Independence Standards (AICPA, *PCAOB Standards and Related Rules*, Interim Standards). In addition, the PCAOB requires compliance with the SEC's independence rules. The PCAOB's Interim Independence Standards are not to be interpreted to supersede the SEC's independence requirements. Therefore, to the extent that a provision of the SEC's rule or policy is more restrictive—or less restrictive—than the PCAOB's Interim Independence Standards, a registered public accounting firm must comply with the more restrictive requirement.

References to GAAS

Auditing Standard No. 1, *References in Auditors' Reports to the Standards of the Public Company Accounting Oversight Board* (AICPA, *PCAOB Standards and Related Rules*, Auditing Standards), changed the requirement in the PCAOB's interim standards that the auditors include in their reports a reference to auditing standards promulgated by the ASB, examples of which include GAAS, U.S. GAAS, auditing standards generally accepted in the United States of America, and standards established by the AICPA. Instead, it requires that auditor's reports on the financial statements of issuers that are issued or reissued after the effective date of Auditing Standard No. 1 include a statement that the engagement was conducted in accordance with "the standards of the Public Company Accounting Oversight Board (United States)."

Conforming amendments resulting from Auditing Standard No. 1 have not yet been reflected in the PCAOB's interim standards. Such conforming changes will be made after the PCAOB issues, and the SEC approves, such conforming amendments.

Standards Applicable If a Nonissuer's Financial Statements Are Audited in Accordance With Both GAAS and PCAOB Auditing Standards

Interpretation No. 18, "Reference to PCAOB Standards in an Audit Report on a Nonissuer," of AU section 508, *Reports on Audited Financial Statements* (AU sec. 9508 par. .89–.92), addresses the applicable standards, and references to those standards in the auditor's report, when an auditor is engaged to perform an audit of a nonissuer in accordance with GAAS and PCAOB auditing standards. The interpretation states that an auditor may indicate that the audit was conducted in accordance with GAAS and another set of auditing standards. If the auditor conducted the audit in accordance with GAAS and the auditing standards of the PCAOB, the auditor may indicate in the auditor's report that the audit was conducted in accordance with both sets of standards. The interpretation provides example report language.

Standards Applicable to an Integrated Audit of a Nonissuer's Financial Statements

In October 2008, the ASB issued SSAE No. 15, *An Examination of an Entity's Internal Control Over Financial Reporting That Is Integrated With an Audit of Its Financial Statements* (AT sec. 501), which establishes standards and provides guidance to practitioners performing an examination of a nonissuer's internal control over financial reporting in the context of an integrated audit (an audit of an entity's financial statements and an examination of its internal control). SSAE No. 15 supersedes extant AT section 501, *Reporting on an Entity's Internal Control Over Financial Reporting*, and converges the standards practitioners use for reporting on a nonissuer's internal control with PCAOB Auditing Standard No. 5, *An Audit of Internal Control Over Financial Reporting That Is Integrated with An Audit of Financial Statements* (AICPA, *PCAOB Standards and Related Rules*, Auditing Standards).

AICPA Standards and the Audits of Issuers

If a registered public accounting firm performs an audit of *an issuer* in accordance with PCAOB standards, the auditor does not need to follow standards promulgated by the ASB. However, AICPA members are required to comply with the AICPA Code in addition to the ethics and independence rules and standards required by the SEC and PCAOB.

AU

CROSS-REFERENCES TO SASs

TABLE OF CONTENTS

Part I

Statements on Auditing Standards and Sources of Sections in Current Text

Statements on Auditing Standards *, †

No.	*Date Issued*	*Title*	*AU Section*
1	**Nov. 1972**	**Codification of Auditing Standards and Procedures**	**See part II** [1]
2	Oct. 1974	Reports on Audited Financial Statements [Superseded by SAS No .58]	
3	Dec. 1974	The Effects of EDP on the Auditor's Study and Evaluation of Internal Control [Superseded by SAS No. 48]	
4	Dec. 1974	Quality Control Considerations for a Firm of Independent Auditors [Superseded by SAS No.25]	
5	July 1975	The Meaning of "Present Fairly in Conformity With Generally Accepted Accounting Principles" in the Independent Auditor's Report [Superseded by SAS No. 69]	
6	July 1975	Related Party Transactions [Superseded by SAS No. 45]	
7	Oct. 1975	Communications Between Predecessor and Successor Auditors [Superseded by SAS No. 84]	
8	Dec. 1975	Other Information in Documents Containing Audited Financial Statements	
9	Dec. 1975	The Effect of an Internal Audit Function on the Scope of the Independent Auditor's Examination [Superseded by SAS No. 65]	
10	Dec. 1975	Limited Review of Interim Financial Information [Superseded by SAS No. 24]	
11	Dec. 1975	Using the Work of a Specialist [Superseded by SAS No. 73]	
12	**Jan. 1976**	**Inquiry of a Client's Lawyer Concerning Litigation, Claims, and Assessments**	337

(continued)

* Pronouncements in effect are indicated in **boldface** type.

† This table lists Statements on Auditing Standards (SASs) issued before SAS No. 122, *Statements on Auditing Standards: Clarification and Recodification*, was issued in October 2011. Refer to the AU-C Cross-References to SASs (preceding the AU-C section) for SASs issued after SAS No. 122.

[1] Portions of SAS No. 1 have been superseded by subsequent pronouncements.

Statements on Auditing Standards—continued

No.	Date Issued	Title	AU Section
13	May 1976	Reports on a Limited Review of Interim Financial Information [Superseded by SAS No. 24]	
14	Dec. 1976	Special Reports [Superseded by SAS No. 62]	
15	Dec. 1976	Reports on Comparative Financial Statements [Superseded by SAS No. 58]	
16	Jan. 1977	The Independent Auditor's Responsibility for the Detection of Errors or Irregularities [Superseded by SAS No. 53]	
17	Jan. 1977	Illegal Acts by Clients [Superseded by SAS No. 54]	
18	May 1977	Unaudited Replacement Cost Information [Withdrawn by the Auditing Standards Board]	
19	June 1977	Client Representations [Superseded by SAS No. 85]	
20	Aug. 1977	Required Communication of Material Weaknesses in Internal Accounting Control [Superseded by SAS No. 60]	
21	Dec. 1977	Segment Information [Rescinded by the Auditing Standards Board] [2]	
22	Mar. 1978	Planning and Supervision [Superseded by SAS No. 108]	
23	Oct. 1978	Analytical Review Procedures [Superseded by SAS No. 56]	
24	Mar. 1979	Review of Interim Financial Information [Superseded by SAS No. 36]	
25	**Nov. 1979**	**The Relationship of Generally Accepted Auditing Standards to Quality Control Standards**	161
26	**Nov. 1979**	**Association With Financial Statements**	504
27	Dec. 1979	Supplementary Information Required by the Financial Accounting Standards Board [Superseded by SAS No. 52]	
28	June 1980	Supplementary Information on the Effects of Changing Prices [Withdrawn by SAS No. 52]	
29	July 1980	Reporting on Information Accompanying the Basic Financial Statements in Auditor-Submitted Documents	

[2] The Auditing Standards Board rescinded SAS No. 21, *Segment Information*, effective for audits of financial statements to which Financial Accounting Standards Board (FASB) Statement No. 131, *Disclosures about Segments of an Enterprise and Related Information*, has been applied. FASB Statement No. 131 became effective for fiscal years beginning after December 15, 1997.

Statements on Auditing Standards—continued

No.	*Date Issued*	*Title*	*AU Section*
30	July 1980	Reporting on Internal Accounting Control [Superseded by SSAE No. 2]	
31	Aug. 1980	Evidential Matter [Superseded by SAS No. 106]	
32	**Oct. 1980**	**Adequacy of Disclosure of Financial Statements**	431
33	Oct. 1980	Supplementary Oil and Gas Reserve Information [Superseded by SAS No. 45]	
34	Mar. 1981	The Auditor's Considerations When a Question Arises About an Entity's Continued Existence [Superseded by SAS No. 59]	
35	April 1981	Special Reports—Applying Agreed-Upon Procedures to Specified Elements, Accounts, or Items of a Financial Statement [Superseded by SAS No. 75]	
36	April 1981	Review of Interim Financial Information [Superseded by SAS No. 71]	
37	**April 1981**	**Filings Under Federal Securities Statutes**	711
38	April 1981	Letters for Underwriters [Superseded by SAS No. 49]	
39	**June 1981**	**Audit Sampling**	350
40	Feb. 1982	Supplementary Mineral Reserve Information [Superseded by SAS No. 52]	
41	April 1982	Working Papers [Superseded by SAS No. 96]	
42	**Sept. 1982**	**Reporting on Condensed Financial Statements and Selected Financial Data**	552
43	**Aug. 1982**	**Omnibus Statement on Auditing Standards**[3]	
44	Dec. 1982	Special-Purpose Reports on Internal Accounting Control at Service Organizations [Superseded by SAS No. 70]	
45	**Aug. 1983**	**Omnibus Statement on Auditing Standards—1983**[4]	
46	**Sept. 1983**	**Consideration of Omitted Procedures After the Report Date**	390

(continued)

[3] SAS No. 43 has been integrated within sections 150 (superseded by SAS No. 95), 320 (superseded by SAS No. 55, as superseded by SAS Nos. 109 and 110), 331.14, 350.47, 420[.18], 901.01, 901.24, and 901.28.

[4] SAS No. 45 has created new sections 313, *Substantive Tests Prior to the Balance-Sheet Date* (superseded by SAS No. 110); 334, *Related Parties*; and 557, *Supplementary Oil and Gas Reserve Information* (withdrawn by the issuance of SAS No. 52).

Statements on Auditing Standards—continued

No.	*Date Issued*	*Title*	*AU Section*
47	Dec. 1983	Audit Risk and Materiality in Conducting an Audit [Superseded by SAS No. 107]	
48	July 1984	The Effects of Computer Processing on the Audit of Financial Statements [Effectively superseded by SAS No. 55, SAS No. 56, SAS No. 106, SAS No. 108, SAS No. 109, and SAS No. 110]	
49	Sept. 1984	Letters for Underwriters [Superseded by SAS No. 72]	
50	**July 1986**	**Reports on the Application of Accounting Principles**	625
51	**July 1986**	**Reporting on Financial Statements Prepared for Use in Other Countries**	534
52	April 1988	Omnibus Statement on Auditing Standards—1987	
53	April 1988	The Auditor's Responsibility to Detect and Report Errors and Irregularities [Superseded by SAS No. 82]	
54	**April 1988**	**Illegal Acts by Clients**	317
55	April 1988	Consideration of Internal Control in a Financial Statement Audit [Superseded by SAS Nos. 109 and 110]	
56	**April 1988**	**Analytical Procedures**	329
57	**April 1988**	**Auditing Accounting Estimates**	342
58	**April 1988**	**Reports on Audited Financial Statements**	508
59	**April 1988**	**The Auditor's Consideration of an Entity's Ability to Continue as a Going Concern**	341
60	April 1988	Communication of Internal Control Related Matters Noted in an Audit [Superseded by SAS No. 112]	
61	April 1988	Communication With Audit Committees [Superseded by SAS No. 114]	
62	**April 1989**	**Special Reports**	623
63	April 1989	Compliance Auditing Applicable to Governmental Entities and Other Recipients of Governmental Financial Assistance [Superseded by SAS No. 68]	
64	**Dec. 1990**	**Omnibus Statement on Auditing Standards—1990**[5]	
65	**April 1991**	**The Auditor's Consideration of the Internal Audit Function in an Audit of Financial Statements**	322

[5] SAS No. 64 has been integrated within sections 341.12, 341.13, 508.74, and 543.16.

Statements on Auditing Standards—continued

No.	*Date Issued*	*Title*	*AU Section*
66	June 1991	Communication of Matters About Interim Financial Information Filed or to Be Filed With Specified Regulatory Agencies—An Amendment to SAS No. 36, *Review of Interim Financial Information* [Superseded by SAS No. 71]	
67	**Nov. 1991**	**The Confirmation Process**	330
68	Dec. 1991	Compliance Auditing Applicable to Governmental Entities and Other Recipients of Governmental Financial Assistance [Superseded by SAS No. 74]	
69	Jan. 1992	The Meaning of *Present Fairly in Conformity With Generally Accepted Accounting Principles* [Withdrawn by the Auditing Standards Board]	
70	**April 1992**	**Service Organizations**[6] [The guidance for service auditors reporting on controls at a service organization is superseded by SSAE No. 16.]	324
71	May 1992	Interim Financial Information [Superseded by SAS No. 100]	
72	**Feb. 1993**	**Letters for Underwriters and Certain Other Requesting Parties**	634
73	**July 1994**	**Using the Work of a Specialist**	336
74	Feb. 1995	Compliance Auditing Considerations in Audits of Governmental Entities and Recipients of Governmental Financial Assistance	
75	Sept. 1995	Engagements to Apply Agreed-Upon Procedures to Specified Elements, Accounts, or Items of a Financial Statement [Withdrawn by SAS No. 93]	
76	**Sept. 1995**	**Amendments to Statement on Auditing Standards No. 72, *Letters for Underwriters and Certain Other Requesting Parties***[7]	
77	**Nov. 1995**	**Amendments to Statements on Auditing Standards No. 22, *Planning and Supervision*, No. 59, *The Auditor's Consideration of an Entity's Ability to Continue as a Going Concern*, and No. 62, *Special Reports***[8]	

(continued)

[6] Title of SAS No. 70 was amended by SAS No. 88.

[7] SAS No. 76 has been integrated within sections 634.01, 634.09, 634.10, 634.64, and AT section 300 (superseded by Statement on Standards for Attestation Engagements [SSAE] No. 10).

[8] SAS No. 77 has been integrated within sections 311 (superseded by SAS No. 108), 341.13, 544.02, 544.04, and 623.05.

Statements on Auditing Standards—continued

No.	*Date Issued*	*Title*	*AU Section*
78	Dec. 1995	Consideration of Internal Control in a Financial Statement Audit: An Amendment to Statement on Auditing Standards No. 55 [Effectively superseded by SAS No. 109 and SAS No. 110]	
79	**Dec. 1995**	**Amendment to Statement on Auditing Standards No. 58, *Reports on Audited Financial Statements*** [9]	
80	Dec. 1996	Amendment to Statement on Auditing Standards No. 31, *Evidential Matter* [Effectively superseded by SAS No. 106]	
81	Dec. 1996	Auditing Investments [Superseded by SAS No. 92]	
82	Feb. 1997	Consideration of Fraud in a Financial Statement Audit [Superseded by SAS No. 99]	
83	Oct. 1997	Establishing an Understanding With the Client [Effectively superseded by SAS No. 108]	
84	**Oct. 1997**	**Communications Between Predecessor and Successor Auditors**	315
85	**Nov. 1997**	**Management Representations**	333
86	**Mar. 1998**	**Amendment to Statement on Auditing Standards No. 72, *Letters for Underwriters and Certain Other Requesting Parties*** [10]	
87	**Sept. 1998**	**Restricting the Use of an Auditor's Report**	532
88	**Dec. 1999**	**Service Organizations and Reporting on Consistency** [11]	
89	**Dec. 1999**	**Audit Adjustments** [12]	
90	Dec. 1999	Audit Committee Communications [Effectively superseded by SAS Nos. 100 and 114]	
91	Apr. 2000	Federal GAAP Hierarchy [Effectively withdrawn upon the withdrawal of SAS No. 69]	

---

[9] SAS No. 79 has been integrated within sections 508.11, 508.19, 508.29–.32, 508.45–.49, 508.61, 508.62, and 508.74–.76.

[10] SAS No. 86 has been integrated within sections 634.20, 634.22, 634.29, 634.33, 634.34, 634.55, 634.57, and 634.64.

[11] SAS No. 88 has been integrated within sections 324 (title), 324.03, 324.06–.10, and 420.07–[.11].

[12] SAS No. 89 has been integrated within sections 310 (superseded by SAS No. 108), 333.06, 333.16, and 380 (superseded by SAS No. 114).

Statements on Auditing Standards—continued

No.	Date Issued	Title	AU Section
92	**Sept. 2000**	**Auditing Derivative Instruments, Hedging Activities, and Investments in Securities**	332
93	**Oct. 2000**	**Omnibus Statement on Auditing Standards—2000**[13]	
94	May 2001	The Effect of Information Technology on the Auditor's Consideration of Internal Control in a Financial Statement Audit [Effectively superseded by SAS No. 109 and SAS No. 110]	
95	**Dec. 2001**	**Generally Accepted Auditing Standards**	150
96	Jan. 2002	Audit Documentation [Superseded by SAS No. 103]	
97	**June 2002**	**Amendment to Statement on Auditing Standards No. 50, *Reports on the Application of Accounting Principles***[14]	
98	**Sept. 2002**	**Omnibus Statement on Auditing Standards—2002**[15]	
99	**Oct. 2002**	**Consideration of Fraud in a Financial Statement Audit**	316
100	**Nov. 2002**	**Interim Financial Information**	722
101	**Jan. 2003**	**Auditing Fair Value Measurements and Disclosures**	328
102	**Dec. 2005**	**Defining Professional Requirements in Statements on Auditing Standards**	120
103	**Dec. 2005**	**Audit Documentation**	339
104	**Mar. 2006**	**Amendment to Statement on Auditing Standards No. 1, *Codification of Auditing Standards and Procedures* ("Due Professional Care in the Performance of Work")**[16]	
105	**Mar. 2006**	**Amendment to Statement on Auditing Standards No. 95, *Generally Accepted Auditing Standards***[17]	

(continued)

[13] SAS No. 93 has been integrated within sections 315.02, 315.12, 411 (title), 411.01 (withdrawn by the Auditing Standards Board), 508.08, and 622.

[14] SAS No. 97 has been integrated within section 625.01–.07 and 625.09–.11.

[15] SAS No. 98 has been integrated within sections 150.05, 161 (headnote), 161.02, 161.03, 312 (superseded by SAS No. 107), 324.57–.61, 9324[.41–.42], 508.65, 530.03–.05, 550A.07, 551A.12, 551A.15, 551A.16 (superseded by SAS No. 118–119), 558A.02, 558A.08–.11 (superseded by SAS No. 120), 560.01, and 561.01–.03.

[16] SAS No. 104 has been integrated within section 230.10.

[17] SAS No. 105 has been integrated within section 150.02.

Statements on Auditing Standards—continued

No.	*Date Issued*	*Title*	*AU Section*
106	**Mar. 2006**	**Audit Evidence**	326
107	**Mar. 2006**	**Audit Risk and Materiality in Conducting an Audit**	312
108	**Mar. 2006**	**Planning and Supervision**	311
109	**Mar. 2006**	**Understanding the Entity and Its Environment and Assessing the Risks of Material Misstatement**	314
110	**Mar. 2006**	**Performing Audit Procedures in Response to Assessed Risks and Evaluating the Audit Evidence Obtained**	318
111	**Mar. 2006**	**Amendment to Statement on Auditing Standards No. 39, *Audit Sampling*** [18]	
112	May 2006	Communicating Internal Control Related Matters Identified in an Audit	
113	**Nov. 2006**	**Omnibus Statement on Auditing Standards—2006** [19]	
114	**Dec. 2006**	**The Auditor's Communication With Those Charged With Governance**	380
115	**Sept. 2008**	**Communicating Internal Control Related Matters Identified in an Audit**	325
116	**Feb. 2009**	**Interim Financial Information**	722
117	**Dec. 2009**	**Compliance Audits**	801
118	**Feb. 2010**	**Other Information in Documents Containing Audited Financial Statements**	550
119	**Feb. 2010**	**Supplementary Information in Relation to the Financial Statements as a Whole**	551
120	**Feb. 2010**	**Required Supplementary Information**	558
121	**Feb. 2011**	**Revised Applicability of Statement on Auditing Standards No. 100, *Interim Financial Information*** [20]	

[18] SAS No. 111 has been integrated within sections 350.08, 350[.09], 350.18, 350.20, 350.23, 350.25, 350.32, 350.42, 350.44, and 350.48.

[19] SAS No. 113 has been integrated within sections 150.02, 150.04, 316.35, 316.46, 328.41, 333.09, 341.02, 342.10, 342.13, and 560.12.

[20] SAS No. 121 has been integrated within section 722.05.

Sources of Sections in Current Text [‡]

AU Section	Contents	Source
100	**Introduction**	
110	Responsibilities and Functions of the Independent Auditor	SAS No. 1[‖]
120	Defining Professional Requirements in Statements on Auditing Standards	SAS No. 102
150	Generally Accepted Auditing Standards	SAS No. 95
161	The Relationship of Generally Accepted Auditing Standards to Quality Control Standards	SAS No. 25
200	**The General Standards**	
201	Nature of the General Standards	SAS No. 1[jj]
210	Training and Proficiency of the Independent Auditor	SAS No. 1[jj]
220	Independence	SAS No. 1[jj]
230	Due Professional Care in the Performance of Work	SAS No. 1[jj]
300	**The Standards of Field Work**	
311	Planning and Supervision	SAS No. 108
312	Audit Risk and Materiality in Conducting an Audit	SAS No. 107
314	Understanding the Entity and Its Environment and Assessing the Risks of Material Misstatement	SAS No. 109
315	Communications Between Predecessor and Successor Auditors	SAS No. 84
316	Consideration of Fraud in a Financial Statement Audit	SAS No. 99
317	Illegal Acts by Clients	SAS No. 54
318	Performing Audit Procedures in Response to Assessed Risks and Evaluating the Audit Evidence Obtained	SAS No. 110
322	The Auditor's Consideration of the Internal Audit Function in an Audit of Financial Statements	SAS No. 65
324	Service Organizations	SAS No. 70[21]

(continued)

‡ This table lists the sources of AU sections only. Refer to the AU-C Cross-References to SASs (preceding the AU-C section) for sources of AU-C sections created after SAS No. 122.

‖ Portions of Statement on Auditing Standards (SAS) No. 1 have been superseded by subsequent pronouncements. See part II.

21 Title of SAS No. 70 has been amended by SAS No. 88.

Sources of Sections in Current Text—continued

AU Section	*Contents*	*Source*
325	Communicating Internal Control Related Matters Identified in an Audit	SAS No. 115
326	Audit Evidence	SAS No. 106
328	Auditing Fair Value Measurements and Disclosures	SAS No. 101
329	Analytical Procedures	SAS No. 56
330	The Confirmation Process	SAS No. 67
331	Inventories	SAS No. 1[‖]
332	Auditing Derivative Instruments, Hedging Activities, and Investments in Securities	SAS No. 92
333	Management Representations	SAS No. 85
334	Related Parties	SAS No. 45
336	Using the Work of a Specialist	SAS No. 73
337	Inquiry of a Client's Lawyer Concerning Litigation, Claims, and Assessments	SAS No. 12
339	Audit Documentation	SAS No. 103
341	The Auditor's Consideration of an Entity's Ability to Continue as a Going Concern	SAS No. 59
342	Auditing Accounting Estimates	SAS No. 57
350	Audit Sampling	SAS No. 39
380	The Auditor's Communication With Those Charged With Governance	SAS No. 114
390	Consideration of Omitted Procedures After the Report Date	SAS No. 46
400	**The First, Second, and Third Standards of Reporting**	
410	Adherence to Generally Accepted Accounting Principles	SAS No. 1[jj]
420	Consistency of Application of Generally Accepted Accounting Principles	SAS No. 1[jj]
431	Adequacy of Disclosure in Financial Statements	SAS No. 32
500	**The Fourth Standard of Reporting**	
504	Association With Financial Statements	SAS No. 26
508	Reports on Audited Financial Statements	SAS No. 58
530	Dating of the Independent Auditor's Report	SAS No. 1[jj]
532	Restricting the Use of an Auditor's Report	SAS No. 87
534	Reporting on Financial Statements Prepared for Use in Other Countries	SAS No. 51
543	Part of Audit Performed by Other Independent Auditors	SAS No. 1[jj]
544	Lack of Conformity With Generally Accepted Accounting Principles	SAS No. 1[jj]

‖ Portions of Statement on Auditing Standards (SAS) No. 1 have been superseded by subsequent pronouncements. See part II.

Sources of Sections in Current Text—continued

AU Section	*Contents*	*Source*
550	Other Information in Documents Containing Audited Financial Statements	SAS No. 118
551	Supplementary Information in Relation to the Financial Statements as a Whole	SAS No. 119
552	Reporting on Condensed Financial Statements and Selected Financial Data	SAS No. 42
558	Required Supplementary Information	SAS No. 120
560	Subsequent Events	SAS No. 1[jj]
561	Subsequent Discovery of Facts Existing at the Date of the Auditor's Report	SAS No. 1[‖]
600	**Other Types of Reports**	
622	Engagements to Apply Agreed-Upon Procedures to Specified Elements, Accounts, or Items of a Financial Statement	SAS No. 75[22]
623	Special Reports	SAS No. 62
625	Reports on the Application of Accounting Principles	SAS No. 50
634	Letters for Underwriters and Certain Other Requesting Parties	SAS No. 72
700	**Special Topics**	
711	Filings Under Federal Securities Statutes	SAS No. 37
722	Interim Financial Information	SAS No. 100
800	**Compliance Auditing**	
801	Compliance Audits	SAS No. 117
900	**Special Reports of the Committee on Auditing Procedure**	
901	Public Warehouses—Controls and Auditing Procedures for Goods Held	SAS No. 1[jj]

‖ Portions of Statement on Auditing Standards (SAS) No. 1 have been superseded by subsequent pronouncements. See part II.

22 The Auditing Standards Board has withdrawn SAS No. 75 and its auditing interpretation, effective for audits of financial statements for periods ending on or after June 30, 2001, in order to consolidate the guidance applicable to agreed-upon procedures engagements in professional standards. For guidance relating to performing and reporting on agreed-upon procedures engagements, practitioners should refer to AT section 201, *Agreed-Upon Procedures Engagements*.

Part II

List of Sections in Statement on Auditing Standards No. 1, Codification of Auditing Standards and Procedures, and List of Statements on Auditing Procedure Nos. 1–54

Statement on Auditing Standards No. 1 *

Section	Title [1]
100	*Introduction*
110	**Responsibilities and Functions of the Independent Auditor**
150	Generally Accepted Auditing Standards [Superseded by SAS No. 95]
200	*The General Standards*
201	**Nature of the General Standards**
210	**Training and Proficiency of the Independent Auditor**
220	**Independence**
230	**Due Professional Care in the Performance of Work**[1]
300	*The Standards of Field Work*
310	Appointment of the Independent Auditor [Superseded by SAS No. 108]
320	The Auditor's Study and Evaluation of Internal Control [Superseded by SAS No. 55]
320A	Appendix A—Relationship of Statistical Sampling to Generally Accepted Auditing Standards [Superseded by SAS No. 39]
320B	Appendix B—Precision and Reliability for Statistical Sampling in Auditing [Superseded by SAS No. 39]
330	Evidential Matter [Superseded by SAS No. 31]
331	**Inventories**[1]
332	Evidential Matter for Long-Term Investments [Superseded by SAS No. 81]
338	Working Papers [Superseded by SAS No. 41]
400	*The First, Second, and Third Standards of Reporting*
410	**Adherence to Generally Accepted Accounting Principles**
420	**Consistency of Application of Generally Accepted Accounting Principles**
430	Adequacy of Disclosure in Financial Statements [Superseded by SAS No. 32]

(continued)

* Pronouncements in effect are indicated in **boldface** type.

[1] Current section titles are listed. Section titles reflect amendments and conforming changes resulting from subsequent pronouncements.

Statement on Auditing Standards No. 1—continued

Section	*Title* [1]
500	*The Fourth Standard of Reporting*
510	Expression of Opinion in the Auditor's Report [Superseded by SAS No. 2]
511	Unqualified Opinion [Superseded by SAS No. 2]
512	Qualified Opinion [Superseded by SAS No. 2]
513	Adverse Opinion [Superseded by SAS No. 2]
514	Disclaimer of Opinion [Superseded by SAS No. 2]
515	Piecemeal Opinion [Superseded by SAS No. 2]
516	Unaudited Financial Statements [Superseded by SAS No. 26]
517	Reporting When a Certified Public Accountant Is Not Independent [Superseded by SAS No. 26]
518	Negative Assurance [Superseded by SAS No. 26]
530	**Dating of the Independent Auditor's Report**
535	Opinions on Prior Year's Statements [Superseded by SAS No. 2]
540	Circumstances Which Require a Departure From the Standard Short-Form Report [Superseded by SAS No. 2]
541	Restrictions Imposed by the Client [Superseded by SAS No. 2]
542	Other Conditions Which Preclude the Application of Necessary Auditing Procedures [Superseded by SAS No. 58]
543	**Part of Audit Performed by Other Independent Auditors**[1]
544	**Lack of Conformity With Generally Accepted Accounting Principles**
545	Inadequate Disclosure [Superseded by SAS No. 58]
546	Reporting on Inconsistency [Superseded by SAS No. 58]
547	Unusual Uncertainties as to the Effect of Future Developments on Certain Items [Superseded by SAS No. 2]
560	**Subsequent Events**
561	**Subsequent Discovery of Facts Existing at the Date of the Auditor's Report**
600	*Other Types of Reports*
610	Long-Form Reports [Superseded by SAS No. 29]
620	Special Reports [Superseded by SAS No. 14]
630	Letters for Underwriters [Superseded by SAS No. 38]
640	Reports on Internal Control [Superseded by SAS No. 30]
641	Reports on Internal Control Based on Criteria Established by Governmental Agencies [Superseded by SAS No. 30]
700	*Special Topics*
710	Filings Under Federal Securities Statutes [Superseded by SAS No. 37]
900	*Special Reports of the Committee on Auditing Procedure*
901	**Public Warehouses—Controls and Auditing Procedures for Goods Held**[1]

[1] Current section titles are listed. Section titles reflect amendments and conforming changes resulting from subsequent pronouncements.

Statements on Auditing Procedure

No.	*Date Issued*	*Title*
1	Oct. 1939	Extensions of Auditing Procedure
2	Dec. 1939	The Auditor's Opinion on the Basis of a Restricted Examination
3	Feb. 1940	Inventories and Receivables of Department Stores, Installment Houses, Chain Stores, and Other Retailers
4	Mar. 1941	Clients' Written Representations Regarding Inventories, Liabilities, and Other Matters
5	Feb. 1941	The Revised SEC Rule on "Accountants' Certificates"
6	Mar. 1941	The Revised SEC Rule on "Accountants' Certificates"
7	Mar. 1941	Contingent Liability Under Policies With Mutual Insurance Companies
8	Sept. 1941	Interim Financial Statements and the Auditor's Report Thereon
9	Dec. 1941	Accountants' Reports on Examinations of Securities and Similar Investments Under the Investment Company Act
10	June 1942	Auditing Under Wartime Conditions
11	Sept. 1942	The Auditor's Opinion on the Basis of a Restricted Examination (No. 2)
12	Oct. 1942	Amendment to Extensions of Auditing Procedure
13	Dec. 1942	The Auditor's Opinion on the Basis of a Restricted Examination (No. 3) Face-Amount Certificate Companies
14	Dec. 1942	Confirmation of Public Utility Accounts Receivable
15	Dec. 1942	Disclosure of the Effect of Wartime Uncertainties on Financial Statements
16	Dec. 1942	Case Studies on Inventories
17	Dec. 1942	Physical Inventories in Wartime
18	Jan. 1943	Confirmation of Receivables From the Government
19	Nov. 1943	Confirmation of Receivables (Positive and Negative Methods)
20	Dec. 1943	Termination of Fixed Price Supply Contracts
21	July 1944	Wartime Government Regulations
22	May 1945	References to the Independent Accountant in Securities Registrations
23	Dec. 1949	Clarification of Accountant's Report When Opinion is Omitted (Revised)
24	Oct. 1948	Revision in Short-Form Accountant's Report or Certificate
25	Oct. 1954	Events Subsequent to the Date of Financial Statements
26	Apr. 1956	Reporting on Use of "Other Procedures"
27	July 1957	Long-Form Reports
28	Oct. 1957	Special Reports

(continued)

Statements on Auditing Procedure—continued

No.	*Date Issued*	*Title*
29	Oct. 1958	Scope of the Independent Auditor's Review of Internal Control
30	Sept. 1960	Responsibilities and Functions of the Independent Auditor in the Examination of Financial Statements
31	Oct. 1961	Consistency
32	Sept. 1962	Qualifications and Disclaimers
33	Dec. 1963	Auditing Standards and Procedures (a codification)
34	Sept. 1965	Long-Term Investments
35	Nov. 1965	Letters for Underwriters
36	Aug. 1966	Revision of "Extensions of Auditing Procedure" Relating to Inventories
37	Sept. 1966	Special Report: Public Warehouses Controls and Auditing Procedures for Goods Held
38	Sept. 1967	Unaudited Financial Statements
39	Sept. 1967	Working Papers
40	Oct. 1968	Reports Following a Pooling of Interests
41	Oct. 1969	Subsequent Discovery of Facts Existing at the Date of the Auditor's Report
42	Jan. 1970	Reporting When a Certified Public Accountant Is Not Independent
43	Sept. 1970	Confirmation of Receivables and Observation of Inventories
44	Apr. 1971	Reports Following a Pooling of Interests
45	July 1971	Using the Work and Reports of Other Auditors
46	July 1971	Piecemeal Opinions
47	Sept. 1971	Subsequent Events
48	Oct. 1971	Letters for Underwriters
49	Nov. 1971	Reports on Internal Control
50	Nov. 1971	Reporting on the Statement of Changes in Financial Position
51	July 1972	Long-Term Investments
52	Oct. 1972	Reports on Internal Control Based on Criteria Established by Governmental Agencies
53	Nov. 1972	Reporting on Consistency and Accounting Changes
54	Nov. 1972	The Auditor's Study and Evaluation of Internal Control

AU Section 100

STATEMENTS ON AUDITING STANDARDS — Introduction

The following is a Codification of currently effective Statements on Auditing Standards (SASs) and related Auditing Interpretations. Statements on Auditing Standards are issued by the Auditing Standards Board (ASB), the senior technical body of the Institute designated to issue pronouncements on auditing matters. Rule 202 of the Institute's Code of Professional Conduct requires adherence to the applicable generally accepted auditing standards promulgated by the ASB. An auditor is required to comply with an unconditional requirement in all cases in which the circumstances exist to which the unconditional requirement applies. An auditor is also required to comply with a presumptively mandatory requirement in all cases in which the circumstances exist to which the presumptively mandatory requirement applies; however, in rare circumstances, an auditor may depart from a presumptively mandatory requirement provided the auditor documents his or her justification for the departure and how the alternative procedures performed in the circumstances were sufficient to achieve the objectives of the presumptively mandatory requirement.

Interpretations are issued under the authority of the Auditing Standards Board to provide recommendations on the application of Statements on Auditing Standards in specific circumstances, including engagements for entities in specialized industries. An auditor should be aware of and consider interpretations applicable to his or her audit. An interpretation is not as authoritative as a pronouncement of the ASB; however, if an auditor does not apply an auditing interpretation, the auditor should be prepared to explain how he or she complied with the SAS provisions addressed by such auditing interpretation. The specific terms used to define professional requirements in the SASs are not intended to apply to interpretations since interpretations are not auditing standards. It is the ASB's intention to make conforming changes to the interpretations over the next several years to remove any language that would imply a professional requirement where none exists.

TABLE OF CONTENTS

AU Section 110

Responsibilities and Functions of the Independent Auditor

Source: SAS No. 1, section 110; SAS No. 78; SAS No. 82.

Issue date, unless otherwise indicated: November, 1972.

.01 The objective of the ordinary audit of financial statements by the independent auditor is the expression of an opinion on the fairness with which they present, in all material respects, financial position, results of operations, and its cash flows in conformity with generally accepted accounting principles. The auditor's report is the medium through which he expresses his opinion or, if circumstances require, disclaims an opinion. In either case, he states whether his audit has been made in accordance with generally accepted auditing standards. These standards require him to state whether, in his opinion, the financial statements are presented in conformity with generally accepted accounting principles and to identify those circumstances in which such principles have not been consistently observed in the preparation of the financial statements of the current period in relation to those of the preceding period.

Distinction Between Responsibilities of Auditor and Management

.02 The auditor has a responsibility to plan and perform the audit to obtain reasonable assurance about whether the financial statements are free of material misstatement, whether caused by error or fraud.[1] Because of the nature of audit evidence and the characteristics of fraud, the auditor is able to obtain reasonable, but not absolute, assurance that material misstatements are detected.[2] The auditor has no responsibility to plan and perform the audit to obtain reasonable assurance that misstatements, whether caused by errors or fraud, that are not material to the financial statements are detected. [Paragraph added, effective for audits of financial statements for periods ending on or after December 15, 1997, by Statement on Auditing Standards No. 82.]

.03 The financial statements are management's responsibility. The auditor's responsibility is to express an opinion on the financial statements. Management is responsible for adopting sound accounting policies and for establishing and maintaining internal control that will, among other things, initiate,

---

[1] See section 312, *Audit Risk and Materiality in Conducting an Audit*, and section 316, *Consideration of Fraud in a Financial Statement Audit*. The auditor's consideration of illegal acts and responsibility for detecting misstatements resulting from illegal acts is defined in section 317, *Illegal Acts by Clients*. For those illegal acts that are defined in that section as having a direct and material effect on the determination of financial statement amounts, the auditor's responsibility to detect misstatements resulting from such illegal acts is the same as that for error or fraud. [Footnote added, effective for audits of financial statements for periods ending on or after December 15, 1997, by Statement on Auditing Standards No. 82.]

[2] See section 230, *Due Professional Care in the Performance of Work*, paragraphs .10 through .13. [Footnote added, effective for audits of financial statements for periods ending on or after December 15, 1997, by Statement on Auditing Standards No. 82.]

authorize, record, process, and report transactions (as well as events and conditions) consistent with management's assertions embodied in the financial statements. The entity's transactions and the related assets, liabilities, and equity are within the direct knowledge and control of management. The auditor's knowledge of these matters and internal control is limited to that acquired through the audit. Thus, the fair presentation of financial statements in conformity with generally accepted accounting principles[3] is an implicit and integral part of management's responsibility. The independent auditor may make suggestions about the form or content of the financial statements or draft them, in whole or in part, based on information from management during the performance of the audit. However, the auditor's responsibility for the financial statements he or she has audited is confined to the expression of his or her opinion on them. [Revised, April 1989, to reflect conforming changes necessary due to the issuance of Statement on Auditing Standards Nos. 53 through 62. As amended, effective for audits of financial statements for periods beginning on or after January 1, 1997, by Statement on Auditing Standards No. 78. Paragraph renumbered by the issuance of Statement on Auditing Standards No. 82, February 1997. Revised, April 2002, to reflect conforming changes necessary due to the issuance of Statement on Auditing Standards No. 94. Revised, March 2006, to reflect conforming changes necessary due to the issuance of Statement on Auditing Standards No. 106.]

Professional Qualifications

.04 The professional qualifications required of the independent auditor are those of a person with the education and experience to practice as such. They do not include those of a person trained for or qualified to engage in another profession or occupation. For example, the independent auditor, in observing the taking of a physical inventory, does not purport to act as an appraiser, a valuer, or an expert in materials. Similarly, although the independent auditor is informed in a general manner about matters of commercial law, he does not purport to act in the capacity of a lawyer and may appropriately rely upon the advice of attorneys in all matters of law. [Paragraph renumbered by the issuance of Statement on Auditing Standards No. 82, February 1997.]

.05 In the observance of generally accepted auditing standards, the independent auditor must exercise his judgment in determining which auditing procedures are necessary in the circumstances to afford a reasonable basis for his opinion. His judgment is required to be the informed judgment of a qualified professional person. [Paragraph renumbered by the issuance of Statement on Auditing Standards No. 82, February 1997.]

Detection of Fraud

[.06–.09] [Superseded January 1977 by Statement on Auditing Standards No. 16, as superseded by Statement on Auditing Standards No. 53, as superseded by section 316. Paragraphs renumbered by the issuance of Statement on Auditing Standards No. 82, February 1997.]

---

[3] The responsibilities and functions of the independent auditor are also applicable to financial statements presented in conformity with a comprehensive basis of accounting other than generally accepted accounting principles; references in this section to financial statements presented in conformity with generally accepted accounting principles also include those presentations. [Footnote added, effective for audits of financial statements for periods beginning on or after January 1, 1997, by Statement on Auditing Standards No. 78. Footnote renumbered by the issuance of Statement on Auditing Standards No. 82, February 1997.]

Responsibility to the Profession

.10 The independent auditor also has a responsibility to his profession, the responsibility to comply with the standards accepted by his fellow practitioners. In recognition of the importance of such compliance, the American Institute of Certified Public Accountants has adopted, as part of its Code of Professional Conduct, rules which support the standards and provide a basis for their enforcement. [Paragraph renumbered by the issuance of Statement on Auditing Standards No. 82, February 1997.]

AU Section 120

Defining Professional Requirements in Statements on Auditing Standards

Source: SAS No. 102.

Effective December 2005.

Introduction

.01 This section sets forth the meaning of certain terms used in Statements on Auditing Standards (SASs) issued by the Auditing Standards Board in describing the professional requirements imposed on auditors.

Professional Requirements

.02 SASs contain professional requirements together with related guidance in the form of explanatory material. Auditors have a responsibility to consider the entire text of a SAS in carrying out their work on an engagement and in understanding and applying the professional requirements of the relevant SASs.

.03 Not every paragraph of a SAS carries a professional requirement that the auditor is expected to fulfill. Rather, the professional requirements are communicated by the language and the meaning of the words used in the SASs.

.04 SASs use two categories of professional requirements, identified by specific terms, to describe the degree of responsibility they impose on auditors, as follows:

- *Unconditional requirements.* The auditor is required to comply with an unconditional requirement in all cases in which the circumstances exist to which the unconditional requirement applies. SASs use the words *must* or *is required* to indicate an unconditional requirement.
- *Presumptively mandatory requirements.* The auditor is also required to comply with a presumptively mandatory requirement in all cases in which the circumstances exist to which the presumptively mandatory requirement applies; however, in rare circumstances, the auditor may depart from a presumptively mandatory requirement provided the auditor documents his or her justification for the departure and how the alternative procedures performed in the circumstances were sufficient to achieve the objectives of the presumptively mandatory requirement. SASs use the word should to indicate a presumptively mandatory requirement.

If a SAS provides that a procedure or action is one that the auditor "should consider," the consideration of the procedure or action is presumptively required, whereas carrying out the procedure or action is not. The professional requirements of a SAS are to be understood and applied in the context of the explanatory material that provides guidance for their application. Section 339, *Audit Documentation*, establishes standards and provides guidance on the form, content, and extent of audit documentation.

Explanatory Material

.05 Explanatory material is defined as the text within a SAS (excluding any related appendixes or interpretations[1]) that may:

- Provide further explanation and guidance on the professional requirements; or
- Identify and describe other procedures or actions relating to the activities of the auditor.

.06 Explanatory material that provides further explanation and guidance on the professional requirements is intended to be descriptive rather than imperative. That is, it explains the objective of the professional requirements (where not otherwise self-evident); it explains why the auditor might consider or employ particular procedures, depending on the circumstances; and it provides additional information for the auditor to consider in exercising professional judgment in performing the engagement.

.07 Explanatory material that identifies and describes other procedures or actions relating to the activities of the auditor is not intended to impose a professional requirement for the auditor to perform the suggested procedures or actions. Rather, these procedures or actions require the auditor's attention and understanding; how and whether the auditor carries out such procedures or actions in the engagement depends on the exercise of professional judgment in the circumstances consistent with the objective of the standard. The words *may*, *might*, and *could* are used to describe these actions and procedures.

Application

.08 The provisions of this section are effective upon issuance.[2]

---

[1] Auditing interpretations and certain appendixes represent interpretive publications, which differ from explanatory material. Interpretive publications, as defined in paragraphs .05 and .06 of section 150, *Generally Accepted Auditing Standards*, as amended, reside outside of the standards section of a SAS and are recommendations on the application of the SAS in specific circumstances, including engagements for entities in specialized industries. In contrast, explanatory material is always contained within the standards sections of the SAS and is meant to be more descriptive in nature. Interpretive publications are issued under the authority of the Auditing Standards Board (ASB) and consist of auditing interpretations of the SASs, appendixes to the SASs (except for previously issued appendixes to original pronouncements that when adopted modified other SASs), auditing guidance included in AICPA Audit and Accounting Guides, and AICPA auditing Statements of Position.

[2] The specific terms used to define professional requirements in this section are not intended to apply to interpretive publications issued under the authority of the ASB, since interpretive publications are not auditing standards. (See footnote 1.) It is the ASB's intention to make conforming changes to the interpretive publications over the next several years to remove any language that would imply a professional requirement where none exists. It is the ASB's intention that such language would only be used in the standards sections of the SASs.

AU Section 150

Generally Accepted Auditing Standards

(Supersedes SAS No. 1, section 150.)

Source: SAS No. 95; SAS No. 98; SAS No. 102; SAS No. 105; SAS No. 113.

Effective for audits of financial statements for periods beginning on or after December 15, 2001, unless otherwise indicated.

.01 An independent auditor plans, conducts, and reports the results of an audit in accordance with generally accepted auditing standards. Auditing standards provide a measure of audit quality and the objectives to be achieved in an audit. Auditing procedures differ from auditing standards. Auditing procedures are acts that the auditor performs during the course of an audit to comply with auditing standards.

Auditing Standards

.02 The general, field work, and reporting standards (the 10 standards) approved and adopted by the membership of the AICPA, as amended by the AICPA Auditing Standards Board (ASB), are as follows:

General Standards

1. The auditor must have adequate technical training and proficiency to perform the audit.

2. The auditor must maintain independence in mental attitude in all matters relating to the audit.

3. The auditor must exercise due professional care in the performance of the audit and the preparation of the report.

Standards of Field Work

1. The auditor must adequately plan the work and must properly supervise any assistants.

2. The auditor must obtain a sufficient understanding of the entity and its environment, including its internal control, to assess the risk of material misstatement of the financial statements whether due to error or fraud, and to design the nature, timing, and extent of further audit procedures.

3. The auditor must obtain sufficient appropriate[1] audit evidence by performing audit procedures to afford a reasonable basis for an opinion regarding the financial statements under audit.

---

[1] See paragraph .06 of section 326, *Audit Evidence*, for the definition of the term *appropriate*. [Footnote added, effective for audits of financial statements for periods beginning on or after December 15, 2006, by Statement on Auditing Standards (SAS) No. 105.]

Standards of Reporting[2]

1. The auditor must state in the auditor's report whether the financial statements are presented in accordance with generally accepted accounting principles.[3]
2. The auditor must identify in the auditor's report those circumstances in which such principles have not been consistently observed in the current period in relation to the preceding period.
3. When the auditor determines that informative disclosures are not reasonably adequate, the auditor must so state in the auditor's report.
4. The auditor must either express an opinion regarding the financial statements, taken as a whole, or state that an opinion cannot be expressed, in the auditor's report. When the auditor cannot express an overall opinion, the auditor should state the reasons therefor in the auditor's report. In all cases where an auditor's name is associated with financial statements, the auditor should clearly indicate the character of the auditor's work, if any, and the degree of responsibility the auditor is taking, in the auditor's report.

[As amended, effective for audits of financial statements for periods beginning on or after December 15, 2006, by Statement on Auditing Standards (SAS) No. 105. As amended, effective for audits of financial statements for periods beginning on or after December 15, 2006, by SAS No. 113.]

.03 Rule 202, *Compliance With Standards*, of the AICPA Code of Professional Conduct [ET section 202.01], requires an AICPA member who performs an audit (the auditor) to comply with standards promulgated by the ASB.[4] The ASB develops and issues standards in the form of SASs through a due process that includes deliberation in meetings open to the public, public exposure of proposed SASs, and a formal vote. The SASs are codified within the framework of the 10 standards.

.04 The nature of the 10 standards and the SASs requires the auditor to exercise professional judgment in applying them. Materiality and audit risk also underlie the application of the 10 standards and the SASs, particularly those related to field work and reporting.[5] When, in rare circumstances, the auditor departs from a presumptively mandatory requirement, the auditor must document in the working papers his or her justification for the departure and

---

[2] The reporting standards apply only when the auditor issues a report. [Footnote added, effective for audits of financial statements for periods beginning on or after December 15, 2006, by SAS No. 113.]

[3] When an auditor reports on financial statements prepared in accordance with a comprehensive basis of accounting other than generally accepted accounting principles (GAAP), the first standard of reporting is satisfied by stating in the auditor's report that the basis of presentation is a comprehensive basis of accounting other than GAAP and by expressing an opinion (or disclaiming an opinion) on whether the financial statements are presented in conformity with the comprehensive basis of accounting used. [Footnote added, effective for audits of financial statements for periods beginning on or after December 15, 2006, by SAS No. 113.]

[4] In certain engagements, the auditor also may be subject to other auditing requirements, such as Government Auditing Standards issued by the comptroller general of the United States, or rules and regulations promulgated by the U.S. Securities and Exchange Commission. [Footnote renumbered by the issuance of SAS No. 105, March 2006. Footnote subsequently renumbered by the issuance of SAS No. 113, November 2006.]

[5] See section 312, *Audit Risk and Materiality in Conducting an Audit*. [Footnote renumbered by the issuance of SAS No. 105, March 2006. Footnote subsequently renumbered by the issuance of SAS No. 113, November 2006.]

how the alternative procedures performed in the circumstances were sufficient to achieve the objectives of the presumptively mandatory requirement. [As amended, effective December 2005, by SAS No. 102. As amended, effective for audits of financial statements for periods beginning on or after December 15, 2006, by SAS No. 113.]

Interpretive Publications

.05 *Interpretive publications* consist of auditing interpretations of the SASs, appendixes to the SASs,[6] auditing guidance included in AICPA Audit and Accounting Guides, and AICPA auditing Statements of Position.[7] Interpretive publications are not auditing standards. Interpretive publications are recommendations on the application of the SASs in specific circumstances, including engagements for entities in specialized industries. An interpretive publication is issued under the authority of the ASB after all ASB members have been provided an opportunity to consider and comment on whether the proposed interpretive publication is consistent with the SASs. [As amended, effective September 2002, by SAS No. 98.]

.06 The auditor should be aware of and consider interpretive publications applicable to his or her audit. If the auditor does not apply the auditing guidance included in an applicable interpretive publication, the auditor should be prepared to explain how he or she complied with the SAS provisions addressed by such auditing guidance.

Other Auditing Publications

.07 *Other auditing publications* include AICPA auditing publications not referred to previously; auditing articles in the *Journal of Accountancy* and other professional journals; auditing articles in the AICPA *CPA Letter*; continuing professional education programs and other instruction materials, textbooks, guide books, audit programs, and checklists; and other auditing publications from state CPA societies, other organizations, and individuals.[8] Other auditing publications have no authoritative status; however, they may help the auditor understand and apply the SASs.

.08 If an auditor applies the auditing guidance included in an other auditing publication, he or she should be satisfied that, in his or her judgment, it is both relevant to the circumstances of the audit, and appropriate. In determining whether an other auditing publication is appropriate, the auditor may wish to consider the degree to which the publication is recognized as being helpful in understanding and applying the SASs and the degree to which the issuer or author is recognized as an authority in auditing matters. Other auditing

---

[6] Appendixes to SASs referred to in paragraph .05 of this section do not include previously issued appendixes to original pronouncements that when adopted modified other SASs. [Footnote added, effective September 2002, by SAS No. 98. Footnote renumbered by the issuance of SAS No. 105, March 2006. Footnote subsequently renumbered by the issuance of SAS No. 113, November 2006.]

[7] Auditing interpretations of the SASs are included in the codified version of the SASs. AICPA Audit and Accounting Guides and auditing Statements of Position are listed in appendix D. [Footnote renumbered by the issuance of SAS No. 98, September 2002. Footnote subsequently renumbered by the issuance of SAS No. 105, March 2006. Footnote subsequently renumbered by the issuance of SAS No. 113, November 2006.]

[8] The auditor is not expected to be aware of the full body of other auditing publications. [Footnote renumbered by the issuance of SAS No. 98, September 2002. Footnote subsequently renumbered by the issuance of SAS No. 105, March 2006. Footnote subsequently renumbered by the issuance of SAS No. 113, November 2006.]

publications published by the AICPA that have been reviewed by the AICPA Audit and Attest Standards staff are presumed to be appropriate.[9]

Effective Date

.09 This section is effective for audits of financial statements for periods beginning on or after December 15, 2001.

[9] Other auditing publications published by the AICPA that have been reviewed by the AICPA Audit and Attest Standards staff are listed in AU appendix F. [Footnote renumbered by the issuance of SAS No. 98, September 2002. Footnote subsequently renumbered by the issuance of SAS No. 105, March 2006. Footnote subsequently renumbered by the issuance of SAS No. 113, November 2006.]

AU Section 161

The Relationship of Generally Accepted Auditing Standards to Quality Control Standards

(Supersedes SAS No. 4.)[1]

Source: SAS No. 25; SAS No. 98.

Issue date, unless otherwise indicated: November, 1979.

.01 The independent auditor is responsible for compliance with generally accepted auditing standards in an audit engagement. Rule 202 [ET section 202.01] of the Rules of Conduct of the Code of Professional Conduct of the American Institute of Certified Public Accountants requires members to comply with such standards when associated with financial statements.

.02 A firm of independent auditors has a responsibility to adopt a system of quality control in conducting an audit practice.[2] Thus, a firm should establish quality control policies and procedures to provide it with reasonable assurance that its personnel comply with generally accepted auditing standards in its audit engagements. The nature and extent of a firm's quality control policies and procedures depend on factors such as its size, the degree of operating autonomy allowed its personnel and its practice offices, the nature of its practice, its organization, and appropriate cost-benefit considerations. [Revised, April 2002, to reflect conforming changes necessary due to the issuance of Statement on Auditing Standards No. 96. As amended, effective September 2002, by Statement on Auditing Standards No. 98.]

.03 Generally accepted auditing standards relate to the conduct of individual audit engagements; quality control standards relate to the conduct of a firm's audit practice as a whole. Thus, generally accepted auditing standards and quality control standards are related, and the quality control policies and procedures that a firm adopts may affect both the conduct of individual audit engagements and the conduct of a firm's audit practice as a whole. However, deficiencies in or instances of noncompliance with a firm's quality control policies and procedures do not, in and of themselves, indicate that a particular audit engagement was not performed in accordance with generally accepted auditing standards. [As amended, effective September 2002, by Statement on Auditing Standards No. 98.]

---

[1] [Footnote deleted by the issuance of Statement on Auditing Standards No. 98, September 2002.]

[2] The elements of quality control are identified in QC section 10B, *A Firm's System of Quality Control*. A system of quality control consists of policies designed to provide the firm with reasonable assurance that the firm and its personnel comply with professional standards and applicable legal and regulatory requirements and that reports issued by the firm are appropriate in the circumstances, and the procedures necessary to implement and monitor compliance with those policies. [Footnote added, effective September 2002, by SAS No. 98. Footnote amended due to the issuance of SQCS No. 7, December 2008.]

(Supersedes SAS No. 4.)||

|| [Footnote deleted by the issuance of Statement on Auditing Standards No. 98, September 2002.]

AU Section 200
THE GENERAL STANDARDS

TABLE OF CONTENTS

AU Section 201

Nature of the General Standards

Source: SAS No. 1, section 201.

Issue date, unless otherwise indicated: November, 1972.

.01 The general standards are personal in nature and are concerned with the qualifications of the auditor and the quality of his work as distinct from those standards which relate to the performance of his field work and to his reporting. These personal, or general, standards apply alike to the areas of field work and reporting.

AU Section 210

Training and Proficiency of the Independent Auditor

Source: SAS No. 1, section 210; SAS No. 5.

Issue date, unless otherwise indicated: November, 1972.

.01 The first general standard is:

The auditor must have adequate technical training and proficiency to perform the audit.

[Revised, November 2006, to reflect conforming changes necessary due to the issuance of Statement on Auditing Standards No. 113.]

.02 This standard recognizes that however capable a person may be in other fields, including business and finance, he cannot meet the requirements of the auditing standards without proper education and experience in the field of auditing.

.03 In the performance of the audit which leads to an opinion, the independent auditor holds himself out as one who is proficient in accounting and auditing. The attainment of that proficiency begins with the auditor's formal education and extends into his subsequent experience. The independent auditor must undergo training adequate to meet the requirements of a professional. This training must be adequate in technical scope and should include a commensurate measure of general education. The junior assistant, just entering upon an auditing career, must obtain his professional experience with the proper supervision and review of his work by a more experienced superior. The nature and extent of supervision and review must necessarily reflect wide variances in practice. The auditor charged with final responsibility for the engagement must exercise a seasoned judgment in the varying degrees of his supervision and review of the work done and judgment exercised by his subordinates, who in turn must meet the responsibility attaching to the varying gradations and functions of their work.

.04 The independent auditor's formal education and professional experience complement one another; each auditor exercising authority upon an engagement should weigh these attributes in determining the extent of his supervision of subordinates and review of their work. It should be recognized that the training of a professional man includes a continual awareness of developments taking place in business and in his profession. He must study, understand, and apply new pronouncements on accounting principles and auditing procedures as they are developed by authoritative bodies within the accounting profession.

.05 In the course of his day-to-day practice, the independent auditor encounters a wide range of judgment on the part of management, varying from true objective judgment to the occasional extreme of deliberate misstatement. He is retained to audit and report upon the financial statements of a business because, through his training and experience, he has become skilled in accounting and auditing and has acquired the ability to consider objectively and to exercise independent judgment with respect to the information recorded in books of account or otherwise disclosed by his audit. [As amended July, 1975 by Statement on Auditing Standards No. 5.]

AU Section 220

Independence

Source: SAS No. 1, section 220.

Issue date, unless otherwise indicated: November, 1972.

.01 The second general standard is:

> The auditor must maintain independence in mental attitude in all matters relating to the audit.

[Revised, November 2006, to reflect conforming changes necessary due to the issuance of Statement on Auditing Standards No. 113.]

.02 This standard requires that the auditor be independent; aside from being in public practice (as distinct from being in private practice), he must be without bias with respect to the client since otherwise he would lack that impartiality necessary for the dependability of his findings, however excellent his technical proficiency may be. However, independence does not imply the attitude of a prosecutor but rather a judicial impartiality that recognizes an obligation for fairness not only to management and owners of a business but also to creditors and those who may otherwise rely (in part, at least) upon the independent auditor's report, as in the case of prospective owners or creditors.

.03 It is of utmost importance to the profession that the general public maintain confidence in the independence of independent auditors. Public confidence would be impaired by evidence that independence was actually lacking, and it might also be impaired by the existence of circumstances which reasonable people might believe likely to influence independence. To *be* independent, the auditor must be intellectually honest; to be *recognized* as independent, he must be free from any obligation to or interest in the client, its management, or its owners. For example, an independent auditor auditing a company of which he was also a director might be intellectually honest, but it is unlikely that the public would accept him as independent since he would be in effect auditing decisions which he had a part in making. Likewise, an auditor with a substantial financial interest in a company might be unbiased in expressing his opinion on the financial statements of the company, but the public would be reluctant to believe that he was unbiased. Independent auditors should not only be independent in fact; they should avoid situations that may lead outsiders to doubt their independence.

.04 The profession has established, through the AICPA's Code of Professional Conduct, precepts to guard against the *presumption* of loss of independence. "Presumption" is stressed because the possession of intrinsic independence is a matter of personal quality rather than of rules that formulate certain objective tests. Insofar as these precepts have been incorporated in the profession's code, they have the force of professional law for the independent auditor.

.05 The Securities and Exchange Commission (SEC) has also adopted requirements for independence of auditors who report on financial statements filed with it that differ from the AICPA requirements in certain respects.[1]

---

[1] [Footnote deleted, December 2001, to acknowledge the dissolution of the Independence Standard Board.]

.06 The independent auditor should administer his practice within the spirit of these precepts and rules if he is to achieve a proper degree of independence in the conduct of his work.

.07 To emphasize independence from management, many corporations follow the practice of having the independent auditor appointed by the board of directors or elected by the stockholders.

AU Section 230

*Due Professional Care in the Performance of Work**

Source: SAS No. 1, section 230; SAS No. 41; SAS No. 82; SAS No. 99; SAS No. 104.

Issue date, unless otherwise indicated: November, 1972.

.01 The third general standard is:

> The auditor must exercise due professional care in the performance of the audit and the preparation of the report.[1]

[As amended, effective for audits of financial statements for periods ending on or after December 15, 1997, by Statement on Auditing Standards No. 82. Revised, November 2006, to reflect conforming changes necessary due to the issuance of Statement on Auditing Standards No. 113.]

.02 This standard requires the independent auditor to plan and perform his or her work with due professional care. Due professional care imposes a responsibility upon each professional within an independent auditor's organization to observe the standards of field work and reporting. [As amended, effective for audits of financial statements for periods ending on or after December 15, 1997, by Statement on Auditing Standards No. 82.]

.03 *Cooley on Torts*, a legal treatise, describes the obligation for due care as follows:

> Every man who offers his services to another and is employed assumes the duty to exercise in the employment such skill as he possesses with reasonable care and diligence. In all these employments where peculiar skill is requisite, if one offers his services, he is understood as holding himself out to the public as possessing the degree of skill commonly possessed by others in the same employment, and if his pretentions are unfounded, he commits a species of fraud upon every man who employs him in reliance on his public profession. But no man, whether skilled or unskilled, undertakes that the task he assumes shall be performed successfully, and without fault or error; he undertakes for good faith and integrity, but not for infallibility, and he is liable to his employer for negligence, bad faith, or dishonesty, but not for losses consequent upon pure errors of judgment.[2]

---

* [Title amended, effective for audits of financial statements for periods ending on or after December 15, 1997, by Statement on Auditing Standards No. 82.]

[1] This amendment revises the third general standard of the ten generally accepted auditing standards. [Footnote added, effective for audits of financial statements for periods ending on or after December 15, 1997, by Statement on Auditing Standards No. 82.]

[2] D. Haggard, *Cooley on Torts*, 472 (4th ed., 1932). [Footnote added, effective for audits of financial statements for periods ending on or after December 15, 1997, by Statement on Auditing Standards No. 82.]

[As amended, effective for audits of financial statements for periods ending on or after December 15, 1997, by Statement on Auditing Standards No. 82.]

.04 The matter of due professional care concerns what the independent auditor does and how well he or she does it. The quotation from *Cooley on Torts* provides a source from which an auditor's responsibility for conducting an audit with due professional care can be derived. The remainder of the section discusses the auditor's responsibility in the context of an audit. [As amended, April 1982, by Statement on Auditing Standards No. 41. As amended, effective for audits of financial statements for periods ending on or after December 15, 1997, by Statement on Auditing Standards No. 82.]

.05 An auditor should possess "the degree of skill commonly possessed" by other auditors and should exercise it with "reasonable care and diligence" (that is, with due professional care). [Paragraph added, effective for audits of financial statements for periods ending on or after December 15, 1997, by Statement on Auditing Standards No. 82.]

.06 Auditors should be assigned to tasks and supervised commensurate with their level of knowledge, skill, and ability so that they can evaluate the audit evidence they are examining. The auditor with final responsibility for the engagement should know, at a minimum, the relevant professional accounting and auditing standards and should be knowledgeable about the client.[3] The auditor with final responsibility is responsible for the assignment of tasks to, and supervision of, assistants.[4] [Paragraph added, effective for audits of financial statements for periods ending on or after December 15, 1997, by Statement on Auditing Standards No. 82.]

Professional Skepticism

.07 Due professional care requires the auditor to exercise *professional skepticism*. Professional skepticism is an attitude that includes a questioning mind and a critical assessment of audit evidence. The auditor uses the knowledge, skill, and ability called for by the profession of public accounting to diligently perform, in good faith and with integrity, the gathering and objective evaluation of evidence. [Paragraph added, effective for audits of financial statements for periods ending on or after December 15, 1997, by Statement on Auditing Standards No. 82.]

.08 Gathering and objectively evaluating audit evidence requires the auditor to consider the competency and sufficiency of the evidence. Since evidence is gathered and evaluated throughout the audit, professional skepticism should be exercised throughout the audit process. [Paragraph added, effective for audits of financial statements for periods ending on or after December 15, 1997, by Statement on Auditing Standards No. 82.]

.09 The auditor neither assumes that management is dishonest nor assumes unquestioned honesty. In exercising professional skepticism, the auditor should not be satisfied with less than persuasive evidence because of a belief that management is honest. [Paragraph added, effective for audits of financial statements for periods ending on or after December 15, 1997, by Statement on Auditing Standards No. 82.]

---

[3] See section 311, *Planning and Supervision*, paragraph .07. [Footnote added, effective for audits of financial statements for periods ending on or after December 15, 1997, by Statement on Auditing Standards No. 82.]

[4] See section 311.11. [Footnote added, effective for audits of financial statements for periods ending on or after December 15, 1997, by Statement on Auditing Standards No. 82.]

Reasonable Assurance

.10 While exercising due professional care, the auditor must plan and perform the audit to obtain sufficient appropriate audit evidence so that audit risk will be limited to a low level that is, in his or her professional judgment, appropriate for expressing an opinion on the financial statements. The high, but not absolute, level of assurance that is intended to be obtained by the auditor is expressed in the auditor's report as obtaining reasonable assurance about whether the financial statements are free of material misstatement (whether caused by error or fraud). Absolute assurance is not attainable because of the nature of audit evidence and the characteristics of fraud. Therefore, an audit conducted in accordance with generally accepted auditing standards may not detect a material misstatement. [Paragraph added, effective for audits of financial statements for periods ending on or after December 15, 1997, by Statement on Auditing Standards No. 82. As amended, effective for audits of financial statements for periods beginning on or after December 15, 2006, by Statement on Auditing Standards No. 104.]

.11 The independent auditor's objective is to obtain sufficient appropriate audit evidence to provide him or her with a reasonable basis for forming an opinion. The nature of most evidence derives, in part, from the concept of selective testing of the data being audited, which involves judgment regarding both the areas to be tested and the nature, timing, and extent of the tests to be performed. In addition, judgment is required in interpreting the results of audit testing and evaluating audit evidence. Even with good faith and integrity, mistakes and errors in judgment can be made. Furthermore, accounting presentations contain accounting estimates, the measurement of which is inherently uncertain and depends on the outcome of future events. The auditor exercises professional judgment in evaluating the reasonableness of accounting estimates based on information that could reasonably be expected to be available prior to the completion of field work.[5] As a result of these factors, in the great majority of cases, the auditor has to rely on evidence that is persuasive rather than convincing.[6] [Paragraph added, effective for audits of financial statements for periods ending on or after December 15, 1997, by Statement on Auditing Standards No. 82. Revised, March 2008, to reflect conforming changes necessary due to the issuance of Statement on Auditing Standards No. 105.]

.12 Because of the characteristics of fraud, a properly planned and performed audit may not detect a material misstatement. Characteristics of fraud include (*a*) concealment through collusion among management, employees, or third parties; (*b*) withheld, misrepresented, or falsified documentation; and (*c*) the ability of management to override or instruct others to override what otherwise appears to be effective controls. For example, auditing procedures may be ineffective for detecting an intentional misstatement that is concealed through collusion among personnel within the entity and third parties or among management or employees of the entity. Collusion may cause the auditor who has properly performed the audit to conclude that evidence provided is persuasive when it is, in fact, false. In addition, an audit conducted in accordance with generally accepted auditing standards rarely involves authentication of documentation, nor are auditors trained as or expected to be experts in such authentication. Furthermore, an auditor may not discover the existence of a

---

[5] See section 342, *Auditing Accounting Estimates*. [Footnote added, effective for audits of financial statements for periods ending on or after December 15, 1997, by Statement on Auditing Standards No. 82.]

[6] See AU section 326, *Audit Evidence*. [Footnote added, effective for audits of financial statements for periods ending on or after December 15, 1997, by Statement on Auditing Standards No. 82.]

modification of documentation through a side agreement that management or a third party has not disclosed. Finally, management has the ability to directly or indirectly manipulate accounting records and present fraudulent financial information by overriding controls in unpredictable ways. [Paragraph added, effective for audits of financial statements for periods ending on or after December 15, 1997, by Statement on Auditing Standards No. 82. As amended, effective for audits of financial statements for periods beginning on or after December 15, 2002, by Statement on Auditing Standards No. 99.]

.13 Since the auditor's opinion on the financial statements is based on the concept of obtaining reasonable assurance, the auditor is not an insurer and his or her report does not constitute a guarantee. Therefore, the subsequent discovery that a material misstatement, whether from error or fraud, exists in the financial statements does not, in and of itself, evidence (*a*) failure to obtain reasonable assurance, (*b*) inadequate planning, performance, or judgment, (*c*) the absence of due professional care, or (*d*) a failure to comply with generally accepted auditing standards. [Paragraph added, effective for audits of financial statements for periods ending on or after December 15, 1997, by Statement on Auditing Standards No. 82.]

AU Section 300

THE STANDARDS OF FIELD WORK

TABLE OF CONTENTS

AU Section 311
Planning and Supervision

(Supersedes SAS No. 22)

Source: SAS No. 108; SAS No. 114.

See section 9311 for interpretations of this section.

Effective for audits of financial statements for periods beginning on or after December 15, 2006. Earlier application is permitted.

.01 The first standard of field work states, "The auditor must adequately plan the work and must properly supervise any assistants." This section establishes standards and provides guidance to the independent auditor conducting an audit in accordance with generally accepted auditing standards on the considerations and activities applicable to planning and supervision. Planning and supervision continue throughout the audit.

.02 Audit planning involves developing an overall audit strategy for the expected conduct, organization, and staffing of the audit. The nature, timing, and extent of planning vary with the size and complexity of the entity, and with the auditor's experience with the entity and understanding of the entity and its environment, including its internal control.

.03 Obtaining an understanding of the entity and its environment, including its internal control, is an essential part of planning and performing an audit in accordance with generally accepted auditing standards.[1] The auditor must plan the audit so that it is responsive to the assessment of the risk of material misstatement based on the auditor's understanding of the entity and its environment, including its internal control. Planning is not a discrete phase of the audit, but rather an iterative process that begins with engagement acceptance and continues throughout the audit as the auditor performs audit procedures and accumulates sufficient appropriate audit evidence to support the audit opinion. As a result of performing planned audit procedures,[2] the auditor may obtain disconfirming evidence that might cause the auditor to revise the overall audit strategy.

---

[1] Section 314, *Understanding the Entity and Its Environment and Assessing the Risks of Material Misstatement*, establishes standards and provides guidance on obtaining an understanding of the entity and its environment, including its internal control, sufficient to assess the risks of material misstatement, whether due to error or fraud, at the financial statement and relevant assertion levels. Section 318, *Performing Audit Procedures in Response to Assessed Risks and Evaluating the Audit Evidence Obtained*, establishes standards and provides guidance on the auditor's overall responses and the nature, timing, and extent of further audit procedures that are responsive to the assessed risks.

[2] Paragraph .03 of section 314 provides guidance with respect to the procedures the auditor performs in obtaining an understanding of the entity and its environment to establish a frame of reference within which the auditor plans the audit and exercises professional judgment about assessing the risk of material misstatement of the financial statements.

.04 The auditor with final responsibility for the audit may delegate portions of the planning and supervision of the audit to other firm personnel.[3] For purposes of this section, (*a*) firm personnel other than the auditor with final responsibility for the audit are referred to as *assistants* and (*b*) the term *auditor* refers to either the auditor with final responsibility for the audit or assistants.

Planning

Appointment of the Independent Auditor

.05 Early appointment of the independent auditor has many advantages to both the auditor and the client. Early appointment enables the auditor to plan the audit prior to the balance-sheet date.

.06 Although early appointment is preferable, an independent auditor may accept an engagement near or after the close of the fiscal year. In such instances, before accepting the engagement, the auditor should ascertain whether circumstances are likely to permit an adequate audit and expression of an unqualified opinion and, if they will not, the auditor should discuss with the client the possible necessity for a qualified opinion or disclaimer of opinion. Sometimes the audit limitations present in such circumstances can be remedied. For example, the taking of the physical inventory can be postponed or another physical inventory, which the auditor can observe, can be taken.

.07 Section 315, *Communications Between Predecessor and Successor Auditors*, provides guidance concerning a change of auditors. Among other matters, it describes communications that a successor auditor should evaluate before accepting an engagement.

Establishing an Understanding With the Client

.08 The auditor should establish an understanding with the client[4] regarding the services to be performed for each engagement[5] and should document the understanding through a written communication with the client. Such an understanding reduces the risk that either the auditor or the client may misinterpret the needs or expectations of the other party. For example, it reduces the risk that the client may inappropriately rely on the auditor to protect the entity against certain risks or to perform certain functions that are the client's responsibility. The understanding should include the objectives of

---

[3] Paragraphs .14 through .20 of section 314 provide guidance about the discussion among the audit team. The objective of this discussion is for members of the audit team to gain a better understanding of the potential for material misstatements of the financial statements resulting from fraud or error in the specific areas assigned to them, and to understand how the results of the audit procedures that they perform may affect other aspects of the audit, including the decisions about the nature, timing, and extent of further audit procedures.

[4] Generally, the auditor establishes an understanding of the services to be performed with the entity's management. In some cases, the auditor may establish such an understanding with those charged with governance. The term *those charged with governance* means the person(s) with responsibility for overseeing the strategic direction of the entity and obligations related to the accountability of the entity. This includes overseeing the financial reporting and disclosure process. In some cases, those charged with governance are responsible for approving the financial statements (in other cases, management has this responsibility). For entities with a board of directors, this term encompasses the term *board of directors* or *audit committees* expressed elsewhere in generally accepted auditing standards.

[5] See paragraph .28 of QC section 10B, *A Firm's System of Quality Control*. [Footnote amended due to the issuance of SQCS No. 7, December 2008.]

the engagement, management's responsibilities, the auditor's responsibilities, and limitations of the engagement.[6]

.09 An understanding with the client regarding an audit of the financial statements generally includes the following matters:

- The objective of the audit is the expression of an opinion on the financial statements.
- Management is responsible for the entity's financial statements and the selection and application of the accounting policies.
- Management is responsible for establishing and maintaining effective internal control over financial reporting.
- Management is responsible for designing and implementing programs and controls to prevent and detect fraud.
- Management is responsible for identifying and ensuring that the entity complies with the laws and regulations applicable to its activities.
- Management is responsible for making all financial records and related information available to the auditor.
- At the conclusion of the engagement, management will provide the auditor with a letter that confirms certain representations made during the audit.
- The auditor is responsible for conducting the audit in accordance with generally accepted auditing standards. Those standards require that the auditor obtain reasonable rather than absolute assurance about whether the financial statements are free of material misstatement, whether caused by error or fraud. Accordingly, a material misstatement may remain undetected. Also, an audit is not designed to detect error or fraud that is immaterial to the financial statements. If, for any reason, the auditor is unable to complete the audit or is unable to form or has not formed an opinion, he or she may decline to express an opinion or decline to issue a report as a result of the engagement.
- An audit includes obtaining an understanding of the entity and its environment, including its internal control, sufficient to assess the risks of material misstatement of the financial statements and to design the nature, timing, and extent of further audit procedures. An audit is not designed to provide assurance on internal control or to identify significant deficiencies. However, the auditor is responsible for ensuring that those charged with governance are aware of any significant deficiencies that come to his or her attention.
- Management is responsible for adjusting the financial statements to correct material misstatements and for affirming to the auditor in the

---

[6] The objectives of certain engagements may differ. The understanding should reflect the effects of those objectives on the responsibilities of management and the auditor, and on the limitations of the engagement. The following are examples:

- Audits of an entity's compliance with applicable compliance requirements performed under section 801, *Compliance Audits*.
- Application of agreed-upon procedures to specified elements, accounts, or items of a financial statement (see AT section 201, *Agreed-Upon Procedures Engagements*).
- Engagements to examine the design and operating effectiveness of an entity's internal control over financial reporting that is integrated with an audit of the entity's financial statements (see AT section 501, *An Examination of an Entity's Internal Control Over Financial Reporting That Is Integrated With an Audit of Its Financial Statements*).

[Footnote revised, December 2010, to reflect conforming changes necessary due to the issuance of SAS No. 117.]

management representation letter that the effects of any uncorrected misstatements[7] aggregated by the auditor during the current engagement and pertaining to the latest period presented are immaterial, both individually and in the aggregate, to the financial statements taken as a whole.

These matters should be communicated in the form of an engagement letter.

.10 An understanding with the client also may include other matters, such as the following:

- The overall audit strategy (see paragraphs .13 through .18)
- Involvement of specialists or internal auditors, if applicable
- Involvement of a predecessor auditor
- Fees and billing
- Any limitation of or other arrangements regarding the liability of the auditor or the client, such as indemnification to the auditor for liability arising from knowing misrepresentations to the auditor by management (regulators may restrict or prohibit such liability limitation arrangements)
- Conditions under which access to audit documentation may be granted to others
- Additional services to be provided relating to regulatory requirements
- Other services to be provided in connection with the engagement, for example, nonattest services, such as accounting assistance and preparation of tax returns subject to the limitations of Ethics Interpretation No. 101–3, "Performance of Nonattest Services," [ET section 101.05], under Rule 101, *Independence*.

Preliminary Engagement Activities

.11 In addition to the procedures related to the appointment of the auditor and establishing an understanding of the terms of the engagement as discussed above, the auditor should perform the following activities at the beginning of the current audit engagement:

- Perform procedures regarding the continuance of the client relationship and the specific audit engagement.
- Evaluate the auditor's compliance with ethical requirements, including independence.

The auditor's consideration of client continuance and ethical requirements, including independence, occurs throughout the performance of the audit engagement as changes in conditions and circumstances occur. However, the auditor's initial procedures on both client continuance and evaluation of the auditor's ethical requirements (including independence) should be performed prior to performing other significant activities for the current audit engagement. For continuing audit engagements, such initial procedures often occur shortly after (or in connection with) the completion of the previous audit. See QC section 10B, *A Firm's System of Quality Control*. [Paragraph amended due to the issuance of SQCS No. 7, December 2008.]

.12 The purpose of performing these preliminary engagement activities is to consider any events or circumstances that may either adversely affect

---

[7] Paragraph .07 of section 312, *Audit Risk and Materiality in Conducting an Audit*, states that a misstatement can result from errors or fraud.

the auditor's ability to plan and perform the audit engagement to reduce audit risk to an acceptably low level or may pose an unacceptable level of risk to the auditor. Performing these preliminary engagement activities helps ensure that the auditor plans an audit engagement for which:

- The auditor maintains the necessary independence and ability to perform the engagement.
- There are no issues with management integrity that may affect the auditor's willingness to continue the engagement.
- There is no misunderstanding with the client as to the terms of the engagement.

The Overall Audit Strategy[8]

.13 The auditor should establish the overall audit strategy for the audit.

.14 In establishing the overall audit strategy, the auditor should:

a. Determine the characteristics of the engagement that define its scope, such as the basis of reporting, industry-specific reporting requirements, and the locations of the entity;

b. Ascertain the reporting objectives of the engagement to plan the timing of the audit and the nature of the communications required, such as deadlines for interim and final reporting, and key dates for expected communications with management and those charged with governance; and

c. Consider the important factors that will determine the focus of the audit team's efforts, such as determination of appropriate materiality levels, preliminary identification of areas where there may be higher risks of material misstatement, preliminary identification of material locations and account balances, evaluation of whether the auditor may plan to obtain evidence regarding the operating effectiveness of internal control, and identification of recent significant entity-specific, industry, financial reporting, or other relevant developments.

In developing the audit strategy, the auditor also should consider the results of preliminary engagement activities (see paragraphs .11 and .12) and, where practicable, experience gained on other engagements performed for the entity. The Appendix [paragraph .34] to this section lists examples of matters the auditor may consider in establishing the overall audit strategy for an engagement.

.15 The process of developing the audit strategy helps the auditor determine the resources necessary to perform the engagement, such as:

- The resources to assign for specific audit areas, such as the use of appropriately experienced team members for high-risk areas or the involvement of experts on complex matters;
- The amount of resources to assign to specific audit areas, such as the number of team members assigned to observe the inventory count at material locations, the extent of review of other auditors' work, or the audit budget in hours to allocate to high-risk areas;
- When these resources are to be assigned, such as whether at an interim audit period or at key cutoff dates;

---

[8] See paragraphs .04 through .06 of section 318 for further guidance on the auditor's overall responses in performing an audit.

- How such resources are to be managed, directed, and supervised, such as when team briefing and debriefing meetings are expected to be held, how the auditor with final responsibility and manager reviews are expected to take place (for example, on-site or off-site), and whether to complete engagement quality control reviews.

.16 The auditor should update and document any significant revisions to the overall audit strategy to respond to changes in circumstances.

.17 Once the audit strategy has been established, the auditor is able to start the development of a more detailed audit plan to address the various matters identified in the audit strategy, taking into account the need to achieve the audit objectives through the efficient use of the auditor's resources. Although the auditor may establish the audit strategy before developing the detailed audit plan, the two planning activities are not necessarily discrete or sequential processes but are closely interrelated since changes in one may result in consequential changes to the other. Paragraphs .19 through .21 provide further guidance on developing the audit plan.

.18 In audits of small entities, the entire audit may be conducted by a very small audit team. Many audits of small entities involve the auditor with final responsibility (who may be a sole practitioner) working with one audit team member (or without any audit team members). With a smaller team, coordination and communication between team members are easier. Establishing the overall audit strategy for the audit of a small entity need not be a complex or time-consuming exercise; it varies according to the size of the entity and the complexity of the audit. For example, a brief memorandum prepared at the completion of the previous audit, based on a review of the audit documentation and highlighting issues identified in the audit just completed, updated, and changed in the current period based on discussions with the owner-manager, can serve as the basis for planning the current audit engagement.

The Audit Plan

.19 The auditor must develop an audit plan in which the auditor documents the audit procedures to be used that, when performed, are expected to reduce audit risk to an acceptably low level.

.20 The audit plan is more detailed than the audit strategy and includes the nature, timing, and extent of audit procedures to be performed by audit team members in order to obtain sufficient appropriate audit evidence to reduce audit risk to an acceptably low level. Documentation of the audit plan also serves as a record of the proper planning and performance of the audit procedures that can be reviewed and approved prior to the performance of further audit procedures.

.21 The audit plan should include:

- A description of the nature, timing, and extent of planned risk assessment procedures sufficient to assess the risks of material misstatement, as determined under section 314, *Understanding the Entity and Its Environment and Assessing the Risks of Material Misstatement*.
- A description of the nature, timing, and extent of planned further audit procedures at the relevant assertion level for each material class of transactions, account balance, and disclosure, as determined under section 318, *Performing Audit Procedures in Response to Assessed Risks and Evaluating the Audit Evidence Obtained*. The plan for further audit procedures reflects the auditor's decision whether to test the operating effectiveness of controls, and the nature, timing, and extent of planned substantive procedures.

- A description of other audit procedures to be carried out for the engagement in order to comply with generally accepted auditing standards (for example, seeking direct communication with the entity's lawyers).

Planning for these audit procedures takes place over the course of the audit as the audit plan for the engagement develops. For example, planning of the auditor's risk assessment procedures may occur early in the audit process. However, planning of the nature, timing, and extent of specific further audit procedures depends on the outcome of those risk assessment procedures. The auditor should document changes to the original audit plan. In addition, the auditor may begin the execution of further audit procedures for some classes of transactions, account balances, and disclosures before completing the more detailed audit plan of all remaining further audit procedures.

Determining the Extent of Involvement of Professionals Possessing Specialized Skills

.22 The auditor should consider whether specialized skills are needed in performing the audit. If specialized skills are needed, the auditor should seek the assistance of a professional possessing such skills, who may be either on the auditor's staff or an outside professional. If the use of such a professional is planned, the auditor should determine whether that professional will effectively function as a member of the audit team. For example, a tax practitioner or a professional with valuation skills employed by the audit firm may be used to perform audit procedures as part of the audit team's work on the audit. If such a professional is part of the audit team, the auditor's responsibilities for supervising that professional are equivalent to those for other assistants (see paragraph .28). In such circumstances, the auditor should have sufficient knowledge to communicate the objectives of the other professional's work; to evaluate whether the specified audit procedures will meet the auditor's objectives; and to evaluate the results of the audit procedures applied as they relate to the nature, timing, and extent of further planned audit procedures.

.23 The use of professionals possessing information technology (IT) skills to determine the effect of IT on the audit, to understand the IT controls, or to design and perform tests of IT controls or substantive procedures is a significant aspect of many audit engagements. In determining whether such a professional is needed on the audit team, the auditor should consider such factors as the following:

- The complexity of the entity's systems and IT controls and the manner in which they are used in conducting the entity's business
- The significance of changes made to existing systems, or the implementation of new systems
- The extent to which data is shared among systems
- The extent of the entity's participation in electronic commerce
- The entity's use of emerging technologies
- The significance of audit evidence that is available only in electronic form

.24 Audit procedures that the auditor may assign to a professional possessing IT skills include inquiring of an entity's IT personnel how data and transactions are initiated, authorized, recorded, processed, and reported and how IT controls are designed; inspecting systems documentation; observing the operation of IT controls; and planning and performing tests of IT controls.

Communication With Those Charged With Governance

.25 Section 380, *The Auditor's Communication With Those Charged With Governance*, requires the auditor to communicate with those charged with governance an overview of the planned scope and timing of the audit. [As amended, effective for audits of financial statements for periods beginning on or after December 15, 2006, by Statement on Auditing Standards No. 114.]

Additional Considerations in Initial Audit Engagements

.26 The auditor should perform the following activities before starting an initial audit:

a. Perform procedures regarding the acceptance of the client relationship and the specific audit engagement (see QC section 10B).

b. Communicate with the previous auditor, where there has been a change of auditors (see section 315)

[Paragraph amended due to the issuance of SQCS No. 7, December 2008.]

.27 The purpose and objective of planning the audit are the same whether the audit is an initial or recurring engagement. However, for an initial audit, the auditor may need to expand the planning activities because the auditor does not ordinarily have the previous experience with the entity that is considered when planning recurring engagements. For initial audits, additional matters the auditor should consider in developing the overall audit strategy and audit plan include the following:

- Arrangements to be made with the previous auditor, for example, to review the previous auditor's audit documentation.
- Any major issues (including the application of accounting principles or of auditing and reporting standards) discussed with management in connection with the initial selection as auditors, the communication of these matters to those charged with governance, and how these matters affect the overall audit strategy and audit plan.
- The planned audit procedures to obtain sufficient appropriate audit evidence regarding opening balances.
- The assignment of firm personnel with appropriate levels of capabilities and competence to respond to anticipated significant risks.
- Other procedures required by the firm's system of quality control for initial audit engagements (for example, the firm's system of quality control may require the involvement of another partner or senior individual to review the overall audit strategy prior to commencing significant audit procedures or to review reports prior to their issuance).

Supervision

.28 Supervision involves directing the efforts of assistants who are involved in accomplishing the objectives of the audit and determining whether those objectives were accomplished. Elements of supervision include instructing assistants, keeping informed of significant issues encountered, reviewing the work performed, and dealing with differences of opinion among firm personnel. The extent of supervision appropriate in a given instance depends on many factors, including the complexity of the subject matter and the qualifications of persons performing the work, including knowledge of the client's business and industry.

.29 The auditor with final responsibility for the audit should communicate with members of the audit team regarding the susceptibility of the entity's financial statements to material misstatement due to error or fraud, with special emphasis on fraud. Such discussion helps all audit team members understand the entity and its environment, including its internal control, and how risks that the entity faces may affect the audit. The discussion should emphasize the need to maintain a questioning mind and to exercise professional skepticism in gathering and evaluating evidence throughout the audit.[9]

.30 In addition, assistants should be informed of their responsibilities and the objectives of the audit procedures they are to perform. They should be informed of matters that may affect the nature, timing, and extent of audit procedures they are to perform, such as the nature of the entity's business as it relates to their assignments and possible accounting and auditing issues. The auditor with final responsibility for the audit should direct assistants to bring to his or her attention accounting and auditing issues raised during the audit that the assistant believes are of significance to the financial statements or auditor's report so the auditor with final responsibility may assess their significance. Assistants also should be directed to bring to the attention of appropriate individuals in the firm difficulties encountered in performing the audit, such as missing documents or resistance from client personnel in providing access to information or in responding to inquiries.

.31 The work performed by each assistant, including the audit documentation, should be reviewed to determine whether it was adequately performed and documented and to evaluate the results, relative to the conclusions to be presented in the auditor's report. The person with final responsibility for the audit may delegate parts of the review responsibility to other assistants, in accordance with the firm's quality control system. See section 339, *Audit Documentation*, for guidance on documenting the review of audit documentation.

.32 Each assistant has a professional responsibility to bring to the attention of appropriate individuals in the firm disagreements or concerns with respect to accounting and auditing issues that the assistant believes are of significance to the financial statements or auditor's report, however those disagreements or concerns may have arisen. The auditor with final responsibility for the audit and assistants should be aware of the procedures to be followed when differences of opinion concerning accounting and auditing issues exist among firm personnel involved in the audit. Such procedures should enable an assistant to document his or her disagreement with the conclusions reached if, after appropriate consultation, he or she believes it necessary to disassociate himself or herself from the resolution of the matter. In this situation, the basis for the final resolution should also be documented.

Effective Date

.33 This section is effective for audits of financial statements for periods beginning on or after December 15, 2006. Earlier application is permitted.

---

[9] For further guidance on the discussion among the audit team, see paragraphs .14 through .18 of section 316, *Consideration of Fraud in a Financial Statement Audit*, and paragraphs .14 through .20 of section 314.

.34

Appendix

Examples of Matters the Auditor May Consider in Establishing the Overall Audit Strategy

A1. This appendix provides examples of matters the auditor may consider in establishing the overall audit strategy. Many of these matters will also influence the auditor's detailed audit plan. The examples provided cover a broad range of matters applicable to many engagements. Not all matters listed here are relevant to every audit engagement and the list is not necessarily complete. In addition, the auditor may consider these matters in an order different from that shown below.

Scope of the Audit Engagement

A2. The auditor may consider the following matters when establishing the scope of the audit engagement:

- The basis of reporting on which the financial information to be audited has been prepared, including any need for reconciliations to another basis of reporting.
- Industry-specific reporting requirements, such as reports mandated by industry regulators.
- The expected audit coverage, including the number and locations to be included.
- The nature of the control relationships between a parent and its subsidiaries that determine how the group is to be consolidated.
- The extent to which locations are audited by other auditors.
- The nature of the subsidiaries or divisions to be audited, including the need for specialized knowledge.
- The reporting currency to be used, including any need for currency translation for the financial information audited.
- The need for statutory or regulatory audit requirements, for example, the Office of Management and Budget (OMB) Circular A-133, *Audits of States, Local Governments, and Non-Profit Organization*.
- The availability of the work of internal auditors and the extent of the auditor's potential reliance on such work.
- The entity's use of service organizations and how the auditor may obtain evidence concerning the design or operation of controls performed by them.
- The expected use of audit evidence obtained in prior audits, for example, audit evidence related to risk assessment procedures and tests of controls.
- The effect of information technology on the audit procedures, including the availability of data and the expected use of computer-assisted audit techniques.

- The coordination of the expected coverage and timing of the audit work with any reviews of interim financial information and the effect on the audit of the information obtained during such reviews.
- The discussion of matters that may affect the audit with firm personnel responsible for performing other services to the entity.
- The availability of client personnel and data.

Reporting Objectives, Timing of the Audit, and Communications Required

A3. The auditor may consider the following matters when ascertaining the reporting objectives of the engagement, the timing of the audit, and the nature of communications required:

- The entity's timetable for reporting, including interim periods.
- The organization of meetings with management and those charged with governance to discuss the nature, extent, and timing of the audit work.
- The discussion with management and those charged with governance regarding the expected type and timing of reports to be issued and other communications, both written and oral, including the auditor's report, management letters, and communications to those charged with governance.
- The discussion with management regarding the expected communications on the status of audit work throughout the engagement and the expected deliverables resulting from the audit procedures.
- Communication with auditors of other locations regarding the expected types and timing of reports to be issued and other communications in connection with the audit of other locations.
- The expected nature and timing of communications among audit team members, including the nature and timing of team meetings and timing of the review of work performed.
- Whether there are any other expected communications with third parties, including any statutory or contractual reporting responsibilities arising from the audit.

Scope of the Audit

A4. The auditor may consider the following matters when setting the scope of the audit:

- With respect to materiality:
  - Setting materiality for planning purposes.
  - Setting and communicating materiality for auditors of other locations.
  - Reconsidering materiality as audit procedures are performed during the course of the audit.
  - Identifying the material locations and account balances.
- Audit areas where there is a higher risk of material misstatement.
- The effect of the assessed risk of material misstatement at the overall financial statement level on scope, supervision, and review.

- The selection of the audit team (including, where necessary, the engagement quality control reviewer) and the assignment of audit work to the team members, including the assignment of appropriately experienced team members to areas where there may be higher risks of material misstatement.
- Engagement budgeting, including considering the appropriate amount of time to set aside for areas where there may be higher risks of material misstatement.
- The manner in which the auditor emphasizes to audit team members the need to maintain a questioning mind and to exercise professional skepticism in gathering and evaluating audit evidence.
- Results of previous audits that involved evaluating the operating effectiveness of internal control, including the nature of identified weaknesses and action taken to address them.
- Management's commitment to the design and operation of internal control.
- Volume of transactions, which may be a factor in determining whether it is more effective for the auditor to rely on internal control.
- Importance attached to internal control throughout the entity to the successful operation of the business.
- Significant business developments affecting the entity, including changes in information technology and business processes; changes in key management; and acquisitions, mergers, and divestments.
- Significant industry developments, such as changes in industry regulations and new reporting requirements.
- Significant accounting changes, such as changes in generally accepted accounting principles.
- Other significant relevant developments, such as changes in the legal environment affecting the entity.

AU Section 9311

Planning and Supervision: Auditing Interpretations of Section 311

1. Communications Between the Auditor and Firm Personnel Responsible for Non-Audit Services

.01 *Question*—Section 311, *Planning and Supervision*, Appendix A, paragraph A2. [section 311.34], lists the following procedure that an auditor may consider in planning an audit: "Discussing matters that may affect the audit with firm personnel responsible for non-audit services to the entity."

.02 What specific things should the auditor consider in performing this procedure?

.03 *Interpretation*—The auditor should consider the nature of non-audit services that have been performed. He should assess whether the services involve matters that might be expected to affect the entity's financial statements or the performance of the audit, for example, tax planning or recommendations on a cost accounting system. If the auditor decides that the performance of the non-audit services or the information likely to have been gained from it may have implications for his audit, he should discuss the matter with personnel who rendered the services and consider how the expected conduct and scope of his audit may be affected. In some cases, the auditor may find it useful to review the pertinent portions of the work papers prepared for the non-audit engagement as an aid in determining the nature of the services rendered or the possible audit implications.

[Issue Date: February, 1980; Revised: March, 2006.]

[2.] Planning Considerations for an Audit of a Federally Assisted Program

[.04–.34] [Withdrawn March 1989.]

[3.] Responsibility of Assistants for the Resolution of Accounting and Auditing Issues

[.35–.37] [Deleted March 2006.]

[4.] Audit Considerations for the Year 2000 Issue

[.38–.47] [Withdrawn July 2000 by the Audit Issues Task Force.]

AU Section 312

Audit Risk and Materiality in Conducting an Audit

(Supersedes SAS No. 47.)

Source: SAS No. 107.

See section 9312 for interpretations of this section.

Effective for audits of financial statements for periods beginning on or after December 15, 2006. Earlier application is permitted.

.01 This section provides guidance on the auditor's consideration of audit risk and materiality when performing an audit of financial statements in accordance with generally accepted auditing standards. Audit risk and materiality affect the application of generally accepted auditing standards, especially the standards of fieldwork and reporting, and are reflected in the auditor's standard report. Audit risk and materiality, among other matters, need to be considered together in designing the nature, timing, and extent of audit procedures and in evaluating the results of those procedures.

.02 The existence of audit risk is recognized in the description of the responsibilities and functions of the independent auditor that states, "Because of the nature of audit evidence and the characteristics of fraud, the auditor is able to obtain reasonable, but not absolute, assurance that material misstatements are detected."[1] Audit risk[2] is the risk that the auditor may unknowingly fail to appropriately modify his or her opinion on financial statements that are materially misstated.[3]

.03 The concept of materiality recognizes that some matters, either individually or in the aggregate, are important for fair presentation of financial statements in conformity with generally accepted accounting principles,[4] while other matters are not important. In performing the audit, the auditor is

---

[1] See section 110, *Responsibilities and Functions of the Independent Auditor* and section 230, *Due Professional Care in the Performance of Work*, for a further discussion of reasonable assurance.

[2] In addition to audit risk, the auditor is also exposed to loss of or injury to his or her professional practice from litigation, adverse publicity, or other events arising in connection with financial statements audited and reported on. This exposure is present even though the auditor has performed the audit in accordance with generally accepted auditing standards and has reported appropriately on those financial statements. Even if an auditor assesses this exposure as low, the auditor does not perform less extensive audit procedures than otherwise is appropriate under generally accepted auditing standards.

[3] This definition of *audit risk* does not include the risk that the auditor might erroneously conclude that the financial statements are materially misstated. In such a situation, the auditor ordinarily reconsiders or extends audit procedures and requests that management perform specific tasks to reevaluate the appropriateness of the financial statements. These steps ordinarily lead the auditor to the correct conclusion. This definition also excludes the risk of an inappropriate reporting decision unrelated to the detection and evaluation of a misstatement in the financial statements, such as an inappropriate decision regarding the form of the auditor's report because of a limitation on the scope of the audit.

[4] The concepts of audit risk and materiality also are applicable to financial statements presented in conformity with a comprehensive basis of accounting other than generally accepted accounting principles as defined in section 623, *Special Reports*. References in this section to financial statements presented in conformity with generally accepted accounting principles also include those presentations.

concerned with matters that, either individually or in the aggregate, could be material to the financial statements. The auditor's responsibility is to plan and perform the audit to obtain reasonable assurance that material misstatements, whether caused by errors or fraud, are detected.

Materiality in the Context of an Audit

.04 The auditor's consideration of materiality is a matter of professional judgment and is influenced by the auditor's perception of the needs of users of financial statements. The perceived needs of users are recognized in the discussion of materiality in Financial Accounting Standards Board (FASB) Statement of Financial Accounting Concepts No. 2, *Qualitative Characteristics of Accounting Information*, which defines *materiality* as "the magnitude of an omission or misstatement of accounting information that, in the light of surrounding circumstances, makes it probable that the judgment of a reasonable person relying on the information would have been changed or influenced by the omission or misstatement." That discussion recognizes that materiality judgments are made in light of surrounding circumstances and necessarily involve both quantitative and qualitative considerations.[5]

Users

.05 In an audit of financial statements, the auditor's judgment as to matters that are material to users of financial statements is based on consideration of the needs of users as a group; the auditor does not consider the possible effect of misstatements on specific individual users, whose needs may vary widely.[6]

.06 The evaluation of whether a misstatement could influence economic decisions of users, and therefore be material, involves consideration of the characteristics of those users. Users are assumed to:

a. Have an appropriate knowledge of business and economic activities and accounting and a willingness to study the information in the financial statements with an appropriate diligence;

b. Understand that financial statements are prepared and audited to levels of materiality;

c. Recognize the uncertainties inherent in the measurement of amounts based on the use of estimates, judgment, and the consideration of future events; and

d. Make appropriate economic decisions on the basis of the information in the financial statements.

The determination of materiality, therefore, takes into account how users with such characteristics could reasonably be expected to be influenced in making economic decisions.

Nature and Causes of Misstatements

.07 The representation in the auditor's standard report regarding fair presentation, in all material respects, in conformity with generally accepted accounting principles indicates the auditor's belief that the financial statements,

---

[5] See paragraphs .59 and .60 for further guidance regarding qualitative considerations in evaluating audit findings.

[6] When determining materiality in audits of financial statements or other historical financial information prepared for a special purpose, the auditor considers the needs of specific users in the context of the objective of the engagement.

taken as a whole, are not materially misstated. Misstatements can result from errors or fraud[7] and may consist of any of the following:

a. An inaccuracy in gathering or processing data from which financial statements are prepared

b. A difference between the amount, classification, or presentation of a reported financial statement element, account, or item and the amount, classification, or presentation that would have been reported under generally accepted accounting principles

c. The omission of a financial statement element, account, or item

d. A financial statement disclosure that is not presented in conformity with generally accepted accounting principles

e. The omission of information required to be disclosed in conformity with generally accepted accounting principles

f. An incorrect accounting estimate arising, for example, from an oversight or misinterpretation of facts; and

g. Management's judgments concerning an accounting estimate or the selection or application of accounting policies that the auditor may consider unreasonable or inappropriate.

.08 Misstatements may be of two types: known and likely, defined as follows:

a. *Known misstatements.* These are specific misstatements identified during the audit arising from the incorrect selection or misapplication of accounting principles or misstatements of facts identified, including, for example, those arising from mistakes in gathering or processing data and the overlooking or misinterpretation of facts.

b. *Likely misstatements.* These are misstatements that:

i. Arise from differences between management's and the auditor's judgments concerning accounting estimates that the auditor considers unreasonable or inappropriate (for example, because an estimate included in the financial statements by management is outside of the range of reasonable outcomes the auditor has determined).

ii. The auditor considers likely to exist based on an extrapolation from audit evidence obtained (for example, the amount obtained by projecting known misstatements identified in an audit sample[8] to the entire population from which the sample was drawn).

.09 The term *errors* refers to unintentional misstatements of amounts or disclosures in financial statements. The term *fraud* refers to an intentional act by one or more individuals among management, those charged with governance, employees, or third parties, involving the use of deception to obtain an unjust or illegal advantage. Two types of misstatements resulting from fraud are relevant to the auditor's consideration in a financial statement audit: misstatements arising from fraudulent financial reporting and misstatements arising

---

[7] The auditor's consideration of illegal acts and responsibility for detecting misstatements resulting from illegal acts are defined in section 317, *Illegal Acts by Clients*. For those illegal acts that are defined in that section as having a direct and material effect on the determination of financial statement amounts, the auditor's responsibility to detect misstatements resulting from such illegal acts is the same as that for errors or fraud.

[8] Audit sample includes statistical and nonstatistical sample. See section 350, *Audit Sampling*.

from misappropriation of assets. These two types of misstatements are further described in section 316, *Consideration of Fraud in a Financial Statement Audit*.

.10 Although the auditor has no responsibility to plan and perform the audit to detect immaterial misstatements, there is a distinction in the auditor's response to detected misstatements depending on whether those misstatements are caused by error or fraud. When the auditor encounters evidence of potential fraud, regardless of its materiality, the auditor should consider the implications for the integrity of management or employees and the possible effect on other aspects of the audit.

Considerations at the Financial Statement Level

.11 The auditor must consider audit risk and must determine a materiality level for the financial statements taken as a whole for the purpose of:

a. Determining the extent and nature of risk assessment procedures

b. Identifying and assessing the risks of material misstatement

c. Determining the nature, timing, and extent of further audit procedures

d. Evaluating whether the financial statements taken as a whole are presented fairly, in all material respects, in conformity with generally accepted accounting principles

.12 Audit risk is a function of the risk that the financial statements prepared by management are materially misstated and the risk that the auditor will not detect such material misstatement. The auditor should consider audit risk in relation to the relevant assertions related to individual account balances, classes of transactions, and disclosures and at the overall financial statement level. The auditor should perform risk assessment procedures to assess the risks of material misstatement both at the financial statement and the relevant assertion levels.[9] The auditor may reduce audit risk by determining overall responses and designing the nature, timing, and extent of further audit procedures based on those assessments.[10]

.13 The auditor should perform the audit to reduce audit risk to a low level that is, in the auditor's professional judgment, appropriate for expressing an opinion on the financial statements. As discussed in paragraph .20, audit risk may be assessed in quantitative or nonquantitative terms.

.14 The considerations of audit risk and materiality are affected by the size and complexity of the entity and the auditor's experience with and knowledge of the entity and its environment, including its internal control. As discussed in paragraphs .17 through .26, certain entity-related factors also affect the nature, timing, and extent of further audit procedures with respect to relevant assertions related to specific account balances, classes of transactions, and disclosures.

.15 In considering audit risk at the overall financial statement level, the auditor should consider risks of material misstatement that relate pervasively to the financial statements taken as a whole and potentially affect many relevant assertions. Risks of this nature often relate to the entity's control environment and are not necessarily identifiable with specific relevant assertions at

---

[9] See paragraph .102 of section 314, *Understanding the Entity and Its Environment and Assessing the Risks of Material Misstatement*. See also paragraphs .14 through .19 of section 326, *Audit Evidence*, for discussion and guidance on the use of assertions in obtaining audit evidence.

[10] See section 318, *Performing Audit Procedures in Response to Assessed Risks and Evaluating the Audit Evidence Obtained*.

the class of transactions, account balance, or disclosure level. Such risks may be especially relevant to the auditor's consideration of the risks of material misstatement arising from fraud, for example, through management override of internal control. In developing responses to the risks of material misstatement at the overall financial statement level, the auditor should consider such matters as the knowledge, skill, and ability of personnel assigned significant engagement responsibilities; whether certain aspects of the engagement need the involvement of a specialist; and the appropriate level of supervision of assistants.

.16 In an audit of an entity with operations in multiple locations or with multiple components, the auditor should consider the extent to which audit procedures should be performed at selected locations or components. The factors an auditor should consider regarding the selection of a particular location or component include (*a*) the nature and amount of assets and transactions executed at the location or component; (*b*) the degree of centralization of records or information processing; (*c*) the effectiveness of the control environment, particularly with respect to management's direct control over the exercise of authority delegated to others and its ability to effectively supervise activities at the location or component; (*d*) the frequency, timing, and scope of monitoring activities by the entity or others at the location or component; (*e*) judgments about materiality of the location or component; and (*f*) risks associated with the location, such as political or economic instability.

Considerations at the Individual Account Balance, Class of Transactions, or Disclosure Level

.17 There is an inverse relationship between audit risk and materiality considerations. For example, the risk that relevant assertions related to a particular account balance, class of transactions, or disclosure could be misstated by an extremely large amount might be very low, but the risk that it could be misstated by an extremely small amount might be very high. Holding other considerations equal, either a decrease in the level of audit risk that the auditor judges to be appropriate in an account balance, class of transactions, or disclosure or a decrease in the amount of misstatements in the balance, class, or disclosure that the auditor believes could be material would require the auditor to do one or more of the following: (*a*) perform more effective audit procedures, (*b*) perform audit procedures closer to year end, or (*c*) increase the extent of particular audit procedures.

.18 In determining the nature, timing, and extent of audit procedures to be applied to a specific account balance, class of transactions, or disclosure, the auditor should design audit procedures to obtain reasonable assurance of detecting misstatements that the auditor believes, based on the judgment about materiality, could be material, when aggregated with misstatements in other balances, classes, or disclosures, to the financial statements taken as a whole. Auditors use various methods to design audit procedures to detect such misstatements.

.19 The auditor should consider audit risk at the individual account balance, class of transactions, or disclosure level because such consideration directly assists in determining the nature, timing, and extent of further audit procedures for the relevant assertions related to balances, classes, or disclosures. For example, the auditor should consider the risk of understatement as well as overstatement at the relevant assertion level such as when a liability may be understated (completeness) or when inventory may be overstated as a result of obsolescence (valuation). The auditor should seek to reduce audit risk at the individual balance, class, or disclosure level in such a way that will enable the auditor, at the completion of the audit, to express an opinion on the financial statements taken as a whole at an appropriately low level of audit risk. Auditors use various approaches to accomplish that objective.

.20 At the account balance, class of transactions, relevant assertion, or disclosure level, audit risk (AR) consists of *(a)* the risk (consisting of inherent risk and control risk) that the relevant assertions related to balances, classes, or disclosures contain misstatements (whether caused by error or fraud) that could be material to the financial statements when aggregated with misstatements in other relevant assertions related to balances, classes, or disclosures and *(b)* the risk (detection risk) that the auditor will not detect such misstatements. These components of audit risk may be assessed in quantitative terms, such as percentages, or in nonquantitative terms such as *high*, *medium*, or *low* risk. The way the auditor should consider these component risks and combines them involves professional judgment and depends on the auditor's approach or methodology.

.21 The risk that the relevant assertions related to account balances, classes of transactions, or disclosures are misstated consists of the following two components:

- *Inherent risk* (IR) is the susceptibility of a relevant assertion to a misstatement that could be material, either individually or when aggregated with other misstatements, assuming that there are no related controls. The risk of such misstatement is greater for some assertions and related account balances, classes of transactions, and disclosures than for others. For example, complex calculations are more likely to be misstated than simple calculations. Cash is more susceptible to theft than an inventory of coal. Accounts consisting of amounts derived from accounting estimates that are subject to significant measurement uncertainty pose greater risks than do accounts consisting of relatively routine, factual data. External circumstances giving rise to business risks[11] also influence inherent risk. For example, technological developments might make a particular product obsolete, thereby causing inventory to be more susceptible to overstatement. In addition to those circumstances that are peculiar to a specific relevant assertion, factors in the entity and its environment that relate to several or all of the classes of transaction, account balances, or disclosures may influence the inherent risk related to a specific relevant assertion. These latter factors include, for example, a lack of sufficient working capital to continue operations or a declining industry characterized by a large number of business failures.
- *Control risk* (CR) is the risk that a misstatement that could occur in a relevant assertion and that could be material, either individually or when aggregated with other misstatements, will not be prevented or detected on a timely basis by the entity's internal control. That risk is a function of the effectiveness of the design and operation of internal control in achieving the entity's objectives relevant to preparation of the entity's financial statements. Some control risk will always exist because of the inherent limitations of internal control.

.22 Inherent risk and control risk are the entity's risks, that is, they exist independently of the audit of financial statements. This section and other

---

[11] See section 314, paragraphs .29 through .33.

sections describe the risk of material misstatement (RMM) as the auditor's combined assessment of inherent risk and control risk; however, the auditor may make separate assessments of inherent risk and control risk. Furthermore, auditors may implement the concepts surrounding the assessment of inherent and control risks and responding to the risk of material misstatement in different ways as long as they achieve the same result.

.23 The auditor should assess the risk of material misstatement at the relevant assertion level as a basis for further audit procedures. Although that assessment is a judgment rather than a precise measurement of risk, the auditor should have an appropriate basis for that assessment. This basis may be obtained through the risk assessment procedures performed to obtain an understanding of the entity and its environment, including its internal control, and through the performance of suitable tests of controls to obtain audit evidence about the operating effectiveness of controls, where appropriate.

.24 *Detection risk* (DR) is the risk that the auditor will not detect a misstatement that exists in a relevant assertion that could be material, either individually or when aggregated with other misstatements. Detection risk is a function of the effectiveness of an audit procedure and of its application by the auditor. Detection risk cannot be reduced to zero because the auditor does not examine 100 percent of an account balance or a class of transactions and because of other factors. Such other factors include the possibility that an auditor might select an inappropriate audit procedure, misapply an appropriate audit procedure, or misinterpret the audit results. These other factors might be addressed through adequate planning, proper assignment of personnel to the engagement team, the application of professional skepticism, supervision and review of the audit work performed, and supervision and conduct of a firm's audit practice in accordance with appropriate quality control standards. Detection risk can be disaggregated into additional components of tests of details risk (TD) and substantive analytical procedures risk (AP).

.25 Detection risk relates to the substantive audit procedures and is managed by the auditor's response to risk of material misstatement. For a given level of audit risk, detection risk should bear an inverse relationship to the risk of material misstatement at the relevant assertion level. The greater the risk of material misstatement, the less the detection risk that can be accepted by the auditor. Conversely, the lower the risk of material misstatement, the greater the detection risk that can be accepted by the auditor. However, the auditor should perform substantive procedures for all relevant assertions related to material classes of transactions, account balances, and disclosures.

.26 The model, AR = RMM x DR,[12] expresses the general relationship of audit risk and the risks associated with the auditor's assessments of risk of material misstatement (inherent and control risks); of the risk that substantive tests of details and substantive analytical procedures would fail to detect a material misstatement that could occur in a relevant assertion, given that such misstatements occur and are not detected by the entity's controls; and of the allowable risk that material error will not be detected by the test of details, given that a material misstatement might occur in a relevant assertion and not be detected by internal control or substantive analytical procedures and other relevant substantive procedures. The model is not intended to be a mathematical formula including all factors that may influence the assessment of audit

---

[12] Risk of material misstatement (RMM) is the product of inherent risk (IR) and control risk (CR); and detection risk (DR) is the product of test of details risk (TD) and substantive analytical procedures risk (AP).

risk; however, some auditors find such a model to be useful when planning appropriate risk levels for audit procedures to reduce the auditor's desired audit risk to an appropriate low level.[13]

Determining Materiality for the Financial Statements Taken as a Whole When Planning the Audit

.27 The auditor should determine a materiality level for the financial statements taken as a whole when establishing the overall audit strategy for the audit (see section 311, *Planning and Supervision*). Determining a materiality level for the financial statements taken as a whole helps guide the auditor's judgments in identifying and assessing the risks of material misstatements and in planning the nature, timing, and extent of further audit procedures. This materiality level does not, however, establish a threshold below which identified misstatements are always considered to be immaterial when evaluating those misstatements and their effect on the financial statements and the auditor's report thereon. As discussed in paragraph .60, the circumstances related to some identified misstatements may cause the auditor to evaluate them as material even if they are below the materiality level determined when establishing the overall audit strategy.

.28 The determination of what is material to the users is a matter of professional judgment. The auditor often may apply a percentage to a chosen benchmark as a step in determining materiality for the financial statements taken as a whole. When identifying an appropriate benchmark, the auditor may consider factors such as:

- The elements of the financial statements (for example, assets, liabilities, equity, income, and expenses) and the financial statement measures defined in generally accepted accounting principles (for example, financial position, financial performance, and cash flows), or other specific requirements.
- Whether there are financial statement items on which, for the particular entity, users' attention tends to be focused (for example, for the purpose of evaluating financial performance).
- The nature of the entity and the industry in which it operates.
- The size of the entity, nature of its ownership, and the way it is financed.

Examples of benchmarks that might be appropriate, depending on the nature and circumstances of the entity, include total revenues, gross profit, and other categories of reported income, such as profit before tax from continuing operations. Profit before tax from continuing operations may be a suitable benchmark for profit-oriented entities but may not be an appropriate benchmark for the determination of materiality when, for example, the entity's earnings are volatile, when the entity is a not-for-profit entity, or when it is an owner-managed business where the owner takes much of the pretax income out of the business in the form of remuneration. For asset-based entities (for example, an investment fund) an appropriate benchmark might be net assets. Other entities (for example, banks and insurance companies) might use other benchmarks.

.29 When determining materiality, the auditor should consider prior periods' financial results and financial positions, the period-to-date financial results

---

[13] Table 2 in the Appendix [paragraph .48] of section 350, *Audit Sampling*, illustrates how this application of the model might work when applying sampling.

and financial position, and budgets or forecasts for the current period, taking account of significant changes in the entity's circumstances (for example, a significant business acquisition) and relevant changes of conditions in the economy as a whole or the industry in which the entity operates. For example, when the auditor usually determines materiality for a particular entity based on a percentage of profit, circumstances that give rise to an exceptional decrease or increase in profit may lead the auditor to conclude that materiality is more appropriately determined using a normalized profit figure based on past results.

.30 Once materiality is established, the auditor should consider materiality when planning and evaluating the same way regardless of the inherent business characteristics of the entity being audited. Materiality is determined based on the auditor's understanding of the user needs and expectations. User expectations may differ based on the degree of inherent uncertainty associated with the measurement of particular items in the financial statements, among other considerations. For example, the fact that the financial statements include very large provisions with a high degree of estimation uncertainty (for example, provisions for insurance claims in the case of an insurance company, oil rig decommissioning costs in the case of an oil company, or, more generally, legal claims against an entity) may influence the user's assessment of materiality. However, for audit purposes, this factor does not cause the auditor to follow different procedures for planning or evaluating misstatements than those outlined for other entities.

Materiality for Particular Items of Lesser Amounts Than the Materiality Level Determined for the Financial Statements Taken as a Whole

.31 When establishing the overall strategy for the audit, the auditor should consider whether, in the specific circumstances of the entity, misstatements of particular items of lesser amounts than the materiality level determined for the financial statements taken as a whole, if any, could, in the auditor's judgment, reasonably be expected to influence economic decisions of users taken on the basis of the financial statements. Any such amounts determined represent lower materiality levels to be considered in relation to the particular items in the financial statements.

.32 In making this judgment, the auditor should consider factors such as the following:

- Whether accounting standards, laws, or regulations affect users' expectations regarding the measurement or disclosure of certain items (for example, related party transactions and the remuneration of management and those charged with governance)
- The key disclosures in relation to the industry and the environment in which the entity operates (for example, research and development costs for a pharmaceutical company)
- Whether attention is focused on the financial performance of a particular subsidiary or division that is separately disclosed in the consolidated financial statements (for example, for a newly acquired business)

.33 In considering whether, in the specific circumstances of the entity, misstatements of particular items of lesser amounts than the materiality level for the financial statements taken as a whole, if any, could reasonably be considered material by the users of the financial statements, the auditor may consider whether the views and expectations of those charged with governance and management[14] might be helpful.

Tolerable Misstatement[15]

.34 *Tolerable misstatement* is the maximum error in a population (for example, the class of transactions or account balance) that the auditor is willing to accept. This term may be referred to as *tolerable error* in other standards.

.35 When assessing the risks of material misstatements and designing and performing further audit procedures to respond to the assessed risks, the auditor should allow for the possibility that some misstatements of lesser amounts than the materiality levels determined in accordance with paragraphs .11 and .31 could, in the aggregate, result in a material misstatement of the financial statements. To do so, the auditor should determine one or more levels of tolerable misstatement. Such levels of tolerable misstatement are normally lower than the materiality levels.

.36 The auditor must perform the audit to obtain reasonable assurance of detecting misstatements that the auditor believes could be large enough, individually or in the aggregate, to be quantitatively material to the financial statements. Although the auditor should be alert for misstatements that could be qualitatively material (see paragraphs .59 and .60), it ordinarily is not practical to design audit procedures to detect them.

Considerations as the Audit Progresses

.37 In some situations, the auditor may consider materiality for planning purposes before the financial statements to be audited are prepared. In those situations, the auditor's judgment about materiality might be based on the entity's annualized interim financial statements or financial statements of one or more prior annual periods, as long as recognition is given to the effects of major changes in the entity's circumstances (for example, a significant merger) and relevant changes in the economy as a whole or the industry in which the entity operates.

.38 Because it is not feasible for the auditor to anticipate all the circumstances that may ultimately influence judgments about materiality in evaluating the audit findings at the completion of the audit, the auditor's judgment about materiality for planning purposes may differ from the judgment about materiality used in evaluating the audit findings. For example, while performing the audit, the auditor may become aware of additional quantitative or qualitative factors that were not initially considered but that could be important to users of the financial statements and that should be considered in making judgments about materiality when evaluating audit findings.

.39 If the auditor concludes that a lower materiality level than that initially determined is appropriate, the auditor should reconsider the related levels of tolerable misstatement and appropriateness of the nature, timing, and extent of further audit procedures.

.40 The auditor should consider whether the overall audit strategy and audit plan need to be revised if the nature of identified misstatements and the circumstances of their occurrence are indicative that other misstatements may

---

[14] Paragraph .25 of section 311, *Planning and Supervision*, provides further discussion and guidance regarding communications with those charged with governance and management.

[15] See section 350 for further discussion and guidance on tolerable misstatement.

exist that, when aggregated with identified misstatements, could be material. The auditor should not assume that a misstatement is an isolated occurrence.[16]

.41 If the aggregate of the misstatements (known and likely) that the auditor has identified approaches the materiality level, the auditor should consider whether there is a greater than acceptably low level of risk that undetected misstatements, when taken with the aggregate identified misstatements, could exceed the materiality level and, if so, the auditor should reconsider the nature and extent of further audit procedures.

Communication of Misstatements to Management

.42 The auditor must accumulate all known and likely misstatements identified during the audit, other than those that the auditor believes are trivial,[17] and communicate them to the appropriate level of management. This communication should occur on a timely basis.

.43 Timely communication of potential misstatements to the appropriate level of management is important for management to evaluate whether the items are misstatements, or to inform the auditor if they disagree, and to take action as necessary. The determination of which level of management is the appropriate one is based on such factors as the nature, size, and frequency of the misstatement and which level of management can take the necessary action.

.44 When communicating details of misstatements, the auditor should distinguish between known misstatements and likely misstatements, as defined in paragraph .08.

.45 The auditor should request management to record the adjustment needed to correct all known misstatements, including the effect of prior period misstatement (see paragraph .53), other than those that the auditor believes are trivial.

.46 Where the auditor evaluates the amount of likely misstatement from a sample in a class of transactions, account balance, or disclosure as material, either individually or in aggregate with other misstatements, the auditor should request management to examine the class of transactions, account balance, or disclosure in order to identify and correct misstatements therein. For example, if an auditor identifies a misstatement while testing the cost prices of raw materials inventory, the auditor should extrapolate this misstatement to the raw materials account balance. If material, the auditor should then request management to examine the entire raw materials account balance to identify and correct any additional misstatements.

.47 Where the auditor has identified a likely misstatement involving differences in estimates such as a difference in a fair value estimate, the auditor should request management to review the assumptions and methods used in developing management's estimate.

.48 After management has (*a*) examined a class of transactions, account balance, or disclosure and corrected misstatements that are found and (*b*) challenged the assumptions and methods used in developing an estimate for which the auditor has identified a likely misstatement, the auditor should reevaluate

---

[16] See section 318, paragraph .73, for further guidance with respect to isolated misstatements.

[17] Matters that are "trivial" are amounts designated by the auditor below which misstatements need not be accumulated. This amount is set so that any such misstatements, either individually or when aggregated with other such misstatements, would not be material to the financial statements, after the possibility of further undetected misstatements is considered.

the amount of likely misstatement. This includes performing additional further audit procedures, if necessary.

.49 If management decides not to correct some or all of the known and likely misstatements communicated to it by the auditor, or identified when management examined a class of transactions, account balance, or disclosure, the auditor should obtain an understanding of management's reasons for not making the corrections and should take that into account when considering the qualitative aspects of the entity's accounting practices (see paragraph .60) and the implications for the auditor's report (see paragraph .67).

Evaluating Audit Findings[18]

.50 In evaluating whether the financial statements are presented fairly, in all material respects, in conformity with generally accepted accounting principles, the auditor must consider the effects, both individually and in the aggregate, of misstatements (known and likely) that are not corrected by the entity. In making this evaluation, in relation to particular classes of transactions, account balances, and disclosures, the auditor should consider the size and nature of the misstatements and the particular circumstances of their occurrence, and determine the effect of such misstatements on the financial statements taken as a whole.

.51 The consideration and aggregation of misstatements should include likely misstatements (the auditor's best estimate of the total misstatements in the account balances or classes of transactions that he or she has examined),[19] not just known misstatements (the amount of misstatements specifically identified).[20] Misstatements should be aggregated in a way that enables the auditor to consider whether, in relation to individual amounts, subtotals, or totals in the financial statements, they materially misstate the financial statements taken as a whole.

.52 Before considering the aggregate effect of identified uncorrected misstatements, the auditor should consider each misstatement separately to evaluate:

a. Its effect in relation to the relevant individual classes of transactions, account balances, or disclosures, including whether materiality levels for particular items of lesser amounts than the materiality level for the financial statements taken as a whole, determined in accordance with paragraph .31, have been exceeded.

b. Whether, in considering the effect of the individual misstatement on the financial statements taken as a whole, it is appropriate to offset misstatements. For example, it may be appropriate to offset misstatements of items within the same account balance in the financial statements.

c. The effect of misstatements related to prior periods. In prior periods, misstatements may not have been corrected by the entity because they

---

[18] This consideration includes any misstatements that remain uncorrected from different entity locations or from audits of portions of the entity that are performed by other auditors.

[19] See paragraphs .68 through .77 of section 316, *Consideration of Fraud in a Financial Statement Audit*, for a further discussion of the auditor's consideration of differences between the accounting records and the underlying facts and circumstances. Those paragraphs provide specific guidance on the auditor's consideration of an audit adjustment that is, or may be, the result of fraud.

[20] If the auditor were to examine all of the items in a balance or a class, the likely misstatement applicable to recorded transactions in the balance or class would be the amount of known misstatements specifically identified.

did not cause the financial statements for those periods to be materially misstated. Those misstatements might also affect the current period's financial statements.[21]

.53 In aggregating misstatements, the auditor should include the effect on the current period's financial statements of those prior period misstatements. When evaluating the aggregate uncorrected misstatements, the auditor should consider the effects of these uncorrected misstatements in determining whether the financial statements are free of material misstatement.

.54 When the auditor tests relevant assertions related to an account balance or a class of transactions by a substantive analytical procedure,[22] the auditor might not specifically identify misstatements but would obtain only an indication of whether misstatement might exist in the balance or class and possibly its approximate magnitude. If the substantive analytical procedure indicates that a misstatement might exist, but not its approximate amount, the auditor should request management to investigate and, if necessary, should expand his or her audit procedures to enable him or her to determine whether a misstatement exists in the account balance or class of transactions.

.55 When an auditor uses audit sampling to test a relevant assertion for an account balance or a class of transactions, he or she should project the amount of known misstatements identified in the sample to the items in the balance or class from which the sample was selected. That projected misstatement, along with the results of other substantive procedures, contributes to the auditor's assessment of likely misstatement in the balance or class.

.56 The risk of material misstatement of the financial statements is generally greater when account balances and classes of transactions are subject to estimation rather than precise measurement because of the inherent subjectivity in estimating future events. Estimates, such as those for inventory obsolescence, uncollectible receivables, and warranty obligations, are subject not only to the unpredictability of future events, but also to misstatements that may arise from using inadequate or inappropriate data or misapplying appropriate data. Because no one accounting estimate can be considered accurate with certainty, the auditor may determine that a difference between an estimated amount best supported by the audit evidence and the estimated amount included in the financial statements may not be significant, and such difference would not be considered to be a likely misstatement. However, if the auditor believes the estimated amount included in the financial statements is unreasonable, he or she should treat the difference between that estimate and the closest reasonable estimate as a likely misstatement.

.57 The "closest reasonable estimate" may be a range of acceptable amounts or a precisely determined point estimate, if that is a better estimate than any other amount. In some cases, the auditor may use a method that produces a range of acceptable amounts to determine the reasonableness of amounts recorded. For example, the auditor's analysis of specific problem accounts receivable and recent trends in bad-debt write-offs as a percent of sales may cause the auditor to conclude that the allowance for doubtful accounts should be between $130,000 and $160,000. If management's recorded estimate[23] falls within that range of acceptable amounts, the auditor may conclude

---

[21] The measurement of the effect, if any, on the current period's financial statements of misstatements uncorrected in prior periods involves accounting considerations and is therefore not addressed.

[22] Section 329, *Analytical Procedures*, provides guidance on the use of analytical procedures.

[23] Section 328, *Auditing Fair Value Measurements and Disclosures*, and section 342, *Auditing Accounting Estimates*, provide guidance with respect to the auditor's procedures to obtain an understanding of management's estimation process.

that the recorded amount is reasonable and no difference would be aggregated. If management's recorded estimate falls outside the auditor's range of acceptable amounts, the difference between the recorded amount and the amount at the closest end of the auditor's range would be aggregated as a likely misstatement.[24]

.58 The auditor should also consider whether the difference between estimates best supported by the audit evidence and the estimates included in the financial statements, which are individually reasonable, indicate a possible bias on the part of the entity's management. For example, if each accounting estimate included in the financial statements was individually reasonable, but the effect of the difference between each estimate and the estimate best supported by the audit evidence was to increase income, the auditor should reconsider the estimates taken as a whole.[25] In these circumstances, the auditor should reconsider whether other recorded estimates reflect a similar bias and should perform additional audit procedures that address those estimates. In addition, the possibility might exist that management's recorded estimates were clustered at one end of the range of acceptable amounts in the preceding year and clustered at the other end of the range of acceptable amounts in the current year, thus indicating the possibility that management is using swings in accounting estimates to offset higher- or lower-than-expected earnings. If the auditor believes that such circumstances exist, he or she should consider whether these matters should be communicated to those charged with governance, as described in paragraphs .34*a*, .37, and .38 of section 380, *The Auditor's Communication With Those Charged With Governance*.

.59 As discussed in paragraph .04, there are quantitative and qualitative materiality considerations. As a result of the interaction of quantitative and qualitative considerations in materiality judgments, misstatements of relatively small amounts that come to the auditor's attention could have a material effect on the financial statements. For example, an illegal payment of an otherwise immaterial amount could be material if there is a reasonable possibility that it could lead to a material contingent liability or a material loss of revenue.[26]

.60 Qualitative considerations also influence the auditor in reaching a conclusion about whether misstatements are material. Qualitative factors that the auditor may consider relevant to his or her consideration of whether misstatements are material include the following:

a. The potential effect of the misstatement on trends, especially trends in profitability.

b. A misstatement that changes a loss into income or vice versa.

c. The potential effect of the misstatement on the entity's compliance with loan covenants, other contractual agreements, and regulatory provisions.

d. The existence of statutory or regulatory reporting requirements that affect materiality thresholds.

---

[24] See Financial Accounting Standards Board *Accounting Standards Codification* 450, *Contingencies*. [Footnote revised, June 2009, to reflect conforming changes necessary due to the issuance of FASB ASC.]

[25] Section 316, paragraph .64, also provides guidance to the auditor in performing a retrospective review of significant accounting estimates reflected in the financial statements of the prior year to determine whether management judgments and assumptions relating to the estimates indicate a possible bias on the part of management.

[26] See section 317.

e. The misstatement masks a change in earnings or other trends, especially in the context of general economic and industry conditions.

f. A misstatement that has the effect of increasing management's compensation, for example, by satisfying the requirements for the award of bonuses or other forms of incentive compensation.

g. The sensitivity of the circumstances surrounding the misstatement, for example, the implications of misstatements involving fraud and possible illegal acts, violations of contractual provisions, and conflicts of interest.

h. The significance of the financial statement element affected by the misstatement, for example, a misstatement affecting recurring earnings as contrasted to one involving a nonrecurring charge or credit, such as an extraordinary item.

i. The effects of misclassifications, for example, misclassification between operating and nonoperating income or recurring and nonrecurring income items or a misclassification between fundraising costs and program activity costs in a not-for-profit organization.

j. The significance of the misstatement relative to reasonable user needs, for example:

- Earnings to investors and the equity amounts to creditors.
- The magnifying effects of a misstatement on the calculation of purchase price in a transfer of interests (buy-sell agreement).
- The effect of misstatements of earnings when contrasted with expectations.

Obtaining the views and expectations of those charged with governance and management may be helpful in gaining or corroborating an understanding of user needs, such as those illustrated above.

k. The definitive character of the misstatement, for example, the precision of an error that is objectively determinable as contrasted with a misstatement that unavoidably involves a degree of subjectivity through estimation, allocation, or uncertainty.

l. The motivation of management with respect to the misstatement, for example, (i) an indication of a possible pattern of bias by management when developing and accumulating accounting estimates, (ii) a misstatement precipitated by management's continued unwillingness to correct weaknesses in the financial reporting process, or (iii) intentional decision not to follow generally accepted accounting principles.

m. The existence of offsetting effects of individually significant but different misstatements.

n. The likelihood that a misstatement that is currently immaterial may have a material effect in future periods because of a cumulative effect, for example, that builds over several periods.

o. The cost of making the correction. It may not be cost-beneficial for the client to develop a system to calculate a basis to record the effect of an immaterial misstatement. On the other hand, if management appears to have developed a system to calculate an amount that represents an immaterial misstatement, it may reflect a motivation of management as noted in item *l* above.

p. The risk that possible additional undetected misstatements would affect the auditor's evaluation.

These circumstances are only examples; not all are likely to be present in all audits, nor is the list necessarily complete. The existence of any circumstances such as these does not necessarily lead to a conclusion that the misstatement is material.

.61 If the auditor believes that a misstatement is, or may be, the result of fraud, the auditor should consider the implications of the misstatement in relation to other aspects of the audit as described in section 316, even if the effect of the misstatement is not material to the financial statements.

Evaluating Whether the Financial Statements Taken as a Whole Are Free of Material Misstatement

.62 The auditor must evaluate whether the financial statements taken as a whole are free of material misstatement. In making this evaluation, the auditor should consider both the evaluation of the uncorrected (known and likely) misstatements required in paragraphs .50 through .53 and the qualitative considerations in paragraphs .60.

.63 When concluding as to whether the effect of misstatements, individually or in the aggregate, is material, an auditor should consider the nature and amount of the misstatements in relation to the nature and amount of items in the financial statements under audit. For example, an amount that is material to the financial statements of one entity may not be material to the financial statements of another entity of a different size or nature. Also, what is material to the financial statements of a particular entity might change from one period to another.

.64 If the auditor believes that the financial statements taken as a whole are materially misstated, the auditor should request management to make the necessary corrections. If management refuses to make the corrections, the auditor must determine the implications for the auditor's report (see paragraph .67).

.65 If the auditor concludes that the effects of uncorrected misstatements, individually or in the aggregate, do not cause the financial statements to be materially misstated, they could still be materially misstated because of further misstatements remaining undetected. As the aggregate misstatements approach materiality, the risk that the financial statements may be materially misstated also increases; consequently, the auditor should also consider the effect of undetected misstatements in concluding whether the financial statements are fairly stated.

.66 The auditor can reduce audit risk by modifying the nature, timing, and extent of planned audit procedures in performing the audit. If the auditor believes that such risk is unacceptably high, the auditor should perform additional audit procedures or satisfy himself or herself that the entity has adjusted the financial statements to reduce audit risk to an appropriate low level.[27]

Evaluating the Overall Effect of Audit Findings on the Auditor's Report

.67 If the auditor concludes that, or is unable to conclude whether, the financial statements are materially misstated, the auditor must determine the

---

[27] See section 318, paragraphs .70 through .76, with respect to the auditor's evaluation of the sufficiency and appropriateness of audit evidence obtained.

implications for the auditor's report on the financial statements. See paragraphs .20 through .63 of section 508, *Reports on Audited Financial Statements*, regarding discussion about departures from unqualified opinions.

Communications With Those Charged With Governance

.68 Standards and guidance regarding communications about materiality and misstatements to those charged with governance are set out in section 380, *The Auditor's Communication With Those Charged With Governance*. In addition, section 325, *Communicating Internal Control Related Matters Identified in an Audit*, requires the auditor to communicate, in writing, to management and those charged with governance, significant deficiencies and material weaknesses identified in an audit. [Revised, May 2006, due to conforming changes necessary due to the issuance of Statement on Standards No. 112.]

Documentation

.69 The auditor should document:

a. The levels of materiality, as discussed in paragraph .27, and tolerable misstatement, including any changes thereto, used in the audit and the basis on which those levels were determined.

b. A summary of uncorrected misstatements, other than those that are trivial, related to known and likely misstatements.

c. The auditor's conclusion as to whether uncorrected misstatements, individually or in aggregate, do or do not cause the financial statements to be materially misstated, and the basis for that conclusion.

d. All known and likely misstatements identified by the auditor during the audit, other than those that are trivial, that have been corrected by management.

.70 Uncorrected misstatements should be documented in a manner that allows the auditor to:

a. Separately consider the effects of known and likely misstatements, including uncorrected misstatements identified in prior periods;

b. Consider the aggregate effect of misstatements on the financial statements; and

c. Consider the qualitative factors that are relevant to the auditor's consideration whether misstatements are material (see paragraph .60).

Effective Date

.71 This section is effective for audits of financial statements for periods beginning on or after December 15, 2006. Earlier application is permitted.

AU Section 9312

Audit Risk and Materiality in Conducting an Audit: Auditing Interpretations of Section 312

[1.] The Meaning of the Term *Misstatement*

[.01–.04][1] [Deleted March 2006.]

[2.] Evaluating Differences in Estimates

[.05–.09][2] [Deleted March 2006.]

[3.] Quantitative Measures of Materiality in Evaluating Audit Findings

[.10–.14][3] [Deleted March 2006.]

[4.] Considering the Qualitative Characteristics of Misstatements

[.15–.17] [Deleted March 2006.]

---

[1] [Footnote deleted to reflect conforming changes necessary due to the issuance of Statements on Auditing Standards No. 107.]

[2] [Footnote deleted to reflect conforming changes necessary due to the issuance of Statements on Auditing Standards No. 107.]

[3] [Footnote deleted to reflect conforming changes necessary due to the issuance of Statements on Auditing Standards No. 107.]

AU Section 314

Understanding the Entity and Its Environment and Assessing the Risks of Material Misstatement

(Supersedes SAS No. 55.)

Source: SAS No. 109.

Effective for audits of financial statements for periods beginning on or after December 15, 2006. Earlier application is permitted.

Introduction

.01 This section establishes standards and provides guidance about implementing the second standard of field work, as follows:

> The auditor must obtain a sufficient understanding of the entity and its environment, including its internal control, to assess the risk of material misstatement of the financial statements whether due to error or fraud, and to design the nature, timing, and extent of further audit procedures.

The importance of the auditor's risk assessment as a basis for further audit procedures is discussed in the explanation of audit risk in section 312, *Audit Risk and Materiality in Conducting an Audit*. See section 326, *Audit Evidence*, for guidance on how the auditor uses relevant assertions [1] in sufficient detail to form a basis for the assessment of risks of material misstatement and to design and perform further audit procedures. The auditor should make risk assessments at the financial statement and relevant assertion levels based on an appropriate understanding of the entity and its environment, including its internal control. Section 318, *Performing Audit Procedures in Response to Assessed Risks and Evaluating the Audit Evidence Obtained*, discusses the auditor's responsibility to determine overall responses and to design and perform further audit procedures whose nature, timing, and extent are responsive to the risk assessments. This section should be applied in conjunction with the standards and guidance provided in other sections. In particular, the auditor's responsibility to consider fraud in an audit of financial statements is discussed in section 316, *Consideration of Fraud in a Financial Statement Audit*.

.02 The following is an overview of this standard:

- *Risk assessment procedures and sources of information about the entity and its environment, including its internal control.* This section explains the audit procedures that the auditor should perform to obtain the understanding of the entity and its environment, including its internal control (risk assessment procedures). The audit team should discuss the susceptibility of the entity's financial statements to material misstatement.

---

[1] *Relevant assertions* are assertions that have a meaningful bearing on whether the account is fairly stated. For example, valuation may not be relevant to the cash account unless currency translation is involved; however, existence and completeness are always relevant. Similarly, valuation may not be relevant to the gross amount of the accounts receivable balance, but is relevant to the related allowance accounts. Additionally, the auditor might, in some circumstances, focus on the presentation and disclosure assertions separately in connection with the period-end financial reporting process.

- *Understanding the entity and its environment, including its internal control.* This section provides guidance to the auditor in understanding specified aspects of the entity and its environment, and components of its internal control, in order to identify and assess risks of material misstatement, and in designing and performing further audit procedures.
- *Assessing the risks of material misstatement.* This section provides guidance to the auditor in assessing the risks of material misstatement at the financial statement and relevant assertion levels. The auditor should:
  - — Identify risks by considering the entity and its environment, including relevant controls, and by considering the classes of transactions, account balances, and disclosures in the financial statements.
  - — Relate the identified risks to what could go wrong at the relevant assertion level.
  - — Consider the significance and the likelihood of material misstatement for each identified risk.

  This section also provides guidance to the auditor in determining whether any of the assessed risks are significant risks that require special audit consideration or risks for which substantive procedures alone do not provide sufficient appropriate audit evidence. The auditor should evaluate the design of the entity's controls, including relevant control activities, over such risks and determine whether they are adequate and have been implemented.
- *Documentation.* This section provides related documentation guidance.

.03 Obtaining an understanding of the entity and its environment is an essential aspect of performing an audit in accordance with generally accepted auditing standards. In particular, that understanding establishes a frame of reference within which the auditor plans the audit and exercises professional judgment about assessing risks of material misstatement of the financial statements and responding to those risks throughout the audit, for example when:

- Establishing materiality for planning purposes and evaluating whether that judgment remains appropriate as the audit progresses.
- Considering the appropriateness of the selection and application of accounting policies and the adequacy of financial statement disclosures.
- Identifying areas where special audit consideration may be necessary, for example, related-party transactions, the appropriateness of management's use of the going-concern assumption, complex or unusual transactions, or considering the business purpose of transactions.
- Developing expectations for use when performing analytical procedures.
- Designing and performing further audit procedures to reduce audit risk to an appropriately low level.
- Evaluating the sufficiency and appropriateness of audit evidence obtained, such as evidence related to the reasonableness of management's assumptions and of management's oral and written representations.

.04 The auditor should use professional judgment to determine the extent of the understanding required of the entity and its environment, including its internal control. The auditor's primary consideration is whether the understanding that has been obtained is sufficient to assess risks of material misstatement of the financial statements and to design and perform further audit procedures. The depth of the overall understanding that the auditor obtains in performing the audit is less than that possessed by management in managing the entity.

Risk Assessment Procedures and Sources of Information About the Entity and Its Environment, Including Its Internal Control

.05 Obtaining an understanding of the entity and its environment, including its internal control, is a continuous, dynamic process of gathering, updating, and analyzing information throughout the audit. Throughout this process, the auditor should also follow the guidance in section 316. As described in section 326, audit procedures to obtain the understanding are referred to as *risk assessment procedures* because some of the information obtained by performing such procedures may be used by the auditor as audit evidence to support assessments of the risks of material misstatement. In addition, in performing risk assessment procedures, the auditor may obtain audit evidence about the relevant assertions related to classes of transactions, account balances, or disclosures and about the operating effectiveness of controls, even though such audit procedures were not specifically planned as substantive procedures or as tests of controls. The auditor also may choose to perform substantive procedures or tests of controls concurrently with risk assessment procedures because it is efficient to do so.

Risk Assessment Procedures

.06 The auditor should perform the following risk assessment procedures to obtain an understanding of the entity and its environment, including its internal control:

a. Inquiries of management and others within the entity

b. Analytical procedures

c. Observation and inspection

The auditor is not required to perform all the risk assessment procedures described above for each aspect of the understanding described in paragraph .21. However, all the risk assessment procedures should be performed by the auditor in the course of obtaining the required understanding.

.07 In addition, the auditor might perform other procedures where the information obtained may be helpful in identifying risks of material misstatement. For example, in cooperation with the entity, the auditor may consider making inquiries of others outside the entity such as the entity's external legal counsel or of valuation experts that the entity has used. Reviewing information obtained from external sources such as reports by analysts, banks, or rating agencies; trade and economic journals; or regulatory or financial publications may also be useful in obtaining information about the entity.

.08 Although much of the information the auditor obtains by inquiries can be obtained from management and those responsible for financial reporting, inquiries of others within the entity, such as production and internal audit personnel, and other employees with different levels of authority, may be useful in providing the auditor with a different perspective in identifying risks of material misstatement. In determining others within the entity to whom inquiries may be directed, or the extent of those inquiries, the auditor should consider what information may be obtained that might help the auditor in identifying risks of material misstatement. For example:

- Inquiries directed toward those charged with governance[2] may help the auditor understand the environment in which the financial statements are prepared.
- Inquiries directed toward internal audit personnel may relate to their activities concerning the design and effectiveness of the entity's internal control and whether management has satisfactorily responded to any findings from these activities.
- Inquiries of employees involved in initiating, authorizing, processing, or recording complex or unusual transactions may help the auditor in evaluating the appropriateness of the selection and application of certain accounting policies.
- Inquiries directed toward in-house legal counsel may relate to such matters as litigation, compliance with laws and regulations, knowledge of fraud or suspected fraud affecting the entity, warranties, post-sales obligations, arrangements (such as joint ventures) with business partners, and the meaning of contract terms.
- Inquiries directed toward marketing, sales, or production personnel may relate to changes in the entity's marketing strategies, sales trends, production strategies, or contractual arrangements with its customers.

.09 Paragraphs .04 and .06 of section 329, *Analytical Procedures*, specify that the auditor should apply analytical procedures in planning the audit to assist in understanding the entity and its environment and to identify areas that may represent specific risks relevant to the audit. For example, analytical procedures may be helpful in identifying the existence of unusual transactions or events, and amounts, ratios, and trends that might indicate matters that have financial statement and audit implications. In performing analytical procedures as risk assessment procedures, the auditor should develop expectations about plausible relationships that are reasonably expected to exist. When comparison of those expectations with recorded amounts or ratios developed from recorded amounts yields unusual or unexpected relationships, the auditor should consider those results in identifying risks of material misstatement. However, when such analytical procedures use data aggregated at a high level (which is often the situation), the results of those analytical procedures provide only a broad initial indication about whether a material misstatement may exist. Accordingly, the auditor should consider the results of such analytical procedures along with other information gathered in identifying the risks of material misstatement.

.10 Observation and inspection may support inquiries of management and others, and also provide information about the entity and its environment. Such audit procedures ordinarily include:

- Observation of entity activities and operations
- Inspection of documents (such as business plans and strategies), records, and internal control manuals
- Reading reports prepared by management (such as quarterly management reports and interim financial statements), those charged with

[2] See footnote 4 of section 311, *Planning and Supervision*, for the definition of and discussion about those charged with governance.

governance (such as minutes of board of directors' meetings), and internal audit

- Visits to the entity's premises and plant facilities
- Tracing transactions through the information system relevant to financial reporting, which may be performed as part of a walk-through

.11 When the auditor intends to use information about the entity and its environment obtained in prior periods, the auditor should determine whether changes have occurred that may affect the relevance of such information in the current audit. For continuing engagements, the auditor's previous experience with the entity contributes to the understanding of the entity. For example, audit procedures performed in previous audits ordinarily provide audit evidence about the entity's organizational structure, business, and controls, as well as information about past misstatements and whether or not they were corrected on a timely basis, which assists the auditor in assessing risks of material misstatement in the current audit. However, such information may have been rendered irrelevant by changes in the entity or its environment. The auditor should make inquiries and perform other appropriate audit procedures, such as walk-throughs of systems, to determine whether changes have occurred that may affect the relevance of such information.

.12 Section 316 specifies that the auditor should specifically assess the risk of material misstatement[3] of the financial statements due to fraud and states that the auditor should consider that assessment in designing audit procedures to be performed. In making this assessment, the auditor should also consider fraud risk factors that relate to either material misstatements arising from fraudulent financial reporting or misstatements arising from misappropriation of assets. Fraud risk factors that relate to fraudulent financial reporting are (*a*) management's characteristics and influence over the control environment, (*b*) industry conditions, and (*c*) operating characteristics and financial stability. Fraud risk factors that relate to misappropriation of assets are (*a*) susceptibility of assets to misappropriations and (*b*) absence of controls. The auditor's response to the assessment of the risk of material misstatement due to fraud is influenced by the nature and significance of the risk factors identified as being present. In some circumstances, the auditor may conclude that the conditions indicate a need to modify audit procedures. In these circumstances, the auditor should consider whether the assessment of the risk of material misstatement due to fraud calls for an overall response, one that is specific to a particular account balance, class of transactions, or disclosures at the relevant assertion level, or both. However, since such risk factors do not necessarily indicate the existence of fraud, the results of the assessment of the risk of material misstatement due to fraud provide only a broad initial indication about whether a material misstatement due to fraud may exist. Accordingly, the auditor should consider the results of the assessment of the risk of material misstatement due to fraud performed during planning along with other information gathered in identifying the risks of material misstatements.

.13 When relevant to the audit, the auditor also should consider other information such as that obtained from the auditor's client acceptance or continuance process or, where practicable, experience gained on other engagements performed for the entity, for example, engagements to review interim financial information.

---

[3] Risk of material misstatement is described as the auditor's combined assessment of inherent risk and control risk. See paragraph .22 of section 312, *Audit Risk and Materiality in Conducting an Audit*, for the definition of and further discussion about risk of material misstatement.

Discussion Among the Audit Team

.14 The members of the audit team, including the auditor with final responsibility for the audit, should discuss the susceptibility of the entity's financial statements to material misstatements. This discussion could be held concurrently with the discussion among the audit team that is specified by section 316 to discuss the susceptibility of the entity's financial statements to fraud. When the entire engagement is performed by a single auditor, the auditor should consider and document the susceptibility of the entity's financial statements to material misstatements. In these circumstances, the auditor should consider other factors that may be necessary in the engagement, such as personnel possessing specialized skills.

.15 Professional judgment should be used to determine which members of the audit team should be included in the discussion, how and when it should occur, and the extent of the discussion. Key members of the audit team, including the auditor with final responsibility, should be involved in the discussion; however, it is not necessary for all team members to have a comprehensive knowledge of all aspects of the audit. The extent of the discussion is influenced by the roles, experience, and information needs of the audit team members. An additional consideration is whether to include specialists assigned to the audit team. For example, the auditor may determine that a professional possessing information technology (IT)[4] or other specialized skills is needed on the audit team and therefore include that individual in the discussion.

.16 The auditor with final responsibility should consider which matters are to be communicated to members of the engagement not involved in the discussion. In a multilocation audit, for example, there may be multiple discussions that involve the key members of the audit team in each significant location.

.17 The objective of this discussion[5] is for members of the audit team to gain a better understanding of the potential for material misstatements of the financial statements resulting from fraud or error in the specific areas assigned to them, and to understand how the results of the audit procedures that they perform may affect other aspects of the audit, including the decisions about the nature, timing, and extent of further audit procedures.

.18 The discussion provides an opportunity for more experienced team members, including the auditor with final responsibility for the audit, to share their insights based on their knowledge of the entity and for the team members to exchange information about the business risks[6] to which the entity is subject and about how and where the financial statements might be susceptible to material misstatement. As specified in section 316, particular emphasis should be given to the susceptibility of the entity's financial statements to material misstatement due to fraud. In addition, the audit team should discuss critical issues, such as areas of significant audit risk; areas susceptible to management override of controls; unusual accounting procedures used by the client; important control systems; materiality at the financial statement level and at the account level; and how materiality will be used to determine the extent of testing. The discussion should also address application of generally accepted

---

[4] Information technology (IT) encompasses automated means of originating, processing, storing, and communicating information, and includes recording devices, communication systems, computer systems (including hardware and software components and data), and other electronic devices. An entity's use of IT may be extensive; however, the auditor is primarily interested in the entity's use of IT to initiate, authorize, record, process, and report transactions or other financial data.

[5] There may be one or more discussions, depending on the circumstances of the engagement.

[6] See paragraphs .29 through .33.

accounting principles to the entity's facts and circumstances and in light of the entity's accounting policies.

.19 The auditor should plan and perform the audit with an attitude of professional skepticism. The discussion among the audit team members should emphasize the need to exercise professional skepticism throughout the engagement, to be alert for information or other conditions that indicate that a material misstatement due to fraud or error may have occurred, and to be rigorous in following up on such indications.

.20 Depending on the circumstances of the audit, there may be multiple discussions in order to facilitate the ongoing exchange of information between audit team members regarding the susceptibility of the entity's financial statements to material misstatements. The purpose is for audit team members to communicate and share information obtained throughout the audit that may affect the assessment of the risks of material misstatement due to fraud or error or the audit procedures performed to address the risks.

Understanding the Entity and Its Environment, Including Its Internal Control

.21 The auditor's understanding of the entity and its environment consists of an understanding of the following aspects:

a. Industry, regulatory, and other external factors
b. Nature of the entity
c. Objectives and strategies and the related business risks that may result in a material misstatement of the financial statements
d. Measurement and review of the entity's financial performance
e. Internal control, which includes the selection and application of accounting policies

.22 Appendix A [paragraph .125] contains examples of matters that the auditor may consider in obtaining an understanding of the entity and its environment relating to categories (*a*) through (*d*) above. Appendix B [paragraph .126] contains a detailed explanation of the internal control components.

.23 The nature, timing, and extent of the risk assessment procedures performed depend on the circumstances of the engagement, such as the size and complexity of the entity and the auditor's experience with it. In addition, identifying significant changes in any of the above aspects of the entity from prior periods is particularly important in gaining a sufficient understanding of the entity to identify and assess risks of material misstatement.

Industry, Regulatory, and Other External Factors

.24 The auditor should obtain an understanding of relevant industry, regulatory, and other external factors. These factors include industry conditions, such as the competitive environment, supplier and customer relationships, and technological developments; the regulatory environment encompassing, among other matters, relevant accounting pronouncements, the legal and political environment, and environmental requirements affecting the industry and the entity; and other external factors, such as general economic conditions.[7]

.25 The industry in which the entity operates may be subject to specific risks of material misstatement arising from the nature of the business, the

[7] See section 317, *Illegal Acts by Clients*, for additional requirements related to the legal and regulatory framework applicable to the entity and the industry.

degree of regulation, or other external forces (such as political, economic, social, technical, and competitive). For example, long-term contracts may involve significant estimates of revenues and costs that give rise to risks of material misstatement of the financial statements. Similarly, regulations may specify certain financial reporting requirements for the industry in which the entity operates. In such cases, the auditor should consider whether the audit team includes members with sufficient relevant knowledge and experience. If management fails to comply with such regulations, its financial statements may be materially misstated.

Nature of the Entity

.26 The auditor should obtain an understanding of the nature of the entity. The nature of an entity refers to the entity's operations, its ownership, governance, the types of investments that it is making and plans to make, the way that the entity is structured, and how it is financed. An understanding of the nature of an entity enables the auditor to understand the classes of transactions, account balances, and disclosures to be expected in the financial statements.

.27 The entity may have a complex structure with subsidiaries or other components in multiple locations. In addition to the difficulties of consolidation in such cases, other issues with complex structures that may give rise to risks of material misstatement include the allocation of goodwill to subsidiaries, and its impairment; whether investments are joint ventures, subsidiaries, or investments accounted for using the equity method; and whether special-purpose entities are accounted for appropriately.

.28 An understanding of the ownership, management, and other key personnel and their relations between owners and other people or entities is also important in determining whether related-party transactions have been identified and accounted for appropriately. Section 334, *Related Parties*, provides additional guidance on the auditor's considerations relevant to related parties.

Objectives and Strategies and Related Business Risks

.29 The auditor should obtain an understanding of the entity's objectives and strategies, and the related business risks that may result in material misstatement of the financial statements. The entity conducts its business in the context of industry, regulatory, and other internal and external factors. To respond to these factors, the entity's management or those charged with governance define objectives, which are the overall plans for the entity. Strategies are the operational approaches by which management intends to achieve its objectives. Business risks result from significant conditions, events, circumstances, actions, or inactions that could adversely affect the entity's ability to achieve its objectives and execute its strategies, or through the setting of inappropriate objectives and strategies. Just as the external environment changes, the conduct of the entity's business is also dynamic and the entity's strategies and objectives change over time.

.30 Business risk is broader than the risk of material misstatement of the financial statements, although it includes the latter. For example, a new entrant to the marketplace with the competitive advantage of brand recognition and economies of scale may represent a business risk to a manufacturer's ability to garner as much shelf space at retailers and compete on price. The potential risk of material misstatement of the financial statements related to such business risk might be obsolescence or overproduction of inventory that could only be sold at discounted amounts. Business risk particularly may arise from change or complexity, although a failure to recognize the need for change may also give rise to risk. Change may arise, for example, from the development of new products that may fail; from an inadequate market, even if successfully developed; or from flaws that may result in liabilities and reputation risk. As an example of complexity, the conduct and management of long-term engineering projects (such as ship construction or the building of a suspension bridge) give rise to risks in the areas of percentage of completion, pricing, costing, design, and performance control. An understanding of business risks increases the likelihood of identifying risks of material misstatement. However, the auditor does not have a responsibility to identify or assess all business risks.

.31 Most business risks will eventually have financial consequences and, therefore, an effect on the financial statements. However, not all business risks give rise to risks of material misstatement. A business risk may have an immediate consequence for the risk of misstatement for classes of transactions, account balances, or disclosures at the relevant assertion level or for the financial statements taken as a whole. For example, the business risk arising from a contracting customer base due to industry consolidation may increase the risk of misstatement associated with the valuation of accounts receivable. Similarly, a business risk may have an immediate consequence for the risk of misstatement of the financial statements taken as a whole. For example, the business risk of significant transactions with related parties may increase the risk of misstatement of a range of significant account balances and relevant assertions. Furthermore, a business objective and related risks may also have a longer-term consequence that the auditor may need to consider when assessing the appropriateness of the going concern assumption. For example, the business risk of a decline in the industry in which the entity operates may affect the entity's ability to continue as a going concern. The auditor's consideration of whether a business risk may result in material misstatement is, therefore, made in light of the entity's circumstances. Examples of conditions and events that may indicate risks of material misstatement are given in Appendix C [paragraph .127].

.32 Usually management identifies business risks and develops approaches to address them. Such a risk assessment process is part of internal control and is discussed in paragraphs .76 to .80.

.33 Smaller entities often do not set their objectives and strategies, or manage the related business risks, through formal plans or processes. In many cases there may be no documentation of such matters. In such entities, the auditor's understanding may be obtained through inquiries of management and observation of how the entity responds to such matters.

Measurement and Review of the Entity's Financial Performance

.34 The auditor should obtain an understanding of the measurement and review of the entity's financial performance. Performance measures and their review indicate to the auditor aspects of the entity's performance that management and others consider to be important. Performance measures, whether external or internal, create pressures on the entity that, in turn, may motivate management to take action to improve the business performance or to misstate the financial statements. Obtaining an understanding of the entity's performance measures assists the auditor in considering whether such pressures result in management actions that may have increased the risks of material misstatement.

.35 Management's measurement and review of the entity's financial performance is to be distinguished from the monitoring of controls (discussed as a component of internal control in paragraphs .97 through .101), although their purposes may overlap. Monitoring of controls, however, is specifically concerned with the effective operation of internal control through consideration of information about the controls. The measurement and review of performance is directed at whether business performance is meeting the objectives set by management (or third parties), but it may be that performance indicators also provide information that enables management to identify deficiencies in internal control.

.36 Internally generated information used by management for this purpose may include key performance indicators (financial and nonfinancial); budgets; variance analysis; subsidiary information and divisional, departmental, or other level performance reports; and comparisons of an entity's performance with that of competitors. External parties may also measure and review the entity's financial performance. For example, external information, such as analysts' reports and credit rating agency reports, may provide information useful to the auditor's understanding of the entity and its environment. Such reports may be obtained from the entity being audited or from websites.

.37 Internal measures may highlight unexpected results or trends requiring management's inquiry of others in order to determine their cause and take corrective action (including, in some cases, the detection and correction of misstatements on a timely basis). Performance measures may also indicate to the auditor a risk of misstatement of related financial statement information. For example, performance measures may indicate that the entity has unusually rapid growth or profitability when compared to that of other entities in the same industry. Such information, particularly if combined with other factors such as performance-based bonus or incentive remuneration, may indicate the potential risk of management bias in the preparation of the financial statements.

.38 Much of the information used in performance measurement may be produced by the entity's information system. If management assumes that data used for reviewing the entity's performance is accurate without having a basis for that assumption, errors may exist in the information, potentially leading management to incorrect conclusions about performance. When the auditor intends to make use of the performance measures for the purpose of the audit (for example, for analytical procedures), the auditor should consider whether the information related to management's review of the entity's performance provides a reliable basis and is sufficiently precise for such a purpose. If making use of performance measures, the auditor should consider whether they are precise enough to detect material misstatements.

.39 Smaller entities ordinarily do not have formal processes to measure and review the entity's financial performance. Management nevertheless often relies on certain key indicators that knowledge and experience of the business suggest are reliable bases for evaluating financial performance and taking appropriate action.

Internal Control[8]

.40 The auditor should obtain an understanding of the five components of internal control sufficient to assess the risk of material misstatement of the financial statements whether due to error or fraud, and to design the nature, timing, and extent of further audit procedures. The auditor should obtain a sufficient understanding by performing risk assessment procedures to evaluate the design of controls relevant to an audit of financial statements and to determine whether they have been implemented. The auditor should use such knowledge to:

---

[8] This section recognizes the definition and description of internal control contained in *Internal Control—Integrated Framework*, published by the Committee of Sponsoring Organizations of the Treadway Commission (COSO Report).

- Identify types of potential misstatements.
- Consider factors that affect the risks of material misstatement.
- Design tests of controls, when applicable, and substantive procedures.

.41 Internal control[9] is a process—effected by those charged with governance, management, and other personnel—designed to provide reasonable assurance about the achievement of the entity's objectives with regard to reliability of financial reporting, effectiveness and efficiency of operations, and compliance with applicable laws and regulations.[10] Internal control over safeguarding of assets against unauthorized acquisition, use, or disposition may include controls relating to financial reporting and operations objectives. Internal control consists of five interrelated components:

a. *Control environment* sets the tone of an organization, influencing the control consciousness of its people. It is the foundation for all other components of internal control, providing discipline and structure.

b. Entity's *risk assessment* is the entity's identification and analysis of relevant risks to achievement of its objectives, forming a basis for determining how the risks should be managed.

c. *Information and communication systems* support the identification, capture, and exchange of information in a form and time frame that enable people to carry out their responsibilities.

d. *Control activities* are the policies and procedures that help ensure that management directives are carried out.

e. *Monitoring* is a process that assesses the quality of internal control performance over time.

Appendix B [paragraph .126] contains a detailed discussion of the internal control components.

.42 The division of internal control into the five components provides a useful framework for auditors to consider how different aspects of an entity's internal control may affect the audit. The division does not necessarily reflect how an entity considers and implements internal control. Also, the auditor's primary consideration is whether, and how, a specific control prevents, or detects and corrects, material misstatements in relevant assertions related to classes of transactions, account balances, or disclosures, rather than its classification into any particular component. Accordingly, auditors may use different terminology or frameworks to describe the various aspects of internal control, and their effect on the audit, than those used in this section, provided all the components described in this section are addressed.

.43 The way in which internal control is designed and implemented varies with an entity's size and complexity. Specifically, smaller entities may use less formal means and simpler processes and procedures to achieve their objectives. For example, smaller entities with active management involvement in the financial reporting process may not have extensive descriptions of accounting procedures or detailed written policies. For some entities, in particular very small entities, the owner-manager[11] may perform functions that in a larger entity would be regarded as belonging to several of the components of internal control. Therefore, the components of internal control may not be clearly distinguished within smaller entities, but their underlying purposes are equally valid.

---

[9] Internal control also may be referred to as internal control structure.

[10] It follows that internal control is designed and effected to address business risks that threaten the achievement of any of these objectives.

[11] This section uses the term *owner-manager* to indicate proprietors of entities who are involved in the running of the entity on a day-to-day basis.

.44 The auditor should obtain an understanding of the entity's selection and application of accounting policies and should consider whether they are appropriate for its business and consistent with generally accepted accounting principles and accounting policies used in the relevant industry,[12] or with a comprehensive basis of accounting other than generally accepted accounting principles.[13] The understanding encompasses the methods the entity uses to account for significant and unusual transactions; the effect of significant accounting policies in controversial or emerging areas for which there is a lack of authoritative guidance or consensus; and changes in the entity's accounting policies. The auditor should also identify financial reporting standards and regulations that are new to the entity and consider when and how the entity will adopt such requirements. Where the entity has changed its selection of or method of applying a significant accounting policy, the auditor should consider the reasons for the change and whether it is appropriate and consistent with generally accepted accounting principles.

.45 The presentation of financial statements in conformity with generally accepted accounting principles should include adequate disclosure of material matters. These matters relate to the form, arrangement, and content of the financial statements and their appended notes, including, for example, the terminology used, the amount of detail given, the classification of items in the statements, and the bases of amounts set forth. The auditor should consider whether the entity has disclosed a particular matter appropriately in light of the circumstances and facts of which the auditor is aware at the time.

.46 For the purposes of this section, the term *internal control* encompasses all five components of internal control stated above. In addition, the term *controls* refers to one or more of the components, or any aspect thereof.

Controls Relevant to Reliable Financial Reporting and to the Audit

.47 There is a direct relationship between an entity's objectives and the internal control components it implements to provide reasonable assurance about their achievement. In addition, internal control is relevant to the entire entity, or to any of its operating units or business functions. This relationship is depicted as follows:

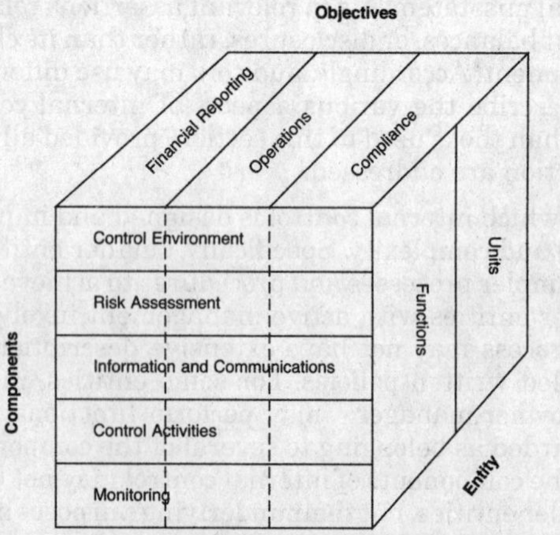

[12] [Footnote deleted, October 2009, to reflect conforming changes necessary due to the withdrawal of SAS No. 69.]

[13] The term *comprehensive basis of accounting other than generally accepted accounting principles* is defined in section 623, *Special Reports*. Hereafter, reference to generally accepted accounting principles in this section includes, where applicable, an other comprehensive basis of accounting.

Although the entity's objectives, and therefore controls, relate to financial reporting, operations, and compliance, as referred to in paragraph .41, not all of these objectives and controls are relevant to the audit. Further, although internal control applies to the entire entity, or to any of its operating units or business functions, an understanding of internal control relating to each of the entity's operating units and business functions may not be necessary to the performance of the audit.

.48 Ordinarily, controls that are relevant to an audit pertain to the entity's objective of preparing financial statements that are fairly presented in conformity with generally accepted accounting principles, including the management of risk that may give rise to a risk of material misstatement in those financial statements. However, it is not necessary to assess all controls in connection with assessing the risks of material misstatement and designing and performing further audit procedures in response to assessed risks. It is a matter of the auditor's professional judgment, as to the controls or combination of controls that should be assessed. However, as stated in paragraph .115, for significant risks, to the extent the auditor has not already done so, the auditor should evaluate the design of the entity's related controls, including relevant control activities, and determine whether they have been implemented. In exercising that judgment, the auditor should consider the circumstances, the applicable component, and factors such as the following:

- Materiality.
- The size of the entity.
- The nature of the entity's business, including its organization and ownership characteristics.
- The diversity and complexity of the entity's operations.
- Applicable legal and regulatory requirements.
- The nature and complexity of the systems that are part of the entity's internal control, including the use of service organizations.

.49 Controls over the completeness and accuracy of information produced by the entity may also be relevant to the audit if the auditor intends to make use of the information in designing and performing further audit procedures. The auditor's previous experience with the entity and information obtained in understanding the entity and its environment and throughout the audit assist the auditor in identifying controls relevant to the audit.

.50 Controls relating to operations and compliance [14] objectives may, however, be relevant to an audit if they pertain to information or data the auditor may evaluate or use in applying audit procedures. For example, controls pertaining to nonfinancial data that the auditor may use in analytical procedures, such as production statistics, or controls pertaining to detecting noncompliance with laws and regulations that may have a direct and material effect on the financial statements, such as controls over compliance with income tax laws and regulations used to determine the income tax provision, may be relevant to an audit.

.51 An entity generally has controls relating to objectives that are not relevant to an audit and therefore need not be considered. For example, an entity may rely on a sophisticated system of automated controls to provide efficient and effective operations (such as a manufacturing plant's computerized

---

[14] An auditor may need to consider controls relevant to compliance objectives when performing an audit in accordance with section 801, *Compliance Audits*. [Footnote revised, December 2010, to reflect conforming changes necessary due to the issuance of SAS No. 117.]

production scheduling system), but these controls ordinarily would not be relevant to the audit.

.52 Internal control over safeguarding of assets against unauthorized acquisition, use, or disposition may include controls relating to financial reporting and operations objectives. In obtaining an understanding of each of the components of internal control, the auditor's consideration of safeguarding controls is generally limited to those relevant to the reliability of financial reporting. For example, use of access controls, such as passwords, that limit access to the data and programs that process cash disbursements may be relevant to a financial statement audit. Conversely, safeguarding controls relating to operations objectives, such as controls to prevent the excessive use of materials in production, generally are not relevant to a financial statement audit.

.53 Controls relevant to the audit may exist in any of the components of internal control and a further discussion of controls relevant to the audit is included under the heading of each internal control component below (see paragraphs .67 through .101). In addition, paragraphs .115 and .117 discuss certain risks for which the auditor should evaluate the design of the entity's controls over such risks and determine whether they have been implemented.

Depth of Understanding of Internal Control

.54 Obtaining an understanding of internal control involves evaluating the design of a control and determining whether it has been implemented. Evaluating the design of a control involves considering whether the control, individually or in combination with other controls, is capable of effectively preventing or detecting and correcting material misstatements. Further explanation is contained in the discussion of each internal control component below (see paragraphs .67 through .101). Implementation of a control means that the control exists and that the entity is using it. The auditor should consider the design of a control in determining whether to consider its implementation. An improperly designed control may represent a material weakness[15] in the entity's internal control and the auditor should consider whether to communicate this to those charged with governance and management.

.55 As stated in paragraph .06, the auditor should perform risk assessment procedures to obtain an understanding of internal control. Procedures to obtain audit evidence about the design and implementation of relevant controls may include inquiring of entity personnel, observing the application of specific controls, inspecting documents and reports, and tracing transactions through the information system relevant to financial reporting. Inquiry alone is not sufficient to evaluate the design of a control relevant to an audit and to determine whether it has been implemented.

.56 Obtaining an understanding of an entity's controls is not sufficient to serve as testing the operating effectiveness of controls, unless there is some automation[16] that provides for the consistent application of the operation of the control (manual and automated elements of internal control relevant to the audit are further described below). For example, obtaining audit evidence about the implementation of a manually operated control at a point in time does not provide audit evidence about the operating effectiveness of the control at other times during the period under audit. However, IT enables an entity to process large volumes of data consistently and enhances the entity's ability to monitor the performance of control activities and to achieve effective segregation of

---

[15] A *material weakness* is a significant deficiency, or combination of significant deficiencies, that results in more than a remote likelihood that a material misstatement of the annual or interim financial statements will not be prevented or detected.

[16] This is assuming effective IT general controls.

duties by implementing security controls in applications, databases, and operating systems. Therefore, because generally, IT processing is inherently consistent, performing audit procedures to determine whether an automated control has been implemented may serve as a test of that control's operating effectiveness, depending on the auditor's assessment and testing of IT general controls, including computer security and program change control. Tests of the operating effectiveness of controls are further described in section 318.

Characteristics of Manual and Automated Elements of Internal Control Relevant to the Auditor's Risk Assessment

.57 ***Effect of information technology on internal control.*** An entity's use of IT may affect any of the five components of internal control relevant to the achievement of the entity's financial reporting, operations, or compliance objectives, and its operating units or business functions. For example, an entity may use IT as part of discrete systems that support only particular business units, functions, or activities, such as a unique accounts receivable system for a particular business unit or a system that controls the operation of factory equipment. Alternatively, an entity may have complex, highly integrated systems that share data and that are used to support all aspects of the entity's financial reporting, operations, and compliance objectives.

.58 The use of IT also affects the fundamental manner in which transactions are initiated, authorized, recorded, processed, and reported.[17] In a manual system, an entity uses manual procedures and records in paper format (for example, individuals may manually record sales orders on paper forms or journals, authorize credit, prepare shipping reports and invoices, and maintain accounts receivable records). Controls in such a system also are manual and may include such procedures as approvals and reviews of activities, and reconciliations and follow-up of reconciling items. Alternatively, an entity may have information systems that use automated procedures to initiate, authorize, record, process, and report transactions, in which case records in electronic format replace such paper documents as purchase orders, invoices, shipping documents, and related accounting records. Controls in systems that use IT consist of a combination of automated controls (for example, controls embedded in computer programs) and manual controls. Further, manual controls may be independent of IT, may use information produced by IT, or may be limited to monitoring the effective functioning of IT and of automated controls, and to handling exceptions. When IT is used to initiate, authorize, record, process, or report transactions, or other financial data for inclusion in financial statements, the systems and programs may include controls related to the corresponding assertions for material accounts or may be critical to the effective functioning of manual controls that depend on IT. An entity's mix of manual and automated controls varies with the nature and complexity of the entity's use of IT.

.59 Generally, IT provides potential benefits of effectiveness and efficiency for an entity's internal control because it enables an entity to:

- Consistently apply predefined business rules and perform complex calculations in processing large volumes of transactions or data.
- Enhance the timeliness, availability, and accuracy of information.
- Facilitate the additional analysis of information.
- Enhance the ability to monitor the performance of the entity's activities and its policies and procedures.
- Reduce the risk that controls will be circumvented.

---

[17] Paragraph B9 of Appendix B [paragraph .126] defines *initiation*, *authorizing*, *recording*, *processing*, and *reporting* as used throughout this section.

- Enhance the ability to achieve effective segregation of duties by implementing security controls in applications, databases, and operating systems.

.60 IT also poses specific risks to an entity's internal control, including:

- Reliance on systems or programs that are processing data inaccurately, processing inaccurate data, or both.
- Unauthorized access to data that may result in destruction of data or improper changes to data, including the recording of unauthorized or nonexistent transactions or inaccurate recording of transactions.
- Unauthorized changes to data in master files.
- Unauthorized changes to systems or programs.
- Failure to make necessary changes to systems or programs.
- Inappropriate manual intervention.
- Potential loss of data or inability to access data as required.

.61 The extent and nature of these risks to internal control vary depending on the nature and characteristics of the entity's information system. For example, multiple users, either external or internal, may access a common database of information that affects financial reporting. In such circumstances, a lack of control at a single user entry point might compromise the security of the entire database, potentially resulting in improper changes to or destruction of data. When IT personnel or users are given, or can gain, access privileges beyond those necessary to perform their assigned duties, a breakdown in segregation of duties can occur. This could result in unauthorized transactions or changes to programs or data that affect the financial statements. Therefore, the nature and characteristics of an entity's use of IT in its information system affect the entity's internal control.

.62 Manual controls of systems may be more suitable where judgment and discretion are required, such as for the following circumstances:

- Large, unusual, or nonrecurring transactions.
- Circumstances where misstatements are difficult to define, anticipate, or predict.
- In changing circumstances that require a control response outside the scope of an existing automated control.
- In monitoring the effectiveness of automated controls.

.63 Manual controls are performed by people, and therefore pose specific risks to the entity's internal control. Manual controls may be less reliable than automated controls because they can be more easily bypassed, ignored, or overridden and they are also more prone to errors and mistakes. Consistency of application of a manual control element cannot therefore be assumed. Manual systems may be less suitable for the following:

- High volume or recurring transactions, or in situations where errors that can be anticipated or predicted can be prevented or detected by control parameters that are automated.
- Control activities where the specific ways to perform the control can be adequately designed and automated.

Limitations of Internal Control

.64 Internal control, no matter how well designed and operated, can provide an entity with reasonable, but not absolute, assurance about achieving an entity's objectives. The likelihood of achievement is affected by limitations inherent to internal control. These include the realities that human judgment in decision making can be faulty and that breakdowns in internal control can occur because of human failures such as simple errors or mistakes. For example, if an entity's information system personnel do not sufficiently understand how an order entry system processes sales transactions, they may design changes to the system that will erroneously process sales for a new line of products. On the other hand, such changes may be correctly designed but misunderstood by individuals who translate the design into program code. Errors also may occur in the use of information produced by IT. For example, automated controls may be designed to report transactions over a specified amount for management review, but individuals responsible for conducting the review may not understand the purpose of such reports and, accordingly, may fail to review them or investigate unusual items.

.65 Additionally, controls, whether manual or automated, can be circumvented by the collusion of two or more people or inappropriate management override of internal control. For example, management may enter into undisclosed agreements with customers that alter the terms and conditions of the entity's standard sales contracts, which may result in improper revenue recognition. Also, edit checks in a software program that are designed to identify and report transactions that exceed specified credit limits may be overridden or disabled.

.66 Smaller entities often have fewer employees, which may limit the extent to which segregation of duties is practicable. However, for key areas, even in a very small entity, it can be practicable to implement some degree of segregation of duties or other form of unsophisticated but effective controls. The potential for override of controls by the owner-manager depends to a great extent on the control environment and, in particular, the owner-manager's attitudes about the importance of internal control.

Internal Control Components

.67 ***Control environment.*** The control environment sets the tone of an organization, influencing the control consciousness of its people. It is the foundation for all other components of internal control, providing discipline and structure.

.68 The primary responsibility for the prevention and detection of fraud and error rests with those charged with governance and the management of the entity. In obtaining an understanding of the control environment, the auditor should consider the design and implementation of entity programs and controls to address the risk of fraud as discussed in section 316. The absence or inadequacy of such programs and controls may constitute a significant deficiency or a material weakness. An example of such programs is a "hotline process" for employees to report on a confidential basis any known or suspected fraudulent activity.

.69 In evaluating the design of the entity's control environment, the auditor should consider the following elements and how they have been incorporated into the entity's processes:

a. *Communication and enforcement of integrity and ethical values.* Essential elements that influence the effectiveness of the design, administration, and monitoring of controls.

b. *Commitment to competence.* Management's consideration of the competence levels for particular jobs and how those levels translate into requisite skills and knowledge.

c. *Participation of those charged with governance.* Independence from management, the experience and stature of its members, the extent of its involvement and scrutiny of activities, the information it receives, the degree to which difficult questions are raised and pursued with management, and its interaction with internal and external auditors.

d. *Management's philosophy and operating style.* Management's approach to taking and managing business risks, and management's attitudes and actions toward financial reporting, information processing and accounting functions, and personnel.

e. *Organizational structure.* The framework within which an entity's activities for achieving its objectives are planned, executed, controlled, and reviewed.

f. *Assignment of authority and responsibility.* How authority and responsibility for operating activities are assigned and how reporting relationships and authorization hierarchies are established.

g. *Human resource policies and practices.* Recruitment, orientation, training, evaluating, counseling, promoting, compensating, and remedial actions.

For example, management's response to internal control deficiencies communicated in prior periods may relate to one or more of the aforementioned elements, such as commitment to competence or management's philosophy and operating style.

.70 The auditor should obtain sufficient knowledge of the control environment to understand the attitudes, awareness, and actions of those charged with governance concerning the entity's internal control and its importance in achieving reliable financial reporting. In understanding the control environment, the auditor should concentrate on the implementation of controls because controls may be established but not acted upon.

.71 The responsibilities of those charged with governance are of considerable importance. This is recognized in codes of practice and other regulations or guidance produced for the benefit of those charged with governance. The basis for management remuneration, especially executive performance-related compensation, places stress on management arising from the conflicting demands of fair reporting and the perceived benefits to shareholders of improved results. It is one, but not the only, role of those charged with governance to counterbalance such pressures. In understanding the control environment, the auditor should consider such matters as the independence of the directors and their ability to evaluate the actions of management. The auditor also should consider whether there is a group of those charged with governance that understands the entity's business transactions and evaluates whether the financial statements are presented fairly in conformity with generally accepted accounting principles.

.72 In understanding the control environment elements, the auditor should consider whether they have been implemented. The auditor should obtain sufficient appropriate audit evidence through a combination of inquiries and other risk assessment procedures, for example, corroborating inquiries through observation or inspection of documents. For example, through inquiries of management and employees, the auditor may obtain an understanding of how management communicates to employees its views on business practices and ethical behavior. The auditor should determine whether controls have been implemented by considering, for example, whether management has established a formal code of conduct and whether it acts in a manner that supports or condones violations of or authorizes exceptions to the code.

.73 Audit evidence for elements of the control environment may not be available in documentary form, in particular for smaller entities where communication between management and other personnel may be informal, yet effective. For example, management's commitment to ethical values and competence are often implemented through the behavior and attitude they demonstrate in managing the entity's business instead of in a written code of conduct. Consequently, management's attitudes, awareness, and actions are of particular importance in the design of a smaller entity's control environment. In addition, the role of those charged with governance is often undertaken by the owner-manager where there are no other owners.

.74 When obtaining an understanding of the control environment, the auditor also should consider the collective effect on the control environment of strengths and weaknesses in various control environment elements. Management's strengths and weaknesses may have a pervasive effect on internal control. For example, owner-manager controls may mitigate a lack of segregation of duties in a small business, or an active and independent board of directors may influence the philosophy and operating style of senior management in larger entities. Alternatively, management's failure to commit sufficient resources to address security risks presented by IT may adversely affect internal control by allowing improper changes to be made to computer programs or to data, or by allowing unauthorized transactions to be processed. Similarly, human resource policies and practices directed toward hiring competent financial, accounting, and IT personnel may not mitigate a strong bias by top management to overstate earnings.

.75 The existence of a satisfactory control environment is a positive factor when the auditor assesses the risks of material misstatement of the financial statements. Although an effective control environment is not an absolute deterrent to fraud because of the limitations of internal control, it may help reduce the risks of fraud. Because of the pervasive effect of the control environment on assessing the risks of material misstatement, the auditor's preliminary judgment about its effectiveness often influences the nature, timing, and extent of the further audit procedures to be performed. For example, weaknesses in the control environment may lead the auditor to perform more substantive procedures as of the date of the balance sheet rather than at an interim date, modify the nature of the tests of controls or substantive procedures to obtain more persuasive evidence, or increase the number of locations to be included in the scope of the audit. Conversely, an effective control environment may allow the auditor to have some degree of increased confidence in internal control and the reliability of evidence generated internally within the entity and thus, for example, allow the auditor to perform tests of controls and substantive procedures at an interim date rather than at the balance sheet date. However, the control environment ordinarily is not specific enough to prevent or detect material misstatements in account balances, classes of transactions, or disclosures and related assertions. The auditor, therefore, should consider the effect of other components of internal control in conjunction with the control environment when assessing the risks of material misstatement, for example, the monitoring of controls and the operation of specific control activities.

.76 ***The entity's risk assessment process.*** An entity's risk assessment process for financial reporting purposes is its identification, analysis, and management of risks relevant to the preparation of financial statements that are presented fairly in conformity with generally accepted accounting principles. For example, risk assessment may address how the entity considers the possibility of unrecorded transactions or identifies and analyzes significant estimates recorded in the financial statements. Risks relevant to reliable financial reporting also relate to specific events or transactions.

.77 Risks relevant to financial reporting include external and internal events and circumstances that may occur and adversely affect an entity's ability to initiate, authorize, record, process, and report financial data consistent with the assertions of management in the financial statements.[18] Risks can arise or change due to circumstances such as the following:

- Changes in operating environment
- New personnel
- New or revamped information systems
- Rapid growth
- New technology
- New business models, products, or activities
- Corporate restructurings
- Expanded foreign operations
- New accounting pronouncements

.78 The auditor should obtain sufficient knowledge of the entity's risk assessment process to understand how management considers risks relevant to financial reporting objectives and decides about actions to address those risks. In evaluating the design and implementation of the entity's risk assessment process, the auditor should consider how management identifies business risks relevant to financial reporting, estimates the significance of the risks, assesses the likelihood of their occurrence, and decides upon actions to manage them. An entity's risk assessment process for financial reporting that encompasses the elements of internal control herein might be part of an entity's risk management framework. As such, auditors should focus on aspects of the framework that affect risks of material misstatements in financial reporting. If the entity's risk assessment process is appropriate to the circumstances, it assists the auditor in identifying risks of material misstatement.

.79 The auditor should inquire about business risks that management has identified and should consider whether they may result in material misstatement of the financial statements. An entity's risk assessment process differs from the auditor's consideration of audit risk in a financial statement audit. The purpose of an entity's risk assessment process is to identify, analyze, and manage risks that affect the entity's objectives. In a financial statement audit, the auditor assesses risks to evaluate the likelihood that material misstatements could occur in the financial statements. Not all of the entity's risks are necessarily audit risks. However, the entity's risk assessment process may affect the auditor's consideration of audit risk. During the audit, the auditor may identify business risks or risks of material misstatement in the financial statements that management failed to identify. In such cases, the auditor should consider why the entity's risk assessment process failed to identify those risks and whether the process is appropriate to its circumstances.

.80 In a smaller entity, management may not have a formal risk assessment process as described in paragraph .76. For such entities, the auditor should discuss with management how risks to the business are identified by management and how they are addressed.

---

[18] These assertions are discussed in section 326, *Audit Evidence*.

.81 ***Information system, including the related business processes relevant to financial reporting, and communication.*** The information system relevant to financial reporting objectives, which includes the accounting system, consists of the procedures, whether automated or manual, and records established to initiate, authorize, record, process, and report entity transactions (as well as events and conditions) and to maintain accountability for the related assets, liabilities, and equity. The quality of system-generated information affects management's ability to make appropriate decisions in controlling the entity's activities and to prepare reliable financial reports.

.82 Communication involves providing an understanding of individual roles and responsibilities pertaining to internal control over financial reporting.

.83 The auditor should obtain sufficient knowledge of the information system, including the related business processes relevant to financial reporting, to understand:

- The classes of transactions in the entity's operations that are significant to the financial statements.
- The procedures, within both automated and manual systems, by which those transactions are initiated, authorized, recorded, processed, and reported in the financial statements.
- The related accounting records, whether electronic or manual, supporting information, and specific accounts in the financial statements involved in initiating, authorizing, recording, processing, and reporting transactions.
- How the information system captures events and conditions, other than classes of transactions, that are significant to the financial statements.
- The financial reporting process used to prepare the entity's financial statements, including significant accounting estimates and disclosures.

.84 When IT is used to initiate, authorize, record, process, or report transactions or other financial data for inclusion in financial statements, the systems and programs may include controls related to the corresponding assertions for significant accounts or may be critical to the effective functioning of manual controls that depend on IT.

.85 The auditor also should obtain an understanding of how the incorrect processing of transactions is resolved. For example, such understanding might include whether there is an automated suspense file, how it is used by the entity to ensure that suspense items are cleared out on a timely basis, and how system overrides or bypasses to controls are processed and accounted for.

.86 In obtaining an understanding of the financial reporting process (including the closing process), the auditor should obtain an understanding of the automated and manual procedures an entity uses to prepare financial statements and related disclosures, and how misstatements may occur. Such procedures include those used to:

- *Enter transaction totals into the general ledger (or equivalent record).* In some information systems, IT may be used to transfer such information automatically from transaction processing systems to general ledger or financial reporting systems. The automated processes and controls in such systems may reduce the risk of inadvertent error but do not overcome the risk that individuals may inappropriately override such automated processes, for example, by changing the amounts being automatically passed to the general ledger or financial reporting system. Furthermore, in planning the audit, the auditor should be aware that when IT is used to transfer information automatically there may be little or no visible evidence of such intervention in the information systems.

- *Initiate, authorize, record, and process journal entries in the general ledger.* An entity's financial reporting process used to prepare the financial statements typically includes the use of standard journal entries that are required on a recurring basis to record transactions such as sales, purchases, and cash disbursements, or to record accounting estimates that are periodically made by management such as changes in the estimate of uncollectible accounts receivable. An entity's financial reporting process also includes the use of nonstandard journal entries to record nonrecurring or unusual transactions or adjustments such as a business combination or disposal, or a nonrecurring estimate such as an asset impairment. In manual, paper-based general ledger systems, such journal entries may be identified through inspection of ledgers, journals, and supporting documentation. However, when IT is used to maintain the general ledger and prepare financial statements, such entries may exist only in electronic form and may be more easily identified through the use of computer-assisted audit techniques.

- *Initiate and record recurring and nonrecurring adjustments to the financial statements.* These are procedures relating to adjustments and reclassifications that are not reflected in formal journal entries.

- *Combine and consolidate general ledger data.* This includes procedures to combine detailed general ledger accounts, prepare the trial balance, and prepare consolidated financial data (for example, transferring general ledger data and adjusting journals into a consolidation system or spreadsheet; performing consolidation routines; and reconciling and reviewing consolidated financial data, including footnote data).

- *Prepare financial statements and disclosures.* These are procedures designed to ensure that information required to be presented and disclosed is accumulated, recorded, processed, summarized, and appropriately reported in the financial statements.

.87 The auditor should obtain an understanding of the entity's information system relevant to financial reporting in a manner that is appropriate to the entity's circumstances. This includes obtaining an understanding of how transactions originate within the entity's business processes. An entity's business processes are the activities designed to develop, purchase, produce, sell, and distribute an entity's products and services; ensure compliance with laws and regulations; and record information, including accounting and financial reporting information.

.88 The auditor should obtain sufficient knowledge of the communication component to understand how the entity communicates financial reporting roles and responsibilities and significant matters relating to financial reporting. Communication involves providing an understanding of individual roles and responsibilities pertaining to internal control over financial reporting and may take such forms as policy manuals and financial reporting manuals. It includes the extent to which personnel understand how their activities in the financial reporting information system relate to the work of others and the means of reporting exceptions to an appropriate higher level within the entity. Open communication channels help ensure that exceptions are reported and acted on. The auditor's understanding of communication pertaining to financial reporting matters also includes communications between management and those charged with governance, particularly the audit committee, as well as external communications, such as those with regulatory authorities.

.89 ***Control activities.*** The auditor should obtain an understanding of those control activities relevant to the audit. Control activities are the policies and procedures that help ensure that management directives are carried out; for example, that necessary actions are taken to address risks that threaten the achievement of the entity's objectives. Control activities, whether automated or manual, have various objectives and are applied at various organizational and functional levels. Examples of specific control activities include the following:

- *Authorization.* Control activities related to the initiation of derivatives and other off-balance sheet transactions may be relevant to the auditor's design of audit procedures related to the completeness assertion.
- *Segregation of duties.* Whether the personnel responsible for recording estimates for uncollectible accounts receivables are independent of personnel authorizing sales transactions may be relevant to the auditor's design of audit procedures related to the valuation assertion.
- *Safeguarding.* Control activities related to whether inventory is securely stored and the movement and access to inventory is limited to authorized individuals may be relevant to the auditor's design of audit procedures related to the existence assertion, in particular, the auditor's consideration as to the number of locations to visit.
- *Asset accountability.* Control activities related to reconciliations of the detailed records to the general ledger are ordinarily necessary to design and perform audit procedures for material classes of transactions and account balances.

.90 The auditor should consider the knowledge about the presence or absence of control activities obtained from the understanding of the other components of internal control in determining whether it is necessary to devote additional attention to obtaining an understanding of control activities. An audit does not require an understanding of all the control activities related to each class of transactions, account balance, and disclosure in the financial statements or to every relevant assertion. Ordinarily, control activities that may be relevant to an audit include those relating to authorization, segregation of duties, safeguarding of assets, and asset accountability, including, for example, reconciliations of the general ledger to the detailed records. The auditor should obtain an understanding of the process of reconciling detail to the general ledger for significant accounts. Also, control activities are relevant to the audit if the auditor is required to evaluate them as discussed in paragraphs .115 through .117.

.91 In obtaining an understanding of control activities, the auditor's primary consideration is whether, and how, a specific control activity, individually or in combination with others, prevents, or detects and corrects, material misstatements in classes of transactions, account balances, or disclosures. Control activities relevant to the audit are those for which the auditor considers it necessary to obtain an understanding in order to assess risks of material misstatement at the assertion level and to design and perform further audit procedures responsive to the assessed risks. The auditor's emphasis is on identifying and obtaining an understanding of control activities that address the areas where the auditor considers that material misstatements are more likely to occur. When multiple control activities achieve the same objective, it is unnecessary to obtain an understanding of each of the control activities related to such objective.

.92 The auditor should obtain an understanding of how IT affects control activities that are relevant to planning the audit. Some entities and auditors may view the IT control activities in terms of application controls and general controls. Application controls apply to the processing of individual applications. Accordingly, application controls relate to the use of IT to initiate, authorize, record, process, and report transactions or other financial data. These controls help ensure that transactions occurred, are authorized, and are completely and accurately recorded and processed. Examples include edit checks of input data, numerical sequence checks, and manual follow-up of exception reports.

.93 Application controls may be performed by IT (for example, automated reconciliation of subsystems) or by individuals. When application controls are performed by people interacting with IT, they may be referred to as user controls. The effectiveness of user controls, such as reviews of computer-produced exception reports or other information produced by IT, may depend on the accuracy of the information produced. For example, a user may review an exception report to identify credit sales over a customer's authorized credit limit without performing procedures to verify its accuracy. In such cases, the effectiveness of the user control (that is, the review of the exception report) depends on both the effectiveness of the user review and the accuracy of the information in the report produced by IT.

.94 General controls are policies and procedures that relate to many applications and support the effective functioning of application controls by helping to ensure the continued proper operation of information systems. General controls commonly include controls over data center and network operations; system software acquisition, change, and maintenance; access security; and application system acquisition, development, and maintenance. While ineffective general controls do not, by themselves, cause misstatements, they may permit application controls to operate improperly and allow misstatements to occur and not be detected. For example, if there are weaknesses in the general controls over access security, and applications are relying on these general controls to prevent unauthorized transactions from being processed, such a general control weakness may have a more severe effect on the effective design and operation of the application control. General controls should be assessed in relation to their effect on applications and data that become part of the financial statements. For example, if no new systems are implemented during the period of the financial statements, weaknesses in the general controls over "systems development" may not be relevant to the financial statements being audited.

.95 The use of IT affects the way that control activities are implemented. For example, when IT is used in an information system, segregation of duties often is achieved by implementing security controls.

.96 The auditor should consider whether the entity has responded adequately to the risks arising from IT by establishing effective controls, including effective general controls upon which application controls depend. From the auditor's perspective, controls over IT systems are effective when they maintain the integrity of information and the security of the data such systems process.

.97 ***Monitoring of controls.*** The auditor should obtain an understanding of the major types of activities that the entity uses to monitor internal control over financial reporting, including the sources of the information related to those activities, and how those activities are used to initiate corrective actions to its controls.

.98 An important management responsibility is to establish and maintain internal control on an ongoing basis. Management's monitoring of controls includes whether they are operating as intended and that they are modified as appropriate for changes in conditions. Monitoring of controls may include activities such as management's review of whether bank reconciliations are being prepared on a timely basis, internal auditors' evaluation of sales personnel's compliance with the entity's policies on terms of sales contracts, and legal department's oversight of compliance with the entity's ethical or business practice policies.

.99 Monitoring of controls is a process to assess the quality of internal control performance over time. It involves assessing the design and operation of controls on a timely basis and taking necessary corrective actions. Monitoring is done to ensure that controls continue to operate effectively. For example, if the timeliness and accuracy of bank reconciliations are not monitored, personnel are likely to stop preparing them. Management accomplishes monitoring of controls through ongoing activities, separate evaluations, or a combination of the two. In many entities, internal auditors or personnel performing similar functions contribute to the monitoring of an entity's activities. When obtaining an understanding of the internal audit function, the auditor should follow the guidance in paragraphs .04 through .08 of section 322, *The Auditor's Consideration of the Internal Audit Function in an Audit of Financial Statements.* Management's monitoring activities may include using information from communications from external parties such as customer complaints and regulator comments that may indicate problems or highlight areas in need of improvement.

.100 In many entities, much of the information used in monitoring may be produced by the entity's information system. If management assumes that data used for monitoring is accurate without having a basis for that assumption, errors may exist in the information, potentially leading management to incorrect conclusions from its monitoring activities. The auditor should obtain an understanding of the sources of the information related to the entity's monitoring activities, and the basis upon which management considers the information to be sufficiently reliable for the purpose.

.101 The auditor's understanding of management's monitoring of controls may assist the auditor in identifying the existence of more detailed controls or other activities that the auditor may consider in making risk assessments.

Assessing the Risks of Material Misstatement

.102 The auditor should identify and assess the risks of material misstatement at the financial statement level and at the relevant assertion level related to classes of transactions, account balances, and disclosures. For this purpose, the auditor should:

- Identify risks throughout the process of obtaining an understanding of the entity and its environment, including relevant controls that relate to the risks, and considering the classes of transactions, account balances, and disclosures in the financial statements.
- Relate the identified risks to what can go wrong at the relevant assertion level.
- Consider whether the risks are of a magnitude that could result in a material misstatement of the financial statements.
- Consider the likelihood that the risks could result in a material misstatement of the financial statements.

.103 The auditor should use information gathered by performing risk assessment procedures, including the audit evidence obtained in evaluating the design of controls and determining whether they have been implemented, as audit evidence to support the risk assessment. The auditor should use the risk assessment to determine the nature, timing, and extent of further audit procedures to be performed. When the risk assessment is based on an expectation that controls are operating effectively to prevent or detect material misstatement, individually or when aggregated, at the relevant assertion level, the auditor should perform tests of the controls that the auditor has determined to be suitably designed to prevent or detect a material misstatement in the relevant assertion to obtain audit evidence that the controls are operating effectively, as described in section 318.

.104 The auditor should determine whether the identified risks of material misstatement relate to specific relevant assertions related to classes of transactions, account balances, and disclosures, or whether they relate more pervasively to the financial statements taken as a whole and potentially affect many relevant assertions. The latter risks (risks at the financial statement level) may derive in particular from a weak control environment.

.105 The nature of the risks arising from a weak control environment is such that they are not likely to be confined to specific individual risks of material misstatement in particular classes of transactions, account balances, and disclosures. Rather, weaknesses such as management's lack of competence may have a more pervasive effect on the financial statements and may require an overall response by the auditor.

.106 In making risk assessments, the auditor should identify the controls that are likely to prevent or detect and correct material misstatements in specific relevant assertions. Generally, the auditor gains an understanding of controls and relates them to relevant assertions in the context of processes and systems in which they exist. Doing so is useful because individual control activities often do not in themselves address a risk. Often only multiple control activities, together with other elements of internal control, will be sufficient to address a risk.

.107 Conversely, some control activities may have a specific effect on an individual relevant assertion embodied in a particular class of transaction or account balance. For example, the control activities that an entity established to ensure that its personnel are properly counting and recording the annual physical inventory relate directly to the existence and completeness assertions for the inventory account balance.

.108 Controls can be either directly or indirectly related to an assertion. The more indirect the relationship, the less effective that control may be in preventing or detecting and correcting misstatements in that assertion. For example, a sales manager's review of a summary of sales activity for specific stores by region ordinarily is only indirectly related to the completeness assertion for sales revenue. Accordingly, it may be less effective in reducing risk for that assertion than controls more directly related to that assertion, such as matching shipping documents with billing documents.

.109 In assessing risks, deficiencies in an entity's internal control may come to the auditor's attention that are significant enough that they are, in the auditor's judgment, significant deficiencies that should be communicated to those charged with governance as required by section 325, *Communication of Internal Control Related Matters Noted in an Audit*. Furthermore, the auditor's understanding of internal control may raise doubts about the auditability of an entity's financial statements. Concerns about the integrity of the entity's management may be so serious as to cause the auditor to conclude that the risk of management misrepresentation in the financial statements is such that an audit cannot be conducted. Also, concerns about the condition and reliability of an entity's records may cause the auditor to conclude that it is unlikely that sufficient appropriate audit evidence will be available to support an unqualified opinion on the financial statements. In such circumstances, the auditor should consider a qualification or disclaimer of opinion, but in some cases the auditor's only recourse may be to withdraw from the engagement.

Significant Risks That Require Special Audit Consideration

.110 As part of the risk assessment described in paragraph .102, the auditor should determine which of the risks identified are, in the auditor's judgment, risks that require special audit consideration (such risks are defined as "significant risks"). Paragraphs .45 and .53 of section 318 describe the consequences for further audit procedures of identifying a risk as significant.

.111 The determination of significant risks, which arise on most audits, is a matter for the auditor's professional judgment. In exercising this judgment, the auditor should consider inherent risk[19] to determine whether the nature of the risk, the likely magnitude of the potential misstatement including the possibility that the risk may give rise to multiple misstatements, and the likelihood of the risk occurring are such that they require special audit consideration. Routine, noncomplex transactions that are subject to systematic processing are less likely to give rise to significant risks because they have lower inherent risks. On the other hand, significant risks are often derived from business risks that may result in a material misstatement. In considering the nature of the risks, the auditor should consider a number of matters, including the following:

- Whether the risk is a risk of fraud
- Whether the risk is related to recent significant economic, accounting, or other developments and, therefore, requires specific attention
- The complexity of transactions
- Whether the risk involves significant transactions with related parties
- The degree of subjectivity in the measurement of financial information related to the risks, especially those involving a wide range of measurement uncertainty
- Whether the risk involves significant nonroutine transactions that are outside the normal course of business for the entity, or that otherwise appear to be unusual

.112 Significant risks often relate to significant nonroutine transactions and judgmental matters. Nonroutine transactions are transactions that are unusual, either due to size or nature, and that therefore occur infrequently. Judgmental matters may include the development of accounting estimates for which there is significant measurement uncertainty.

.113 Risks of material misstatement may be greater for risks relating to significant nonroutine transactions arising from matters such as the following:

- Greater management intervention to specify the accounting treatment
- Greater manual intervention for data collection and processing
- Complex calculations or accounting principles

---

[19] The auditor does this before considering the effect of identified controls related to the risk.

- The nature of nonroutine transactions, which may make it difficult for the entity to implement effective controls over the risks
- Significant related-party transactions

.114 Risks of material misstatement may be greater for risks relating to significant judgmental matters that require the development of accounting estimates arising from matters such as the following:

- Accounting principles for accounting estimates or revenue recognition may be subject to differing interpretation.
- Required judgment may be subjective or complex, or may require assumptions about the effects of future events, for example, judgment about fair value.

.115 For significant risks, to the extent the auditor has not already done so, the auditor should evaluate the design of the entity's related controls, including relevant control activities, and determine whether they have been implemented. An understanding of the entity's controls related to significant risks should provide the auditor with adequate information to develop an effective audit approach. Management ought to be aware of significant risks; however, risks relating to significant nonroutine or judgmental matters are often less likely to be subject to routine controls. Therefore, the auditor's understanding of whether the entity has designed and implemented controls for such significant risks includes whether and how management responds to the risks and whether control activities such as a review of assumptions by senior management or experts, formal processes for estimations, or approval by those charged with governance have been implemented to address the risks. For example, where there are nonrecurring events such as the receipt of notice of a significant lawsuit, consideration of the entity's response will include such matters as whether it has been referred to appropriate experts (such as internal or external legal counsel), whether an assessment has been made of the potential effect, and how it is proposed that the circumstances are to be disclosed in the financial statements.

.116 If management has not appropriately responded by implementing controls over significant risks and if, as a result, the auditor judges that there is a significant deficiency or material weakness in the entity's internal control over financial reporting, the auditor should communicate this matter to those charged with governance. In these circumstances, the auditor also should consider the implications for the auditor's risk assessment.

Risks for Which Substantive Procedures Alone Do Not Provide Sufficient Appropriate Audit Evidence

.117 As part of the risk assessment described in paragraph .102, the auditor should evaluate the design and determine the implementation of the entity's controls, including relevant control activities, over those risks for which, in the auditor's judgment, it is not possible or practicable to reduce detection risk at the relevant assertion level to an acceptably low level with audit evidence obtained only from substantive procedures. The consequences for further audit procedures of identifying such risks are described in paragraph .24 of section 318.

.118 The understanding of the entity's information system relevant to financial reporting enables the auditor to identify risks of material misstatement that relate directly to the recording of routine classes of transactions or account balances and the preparation of reliable financial statements; these include risks of inaccurate or incomplete processing. Ordinarily, such risks relate to significant classes of transactions, such as an entity's revenue, purchases, and cash receipts or cash payments.

.119 The characteristics of routine day-to-day business transactions often permit highly automated processing with little or no manual intervention. In such circumstances, it may not be possible to perform only substantive procedures in relation to the risk. For example, in circumstances where a significant amount of an entity's information is initiated, authorized, recorded, processed, or reported electronically, such as in an integrated system, the auditor may determine that it is not possible to design effective substantive procedures that by themselves would provide sufficient appropriate audit evidence that relevant classes of transactions or account balances are not materially misstated. In such cases, audit evidence may be available only in electronic form, and its appropriateness and sufficiency usually depend on the effectiveness of controls over its accuracy and completeness. Furthermore, the potential for improper initiation or alteration of information to occur and not be detected may be greater if information is initiated, authorized, recorded, processed, or reported only in electronic form and appropriate controls are not operating effectively.

.120 Examples of situations in which the auditor may find it impossible to design effective substantive procedures that by themselves provide sufficient appropriate audit evidence that certain relevant assertions are not materially misstated include the following:

- An entity that conducts its business using IT to initiate orders for the purchase and delivery of goods based on predetermined rules of what to order and in what quantities and to pay the related accounts payable based on system-generated decisions initiated upon the confirmed receipt of goods and terms of payment. No other documentation of orders placed or goods received is produced or maintained, other than through the IT system.

- An entity that provides services to customers via electronic media (for example, an Internet service provider or a telecommunications company) and uses IT to create a log of the services provided to its customers, to initiate and process its billings for the services, and to automatically record such amounts in electronic accounting records that are part of the system used to produce the entity's financial statements.

Revision of Risk Assessment

.121 The auditor's assessment of the risks of material misstatement at the relevant assertion level is based on available audit evidence and may change during the course of the audit as additional audit evidence is obtained. In particular, the risk assessment may be based on an expectation that controls are operating effectively to prevent or detect and correct a material misstatement at the relevant assertion level. In performing tests of controls to obtain audit evidence about their operating effectiveness, the auditor may obtain audit evidence that controls are not operating effectively at relevant times during the audit. Similarly, in performing substantive procedures, the auditor may detect misstatements in amounts or frequency that is greater than is consistent with the auditor's risk assessment. When the auditor obtains audit evidence from performing further audit procedures that tends to contradict the audit evidence on which the auditor originally based the assessment, the auditor should revise the assessment and should further modify planned audit procedures accordingly. See paragraphs .70 and .74 of section 318 for further guidance.

Documentation

.122 The auditor should document:

a. The discussion among the audit team regarding the susceptibility of the entity's financial statements to material misstatement due to error or fraud, including how and when the discussion occurred, the subject matter discussed, the audit team members who participated, and significant decisions reached concerning planned responses at the financial statement and relevant assertion levels.

b. Key elements of the understanding obtained regarding each of the aspects of the entity and its environment identified in paragraph .21, including each of the components of internal control identified in paragraph .41, to assess the risks of material misstatement of the financial statements; the sources of information from which the understanding was obtained; and the risk assessment procedures.

c. The assessment of the risks of material misstatement both at the financial statement level and at the relevant assertion level as required by paragraph .102 and the basis for the assessment.

d. The risks identified and related controls evaluated as a result of the requirements in paragraphs .110 and .117.

.123 The manner in which these matters are documented is for the auditor to determine using professional judgment. Section 339, *Audit Documentation*, provides general guidance regarding the purpose, content, and ownership and confidentiality of audit documentation. Examples of common techniques used alone or in combination include narrative descriptions, questionnaires, checklists, and flowcharts. Such techniques may also be useful in documenting the auditor's assessment of the risks of material misstatement at the overall financial statement and relevant assertions level. The form and extent of this documentation are influenced by the nature, size, and complexity of the entity and its environment, including its internal control, and the availability of information from the entity and the specific audit methodology and technology used in the course of the audit. For example, documentation of the understanding of a complex information system in which a large volume of transactions are electronically initiated, authorized, recorded, processed, or reported may include flowcharts, questionnaires, or decision tables. For an information system making limited or no use of IT or for which few transactions are processed (for example, long-term debt), documentation in the form of a memorandum may be sufficient. Generally, the more complex the entity and its environment, including its internal control, and the more extensive the audit procedures performed by the auditor, the more extensively the auditor should document his or her work. The specific audit methodology and technology used in the course of the audit will also affect the form and extent of documentation.

Effective Date

.124 This section is effective for audits of financial statements for periods beginning on or after December 15, 2006. Earlier application is permitted.

.125

Appendix A

Understanding the Entity and Its Environment

A1. This Appendix provides additional guidance on matters the auditor may consider when obtaining an understanding of the industry, regulatory, and other external factors that affect the entity; the nature of the entity; objectives and strategies and related business risks; and measurement and review of the entity's financial performance. The examples provided cover a broad range of matters applicable to many engagements; however, not all matters are relevant to every engagement and the list of examples is not necessarily complete. Additional guidance on internal control is contained in Appendix B [paragraph .126].

Industry, Regulatory, and Other External Factors

A2. Examples of matters an auditor may consider include the following:

- Industry conditions
  - — The market and competition, including demand, capacity, and price competition
  - — Cyclical or seasonal activity
  - — Product technology relating to the entity's products
  - — Supply availability and cost
- Regulatory environment
  - — Accounting principles and industry-specific practices
  - — Regulatory framework for a regulated industry
  - — Legislation and regulation that significantly affect the entity's operations
    - Regulatory requirements
    - Direct supervisory activities
  - — Taxation (corporate and other)
  - — Government policies currently affecting the conduct of the entity's business
    - Monetary, including foreign exchange controls
    - Fiscal
    - Financial incentives (for example, government aid programs)
    - Tariffs and trade restrictions
  - — Environmental requirements affecting the industry and the entity's business
- Other external factors currently affecting the entity's business
  - — General level of economic activity (for example, recession, growth)
  - — Interest rates and availability of financing
  - — Inflation and currency revaluation

Nature of the Entity

A3. Examples of matters an auditor may consider include the following:

- Business operations
  - — Nature of revenue sources (for example, manufacturer; wholesaler; banking, insurance, or other financial services; import-export trading, utility, transportation, and technology products and services)
  - — Products or services and markets (for example, major customers and contracts, terms of payment, profit margins, market share, competitors, exports, pricing policies, reputation of products, warranties, backlog, trends, marketing strategy and objectives, and manufacturing processes)
  - — Conduct of operations (for example, stages and methods of production, subsidiaries or divisions, delivery of products and services, and details of declining or expanding operations)
  - — Alliances, joint ventures, and outsourcing activities
  - — Involvement in e-commerce, including Internet sales and marketing activities
  - — Geographic dispersion and industry segmentation
  - — Location of production facilities, warehouses, and offices
  - — Key customers
  - — Important suppliers of goods and services (for example, long-term contracts, stability of supply, terms of payment, imports, and methods of delivery, such as "just-in-time")
  - — Employment (for example, by location, supply, wage levels, union contracts, pension and other postemployment benefits, stock option or incentive bonus arrangements, and government regulation related to employment matters)
  - — Research and development activities and expenditures
  - — Transactions with related parties
- Investments
  - — Acquisitions, mergers, or disposals of business activities (planned or recently executed)
  - — Investments and dispositions of securities and loans
  - — Capital investment activities, including investments in plant and equipment and technology, and any recent or planned changes
  - — Investments in nonconsolidated entities, including partnerships, joint ventures, and special-purpose entities
  - — Life cycle stage of enterprise (start-up, growing, mature, declining)
- Financing
  - — Group structure—major subsidiaries and associated entities, including consolidated and nonconsolidated structures
  - — Debt structure, including covenants, restrictions, guarantees, and off-balance-sheet financing arrangements
  - — Leasing of property, plant, or equipment for use in the business
  - — Beneficial owners (local and foreign business reputation and experience)
  - — Related parties

— Use of derivative financial instruments

- Financial reporting
  - — Accounting principles and industry-specific practices
  - — Revenue recognition practices
  - — Accounting for fair values
  - — Inventories (for example, locations and quantities)
  - — Foreign currency assets, liabilities, and transactions
  - — Industry-specific significant categories (for example, loans and investments for banks, accounts receivable and inventory for manufacturers, research and development for pharmaceuticals)
  - — Accounting for unusual or complex transactions including those in controversial or emerging areas (for example, accounting for stock-based compensation)
  - — Financial statement presentation and disclosure

Objectives and Strategies and Related Business Risks

A4. Examples of matters an auditor may consider include the following:

- Existence of objectives (that is, how the entity addresses industry, regulatory, and other external factors) relating to, for example, the following:
  - — Industry developments (a potential related business risk might be, for example, that the entity does not have the personnel or expertise to deal with the changes in the industry)
  - — New products and services (a potential related business risk might be, for example, that there is increased product liability)
  - — Expansion of the business (a potential related business risk might be, for example, that the demand has not been accurately estimated)
  - — New accounting requirements (a potential related business risk might be, for example, incomplete or improper implementation, or increased costs)
  - — Regulatory requirements (a potential related business risk might be, for example, that there is increased legal exposure)
  - — Current and prospective financing requirements (a potential related business risk might be, for example, the loss of financing due to the entity's inability to meet requirements)
  - — Use of information technology (IT) (a potential related business risk might be, for example, that systems and processes are not compatible)
  - — Risk appetite of managers and stakeholders
- Effects of implementing a strategy, particularly any effects that will lead to new accounting requirements (a potential related business risk might be, for example, incomplete or improper implementation)

Measurement and Review of the Entity's Financial Performance

A5. Examples of matters an auditor may consider include:

- Key ratios and operating statistics
- Key performance indicators

- Employee performance measures and incentive compensation policies
- Trends
- Use of forecasts, budgets, and variance analysis
- Analyst reports and credit rating reports
- Competitor analysis
- Period-on-period financial performance (revenue growth, profitability, and leverage)

.126

Appendix B

Internal Control Components

B1. As set forth in paragraph .41 and described in .67 through .101, internal control consists of the following components:

a. Control environment

b. Risk assessment

c. Information and communication systems

d. Control activities

e. Monitoring

This Appendix further explains these components as they relate to the financial statement audit.

Control Environment

B2. The control environment sets the tone of an organization, influencing the control consciousness of its people. It is the foundation for effective internal control, providing discipline and structure.

B3. The control environment encompasses the following elements:

a. *Communication and enforcement of integrity and ethical values.* The effectiveness of controls cannot rise above the integrity and ethical values of the people who create, administer, and monitor them. Integrity and ethical values are essential elements of the control environment that influence the effectiveness of the design, administration, and monitoring of other components of internal control. Integrity and ethical behavior are the product of the entity's ethical and behavioral standards, how they are communicated, and how they are reinforced in practice. They include management's actions to remove or reduce incentives and temptations that might prompt personnel to engage in dishonest, illegal, or unethical acts. They also include the communication of entity values and behavioral standards to personnel through policy statements and codes of conduct and by example.

b. *Commitment to competence.* Competence is the knowledge and skills necessary to accomplish tasks that define the individual's job. Commitment to competence includes management's consideration of the competence levels for particular jobs and how those levels translate into requisite skills and knowledge.

c. *Participation of those charged with governance.* An entity's control consciousness is significantly influenced by those charged with governance. Attributes include those charged with governance's independence from management, the experience and stature of its members, the extent of its involvement and scrutiny of activities, the appropriateness of its actions, the information it receives, the degree to which difficult questions are raised and pursued with management, and its interaction with internal and external auditors. The importance of responsibilities of those charged with governance is recognized in codes of practice and other regulations or guidance produced for the benefit of those charged with governance. Other responsibilities of those charged with governance include oversight of the design and effective operation of whistle-blower procedures and of the process for reviewing the effectiveness of the entity's internal control.

d. *Management's philosophy and operating style.* Management's philosophy and operating style encompass a broad range of characteristics. Such characteristics may include the following: management's approach to taking and monitoring business risks; management's attitudes and actions toward financial reporting (conservative or aggressive selection from available alternative accounting principles, and conscientiousness and conservatism with which accounting estimates are developed); and management's attitudes toward information processing and accounting functions and personnel.

e. *Organizational structure.* An entity's organizational structure provides the framework within which its activities for achieving entity-wide objectives are planned, executed, controlled, and reviewed. Establishing a relevant organizational structure includes considering key areas of authority and responsibility and appropriate lines of reporting. An entity develops an organizational structure suited to its needs. The appropriateness of an entity's organizational structure depends in part on its size and the nature of its activities.

f. *Assignment of authority and responsibility.* This factor includes how authority and responsibility for operating activities are assigned and how reporting relationships and authorization hierarchies are established. It also includes policies relating to appropriate business practices, knowledge and experience of key personnel, and resources provided for carrying out duties. In addition, it includes policies and communications directed at ensuring that all personnel understand the entity's objectives, know how their individual actions interrelate and contribute to those objectives, and recognize how and for what they will be held accountable.

g. *Human resource policies and practices.* Human resource policies and practices relate to recruitment, orientation, training, evaluating, counseling, promoting, compensating, and remedial actions. For example, standards for recruiting the most qualified individuals—with emphasis on educational background, prior work experience, past accomplishments, and evidence of integrity and ethical behavior—demonstrate an entity's commitment to competent and trustworthy people. Training policies that communicate prospective roles and responsibilities and include practices such as training schools and seminars illustrate expected levels of performance and behavior. Promotions driven by periodic performance appraisals demonstrate the entity's commitment to the advancement of qualified personnel to higher levels of responsibility.

Application to Small and Midsized Entities

B4. Small and midsized entities may implement the control environment elements differently than larger entities. For example, smaller entities might not have a written code of conduct but, instead, develop a culture that emphasizes the importance of integrity and ethical behavior through oral communication and by management example. Similarly, those charged with governance in smaller entities may not include independent or outside members.

Entity's Risk Assessment Process

B5. An entity's risk assessment process is its process for identifying and responding to business risks and the results thereof. For financial reporting purposes, the entity's risk assessment process includes how management identifies risks relevant to the preparation of financial statements that are presented fairly in conformity with generally accepted accounting principles, estimates their significance, assesses the likelihood of their occurrence, and decides upon actions to manage them. For example, the entity's risk assessment process may address how the entity considers the possibility of unrecorded transactions or identifies and analyzes significant estimates recorded in the financial statements. Risks relevant to reliable financial reporting also relate to specific events or transactions.

B6. Risks relevant to financial reporting include external and internal events and circumstances that may occur and adversely affect an entity's ability to initiate, authorize, record, process, and report financial data consistent with the assertions of management in the financial statements. Once risks are identified, management considers their significance, the likelihood of their occurrence, and how they should be managed. Management may initiate plans, programs, or actions to address specific risks, or it may decide to accept a risk because of cost or other considerations. Risks can arise or change due to such circumstances as the following:

- *Changes in operating environment.* Changes in the regulatory or operating environment can result in changes in competitive pressures and significantly different risks.
- *New personnel.* New personnel may have a different focus on or understanding of internal control.
- *New or revamped information systems.* Significant and rapid changes in information systems can change the risk relating to internal control.
- *Rapid growth.* Significant and rapid expansion of operations can strain controls and increase the risk of a breakdown in controls.
- *New technology.* Incorporating new technologies into production processes or information systems may change the risk associated with internal control.
- *New business models, products, or activities.* Entering into business areas or transactions with which an entity has little experience may introduce new risks associated with internal control.
- *Corporate restructurings.* Restructurings may be accompanied by staff reductions and changes in supervision and segregation of duties that may change the risk associated with internal control.
- *Expanded foreign operations.* The expansion or acquisition of foreign operations carries new and often unique risks that may affect internal control, for example, additional or changed risks from foreign currency transactions.
- *New accounting pronouncements.* Adoption of new accounting principles or changing accounting principles may affect risks in preparing financial statements.

Application to Small and Midsized Entities

B7. The basic concepts of the entity's risk assessment process are relevant to every entity, regardless of size, but the risk assessment process is likely to be less formal and less structured in small and midsized entities than in larger ones. All entities should have established financial reporting objectives, but they may be recognized implicitly rather than explicitly in smaller entities. Management may be able to learn about risks related to these objectives through direct personal involvement with employees and outside parties.

Information System, Including the Related Business Processes Relevant to Financial Reporting, and Communication

B8. An information system consists of infrastructure (physical and hardware components), software, people, procedures (manual and information technology [IT]), and data. Infrastructure and software will be absent, or have less significance, in systems that are exclusively or primarily manual. Many information systems rely extensively on IT.

B9. The information system relevant to financial reporting objectives, which includes the accounting system, consists of the procedures, whether IT or manual, and records established to initiate, authorize, record, process, and report entity transactions (as well as events and conditions) and to maintain accountability for the related assets, liabilities, and equity. Transactions may be initiated manually or automatically by programmed procedures. Authorization includes the process of approving transactions by the appropriate level of management. Recording includes identifying and capturing the relevant information for transactions or events. Processing includes functions such as edit and validation, calculation, measurement, valuation, summarization, and reconciliation, whether performed by IT or manual procedures. Reporting relates to the preparation of financial reports as well as other information, in electronic or printed format, that the entity uses in measuring and reviewing the entity's financial performance and in other functions. The quality of system-generated information affects management's ability to make appropriate decisions in managing and controlling the entity's activities and to prepare reliable financial reports.

B10. Accordingly, an information system encompasses methods and records that:

- Identify and record all valid transactions.
- Describe on a timely basis the transactions in sufficient detail to permit proper classification of transactions for financial reporting.
- Measure the value of transactions in a manner that permits recording their proper monetary value in the financial statements.
- Determine the time period in which transactions occurred to permit recording of transactions in the proper accounting period.
- Present properly the transactions and related disclosures in the financial statements.

B11. Communication involves providing an understanding of individual roles and responsibilities pertaining to internal control over financial reporting. It includes the extent to which personnel understand how their activities in the financial reporting information system relate to the work of others and the means of reporting exceptions to an appropriate higher level within the entity. Open communication channels help ensure that exceptions are reported and acted on.

B12. Communication takes such forms as policy manuals, accounting and financial reporting manuals, and memoranda. Communication also can be made electronically, orally, and through the actions of management.

Application to Small and Midsized Entities

B13. Information systems and related business processes relevant to financial reporting in small or midsized organizations are likely to be less formal than in larger organizations, but their role is just as significant. Smaller entities with active management involvement may not need extensive descriptions of accounting procedures, sophisticated accounting records, or written policies. Communication may be less formal and easier to achieve in a small or midsized company than in a larger enterprise due to the smaller organization's size and fewer levels as well as management's greater visibility and availability.

Control Activities

B14. Control activities are the policies and procedures that help ensure that management directives are carried out, for example, that necessary actions are taken to address risks that threaten the achievement of the entity's objectives. Control activities, whether automated or manual, have various objectives and are applied at various organizational and functional levels.

B15. Generally, control activities that may be relevant to an audit may be categorized as policies and procedures that pertain to the following:

- *Performance reviews.* These control activities include reviewing and analyzing actual performance versus budgets, forecasts, and prior-period performance; relating different sets of data—operating or financial—to one another, together with analyses of the relationships and investigative and corrective actions; comparing internal data with external sources of information, and reviewing functional or activity performance, such as a bank's consumer loan manager's review of reports by branch, region, and loan type for loan approvals and collections.
- *Information processing.* A variety of controls are performed to check accuracy, completeness, and authorization of transactions. The two broad groupings of information systems control activities are application controls and general controls. Application controls apply to the processing of individual applications. These controls help ensure that transactions occurred, are authorized, and are completely and accurately recorded and processed. Examples of application controls include checking the arithmetical accuracy of records, maintaining and reviewing accounts and trial balances, automated controls such as edit checks of input data and numerical sequence checks, and manual follow-up of exception reports. General controls are policies and procedures that relate to many applications and support the effective functioning of application controls by helping to ensure the continued proper operation of information systems. General controls commonly include controls over data center and network operations; system software acquisition, change, and maintenance; access security; and application system acquisition, development, and maintenance. These controls apply to mainframe, miniframe, and end-user environments. Examples of such general controls are program change controls, controls that restrict access to programs or data, controls over the implementation of new releases of packaged software applications, and controls over system software that restrict access to or monitor the use of system utilities that could change financial data or records without leaving an audit trail.
- *Physical controls.* These activities encompass the physical security of assets, including adequate safeguards such as secured facilities to

limit access to assets and records; authorization for access to computer programs and data files; and periodic counting and comparison with amounts shown on control records (for example, comparing the results of cash, security, and inventory counts with accounting records). The extent to which physical controls intended to prevent theft of assets are relevant to the reliability of financial statement preparation, and therefore the audit, depends on circumstances such as when assets are highly susceptible to misappropriation. For example, these controls would ordinarily not be relevant when any inventory losses would be detected pursuant to periodic physical inspection and recorded in the financial statements. However, if for financial reporting purposes management relies solely on perpetual inventory records, the physical security controls would be relevant to the audit.

- *Segregation of duties.* Assigning different people the responsibilities of authorizing transactions, recording transactions, and maintaining custody of assets is intended to reduce the opportunities to allow any person to be in a position to both perpetrate and conceal errors or fraud in the normal course of his or her duties. Examples of segregation of duties include reporting, reviewing and approving reconciliations, and approval and control of documents.

B16. Certain control activities may depend on the existence of appropriate higher-level policies established by management or those charged with governance. For example, authorization controls may be delegated under established guidelines, such as investment criteria set by those charged with governance; alternatively, nonroutine transactions such as major acquisitions or divestments may require specific high-level approval, including in some cases that of shareholders.

Application to Small and Midsized Entities

B17. The concepts underlying control activities in small or midsized organizations are likely to be similar to those in larger entities, but the formality with which they operate varies. Further, smaller entities may find that certain types of control activities are not relevant because of controls applied by management. For example, management's retention of authority for approving credit sales, significant purchases, and draw-downs on lines of credit can provide strong control over those activities, lessening or removing the need for more detailed control activities. An appropriate segregation of duties often appears to present difficulties in smaller organizations. Even companies that have only a few employees, however, may be able to assign responsibilities to achieve appropriate segregation or, if that is not possible, to use management oversight of the incompatible activities to achieve control objectives.

Monitoring of Controls

B18. An important management responsibility is to establish and maintain internal control on an ongoing basis. Management's monitoring of controls includes considering whether they are operating as intended and that they are modified as appropriate for changes in conditions. Monitoring of controls may include activities such as management's review of whether bank reconciliations are being prepared on a timely basis, internal auditors' evaluation of sales personnel's compliance with the entity's policies on terms of sales contracts, and a legal department's oversight of compliance with the entity's ethical or business practice policies.

B19. Monitoring of controls is a process to assess the quality of internal control performance over time. It involves assessing the design and operation of controls on a timely basis and taking necessary corrective actions. Monitoring is done to ensure that controls continue to operate effectively. For example, if the timeliness and accuracy of bank reconciliations are not monitored, personnel are likely to stop preparing them. Monitoring of controls is accomplished through ongoing monitoring activities, separate evaluations, or a combination of the two.

B20. Ongoing monitoring activities are built into the normal recurring activities of an entity and include regular management and supervisory activities. Managers of sales, purchasing, and production at divisional and corporate levels are in touch with operations and may question reports that differ significantly from their knowledge of operations.

B21. In many entities, internal auditors or personnel performing similar functions contribute to the monitoring of an entity's controls through separate evaluations. They regularly provide information about the functioning of internal control, focusing considerable attention on evaluating the design and operation of internal control. They communicate information about strengths and weaknesses and recommendations for improving internal control.

B22. Monitoring activities may include using information from communications from external parties that may indicate problems or highlight areas in need of improvement. Customers implicitly corroborate billing data by paying their invoices or complaining about their charges. In addition, regulators may communicate with the entity concerning matters that affect the functioning of internal control, for example, communications concerning examinations by bank regulatory agencies. Also, management may consider communications relating to internal control from external auditors in performing monitoring activities.

Application to Small and Midsized Entities

B23. Ongoing monitoring activities of small and midsized entities are more likely to be informal and are typically performed as a part of the overall management of the entity's operations. Management's close involvement in operations often will identify significant variances from expectations and inaccuracies in financial data.

.127

Appendix C

Conditions and Events That May Indicate Risks of Material Misstatement

C1. The following are examples of conditions and events that may indicate the existence of risks of material misstatement. The examples provided cover a broad range of conditions and events; however, not all conditions and events are relevant to every audit engagement and the list of examples is not necessarily complete.

- Operations in regions that are economically unstable, for example, countries with significant currency devaluation or highly inflationary economies.
- Operations exposed to volatile markets, for example, futures trading.
- High degree of complex regulation.
- Going concern and liquidity issues, including loss of significant customers.
- Marginally achieving explicitly stated strategic objectives.
- Constraints on the availability of capital and credit.
- Changes in the industry in which the entity operates.
- Changes in the supply chain.
- Developing or offering new products or services, or moving into new lines of business.
- Expanding into new locations.
- Changes in the entity, such as large acquisitions, reorganizations, or other unusual events.
- Entities or divisions likely to be sold.
- Complex alliances and joint ventures.
- Use of off-balance-sheet finance, special-purpose entities, and other complex financing arrangements.
- Significant transactions with related parties.
- Lack of personnel with appropriate accounting and financial reporting skills.
- Changes in key personnel, including departure of key executives.
- Weaknesses in internal control, especially those not addressed by management.
- Inconsistencies between the entity's information technology (IT) strategy and its business strategies.
- Changes in the IT environment.
- Installation of significant new IT systems related to financial reporting.

- Inquiries into the entity's operations or financial results by regulatory or government bodies.
- Past misstatements, history of errors, or a significant amount of adjustments at period end.
- Significant amount of nonroutine or nonsystematic transactions, including intercompany transactions and large revenue transactions at period end.
- Transactions that are recorded based on management's intent, for example, debt refinancing, assets to be sold, and classification of marketable securities.
- Application of new accounting pronouncements.
- Complex processes related to accounting measurements.
- Events or transactions that result in significant measurement uncertainty, including accounting estimates.
- Pending litigation and contingent liabilities, for example, sales warranties, financial guarantees, and environmental remediation.

AU Section 315

Communications Between Predecessor and Successor Auditors

(Supersedes SAS No. 7.)

Source: SAS No. 84; SAS No. 93.

Effective with respect to acceptance of an engagement after March 31, 1998, unless otherwise indicated.

Introduction

.01 This section provides guidance on communications between predecessor and successor auditors when a change of auditors is in process or has taken place. It also provides communications guidance when possible misstatements are discovered in financial statements reported on by a predecessor auditor. This section applies whenever an independent auditor is considering accepting an engagement to audit or reaudit (see paragraph .14 of this section) financial statements in accordance with generally accepted auditing standards, and after such auditor has been appointed to perform such an engagement.

.02 For the purposes of this section, the term *predecessor auditor* refers to an auditor who (*a*) has reported on the most recent audited financial statements[1] or was engaged to perform but did not complete an audit of the financial statements[2] and (*b*) has resigned, declined to stand for reappointment, or been notified that his or her services have been, or may be, terminated. The term *successor auditor* refers to an auditor who is considering accepting an engagement to audit financial statements but has not communicated with the predecessor auditor as provided in paragraphs .07 through .10 and to an auditor who has accepted such an engagement. [As amended, effective for audits of financial statements for periods ending on or after June 30, 2001, by Statement on Auditing Standards No. 93.]

Change of Auditors

.03 An auditor should not accept an engagement until the communications described in paragraphs .07 through .10 have been evaluated.[3] However, an auditor may make a proposal for an audit engagement before communicating with the predecessor auditor. The auditor may wish to advise the prospective

---

[1] The provisions of this section are not required if the most recent audited financial statements are more than two years prior to the beginning of the earliest period to be audited by the successor auditor.

[2] There may be two predecessor auditors: the auditor who reported on the most recent audited financial statements and the auditor who was engaged to perform but did not complete an audit of any subsequent financial statements. [As amended, effective for audits of financial statements for periods ending on or after June 30, 2001, by Statement on Auditing Standards No. 93.]

[3] When the most recent financial statements have been compiled or reviewed in accordance with the Statements on Standards for Accounting and Review Services, the accountant who reported on those financial statements is not a predecessor auditor. Although not required by this section, in these circumstances the successor auditor may find the matters described in paragraphs .08 and .09 useful in determining whether to accept the engagement.

client (for example, in a proposal) that acceptance cannot be final until the communications have been evaluated.

.04 Other communications between the successor and predecessor auditors, described in paragraph .11, are advisable to assist in the planning of the engagement. However, the timing of these other communications is more flexible. The successor auditor may initiate these other communications either prior to acceptance of the engagement or subsequent thereto.

.05 When more than one auditor is considering accepting an engagement, the predecessor auditor should not be expected to be available to respond to inquiries until a successor auditor has been selected by the prospective client and has accepted the engagement subject to the evaluation of the communications with the predecessor auditor as provided in paragraphs .07 through .10.

.06 The initiative for communicating rests with the successor auditor. The communication may be either written or oral. Both the predecessor and successor auditors should hold in confidence information obtained from each other. This obligation applies whether or not the successor auditor accepts the engagement.

Communications Before Successor Auditor Accepts Engagement

.07 Inquiry of the predecessor auditor is a necessary procedure because the predecessor auditor may be able to provide information that will assist the successor auditor in determining whether to accept the engagement. The successor auditor should bear in mind that, among other things, the predecessor auditor and the client may have disagreed about accounting principles, auditing procedures, or similarly significant matters.

.08 The successor auditor should request permission from the prospective client to make an inquiry of the predecessor auditor prior to final acceptance of the engagement. Except as permitted by the Rules of the Code of Professional Conduct, an auditor is precluded from disclosing confidential information obtained in the course of an engagement unless the client specifically consents. Thus, the successor auditor should ask the prospective client to authorize the predecessor auditor to respond fully to the successor auditor's inquiries. If a prospective client refuses to permit the predecessor auditor to respond or limits the response, the successor auditor should inquire as to the reasons and consider the implications of that refusal in deciding whether to accept the engagement.

.09 The successor auditor should make specific and reasonable inquiries of the predecessor auditor regarding matters that will assist the successor auditor in determining whether to accept the engagement. Matters subject to inquiry should include—

- Information that might bear on the integrity of management.
- Disagreements with management as to accounting principles, auditing procedures, or other similarly significant matters.
- Communications to those charged with governance regarding fraud and illegal acts by clients.[4]

---

[4] [Footnote deleted to reflect conforming changes necessary due to the issuance of Statement on Auditing Standards No. 114.]

- Communications to management and those charged with governance regarding significant deficiencies and material weaknesses in internal control.[5]
- The predecessor auditor's understanding as to the reasons for the change of auditors.

The successor auditor may wish to consider other reasonable inquiries. [Revised, May 2006, to reflect conforming changes necessary due to the issuance of Statement on Auditing Standards No. 112. Revised, April 2007, to reflect conforming changes necessary due to the issuance of Statement on Auditing Standards No. 114.]

.10 The predecessor auditor should respond promptly and fully, on the basis of known facts, to the successor auditor's reasonable inquiries. However, should the predecessor auditor decide, due to unusual circumstances such as impending, threatened, or potential litigation; disciplinary proceedings; or other unusual circumstances, not to respond fully to the inquiries, the predecessor auditor should clearly state that the response is limited. If the successor auditor receives a limited response, its implications should be considered in deciding whether to accept the engagement.

Other Communications

.11 The successor auditor should request that the client authorize the predecessor auditor to allow a review of the predecessor auditor's working papers. The predecessor auditor may wish to request a consent and acknowledgment letter from the client to document this authorization in an effort to reduce misunderstandings about the scope of the communications being authorized.[6] It is customary in such circumstances for the predecessor auditor to make himself or herself available to the successor auditor and make available for review certain of the working papers. The predecessor auditor should determine which working papers are to be made available for review and which may be copied. The predecessor auditor should ordinarily permit the successor auditor to review working papers, including documentation of planning, internal control, audit results, and other matters of continuing accounting and auditing significance, such as the working paper analysis of balance sheet accounts, and those relating to contingencies. Also, the predecessor auditor should reach an understanding with the successor auditor as to the use of the working papers.[7] The extent, if any, to which a predecessor auditor permits access to the working papers is a matter of judgment.

Successor Auditor's Use of Communications

.12 The successor auditor must obtain sufficient appropriate audit evidence to afford a reasonable basis for expressing an opinion on the financial statements he or she has been engaged to audit, including evaluating the consistency of the application of accounting principles. The audit evidence used in analyzing the impact of the opening balances on the current-year financial statements and consistency of accounting principles is a matter of professional judgment. Such audit evidence may include the most recent audited financial

---

[5] See section 316, *Consideration of Fraud in a Financial Statement Audit*; section 317, *Illegal Acts by Clients*; and section 325, *Communicating Internal Control Related Matters Identified in an Audit*. [Footnote revised, May 2006, to reflect conforming changes necessary due to the issuance of Statement on Auditing Standards No. 112.]

[6] Appendix A [paragraph .24] contains an illustrative client consent and acknowledgment letter.

[7] Before permitting access to the working papers, the predecessor auditor may wish to obtain a written communication from the successor auditor regarding the use of the working papers. Appendix B [paragraph .25] contains an illustrative successor auditor acknowledgment letter.

statements, the predecessor auditor's report thereon,[8] the results of inquiry of the predecessor auditor, the results of the successor auditor's review of the predecessor auditor's working papers relating to the most recently completed audit, and audit procedures performed on the current period's transactions that may provide evidence about the opening balances or consistency. For example, evidence gathered during the current year's audit may provide information about the realizability and existence of receivables and inventory recorded at the beginning of the year. The successor auditor may also apply appropriate auditing procedures to account balances at the beginning of the period under audit and to transactions in prior periods. [As amended, effective for audits of financial statements for periods ending on or after June 30, 2001, by Statement on Auditing Standards No. 93. Revised, March 2006, to reflect conforming changes necessary due to the issuance of Statement on Auditing Standards No. 105.]

.13 The successor auditor's review of the predecessor auditor's working papers may affect the nature, timing, and extent of the successor auditor's procedures with respect to the opening balances and consistency of accounting principles. However, the nature, timing, and extent of audit work performed and the conclusions reached in both these areas are solely the responsibility of the successor auditor. In reporting on the audit, the successor auditor should not make reference to the report or work of the predecessor auditor as the basis, in part, for the successor auditor's own opinion.

Audits of Financial Statements That Have Been Previously Audited

.14 If an auditor is asked to audit and report on financial statements that have been previously audited and reported on (henceforth referred to as a reaudit), the auditor considering acceptance of the reaudit engagement is also a successor auditor, and the auditor who previously reported is also a predecessor auditor. In addition to the communications described in paragraphs .07 through .10, the successor auditor should state that the purpose of the inquiries is to obtain information about whether to accept an engagement to perform a reaudit.

.15 If the successor auditor accepts the reaudit engagement, he or she may consider the information obtained from inquiries of the predecessor auditor and review of the predecessor auditor's report and working papers in planning the reaudit. However, the information obtained from those inquiries and any review of the predecessor auditor's report and working papers is not sufficient to afford a basis for expressing an opinion. The nature, timing, and extent of the audit work performed and the conclusions reached in the reaudit are solely the responsibility of the successor auditor performing the reaudit.

.16 The successor auditor should plan and perform the reaudit in accordance with generally accepted auditing standards. The successor auditor should not assume responsibility for the predecessor auditor's work or issue a report that reflects divided responsibility as described in section 543, *Part of Audit Performed by Other Independent Auditors*. Furthermore, the predecessor auditor is not a specialist as defined in section 336, *Using the Work of a Specialist*, or an internal auditor as defined in section 322, *The Auditor's Consideration of the Internal Audit Function in an Audit of Financial Statements*.

.17 If the successor auditor has audited the current period, the results of that audit may be considered in planning and performing the reaudit of the

---

[8] The successor auditor may wish to make inquiries about the professional reputation and standing of the predecessor auditor. See section 543, *Part of Audit Performed by Other Independent Auditors*, paragraph .10*a*.

preceding period or periods and may provide audit evidence that is useful in performing the reaudit. [Revised, March 2006, to reflect conforming changes necessary due to the issuance of Statement on Auditing Standards No. 105.]

.18 If, in a reaudit engagement, the successor auditor is unable to obtain sufficient appropriate audit evidence to express an opinion on the financial statements, the successor auditor should qualify or disclaim an opinion because of the inability to perform procedures the successor auditor considers necessary in the circumstances. [Revised, March 2006, to reflect conforming changes necessary due to the issuance of Statement on Auditing Standards No. 105.]

.19 The successor auditor should request working papers for the period or periods under reaudit and the period prior to the reaudit period. However, the extent, if any, to which the predecessor auditor permits access to the working papers is a matter of judgment. (See paragraph .11 of this section.)

.20 In a reaudit, the successor auditor generally will be unable to observe inventory or make physical counts at the reaudit date or dates in the manner discussed in paragraphs .09 through .11 of section 331, *Inventories*. In such cases, the successor auditor may consider the knowledge obtained from his or her review of the predecessor auditor's working papers and inquiries of the predecessor auditor to determine the nature, timing, and extent of procedures to be applied in the circumstances. The successor auditor performing the reaudit should, if material, observe or perform some physical counts of inventory at a date subsequent to the period of the reaudit, in connection with a current audit or otherwise, and apply appropriate tests of intervening transactions. Appropriate procedures may include tests of prior transactions, reviews of records of prior counts, and the application of analytical procedures, such as gross profit tests.

Discovery of Possible Misstatements in Financial Statements Reported on by a Predecessor Auditor

.21 If during the audit or reaudit, the successor auditor becomes aware of information that leads him or her to believe that financial statements reported on by the predecessor auditor may require revision, the successor auditor should request that the client inform the predecessor auditor of the situation and arrange for the three parties to discuss this information and attempt to resolve the matter. The successor auditor should communicate to the predecessor auditor any information that the predecessor auditor may need to consider in accordance with section 561, *Subsequent Discovery of Facts Existing at the Date of the Auditor's Report*, which sets out the procedures that an auditor should follow when the auditor subsequently discovers facts that may have affected the audited financial statements previously reported on.[9]

.22 If the client refuses to inform the predecessor auditor or if the successor auditor is not satisfied with the resolution of the matter, the successor auditor should evaluate (*a*) possible implications on the current engagement and (*b*) whether to resign from the engagement. Furthermore, the successor auditor may wish to consult with his or her legal counsel in determining an appropriate course of further action.

Effective Date

.23 This section will be effective with respect to acceptance of an engagement after March 31, 1998. Earlier application is permitted.

---

[9] See section 508, *Reports on Audited Financial Statements*, paragraphs .70 through .74, for reporting guidance.

.24

Appendix A

Illustrative Client Consent and Acknowledgment Letter

1. Paragraph .11 of this section states, "The successor auditor should request that the client authorize the predecessor auditor to allow a review of the predecessor auditor's working papers. The predecessor auditor may wish to request a consent and acknowledgment letter from the client to document this authorization in an effort to reduce misunderstandings about the scope of the communications being authorized." The following letter is presented for illustrative purposes only and is not required by professional standards.

[*Date*]

ABC Enterprises

[*Address*]

You have given your consent to allow [*name of successor CPA firm*], as successor independent auditors for ABC Enterprises (ABC), access to our working papers for our audit of the December 31, 19X1, financial statements of ABC. You also have given your consent to us to respond fully to [*name of successor CPA firm*] inquiries. You understand and agree that the review of our working papers is undertaken solely for the purpose of obtaining an understanding about ABC and certain information about our audit to assist [*name of successor CPA firm*] in planning the audit of the December 31, 19X2, financial statements of ABC.

Please confirm your agreement with the foregoing by signing and dating a copy of this letter and returning it to us.

Attached is the form of the letter we will furnish [*name of successor CPA firm*] regarding the use of the working papers.

Very truly yours,

[*Predecessor Auditor*]

By: ______________

Accepted:

ABC Enterprises

By: ______________

Date: ____________

.25

Appendix B

Illustrative Successor Auditor Acknowledgment Letter

1. Paragraph .11, footnote 7, of this section states, "Before permitting access to the working papers, the predecessor auditor may wish to obtain a written communication from the successor auditor regarding the use of the working papers." The following letter is presented for illustrative purposes only and is not required by professional standards.

[*Date*]

[*Successor Auditor*]

[*Address*]

We have previously audited, in accordance with auditing standards generally accepted in the United States of America, the December 31, 20X1, financial statements of ABC Enterprises (ABC). We rendered a report on those financial statements and have not performed any audit procedures subsequent to the audit report date. In connection with your audit of ABC's 20X2 financial statements, you have requested access to our working papers prepared in connection with that audit. ABC has authorized our firm to allow you to review those working papers.

Our audit, and the working papers prepared in connection therewith, of ABC's financial statements were not planned or conducted in contemplation of your review. Therefore, items of possible interest to you may not have been specifically addressed. Our use of professional judgment and the assessment of audit risk and materiality for the purpose of our audit mean that matters may have existed that would have been assessed differently by you. We make no representation as to the sufficiency or appropriateness of the information in our working papers for your purposes.

We understand that the purpose of your review is to obtain information about ABC and our 19X1 audit results to assist you in planning your 19X2 audit of ABC. For that purpose only, we will provide you access to our working papers that relate to that objective.

Upon request, we will provide copies of those working papers that provide factual information about ABC. You agree to subject any such copies or information otherwise derived from our working papers to your normal policy for retention of working papers and protection of confidential client information. Furthermore, in the event of a third-party request for access to your working papers prepared in connection with your audits of ABC, you agree to obtain our permission before voluntarily allowing any such access to our working papers or information otherwise derived from our working papers, and to obtain on our behalf any releases that you obtain from such third party. You agree to advise us promptly and provide us a copy of any subpoena, summons, or other court order for access to your working papers that include copies of our working papers or information otherwise derived therefrom.

Please confirm your agreement with the foregoing by signing and dating a copy of this letter and returning it to us.

Very truly yours,

[*Predecessor Auditor*]

By: ________________

Accepted:

[*Successor Auditor*]

By: ________________

Date: ________

Even with the client's consent, access to the predecessor auditor's working papers may still be limited. Experience has shown that the predecessor auditor may be willing to grant broader access if given additional assurance concerning the use of the working papers. Accordingly, the successor auditor might consider agreeing to the following limitations on the review of the predecessor auditor's working papers in order to obtain broader access:

- The successor auditor will not comment, orally or in writing, to anyone as a result of the review as to whether the predecessor auditor's engagement was performed in accordance with generally accepted auditing standards.
- The successor auditor will not provide expert testimony or litigation support services or otherwise accept an engagement to comment on issues relating to the quality of the predecessor auditor's audit.
- The successor auditor will not use the audit procedures or results thereof documented in the predecessor auditor's working papers as audit evidence in rendering an opinion on the 19X2 financial statements of ABC Enterprises, except as contemplated in Statement on Auditing Standards No. 84.

The following paragraph illustrates the above:

> Because your review of our working papers is undertaken solely for the purpose described above and may not entail a review of all our working papers, you agree that (1) the information obtained from the review will not be used by you for any other purpose, (2) you will not comment, orally or in writing, to anyone as a result of that review as to whether our audit was performed in accordance with generally accepted auditing standards, (3) you will not provide expert testimony or litigation support services or otherwise accept an engagement to comment on issues relating to the quality of our audit, and (4) you will not use the audit procedures or results thereof documented in our working papers as audit evidence in rendering your opinion on the 19X2 financial statements of ABC, except as contemplated in Statement on Auditing Standards No. 84.

[Revised, October 2000, to reflect conforming changes necessary due to the issuance of Statement on Auditing Standards No. 93. Revised, March 2006, to reflect conforming changes necessary due to the issuance of Statement on Auditing Standards No. 105.]

AU Section 316

Consideration of Fraud in a Financial Statement Audit

(Supersedes SAS No. 82.)

Source: SAS No. 99; SAS No. 113.

Effective for audits of financial statements for periods beginning on or after December 15, 2002, unless otherwise indicated.

Introduction and Overview

.01 Section 110, *Responsibilities and Functions of the Independent Auditor*, paragraph .02, states, "The auditor has a responsibility to plan and perform the audit to obtain reasonable assurance about whether the financial statements are free of material misstatement, whether caused by error or fraud. [footnote omitted]"[1] This section establishes standards and provides guidance to auditors in fulfilling that responsibility, as it relates to fraud, in an audit of financial statements conducted in accordance with generally accepted auditing standards (GAAS).[2]

.02 The following is an overview of the organization and content of this section:

- *Description and characteristics of fraud.* This section describes fraud and its characteristics. (See paragraphs .05 through .12.)
- *The importance of exercising professional skepticism.* This section discusses the need for auditors to exercise professional skepticism when considering the possibility that a material misstatement due to fraud could be present. (See paragraph .13.)
- *Discussion among engagement personnel regarding the risks of material misstatement due to fraud.* This section requires, as part of planning the audit, that there be a discussion among the audit team members to consider how and where the entity's financial statements might be susceptible to material misstatement due to fraud and to reinforce the importance of adopting an appropriate mindset of professional skepticism. (See paragraphs .14 through .18.)

---

[1] The auditor's consideration of illegal acts and responsibility for detecting misstatements resulting from illegal acts is defined in section 317, *Illegal Acts by Clients*. For those illegal acts that are defined in that section as having a direct and material effect on the determination of financial statement amounts, the auditor's responsibility to detect misstatements resulting from such illegal acts is the same as that for errors (see section 312, *Audit Risk and Materiality in Conducting an Audit*, or fraud).

[2] Auditors are sometimes requested to perform other services related to fraud detection and prevention, for example, special investigations to determine the extent of a suspected or detected fraud. These other services usually include procedures that extend beyond or are different from the procedures ordinarily performed in an audit of financial statements in accordance with generally accepted auditing standards (GAAS). AT section 101, *Attest Engagements*, and CS section 100, *Consulting Services: Definitions and Standards*, provide guidance to accountants relating to the performance of such services.

- *Obtaining the information needed to identify risks of material misstatement due to fraud.* This section requires the auditor to gather information necessary to identify risks of material misstatement due to fraud, by
    a. Inquiring of management and others within the entity about the risks of fraud. (See paragraphs .20 through .27.)
    b. Considering the results of the analytical procedures performed in planning the audit. (See paragraphs .28 through .30.)
    c. Considering fraud risk factors. (See paragraphs .31 through .33, and the Appendix, "Examples of Fraud Risk Factors" [paragraph .85].)
    d. Considering certain other information. (See paragraph .34.)
- *Identifying risks that may result in a material misstatement due to fraud.* This section requires the auditor to use the information gathered to identify risks that may result in a material misstatement due to fraud. (See paragraphs .35 through .42.)
- *Assessing the identified risks after taking into account an evaluation of the entity's programs and controls.* This section requires the auditor to evaluate the entity's programs and controls that address the identified risks of material misstatement due to fraud, and to assess the risks taking into account this evaluation. (See paragraphs .43 through .45.)
- *Responding to the results of the assessment.* This section emphasizes that the auditor's response to the risks of material misstatement due to fraud involves the application of professional skepticism when gathering and evaluating audit evidence. (See paragraph .46 through .49.) The section requires the auditor to respond to the results of the risk assessment in three ways:
    a. A response that has an overall effect on how the audit is conducted, that is, a response involving more general considerations apart from the specific procedures otherwise planned. (See paragraph .50.)
    b. A response to identified risks that involves the nature, timing, and extent of the auditing procedures to be performed. (See paragraphs .51 through .56.)
    c. A response involving the performance of certain procedures to further address the risk of material misstatement due to fraud involving management override of controls. (See paragraphs .57 through .67.)
- *Evaluating audit evidence.* This section requires the auditor to assess the risks of material misstatement due to fraud throughout the audit and to evaluate at the completion of the audit whether the accumulated results of auditing procedures and other observations affect the assessment. (See paragraphs .68 through .74.) It also requires the auditor to consider whether identified misstatements may be indicative of fraud and, if so, directs the auditor to evaluate their implications. (See paragraphs .75 through .78.)
- *Communicating about fraud to management, those charged with governance, and others.* This section provides guidance regarding the auditor's communications about fraud to management, those charged with governance, and others. (See paragraphs .79 through .82.)
- *Documenting the auditor's consideration of fraud.* This section describes related documentation requirements. (See paragraph .83.)

[Revised, April 2007, to reflect conforming changes necessary due to the issuance of Statement on Auditing Standards No. 114.]

.03 The requirements and guidance set forth in this section are intended to be integrated into an overall audit process, in a logical manner that is consistent with the requirements and guidance provided in other sections, including section 311, *Planning and Supervision*; section 312, *Audit Risk and Materiality in Conducting an Audit*; section 314, *Understanding the Entity and Its Environment and Assessing the Risks of Material Misstatement*, and section 318 *Performing Audit Procedures in Response to Assessed Risks and Evaluating the Audit Evidence Obtained*. Even though some requirements and guidance set forth in this section are presented in a manner that suggests a sequential audit process, auditing in fact involves a continuous process of gathering, updating, and analyzing information throughout the audit. Accordingly the sequence of the requirements and guidance in this section may be implemented differently among audit engagements. [Revised, March 2006, to reflect conforming changes necessary due to the issuance of Statements on Auditing Standards No. 109 and No. 110.]

.04 Although this section focuses on the auditor's consideration of fraud in an audit of financial statements, it is management's responsibility to design and implement programs and controls to prevent, deter, and detect fraud.[3] That responsibility is described in section 110.03, which states, "Management is responsible for adopting sound accounting policies and for establishing and maintaining internal control that will, among other things, authorize, record, process, and report transactions (as well as events and conditions) consistent with management's assertions embodied in the financial statements." Management, along with those charged with governance, should set the proper tone; create and maintain a culture of honesty and high ethical standards; and establish appropriate controls to prevent, deter, and detect fraud. When management and those charged with governance fulfill those responsibilities, the opportunities to commit fraud can be reduced significantly. [Revised, March 2006, to reflect conforming changes necessary due to the issuance of Statement on Auditing Standards No. 106. Revised, April 2007, to reflect conforming changes necessary due to the issuance of Statement on Auditing Standards No. 114.]

Description and Characteristics of Fraud

.05 Fraud is a broad legal concept and auditors do not make legal determinations of whether fraud has occurred. Rather, the auditor's interest specifically relates to acts that result in a material misstatement of the financial statements. The primary factor that distinguishes fraud from error is whether the underlying action that results in the misstatement of the financial statements is intentional or unintentional. For purposes of the section, *fraud* is an intentional act that results in a material misstatement in financial statements that are the subject of an audit.[4]

---

[3] In its October 1987 report, the National Commission on Fraudulent Financial Reporting, also known as the Treadway Commission, noted, "The responsibility for reliable financial reporting resides first and foremost at the corporate level. Top management, starting with the chief executive officer, sets the tone and establishes the financial reporting environment. Therefore, reducing the risk of fraudulent financial reporting must start with the reporting company."

[4] Intent is often difficult to determine, particularly in matters involving accounting estimates and the application of accounting principles. For example, unreasonable accounting estimates may be unintentional or may be the result of an intentional attempt to misstate the financial statements. Although an audit is not designed to determine intent, the auditor has a responsibility to plan and perform the audit to obtain reasonable assurance about whether the financial statements are free of material misstatement, whether the misstatement is intentional or not.

.06 Two types of misstatements are relevant to the auditor's consideration of fraud—misstatements arising from fraudulent financial reporting and misstatements arising from misappropriation of assets.

- *Misstatements arising from fraudulent financial reporting* are intentional misstatements or omissions of amounts or disclosures in financial statements designed to deceive financial statement users where the effect causes the financial statements not to be presented, in all material respects, in conformity with generally accepted accounting principles (GAAP).[5] Fraudulent financial reporting may be accomplished by the following:
  - — Manipulation, falsification, or alteration of accounting records or supporting documents from which financial statements are prepared
  - — Misrepresentation in or intentional omission from the financial statements of events, transactions, or other significant information
  - — Intentional misapplication of accounting principles relating to amounts, classification, manner of presentation, or disclosure

  Fraudulent financial reporting need not be the result of a grand plan or conspiracy. It may be that management representatives rationalize the appropriateness of a material misstatement, for example, as an aggressive rather than indefensible interpretation of complex accounting rules, or as a temporary misstatement of financial statements, including interim statements, expected to be corrected later when operational results improve.

- *Misstatements arising from misappropriation of assets* (sometimes referred to as theft or defalcation) involve the theft of an entity's assets where the effect of the theft causes the financial statements not to be presented, in all material respects, in conformity with GAAP. Misappropriation of assets can be accomplished in various ways, including embezzling receipts, stealing assets, or causing an entity to pay for goods or services that have not been received. Misappropriation of assets may be accompanied by false or misleading records or documents, possibly created by circumventing controls. The scope of this section includes only those misappropriations of assets for which the effect of the misappropriation causes the financial statements not to be fairly presented, in all material respects, in conformity with GAAP.

.07 Three conditions generally are present when fraud occurs. First, management or other employees have an *incentive* or are under *pressure*, which provides a reason to commit fraud. Second, circumstances exist—for example, the absence of controls, ineffective controls, or the ability of management to override controls—that provide an *opportunity* for a fraud to be perpetrated. Third, those involved are able to *rationalize* committing a fraudulent act. Some individuals possess an *attitude*, character, or set of ethical values that allow them to knowingly and intentionally commit a dishonest act. However, even otherwise honest individuals can commit fraud in an environment that imposes sufficient pressure on them. The greater the incentive or pressure, the more likely an individual will be able to rationalize the acceptability of committing fraud.

---

[5] Reference to generally accepted accounting principles (GAAP) includes, where applicable, a comprehensive basis of accounting other than GAAP as defined in section 623, *Special Reports*, paragraph .04.

.08 Management has a unique ability to perpetrate fraud because it frequently is in a position to directly or indirectly manipulate accounting records and present fraudulent financial information. Fraudulent financial reporting often involves management override of controls that otherwise may appear to be operating effectively.[6] Management can either direct employees to perpetrate fraud or solicit their help in carrying it out. In addition, management personnel at a component of the entity may be in a position to manipulate the accounting records of the component in a manner that causes a material misstatement in the consolidated financial statements of the entity. Management override of controls can occur in unpredictable ways.

.09 Typically, management and employees engaged in fraud will take steps to conceal the fraud from the auditors and others within and outside the organization. Fraud may be concealed by withholding evidence or misrepresenting information in response to inquiries or by falsifying documentation. For example, management that engages in fraudulent financial reporting might alter shipping documents. Employees or members of management who misappropriate cash might try to conceal their thefts by forging signatures or falsifying electronic approvals on disbursement authorizations. An audit conducted in accordance with GAAS rarely involves the authentication of such documentation, nor are auditors trained as or expected to be experts in such authentication. In addition, an auditor may not discover the existence of a modification of documentation through a side agreement that management or a third party has not disclosed.

.10 Fraud also may be concealed through collusion among management, employees, or third parties. Collusion may cause the auditor who has properly performed the audit to conclude that evidence provided is persuasive when it is, in fact, false. For example, through collusion, false evidence that controls have been operating effectively may be presented to the auditor, or consistent misleading explanations may be given to the auditor by more than one individual within the entity to explain an unexpected result of an analytical procedure. As another example, the auditor may receive a false confirmation from a third party that is in collusion with management.

.11 Although fraud usually is concealed and management's intent is difficult to determine, the presence of certain conditions may suggest to the auditor the possibility that fraud may exist. For example, an important contract may be missing, a subsidiary ledger may not be satisfactorily reconciled to its control account, or the results of an analytical procedure performed during the audit may not be consistent with expectations. However, these conditions may be the result of circumstances other than fraud. Documents may legitimately have been lost or misfiled; the subsidiary ledger may be out of balance with its control account because of an unintentional accounting error; and unexpected analytical relationships may be the result of unanticipated changes in underlying economic factors. Even reports of alleged fraud may not always be reliable because an employee or outsider may be mistaken or may be motivated for unknown reasons to make a false allegation.

.12 As indicated in paragraph .01, the auditor has a responsibility to plan and perform the audit to obtain reasonable assurance about whether the financial statements are free of material misstatement, whether caused by fraud or

---

[6] Frauds have been committed by management override of existing controls using such techniques as (*a*) recording fictitious journal entries, particularly those recorded close to the end of an accounting period to manipulate operating results, (*b*) intentionally biasing assumptions and judgments used to estimate account balances, and (*c*) altering records and terms related to significant and unusual transactions.

error.[7] However, absolute assurance is not attainable and thus even a properly planned and performed audit may not detect a material misstatement resulting from fraud. A material misstatement may not be detected because of the nature of audit evidence or because the characteristics of fraud as discussed above may cause the auditor to rely unknowingly on audit evidence that appears to be valid, but is, in fact, false and fraudulent. Furthermore, audit procedures that are effective for detecting an error may be ineffective for detecting fraud.

The Importance of Exercising Professional Skepticism

.13 Due professional care requires the auditor to exercise professional skepticism. See section 230, *Due Professional Care in the Performance of Work*, paragraphs .07 through .09. Because of the characteristics of fraud, the auditor's exercise of professional skepticism is important when considering the risk of material misstatement due to fraud. Professional skepticism is an attitude that includes a questioning mind and a critical assessment of audit evidence. The auditor should conduct the engagement with a mindset that recognizes the possibility that a material misstatement due to fraud could be present, regardless of any past experience with the entity and regardless of the auditor's belief about management's honesty and integrity. Furthermore, professional skepticism requires an ongoing questioning of whether the information and evidence obtained suggests that a material misstatement due to fraud has occurred. In exercising professional skepticism in gathering and evaluating evidence, the auditor should not be satisfied with less-than-persuasive evidence because of a belief that management is honest.

Discussion Among Engagement Personnel Regarding the Risks of Material Misstatement Due to Fraud

.14 Prior to or in conjunction with the information-gathering procedures described in paragraphs .19 through .34 of this section, members of the audit team should discuss the potential for material misstatement due to fraud. The discussion should include:

- An exchange of ideas or "brainstorming" among the audit team members, including the auditor with final responsibility for the audit, about how and where they believe the entity's financial statements might be susceptible to material misstatement due to fraud, how management could perpetrate and conceal fraudulent financial reporting, and how assets of the entity could be misappropriated. (See paragraph .15.)
- An emphasis on the importance of maintaining the proper state of mind throughout the audit regarding the potential for material misstatement due to fraud. (See paragraph .16.)

.15 The discussion among the audit team members about the susceptibility of the entity's financial statements to material misstatement due to fraud should include a consideration of the known external and internal factors affecting the entity that might (*a*) create incentives/pressures for management and others to commit fraud, (*b*) provide the opportunity for fraud to be perpetrated, and (*c*) indicate a culture or environment that enables management to rationalize committing fraud. The discussion should occur with an attitude that includes a questioning mind as described in paragraph .16 and, for this purpose,

[7] For a further discussion of the concept of reasonable assurance, see section 230, *Due Professional Care in the Performance of Work*, paragraphs .10 through .13.

setting aside any prior beliefs the audit team members may have that management is honest and has integrity. In this regard, the discussion should include a consideration of the risk of management override of controls.[8] Finally, the discussion should include how the auditor might respond to the susceptibility of the entity's financial statements to material misstatement due to fraud.

.16 The discussion among the audit team members should emphasize the need to maintain a questioning mind and to exercise professional skepticism in gathering and evaluating evidence throughout the audit, as described in paragraph .13. This should lead the audit team members to continually be alert for information or other conditions (such as those presented in paragraph .68) that indicate a material misstatement due to fraud may have occurred. It should also lead audit team members to thoroughly probe the issues, acquire additional evidence as necessary, and consult with other team members and, if appropriate, experts in the firm, rather than rationalize or dismiss information or other conditions that indicate a material misstatement due to fraud may have occurred.

.17 Although professional judgment should be used in determining which audit team members should be included in the discussion, the discussion ordinarily should involve the key members of the audit team. A number of factors will influence the extent of the discussion and how it should occur. For example, if the audit involves more than one location, there could be multiple discussions with team members in differing locations. Another factor to consider in planning the discussions is whether to include specialists assigned to the audit team. For example, if the auditor has determined that a professional possessing information technology skills is needed on the audit team (see section 311.31), it may be useful to include that individual in the discussion. [Revised, March 2006, to reflect conforming changes necessary due to the issuance of Statement on Auditing Standards No. 108.]

.18 Communication among the audit team members about the risks of material misstatement due to fraud also should continue throughout the audit—for example, in evaluating the risks of material misstatement due to fraud at or near the completion of the field work. (See paragraph .74 and footnote 28.)

Obtaining the Information Needed to Identify the Risks of Material Misstatement Due to Fraud

.19 Section 314 provides guidance about how the auditor obtains an understanding of the entity and its environment, including its internal control. In performing that work, information may come to the auditor's attention that should be considered in identifying risks of material misstatement due to fraud. As part of this work, the auditor should perform the following procedures to obtain information that is used (as described in paragraphs .35 through .42) to identify the risks of material misstatement due to fraud:

a. Make inquiries of management and others within the entity to obtain their views about the risks of fraud and how they are addressed. (See paragraphs .20 through .27.)

b. Consider any unusual or unexpected relationships that have been identified in performing analytical procedures in planning the audit. (See paragraphs .28 through .30.)

[8] See footnote 6.

c. Consider whether one or more fraud risk factors exist. (See paragraphs .31 through .33, and the Appendix [paragraph .85].)

d. Consider other information that may be helpful in the identification of risks of material misstatement due to fraud. (See paragraph .34.)

[Revised, March 2006, to reflect conforming changes necessary due to the issuance of Statement on Auditing Standards No. 109.]

Making Inquiries of Management and Others Within the Entity About the Risks of Fraud

.20 The auditor should inquire of management about:[9]

- Whether management has knowledge of any fraud or suspected fraud affecting the entity
- Whether management is aware of allegations of fraud or suspected fraud affecting the entity, for example, received in communications from employees, former employees, analysts, regulators, short sellers, or others
- Management's understanding about the risks of fraud in the entity, including any specific fraud risks the entity has identified or account balances or classes of transactions for which a risk of fraud may be likely to exist
- Programs and controls[10] the entity has established to mitigate specific fraud risks the entity has identified, or that otherwise help to prevent, deter, and detect fraud, and how management monitors those programs and controls. For examples of programs and controls an entity may implement to prevent, deter, and detect fraud, see the exhibit titled "Management Antifraud Programs and Controls" [paragraph .86] at the end of this section.
- For an entity with multiple locations, (*a*) the nature and extent of monitoring of operating locations or business segments, and (*b*) whether there are particular operating locations or business segments for which a risk of fraud may be more likely to exist
- Whether and how management communicates to employees its views on business practices and ethical behavior

.21 The inquiries of management also should include whether management has reported to those charged with governance[11] on how the entity's internal control[12] serves to prevent, deter, or detect material misstatements due to fraud. [Revised, April 2007, to reflect conforming changes necessary due to the issuance of Statement on Auditing Standards No. 114.]

.22 The auditor also should inquire directly of those charged with governance (or the audit committee or at least its chair) regarding their views about

---

[9] In addition to these inquiries, section 333, *Management Representations*, requires the auditor to obtain selected written representations from management regarding fraud.

[10] Section 314, *Understanding the Entity and Its Environment and Assessing the Risks of Material Misstatement*, paragraph .41, defines internal control and its five interrelated components (the control environment, risk assessment, control activities, information and communication, and monitoring). Entity programs and controls intended to address the risks of fraud may be part of any of the five components discussed in section 314. [Footnote revised, March 2006, to reflect conforming changes necessary due to the issuance of Statement on Auditing Standards No. 109.]

[11] [Footnote deleted due to conforming changes necessary due to the issuance of Statement on Auditing Standards No. 114.]

[12] See footnote 10.

the risks of fraud and whether those charged with governance have knowledge of any fraud or suspected fraud affecting the entity. An entity's audit committee sometimes assumes an active role in oversight of the entity's assessment of the risks of fraud and the programs and controls the entity has established to mitigate these risks. The auditor should obtain an understanding of how the audit committee exercises oversight activities in that area. [Revised, April 2007, to reflect conforming changes necessary due to the issuance of Statement on Auditing Standards No. 114.]

.23 For entities that have an internal audit function, the auditor also should inquire of appropriate internal audit personnel about their views about the risks of fraud, whether they have performed any procedures to identify or detect fraud during the year, whether management has satisfactorily responded to any findings resulting from these procedures, and whether the internal auditors have knowledge of any fraud or suspected fraud.

.24 In addition to the inquiries outlined in paragraphs .20 through .23, the auditor should inquire of others within the entity about the existence or suspicion of fraud. The auditor should use professional judgment to determine those others within the entity to whom inquiries should be directed and the extent of such inquiries. In making this determination, the auditor should consider whether others within the entity may be able to provide information that will be helpful to the auditor in identifying risks of material misstatement due to fraud—for example, others who may have additional knowledge about or be able to corroborate risks of fraud identified in the discussions with management (see paragraph .20) or those charged with governance (see paragraph .22). [Revised, April 2007, to reflect conforming changes necessary due to the issuance of Statement on Auditing Standards No. 114.]

.25 Examples of others within the entity to whom the auditor may wish to direct these inquiries include:

- Employees with varying levels of authority within the entity, including, for example, entity personnel with whom the auditor comes into contact during the course of the audit in obtaining (*a*) an understanding of the entity's systems and internal control, (*b*) in observing inventory or performing cutoff procedures, or (*c*) in obtaining explanations for fluctuations noted as a result of analytical procedures
- Operating personnel not directly involved in the financial reporting process
- Employees involved in initiating, recording, or processing complex or unusual transactions—for example, a sales transaction with multiple elements, or a significant related party transaction
- In-house legal counsel

.26 The auditor's inquiries of management and others within the entity are important because fraud often is uncovered through information received in response to inquiries. One reason for this is that such inquiries may provide individuals with an opportunity to convey information to the auditor that otherwise might not be communicated. Making inquiries of others within the entity, in addition to management, may be useful in providing the auditor with a perspective that is different from that of individuals involved in the financial reporting process. The responses to these other inquiries might serve to corroborate responses received from management, or alternatively, might provide information regarding the possibility of management override of controls—for example, a response from an employee indicating an unusual change in the way transactions have been processed. In addition, the auditor may obtain information from these inquiries regarding how effectively management has communicated standards of ethical behavior to individuals throughout the organization.

.27 The auditor should be aware when evaluating management's responses to the inquiries discussed in paragraph .20 that management is often in the best position to perpetrate fraud. The auditor should use professional judgment in deciding when it is necessary to corroborate responses to inquiries with other information. However, when responses are inconsistent among inquiries, the auditor should obtain additional audit evidence to resolve the inconsistencies.

Considering the Results of the Analytical Procedures Performed in Planning the Audit

.28 Section 329, *Analytical Procedures*, paragraphs .04 and .06, requires that analytical procedures be performed in planning the audit with an objective of identifying the existence of unusual transactions or events, and amounts, ratios, and trends that might indicate matters that have financial statement and audit planning implications. In performing analytical procedures in planning the audit, the auditor develops expectations about plausible relationships that are reasonably expected to exist, based on the auditor's understanding of the entity and its environment. When comparison of those expectations with recorded amounts or ratios developed from recorded amounts yields unusual or unexpected relationships, the auditor should consider those results in identifying the risks of material misstatement due to fraud.

.29 In planning the audit, the auditor also should perform analytical procedures relating to revenue with the objective of identifying unusual or unexpected relationships involving revenue accounts that may indicate a material misstatement due to fraudulent financial reporting. An example of such an analytical procedure that addresses this objective is a comparison of sales volume, as determined from recorded revenue amounts, with production capacity. An excess of sales volume over production capacity may be indicative of recording fictitious sales. As another example, a trend analysis of revenues by month and sales returns by month during and shortly after the reporting period may indicate the existence of undisclosed side agreements with customers to return goods that would preclude revenue recognition.[13]

.30 Analytical procedures performed during planning may be helpful in identifying the risks of material misstatement due to fraud. However, because such analytical procedures generally use data aggregated at a high level, the results of those analytical procedures provide only a broad initial indication about whether a material misstatement of the financial statements may exist. Accordingly, the results of analytical procedures performed during planning should be considered along with other information gathered by the auditor in identifying the risks of material misstatement due to fraud.

Considering Fraud Risk Factors

.31 Because fraud is usually concealed, material misstatements due to fraud are difficult to detect. Nevertheless, the auditor may identify events or conditions that indicate incentives/pressures to perpetrate fraud, opportunities to carry out the fraud, or attitudes/rationalizations to justify a fraudulent action. Such events or conditions are referred to as "fraud risk factors." Fraud risk factors do not necessarily indicate the existence of fraud; however, they often are present in circumstances where fraud exists.

---

[13] See paragraph .70 for a discussion of the need to update these analytical procedures during the overall review stage of the audit.

.32 When obtaining information about the entity and its environment, the auditor should consider whether the information indicates that one or more fraud risk factors are present. The auditor should use professional judgment in determining whether a risk factor is present and should be considered in identifying and assessing the risks of material misstatement due to fraud.

.33 Examples of fraud risk factors related to fraudulent financial reporting and misappropriation of assets are presented in the Appendix [paragraph .85]. These illustrative risk factors are classified based on the three conditions generally present when fraud exists: *incentive/pressure* to perpetrate fraud, an *opportunity* to carry out the fraud, and *attitude/rationalization* to justify the fraudulent action. Although the risk factors cover a broad range of situations, they are only examples and, accordingly, the auditor may wish to consider additional or different risk factors. Not all of these examples are relevant in all circumstances, and some may be of greater or lesser significance in entities of different size or with different ownership characteristics or circumstances. Also, the order of the examples of risk factors provided is not intended to reflect their relative importance or frequency of occurrence.

Considering Other Information That May Be Helpful in Identifying Risks of Material Misstatement Due to Fraud

.34 The auditor should consider other information that may be helpful in identifying risks of material misstatement due to fraud. Specifically, the discussion among the engagement team members (see paragraphs .14 through .18) may provide information helpful in identifying such risks. In addition, the auditor should consider whether information from the results of (*a*) procedures relating to the acceptance and continuance of clients and engagements[14] and (*b*) reviews of interim financial statements may be relevant in the identification of such risks. Finally, as part of the consideration of audit risk at the individual account balance or class of transaction level (see section 312.17 through .26), the auditor should consider whether identified inherent risks would provide useful information in identifying the risks of material misstatement due to fraud (see paragraph .39). [Revised, March 2006, to reflect conforming changes necessary due to the issuance of Statement on Auditing Standards No. 107.]

Identifying Risks That May Result in a Material Misstatement Due to Fraud[15]

Using the Information Gathered to Identify Risk of Material Misstatements Due to Fraud

.35 In identifying risks of material misstatement due to fraud, it is helpful for the auditor to consider the information that has been gathered (see paragraphs .19 through .34) in the context of the three conditions present when a material misstatement due to fraud occurs—that is, incentives/pressures,

---

[14] See paragraphs .27–.36 of QC section 10B, *A Firm's System of Quality Control*. [Footnote amended due to issuance of SQCS No. 7, December 2008.]

[15] Section 314, *Understanding the Entity and its Environment and Assessing the Risks of Material Misstatement*, requires the auditor to identify and assess the risk of material misstatement at the financial statement level and at the relevant assertion level related to classes of transactions, account balances and disclosures. See section 314.102. [Footnote added, effective for audits of financial statements for periods beginning on or after December 15, 2006, by Statement on Auditing Standards No. 113.]

opportunities, and attitudes/rationalizations (see paragraph .07). However, the auditor should not assume that all three conditions must be observed or evident before concluding that there are identified risks. Although the risk of material misstatement due to fraud may be greatest when all three fraud conditions are observed or evident, the auditor cannot assume that the inability to observe one or two of these conditions means there is no risk of material misstatement due to fraud. In fact, observing that individuals have the requisite attitude to commit fraud, or identifying factors that indicate a likelihood that management or other employees will rationalize committing a fraud, is difficult at best.

.36 In addition, the extent to which each of the three conditions referred to above are present when fraud occurs may vary. In some instances the significance of incentives/pressures may result in a risk of material misstatement due to fraud, apart from the significance of the other two conditions. For example, an incentive/pressure to achieve an earnings level to preclude a loan default, or to "trigger" incentive compensation plan awards, may alone result in a risk of material misstatement due to fraud. In other instances, an easy opportunity to commit the fraud because of a lack of controls may be the dominant condition precipitating the risk of fraud, or an individual's attitude or ability to rationalize unethical actions may be sufficient to motivate that individual to engage in fraud, even in the absence of significant incentives/pressures or opportunities.

.37 The auditor's identification of fraud risks also may be influenced by characteristics such as the size, complexity, and ownership attributes of the entity. For example, in the case of a larger entity, the auditor ordinarily considers factors that generally constrain improper conduct by management, such as the effectiveness of the audit committee and the internal audit function, and the existence and enforcement of a formal code of conduct. In the case of a smaller entity, some or all of these considerations may be inapplicable or less important, and management may have developed a culture that emphasizes the importance of integrity and ethical behavior through oral communication and management by example. Also, the risks of material misstatement due to fraud may vary among operating locations or business segments of an entity, requiring an identification of the risks related to specific geographic areas or business segments, as well as for the entity as a whole.[16]

.38 The auditor should evaluate whether identified risks of material misstatement due to fraud can be related to specific financial-statement account balances or classes of transactions and related assertions, or whether they relate more pervasively to the financial statements as a whole. Relating the risks of material misstatement due to fraud to the individual accounts, classes of transactions, and assertions will assist the auditor in subsequently designing appropriate auditing procedures.

.39 Certain accounts, classes of transactions, and assertions that have high inherent risk because they involve a high degree of management judgment and subjectivity also may present risks of material misstatement due to fraud because they are susceptible to manipulation by management. For example, liabilities resulting from a restructuring may be deemed to have high inherent risk because of the high degree of subjectivity and management judgment involved in their estimation. Similarly, revenues for software developers may be deemed to have high inherent risk because of the complex accounting principles

---

[16] Section 312.16 provides guidance on the auditor's consideration of the extent to which auditing procedures should be performed at selected locations or components. [Footnote revised, March 2006, to reflect conforming changes necessary due to the issuance of Statement on Auditing Standards No. 107. Footnote renumbered by the issuance of Statement on Auditing Standards No. 113, November 2006.]

applicable to the recognition and measurement of software revenue transactions. Assets resulting from investing activities may be deemed to have high inherent risk because of the subjectivity and management judgment involved in estimating fair values of those investments.

.40 In summary, the identification of a risk of material misstatement due to fraud involves the application of professional judgment and includes the consideration of the attributes of the risk, including:

- The *type* of risk that may exist, that is, whether it involves fraudulent financial reporting or misappropriation of assets
- The *significance* of the risk, that is, whether it is of a magnitude that could lead to result in a possible material misstatement of the financial statements
- The *likelihood* of the risk, that is, the likelihood that it will result in a material misstatement in the financial statements[17]
- The *pervasiveness* of the risk, that is, whether the potential risk is pervasive to the financial statements as a whole or specifically related to a particular assertion, account, or class of transactions.

A Presumption That Improper Revenue Recognition Is a Fraud Risk

.41 Material misstatements due to fraudulent financial reporting often result from an overstatement of revenues (for example, through premature revenue recognition or recording fictitious revenues) or an understatement of revenues (for example, through improperly shifting revenues to a later period). Therefore, the auditor should ordinarily presume that there is a risk of material misstatement due to fraud relating to revenue recognition. (See paragraph .54 for examples of auditing procedures related to the risk of improper revenue recognition.)[18]

A Consideration of the Risk of Management Override of Controls

.42 Even if specific risks of material misstatement due to fraud are not identified by the auditor, there is a possibility that management override of controls could occur, and accordingly, the auditor should address that risk (see paragraph .57) apart from any conclusions regarding the existence of more specifically identifiable risks.

Assessing the Identified Risks After Taking Into Account an Evaluation of the Entity's Programs and Controls That Address the Risks

.43 Section 314 requires the auditor to obtain an understanding of each of the five components of internal control sufficient to plan the audit. It also notes

---

[17] The occurrence of material misstatements of financial statements due to fraud is relatively infrequent in relation to the total population of published financial statements. However, the auditor should not use this as a basis to conclude that one or more risks of a material misstatement due to fraud are not present in a particular entity. [Footnote renumbered by the issuance of Statement on Auditing Standards No. 113, November 2006.]

[18] For a discussion of indicators of improper revenue recognition and common techniques for overstating revenue and illustrative audit procedures, see the AICPA Audit Guide *Auditing Revenue in Certain Industries*. [Footnote renumbered by the issuance of Statement on Auditing Standards No. 113, November 2006.]

that such knowledge should be used to identify types of potential misstatements, consider factors that affect the risk of material misstatement, design tests of controls when applicable, and design substantive tests. Additionally, section 314 notes that controls, whether manual or automated, can be circumvented by collusion of two or more people or inappropriate management override of internal control. [Revised, March 2006, to reflect conforming changes necessary due to the issuance of Statement on Auditing Standards No. 109.]

.44 As part of the understanding of internal control sufficient to plan the audit, the auditor should evaluate whether entity programs and controls that address identified risks of material misstatement due to fraud have been suitably designed and placed in operation.[19] These programs and controls may involve (*a*) specific controls designed to mitigate specific risks of fraud—for example, controls to address specific assets susceptible to misappropriation, and (*b*) broader programs designed to prevent, deter, and detect fraud—for example, programs to promote a culture of honesty and ethical behavior. The auditor should consider whether such programs and controls mitigate the identified risks of material misstatement due to fraud or whether specific control deficiencies may exacerbate the risks (see paragraph .80). The exhibit at the end of this section [paragraph .88] discusses examples of programs and controls an entity might implement to create a culture of honesty and ethical behavior, and that help to prevent, deter, and detect fraud.

.45 After the auditor has evaluated whether the entity's programs and controls that address identified risks of material misstatement due to fraud have been suitably designed and placed in operation, the auditor should assess these risks taking into account that evaluation. This assessment should be considered when developing the auditor's response to the identified risks of material misstatement due to fraud (see paragraphs .46 through .67).[20]

Responding to the Results of the Assessment[21]

.46 The auditor's response to the assessment of the risks of material misstatement due to fraud involves the application of professional skepticism in gathering and evaluating audit evidence. As noted in paragraph .13, professional skepticism is an attitude that includes a critical assessment of the competency and sufficiency of audit evidence. Examples of the application of professional skepticism in response to the risks of material misstatement due to fraud are (*a*) designing additional or different auditing procedures to obtain more reliable evidence in support of specified financial statement account balances, classes of transactions, and related assertions, and (*b*) obtaining additional corroboration of management's explanations or representations concerning material matters, such as through third-party confirmation, the use of a specialist, analytical procedures, examination of documentation from independent sources, or inquiries of others within or outside the entity.

---

[19] See footnote 10. [Footnote renumbered by the issuance of Statement on Auditing Standards No. 113, November 2006.]

[20] Notwithstanding that the auditor assesses identified risks of material misstatement due to fraud, the assessment need not encompass an overall judgment about whether risk for the entity is classified as *high*, *medium*, or *low* because such a judgment is too broad to be useful in developing the auditor's response described in paragraphs .46 through .67. [Footnote renumbered by the issuance of Statement on Auditing Standards No. 113, November 2006.]

[21] Section 318, *Performing Audit Procedures in Response to Assessed Risks and Evaluating the Audit Evidence Obtained*, requires the auditor to determine overall responses and design and perform further audit procedures to respond to the assessed risks of material misstatement at the financial statement and relevant assertion levels in a financial statement audit. See paragraphs .04 and .07 of section 318. [Footnote added, effective for audits of financial statements for periods beginning on or after December 15, 2006, by Statement on Auditing Standards No. 113.]

.47 The auditor's response to the assessment of the risks of material misstatement of the financial statements due to fraud is influenced by the nature and significance of the risks identified as being present (paragraphs .35 through .42) and the entity's programs and controls that address these identified risks (paragraphs .43 through .45).

.48 The auditor responds to risks of material misstatement due to fraud in the following three ways:

a. A response that has an overall effect on how the audit is conducted—that is, a response involving more general considerations apart from the specific procedures otherwise planned (see paragraph .50).

b. A response to identified risks involving the nature, timing, and extent of the auditing procedures to be performed (see paragraphs .51 through .56).

c. A response involving the performance of certain procedures to further address the risk of material misstatement due to fraud involving management override of controls, given the unpredictable ways in which such override could occur (see paragraphs .57 through .67).

.49 The auditor may conclude that it would not be practicable to design auditing procedures that sufficiently address the risks of material misstatement due to fraud. In that case, withdrawal from the engagement with communication to the appropriate parties may be an appropriate course of action (see paragraph .78).

Overall Responses to the Risk of Material Misstatement

.50 Judgments about the risk of material misstatement due to fraud have an overall effect on how the audit is conducted in the following ways:

- *Assignment of personnel and supervision.* The knowledge, skill, and ability of personnel assigned significant engagement responsibilities should be commensurate with the auditor's assessment of the risks of material misstatement due to fraud for the engagement (see section 210, *Training and Proficiency of the Independent Auditor*, paragraph .03). For example, the auditor may respond to an identified risk of material misstatement due to fraud by assigning additional persons with specialized skill and knowledge, such as forensic and information technology (IT) specialists, or by assigning more experienced personnel to the engagement. In addition, the extent of supervision should reflect the risks of material misstatement due to fraud (see section 311.28).
- *Accounting principles.* The auditor should consider management's selection and application of significant accounting principles, particularly those related to subjective measurements and complex transactions. In this respect, the auditor may have a greater concern about whether the accounting principles selected and policies adopted are being applied in an inappropriate manner to create a material misstatement of the financial statements. In developing judgments about the quality of such principles (see section 380, *The Auditor's Communication With Those Charged With Governance*, paragraph .11), the auditor should consider whether their collective application indicates a bias that may create such a material misstatement of the financial statements.
- *Predictability of auditing procedures.* The auditor should incorporate an element of unpredictability in the selection from year to

year of auditing procedures to be performed—for example, performing substantive tests of selected account balances and assertions not otherwise tested due to their materiality or risk, adjusting the timing of testing from that otherwise expected, using differing sampling methods, and performing procedures at different locations or at locations on an unannounced basis.

[Revised, March 2006, to reflect conforming changes necessary due to the issuance of Statement on Auditing Standards No. 108. Revised, April 2007, to reflect conforming changes necessary due to the issuance of Statement on Auditing Standards No. 114.]

Responses Involving the Nature, Timing, and Extent of Procedures to Be Performed to Address the Identified Risks

.51 The auditing procedures performed in response to identified risks of material misstatement due to fraud will vary depending upon the types of risks identified and the account balances, classes of transactions, and related assertions that may be affected. These procedures may involve both substantive tests and tests of the operating effectiveness of the entity's programs and controls. However, because management may have the ability to override controls that otherwise appear to be operating effectively (see paragraph .08), it is unlikely that audit risk can be reduced to an appropriately low level by performing only tests of controls.

.52 The auditor's responses to address specifically identified risks of material misstatement due to fraud may include changing the nature, timing, and extent of auditing procedures in the following ways:

- The *nature* of auditing procedures performed may need to be changed to obtain evidence that is more reliable or to obtain additional corroborative information. For example, more audit evidence may be needed from independent sources outside the entity, such as public-record information about the existence and nature of key customers, vendors, or counterparties in a major transaction. Also, physical observation or inspection of certain assets may become more important (see section 326, *Audit Evidence*, paragraphs .06 through .13). Furthermore, the auditor may choose to employ computer-assisted audit techniques to gather more extensive evidence about data contained in significant accounts or electronic transaction files. Finally, inquiry of additional members of management or others may be helpful in identifying issues and corroborating other audit evidence (see paragraphs .24 through .26 and paragraph .53).
- The *timing* of substantive tests may need to be modified. The auditor might conclude that substantive testing should be performed at or near the end of the reporting period to best address an identified risk of material misstatement due to fraud (see section 318, *Performing Procedures in Response to Assessed Risks and Evaluating the Audit Evidence Obtained*). That is, the auditor might conclude that, given the risks of intentional misstatement or manipulation, tests to extend audit conclusions from an interim date to the period-end reporting date would not be effective.

  In contrast, because an intentional misstatement—for example, a misstatement involving inappropriate revenue recognition—may have been initiated in an interim period, the auditor might elect to apply substantive tests to transactions occurring earlier in or throughout the reporting period.

- The *extent* of the procedures applied should reflect the assessment of the risks of material misstatement due to fraud. For example, increasing sample sizes or performing analytical procedures at a more detailed level may be appropriate (see section 350, *Audit Sampling*, paragraph .22, and section 329). Also, computer-assisted audit techniques may enable more extensive testing of electronic transactions and account files. Such techniques can be used to select sample transactions from key electronic files, to sort transactions with specific characteristics, or to test an entire population instead of a sample.

[Revised, March 2006, to reflect conforming changes necessary due to the issuance of Statements on Auditing Standards No. 105, No. 106, No. 110 and No. 111.]

.53 The following are examples of modification of the nature, timing, and extent of tests in response to identified risks of material misstatements due to fraud.

- Performing procedures at locations on a surprise or unannounced basis, for example, observing inventory on unexpected dates or at unexpected locations or counting cash on a surprise basis.
- Requesting that inventories be counted at the end of the reporting period or on a date closer to period end to minimize the risk of manipulation of balances in the period between the date of completion of the count and the end of the reporting period.
- Making oral inquiries of major customers and suppliers in addition to sending written confirmations, or sending confirmation requests to a specific party within an organization.
- Performing substantive analytical procedures using disaggregated data, for example, comparing gross profit or operating margins by location, line of business, or month to auditor-developed expectations.[22]
- Interviewing personnel involved in activities in areas where a risk of material misstatement due to fraud has been identified to obtain their insights about the risk and how controls address the risk (also see paragraph .24).
- If other independent auditors are auditing the financial statements of one or more subsidiaries, divisions, or branches, discussing with them the extent of work that needs to be performed to address the risk of material misstatement due to fraud resulting from transactions and activities among these components.

Additional Examples of Responses to Identified Risks of Misstatements Arising From Fraudulent Financial Reporting

.54 The following are additional examples of responses to identified risks of material misstatements relating to fraudulent financial reporting:

- *Revenue recognition.* Because revenue recognition is dependent on the particular facts and circumstances, as well as accounting principles

[22] Section 329, *Analytical Procedures*, provides guidance on performing analytical procedures as substantive tests. [Footnote renumbered by the issuance of Statement on Auditing Standards No. 113, November 2006.]

and practices that can vary by industry, the auditor ordinarily will develop auditing procedures based on the auditor's understanding of the entity and its environment, including the composition of revenues, specific attributes of the revenue transactions, and unique industry considerations. If there is an identified risk of material misstatement due to fraud that involves improper revenue recognition, the auditor also may want to consider:

- — Performing substantive analytical procedures relating to revenue using disaggregated data, for example, comparing revenue reported by month and by product line or business segment during the current reporting period with comparable prior periods. Computer-assisted audit techniques may be useful in identifying unusual or unexpected revenue relationships or transactions.
- — Confirming with customers certain relevant contract terms and the absence of side agreements, because the appropriate accounting often is influenced by such terms or agreements.[23] For example, acceptance criteria, delivery and payment terms, the absence of future or continuing vendor obligations, the right to return the product, guaranteed resale amounts, and cancellation or refund provisions often are relevant in such circumstances.
- — Inquiring of the entity's sales and marketing personnel or in-house legal counsel regarding sales or shipments near the end of the period and their knowledge of any unusual terms or conditions associated with these transactions.
- — Being physically present at one or more locations at period end to observe goods being shipped or being readied for shipment (or returns awaiting processing) and performing other appropriate sales and inventory cutoff procedures.
- — For those situations for which revenue transactions are electronically initiated, authorized, processed, and recorded, testing controls to determine whether they provide assurance that recorded revenue transactions occurred and are properly recorded.

- *Inventory quantities.* If there is an identified risk of material misstatement due to fraud that affects inventory quantities, examining the entity's inventory records may help identify locations or items that require specific attention during or after the physical inventory count. Such a review may lead to a decision to observe inventory counts at certain locations on an unannounced basis (see paragraph .53) or to conduct inventory counts at all locations on the same date. In addition, it may be appropriate for inventory counts to be conducted at or near the end of the reporting period to minimize the risk of inappropriate manipulation during the period between the count and the end of the reporting period.

  It also may be appropriate for the auditor to perform additional procedures during the observation of the count, for example, more rigorously examining the contents of boxed items, the manner in which the goods are stacked (for example, hollow squares) or labeled, and the quality (that is, purity, grade, or concentration) of liquid substances

---

[23] Section 330, *The Confirmation Process*, provides guidance about the confirmation process in audits performed in accordance with GAAS. [Footnote renumbered by the issuance of Statement on Auditing Standards No. 113, November 2006.]

such as perfumes or specialty chemicals. Using the work of a specialist may be helpful in this regard.[24] Furthermore, additional testing of count sheets, tags, or other records, or the retention of copies of these records, may be warranted to minimize the risk of subsequent alteration or inappropriate compilation.

Following the physical inventory count, the auditor may want to employ additional procedures directed at the quantities included in the priced out inventories to further test the reasonableness of the quantities counted—for example, comparison of quantities for the current period with prior periods by class or category of inventory, location or other criteria, or comparison of quantities counted with perpetual records. The auditor also may consider using computer-assisted audit techniques to further test the compilation of the physical inventory counts—for example, sorting by tag number to test tag controls or by item serial number to test the possibility of item omission or duplication.

- *Management estimates.* The auditor may identify a risk of material misstatement due to fraud involving the development of management estimates. This risk may affect a number of accounts and assertions, including asset valuation, estimates relating to specific transactions (such as acquisitions, restructurings, or disposals of a segment of the business), and other significant accrued liabilities (such as pension and other postretirement benefit obligations, or environmental remediation liabilities). The risk may also relate to significant changes in assumptions relating to recurring estimates. As indicated in section 342, *Auditing Accounting Estimates*, estimates are based on subjective as well as objective factors and there is a potential for bias in the subjective factors, even when management's estimation process involves competent personnel using relevant and reliable data.

  In addressing an identified risk of material misstatement due to fraud involving accounting estimates, the auditor may want to supplement the audit evidence otherwise obtained (see section 342.09 through .14). In certain circumstances (for example, evaluating the reasonableness of management's estimate of the fair value of a derivative), it may be appropriate to engage a specialist or develop an independent estimate for comparison to management's estimate. Information gathered about the entity and its environment may help the auditor evaluate the reasonableness of such management estimates and underlying judgments and assumptions.

  A retrospective review of similar management judgments and assumptions applied in prior periods (see paragraphs .63 through .65) may also provide insight about the reasonableness of judgments and assumptions supporting management estimates.

[Revised, March 2006, to reflect conforming changes necessary due to the issuance of Statement on Auditing Standards No. 106.]

---

[24] Section 336, *Using the Work of a Specialist*, provides guidance to an auditor who uses the work of a specialist in performing an audit in accordance with GAAS. [Footnote renumbered by the issuance of Statement on Auditing Standards No. 113, November 2006.]

Examples of Responses to Identified Risks of Misstatements Arising From Misappropriations of Assets

.55 The auditor may have identified a risk of material misstatement due to fraud relating to misappropriation of assets. For example, the auditor may conclude that the risk of asset misappropriation at a particular operating location is significant because a large amount of easily accessible cash is maintained at that location, or there are inventory items such as laptop computers at that location that can easily be moved and sold.

.56 The auditor's response to a risk of material misstatement due to fraud relating to misappropriation of assets usually will be directed toward certain account balances. Although some of the audit responses noted in paragraphs .52 through .54 may apply in such circumstances, such as the procedures directed at inventory quantities, the scope of the work should be linked to the specific information about the misappropriation risk that has been identified. For example, if a particular asset is highly susceptible to misappropriation and a potential misstatement would be material to the financial statements, obtaining an understanding of the controls related to the prevention and detection of such misappropriation and testing the operating effectiveness of such controls may be warranted. In certain circumstances, physical inspection of such assets (for example, counting cash or securities) at or near the end of the reporting period may be appropriate. In addition, the use of substantive analytical procedures, such as the development by the auditor of an expected dollar amount at a high level of precision, to be compared with a recorded amount, may be effective in certain circumstances.

Responses to Further Address the Risk of Management Override of Controls

.57 As noted in paragraph .08, management is in a unique position to perpetrate fraud because of its ability to directly or indirectly manipulate accounting records and prepare fraudulent financial statements by overriding established controls that otherwise appear to be operating effectively. By its nature, management override of controls can occur in unpredictable ways. Accordingly, in addition to overall responses (paragraph .50) and responses that address specifically identified risks of material misstatement due to fraud (see paragraphs .51 through .56), the procedures described in paragraphs .58 through .67 should be performed to further address the risk of management override of controls.

.58 ***Examining journal entries and other adjustments for evidence of possible material misstatement due to fraud.*** Material misstatements of financial statements due to fraud often involve the manipulation of the financial reporting process by (*a*) recording inappropriate or unauthorized journal entries throughout the year or at period end, or (*b*) making adjustments to amounts reported in the financial statements that are not reflected in formal journal entries, such as through consolidating adjustments, report combinations, and reclassifications. Accordingly, the auditor should design procedures to test the appropriateness of journal entries recorded in the general ledger and other adjustments (for example, entries posted directly to financial statement drafts) made in the preparation of the financial statements. More specifically, the auditor should:

a. Obtain an understanding of the entity's financial reporting process[25] and the controls over journal entries and other adjustments. (See paragraphs .59 and .60.)

b. Identify and select journal entries and other adjustments for testing. (See paragraph .61.)

c. Determine the timing of the testing. (See paragraph .62.)

d. Inquire of individuals involved in the financial reporting process about inappropriate or unusual activity relating to the processing of journal entries and other adjustments.

.59 The auditor's understanding of the entity's financial reporting process may help in identifying the type, number, and monetary value of journal entries and other adjustments that typically are made in preparing the financial statements. For example, the auditor's understanding may include the sources of significant debits and credits to an account, who can initiate entries to the general ledger or transaction processing systems, what approvals are required for such entries, and how journal entries are recorded (for example, entries may be initiated and recorded online with no physical evidence, or may be created in paper form and entered in batch mode).

.60 An entity may have implemented specific controls over journal entries and other adjustments. For example, an entity may use journal entries that are preformatted with account numbers and specific user approval criteria, and may have automated controls to generate an exception report for any entries that were unsuccessfully proposed for recording or entries that were recorded and processed outside of established parameters. The auditor should obtain an understanding of the design of such controls over journal entries and other adjustments and determine whether they are suitably designed and have been placed in operation.

.61 The auditor should use professional judgment in determining the nature, timing, and extent of the testing of journal entries and other adjustments. For purposes of identifying and selecting specific entries and other adjustments for testing, and determining the appropriate method of examining the underlying support for the items selected, the auditor should consider:

- *The auditor's assessment of the risk of material misstatement due to fraud.* The presence of fraud risk factors or other conditions may help the auditor to identify specific classes of journal entries for testing and indicate the extent of testing necessary.

- *The effectiveness of controls that have been implemented over journal entries and other adjustments.* Effective controls over the preparation and posting of journal entries and adjustments may affect the extent of substantive testing necessary, provided that the auditor has tested the operating effectiveness of those controls. However, even though controls might be implemented and operating effectively, the auditor's

---

[25] Section 314 requires the auditor to obtain an understanding of the automated and manual procedures an entity uses to prepare financial statements and related disclosures, and how misstatements may occur. This understanding includes (*a*) the procedures used to enter transaction totals into the general ledger; (*b*) the procedures used to initiate, record, and process journal entries in the general ledger; and (*c*) other procedures used to record recurring and nonrecurring adjustments to the financial statements. [Footnote revised, March 2006, to reflect conforming changes necessary due to the issuance of Statement on Auditing Standards No. 109. Footnote renumbered by the issuance of Statement on Auditing Standards No. 113, November 2006.]

procedures for testing journal entries and other adjustments should include the identification and testing of specific items.

- *The entity's financial reporting process and the nature of the evidence that can be examined.* The auditor's procedures for testing journal entries and other adjustments will vary based on the nature of the financial reporting process. For many entities, routine processing of transactions involves a combination of manual and automated steps and procedures. Similarly, the processing of journal entries and other adjustments might involve both manual and automated procedures and controls. Regardless of the method, the auditor's procedures should include selecting from the general ledger journal entries to be tested and examining support for those items. In addition, the auditor should be aware that journal entries and other adjustments might exist in either electronic or paper form. When information technology (IT) is used in the financial reporting process, journal entries and other adjustments might exist only in electronic form. Electronic evidence often requires extraction of the desired data by an auditor with IT knowledge and skills or the use of an IT specialist. In an IT environment, it may be necessary for the auditor to employ computer-assisted audit techniques (for example, report writers, software or data extraction tools, or other systems-based techniques) to identify the journal entries and other adjustments to be tested.

- *The characteristics of fraudulent entries or adjustments.* Inappropriate journal entries and other adjustments often have certain unique identifying characteristics. Such characteristics may include entries (*a*) made to unrelated, unusual, or seldom-used accounts, (*b*) made by individuals who typically do not make journal entries, (*c*) recorded at the end of the period or as post-closing entries that have little or no explanation or description, (*d*) made either before or during the preparation of the financial statements that do not have account numbers, or (*e*) containing round numbers or a consistent ending number.

- *The nature and complexity of the accounts.* Inappropriate journal entries or adjustments may be applied to accounts that (*a*) contain transactions that are complex or unusual in nature, (*b*) contain significant estimates and period-end adjustments, (*c*) have been prone to errors in the past, (*d*) have not been reconciled on a timely basis or contain unreconciled differences, (*e*) contain intercompany transactions, or (*f*) are otherwise associated with an identified risk of material misstatement due to fraud. The auditor should recognize, however, that inappropriate journal entries and adjustments also might be made to other accounts. In audits of entities that have several locations or components, the auditor should consider the need to select journal entries from locations based on the factors set forth in section 312.16.

- *Journal entries or other adjustments processed outside the normal course of business.* Standard journal entries used on a recurring basis to record transactions such as monthly sales, purchases, and cash disbursements, or to record recurring periodic accounting estimates generally are subject to the entity's internal controls. Nonstandard entries (for example, entries used to record nonrecurring transactions, such as a business combination, or entries used to record a nonrecurring estimate, such as an asset impairment) might not be subject to the same level of internal control. In addition, other adjustments such as consolidating adjustments, report combinations, and reclassifications generally are not reflected in formal journal entries and might not be subject to the entity's internal controls. Accordingly, the auditor should consider placing additional emphasis on identifying and testing items processed outside of the normal course of business.

[Revised, March 2006, to reflect conforming changes necessary due to the issuance of Statement on Auditing Standards No. 107.]

.62 Because fraudulent journal entries often are made at the end of a reporting period, the auditor's testing ordinarily should focus on the journal entries and other adjustments made at that time. However, because material misstatements in financial statements due to fraud can occur throughout the period and may involve extensive efforts to conceal how it is accomplished, the auditor should consider whether there also is a need to test journal entries throughout the period under audit.

.63 ***Reviewing accounting estimates for biases that could result in material misstatement due to fraud.*** In preparing financial statements, management is responsible for making a number of judgments or assumptions that affect significant accounting estimates[26] and for monitoring the reasonableness of such estimates on an ongoing basis. Fraudulent financial reporting often is accomplished through intentional misstatement of accounting estimates. As discussed in section 312.58, the auditor should consider whether differences between estimates best supported by the audit evidence and the estimates included in the financial statements, even if they are individually reasonable, indicate a possible bias on the part of the entity's management, in which case the auditor should reconsider the estimates taken as a whole. [Revised, March 2006, to reflect conforming changes necessary due to the issuance of Statement on Auditing Standards No. 107.]

.64 The auditor also should perform a retrospective review of significant accounting estimates reflected in the financial statements of the prior year to determine whether management judgments and assumptions relating to the estimates indicate a possible bias on the part of management. The significant accounting estimates selected for testing should include those that are based on highly sensitive assumptions or are otherwise significantly affected by judgments made by management. With the benefit of hindsight, a retrospective review should provide the auditor with additional information about whether there may be a possible bias on the part of management in making the current-year estimates. This review, however, is not intended to call into question the auditor's professional judgments made in the prior year that were based on information available at the time.

.65 If the auditor identifies a possible bias on the part of management in making accounting estimates, the auditor should evaluate whether circumstances producing such a bias represent a risk of a material misstatement due to fraud. For example, information coming to the auditor's attention may indicate a risk that adjustments to the current-year estimates might be recorded at the instruction of management to arbitrarily achieve a specified earnings target.

.66 ***Evaluating the business rationale for significant unusual transactions.*** During the course of the audit, the auditor may become aware of significant transactions that are outside the normal course of business for the entity, or that otherwise appear to be unusual given the auditor's understanding of the entity and its environment. The auditor should gain an understanding

---

[26] See section 342, *Auditing Accounting Estimates*, paragraphs .02 and .16, for a definition of accounting estimates and a listing of examples. [Footnote renumbered by the issuance of Statement on Auditing Standards No. 113, November 2006.]

of the business rationale for such transactions and whether that rationale (or the lack thereof) suggests that the transactions may have been entered into to engage in fraudulent financial reporting or conceal misappropriation of assets.

.67 In understanding the business rationale for the transactions, the auditor should consider:

- Whether the form of such transactions is overly complex (for example, involves multiple entities within a consolidated group or unrelated third parties).
- Whether management has discussed the nature of and accounting for such transactions with those charged with governance.
- Whether management is placing more emphasis on the need for a particular accounting treatment than on the underlying economics of the transaction.
- Whether transactions that involve unconsolidated related parties, including special purpose entities, have been properly reviewed and approved by those charged with governance.
- Whether the transactions involve previously unidentified related parties[27] or parties that do not have the substance or the financial strength to support the transaction without assistance from the entity under audit.

[Revised, April 2007, to reflect conforming changes necessary due to the issuance of Statement on Auditing Standards No. 114.]

Evaluating Audit Evidence

.68 ***Assessing risks of material misstatement due to fraud throughout the audit.*** The auditor's assessment of the risks of material misstatement due to fraud should be ongoing throughout the audit. Conditions may be identified during fieldwork that change or support a judgment regarding the assessment of the risks, such as the following:

- Discrepancies in the accounting records, including:
  - — Transactions that are not recorded in a complete or timely manner or are improperly recorded as to amount, accounting period, classification, or entity policy
  - — Unsupported or unauthorized balances or transactions
  - — Last-minute adjustments that significantly affect financial results
  - — Evidence of employees' access to systems and records inconsistent with that necessary to perform their authorized duties
  - — Tips or complaints to the auditor about alleged fraud
- Conflicting or missing audit evidence, including:
  - — Missing documents
  - — Documents that appear to have been altered[28]

---

[27] Section 334, *Related Parties*, provides guidance with respect to the identification of related-party relationships and transactions, including transactions that may be outside the ordinary course of business (see, in particular, section 334.06). [Footnote renumbered by the issuance of Statement on Auditing Standards No. 113, November 2006.]

[28] As discussed in paragraph .09, auditors are not trained as or expected to be experts in the authentication of documents; however, if the auditor believes that documents may not be authentic, he or she should investigate further and consider using the work of a specialist to determine the authenticity. [Footnote renumbered by the issuance of Statement on Auditing Standards No. 113, November 2006.]

- — Unavailability of other than photocopied or electronically transmitted documents when documents in original form are expected to exist
- — Significant unexplained items on reconciliations
- — Inconsistent, vague, or implausible responses from management or employees arising from inquiries or analytical procedures (See paragraph .72.)
- — Unusual discrepancies between the entity's records and confirmation replies
- — Missing inventory or physical assets of significant magnitude
- — Unavailable or missing electronic evidence, inconsistent with the entity's record retention practices or policies
- — Inability to produce evidence of key systems development and program change testing and implementation activities for current-year system changes and deployments

- Problematic or unusual relationships between the auditor and management, including:
  - — Denial of access to records, facilities, certain employees, customers, vendors, or others from whom audit evidence might be sought[29]
  - — Undue time pressures imposed by management to resolve complex or contentious issues
  - — Complaints by management about the conduct of the audit or management intimidation of audit team members, particularly in connection with the auditor's critical assessment of audit evidence or in the resolution of potential disagreements with management
  - — Unusual delays by the entity in providing requested information
  - — Unwillingness to facilitate auditor access to key electronic files for testing through the use of computer-assisted audit techniques
  - — Denial of access to key IT operations staff and facilities, including security, operations, and systems development personnel
  - — An unwillingness to add or revise disclosures in the financial statements to make them more complete and transparent

[Revised, March 2006, to reflect conforming changes necessary due to the issuance of Statement on Auditing Standards No. 105.]

.69 ***Evaluating whether analytical procedures performed as substantive tests or in the overall review stage of the audit indicate a previously unrecognized risk of material misstatement due to fraud.*** As discussed in paragraphs .28 through .30, the auditor should consider whether analytical procedures performed in planning the audit result in identifying any unusual or unexpected relationships that should be considered in assessing the risks of material misstatement due to fraud. The auditor also should evaluate whether analytical procedures that were performed as substantive tests or in the overall review stage of the audit (see section 329) indicate a previously unrecognized risk of material misstatement due to fraud.

---

[29] Denial of access to information may constitute a limitation on the scope of the audit that may require the auditor to consider qualifying or disclaiming an opinion on the financial statements. (See section 508, *Reports on Audited Financial Statements*, paragraph .24.) [Footnote renumbered by the issuance of Statement on Auditing Standards No. 113, November 2006.]

.70 If not already performed during the overall review stage of the audit, the auditor should perform analytical procedures relating to revenue, as discussed in paragraph .29, through the end of the reporting period.

.71 Determining which particular trends and relationships may indicate a risk of material misstatement due to fraud requires professional judgment. Unusual relationships involving year-end revenue and income often are particularly relevant. These might include, for example, (*a*) uncharacteristically large amounts of income being reported in the last week or two of the reporting period from unusual transactions, as well as (*b*) income that is inconsistent with trends in cash flow from operations.

.72 Some unusual or unexpected analytical relationships may have been identified and may indicate a risk of material misstatement due to fraud because management or employees generally are unable to manipulate certain information to create seemingly normal or expected relationships. Some examples are as follows:

- The relationship of net income to cash flows from operations may appear unusual because management recorded fictitious revenues and receivables but was unable to manipulate cash.
- Changes in inventory, accounts payable, sales, or cost of sales from the prior period to the current period may be inconsistent, indicating a possible employee theft of inventory, because the employee was unable to manipulate all of the related accounts.
- A comparison of the entity's profitability to industry trends, which management cannot manipulate, may indicate trends or differences for further consideration when identifying risks of material misstatement due to fraud.
- A comparison of bad debt write-offs to comparable industry data, which employees cannot manipulate, may provide unexplained relationships that could indicate a possible theft of cash receipts.
- An unexpected or unexplained relationship between sales volume as determined from the accounting records and production statistics maintained by operations personnel—which may be more difficult for management to manipulate—may indicate a possible misstatement of sales.

.73 The auditor also should consider whether responses to inquiries throughout the audit about analytical relationships have been vague or implausible, or have produced evidence that is inconsistent with other audit evidence accumulated during the audit. [Revised, March 2006, to reflect conforming changes necessary due to the issuance of Statement on Auditing Standards No. 105.]

.74 ***Evaluating the risks of material misstatement due to fraud at or near the date of the auditor's report.*** At or near the completion of fieldwork, the auditor should evaluate whether the accumulated results of auditing procedures and other observations (for example, conditions and analytical relationships noted in paragraphs .69 through .73) affect the assessment of the risks of material misstatement due to fraud made earlier in the audit. This evaluation primarily is a qualitative matter based on the auditor's judgment. Such an evaluation may provide further insight about the risks of material misstatement due to fraud and whether there is a need to perform additional or different audit procedures. As part of this evaluation, the auditor with final responsibility for the audit should ascertain that there has been appropriate communication with the other audit team members throughout the audit regarding information or conditions indicative of risks of material misstatement due to fraud.[30]

.75 ***Responding to misstatements that may be the result of fraud.*** When audit test results identify misstatements in the financial statements, the auditor should consider whether such misstatements may be indicative of fraud.[31] That determination affects the auditor's evaluation of materiality and the related responses necessary as a result of that evaluation.[32]

.76 If the auditor believes that misstatements are or may be the result of fraud, but the effect of the misstatements is not material to the financial statements, the auditor nevertheless should evaluate the implications, especially those dealing with the organizational position of the person(s) involved. For example, fraud involving misappropriations of cash from a small petty cash fund normally would be of little significance to the auditor in assessing the risk of material misstatement due to fraud because both the manner of operating the fund and its size would tend to establish a limit on the amount of potential loss, and the custodianship of such funds normally is entrusted to a nonmanagement employee.[33] Conversely, if the matter involves higher-level management, even though the amount itself is not material to the financial statements, it may be indicative of a more pervasive problem, for example, implications about the integrity of management.[34] In such circumstances, the auditor should reevaluate the assessment of the risk of material misstatement due to fraud and its resulting impact on (*a*) the nature, timing, and extent of the tests of balances or transactions and (*b*) the assessment of the effectiveness of controls if control risk was assessed below the maximum.

.77 If the auditor believes that the misstatement is or may be the result of fraud, and either has determined that the effect could be material to the financial statements or has been unable to evaluate whether the effect is material, the auditor should:

a. Attempt to obtain additional audit evidence to determine whether material fraud has occurred or is likely to have occurred, and, if so, its effect on the financial statements and the auditor's report thereon.[35]

---

[30] To accomplish this communication, the auditor with final responsibility for the audit may want to arrange another discussion among audit team members about the risks of material misstatement due to fraud (see paragraphs .14 through .18). [Footnote renumbered by the issuance of Statement on Auditing Standards No. 113, November 2006.]

[31] See footnote 4. [Footnote renumbered by the issuance of Statement on Auditing Standards No. 113, November 2006.]

[32] Section 312.60 states in part, "Qualitative considerations also influence the auditor in reaching a conclusion as to whether misstatements are material." Section 312.59 states, "As a result of the interaction of quantitative and qualitative considerations in materiality judgments, misstatements of relatively small amounts that come to the auditor's attention could have a material effect on the financial statements." [Footnote revised, March 2006, to reflect conforming changes necessary due to the issuance of Statement on Auditing Standards No. 107. Footnote renumbered by the issuance of Statement on Auditing Standards No. 113, November 2006.]

[33] However, see paragraphs .79 through .82 of this section for a discussion of the auditor's communication responsibilities. [Footnote renumbered by the issuance of Statement on Auditing Standards No. 113, November 2006.]

[34] Section 312.10 states that there is a distinction between the auditor's response to detected misstatements due to error and those due to fraud. When fraud is detected, the auditor should consider the implications for the integrity of management or employees and the possible effect on other aspects of the audit. [Footnote revised, March 2006, to reflect conforming changes necessary due to the issuance of Statement on Auditing Standards No. 107. Footnote renumbered by the issuance of Statement on Auditing Standards No. 113, November 2006.]

[35] See section 508 for guidance on auditors' reports issued in connection with audits of financial statements. [Footnote renumbered by the issuance of Statement on Auditing Standards No. 113, November 2006.]

b. Consider the implications for other aspects of the audit (see paragraph .76).

c. Discuss the matter and the approach for further investigation with an appropriate level of management that is at least one level above those involved, and with senior management and those charged with governance.[36]

d. If appropriate, suggest that the client consult with legal counsel.

[Revised, March 2006, to reflect conforming changes necessary due to the issuance of Statement on Auditing Standards No. 105. Revised, April 2007, to reflect conforming changes necessary due to the issuance of Statement on Auditing Standards No. 114.]

.78 The auditor's consideration of the risks of material misstatement and the results of audit tests may indicate such a significant risk of material misstatement due to fraud that the auditor should consider withdrawing from the engagement and communicating the reasons for withdrawal to those charged with governance.[37] Whether the auditor concludes that withdrawal from the engagement is appropriate may depend on (*a*) the implications about the integrity of management and (*b*) the diligence and cooperation of management or the board of directors in investigating the circumstances and taking appropriate action. Because of the variety of circumstances that may arise, it is not possible to definitively describe when withdrawal is appropriate.[38] The auditor may wish to consult with legal counsel when considering withdrawal from an engagement. [Revised, April 2007, to reflect conforming changes necessary due to the issuance of Statement on Auditing Standards No. 114.]

Communicating About Possible Fraud to Management, Those Charged With Governance, and Others[39]

.79 Whenever the auditor has determined that there is evidence that fraud may exist, that matter should be brought to the attention of an appropriate level of management. This is appropriate even if the matter might be considered inconsequential, such as a minor defalcation by an employee at a low level in the entity's organization. Fraud involving senior management and fraud (whether caused by senior management or other employees) that causes

---

[36] If the auditor believes senior management may be involved, discussion of the matter directly with those charged with governance may be appropriate. [Footnote renumbered by the issuance of Statement on Auditing Standards No. 113, November 2006. Footnote revised, April 2007, to reflect conforming changes necessary due to the issuance of Statement on Auditing Standards No. 114.]

[37] [Footnote renumbered by the issuance of Statement on Auditing Standards No. 113, November 2006. Footnote deleted due to conforming changes necessary due to the issuance of Statement on Auditing Standards No. 114.]

[38] If the auditor, subsequent to the date of the report on the audited financial statements, becomes aware that facts existed at that date that might have affected the report had the auditor been aware of such facts, the auditor should refer to section 561, *Subsequent Discovery of Facts Existing at the Date of the Auditor's Report*, for guidance. Furthermore, section 315, *Communications Between Predecessor and Successor Auditors*, paragraphs .21 and .22, provide guidance regarding communication with a predecessor auditor. [Footnote renumbered by the issuance of Statement on Auditing Standards No. 113, November 2006.]

[39] The requirements to communicate noted in paragraphs .79 through .82 extend to any intentional misstatement of financial statements (see paragraph .03). However, the communication may use terms other than fraud—for example, irregularity, intentional misstatement, misappropriation, or defalcations—if there is possible confusion with a legal definition of fraud or other reason to prefer alternative terms. [Footnote renumbered by the issuance of Statement on Auditing Standards No. 113, November 2006.]

a material misstatement of the financial statements should be reported directly to those charged with governance. In addition, the auditor should reach an understanding with those charged with governance regarding the nature and extent of communications with them about misappropriations perpetrated by lower-level employees. [Revised, April 2007, to reflect conforming changes necessary due to the issuance of Statement on Auditing Standards No. 114.]

.80 If the auditor, as a result of the assessment of the risks of material misstatement, has identified risks of material misstatement due to fraud that have continuing control implications (whether or not transactions or adjustments that could be the result of fraud have been detected), the auditor should consider whether these risks represent significant deficiencies or material weaknesses in the entity's internal control that should be communicated to management and those charged with governance.[40] (See section 325, *Communicating Internal Control Related Matters Identified in an Audit*, paragraph .04). The auditor also should consider whether the absence of or deficiencies in programs and controls to mitigate specific risks of fraud or to otherwise help prevent, deter, and detect fraud (see paragraph .44) represent significant deficiencies or material weaknesses that should be communicated to management and those charged with governance. [Revised, May 2006, to reflect conforming changes necessary due to the issuance of Statement on Auditing Standards No. 112.]

.81 The auditor also may wish to communicate other risks of fraud identified as a result of the assessment of the risks of material misstatements due to fraud. Such a communication may be a part of an overall communication with those charged with governance of business and financial statement risks affecting the entity and/or in conjunction with the auditor communication about the quality of the entity's accounting principles (see section 380.11). [Revised, April 2007, to reflect conforming changes necessary due to the issuance of Statement on Auditing Standards No. 114.]

.82 The disclosure of possible fraud to parties other than the client's senior management and those charged with governance ordinarily is not part of the auditor's responsibility and ordinarily would be precluded by the auditor's ethical or legal obligations of confidentiality unless the matter is reflected in the auditor's report. The auditor should recognize, however, that in the following circumstances a duty to disclose to parties outside the entity may exist:

a. To comply with certain legal and regulatory requirements[41]

b. To a successor auditor when the successor makes inquiries in accordance with section 315, *Communications Between Predecessor and Successor Auditors*[42]

c. In response to a subpoena

---

[40] [Footnote deleted to reflect conforming changes necessary due to the issuance of Statement on Auditing Standards No. 112. Footnote renumbered by the issuance of Statement on Auditing Standards No. 113, November 2006.]

[41] These requirements include reports in connection with the termination of the engagement, such as when the entity reports an auditor change on Form 8-K and the fraud or related risk factors constitute a *reportable event* or is the source of a *disagreement*, as these terms are defined in Item 304 of Regulation S-K. These requirements also include reports that may be required, under certain circumstances, pursuant to Section 10A(b)1 of the Securities Exchange Act of 1934 relating to an illegal act that has a material effect on the financial statements. [Footnote renumbered by the issuance of Statement on Auditing Standards No. 113, November 2006.]

[42] Section 315 requires the specific permission of the client. [Footnote renumbered by the issuance of Statement on Auditing Standards No. 113, November 2006.]

d. To a funding agency or other specified agency in accordance with requirements for the audits of entities that receive governmental financial assistance[43]

Because potential conflicts between the auditor's ethical and legal obligations for confidentiality of client matters may be complex, the auditor may wish to consult with legal counsel before discussing matters covered by paragraphs .79 through .81 with parties outside the client. [Revised, April 2007, to reflect conforming changes necessary due to the issuance of Statement on Auditing Standards No. 114.]

Documenting the Auditor's Consideration of Fraud

.83 The auditor should document the following:

- The discussion among engagement personnel in planning the audit regarding the susceptibility of the entity's financial statements to material misstatement due to fraud, including how and when the discussion occurred, the audit team members who participated, and the subject matter discussed (See paragraphs .14 through .17.)
- The procedures performed to obtain information necessary to identify and assess the risks of material misstatement due to fraud (See paragraphs .19 through .34.)
- Specific risks of material misstatement due to fraud that were identified (see paragraphs .35 through .45), and a description of the auditor's response to those risks (See paragraphs .46 through .56.)
- If the auditor has not identified in a particular circumstance, improper revenue recognition as a risk of material misstatement due to fraud, the reasons supporting the auditor's conclusion (See paragraph .41.)
- The results of the procedures performed to further address the risk of management override of controls (See paragraphs .58 through .67.)
- Other conditions and analytical relationships that caused the auditor to believe that additional auditing procedures or other responses were required and any further responses the auditor concluded were appropriate, to address such risks or other conditions (See paragraphs .68 through .73.)
- The nature of the communications about fraud made to management, those charged with governance, and others (See paragraphs .79 through .82.)

[Revised, April 2007, to reflect conforming changes necessary due to the issuance of Statement on Auditing Standards No. 114.]

Effective Date

.84 This section is effective for audits of financial statements for periods beginning on or after December 15, 2002. Early application of the provisions of this section is permissible.

---

[43] For example, *Government Auditing Standards* (the Yellow Book) require auditors to report fraud or illegal acts directly to parties outside the audited entity in certain circumstances. [Footnote renumbered by the issuance of Statement on Auditing Standards No. 113, November 2006.]

.85

Appendix

Examples of Fraud Risk Factors

A.1 This appendix contains examples of risk factors discussed in paragraphs .31 through .33 of the section. Separately presented are examples relating to the two types of fraud relevant to the auditor's consideration—that is, fraudulent financial reporting and misappropriation of assets. For each of these types of fraud, the risk factors are further classified based on the three conditions generally present when material misstatements due to fraud occur: (*a*) incentives/pressures, (*b*) opportunities, and (*c*) attitudes/rationalizations. Although the risk factors cover a broad range of situations, they are only examples and, accordingly, the auditor may wish to consider additional or different risk factors. Not all of these examples are relevant in all circumstances, and some may be of greater or lesser significance in entities of different size or with different ownership characteristics or circumstances. Also, the order of the examples of risk factors provided is not intended to reflect their relative importance or frequency of occurrence.

Risk Factors Relating to Misstatements Arising From Fraudulent Financial Reporting

A.2 The following are examples of risk factors relating to misstatements arising from fraudulent financial reporting.

Incentives/Pressures

a. Financial stability or profitability is threatened by economic, industry, or entity operating conditions, such as (or as indicated by):

— High degree of competition or market saturation, accompanied by declining margins

— High vulnerability to rapid changes, such as changes in technology, product obsolescence, or interest rates

— Significant declines in customer demand and increasing business failures in either the industry or overall economy

— Operating losses making the threat of bankruptcy, foreclosure, or hostile takeover imminent

— Recurring negative cash flows from operations and an inability to generate cash flows from operations while reporting earnings and earnings growth

— Rapid growth or unusual profitability, especially compared to that of other companies in the same industry

— New accounting, statutory, or regulatory requirements

b. Excessive pressure exists for management to meet the requirements or expectations of third parties due to the following:

— Profitability or trend level expectations of investment analysts, institutional investors, significant creditors, or other external parties (particularly expectations that are unduly aggressive or unrealistic), including expectations created by management in, for example, overly optimistic press releases or annual report messages

— Need to obtain additional debt or equity financing to stay competitive—including financing of major research and development or capital expenditures

— Marginal ability to meet exchange listing requirements or debt repayment or other debt covenant requirements

— Perceived or real adverse effects of reporting poor financial results on significant pending transactions, such as business combinations or contract awards

c. Information available indicates that management's or those charged with governance's personal financial situation is threatened by the entity's financial performance arising from the following:

— Significant financial interests in the entity

— Significant portions of their compensation (for example, bonuses, stock options, and earn-out arrangements) being contingent upon achieving aggressive targets for stock price, operating results, financial position, or cash flow[1]

— Personal guarantees of debts of the entity

d. There is excessive pressure on management or operating personnel to meet financial targets set up by those charged with governance or management, including sales or profitability incentive goals.

Opportunities

a. The nature of the industry or the entity's operations provides opportunities to engage in fraudulent financial reporting that can arise from the following:

— Significant related-party transactions not in the ordinary course of business or with related entities not audited or audited by another firm

— A strong financial presence or ability to dominate a certain industry sector that allows the entity to dictate terms or conditions to suppliers or customers that may result in inappropriate or non-arm's-length transactions

— Assets, liabilities, revenues, or expenses based on significant estimates that involve subjective judgments or uncertainties that are difficult to corroborate

— Significant, unusual, or highly complex transactions, especially those close to period end that pose difficult "substance over form" questions

— Significant operations located or conducted across international borders in jurisdictions where differing business environments and cultures exist

— Significant bank accounts or subsidiary or branch operations in tax-haven jurisdictions for which there appears to be no clear business justification

---

[1] Management incentive plans may be contingent upon achieving targets relating only to certain accounts or selected activities of the entity, even though the related accounts or activities may not be material to the entity as a whole.

b. There is ineffective monitoring of management as a result of the following:
- — Domination of management by a single person or small group (in a nonowner-managed business) without compensating controls
- — Ineffective oversight over the financial reporting process and internal control by those charged with governance

c. There is a complex or unstable organizational structure, as evidenced by the following:
- — Difficulty in determining the organization or individuals that have controlling interest in the entity
- — Overly complex organizational structure involving unusual legal entities or managerial lines of authority
- — High turnover of senior management, counsel, or board members

d. Internal control components are deficient as a result of the following:
- — Inadequate monitoring of controls, including automated controls and controls over interim financial reporting (where external reporting is required)
- — High turnover rates or employment of ineffective accounting, internal audit, or information technology staff
- — Ineffective accounting and information systems, including situations involving significant deficiencies or material weaknesses in internal control

Attitudes/Rationalizations

Risk factors reflective of attitudes/rationalizations by those charged with governance, management, or employees, that allow them to engage in and/or justify fraudulent financial reporting, may not be susceptible to observation by the auditor. Nevertheless, the auditor who becomes aware of the existence of such information should consider it in identifying the risks of material misstatement arising from fraudulent financial reporting. For example, auditors may become aware of the following information that may indicate a risk factor:

- Ineffective communication, implementation, support, or enforcement of the entity's values or ethical standards by management or the communication of inappropriate values or ethical standards
- Nonfinancial management's excessive participation in or preoccupation with the selection of accounting principles or the determination of significant estimates
- Known history of violations of securities laws or other laws and regulations, or claims against the entity, its senior management, or board members alleging fraud or violations of laws and regulations
- Excessive interest by management in maintaining or increasing the entity's stock price or earnings trend
- A practice by management of committing to analysts, creditors, and other third parties to achieve aggressive or unrealistic forecasts
- Management failing to correct known significant deficiencies or material weaknesses in internal control on a timely basis
- An interest by management in employing inappropriate means to minimize reported earnings for tax-motivated reasons

- Recurring attempts by management to justify marginal or inappropriate accounting on the basis of materiality
- The relationship between management and the current or predecessor auditor is strained, as exhibited by the following:
  - — Frequent disputes with the current or predecessor auditor on accounting, auditing, or reporting matters
  - — Unreasonable demands on the auditor, such as unreasonable time constraints regarding the completion of the audit or the issuance of the auditor's report
  - — Formal or informal restrictions on the auditor that inappropriately limit access to people or information or the ability to communicate effectively with those charged with governance
  - — Domineering management behavior in dealing with the auditor, especially involving attempts to influence the scope of the auditor's work or the selection or continuance of personnel assigned to or consulted on the audit engagement

Risk Factors Relating to Misstatements Arising From Misappropriation of Assets

A.3 Risk factors that relate to misstatements arising from misappropriation of assets are also classified according to the three conditions generally present when fraud exists: incentives/pressures, opportunities, and attitudes/rationalizations. Some of the risk factors related to misstatements arising from fraudulent financial reporting also may be present when misstatements arising from misappropriation of assets occur. For example, ineffective monitoring of management and weaknesses in internal control may be present when misstatements due to either fraudulent financial reporting or misappropriation of assets exist. The following are examples of risk factors related to misstatements arising from misappropriation of assets.

Incentives/Pressures

a. Personal financial obligations may create pressure on management or employees with access to cash or other assets susceptible to theft to misappropriate those assets.

b. Adverse relationships between the entity and employees with access to cash or other assets susceptible to theft may motivate those employees to misappropriate those assets. For example, adverse relationships may be created by the following:
  - — Known or anticipated future employee layoffs
  - — Recent or anticipated changes to employee compensation or benefit plans
  - — Promotions, compensation, or other rewards inconsistent with expectations

Opportunities

a. Certain characteristics or circumstances may increase the susceptibility of assets to misappropriation. For example, opportunities to misappropriate assets increase when there are the following:
  - — Large amounts of cash on hand or processed
  - — Inventory items that are small in size, of high value, or in high demand

— Easily convertible assets, such as bearer bonds, diamonds, or computer chips
— Fixed assets that are small in size, marketable, or lacking observable identification of ownership

b. Inadequate internal control over assets may increase the susceptibility of misappropriation of those assets. For example, misappropriation of assets may occur because there is the following:

— Inadequate segregation of duties or independent checks
— Inadequate management oversight of employees responsible for assets, for example, inadequate supervision or monitoring of remote locations
— Inadequate job applicant screening of employees with access to assets
— Inadequate recordkeeping with respect to assets
— Inadequate system of authorization and approval of transactions (for example, in purchasing)
— Inadequate physical safeguards over cash, investments, inventory, or fixed assets
— Lack of complete and timely reconciliations of assets
— Lack of timely and appropriate documentation of transactions, for example, credits for merchandise returns
— Lack of mandatory vacations for employees performing key control functions
— Inadequate management understanding of information technology, which enables information technology employees to perpetrate a misappropriation
— Inadequate access controls over automated records, including controls over and review of computer systems event logs.

Attitudes/Rationalizations

Risk factors reflective of employee attitudes/rationalizations that allow them to justify misappropriations of assets, are generally not susceptible to observation by the auditor. Nevertheless, the auditor who becomes aware of the existence of such information should consider it in identifying the risks of material misstatement arising from misappropriation of assets. For example, auditors may become aware of the following attitudes or behavior of employees who have access to assets susceptible to misappropriation:

- Disregard for the need for monitoring or reducing risks related to misappropriations of assets
- Disregard for internal control over misappropriation of assets by overriding existing controls or by failing to correct known internal control deficiencies
- Behavior indicating displeasure or dissatisfaction with the company or its treatment of the employee
- Changes in behavior or lifestyle that may indicate assets have been misappropriated

[Revised, May 2006, to reflect conforming changes necessary due to the issuance of Statement on Auditing Standards No. 112. Revised, April 2007, to reflect conforming changes necessary due to the issuance of Statement on Auditing Standards No. 114.]

.86

Exhibit

Management Antifraud Programs and Controls

Guidance to Help Prevent, Deter, and Detect Fraud

(This exhibit is reprinted for the reader's convenience but is not an integral part of the section.)

This document is being issued jointly by the following organizations:

American Institute of Certified Public Accountants

Association of Certified Fraud Examiners

Financial Executives International

Information Systems Audit and Control Association

The Institute of Internal Auditors

Institute of Management Accountants

Society for Human Resource Management

In addition, we would also like to acknowledge the American Accounting Association, the Defense Industry Initiative, and the National Association of Corporate Directors for their review of the document and helpful comments and materials.

We gratefully acknowledge the valuable contribution provided by the Anti-Fraud Detection Subgroup:

Daniel D. Montgomery, *Chair*
Toby J.F. Bishop
Dennis H. Chookaszian
Susan A. Finn
Dana Hermanson
David L. Landsittel
Carol A. Langelier
Joseph T. Wells
Janice Wilkins

Finally, we thank the staff of the American Institute of Certified Public Accountants for their support on this project:

Charles E. Landes
Director
Audit and Attest Standards

Richard Lanza
Senior Program Manager
Chief Operating Office

Kim M. Gibson
Senior Technical Manager
Audit and Attest Standards

Hugh Kelsey
Program Manager
Knowledge Management

This document was commissioned by the Fraud Task Force of the AICPA's Auditing Standards Board. This document has not been adopted, approved, disapproved, or otherwise acted upon by a board, committee, governing body, or membership of the above issuing organizations.

Preface

Some organizations have significantly lower levels of misappropriation of assets and are less susceptible to fraudulent financial reporting than other organizations because these organizations take proactive steps to prevent or deter fraud. It is only those organizations that seriously consider fraud risks and take proactive steps to create the right kind of climate to reduce its occurrence that have success in preventing fraud. This document identifies the key participants in this antifraud effort, including the board of directors, management, internal and independent auditors, and certified fraud examiners.

Management may develop and implement some of these programs and controls in response to specific identified risks of material misstatement of financial statements due to fraud. In other cases, these programs and controls may be a part of the entity's enterprise-wide risk management activities.

Management is responsible for designing and implementing systems and procedures for the prevention and detection of fraud and, along with the board of directors, for ensuring a culture and environment that promotes honesty and ethical behavior. However, because of the characteristics of fraud, a material misstatement of financial statements due to fraud may occur notwithstanding the presence of programs and controls such as those described in this document.

Introduction

Fraud can range from minor employee theft and unproductive behavior to misappropriation of assets and fraudulent financial reporting. Material financial statement fraud can have a significant adverse effect on an entity's market value, reputation, and ability to achieve its strategic objectives. A number of highly publicized cases have heightened the awareness of the effects of fraudulent financial reporting and have led many organizations to be more proactive in taking steps to prevent or deter its occurrence. Misappropriation of assets, though often not material to the financial statements, can nonetheless result in substantial losses to an entity if a dishonest employee has the incentive and opportunity to commit fraud.

The risk of fraud can be reduced through a combination of prevention, deterrence, and detection measures. However, fraud can be difficult to detect because it often involves concealment through falsification of documents or collusion among management, employees, or third parties. Therefore, it is important to place a strong emphasis on fraud prevention, which may reduce opportunities for fraud to take place, and fraud deterrence, which could persuade individuals that they should not commit fraud because of the likelihood of detection and punishment. Moreover, prevention and deterrence measures are much less costly than the time and expense required for fraud detection and investigation.

An entity's management has both the responsibility and the means to implement measures to reduce the incidence of fraud. The measures an organization takes to prevent and deter fraud also can help create a positive workplace environment that can enhance the entity's ability to recruit and retain high-quality employees.

Research suggests that the most effective way to implement measures to reduce wrongdoing is to base them on a set of core values that are embraced by the entity. These values provide an overarching message about the key principles guiding all employees' actions. This provides a platform upon which a more detailed code of conduct can be constructed, giving more specific guidance about permitted and prohibited behavior, based on applicable laws and the organization's values. Management needs to clearly articulate that all employees will be held accountable to act within the organization's code of conduct.

This document identifies measures entities can implement to prevent, deter, and detect fraud. It discusses these measures in the context of three fundamental elements. Broadly stated, these fundamental elements are (1) create and maintain a *culture* of honesty and high ethics; (2) *evaluate* the risks of fraud and implement the processes, procedures, and controls needed to mitigate the risks and reduce the opportunities for fraud; and (3) develop an appropriate *oversight* process. Although the entire management team shares the responsibility for implementing and monitoring these activities, with oversight from the board of directors, the entity's chief executive officer (CEO) should initiate and support such measures. Without the CEO's active support, these measures are less likely to be effective.

The information presented in this document generally is applicable to entities of all sizes. However, the degree to which certain programs and controls are applied in smaller, less-complex entities and the formality of their application are likely to differ from larger organizations. For example, management of a smaller entity (or the owner of an owner-managed entity), along with those charged with governance of the financial reporting process, are responsible for creating a culture of honesty and high ethics. Management also is responsible for implementing a system of internal controls commensurate with the nature and size of the organization, but smaller entities may find that certain types of control activities are not relevant because of the involvement of and controls applied by management. However, all entities must make it clear that unethical or dishonest behavior will not be tolerated.

Creating a Culture of Honesty and High Ethics

It is the organization's responsibility to create a culture of honesty and high ethics and to clearly communicate acceptable behavior and expectations of each employee. Such a culture is rooted in a strong set of core values (or value system) that provides the foundation for employees as to how the organization conducts its business. It also allows an entity to develop an ethical framework that covers (1) fraudulent financial reporting, (2) misappropriation of assets, and (3) corruption as well as other issues.[1]

Creating a culture of honesty and high ethics should include the following.

Setting the Tone at the Top

Directors and officers of corporations set the "tone at the top" for ethical behavior within any organization. Research in moral development strongly suggests that honesty can best be reinforced when a proper example is set—sometimes referred to as the tone at the top. The management of an entity cannot act one way and expect others in the entity to behave differently.

In many cases, particularly in larger organizations, it is necessary for management to both behave ethically and openly communicate its expectations for ethical behavior because most employees are not in a position to observe management's actions. Management must show employees through its words and actions that dishonest or unethical behavior will not be tolerated, even if the result of the action benefits the entity. Moreover, it should be evident that all employees will be treated equally, regardless of their position.

For example, statements by management regarding the absolute need to meet operating and financial targets can create undue pressures that may lead employees to commit fraud to achieve them. Setting unachievable goals for employees can give them two unattractive choices: fail or cheat. In contrast, a statement from management that says, "We are aggressive in pursuing our targets, while requiring truthful financial reporting at all times," clearly indicates to employees that integrity is a requirement. This message also conveys that the entity has "zero tolerance" for unethical behavior, including fraudulent financial reporting.

The cornerstone of an effective antifraud environment is a culture with a strong value system founded on integrity. This value system often is reflected in a code of conduct.[2] The code of conduct should reflect the core values of the entity and guide employees in making appropriate decisions during their workday. The code of conduct might include such topics as ethics, confidentiality, conflicts of interest, intellectual property, sexual harassment, and fraud.[3] For a code of

---

[1] Corruption includes bribery and other illegal acts.

[2] An entity's value system also could be reflected in an ethics policy, a statement of business principles, or some other concise summary of guiding principles.

[3] Although the discussion in this document focuses on fraud, the subject of fraud often is considered in the context of a broader set of principles that govern an organization. Some organizations, however, may elect to develop a fraud policy separate from an ethics policy. Specific examples of topics in a fraud policy might include a requirement to comply with all laws and regulations and explicit guidance regarding making payments to obtain contracts, holding pricing discussions with competitors, environmental discharges, relationships with vendors, and maintenance of accurate books and records.

conduct to be effective, it should be communicated to all personnel in an understandable fashion. It also should be developed in a participatory and positive manner that will result in both management and employees taking ownership of its content. Finally, the code of conduct should be included in an employee handbook or policy manual, or in some other formal document or location (for example, the entity's intranet) so it can be referred to when needed.

Senior financial officers hold an important and elevated role in corporate governance. While members of the management team, they are uniquely capable and empowered to ensure that all stakeholders' interests are appropriately balanced, protected, and preserved. For examples of codes of conduct, see Attachment 1, "AICPA 'CPA's Handbook of Fraud and Commercial Crime Prevention,' An Organizational Code of Conduct," and Attachment 2, "Financial Executives International Code of Ethics Statement" provided by Financial Executives International. In addition, visit the Institute of Management Accountant's Ethics Center at www.imanet.org for their members' standards of ethical conduct.

Creating a Positive Workplace Environment

Research results indicate that wrongdoing occurs less frequently when employees have positive feelings about an entity than when they feel abused, threatened, or ignored. Without a positive workplace environment, there are more opportunities for poor employee morale, which can affect an employee's attitude about committing fraud against an entity. Factors that detract from a positive work environment and may increase the risk of fraud include:

- Top management that does not seem to care about or reward appropriate behavior
- Negative feedback and lack of recognition for job performance
- Perceived inequities in the organization
- Autocratic rather than participative management
- Low organizational loyalty or feelings of ownership
- Unreasonable budget expectations or other financial targets
- Fear of delivering "bad news" to supervisors and/or management
- Less-than-competitive compensation
- Poor training and promotion opportunities
- Lack of clear organizational responsibilities
- Poor communication practices or methods within the organization

The entity's human resources department often is instrumental in helping to build a corporate culture and a positive work environment. Human resource professionals are responsible for implementing specific programs and initiatives, consistent with management's strategies, that can help to mitigate many of the detractors mentioned above. Mitigating factors that help create a positive work environment and reduce the risk of fraud may include:

- Recognition and reward systems that are in tandem with goals and results
- Equal employment opportunities
- Team-oriented, collaborative decision-making policies
- Professionally administered compensation programs
- Professionally administered training programs and an organizational priority of career development

Employees should be empowered to help create a positive workplace environment and support the entity's values and code of conduct. They should be given the opportunity to provide input to the development and updating of the entity's code of conduct, to ensure that it is relevant, clear, and fair. Involving employees in this fashion also may effectively contribute to the oversight of the entity's code of conduct and an environment of ethical behavior (see the section titled "Developing an Appropriate Oversight Process").

Employees should be given the means to obtain advice internally before making decisions that appear to have significant legal or ethical implications. They should also be encouraged and given the means to communicate concerns, anonymously if preferred, about potential violations of the entity's code of conduct, without fear of retribution. Many organizations have implemented a process for employees to report on a confidential basis any actual or suspected wrongdoing, or potential violations of the code of conduct or ethics policy. For example, some organizations use a telephone "hotline" that is directed to or monitored by an ethics officer, fraud officer, general counsel, internal audit director, or another trusted individual responsible for investigating and reporting incidents of fraud or illegal acts.

Hiring and Promoting Appropriate Employees

Each employee has a unique set of values and personal code of ethics. When faced with sufficient pressure and a perceived opportunity, some employees will behave dishonestly rather than face the negative consequences of honest behavior. The threshold at which dishonest behavior starts, however, will vary among individuals. If an entity is to be successful in preventing fraud, it must have effective policies that minimize the chance of hiring or promoting individuals with low levels of honesty, especially for positions of trust.

Proactive hiring and promotion procedures may include:

- Conducting background investigations on individuals being considered for employment or for promotion to a position of trust[4]
- Thoroughly checking a candidate's education, employment history, and personal references
- Periodic training of all employees about the entity's values and code of conduct, (training is addressed in the following section)
- Incorporating into regular performance reviews an evaluation of how each individual has contributed to creating an appropriate workplace environment in line with the entity's values and code of conduct
- Continuous objective evaluation of compliance with the entity's values and code of conduct, with violations being addressed immediately

Training

New employees should be trained at the time of hiring about the entity's values and its code of conduct. This training should explicitly cover expectations of all employees regarding (1) their duty to communicate certain matters; (2) a list of the types of matters, including actual or suspected fraud, to be communicated along with specific examples; and (3) information on how to communicate those matters. There also should be an affirmation from senior management regarding employee expectations and communication responsibilities. Such training should include an element of "fraud awareness," the tone of which should be

[4] Some organizations also have considered follow-up investigations, particularly for employees in positions of trust, on a periodic basis (for example, every five years) or as circumstances dictate.

positive but nonetheless stress that fraud can be costly (and detrimental in other ways) to the entity and its employees.

In addition to training at the time of hiring, employees should receive refresher training periodically thereafter. Some organizations may consider ongoing training for certain positions, such as purchasing agents or employees with financial reporting responsibilities. Training should be specific to an employee's level within the organization, geographic location, and assigned responsibilities. For example, training for senior manager level personnel would normally be different from that of nonsupervisory employees, and training for purchasing agents would be different from that of sales representatives.

Confirmation

Management needs to clearly articulate that all employees will be held accountable to act within the entity's code of conduct. All employees within senior management and the finance function, as well as other employees in areas that might be exposed to unethical behavior (for example, procurement, sales and marketing) should be required to sign a code of conduct statement annually, at a minimum.

Requiring periodic confirmation by employees of their responsibilities will not only reinforce the policy but may also deter individuals from committing fraud and other violations and might identify problems before they become significant. Such confirmation may include statements that the individual understands the entity's expectations, has complied with the code of conduct, and is not aware of any violations of the code of conduct other than those the individual lists in his or her response. Although people with low integrity may not hesitate to sign a false confirmation, most people will want to avoid making a false statement in writing. Honest individuals are more likely to return their confirmations and to disclose what they know (including any conflicts of interest or other personal exceptions to the code of conduct). Thorough follow-up by internal auditors or others regarding nonreplies may uncover significant issues.

Discipline

The way an entity reacts to incidents of alleged or suspected fraud will send a strong deterrent message throughout the entity, helping to reduce the number of future occurrences. The following actions should be taken in response to an alleged incident of fraud:

- A thorough investigation of the incident should be conducted.[5]
- Appropriate and consistent actions should be taken against violators.
- Relevant controls should be assessed and improved.
- Communication and training should occur to reinforce the entity's values, code of conduct, and expectations.

Expectations about the consequences of committing fraud must be clearly communicated throughout the entity. For example, a strong statement from management that dishonest actions will not be tolerated, and that violators may be terminated and referred to the appropriate authorities, clearly establishes consequences and can be a valuable deterrent to wrongdoing. If wrongdoing occurs

---

[5] Many entities of sufficient size are employing antifraud professionals, such as certified fraud examiners, who are responsible for resolving allegations of fraud within the organization and who also assist in the detection and deterrence of fraud. These individuals typically report their findings internally to the corporate security, legal, or internal audit departments. In other instances, such individuals may be empowered directly by the board of directors or its audit committee.

and an employee is disciplined, it can be helpful to communicate that fact, on a no-name basis, in an employee newsletter or other regular communication to employees. Seeing that other people have been disciplined for wrongdoing can be an effective deterrent, increasing the perceived likelihood of violators being caught and punished. It also can demonstrate that the entity is committed to an environment of high ethical standards and integrity.

Evaluating Antifraud Processes and Controls

Neither fraudulent financial reporting nor misappropriation of assets can occur without a perceived opportunity to commit and conceal the act. Organizations should be proactive in reducing fraud opportunities by (1) identifying and measuring fraud risks, (2) taking steps to mitigate identified risks, and (3) implementing and monitoring appropriate preventive and detective internal controls and other deterrent measures.

Identifying and Measuring Fraud Risks

Management has primary responsibility for establishing and monitoring all aspects of the entity's fraud risk-assessment and prevention activities.[6] Fraud risks often are considered as part of an enterprise-wide risk management program, though they may be addressed separately.[7] The fraud risk-assessment process should consider the vulnerability of the entity to fraudulent activity (fraudulent financial reporting, misappropriation of assets, and corruption) and whether any of those exposures could result in a material misstatement of the financial statements or material loss to the organization. In identifying fraud risks, organizations should consider organizational, industry, and country-specific characteristics that influence the risk of fraud.

The nature and extent of management's risk assessment activities should be commensurate with the size of the entity and complexity of its operations. For example, the risk assessment process is likely to be less formal and less structured in smaller entities. However, management should recognize that fraud can occur in organizations of any size or type, and that almost any employee may be capable of committing fraud given the right set of circumstances. Accordingly, management should develop a heightened "fraud awareness" and an appropriate fraud risk-management program, with oversight from those charged with governance.

Mitigating Fraud Risks

It may be possible to reduce or eliminate certain fraud risks by making changes to the entity's activities and processes. An entity may choose to sell certain segments of its operations, cease doing business in certain locations, or reorganize its business processes to eliminate unacceptable risks. For example, the risk of misappropriation of funds may be reduced by implementing a central lockbox at a bank to receive payments instead of receiving money at the entity's various locations. The risk of corruption may be reduced by closely monitoring the

---

[6] Management may elect to have internal audit play an active role in the development, monitoring, and ongoing assessment of the entity's fraud risk-management program. This may include an active role in the development and communication of the entity's code of conduct or ethics policy, as well as in investigating actual or alleged instances of noncompliance.

[7] Some organizations may perform a periodic self-assessment using questionnaires or other techniques to identify and measure risks. Self-assessment may be less reliable in identifying the risk of fraud due to a lack of experience with fraud (although many organizations experience some form of fraud and abuse, material financial statement fraud or misappropriation of assets is a rare event for most) and because management may be unwilling to acknowledge openly that they might commit fraud given sufficient pressure and opportunity.

entity's procurement process. The risk of financial statement fraud may be reduced by implementing shared services centers to provide accounting services to multiple segments, affiliates, or geographic locations of an entity's operations. A shared services center may be less vulnerable to influence by local operations managers and may be able to implement more extensive fraud detection measures cost-effectively.

Implementing and Monitoring Appropriate Internal Controls

Some risks are inherent in the environment of the entity, but most can be addressed with an appropriate system of internal control. Once fraud risk assessment has taken place, the entity can identify the processes, controls, and other procedures that are needed to mitigate the identified risks. Effective internal control will include a well-developed control environment, an effective and secure information system, and appropriate control and monitoring activities.[8] Because of the importance of information technology in supporting operations and the processing of transactions, management also needs to implement and maintain appropriate controls, whether automated or manual, over computer-generated information.

In particular, management should evaluate whether appropriate internal controls have been implemented in any areas management has identified as posing a higher risk of fraudulent activity, as well as controls over the entity's financial reporting process. Because fraudulent financial reporting may begin in an interim period, management also should evaluate the appropriateness of internal controls over interim financial reporting.

Fraudulent financial reporting by upper-level management typically involves override of internal controls within the financial reporting process. Because management has the ability to override controls, or to influence others to perpetrate or conceal fraud, the need for a strong value system and a culture of ethical financial reporting becomes increasingly important. This helps create an environment in which other employees will decline to participate in committing a fraud and will use established communication procedures to report any requests to commit wrongdoing. The potential for management override also increases the need for appropriate oversight measures by those charged with governance, as discussed in the following section.

Fraudulent financial reporting by lower levels of management and employees may be deterred or detected by appropriate monitoring controls, such as having higher-level managers review and evaluate the financial results reported by individual operating units or subsidiaries. Unusual fluctuations in results of particular reporting units, or the lack of expected fluctuations, may indicate potential manipulation by departmental or operating unit managers or staff.

Developing an Appropriate Oversight Process

To effectively prevent or deter fraud, an entity should have an appropriate oversight function in place. Oversight can take many forms and can be performed by many within and outside the entity, under the overall oversight of the audit committee (or those charged with governance, such as the board of directors, where no audit committee exists).

---

[8] The report of the Committee of Sponsoring Organizations (COSO) of the Treadway Commission, *Internal Control—Integrated Framework*, provides reasonable criteria for management to use in evaluating the effectiveness of the entity's system of internal control.

Audit Committee or Those Charged With Governance

The audit committee (or those charged with governance where no audit committee exists) should evaluate management's identification of fraud risks, implementation of antifraud measures, and creation of the appropriate "tone at the top." Active oversight by the audit committee can help to reinforce management's commitment to creating a culture with "zero tolerance" for fraud. An entity's audit committee also should ensure that senior management (in particular, the CEO) implements appropriate fraud deterrence and prevention measures to better protect investors, employees, and other stakeholders. The audit committee's evaluation and oversight not only helps make sure that senior management fulfills its responsibility, but also can serve as a deterrent to senior management engaging in fraudulent activity (that is, by ensuring an environment is created whereby any attempt by senior management to involve employees in committing or concealing fraud would lead promptly to reports from such employees to appropriate persons, including the audit committee).

The audit committee also plays an important role in helping those charged with governance fulfill their oversight responsibilities with respect to the entity's financial reporting process and the system of internal control.[9] In exercising this oversight responsibility, the audit committee should consider the potential for management override of controls or other inappropriate influence over the financial reporting process. For example, the audit committee may obtain from the internal auditors and independent auditors their views on management's involvement in the financial reporting process and, in particular, the ability of management to override information processed by the entity's financial reporting system (for example, the ability for management or others to initiate or record nonstandard journal entries). The audit committee also may consider reviewing the entity's reported information for reasonableness compared with prior or forecasted results, as well as with peers or industry averages. In addition, information received in communications from the independent auditors[10] can assist the audit committee in assessing the strength of the entity's internal control and the potential for fraudulent financial reporting.

As part of its oversight responsibilities, the audit committee should encourage management to provide a mechanism for employees to report concerns about unethical behavior, actual or suspected fraud, or violations of the entity's code of conduct or ethics policy. The committee should then receive periodic reports describing the nature, status, and eventual disposition of any fraud or unethical conduct. A summary of the activity, follow-up and disposition also should be provided to all of those charged with governance.

If senior management is involved in fraud, the next layer of management may be the most likely to be aware of it. As a result, the audit committee (and others of those charged with governance) should consider establishing an open line of communication with members of management one or two levels below senior management to assist in identifying fraud at the highest levels of the

---

[9] See the Report of the NACD Blue Ribbon Commission on the Audit Committee, (Washington, D.C.: National Association of Corporate Directors, 2000). For the board's role in the oversight of risk management, see Report of the NACD Blue Ribbon Commission on Risk Oversight, (Washington, D.C.: National Association of Corporate Directors, 2002).

[10] See section 325, *Communicating Internal Control Related Matters Identified in an Audit*, and section 380, *The Auditor's Communication With Those Charged With Governance*. [Footnote revised, May 2006, due to conforming changes necessary due to the issuance of Statement on Standards No. 112. Footnote revised, April 2007, due to conforming changes necessary due to the issuance of Statement on Standards No. 114.]

organization or investigating any fraudulent activity that might occur.[11] The audit committee typically has the ability and authority to investigate any alleged or suspected wrongdoing brought to its attention. Most audit committee charters empower the committee to investigate any matters within the scope of its responsibilities, and to retain legal, accounting, and other professional advisers as needed to advise the committee and assist in its investigation.

All audit committee members should be financially literate, and each committee should have at least one financial expert. The financial expert should possess:

- An understanding of generally accepted accounting principles and audits of financial statements prepared under those principles. Such understanding may have been obtained either through education or experience. It is important for someone on the audit committee to have a working knowledge of those principles and standards.
- Experience in the preparation and/or the auditing of financial statements of an entity of similar size, scope and complexity as the entity on whose board the committee member serves. The experience would generally be as a chief financial officer, chief accounting officer, controller, or auditor of a similar entity. This background will provide a necessary understanding of the transactional and operational environment that produces the issuer's financial statements. It will also bring an understanding of what is involved in, for example, appropriate accounting estimates, accruals, and reserve provisions, and an appreciation of what is necessary to maintain a good internal control environment.
- Experience in internal governance and procedures of audit committees, obtained either as an audit committee member, a senior corporate manager responsible for answering to the audit committee, or an external auditor responsible for reporting on the execution and results of annual audits.

Management

Management is responsible for overseeing the activities carried out by employees, and typically does so by implementing and monitoring processes and controls such as those discussed previously. However, management also may initiate, participate in, or direct the commission and concealment of a fraudulent act. Accordingly, the audit committee (or those charged with governance where no audit committee exists) has the responsibility to oversee the activities of senior management and to consider the risk of fraudulent financial reporting involving the override of internal controls or collusion (see discussion on the audit committee and board of directors above).

Public companies should include a statement in the annual report acknowledging management's responsibility for the preparation of the financial statements and for establishing and maintaining an effective system of internal control. This will help improve the public's understanding of the respective roles of management and the auditor. This statement has also been generally referred to as a "Management Report" or "Management Certificate." Such a statement can provide a convenient vehicle for management to describe the nature and manner of preparation of the financial information and the adequacy of the

---

[11] *Report of the NACD Best Practices Council: Coping with Fraud and Other Illegal Activity, A Guide for Directors, CEOs, and Senior Managers* (1998) sets forth "basic principles" and "implementation approaches" for dealing with fraud and other illegal activity.

internal accounting controls. Logically, the statement should be presented in close proximity to the formal financial statements. For example, it could appear near the independent auditor's report, or in the financial review or management analysis section.

Internal Auditors

An effective internal audit team can be extremely helpful in performing aspects of the oversight function. Their knowledge about the entity may enable them to identify indicators that suggest fraud has been committed. The *Standards for the Professional Practice of Internal Auditing* (IIA Standards), issued by the Institute of Internal Auditors, state, "The internal auditor should have sufficient knowledge to identify the indicators of fraud but is not expected to have the expertise of a person whose primary responsibility is detecting and investigating fraud." Internal auditors also have the opportunity to evaluate fraud risks and controls and to recommend action to mitigate risks and improve controls. Specifically, the IIA Standards require internal auditors to assess risks facing their organizations. This risk assessment is to serve as the basis from which audit plans are devised and against which internal controls are tested. The IIA Standards require the audit plan to be presented to and approved by the audit committee (or board of directors where no audit committee exists). The work completed as a result of the audit plan provides assurance on which management's assertion about controls can be made.

Internal audits can be both a detection and a deterrence measure. Internal auditors can assist in the deterrence of fraud by examining and evaluating the adequacy and the effectiveness of the system of internal control, commensurate with the extent of the potential exposure or risk in the various segments of the organization's operations. In carrying out this responsibility, internal auditors should, for example, determine whether:

- The organizational environment fosters control consciousness.
- Realistic organizational goals and objectives are set.
- Written policies (for example, a code of conduct) exist that describe prohibited activities and the action required whenever violations are discovered.
- Appropriate authorization policies for transactions are established and maintained.
- Policies, practices, procedures, reports, and other mechanisms are developed to monitor activities and safeguard assets, particularly in high-risk areas.
- Communication channels provide management with adequate and reliable information.
- Recommendations need to be made for the establishment or enhancement of cost-effective controls to help deter fraud.

Internal auditors may conduct proactive auditing to search for corruption, misappropriation of assets, and financial statement fraud. This may include the use of computer-assisted audit techniques to detect particular types of fraud. Internal auditors also can employ analytical and other procedures to isolate anomalies and perform detailed reviews of high-risk accounts and transactions to identify potential financial statement fraud. The internal auditors should have an independent reporting line directly to the audit committee, to enable them to express any concerns about management's commitment to appropriate internal controls or to report suspicions or allegations of fraud involving senior management.

Independent Auditors

Independent auditors can assist management and the board of directors (or audit committee) by providing an assessment of the entity's process for identifying, assessing, and responding to the risks of fraud. Those charged with governance, such as the board of directors or audit committee, should have an open and candid dialogue with the independent auditors regarding management's risk assessment process and the system of internal control. Such a dialogue should include a discussion of the susceptibility of the entity to fraudulent financial reporting and the entity's exposure to misappropriation of assets.

Certified Fraud Examiners

Certified fraud examiners may assist the audit committee and board of directors with aspects of the oversight process either directly or as part of a team of internal auditors or independent auditors. Certified fraud examiners can provide extensive knowledge and experience about fraud that may not be available within a corporation. They can provide more objective input into management's evaluation of the risk of fraud (especially fraud involving senior management, such as financial statement fraud) and the development of appropriate antifraud controls that are less vulnerable to management override. They can assist the audit committee and board of directors in evaluating the fraud risk assessment and fraud prevention measures implemented by management. Certified fraud examiners also conduct examinations to resolve allegations or suspicions of fraud, reporting either to an appropriate level of management or to the audit committee or board of directors, depending upon the nature of the issue and the level of personnel involved.

Other Information

To obtain more information on fraud and implementing antifraud programs and controls, please go to the following websites where additional materials, guidance, and tools can be found.

American Institute of Certified Public Accountants	www.aicpa.org
Association of Certified Fraud Examiners	www.cfenet.com
Financial Executives International	www.fei.org
Information Systems Audit and Control Association	www.isaca.org
The Institute of Internal Auditors	www.theiia.org
Institute of Management Accountants	www.imanet.org
National Association of Corporate Directors	www.nacdonline.org
Society for Human Resource Management	www.shrm.org

Attachment 1: AICPA "CPA's Handbook of Fraud and Commercial Crime Prevention," An Organizational Code of Conduct

The following is an example of an organizational code of conduct, which includes definitions of what is considered unacceptable, and the consequences of any breaches thereof. The specific content and areas addressed in an entity's code of conduct should be specific to that entity.

Organizational Code of Conduct

The Organization and its employees must, at all times, comply with all applicable laws and regulations. The Organization will not condone the activities of employees who achieve results through violation of the law or unethical business dealings. This includes any payments for illegal acts, indirect contributions, rebates, and bribery. The Organization does not permit any activity that fails to stand the closest possible public scrutiny.

All business conduct should be well above the minimum standards required by law. Accordingly, employees must ensure that their actions cannot be interpreted as being, in any way, in contravention of the laws and regulations governing the Organization's worldwide operations.

Employees uncertain about the application or interpretation of any legal requirements should refer the matter to their superior, who, if necessary, should seek the advice of the legal department.

General Employee Conduct

The Organization expects its employees to conduct themselves in a businesslike manner. Drinking, gambling, fighting, swearing, and similar unprofessional activities are strictly prohibited while on the job.

Employees must not engage in sexual harassment, or conduct themselves in a way that could be construed as such, for example, by using inappropriate language, keeping or posting inappropriate materials in their work area, or accessing inappropriate materials on their computer.

Conflicts of Interest

The Organization expects that employees will perform their duties conscientiously, honestly, and in accordance with the best interests of the Organization. Employees must not use their position or the knowledge gained as a result of their position for private or personal advantage. Regardless of the circumstances, if employees sense that a course of action they have pursued, are presently pursuing, or are contemplating pursuing may involve them in a conflict of interest with their employer, they should immediately communicate all the facts to their superior.

Outside Activities, Employment, and Directorships

All employees share a serious responsibility for the Organization's good public relations, especially at the community level. Their readiness to help with religious, charitable, educational, and civic activities brings credit to the Organization and is encouraged. Employees must, however, avoid acquiring any business interest or participating in any other activity outside the Organization that would, or would appear to:

- Create an excessive demand upon their time and attention, thus depriving the Organization of their best efforts on the job.
- Create a conflict of interest—an obligation, interest, or distraction—that may interfere with the independent exercise of judgment in the Organization's best interest.

Relationships With Clients and Suppliers

Employees should avoid investing in or acquiring a financial interest for their own accounts in any business organization that has a contractual relationship with the Organization, or that provides goods or services, or both to the Organization, if such investment or interest could influence or create the impression of influencing their decisions in the performance of their duties on behalf of the Organization.

Gifts, Entertainment, and Favors

Employees must not accept entertainment, gifts, or personal favors that could, in any way, influence, or appear to influence, business decisions in favor of any person or organization with whom or with which the Organization has, or is likely to have, business dealings. Similarly, employees must not accept any other preferential treatment under these circumstances because their position with the Organization might be inclined to, or be perceived to, place them under obligation.

Kickbacks and Secret Commissions

Regarding the Organization's business activities, employees may not receive payment or compensation of any kind, except as authorized under the Organization's remuneration policies. In particular, the Organization strictly prohibits the acceptance of kickbacks and secret commissions from suppliers or others. Any breach of this rule will result in immediate termination and prosecution to the fullest extent of the law.

Organization Funds and Other Assets

Employees who have access to Organization funds in any form must follow the prescribed procedures for recording, handling, and protecting money as detailed in the Organization's instructional manuals or other explanatory materials, or both. The Organization imposes strict standards to prevent fraud and dishonesty. If employees become aware of any evidence of fraud and dishonesty, they should immediately advise their superior or the Law Department so that the Organization can promptly investigate further.

When an employee's position requires spending Organization funds or incurring any reimbursable personal expenses, that individual must use good judgment on the Organization's behalf to ensure that good value is received for every expenditure.

Organization funds and all other assets of the Organization are for Organization purposes only and not for personal benefit. This includes the personal use of organizational assets, such as computers.

Organization Records and Communications

Accurate and reliable records of many kinds are necessary to meet the Organization's legal and financial obligations and to manage the affairs of the Organization. The Organization's books and records must reflect in an accurate and timely manner all business transactions. The employees responsible for accounting and recordkeeping must fully disclose and record all assets, liabilities, or both, and must exercise diligence in enforcing these requirements.

Employees must not make or engage in any false record or communication of any kind, whether internal or external, including but not limited to:

- False expense, attendance, production, financial, or similar reports and statements
- False advertising, deceptive marketing practices, or other misleading representations

Dealing With Outside People and Organizations

Employees must take care to separate their personal roles from their Organization positions when communicating on matters not involving Organization business. Employees must not use organization identification, stationery, supplies, and equipment for personal or political matters.

When communicating publicly on matters that involve Organization business, employees must not presume to speak for the Organization on any topic, unless they are certain that the views they express are those of the Organization, and it is the Organization's desire that such views be publicly disseminated.

When dealing with anyone outside the Organization, including public officials, employees must take care not to compromise the integrity or damage the reputation of either the Organization, or any outside individual, business, or government body.

Prompt Communications

In all matters relevant to customers, suppliers, government authorities, the public and others in the Organization, all employees must make every effort to achieve complete, accurate, and timely communications—responding promptly and courteously to all proper requests for information and to all complaints.

Privacy and Confidentiality

When handling financial and personal information about customers or others with whom the Organization has dealings, observe the following principles:

1. Collect, use, and retain only the personal information necessary for the Organization's business. Whenever possible, obtain any relevant information directly from the person concerned. Use only reputable and reliable sources to supplement this information.
2. Retain information only for as long as necessary or as required by law. Protect the physical security of this information.
3. Limit internal access to personal information to those with a legitimate business reason for seeking that information. Use only personal information for the purposes for which it was originally obtained. Obtain the consent of the person concerned before externally disclosing any personal information, unless legal process or contractual obligation provides otherwise.

Attachment 2: Financial Executives International Code of Ethics Statement

The mission of Financial Executives International (FEI) includes significant efforts to promote ethical conduct in the practice of financial management throughout the world. Senior financial officers hold an important and elevated role in corporate governance. While members of the management team, they are uniquely capable and empowered to ensure that all stakeholders' interests are appropriately balanced, protected, and preserved. This code provides principles that members are expected to adhere to and advocate. They embody rules regarding individual and peer responsibilities, as well as responsibilities to employers, the public, and other stakeholders.

All members of FEI will:

1. Act with honesty and integrity, avoiding actual or apparent conflicts of interest in personal and professional relationships.
2. Provide constituents with information that is accurate, complete, objective, relevant, timely, and understandable.
3. Comply with rules and regulations of federal, state, provincial, and local governments, and other appropriate private and public regulatory agencies.
4. Act in good faith; responsibly; and with due care, competence, and diligence, without misrepresenting material facts or allowing one's independent judgment to be subordinated.
5. Respect the confidentiality of information acquired in the course of one's work except when authorized or otherwise legally obligated to disclose. Confidential information acquired in the course of one's work will not be used for personal advantage.
6. Share knowledge and maintain skills important and relevant to constituents' needs.
7. Proactively promote ethical behavior as a responsible partner among peers, in the work environment, and in the community.
8. Achieve responsible use of and control over all assets and resources employed or entrusted.

[Revised, April 2007, to reflect conforming changes necessary due to the issuance of Statement on Auditing Standards No. 114.]

AU Section 317

Illegal Acts by Clients

(Supersedes section 328.)

Source: SAS No. 54.

See section 9317 for interpretations of this section.

Effective for audits of financial statements for periods beginning on or after January 1, 1989, unless otherwise indicated.

.01 This section prescribes the nature and extent of the consideration an independent auditor should give to the possibility of illegal acts by a client in an audit of financial statements in accordance with generally accepted auditing standards. The section also provides guidance on the auditor's responsibilities when a possible illegal act is detected.

Definition of Illegal Acts

.02 The term *illegal acts*, for purposes of this section, refers to violations of laws or governmental regulations. Illegal acts by clients are acts attributable to the entity whose financial statements are under audit or acts by management or employees acting on behalf of the entity. Illegal acts by clients do not include personal misconduct by the entity's personnel unrelated to their business activities.

Dependence on Legal Judgment

.03 Whether an act is, in fact, illegal is a determination that is normally beyond the auditor's professional competence. An auditor, in reporting on financial statements, presents himself as one who is proficient in accounting and auditing. The auditor's training, experience, and understanding of the client and its industry may provide a basis for recognition that some client acts coming to his attention may be illegal. However, the determination as to whether a particular act is illegal would generally be based on the advice of an informed expert qualified to practice law or may have to await final determination by a court of law.

Relation to Financial Statements

.04 Illegal acts vary considerably in their relation to the financial statements. Generally, the further removed an illegal act is from the events and transactions ordinarily reflected in financial statements, the less likely the auditor is to become aware of the act or to recognize its possible illegality.

.05 The auditor considers laws and regulations that are generally recognized by auditors to have a direct and material effect on the determination of financial statement amounts. For example, tax laws affect accruals and the amount recognized as expense in the accounting period; applicable laws and regulations may affect the amount of revenue accrued under government contracts.

However, the auditor considers such laws or regulations from the perspective of their known relation to audit objectives derived from financial statements assertions rather than from the perspective of legality *per se*. The auditor's responsibility to detect and report misstatements resulting from illegal acts having a direct and material effect on the determination of financial statement amounts is the same as that for misstatements caused by error or fraud as described in section 110, *Responsibilities and Functions of the Independent Auditor*.

.06 Entities may be affected by many other laws or regulations, including those related to securities trading, occupational safety and health, food and drug administration, environmental protection, equal employment, and price-fixing or other antitrust violations. Generally, these laws and regulations relate more to an entity's operating aspects than to its financial and accounting aspects, and their financial statement effect is indirect. An auditor ordinarily does not have sufficient basis for recognizing possible violations of such laws and regulations. Their indirect effect is normally the result of the need to disclose a contingent liability because of the allegation or determination of illegality. For example, securities may be purchased or sold based on inside information. While the direct effects of the purchase or sale may be recorded appropriately, their indirect effect, the possible contingent liability for violating securities laws, may not be appropriately disclosed. Even when violations of such laws and regulations can have consequences material to the financial statements, the auditor may not become aware of the existence of the illegal act unless he is informed by the client, or there is evidence of a governmental agency investigation or enforcement proceeding in the records, documents, or other information normally inspected in an audit of financial statements.

The Auditor's Consideration of the Possibility of Illegal Acts

.07 As explained in paragraph .05, certain illegal acts have a direct and material effect on the determination of financial statement amounts. Other illegal acts, such as those described in paragraph .06, may, in particular circumstances, be regarded as having material but indirect effects on financial statements. The auditor's responsibility with respect to detecting, considering the financial statement effects of, and reporting these other illegal acts is described in this section. These other illegal acts are hereinafter referred to simply as *illegal acts*. The auditor should be aware of the possibility that such illegal acts may have occurred. If specific information comes to the auditor's attention that provides evidence concerning the existence of possible illegal acts that could have a material indirect effect on the financial statements, the auditor should apply audit procedures specifically directed to ascertaining whether an illegal act has occurred. However, because of the characteristics of illegal acts explained above, an audit made in accordance with generally accepted auditing standards provides no assurance that illegal acts will be detected or that any contingent liabilities that may result will be disclosed.

Audit Procedures in the Absence of Evidence Concerning Possible Illegal Acts

.08 Normally, an audit in accordance with generally accepted auditing standards does not include audit procedures specifically designed to detect illegal acts. However, procedures applied for the purpose of forming an opinion on the financial statements may bring possible illegal acts to the auditor's attention. For example, such procedures include reading minutes; inquiring of the client's management and legal counsel concerning litigation, claims, and assessments; performing substantive tests of details of transactions or balances. The auditor should make inquiries of management concerning the client's compliance with laws and regulations. Where applicable, the auditor should also inquire of management concerning—

- The client's policies relative to the prevention of illegal acts.
- The use of directives issued by the client and periodic representations obtained by the client from management at appropriate levels of authority concerning compliance with laws and regulations.

The auditor also obtains written representations from management concerning the absence of violations or possible violations of laws or regulations whose effects should be considered for disclosure in the financial statements or as a basis for recording a loss contingency. (See section 333, *Management Representations*.) The auditor need perform no further procedures in this area absent specific information concerning possible illegal acts.

Specific Information Concerning Possible Illegal Acts

.09 In applying audit procedures and evaluating the results of those procedures, the auditor may encounter specific information that may raise a question concerning possible illegal acts, such as the following:

- Unauthorized transactions, improperly recorded transactions, or transactions not recorded in a complete or timely manner in order to maintain accountability for assets
- Investigation by a governmental agency, an enforcement proceeding, or payment of unusual fines or penalties
- Violations of laws or regulations cited in reports of examinations by regulatory agencies that have been made available to the auditor
- Large payments for unspecified services to consultants, affiliates, or employees
- Sales commissions or agents' fees that appear excessive in relation to those normally paid by the client or to the services actually received
- Unusually large payments in cash, purchases of bank cashiers' checks in large amounts payable to bearer, transfers to numbered bank accounts, or similar transactions
- Unexplained payments made to government officials or employees
- Failure to file tax returns or pay government duties or similar fees that are common to the entity's industry or the nature of its business

Audit Procedures in Response to Possible Illegal Acts

.10 When the auditor becomes aware of information concerning a possible illegal act, the auditor should obtain an understanding of the nature of the act, the circumstances in which it occurred, and sufficient other information to evaluate the effect on the financial statements. In doing so, the auditor should inquire of management at a level above those involved, if possible. If management does not provide satisfactory information that there has been no illegal act, the auditor should—

a. Consult with the client's legal counsel or other specialists about the application of relevant laws and regulations to the circumstances and the possible effects on the financial statements. Arrangements for such consultation with client's legal counsel should be made by the client.

b. Apply additional procedures, if necessary, to obtain further understanding of the nature of the acts.

.11 The additional audit procedures considered necessary, if any, might include procedures such as the following:

a. Examine supporting documents, such as invoices, canceled checks, and agreements and compare with accounting records.

b. Confirm significant information concerning the matter with the other party to the transaction or with intermediaries, such as banks or lawyers.

c. Determine whether the transaction has been properly authorized.

d. Consider whether other similar transactions or events may have occurred, and apply procedures to identify them.

The Auditor's Response to Detected Illegal Acts

.12 When the auditor concludes, based on information obtained and, if necessary, consultation with legal counsel, that an illegal act has or is likely to have occurred, the auditor should consider the effect on the financial statements as well as the implications for other aspects of the audit.

The Auditor's Consideration of Financial Statement Effect

.13 In evaluating the materiality of an illegal act that comes to his attention, the auditor should consider both the quantitative and qualitative materiality of the act. For example, section 312, *Audit Risk and Materiality in Conducting an Audit*, paragraph .59, states that "an illegal payment of an otherwise immaterial amount could be material if there is a reasonable possibility that it could lead to a material contingent liability or a material loss of revenue." [Revised, March 2006, to reflect conforming changes necessary due to the issuance of Statement on Auditing Standards No. 107.]

.14 The auditor should consider the effect of an illegal act on the amounts presented in financial statements including contingent monetary effects, such as fines, penalties and damages. Loss contingencies resulting from illegal acts that may be required to be disclosed should be evaluated in the same manner as other loss contingencies. Examples of loss contingencies that may arise from an illegal act are: threat of expropriation of assets, enforced discontinuance of operations in another country, and litigation.

.15 The auditor should evaluate the adequacy of disclosure in the financial statements of the potential effects of an illegal act on the entity's operations. If material revenue or earnings are derived from transactions involving illegal acts, or if illegal acts create significant unusual risks associated with material revenue or earnings, such as loss of a significant business relationship, that information should be considered for disclosure.

Implications for Audit

.16 The auditor should consider the implications of an illegal act in relation to other aspects of the audit, particularly the reliability of representations of management. The implications of particular illegal acts will depend on the relationship of the perpetration and concealment, if any, of the illegal act to specific control procedures and the level of management or employees involved.

Communication With Those Charged With Governance

.17 The auditor should assure himself that those charged with governance are adequately informed with respect to illegal acts that come to the auditor's attention.[[1]] The auditor need not communicate matters that are clearly inconsequential and may reach agreement in advance with the audit committee on the nature of such matters to be communicated. The communication should describe the act, the circumstances of its occurrence, and the effect on the financial statements. Senior management may wish to have its remedial actions communicated to the audit committee simultaneously. Possible remedial actions include disciplinary action against involved personnel, seeking restitution, adoption of preventive or corrective company policies, and modifications of specific control activities. If senior management is involved in an illegal act, the auditor should communicate directly with those charged with governance. The communication may be oral or written. If the communication is oral, the auditor should document it. [Revised, April 2007, to reflect conforming changes necessary due to the issuance of Statement on Auditing Standards No. 114.]

Effect on the Auditor's Report

.18 If the auditor concludes that an illegal act has a material effect on the financial statements, and the act has not been properly accounted for or disclosed, the auditor should express a qualified opinion or an adverse opinion on the financial statements taken as a whole, depending on the materiality of the effect on the financial statements.

.19 If the auditor is precluded by the client from obtaining sufficient appropriate audit evidence to evaluate whether an illegal act that could be material to the financial statements has, or is likely to have, occurred, the auditor generally should disclaim an opinion on the financial statements. [Revised, March 2006, to reflect conforming changes necessary due to the issuance of Statement on Auditing Standards No. 105.]

.20 If the client refuses to accept the auditor's report as modified for the circumstances described in paragraphs .18 and .19, the auditor should withdraw from the engagement and indicate the reasons for withdrawal in writing to those charged with governance. [Revised, April 2007, to reflect conforming changes necessary due to the issuance of Statement on Auditing Standards No. 114.]

.21 The auditor may be unable to determine whether an act is illegal because of limitations imposed by the circumstances rather than by the client or because of uncertainty associated with interpretation of applicable laws or regulations or surrounding facts. In these circumstances, the auditor should consider the effect on his report.[2]

[[1]] [Footnote deleted to reflect conforming changes necessary due to the issuance of Statement on Auditing Standards No. 114.]

[2] See section 508, *Reports on Audited Financial Statements*.

Other Considerations in an Audit in Accordance With Generally Accepted Auditing Standards

.22 In addition to the need to withdraw from the engagement, as described in paragraph .20, the auditor may conclude that withdrawal is necessary when the client does not take the remedial action that the auditor considers necessary in the circumstances even when the illegal act is not material to the financial statements. Factors that should affect the auditor's conclusion include the implications of the failure to take remedial action, which may affect the auditor's ability to rely on management representations, and the effects of continuing association with the client. In reaching a conclusion on such matters, the auditor may wish to consult with his own legal counsel.

.23 Disclosure of an illegal act to parties other than the client's senior management and those charged with governance is not ordinarily part of the auditor's responsibility, and such disclosure would be precluded by the auditor's ethical or legal obligation of confidentiality, unless the matter affects his opinion on the financial statements. The auditor should recognize, however, that in the following circumstances a duty to notify parties outside the client may exist:[3]

a. When the entity reports an auditor change under the appropriate securities law on Form 8-K[4]

b. To a successor auditor when the successor makes inquiries in accordance with section 315, *Communications Between Predecessor and Successor Auditors*[5]

c. In response to a subpoena

d. To a funding agency or other specified agency in accordance with requirements for the audits of entities that receive financial assistance from a government agency

Because potential conflicts with the auditor's ethical and legal obligations for confidentiality may be complex, the auditor may wish to consult with legal counsel before discussing illegal acts with parties outside the client. [Revised, April 2007, to reflect conforming changes necessary due to the issuance of Statement on Auditing Standards No. 114.]

Responsibilities in Other Circumstances

.24 An auditor may accept an engagement that entails a greater responsibility for detecting illegal acts than that specified in this section. For example, a governmental unit may engage an independent auditor to perform an audit in accordance with the Single Audit Act of 1984. In such an engagement,

---

[3] Auditors may be required, under certain circumstances, pursuant to the Private Securities Litigation Reform Act of 1995 (codified in section 10A(b)1 of the Securities Exchange Act of 1934) to make a report to the Securities and Exchange Commission relating to an illegal act that has a material effect on the financial statements. [Footnote added, July 1997, to reflect conforming changes necessary due to the issuance of the Private Securities Litigation Reform Act of 1995.]

[4] Disclosure to the Securities and Exchange Commission may be necessary if, among other matters, the auditor withdraws because the board of directors has not taken appropriate remedial action. Such failure may be a reportable disagreement on Form 8-K. [Footnote renumbered, July 1997, to reflect conforming changes necessary due to the issuance of the Private Securities Litigation Reform Act of 1995.]

[5] In accordance with section 315, communications between predecessor and successor auditors require the specific permission of the client. [Footnote renumbered, July 1997, to reflect conforming changes necessary due to the issuance of the Private Securities Litigation Reform Act of 1995.]

the independent auditor is responsible for testing and reporting on the governmental unit's compliance with certain laws and regulations applicable to Federal financial assistance programs. Also, an independent auditor may undertake a variety of other special engagements. For example, a corporation's board of directors or its audit committee may engage an auditor to apply agreed-upon procedures and report on compliance with the corporation's code of conduct under the attestation standards.

Effective Date

.25 This section is effective for audits of financial statements for periods beginning on or after January 1, 1989. Early application of the provisions of this section is permissible.

AU Section 9317

Illegal Acts by Clients: Auditing Interpretations of Section 317

[1.] Consideration of Internal Control in a Financial Statement Audit and the Foreign Corrupt Practices Act

[.01–.02] [Deleted November 2006.]

[2.] Material Weaknesses in Internal Control and the Foreign Corrupt Practices Act [1]

[.03–.06] [Deleted March 2009.]

---

[1] [Footnote deleted March 2009.]

AU Section 318

Performing Audit Procedures in Response to Assessed Risks and Evaluating the Audit Evidence Obtained

(Supersedes SAS No. 55.)

Source: SAS No. 110.

Effective for audits of financial statements for periods beginning on or after December 15, 2006. Earlier application is permitted.

Introduction

.01 This section establishes standards and provides guidance on determining overall responses and designing and performing further audit procedures to respond to the assessed risks of material misstatement[1] at the financial statement and relevant assertion levels in a financial statement audit, and on evaluating the sufficiency and appropriateness of the audit evidence obtained. In particular, this section provides guidance about implementing the third standard of field work, as follows:

> The auditor must obtain sufficient appropriate audit evidence by performing audit procedures to afford a reasonable basis for an opinion regarding the financial statements under audit.

.02 The following is an overview of this standard:

- *Overall responses.* This section provides guidance to the auditor in determining overall responses to address risks of material misstatement at the financial statement level and provides guidance on the nature of those responses.
- *Audit procedures responsive to risks of material misstatement at the relevant assertion level.* This section provides guidance to the auditor in designing and performing further audit procedures, including tests of the operating effectiveness of controls, where relevant or necessary, and substantive procedures, whose nature, timing, and extent are responsive to the assessed risks of material misstatement at the relevant assertion level. In addition, this section includes matters the auditor should consider in determining the nature, timing, and extent of such further audit procedures.
- *Evaluating the sufficiency and appropriateness of the audit evidence obtained.* This section provides guidance to the auditor in evaluating whether the risk assessments remain appropriate and to conclude whether sufficient appropriate audit evidence has been obtained.
- *Documentation.* This section provides related documentation guidance.

---

[1] Risk of material misstatement is described as the auditor's combined assessment of inherent risk and control risk. See paragraph .22 of section 312, *Audit Risk and Materiality in Conducting an Audit*, for the definition of and discussion about risk of material misstatement.

.03 To reduce audit risk to an acceptably low level, the auditor should determine overall responses to address the assessed risks of material misstatement at the financial statement level and should design and perform further audit procedures whose nature, timing, and extent are responsive to the assessed risks of material misstatement at the relevant assertion level[2] The overall responses and the nature, timing, and extent of the further audit procedures to be performed are matters for the professional judgment of the auditor.

Overall Responses[3]

.04 The auditor's overall responses to address the assessed risks of material misstatement at the financial statement level may include emphasizing to the audit team the need to maintain professional skepticism in gathering and evaluating audit evidence, assigning more experienced staff or those with specialized skills or using specialists, providing more supervision, or incorporating additional elements of unpredictability in the selection of further audit procedures to be performed. Additionally, the auditor may make general changes to the nature, timing, or extent of further audit procedures as an overall response, for example, performing substantive procedures at period end instead of at an interim date.

.05 The assessment of the risks of material misstatement at the financial statement level is affected by the auditor's understanding of the control environment. An effective control environment may allow the auditor to have more confidence in internal control and the reliability of audit evidence generated internally within the entity and thus, for example, allow the auditor to perform some audit procedures at an interim date rather than at period end. If there are weaknesses in the control environment, the auditor should consider an appropriate response. For example, the auditor could perform audit procedures as of the period end rather than at an interim date, seek more extensive audit evidence from substantive procedures, modify the nature of audit procedures to obtain more persuasive audit evidence, or increase the number of locations to be included in the audit scope.

.06 Such considerations, therefore, have a significant bearing on the auditor's general approach, for example, an emphasis on substantive procedures (substantive approach), or an approach that uses tests of controls as well as substantive procedures (combined approach).

Audit Procedures Responsive to Risks of Material Misstatement at the Relevant Assertion Level

.07 The auditor should design and perform further audit procedures whose nature, timing, and extent are responsive to the assessed risks of material misstatement at the relevant assertion level. The purpose is to provide a clear linkage between the nature, timing, and extent of the auditor's further audit procedures and the risk assessments. In designing further audit procedures, the auditor should consider such matters as:

- The significance of the risk
- The likelihood that a material misstatement will occur

---

[2] See paragraph .102 of section 314, *Understanding the Entity and Its Environment and Assessing the Risks of Material Misstatement*.

[3] See paragraphs .13 through .18 of section 311, *Planning and Supervision*, for further guidance on the auditor's overall audit strategy.

- The characteristics of the class of transactions, account balance, or disclosure involved
- The nature of the specific controls used by the entity, in particular, whether they are manual or automated
- Whether the auditor expects to obtain audit evidence to determine if the entity's controls are effective in preventing or detecting material misstatements

The nature of the audit procedures is of most importance in responding to the assessed risks.

.08 The auditor's assessment of the identified risks at the relevant assertion level provides a basis for considering the appropriate audit approach for designing and performing further audit procedures. In some cases, the auditor may determine that performing only substantive procedures is appropriate for specific relevant assertions and risks. In those circumstances, the auditor may exclude the effect of controls from the relevant risk assessment. This may be because the auditor's risk assessment procedures[4] have not identified any effective controls relevant to the assertion or because testing the operating effectiveness of controls would be inefficient. However, the auditor needs to be satisfied that performing only substantive procedures for the relevant assertions would be effective in reducing detection risk to an acceptably low level.[5] The auditor often will determine that a combined audit approach using both tests of the operating effectiveness of controls and substantive procedures is an effective audit approach.

.09 Regardless of the audit approach selected, the auditor should design and perform substantive procedures for all relevant assertions related to each material class of transactions, account balance, and disclosure as specified by paragraph .51. Because effective internal controls generally reduce, but do not eliminate, risk of material misstatement, tests of controls reduce, but do not eliminate, the need for substantive procedures. In addition, analytical procedures alone may not be sufficient in some cases. For example, when auditing certain estimation processes such as examining the allowance for doubtful accounts, the auditor may perform substantive procedures beyond analytical procedures (for example, examining cash collections subsequent to period end) due to the risk of management override of controls or the subjectivity of the account balance.

.10 In the case of very small entities, there may not be many control activities that could be identified by the auditor. For this reason, the auditor's further audit procedures are likely to be primarily substantive procedures. In such cases, in addition to the matters referred to in paragraph .07, the auditor should consider whether in the absence of controls it is possible to obtain sufficient appropriate audit evidence.

Considering the Nature, Timing, and Extent of Further Audit Procedures

Nature

.11 The nature of further audit procedures refers to their purpose (tests of controls or substantive procedures) and their type, that is, inspection,

---

[4] Audit procedures performed for the purpose of assessing risk (risk assessment procedures) are discussed in paragraphs .06 through .13 of section 314.

[5] Paragraphs .117 through .120 of section 314 describe circumstances in which the auditor may determine that it is not possible or practicable to reduce detection risk at the relevant assertion level to an appropriately low level with audit evidence obtained only from substantive procedures.

observation, inquiry, confirmation, recalculation, reperformance, or analytical procedures. Certain audit procedures may be more appropriate for some assertions than others. For example, in relation to revenue, tests of controls may be most responsive to the assessed risk of misstatement of the completeness assertion, whereas substantive procedures may be most responsive to the assessed risk of misstatement of the occurrence assertion.

.12 The auditor's selection of audit procedures is based on the risk of material misstatement. The higher the auditor's assessment of risk, the more reliable and relevant is the audit evidence sought by the auditor from substantive procedures. This may affect both the types of audit procedures to be performed and their combination. For example, the auditor may confirm the completeness of the terms of a contract with a third party, in addition to inspecting the document and obtaining management's representation.

.13 In determining the audit procedures to be performed, the auditor should consider the reasons for the assessment of the risk of material misstatement at the relevant assertion level for each class of transactions, account balance, and disclosure. This includes considering both the particular characteristics of each class of transactions, account balance, or disclosure (that is, the inherent risks) and whether the auditor's risk assessment takes account of the entity's controls (that is, the control risk). For example, if the auditor considers that there is a lower risk that a material misstatement may occur because of the particular characteristics of a class of transactions (without consideration of the related controls), the auditor may determine that substantive analytical procedures alone may provide sufficient appropriate audit evidence. On the other hand, if the auditor expects that there is a lower risk that a material misstatement may occur because an entity has effective controls and the auditor intends to design substantive procedures based on the effective operation of those controls, then the auditor should perform tests of controls to obtain audit evidence about their operating effectiveness. This may be the case for a class of transactions of reasonably uniform, noncomplex characteristics that are routinely processed and controlled by the entity's information system.

.14 The auditor should obtain audit evidence about the accuracy and completeness of information produced by the entity's information system when that information is used in performing audit procedures. For example, if the auditor uses nonfinancial information or budget data produced by the entity's information system in performing audit procedures, such as substantive analytical procedures or tests of controls, the auditor should obtain audit evidence about the accuracy and completeness of such information. See paragraph .57 of this section and paragraph .10 of section 326, *Audit Evidence*, for further guidance.

Timing

.15 Timing refers to when audit procedures are performed or the period or date to which the audit evidence applies.

.16 The auditor may perform tests of controls or substantive procedures at an interim date or at period end. The higher the risk of material misstatement, the more likely it is that the auditor may decide it is more effective to perform substantive procedures nearer to, or at, the period end rather than at an earlier date, or to perform audit procedures unannounced or at unpredictable times (for example, performing audit procedures at selected locations on an unannounced basis). On the other hand, performing audit procedures before the period end may assist the auditor in identifying significant matters at an early stage of the audit, and consequently resolving them with the assistance of management or developing an effective audit approach to address such matters. If the auditor performs tests of the operating effectiveness of controls or substantive procedures before period end, the auditor should consider the additional evidence that is necessary for the remaining period (see paragraphs .37 through .39, and .58 through .65).

.17 In considering when to perform audit procedures, the auditor should also consider such matters as:

- The control environment
- When relevant information is available (for example, electronic files may subsequently be overwritten, or procedures to be observed may occur only at certain times)
- The nature of the risk (for example, if there is a risk of inflated revenues to meet earnings expectations by subsequent creation of false sales agreements, the auditor may examine contracts available on the date of the period end)
- The period or date to which the audit evidence relates

.18 Certain audit procedures can be performed only at or after period end, for example, agreeing the financial statements to the accounting records, or examining adjustments made during the course of preparing the financial statements. If there is a risk that the entity may have entered into improper sales contracts or that transactions may not have been finalized at period end, the auditor should perform procedures to respond to that specific risk. For example, when transactions are individually material or an error in cutoff may lead to material misstatement, the auditor should inspect transactions near the period end.

Extent

.19 Extent refers to the quantity of a specific audit procedure to be performed, for example, a sample size or the number of observations of a control activity. The extent of an audit procedure is determined by the judgment of the auditor after considering the tolerable misstatement, the assessed risk of material misstatement, and the degree of assurance the auditor plans to obtain. In particular, the auditor may increase the extent of audit procedures as the risk of material misstatement increases. However, increasing the extent of an audit procedure is effective only if the audit procedure itself is relevant to the specific risk and reliable; therefore, the nature of the audit procedure is the most important consideration.

.20 An auditor may use techniques such as computer-assisted audit techniques (CAATs) to enable him or her to extensively test electronic transactions and account files. Such techniques can be used to select sample transactions from key electronic files, to identify transactions with specific characteristics, or to test an entire population instead of a sample.

.21 Valid conclusions may ordinarily be drawn using sampling approaches. However, if the sample size is too small, the sampling approach or the method of selection is not appropriate to achieve the specific audit objective, or exceptions are not appropriately followed up, there will be an unacceptable risk that the auditor's conclusion based on a sample may be different from the conclusion reached if the entire population was subjected to the same audit procedure. Section 350, *Audit Sampling*, provides guidance on planning, performing, and evaluating audit samples.

.22 This section regards the use of different audit procedures in combination as an aspect of the nature of testing as discussed above. However, the auditor should consider whether the extent of testing is appropriate when performing different audit procedures in combination.

Tests of Controls

.23 The auditor should perform tests of controls when the auditor's risk assessment[6] includes an expectation of the operating effectiveness of controls or when substantive procedures alone do not provide sufficient appropriate audit evidence at the relevant assertion level.

.24 When, in accordance with paragraph .117 of section 314, *Understanding the Entity and Its Environment and Assessing the Risks of Material Misstatement*, the auditor has determined that it is not possible or practicable to reduce the detection risks at the relevant assertion level to an acceptably low level with audit evidence obtained only from substantive procedures, he or she should perform tests of controls to obtain audit evidence about their operating effectiveness. For example, as discussed in paragraphs .119 and .120 of section 314, the auditor may find it impossible to design effective substantive procedures that by themselves provide sufficient appropriate audit evidence at the relevant assertion level when an entity conducts its business using information technology (IT) and no documentation of transactions is produced or maintained, other than through the IT system.

.25 Tests of the operating effectiveness of controls are performed only on those controls that the auditor has determined are suitably designed to prevent or detect a material misstatement in a relevant assertion. Paragraphs .106 through .108 of section 314 discuss the identification of controls at the relevant assertion level likely to prevent or detect a material misstatement in a class of transactions, account balance, or disclosure.

.26 Testing the operating effectiveness of controls is different from obtaining audit evidence that controls have been implemented. When obtaining audit evidence of implementation by performing risk assessment procedures,[7] the auditor should determine that the relevant controls exist and that the entity is using them. When performing tests of controls, the auditor should obtain audit evidence that controls operate effectively. This includes obtaining audit evidence about how controls were applied at relevant times during the period under audit, the consistency with which they were applied, and by whom or by what means they were applied. If substantially different controls were used at different times during the period under audit, the auditor should consider each separately. The auditor may determine that testing the operating effectiveness of controls at the same time as evaluating their design and obtaining audit evidence of their implementation is efficient.

.27 Although some risk assessment procedures that the auditor performs to evaluate the design of controls and to determine that they have been implemented may not have been specifically designed as tests of controls, they may nevertheless provide audit evidence about the operating effectiveness of the controls and, consequently, serve as tests of controls. For example, because, generally, IT processing is inherently consistent, performing risk assessment procedures to determine whether an automated control has been implemented may serve as a test of that control's operating effectiveness, depending on the auditor's assessment and testing of IT general controls including computer security and program change control (see paragraph .49). Also, in obtaining an understanding of the control environment, the auditor may have made inquiries

---

[6] The auditor's strategy reflects the level of assurance the auditor plans to obtain regarding controls.

[7] Paragraph .06 of section 314 discusses the use of risk assessment procedures to obtain an understanding of the entity and its environment, including its internal control, that the auditor uses to support assessments of the risks of material misstatement of the financial statements.

about management's use of budgets, observed management's comparison of monthly budgeted and actual expenses, and inspected reports pertaining to the investigation of variances between budgeted and actual amounts. These audit procedures provide knowledge about the design of the entity's budgeting policies and whether they have been implemented and may also provide audit evidence about the effectiveness of the operation of budgeting policies in preventing or detecting material misstatements in the classification of expenses. In such circumstances, the auditor should consider whether the audit evidence provided by those audit procedures is sufficient.

Nature of Tests of Controls

.28 The auditor should select audit procedures to obtain assurance about the operating effectiveness of controls. As the planned level of assurance increases, the auditor should seek more reliable or more extensive audit evidence. In circumstances in which the auditor adopts an approach consisting primarily of tests of controls, in particular related to those risks where it is not possible or practicable to obtain sufficient appropriate audit evidence only from substantive procedures, the auditor should perform tests of controls to obtain a higher level of assurance about their operating effectiveness. Tests of the operating effectiveness of controls ordinarily include procedures such as inquiries of appropriate entity personnel; inspection of documents, reports, or electronic files, indicating performance of the control; observation of the application of the control; and reperformance of the application of the control by the auditor.

.29 The auditor should perform other audit procedures in combination with inquiry to test the operating effectiveness of controls. Tests of the operating effectiveness of controls ordinarily include the same types of audit procedures used to evaluate the design and implementation of controls, and may also include reperformance of the application of the control by the auditor. Since inquiry alone is not sufficient, the auditor should use a combination of audit procedures to obtain sufficient appropriate audit evidence regarding the operating effectiveness of controls. Those controls subject to testing by performing inquiry combined with inspection or reperformance ordinarily provide more assurance than those controls for which the audit evidence consists solely of inquiry and observation. For example, an auditor may inquire about and observe the entity's procedures for opening the mail and processing cash receipts to test the operating effectiveness of controls over cash receipts. Because an observation is pertinent only at the point in time at which it is made, the auditor should supplement the observation with inquiries of entity personnel and may also inspect documentation about the operation of such controls at other times during the audit period in order to obtain sufficient appropriate audit evidence.

.30 The nature of the particular control influences the type of audit procedure necessary to obtain audit evidence about whether the control was operating effectively at relevant times during the period under audit. For some controls, operating effectiveness is evidenced by documentation. In such circumstances, the auditor may decide to inspect the documentation to obtain audit evidence about operating effectiveness. For other controls, however, such documentation may not be available or relevant. For example, documentation of operation may not exist for some factors in the control environment, such as assignment of authority and responsibility, or for some types of control activities, such as control activities performed by a computer. In such circumstances, audit evidence about operating effectiveness may be obtained through inquiry in combination with other audit procedures such as observation or the use of CAATs.

.31 In designing tests of controls, the auditor should consider the need to obtain audit evidence supporting the effective operation of controls directly related to the relevant assertions as well as other indirect controls on which these controls depend. For example, the auditor may identify a user review of an exception report of credit sales over a customer's authorized credit limit as a direct control related to an assertion. In this case, the auditor should consider the effectiveness of the user's review of the report and also the controls related to the accuracy of the information in the report (for example, the IT general and application controls).

.32 In the case of an automated application control, because of the inherent consistency of IT processing, audit evidence about the implementation of the control, when considered in combination with audit evidence obtained regarding the operating effectiveness of the entity's IT general controls (and in particular, security and change controls), may provide substantial audit evidence about its operating effectiveness during the relevant period.

.33 When responding to the risk assessment, the auditor may design a test of controls to be performed concurrently with a test of details on the same transaction. The objective of tests of controls is to evaluate whether a control operated effectively. The objective of tests of details is to support relevant assertions or detect material misstatements at the relevant assertion level. Although these objectives are different, both may be accomplished concurrently through performance of a test of controls and a test of details on the same transaction, known as a dual-purpose test. For example, the auditor may examine an invoice to determine whether it has been approved and to provide substantive evidence of a transaction. The auditor should carefully consider the design and evaluation of such tests in order to accomplish both objectives. Furthermore, when performing such tests the auditor should consider how the outcome of the tests of controls may affect the auditor's determination about the extent of substantive procedures to be performed. For example, if controls are found to be ineffective, the auditor should consider whether the sample size for substantive procedures should be increased from that originally planned.

.34 The absence of misstatements detected by a substantive procedure does not provide audit evidence that controls related to the relevant assertion being tested are effective; however, misstatements that the auditor detects by performing substantive procedures should be considered by the auditor when assessing the operating effectiveness of related controls. A misstatement detected by the auditor's procedures that was not identified by the entity is evidence of a deficiency in internal control and may be a significant deficiency or a material weakness. Such a misstatement, if material, is an indicator of a material weakness in internal control. [Revised December 2008 to reflect conforming changes due to the issuance of SAS No. 115.][8]

Timing of Tests of Controls

.35 The timing of tests of controls depends on the auditor's objective and the period of reliance on those controls. When the auditor tests controls at a particular time, the auditor may obtain audit evidence that the controls operated effectively only at that time. However, when the auditor tests controls throughout a period, the auditor may obtain audit evidence of the effectiveness of the operation of the controls during that period.

---

[8] See paragraph .15 of AU section 325, *Communicating Internal Control Related Matters Identified in an Audit*. [Revised December 2008 to reflect conforming changes due to the issuance of SAS No. 115.]

.36 The auditor should test controls for the particular time, or throughout the period, for which the auditor intends to rely on those controls. Audit evidence pertaining only to a point in time may be sufficient for the auditor's purpose, for example, when testing controls over the entity's physical inventory counting at the period end. If, on the other hand, the auditor needs audit evidence of the effectiveness of a control over a period, audit evidence pertaining only to a point in time may be insufficient, and the auditor should supplement those tests with other tests of controls that are capable of providing audit evidence that the control operated effectively at relevant times during the period under audit. For example, for a control embedded in a computer program, the auditor may test the operation of the control at a particular point in time to obtain audit evidence about whether the control is operating effectively at that point in time. The auditor then may perform tests of controls directed toward obtaining audit evidence about whether the control operated consistently during the audit period, such as tests of general controls pertaining to the modification and use of that computer program during the audit period. Such additional tests may be made as part of the tests of controls over the entity's monitoring of controls.

.37 When the auditor obtains audit evidence about the operating effectiveness of controls during an interim period, the auditor should determine what additional audit evidence should be obtained for the remaining period.

.38 In making that determination, the auditor should consider the significance of the assessed risks of material misstatement at the relevant assertion level, the specific controls that were tested during the interim period, the degree to which audit evidence about the operating effectiveness of those controls was obtained, the length of the remaining period, the extent to which the auditor intends to reduce further substantive procedures based on the reliance of controls, and the control environment. The auditor should obtain audit evidence about the nature and extent of any significant changes in internal control, including changes in the information system, processes, and personnel that occur subsequent to the interim period.

.39 Additional audit evidence may be obtained, for example, by extending the testing of the operating effectiveness of controls over the remaining period, or testing the entity's monitoring of controls.

.40 If the auditor plans to use audit evidence about the operating effectiveness of controls obtained in prior audits, the auditor should obtain audit evidence about whether changes in those specific controls have occurred subsequent to the prior audit. The auditor should obtain audit evidence about whether such changes have occurred by a combination of observation, inquiry, and inspection to confirm the understanding of those specific controls. Paragraph .24 of section 326 states that the auditor should perform audit procedures to establish the continuing relevance of audit evidence obtained in prior periods when the auditor plans to use such audit evidence in the current period. For example, in performing the prior audit, the auditor may have determined that an automated control was functioning as intended. The auditor should obtain audit evidence to determine whether changes to the automated control have been made that affect its continued effective functioning, for example, through inquiries of management and the inspection of logs to indicate whether controls have been changed. Consideration of audit evidence about these changes may support either increasing or decreasing the expected audit evidence to be obtained in the current period about the operating effectiveness of the controls.

.41 If the auditor plans to rely on controls that have changed since they were last tested, the auditor should test the operating effectiveness of such controls in the current audit. Changes may affect the relevance of the audit evidence obtained in prior periods such that it may no longer be a basis for continued reliance. For example, changes in a system that enable an entity to receive a new report from the system probably do not affect the relevance of prior-period audit evidence; however, a change that causes data to be accumulated or calculated differently does affect it.

.42 If, based on the understanding of the entity and its environment, the auditor plans to rely on controls that have not changed since they were last tested, the auditor should test the operating effectiveness of such controls at least once in every third year in an annual audit.[9] As indicated in paragraphs .40 and .45, the auditor may not rely on audit evidence about the operating effectiveness of controls obtained in prior audits for controls that have changed since they were last tested or for controls that mitigate a significant risk. The auditor's decision about whether to rely on audit evidence obtained in prior audits for other controls is a matter of professional judgment. In addition, the length of time between retesting such controls is also a matter of professional judgment, but it should not exceed more than two years. The auditor should test a control at least once in every third year in an annual audit, because as time elapses between testing a control, the audit evidence provided in the current audit period about the operating effectiveness of a control tested in a prior audit becomes less relevant and reliable (see paragraph .44).

.43 In considering whether it is appropriate to use audit evidence about the operating effectiveness of controls obtained in prior audits and, if so, the length of time that may elapse before retesting a control, the auditor should consider:

- The effectiveness of other elements of internal control, including the control environment, the entity's monitoring of controls, and the entity's risk assessment process.
- The risks arising from the characteristics of the control, including whether controls are manual or automated (see paragraphs .57 through .63 of section 314 for a discussion of specific risks arising from manual and automated elements of a control).
- The effectiveness of IT general controls.
- The effectiveness of the control and its application by the entity, including the nature and extent of deviations in the application of the control from tests of operating effectiveness in prior audits.
- Whether the lack of a change in a particular control poses a risk due to changing circumstances.
- The risk of material misstatement and the extent of reliance on the control.

In general, the higher the risk of material misstatement, or the greater the reliance on controls, the shorter the time elapsed, if any, is likely to be. Factors that ordinarily decrease the period for retesting a control, or result in not relying on audit evidence obtained in prior audits at all, include:

- A weak control environment.
- Weak monitoring controls.
- A significant manual element to the relevant controls.
- Personnel changes that significantly affect the application of the control.

---

[9] This guidance may not be appropriate for audits not performed at least on an annual basis.

- Changing circumstances that indicate the need for changes in the control.
- Weak IT general controls.

.44 When there are a number of controls for which the auditor determines that it is appropriate to use audit evidence obtained in prior audits, the auditor should test the operating effectiveness of some controls each year. The purpose of such tests of operating effectiveness is to avoid the possibility that the auditor might apply the approach of paragraph .42 to all controls on which the auditor proposes to rely, but test all those controls in a single audit period with no testing of controls in the subsequent two audit periods. In addition to providing audit evidence about the operating effectiveness of the controls being tested in the current audit, such tests provide collateral evidence about the continuing effectiveness of the control environment and therefore contribute to the decision about whether it is appropriate to rely on audit evidence obtained in prior audits. Therefore, when the auditor determines in accordance with paragraphs .40 through .43 that it is appropriate to use audit evidence obtained in prior audits for a number of controls, the auditor should plan to test a sufficient portion of the controls in each audit period, so that at a minimum, each control is tested at least every third audit.

.45 When, in accordance with paragraph .110 of section 314, the auditor has determined that an assessed risk of material misstatement at the relevant assertion level is a significant risk, and if the auditor plans to rely on the operating effectiveness of controls intended to mitigate that significant risk, the auditor should obtain audit evidence about the operating effectiveness of those controls from tests of controls performed in the current period. The greater the risk of material misstatement, the more audit evidence the auditor should obtain that controls are operating effectively. Accordingly, although the auditor should consider information obtained in prior audits in designing tests of controls to mitigate a significant risk, the auditor should not rely on audit evidence about the operating effectiveness of controls over such risks obtained in a prior audit, but instead should obtain audit evidence about the operating effectiveness of controls over such risks in the current period.

Extent of Tests of Controls

.46 The auditor should design sufficient tests of controls to obtain sufficient appropriate audit evidence that the controls are operating effectively throughout the period of reliance. Factors that the auditor may consider in determining the extent of tests of controls include the following:

- The frequency of the performance of the control by the entity during the period.
- The length of time during the audit period that the auditor is relying on the operating effectiveness of the control.
- The relevance and reliability of the audit evidence to be obtained in supporting that the control prevents, or detects and corrects, material misstatements at the relevant assertion level.
- The extent to which audit evidence is obtained from tests of other controls related to the relevant assertion.
- The extent to which the auditor plans to rely on the operating effectiveness of the control in the assessment of risk (and thereby reduce substantive procedures based on the reliance of such control).
- The expected deviation from the control.

Considering the above factors, when a control is applied on a transaction basis (for example, matching approved purchase orders to supplier invoices) and if the control operates frequently, the auditor should consider using an audit sampling technique to obtain reasonable assurance of the operation of the control. When a control is applied on a periodic basis (for example, monthly reconciliation of accounts receivable subsidiary ledger to the general ledger) the auditor should consider guidance appropriate for testing smaller populations (for example, testing the control application for two months and reviewing evidence the control operated in other months or reviewing other months for unusual items). Refer further to section 350, *Audit Sampling*, and the related Audit Guide.

.47 To reduce the extent of substantive procedures in an audit, the tests of controls performed by the auditor need to be sufficient to determine the operating effectiveness of the controls at the relevant assertion level and the level of planned reliance (see paragraph .50).

.48 The auditor should increase the extent of tests of controls the more the auditor relies on the operating effectiveness of controls in the assessment of risk. In addition, as the rate of expected deviation from a control increases, the auditor should increase the extent of testing of the control. However, the auditor should consider whether the rate of expected deviation indicates that obtaining audit evidence from the performance of tests of controls will not be sufficient to reduce the control risk at the relevant assertion level. If the rate of expected deviation is expected to be too high, the auditor may determine that tests of controls for a particular assertion may be inappropriate.

.49 Generally, IT processing is inherently consistent; therefore, the auditor may be able to limit the testing to one or a few instances of the control operation. An automated control should function consistently unless the program (including the tables, files, or other permanent data used by the program) is changed. Once the auditor determines that an automated control is functioning as intended (which could be done at the time the control is initially implemented or at some other date), the auditor should perform tests to determine that the control continues to function effectively. Such tests might include determining that changes to the program are not made without being subject to the appropriate program change controls, that the authorized version of the program is used for processing transactions, and that other relevant general controls are effective. Such tests also might include determining that changes to the programs have not been made, as may be the case when the entity uses packaged software applications without modifying or maintaining them. For example, the auditor may test the administration of IT security to obtain audit evidence that unauthorized access has not occurred during the period.

Substantive Procedures

.50 Substantive procedures are performed to detect material misstatements at the relevant assertion level, and include tests of details of classes of transactions, account balances, and disclosures and substantive analytical procedures. The auditor should plan and perform substantive procedures to be responsive to the related assessment of the risk of material misstatement.

.51 Regardless of the assessed risk of material misstatement, the auditor should design and perform substantive procedures for all relevant assertions related to each material class of transactions, account balance, and disclosure. This reflects the fact that the auditor's assessment of risk is judgmental and may not be sufficiently precise to identify all risks of material misstatement. Further, there are inherent limitations to internal control, including management override, and even effective internal controls generally reduce, but do not eliminate, the risk of material misstatement.

.52 The auditor's substantive procedures should include the following audit procedures related to the financial statement reporting process:

- Agreeing the financial statements, including their accompanying notes, to the underlying accounting records; and
- Examining material journal entries and other adjustments made during the course of preparing the financial statements.

The nature and extent of the auditor's examination of journal entries and other adjustments depend on the nature and complexity of the entity's financial reporting system and the associated risks of material misstatement.

.53 When, in accordance with paragraph .110 of section 314, the auditor has determined that an assessed risk of material misstatement at the relevant assertion level is a significant risk, the auditor should perform substantive procedures that are specifically responsive to that risk. For example, if the auditor identifies that management is under pressure to meet earnings expectations, there may be a risk that management is inflating sales by improperly recognizing revenue related to sales agreements with terms that preclude revenue recognition or by invoicing sales before shipment. In these circumstances, the auditor may, for example, design external written confirmation requests not only to confirm outstanding amounts, but also to confirm the details of the sales agreements, including date, any rights of return, and delivery terms. In addition, the auditor may find it effective to supplement such external written confirmations with inquiries of nonfinancial personnel in the entity regarding any changes in sales agreements and delivery terms.

.54 When the approach to significant risks consists only of substantive procedures, the audit procedures appropriate to address such significant risks consist of tests of details only, or a combination of tests of details and substantive analytical procedures. The auditor should consider the guidance in paragraphs .55 through .68 in designing the nature, timing, and extent of substantive procedures for significant risks. To obtain sufficient appropriate audit evidence, the substantive procedures related to significant risks are most often designed to obtain audit evidence with higher reliability.

Nature of Substantive Procedures

.55 Substantive procedures include tests of details and substantive analytical procedures. Substantive analytical procedures are generally more applicable to large volumes of transactions that tend to be predictable over time. Tests of details are ordinarily more appropriate to obtain audit evidence regarding certain relevant assertions about account balances, including existence and valuation. The auditor should plan substantive procedures to be responsive to the planned level of detection risk. In some situations, the auditor may determine that performing only substantive analytical procedures may be sufficient to reduce the planned level of detection risk to an acceptably low level. For example, the auditor may determine that performing only substantive analytical procedures is responsive to the planned level of detection risk for an individual class of transactions where the auditor's assessment of risk has been reduced by obtaining audit evidence from performance of tests of the operating effectiveness of controls. In other situations, the auditor may determine that tests of details only are appropriate, or that a combination of substantive analytical procedures and tests of details is most responsive to the assessed risks. The auditor's determination as to the substantive procedures that are most responsive to the planned level of detection risk is affected by whether the auditor has obtained audit evidence about the operating effectiveness of controls. The Appendix [paragraph .79] includes examples of substantive procedures that may be performed on inventories of a manufacturing entity.

.56 The auditor should design tests of details responsive to the assessed risk with the objective of obtaining sufficient appropriate audit evidence to achieve the planned level of assurance at the relevant assertion level. In designing substantive procedures related to the existence or occurrence assertion, the auditor should select from items contained in a financial statement amount and should obtain the relevant audit evidence. On the other hand, in designing audit procedures related to the completeness assertion, the auditor should select from audit evidence indicating that an item should be included in the relevant financial statement amount and should investigate whether that item is so included. The knowledge gained when understanding the business and its environment should be helpful in selecting the nature, timing, and extent of audit procedures related to the completeness assertion. For example, the auditor might inspect subsequent cash disbursements and compare them with the recorded accounts payable to determine whether any purchases had been omitted from accounts payable.

.57 In designing substantive analytical procedures, the auditor should consider such matters as:

- The suitability of using substantive analytical procedures, given the assertions
- The reliability of the data, whether internal or external, from which the expectation of recorded amounts or ratios is developed
- Whether the expectation is sufficiently precise to identify the possibility of a material misstatement at the desired level of assurance
- The amount of any difference in recorded amounts from expected values that is acceptable

The auditor should consider testing the controls, if any, over the entity's preparation of information to be used by the auditor in applying analytical procedures. When such controls are effective, the auditor has greater confidence in the reliability of the information and, therefore, in the results of analytical procedures. When designing substantive analytical procedures, the auditor should evaluate the risk of management override of controls. As part of this process, the auditor should evaluate whether such an override might have allowed adjustments outside of the normal period-end financial reporting process to have been made to the financial statements. Such adjustments might have resulted in artificial changes to the financial statement relationships being analyzed, causing the auditor to draw erroneous conclusions. For this reason, substantive analytical procedures alone are not well suited to detecting some types of fraud. Alternatively, the auditor may consider whether the information was subjected to audit testing in the current or prior period. In determining the audit procedures to apply to the information upon which the expectation for substantive analytical procedures is based, the auditor should consider the guidance in paragraph .14.

Timing of Substantive Procedures

.58 In some circumstances, substantive procedures may be performed at an interim date. When substantive procedures are performed at an interim date, the auditor should perform further substantive procedures or substantive procedures combined with tests of controls to cover the remaining period that provide a reasonable basis for extending the audit conclusions from the interim date to the period end.

.59 Performing substantive procedures at an interim date increases the risk that misstatements that may exist at the period end are not detected by the auditor. This risk increases as the remaining period is lengthened. In considering whether to perform substantive procedures at an interim date, the auditor should consider such factors as:

- The control environment and other relevant controls
- The availability of information at a later date that is necessary for the auditor's procedures
- The objective of the substantive procedure
- The assessed risk of material misstatement
- The nature of the class of transactions or account balance and relevant assertions
- The ability of the auditor to reduce the risk that misstatements that exist at the period end are not detected by performing appropriate substantive procedures or substantive procedures combined with tests of controls to cover the remaining period in order to reduce the risk that misstatements that exist at period end are not detected

.60 Although it is not necessary to obtain audit evidence about the operating effectiveness of controls in order to have a reasonable basis for extending audit conclusions from an interim date to the period end, the auditor should consider whether performing only substantive procedures to cover the remaining period is sufficient. If the auditor concludes that substantive procedures alone would not be sufficient to cover the remaining period, tests of the operating effectiveness of relevant controls should be performed or the substantive procedures should be performed as of the period end.

.61 In circumstances in which the auditor has identified risks of material misstatement due to fraud, the auditor's responses to address those risks may include changing the timing of audit procedures. For example, the auditor might conclude that, given the risks of intentional misstatement or manipulation, audit procedures to extend audit conclusions from an interim date to the period-end reporting date would not be effective. In such circumstances, the auditor might conclude that substantive procedures should be performed at or near the end of the reporting period to best address an identified risk of material misstatement due to fraud.[10]

.62 When performing substantive procedures at an interim date, the auditor may compare and may reconcile information concerning the balance at the period end with the comparable information at the interim date to identify amounts that appear unusual, investigates any such amounts, and may perform substantive analytical procedures or tests of details to test the intervening period. When the auditor plans to perform substantive analytical procedures with respect to the intervening period, the auditor should consider whether the period-end balances of the particular classes of transactions or account balances are reasonably predictable with respect to amount, relative significance, and composition. The auditor should also consider whether the entity's procedures for analyzing and adjusting such classes of transactions or account balances at interim dates and for establishing proper accounting cutoffs are appropriate. In addition, the auditor should consider whether the information system relevant to financial reporting will provide information concerning the balances at the period end and the transactions in the remaining period that is sufficient to

---

[10] See paragraph .52 of section 316, *Consideration of Fraud in a Financial Statement Audit.*

permit investigation of (*a*) significant unusual transactions or entries (including those at or near the period end); (*b*) other causes of significant fluctuations, or expected fluctuations that did not occur; and (*c*) changes in the composition of the classes of transactions or account balances.

.63 If misstatements are detected in classes of transactions or account balances at an interim date, the auditor should consider modifying the related assessment of risk and the planned nature, timing, or extent of the substantive procedures covering the remaining period that relate to such classes of transactions or account balances, or the auditor may extend or may repeat such audit procedures at the period end.

.64 The use of audit evidence from the performance of substantive procedures in a prior audit is not sufficient to reduce detection risk to an acceptably low level in the current period. In most cases, audit evidence from the performance of substantive procedures in a prior audit provides little or no audit evidence for the current period. In order for audit evidence obtained in a prior audit to be used in the current period as substantive audit evidence, the audit evidence and the related subject matter must not fundamentally change. An example of audit evidence obtained from the performance of substantive procedures in a prior period that may be relevant in the current year is prior audit evidence substantiating the purchase cost of a building or building addition. As specified by paragraph .24 of section 326, if the auditor plans to use audit evidence obtained from the performance of substantive procedures in a prior audit, the auditor should perform audit procedures during the current period to establish the continuing relevance of the audit evidence.

.65 The timing of audit procedures also involves consideration of whether related audit procedures are properly coordinated. This includes, for example:

a. Coordinating the audit procedures applied to related-party transactions and balances.[11]

b. Coordinating the testing of interrelated accounts and accounting cutoffs.

c. Maintaining temporary audit control over assets that are readily negotiable and simultaneously testing such assets and cash on hand and in banks, bank loans, and other related items.

Decisions about coordinating related audit procedures should be made in the light of the risks of material misstatement and of the particular audit procedures that could be applied, either for the remaining period or at period end, or both.

Extent of the Performance of Substantive Procedures

.66 The greater the risk of material misstatement, the less detection risk that can be accepted; consequently, the greater the extent of substantive procedures. Because the risk of material misstatement includes consideration of the effectiveness of internal control, the extent of substantive procedures may be reduced by satisfactory results from tests of the operating effectiveness of controls. However, increasing the extent of an audit procedure is appropriate only if the audit procedure itself is relevant to the specific risk.

.67 In designing tests of details, the extent of testing is ordinarily thought of in terms of the sample size, which is affected by the planned level of detection risk, tolerable misstatement, expected misstatement, and nature of the

---

[11] See section 334, *Related Parties*.

population. However, the auditor should also consider other matters, including whether it is more effective to use other selective means of testing, such as selecting large or unusual items from a population as opposed to performing sampling or stratifying the population into homogeneous sub-populations for sampling. Section 350 contains guidance on the use of sampling and other means of selecting items for testing.

.68 In planning substantive analytical procedures, the auditor should consider the amount of difference from the expectation that can be accepted without further investigation. This consideration is influenced primarily by tolerable misstatement and should be consistent with the desired level of assurance. Determination of this amount involves considering the possibility that a combination of misstatements in the specific account balance, class of transactions, or disclosure could aggregate to an unacceptable amount. In designing substantive analytical procedures, the auditor should increase the desired level of assurance as the risk of material misstatement increases. Section 329, *Analytical Procedures*, contains guidance on the application of analytical procedures during an audit.

Adequacy of Presentation and Disclosure

.69 The auditor should perform audit procedures to evaluate whether the overall presentation of the financial statements, including the related disclosures, are in accordance with generally accepted accounting principles. The auditor should consider whether the individual financial statements are presented in a manner that reflects the appropriate classification and description of financial information. The presentation of financial statements in conformity with generally accepted accounting principles also includes adequate disclosure of material matters. These matters relate to the form, arrangement, and content of the financial statements and their related notes, including, for example, the terminology used, the amount of detail given, the classification of items in the financial statements, and the bases of amounts set forth. The auditor should consider whether management should have disclosed a particular matter in light of the circumstances and facts of which the auditor is aware at the time. In performing the evaluation of the overall presentation of the financial statements, including the related disclosures, the auditor should consider the assessed risk of material misstatement at the relevant assertion level. See paragraph .15 of section 326 for a description of the relevant assertions related to presentation and disclosure.

Evaluating the Sufficiency and Appropriateness of the Audit Evidence Obtained[12]

.70 Based on the audit procedures performed and the audit evidence obtained, the auditor should evaluate whether the assessments of the risks of material misstatement at the relevant assertion level remain appropriate.

.71 An audit of financial statements is a cumulative and iterative process. As the auditor performs planned audit procedures, the audit evidence obtained may cause the auditor to modify the nature, timing, or extent of other planned audit procedures. Information may come to the auditor's attention that differs significantly from the information on which the risk assessments were based. For example, the extent of misstatements that the auditor detects by performing substantive procedures may alter the auditor's judgment about the risk

---

[12] See paragraph .67 of section 312.

assessments and may indicate a material weakness in internal control. In addition, analytical procedures performed at the overall review stage of the audit may indicate a previously unrecognized risk of material misstatement (see section 329). In such circumstances, the auditor should reevaluate the planned audit procedures based on the revised consideration of assessed risks for all or some of the relevant assertions related to classes of transactions, account balances, or disclosures. Paragraph .121 of section 314 contains further guidance on revising the auditor's risk assessment.

.72 The concept of effectiveness of the operation of controls recognizes that some deviations in the way controls are applied by the entity may occur. Deviations from prescribed controls may be caused by such factors as changes in key personnel, significant seasonal fluctuations in volume of transactions, and human error. When such deviations are detected during the performance of tests of controls, the auditor should make specific inquiries to understand these matters and their potential consequences, for example, by inquiring about the timing of personnel changes in key internal control functions. In addition, the auditor should consider whether any misstatements detected from the performance of substantive procedures alter the auditor's judgment as to the effectiveness of the related controls. The auditor should determine whether the tests of controls performed provide an appropriate basis for reliance on the controls, whether additional tests of controls are necessary, or whether the potential risks of misstatement need to be addressed using substantive procedures.

.73 The auditor should not assume that an instance of fraud or error is an isolated occurrence, and therefore should consider how the detection of such misstatement affects the assessed risks of material misstatement. Before the conclusion of the audit, the auditor should evaluate whether audit risk has been reduced to an appropriately low level and whether the nature, timing, and extent of the audit procedures may need to be reconsidered. For example, the auditor should reconsider:

- The nature, timing, and extent of substantive procedures
- The audit evidence of the operating effectiveness of relevant controls, including the entity's risk assessment process

.74 The auditor should conclude whether sufficient appropriate audit evidence has been obtained to reduce to an appropriately low level the risk of material misstatement in the financial statements. In developing an opinion, the auditor should consider all relevant audit evidence, regardless of whether it appears to corroborate or to contradict the relevant assertions in the financial statements.

.75 The sufficiency and appropriateness of audit evidence to support the auditor's conclusions throughout the audit are a matter of professional judgment. The auditor's judgment as to what constitutes sufficient appropriate audit evidence is influenced by such factors as the:

- Significance of the potential misstatement in the relevant assertion and the likelihood of its having a material effect, individually or aggregated with other potential misstatements, on the financial statements.
- Effectiveness of management's responses and controls to address the risks.
- Experience gained during previous audits with respect to similar potential misstatements.
- Results of audit procedures performed, including whether such audit procedures identified specific instances of fraud or error.

- Source and reliability of available information.
- Persuasiveness of the audit evidence.
- Understanding of the entity and its environment, including its internal control.

.76 If the auditor has not obtained sufficient appropriate audit evidence as to a material financial statement assertion, the auditor should attempt to obtain further audit evidence. If the auditor is unable to obtain sufficient appropriate audit evidence, the auditor should express a qualified opinion or a disclaimer of opinion.[13]

Documentation

.77 The auditor should document:

a. The overall responses to address the assessed risks of misstatement at the financial statement level

b. The nature, timing, and extent of the further audit procedures

c. The linkage of those procedures with the assessed risks at the relevant assertion level

d. The results of the audit procedures

e. The conclusions reached with regard to the use in the current audit of audit evidence about the operating effectiveness of controls that was obtained in a prior audit

The manner in which these matters are documented is based on the auditor's professional judgment. Section 339, *Audit Documentation*, establishes standards and provides guidance regarding documentation in the context of the audit of financial statements.

Effective Date

.78 This section is effective for audits of financial statements for periods beginning on or after December 15, 2006. Earlier application is permitted.

---

[13] See paragraphs .20 through .34 and .61 through .63 of section 508, *Reports on Audited Financial Statements*, for further guidance on expression of a qualified opinion or a disclaimer of opinion.

.79

Appendix

Illustrative Financial Statement Assertions and Examples of Substantive Procedures Illustrations for Inventories of a Manufacturing Company

A1. This Appendix illustrates the use of assertions in designing substantive procedures and does not illustrate tests of controls. The following examples of substantive procedures are not intended to be all-inclusive, nor is it expected that all of the procedures would be applied in an audit. The particular substantive procedures to be used in each circumstance depend on the auditor's risk assessments and tests of controls.

Illustrative Assertions About Account Balances	*Examples of Substantive Procedures*
Existence	
Inventories included in the balance sheet physically exist.	• Physical examination of inventory items. • Obtaining confirmation of inventories at locations outside the entity. • Inspection of documents relating to inventory transactions between a physical inventory date and the balance sheet date.
Inventories represent items held for sale or use in the normal course of business.	• Inspecting perpetual inventory records, production records, and purchasing records for indications of current activity. • Reconciling items in the inventory listing to a current computer-maintained sales catalog and subsequent sales and delivery reports using computer-assisted audit techniques (CAATs). • Inquiry of production and sales personnel. • Using the work of specialists to corroborate the nature of specialized products.
Rights and Obligations	
The entity has legal title or similar rights of ownership to the inventories.	• Examining paid vendors' invoices, consignment agreements, and contracts. • Obtaining confirmation of inventories at locations outside the entity.

Illustrative Assertions About Account Balances	*Examples of Substantive Procedures*
Inventories exclude items billed to customers or owned by others.	• Examining paid vendors' invoices, consignment agreements, and contracts. • Inspecting shipping and receiving transactions near year end for recording in the proper period.
Completeness	
Inventory quantities include all products, materials, and supplies on hand.	• Observing physical inventory counts. • Analytically comparing the relationship of inventory balances to recent purchasing, production, and sales activities. • Inspecting shipping and receiving transactions near year end for recording in the proper period.
Inventory quantities include all products, materials, and supplies owned by the company that are in transit or stored at outside locations.	• Obtaining confirmation of inventories at locations outside the entity. • Analytically comparing the relationship of inventory balances to recent purchasing, production, and sales activities.
Inventory listings are accurately compiled and the totals are properly included in the inventory accounts.	• Inspecting shipping and receiving transactions near year end for recording in the proper period. • Examining the inventory listing for inclusion of test counts recorded during the physical inventory observation. • Reconciliation of all inventory tags and count sheets used in recording the physical inventory counts using CAATs. • Recalculation of inventory listing for clerical accuracy using CAATs. • Reconciling physical counts to perpetual records and general ledger balances and investigating significant fluctuations using CAATs.
Valuation and Allocation	
Inventories are properly stated at cost (except when market is lower).	• Examining paid vendors' invoices and comparing product prices to standard cost build-ups. • Analytically comparing direct labor rates to production records. • Recalculation of the computation of standard overhead rates. • Examining analyses of purchasing and manufacturing standard cost variances.

(continued)

Illustrative Assertions About Account Balances	*Examples of Substantive Procedures*
Slow-moving, excess, defective, and obsolete items included in inventories are properly identified.	• Examining an analysis of inventory turnover. • Analyzing industry experience and trends. • Analytically comparing the relationship of inventory balances to anticipated sales volume. • Walk-through of the plant for indications of products not being used. • Inquiring of production and sales personnel concerning possible excess, or defective or obsolete inventory items. • Logistic and distribution business process (e.g., cycle time, volume of returns, or problems with suppliers).
Inventories are reduced, when appropriate, to replacement cost or net realizable value.	• Inspecting sales catalogs or industry publications for current market value quotations. • Recalculation of inventory valuation reserves. • Analyzing current production costs. • Examining sales after year end and open purchase order commitments.

Illustrative Assertions About Presentation and Disclosure	*Examples of Substantive Procedures*
Rights and Obligations	
The pledge or assignment of any inventories is appropriately disclosed.	• Obtaining confirmation of inventories pledged under loan agreements.
Completeness	
The financial statements include all disclosures related to inventories specified by generally accepted accounting principles.	• Using a disclosure checklist to determine whether the disclosures included in generally accepted accounting principles were made.
Understandability	
Inventories are properly classified in the balance sheet as current assets.	• Examining drafts of the financial statements for appropriate balance sheet classification.
Disclosures related to inventories are understandable.	• Reading disclosures for clarity.

Illustrative Assertions About Presentation and Disclosure	*Examples of Substantive Procedures*
Accuracy and Valuation	
The major categories of inventories and their bases of valuation are accurately disclosed in the financial statements.	• Examining drafts of the financial statements for appropriate disclosures. • Reconciling the categories of inventories disclosed in the draft financial statements to the categories recorded during the physical inventory observation.

AU Section 322

The Auditor's Consideration of the Internal Audit Function in an Audit of Financial Statements

(Supersedes SAS No. 9.)

Source: SAS No. 65.

Effective for audits of financial statements for periods ending after December 15, 1991, unless otherwise indicated.

.01 The auditor considers many factors in determining the nature, timing, and extent of auditing procedures to be performed in an audit of an entity's financial statements. One of the factors is the existence of an internal audit function.[1] This section provides the auditor with guidance on considering the work of internal auditors and on using internal auditors to provide direct assistance to the auditor in an audit performed in accordance with generally accepted auditing standards.

Roles of the Auditor and the Internal Auditors

.02 One of the auditor's responsibilities in an audit conducted in accordance with generally accepted auditing standards is to obtain sufficient appropriate audit evidence to provide a reasonable basis for the opinion on the entity's financial statements. In fulfilling this responsibility, the auditor maintains independence from the entity. [Revised, March 2006, to reflect conforming changes necessary due to the issuance of Statement on Auditing Standards No. 105.][2]

.03 Internal auditors are responsible for providing analyses, evaluations, assurances, recommendations, and other information to the entity's management and those charged with governance. To fulfill this responsibility, internal auditors maintain objectivity with respect to the activity being audited. [Revised, April 2007, to reflect conforming changes necessary due to the issuance of Statement on Auditing Standards No. 114.]

Obtaining an Understanding of the Internal Audit Function

.04 An important responsibility of the internal audit function is to monitor the performance of an entity's controls. When obtaining an understanding of

---

[1] An *internal audit function* may consist of one or more individuals who perform internal auditing activities within an entity. This section is not applicable to personnel who have the title *internal auditor* but who do not perform internal auditing activities as described herein.

[2] Although internal auditors are not independent from the entity, The Institute of Internal Auditors' *Standards for the Professional Practice of Internal Auditing* defines internal auditing as an independent appraisal function and requires internal auditors to be independent of the activities they audit. This concept of independence is different from the independence the auditor maintains under the AICPA Code of Professional Conduct.

internal control,[3] the auditor should obtain an understanding of the internal audit function sufficient to identify those internal audit activities that are relevant to planning the audit. The extent of the procedures necessary to obtain this understanding will vary, depending on the nature of those activities.

.05 The auditor ordinarily should make inquiries of appropriate management and internal audit personnel about the internal auditors'—

a. Organizational status within the entity.

b. Application of professional standards (see paragraph .11).

c. Audit plan, including the nature, timing, and extent of audit work.

d. Access to records and whether there are limitations on the scope of their activities.

In addition, the auditor might inquire about the internal audit function's charter, mission statement, or similar directive from management or those charged with governance. This inquiry will normally provide information about the goals and objectives established for the internal audit function. [Revised, April 2007, to reflect conforming changes necessary due to the issuance of Statement on Auditing Standards No. 114.]

.06 Certain internal audit activities may not be relevant to an audit of the entity's financial statements. For example, the internal auditors' procedures to evaluate the efficiency of certain management decision-making processes are ordinarily not relevant to a financial statement audit.

.07 Relevant activities are those that provide evidence about the design and effectiveness of controls that pertain to the entity's ability to initiate, authorize, record, process, and report financial data consistent with the assertions embodied in the financial statements or that provide direct evidence about potential misstatements of such data. The auditor may find the results of the following procedures helpful in assessing the relevancy of internal audit activities:

a. Considering knowledge from prior-year audits

b. Reviewing how the internal auditors allocate their audit resources to financial or operating areas in response to their risk-assessment process

c. Reading internal audit reports to obtain detailed information about the scope of internal audit activities

[Revised, April 2002, to reflect conforming changes necessary due to the issuance of Statement on Auditing Standards No. 94. Revised, March 2006, to reflect conforming changes necessary due to the issuance of Statement on Auditing Standards No. 106.]

.08 If, after obtaining an understanding of the internal audit function, the auditor concludes that the internal auditors' activities are not relevant to the financial statement audit, the auditor does not have to give further consideration to the internal audit function unless the auditor requests direct assistance from the internal auditors as described in paragraph .27. Even if some of the internal auditors' activities are relevant to the audit, the auditor may conclude that it would not be efficient to consider further the work of the internal auditors. If the auditor decides that it would be efficient to consider how the internal auditors' work might affect the nature, timing, and extent of audit

---

[3] Section 314, *Understanding the Entity and Its Environment and Assessing the Risks of Material Misstatement*, describes the procedures the auditor follows to obtain an understanding of internal control and indicates that the internal audit function is part of the entity's monitoring component. [Footnote revised, March 2006, to reflect conforming changes necessary due to the issuance of Statement on Auditing Standards No. 109.]

procedures, the auditor should assess the competence and objectivity of the internal audit function in light of the intended effect of the internal auditors' work on the audit.

Assessing the Competence and Objectivity of the Internal Auditors

Competence of the Internal Auditors

.09 When assessing the internal auditors' competence, the auditor should obtain or update information from prior years about such factors as—

- Educational level and professional experience of internal auditors.
- Professional certification and continuing education.
- Audit policies, programs, and procedures.
- Practices regarding assignment of internal auditors.
- Supervision and review of internal auditors' activities.
- Quality of working-paper documentation, reports, and recommendations.
- Evaluation of internal auditors' performance.

Objectivity of the Internal Auditors

.10 When assessing the internal auditors' objectivity, the auditor should obtain or update information from prior years about such factors as—

- The organizational status of the internal auditor responsible for the internal audit function, including—
  - — Whether the internal auditor reports to an officer of sufficient status to ensure broad audit coverage and adequate consideration of, and action on, the findings and recommendations of the internal auditors.
  - — Whether the internal auditor has direct access and reports regularly to those charged with governance.
  - — Whether those charged with governance oversee employment decisions related to the internal auditor.
- Policies to maintain internal auditors' objectivity about the areas audited, including—
  - — Policies prohibiting internal auditors from auditing areas where relatives are employed in important or audit-sensitive positions.
  - — Policies prohibiting internal auditors from auditing areas where they were recently assigned or are scheduled to be assigned on completion of responsibilities in the internal audit function.

[Revised, April 2007, to reflect conforming changes necessary due to the issuance of Statement on Auditing Standards No. 114.]

Assessing Competence and Objectivity

.11 In assessing competence and objectivity, the auditor usually considers information obtained from previous experience with the internal audit function, from discussions with management personnel, and from a recent external quality review, if performed, of the internal audit function's activities. The auditor may also use professional internal auditing standards[4] as criteria in making the assessment. The auditor also considers the need to test the effectiveness of the factors described in paragraphs .09 and .10. The extent of such testing will vary in light of the intended effect of the internal auditors' work on the audit. If the auditor determines that the internal auditors are sufficiently competent and objective, the auditor should then consider how the internal auditors' work may affect the audit.

Effect of the Internal Auditors' Work on the Audit

.12 The internal auditors' work may affect the nature, timing, and extent of the audit, including—

- Procedures the auditor performs when obtaining an understanding of the entity's internal control (paragraph .13).
- Procedures the auditor performs when assessing risk (paragraphs .14 through .16).
- Substantive procedures the auditor performs (paragraph .17).

When the work of the internal auditors is expected to affect the audit, the guidance in paragraphs .18 through .26 should be followed for considering the extent of the effect, coordinating audit work with internal auditors, and evaluating and testing the effectiveness of internal auditors' work.

Understanding of Internal Control

.13 The auditor obtains a sufficient understanding of the design of controls relevant to the audit of financial statements to plan the audit and to determine whether they have been placed in operation. Since a primary objective of many internal audit functions is to review, assess, and monitor controls, the procedures performed by the internal auditors in this area may provide useful information to the auditor. For example, internal auditors may develop a flowchart of a new computerized sales and receivables system. The auditor may review the flowchart to obtain information about the design of the related controls. In addition, the auditor may consider the results of procedures performed by the internal auditors on related controls to obtain information about whether the controls have been placed in operation. [Revised, February 1997, to reflect conforming changes necessary due to the issuance of Statement on Auditing Standards No. 78.]

Risk Assessment

.14 The auditor assesses the risk of material misstatement at both the financial-statement level and the account-balance or class-of-transaction level.

Financial-Statement Level

.15 At the financial-statement level, the auditor makes an overall assessment of the risk of material misstatement. When making this assessment, the auditor should recognize that certain controls may have a pervasive effect on many financial statement assertions. The control environment and accounting system often have a pervasive effect on a number of account balances and transaction classes and therefore can affect many assertions. The auditor's assessment of risk at the financial-statement level often affects the overall audit

---

[4] Standards have been developed for the professional practice of internal auditing by The Institute of Internal Auditors and the General Accounting Office. These standards are meant to (*a*) impart an understanding of the role and responsibilities of internal auditing to all levels of management, boards of directors, public bodies, external auditors, and related professional organizations; (*b*) permit measurement of internal auditing performance; and (*c*) improve the practice of internal auditing.

strategy. The entity's internal audit function may influence this overall assessment of risk as well as the auditor's resulting decisions concerning the nature, timing, and extent of auditing procedures to be performed. For example, if the internal auditors' plan includes relevant audit work at various locations, the auditor may coordinate work with the internal auditors (see paragraph .23) and reduce the number of the entity's locations at which the auditor would otherwise need to perform auditing procedures.

Account-Balance or Class-of-Transaction Level

.16 At the account-balance or class-of-transaction level, the auditor performs procedures to obtain and evaluate audit evidence concerning management's assertions. The auditor assesses control risk for each of the significant assertions and performs tests of controls to support assessments below the maximum. When planning and performing tests of controls, the auditor may consider the results of procedures planned or performed by the internal auditors. For example, the internal auditors' scope may include tests of controls for the completeness of accounts payable. The results of internal auditors' tests may provide appropriate information about the effectiveness of controls and change the nature, timing, and extent of testing the auditor would otherwise need to perform. [Revised, March 2006, to reflect conforming changes necessary due to the issuance of Statement on Auditing Standards No. 105.]

Substantive Procedures

.17 Some procedures performed by the internal auditors may provide direct evidence about material misstatements in assertions about specific account balances or classes of transactions. For example, the internal auditors, as part of their work, may confirm certain accounts receivable and observe certain physical inventories. The results of these procedures can provide evidence the auditor may consider in restricting detection risk for the related assertions. Consequently, the auditor may be able to change the timing of the confirmation procedures, the number of accounts receivable to be confirmed, or the number of locations of physical inventories to be observed.

Extent of the Effect of the Internal Auditors' Work

.18 Even though the internal auditors' work may affect the auditor's procedures, the auditor should perform procedures to obtain sufficient appropriate audit evidence to support the auditor's report. Evidence obtained through the auditor's direct personal knowledge, including physical examination, observation, computation, and inspection, is generally more persuasive than information obtained indirectly. [Revised, March 2006, to reflect conforming changes necessary due to the issuance of Statement on Auditing Standards No. 105.][5]

.19 The responsibility to report on the financial statements rests solely with the auditor. Unlike the situation in which the auditor uses the work of other independent auditors,[6] this responsibility cannot be shared with the internal auditors. Because the auditor has the ultimate responsibility to express an opinion on the financial statements, judgments about assessments of inherent and control risks, the materiality of misstatements, the sufficiency of tests performed, the evaluation of significant accounting estimates, and other matters affecting the auditor's report should always be those of the auditor.

---

[5] See section 326, *Audit Evidence*, paragraph .13. [Footnote revised, March 2006, to reflect conforming changes necessary due to the issuance of Statement on Auditing Standards No. 106.]

[6] See section 543, *Part of Audit Performed by Other Independent Auditors*.

.20 In making judgments about the extent of the effect of the internal auditors' work on the auditor's procedures, the auditor considers—

a. The materiality of financial statement amounts—that is, account balances or classes of transactions.

b. The risk (consisting of inherent risk and control risk) of material misstatement of the assertions related to these financial statement amounts.

c. The degree of subjectivity involved in the evaluation of the audit evidence gathered in support of the assertions.[7]

As the materiality of the financial statement amounts increases and either the risk of material misstatement or the degree of subjectivity increases, the need for the auditor to perform his or her own tests of the assertions increases. As these factors decrease, the need for the auditor to perform his or her own tests of the assertions decreases.

.21 For assertions related to material financial statement amounts where the risk of material misstatement or the degree of subjectivity involved in the evaluation of the audit evidence is high, the auditor should perform sufficient procedures to fulfill the responsibilities described in paragraphs .18 and .19. In determining these procedures, the auditor gives consideration to the results of work (either tests of controls or substantive tests) performed by internal auditors on those particular assertions. However, for such assertions, the consideration of internal auditors' work cannot alone reduce audit risk to an acceptable level to eliminate the necessity to perform tests of those assertions directly by the auditor. Assertions about the valuation of assets and liabilities involving significant accounting estimates, and about the existence and disclosure of related-party transactions, contingencies, uncertainties, and subsequent events, are examples of assertions that might have a high risk of material misstatement or involve a high degree of subjectivity in the evaluation of audit evidence.

.22 On the other hand, for certain assertions related to less material financial statement amounts where the risk of material misstatement or the degree of subjectivity involved in the evaluation of the audit evidence is low, the auditor may decide, after considering the circumstances and the results of work (either tests of controls or substantive tests) performed by internal auditors on those particular assertions, that audit risk has been reduced to an acceptable level and that testing of the assertions directly by the auditor may not be necessary. Assertions about the existence of cash, prepaid assets, and fixed-asset additions are examples of assertions that might have a low risk of material misstatement or involve a low degree of subjectivity in the evaluation of audit evidence.

Coordination of the Audit Work With Internal Auditors

.23 If the work of the internal auditors is expected to have an effect on the auditor's procedures, it may be efficient for the auditor and the internal auditors to coordinate their work by—

- Holding periodic meetings.
- Scheduling audit work.
- Providing access to internal auditors' working papers.

[7] For some assertions, such as existence and occurrence, the evaluation of audit evidence is generally objective. More subjective evaluation of the audit evidence is often required for other assertions, such as the valuation and disclosure assertions.

- Reviewing audit reports.
- Discussing possible accounting and auditing issues.

Evaluating and Testing the Effectiveness of Internal Auditors' Work

.24 The auditor should perform procedures to evaluate the quality and effectiveness of the internal auditors' work, as described in paragraphs .12 through .17, that significantly affects the nature, timing, and extent of the auditor's procedures. The nature and extent of the procedures the auditor should perform when making this evaluation are a matter of judgment depending on the extent of the effect of the internal auditors' work on the auditor's procedures for significant account balances or classes of transactions.

.25 In developing the evaluation procedures, the auditor should consider such factors as whether the internal auditors'—

- Scope of work is appropriate to meet the objectives.
- Audit programs are adequate.
- Working papers adequately document work performed, including evidence of supervision and review.
- Conclusions are appropriate in the circumstances.
- Reports are consistent with the results of the work performed.

.26 In making the evaluation, the auditor should test some of the internal auditors' work related to the significant financial statement assertions. These tests may be accomplished by either (*a*) examining some of the controls, transactions, or balances that the internal auditors examined or (*b*) examining similar controls, transactions, or balances not actually examined by the internal auditors. In reaching conclusions about the internal auditors' work, the auditor should compare the results of his or her tests with the results of the internal auditors' work. The extent of this testing will depend on the circumstances and should be sufficient to enable the auditor to make an evaluation of the overall quality and effectiveness of the internal audit work being considered by the auditor.

Using Internal Auditors to Provide Direct Assistance to the Auditor

.27 In performing the audit, the auditor may request direct assistance from the internal auditors. This direct assistance relates to work the auditor specifically requests the internal auditors to perform to complete some aspect of the auditor's work. For example, internal auditors may assist the auditor in obtaining an understanding of internal control or in performing tests of controls or substantive tests, consistent with the guidance about the auditor's responsibility in paragraphs .18 through .22. When direct assistance is provided, the auditor should assess the internal auditors' competence and objectivity (see paragraphs .09 through .11) and supervise,[8] review, evaluate, and test the work performed by internal auditors to the extent appropriate in the circumstances. The auditor should inform the internal auditors of their responsibilities, the

---

[8] See section 311, *Planning and Supervision*, paragraphs .28 through .32, for the type of supervisory procedures to apply. [Footnote revised, March 2006, to reflect conforming changes necessary due to the issuance of Statement on Auditing Standards No. 108.]

objectives of the procedures they are to perform, and matters that may affect the nature, timing, and extent of audit procedures, such as possible accounting and auditing issues. The auditor should also inform the internal auditors that all significant accounting and auditing issues identified during the audit should be brought to the auditor's attention.

Effective Date

.28 This section is effective for audits of financial statements for periods ending after December 15, 1991. Early application of the provisions of this section is permissible.

.29

Appendix

The Auditor's Consideration of the Internal Audit Function in an Audit of Financial Statements

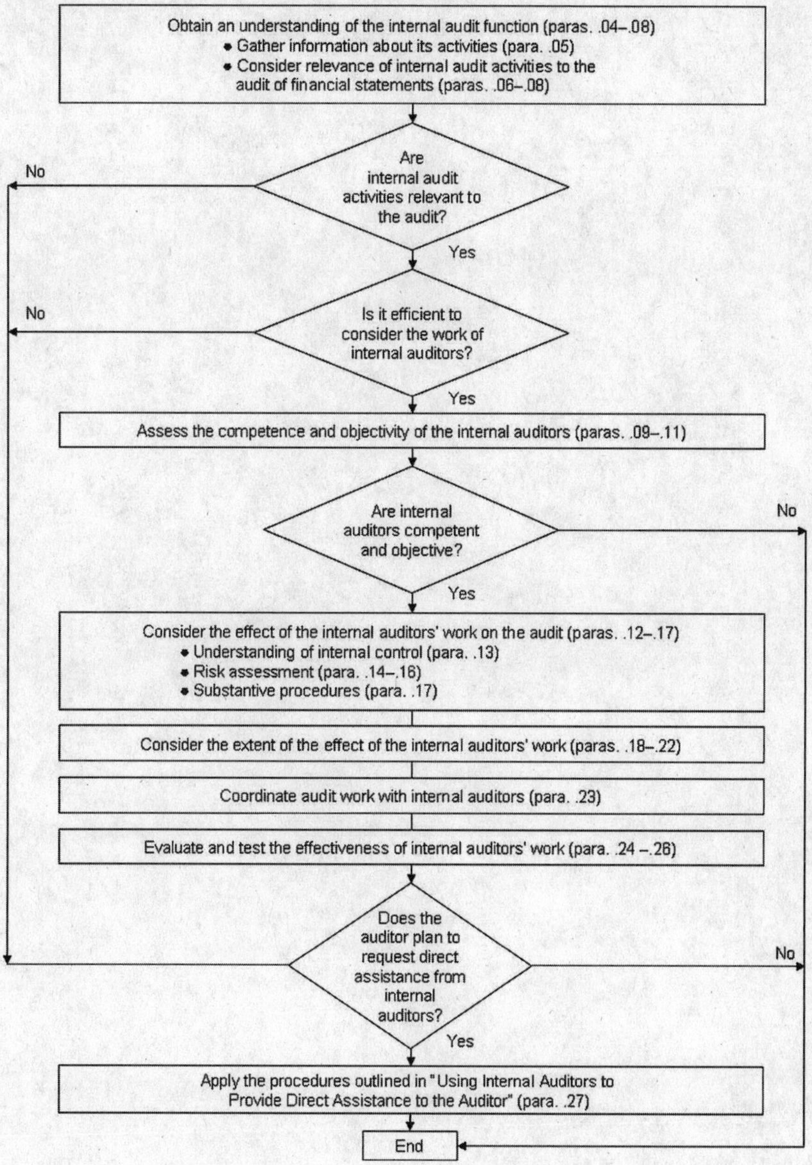

AU Section 324

Service Organizations *

(Supersedes SAS No. 44.)

Sources: SAS No. 70; SAS No. 78; SAS No. 88; SAS No. 98.

See section 9324 for interpretations of this section.

Effective for service auditors' reports dated after March 31, 1993, unless otherwise indicated.

SSAE No. 16, *Reporting on Controls at a Service Organization*, supersedes the guidance for service auditors in this AU section for service auditors' reports for periods ending on or after June 15, 2011. Earlier implementation of SSAE No. 16 is permitted. The guidance for user auditors in this section remains in effect until the clarified SAS *Audit Considerations Relating to an Entity Using a Service Organization* becomes effective and supersedes the guidance for user auditors in this AU section. The new clarified SAS is effective for audits of financial statements for periods ending on or after December 15, 2012. [Revised, August 2011, to reflect conforming changes necessary due to the issuance of SSAE No. 16.]

Introduction and Applicability

.01 This section provides guidance on the factors an independent auditor should consider when auditing the financial statements of an entity that uses a service organization to process certain transactions. This section also provides guidance for independent auditors who issue reports on the processing of transactions by a service organization for use by other auditors.

.02 For purposes of this section, the following definitions apply.

- *User organization*—The entity that has engaged a service organization and whose financial statements are being audited
- *User auditor*—The auditor who reports on the financial statements of the user organization
- *Service organization*—The entity (or segment of an entity) that provides services to a user organization that are part of the user organization's information system
- *Service auditor*—The auditor who reports on controls of a service organization that may be relevant to a user organization's internal control as it relates to an audit of financial statements
- *Report on controls placed in operation*—A service auditor's report on a service organization's description of its controls that may be relevant to a user organization's internal control as it relates to an audit of financial statements, on whether such controls were suitably designed to achieve specified control objectives, and on whether they had been placed in operation as of a specific date

* Title amended, effective December 1999, by Statement on Auditing Standards No. 88.

- *Report on controls placed in operation and tests of operating effectiveness*—A service auditor's report on a service organization's description of its controls that may be relevant to a user organization's internal control as it relates to an audit of financial statements, [1] on whether such controls were suitably designed to achieve specified control objectives, on whether they had been placed in operation as of a specific date, and on whether the controls that were tested were operating with sufficient effectiveness to provide reasonable, but not absolute, assurance that the related control objectives were achieved during the period specified

[Revised, April 2002, to reflect conforming changes necessary due to the issuance of Statement on Auditing Standards No. 94.]

.03 The guidance in this section is applicable to the audit of the financial statements of an entity that obtains services from another organization that are part of its information system. A service organization's services are part of an entity's information system if they affect any of the following:

- The classes of transactions in the entity's operations that are significant to the entity's financial statements
- The procedures, both automated and manual, by which the entity's transactions are initiated, authorize, recorded, processed, and reported from their occurrence to their inclusion in the financial statements
- The related accounting records, whether electronic or manual, supporting information, and specific accounts in the entity's financial statements involved in initiating, recording, processing and reporting the entity's transactions
- How the entity's information system captures other events and conditions that are significant to the financial statements
- The financial reporting process used to prepare the entity's financial statements, including significant accounting estimates and disclosures

Service organizations that provide such services include, for example, bank trust departments that invest and service assets for employee benefit plans or for others, mortgage bankers that service mortgages for others, and application service providers that provide packaged software applications and a technology environment that enables customers to process financial and operational transactions. The guidance in this section may also be relevant to situations in which an organization develops, provides, and maintains the software used by client organizations. The provisions of this section are not intended to apply to situations in which the services provided are limited to executing client organization transactions that are specifically authorized by the client, such as the processing of checking account transactions by a bank or the execution of securities transactions by a broker. This section also is not intended to apply to the audit of transactions arising from financial interests in partnerships, corporations, and joint ventures, such as working interests in oil and gas ventures, when proprietary interests are accounted for and reported to interest holders. [As amended, effective December 1999, by Statement on Auditing Standards No. 88. Revised, April 2002, to reflect conforming changes necessary due to the issuance of Statement on Auditing Standards No. 94. Revised, March 2006,

[1] In this section, a service organization's controls that may be relevant to a user organization's internal control as it relates to an audit of financial statements will be referred to as a service organization's *controls*.

to reflect conforming changes necessary due to the issuance of Statement on Auditing Standards No. 106.]

.04 This section is organized into the following sections.

a. The user auditor's consideration of the effect of the service organization on the user organization's internal control and the availability of evidence to:

- Obtain the necessary understanding of the user organization's internal control to assess the risks of material misstatement.
- Assess the risks of material misstatement at the user organization.
- Perform further audit procedures.

b. Considerations in using a service auditor's report.

c. Responsibilities of service auditors.

[Revised, May 2007, to reflect conforming changes necessary due to the issuance of Statement on Auditing Standards No. 109.]

The User Auditor's Consideration of the Effect of the Service Organization on the User Organization's Internal Control and the Availability of Audit Evidence

.05 The user auditor should consider the discussion in paragraphs .06–.21 when obtaining an understanding of the entity and its environment, including its internal controls and performing the audit of an entity that uses a service organization to process its transactions. [Revised, May 2007, to reflect conforming changes necessary due to the issuance of Statement on Auditing Standards No. 109.]

The Effect of Use of a Service Organization on a User Organization's Internal Control

.06 When a user organization uses a service organization, transactions that affect the user organization's financial statements are subjected to controls that are, at least in part, physically and operationally separate from the user organization. The significance of the controls of the service organization to those of the user organization depends on the nature of the services provided by the service organization, primarily the nature and materiality of the transactions it processes for the user organization and the degree of interaction between its activities and those of the user organization. To illustrate how the degree of interaction affects user organization controls, when the user organization initiates transactions and the service organization executes and does the accounting processing of those transactions, there is a high degree of interaction between the activities at the user organization and those at the service organization. In these circumstances, it may be practicable for the user organization to implement effective controls for those transactions. However, when the service organization initiates, executes, and does the accounting processing of the user organization's transactions, there is a lower degree of interaction and it may not be practicable for the user organization to implement effective controls for those transactions. [As amended, effective December 1999, by Statement on Auditing Standards No. 88.]

Planning the Audit

.07 Section 314, *Understanding the Entity and its Environment and Assessing the Risks of Material Misstatement*, states that an auditor should obtain an understanding of each of the five components of the entity's internal control sufficient to assess the risks of material misstatement and to design the nature, timing, and extent of further audit procedures. This understanding may encompass controls placed in operation by the entity and by service organizations whose services are part of the entity's information system. The auditor should use such knowledge to:

- Identify types of potential misstatements.
- Consider factors that affect the risks of material misstatement.
- Design tests of controls, when applicable. Paragraphs .23–.27 of section 318 discuss factors the auditor considers in determining whether to perform tests of controls
- Design substantive tests.

[As amended, effective for service auditor's reports covering descriptions as of or after January 1, 1997, by Statement on Auditing Standards No. 78. As amended, effective December 1999, by Statement on Auditing Standards No. 88. Revised, May 2001, to reflect conforming changes necessary due to the issuance of Statement on Auditing Standards No. 94. Revised, March 2006 and May 2007, to reflect conforming changes necessary due to the issuance of Statements on Auditing Standards No. 109 and No. 110.]

[.08] [Paragraph deleted by the issuance of Statement on Auditing Standards No. 88, December 1999.]

.09 Information about the nature of the services provided by a service organization that are part of the user organization's information system and the service organization's controls over those services may be available from a wide variety of sources, such as user manuals, system overviews, technical manuals, the contract between the user organization and the service organization, and reports by service auditors, internal auditors, or regulatory authorities on the service organization's controls. If the services and the service organization's controls over those services are highly standardized, information obtained through the user auditor's prior experience with the service organization may be helpful in assessing the risks of material misstatement. [As amended, effective December 1999, by Statement on Auditing Standards No. 88. Revised, May 2007, to reflect conforming changes necessary due to the issuance of Statement on Auditing Standards No. 109.]

.10 After considering the available information, the user auditor may conclude that he or she has the means to obtain a sufficient understanding of internal control to assess the risks of material misstatement. If the user auditor concludes that information is not available to obtain a sufficient understanding to assess the risks of material misstatement, he or she may consider contacting the service organization, through the user organization, to obtain specific information or request that a service auditor be engaged to perform procedures that will supply the necessary information, or the user auditor may visit the service organization and perform such procedures. If the user auditor is unable to obtain sufficient audit evidence to achieve his or her audit objectives, the user auditor should qualify his or her opinion or disclaim an opinion on the financial statements because of a scope limitation. [As amended, effective December 1999, by Statement on Auditing Standards No. 88. Revised, May 2007, to reflect conforming changes necessary due to the issuance of Statement on Auditing Standards No. 109.]

Assessing Control Risk at the User Organization

.11 The user auditor uses his or her understanding of the internal control to assess control risk for the as-sertions embodied in the account balances and classes of transactions, including those that are affected by the activities of the service organization. In doing so, the user auditor may identify certain user organization controls that, if effective, would permit the user auditor to assess control risk as low or moderate for particular assertions. Such controls may be applied at either the user organization or the service organization. The user auditor may conclude that it would be efficient to obtain audit evidence about the operating effectiveness of controls to provide a basis for assessing control risk as low or moderate. [Revised, April 2002, to reflect conforming changes necessary due to the issuance of Statement on Auditing Standards No. 94. Revised, March 2006, to reflect conforming changes necessary due to the issuance of Statement on Auditing Standards No. 105. Revised, May 2007, to reflect conforming changes necessary due to the issuance of Statement on Auditing Standards No. 109.]

.12 A service auditor's report on controls placed in operation at the service organization should be helpful in providing a sufficient understanding to assess the risks of material misstatement of the user organization. Such a report, however, is not intended to provide any evidence of the operating effectiveness of the relevant controls that would allow the user auditor to reduce the assessed level of control risk as low or moderate. Such audit evidence should be derived from one or more of the following:

a. Tests of the user organization's controls over the activities of the service organization (for example, the user auditor may test the user organization's independent reperformance of selected items processed by a service organization or test the user organization's reconciliation of output reports with source documents)

b. A service auditor's report on controls placed in operation and tests of operating effectiveness, or a report on the application of agreed-upon procedures that describes relevant tests of controls

c. Appropriate tests of controls performed by the user auditor at the service organization

[Revised, March 2006, to reflect conforming changes necessary due to the issuance of Statement on Auditing Standards No. 105. Revised, May 2007, to reflect conforming changes necessary due to the issuance of Statement on Auditing Standards No. 109.]

.13 The user organization may establish effective controls over the service organization's activities that may be tested and that may enable the user auditor to reduce the assessed level of control risk as low or moderate for some or all of the relevant assertions. If a user organization, for example, uses a service organization to process its payroll transactions, the user organization may establish controls over the submission and receipt of payroll information that could prevent or detect material misstatements. The user organization might reperform the service organization's payroll calculations on a test basis. In this situation, the user auditor should obtain a sufficient understanding of the user organization's controls over payroll processing to (1) evaluate the design of such controls and (2) determine whether they have been implemented. The understanding of the user organization's controls over payroll processing would provide a basis for assessing control risk for the assertions related to payroll transactions. [Revised, April 2002, to reflect conforming changes necessary due to the issuance of Statement on Auditing Standards No. 94. Revised, May 2007,

to reflect conforming changes necessary due to the issuance of Statement on Auditing Standards No. 109.]

.14 The user auditor may find that controls relevant to assessing control risk as low or moderate for particular assertions are applied only at the service organization. If the user auditor plans to assess control risk as low or moderate for those assertions, he or she should evaluate the operating effectiveness of those controls by obtaining a service auditor's report that describes the results of the service auditor's tests of those controls (that is, a report on controls placed in operation and tests of operating effectiveness, or an agreed-upon procedures report)[2] or by performing tests of controls at the service organization. If the user auditor decides to use a service auditor's report, the user auditor should consider the extent of the evidence provided by the report about the effectiveness of controls intended to prevent or detect material misstatements in the particular assertions. The user auditor remains responsible for evaluating the evidence presented by the service auditor and for determining its effect on the assessment of control risk at the user organization. [Revised, May 2007, to reflect conforming changes necessary due to the issuance of Statement on Auditing Standards No. 109.]

.15 The user auditor's assessments of control risk regarding assertions about account balances or classes of transactions are based on the combined evidence provided by the service auditor's report and the user auditor's own procedures. In making these assessments, the user auditor should consider the nature, source, and interrelationships among the evidence, as well as the period covered by the tests of controls. The user auditor uses the assessed levels of control risk, as well as his or her understanding of internal control, in determining the nature, timing, and extent of substantive tests for particular assertions.

.16 The guidance in section 326.06, regarding the auditor's consideration of the sufficiency of audit evidence to support a specific assessed level of control risk is applicable to user auditors considering audit evidence provided by a service auditor's report on controls placed in operation and tests of operating effectiveness. Because the report may be intended to satisfy the needs of several different user auditors, a user auditor should determine whether the specific tests of controls and results in the service auditor's report are relevant to assertions that are significant in the user organization's financial statements. For those tests of controls and results that are relevant, a user auditor should consider whether the nature, timing, and extent of such tests of controls and results provide appropriate evidence about the effectiveness of the controls to support the user auditor's assessed level of control risk. In evaluating these factors, user auditors should also keep in mind that, for certain assertions, the shorter the period covered by a specific test and the longer the time elapsed since the performance of the test, the less support for control risk reduction the test may provide. [Revised, May 2001, to reflect conforming changes necessary due to the issuance of Statement on Auditing Standards No. 94. Revised, March 2006, to reflect conforming changes necessary due to the issuance of Statements on Auditing Standards No. 105 and No. 106.]

---

[2] See AT section 201, *Agreed-Upon Procedures Engagements*, for guidance on performing and reporting on agreed-upon procedures engagements. [Footnote added, April 2002, to reflect conforming changes necessary due to the issuance of Statement on Standards for Attestation Engagements No. 10.]

Audit Evidence From Substantive Audit Procedures Performed by Service Auditors

.17 Service auditors may be engaged to perform procedures that are substantive in nature for the benefit of user auditors. Such engagements may involve the performance, by the service auditor, of procedures agreed upon by the user organization and its auditor and by the service organization and its auditor. In addition, there may be requirements imposed by governmental authorities or through contractual arrangements whereby service auditors perform designated procedures that are substantive in nature. The results of the application of the required procedures to balances and transactions processed by the service organization may be used by user auditors as part of the evidence necessary to support their opinions.

Considerations in Using a Service Auditor's Report

.18 In considering whether the service auditor's report is satisfactory for his or her purposes, the user auditor should make inquiries concerning the service auditor's professional reputation. Appropriate sources of information concerning the professional reputation of the service auditor are discussed in section 543, *Part of Audit Performed by Other Independent Auditors*, paragraph .10*a*.

.19 In considering whether the service auditor's report is sufficient to meet his or her objectives, the user auditor should give consideration to the guidance in section 543.12. If the user auditor believes that the service auditor's report may not be sufficient to meet his or her objectives, the user auditor may supplement his or her understanding of the service auditor's procedures and conclusions by discussing with the service auditor the scope and results of the service auditor's work. Also, if the user auditor believes it is necessary, he or she may contact the service organization, through the user organization, to request that the service auditor perform agreed-upon procedures at the service organization, or the user auditor may perform such procedures.

.20 When assessing a service organization's controls and how they interact with a user organization's controls, the user auditor may become aware of the existence of significant deficiencies or material weaknesses in internal control. In such circumstances, the user auditor should consider the guidance provided in section 325, *Communicating Internal Control Related Matters Identified in an Audit*. [Revised, May 2006, to reflect conforming changes necessary due to the issuance of Statement on Auditing Standards No. 112.]

.21 The user auditor should not make reference to the report of the service auditor as a basis, in part, for his or her own opinion on the user organization's financial statements. The service auditor's report is used in the audit, but the service auditor is not responsible for examining any portion of the financial statements as of any specific date or for any specified period. Thus, there cannot be a division of responsibility for the audit of the financial statements.

Responsibilities of Service Auditors

.22 The service auditor is responsible for the representations in his or her report and for exercising due care in the application of procedures that support those representations. Although a service auditor's engagement differs from an audit of financial statements conducted in accordance with generally accepted auditing standards, it should be performed in accordance with the general standards and with the relevant fieldwork and reporting standards. Although the service auditor should be independent from the service organization, it is not necessary for the service auditor to be independent from each user organization.

.23 As a result of procedures performed at the service organization, the service auditor may become aware of illegal acts, fraud, or uncorrected errors attributable to the service organization's management or employees that may affect one or more user organizations. The terms *errors*, *fraud*, and *illegal acts* are discussed in section 312, *Audit Risk and Materiality in Conducting an Audit*, and section 317, *Illegal Acts by Clients*; the discussions therein are relevant to this section. When the service auditor becomes aware of such matters, he or she should determine from the appropriate level of management of the service organization whether this information has been communicated appropriately to affected user organizations, unless those matters are clearly inconsequential. If the management of the service organization has not communicated the information to affected user organizations and is unwilling to do so, the service auditor should inform those charged with governance of the service organization. If those charged with governance do not respond appropriately to the service auditor's communication, the service auditor should consider whether to resign from the engagement. The service auditor may wish to consult with his or her attorney in making this decision. [Revised, April 2007, to reflect conforming changes necessary due to the issuance of Statement on Auditing Standards No. 114.]

.24 The type of engagement to be performed and the related report to be prepared should be established by the service organization. However, when circumstances permit, discussions between the service organization and the user organizations are advisable to determine the type of report that will be most suitable for the user organizations' needs. This section provides guidance on the two types of reports that may be issued:

a. *Reports on controls placed in operation*—A service auditor's report on a service organization's description of the controls that may be relevant to a user organization's internal control as it relates to an audit of financial statements, on whether such controls were suitably designed to achieve specified control objectives, and on whether they had been placed in operation as of a specific date. Such reports may be useful in providing a user auditor with an understanding of the controls necessary to assess the risks of material misstatement and to design effective tests of controls and substantive tests at the user organization, but they are not intended to provide the user auditor with a basis for reducing his or her assessments of control risk as low or moderate.

b. *Reports on controls placed in operation and tests of operating effectiveness*—A service auditor's report on a service organization's description of the controls that may be relevant to a user organization's internal control as it relates to an audit of financial statements, on whether such controls were suitably designed to achieve specified control objectives, on whether they had been placed in operation as of a specific date, and on whether the controls that were tested were operating with sufficient effectiveness to provide reasonable, but not absolute, assurance that the related control objectives were achieved during the period specified. Such reports may be useful in providing the user auditor with an understanding of the controls necessary to plan the audit and may also provide the user auditor with a basis for reducing his or her assessments of control risk as low or moderate.

[Revised, May 2007, to reflect conforming changes necessary due to the issuance of Statement on Auditing Standards No. 109.]

Reports on Controls Placed in Operation

.25 The information necessary for a report on controls placed in operation ordinarily is obtained through discussions with appropriate service organization personnel and through reference to various forms of documentation, such as system flowcharts and narratives.

.26 After obtaining a description of the relevant controls, the service auditor should determine whether the description provides sufficient information for user auditors to obtain an understanding of those aspects of the service organization's controls that may be relevant to a user organization's internal control. The description should contain a discussion of the features of the service organization's controls that would have an effect on a user organization's internal control. Such features are relevant when they directly affect the service provided to the user organization. They may include controls within the control environment, risk assessment, control activities, information and communication, and monitoring components of internal control. The control environment may include hiring practices and key areas of authority and responsibility. Risk assessment may include the identification of risks associated with processing specific transactions. Control activities may include policies and procedures over the modification of computer programs and are ordinarily designed to meet specific control objectives. The specific control objectives of the service organization should be set forth in the service organization's description of controls. Information and communication may include ways in which user transactions are initiated and processed. Monitoring may include the involvement of internal auditors. [As amended, effective for service auditor's reports covering descriptions as of or after January 1, 1997, by Statement on Auditing Standards No. 78.]

.27 Evidence of whether controls have been placed in operation is ordinarily obtained through previous experience with the service organization and through procedures such as inquiry of appropriate management, supervisory, and staff personnel; inspection of service organization documents and records; and observation of service organization activities and operations. For the type of report described in paragraph .24*a*, these procedures need not be supplemented by tests of the operating effectiveness of the service organization's controls.

.28 Although a service auditor's report on controls placed in operation is as of a specified date, the service auditor should inquire about changes in the service organization's controls that may have occurred before the beginning of fieldwork. If the service auditor believes that the changes would be considered significant by user organizations and their auditors, those changes should be included in the description of the service organization's controls. If the service auditor concludes that the changes would be considered significant by user organization's and their auditors and the changes are not included in the description of the service organization's controls, the service auditor should describe the changes in his or her report. Such changes might include:

- Procedural changes made to accommodate provisions of a new FASB Statement of Financial Accounting Standards.
- Major changes in an application to permit on-line processing.
- Procedural changes to eliminate previously identified deficiencies.

Changes that occurred more than twelve months before the date being reported on normally would not be considered significant, because they generally would not affect user auditors' considerations.

.29 A service auditor's report expressing an opinion on a description of controls placed in operation at a service organization should contain:

a. A specific reference to the applications, services, products, or other aspects of the service organization covered.

b. A description of the scope and nature of the service auditor's procedures.

c. Identification of the party specifying the control objectives.

d. An indication that the purpose of the service auditor's engagement was to obtain reasonable assurance about whether (1) the service organization's description presents fairly, in all material respects, the aspects of the service organization's controls that may be relevant to a user organization's internal control as it relates to an audit of financial statements, (2) the controls were suitably designed to achieve specified control objectives, and (3) such controls had been placed in operation as of a specific date.

e. A disclaimer of opinion on the operating effectiveness of the controls.

f. The service auditor's opinion on whether the description presents fairly, in all material respects, the relevant aspects of the service organization's controls that had been placed in operation as of a specific date and whether, in the service auditor's opinion, the controls were suitably designed to provide reasonable assurance that the specified control objectives would be achieved if those controls were complied with satisfactorily.

g. A statement of the inherent limitations of the potential effectiveness of controls at the service organization and of the risk of projecting to future periods any evaluation of the description.

h. Identification of the parties for whom the report is intended.

.30 If the service auditor believes that the description is inaccurate or insufficiently complete for user auditors, the service auditor's report should so state and should contain sufficient detail to provide user auditors with an appropriate understanding.

.31 It may become evident to the service auditor, when considering the service organization's description of controls placed in operation, that the system was designed with the assumption that certain controls would be implemented by the user organization. If the service auditor is aware of the need for such complementary user organization controls, these should be delineated in the description of controls. If the application of controls by user organizations is necessary to achieve the stated control objectives, the service auditor's report should be modified to include the phrase "and user organizations applied the controls contemplated in the design of the Service Organization's controls" following the words "complied with satisfactorily" in the scope and opinion paragraphs.

.32 The service auditor should consider conditions that come to his or her attention that, in the service auditor's judgment, represent significant deficiencies in the design or operation of the service organization's controls that preclude the service auditor from obtaining reasonable assurance that specified control objectives would be achieved. The service auditor should also consider whether any other information, irrespective of specified control objectives, has come to his or her attention that causes him or her to conclude (*a*) that design deficiencies exist that could adversely affect the ability to initiate, authorize, record, process, or report financial data to user organizations without error, and (*b*) that user organizations would not generally be expected to have controls in place to mitigate such design deficiencies. [Revised, April 2002, to reflect conforming changes necessary due to the issuance of Statement on Auditing

Standards No. 94. Revised, March 2006, to reflect conforming changes necessary due to the issuance of Statement on Auditing Standards No. 106.]

.33 The description of controls and control objectives required for these reports may be prepared by the service organization. If the service auditor prepares the description of controls and control objectives, the representations in the description remain the responsibility of the service organization.

.34 For the service auditor to express an opinion on whether the controls were suitably designed to achieve the specified control objectives, it is necessary that:

a. The service organization identify and appropriately describe such control objectives and the relevant controls.

b. The service auditor consider the linkage of the controls to the stated control objectives.

c. The service auditor obtain sufficient appropriate audit evidence to reach an opinion.

.35 The control objectives may be designated by the service organization or by outside parties such as regulatory authorities, a user group, or others. When the control objectives are not established by outside parties, the service auditor should be satisfied that the control objectives, as set forth by the service organization, are reasonable in the circumstances and consistent with the service organization's contractual obligations.

.36 The service auditor's report should state whether the controls were suitably designed to achieve the specified control objectives. The report should not state whether they were suitably designed to achieve objectives beyond the specifically identified control objectives.

.37 The service auditor's opinion on whether the controls were suitably designed to achieve the specified control objectives is not intended to provide evidence of operating effectiveness or to provide the user auditor with a basis for concluding that control risk may be assessed as low or moderate. [Revised, May 2007, to reflect conforming changes necessary due to the issuance of Statement on Auditing Standards No. 109.]

.38 The following is a sample report on controls placed in operation at a service organization. The report should have, as an attachment, a description of the service organization's controls that may be relevant to a user organization's internal control as it relates to an audit of financial statements. This report is illustrative only and should be modified as appropriate to suit the circumstances of individual engagements.

To XYZ Service Organization:

We have examined the accompanying description of controls related to the __ application of XYZ Service Organization. Our examination included procedures to obtain reasonable assurance about whether (1) the accompanying description presents fairly, in all material respects, the aspects of XYZ Service Organization's controls that may be relevant to a user organization's internal control as it relates to an audit of financial statements, (2) the controls included in the description were suitably designed to achieve the control objectives specified in the description, if those controls were complied with satisfactorily,[3] and (3)

---

[3] If the application of controls by user organizations is necessary to achieve the stated control objectives, the service auditor's report should be modified to include the phrase "and user organizations applied the controls contemplated in the design of XYZ Service Organization's controls" following the words "complied with satisfactorily" in the scope and opinion paragraphs. [Footnote renumbered,

(continued)

such controls had been placed in operation as of ____. The control objectives were specified by ___. Our examination was performed in accordance with standards established by the American Institute of Certified Public Accountants and included those procedures we considered necessary in the circumstances to obtain a reasonable basis for rendering our opinion.

We did not perform procedures to determine the operating effectiveness of controls for any period. Accordingly, we express no opinion on the operating effectiveness of any aspects of XYZ Service Organization's controls, individually or in the aggregate.

In our opinion, the accompanying description of the aforementioned application presents fairly, in all material respects, the relevant aspects of XYZ Service Organization's controls that had been placed in operation as of ___. Also, in our opinion, the controls, as described, are suitably designed to provide reasonable assurance that the specified control objectives would be achieved if the described controls were complied with satisfactorily.

The description of controls at XYZ Service Organization is as of ___ and any projection of such information to the future is subject to the risk that, because of change, the description may no longer portray the controls in existence. The potential effectiveness of specific controls at the Service Organization is subject to inherent limitations and, accordingly, errors or fraud may occur and not be detected. Furthermore, the projection of any conclusions, based on our findings, to future periods is subject to the risk that changes may alter the validity of such conclusions.

This report is intended solely for use by the management of XYZ Service Organization, its customers, and the independent auditors of its customers ___.

.39 If the service auditor concludes that the description is inaccurate or insufficiently complete for user auditors, the service auditor should so state in an explanatory paragraph preceding the opinion paragraph. An example of such an explanatory paragraph follows:

The accompanying description states that XYZ Service Organization uses operator identification numbers and passwords to prevent unauthorized access to the system. Based on inquiries of staff personnel and inspections of activities, we determined that such procedures are employed in Applications A and B but are not required to access the system in Applications C and D.

In addition, the first sentence of the opinion paragraph would be modified to read as follows:

In our opinion, except for the matter referred to in the preceding paragraph, the accompanying description of the aforementioned application presents fairly, in all material respects, the relevant aspects of XYZ Service Organization's controls that had been placed in operation as of.

.40 If, after applying the criteria in paragraph .32, the service auditor concludes that there are significant deficiencies in the design or operation of the service organization's controls, the service auditor should report those conditions in an explanatory paragraph preceding the opinion paragraph. An example of an explanatory paragraph describing a significant deficiency in the design or operation of the service organization's controls follows:

(footnote continued)

April 2002, to reflect conforming changes necessary due to the issuance of Statement on Standards for Attestation Engagements No. 10.]

> As discussed in the accompanying description, from time to time the Service Organization makes changes in application programs to correct deficiencies or to enhance capabilities. The procedures followed in determining whether to make changes, in designing the changes, and in implementing them do not include review and approval by authorized individuals who are independent from those involved in making the changes. There are also no specified requirements to test such changes or provide test results to an authorized reviewer prior to implementing the changes.

In addition, the second sentence of the opinion paragraph would be modified to read as follows:

> Also in our opinion, except for the deficiency referred to in the preceding paragraph, the controls, as described, are suitably designed to provide reasonable assurance that the specified control objectives would be achieved if the described controls were complied with satisfactorily.

Reports on Controls Placed in Operation and Tests of Operating Effectiveness

Paragraphs .41–.56 repeat some of the information contained in paragraphs .25–.40 to provide readers with a comprehensive, stand-alone presentation of the relevant considerations for each type of report.

.41 The information necessary for a report on controls placed in operation and tests of operating effectiveness ordinarily is obtained through discussions with appropriate service organization personnel, through reference to various forms of documentation, such as system flowcharts and narratives, and through the performance of tests of controls. Evidence of whether controls have been placed in operation is ordinarily obtained through previous experience with the service organization and through procedures such as inquiry of appropriate management, supervisory, and staff personnel; inspection of service organization documents and records; and observation of service organization activities and operations. The service auditor applies tests of controls to determine whether specific controls are operating with sufficient effectiveness to achieve specified control objectives. Section 350, *Audit Sampling*, as amended, provides guidance on the application and evaluation of audit sampling in performing tests of controls.

.42 After obtaining a description of the relevant controls, the service auditor should determine whether the description provides sufficient information for user auditors to obtain an understanding of those aspects of the service organization's controls that may be relevant to a user organization's internal control. The description should contain a discussion of the features of the service organization's controls that would have an effect on a user organization's internal control. Such features are relevant when they directly affect the service provided to the user organization. They may include controls within the control environment, risk assessment, control activities, information and communication, and monitoring components of internal control. The control environment may include hiring practices and key areas of authority and responsibility. Risk assessment may include the identification of risks associated with processing specific transactions. Control activities may include policies and procedures over the modification of computer programs and are ordinarily designed to meet specific control objectives. The specific control objectives of the service organization should be set forth in the service organization's description of controls. Information and communication may include ways in which user transactions are initiated and processed. Monitoring may include the involvement of internal auditors. [As amended, effective for service auditor's reports covering descriptions as of or after January 1, 1997, by Statement on Auditing Standards No. 78.]

.43 The service auditor should inquire about changes in the service organization's controls that may have occurred before the beginning of fieldwork. If the service auditor believes the changes would be considered significant by user organizations and their auditors, those changes should be included in the description of the service organization's controls. If the service auditor concludes that the changes would be considered significant by user organizations and their auditors and the changes are not included in the description of the service organization's controls, the service auditor should describe the changes in his or her report. Such changes might include:

- Procedural changes made to accommodate provisions of a new FASB Statement of Financial Accounting Standards.
- Major changes in an application to permit on-line processing.
- Procedural changes to eliminate previously identified deficiencies.

Changes that occurred more than twelve months before the date being reported on normally would not be considered significant, because they generally would not affect user auditors' considerations.

.44 A service auditor's report expressing an opinion on a description of controls placed in operation at a service organization and tests of operating effectiveness should contain:

a. A specific reference to the applications, services, products, or other aspects of the service organization covered.

b. A description of the scope and nature of the service auditor's procedures.

c. Identification of the party specifying the control objectives.

d. An indication that the purpose of the service auditor's engagement was to obtain reasonable assurance about whether (1) the service organization's description presents fairly, in all material respects, the aspects of the service organization's controls that may be relevant to a user organization's internal control as it relates to an audit of financial statements, (2) the controls were suitably designed to achieve specified control objectives, and (3) such controls had been placed in operation as of a specific date.

e. The service auditor's opinion on whether the description presents fairly, in all material respects, the relevant aspects of the service organization's controls that had been placed in operation as of a specific date and whether, in the service auditor's opinion, the controls were suitably designed to provide reasonable assurance that the specified control objectives would be achieved if those controls were complied with satisfactorily.

f. A reference to a description of tests of specific service organization controls designed to obtain evidence about the operating effectiveness of those controls in achieving specified control objectives. The description should include the controls that were tested, the control objectives the controls were intended to achieve, the tests applied, and the results of the tests. The description should include an indication of the nature, timing, and extent of the tests, as well as sufficient detail to enable user auditors to determine the effect of such tests on user auditors' assessments of control risk. To the extent that the service auditor identified causative factors for exceptions, determined the current status of corrective actions, or obtained other relevant qualitative information about exceptions noted, such information should be provided.

g. A statement of the period covered by the service auditor's report on the operating effectiveness of the specific controls tested.

h. The service auditor's opinion on whether the controls that were tested were operating with sufficient effectiveness to provide reasonable, but not absolute, assurance that the related control objectives were achieved during the period specified.

i. When all of the control objectives listed in the description of controls placed in operation are not covered by tests of operating effectiveness, a statement that the service auditor does not express an opinion on control objectives not listed in the description of tests performed at the service organization.

j. A statement that the relative effectiveness and significance of specific service organization controls and their effect on assessments of control risk at user organizations are dependent on their interaction with the controls and other factors present at individual user organizations.

k. A statement that the service auditor has performed no procedures to evaluate the effectiveness of controls at individual user organizations.

l. A statement of the inherent limitations of the potential effectiveness of controls at the service organization and of the risk of projecting to the future any evaluation of the description or any conclusions about the effectiveness of controls in achieving control objectives.

m. Identification of the parties for whom the report is intended.

.45 If the service auditor believes that the description is inaccurate or insufficiently complete for user auditors, the service auditor's report should so state and should contain sufficient detail to provide user auditors with an appropriate understanding.

.46 It may become evident to the service auditor, when considering the service organization's description of controls placed in operation, that the system was designed with the assumption that certain controls would be implemented by the user organization. If the service auditor is aware of the need for such complementary user organization controls, these should be delineated in the description of controls. If the application of controls by user organizations is necessary to achieve the stated control objectives, the service auditor's report should be modified to include the phrase "and user organizations applied the controls contemplated in the design of the Service Organization's controls" following the words "complied with satisfactorily" in the scope and opinion paragraphs. Similarly, if the operating effectiveness of controls at the service organization is dependent on the application of controls at user organizations, this should be delineated in the description of tests performed.

.47 The service auditor should consider conditions that come to his or her attention that, in the service auditor's judgment, represent significant deficiencies in the design or operation of the service organization's controls that preclude the service auditor from obtaining reasonable assurance that specified control objectives would be achieved. The service auditor should also consider whether any other information, irrespective of specified control objectives, has come to his or her attention that causes him or her to conclude (*a*) that design deficiencies exist that could adversely affect the ability to initiate, authorize, record, process, or report financial data to user organizations without error, and (*b*) that user organizations would not generally be expected to have controls in place to mitigate such design deficiencies. [Revised, April 2002, to reflect conforming changes necessary due to the issuance of Statement on Auditing

Standards No. 94. Revised, March 2006, to reflect conforming changes necessary due to the issuance of Statement on Auditing Standards No. 106.]

.48 The description of controls and control objectives required for these reports may be prepared by the service organization. If the service auditor prepares the description of controls and control objectives, the representations in the description remain the responsibility of the service organization.

.49 For the service auditor to express an opinion on whether the controls were suitably designed to achieve the specified control objectives, it is necessary that:

a. The service organization identify and appropriately describe such control objectives and the relevant controls.

b. The service auditor consider the linkage of the controls to the stated control objectives.

c. The service auditor obtain sufficient appropriate audit evidence to reach an opinion.

.50 The control objectives may be designated by the service organization or by outside parties such as regulatory authorities, a user group, or others. When the control objectives are not established by outside parties, the service auditor should be satisfied that the control objectives, as set forth by the service organization, are reasonable in the circumstances and consistent with the service organization's contractual obligations.

.51 The service auditor's report should state whether the controls were suitably designed to achieve the specified control objectives. The report should not state whether they were suitably designed to achieve objectives beyond the specifically identified control objectives.

.52 The service auditor's opinion on whether the controls were suitably designed to achieve the specified control objectives is not intended to provide evidence of operating effectiveness or to provide the user auditor with a basis for concluding that control risk may be assessed as low or moderate. Evidence that may enable the user auditor to conclude that control risk may be assessed as low or moderate may be obtained from the results of specific tests of operating effectiveness. [Revised, May 2007, to reflect conforming changes necessary due to the issuance of Statement on Auditing Standards No. 109.]

.53 The management of the service organization specifies whether all or selected applications and control objectives will be covered by the tests of operating effectiveness. The service auditor determines which controls are, in his or her judgment, necessary to achieve the control objectives specified by management. The service auditor then determines the nature, timing, and extent of the tests of controls needed to evaluate operating effectiveness. Testing should be applied to controls in effect throughout the period covered by the report. To be useful to user auditors, the report should ordinarily cover a minimum reporting period of six months.

.54 The following is a sample report on controls placed in operation at a service organization and tests of operating effectiveness. It should be assumed that the report has two attachments: (*a*) a description of the service organization's controls that may be relevant to a user organization's internal control as it relates to an audit of financial statements and (*b*) a description of controls for which tests of operating effectiveness were performed, the control objectives the controls were intended to achieve, the tests applied, and the results of those tests. This report is illustrative only and should be modified as appropriate to suit the circumstances of individual engagements.

To XYZ Service Organization:

We have examined the accompanying description of controls related to the ___ application of XYZ Service Organization. Our examination included procedures to obtain reasonable assurance about whether (1) the accompanying description presents fairly, in all material respects, the aspects of XYZ Service Organization's controls that may be relevant to a user organization's internal control as it relates to an audit of financial statements, (2) the controls included in the description were suitably designed to achieve the control objectives specified in the description, if those controls were complied with satisfactorily,[4] and (3) such controls had been placed in operation as of ____. The control objectives were specified by ___. Our examination was performed in accordance with standards established by the American Institute of Certified Public Accountants and included those procedures we considered necessary in the circumstances to obtain a reasonable basis for rendering our opinion.

In our opinion, the accompanying description of the aforementioned application presents fairly, in all material respects, the relevant aspects of XYZ Service Organization's controls that had been placed in operation as of ___. Also, in our opinion, the controls, as described, are suitably designed to provide reasonable assurance that the specified control objectives would be achieved if the described controls were complied with satisfactorily.

In addition to the procedures we considered necessary to render our opinion as expressed in the previous paragraph, we applied tests to specific controls, listed in Schedule X, to obtain evidence about their effectiveness in meeting the control objectives, described in Schedule X, during the period from ___ to ___. The specific controls and the nature, timing, extent, and results of the tests are listed in Schedule X. This information has been provided to user organizations of XYZ Service Organization and to their auditors to be taken into consideration, along with information about the internal control at user organizations, when making assessments of control risk for user organizations. In our opinion the controls that were tested, as described in Schedule X, were operating with sufficient effectiveness to provide reasonable, but not absolute, assurance that the control objectives specified in Schedule X were achieved during the period from ___ to ___. [However, the scope of our engagement did not include tests to determine whether control objectives not listed in Schedule X were achieved; accordingly, we express no opinion on the achievement of control objectives not included in Schedule X.][5]

The relative effectiveness and significance of specific controls at XYZ Service Organization and their effect on assessments of control risk at user organizations are dependent on their interaction with the controls and other factors present at individual user organizations. We have performed no procedures to evaluate the effectiveness of controls at individual user organizations.

The description of controls at XYZ Service Organization is as of ____, and information about tests of the operating effectiveness of specific controls covers

---

[4] If the application of controls by user organizations is necessary to achieve the stated control objectives, the service auditor's report should be modified to include the phrase "and user organizations applied the controls contemplated in the design of XYZ Service Organization's controls" following the words "complied with satisfactorily" in the scope and opinion paragraphs. [Footnote renumbered, April 2002, to reflect conforming changes necessary due to the issuance of Statement on Standards for Attestation Engagements No. 10.]

[5] This sentence should be added when all of the control objectives listed in the description of controls placed in operation are not covered by the tests of operating effectiveness. This sentence would be omitted when all of the control objectives listed in the description of controls placed in operation are included in the tests of operating effectiveness. [Footnote renumbered, April 2002, to reflect conforming changes necessary due to the issuance of Statement on Standards for Attestation Engagements No. 10.]

the period from ___ to ___. Any projection of such information to the future is subject to the risk that, because of change, the description may no longer portray the controls in existence. The potential effectiveness of specific controls at the Service Organization is subject to inherent limitations and, accordingly, errors or fraud may occur and not be detected. Furthermore, the projection of any conclusions, based on our findings, to future periods is subject to the risk that changes may alter the validity of such conclusions.

This report is intended solely for use by the management of XYZ Service Organization, its customers, and the independent auditors of its customers.

.55 If the service auditor concludes that the description is inaccurate or insufficiently complete for user auditors, the service auditor should so state in an explanatory paragraph preceding the opinion paragraph. An example of such an explanatory paragraph follows:

The accompanying description states that XYZ Service Organization uses operator identification numbers and passwords to prevent unauthorized access to the system. Based on inquiries of staff personnel and inspection of activities, we determined that such procedures are employed in Applications A and B but are not required to access the system in Applications C and D.

In addition, the first sentence of the opinion paragraph would be modified to read as follows:

In our opinion, except for the matter referred to in the preceding paragraph, the accompanying description of the aforementioned application presents fairly, in all material respects, the relevant aspects of XYZ Service Organization's controls that had been placed in operation as of ___.

.56 If, after applying the criteria in paragraph .47, the service auditor concludes that there are significant deficiencies in the design or operation of the service organization's controls, the service auditor should report those conditions in an explanatory paragraph preceding the opinion paragraph. An example of an explanatory paragraph describing a significant deficiency in the design or operation of the service organization's controls follows:

As discussed in the accompanying description, from time to time the Service Organization makes changes in application programs to correct deficiencies or to enhance capabilities. The procedures followed in determining whether to make changes, in designing the changes, and in implementing them do not include review and approval by authorized individuals who are independent from those involved in making the changes. There are also no specified requirements to test such changes or provide test results to an authorized reviewer prior to implementing the changes.

In addition, the second sentence of the opinion paragraph would be modified to read as follows:

Also in our opinion, except for the deficiency referred to in the preceding paragraph, the controls, as described, are suitably designed to provide reasonable assurance that the related control objectives would be achieved if the described controls were complied with satisfactorily.

Responsibilities of Service Organizations and Service Auditors With Respect to Subsequent Events

.57 Changes in a service organization's controls that could affect user organizations' information systems may occur subsequent to the period covered by the service auditor's report but before the date of the service auditor's report. These occurrences are referred to as subsequent events. A service auditor should consider information about two types of subsequent events that come to his or her attention. [Paragraph added, effective for reports issued on or after January 1, 2003, by Statement on Auditing Standards No. 98.]

.58 The first type consists of events that provide additional information about conditions that existed during the period covered by the service auditor's report. This information should be used by the service auditor in determining whether controls at the service organization that could affect user organizations' information systems were placed in operation, suitably designed, and, if applicable, operating effectively during the period covered by the engagement. [Paragraph added, effective for reports issued on or after January 1, 2003, by Statement on Auditing Standards No. 98.]

.59 The second type consists of those events that provide information about conditions that arose subsequent to the period covered by the service auditor's report that are of such a nature and significance that their disclosure is necessary to prevent users from being misled. This type of information ordinarily will not affect the service auditor's report if the information is adequately disclosed by management in a section of the report containing "Other Information Provided by the Service Organization." If this information is not disclosed by the service organization, the service auditor should disclose it in a section of the report containing "Other Information Provided by the Service Auditor" and/or in the service auditor's report. [Paragraph added, effective for reports issued on or after January 1, 2003, by Statement on Auditing Standards No. 98.]

.60 Although a service auditor has no responsibility to detect subsequent events, the service auditor should inquire of management as to whether it is aware of any subsequent events through the date of the service auditor's report that would have a significant effect on user organizations. In addition, a service auditor should obtain a representation from management regarding subsequent events. [Paragraph added, effective for reports issued on or after January 1, 2003, by Statement on Auditing Standards No. 98.]

Written Representations of the Service Organization's Management

.61 Regardless of the type of report issued, the service auditor should obtain written representations from the service organization's management that:

- Acknowledge management's responsibility for establishing and maintaining appropriate controls relating to the processing of transactions for user organizations.
- Acknowledge the appropriateness of the specified control objectives.
- State that the description of controls presents fairly, in all material respects, the aspects of the service organization's controls that may be relevant to a user organization's internal control.
- State that the controls, as described, had been placed in operation as of a specific date.
- State that management believes its controls were suitably designed to achieve the specified control objectives.
- State that management has disclosed to the service auditor any significant changes in controls that have occurred since the service organization's last examination.

- State that management has disclosed to the service auditor any illegal acts, fraud, or uncorrected errors attributable to the service organization's management or employees that may affect one or more user organizations.
- State that management has disclosed to the service auditor all design deficiencies in controls of which it is aware, including those for which management believes the cost of corrective action may exceed the benefits.
- State that management has disclosed to the service auditor any subsequent events that would have a significant effect on user organizations.

If the scope of the work includes tests of operating effectiveness, the service auditor should obtain a written representation from the service organization's management stating that management has disclosed to the service auditor all instances, of which it is aware, when controls have not operated with sufficient effectiveness to achieve the specified control objectives. [Paragraph renumbered and amended, effective for reports issued on or after January 1, 2003, by Statement on Auditing Standards No. 98.]

Reporting on Substantive Procedures

.62 The service auditor may be requested to apply substantive procedures to user transactions or assets at the service organization. In such circumstances, the service auditor may make specific reference in his or her report to having carried out the designated procedures or may provide a separate report in accordance with AT section 201, *Agreed-Upon Procedures Engagements*. Either form of reporting should include a description of the nature, timing, extent, and results of the procedures in sufficient detail to be useful to user auditors in deciding whether to use the results as evidence to support their opinions. [Revised, January 2001, to reflect conforming changes necessary due to the issuance of Statement on Standards for Attestation Engagements No. 10. Paragraph renumbered by the issuance of Statement on Auditing Standards No. 98, September 2002.]

Effective Date

.63 This section is effective for service auditors' reports dated after March 31, 1993. Earlier application of this section is encouraged. [Paragraph renumbered by the issuance of Statement on Auditing Standards No. 98, September 2002.]

AU Section 9324

Service Organizations: Auditing Interpretations of Section 324

1. Describing Tests of Operating Effectiveness and the Results of Such Tests

.01 *Question*—Paragraph .44*f* of section 324, *Service Organizations*, specifies the elements that should be included in a description of tests of operating effectiveness, which is part of a report on controls placed in operation and tests of operating effectiveness. Section 324.44*f* states:

> "...The description should include the controls that were tested, the control objectives the controls were intended to achieve, the tests applied and the results of the tests. The description should include an indication of the nature, timing, and extent of the tests, as well as sufficient detail to enable user auditors to determine the effect of such tests on user auditors' assessments of control risk. To the extent that the service auditor identified causative factors for exceptions, determined the current status of corrective actions, or obtained other relevant qualitative information about exceptions noted, such information should be provided."

When a service auditor performs an engagement that includes tests of operating effectiveness, what information and how much detail should be included in the description of the "tests applied" and the "results of the tests"?

.02 *Interpretation*—In all cases, for each control objective tested, the description of tests of operating effectiveness should include all of the elements listed in section 324.44*f*, whether or not the service auditor concludes that the control objective has been achieved. The description should provide sufficient information to enable user auditors to assess control risk for financial statement assertions affected by the service organization. The description need not be a duplication of the service auditor's detailed audit program, which in some cases would make the report too voluminous for user auditors and would provide more than the required level of detail.

.03 In describing the nature, timing, and extent of the tests applied, the service auditor also should indicate whether the items tested represent a sample or all of the items in the population, but need not indicate the size of the population. In describing the results of the tests, the service auditor should include exceptions and other information that in the service auditor's judgment could be relevant to user auditors. Such exceptions and other information should be included for each control objective, whether or not the service auditor concludes that the control objective has been achieved. When exceptions that could be relevant to user auditors are noted, the description also should include the following information:

- The size of the sample, when sampling has been used
- The number of exceptions noted
- The nature of the exceptions

If no exceptions or other information that could be relevant to user auditors are identified by the tests, the service auditor should indicate that finding (for example, "No relevant exceptions noted").

[Issue Date: April, 1995.]

2. Service Organizations That Use the Services of Other Service Organizations (Subservice Organizations)

.04 *Question*—A service organization may use the services of another service organization, such as a bank trust department that uses an independent computer processing service organization to perform its data processing. In this situation, the bank trust department is a service organization and the computer processing service organization is considered a subservice organization. How are a user auditor's and a service auditor's procedures affected when a service organization uses a subservice organization?

.05 *Interpretation*—When a service organization uses a subservice organization, the user auditor should determine whether the processing performed by the subservice organization affects assertions in the user organization's financial statements and whether those assertions are significant to the user organization's financial statements. To plan the audit and assess control risk, a user auditor may need to consider the controls at both the service organization and the subservice organization. Paragraphs .06–.17 of section 324, *Service Organizations*, provide guidance to user auditors on considering the effect of a service organization on a user organization's internal control. Although section 324.06–.17 do not specifically refer to subservice organizations, when a subservice organization provides services to a service organization, the guidance in these paragraphs should be interpreted to include the subservice organization. For example, in situations where subservice organizations are used, the interaction between the user organization and the service organization described in section 324.06 would be expanded to include the interaction between the user organization, the service organization and the subservice organization.

.06 Similarly, a service auditor engaged to examine the controls of a service organization and issue a service auditor's report may need to consider functions performed by the subservice organization and the effect of the subservice organization's controls on the service organization.

.07 The degree of interaction and the nature and materiality of the transactions processed by the service organization and the subservice organization are the most important factors to consider in determining the significance of the subservice organization's controls to the user organization's internal control. Section 324.11–.16 describe how a user auditor's assessment of control risk is affected when a user organization uses a service organization. When a subservice organization is involved, the user auditor may need to consider activities at both the service organization and the subservice organization in applying the guidance in these paragraphs.

.08 *Question*—How does a user auditor obtain information about controls at a subservice organization?

.09 *Interpretation*—If a user auditor concludes that he or she needs information about the subservice organization to plan the audit or to assess control risk, the user auditor (*a*) may contact the service organization through the user organization and may contact the subservice organization either through the user organization or the service organization to obtain specific information or (*b*) may request that a service auditor be engaged to perform procedures that will supply the necessary information. Alternatively, the user auditor may visit the service organization or subservice organization and perform such procedures.

.10 *Question*—When a service organization uses a subservice organization, what information about the subservice organization should be included in the service organization's description of controls?

.11 *Interpretation*—A service organization's description of controls should include a description of the functions and nature of the processing performed by the subservice organization in sufficient detail for user auditors to understand the significance of the subservice organization's functions to the processing of the user organizations' transactions. Ordinarily, disclosure of the identity of the subservice organization is not required. However, if the service organization determines that the identity of the subservice organization would be relevant to user organizations, the name of the subservice organization may be included in the description. The purpose of the description of the functions and nature of the processing performed by the subservice organization is to alert user organizations and their auditors to the fact that another entity (that is, the subservice organization) is involved in the processing of the user organizations' transactions and to summarize the functions the subservice organization performs.

.12 When a subservice organization performs services for a service organization, there are two alternative methods of presenting the description of controls. The service organization determines which method will be used.

a. *The Carve-Out Method*—The subservice organization's relevant control objectives and controls are excluded from the description and from the scope of the service auditor's engagement. The service organization states in the description that the subservice organization's control objectives and related controls are omitted from the description and that the control objectives in the report include only the objectives the service organization's controls are intended to achieve.

b. *The Inclusive Method*—The subservice organization's relevant controls are included in the description and in the scope of the engagement. The description should clearly differentiate between controls of the service organization and controls of the subservice organization. The set of control objectives includes all of the objectives a user auditor would expect both the service organization and the subservice organization to achieve. To accomplish this, the service organization should coordinate the preparation and presentation of the description of controls with the subservice organization.

In either method, the service organization includes in its description of controls a description of the functions and nature of the processing performed by the subservice organization, as set forth in paragraph .11.

.13 If the functions and processing performed by the subservice organization are significant to the processing of user organization transactions, and the service organization does not disclose the existence of the subservice organization and the functions it performs, the service auditor may need to issue a qualified or adverse opinion as to the fairness of the presentation of the description of controls.

.14 *Question*—How is the service auditor's report affected by the method of presentation selected?

.15 *Interpretation*—If the service organization has adopted the carve-out method, the service auditor should modify the scope paragraph of the service auditor's report to briefly summarize the functions and nature of the processing performed by the subservice organization. This summary ordinarily would be briefer than the information provided by the service organization in its description of the functions and nature of the processing performed by the subservice organization. The service auditor should include a statement in the scope paragraph of the service auditor's report indicating that the description of controls includes only the control objectives and related controls of the service organization; accordingly, the service auditor's examination does not extend to controls at the subservice organization.

.16 An example of the scope paragraph of a service auditor's report using the carve-out method is presented below. Additional or modified report language is shown in ***boldface italics***.

Sample Scope Paragraph of a Service Auditor's Report Using the Carve-Out Method

Independent Service Auditor's Report

To the Board of Directors of Example Trust Company:

We have examined the accompanying description of the controls of Example Trust Company applicable to the processing of transactions for users of the Institutional Trust Division. Our examination included procedures to obtain reasonable assurance about whether (1) the accompanying description presents fairly, in all material respects, the aspects of Example Trust Company's controls that may be relevant to a user organization's internal control as it relates to an audit of financial statements; (2) the controls included in the description were suitably designed to achieve the control objectives specified in the description, if those controls were complied with satisfactorily, and user organizations applied the controls contemplated in the design of Example Trust Company's controls; and (3) such controls had been placed in operation as of June 30, 20XX. ***Example Trust Company uses a computer processing service organization for all of its computerized application processing. The accompanying description includes only those control objectives and related controls of Example Trust Company and does not include control objectives and related controls of the computer processing service organization. Our examination did not extend to controls of the computer processing service organization.*** The control objectives were specified by the management of Example Trust Company. Our examination was performed in accordance with standards established by the American Institute of Certified Public Accountants and included those procedures we considered necessary in the circumstances to obtain a reasonable basis for rendering our opinion.

[The remainder of the report is the same as the standard service auditor's report illustrated in section 324.38 and .54.]

.17 If the service organization has used the inclusive method, the service auditor should perform procedures comparable to those described in section 324.12. Such procedures may include performing tests of the service organization's controls over the activities of the subservice organization or performing procedures at the subservice organization. If the service auditor will be performing procedures at the subservice organization, the service organization should arrange for such procedures. The service auditor should recognize that the subservice organization generally is not the client for the engagement. Accordingly, in these circumstances the service auditor should determine whether it will be possible to obtain the required evidence to support the portion of the opinion covering the subservice organization and whether it will be possible to obtain an appropriate letter of representations regarding the subservice organization's controls.

.18 An example of a service auditor's report using the inclusive method is presented below. Additional or modified report language is shown in ***boldface italics***.

Sample Service Auditor's Report Using the Inclusive Method

Independent Service Auditor's Report

To the Board of Directors of Example Trust Company:

We have examined the accompanying description of the controls of Example Trust Company ***and Computer Processing Service Organization, an independent service organization that provides computer processing services to Example Trust Company,*** applicable to the processing of transactions for users of the Institutional Trust Division. Our examination included procedures to obtain reasonable assurance about whether (1) the accompanying description presents fairly, in all material respects, the aspects of Example Trust Company's ***and Computer Processing Service Organization's*** controls that may be relevant to a user organization's internal control as it relates to an audit of financial statements; (2) the controls included in the description were suitably designed to achieve the control objectives specified in the description, if those controls were complied with satisfactorily, and user organizations applied the controls contemplated in the design of Example Trust Company's controls; and (3) the controls had been placed in operation as of June 30, 20XX. The control objectives were specified by the management of Example Trust Company. Our examination was performed in accordance with standards established by the American Institute of Certified Public Accountants and included those procedures we considered necessary in the circumstances to obtain a reasonable basis for rendering our opinion.

In our opinion, the accompanying description of the aforementioned controls presents fairly, in all material respects, the relevant aspects of Example Trust Company's ***and Computer Processing Service Organization's*** controls that had been placed in operation as of June 30, 20XX. Also, in our opinion, the controls, as described, are suitably designed to provide reasonable assurance that the specified control objectives would be achieved if the described controls were complied with satisfactorily and user organizations applied the controls contemplated in the design of Example Trust Company's controls.

In addition to the procedures we considered necessary to render our opinion as expressed in the previous paragraph, we applied tests to specific controls, listed in Schedule X to obtain evidence about their effectiveness in meeting the control objectives, described in Schedule X, during the period from January 1, 20XX, to June 30, 20XX. The specific controls and the nature, timing, extent, and results of the tests are listed in Schedule X. This information has been provided to user organizations of Example Trust Company and to their auditors to be taken into consideration, along with information about internal control at user organizations, when making assessments of control risk for user organizations.

In our opinion the controls that were tested, as described in Schedule X, were operating with sufficient effectiveness to provide reasonable, but not absolute, assurance that the control objectives specified in Schedule X were achieved during the period from January 1, 20XX, to June 30, 20XX.

The relative effectiveness and significance of specific controls at Example Trust Company ***and Computer Processing Service Organization***, and their effect on assessments of control risk at user organizations are dependent on their interaction with the controls and other factors present at individual user organizations. We have performed no procedures to evaluate the effectiveness of controls at individual user organizations.

The description of controls at Example Trust Company ***and Computer Processing Service Organization*** is as of June 30, 20XX, and information about tests of the operating effectiveness of specific controls covers the period from January 1, 20XX, to June 30, 20XX. Any projection of such information to the future is subject to the risk that, because of change, the description may no longer portray the controls in existence. The potential effectiveness of specific controls at the Service Organization ***and Computer Processing Service Organization*** is subject to inherent limitations and, accordingly, errors or fraud may occur and not be detected. Furthermore, the projection of any conclusions, based on our findings, to future periods is subject to the risk that changes may alter the validity of such conclusions.[1]

This report is intended solely for use by the management of Example Trust Company, its users, and the independent auditors of its users.

July 10, 20XX

[Issue Date: April, 1995; Revised: February, 1997; Revised: April, 2002.]

[3.] Responsibilities of Service Organizations and Service Auditors With Respect to Information About the Year 2000 Issue in a Service Organization's Description of Controls

[.19–.34] [Withdrawn July 2000 by the Audit Issues Task Force.]

4. Responsibilities of Service Organizations and Service Auditors With Respect to Forward-Looking Information in a Service Organization's Description of Controls

.35 *Question*—Section 324.32 requires a service auditor to consider "whether any other information, irrespective of specified control objectives, has come to his or her attention that causes him or her to conclude (*a*) that design deficiencies exist that could adversely affect the ability to initiate, authorize, record, process, or report financial data to user organizations without error, and (*b*) that user organizations would not generally be expected to have controls in place to mitigate such design deficiencies." A service auditor performing a service auditor's engagement may become aware that a service organization, whose system is correctly processing data during the period covered by the service auditor's examination, has not performed contingency planning or made adequate provision for disaster recovery, and may not be able to retrieve or process data in future periods. Does section 324.32 require a service

[1] This sentence has been expanded to describe the risks of projecting any evaluation of the controls to future periods because of the failure to make needed changes to a system or controls, as provided for in Interpretation No. 5, "Statements About the Risk of Projecting Evaluations of the Effectiveness of Controls to Future Periods" (paragraphs .38–.40).

auditor to identify, in his or her report, design deficiencies that do not affect processing during the period covered by the service auditor's examination but may represent potential problems in future periods?

.36 *Interpretation*—No. Section 324.32 addresses design deficiencies that could adversely affect processing *during the period covered by the service auditor's examination*. Section 324.32 does not apply to design deficiencies that potentially could affect processing *in future periods*. If the computer programs are correctly processing data during the period covered by the service auditor's examination, and such design deficiencies currently do not affect user organizations' abilities to initiate, authorize, record, process, or report financial data, the service auditor would not be required to report such design deficiencies in his or her report, based on the requirements in section 324.32. However, if a service auditor becomes aware of design deficiencies at the service organization that could potentially affect the processing of user organizations' transactions in future periods, the service auditor, in his or her judgment, may choose to communicate this information to the service organization's management and advise management to disclose this information and its plans for correcting the design deficiencies in a section of the service auditor's document titled "Other Information Provided by the Service Organization."[2]

.37 If the service organization includes information about the design deficiencies in the section of the document titled "Other Information Provided by the Service Organization," the service auditor should read the information and consider applying by analogy the guidance in section 550, *Other Information in Documents Containing Audited Financial Statements*. In addition, the service auditor should include a paragraph in his or her report disclaiming an opinion on the information provided by the service organization. The following is an example of such a paragraph.

> The information in section 4 describing XYZ Service Organization's plans to modify its disaster recovery plan is presented by the Service Organization to provide additional information and is not a part of the Service Organization's description of controls that may be relevant to a user organization's internal control. Such information has not been subjected to the procedures applied in the examination of the description of the controls applicable to the processing of transactions for user organizations and, accordingly, we do not express an opinion or provide any assurance on it.

A service auditor also may consider communicating information about the design deficiencies in the section of the service auditor's document titled "Other Information Provided by the Service Auditor."

[Issue Date: February 2002; Revised: March 2006. Revised: December 2010.]

5. Statements About the Risk of Projecting Evaluations of the Effectiveness of Controls to Future Periods

.38 *Question*—Section 324.29*g* and .44*l* state that a service auditor's report should contain a statement of the inherent limitations of the potential

---

[2] Chapter 2 of the AICPA Audit Guide *Service Organizations: Applying SAS No. 70, as Amended*, proposes four sections of a service auditor's document.

1. Independent service auditor's report (the letter from the service auditor expressing his or her opinion)
2. Service organization's description of controls
3. Information provided by the independent service auditor (This section generally contains a description of the service auditor's tests of operating effectiveness and the results of those tests.)
4. Other information provided by the service organization

effectiveness of controls at the service organization and of the risk of projecting to future periods any evaluation of the description. Section 324.44*l* goes on to state that the report also should refer to the risk of projecting to the future "any conclusions about the effectiveness of controls in achieving control objectives." The sample service auditor's reports in section 324.38 and .54 include illustrative paragraphs that illustrate this caveat. The following excerpt is from section 324.54:

> The description of controls at XYZ Service Organization is as of________, and information about tests of the operating effectiveness of specific controls covers the period from ________to ________. Any projection of such information to the future is subject to the risk that, because of change, the description may no longer portray the controls in existence. The potential effectiveness of specific controls at the Service Organization is subject to inherent limitations and, accordingly, errors or fraud may occur and not be detected. Furthermore, the projection of any conclusions, based on our findings, to future periods is subject to the risk that changes may alter the validity of such conclusions.

The validity of projections to the future about the effectiveness of controls may be affected by changes made to the system and the controls, and also by the failure to make needed changes, for example, changes to accommodate new processing requirements. May a service auditor's report be expanded to describe the risk of projecting to the future conclusions about the effectiveness of controls?

.39 *Interpretation*—The sample reports in section 324.38 and .54 may be expanded to describe this risk. The first and second sentences of the illustrative paragraph above address the potential effect of change on the description of controls as of a specified date; accordingly, they do not require modification because new processing requirements would not affect the description as of the specified date. However, the last sentence in the sample report paragraph above could be expanded to describe the risk of projecting an evaluation of the controls to future periods because of changes to the system or controls, or the failure to make needed changes to the system or controls.

.40 Suggested additions to the paragraph in the illustrative service auditor's reports in section 324.38 and .54 are the following (new language is shown in italics.):

> The description of controls at XYZ Service Organization is as of ________, and information about tests of the operating effectiveness of specific controls covers the period from ________ to ________. Any projection of such information to the future is subject to the risk that, because of change, the description may no longer portray the controls in existence. The potential effectiveness of specific controls at the Service Organization is subject to inherent limitations and, accordingly, errors or fraud may occur and not be detected. Furthermore, the projection of any conclusions, based on our findings, to future periods is subject to the risk that changes *made to the system or controls, or the failure to make needed changes to the system or controls*, may alter the validity of such conclusions.

[Issue Date: February, 2002.]

[6.] Responsibilities of Service Organizations and Service Auditors With Respect to Subsequent Events in a Service Auditor's Engagement

[.41–.42] [Rescinded September 2002, by Statement on Auditing Standards No. 98.]

AU Section 325

Communicating Internal Control Related Matters Identified in an Audit

(Supersedes SAS No. 112.)

Source: SAS No. 115.

Effective for audits of financial statements for periods ending on or after December 15, 2009. Earlier implementation is permitted.

Applicability

.01 This section establishes standards and provides guidance on communicating matters related to an entity's internal control over financial reporting identified in an audit of financial statements. It is applicable whenever an auditor expresses or disclaims an opinion on financial statements. In particular, this section

- defines the terms *deficiency in internal control*, *significant deficiency*, and *material weakness*.
- provides guidance on evaluating the severity of deficiencies in internal control identified in an audit of financial statements.
- requires the auditor to communicate, in writing, to management and those charged with governance,[1] significant deficiencies and material weaknesses identified in an audit.

.02 This section is not applicable if the auditor is engaged to examine the design and operating effectiveness of an entity's internal control over financial reporting that is integrated with an audit of the entity's financial statements under AT section 501, *An Examination of an Entity's Internal Control Over Financial Reporting That Is Integrated With an Audit of Its Financial Statements*.

Introduction

.03 Internal control is a process—effected by those charged with governance, management, and other personnel—designed to provide reasonable assurance about the achievement of the entity's objectives with regard to the reliability of financial reporting, effectiveness and efficiency of operations, and compliance with applicable laws and regulations. Internal control over the safeguarding of assets against unauthorized acquisition, use, or disposition may include controls related to financial reporting and operations objectives. Generally, controls that are relevant to an audit of financial statements are those

---

[1] The term *those charged with governance* is defined in paragraph .03 of section 380, *The Auditor's Communication With Those Charged With Governance*, as "the person(s) with responsibility for overseeing the strategic direction of the entity and obligations related to the accountability of the entity. This includes overseeing the financial reporting process. In some cases, those charged with governance are responsible for approving the entity's financial statements (in other cases management has this responsibility). For entities with a board of directors, this term encompasses the term *board of directors* or *audit committee* used elsewhere in generally accepted auditing standards."

that pertain to the entity's objective of reliable financial reporting. In this section, the term *financial reporting* relates to the preparation of reliable financial statements that are fairly presented in conformity with generally accepted accounting principles (GAAP).[2] The design and formality of an entity's internal control will vary depending on the entity's size, the industry in which it operates, its culture, and management's philosophy.

.04 In an audit of financial statements, the auditor is not required to perform procedures to identify deficiencies in internal control[3,4] or to express an opinion on the effectiveness of the entity's internal control. However, during the course of an audit, the auditor may become aware of deficiencies in internal control while obtaining an understanding of the entity and its environment, including its internal control, assessing the risks of material misstatement of the financial statements due to error or fraud, performing further audit procedures to respond to assessed risks, communicating with management or others (for example, internal auditors or governmental authorities), or otherwise. The auditor's awareness of deficiencies in internal control varies with each audit and is influenced by the nature, timing, and extent of audit procedures performed, as well as other factors.

Definitions

.05 A deficiency in internal control exists when the design or operation of a control does not allow management or employees, in the normal course of performing their assigned functions, to prevent, or detect and correct misstatements on a timely basis.

A deficiency in *design* exists when

- a control necessary to meet the control objective is missing; or
- an existing control is not properly designed so that, even if the control operates as designed, the control objective would not be met.

A deficiency in *operation* exists when

- a properly designed control does not operate as designed; or
- the person performing the control does not possess the necessary authority or competence to perform the control effectively.

.06 A material weakness is a deficiency, or combination of deficiencies, in internal control, such that there is a reasonable possibility[5] that a material misstatement of the entity's financial statements will not be prevented, or detected and corrected on a timely basis.

.07 A significant deficiency is a deficiency, or a combination of deficiencies, in internal control that is less severe than a material weakness, yet important enough to merit attention by those charged with governance.

---

[2] Reference to generally accepted accounting principles includes, where applicable, a comprehensive basis of accounting other than generally accepted accounting principles, as that term is defined in paragraph .04 of section 623, *Special Reports*, as amended.

[3] Hereinafter in this section, the term *internal control* means internal control over financial reporting.

[4] Section 314, *Understanding the Entity and its Environment and Assessing the Risks of Material Misstatement*, contains a detailed discussion of internal control and identifies the following five interrelated components of internal control: (*a*) the control environment, (*b*) the entity's risk assessment, (*c*) information and communication systems, (*d*) control activities, and (*e*) monitoring.

[5] In this section, a reasonable possibility exists when the likelihood of the event is either *reasonably possible* or *probable* as those terms are defined in the Financial Accounting Standards Board *Accounting Standards Codification* glossary. [Footnote revised, June 2009, to reflect conforming changes necessary due to the issuance of FASB ASC.]

Evaluating Deficiencies Identified as Part of the Audit

.08 The auditor should evaluate the severity of each deficiency in internal control[6] identified during the audit to determine whether the deficiency, individually or in combination, is a significant deficiency or a material weakness. The severity of a deficiency depends on

- the magnitude of the potential misstatement resulting from the deficiency or deficiencies; and
- whether there is a reasonable possibility that the entity's controls will fail to prevent, or detect and correct a misstatement of an account balance or disclosure.

The severity of a deficiency does not depend on whether a misstatement actually occurred.

.09 Factors that affect the magnitude of a misstatement that might result from a deficiency or deficiencies include, but are not limited to, the following:

- The financial statement amounts or total of transactions exposed to the deficiency
- The volume of activity (in the current period or expected in future periods) in the account or class of transactions exposed to the deficiency

.10 In evaluating the magnitude of the potential misstatement, the maximum amount by which an account balance or total of transactions can be overstated generally is the recorded amount, whereas understatements could be larger.

.11 Risk factors affect whether there is a reasonable possibility that a deficiency, or a combination of deficiencies, will result in a misstatement of an account balance or disclosure. The factors include, but are not limited to, the following:

- The nature of the financial statement accounts, classes of transactions, disclosures, and assertions involved
- The susceptibility of the related asset or liability to loss or fraud
- The subjectivity, complexity, or extent of judgment required to determine the amount involved
- The interaction or relationship of the control with other controls
- The interaction among the deficiencies
- The possible future consequences of the deficiency

.12 The evaluation of whether a deficiency presents a reasonable possibility of misstatement may be made without quantifying the probability of occurrence as a specific percentage or range. Also, in many cases, the probability of a small misstatement will be greater than the probability of a large misstatement.

.13 Multiple deficiencies that affect the same significant account or disclosure, relevant assertion, or component of internal control increase the likelihood of material misstatement and may, in combination, constitute a significant deficiency or a material weakness, even though such deficiencies individually may

---

[6] Hereinafter in this section, the term *deficiency in internal control* is referred to as a *deficiency* or *deficiencies*.

be less severe. Therefore, the auditor should determine whether deficiencies that affect the same significant account or disclosure, relevant assertion, or component of internal control collectively result in a significant deficiency or a material weakness.

.14 When performing substantive procedures or tests of the operating effectiveness of controls, the auditor may obtain evidence that a control does not operate effectively; for example, by identifying a misstatement that was not prevented, or detected and corrected by the control. Management may inform the auditor, or the auditor may otherwise become aware, of the existence of compensating controls that, if effective, may limit the severity of the deficiency and prevent it from being a significant deficiency or a material weakness. In these circumstances, although the auditor is not required to consider the effects of compensating controls for purposes of this section, the auditor may consider the effects of compensating controls related to a deficiency in operation provided the auditor has tested the compensating controls for operating effectiveness as part of the financial statement audit. Compensating controls can limit the severity of the deficiency, but do not eliminate the deficiency.

.15 Indicators of material weaknesses in internal control include

- identification of fraud, whether or not material, on the part of senior management;
- restatement of previously issued financial statements to reflect the correction of a material misstatement due to error or fraud;
- identification by the auditor of a material misstatement of the financial statements under audit in circumstances that indicate that the misstatement would not have been detected by the entity's internal control; and
- ineffective oversight of the entity's financial reporting and internal control by those charged with governance.

.16 If the auditor determines that a deficiency, or a combination of deficiencies, is not a material weakness, the auditor should consider whether prudent officials, having knowledge of the same facts and circumstances, would likely reach the same conclusion.

Communication—Form, Content, and Timing

.17 Deficiencies identified during the audit that upon evaluation are considered significant deficiencies or material weaknesses under this section should be communicated, in writing, to management and those charged with governance as a part of each audit, including significant deficiencies and material weaknesses that were communicated to management and those charged with governance in previous audits and have not yet been remediated. Significant deficiencies and material weaknesses that previously were communicated and have not yet been remediated may be communicated, in writing, by referring to the previously issued written communication and the date of that communication.

.18 The written communication referred to in paragraph .17 is best made by the report release date,[7] which is the date the auditor grants the entity permission to use the auditor's report in connection with the financial statements, but should be made no later than 60 days following the report release date.

---

[7] See paragraph .23 of section 339, *Audit Documentation*, for additional guidance related to the report release date.

.19 For some matters, early communication to management or those charged with governance may be important because of their relative significance and the urgency for corrective follow-up action. Accordingly, the auditor may decide to communicate certain matters during the audit. These matters need not be communicated in writing during the audit, but significant deficiencies and material weaknesses should ultimately be included in a written communication in accordance with paragraphs .17–.18, even if such significant deficiencies or material weaknesses were remediated during the audit.

.20 The existence of significant deficiencies or material weaknesses may already be known to management and may represent a conscious decision by management or those charged with governance to accept the risk associated with the deficiencies because of cost or other considerations. Management is responsible for making decisions concerning costs to be incurred and related benefits. The auditor's responsibility to communicate significant deficiencies and material weaknesses exists regardless of management's decisions.

.21 Nothing precludes the auditor from communicating to management and those charged with governance other matters related to an entity's internal control. For example, the auditor may communicate

- matters the auditor believes to be of potential benefit to the entity, such as recommendations for operational or administrative efficiency, or for improving controls.
- deficiencies that are not significant deficiencies or material weaknesses.

If other matters are communicated orally, the auditor should document the communication.

.22 The written communication regarding significant deficiencies and material weaknesses identified during the audit of financial statements should

- include a statement that indicates the purpose of the auditor's consideration of internal control was to express an opinion on the financial statements, but not to express an opinion on the effectiveness of the entity's internal control.
- include a statement that indicates the auditor is not expressing an opinion on the effectiveness of internal control.
- include a statement that indicates that the auditor's consideration of internal control was not designed to identify all deficiencies in internal control that might be significant deficiencies or material weaknesses.
- include the definition of the term material weakness and, where relevant, the definition of the term significant deficiency.
- identify the matters that are considered to be significant deficiencies and those that are considered to be material weaknesses.
- include a statement that indicates the communication is intended solely for the information and use of management, those charged with governance, and others within the organization and is not intended to be and should not be used by anyone other than these specified parties. If an entity is required to furnish such auditor communications to a governmental authority, specific reference to such governmental authorities may be made.

.23 The auditor may include additional statements in the communication regarding the general inherent limitations of internal control, including the possibility of management override of controls, or the specific nature and extent of the auditor's consideration of internal control during the audit.

.24 Management or those charged with governance may ask the auditor to issue a communication indicating that no material weaknesses were identified during the audit of the financial statements to submit to governmental authorities. Exhibit A includes an illustrative communication when the auditor has not identified any material weaknesses and decides, or has been requested, to advise management and those charged with governance that no material weaknesses were identified.

.25 The auditor should not issue a written communication stating that no significant deficiencies were identified during the audit.

.26 Management may wish to, or may be required by a regulator to, prepare a written response to the auditor's communication regarding significant deficiencies or material weaknesses identified during the audit. Such management communications may include a description of corrective actions taken by the entity, the entity's plans to implement new controls, or a statement indicating that management believes the cost of correcting a significant deficiency or material weakness would exceed the benefits to be derived from doing so. If such a written response is included in a document containing the auditor's written communication to management and those charged with governance concerning identified significant deficiencies or material weaknesses, the auditor may add a paragraph to his or her written communication disclaiming an opinion on such information. Following is an example of such a paragraph:

> ABC Company's written response to the significant deficiencies [*and material weaknesses*] identified in our audit was not subjected to the auditing procedures applied in the audit of the financial statements and, accordingly, we express no opinion on it.

Effective Date

.27 This section is effective for audits of financial statements for periods ending on or after December 15, 2009. Earlier implementation is permitted.

.28

Exhibit A

Illustrative Written Communications

1. The following is an illustrative written communication encompassing the requirements in paragraph .22 of this section:

In planning and performing our audit of the financial statements of ABC Company (the "Company") as of and for the year ended December 31, 20XX, in accordance with auditing standards generally accepted in the United States of America, we considered the Company's internal control over financial reporting (internal control) as a basis for designing our auditing procedures for the purpose of expressing our opinion on the financial statements, but not for the purpose of expressing an opinion on the effectiveness of the Company's internal control. Accordingly, we do not express an opinion on the effectiveness of the Company's internal control.

Our consideration of internal control was for the limited purpose described in the preceding paragraph and was not designed to identify all deficiencies in internal control that might be significant deficiencies or material weaknesses and therefore, there can be no assurance that all deficiencies, significant deficiencies, or material weaknesses have been identified. However, as discussed below, we identified certain deficiencies in internal control that we consider to be material weaknesses [*and other deficiencies that we consider to be significant deficiencies*].

A deficiency in internal control exists when the design or operation of a control does not allow management or employees, in the normal course of performing their assigned functions, to prevent, or detect and correct misstatements on a timely basis. A material weakness is a deficiency, or a combination of deficiencies, in internal control, such that there is a reasonable possibility that a material misstatement of the entity's financial statements will not be prevented, or detected and corrected on a timely basis. [*We consider the following deficiencies in the Company's internal control to be material weaknesses:*]

[*Describe the material weaknesses that were identified.*]

[*A significant deficiency is a deficiency, or a combination of deficiencies, in internal control that is less severe than a material weakness, yet important enough to merit attention by those charged with governance. We consider the following deficiencies in the Company's internal control to be significant deficiencies:*]

[*Describe the significant deficiencies that were identified.*]

This communication is intended solely for the information and use of management, [*identify the body or individuals charged with governance*], others within the organization, and [*identify any specified governmental authorities*] and is not intended to be and should not be used by anyone other than these specified parties.

2. The following is an illustrative written communication indicating that no material weaknesses were identified during the audit.

In planning and performing our audit of the financial statements of ABC Company (the "Company") as of and for the year ended December 31, 20XX, in accordance with auditing standards generally accepted in the United States of America, we considered the Company's internal control over financial reporting (internal control) as a basis for designing our auditing procedures for the purpose of expressing our opinion on the financial statements, but not for the purpose of expressing an opinion on the effectiveness of the Company's internal control. Accordingly, we do not express an opinion on the effectiveness of the Company's internal control.

A deficiency in internal control exists when the design or operation of a control does not allow management or employees, in the normal course of performing their assigned functions, to prevent, or detect and correct misstatements on a timely basis. A material weakness is a deficiency, or combination of deficiencies, in internal control, such that there is a reasonable possibility that a material misstatement of the entity's financial statements will not be prevented, or detected and corrected on a timely basis.

Our consideration of internal control was for the limited purpose described in the first paragraph and was not designed to identify all deficiencies in internal control that might be deficiencies, significant deficiencies, or material weaknesses. We did not identify any deficiencies in internal control that we consider to be material weaknesses, as defined above.

This communication is intended solely for the information and use of management, [*identify the body or individuals charged with governance*], others within the organization, and [*identify any specified governmental authorities*] and is not intended to be and should not be used by anyone other than these specified parties.

If one or more significant deficiencies have been identified, the auditor may add the following sentence to the third paragraph of the communication:

However, we identified certain deficiencies in internal control that we consider to be significant deficiencies, and communicated them in writing to management and those charged with governance on [*date*]. A significant deficiency is a deficiency, or a combination of deficiencies, in internal control that is less severe than a material weakness, yet important enough to merit attention by those charged with governance.

.29

Exhibit B

Examples of Circumstances That May Be Deficiencies, Significant Deficiencies, or Material Weaknesses

Paragraph .15 of this section identifies indicators of material weaknesses in internal control. The following are examples of circumstances that may be deficiencies, significant deficiencies, or material weaknesses:

Deficiencies in the Design of Controls

- Inadequate design of controls over the preparation of the financial statements being audited.
- Inadequate design of controls over a significant account or process.
- Inadequate documentation of the components of internal control.
- Insufficient control consciousness within the organization; for example, the tone at the top and the control environment.
- Absent or inadequate segregation of duties within a significant account or process.
- Absent or inadequate controls over the safeguarding of assets (this applies to controls that the auditor determines would be necessary for effective internal control over financial reporting).
- Inadequate design of IT general and application controls that prevent the information system from providing complete and accurate information consistent with financial reporting objectives and current needs.
- Employees or management who lack the qualifications and training to fulfill their assigned functions. For example, in an entity that prepares financial statements in accordance with generally accepted accounting principles (GAAP), the person responsible for the accounting and reporting function lacks the skills and knowledge to apply GAAP in recording the entity's financial transactions or preparing its financial statements.
- Inadequate design of monitoring controls used to assess the design and operating effectiveness of the entity's internal control over time.
- The absence of an internal process to report deficiencies in internal control to management on a timely basis.

Failures in the Operation of Internal Control

- Failure in the operation of effectively designed controls over a significant account or process; for example, the failure of a control such as dual authorization for significant disbursements within the purchasing process.
- Failure of the information and communication component of internal control to provide complete and accurate output because of deficiencies in timeliness, completeness, or accuracy; for example, the failure to obtain timely and accurate consolidating information from remote locations that is needed to prepare the financial statements.
- Failure of controls designed to safeguard assets from loss, damage, or misappropriation. This circumstance may need careful consideration before it is evaluated as a significant deficiency or material weakness. For example, assume that a company uses security devices to safeguard

its inventory (preventive controls) and also performs periodic physical inventory counts (detective control) timely in relation to its financial reporting. Although the physical inventory count does not safeguard the inventory from theft or loss, it prevents a material misstatement of the financial statements if performed effectively and timely. Therefore, given that the definitions of material weakness and significant deficiency relate to likelihood of misstatement of the financial statements, the failure of a preventive control such as inventory tags will not result in a significant deficiency or material weakness if the detective control (physical inventory) prevents a misstatement of the financial statements. Material weaknesses relating to controls over the safeguarding of assets would only exist if the company does not have effective controls (considering both safeguarding and other controls) to prevent, or detect and correct a material misstatement of the financial statements.

- Failure to perform reconciliations of significant accounts. For example, accounts receivable subsidiary ledgers are not reconciled to the general ledger account in a timely or accurate manner.
- Undue bias or lack of objectivity by those responsible for accounting decisions; for example, consistent understatement of expenses or overstatement of allowances at the direction of management.
- Misrepresentation by entity personnel to the auditor (an indicator of fraud).
- Management override of controls.
- Failure of an application control caused by a deficiency in the design or operation of an IT general control.
- An observed deviation rate that exceeds the number of deviations expected by the auditor in a test of the operating effectiveness of a control. For example, if the auditor designs a test in which he or she selects a sample and expects no deviations, the finding of one deviation is a nonnegligible deviation rate because, based on the results of the auditor's test of the sample, the desired level of confidence was not obtained.

AU Section 9325

Communicating Internal Control Related Matters Identified in an Audit: Auditing Interpretations of Section 325

1. Communicating Deficiencies in Internal Control Over Compliance in an Office of Management and Budget Circular A-133 Audit

.01 *Question*—Section 325, *Communicating Internal Control Related Matters Identified in an Audit*, establishes standards and provides guidance on communicating matters related to an entity's internal control over financial reporting identified in an audit of financial statements. In an audit performed under Office of Management and Budget (OMB) Circular A-133, *Audits of States, Local Governments, and Non-Profit Organizations* (Circular A-133), as amended in a Federal Register Notice on June 26, 2007 (also referred to as a single audit), the auditor also is responsible for reporting significant deficiencies and material weaknesses in internal control over compliance as it relates to major programs.[1] How should the definitions of the terms *deficiency in internal control*, *significant deficiency*, and *material weakness* found in section 325 be adapted and applied in the context of reporting on internal control over compliance in a single audit?

.02 *Interpretation*—Circular A-133 includes guidelines for reporting significant deficiencies and material weaknesses. On March 11, 2010, the OMB issued a statement on its website (in the introductory section of Circular A-133) clarifying that these terms are to be used as defined in generally accepted auditing standards issued by the AICPA and *Government Auditing Standards* issued by the Government Accountability Office. Therefore, the following definitions should be used when an auditor reports on internal control over compliance in a single audit.[2]

> A *deficiency in internal control* over compliance exists when the design or operation of a control over compliance does not allow management or employees, in the normal course of performing their assigned functions, to prevent, or detect and correct, noncompliance with a type of compliance[3] requirement of a federal program on a timely basis.

---

[1] The Federal Register Notice can be found on the Office of Management and Budget (OMB) website at www.whitehouse.gov/omb/fedreg/2007/062607_audits.pdf.

[2] This interpretation does not modify or replace an auditor's responsibility for communicating internal control over financial reporting matters under section 325, *Communicating Internal Control Related Matters Identified in an Audit*, or reporting such matters as required by *Government Auditing Standards* issued by the U.S. Government Accountability Office.

[3] Under Section 510(a)(1) of OMB Circular A-133, *Audits of States, Local Governments, and Non-Profit Organizations*, the auditor's determination of whether a deficiency in internal control over compliance is a material weakness or significant deficiency for the purpose of reporting an audit finding is in relation to a type of compliance requirement for a major program or an audit objective identified in the *OMB Circular A-133 Compliance Supplement* (the *Compliance Supplement*). This reference to "type of compliance requirement" refers to the 14 types of compliance requirements (identified as A-N) described in part 3 of the *Compliance Supplement*. For purposes of reporting audit findings, auditors are alerted that certain of the types of compliance requirements may include multiple compliance requirements with multiple audit objectives (for example, compliance requirement "G" covers 3 separate requirements—matching, level of effort, and earmarking; and "N" covers separate requirements specific to each individual special test and provision).

A *material weakness* in internal control over compliance is a deficiency, or combination of deficiencies, in internal control over compliance, such that there is a reasonable possibility[4] that material noncompliance with a type of compliance requirement[5] of a federal program will not be prevented, or detected and corrected, on a timely basis.

A *significant deficiency* in internal control over compliance is a deficiency, or a combination of deficiencies, in internal control over compliance with a type of compliance requirement[6] of a federal program that is less severe than a material weakness in internal control over compliance, yet important enough to merit attention by those charged with governance.

.03 See also the AICPA Audit Guide Government Auditing Standards *and Circular A-133 Audits* for additional guidance on performing single audits.

[Issue Date: June 2007; Revised: March 2010.]

2. Communication of Significant Deficiencies and Material Weaknesses Prior to the Completion of the Compliance Audit for Participants in Office of Management and Budget Single Audit Pilot Project

.04 *Question*—On October 7, 2009, the Office of Management and Budget (OMB) published the parameters of a pilot project, which is a collaborative effort between volunteer nonfederal entities expending American Recovery and Reinvestment Act of 2009 (ARRA) awards (auditees), the auditors performing compliance audits of auditees with ARRA expenditures under OMB Circular A-133, *Audits of States, Local Governments, and Non-Profit Organizations*, and the federal government. For auditees that volunteer, the pilot project requires their auditors to issue to management an early written communication of significant deficiencies and material weaknesses in internal control over compliance at an interim date, prior to the completion of the compliance audit. Such communication would be based on internal control work performed on specified compliance requirements for two major programs with ARRA expenditures chosen from a list of approved ARRA pilot project programs. This communication also would be required to be submitted by management to the cognizant agency for audit. May an auditor issue such an interim communication in accordance with section 325, *Communicating Internal Control Related Matters Identified in an Audit*?

.05 *Interpretation*—Yes. Section 325 permits an auditor to communicate to management identified significant deficiencies and material weaknesses before the completion of a financial statement audit. It would be equally appropriate for a compliance audit. Regardless of how the early communication is delivered, the auditor should communicate all significant deficiencies and material weaknesses in writing to management and those charged with governance in accordance with paragraphs .17–.18 of section 325.

.06 The following is an illustrative communication that an auditor may use to comply with the pilot project communication requirement to inform management and those charged with governance of deficiencies in internal control over compliance related to ARRA funding that have been identified at an interim

---

[4] In this section, a reasonable possibility exists when the likelihood of the event is either *reasonably possible* or *probable* as those terms are defined in the Financial Accounting Standards Board *Accounting Standards Codification* glossary.

[5] See footnote 3.

[6] See footnote 3.

date prior to the completion of the compliance audit and are, or likely to be, in the auditor's judgment, significant deficiencies or material weaknesses in internal control over compliance:

> This communication is provided pursuant to the parameters of the 2009 Office of Management and Budget (OMB) pilot project. Such project requires auditors of entities that volunteer for the project to issue, in writing, an early communication of significant deficiencies and material weaknesses in internal control over compliance for certain federal programs having expenditures of American Recovery and Reinvestment Act of 2009 (ARRA) funding at an interim date, prior to the completion of the compliance audit. Accordingly, this communication is based on our audit procedures performed through [insert "as of date"], an interim period. Because we have not completed our compliance audit, additional significant deficiencies and material weaknesses may be identified and communicated in our final report on compliance and internal control over compliance issued to meet the reporting requirements of OMB Circular A-133, *Audits of States, Local Governments, and Non-Profit Organizations.*
>
> In planning and performing our audit through [insert "as of date"] of [identify the federal programs selected to be tested as a major program from the federal list of approved ARRA pilot project programs], we are considering [Example Entity's] compliance with [list the applicable types of compliance requirements subject to the communication requirement in the pilot project (for example, activities allowed or unallowed, allowable costs and cost principles, cash management, eligibility, reporting, and special tests and provisions)] as described in the *OMB Circular A-133 Compliance Supplement* for the year ended June 30, 2009. We are also considering [Example Entity's] internal control over compliance with the requirements previously described that could have a direct and material effect on [identify the federal programs selected to be tested as a major program from the federal list of approved ARRA pilot project programs] in order to determine our auditing procedures for the purpose of expressing our opinion on compliance and to test and report on internal control over compliance in accordance with OMB Circular A-133, but not for the purpose of expressing an opinion on the effectiveness of internal control over compliance. Accordingly, we do not express an opinion on the effectiveness of the [Example Entity's] internal control over compliance.
>
> Our consideration of internal control over compliance is for the limited purpose described in the preceding paragraph and would not necessarily identify all deficiencies in the entity's internal control that might be significant deficiencies or material weaknesses as defined in the following paragraph. However, as discussed subsequently, based on the audit procedures performed through [insert "as of date"], we identified certain deficiencies in internal control over compliance that we consider to be significant deficiencies and other deficiencies that we consider to be material weaknesses.
>
> A *deficiency in internal control* over compliance exists when the design or operation of a control over compliance does not allow management or employees, in the normal course of performing their assigned functions, to prevent, or detect and correct, noncompliance with a type of compliance requirement [7] of a federal program on a timely basis. A *material weakness* in internal control over compliance is a deficiency, or a combination of deficiencies, in internal control over compliance, such that there is a reasonable possibility that material noncompliance with a type of compliance requirement of a federal program will not be prevented, or detected and corrected, on a timely basis. We consider the following deficiencies in internal control over compliance to be material weaknesses:

---

[7] See footnote 3.

[Describe the material weaknesses that were identified either here or by reference to a separate schedule.] [8]

A *significant deficiency* in internal control over compliance is a deficiency, or a combination of deficiencies, in internal control over compliance with a type of compliance requirement of a federal program that is less severe than a material weakness in internal control over compliance, yet important enough to merit attention by those charged with governance. We consider the following deficiencies in internal control over compliance to be significant deficiencies:

[Describe the significant deficiencies that were identified either here or by reference to a separate schedule.] [9]

[Example Entity's] responses to our findings are described [insert either "in the preceding paragraph" or "in the accompanying schedule"]. We did not audit [Example Entity's] responses and, accordingly, we express no opinion on the responses. [10]

This interim communication is intended solely for the information and use of management, [identify the body or individuals charged with governance], others within the entity, [identify the legislative or regulatory body], federal awarding agencies, and pass-through entities and is not intended to be and should not be used by anyone other than these specified parties.

[Issue Date: November 2009; Revised: March 2010.]

3. Communication of Significant Deficiencies and Material Weaknesses Prior to the Completion of the Compliance Audit for Auditors That Are Not Participants in Office of Management and Budget Pilot Project

.07 *Question*—Part 6, "Internal Control," of the *Office of Management and Budget (OMB) Circular A-133 Compliance Supplement* stresses the importance of internal control testwork over major programs with American Recovery and Reinvestment Act of 2009 (ARRA) expenditures and encourages early communication to management and those charged with governance of any significant deficiencies or material weaknesses in internal control:

Early communication by auditors to management, and those charged with governance, of identified control deficiencies related to ARRA funding that are, or likely to be, significant deficiencies or material weaknesses in internal control will allow management to expedite corrective action and mitigate the risk of improper expenditure of ARRA awards. Therefore, auditors are encouraged to promptly inform auditee management and those charged with governance during the audit engagement about control deficiencies related to ARRA funding that are, or likely to be, significant deficiencies or material weaknesses in internal control. The auditor should use professional judgment regarding the form of such interim communications.

.08 Although not required, if an auditor decides to make such a communication in writing at an interim date, may the auditor issue the interim

---

[8] The OMB pilot project requires the auditee, upon receipt of the interim communication from the auditor, to provide it to the federal cognizant agency for audit. Federal agencies are required to follow-up with the auditee concerning actions taken or needed to correct the finding. Therefore, to assist the federal agencies with this responsibility, significant deficiency and material weakness finding descriptions should include the level of detail required by both *Government Auditing Standards* and Section 510(b) of OMB Circular A-133. This would require the inclusion of, among other things, the views of responsible officials (see footnote 10).

[9] See footnote 8.

[10] The OMB pilot project requires the auditor to obtain management responses to the internal control matters identified and to include them in the interim communication.

communication in accordance with section 325, *Communicating Internal Control Related Matters Identified in an Audit*?

.09 *Interpretation*—Yes. As noted in the previous question, section 325 permits an auditor to communicate to management and those charged with governance identified significant deficiencies and material weaknesses before the completion of a financial statement audit. It would be equally appropriate for a compliance audit. The auditor is reminded that, regardless of how the early communication is delivered, the auditor should communicate all significant deficiencies and material weaknesses in writing to management and those charged with governance in accordance with paragraphs .17–.18 of section 325.

.10 If the auditor decides to make the interim communication encouraged in part 6 of the *OMB Circular A-133 Compliance Supplement* in writing, the following is an illustrative communication that an auditor may use to inform management and those charged with governance of deficiencies in internal control over compliance related to ARRA funding that have been identified at an interim date prior to the completion of the compliance audit and that are, or likely to be, in the auditor's judgment, significant deficiencies or material weaknesses in internal control:

> This communication is provided pursuant to the *Office of Management and Budget (OMB) Circular A-133 Compliance Supplement*, which encourages auditors to communicate, at an interim date, control deficiencies related to federal programs with expenditures of American Recovery and Reinvestment Act of 2009 (ARRA) funding that are, or likely to be, significant deficiencies or material weaknesses in internal control over compliance. Accordingly, this communication is based on our audit procedures performed through [insert "as of date"], an interim period. Because we have not completed our compliance audit, additional significant deficiencies and material weaknesses may be identified and communicated in our final report on compliance and internal control over compliance issued to meet the reporting requirements of OMB Circular A-133, *Audits of States, Local Governments, and Non-Profit Organizations*.
>
> In planning and performing our audit through [insert "as of date"] of [identify the federal programs with ARRA expenditures selected by the auditor to be tested as a major program], we are considering [Example Entity's] compliance with the applicable types of compliance requirements as described in the *OMB Circular A-133 Compliance Supplement* for the year ended June 30, 20XX. We are also considering [Example Entity's] internal control over compliance with the requirements previously described that could have a direct and material effect on [identify the federal programs with ARRA expenditures selected by the auditor to be tested as a major program] in order to determine our auditing procedures for the purpose of expressing our opinion on compliance and to test and report on internal control over compliance in accordance with OMB Circular A-133, but not for the purpose of expressing an opinion on the effectiveness of internal control over compliance. Accordingly, we do not express an opinion on the effectiveness of the [Example Entity's] internal control over compliance.
>
> Our consideration of internal control over compliance is for the limited purpose described in the preceding paragraph and would not necessarily identify all deficiencies in the entity's internal control that might be significant deficiencies or material weaknesses as defined in the following paragraph. However, as discussed subsequently, based on the audit procedures performed through [insert "as of date"], we identified certain deficiencies in internal control over compliance that we consider to be significant deficiencies and other deficiencies that we consider to be material weaknesses.
>
> A *deficiency in internal control* over compliance exists when the design or operation of a control over compliance does not allow management or employees, in the normal course of performing their assigned functions, to prevent, or

detect and correct, noncompliance with a type of compliance requirement [11] of a federal program on a timely basis. A *material weakness* in internal control over compliance is a deficiency, or combination of deficiencies, in internal control over compliance, such that there is a reasonable possibility that material noncompliance with a type of compliance requirement of a federal program will not be prevented, or detected and corrected, on a timely basis. We consider the following deficiencies in internal control over compliance to be material weaknesses:

[Describe the material weaknesses that were identified either here or by reference to a separate schedule.]

A *significant deficiency* in internal control over compliance is a deficiency, or a combination of deficiencies, in internal control over compliance with a type of compliance requirement of a federal program that is less severe than a material weakness in internal control over compliance, yet important enough to merit attention by those charged with governance. We consider the following deficiencies in internal control over compliance to be significant deficiencies:

[Describe the significant deficiencies that were identified either here or by reference to a separate schedule.]

This interim communication is intended solely for the information and use of management, [identify the body or individuals charged with governance], others within the entity, [identify the legislative or regulatory body], federal awarding agencies, and pass-through entities and is not intended to be and should not be used by anyone other than these specified parties.

[Issue Date: November 2009; Revised: March 2010.]

4. Appropriateness of Identifying No Significant Deficiencies or No Material Weaknesses in an Interim Communication

.11 *Question*—In either of the previously described scenarios, may the auditor issue an interim communication in accordance with section 325, *Communicating Internal Control Related Matters Identified in an Audit*, stating that as of the interim communication date, no significant deficiencies or material weaknesses have been noted?

.12 *Interpretation*—No. Paragraph .25 of section 325 states that the auditor should not issue a written communication stating that no significant deficiencies were identified during the audit. Such guidance would also apply to the interim communication contemplated in the previous two questions. Therefore, it would not be appropriate for an auditor to issue an interim communication stating that no significant deficiencies were identified.

.13 Although section 325 would permit the auditor to issue a communication at the end of an audit stating that no material weaknesses were identified by the auditor (see paragraph .24 of section 325), it would not be appropriate for an auditor to do so at an interim date. Making such a communication at an interim date could lead to misinterpretation by management and those charged with governance, that there are no identified material weaknesses when, in fact, material weaknesses could be identified before completion of the compliance audit.

[Issue Date: November 2009; Revised: March 2010.]

---

[11] See footnote 3.

AU Section 326

Audit Evidence

(Supersedes SAS No. 31.)

Source: SAS No. 106.

See section 9326 for interpretations of this section.

Effective for audits of financial statements for periods beginning on or after December 15, 2006. Earlier application is permitted.

Introduction

.01 This section provides guidance about concepts underlying the third standard of field work: "The auditor must obtain sufficient appropriate audit evidence by performing audit procedures to afford a reasonable basis for an opinion regarding the financial statements under audit." This section:

- Defines *audit evidence*;
- Defines *relevant assertions* and discusses their use in assessing risks and designing appropriate further audit procedures;[1]
- Discusses qualitative aspects that the auditor considers in determining the sufficiency and appropriateness of audit evidence; and
- Describes various audit procedures and discusses the purposes for which they may be performed.

Concept of Audit Evidence

.02 *Audit evidence* is all the information used by the auditor in arriving at the conclusions on which the audit opinion is based and includes the information contained in the accounting records underlying the financial statements and other information. Auditors are not expected to examine all information that may exist.[2] Audit evidence, which is cumulative in nature, includes audit evidence obtained from audit procedures performed during the course of the audit and may include audit evidence obtained from other sources, such as previous audits and a firm's quality control procedures for client acceptance and continuance.

.03 Accounting records generally include the records of initial entries and supporting records, such as checks and records of electronic fund transfers; invoices; contracts; the general and subsidiary ledgers, journal entries, and other adjustments to the financial statements that are not reflected in formal journal entries; and records such as worksheets and spreadsheets supporting cost allocations, computations, reconciliations, and disclosures. The entries in the accounting records are often initiated, authorized, recorded, processed, and

---

[1] Further audit procedures include tests of the operating effectiveness of controls and substantive procedures whose nature, timing, and extent are responsive to the assessed risks of material misstatement. See paragraph .07 of section 318, *Performing Audit Procedures in Response to Assessed Risks and Evaluating the Audit Evidence Obtained.*

[2] See paragraph .13.

reported in electronic form. In addition, the accounting records may be part of integrated systems that share data and support all aspects of the entity's financial reporting, operations, and compliance objectives.

.04 Management is responsible for the preparation of the financial statements based on the accounting records of the entity. The auditor should obtain audit evidence by testing the accounting records, for example, through analysis and review, reperforming procedures followed in the financial reporting process, and reconciling related types and applications of the same information. Through the performance of such audit procedures, the auditor may determine that the accounting records are internally consistent and agree to the financial statements. However, because accounting records alone do not provide sufficient appropriate audit evidence on which to base an audit opinion on the financial statements, the auditor should obtain other audit evidence.

.05 Other information that the auditor may use as audit evidence includes minutes of meetings; confirmations from third parties; industry analysts' reports; comparable data about competitors (benchmarking); controls manuals; information obtained by the auditor from such audit procedures as inquiry, observation, and inspection; and other information developed by or available to the auditor that permits the auditor to reach conclusions through valid reasoning.

Sufficient Appropriate Audit Evidence

.06 *Sufficiency* is the measure of the quantity of audit evidence. *Appropriateness* is the measure of the quality of audit evidence, that is, its relevance and its reliability in providing support for, or detecting misstatements in, the classes of transactions, account balances, and disclosures and related assertions. The auditor should consider the sufficiency and appropriateness of audit evidence to be obtained when assessing risks and designing further audit procedures. The quantity of audit evidence needed is affected by the risk of misstatement (the greater the risk, the more audit evidence is likely to be required) and also by the quality of such audit evidence (the higher the quality, the less the audit evidence that may be required). Accordingly, the sufficiency and appropriateness of audit evidence are interrelated. However, merely obtaining more audit evidence may not compensate if it is of a lower quality.

.07 A given set of audit procedures may provide audit evidence that is relevant to certain assertions but not to others. For example, inspection of records and documents related to the collection of receivables after the period end may provide audit evidence regarding both existence and valuation, although not necessarily the appropriateness of period-end cutoffs. On the other hand, the auditor often obtains audit evidence from different sources or of a different nature that is relevant to the same assertion. For example, the auditor may analyze the aging of accounts receivable and the subsequent collection of receivables to obtain audit evidence relating to the valuation of the allowance for doubtful accounts. Furthermore, obtaining audit evidence relating to a particular assertion, for example, the physical existence of inventory, is not a substitute for obtaining audit evidence regarding another assertion, for example, rights and obligations.

.08 The reliability of audit evidence is influenced by its source and by its nature and is dependent on the individual circumstances under which it is obtained. Generalizations about the reliability of various kinds of audit evidence can be made; however, such generalizations are subject to important exceptions. Even when audit evidence is obtained from sources external to the entity, circumstances may exist that could affect the reliability of the information obtained. For example, audit evidence obtained from an independent external source may not be reliable if the source is not knowledgeable. While recognizing that exceptions may exist, the following generalizations about the reliability of audit evidence are useful:

- Audit evidence is more reliable when it is obtained from knowledgeable independent sources outside the entity.
- Audit evidence that is generated internally is more reliable when the related controls imposed by the entity are effective.
- Audit evidence obtained directly by the auditor (for example, observation of the application of a control) is more reliable than audit evidence obtained indirectly or by inference (for example, inquiry about the application of a control).
- Audit evidence is more reliable when it exists in documentary form, whether paper, electronic, or other medium (for example, a contemporaneously written record of a meeting is more reliable than a subsequent oral representation of the matters discussed).
- Audit evidence provided by original documents is more reliable than audit evidence provided by photocopies or facsimiles.

.09 The auditor should consider the reliability of the information to be used as audit evidence, for example, photocopies; facsimiles; or filmed, digitized, or other electronic documents, including consideration of controls over their preparation and maintenance where relevant. However, an audit rarely involves the authentication of documentation, nor is the auditor trained as or expected to be an expert in such authentication.

.10 When information produced by the entity is used by the auditor to perform further audit procedures, the auditor should obtain audit evidence about the accuracy and completeness of the information.[3] In order for the auditor to obtain reliable audit evidence, the information upon which the audit procedures are based needs to be sufficiently complete and accurate. For example, in auditing revenue by applying standard prices to records of sales volume, the auditor should consider the accuracy of the price information and the completeness and accuracy of the sales volume data. Obtaining audit evidence about the completeness and accuracy of the information produced by the entity's information system may be performed concurrently with the actual audit procedure applied to the information when obtaining such audit evidence is an integral part of the audit procedure itself. In other situations, the auditor may have obtained audit evidence of the accuracy and completeness of such information by testing controls over the production and maintenance of the information. However, in some situations the auditor may determine that additional audit procedures are needed. For example, these additional procedures may include using computer-assisted audit techniques (CAATs) to recalculate the information.

.11 The auditor ordinarily obtains more assurance from consistent audit evidence obtained from different sources or of a different nature than from items of audit evidence considered individually. In addition, obtaining audit evidence from different sources or of a different nature may indicate that an individual item of audit evidence is not reliable. For example, corroborating information obtained from a source independent of the entity may increase the assurance the auditor obtains from a management representation. Conversely, when audit evidence obtained from one source is inconsistent with that obtained

---

[3] See paragraphs .14 and .57 of section 318.

from another, the auditor should determine what additional audit procedures are necessary to resolve the inconsistency.

.12 The auditor may consider the relationship between the cost of obtaining audit evidence and the usefulness of the information obtained. However, the matter of difficulty or expense involved is not in itself a valid basis for omitting an audit procedure for which there is no appropriate alternative.

.13 In forming the audit opinion, the auditor does not examine all the information available (evidence) because conclusions ordinarily can be reached by using sampling approaches and other means of selecting items for testing. Also, the auditor may find it necessary to rely on audit evidence that is persuasive rather than conclusive; however, to obtain reasonable assurance,[4] the auditor must not be satisfied with audit evidence that is less than persuasive. The auditor should use professional judgment and should exercise professional skepticism in evaluating the quantity and quality of audit evidence, and thus its sufficiency and appropriateness, to support the audit opinion.

The Use of Assertions in Obtaining Audit Evidence

.14 Management is responsible for the fair presentation of financial statements that reflect the nature and operations of the entity.[5] In representing that the financial statements are fairly presented in conformity with generally accepted accounting principles,[6] management implicitly or explicitly makes assertions regarding the recognition, measurement, presentation, and disclosure of information in the financial statements and related disclosures.

.15 Assertions used by the auditor (see paragraph .16) fall into the following categories:

a. Assertions about classes of transactions and events for the period under audit:

- *i.* *Occurrence.* Transactions and events that have been recorded have occurred and pertain to the entity.
- *ii.* *Completeness.* All transactions and events that should have been recorded have been recorded.
- *iii.* *Accuracy.* Amounts and other data relating to recorded transactions and events have been recorded appropriately.
- *iv.* *Cutoff.* Transactions and events have been recorded in the correct accounting period.
- *v.* *Classification.* Transactions and events have been recorded in the proper accounts.

b. Assertions about account balances at the period end:

- *i.* *Existence.* Assets, liabilities, and equity interests exist.
- *ii.* *Rights and obligations.* The entity holds or controls the rights to assets, and liabilities are the obligations of the entity.
- *iii.* *Completeness.* All assets, liabilities, and equity interests that should have been recorded have been recorded.

---

[4] Section 230, paragraphs .10 through .13, provides guidance on reasonable assurance as it relates to an audit of financial statements.

[5] See section 110, paragraph .03.

[6] Reference to generally accepted accounting principles in this section includes, where applicable, a comprehensive basis of accounting other than generally accepted accounting principles as defined in section 623, *Special Reports*.

iv. *Valuation and allocation.* Assets, liabilities, and equity interests are included in the financial statements at appropriate amounts and any resulting valuation or allocation adjustments are appropriately recorded.

c. Assertions about presentation and disclosure:

i. *Occurrence and rights and obligations.* Disclosed events and transactions have occurred and pertain to the entity.

ii. *Completeness.* All disclosures that should have been included in the financial statements have been included.

iii. *Classification and understandability.* Financial information is appropriately presented and described and disclosures are clearly expressed.

iv. *Accuracy and valuation.* Financial and other information are disclosed fairly and at appropriate amounts.

.16 The auditor may use the relevant assertions as they are described above or may express them differently provided aspects described above have been covered. For example, the auditor may choose to combine the assertions about transactions and events with the assertions about account balances. As another example, there may not be a separate assertion related to cutoff of transactions and events when the occurrence and completeness assertions include appropriate consideration of recording transactions in the correct accounting period.

.17 The auditor should use relevant assertions for classes of transactions, account balances, and presentation and disclosures in sufficient detail to form a basis for the assessment of risks of material misstatement and the design and performance of further audit procedures. The auditor should use relevant assertions in assessing risks by considering the different types of potential misstatements that may occur, and then designing further audit procedures that are responsive to the assessed risks.

.18 Relevant assertions are assertions that have a meaningful bearing on whether the account is fairly stated. For example, valuation may not be relevant to the cash account unless currency translation is involved; however, existence and completeness are always relevant. Similarly, valuation may not be relevant to the gross amount of the accounts receivable balance but is relevant to the related allowance accounts. Additionally, the auditor might, in some circumstances, focus on the presentation and disclosure assertion separately in connection with the period-end financial reporting process.

.19 For each significant class of transactions, account balance, and presentation and disclosure, the auditor should determine the relevance of each of the financial statement assertions. To identify relevant assertions, the auditor should determine the source of likely potential misstatements in each significant class of transactions, account balance, and presentation and disclosure. In determining whether a particular assertion is relevant to a significant account balance or disclosure, the auditor should evaluate:

a. The nature of the assertion;

b. The volume of transactions or data related to the assertion; and

c. The nature and complexity of the systems, including the use of information technology, by which the entity processes and controls information supporting the assertion.

Audit Procedures for Obtaining Audit Evidence

.20 The auditor should obtain audit evidence to draw reasonable conclusions on which to base the audit opinion by performing audit procedures to:

a. Obtain an understanding of the entity and its environment, including its internal control, to assess the risks of material misstatement at the financial statement and relevant assertion levels (audit procedures performed for this purpose are referred to as *risk assessment procedures*);

b. When necessary, or when the auditor has determined to do so, test the operating effectiveness of controls in preventing or detecting material misstatements at the relevant assertion level (audit procedures performed for this purpose are referred to as *tests of controls*); and

c. Detect material misstatements at the relevant assertion level (audit procedures performed for this purpose are referred to as *substantive procedures* and include tests of details of classes of transactions, account balances, and disclosures, and substantive analytical procedures).

.21 The auditor must perform risk assessment procedures[7] to provide a satisfactory basis for the assessment of risks at the financial statement and relevant assertion levels. Risk assessment procedures by themselves do not provide sufficient appropriate audit evidence on which to base the audit opinion and must be supplemented by further audit procedures in the form of tests of controls, when relevant or necessary, and substantive procedures.

.22 Tests of controls are necessary in two circumstances. When the auditor's risk assessment includes an expectation of the operating effectiveness of controls, the auditor should test those controls to support the risk assessment. In addition, when the substantive procedures alone do not provide sufficient appropriate audit evidence, the auditor should perform tests of controls to obtain audit evidence about their operating effectiveness.[8]

.23 As described in section 318, *Performing Audit Procedures in Response to Assessed Risks and Evaluating the Audit Evidence Obtained*, the auditor should plan and should perform substantive procedures to be responsive to the related planned level of detection risk, which includes the results of tests of controls, if any. The auditor's risk assessment is judgmental, however, and may not be sufficiently precise to identify all risks of material misstatement.[9] Further, there are inherent limitations in internal control, including the risk of management override, the possibility of human error, and the effect of systems changes. Therefore, regardless of the assessed risk of material misstatement, the auditor should design and perform substantive procedures for all relevant assertions related to each material class of transactions, account balance, and disclosure to obtain sufficient appropriate audit evidence.

.24 The auditor should use one or more types of the audit procedures described in paragraphs .27 through .41 of this section. These audit procedures, or combinations thereof, may be used as risk assessment procedures, tests of controls, or substantive procedures, depending on the context in which they are applied by the auditor. Paragraph .05 of section 314, *Understanding the*

---

[7] See paragraph .05 of section 314, *Understanding the Entity and Its Environment and Assessing the Risks of Material Misstatement*, for an explanation of risk assessment procedures.

[8] See paragraphs .117 through .120 of section 314 and paragraph .24 of section 318.

[9] See paragraph .22 of section 312, *Audit Risk and Materiality in Conducting an Audit*, for definition of *risk of material misstatement*.

Entity and Its Environment and Assessing the Risks of Material Misstatement, provides guidance to the auditor to perform a combination of audit procedures when performing risk assessment procedures. In addition, a combination of two or more of these audit procedures may be necessary to obtain sufficient appropriate audit evidence when performing tests of controls or substantive procedures at the relevant assertion level. In certain circumstances, audit evidence obtained from previous audits may provide audit evidence where the auditor should perform audit procedures to establish its continuing relevance.[10]

.25 The nature and timing of the audit procedures to be used may be affected by the fact that some of the accounting data and other information may be available only in electronic form or only at certain points or periods in time.[11] Source documents, such as purchase orders, bills of lading, invoices, and checks, may be replaced with electronic messages. For example, entities may use electronic commerce or image processing systems. In electronic commerce, the entity and its customers or suppliers use connected computers over a public network, such as the Internet, to transact business electronically. Purchasing, shipping, billing, cash receipt, and cash disbursement transactions are often consummated entirely by the exchange of electronic messages between the parties. In image processing systems, documents are scanned and converted into electronic images to facilitate storage and reference, and the source documents may not be retained after conversion. Certain electronic information may exist at a certain point in time. However, such information may not be retrievable after a specified period of time if files are changed and if backup files do not exist. An entity's data retention policies may require the auditor to request retention of some information for the auditor's review or to perform audit procedures at a time when the information is available.

.26 When the information is in electronic form, the auditor may carry out through CAATs certain of the audit procedures described in the following sections.

Inspection of Records or Documents

.27 Inspection consists of examining records or documents, whether internal or external, in paper form, electronic form, or other media. Inspection of records and documents provides audit evidence of varying degrees of reliability, depending on their nature and source and, in the case of internal records and documents, on the effectiveness of the controls over their production. An example of inspection used as a test of controls is inspection of records or documents for evidence of authorization.

.28 Some documents represent direct audit evidence of the existence of an asset, for example, a document constituting a financial instrument such as a stock or bond. Inspection of such documents may not necessarily provide audit evidence about ownership or value. In addition, inspecting an executed contract may provide audit evidence relevant to the entity's application of accounting principles, such as revenue recognition.

Inspection of Tangible Assets

.29 Inspection of tangible assets consists of physical examination of the assets. Inspection of tangible assets may provide appropriate audit evidence with respect to their existence, but not necessarily about the entity's rights and

---

[10] See paragraph .64 of section 318.

[11] See paragraphs .57 through .63 of section 314.

obligations or the valuation of the assets. Inspection of individual inventory items ordinarily accompanies the observation of inventory counting. For example, when observing an inventory count, the auditor may inspect individual inventory items (such as opening containers included in the inventory count to ensure that they are not empty) to verify their existence.

Observation

.30 Observation consists of looking at a process or procedure being performed by others. Examples include observation of the counting of inventories by the entity's personnel and observation of the performance of control activities. Observation provides audit evidence about the performance of a process or procedure but is limited to the point in time at which the observation takes place and by the fact that the act of being observed may affect how the process or procedure is performed. See section 331, *Inventories*, for further guidance on observation of the counting of inventory.

Inquiry

.31 Inquiry consists of seeking information of knowledgeable persons, both financial and nonfinancial, inside or outside the entity. Inquiry is an audit procedure that is used extensively throughout the audit and often is complementary to performing other audit procedures. Inquiries may range from formal written inquiries to informal oral inquiries. Evaluating responses to inquiries is an integral part of the inquiry process.

.32 Inquiry normally involves:

- Considering the knowledge, objectivity, experience, responsibility, and qualifications of the individual to be questioned.
- Asking clear, concise, and relevant questions.
- Using open or closed questions appropriately.
- Listening actively and effectively.
- Considering the reactions and responses and asking follow-up questions.
- Evaluating the response.

.33 In some cases, the auditor should obtain replies to inquiries in the form of written representations from management. For example, when obtaining oral responses to inquiries, the nature of the response may be so significant that it warrants obtaining written representation from the source. See section 333, *Management Representations*, for further guidance on written representations.

.34 Responses to inquiries may provide the auditor with information not previously possessed or with corroborative audit evidence. Alternatively, responses might provide information that differs significantly from other information that the auditor has obtained, for example, information regarding the possibility of management override of controls. In some cases, responses to inquiries provide a basis for the auditor to modify or perform additional audit procedures. The auditor should resolve any significant inconsistencies in the information obtained.

.35 The auditor should perform audit procedures in addition to the use of inquiry to obtain sufficient appropriate audit evidence. Inquiry alone ordinarily does not provide sufficient appropriate audit evidence to detect a material misstatement at the relevant assertion level. Moreover, inquiry alone is not sufficient to test the operating effectiveness of controls.

.36 Although corroboration of evidence obtained through inquiry is often of particular importance, in the case of inquiries about management's intent, the information available to support management's intent may be limited. In these cases, understanding management's past history of carrying out its stated intentions with respect to assets or liabilities, management's stated reasons for choosing a particular course of action, and management's ability to pursue a specific course of action may provide relevant information about management's intent.

Confirmation

.37 Confirmation, which is a specific type of inquiry, is the process of obtaining a representation of information or of an existing condition directly from a third party. For example, the auditor may seek direct confirmation of receivables by communication with debtors. Confirmations are frequently used in relation to account balances and their components but need not be restricted to these items. A confirmation request can be designed to ask if any modifications have been made to the agreement, and if so, what the relevant details are. For example, the auditor may request confirmation of the terms of agreements or transactions an entity has with third parties. Confirmations also are used to obtain audit evidence about the absence of certain conditions, for example, the absence of an undisclosed agreement that may influence revenue recognition. See section 330, *The Confirmation Process*, for further guidance on confirmations.

Recalculation

.38 Recalculation consists of checking the mathematical accuracy of documents or records. Recalculation can be performed through the use of information technology, for example, by obtaining an electronic file from the entity and using CAATs to check the accuracy of the summarization of the file.

Reperformance

.39 Reperformance is the auditor's independent execution of procedures or controls that were originally performed as part of the entity's internal control, either manually or through the use of CAATs, for example, reperforming the aging of accounts receivable.

Analytical Procedures

.40 Analytical procedures consist of evaluations of financial information made by a study of plausible relationships among both financial and nonfinancial data. Analytical procedures also encompass the investigation of identified fluctuations and relationships that are inconsistent with other relevant information or deviate significantly from predicted amounts. See section 329, *Analytical Procedures*, for further guidance on analytical procedures.

.41 An analytical procedure might be scanning, which is the auditor's use of professional judgment to review accounting data to identify significant or unusual items and then to test those items. This includes the identification of anomalous individual items within account balances or other data through the reading or analysis of entries in transaction listings, subsidiary ledgers, general ledger control accounts, adjusting entries, suspense accounts, reconciliations, and other detailed reports. Scanning includes searching for large or unusual items in the accounting records (for example, nonstandard journal entries), as well as in transaction data (for example, suspense accounts, adjusting journal entries) for indications of misstatements that have occurred. CAATS may assist an auditor in identifying anomalies. Since the auditor tests the items selected by scanning, the auditor obtains audit evidence about those items. The auditor's scanning also may provide some audit evidence about the items not selected since the auditor has used professional judgment to determine that the items not selected are less likely to be misstated.

Effective Date

.42 This section is effective for audits of financial statements for periods beginning on or after December 15, 2006. Earlier application is permitted.

AU Section 9326

Audit Evidence: Auditing Interpretations of Section 326

1. Audit Evidence for an Audit of Interim Financial Statements

.01 *Question*—Financial Accounting Standards Board (FASB) *Accounting Standards Codification* (ASC) 270-10-45-2 states that "certain accounting principles and practices followed for annual reporting purposes may require modification at interim reporting dates so that the reported results for the interim period may better relate to the results of operations for the annual period." The modifications introduce a need for estimates to a greater extent than is necessary for annual financial information. Does this imply a relaxation of the third standard of field work, which requires that sufficient appropriate audit evidence be obtained to afford a reasonable basis for an opinion regarding the financial statements under audit?

.02 *Interpretation*—No. The third standard of field work applies to all engagements leading to an expression of opinion on financial statements or financial information.

.03 The objective of the independent auditor's engagement is to obtain sufficient appropriate audit evidence to provide him with a reasonable basis for forming an opinion. The auditor develops specific audit objectives in light of assertions by management that are embodied in financial statement components. Section 326 paragraph .17 states, "the auditor should use relevant assertions for classes of transactions, account balances, and presentation and disclosures in sufficient detail to form a basis for the assessment of risks of material misstatement and the design and performance of further audit procedures. The auditor should use relevant assertions in assessing risks by considering the different types of potential misstatements that may occur, and then designing further audit procedures that are responsive to the assessed risks."

.04 Audit evidence obtained for an audit of annual financial statements may also be useful in an audit of interim financial statements, and audit evidence obtained for an audit of interim financial statements may also be useful in an audit of annual financial statements. Section 318 paragraph .16 states that "The auditor may perform tests of controls or substantive procedures at an interim date or at period end. The higher the risk of material misstatement, the more likely it is that the auditor may decide it is more effective to perform substantive procedures nearer to, or at, the period end rather than at an earlier date, or to perform audit procedures unannounced or at unpredictable times (for example, performing audit procedures at selected locations on an unannounced basis). On the other hand, performing audit procedures before the period end may assist the auditor in identifying significant matters at an early stage of the audit, and consequently resolving them with the assistance of management or developing an effective audit approach to address such matters."[1]

---

[1] [Footnote deleted to reflect conforming changes necessary due to the issuance of Statement on Auditing Standards No. 106.]

.05 The introduction by FASB ASC 270, *Interim Reporting*, of a need for additional estimates in measuring certain items for interim financial information may lead to a need for evidence in examining those items that differs from the evidence required in an audit of annual financial information. For example, computing the provision for federal income taxes in interim information involves estimating the effective tax rate expected to be applicable for the full fiscal year, and the auditor should examine evidence as to the basis for estimating that rate. Since the effective tax rate for the full year ordinarily is known at year-end, similar evidence is not usually required in examining annual information.

[Issue Date: February 1974; Modified: October 1980; Revised: March 2006; Revised: June 2009.]

2. The Effect of an Inability to Obtain Audit Evidence Relating to Income Tax Accruals

.06 *Question*—The Internal Revenue Service's audit manual instructs its examiners on how to secure from corporate officials "tax accrual workpapers" or the "tax liability contingency analysis," including, "a memorandum discussing items reflected in the financial statements as income or expense where the ultimate tax treatment is unclear." The audit manual states that the examiner may question or summons a corporate officer or manager concerning the "knowledge of the items that make up the corporation's contingent reserve accounts." It also states that "in unusual circumstances, access may be had to the audit or tax workpapers" of an independent accountant or an accounting firm after attempting to obtain the information from the taxpayer. IRS policy also includes specific procedures to be followed in circumstances involving "Listed Transactions," to help address what the IRS considers to be abusive tax avoidance transactions (Internal Revenue Manual, section 4024.2-.5, 5/14/81, and Internal Revenue Service Announcement 2002-63, 6/17/02).

.07 Concern over IRS access to tax accrual working papers might cause some clients to not prepare or maintain appropriate documentation of the calculation or contents of the accrual for income taxes included in the financial statements, or to deny the independent auditor access to such information.

.08 What effect does this situation have on the auditor's opinion on the financial statements?

.09 *Interpretation*—The client is responsible for its tax accrual, the underlying support for the accrual, and the related disclosures. Limitations on the auditor's access to information considered necessary to audit the tax accrual will affect the auditor's ability to issue an unqualified opinion on the financial statements. Thus, if the client does not have appropriate documentation of the calculation or contents of the accrual for income taxes and denies the auditor access to client personnel responsible for making the judgments and estimates relating to the accrual, the auditor should assess the importance of that inadequacy in the accounting records and the client imposed limitation on his or her ability to form an opinion on the financial statements. Also, if the client has appropriate documentation but denies the auditor access to it and to client personnel who possess the information, the auditor should assess the importance of the client-imposed scope limitation on his or her ability to form an opinion.

.10 The third standard of field work requires the auditor to obtain sufficient appropriate audit evidence through, among other things, inspection and inquiries to afford a reasonable basis for an opinion on the financial statements. Section 318, *Performing Audit Procedures in Response to Assessed Risks and Evaluating the Audit Evidence Obtained*, paragraph .76, requires the auditor to obtain sufficient appropriate audit evidence about material financial statement assertions or else to qualify or disclaim his or her opinion on the statements. Section 508, *Reports on Audited Financial Statements*, paragraph .24, states that, "When restrictions that significantly limit the scope of the audit are imposed by the client, ordinarily the auditor should disclaim an opinion on the financial statements." Also, section 333 on *Management Representations* requires the auditor to obtain written representations from management. Section 333 paragraph .06 states that specific representations should relate to the following matters, "availability of all financial records and related data," and section 333 paragraph .08 states that a materiality limit does not apply to that representation. Section 333 paragraph .13 states that "management's refusal to furnish a written representation" constitutes a limitation on the scope of the audit sufficient to preclude an unqualified opinion.

.11 *Question*—A client may allow the auditor to inspect its tax accrual workpapers, but request that copies not be retained for audit documentation, particularly copies of the tax liability contingency analysis. The client also may suggest that the auditor not prepare and maintain similar documentation of his or her own. What should the auditor consider in deciding a response to such a request?

.12 *Interpretation*—Section 339, *Audit Documentation*, states that audit documentation is the principal record of auditing procedures applied, evidence obtained, and conclusions reached by the auditor in the engagement. Audit documentation should include sufficient appropriate audit evidence to afford a reasonable basis for an opinion. In addition, audit documentation should be sufficient to enable an experienced auditor to understand the nature, timing, extent, and results of auditing procedures performed, and the evidence obtained. Section 326, *Audit Evidence*, paragraph .05, states that other information includes information obtained by the auditor from inquiry, observation, inspection, and physical examination. The quantity, type, and content of audit documentation are matters of the auditor's professional judgment (see section 339).

.13 The auditor's documentation of the results of auditing procedures directed at the tax accounts and related disclosures also should include sufficient appropriate audit evidence about the significant elements of the client's tax liability contingency analysis. This documentation should include copies of the client's documents, schedules, or analyses (or auditor-prepared summaries thereof) to enable the auditor to support his or her conclusions regarding the appropriateness of the client's accounting and disclosure of significant tax-related contingency matters. The audit documentation should reflect the procedures performed and conclusions reached by the auditor and, for significant matters, include the client's documentary support for its financial statement amounts and disclosures.

.14 The audit documentation should include the significant elements of the client's analysis of tax contingencies or reserves, including roll-forward of material changes to such reserves. In addition, the documentation should provide the client's position and support for income tax related disclosures, such as its effective tax rate reconciliation, and support for its intra-period allocation of income tax expense or benefit to continuing operations and to items other than continuing operations. Where applicable, the documentation also should include the client's basis for assessing deferred tax assets and related valuation allowances and its support for applying the "indefinite reversal criteria" in FASB ASC 740-30-25-17, including its specific plans for reinvestment of undistributed foreign earnings.

.15 *Question*—In some situations, a client may furnish its outside legal counsel or in-house legal or tax counsel with information concerning the tax contingencies covered by the accrual for income taxes included in the financial statements and ask counsel to provide the auditor an opinion on the adequacy of the accrual for those contingencies.

.16 In such circumstances, rather than inspecting and obtaining documentary evidence of the client's tax liability contingency analysis and making inquiries of the client, may the auditor consider the counsel as a specialist within the meaning of AU section 336, *Using the Work of a Specialist*, and rely solely on counsel's opinion as an appropriate procedure for obtaining audit evidence to support his or her opinion on the financial statements?

.17 *Interpretation*—No. The opinion of legal counsel in this situation would not provide sufficient appropriate audit evidence to afford a reasonable basis for an opinion on the financial statements.

.18 Section 336 paragraph .01 defines a specialist as "a person (or firm) possessing special skill or knowledge in a particular field other than accounting or auditing." It is intended to apply to situations requiring special knowledge of matters about which the auditor does not have adequate technical training and proficiency. The auditor's education, training, and experience, on the other hand, do enable him or her to be knowledgeable concerning income tax matters and competent to assess their presentation in the financial statements.

.19 The opinion of legal counsel on specific tax issues that he or she is asked to address and to which he or she has devoted substantive attention, as contemplated by section 337, *Inquiry of a Client's Lawyer Concerning Litigation, Claims, and Assessments*, can be useful to the auditor in forming his or her own opinion. However, the audit of income tax accounts requires a combination of tax expertise and knowledge about the client's business that is accumulated during all aspects of an audit. Therefore, as previously stated, it is not appropriate for the auditor to rely solely on such legal opinion.

.20 *Question*—A client may have obtained the advice or opinion of an outside tax adviser related to the tax accrual or matters affecting it, including tax contingencies, and further may attempt to limit the auditor's access to such advice or opinion, or limit the auditor's documentation of such advice or opinion. This limitation on the auditor's access may be proposed on the basis that such information is privileged. Can the auditor rely solely on the conclusions of third party tax advisers? What audit evidence should the auditor obtain and include in the audit documentation?

.21 *Interpretation*—As discussed in paragraphs .17–.19, the auditor cannot accept a client's or a third party's analysis or opinion with respect to tax matters without careful consideration and application of the auditor's tax expertise and knowledge about the client's business. As a result of applying such knowledge to the facts, the auditor may encounter situations in which the auditor either disagrees with the position taken by the client, or its advisers, or does not have sufficient appropriate audit evidence to support his or her opinion.

.22 If the client's support for the tax accrual or matters affecting it, including tax contingencies, is based upon an opinion issued by an outside adviser with respect to a potentially material matter, the auditor should obtain access to the opinion, notwithstanding potential concerns regarding attorney-client or other forms of privilege. The audit documentation should include either the actual advice or opinions rendered by an outside adviser, or other sufficient documentation or abstracts supporting both the transactions or facts addressed as well as the analysis and conclusions reached by the client and adviser. Alternatives such as redacted or modified opinions may be considered, but must nonetheless include sufficient content to articulate and document the client's position so that the auditor can formulate his or her conclusion. Similarly, it may be possible to accept a client's analysis summarizing an outside adviser's opinion, but the client's analysis must provide sufficient appropriate audit evidence for the auditor to formulate his or her conclusion. In addition, client representations may be obtained stating that the client has not received any advice or opinions that are contradictory to the client's support for the tax accrual.

.23 If the auditor is unable to accumulate sufficient appropriate audit evidence about whether there is a supported and reasonable basis for the client's position, the auditor should consider the effect of this scope limitation on his or her report.

[Issue Date: March 1981; Amended: April 9, 2003; Revised: December 2005; Revised: March 2006; Revised: March 2008; Revised: June 2009.]

3. The Auditor's Consideration of the Completeness Assertion

.24 *Question*—Section 326, *Audit Evidence*, paragraphs .14–.19, discusses the use of assertions that are embodied in financial statement components. In obtaining audit evidence about certain assertions such as, existence or occurrence, rights and obligations, valuation or allocation, and presentation and disclosure, the auditor may consider classes of transactions, account balances and disclosures that are included in the financial statements. In contrast, in obtaining audit evidence about the completeness assertion related to classes of transactions, account balances and disclosures, the auditor may consider whether transactions, accounts and disclosures have been improperly excluded from the financial statements. May management's written representations and the auditor's assessment of control risk constitute sufficient audit evidence about the completeness assertion? [Paragraph renumbered by the amendment to Interpretation No. 2, April 2003.]

.25 *Interpretation*—Written representations from management are a part of the audit evidence the auditor may obtain in an audit performed in accordance with generally accepted auditing standards. Management's representations about the completeness assertion, whether considered alone or in combination with the auditor's assessment of control risk, do not constitute sufficient appropriate audit evidence to support that assertion. Obtaining such representations complements but does not replace other auditing procedures that the auditor should perform. [Paragraph renumbered by the amendment to Interpretation No. 2, April 2003.]

.26 In planning audit procedures to obtain evidence about the completeness assertion, the auditor should consider the inherent risk that transactions and accounts have been improperly omitted from the financial statements. When the auditor assesses the inherent risk of omission for a particular account balance or class of transactions to be such that he believes omissions could exist that might be material when aggregated with errors in other balances or classes, he should restrict the audit risk of omission by performing substantive tests designed to obtain evidence about the completeness assertion. Substantive tests designed primarily to obtain evidence about the completeness assertion include analytical procedures and tests of details of *related populations*.[2] [Paragraph renumbered by the amendment to Interpretation No. 2, April 2003.]

---

[2] For purposes of this interpretation, a related population is a population other than the recorded account balance or class of transactions being audited that would be expected to contain evidence of whether all accounts or transactions that should be presented in that balance or class are so included.

.27 The extent of substantive tests of completeness may properly vary in relation to the assessed level of control risk. Because of the unique nature of the completeness assertion, an assessed level of control risk below the maximum may be an effective means for the auditor to obtain evidence about that assertion. Although an assessed level of control risk below the maximum is not required to satisfy the auditor's objectives with respect to the completeness assertion, the auditor should consider that for some transactions (for example, revenues that are received primarily in cash, such as those of a casino or of some charitable organizations) it may be difficult to limit audit risk for those assertions to an acceptable level without an assessed level of control risk below the maximum. [Paragraph renumbered by the amendment to Interpretation No. 2, April 2003.]

[Issue Date: April 1986; Revised: March 2006.]

[4.] Applying Auditing Procedures to Segment Disclosures in Financial Statements

[.28–.41] [3] [Deleted March 2006.]

---

[3] [Footnote deleted to reflect conforming changes necessary due to the issuance of Statement on Auditing Standards No. 106.]

AU Section 328

Auditing Fair Value Measurements and Disclosures

Source: SAS No. 101; SAS No. 113.

Effective for audits of financial statements for periods beginning on or after June 15, 2003, unless otherwise indicated.

See section 9328 for interpretations of this section.

Introduction

.01 The purpose of this section is to establish standards and provide guidance on auditing fair value measurements and disclosures contained in financial statements. In particular, this section addresses audit considerations relating to the measurement and disclosure of assets, liabilities, and specific components of equity presented or disclosed at fair value in financial statements. Fair value measurements of assets, liabilities, and components of equity may arise from both the initial recording of transactions and later changes in value. Changes in fair value measurements that occur over time may be treated in different ways under generally accepted accounting principles (GAAP). For example, GAAP may require that some fair value changes be reflected in net income and that other fair value changes be reflected in other comprehensive income and equity.

.02 While this section provides guidance on auditing fair value measurements and disclosures, evidence obtained from other audit procedures also may provide evidence relevant to the measurement and disclosure of fair values. For example, inspection procedures to verify existence of an asset measured at fair value also may provide relevant evidence about its valuation, such as the physical condition of the asset.

.03 The auditor should obtain sufficient appropriate audit evidence to provide reasonable assurance that fair value measurements and disclosures are in conformity with GAAP. GAAP requires that certain items be measured at fair value. Financial Accounting Standards Board (FASB) *Accounting Standards Codification* (ASC) glossary term *fair value* is defined as the price that would be received to sell an asset or paid to transfer a liability in an orderly transaction between market participants at the measurement date. [1] Although GAAP may not prescribe the method for measuring the fair value of an item, it expresses a preference for the use of observable market prices to make that determination. In the absence of observable market prices, GAAP requires fair value to be based on the best information available in the circumstances.

---

[1] Governmental Accounting Standards Board Statement of Governmental Accounting Standards No. 31, *Accounting and Financial Reporting for Certain Investments and for External Investment Pools*, defines *fair value* as "the amount at which an investment could be exchanged in a current transaction between willing parties, other than in a forced or liquidation sale." [Footnote revised, June 2009, to reflect conforming changes necessary due to the issuance of FASB ASC.]

[Revised, March 2008, to reflect conforming changes necessary due to the issuance of Statement on Auditing Standards No. 105. Revised, June 2009, to reflect conforming changes necessary due to the issuance of FASB ASC.]

.04 Management is responsible for making the fair value measurements and disclosures included in the financial statements. As part of fulfilling its responsibility, management needs to establish an accounting and financial reporting process for determining the fair value measurements and disclosures, select appropriate valuation methods, identify and adequately support any significant assumptions used, prepare the valuation, and ensure that the presentation and disclosure of the fair value measurements are in accordance with GAAP.

.05 Fair value measurements for which observable market prices are not available are inherently imprecise. That is because, among other things, those fair value measurements may be based on assumptions about future conditions, transactions, or events whose outcome is uncertain and will therefore be subject to change over time. The auditor's consideration of such assumptions is based on information available to the auditor at the time of the audit. The auditor is not responsible for predicting future conditions, transactions, or events that, had they been known at the time of the audit, may have had a significant effect on management's actions or management's assumptions underlying the fair value measurements and disclosures.[2]

.06 Assumptions used in fair value measurements are similar in nature to those required when developing other accounting estimates. However, if observable market prices are not available, GAAP requires that valuation methods incorporate assumptions that marketplace participants would use in their estimates of fair value whenever that information is available without undue cost and effort. If information about market assumptions is not available, an entity may use its own assumptions as long as there are no contrary data indicating that marketplace participants would use different assumptions. These concepts generally are not relevant for accounting estimates made under measurement bases other than fair value. Section 342, *Auditing Accounting Estimates*, provides guidance on auditing accounting estimates in general. This section addresses considerations similar to those in section 342 as well as others in the specific context of fair value measurements and disclosures in accordance with GAAP.

.07 GAAP requires or permits a variety of fair value measurements and disclosures in financial statements. GAAP also varies in the level of guidance that it provides on measuring fair values and disclosures. While this section provides guidance on auditing fair value measurements and disclosures, it does not address specific types of assets, liabilities, components of equity, transactions, or industry-specific practices.[3]

.08 The measurement of fair value may be relatively simple for certain assets or liabilities, for example, investments that are bought and sold in active markets that provide readily available and reliable information on the prices at which actual exchanges occur. For those items, the existence of published

---

[2] For purposes of this section, management's assumptions include assumptions developed by management under the guidance of those charged with governance and assumptions developed by a specialist engaged or employed by management. [Footnote revised, April 2007, to reflect conforming changes necessary due to the issuance of Statement on Auditing Standards No. 114.]

[3] See, for example, section 332, *Auditing Derivative Instruments, Hedging Activities, and Investments in Securities*.

price quotations in an active market is the best evidence of fair value. The measurement of fair value for other assets or liabilities may be more complex. A specific asset may not have an observable market price or may possess such characteristics that it becomes necessary for management to estimate its fair value based on the best information available in the circumstances (for example, a complex derivative financial instrument). The estimation of fair value may be achieved through the use of a valuation method (for example, a model premised on discounting of estimated future cash flows).

Understanding the Entity's Process for Determining Fair Value Measurements and Disclosures and the Relevant Controls, and Assessing Risk

.09 The auditor should obtain an understanding of the entity's process for determining fair value measurements and disclosures and of the relevant controls sufficient to develop an effective audit approach.

.10 Management is responsible for establishing an accounting and financial reporting process for determining fair value measurements. In some cases, the measurement of fair value and therefore the process set up by management to determine fair value may be simple and reliable. For example, management may be able to refer to published price quotations in an active market to determine fair value for marketable securities held by the entity. Some fair value measurements, however, are inherently more complex than others and involve uncertainty about the occurrence of future events or their outcome, and therefore assumptions that may involve the use of judgment need to be made as part of the measurement process.

.11 Section 314, *Understanding the Entity and its Environment and Assessing the Risks of Material Misstatement*, requires the auditor to obtain an understanding of each of the five components of internal control sufficient to assess the risk of material misstatement. In the specific context of this section, the auditor obtains such an understanding related to the determination of the entity's fair value measurements and disclosures in order to plan the nature, timing, and extent of the audit procedures. [Revised, March 2006, to reflect conforming changes necessary due to the issuance of Statement on Auditing Standards No. 109.]

.12 When obtaining an understanding of the entity's process for determining fair value measurements and disclosures, the auditor considers, for example:

- Controls over the process used to determine fair value measurements, including, for example, controls over data and the segregation of duties between those committing the entity to the underlying transactions and those responsible for undertaking the valuations.
- The expertise and experience of those persons determining the fair value measurements.
- The role that information technology has in the process.
- The types of accounts or transactions requiring fair value measurements or disclosures (for example, whether the accounts arise from the recording of routine and recurring transactions or whether they arise from nonroutine or unusual transactions).
- The extent to which the entity's process relies on a service organization to provide fair value measurements or the data that supports the

measurement. When an entity uses a service organization, the auditor considers the requirements for user auditors in section 324, *Service Organizations*.[4]

- The extent to which the entity engages or employs specialists in determining fair value measurements and disclosures.
- The significant management assumptions used in determining fair value.
- The documentation supporting management's assumptions.
- The process used to develop and apply management assumptions, including whether management used available market information to develop the assumptions.
- The process used to monitor changes in management's assumptions.
- The integrity of change controls and security procedures for valuation models and relevant information systems, including approval processes.
- The controls over the consistency, timeliness, and reliability of the data used in valuation models.

[Revised, August 2011, to reflect conforming changes necessary due to the issuance of SSAE No. 16.]

.13 The auditor uses his or her understanding of the entity's process, including its complexity, and of the controls when assessing the risk of material misstatement. Based on that risk assessment, the auditor determines the nature, timing, and extent of the audit procedures. The risk of material misstatement may increase as the accounting and financial reporting requirements for fair value measurements become more complex.

.14 Section 314 discusses the inherent limitations of internal control. As fair value determinations often involve subjective judgments by management, this may affect the nature of controls that are capable of being implemented, including the possibility of management override of controls (see section 316, *Consideration of Fraud in a Financial Statement Audit*). The auditor considers the inherent limitations of internal control in such circumstances in assessing control risk. [Revised, March 2006, to reflect conforming changes necessary due to the issuance of Statement on Auditing Standards No. 109.]

Evaluating Conformity of Fair Value Measurements and Disclosures With GAAP

.15 The auditor should evaluate whether the fair value measurements and disclosures in the financial statements are in conformity with GAAP. The auditor's understanding of the requirements of GAAP and knowledge of the business and industry, together with the results of other audit procedures, are used to evaluate the accounting for assets or liabilities requiring fair value measurements, and the disclosures about the basis for the fair value measurements and significant uncertainties related thereto.

---

[4] Section 324, *Service Organizations*, contains the requirements and guidance for auditors of the financial statements of entities that use a service organization (user auditors). The requirements and guidance in section 324 for service auditors reporting on controls at a service organization has been superseded by AT section 801, *Reporting on Controls at a Service Organization*. [Footnote added, August 2011, to reflect conforming changes necessary due to the issuance of SSAE No. 16.]

.16 The evaluation of the entity's fair value measurements and of the audit evidence depends, in part, on the auditor's knowledge of the nature of the business. This is particularly true where the asset or liability or the valuation method is highly complex. For example, derivative financial instruments may be highly complex, with a risk that differing assumptions used in determining fair values will result in different conclusions. The measurement of the fair value of some items, for example "in process research and development" or intangible assets acquired in a business combination, may involve special considerations that are affected by the nature of the entity and its operations. Also, the auditor's knowledge of the business, together with the results of other audit procedures, may help identify assets for which management should assess the need to recognize an impairment loss under applicable GAAP.

.17 The auditor should evaluate management's intent to carry out specific courses of action where intent is relevant to the use of fair value measurements, the related requirements involving presentation and disclosures, and how changes in fair values are reported in financial statements. The auditor also should evaluate management's ability to carry out those courses of action. Management often documents plans and intentions relevant to specific assets or liabilities and GAAP may require it to do so. While the extent of evidence to be obtained about management's intent and ability is a matter of professional judgment, the auditor's procedures ordinarily include inquiries of management, with appropriate corroboration of responses, for example, by:

- Considering management's past history of carrying out its stated intentions with respect to assets or liabilities.
- Reviewing written plans and other documentation, including, where applicable, budgets, minutes, and other such items.
- Considering management's stated reasons for choosing a particular course of action.
- Considering management's ability to carry out a particular course of action given the entity's economic circumstances, including the implications of its contractual commitments.

.18 When there are no observable market prices and the entity estimates fair value using a valuation method, the auditor should evaluate whether the entity's method of measurement is appropriate in the circumstances. That evaluation requires the use of professional judgment. It also involves obtaining an understanding of management's rationale for selecting a particular method by discussing with management its reasons for selecting the valuation method. The auditor considers whether:

a. Management has sufficiently evaluated and appropriately applied the criteria, if any, provided by GAAP to support the selected method.

b. The valuation method is appropriate in the circumstances given the nature of the item being valued.

c. The valuation method is appropriate in relation to the business, industry, and environment in which the entity operates.

Management may have determined that different valuation methods result in a range of significantly different fair value measurements. In such cases, the auditor evaluates how the entity has investigated the reasons for these differences in establishing its fair value measurements.

.19 The auditor should evaluate whether the entity's method for determining fair value measurements is applied consistently and if so, whether the consistency is appropriate considering possible changes in the environment or circumstances affecting the entity, or changes in accounting principles. If management has changed the method for determining fair value, the auditor considers whether management can adequately demonstrate that the method to which it has changed provides a more appropriate basis of measurement or whether the change is supported by a change in the GAAP requirements or a change in circumstances.[5] For example, the introduction of an active market for an equity security may indicate that the use of the discounted cash flows method to estimate the fair value of the security is no longer appropriate.

Engaging a Specialist

.20 The auditor should consider whether to engage a specialist and use the work of that specialist as audit evidence in performing substantive tests to evaluate material financial statement assertions. The auditor may have the necessary skill and knowledge to plan and perform audit procedures related to fair values or may decide to use the work of a specialist. If the use of such a specialist is planned, the auditor should consider the guidance in section 336, *Using the Work of a Specialist*. [Revised, March 2006, to reflect conforming changes necessary due to the issuance of Statement on Auditing Standards No. 105.]

.21 When planning to use the work of a specialist in auditing fair value measurements, the auditor considers whether the specialist's understanding of the definition of fair value and the method that the specialist will use to determine fair value are consistent with those of management and with GAAP. For example, the method used by a specialist for estimating the fair value of real estate or a complex derivative may not be consistent with the measurement principles specified in GAAP. Accordingly, the auditor considers such matters, often through discussions with the specialist or by reading the report of the specialist.

.22 Section 336 provides that, while the reasonableness of assumptions and the appropriateness of the methods used and their application are the responsibility of the specialist, the auditor obtains an understanding of the assumptions and methods used. However, if the auditor believes the findings are unreasonable, he or she applies additional procedures as required in section 336.

Testing the Entity's Fair Value Measurements and Disclosures

.23 Based on the auditor's assessment of the risk of material misstatement, the auditor should test the entity's fair value measurements and disclosures. Because of the wide range of possible fair value measurements, from relatively simple to complex, and the varying levels of risk of material misstatement associated with the process for determining fair values, the auditor's planned audit procedures can vary significantly in nature, timing, and extent. For example, substantive tests of the fair value measurements may involve (*a*) testing management's significant assumptions, the valuation model, and the

---

[5] Paragraphs 1–2 of Financial Accounting Standards Board (FASB) *Accounting Standards Codification* (ASC) 250-10-45 state that a presumption exists that an accounting principle once adopted shall not be changed in accounting for events and transactions of a similar type. Consistent use of the same accounting principle from one accounting period to another enhances the utility of financial statements for users by facilitating analysis and understanding of comparative accounting data. A reporting entity shall change an accounting principle only if either of the following apply:

a. The change is required by a newly issued codification update.

b. The entity can justify the use of an allowable alternative accounting principle on the basis that it is preferable.

[Footnote revised, June 2009, to reflect conforming changes necessary due to the issuance of FASB ASC. Footnote renumbered, August 2011, to reflect conforming changes necessary due to the issuance of SSAE No. 16.]

underlying data (see paragraphs .26 through .39), (*b*) developing independent fair value estimates for corroborative purposes (see paragraph .40), or (*c*) reviewing subsequent events and transactions (see paragraphs .41 and .42).

.24 Some fair value measurements are inherently more complex than others. This complexity arises either because of the nature of the item being measured at fair value or because of the valuation method used to determine fair value. For example, in the absence of quoted prices in an active market, an estimate of a security's fair value may be based on valuation methods such as the discounted cash flow method or the transactions method. Complex fair value measurements normally are characterized by greater uncertainty regarding the reliability of the measurement process. This greater uncertainty may be a result of:

- The length of the forecast period
- The number of significant and complex assumptions associated with the process
- A higher degree of subjectivity associated with the assumptions and factors used in the process
- A higher degree of uncertainty associated with the future occurrence or outcome of events underlying the assumptions used
- Lack of objective data when highly subjective factors are used

.25 The auditor uses both the understanding of management's process for determining fair value measurements and his or her assessment of the risk of material misstatement to determine the nature, timing, and extent of the audit procedures. The following are examples of considerations in the development of audit procedures:

- The fair value measurement (for example, a valuation by an independent appraiser) may be made at a date that does not coincide with the date at which the entity is required to measure and report that information in its financial statements. In such cases, the auditor obtains evidence that management has taken into account the effect of events, transactions, and changes in circumstances occurring between the date of the fair value measurement and the reporting date.
- Collateral often is assigned for certain types of investments in debt instruments that either are required to be measured at fair value or are evaluated for possible impairment. If the collateral is an important factor in measuring the fair value of the investment or evaluating its carrying amount, the auditor obtains sufficient appropriate audit evidence regarding the existence, value, rights, and access to or transferability of such collateral, including consideration of whether all appropriate liens have been filed, and considers whether appropriate disclosures about the collateral have been made.
- In some situations, additional procedures, such as the inspection of an asset by the auditor, may be necessary to obtain sufficient appropriate audit evidence about the appropriateness of a fair value measurement. For example, inspection of the asset may be necessary to obtain information about the current physical condition of the asset relevant to its fair value, or inspection of a security may reveal a restriction on its marketability that may affect its value.

[Revised, March 2008, to reflect conforming changes necessary due to the issuance of Statement on Auditing Standards No. 105.]

Testing Management's Significant Assumptions, the Valuation Model, and the Underlying Data

.26 The auditor's understanding of the reliability of the process used by management to determine fair value is an important element in support of the resulting amounts and therefore affects the nature, timing, and extent of audit procedures. When testing the entity's fair value measurements and disclosures, the auditor evaluates whether:

a. Management's assumptions are reasonable and reflect, or are not inconsistent with, market information (see paragraph .06).

b. The fair value measurement was determined using an appropriate model, if applicable.

c. Management used relevant information that was reasonably available at the time.

.27 Estimation methods and assumptions, and the auditor's consideration and comparison of fair value measurements determined in prior periods, if any, to results obtained in the current period, may provide evidence of the reliability of management's processes. However, the auditor also considers whether variances from the prior-period fair value measurements result from changes in market or economic circumstances.

.28 Where applicable, the auditor should evaluate whether the significant assumptions used by management in measuring fair value, taken individually and as a whole, provide a reasonable basis for the fair value measurements and disclosures in the entity's financial statements.

.29 Assumptions are integral components of more complex valuation methods, for example, valuation methods that employ a combination of estimates of expected future cash flows together with estimates of the values of assets or liabilities in the future, discounted to the present. Auditors pay particular attention to the significant assumptions underlying a valuation method and evaluate whether such assumptions are reasonable and reflect, or are not inconsistent with, market information (see paragraph .06).

.30 Specific assumptions will vary with the characteristics of the item being valued and the valuation approach used (for example, cost, market, or income). For example, where the discounted cash flows method (a method under the income approach) is used, there will be assumptions about the level of cash flows, the period of time used in the analysis, and the discount rate.

.31 Assumptions ordinarily are supported by differing types of evidence from internal and external sources that provide objective support for the assumptions used. The auditor evaluates the source and reliability of evidence supporting management's assumptions, including consideration of the assumptions in light of historical and market information.

.32 Audit procedures dealing with management's assumptions are performed in the context of the audit of the entity's financial statements. The objective of the audit procedures is therefore not intended to obtain sufficient appropriate audit evidence to provide an opinion on the assumptions themselves. Rather, the auditor performs procedures to evaluate whether the assumptions provide a reasonable basis for measuring fair values in the context of an audit of the financial statements taken as a whole. [Revised, March 2008, to reflect conforming changes necessary due to the issuance of Statement on Auditing Standards No. 105.]

.33 Identifying those assumptions that appear to be significant to the fair value measurement requires the exercise of judgment by management.

The auditor focuses attention on the significant assumptions that management has identified. Generally, significant assumptions cover matters that materially affect the fair value measurement and may include those that are:

a. Sensitive to variation or uncertainty in amount or nature. For example, assumptions about short-term interest rates may be less susceptible to significant variation compared to assumptions about long-term interest rates.

b. Susceptible to misapplication or bias.

.34 The auditor considers the sensitivity of the valuation to changes in significant assumptions, including market conditions that may affect the value. Where applicable, the auditor encourages management to use techniques such as sensitivity analysis to help identify particularly sensitive assumptions. If management has not identified particularly sensitive assumptions, the auditor considers whether to employ techniques to identify those assumptions.

.35 The evaluation of whether the assumptions provide a reasonable basis for the fair value measurements relates to the whole set of assumptions as well as to each assumption individually. Assumptions are frequently interdependent and therefore need to be internally consistent. A particular assumption that may appear reasonable when taken in isolation may not be reasonable when used in conjunction with other assumptions. The auditor considers whether management has identified the significant assumptions and factors influencing the measurement of fair value.

.36 To be reasonable, the assumptions on which the fair value measurements are based (for example, the discount rate used in calculating the present value of future cash flows),[6] individually and taken as a whole, need to be realistic and consistent with:

a. The general economic environment, the economic environment of the specific industry, and the entity's economic circumstances;

b. Existing market information;

c. The plans of the entity, including what management expects will be the outcome of specific objectives and strategies;

d. Assumptions made in prior periods, if appropriate;

e. Past experience of, or previous conditions experienced by, the entity to the extent currently applicable;

f. Other matters relating to the financial statements, for example, assumptions used by management in accounting estimates for financial statement accounts other than those relating to fair value measurements and disclosures; and

g. The risk associated with cash flows, if applicable, including the potential variability in the amount and timing of the cash flows and the related effect on the discount rate.

Where assumptions are reflective of management's intent and ability to carry out specific courses of action, the auditor considers whether they are consistent with the entity's plans and past experience.

.37 If management relies on historical financial information in the development of assumptions, the auditor considers the extent to which such reliance

---

[6] The auditor also should consider requirements of FASB ASC 820, *Fair Value Measurements and Disclosures*. [Footnote revised, June 2009, to reflect conforming changes necessary due to the issuance of FASB ASC. Footnote renumbered, August 2011, to reflect conforming changes necessary due to the issuance of SSAE No. 16.]

is justified. However, historical information might not be representative of future conditions or events, for example, if management intends to engage in new activities or circumstances change.

.38 For items valued by the entity using a valuation model, the auditor does not function as an appraiser and is not expected to substitute his or her judgment for that of the entity's management. Rather, the auditor reviews the model and evaluates whether the assumptions used are reasonable and the model is appropriate considering the entity's circumstances. For example, it may be inappropriate to use discounted cash flows for valuing an equity investment in a start-up enterprise if there are no current revenues on which to base the forecast of future earnings or cash flows.

.39 The auditor should test the data used to develop the fair value measurements and disclosures and evaluate whether the fair value measurements have been properly determined from such data and management's assumptions. Specifically, the auditor evaluates whether the data on which the fair value measurements are based, including the data used in the work of a specialist, is accurate, complete, and relevant; and whether fair value measurements have been properly determined using such data and management's assumptions. The auditor's tests also may include, for example, procedures such as verifying the source of the data, mathematical recomputation of inputs, and reviewing of information for internal consistency, including whether such information is consistent with management's intent and ability to carry out specific courses of action discussed in paragraph .17.

Developing Independent Fair Value Estimates for Corroborative Purposes

.40 The auditor may make an independent estimate of fair value (for example, by using an auditor-developed model) to corroborate the entity's fair value measurement.[7] When developing an independent estimate using management's assumptions, the auditor evaluates those assumptions as discussed in paragraphs .28 to .37. Instead of using management's assumptions, the auditor may develop his or her own assumptions to make a comparison with management's fair value measurements. In that situation, the auditor nevertheless understands management's assumptions. The auditor uses that understanding to ensure that his or her independent estimate takes into consideration all significant variables and to evaluate any significant difference from management's estimate. The auditor also should test the data used to develop the fair value measurements and disclosures as discussed in paragraph .39.

Reviewing Subsequent Events and Transactions

.41 Events and transactions that occur after the balance-sheet date but before the date of the auditor's report (for example, a sale of an investment shortly after the balance-sheet date) may provide audit evidence regarding management's fair value measurements as of the balance-sheet date.[8] In such circumstances, the audit procedures described in paragraphs .26 through .40 may be minimized or unnecessary because the subsequent event or transaction

---

[7] See section 329, *Analytical Procedures*. [Footnote renumbered, August 2011, to reflect conforming changes necessary due to the issuance of SSAE No. 16.]

[8] The auditor's consideration of a subsequent event or transaction, as contemplated in this paragraph, is a substantive test and thus differs from the review of subsequent events performed pursuant to section 560, *Subsequent Events*. [Footnote renumbered, August 2011, to reflect conforming changes necessary due to the issuance of SSAE No. 16.]

can be used to substantiate the fair value measurement. [As amended, effective for audits of financial statements for periods ending on or after December 15, 2006, by Statement on Auditing Standards No. 113.]

.42 Some subsequent events or transactions may reflect changes in circumstances occurring after the balance-sheet date and thus do not constitute appropriate audit evidence of the fair value measurement at the balance-sheet date (for example, the prices of actively traded marketable securities that change after the balance-sheet date). When using a subsequent event or transaction to substantiate a fair value measurement, the auditor considers only those events or transactions that reflect circumstances existing at the balance-sheet date.

Disclosures About Fair Values

.43 The auditor should evaluate whether the disclosures about fair values made by the entity are in conformity with GAAP.[9] Disclosure of fair value information is an important aspect of financial statements. Often, fair value disclosure is required because of the relevance to users in the evaluation of an entity's performance and financial position. In addition to the fair value information required under GAAP, some entities disclose voluntary additional fair value information in the notes to the financial statements.

.44 When auditing fair value measurements and related disclosures included in the notes to the financial statements, whether required by GAAP or disclosed voluntarily, the auditor ordinarily performs essentially the same types of audit procedures as those employed in auditing a fair value measurement recognized in the financial statements. The auditor obtains sufficient appropriate audit evidence that the valuation principles are appropriate under GAAP and are being consistently applied, and that the method of estimation and significant assumptions used are adequately disclosed in accordance with GAAP. [Revised, March 2008, to reflect conforming changes necessary due to the issuance of Statement on Auditing Standards No. 105.]

.45 The auditor evaluates whether the entity has made adequate disclosures about fair value information. If an item contains a high degree of measurement uncertainty, the auditor assesses whether the disclosures are sufficient to inform users of such uncertainty.[10]

.46 When disclosure of fair value information under GAAP is omitted because it is not practicable to determine fair value with sufficient reliability, the auditor evaluates the adequacy of disclosures required in these circumstances. If the entity has not appropriately disclosed fair value information required by GAAP, the auditor evaluates whether the financial statements are materially misstated.

Evaluating the Results of Audit Procedures

.47 The auditor should evaluate the sufficiency and competence of the audit evidence obtained from auditing fair value measurements and disclosures as well as the consistency of that evidence with other audit evidence obtained and evaluated during the audit. The auditor's evaluation of whether the fair value measurements and disclosures in the financial statements are in conformity with GAAP is performed in the context of the financial statements taken

---

[9] See also section 431, *Adequacy of Disclosure in Financial Statements*. [Footnote renumbered, August 2011, to reflect conforming changes necessary due to the issuance of SSAE No. 16.]

[10] See FASB ASC 275, *Risks and Uncertainties*. [Footnote revised, June 2009, to reflect conforming changes necessary due to the issuance of FASB ASC. Footnote renumbered, August 2011, to reflect conforming changes necessary due to the issuance of SSAE No. 16.]

as a whole (see section 312, *Audit Risk and Materiality in Conducting an Audit*, paragraphs .50 through .61). [Revised, March 2006, to reflect conforming changes necessary due to the issuance of Statement on Auditing Standards No. 107.]

Management Representations

.48 Section 333, *Management Representations*, requires that the independent auditor obtain written representations from management as a part of an audit of financial statements performed in accordance with generally accepted auditing standards and provides guidance concerning the representations to be obtained. The auditor ordinarily should obtain written representations from management regarding the reasonableness of significant assumptions, including whether they appropriately reflect management's intent and ability to carry out specific courses of action on behalf of the entity where relevant to the use of fair value measurements or disclosures.

.49 Depending on the nature, materiality, and complexity of fair values, management representations about fair value measurements and disclosures contained in the financial statements also may include representations about:

- The appropriateness of the measurement methods, including related assumptions, used by management in determining fair value and the consistency in application of the methods.
- The completeness and adequacy of disclosures related to fair values.
- Whether subsequent events require adjustment to the fair value measurements and disclosures included in the financial statements.

Communication With Those Charged With Governance

.50 Section 380, *The Auditor's Communication With Those Charged With Governance*, requires auditors to determine that certain matters related to the conduct of an audit are communicated to those charged with governance. Certain accounting estimates are particularly sensitive because of their significance to the financial statements and because of the possibility that future events affecting them may differ markedly from management's current judgments. For example, the auditor considers communicating the nature of significant assumptions used in fair value measurements, the degree of subjectivity involved in the development of the assumptions, and the relative materiality of the items being measured at fair value to the financial statements as a whole. The auditor considers the guidance contained in section 380 when determining the nature and form of communication. [Revised, April 2007, to reflect conforming changes necessary due to the issuance of Statement on Auditing Standards No. 114.]

Effective Date

.51 This section is effective for audits of financial statements for periods beginning on or after June 15, 2003. Earlier application of the provisions of this section is permitted.

AU Section 9328

Auditing Fair Value Measurements and Disclosures: Auditing Interpretations of Section 328

1. Auditing Interests in Trusts Held by a Third-Party Trustee and Reported at Fair Value

.01 *Question*—Entities may have interests in trusts held by a third-party trustee. For example, a not-for-profit organization (NPO) may have an interest in a trust established by a donor for the benefit of the NPO. Further, that interest may be required to be reported at fair value because it is a beneficial interest pursuant to Financial Accounting Standards Board *Accounting Standards Codification* 958, *Not-for-Profit Entities*. Further, the fair value of that beneficial interest may be estimated, at least in part, because a readily determinable fair value does not exist. For example, the NPO may have an unconditional right to receive all or a portion of the specified cash flows from a charitable trust that has investments in limited partnership interests or other private equity securities for which a readily determinable fair value does not exist. In such circumstances, the auditor typically would satisfy the existence assertion through confirmation, examination of legal documents, or other means. In confirming the existence, the auditor may request the trustee to indicate or to confirm the trust's fair value, including the fair value of investments held in the trust. In some circumstances, the trustee will not provide management or the auditor detailed information about the basis and method for measuring those investments, nor will they provide information about the specific investments held by the trust. For example, in some circumstances the trustee may inform management or the auditor that investments are held by the trust as follows:

- In aggregate, such as "$XXX of total investments"
- In aggregate, such as "$XXX of total investments in private equity securities, $YYY of total investments in interests in limited partnerships, and $ZZZ of total investments in debt securities"
- On an investment-by-investment basis, such as "AA shares of common stock of private company A, with a fair value of $AAA; BB shares of preferred stock of private company B, with a fair value of $BBB; CC units of limited partnership interest CCC, with a fair value of $CCC; and real estate property DDD, with a fair value of $DDDD"

In circumstances in which the auditor determines that the nature and extent of auditing procedures should include verifying the existence and testing the measurement of investments held by a trust, does receiving a confirmation from the trustee, either in aggregate or on an investment-by-investment basis, constitute adequate audit evidence with respect to the existence assertion and auditing fair value measurements in accordance with section 328, *Auditing Fair Value Measurements and Disclosures*?

.02 *Interpretation*—In circumstances in which the auditor determines that the nature and extent of auditing procedures should include verifying the existence and testing the measurement of investments held by a trust, simply receiving a confirmation from the trustee, either in aggregate or on an investment-by-investment basis, does not in and of itself constitute adequate audit evidence with respect to the requirements for auditing the fair value of the interest in the trust under section 328. In addition, receiving confirmation from the trustee for investments in aggregate (illustrated by the first two bullets in the preceding paragraph) does not constitute adequate audit evidence with respect to the existence assertion. Receiving confirmation from the trustee on an investment-by-investment basis (illustrated by the third bullet in the preceding paragraph), however, typically would constitute adequate audit evidence with respect to the existence assertion. Also, as noted in section 328 paragraph .04, in discussing management's responsibility for making fair value measurements:

> Management is responsible for making the fair value measurements and disclosures included in the financial statements. As part of fulfilling its responsibility, management needs to establish an accounting and financial reporting process for determining the fair value measurements and disclosures, select appropriate valuation methods, identify and adequately support any significant assumptions used, prepare the valuation, and ensure that the presentation and disclosure of the fair value measurements are in accordance with GAAP.

.03 In addition, section 328 discusses the auditor's responsibility dealing with:

- Understanding the entity's process for determining fair value measurements and disclosures and the relevant controls, and assessing risk
- Evaluating conformity of fair value measurements and disclosures with GAAP
- Engaging a specialist, where necessary
- Testing the entity's fair value measurements and disclosures
- Disclosures about fair values
- Evaluating the results of audit procedures
- Management representations
- Communication with those charged with governance

.04 In circumstances in which the auditor is unable to audit the existence or measurement of interests in trusts at the financial statement date, the auditor should consider whether that scope limitation requires the auditor to either qualify his or her opinion or to disclaim an opinion, as discussed in section 508, *Reports on Audited Financial Statements*, paragraphs .22–.26.

[Issue Date: July 2005; Revised: April 2007; Revised: June 2009.]

AU Section 329

Analytical Procedures

(Supersedes section 318.)

Source: SAS No. 56; SAS No. 96.

Effective for audits of financial statements for periods beginning on or after January 1, 1989, unless otherwise indicated.

.01 This section provides guidance on the use of analytical procedures and requires the use of analytical procedures in the planning and overall review stages of all audits.

.02 Analytical procedures are an important part of the audit process and consist of evaluations of financial information made by a study of plausible relationships among both financial and nonfinancial data. Analytical procedures range from simple comparisons to the use of complex models involving many relationships and elements of data. A basic premise underlying the application of analytical procedures is that plausible relationships among data may reasonably be expected to exist and continue in the absence of known conditions to the contrary. Particular conditions that can cause variations in these relationships include, for example, specific unusual transactions or events, accounting changes, business changes, random fluctuations, or misstatements.

.03 Understanding financial relationships is essential in planning and evaluating the results of analytical procedures, and generally requires knowledge of the client and the industry or industries in which the client operates. An understanding of the purposes of analytical procedures and the limitations of those procedures is also important. Accordingly, the identification of the relationships and types of data used, as well as conclusions reached when recorded amounts are compared to expectations, requires judgment by the auditor.

.04 Analytical procedures are used for the following purposes:

a. To assist the auditor in planning the nature, timing, and extent of other auditing procedures

b. As a substantive test to obtain audit evidence about particular assertions related to account balances or classes of transactions

c. As an overall review of the financial information in the final review stage of the audit

Analytical procedures should be applied to some extent for the purposes referred to in (*a*) and (*c*) above for all audits of financial statements made in accordance with generally accepted auditing standards. In addition, in some cases, analytical procedures can be more effective or efficient than tests of details for achieving particular substantive testing objectives. [Revised, March, 2006, to reflect conforming changes necessary due to the issuance of Statement on Auditing Standards No. 105.]

.05 Analytical procedures involve comparisons of recorded amounts, or ratios developed from recorded amounts, to expectations developed by the auditor. The auditor develops such expectations by identifying and using plausible relationships that are reasonably expected to exist based on the auditor's understanding of the client and of the industry in which the client operates. Following are examples of sources of information for developing expectations:

a. Financial information for comparable prior period(s) giving consideration to known changes

b. Anticipated results—for example, budgets, or forecasts including extrapolations from interim or annual data

c. Relationships among elements of financial information within the period

d. Information regarding the industry in which the client operates—for example, gross margin information

e. Relationships of financial information with relevant nonfinancial information

Analytical Procedures in Planning the Audit

.06 The purpose of applying analytical procedures in planning the audit is to assist in planning the nature, timing, and extent of auditing procedures that will be used to obtain audit evidence for specific account balances or classes of transactions. To accomplish this, the analytical procedures used in planning the audit should focus on (*a*) enhancing the auditor's understanding of the client's business and the transactions and events that have occurred since the last audit date, and (*b*) identifying areas that may represent specific risks relevant to the audit. Thus, the objective of the procedures is to identify such things as the existence of unusual transactions and events, and amounts, ratios and trends that might indicate matters that have financial statement and audit planning ramifications. [Revised, March, 2006, to reflect conforming changes necessary due to the issuance of Statement on Auditing Standards No. 105.]

.07 Analytical procedures used in planning the audit generally use data aggregated at a high level. Furthermore, the sophistication, extent and timing of the procedures, which are based on the auditor's judgment, may vary widely depending on the size and complexity of the client. For some entities, the procedures may consist of reviewing changes in account balances from the prior to the current year using the general ledger or the auditor's preliminary or unadjusted working trial balance. In contrast, for other entities, the procedures might involve an extensive analysis of quarterly financial statements. In both cases, the analytical procedures, combined with the auditor's knowledge of the business, serve as a basis for additional inquiries and effective planning.

.08 Although analytical procedures used in planning the audit often use only financial data, sometimes relevant nonfinancial information is considered as well. For example, number of employees, square footage of selling space, volume of goods produced, and similar information may contribute to accomplishing the purpose of the procedures.

Analytical Procedures Used as Substantive Tests

.09 The auditor's reliance on substantive tests to achieve an audit objective related to a particular assertion[1] may be derived from tests of details, from

---

[1] Assertions are representations by management that are embodied in financial statement components. See section 326, *Audit Evidence*. [Revised, March 2006, to reflect conforming changes necessary due to the issuance of Statement on Auditing Standards No. 106.]

analytical procedures, or from a combination of both. The decision about which procedure or procedures to use to achieve a particular audit objective is based on the auditor's judgment on the expected effectiveness and efficiency of the available procedures.

.10 The auditor considers the level of assurance, if any, he wants from substantive testing for a particular audit objective and decides, among other things, which procedure, or combination of procedures, can provide that level of assurance. For some assertions, analytical procedures are effective in providing the appropriate level of assurance. For other assertions, however, analytical procedures may not be as effective or efficient as tests of details in providing the desired level of assurance.

.11 The expected effectiveness and efficiency of an analytical procedure in identifying potential misstatements depends on, among other things, (*a*) the nature of the assertion, (*b*) the plausibility and predictability of the relationship, (*c*) the availability and reliability of the data used to develop the expectation, and (*d*) the precision of the expectation.

Nature of Assertion

.12 Analytical procedures may be effective and efficient tests for assertions in which potential misstatements would not be apparent from an examination of the detailed evidence or in which detailed evidence is not readily available. For example, comparisons of aggregate salaries paid with the number of personnel may indicate unauthorized payments that may not be apparent from testing individual transactions. Differences from expected relationships may also indicate potential omissions when independent evidence that an individual transaction should have been recorded may not be readily available.

Plausibility and Predictability of the Relationship

.13 It is important for the auditor to understand the reasons that make relationships plausible because data sometimes appear to be related when they are not, which could lead the auditor to erroneous conclusions. In addition, the presence of an unexpected relationship can provide important evidence when appropriately scrutinized.

.14 As higher levels of assurance are desired from analytical procedures, more predictable relationships are required to develop the expectation. Relationships in a stable environment are usually more predictable than relationships in a dynamic or unstable environment. Relationships involving income statement accounts tend to be more predictable than relationships involving only balance sheet accounts since income statement accounts represent transactions over a period of time, whereas balance sheet accounts represent amounts as of a point in time. Relationships involving transactions subject to management discretion are sometimes less predictable. For example, management may elect to incur maintenance expense rather than replace plant and equipment, or they may delay advertising expenditures.

Availability and Reliability of Data

.15 Data may or may not be readily available to develop expectations for some assertions. For example, to test the completeness assertion, expected sales for some entities might be developed from production statistics or square feet of selling space. For other entities, data relevant to the assertion of completeness of sales may not be readily available, and it may be more effective or efficient to use the details of shipping records to test that assertion.

.16 The auditor obtains assurance from analytical procedures based upon the consistency of the recorded amounts with expectations developed from data derived from other sources. The reliability of the data used to develop the expectations should be appropriate for the desired level of assurance from the analytical procedure. The auditor should assess the reliability of the data by considering the source of the data and the conditions under which it was gathered, as well as other knowledge the auditor may have about the data. The following factors influence the auditor's consideration of the reliability of data for purposes of achieving audit objectives:

- Whether the data was obtained from independent sources outside the entity or from sources within the entity
- Whether sources within the entity were independent of those who are responsible for the amount being audited
- Whether the data was developed under a reliable system with adequate controls
- Whether the data was subjected to audit testing in the current or prior year
- Whether the expectations were developed using data from a variety of sources

Precision of the Expectation

.17 The expectation should be precise enough to provide the desired level of assurance that differences that may be potential material misstatements, individually or when aggregated with other misstatements, would be identified for the auditor to investigate (see paragraph .20). As expectations become more precise, the range of expected differences becomes narrower and, accordingly, the likelihood increases that significant differences from the expectations are due to misstatements. The precision of the expectation depends on, among other things, the auditor's identification and consideration of factors that significantly affect the amount being audited and the level of detail of data used to develop the expectation.

.18 Many factors can influence financial relationships. For example, sales are affected by prices, volume and product mix. Each of these, in turn, may be affected by a number of factors, and offsetting factors can obscure misstatements. More effective identification of factors that significantly affect the relationship is generally needed as the desired level of assurance from analytical procedures increases.

.19 Expectations developed at a detailed level generally have a greater chance of detecting misstatement of a given amount than do broad comparisons. Monthly amounts will generally be more effective than annual amounts and comparisons by location or line of business usually will be more effective than company-wide comparisons. The level of detail that is appropriate will be influenced by the nature of the client, its size and its complexity. Generally, the risk that material misstatement could be obscured by offsetting factors increases as a client's operations become more complex and more diversified. Disaggregation helps reduce this risk.

Investigation and Evaluation of Significant Differences

.20 In planning the analytical procedures as a substantive test, the auditor should consider the amount of difference from the expectation that can be accepted without further investigation. This consideration is influenced primarily by materiality and should be consistent with the level of assurance desired from the procedures. Determination of this amount involves considering the possibility that a combination of misstatements in the specific account balances, or class of transactions, or other balances or classes could aggregate to an unacceptable amount.[2]

.21 The auditor should evaluate significant unexpected differences. Reconsidering the methods and factors used in developing the expectation and inquiry of management may assist the auditor in this regard. Management responses, however, should ordinarily be corroborated with other audit evidence. In those cases when an explanation for the difference cannot be obtained, the auditor should obtain sufficient appropriate audit evidence about the assertion by performing other audit procedures to satisfy himself as to whether the difference is a likely misstatement.[3] In designing such other procedures, the auditor should consider that unexplained differences may indicate an increased risk of material misstatement. (See section 316, *Consideration of Fraud in a Financial Statement Audit*.) [Revised, March, 2006, to reflect conforming changes necessary due to the issuance of Statement on Auditing Standards No. 105.]

Documentation of Substantive Analytical Procedures

.22 When an analytical procedure is used as the principal substantive test of a significant financial statement assertion, the auditor should document all of the following:

a. The expectation, where that expectation is not otherwise readily determinable from the documentation of the work performed, and factors considered in its development

b. Results of the comparison of the expectation to the recorded amounts or ratios developed from recorded amounts

c. Any additional auditing procedures performed in response to significant unexpected differences arising from the analytical procedure and the results of such additional procedures

[Paragraph added, effective for audits of financial statements for periods beginning on or after May 15, 2002, by Statement on Auditing Standards No. 96.]

Analytical Procedures Used in the Overall Review

.23 The objective of analytical procedures used in the overall review stage of the audit is to assist the auditor in assessing the conclusions reached and in the evaluation of the overall financial statement presentation. A wide variety of analytical procedures may be useful for this purpose. The overall review would generally include reading the financial statements and notes and considering (*a*) the adequacy of evidence gathered in response to unusual or unexpected balances identified in planning the audit or in the course of the audit and (*b*) unusual or unexpected balances or relationships that were not previously identified. Results of an overall review may indicate that additional evidence may be needed. [Paragraph renumbered by the issuance of Statement on Auditing Standards No. 96, January 2002.]

---

[2] See section 312, *Audit Risk and Materiality in Conducting an Audit*, paragraphs .24 through .26.

[3] See section 312.35.

Effective Date

.24 This section is effective for audits of financial statements for periods beginning on or after January 1, 1989. Early application of the provisions of this section is permissible. [Paragraph renumbered by the issuance of Statement on Auditing Standards No. 96, January 2002.]

AU Section 9329

Analytical Procedures: Auditing Interpretations of Section 329

[1.] Corroboration of Replies to Inquiries in Applying Analytical Review Procedures

[.01–.02] [Withdrawn March 1989.]

AU Section 330

The Confirmation Process

(Supersedes section 331.03–.08.)

Source: SAS No. 67.

Effective for audits of fiscal periods ending after June 15, 1992, unless otherwise indicated.

Introduction and Applicability

.01 This section provides guidance about the confirmation process in audits performed in accordance with generally accepted auditing standards. This section—

- Defines the confirmation process (see paragraph .04).
- Discusses the relationship of confirmation procedures to the auditor's assessment of audit risk (see paragraphs .05 through .10).
- Describes certain factors that affect the reliability of confirmations (see paragraphs .16 through .27).
- Provides guidance on performing alternative procedures when responses to confirmation requests are not received (see paragraphs .31 and .32).
- Provides guidance on evaluating the results of confirmation procedures (see paragraph .33).
- Specifically addresses the confirmation of accounts receivable and supersedes section 331, *Inventories*, paragraphs .03–.08 and the portion of section 331.01 that addresses the confirmation of receivables (see paragraphs .34 and .35). This section does not supersede the portion of section 331.01 that addresses the observation of inventories.

.02 This section does not address the extent or timing of confirmation procedures. Guidance on the extent of audit procedures (that is, considerations involved in determining the number of items to confirm) is found in section 350, *Audit Sampling*, and section 312, *Audit Risk and Materiality in Conducting an Audit*. Guidance on the timing of audit procedures is included in section 318, *Performing Audit Procedures in Response to Assessed Risks and Evaluating the Audit Evidence Obtained*. [Revised, March 2006, to reflect conforming changes necessary due to the issuance of Statement on Auditing Standards No. 110.]

.03 In addition, this section does not address matters described in section 336, *Using the Work of a Specialist*, or in section 337, *Inquiry of a Client's Lawyer Concerning Litigation, Claims, and Assessments*.

Definition of the Confirmation Process

.04 Confirmation is the process of obtaining and evaluating a direct communication from a third party in response to a request for information about a particular item affecting financial statement assertions. The process includes—

- Selecting items for which confirmations are to be requested.
- Designing the confirmation request.
- Communicating the confirmation request to the appropriate third party.
- Obtaining the response from the third party.
- Evaluating the information, or lack thereof, provided by the third party about the audit objectives, including the reliability of that information.

Relationship of Confirmation Procedures to the Auditor's Assessment of Audit Risk

.05 Section 312 discusses the audit risk model. It describes the concept of assessing inherent and control risks, determining the acceptable level of detection risk, and designing an audit program to achieve an appropriately low level of audit risk. The auditor uses the audit risk assessment in determining the audit procedures to be applied, including whether they should include confirmation.

.06 Confirmation is undertaken to obtain evidence from third parties about financial statement assertions made by management. Section 326, *Audit Evidence*, states that, in general, it is presumed that "Audit evidence is more reliable when it is obtained from knowledgeable independent sources outside the entity." [Revised, March 2006, to reflect conforming changes necessary due to the issuance of Statement on Auditing Standards No. 106.]

.07 The greater the combined assessed level of inherent and control risk, the greater the assurance that the auditor needs from substantive tests related to a financial statement assertion. Consequently, as the combined assessed level of inherent and control risk increases, the auditor designs substantive tests to obtain more or different evidence about a financial statement assertion. In these situations, the auditor might use confirmation procedures rather than or in conjunction with tests directed toward documents or parties within the entity.

.08 Unusual or complex transactions may be associated with high levels of inherent risk and control risk. If the entity has entered into an unusual or complex transaction and the combined assessed level of inherent and control risk is high, the auditor should consider confirming the terms of the transaction with the other parties in addition to examining documentation held by the entity. For example, if the combined assessed level of inherent and control risk over the occurrence of revenue related to an unusual, year-end sale is high, the auditor should consider confirming the terms of that sale.

.09 The auditor should assess whether the evidence provided by confirmations reduces audit risk for the related assertions to an acceptably low level. In making that assessment, the auditor should consider the materiality of the account balance and his or her inherent and control risk assessments. When the auditor concludes that evidence provided by confirmations alone is not sufficient, additional procedures should be performed. For example, to achieve an appropriately low level of audit risk related to the completeness and existence assertions for accounts receivable, an auditor may perform sales cutoff tests in addition to confirming accounts receivable.

.10 The lower the combined assessed level of inherent and control risk, the less assurance the auditor needs from substantive tests to form a conclusion about a financial statement assertion. Consequently, as the combined assessed level of inherent and control risk decreases for a particular assertion, the auditor may modify substantive tests by changing their nature from more effective (but costly) tests to less effective (and less costly) tests. For example, if the combined assessed level of inherent and control risk over the existence of cash is low, the auditor might limit substantive procedures to inspecting client-provided bank statements rather than confirming cash balances.

Assertions Addressed by Confirmations

.11 For the audit evidence obtained to be appropriate, it must be reliable and relevant. Factors affecting the reliability of confirmations are discussed in paragraphs .16 through .27. The relevance of audit evidence depends on its relationship to the financial statement assertion being addressed. Section 326 classifies financial statement assertions into five categories:

a. Existence or occurrence

b. Completeness

c. Rights and obligations

d. Valuation or allocation

e. Presentation and disclosure

.12 Confirmation requests, if properly designed by the auditor, may address any one or more of those assertions. However, confirmations do not address all assertions equally well. Confirmation of goods held on consignment with the consignee would likely be more effective for the existence and the rights-and-obligations assertions than for the valuation assertion. Accounts receivable confirmations are likely to be more effective for the existence assertion than for the completeness and valuation assertions. Thus, when obtaining evidence for assertions not adequately addressed by confirmations, auditors should consider other audit procedures to complement confirmation procedures or to be used instead of confirmation procedures.

.13 Confirmation requests can be designed to elicit evidence that addresses the completeness assertion: that is, if properly designed, confirmations may provide evidence to aid in assessing whether all transactions and accounts that should be included in the financial statements are included. Their effectiveness in addressing the completeness assertion depends, in part, on whether the auditor selects from an appropriate population for testing. For example, when using confirmations to provide evidence about the completeness assertion for accounts payable, the appropriate population might be a list of vendors rather than the amounts recorded in the accounts payable subsidiary ledger.

.14 Some confirmation requests are not designed to elicit evidence regarding the completeness assertion. For example, the AICPA Standard Form to Confirm Account Balance Information With Financial Institutions is designed to substantiate information that is stated on the confirmation request; the form is not designed to provide assurance that information about accounts not listed on the form will be reported.

The Confirmation Process

.15 The auditor should exercise an appropriate level of professional skepticism throughout the confirmation process (see section 230, *Due Professional*

Care in the Performance of Work). Professional skepticism is important in designing the confirmation request, performing the confirmation procedures, and evaluating the results of the confirmation procedures.

Designing the Confirmation Request

.16 Confirmation requests should be tailored to the specific audit objectives. Thus, when designing the confirmation requests, the auditor should consider the assertion(s) being addressed and the factors that are likely to affect the reliability of the confirmations. Factors such as the form of the confirmation request, prior experience on the audit or similar engagements, the nature of the information being confirmed, and the intended respondent should affect the design of the requests because these factors have a direct effect on the reliability of the evidence obtained through confirmation procedures.

Form of Confirmation Request

.17 There are two types of confirmation requests: the positive form and the negative form. Some positive forms request the respondent to indicate whether he or she agrees with the information stated on the request. Other positive forms, referred to as blank forms, do not state the amount (or other information) on the confirmation request, but request the recipient to fill in the balance or furnish other information.

.18 Positive forms provide audit evidence only when responses are received from the recipients; nonresponses do not provide audit evidence about the financial statement assertions being addressed.

.19 Since there is a risk that recipients of a positive form of confirmation request with the information to be confirmed contained on it may sign and return the confirmation without verifying that the information is correct, blank forms may be used as one way to mitigate this risk. Thus, the use of blank confirmation requests may provide a greater degree of assurance about the information confirmed. However, blank forms might result in lower response rates because additional effort may be required of the recipients; consequently, the auditor may have to perform more alternative procedures.

.20 The negative form requests the recipient to respond only if he or she disagrees with the information stated on the request. Negative confirmation requests may be used to reduce audit risk to an acceptable level when (*a*) the combined assessed level of inherent and control risk is low, (*b*) a large number of small balances is involved, and (*c*) the auditor has no reason to believe that the recipients of the requests are unlikely to give them consideration. For example, in the examination of demand deposit accounts in a financial institution, it may be appropriate for an auditor to include negative confirmation requests with the customers' regular statements when the combined assessed level of inherent and control risk is low and the auditor has no reason to believe that the recipients will not consider the requests. The auditor should consider performing other substantive procedures to supplement the use of negative confirmations.

.21 Negative confirmation requests may generate responses indicating misstatements, and are more likely to do so if the auditor sends a large number of negative confirmation requests and such misstatements are widespread. The auditor should investigate relevant information provided on negative confirmations that have been returned to the auditor to determine the effect such information may have on the audit. If the auditor's investigation of responses to negative confirmation requests indicates a pattern of misstatements, the auditor should reconsider his or her combined assessed level of inherent and control risk and consider the effect on planned audit procedures.

.22 Although returned negative confirmations may provide evidence about the financial statement assertions, unreturned negative confirmation requests rarely provide significant evidence concerning financial statement assertions other than certain aspects of the existence assertion. For example, negative confirmations may provide some evidence of the existence of third parties if they are not returned with an indication that the addressees are unknown. However, unreturned negative confirmations do not provide explicit evidence that the intended third parties received the confirmation requests and verified that the information contained on them is correct.

Prior Experience

.23 In determining the effectiveness and efficiency of employing confirmation procedures, the auditor may consider information from prior years' audits or audits of similar entities. This information includes response rates, knowledge of misstatements identified during prior years' audits, and any knowledge of inaccurate information on returned confirmations. For example, if the auditor has experienced poor response rates to properly designed confirmation requests in prior audits, the auditor may instead consider obtaining audit evidence from other sources.

Nature of Information Being Confirmed

.24 When designing confirmation requests, the auditor should consider the types of information respondents will be readily able to confirm, since the nature of the information being confirmed may directly affect the competence of the evidence obtained as well as the response rate. For example, certain respondents' accounting systems may facilitate the confirmation of single transactions rather than of entire account balances. In addition, respondents may not be able to confirm the balances of their installment loans, but they may be able to confirm whether their payments are up-to-date, the amount of the payment, and the key terms of their loans.

.25 The auditor's understanding of the client's arrangements and transactions with third parties is key to determining the information to be confirmed. The auditor should obtain an understanding of the substance of such arrangements and transactions to determine the appropriate information to include on the confirmation request. The auditor should consider requesting confirmation of the terms of unusual agreements or transactions, such as bill and hold sales,[1] in addition to the amounts. The auditor also should consider whether there may be oral modifications to agreements, such as unusual payment terms or liberal rights of return. When the auditor believes there is a moderate or high degree of risk that there may be significant oral modifications, he or she should inquire about the existence and details of any such modifications to written agreements. One method of doing so is to confirm both the terms of the agreements and whether any oral modifications exist.

Respondent

.26 The auditor should direct the confirmation request to a third party who the auditor believes is knowledgeable about the information to be confirmed.

---

[1] Bill and hold sales are sales of merchandise that are billed to customers before delivery and are held by the entity for the customers.

For example, to confirm a client's oral and written guarantees with a financial institution, the auditor should direct the request to a financial institution official who is responsible for the financial institution's relationship with the client or is knowledgeable about the transactions or arrangements.

.27 If information about the respondent's competence, knowledge, motivation, ability, or willingness to respond, or about the respondent's objectivity and freedom from bias with respect to the audited entity[2] comes to the auditor's attention, the auditor should consider the effects of such information on designing the confirmation request and evaluating the results, including determining whether other procedures are necessary. In addition, there may be circumstances (such as for significant, unusual year-end transactions that have a material effect on the financial statements or where the respondent is the custodian of a material amount of the audited entity's assets) in which the auditor should exercise a heightened degree of professional skepticism relative to these factors about the respondent. In these circumstances, the auditor should consider whether there is sufficient basis for concluding that the confirmation request is being sent to a respondent from whom the auditor can expect the response will provide meaningful and appropriate audit evidence.

Performing Confirmation Procedures

.28 During the performance of confirmation procedures, the auditor should maintain control over the confirmation requests and responses. Maintaining control[3] means establishing direct communication between the intended recipient and the auditor to minimize the possibility that the results will be biased because of interception and alteration of the confirmation requests or responses.

.29 There may be situations in which the respondent, because of timeliness or other considerations, responds to a confirmation request other than in a written communication mailed to the auditor. When such responses are received, additional evidence may be required to support their validity. For example, facsimile responses involve risks because of the difficulty of ascertaining the sources of the responses. To restrict the risks associated with facsimile responses and treat the confirmations as valid audit evidence, the auditor should consider taking certain precautions, such as verifying the source and contents of a facsimile response in a telephone call to the purported sender. In addition, the auditor should consider requesting the purported sender to mail the *original* confirmation directly to the auditor. Oral confirmations should be documented in the workpapers. If the information in the oral confirmations is significant, the auditor should request the parties involved to submit written confirmation of the specific information directly to the auditor.

.30 When using confirmation requests other than the negative form, the auditor should generally follow up with a second and sometimes a third request to those parties from whom replies have not been received.

---

[2] Section 334, *Related Parties*, paragraphs .09 and .10, provide guidance on examining related-party transactions that have been identified by the auditor.

[3] The need to maintain control does not preclude the use of internal auditors in the confirmation process. Section 322, *The Auditor's Consideration of the Internal Audit Function in an Audit of Financial Statements*, provides guidance on considering the work of internal auditors and on using internal auditors to provide direct assistance to the auditor.

Alternative Procedures

.31 When the auditor has not received replies to positive confirmation requests, he or she should apply alternative procedures to the nonresponses to obtain the evidence necessary to reduce audit risk to an acceptably low level. However, the omission of alternative procedures may be acceptable (*a*) when the auditor has not identified unusual qualitative factors or systematic characteristics related to the nonresponses, such as that all nonresponses pertain to year-end transactions, and (*b*) when testing for overstatement of amounts, the nonresponses in the aggregate, when projected as 100 percent misstatements to the population and added to the sum of all other unadjusted differences, would not affect the auditor's decision about whether the financial statements are materially misstated.

.32 The nature of alternative procedures varies according to the account and assertion in question. In the examination of accounts receivable, for example, alternative procedures may include examination of subsequent cash receipts (including matching such receipts with the actual items being paid), shipping documents, or other client documentation to provide evidence for the existence assertion. In the examination of accounts payable, for example, alternative procedures may include examination of subsequent cash disbursements, correspondence from third parties, or other records to provide evidence for the completeness assertion.

Evaluating the Results of Confirmation Procedures

.33 After performing any alternative procedures, the auditor should evaluate the combined audit evidence provided by the confirmations and the alternative procedures to determine whether sufficient audit evidence has been obtained about all the applicable financial statement assertions. In performing that evaluation, the auditor should consider (*a*) the reliability of the confirmations and alternative procedures; (*b*) the nature of any exceptions, including the implications, both quantitative and qualitative, of those exceptions; (*c*) the audit evidence provided by other procedures; and (*d*) whether additional audit evidence is needed. If the combined audit evidence provided by the confirmations, alternative procedures, and other procedures is not sufficient, the auditor should request additional confirmations or extend other tests, such as tests of details or analytical procedures.

Confirmation of Accounts Receivable

.34 For the purpose of this section, *accounts receivable* means—

a. The entity's claims against customers that have arisen from the sale of goods or services in the normal course of business, and

b. A financial institution's loans.

Confirmation of accounts receivable is a generally accepted auditing procedure. As discussed in paragraph .06, it is generally presumed that evidence obtained from third parties will provide the auditor with higher-quality audit evidence than is typically available from within the entity. Thus, there is a presumption that the auditor will request the confirmation of accounts receivable during an audit unless one of the following is true:

- Accounts receivable are immaterial to the financial statements.

- The use of confirmations would be ineffective.[4]
- The auditor's combined assessed level of inherent and control risk is low, and the assessed level, in conjunction with the evidence expected to be provided by analytical procedures or other substantive tests of details, is sufficient to reduce audit risk to an acceptably low level for the applicable financial statement assertions. In many situations, both confirmation of accounts receivable and other substantive tests of details are necessary to reduce audit risk to an acceptably low level for the applicable financial statement assertions.

.35 An auditor who has not requested confirmations in the examination of accounts receivable should document how he or she overcame this presumption.

Effective Date

.36 This section is effective for audits of fiscal periods ending after June 15, 1992. Early application of this section is permissible.

---

[4] For example, if, based on prior years' audit experience or on experience with similar engagements, the auditor concludes that response rates to properly designed confirmation requests will be inadequate, or if responses are known or expected to be unreliable, the auditor may determine that the use of confirmations would be ineffective.

AU Section 9330

The Confirmation Process: Auditing Interpretations of Section 330

1. Use of Electronic Confirmations

.01 *Question*—Section 330, *The Confirmation Process*, uses phrases such as *written communication* and *mail the original confirmation* when describing the confirmation process. Increasingly, there are situations in which the auditor transmits, or the respondent responds to, a confirmation request other than in a written communication mailed directly between the respondent and the auditor. For example, the auditor may transmit the confirmation request via e-mail using a scanned electronic copy of a document that has been signed by a client either physically on the original document or with an electronic signature. The response to a confirmation request may also be facilitated through a process whereby a respondent provides the auditor access to a secure website, hosted either by the respondent or by a third party, where the requested information about a particular item affecting financial statement assertions has been made available by the respondent. Therefore, the following questions arise:

- Can the auditor transmit a confirmation request electronically?
- Can information obtained electronically from third parties, sometimes referred to as an electronic confirmation, be considered to be reliable audit evidence?

.02 *Interpretation*—Yes. The transmission or receipt of electronic confirmations or the use of an electronic confirmation process is not precluded by section 330.

.03 The auditor's consideration of the reliability of the information obtained through the confirmation process to be used as audit evidence includes consideration of the risks that

- the information obtained may not be from an authentic source;
- a respondent may not be knowledgeable about the information to be confirmed; or
- the integrity of the information may have been compromised.

No confirmation process with a third party is without some risk of interception or alteration, including the risk that the confirmation respondent will not be the intended respondent. Such risk exists regardless of whether a response is obtained in paper form, by electronic correspondence, or through some other medium. Factors that may indicate increased risk relating to the reliability of a response include that it

- was received by the auditor indirectly; or
- appeared not to come from the originally intended confirming party.

Responses received electronically, for example by facsimile or e-mail, involve risks relating to reliability because proof of origin and knowledge of the respondent may be difficult to establish and alterations may be difficult to detect. An electronic confirmation process that creates a secure confirmation environment may mitigate the risks of interception or alteration. The key to creating a secure confirmation environment lies in the process or mechanism used by the auditor and the respondent to minimize the possibility that the results will be compromised because of interception or alteration of the confirmation.

.04 Paragraph .04 of section 330 discusses the confirmation process, which includes the auditor's communication of the confirmation request to the appropriate third party. Paragraph .28 states that the auditor should maintain control over the confirmation requests and responses. Maintaining control includes performing procedures to verify that the confirmation is being directed to the intended recipient. For example, just as the auditor might perform procedures to verify the physical address of a recipient for a confirmation to be sent through the postal service, the auditor would perform similar procedures to verify the e-mail address supplied by the auditor's client for a confirmation request to be sent to that recipient's e-mail address. If another electronic process is used, the auditor may perform other procedures to determine that the request is directed to the intended recipient.

.05 Paragraph .09 of section 326, *Audit Evidence*, states that the auditor should consider the reliability of the information to be used as audit evidence. Confirmations obtained electronically can be considered to be reliable audit evidence if the auditor is satisfied that (*a*) the electronic confirmation process is secure and properly controlled, (*b*) the information obtained is a direct communication in response to a request, and (*c*) the information is obtained from a third party who is the intended respondent.

.06 Various means might be used to validate the source of the electronic information and the respondent's knowledge about the requested information. For example, the use of encryption,[1] electronic digital signatures,[2] and procedures to verify website authenticity[3] may improve the security of the electronic confirmation process.

.07 If a system or process that facilitates electronic confirmation between the auditor and the confirmation respondent is in place and the auditor plans to rely on such a system or process, an assurance trust services report (for example, SysTrust), or another auditor's report on that process, may assist the auditor in assessing the design and operating effectiveness of the electronic and manual controls with respect to that process. Such a report would usually address the risks described in paragraph .03. If these risks are not adequately addressed in the report, the auditor may perform additional procedures to address those risks.

.08 In some cases, the auditor may determine that it is appropriate to address the risks related to the reliability of the information received electronically by directly contacting the purported sender (for example, by telephone) rather than by using alternative means to validate the source of the electronic information. For example, if significant information is provided via an e-mail response, the auditor may perform alternative procedures, including procedures

---

[1] Encryption is the process of encoding electronic data in such a way that it cannot be read without the second party employing a matching encryption key. Use of encryption reduces the risk of unintended intervention in a communication.

[2] Digital signatures may use the encryption of codes, text, or other means to ensure that only the claimed signer of the document could have affixed the symbol. The signature and its characteristics are uniquely linked to the signer. Digital signature routines allow for the creation of the signature and the checking of the signature at a later date for authenticity.

[3] Website authenticity routines may use various means, including mathematical algorithms to monitor data or a website, to ensure that its content has not been altered without authorization. WebTrust or VeriSign certifications may be earned and affixed to a website, indicating an active program of protecting the underlying content of the information.

to verify the authenticity of information such as the e-mail address of the purported sender. The auditor may also contact the purported sender directly by telephone to verify that the information received by the auditor was sent by the confirming party and also that what was received by the auditor corresponds to the information transmitted by the purported sender. The auditor's determination of procedures appropriate in the circumstances depend on the auditor's assessment of the risks described in paragraph .03.

[Issue Date: April, 2007; Revised: November, 2008.]

AU Section 331

*Inventories**

Source: SAS No. 1, section 331; SAS No. 43; SAS No. 67.

Issue date, unless otherwise indicated: November, 1972.

.01 Observation of inventories is a generally accepted auditing procedure. The independent auditor who issues an opinion when he has not employed them must bear in mind that he has the burden of justifying the opinion expressed. [As amended, effective for fiscal periods ending after June 15, 1992, by Statement on Auditing Standards No. 67.]

.02 The purpose of this section is to provide guidelines for the independent auditor in observing inventories. This section relates only to observation of inventories and does not deal with other important auditing procedures which generally are required for the independent auditor to satisfy himself as to these assets. [Revised, December 1991, to reflect conforming changes necessary due to the issuance of Statement on Auditing Standards No. 67.]

Receivables

[.03–.08] [Superseded November 1991 by Statement on Auditing Standards No. 67.][1–2]

Inventories

.09 When inventory quantities are determined solely by means of a physical count, and all counts are made as of the balance-sheet date or as of a single date within a reasonable time before or after the balance-sheet date, it is ordinarily necessary for the independent auditor to be present at the time of count and, by suitable observation, tests, and inquiries, satisfy himself respecting the effectiveness of the methods of inventory-taking and the measure of reliance which may be placed upon the client's representations about the quantities and physical condition of the inventories.

.10 When the well-kept perpetual inventory records are checked by the client periodically by comparisons with physical counts, the auditor's observation procedures usually can be performed either during or after the end of the period under audit.

.11 In recent years, some companies have developed inventory controls or methods of determining inventories, including statistical sampling, which are highly effective in determining inventory quantities and which are sufficiently reliable to make unnecessary an annual physical count of each item of inventory. In such circumstances, the independent auditor must satisfy himself that

---

* Title amended, effective for audits of fiscal periods ending after June 15, 1992, by Statement on Auditing Standards No. 67.

[1–2] [Superseded November 1991, by Statement on Auditing Standards No. 67.]

the client's procedures or methods are sufficiently reliable to produce results substantially the same as those which would be obtained by a count of all items each year. The auditor must be present to observe such counts as he deems necessary and must satisfy himself as to the effectiveness of the counting procedures used. If statistical sampling methods are used by the client in the taking of the physical inventory, the auditor must be satisfied that the sampling plan is reasonable and statistically valid, that it has been properly applied, and that the results are reasonable in the circumstances. [Revised, June 1981, to reflect conforming changes necessary due to the issuance of Statement on Auditing Standards No. 39.]

.12 When the independent auditor has not satisfied himself as to inventories in the possession of the client through the procedures described in paragraphs .09 through .11, tests of the accounting records alone will not be sufficient for him to become satisfied as to quantities; it will always be necessary for the auditor to make, or observe, some physical counts of the inventory and apply appropriate tests of intervening transactions. This should be coupled with inspection of the records of any client's counts and procedures relating to the physical inventory on which the balance-sheet inventory is based.

.13 The independent auditor may be asked to audit financial statements covering the current period and one or more periods for which he had not observed or made some physical counts of prior inventories. He may, nevertheless, be able to become satisfied as to such prior inventories through appropriate procedures, such as tests of prior transactions, reviews of the records of prior counts, and the application of gross profit tests, provided that he has been able to become satisfied as to the current inventory.

Inventories Held in Public Warehouses[3]

.14 If inventories are in the hands of public warehouses or other outside custodians, the auditor ordinarily would obtain direct confirmation in writing from the custodian. If such inventories represent a significant proportion of current or total assets, to obtain reasonable assurance with respect to their existence, the auditor should apply one or more of the following procedures as he considers necessary in the circumstances.

a. Test the owner's procedures for investigating the warehouseman and evaluating the warehouseman's performance.

b. Obtain an independent accountant's report on the warehouseman's control procedures relevant to custody of goods and, if applicable, pledging of receipts, or apply alternative procedures at the warehouse to gain reasonable assurance that information received from the warehouseman is reliable.

c. Observe physical counts of the goods, if practicable and reasonable.

d. If warehouse receipts have been pledged as collateral, confirm with lenders pertinent details of the pledged receipts (on a test basis, if appropriate).

[As amended, effective after August 31, 1982, by Statement on Auditing Standards No. 43.]

---

[3] See section 901 for Special Report of Committee on Auditing Procedure.

Effect on the Auditor's Report

.15 For a discussion of the circumstances relating to receivables and inventories affecting the independent auditor's report, see sections 508.24 and 508.67. [As amended, effective for periods ending on or after December 31, 1974, by Statement on Auditing Standards No. 2. Paragraph renumbered by the issuance of Statement on Auditing Standards No. 43, effective after August 1982.]

Effect on the Auditor's Report

.11 For a discussion of the circumstances relating to receivables and inventories affecting the independent auditor's report, see sections 508.24 and 509.67. [As amended, effective for periods ending on or after December 31, 1974, by Statement on Auditing Standards No. 2. Paragraph renumbered by the issuance of Statement on Auditing Standards No. 43, effective after August 1982.]

AU Section 9331

Inventories: Auditing Interpretations of Section 331

[1.] Evidential Matter for Inventories at Interim Dates

[.01–.05] [Withdrawn December, 1992.]

AU Section 332

Auditing Derivative Instruments, Hedging Activities, and Investments in Securities[1]

(Supersedes SAS No. 81.)

Source: SAS No. 92.

See section 9332 for interpretations of this section.

Effective for audits of financial statements for fiscal years ending on or after June 30, 2001. Early application is permitted.

Applicability

.01 This section provides guidance to auditors in planning and performing auditing procedures for assertions about derivative instruments, hedging activities, and investments in securities[2] that are made in an entity's financial statements.[3] Those assertions[4] are classified according to three broad categories that are discussed in section 326, *Audit Evidence*, paragraphs .14–.19, as follows:

a. Assertions about classes of transactions and events for the period under audit:

i. *Occurrence*. Transactions and events that have been recorded have occurred and pertain to the entity.

ii. *Completeness*. All transactions and events that should have been recorded have been recorded.

iii. *Accuracy*. Amounts and other data relating to recorded transactions and events have been recorded appropriately.

iv. *Cutoff*. Transactions and events have been recorded in the correct accounting period.

v. *Classification*. Transactions and events have been recorded in the proper accounts.

b. Assertions about account balances at the period end:

i. *Existence*. Assets, liabilities, and equity interests exist.

ii. *Rights and obligations*. The entity holds or controls the rights to assets, and liabilities are the obligations of the entity.

---

1 The AICPA Audit Guide *Auditing Derivative Instruments, Hedging Activities, and Investments in Securities* provides practical guidance for implementing this section.

2 Throughout the remainder of this section, the word *security* or *securities* refers to an entity's investment in a security or securities.

3 The guidance provided in this section applies to audits of financial statements prepared in accordance with generally accepted accounting principles or a comprehensive basis of accounting other than generally accepted accounting principles. Such other bases of accounting are described in section 623, *Special Reports*, paragraph .04. References in this section to generally accepted accounting principles are intended to also refer to other comprehensive bases of accounting when the reference is relevant to the basis of accounting used.

4 Throughout the remainder of this section, the word *assertion* refers to an assertion made in an entity's financial statements.

- *iii.* *Completeness*. All assets, liabilities, and equity interests that should have been recorded have been recorded.
- *iv.* *Valuation and allocation*. Assets, liabilities, and equity interests are included in the financial statements at appropriate amounts and any resulting valuation or allocation adjustments are appropriately recorded.

c. Assertions about presentation and disclosure:

- *i.* *Occurrence and rights and obligations*. Disclosed events and transactions have occurred and pertain to the entity.
- *ii.* *Completeness*. All disclosures that should have been included in the financial statements have been included.
- *iii.* *Classification and understandability*. Financial information is appropriately presented and described and disclosures are clearly expressed.
- *iv.* *Accuracy and valuation*. Financial and other information are disclosed fairly and at appropriate amounts.

[Revised, March 2006, to reflect conforming changes necessary due to the issuance of Statement on Auditing Standards No. 106.]

Derivative Instruments and Hedging Activities Included in the Scope of this Section

.02 The guidance in this section applies to derivative instruments, including certain derivative instruments embedded in other contracts (collectively referred to as derivatives), of all entities. This section uses the definition of a derivative instrument that is in Financial Accounting Standards Board (FASB) *Accounting Standards Codification* (ASC) 815, *Derivatives and Hedging*. FASB ASC 815 addresses the accounting for derivatives that are either freestanding or embedded in contracts or agreements. For purposes of applying the guidance in this section, a derivative instrument is a financial instrument or other contract with all three of the characteristics listed in FASB ASC 815-10-15-83, which are the following.

a. *Underlying, notional amount, payment provision*. The contract has both of the following terms, which determine the amount of the settlement or settlements, and, in some cases, whether or not a settlement is required:

(1) One or more underlyings

(2) One or more notional amounts or payment provisions or both

b. *Initial net investment*. The contract requires no initial net investment or an initial net investment that is smaller than would be required for other types of contracts that would be expected to have a similar response to changes in market factors.

c. *Net settlement*. The contract can be settled net by any of the following means:

(1) Its terms implicitly or explicitly require or permit net settlement.

(2) It can readily be settled net by a means outside the contract.

(3) It provides for delivery of an asset that puts the recipient in a position not substantially different from net settlement.

[Revised, June 2009, to reflect conforming changes necessary due to the issuance of FASB ASC.]

.03 An entity may enter into a derivative[5] for investment purposes or to designate it as a hedge of exposure to changes in fair value (referred to as a *fair value hedge*), exposure to variability in cash flows (referred to as a *cash flow hedge*), or foreign currency exposure. The guidance in this section applies to hedging activities in which the entity designates a derivative or a nonderivative financial instrument as a hedge of exposure for which FASB ASC 815 permits hedge accounting. [Revised, June 2009, to reflect conforming changes necessary due to the issuance of FASB ASC.]

Securities Included in the Scope of this Section

.04 The guidance in this section applies to all securities. There are two types of securities—debt securities and equity securities. This section uses the definitions of *debt security* and *equity security* that are in the FASB ASC glossary. This section applies to debt and equity securities without regard to whether they are subject to the accounting requirements of FASB ASC 320, *Investments—Debt and Equity Securities*. For example, it applies to assertions about securities accounted for under the equity method following the requirements of FASB ASC 323, *Investments—Equity Method and Joint Ventures*. [Revised, June 2009, to reflect conforming changes necessary due to the issuance of FASB ASC.]

The Need for Special Skill or Knowledge to Plan and Perform Auditing Procedures

.05 The auditor may need special skill or knowledge to plan and perform auditing procedures for certain assertions about derivatives and securities. Examples of such auditing procedures and the special skill or knowledge required include—

- Obtaining an understanding of an entity's information system for derivatives and securities, including services provided by a service organization, which may require that the auditor have special skill or knowledge with respect to computer applications when significant information about derivatives and securities is transmitted, processed, maintained, or accessed electronically.
- Identifying controls placed in operation by a service organization that provides services to an entity that are part of the entity's information system for derivatives and securities, which may require that the auditor have an understanding of the operating characteristics of entities in a certain industry.
- Understanding the application of generally accepted accounting principles for assertions about derivatives, which might require that the auditor have special knowledge because of the complexity of those principles. In addition, a derivative may have complex features that require the auditor to have special knowledge to evaluate the measurement and disclosure of the derivative in conformity with generally accepted accounting principles. For example, features embedded in contracts or agreements may require separate accounting as a derivative, and complex pricing structures may increase the complexity of the assumptions used in estimating the fair value of a derivative.

---

[5] To simplify the use of terminology, the remainder of this section often uses the term *derivative* to refer to both the derivative and the purpose for which the entity uses it.

- Understanding the determination of the fair values of derivatives and securities, including the appropriateness of various types of valuation models and the reasonableness of key factors and assumptions, which may require knowledge of valuation concepts.
- Assessing inherent risk and control risk for assertions about derivatives used in hedging activities, which may require an understanding of general risk management concepts and typical asset/liability management strategies.

.06 The auditor may plan to seek the assistance of employees of the auditor's firm, or others outside the firm, with the necessary skill or knowledge. Section 311, *Planning and Supervision*, provides guidance on the use of individuals who serve as members of the audit team and assist the auditor in planning and performing auditing procedures. The auditor also may plan to use the work of a specialist. Section 336, *Using the Work of a Specialist*, provides guidance on the use of the work of specialists as audit evidence. [Revised, March 2006, to reflect conforming changes necessary due to the issuance of Statement on Auditing Standards No. 105.]

Audit Risk and Materiality

.07 Section 312, *Audit Risk and Materiality in Conducting an Audit*, provides guidance on the auditor's consideration of audit risk and materiality when planning and performing an audit of financial statements in accordance with generally accepted auditing standards. It requires the auditor to design procedures to obtain reasonable assurance of detecting misstatements of assertions about derivatives and securities that, when aggregated with misstatements of other assertions, could cause the financial statements taken as a whole to be materially misstated. When designing such procedures, the auditor should consider the inherent risk and control risk for these assertions. The auditor may also consider the work performed by the entity's internal auditors in designing procedures. Guidance on considering the work performed by internal auditors is found in section 322, *The Auditor's Consideration of the Internal Audit Function in an Audit of Financial Statements*.

Inherent Risk Assessment

.08 The inherent risk for an assertion about a derivative or security is its susceptibility to a material misstatement, assuming there are no related controls. Examples of considerations that might affect the auditor's assessment of inherent risk for assertions about a derivative or security include the following.

- *Management's objectives.* Accounting requirements based on management's objectives may increase the inherent risk for certain assertions. For example, in response to management's objective of minimizing the risk of loss from changes in market conditions, the entity may enter into derivatives as hedges. The use of hedges is subject to the risk that market conditions will change in a manner other than expected when the hedge was implemented so that the hedge is no longer effective. That increases the inherent risk for certain assertions about the derivatives because in such circumstances continued application of hedge accounting would not be in conformity with generally accepted accounting principles.
- *The complexity of the features of the derivative or security.* The complexity of the features of the derivative or security may increase the complexity of measurement and disclosure considerations required by

generally accepted accounting principles. For example, interest payments on a structured note may be based on two or more factors, such as one or more interest rates and the market price of certain equity securities. A formula may dictate the interaction of the factors, such as a prescribed interest rate less a multiple of another rate. The number and interaction of the factors may increase the inherent risk for assertions about the fair value of the note.

- *Whether the transaction that gave rise to the derivative or security involved the exchange of cash.* Derivatives that do not involve an initial exchange of cash are subject to an increased risk that they will not be identified for valuation and disclosure considerations. For example, a foreign exchange forward contract that is not recorded at its inception because the entity does not pay cash to enter into the contract is subject to an increased risk that it will not be identified for subsequent adjustment to fair value. Similarly, a stock warrant for a traded security that is donated to an entity is subject to an increased risk that it will not be identified for initial or continuing measurement at fair value.

- *The entity's experience with the derivative or security.* An entity's inexperience with a derivative or security increases the inherent risk for assertions about it. For example, under a new arrangement, an entity may pay a small deposit to enter into a futures contract for foreign currency to pay for purchases from an overseas supplier. The entity's inexperience with such derivatives may lead it to incorrectly account for the deposit, such as treating it as inventory cost, thereby increasing the risk that the contract will not be identified for subsequent adjustment to fair value.

- *Whether a derivative is freestanding or an embedded feature of an agreement.* Embedded derivatives are less likely to be identified by management, which increases the inherent risk for certain assertions. For example, an option to convert the principal outstanding under a loan agreement into equity securities is less likely to be identified for valuation and disclosure considerations if it is a clause in a loan agreement than if it is a freestanding agreement. Similarly, a structured note may include a provision for payments related to changes in a stock index or commodities prices that requires separate accounting.

- *Whether external factors affect the assertion.* Assertions about derivatives and securities may be affected by a variety of risks related to external factors, such as—
  - *Credit risk*, which exposes the entity to the risk of loss as a result of the issuer of a debt security or the counterparty to a derivative failing to meet its obligation.
  - *Market risk*, which exposes the entity to the risk of loss from adverse changes in market factors that affect the fair value of a derivative or security, such as interest rates, foreign exchange rates, and market indexes for equity securities.
  - *Basis risk*, which exposes the entity to the risk of loss from ineffective hedging activities. Basis risk is the difference between the fair value (or cash flows) of the hedged item and the fair value (or cash flows) of the hedging derivative. The entity is subject to the risk that fair values (or cash flows) will change so that the hedge will no longer be effective.

- — *Legal risk*, which exposes the entity to the risk of loss from a legal or regulatory action that invalidates or otherwise precludes performance by one or both parties to the derivative or security.

  Following are examples of how changes in external factors can affect assertions about derivatives and securities.

  - — The increase in credit risk associated with amounts due under debt securities issued by entities that operate in declining industries increases the inherent risk for valuation assertions about those securities.
  - — Significant changes in and the volatility of general interest rates increase the inherent risk for the valuation of derivatives whose value is significantly affected by interest rates.
  - — Significant changes in default rates and prepayments increase the inherent risk for the valuation of retained interests in a securitization.
  - — The fair value of a foreign currency forward contract will be affected by changes in the exchange rate, and the fair value of a put option for an available-for-sale security will be affected by changes in the fair value of the underlying security.

- *The evolving nature of derivatives and the applicable generally accepted accounting principles.* As new forms of derivatives are developed, interpretive accounting guidance for them may not be issued until after the derivatives are broadly used in the marketplace. In addition, generally accepted accounting principles for derivatives may be subject to frequent interpretation by various standard-setting bodies. Evolving interpretative guidance and its applicability increase the inherent risk for valuation and other assertions about existing forms of derivatives.

- *Significant reliance on outside parties.* An entity that relies on external expertise may be unable to appropriately challenge the specialist's methodology or assumptions. This may occur, for example, when a valuation specialist values a derivative.

- *Generally accepted accounting principles may require developing assumptions about future conditions.* As the number and subjectivity of those assumptions increase, the inherent risk of material misstatement increases for certain assertions. For example, the inherent risk for valuation assertions based on assumptions about debt securities whose value fluctuates with changes in prepayments (for example, interest-only strips) increases as the expected holding period lengthens. Similarly, the inherent risk for assertions about cash flow hedges fluctuates with the subjectivity of the assumptions about probability, timing, and amounts of future cash flows.

Control Risk Assessment

Obtaining an Understanding of Internal Control to Plan the Audit

.09 Section 314, *Understanding the Entity and Its Environment and Assessing the Risks of Material Misstatement*, requires the auditor to obtain an understanding of internal control that will enable the auditor to—

a. Identify the risk of material misstatement at the assertion level.

b. Assess the risk of material misstatement at the assertion level.

c. Evaluate the design of internal controls and determine whether they are implemented.

[Revised, May 2001, to reflect conforming changes necessary due to the issuance of Statement on Auditing Standards No. 94. Revised, March 2006, to reflect conforming changes necessary due to the issuance of Statement on Auditing Standards No. 109.]

.10 Controls should be related to management's objectives for financial reporting, operations, and compliance.[6] For example, to achieve its objectives, management of an entity with extensive derivatives transactions may implement controls that call for—

a. Monitoring by a control staff that is fully independent of derivatives activities.

b. Derivatives personnel to obtain, prior to exceeding limits, at least oral approval from members of senior management who are independent of derivatives activities.

c. Senior management to properly address limit excesses and divergences from approved derivatives strategies.

d. The accurate transmittal of derivatives positions to the risk measurement systems.

e. The performance of appropriate reconciliations to ensure data integrity across the full range of derivatives, including any new or existing derivatives that may be monitored apart from the main processing networks.

f. Derivatives traders, risk managers, and senior management to define constraints on derivatives activities and justify identified excesses.

g. Senior management, an independent group, or an individual that management designates to perform a regular review of the identified controls and financial results of the derivatives activities to determine whether controls are being effectively implemented and the entity's business objectives and strategies are being achieved.

h. A review of limits in the context of changes in strategy, risk tolerance of the entity, and market conditions.

.11 The extent of the understanding of internal control over derivatives and securities obtained by the auditor depends on how much information the auditor needs to identify and assess the risk of material misstatement at the assertion level. The understanding obtained may include controls over derivatives and securities transactions from their initiation to their inclusion in the financial statements. It may encompass controls placed in operation by the entity and by service organizations whose services are part of the entity's information system. Section 314 paragraph .81 defines the information system as the procedures, whether automated or manual, and records established by an entity to initiate, authorize, record, process, and report entity transactions

---

[6] The AICPA issued an Audit Guide concurrent with this section entitled *Auditing Derivative Instruments, Hedging Activities, and Investments in Securities* (the Guide). Chapter 5 of the Guide, "Control Risk Assessment," provides sample control objectives for derivatives, hedging activities, and securities which may be useful to auditors in assessing control risk for relevant assertions. Additionally, in 1996, The Committee of Sponsoring Organizations of the Treadway Commission (COSO) issued *Internal Control Issues in Derivatives Usage: An Information Tool for Considering the COSO Internal Control—Integrated Framework in Derivatives Applications*. Although the document precedes Financial Accounting Standards Board (FASB) *Accounting Standards Codification* (ASC) 815, *Derivatives and Hedging*, its guidance may be useful to entities in developing controls over derivatives transactions and to auditors in assessing control risk for assertions about those transactions. [Footnote revised, June 2009, to reflect conforming changes necessary due to the issuance of FASB ASC.]

and to maintain accountability for the related assets, liabilities, and equity. Following the guidance in section 324, *Service Organizations*, [7] a service organization's services are part of an entity's information system for derivatives and securities if they affect any of the following:

a. How the entity's derivatives and securities transactions are initiated.

b. The accounting records, supporting information, and specific accounts in the financial statements involved in the processing and reporting of the entity's derivatives and securities transactions

c. The accounting processing involved from the initiation of those transactions to their inclusion in the financial statements, including electronic means (such as computers and electronic data interchange) used to transmit, process, maintain, and access information

d. The process the entity uses to report information about derivatives and securities transactions in its financial statements, including significant accounting estimates and disclosures

[Revised, May 2001, to reflect conforming changes necessary due to the issuance of Statement on Auditing Standards No. 94. Revised, March 2006, to reflect conforming changes necessary due to the issuance of Statements on Auditing Standards No. 106, and No. 109.]

.12 Examples of a service organization's services that would be part of an entity's information system include—

- The initiation of the purchase or sale of equity securities by a service organization acting as investment adviser or manager.
- Services that are ancillary to holding[8] an entity's securities such as—
  - — Collecting dividend and interest income and distributing that income to the entity.
  - — Receiving notification of corporate actions.
  - — Receiving notification of security purchase and sale transactions.
  - — Receiving payments from purchasers and disbursing proceeds to sellers for security purchase and sale transactions.
  - — Maintaining records of securities transactions for the entity.
- A pricing service providing fair values of derivatives and securities through paper documents or electronic downloads that the entity uses to value its derivatives and securities for financial statement reporting.

.13 Examples of a service organization's services that would not be part of an entity's information system are the following:

- The execution by a securities broker of trades that are initiated by either the entity or its investment adviser
- The holding of an entity's securities

.14 An auditor who needs information about the nature of a service organization's services that are part of an entity's information system for derivatives and securities transactions, or its controls over those services, to plan the audit

---

[7] Section 324, *Service Organizations*, contains the requirements and guidance for auditors auditing the financial statements of an entity that uses a service organization (user auditors). [Footnote added, August 2011, to reflect conforming changes necessary due to the issuance of SSAE No. 16.]

[8] In this section, maintaining custody of securities, either in physical or electronic form, is referred to as *holding* securities, and performing ancillary services is referred to as *servicing* securities. [Footnote renumbered, August 2011, to reflect conforming changes necessary due to the issuance of SSAE No. 16.]

may be able to gather the information from a variety of sources, such as the following:

- User manuals
- System overviews
- Technical manuals
- The contract between the entity and the service organization
- Reports by auditors,[9] internal auditors, or regulatory authorities on the information system and other controls placed in operation by a service organization
- Inquiry or observation of personnel at the entity or at the service organization

In addition, if the services and the service organization's controls over those services are highly standardized, information about the service organization's services, or its controls over those services, obtained through the auditor's prior experience with the service organization may be helpful in planning the audit.

Assessing Control Risk

.15 After obtaining the understanding of internal control over derivatives and securities transactions, the auditor should assess control risk for the related assertions. Guidance on that assessment is found in section 314. [Revised, March 2006, to reflect conforming changes necessary due to the issuance of Statement on Auditing Standards No. 109.]

.16 If the auditor plans to assess control risk at less than maximum for one or more assertions about derivatives and securities, the auditor should identify specific controls relevant to the assertions that are likely to prevent or detect material misstatements and that have been placed in operation by either the entity or the service organization, and gather audit evidence about their operating effectiveness. Audit evidence about the operating effectiveness of a service organization's controls may be gathered through tests performed by the auditor or by an auditor engaged by either the auditor or the service organization—

a. As part of an engagement in which a service auditor reports on management's description of a service organization's system and the suitability of the design and operating effectiveness of controls (a type 2 report), as described in AT section 801, *Reporting on Controls at a Service Organization*.

b. An agreed-upon procedures engagement.[10]

c. To work under the direction of the auditor of the entity's financial statements.

Confirmations of balances or transactions from a service organization do not provide audit evidence about its controls. [Revised, March 2006, to reflect conforming changes necessary due to the issuance of Statement on Auditing

---

[9] AT section 801, *Reporting on Controls at a Service Organization*, establishes the requirements and application guidance for reporting on controls at a service organization relevant to user entities' internal control over financial reporting, and describes the contents of such reports. [Footnote revised and renumbered, August 2011, to reflect conforming changes necessary due to the issuance of SSAE No. 16.]

[10] AT section 201, *Agreed-Upon Procedures Engagements*, provides guidance on applying agreed-upon procedures to controls. [Footnote revised, January 2001, to reflect conforming changes necessary due to the issuance of Statement on Standards for Attestation Engagements No. 10. Footnote renumbered, August 2011, to reflect conforming changes necessary due to the issuance of SSAE No. 16.]

Standards No. 105. Revised, August 2011, to reflect conforming changes necessary due to the issuance of SSAE No. 16.]

.17 The auditor should consider the size of the entity, the entity's organizational structure, the nature of its operations, the types, frequency, and complexity of its derivatives and securities transactions, and its controls over those transactions in designing auditing procedures for assertions about derivatives and securities. For example, if the entity has a variety of derivatives and securities that are reported at fair value estimated using valuation models, the auditor may be able to reduce the substantive procedures for valuation assertions by gathering audit evidence about the controls over the design and use of the models (including the significant assumptions) and evaluating their operating effectiveness. [Revised, March 2006, to reflect conforming changes necessary due to the issuance of Statement on Auditing Standards No. 105.]

.18 In some circumstances, it may not be practicable or possible for the auditor to reduce audit risk to an acceptable level without identifying controls placed in operation by the entity or a service organization and gathering audit evidence about the operating effectiveness of those controls. For example, if the entity has a large number of derivatives or securities transactions, the auditor likely would be unable to reduce audit risk to an acceptable level for assertions about the occurrence of earnings on those securities, including gains and losses from sales, without identifying controls over the authorization, recording, custody, and segregation of duties for those transactions and gathering audit evidence about their operating effectiveness.[11] [Revised, March 2006, to reflect conforming changes necessary due to the issuance of Statement on Auditing Standards No. 105.]

Designing Substantive Procedures Based on Risk Assessments

.19 The auditor should use the assessed levels of inherent risk and control risk for assertions about derivatives and securities to determine the nature, timing, and extent of the substantive procedures to be performed to detect material misstatements of the financial statement assertions. Some substantive procedures address more than one assertion about a derivative or security. Whether one or a combination of substantive procedures should be used to address an assertion depends on the auditor's assessment of the inherent and control risk associated with it as well as the auditor's judgment about a procedure's effectiveness. Paragraphs .21 through .58 provide examples of substantive procedures that address assertions about derivatives and securities. In addition, the auditor should consider whether the results of other audit procedures conflict with management's assertions about derivatives and securities. The auditor should consider the impact of any such identified matters on management's assertions about derivatives and securities. Additionally, the auditor should consider the impact of such matters on the sufficiency of the audit evidence evaluated by the auditor in support of the assertions. [Revised, March 2006, to reflect conforming changes necessary due to the issuance of Statement on Auditing Standards No. 105.]

.20 The provision by a service organization of services that are part of an entity's information system may affect the nature, timing, and extent of the auditor's substantive procedures for assertions about derivatives and securities in a variety of ways. Following are examples of such services and how

---

[11] See footnote 6. [Footnote renumbered, August 2011, to reflect conforming changes necessary due to the issuance of SSAE No. 16.]

they may affect the nature, timing, and extent of the auditor's substantive procedures.

- Supporting documentation, such as derivative contracts and securities purchases and sales advices, may be located at the service organization's facilities. As a result, either the auditor of the entity's financial statements, an auditor working under the direction of that auditor, or an auditor engaged by the service organization may need to visit the facilities to inspect the documentation.

- Data processors, investment advisers, holders of securities, recordkeepers, and other service organizations may electronically transmit, process, maintain, or access significant information about an entity's securities. In such situations, it may not be practicable or possible for the auditor to reduce audit risk to an acceptable level without identifying controls placed in operation by the service organization or the entity and gathering audit evidence about the operating effectiveness of those controls.

- Service organizations may initiate securities transactions for an entity and hold and service the securities. In determining the level of detection risk for substantive tests, the auditor should consider whether there is a segregation of duties and other controls for the services provided. Examples include—

    — When one service organization initiates transactions as an investment adviser and another service organization holds and services those securities, the auditor may corroborate the information provided by the two organizations. For example, the auditor may confirm holdings with the holder of the securities and apply other substantive tests to transactions reported by the entity based on information provided by the investment adviser. Depending on the facts and circumstances, the auditor also may confirm transactions or holdings with the investment adviser and review the reconciliation of differences. Paragraph .24 provides additional guidance on the auditor's considerations.

    — If one service organization initiates transactions as an investment adviser and also holds and services the securities, all of the information available to the auditor is based on the service organization's information. The auditor may be unable to sufficiently limit audit risk without obtaining audit evidence about the operating effectiveness of one or more of the service organization's controls. An example of such controls is establishing independent departments that provide the investment advisory services and the holding and servicing of securities, then reconciling the information about the securities that is provided by each department.

[Revised, March 2006, to reflect conforming changes necessary due to the issuance of Statement on Auditing Standards No. 105.]

Financial Statement Assertions

Existence or Occurrence

.21 Existence assertions address whether the derivatives and securities reported in the financial statements through recognition or disclosure exist at the date of the statement of financial position. Occurrence assertions address whether derivatives and securities transactions reported in the financial statements, as a part of earnings, other comprehensive income, or cash flows or through disclosure, occurred. Paragraph .19 provides guidance on the auditor's determination of the nature, timing, and extent of substantive procedures to be performed. Examples of substantive procedures for existence or occurrence assertions about derivatives and securities include—

- Confirmation with the issuer of the security.
- Confirmation with the holder of the security, including securities in electronic form, or with the counterparty to the derivative.[12]
- Confirmation of settled transactions with the broker-dealer or counterparty.
- Confirmation of unsettled transactions with the broker-dealer or counterparty.
- Physical inspection of the security or derivative contract.
- Reading executed partnership or similar agreements.
- Inspecting underlying agreements and other forms of supporting documentation, in paper or electronic form, for the following:
  - — Amounts reported
  - — Evidence that would preclude the sales treatment of a transfer
  - — Unrecorded repurchase agreements
- Inspecting supporting documentation for subsequent realization or settlement after the end of the reporting period.
- Performing analytical procedures.[13] For example, the absence of a material difference from an expectation that interest income will be a fixed percentage of a debt security based on the effective interest rate determined when the entity purchased the security provides evidence about existence of the security.

Completeness

.22 Completeness assertions address whether all of the entity's derivatives and securities are reported in the financial statements through recognition or disclosure. They also address whether all derivatives and securities transactions are reported in the financial statements as a part of earnings, other comprehensive income, or cash flows or through disclosure. The extent of substantive procedures for completeness may properly vary in relation to the assessed level of control risk. In addition, the auditor should consider that since derivatives may not involve an initial exchange of tangible consideration,

---

[12] Section 330, provides guidance to auditors in using confirmations as substantive tests of financial statement assertions. Confirmations may be used as a substantive test of various financial statement assertions about derivatives and securities. For example, a confirmation may be designed to—

- Obtain information about valuation assertions or assumptions underlying valuations.
- Determine whether there are any side agreements that affect assertions about the entity's rights and obligations associated with a transaction, such as an agreement to repurchase securities sold or an agreement to pledge securities as collateral for a loan.
- Determine whether the holder of the entity's securities agrees to deliver the securities reported or their value when required by the entity.

[Footnote renumbered, August 2011, to reflect conforming changes necessary due to the issuance of SSAE No. 16.]

[13] Section 329, provides guidance to auditors in using analytical procedures as substantive tests. [Footnote renumbered, August 2011, to reflect conforming changes necessary due to the issuance of SSAE No. 16.]

it may be difficult to limit audit risk for assertions about the completeness of derivatives to an acceptable level with an assessed level of control risk at the maximum. Paragraph .19 provides guidance on the auditor's determination of the nature, timing, and extent of substantive procedures to be performed. Examples of substantive procedures for completeness assertions about derivatives and securities are—

- Requesting the counterparty to a derivative or the holder of a security to provide information about it, such as whether there are any side agreements or agreements to repurchase securities sold.
- Requesting counterparties or holders who are frequently used, but with whom the accounting records indicate there are presently no derivatives or securities, to state whether they are counterparties to derivatives with the entity or holders of its securities.[14]
- Inspecting financial instruments and other agreements to identify embedded derivatives.
- Inspecting documentation in paper or electronic form for activity subsequent to the end of the reporting period.
- Performing analytical procedures. For example, a difference from an expectation that interest expense is a fixed percentage of a note based on the interest provisions of the underlying agreement may indicate the existence of an interest rate swap agreement.
- Comparing previous and current account detail to identify assets that have been removed from the accounts and testing those items further to determine that the criteria for sales treatment have been met.
- Reading other information, such as minutes of meetings of the board of directors or finance, asset/liability, investment, or other committees.

.23 One of the characteristics of derivatives is that they may involve only a commitment to perform under a contract and not an initial exchange of tangible consideration. Therefore, auditors designing tests related to the completeness assertion should not focus exclusively on evidence relating to cash receipts and disbursements. When testing for completeness, auditors should consider making inquiries, inspecting agreements, and reading other information, such as minutes of meetings of the board of directors or finance, asset/liability, investment, or other committees. Auditors should also consider making inquiries about aspects of operating activities that might present risks hedged using derivatives. For example, if the entity conducts business with foreign entities, the auditor should inquire about any arrangements the entity has made for purchasing foreign currency. Similarly, if an entity is in an industry in which commodity contracts are common, the auditor should inquire about any commodity contracts with fixed prices that run for unusual durations or involve unusually large quantities. The auditor also should consider inquiring as to whether the entity has converted interest-bearing debt from fixed to variable, or vice versa, using derivatives.

.24 Derivatives may not involve an initial exchange of tangible consideration, as discussed in paragraphs .22 and .23. If one or more service organizations provide services that are part of the entity's information system for derivatives, the auditor may be unable to sufficiently limit audit risk for assertions about

---

[14] Section 317 paragraph .17 discusses the blank form of positive confirmation in which the auditor does not state the amount or other information but instead asks the respondent to provide information. [Footnote renumbered, August 2011, to reflect conforming changes necessary due to the issuance of SSAE No. 16.]

the completeness of derivatives without obtaining audit evidence about the operating effectiveness of controls at one or more of the service organizations. Since the auditor's concern is that derivatives that do not require an initial exchange of tangible consideration may not have been recorded, testing reconciliations of information provided by two or more of the service organizations as discussed in paragraph .20 of this section may not sufficiently limit audit risk for assertions about the completeness of derivatives. [Revised, March 2006, to reflect conforming changes necessary due to the issuance of Statement on Auditing Standards No. 105.]

Rights and Obligations

.25 Assertions about rights and obligations address whether the entity has the rights and obligations associated with derivatives and securities, including pledging arrangements, reported in the financial statements. Paragraph .19 provides guidance on the auditor's determination of the nature, timing, and extent of substantive procedures to be performed. Examples of substantive procedures for assertions about rights and obligations associated with derivatives and securities are—

- Confirming significant terms with the counterparty to a derivative or the holder of a security, including the absence of any side agreements.
- Inspecting underlying agreements and other forms of supporting documentation, in paper or electronic form.
- Considering whether the findings of other auditing procedures, such as reviewing minutes of meetings of the board of directors and reading contracts and other agreements, provide evidence about rights and obligations, such as pledging of securities as collateral or selling securities with a commitment to repurchase them.

Valuation

.26 Assertions about the valuation of derivatives and securities address whether the amounts reported in the financial statements through measurement or disclosure were determined in conformity with generally accepted accounting principles. Tests of valuation assertions should be designed according to the valuation method used for the measurement or disclosure. Generally accepted accounting principles may require that a derivative or security be valued based on cost, the investee's financial results, or fair value. They also may require disclosures about the value of a derivative or security and specify that impairment losses should be recognized in earnings prior to their realization. Also, generally accepted accounting principles for securities may vary depending on the type of security, the nature of the transaction, management's objectives related to the security, and the type of entity. Procedures for evaluating management's consideration of the need to recognize impairment losses are discussed in paragraphs .47 and .48 of this section.

.27 *Valuation Based on Cost.* Procedures to obtain evidence about the cost of securities may include inspection of documentation of the purchase price, confirmation with the issuer or holder, and testing discount or premium amortization, either by recomputation or analytical procedures. The auditor should evaluate management's conclusion about the need to recognize an impairment loss for a decline in the security's fair value below its cost that is other than temporary.

.28 *Valuation Based on an Investee's Financial Results.* For valuations based on an investee's financial results, including but not limited to the equity method of accounting, the auditor should obtain sufficient appropriate audit evidence in support of the investee's financial results. The auditor should read available financial statements of the investee and the accompanying audit report, if any. Financial statements of the investee that have been audited by an auditor whose report is satisfactory, for this purpose,[15] to the investor's auditor may constitute appropriate audit evidence. [Revised, March 2006, to reflect conforming changes necessary due to the issuance of Statement on Auditing Standards No. 105.]

.29 If in the auditor's judgment additional audit evidence is needed, the auditor should perform procedures to gather such evidence. For example, the auditor may conclude that additional audit evidence is needed because of significant differences in fiscal year-ends, significant differences in accounting principles, changes in ownership, changes in conditions affecting the use of the equity method, or the materiality of the investment to the investor's financial position or results of operations. Examples of procedures the auditor may perform are reviewing information in the investor's files that relates to the investee such as investee minutes and budgets and cash flows information about the investee and making inquiries of investor management about the investee's financial results. [Revised, March 2006, to reflect conforming changes necessary due to the issuance of Statement on Auditing Standards No. 105.]

.30 If the investee's financial statements are not audited, or if the investee auditor's report is not satisfactory to the investor's auditor for this purpose, the investor's auditor should apply, or should request that the investor arrange with the investee to have another auditor apply, appropriate auditing procedures to such financial statements, considering the materiality of the investment in relation to the financial statements of the investor.

.31 If the carrying amount of the security reflects factors that are not recognized in the investee's financial statements or fair values of assets that are materially different from the investee's carrying amounts, the auditor should obtain sufficient evidence in support of these amounts. Paragraphs .35 through .46 of this section provide guidance on audit evidence that may be used to corroborate assertions about the fair value of derivatives and securities, and paragraphs .47 and .48 provide guidance on procedures for evaluating management's consideration of the need to recognize impairment losses.

.32 There may be a time lag in reporting between the date of the financial statements of the investor and that of the investee. A time lag in reporting should be consistent from period to period. If a time lag between the date of the entity's financial statements and those of the investee has a material effect on the entity's financial statements, the auditor should determine whether the entity's management has properly considered the lack of comparability. The effect may be material, for example, because the time lag is not consistent with the prior period in comparative statements or because a significant transaction occurred during the time lag. If a change in time lag occurs that has a material effect on the investor's financial statements, an explanatory paragraph should be added to the auditor's report because of the change in reporting period.[16]

---

[15] In determining whether the report of another auditor is satisfactory for this purpose, the auditor may consider performing procedures such as making inquiries as to the professional reputation and standing of the other auditor, visiting the other auditor and discussing the audit procedures followed and the results thereof, and reviewing the audit program and/or working papers of the other auditor. [Footnote renumbered, August 2011, to reflect conforming changes necessary due to the issuance of SSAE No. 16.]

[16] See section 508, *Reports on Audited Financial Statements*, paragraphs .16–.18. [Footnote renumbered, August 2011, to reflect conforming changes necessary due to the issuance of SSAE No. 16.]

.33 The auditor should evaluate management's conclusion about the need to recognize an impairment loss for a decline in the security's fair value below its carrying amount that is other than temporary. In addition, with respect to subsequent events and transactions of the investee occurring after the date of the investee's financial statements but before the date of the investor auditor's report, the auditor should read available interim financial statements of the investee and make appropriate inquiries of the investor to identify subsequent events and transactions that are material to the investor's financial statements. Such events or transactions of the type contemplated in section 560, *Subsequent Events*, paragraphs .05–.06), should be disclosed in the notes to the investor's financial statements and (where applicable) labeled as unaudited information. For the purpose of recording the investor's share of the investee's results of operations, recognition should be given to events or transactions of the type contemplated in section 560 paragraph .03.

.34 Evidence relating to material transactions between the entity and the investee should be obtained to evaluate (*a*) the propriety of the elimination of unrealized profits and losses on transactions between the entity and the investee that is required when the equity method of accounting is used to account for an investment under generally accepted accounting principles and (*b*) the adequacy of disclosures about material related party transactions.

.35 *Valuation Based on Fair Value.* The auditor should obtain evidence supporting management's assertions about the fair value of derivatives and securities measured or disclosed at fair value. The method for determining fair value may be specified by generally accepted accounting principles and may vary depending on the industry in which the entity operates or the nature of the entity. Such differences may relate to the consideration of price quotations from inactive markets and significant liquidity discounts, control premiums, and commissions and other costs that would be incurred to dispose of the derivative or security. The auditor should determine whether generally accepted accounting principles specify the method to be used to determine the fair value of the entity's derivatives and securities and evaluate whether the determination of fair value is consistent with the specified valuation method. Paragraphs .35–.46 of this section provide guidance on audit evidence that may be used to support assertions about fair value; that guidance should be considered in the context of specific accounting requirements. If the determination of fair value requires the use of estimates, the auditor should consider the guidance in section 342, *Auditing Accounting Estimates*. In addition, section 312 paragraph .56 provides guidance on considering a difference between an estimated amount best supported by the audit evidence and the estimated amount included in the financial statements. [Revised, March 2006, to reflect conforming changes necessary due to the issuance of Statement on Auditing Standards No. 107.]

.36 Quoted market prices for derivatives and securities listed on national exchanges or over-the-counter markets are available from sources such as financial publications, the exchanges, the National Association of Securities Dealers Automated Quotations System (NASDAQ), or pricing services based on sources such as those. Quoted market prices obtained from those sources are generally considered to provide sufficient evidence of the fair value of the derivatives and securities.

.37 For certain other derivatives and securities, quoted market prices may be obtained from broker-dealers who are market makers in them or through the National Quotation Bureau. However, using such a price quote to test valuation assertions may require special knowledge to understand the circumstances in which the quote was developed. For example, quotations published by the

National Quotation Bureau may not be based on recent trades and may only be an indication of interest and not an actual price for which a counterparty will purchase or sell the underlying derivative or security.

.38 If quoted market prices are not available for the derivative or security, estimates of fair value frequently can be obtained from broker-dealers or other third-party sources based on proprietary valuation models or from the entity based on internally or externally developed valuation models (for example, the Black-Scholes option pricing model). The auditor should understand the method used by the broker-dealer or other third-party source in developing the estimate, for example, whether a pricing model or a cash flow projection was used. The auditor may also determine that it is necessary to obtain estimates from more than one pricing source. For example, this may be appropriate if either of the following occurs.

- The pricing source has a relationship with an entity that might impair its objectivity, such as an affiliate or a counterparty involved in selling or structuring the product.
- The valuation is based on assumptions that are highly subjective or particularly sensitive to changes in the underlying circumstances.

.39 For fair-value estimates obtained from broker-dealers and other third-party sources, the auditor should consider the applicability of the guidance in section 336 or section 324. The auditor's decision about whether such guidance is applicable and which guidance is applicable will depend on the circumstances. The guidance in section 336 may be applicable if the third-party source derives the fair value of the derivative or security by using modeling or similar techniques. If the entity uses a pricing service to obtain prices of securities and derivatives, the guidance in section 324 may be appropriate.

.40 If the derivative or security is valued by the entity using a valuation model, the auditor does not function as an appraiser and is not expected to substitute his or her judgment for that of the entity's management.[17] Examples of valuation models include the present value of expected future cash flows, option-pricing models, matrix pricing, option-adjusted spread models, and fundamental analysis.

The auditor should obtain evidence supporting management's assertions about fair value determined using a model by performing procedures such as—

- Assessing the reasonableness and appropriateness of the model. The auditor should determine whether the valuation model is appropriate for the derivative or security to which it is applied and whether the assumptions used are reasonable and appropriately supported. Estimates of expected future cash flows, for example, to determine the fair value of debt securities should be based on reasonable and supportable assumptions. The evaluation of the appropriateness of valuation models and each of the assumptions used in the models may require considerable judgment and knowledge of valuation techniques, market factors that affect value, and actual and expected market conditions,

---

[17] Independence Standards Board Interpretation 99-1, *FAS 133 Assistance*, provides guidance to auditors of public companies on services an auditor may provide management to assist with the application of FASB ASC 815 that would and would not impair the auditor's independence. Ethics Interpretation 101-3, *Performance of Nonattest Services* [ET section 101.05], provides general guidance to auditors of all entities on the effect of nonattest services on the auditor's independence. [Footnote revised, September 2003, to reflect conforming changes necessary due to the revision of Ethics Interpretation No. 101-3. Footnote revised, June 2009, to reflect conforming changes necessary due to the issuance of FASB ASC. Footnote renumbered, August 2011, to reflect conforming changes necessary due to the issuance of SSAE No. 16.]

particularly in relation to similar derivatives and securities that are traded. Accordingly, the auditor may consider it necessary to involve a specialist in assessing the model.

- Calculating the value, for example using a model developed by the auditor or by a specialist engaged by the auditor, to develop an independent expectation to corroborate the reasonableness of the value calculated by the entity.
- Comparing the fair value with subsequent or recent transactions.

However, a valuation model should not be used to determine fair value when generally accepted accounting principles require that the fair value of a security be determined using quoted market prices.

.41 Evaluating audit evidence for assertions about derivatives and securities may require the auditor to use considerable judgment. That may be because the assertions, especially those about valuation, are based on highly subjective assumptions or are particularly sensitive to changes in the underlying circumstances. Valuation assertions may be based on assumptions about the occurrence of future events for which expectations are difficult to develop or on assumptions about conditions expected to exist over a long period; for example, default rates or prepayment rates. Accordingly, competent persons could reach different conclusions about estimates of fair values or estimates of ranges of fair values. [Revised, March 2006, to reflect conforming changes necessary due to the issuance of Statement on Auditing Standards No. 105.]

.42 Considerable judgment may also be required in evaluating audit evidence for assertions based on features of the derivative or security and applicable accounting principles, including underlying criteria such as for hedge accounting, that are extremely complex. For example, determining the fair value of a structured note may require consideration of a variety of features of the note that react differently to changes in economic conditions. In addition, one or more other derivatives may be designated to hedge changes in cash flows under the note. Evaluating audit evidence to support the fair value of the note, the determination of whether the hedge is highly effective, and the allocation of changes in fair value to earnings and other comprehensive income may require considerable judgment. [Revised, March 2006, to reflect conforming changes necessary due to the issuance of Statement on Auditing Standards No. 105.]

.43 In situations requiring considerable judgment, the auditor should consider the guidance in—

a. Section 342 on obtaining and evaluating sufficient appropriate audit evidence to support significant accounting estimates.

b. Section 336 on the use of the work of a specialist in performing substantive procedures.

[Revised, March 2006, to reflect conforming changes necessary due to the issuance of Statement on Auditing Standards No. 105.]

.44 Negotiable securities, real estate, chattels, or other property is often assigned as collateral for debt securities. If the collateral is an important factor in evaluating the fair value and collectibility of the security, the auditor should obtain evidence regarding the existence, fair value, and transferability of such collateral as well as the investor's rights to the collateral.

.45 Generally accepted accounting principles may specify how to account for unrealized appreciation and depreciation in the fair value of the entity's derivatives and securities. For example, generally accepted accounting principles require the entity to report a change in the unrealized appreciation or depreciation in the fair value of—

- A derivative that is designated as a fair value hedge in earnings, with disclosure of the ineffective portion of the hedge.
- A derivative that is designated as a cash flow hedge in two components, with the ineffective portion reported in earnings and the effective portion reported in other comprehensive income.
- A derivative that was previously designated as a hedge but is no longer highly effective, or a derivative that is not designated as a hedge, in earnings.
- An available-for-sale security in other comprehensive income.

Generally accepted accounting principles may also require the entity to reclassify amounts from accumulated other comprehensive income to earnings. For example, such reclassifications may be required because a hedged transaction is determined to no longer be probable of occurring, a hedged forecasted transaction affects earnings for the period, or a decline in fair value is determined to be other than temporary.

.46 The auditor should evaluate management's conclusion about the need to recognize in earnings an impairment loss for a decline in fair value that is other than temporary as discussed in paragraphs .47 and .48 of this section. The auditor should also gather audit evidence to support the amount of unrealized appreciation or depreciation in the fair value of a derivative that is recognized in earnings or other comprehensive income or that is disclosed because of the ineffectiveness of a hedge. That requires an understanding of the methods used to determine whether the hedge is highly effective and to determine the ineffective portion of the hedge. [Revised, March 2006, to reflect conforming changes necessary due to the issuance of Statement on Auditing Standards No. 105.]

.47 *Impairment Losses.* Regardless of the valuation method used, generally accepted accounting principles might require recognizing in earnings an impairment loss for a decline in fair value that is other than temporary. Determinations of whether losses are other than temporary often involve estimating the outcome of future events. Accordingly, judgment is required in determining whether factors exist that indicate that an impairment loss has been incurred at the end of the reporting period. These judgments are based on subjective as well as objective factors, including knowledge and experience about past and current events and assumptions about future events. The following are examples of such factors.

- Fair value is significantly below cost and—
  - — The decline is attributable to adverse conditions specifically related to the security or to specific conditions in an industry or in a geographic area.
  - — The decline has existed for an extended period of time.
  - — Management does not possess both the intent and the ability to hold the security for a period of time sufficient to allow for any anticipated recovery in fair value.
- The security has been downgraded by a rating agency.
- The financial condition of the issuer has deteriorated.
- Dividends have been reduced or eliminated, or scheduled interest payments have not been made.
- The entity recorded losses from the security subsequent to the end of the reporting period.

.48 The auditor should evaluate (*a*) whether management has considered relevant information in determining whether factors such as those listed in paragraph .47 exist and (*b*) management's conclusions about the need to recognize an impairment loss. That evaluation requires the auditor to obtain evidence about such factors that tend to corroborate or conflict with management's conclusions. When the entity has recognized an impairment loss, the auditor should gather evidence supporting the amount of the impairment adjustment recorded and determine whether the entity has appropriately followed generally accepted accounting principles.

Presentation and Disclosure

.49 Assertions about presentation and disclosure address whether the classification, description, and disclosure of derivatives and securities in the entity's financial statements are in conformity with generally accepted accounting principles. The auditor should evaluate whether the presentation and disclosure of derivatives and securities are in conformity with generally accepted accounting principles.

[Title of section 411 amended, effective for reports issued or reissued on or after June 30, 2001, by Statement on Auditing Standards No. 93. Revised, October 2009, to reflect conforming changes necessary due to the withdrawal of SAS No. 69.]

.50 For some derivatives and securities, generally accepted accounting principles may prescribe presentation and disclosure requirements. For example—

- Whether changes in the fair value of derivatives used to hedge risks are required to be reported as a component of earnings or other comprehensive income depends on whether they are intended to hedge the risk of changes in the fair value of assets and liabilities or changes in expected future cash flows and on the degree of effectiveness of the hedge.
- Certain securities are required to be classified into categories according to management's intent and ability, such as held-to-maturity.
- Specific information is required to be disclosed about derivatives and securities.

.51 In evaluating the adequacy of presentation and disclosure, the auditor should consider the form, arrangement, and content of the financial statements and their notes, including, for example, the terminology used, the amount of detail given, the classification of items in the statements, and the bases of amounts reported. The auditor should compare the presentation and disclosure with the requirements of generally accepted accounting principles. However, the auditor should also follow the guidance in section 431, *Adequacy of Disclosure in Financial Statements*, in evaluating the adequacy of disclosure that is not specifically required by generally accepted accounting principles.

Additional Considerations About Hedging Activities

.52 To account for a derivative as a hedge, generally accepted accounting principles require management at the inception of the hedge to designate the derivative as a hedge and contemporaneously formally document[18] the hedging

---

[18] FASB ASC 815 requires formal documentation of prescribed aspects of hedging relationships at the inception of the hedge. [Footnote revised, June 2009, to reflect conforming changes necessary due to the issuance of FASB ASC. Footnote renumbered, August 2011, to reflect conforming changes necessary due to the issuance of SSAE No. 16.]

relationship, the entity's risk management objective and strategy for undertaking the hedge, and the method of assessing the effectiveness of the hedge. In addition, to qualify for hedge accounting, generally accepted accounting principles require that management have an expectation, both at the inception of the hedge and on an ongoing basis, that the hedging relationship will be highly effective in achieving the hedging strategy.[19]

.53 The auditor should gather audit evidence to determine whether management complied with the hedge accounting requirements of generally accepted accounting principles, including designation and documentation requirements. In addition, the auditor should gather audit evidence to support management's expectation at the inception of the hedge that the hedging relationship will be highly effective and its periodic assessment of the ongoing effectiveness of the hedging relationship as required by generally accepted accounting principles. [Revised, March 2006, to reflect conforming changes necessary due to the issuance of Statement on Auditing Standards No. 105.]

.54 When the entity designates a derivative as a fair value hedge, generally accepted accounting principles require that the entity adjust the carrying amount of the hedged item for the change in the hedged item's fair value that is attributable to the hedged risk. The auditor should gather audit evidence supporting the recorded change in the hedged item's fair value that is attributable to the hedged risk. Additionally, the auditor should gather audit evidence to determine whether management has properly applied generally accepted accounting principles to the hedged item. [Revised, March 2006, to reflect conforming changes necessary due to the issuance of Statement on Auditing Standards No. 105.]

.55 For a cash flow hedge of a forecasted transaction, generally accepted accounting principles require management to determine that the forecasted transaction is probable of occurring. Those principles require that the likelihood that the transaction will take place not be based solely on management's intent. Instead, the transaction's probability should be supported by observable facts and the attendant circumstances, such as the following:

- The frequency of similar past transactions
- The financial and operational ability of the entity to carry out the transaction
- The extent of loss that could result if the transaction does not occur
- The likelihood that transactions with substantially different characteristics might be used to achieve the same business purpose

The auditor should evaluate management's determination of whether a forecasted transaction is probable.

Assertions About Securities Based on Management's Intent and Ability

.56 Generally accepted accounting principles require that management's intent and ability be considered in valuing certain securities; for example, whether—

---

[19] FASB ASC 815 requires management to periodically reassess the effectiveness of hedging relationships whenever financial statements or earnings are reported, and at least every three months. It also requires that all assessments of effectiveness be consistent with the risk management strategy documented for the particular hedging relationship. [Footnote revised, June 2009, to reflect conforming changes necessary due to the issuance of FASB ASC. Footnote renumbered, August 2011, to reflect conforming changes necessary due to the issuance of SSAE No. 16.]

- Debt securities are classified as held-to-maturity and reported at their cost depends on management's intent and ability to hold them to their maturity.
- Equity securities are reported using the equity method depends on management's ability to significantly influence the investee.
- Equity securities are classified as trading or available-for-sale depends on management's intent and objectives in investing in the securities.

.57 In evaluating management's intent and ability, the auditor should—

a. Obtain an understanding of the process used by management to classify securities as trading, available-for-sale, or held-to-maturity.

b. For an investment accounted for using the equity method, inquire of management as to whether the entity has the ability to exercise significant influence over the operating and financial policies of the investee and evaluate the attendant circumstances that serve as a basis for management's conclusions.

c. If the entity accounts for the investment contrary to the presumption established by generally accepted accounting principles for use of the equity method, obtain sufficient appropriate audit evidence about whether that presumption has been overcome and whether appropriate disclosure is made regarding the reasons for not accounting for the investment in keeping with that presumption.

d. Consider whether management's activities corroborate or conflict with its stated intent. For example, the auditor should evaluate an assertion that management intends to hold debt securities to their maturity by examining evidence such as documentation of management's strategies and sales and other historical activities with respect to those securities and similar securities.

e. Determine whether generally accepted accounting principles require management to document its intentions and specify the content and timeliness of that documentation.[20] The auditor should inspect the documentation and obtain audit evidence about its timeliness. Unlike the formal documentation required for hedging activities, audit evidence supporting the classification of debt and equity securities may be more informal.

f. Determine whether management's activities, contractual agreements, or the entity's financial condition provide evidence of its ability. Examples follow.

(1) The entity's financial position, working capital needs, operating results, debt agreements, guarantees, alternate sources of liquidity, and other relevant contractual obligations, as well as laws and regulations, may provide evidence about an entity's ability to hold debt securities to their maturity.

(2) Management's cash flow projections may suggest that it does not have the ability to hold debt securities to their maturity.

---

[20] FASB ASC 320-10-25-1 requires an investor to document the classification of debt and equity securities into one of three categories—held-to-maturity, available-for-sale, or trading—at their acquisition. [Footnote revised, June 2009, to reflect conforming changes necessary due to the issuance of FASB ASC. Footnote renumbered, August 2011, to reflect conforming changes necessary due to the issuance of SSAE No. 16.]

(3) Management's inability to obtain information from an investee may suggest that it does not have the ability to significantly influence the investee.

(4) If the entity asserts that it maintains effective control over securities transferred under a repurchase agreement, the contractual agreement may be such that the entity actually surrendered control over the securities and therefore should account for the transfer as a sale instead of a secured borrowing.

[Revised, March 2006, to reflect conforming changes necessary due to the issuance of Statement on Auditing Standards No. 105.]

Management Representations

.58 Section 333, *Management Representations*, provides guidance to auditors in obtaining written representations from management. The auditor ordinarily should obtain written representations from management confirming aspects of management's intent and ability that affect assertions about derivatives and securities, such as its intent and ability to hold a debt security until its maturity or to enter into a forecasted transaction for which hedge accounting is applied. In addition, the auditor should consider obtaining written representations from management confirming other aspects of derivatives and securities transactions that affect assertions about them.[21]

Effective Date

.59 This section is effective for audits of financial statements for fiscal years ending on or after June 30, 2001. Early application is permitted.

---

[21] Section 333 paragraph .17 provides illustrative representations about derivatives and securities transactions. [Footnote renumbered, August 2011, to reflect conforming changes necessary due to the issuance of SSAE No. 16.]

AU Section 9332

Auditing Derivative Instruments, Hedging Activities, and Investments in Securities: Auditing Interpretations of Section 332

1. Auditing Investments in Securities Where a Readily Determinable Fair Value Does Not Exist

.01 *Question*—Entities may make investments in securities, required by generally accepted accounting principals to be accounted for at fair value, where a readily determinable fair value for those securities does not exist. For example, an entity may have an investment in a hedge fund that it reports at fair value, but for which a readily determinable fair value does not exist. Further, the hedge fund may own interests in investments in limited partnership interests or other private equity securities for which a readily determinable fair value does not exist. As part of an auditor's procedures in accordance with section 332, *Auditing Derivative Instruments, Hedging Activities, and Investments in Securities*, he or she typically would satisfy the existence assertion through either confirmation with the hedge fund, examination of legal documents, or other means as discussed in section 332. In confirming the existence, the auditor may request the hedge fund to indicate or to confirm the fair value of the entity's investment in the hedge fund, including the fair value of investments held by the hedge fund. In some circumstances, the hedge fund will not provide management or the auditor detailed information about the basis and method for measuring the entity's investment in the hedge fund, nor will they provide information about the specific investments held by the hedge fund. For example, in some circumstances the hedge fund may inform management or the auditor that investments are held by the hedge fund as follows:

- In aggregate, such as "$XXX of total investments"
- In aggregate, such as "$XXX of total investments in private equity securities, $YYY of total investments in interests in limited partnerships, and $ZZZ of total investments in debt securities"
- On an investment-by-investment basis, such as "AA shares of common stock of private company A, with a fair value of $AAA; BB shares of preferred stock of private company B, with a fair value of $BBB; CC units of limited partnership interest CCC, with a fair value of $CCC; and real estate property DDD, with a fair value of $DDDD"

In circumstances in which the auditor determines that the nature and extent of auditing procedures should include verifying the existence and testing the measurement of investments in securities, does receiving a confirmation from a third party, either in aggregate or on a security-by-security basis, constitute adequate audit evidence with respect to the existence and valuation assertions in section 332?

.02 *Interpretation*—In circumstances in which the auditor determines that the nature and extent of auditing procedures should include verifying the existence and testing the measurement of investments in securities, simply receiving a confirmation from a third party, either in aggregate or on a security-by-security basis, does not in and of itself constitute adequate audit evidence with respect to the valuation assertion in section 332. In addition, receiving confirmation from a third party for investments in aggregate (illustrated by the first two bullets above) does not constitute adequate audit evidence with respect to the existence assertion under section 332. Receiving confirmation from a third party on a security-by-security basis (illustrated by the third bullet above), however, typically would constitute adequate audit evidence with respect to the existence assertion under section 332. Also, as noted in section 328, *Auditing Fair Value Measurements and Disclosures*, paragraph .04, in discussing management's responsibility for making fair value measurements:

> Management is responsible for making the fair value measurements and disclosures included in the financial statements. As part of fulfilling its responsibility, management needs to establish an accounting and financial reporting process for determining the fair value measurements and disclosures, select appropriate valuation methods, identify and adequately support any significant assumptions used, prepare the valuation, and ensure that the presentation and disclosure of the fair value measurements are in accordance with GAAP.

.03 In addition, section 328 discusses the auditor's responsibility dealing with:

- Understanding the entity's process for determining fair value measurements and disclosures and the relevant controls, and assessing risk
- Evaluating conformity of fair value measurements and disclosures with GAAP
- Engaging a specialist, where necessary
- Testing the entity's fair value measurements and disclosures
- Disclosures about fair values
- Evaluating the results of audit procedures
- Management representations
- Communication with those charged with governance

.04 In circumstances in which the auditor is unable to audit the existence or measurement of interests in investments in securities at the financial statement date, the auditor should consider whether that scope limitation requires the auditor to either qualify his or her opinion or to disclaim an opinion, as discussed in section 508, *Reports on Audited Financial Statements*, paragraphs .22 to .26.

[Issue Date: July, 2005; Revised: April, 2007.]

AU Section 333

Management Representations

(Supersedes SAS No. 19.)

Source: SAS No. 85; SAS No. 89; SAS No. 99; SAS No. 113.

See section 9333 for interpretations of this section.

Effective for audits of financial statements for periods ending on or after June 30, 1998, unless otherwise indicated.

Introduction

.01 This section establishes a requirement that the independent auditor obtain written representations from management as a part of an audit of financial statements performed in accordance with generally accepted auditing standards and provides guidance concerning the representations to be obtained.

Reliance on Management Representations

.02 During an audit, management makes many representations to the auditor, both oral and written, in response to specific inquiries or through the financial statements. Such representations from management are part of the audit evidence the independent auditor obtains, but they are not a substitute for the application of those auditing procedures necessary to afford a reasonable basis for an opinion regarding the financial statements under audit. Written representations from management ordinarily confirm representations explicitly or implicitly given to the auditor, indicate and document the continuing appropriateness of such representations, and reduce the possibility of misunderstanding concerning the matters that are the subject of the representations. [Revised, March 2006, to reflect conforming changes necessary due to the issuance of Statement on Auditing Standards No. 105.][1]

.03 The auditor obtains written representations from management to complement other auditing procedures. In many cases, the auditor applies auditing procedures specifically designed to obtain audit evidence concerning matters that also are the subject of written representations. For example, after the auditor performs the procedures prescribed in section 334, *Related Parties*, even if the results of those procedures indicate that transactions with related parties have been properly disclosed, the auditor should obtain a written representation to document that management has no knowledge of any such transactions that have not been properly disclosed. In some circumstances, audit evidence that can be obtained by the application of auditing procedures other than inquiry is limited; therefore, the auditor obtains written representations to provide additional audit evidence. For example, if an entity plans to discontinue a line of business and the auditor is not able to obtain sufficient information through other auditing procedures to corroborate the plan or intent,

---

[1] Section 230, *Due Professional Care in the Performance of Work*, states, "The auditor neither assumes that management is dishonest nor assumes unquestioned honesty. In exercising professional skepticism, the auditor should not be satisfied with less than persuasive evidence because of a belief that management is honest."

the auditor obtains a written representation to provide evidence of management's intent. [Revised, March 2006, to reflect conforming changes necessary due to the issuance of Statement on Auditing Standards No. 105.]

.04 If a representation made by management is contradicted by other audit evidence, the auditor should investigate the circumstances and consider the reliability of the representation made. Based on the circumstances, the auditor should consider whether his or her reliance on management's representations relating to other aspects of the financial statements is appropriate and justified.

Obtaining Written Representations

.05 Written representations from management should be obtained for all financial statements and periods covered by the auditor's report.[2] For example, if comparative financial statements are reported on, the written representations obtained at the completion of the most recent audit should address all periods being reported on. The specific written representations obtained by the auditor will depend on the circumstances of the engagement and the nature and basis of presentation of the financial statements.

.06 In connection with an audit of financial statements presented in accordance with generally accepted accounting principles, specific representations should relate to the following matters:[3]

Financial Statements

a. Management's acknowledgment of its responsibility for the fair presentation in the financial statements of financial position, results of operations, and cash flows in conformity with generally accepted accounting principles.

b. Management's belief that the financial statements are fairly presented in conformity with generally accepted accounting principles.

Completeness of Information

c. Availability of all financial records and related data.

d. Completeness and availability of all minutes of meetings of stockholders, directors, and committees of directors.

e. Communications from regulatory agencies concerning noncompliance with or deficiencies in financial reporting practices.

f. Absence of unrecorded transactions.

Recognition, Measurement, and Disclosure

g. Management's belief that the effects of any uncorrected financial statement misstatements[4] aggregated by the auditor during the current engagement and pertaining to the latest period presented are immaterial, both individually and in the aggregate, to the financial statements

---

[2] An illustrative representation letter from management is contained in paragraph .16 of appendix A, "Illustrative Management Representation Letter".

[3] Specific representations also are applicable to financial statements presented in conformity with a comprehensive basis of accounting other than generally accepted accounting principles. The specific representations to be obtained should be based on the nature and basis of presentation of the financial statements being audited.

[4] Paragraph .07 of section 312, *Audit Risk and Materiality in Conducting an Audit*, states that a misstatement can result from errors or fraud, and provides guidance for the auditor's evaluation of audit findings (paragraphs 50-.61 of section 312). [Footnote added, effective for audits of financial statements for periods beginning on or after December 15, 1999, by Statement on Auditing Standards No. 89.]

taken as a whole.[5] (A summary of such items should be included in or attached to the letter.)[6, 7]

h. Management's acknowledgment of its responsibility for the design and implementation of programs and controls to prevent and detect fraud.

i. Knowledge of fraud or suspected fraud affecting the entity involving (1) management, (2) employees who have significant roles in internal control, or (3) others where the fraud could have a material effect on the financial statements.[8]

j. Knowledge of any allegations of fraud or suspected fraud affecting the entity received in communications from employees, former employees, analysts, regulators, short sellers, or others.

k. Plans or intentions that may affect the carrying value or classification of assets or liabilities.

l. Information concerning related-party transactions and amounts receivable from or payable to related parties.[9]

m. Guarantees, whether written or oral, under which the entity is contingently liable.

n. Significant estimates and material concentrations known to management that are required to be disclosed in accordance with Financial Accounting Standards Board (FASB) *Accounting Standards Codification* (ASC) 275, *Risks and Uncertainties*.

o. Violations or possible violations of laws or regulations whose effects should be considered for disclosure in the financial statements or as a basis for recording a loss contingency.[10]

p. Unasserted claims or assessments that the entity's lawyer has advised are probable of assertion and must be disclosed in accordance with FASB ASC 450, *Contingencies*.[11]

---

[5] If management believes that certain of the identified items are not misstatements, management's belief may be acknowledged by adding to the representation, for example, "We do not agree that items XX and XX constitute misstatements because [description of reasons]." [Footnote added, effective for audits of financial statements for periods beginning on or after December 15, 1999, by Statement on Auditing Standards No. 89.]

[6] Paragraph .42 of section 312 states that the auditor may designate an amount below which misstatements need not be accumulated. Similarly, the summary of uncorrected misstatements included in or attached to the representation letter need not include such misstatements. The summary should include sufficient information to provide management with an understanding of the nature, amount, and effect of the uncorrected misstatements. Similar items may be aggregated. [Footnote added, effective for audits of financial statements for periods beginning on or after December 15, 1999, by Statement on Auditing Standards No. 89.]

[7] The communication to management of immaterial misstatements aggregated by the auditor does not constitute a communication pursuant to paragraph .17 of section 317, *Illegal Acts by Clients*, Section 10A of the Securities Exchange Act of 1934, or paragraphs .38–.40 of section 316, *Consideration of Fraud in a Financial Statement Audit*. The auditor may have additional communication responsibilities pursuant to section 317, Section 10A of the Securities Exchange Act of 1934, or section 316. [Footnote added, effective for audits of financial statements for periods beginning on or after December 15, 1999, by Statement on Auditing Standards No. 89. Footnote renumbered by the issuance of Statement on Auditing Standards No. 89, December 1999.]

[8] [Footnote deleted by the issuance of Statement on Auditing Standards No. 99, October 2002.]

[9] See section 334. [Footnote renumbered by the issuance of Statement on Auditing Standards No. 89, December 1999.]

[10] See section 317. [Footnote renumbered by the issuance of Statement on Auditing Standards No. 89, December 1999.]

[11] See paragraph .05 of section 337, *Inquiry of a Client's Lawyer Concerning Litigation, Claims, and Assessments*. If the entity has not consulted a lawyer regarding litigation, claims, and

(continued)

q. Other liabilities and gain or loss contingencies that are required to be accrued or disclosed by FASB ASC 450.[12]

r. Satisfactory title to assets, liens or encumbrances on assets, and assets pledged as collateral.

s. Compliance with aspects of contractual agreements that may affect the financial statements.

Subsequent Events

t. Information concerning subsequent events.[13]

[As amended, effective for audits of financial statements for periods beginning on or after December 15, 1999, by Statement on Auditing Standards No. 89. As amended, effective for audits of financial statements for periods beginning on or after December 15, 2002, by Statement on Auditing Standards No. 99. Revised, June 2009, to reflect conforming changes necessary due to the issuance of FASB ASC.]

.07 The representation letter ordinarily should be tailored to include additional appropriate representations from management relating to matters specific to the entity's business or industry.[14] Examples of additional representations that may be appropriate are provided in paragraph .17 appendix B, "Additional Illustrative Representations."

.08 Management's representations may be limited to matters that are considered either individually or collectively material to the financial statements, provided management and the auditor have reached an understanding on materiality for this purpose. Materiality may be different for different representations. A discussion of materiality may be included explicitly in the representation letter, in either qualitative or quantitative terms. Materiality considerations would not apply to those representations that are not directly related to amounts included in the financial statements, for example, items (*a*), (*c*), (*d*), and (*e*) above. In addition, because of the possible effects of fraud on other aspects of the audit, materiality would not apply to item (*h*) above with respect to management or those employees who have significant roles in internal control.

.09 The written representations should be addressed to the auditor. Because the auditor is concerned with events occurring through the date of his or her report that may require adjustment to or disclosure in the financial statements, the representations should be made as of the date of the auditor's report. [If the auditor "dual dates" his or her report, the auditor should consider whether obtaining additional representations relating to the subsequent event is appropriate. See paragraph .05 of section 530, *Dating of the Independent Auditor's Report*.] The letter should be signed by those members of management

(footnote continued)

assessments, the auditor normally would rely on the review of internally available information and obtain a written representation by management regarding the lack of litigation, claims, and assessments; see auditing Interpretation No. 6, "Client Has Not Consulted a Lawyer" (paragraphs .15–.17 of section 9337). [Footnote renumbered by the issuance of Statement on Auditing Standards No. 89, December 1999.]

[12] See paragraph .05*b* of section 337. [Footnote renumbered by the issuance of Statement on Auditing Standards No. 89, December 1999.]

[13] See paragraph .12 of section 560, *Subsequent Events*; paragraph .10 of section 711, *Filings Under Federal Securities Statutes*; and paragraph .45, footnote 31 of section 634, *Letters for Underwriters and Certain Other Requesting Parties*. [Footnote renumbered by the issuance of Statement on Auditing Standards No. 89, December 1999.]

[14] Certain AICPA Audit Guides recommend that the auditor obtain written representations concerning matters that are unique to a particular industry. [Footnote renumbered by the issuance of Statement on Auditing Standards No. 89, December 1999.]

with overall responsibility for financial and operating matters whom the auditor believes are responsible for and knowledgeable about, directly or through others in the organization, the matters covered by the representations. Such members of management normally include the chief executive officer and chief financial officer or others with equivalent positions in the entity. [As amended, effective for audits of financial statements for periods ending on or after December 15, 2006, by Statement on Auditing Standards No. 113.]

.10 If current management was not present during all periods covered by the auditor's report, the auditor should nevertheless obtain written representations from current management on all such periods. The specific written representations obtained by the auditor will depend on the circumstances of the engagement and the nature and basis of presentation of the financial statements. As discussed in paragraph .08, management's representations may be limited to matters that are considered either individually or collectively material to the financial statements.

.11 In certain circumstances, the auditor may want to obtain written representations from other individuals. For example, he or she may want to obtain written representations about the completeness of the minutes of the meetings of stockholders, directors, and committees of directors from the person responsible for keeping such minutes. Also, if the independent auditor performs an audit of the financial statements of a subsidiary but does not audit those of the parent company, he or she may want to obtain representations from management of the parent company concerning matters that may affect the subsidiary, such as related-party transactions or the parent company's intention to provide continuing financial support to the subsidiary.

.12 There are circumstances in which an auditor should obtain updating representation letters from management. If a predecessor auditor is requested by a former client to reissue (or consent to the reuse of) his or her report on the financial statements of a prior period, and those financial statements are to be presented on a comparative basis with audited financial statements of a subsequent period, the predecessor auditor should obtain an updating representation letter from the management of the former client.[15] Also, when performing subsequent events procedures in connection with filings under the Securities Act of 1933, the auditor should obtain certain written representations.[16] The updating management representation letter should state (*a*) whether any information has come to management's attention that would cause them to believe that any of the previous representations should be modified, and (*b*) whether any events have occurred subsequent to the balance-sheet date of the latest financial statements reported on by the auditor that would require adjustment to or disclosure in those financial statements.[17]

Scope Limitations

.13 Management's refusal to furnish written representations constitutes a limitation on the scope of the audit sufficient to preclude an unqualified opinion and is ordinarily sufficient to cause an auditor to disclaim an opinion

---

[15] See paragraph .71 of section 508, *Reports on Audited Financial Statements*. [Footnote renumbered by the issuance of Statement on Auditing Standards No. 89, December 1999.]

[16] See paragraph .10 of section 711. [Footnote renumbered by the issuance of Statement on Auditing Standards No. 89, December 1999.]

[17] An illustrative updating management representation letter is contained in paragraph .18 of appendix C, "Illustrative Updating Management Representation Letter." [Footnote renumbered by the issuance of Statement on Auditing Standards No. 89, December 1999.]

or withdraw from the engagement.[18] However, based on the nature of the representations not obtained or the circumstances of the refusal, the auditor may conclude that a qualified opinion is appropriate. Further, the auditor should consider the effects of the refusal on his or her ability to rely on other management representations.

.14 If the auditor is precluded from performing procedures he or she considers necessary in the circumstances with respect to a matter that is material to the financial statements, even though management has given representations concerning the matter, there is a limitation on the scope of the audit, and the auditor should qualify his or her opinion or disclaim an opinion.

Effective Date

.15 This section is effective for audits of financial statements for periods ending on or after June 30, 1998. Earlier application is permitted.

---

[18] See paragraphs .22–.34 of section 508. [Footnote renumbered by the issuance of Statement on Auditing Standards No. 89, December 1999.]

.16

Appendix A

Illustrative Management Representation Letter

1. The following letter, which relates to an audit of financial statements prepared in conformity with generally accepted accounting principles, is presented for illustrative purposes only. The introductory paragraph should specify the financial statements and periods covered by the auditor's report, for example, "balance sheets of XYZ Company as of December 31, 19X1 and 19X0, and the related statements of income and retained earnings and cash flows for the years then ended." The written representations to be obtained should be based on the circumstances of the engagement and the nature and basis of presentation of the financial statements being audited. (See paragraph .17 of appendix B.)

2. If matters exist that should be disclosed to the auditor, they should be indicated by modifying the related representation. For example, if an event subsequent to the date of the balance sheet has been disclosed in the financial statements, the final paragraph could be modified as follows: "To the best of our knowledge and belief, except as discussed in Note X to the financial statements, no events have occurred. . . ." In appropriate circumstances, item 9 could be modified as follows: "The company has no plans or intentions that may materially affect the carrying value or classification of assets and liabilities, except for its plans to dispose of segment A, as disclosed in Note X to the financial statements, which are discussed in the minutes of the December 7, 20X1, meeting of the board of directors." Similarly, if management has received a communication regarding an allegation of fraud or suspected fraud, item 8 could be modified as follows: "Except for the allegation discussed in the minutes of the December 7, 20X1, meeting of the board of directors (or disclosed to you at our meeting on October 15, 20X1), we have no knowledge of any allegations of fraud or suspected fraud affecting the company received in communications from employees, former employees, analysts, regulators, short sellers, or others."

3. The qualitative discussion of materiality used in the illustrative letter is adapted from FASB Statement of Financial Accounting Concepts No. 2, *Qualitative Characteristics of Accounting Information*.

4. Certain terms are used in the illustrative letter that are described elsewhere in authoritative literature. Examples are fraud, in section 316, and related parties, in section 334 footnote 1. To avoid misunderstanding concerning the meaning of such terms, the auditor may wish to furnish those definitions to management or request that the definitions be included in the written representations.

5. The illustrative letter assumes that management and the auditor have reached an understanding on the limits of materiality for purposes of the written representations. However, it should be noted that a materiality limit would not apply for certain representations, as explained in paragraph .08 of this section.

6.

[*Date*]

To [*Independent Auditor*]

We are providing this letter in connection with your audit(s) of the [*identification of financial statements*] of [*name of entity*] as of [*dates*] and for the [*periods*] for the purpose of expressing an opinion as to whether the [*consolidated*] financial statements present fairly, in all material respects, the financial position, results of operations, and cash flows of [*name of entity*] in conformity with accounting principles generally accepted in the United States of America. We confirm that we are responsible for the fair presentation in the [*consolidated*] financial statements of financial position, results of operations, and cash flows in conformity with generally accepted accounting principles.

Certain representations in this letter are described as being limited to matters that are material. Items are considered material, regardless of size, if they involve an omission or misstatement of accounting information that, in the light of surrounding circumstances, makes it probable that the judgment of a reasonable person relying on the information would be changed or influenced by the omission or misstatement.

We confirm, to the best of our knowledge and belief, [*as of (date of auditor's report),*] the following representations made to you during your audit(s).

1. The financial statements referred to above are fairly presented in conformity with accounting principles generally accepted in the United States of America.
2. We have made available to you all—
   a. Financial records and related data.
   b. Minutes of the meetings of stockholders, directors, and committees of directors, or summaries of actions of recent meetings for which minutes have not yet been prepared.
3. There have been no communications from regulatory agencies concerning noncompliance with or deficiencies in financial reporting practices.
4. There are no material transactions that have not been properly recorded in the accounting records underlying the financial statements.
5. We believe that the effects of the uncorrected financial statement misstatements summarized in the accompanying schedule are immaterial, both individually and in the aggregate, to the financial statements taken as a whole.[1]
6. We acknowledge our responsibility for the design and implementation of programs and controls to prevent and detect fraud.
7. We have no knowledge of any fraud or suspected fraud affecting the entity involving—
   a. Management,
   b. Employees who have significant roles in internal control, or
   c. Others where the fraud could have a material effect on the financial statements.
8. We have no knowledge of any allegations of fraud or suspected fraud affecting the entity received in communications from employees, former employees, analysts, regulators, short sellers, or others.
9. The company has no plans or intentions that may materially affect the carrying value or classification of assets and liabilities.
10. The following have been properly recorded or disclosed in the financial statements:
    a. Related-party transactions, including sales, purchases, loans, transfers, leasing arrangements, and guarantees, and amounts receivable from or payable to related parties.

---

[1] If management believes that certain of the identified items are not misstatements, management's belief may be acknowledged by adding to the representation, for example, "We do not agree that items XX and XX constitute misstatements because [*description of reasons*]." [Footnote added effective for audits of financial statements for periods beginning on or after December 15, 1999, by Statement on Auditing Standards No. 89.]

b. Guarantees, whether written or oral, under which the company is contingently liable.

c. Significant estimates and material concentrations known to management that are required to be disclosed in accordance with Financial Accounting Standards Board (FASB) *Accounting Standards Codification* (ASC) 275, *Risks and Uncertainties. [Significant estimates are estimates at the balance sheet date that could change materially within the next year. Concentrations refer to volumes of business, revenues, available sources of supply, or markets or geographic areas for which events could occur that would significantly disrupt normal finances within the next year.*]

11. There are no—

a. Violations or possible violations of laws or regulations whose effects should be considered for disclosure in the financial statements or as a basis for recording a loss contingency.

b. Unasserted claims or assessments that our lawyer has advised us are probable of assertion and must be disclosed in accordance with FASB ASC 450, *Contingencies.* [2]

c. Other liabilities or gain or loss contingencies that are required to be accrued or disclosed by FASB ASC 450.

12. The company has satisfactory title to all owned assets, and there are no liens or encumbrances on such assets nor has any asset been pledged as collateral.

13. The company has complied with all aspects of contractual agreements that would have a material effect on the financial statements in the event of noncompliance.

[*Add additional representations that are unique to the entity's business or industry. See paragraph .07 and appendix B, paragraph .17 of this section.*]

To the best of our knowledge and belief, no events have occurred subsequent to the balance-sheet date and through the date of this letter that would require adjustment to or disclosure in the aforementioned financial statements.

____

[*Name of Chief Executive Officer and Title*]

____

[*Name of Chief Financial Officer and Title*]

[As amended, effective for audits of financial statements for periods beginning on or after December 15, 1999 by Statement on Auditing Standards No. 89. As amended, effective for audits of financial statements for periods beginning on or after December 15, 2002, by Statement on Auditing Standards No. 99. Revised, June 2009, to reflect conforming changes necessary due to the issuance of FASB ASC.]

---

[2] In the circumstance discussed in footnote 11 of this section, this representation might be worded as follows:

> We are not aware of any pending or threatened litigation, claims, or assessments or unasserted claims or assessments that are required to be accrued or disclosed in the financial statements in accordance with Financial Accounting Standards Board *Accounting Standards Codification* 450, *Contingencies*, and we have not consulted a lawyer concerning litigation, claims, or assessments.

[Footnote renumbered by the issuance of Statement on Auditing Standards No. 89, December 1999. Footnote revised, June 2009, to reflect conforming changes necessary due to the issuance of FASB ASC.]

.17

Appendix B

Additional Illustrative Representations

1. As discussed in paragraph .07 of this section, representation letters ordinarily should be tailored to include additional appropriate representations from management relating to matters specific to the entity's business or industry. The auditor also should be aware that certain AICPA Audit Guides recommend that the auditor obtain written representations concerning matters that are unique to a particular industry. The following is a list of additional representations that may be appropriate in certain situations. This list is not intended to be all-inclusive. The auditor also should consider the effects of pronouncements issued subsequent to the issuance of this section.

General

Condition	*Illustrative Example*
Unaudited interim information accompanies the financial statements.	The unaudited interim financial information accompanying [*presented in Note X to*] the financial statements for the [*identify all related periods*] has been prepared and presented in conformity with generally accepted accounting principles applicable to interim financial information [*and with Item 302(a) of Regulation S-K*]. The accounting principles used to prepare the unaudited interim financial information are consistent with those used to prepare the audited financial statements.
The impact of a new accounting principle is not known.	We have not completed the process of evaluating the impact that will result from adopting the guidance in Financial Accounting Standards Board (FASB) *Accounting Standards Codification* (ASC) Update 20YY-XX, as discussed in Note [X]. The company is therefore unable to disclose the impact that adopting the guidance in FASB ASC Update 20YY-XX will have on its financial position and the results of operations when such guidance is adopted.
There is justification for a change in accounting principles.	We believe that [*describe the newly adopted accounting principle*] is preferable to [*describe the former accounting principle*] because [*describe management's justification for the change in accounting principles*].

Condition	*Illustrative Example*
Financial circumstances are strained, with disclosure of management's intentions and the entity's ability to continue as a going concern.	Note [*X*] to the financial statements discloses all of the matters of which we are aware that are relevant to the company's ability to continue as a going concern, including significant conditions and events, and management's plans.
The possibility exists that the value of specific significant long-lived assets or certain identifiable intangibles may be impaired.	We have reviewed long-lived assets and certain identifiable intangibles to be held and used for impairment whenever events or changes in circumstances have indicated that the carrying amount of its assets might not be recoverable and have appropriately recorded the adjustment.
The entity has a variable interest in another entity.	Variable interest entities (VIEs) and potential VIEs and transactions with VIEs and potential VIEs have been properly recorded and disclosed in the financial statements in accordance with US GAAP. We have considered both implicit and explicit variable interests in (*a*) determining whether potential VIEs should be considered VIEs, (*b*) calculating expected losses and residual returns, and (*c*) determining which party, if any, is the primary beneficiary. We have provided you with lists of all identified variable interests in (i) VIEs, (ii) potential VIEs that we considered but judged not to be VIEs, and (iii) entities that were afforded the scope exceptions of Financial Accounting Standards Board (FASB) *Accounting Standards Codification* (ASC) 810, *Consolidation*. We have advised you of all transactions with identified VIEs, potential VIEs, or entities afforded the scope exceptions of FASB ASC 810. We have made available all relevant information about financial interests and contractual arrangements with related parties, de facto agents and other entities, including but not limited to, their governing documents, equity and debt instruments, contracts, leases, guarantee arrangements, and other financial contracts and arrangements.

(continued)

Condition	*Illustrative Example*
	The information we provided about financial interests and contractual arrangements with related parties, de facto agents and other entities includes information about all transactions, unwritten understandings, agreement modifications, and written and oral side agreements. Our computations of expected losses and expected residual returns of entities that are VIEs and potential VIEs are based on the best information available and include all reasonably possible outcomes. Regarding entities in which the Company has variable interests (implicit and explicit), we have provided all information about events and changes in circumstances that could potentially cause reconsideration about whether the entities are VIEs or whether the Company is the primary beneficiary or has a significant variable interest in the entity. We have made and continue to make exhaustive efforts to obtain information about entities in which the Company has an implicit or explicit interest but that were excluded from complete analysis under FASB ASC 810 due to lack of essential information to determine one or more of the following: whether the entity is a VIE, whether the Company is the primary beneficiary, or the accounting required to consolidate the entity.
The work of a specialist has been used by the entity.	We agree with the findings of specialists in evaluating the [*describe assertion*] and have adequately considered the qualifications of the specialist in determining the amounts and disclosures used in the financial statements and underlying accounting records. We did not give or cause any instructions to be given to specialists with respect to the values

Condition	Illustrative Example
	or amounts derived in an attempt to bias their work, and we are not otherwise aware of any matters that have had an impact on the independence or objectivity of the specialists.

Assets

Condition	Illustrative Examples
Cash	
Disclosure is required of compensating balances or other arrangements involving restrictions on cash balances, line of credit, or similar arrangements.	Arrangements with financial institutions involving compensating balances or other arrangements involving restrictions on cash balances, line of credit, or similar arrangements have been properly disclosed.
Financial Instruments	
Management intends to and has the ability to hold to maturity debt securities classified as held-to-maturity.	Debt securities that have been classified as held-to-maturity have been so classified due to the company's intent to hold such securities, to maturity and the company's ability to do so. All other debt securities have been classified as available-for-sale or trading.
Management considers the decline in value of debt or equity securities to be temporary.	We consider the decline in value of debt or equity securities classified as either available-for-sale or held-to-maturity to be temporary.
Management has determined the fair value of significant financial instruments that do not have readily determinable market values.	The methods and significant assumptions used to determine fair values of financial instruments are as follows: [*describe methods and significant assumptions used to determine fair values of financial instruments]*. The methods and significant assumptions used result in a measure of fair value appropriate for financial statement measurement and disclosure purposes.
There are financial instruments with off-balance-sheet risk and financial instruments with concentrations of credit risk.	The following information about financial instruments with off-balance-sheet risk and financial instruments with concentrations of credit risk has been properly disclosed in the financial statements: 1. The extent, nature, and terms of financial instruments with off-balance-sheet risk

(continued)

Condition	*Illustrative Examples*
	2. The amount of credit risk of financial instruments with off-balance-sheet risk and information about the collateral supporting such financial instruments 3. Significant concentrations of credit risk arising from all financial instruments and information about the collateral supporting such financial instruments
Receivables Receivables have been recorded in the financial statements.	Receivables recorded in the financial statements represent valid claims against debtors for sales or other charges arising on or before the balance-sheet date and have been appropriately reduced to their estimated net realizable value.
Inventories Excess or obsolete inventories exist.	Provision has been made to reduce excess or obsolete inventories to their estimated net realizable value.
Investments There are unusual considerations involved in determining the application of equity accounting.	*[For investments in common stock that are either nonmarketable or of which the entity has a 20 percent or greater ownership interest, select the appropriate representation from the following:]* • The equity method is used to account for the company's investment in the common stock of [*investee*] because the company has the ability to exercise significant influence over the investee's operating and financial policies. • The cost method is used to account for the company's investment in the common stock of [investee] because the company does not have the ability to exercise significant influence over the investee's operating and financial policies.
Deferred Charges Material expenditures have been deferred.	We believe that all material expenditures that have been deferred to future periods will be recoverable.

Condition	*Illustrative Examples*
Deferred Tax Assets	
A deferred tax asset exists at the balance-sheet date.	The valuation allowance has been determined pursuant to the provisions of Financial Accounting Standards Board *Accounting Standards Codification* 740, *Income Taxes*, including the company's estimation of future taxable income, if necessary, and is adequate to reduce the total deferred tax asset to an amount that will more likely than not be realized. [*Complete with appropriate wording detailing how the entity determined the valuation allowance against the deferred tax asset.*] or A valuation allowance against deferred tax assets at the balance-sheet date is not considered necessary because it is more likely than not the deferred tax asset will be fully realized.

Liabilities

Condition	*Illustrative Examples*
Debt	
Short-term debt could be refinanced on a long-term basis and management intends to do so.	The company has excluded short-term obligations totaling $[*amount*] from current liabilities because it intends to refinance the obligations on a long-term basis. [*Complete with appropriate wording detailing how amounts will be refinanced as follows:*] • The company has issued a long-term obligation [*debt security*] after the date of the balance sheet but prior to the issuance of the financial statements for the purpose of refinancing the short-term obligations on a long-term basis. • The company has the ability to consummate the refinancing, by using the financing agreement referred to in Note [*X*] to the financial statements.
Tax-exempt bonds have been issued.	Tax-exempt bonds issued have retained their tax-exempt status.

(continued)

Condition	Illustrative Examples
Taxes	
Management intends to reinvest undistributed earnings of a foreign subsidiary.	We intend to reinvest the undistributed earnings of [*name of foreign subsidiary*].
Contingencies	
Estimates and disclosures have been made of environmental remediation liabilities and related loss contingencies.	Provision has been made for any material loss that is probable from environmental remediation liabilities associated with [*name of site*]. We believe that such estimate is reasonable based on available information and that the liabilities and related loss contingencies and the expected outcome of uncertainties have been adequately described in the company's financial statements.
Agreements may exist to repurchase assets previously sold.	Agreements to repurchase assets previously sold have been properly disclosed.
Pension and Postretirement Benefits	
An actuary has been used to measure pension liabilities and costs.	We believe that the actuarial assumptions and methods used to measure pension liabilities and costs for financial accounting purposes are appropriate in the circumstances.
There is involvement with a multiemployer plan.	We are unable to determine the possibility of a withdrawal liability in a multiemployer benefit plan. or We have determined that there is the possibility of a withdrawal liability in a multiemployer plan in the amount of $[*XX*].
Postretirement benefits have been eliminated.	We do not intend to compensate for the elimination of postretirement benefits by granting an increase in pension benefits. or We plan to compensate for the elimination of postretirement benefits by granting an increase in pension benefits in the amount of $[*XX*].
Employee layoffs that would otherwise lead to a curtailment of a benefit plan are intended to be temporary.	Current employee layoffs are intended to be temporary.

Condition	Illustrative Examples
Management intends to either continue to make or not make frequent amendments to its pension or other postretirement benefit plans, which may affect the amortization period of prior service cost, or has expressed a substantive commitment to increase benefit obligations.	We plan to continue to make frequent amendments to its pension or other postretirement benefit plans, which may affect the amortization period of prior service cost. or We do not plan to make frequent amendments to its pension or other postretirement benefit plans.

Equity

Condition	Illustrative Example
There are capital stock repurchase options or agreements or capital stock reserved for options, warrants, conversions, or other requirements.	Capital stock repurchase options or agreements or capital stock reserved for options, warrants, conversions, or other requirements have been properly disclosed.

Income Statement

Condition	Illustrative Example
There may be a loss from sales commitments.	Provisions have been made for losses to be sustained in the fulfillment of or from inability to fulfill any sales commitments.
There may be losses from purchase commitments.	Provisions have been made for losses to be sustained as a result of purchase commitments for inventory quantities in excess of normal requirements or at prices in excess of prevailing market prices.
Nature of the product or industry indicates the possibility of undisclosed sales terms.	We have fully disclosed to you all sales terms, including all rights of return or price adjustments and all warranty provisions.

[Revised, April 2002, to reflect conforming changes necessary due to the issuance of recent guidance on special purpose entity transactions. Revised, January 2006, to reflect conforming changes necessary due to the issuance of FASB Interpretation No. 46 (revised 2003). Revised, June 2009, to reflect conforming changes necessary due to the issuance of FASB ASC.]

.18

Appendix C

Illustrative Updating Management Representation Letter

1. The following letter is presented for illustrative purposes only. It may be used in the circumstances described in paragraph .12 of this section. Management need not repeat all of the representations made in the previous representation letter.

2. If matters exist that should be disclosed to the auditor, they should be indicated by listing them following the representation. For example, if an event subsequent to the date of the balance sheet has been disclosed in the financial statements, the final paragraph could be modified as follows: "To the best of our knowledge and belief, except as discussed in Note X to the financial statements, no events have occurred. . . ."

3.

[*Date*]

To [*Auditor*]

In connection with your audit(s) of the [*identification of financial statements*] of [*name of entity*] as of [*dates*] and for the [*periods*] for the purpose of expressing an opinion as to whether the [*consolidated*] financial statements present fairly, in all material respects, the financial position, results of operations, and cash flows of [*name of entity*] in conformity with accounting principles generally accepted in the United States of America, you were previously provided with a representation letter under date of [*date of previous representation letter*]. No information has come to our attention that would cause us to believe that any of those previous representations should be modified.

To the best of our knowledge and belief, no events have occurred subsequent to [*date of latest balance sheet reported on by the auditor*] and through the date of this letter that would require adjustment to or disclosure in the aforementioned financial statements.

____

[*Name of Chief Executive Officer and Title*]

____

[*Name of Chief Financial Officer and Title*]

[Revised, October 2000, to reflect conforming changes necessary due to the issuance of Statement on Auditing Standards No. 93.]

AU Section 9333

Management Representations: Auditing Interpretations of Section 333

1. Management Representations on Violations and Possible Violations of Laws and Regulations

.01 *Question*—Section 333, *Management Representations*, lists matters for which the auditor ordinarily obtains written representations from management. One of those matters is: Violations or possible violations of laws or regulations whose effects should be considered for disclosure in financial statements or as a basis for recording a loss contingency.

.02 Guidance on evaluating the need to disclose litigation, claims, and assessments that may result from possible violations is provided by Financial Accounting Standards Board (FASB) *Accounting Standards Codification* (ASC) 450, *Contingencies*. Section 317, *Illegal Acts by Clients*, provides guidance on evaluating the materiality of illegal acts. Does the representation regarding "possible violations" include matters beyond those described in FASB ASC 450 and section 317?

.03 *Interpretation*—No. Section 333 did not change the relevant criteria for evaluating the need for disclosure of violations and possible violations of laws or regulations. In requesting the representation on possible violations, the auditor is not asking for management's speculation on all possibilities of legal challenges to its actions.

.04 The representation concerns matters that have come to management's attention and that are significant enough that they should be considered in determining whether financial statement disclosures are necessary. It recognizes that these are matters of judgment and that the need for disclosure is not always readily apparent.

[Issue Date: March 1979; Revised: June 2009.]

AU Section 334

Related Parties

(Supersedes Statement on Auditing Standards No. 6, AU sec. 335.01–.19.) *

Source: SAS No. 45.

See section 9334 for interpretations of this section.

Effective for periods ended after September 30, 1983, unless otherwise indicated.

.01 This section provides guidance on procedures that should be considered by the auditor when he is performing an audit of financial statements in accordance with generally accepted auditing standards to identify related party relationships and transactions and to satisfy himself concerning the required financial statement accounting and disclosure.[1] The procedures set forth in this section should not be considered all-inclusive. Also, not all of them may be required in every audit.

Accounting Considerations

.02 Financial Accounting Standards Board (FASB) *Accounting Standards Codification* (ASC) 850, *Related Party Disclosures*, gives the requirements for

---

* This section also withdraws the following auditing interpretations dated March 1976 (AU sec. 9335.01–.11):
- Evaluating the Adequacy of Disclosure of Related Party Transactions
- Disclosure of Commonly Controlled Parties
- Definition of "Immediate Family"

[1] Financial Accounting Standards Board (FASB) Accounting Standards Codification (ASC) 850-10-50 contains the disclosure requirements for related party relationships and transactions. The FASB ASC glossary defines *related parties* as

a. Affiliates of the entity

b. Entities for which investments in their equity securities would be required, absent the election of the fair value option under the Fair Value Option Subsection of Section 825–10–15, to be accounted for by the equity method by the investing entity

c. Trusts for the benefit of employees, such as pension and profit-sharing trusts that are managed by or under the trusteeship of management

d. Principal owners of the entity and members of their immediate families

e. Management of the entity and members of their immediate families

f. Other parties with which the entity may deal if one party controls or can significantly influence the management or operating policies of the other to an extent that one of the transacting parties might be prevented from fully pursuing its own separate interests

g. Other parties that can significantly influence the management or operating policies of the transacting parties or that have an ownership interest in one of the transacting parties and can significantly influence the other to an extent that one or more of the transacting parties might be prevented from fully pursuing its own separate interests. The FASB ASC glossary also defines the terms *affiliate*, *control*, *immediate family*, *management*, and *principal owners*. FASB ASC 850-10-05-3 provides examples of related party transactions.

[Footnote revised, June 2009, to reflect conforming changes necessary due to the issuance of FASB ASC.]

related party disclosures. Certain accounting pronouncements prescribe the accounting treatment when related parties are involved; however, established accounting principles ordinarily do not require transactions with related parties to be accounted for on a basis different from that which would be appropriate if the parties were not related. The auditor should view related party transactions within the framework of existing pronouncements, placing primary emphasis on the adequacy of disclosure. In addition, the auditor should be aware that the substance of a particular transaction could be significantly different from its form and that financial statements should recognize the substance of particular transactions rather than merely their legal form.[2] [Revised, June 2009, to reflect conforming changes necessary due to the issuance of FASB ASC.]

.03 Transactions that because of their nature may be indicative of the existence of related parties include[3] —

a. Borrowing or lending on an interest-free basis or at a rate of interest significantly above or below market rates prevailing at the time of the transaction.

b. Selling real estate at a price that differs significantly from its appraised value.

c. Exchanging property for similar property in a nonmonetary transaction.

d. Making loans with no scheduled terms for when or how the funds will be repaid.

Audit Procedures

.04 An audit performed in accordance with generally accepted auditing standards cannot be expected to provide assurance that all related party transactions will be discovered. Nevertheless, during the course of his audit, the auditor should be aware of the possible existence of material related party transactions that could affect the financial statements and of common ownership or management control relationships for which FASB ASC 850-10-50 requires disclosure. Many of the procedures outlined in the following paragraphs are normally performed in an audit in accordance with generally accepted auditing standards, even if the auditor has no reason to suspect that related party transactions or control relationships exist. Other audit procedures set forth in this section are specifically directed to related party transactions. [Revised, June 2009, to reflect conforming changes necessary due to the issuance of FASB ASC.]

.05 In determining the scope of work to be performed with respect to possible transactions with related parties, the auditor should obtain an

---

[2] Some pronouncements specify criteria for determining, presenting, and accounting for the substance of certain transactions and events. Examples include (1) presenting consolidated financial statements instead of separate statements of the component legal entities (FASB ASC 810, *Consolidation*); (2) capitalizing leases (FASB ASC 840, *Leases*); and (3) imputing an appropriate interest rate when the face amount of a note does not reasonably represent the present value of the consideration given or received in exchange for it (FASB ASC 835, *Interest*). [Footnote revised, June 1993, to reflect conforming changes necessary due to the issuance of Statement of Position 93-3. Footnote revised, June 2009, to reflect conforming changes necessary due to the issuance of FASB ASC.]

[3] FASB ASC 850-10-05-4 gives other examples of common types of transactions with related parties. FASB ASC 850-10-05-5 states that "transactions between related parties are considered to be related party transactions even though they may not be given accounting recognition. For example, an entity may received services from a related party without charge and not record receipt of the services. While not providing accounting or measurement guidance for such transactions, FASB ASC 850 requires their disclosure nonetheless." [Footnote revised, June 2009, to reflect conforming changes necessary due to the issuance of FASB ASC.]

understanding of management responsibilities and the relationship of each component to the total entity. He should consider controls over management activities, and he should consider the business purpose served by the various components of the entity. Normally, the business structure and style of operating are based on the abilities of management, tax and legal considerations, product diversification, and geographical location. Experience has shown, however, that business structure and operating style are occasionally deliberately designed to obscure related party transactions.

.06 In the absence of evidence to the contrary, transactions with related parties should not be assumed to be outside the ordinary course of business. The auditor should, however, be aware of the possibility that transactions with related parties may have been motivated solely, or in large measure, by conditions similar to the following:

a. Lack of sufficient working capital or credit to continue the business

b. An urgent desire for a continued favorable earnings record in the hope of supporting the price of the company's stock

c. An overly optimistic earnings forecast

d. Dependence on a single or relatively few products, customers, or transactions for the continuing success of the venture

e. A declining industry characterized by a large number of business failures

f. Excess capacity

g. Significant litigation, especially litigation between stockholders and management

h. Significant obsolescence dangers because the company is in a high-technology industry

Determining the Existence of Related Parties

.07 The auditor should place emphasis on testing material transactions with parties he knows are related to the reporting entity. Certain relationships, such as parent-subsidiary or investor-investee, may be clearly evident. Determining the existence of others requires the application of specific audit procedures, which may include the following:

a. Evaluate the company's procedures for identifying and properly accounting for related party transactions.

b. Request from appropriate management personnel the names of all related parties and inquire whether there were any transactions with these parties during the period.

c. Review filings by the reporting entity with the Securities and Exchange Commission and other regulatory agencies for the names of related parties and for other businesses in which officers and directors occupy directorship or management positions.

d. Determine the names of all pension and other trusts established for the benefit of employees and the names of their officers and trustees.[4]

e. Review stockholder listings of closely held companies to identify principal stockholders.

---

[4] FASB ASC glossary term *related parties* includes "trusts for the benefit of employees, such as pension and profit-sharing trusts that are managed by or under the trusteeship of management." [Footnote revised, June 2009, to reflect conforming changes necessary due to the issuance of FASB ASC.]

f. Review prior years' working papers for the names of known related parties.

g. Inquire of predecessor, principal, or other auditors of related entities concerning their knowledge of existing relationships and the extent of management involvement in material transactions.

h. Review material investment transactions during the period under audit to determine whether the nature and extent of investments during the period create related parties.

Identifying Transactions With Related Parties

.08 The following procedures are intended to provide guidance for identifying material transactions with parties known to be related and for identifying material transactions that may be indicative of the existence of previously undetermined relationships:

a. Provide audit personnel performing segments of the audit or auditing and reporting separately on the accounts of related components of the reporting entity with the names of known related parties so that they may become aware of transactions with such parties during their audits.

b. Review the minutes of meetings of the board of directors and executive or operating committees for information about material transactions authorized or discussed at their meetings.

c. Review proxy and other material filed with the Securities and Exchange Commission and comparable data filed with other regulatory agencies for information about material transactions with related parties.

d. Review conflict-of-interests statements obtained by the company from its management.[5]

e. Review the extent and nature of business transacted with major customers, suppliers, borrowers, and lenders for indications of previously undisclosed relationships.

f. Consider whether transactions are occurring, but are not being given accounting recognition, such as receiving or providing accounting, management or other services at no charge or a major stockholder absorbing corporate expenses.

g. Review accounting records for large, unusual, or nonrecurring transactions or balances, paying particular attention to transactions recognized at or near the end of the reporting period.

h. Review confirmations of compensating balance arrangements for indications that balances are or were maintained for or by related parties.

i. Review invoices from law firms that have performed regular or special services for the company for indications of the existence of related parties or related party transactions.

j. Review confirmations of loans receivable and payable for indications of guarantees. When guarantees are indicated, determine their nature and the relationships, if any, of the guarantors to the reporting entity.

---

[5] Conflict-of-interests statements are intended to provide those charged with governance with information about the existence or nonexistence of relationships between the reporting persons and parties with whom the company transacts business. [Footnote revised, April 2007, to reflect conforming changes necessary due to the issuance of Statement on Auditing Standards No. 114.]

Examining Identified Related Party Transactions

.09 After identifying related party transactions, the auditor should apply the procedures he considers necessary to obtain satisfaction concerning the purpose, nature, and extent of these transactions and their effect on the financial statements. The procedures should be directed toward obtaining and evaluating sufficient appropriate audit evidence and should extend beyond inquiry of management. Procedures that should be considered include the following:

a. Obtain an understanding of the business purpose of the transaction.[6]

b. Examine invoices, executed copies of agreements, contracts, and other pertinent documents, such as receiving reports and shipping documents.

c. Determine whether the transaction has been approved by those charged with governance.

d. Test for reasonableness the compilation of amounts to be disclosed, or considered for disclosure, in the financial statements.

e. Arrange for the audits of intercompany account balances to be performed as of concurrent dates, even if the fiscal years differ, and for the examination of specified, important, and representative related party transactions by the auditors for each of the parties, with appropriate exchange of relevant information.

f. Inspect or confirm and obtain satisfaction concerning the transferability and value of collateral.

[Revised, March 2006, to reflect conforming changes necessary due to the issuance of Statement on Auditing Standards No. 105. Revised, April 2007, to reflect conforming changes necessary due to the issuance of Statement on Auditing Standards No. 114.]

.10 When necessary to fully understand a particular transaction, the following procedures, which might not otherwise be deemed necessary to comply with generally accepted auditing standards, should be considered.[7]

a. Confirm transaction amount and terms, including guarantees and other significant data, with the other party or parties to the transaction.

b. Inspect evidence in possession of the other party or parties to the transaction.

c. Confirm or discuss significant information with intermediaries, such as banks, guarantors, agents, or attorneys, to obtain a better understanding of the transaction.

d. Refer to financial publications, trade journals, credit agencies, and other information sources when there is reason to believe that unfamiliar customers, suppliers, or other business enterprises with which material amounts of business have been transacted may lack substance.

e. With respect to material uncollected balances, guarantees, and other obligations, obtain information about the financial capability of the

---

[6] Until the auditor understands the business sense of material transactions, he cannot complete his audit. If he lacks sufficient specialized knowledge to understand a particular transaction, he should consult with persons who do have the requisite knowledge.

[7] Arrangements for certain procedures should be made or approved in advance by appropriate client officials.

other party or parties to the transaction. Such information may be obtained from audited financial statements, unaudited financial statements, income tax returns, and reports issued by regulatory agencies, taxing authorities, financial publications, or credit agencies. The auditor should decide on the degree of assurance required and the extent to which available information provides such assurance.

Disclosure

.11 For each material related party transaction (or aggregation of similar transactions) or common ownership or management control relationship for which FASB ASC 850-10-50 requires disclosure, the auditor should consider whether he has obtained sufficient appropriate audit evidence to understand the relationship of the parties and, for related party transactions, the effects of the transaction on the financial statements. He should then evaluate all the information available to him concerning the related party transaction or control relationship and satisfy himself on the basis of his professional judgment that it is adequately disclosed in the financial statements. [Revised, March 2006, to reflect conforming changes necessary due to the issuance of Statement on Auditing Standards No. 105. Revised, June 2009, to reflect conforming changes necessary due to the issuance of FASB ASC.][8]

.12 Except for routine transactions, it will generally not be possible to determine whether a particular transaction would have taken place if the parties had not been related, or assuming it would have taken place, what the terms and manner of settlement would have been. Accordingly, it is difficult to substantiate representations that a transaction was consummated on terms equivalent to those that prevail in arm's-length transactions.[9] If such a representation is included in the financial statements and the auditor believes that the representation is unsubstantiated by management, he should express a qualified or adverse opinion because of a departure from generally accepted accounting principles, depending on materiality (see section 508.35 and .36).

---

[8] Also, see section 431, *Adequacy of Disclosure in Financial Statements*. [Footnote revised, June 2009, to reflect conforming changes necessary due to the issuance of FASB ASC.]

[9] FASB ASC 850-10-50-5 states that if representations are made about transactions with related parties, the representations "shall not imply that the related party transactions were consummated on terms equivalent to those that prevail in arm's-length transactions unless such representations can be substantiated." [Footnote revised, June 2009, to reflect conforming changes necessary due to the issuance of FASB ASC.]

AU Section 9334*

Related Parties: Auditing Interpretations of Section 334

[1.] Evaluating the Adequacy of Disclosure of Related Party Transactions

[.01–.05] [Withdrawn August 1983, by SAS No. 45.] (See section 334.)

[2.] Disclosure of Commonly Controlled Parties

[.06–.09] [Withdrawn August 1983, by SAS No. 45.] (See section 334.)

[3.] Definition of "Immediate Family"

[.10–.11] [Withdrawn August 1983, by SAS No. 45.] (See section 334.)

4. Exchange of Information Between the Principal and Other Auditor on Related Parties

.12 *Question*—Section 334, *Related Parties*, paragraphs .04–.07, states that "during the course of his audit, the auditor should be aware of the possible existence of material related party transactions," and that determining the existence of related party transactions may require the inquiry of the "principal, or other auditors of related entities concerning their knowledge of existing relationships and the extent of management involvement in material transactions." When should that inquiry be made?

.13 *Interpretation*—The principal auditor and the other auditor should each obtain from the other the names of known related parties and the other information referred to above. Ordinarily, that exchange of information should be made at an early stage of the audit.

[Issue Date: April 1979.]

5. Examination of Identified Related Party Transactions with a Component

.14 *Question*—According to section 334 paragraph .09, once related party transactions have been identified, "the auditor should apply the procedures he considers necessary to obtain satisfaction concerning the purpose, nature and extent of these transactions and their effect on the financial statements." When there is a principal auditor-other auditor relationship, how may the auditors obtain that satisfaction regarding transactions that may involve not only the components[1] they are auditing, but also, other components?

---

* [Section number changed August 1983, to correspond to section 334, *Related Parties*.]

[1] For the purpose of this interpretation, the entities whose separate financial statements collectively comprise the consolidated or other financial statements are referred to as components.

.15 *Interpretation*—Audit procedures may sometimes have to be applied to records of components being audited by the other. One auditor may arrange to perform those procedures himself, or he may request the other to do so.[2] There may be circumstances when there are unusual or complex related party transactions and an auditor believes that access to relevant portions of the other's work papers is essential to his understanding of the effects of those transactions on the financial statements he is auditing. In those circumstances, access ordinarily should be provided.[3]

[Issue Date: April 1979.]

6. The Nature and Extent of Auditing Procedures for Examining Related Party Transactions

.16 *Question*—Section 334, *Related Parties*, provides general guidance about the types of procedures an auditor might apply to identified related party transactions. How extensive should the auditor's procedures be to examine related party transactions?

.17 *Interpretation*—The auditor's procedures should be sufficient to provide reasonable assurance that related party transactions are adequately disclosed and that identified related party transactions do not contain misstatements that, when aggregated with misstatements in other balances or classes of transactions, could be material to the financial statements taken as a whole. As in examining any other material account balance or class of transactions, the auditor needs to consider audit risk[4] and design and apply appropriate substantive tests to evaluate management's assertions.

.18 The risk associated with management's assertions about related party transactions is often assessed as higher than for many other types of transactions because of the possibility that the parties to the transaction are motivated by reasons other than those that exist for most business transactions.[5]

.19 The higher the auditor's assessment of risk regarding related party transactions, the more extensive or effective the audit tests should be. For example, the auditor's tests regarding valuation of a receivable from an entity under common control might be more extensive than for a trade receivable of the same size because the common parent may be motivated to obscure the substance of the transaction. In assessing the risk of the related party transactions the auditor obtains an understanding of the business purpose of the transactions. Until the auditor understands the business sense of material transactions, he cannot complete his audit. If he lacks sufficient specialized knowledge to obtain that understanding for a particular transaction, he should consult with persons who do have the requisite knowledge. In addition, to understand the transaction, or obtain evidence regarding it, the auditor may have to refer to audited or unaudited financial statements of the related party, apply procedures at the related party, or in some cases audit the financial statements of the related party.

---

[2] In this case, the auditor should follow the guidance in Interpretation No. 1, "Specific Procedures Performed by Other Auditors at the Principal Auditor's Request," of section 543, *Part of Audit Performed by Other Independent Auditors* (sec. 9543 par. .01–.03).

[3] There is no intention in this interpretation to modify section 543 paragraph .12*c* regarding the principal auditor's consideration of review of the other auditor's workpapers when he decides not to make reference to the other auditor.

[4] Audit risk and its components are described in section 312, *Audit Risk and Materiality in Conducting an Audit*.

[5] See section 334 in paragraph .06.

.20 *Question*—Section 334, *Related Parties*, paragraph .07 states that specific audit procedures should be applied to determine if related parties exist. That paragraph also suggests some specific audit procedures to identify related parties that the auditor should consider. What other audit procedures for determining the existence of related parties should the auditor consider?

.21 *Interpretation*—The auditor should consider obtaining representations from the entity's senior management and its board of directors about whether they or any other related parties engaged in any transactions with the entity during the period.

[Issue Date: May 1986.]

7. Management's and Auditor's Responsibilities With Regard to Related Party Disclosures Prefaced by Terminology Such As "Management Believes That"

.22 *Question*—Management discloses in its financial statements that a related party transaction was consummated on terms equivalent to those that prevail in arm's length transactions, and prefaces the representation with a phrase such as "Management believes that" or "It is the Company's belief that." Does the use of such terminology change management's responsibility to substantiate the representation?

.23 *Interpretation*—No. Financial Accounting Standards Board *Accounting Standards Codification* 850-10-50-5 states that the representations about a related party transaction "shall not imply that the related party transactions were consummated on terms equivalent to those that prevail in arm's-length transactions unless such representations can be substantiated. "A preface to a disclosure such as "Management believes that" or "It is the Company's belief that" does not change management's responsibility to substantiate the representation. Section 334, *Related Parties*, paragraph .12 indicates that if such a representation is included in the financial statements and the auditor believes that the representation is unsubstantiated by management, he should express a qualified or adverse opinion because of a departure from generally accepted accounting principles, depending on materiality.

[Issue Date: May 2000; Revised: June 2009.]

AU Section 336

Using the Work of a Specialist

(Supersedes SAS No. 11.)

Source: SAS No. 73.

See section 9336 for interpretations of this section.

Effective for audits of periods ending on or after December 15, 1994.

Introduction and Applicability

.01 The purpose of this section is to provide guidance to the auditor who uses the work of a specialist in performing an audit in accordance with generally accepted auditing standards. For purposes of this section, a specialist is a person (or firm) possessing special skill or knowledge in a particular field other than accounting or auditing.[1]

.02 Specialists to which this section applies include, but are not limited to, actuaries, appraisers, engineers, environmental consultants, and geologists. This section also applies to attorneys engaged as specialists in situations other than to provide services to a client concerning litigation, claims, or assessments to which section 337, *Inquiry of a Client's Lawyer Concerning Litigation, Claims, and Assessments*, applies. For example, attorneys may be engaged by a client or by the auditor as specialists in a variety of other circumstances, including interpreting the provisions of a contractual agreement.

.03 The guidance in this section is applicable when—

a. Management engages or employs a specialist and the auditor uses that specialist's work as audit evidence in performing substantive tests to evaluate material financial statement assertions.

b. Management engages a specialist employed by the auditor's firm to provide advisory services[2] and the auditor uses that specialist's work as audit evidence in performing substantive tests to evaluate material financial statement assertions.

c. The auditor engages a specialist and uses that specialist's work as audit evidence in performing substantive tests to evaluate material financial statement assertions.

[Revised, March 2006, to reflect conforming changes necessary due to the issuance of Statement on Auditing Standards No. 105.]

.04 The guidance provided in this section applies to audits of financial statements prepared in conformity with generally accepted accounting principles (GAAP)[3] and to engagements performed under section 623, *Special Reports*, including a comprehensive basis of accounting other than GAAP.

---

[1] In general, the auditor's education, training, and experience enable him or her to be knowledgeable concerning income tax matters and to be competent to assess their presentation in the financial statements.

[2] The auditor should consider the effect, if any, that using the work of a specialist employed by the auditor's firm has on independence.

[3] References in this section to "financial statements" and to "generally accepted accounting principles" include special reports covered under section 623, *Special Reports*.

.05 This section does not apply to situations covered by section 311, *Planning and Supervision*, in which a specialist employed by the auditor's firm participates in the audit.

Decision to Use the Work of a Specialist

.06 The auditor's education and experience enable him or her to be knowledgeable about business matters in general, but the auditor is not expected to have the expertise of a person trained for or qualified to engage in the practice of another profession or occupation. During the audit, however, an auditor may encounter complex or subjective matters potentially material to the financial statements. Such matters may require special skill or knowledge and in the auditor's judgment require using the work of a specialist to obtain appropriate audit evidence. [Revised, March 2006, to reflect conforming changes necessary due to the issuance of Statement on Auditing Standards No. 105.]

.07 Examples of the types of matters that the auditor may decide require him or her to consider using the work of a specialist include, but are not limited to, the following:

a. Valuation (for example, special-purpose inventories, high-technology materials or equipment, pharmaceutical products, complex financial instruments, real estate, restricted securities, works of art, and environmental contingencies)

b. Determination of physical characteristics relating to quantity on hand or condition (for example, quantity or condition of minerals, mineral reserves, or materials stored in stockpiles)

c. Determination of amounts derived by using specialized techniques or methods (for example, actuarial determinations for employee benefits obligations and disclosures, and determinations for insurance loss reserves[4])

d. Interpretation of technical requirements, regulations, or agreements (for example, the potential significance of contracts or other legal documents or legal title to property)

Qualifications and Work of a Specialist

.08 The auditor should consider the following to evaluate the professional qualifications of the specialist in determining that the specialist possesses the necessary skill or knowledge in the particular field:

a. The professional certification, license, or other recognition of the competence of the specialist in his or her field, as appropriate

b. The reputation and standing of the specialist in the views of peers and others familiar with the specialist's capability or performance

c. The specialist's experience in the type of work under consideration

.09 The auditor should obtain an understanding of the nature of the work performed or to be performed by the specialist. This understanding should cover the following:

---

[4] In the specific situation involving the audit of an insurance entity's loss reserves, an outside loss reserve specialist—that is, one who is not an employee or officer of the insurance entity—should be used. When the auditor has the requisite knowledge and experience, the auditor may serve as the loss reserve specialist. [Footnote revised, June 2009, to reflect conforming changes necessary due to the issuance of recent authoritative literature.]

a. The objectives and scope of the specialist's work

b. The specialist's relationship to the client (see paragraphs .10 and .11)

c. The methods or assumptions used

d. A comparison of the methods or assumptions used with those used in the preceding period

e. The appropriateness of using the specialist's work for the intended purpose[5]

f. The form and content of the specialist's findings that will enable the auditor to make the evaluation described in paragraph .12

Relationship of the Specialist to the Client

.10 The auditor should evaluate the relationship[6] of the specialist to the client, including circumstances that might impair the specialist's objectivity. Such circumstances include situations in which the client has the ability—through employment, ownership, contractual right, family relationship, or otherwise—to directly or indirectly control or significantly influence the specialist.

.11 When a specialist does not have a relationship with the client, the specialist's work usually will provide the auditor with greater assurance of reliability. However, the work of a specialist who has a relationship with the client may be acceptable under certain circumstances. If the specialist has a relationship with the client, the auditor should assess the risk that the specialist's objectivity might be impaired. If the auditor believes the relationship might impair the specialist's objectivity, the auditor should perform additional procedures with respect to some or all of the specialist's assumptions, methods, or findings to determine that the findings are not unreasonable or should engage another specialist for that purpose.

Using the Findings of the Specialist

.12 The appropriateness and reasonableness of methods and assumptions used and their application are the responsibility of the specialist. The auditor should (*a*) obtain an understanding of the methods and assumptions used by the specialist, (*b*) make appropriate tests of data provided to the specialist, taking into account the auditor's assessment of control risk, and (*c*) evaluate whether the specialist's findings support the related assertions in the financial statements. Ordinarily, the auditor would use the work of the specialist unless the auditor's procedures lead him or her to believe the findings are unreasonable in the circumstances. If the auditor believes the findings are unreasonable, he or she should apply additional procedures, which may include obtaining the opinion of another specialist.

Effect of the Specialist's Work on the Auditor's Report

.13 If the auditor determines that the specialist's findings support the related assertions in the financial statements, he or she reasonably may conclude

---

[5] In some cases, the auditor may decide it is necessary to contact the specialist to determine that the specialist is aware that his or her work will be used for evaluating the assertions in the financial statements.

[6] The term *relationship* includes, but is not limited to, those situations discussed in section 334, *Related Parties*, footnote 1.

that sufficient appropriate audit evidence has been obtained. If there is a material difference between the specialist's findings and the assertions in the financial statements, he or she should apply additional procedures. If after applying any additional procedures that might be appropriate the auditor is unable to resolve the matter, the auditor should obtain the opinion of another specialist, unless it appears to the auditor that the matter cannot be resolved. A matter that has not been resolved ordinarily will cause the auditor to conclude that he or she should qualify the opinion or disclaim an opinion because the inability to obtain sufficient appropriate audit evidence as to an assertion of material significance in the financial statements constitutes a scope limitation. (See section 508, *Reports on Audited Financial Statements*, paragraphs .22 and .23.) [Revised, March 2006, to reflect conforming changes necessary due to the issuance of Statement on Auditing Standards No. 105.]

.14 The auditor may conclude after performing additional procedures, including possibly obtaining the opinion of another specialist, that the assertions in the financial statements are not in conformity with GAAP. In that event, the auditor should express a qualified or adverse opinion. (See section 508.35, .36, and .41.)

Reference to the Specialist in the Auditor's Report

.15 Except as discussed in paragraph .16, the auditor should not refer to the work or findings of the specialist. Such a reference might be misunderstood to be a qualification of the auditor's opinion or a division of responsibility, neither of which is intended. Further, there may be an inference that the auditor making such reference performed a more thorough audit than an auditor not making such reference.

.16 The auditor may, as a result of the report or findings of the specialist, decide to add explanatory language to his or her standard report or depart from an unqualified opinion. Reference to and identification of the specialist may be made in the auditor's report if the auditor believes such reference will facilitate an understanding of the reason for the explanatory paragraph or the departure from the unqualified opinion.

Effective Date

.17 This section is effective for audits of periods ending on or after December 15, 1994. Early application of the provisions of this section is encouraged.

AU Section 9336

Using the Work of a Specialist: Auditing Interpretations of Section 336

1. The Use of Legal Interpretations As Audit Evidence to Support Management's Assertion That a Transfer of Financial Assets Has Met the Isolation Criterion in Paragraphs 7–14 of FASB ASC 860-10-40

.01 *Introduction*—Financial Accounting Standards Board (FASB) *Accounting Standards Codification* (ASC) 860,[1] *Transfers and Servicing*, requires that a transferor of financial assets must surrender control over the financial assets to account for the transfer as a sale. FASB ASC 860-10-40-5(a) states one of several conditions that must be met to provide evidence of surrender of control:

> The transferred assets have been isolated from the transferor—put presumptively beyond the reach of the transferor and its creditors, even in bankruptcy or other receivership.

Paragraphs 8–10 of FASB ASC 860-10-40 describe in greater detail the evidence required to support management's assertion that transferred financial assets have been isolated:

> Derecognition of transferred assets is appropriate only if the available evidence provides reasonable assurance that the transferred assets would be beyond the reach of the powers of a bankruptcy trustee or other receiver for the transferor or any *consolidated affiliate of the transferor* [2] that is not a special-purpose corporation or other entity designed to make remote the possibility that it would enter bankruptcy or other receivership (see FASB ASC 860-10-55-23[c]).The nature and extent of supporting evidence required for an assertion in financial statements that transferred financial assets have been isolated—put presumptively beyond the reach of the transferor and its creditors, either by a single transaction or a series of transactions taken as a whole—depend on the facts and circumstances. FASB ASC 860 does not provide guidance as to the type and amount of evidence that must be obtained to conclude that transferred financial assets have been isolated from the transferor. All available evidence that either supports or questions an assertion shall be considered. That consideration includes making judgments about whether the contract or circumstances permit the transferor to revoke the transfer. It also may include making judgments about the kind of bankruptcy or other receivership into which a transferor or SPE might be placed, whether a transfer of financial assets would likely be deemed a true sale at law, whether the transferor is affiliated with the transferee, and other factors pertinent under applicable law.

---

[1] [Footnote deleted, June 2009, to reflect conforming changes necessary due to the issuance of FASB ASC.]

2 The Financial Accounting Standards Board (FASB) *Accounting Standards Codification* (ASC) glossary defines *consolidated affiliate of the transferor* as "an entity whose assets and liabilities are included with those of the transferor in the consolidated, combined, or other financial statements being presented". [Footnote added, June 2009, to reflect conforming changes necessary due to the issuance of FASB ASC.]

A determination about whether the isolation criterion has been met to support a conclusion regarding surrender of control is largely a matter of law. This aspect of surrender of control, therefore, is assessed primarily from a legal perspective.

.02 *Effective Date and Applicability*—This interpretation is effective for auditing procedures related to transfers of financial assets that are required to be accounted for under FASB ASC 860.[3]

.03 *Question*—What should the auditor consider in determining whether to use the work of a legal specialist[4] to obtain persuasive evidence to support management's assertion that a transfer of financial assets meets the isolation criterion of FASB ASC 860-10-40-5(a)?

.04 *Interpretation*—Section 336, *Using the Work of a Specialist*, paragraph .06 states that "during the audit . . . an auditor may encounter complex or subjective matters potentially material to the financial statements. Such matters may require special skill or knowledge and in the auditor's judgment require using the work of a specialist to obtain appropriate audit evidence."

.05 Use of a legal specialist may not be necessary to obtain appropriate audit evidence to support management's assertion that the isolation criterion is met in certain situations, such as when there is a routine transfer of financial assets that does not result in any continuing involvement by the transferor.[5]

.06 Many transfers of financial assets involve complex legal structures, continuing involvement by the transferor, or other legal issues that, in the auditor's judgment, make it difficult to determine whether the isolation criterion is met. In these situations, use of a legal specialist usually is necessary. A legal specialist formulating an opinion as to whether a transfer isolates the transferred assets beyond the reach of the transferor and its creditors may consider, among other things, the structure of the transaction taken as a whole, the nature of any continuing involvement, the type of insolvency or other receivership proceedings to which the transferor might become subject, and other factors pertinent under applicable law.

.07 If a legal opinion is used as evidence to support the accounting conclusion related to multiple transfers under a single structure, and such transfers occur over an extended period of time under that structure, the auditor should evaluate the need for management to obtain periodic updates of that opinion to confirm that there have been no subsequent changes in relevant law or applicable regulations that may change the applicability of the previous opinion to such transfers. The auditor also should evaluate the need for management to obtain periodic updates of an opinion to confirm that there have been no subsequent changes in relevant law or applicable regulations that may affect the conclusions reached in the previous opinion in the case of other transfers (see FASB ASC 860-10-40-41 and FASB ASC 860-20-25).

---

[3] [Footnote deleted and renumbered, June 2009, to reflect conforming changes necessary due to the issuance of FASB ASC.]

[4] Client's internal or external attorney who is knowledgeable about relevant sections of the U.S. Bankruptcy Code and other federal, state, or foreign laws, as applicable. [Footnote renumbered, June 2009, to reflect conforming changes necessary due to the issuance of FASB ASC.]

[5] FASB ASC 860-10-55-28 characterizes no continuing involvement with the transferred assets as "no servicing responsibilities, no participation in future cash flows, no recourse obligations other than standard representations and warranties that the financial assets transferred met the delivery requirements under the arrangement, no further involvement of any kind. The transferee is significantly limited in its ability to pledge or exchange the transferred assets."

If a contractual provision (such as a call or removal of accounts provision) gives the transferor the unilateral ability to require the return of specific financial assets, the auditor should consider the effect of FASB ASC 860-10-40-5(c). [Footnote revised and renumbered, June 2009, to reflect conforming changes necessary due to the issuance of FASB ASC.]

.08 If management's assertion with respect to a new transaction is that the transaction structure is the same as a prior structure for which a legal opinion that complies with this interpretation was used as evidence to support an assertion that the transfer of assets met the isolation criterion, the auditor should evaluate the need for management to obtain an update of that opinion to confirm that there have been no changes in relevant law, applicable regulations, or in the pertinent facts of the transaction that may affect the applicability of the previous opinion to the new transaction.

.09 *Question*—If the auditor determines that the use of a legal specialist is required, what should he or she consider in assessing the adequacy of the legal opinion?

.10 *Interpretation*—In assessing the adequacy of the legal opinion, the auditor should consider whether the legal specialist has experience with relevant matters, including knowledge of the U.S. Bankruptcy Code, and other federal, state, or foreign law, as applicable, as well as knowledge of the transaction upon which management's assertion is based. For transactions that may be affected by provisions of the Federal Deposit Insurance Act, the auditor should consider whether the legal specialist has experience with the rights and powers of receivers, conservators, and liquidating agents under that act. The auditor should obtain an understanding of the assumptions that are used by the legal specialist, and make appropriate tests of any information that management provides to the legal specialist and upon which the specialist indicates it relied. For example, testing management's information underlying a legal specialist's assumption regarding the adequacy of consideration received may depend on the nature of the transaction and the relationship of the parties. When the legal specialist's opinion has assumed the adequacy of consideration for transfers from a particular legal entity to its wholly owned subsidiary, changes in the subsidiary's capital accounts plus other consideration generally would be sufficient audit evidence as to the adequacy of consideration. In the case of other transfers, such as those that are not to a wholly owned subsidiary of a particular legal entity that is the transferor, obtaining additional audit evidence may be necessary to evaluate management's assertion with regard to the adequacy of consideration upon which the legal specialist relied, because changes in the transferee's capital accounts do not solely benefit the transferring entity.

.11 The auditor also should consider the form and content of the documentation that the legal specialist provides and evaluate whether the legal specialist's findings support management's assertions with respect to the isolation criterion. Section 336 paragraph .13 states that "if the auditor determines that the specialist's findings support the related assertions in the financial statements, he or she reasonably may conclude that sufficient appropriate audit evidence has been obtained." FASB ASC 860's requirement regarding reasonable assurance that the transferred assets would be isolated provides the basis for what auditors should consider in evaluating the work of a legal specialist.

.12 Findings of a legal specialist that relate to the isolation of transferred financial assets are often in the form of a reasoned legal opinion that is restricted to particular facts and circumstances relevant to the specific transaction. The reasoning of such opinion may rely upon analogy to legal precedents that may not involve facts and circumstances that are comparable to that specific transaction. The auditor also should consider the effect of any limitations or disclaimers of opinion in assessing the adequacy of any legal opinion.

.13 An example of the conclusions in a legal opinion for an entity that is subject to the U.S. Bankruptcy Code that provides persuasive evidence, in the absence of contradictory evidence, to support management's assertion that the transferred financial assets have been put presumptively beyond the reach of the entity and its creditors, even in bankruptcy or other receivership, follows:

> *We believe (or it is our opinion) that* in a properly presented and argued case, as a legal matter, in the event the Seller were to become a Debtor, the transfer of the Financial Assets from the Seller to the Purchaser *would be considered to be a sale* (or a true sale) of the Financial Assets from the Seller to the Purchaser and not a loan and, accordingly, the Financial Assets and the proceeds thereof transferred to the Purchaser by the Seller in accordance with the Purchase Agreement would not be deemed to be property of the Seller's estate for purposes of [the relevant sections] of the U.S. Bankruptcy Code.

The following additional paragraph addressing substantive consolidation applies when the entity to which the assets are sold (as described in the opinion) is an affiliate of the selling entity and may also apply in other situations as noted by the legal specialist. For example, if a so-called "two-step" structure has been used to achieve isolation, this paragraph usually will be required with respect to the transferee in the first step of such structure (see paragraph .15 and related footnotes for additional guidance on the second step of a two-step structure as described in paragraphs 22–23 of FASB ASC 860-10-55). When the transferor has entered into transactions with an affiliate that could affect the issue of substantive consolidation, the opinion should address the effect of that involvement on the opinion.

> "Based upon the assumptions of fact and the discussion set forth previously, and on a reasoned analysis of analogous case law, *we are of the opinion that* in a properly presented and argued case, as a legal matter, in a proceeding under the U.S. Bankruptcy Code,[6] in which the Seller is a Debtor, a court *would not* grant an order consolidating the assets and liabilities of the Purchaser with those of the Seller in a case involving the insolvency of the Seller under the doctrine of substantive consolidation."

In the case of a transferor that is not entitled to become a debtor under the U.S. Bankruptcy Code, a legal opinion regarding whether the isolation criterion is met would consider whether isolation is satisfactorily achieved under the insolvency or receivership laws that apply to the transferor.

.14 Following are two examples of the conclusions in a legal opinion for an entity that is subject to receivership or conservatorship under provisions of the Federal Deposit Insurance Act. The conclusions in these two examples provide persuasive evidence, in the absence of contradictory evidence, to support management's assertion that the transferred financial assets have been put presumptively beyond the reach of the entity and its creditors, even in conservatorship or receivership. Insolvency and receivership laws applicable to depository institutions, and how those laws affect the legal isolation criterion, differ depending upon the nature of the depository institution and its chartering authority. Accordingly, legal opinions addressing the legal isolation criterion may be formulated in different ways to accommodate those differences.[7]

---

[6] For an entity subject to additional regulation (for example, a broker-dealer subject to the Securities Investor Protection Act), the legal opinion also generally should address the effect of such regulation and the policies of the regulators implementing such regulations (for example, the Securities Investor Protection Corporation). [Footnote renumbered, June 2009, to reflect conforming changes necessary due to the issuance of FASB ASC.]

[7] For an entity subject to conservatorship or liquidation under the National Credit Union Act, the examples and discussion in this paragraph would be modified to make appropriate references to "liquidation" and "liquidating agent" and additional information relating to rights and regulations of the National Credit Union Administration. [Footnote renumbered, June 2009, to reflect conforming changes necessary due to the issuance of FASB ASC.]

Example 1: "*We believe (or it is our opinion) that* in a properly presented and argued case, as a legal matter, in the event the Seller were to become subject to receivership or conservatorship, the transfer of the Financial Assets from the Seller to the Purchaser *would be considered to be a sale* (or a true sale) of the Financial Assets from the Seller to the Purchaser and not a loan and, accordingly, the Financial Assets and the proceeds thereof transferred to the Purchaser by the Seller in accordance with the Purchase Agreement would not be deemed to be property of, or subject to repudiation, reclamation, recovery, or recharacterization by, the receiver or conservator appointed with respect to the Seller."[8]

Example 2: "The Federal Deposit Insurance Corporation (FDIC) has issued a regulation, 'Treatment by the Federal Deposit Insurance Corporation as Conservator or Receiver of Financial Assets Transferred by an Insured Depository Institution in Connection with a Securitization or Participation,' 12 CFR section 360.6 (the Rule). Based on and subject to the discussion, assumptions, and qualifications herein, it is our opinion that:

A. Following the appointment of the FDIC as the conservator or receiver for the Bank:

(i) The Rule will apply to the Transfers,

(ii) Under the Rule, the FDIC acting as conservator or receiver for the Bank could not, by exercise of its authority to disaffirm or repudiate contracts under 12 U.S.C. §1821(e), reclaim or recover the Transferred Assets from the Issuer or recharacterize the Transferred Assets as property of the Bank or of the conservatorship or receivership for the Bank,

(iii) Neither the FDIC (acting for itself as a creditor or as representative of the Bank or its shareholders or creditors) nor any creditor of the Bank would have the right, under any bankruptcy or insolvency law applicable in the conservatorship or receivership of the Bank, to avoid the Transfers, to recover the Transferred Assets, or to require the Transferred Assets to be turned over to the FDIC or such creditor, and

(iv) There is no other power exercisable by the FDIC as conservator or receiver for the Bank that would permit the FDIC as such conservator or receiver to reclaim or recover the Transferred Assets from the Issuer, or to recharacterize the Transferred Assets as property of the Bank or of the conservatorship or receivership for the Bank; provided, however, that we offer no opinion as to whether, in receivership, the FDIC or any creditor of the Bank may take any such actions if the Holders [*holders of beneficial interests in the transferred assets*] receive payment of the principal amount of the Interests and the interest earned thereon (at the contractual yield) through the date the Holders are so paid; and

B. Prior to the appointment of the FDIC as conservator or receiver for the Bank, the Bank and its other creditors would not have the right to reclaim or recover the Transferred Assets from the Issuer, except by the exercise of a contractual provision [insert appropri-

---

[8] When the opinion indicates that isolation is achieved without reference to a true sale, the opinion also should provide reasonable assurance that the transferred assets are beyond the reach of the transferor and its creditors other than the transferee to the same extent that is provided in example 2 paragraph B. [Footnote renumbered, June 2009, to reflect conforming changes necessary due to the issuance of FASB ASC.]

ate citation] to require the transfer, or return, of the Transferred Assets that exists solely as a result of the contract between the Bank and the Issuer."[9]

The following additional paragraph addressing substantive consolidation applies when the entity to which the assets are sold or transferred (as described in the opinion) is an affiliate of the selling entity and may also apply in other situations as noted by the legal specialist.[10] For example, if a so-called two-step structure has been used to achieve isolation, the following paragraph usually will be required with respect to the transferee in the first step of the structure (see paragraph .15 and related footnotes for additional guidance on the second step of a two-step structure as described in paragraphs 22–23 of FASB ASC 860-10-55). When the transferor has entered into transactions with an affiliate that could affect the issue of substantive consolidation, the opinion should address the effect of that involvement on the opinion:

> Based upon the assumptions of fact and the discussion set forth previously, and on a reasoned analysis of analogous case law, *we are of the opinion that* in a properly presented and argued case, as a legal matter, in a receivership, conservatorship, or liquidation proceeding in respect of the Seller, a court *would not* grant an order consolidating the assets and liabilities of the Purchaser with those of the Seller.

Certain powers to repudiate contracts, recover, reclaim, or recharacterize transferred assets as property of a transferor that are exercisable by the FDIC under the Federal Deposit Insurance Act may, as of the date of the transfer, be limited by a regulation that may be repealed or amended only in respect of transfers occurring on or after the effective date of such repeal or amendment.[11] With respect to the powers of a receiver or conservator that may not be exercised under that regulation, it is acceptable for attorneys to rely upon the effectiveness of the limitation on such powers set forth in the applicable regulation, provided that the attorney states, based on reasonable assumptions, that: (*a*) the affected transfer of financial assets meets all qualification requirements of the regulation, and (*b*) the regulation had not, as of the date of the opinion, been amended, repealed, or held inapplicable by a court with jurisdiction with respect to such transfer. The opinion should separately address any powers of repudiation, recovery, reclamation, or recharacterization exercisable by a receiver or conservator notwithstanding that regulation (for example, rights, powers, or remedies regarding transfers specifically excluded from the regulation) in a manner that provides the same level of assurance as would be provided in the case of opinions that conform with requirements of paragraph .13, except that such opinion shall address powers arising under the Federal Deposit Insurance Act. The considerations in the immediately preceding three sentences are adequately addressed either by the example 1 opinion or the

---

[9] See the second paragraph of footnote 5.

Paragraph B is not required if the opinion includes both a conclusion, as set forth in example 1, that the transfer constitutes a "true sale" and the conclusions set forth of example 2 paragraph A. It is not necessary to include any provision of Example 2 if the opinion is as set forth in example 1. [Footnote revised and renumbered, June 2009, to reflect conforming changes necessary due to the issuance of FASB ASC.]

[10] An additional substantive consolidation opinion is not required if the opinion states that its conclusion includes the inability to recover the transferred financial assets or recharacterize the transfer by application of the doctrine of "substantive consolidation." [Footnote renumbered, June 2009, to reflect conforming changes necessary due to the issuance of FASB ASC.]

[11] The applicable regulation is 12 U.S. *Code of Federal Regulations* 360.6, effective September 11, 2000. [Footnote renumbered, June 2009, to reflect conforming changes necessary due to the issuance of FASB ASC.]

example 2 opinion described in this paragraph or by the variations described in the second paragraph of footnote 9 and in footnote 10.

.15 A legal letter that includes an inadequate opinion, inappropriate limitations, or a disclaimer of opinion, or that effectively limits the scope of the opinion to facts and circumstances that are not applicable to the transaction, does not provide persuasive evidence to support the entity's assertion that the transferred assets have been put presumptively beyond the reach of the transferor and its creditors, even in bankruptcy or other receivership. Likewise, a legal letter that includes conclusions that are expressed using some of the following language would not provide persuasive evidence that a transfer of financial assets has met the isolation criterion of FASB ASC 860-10-40-5(a) (see paragraphs .20–.21 of this interpretation):

- "We are unable to express an opinion..."
- "It is our opinion, based upon limited facts..."
- "We are of the view..." or "it appears..."
- "There is a reasonable basis to conclude that..."
- "In our opinion, the transfer would *either* be a sale *or* a grant of a perfected security interest..."[12]
- "In our opinion, there is a reasonable possibility..."
- "In our opinion, the transfer *should* be considered a sale..."
- "It is our opinion that the company will be able to assert meritorious arguments..."
- "In our opinion, it is more likely than not ..."
- "In our opinion, the transfer would *presumptively* be..."
- "In our opinion, it is probable that..."

Furthermore, conclusions about hypothetical transactions may not be relevant to the transaction that is the subject of management's assertions. Section 326, *Audit Evidence*, paragraph .06 states "The auditor should consider the sufficiency and appropriateness of audit evidence to be obtained when assessing risks and designing further audit procedures." Additionally, conclusions about hypothetical transactions may not contemplate all of the facts and circumstances or the provisions in the agreements of the transaction that is the subject of management's assertions, and generally would not provide persuasive evidence.[13]

---

[12] Certain transferors are subject only to receivership (and not to proceedings under the U.S. Bankruptcy Code or the Federal Deposit Insurance Act) under laws that do not allow a receiver to reach assets in which a security interest has been granted. In such circumstances, an opinion that concludes that the transfer would either be a sale or a grant of a security interest that puts the transferred assets beyond the reach of such receiver and other creditors would provide persuasive evidence that the isolation criterion is met.

In certain circumstances, a legal specialist may provide an opinion on both steps of a two-step structure. Such language would be acceptable in an opinion for a transfer of assets in the second step of a two-step structure as described in paragraphs 22–23 of FASB ASC 860-10-55 provided that the opinion on the transfer in the first step is consistent with paragraphs .13 or .14 of this interpretation. [Footnote revised and renumbered, June 2009, to reflect conforming changes necessary due to the issuance of FASB ASC.]

[13] For example, a memorandum of law from a legal specialist usually analyzes (and may make conclusions about) a transaction that may be completed subsequently. Such memorandum generally would not provide persuasive evidence unless the conclusions conform with this interpretation and a legal specialist opines that such conclusions apply to a completed transaction that is the subject of management's assertion. [Footnote renumbered, June 2009, to reflect conforming changes necessary due to the issuance of FASB ASC.]

.16 *Question*—Are legal opinions that restrict the use of the opinion to the client, or to third parties other than the auditor, acceptable audit evidence?

.17 *Interpretation*—No. Footnote 5 to section 336 paragraph .09 states: "In some cases, the auditor may decide it is necessary to contact the specialist to determine that the specialist is aware that his or her work will be used for evaluating the assertions in the financial statements." Given the importance of the legal opinion to the assertion in this case, and the precision that legal specialists use in drafting such opinions, an auditor should not use as evidence a legal opinion that he or she deems otherwise adequate if the letter restricts use of the findings expressed therein to the client or to third parties other than the auditor. In that event, the auditor should request that the client obtain the legal specialist's written permission for the auditor to use the opinion for the purpose of evaluating management's assertion that a transfer of financial assets meets the isolation criterion of FASB ASC 860-10-40-5(a).

.18 An example of a letter from a legal specialist to a client that adequately communicates permission for the auditor to use the legal specialist's opinion for the purpose of evaluating management's assertion that a transfer of financial assets meets the isolation criterion of FASB ASC 860-10-40-5(a) is as follows:

> Notwithstanding any language to the contrary in our opinions of even date with respect to certain bankruptcy issues relating to the previously referenced transaction, you are authorized to make available to your auditors such opinions solely as audit evidence in support of their evaluation of management's assertion that the transfer of the receivables meets the isolation criterion of Financial Accounting Standards Board *Accounting Standards Codification* 860-10-40-5(a), provided a copy of this letter is furnished to them in connection therewith. In authorizing you to make copies of such opinions available to your auditors for such purpose, we are not undertaking or assuming any duty or obligation to your auditors or establishing any lawyer-client relationship with them. Further, we do not undertake or assume any responsibility with respect to financial statements of you or your affiliates.[14]

.19 A letter from a legal specialist to a client might authorize the client to make copies of the legal opinion available to the auditor to use in his or her evaluation of management's assertion that a transfer of financial assets meets the isolation criterion of FASB ASC 860-10-40-5(a), but then state that the auditor is not authorized to rely thereon. Such "use but not rely on" language, or other language that similarly restricts the auditor's use of the legal specialist's opinion, does not adequately communicate permission for the auditor to use the legal specialist's opinion as audit evidence. The auditor may wish to consult with his or her legal counsel in circumstances where it is not clear that the auditor may use the legal specialist's opinion.

.20 *Question*—If the auditor determines that it is appropriate to use the work of a legal specialist, and either the resulting legal response does not provide persuasive evidence that a transfer of assets has met the isolation criterion, or the legal specialist does not grant permission for the auditor to use a legal opinion that is restricted to the client or to third parties other than the auditor, what other steps might an auditor consider?

.21 *Interpretation*—When other relevant audit evidence exists, the auditor should consider it before reaching a conclusion about the appropriateness of

---

[14] This language may appear in the legal specialist's opinion rather than in a separate letter. In that case, the wording would be modified slightly to indicate the context. [Footnote renumbered, June 2009, to reflect conforming changes necessary due to the issuance of FASB ASC.]

management's accounting for a transfer.[15] However, since the isolation aspect of surrender of control is assessed primarily from a legal perspective, the auditor usually will not be able to obtain persuasive evidence in a form other than a legal opinion. In the absence of persuasive evidence that a transfer has met the isolation criterion, derecognition of the transferred assets is not in conformity with generally accepted accounting principles and the auditor should consider the need to express a qualified or adverse opinion in accordance with section 508, *Reports on Audited Financial Statements*, paragraphs .35–.60. However, if permission for the auditor to use a legal opinion that he or she deems otherwise adequate is not granted, this would be a scope limitation and the auditor should consider the need to express a qualified opinion or to disclaim an opinion in accordance with section 508 paragraphs .22–.26 and .61–.63.

[Issue Date: December 2001; Revised: March 2006; Revised: June 2009.]

---

[15] See section 336 paragraph .13 as to additional procedures that may be applied. [Footnote renumbered, June 2009, to reflect conforming changes necessary due to the issuance of FASB ASC.]

AU Section 337

Inquiry of a Client's Lawyer Concerning Litigation, Claims, and Assessments[1]

Source: SAS No. 12.

See section 9337 for interpretations of this section.

Issue date, unless otherwise indicated: January, 1976.

.01 This section provides guidance on the procedures an independent auditor should consider for identifying litigation, claims, and assessments and for satisfying himself as to the financial accounting and reporting for such matters when he is performing an audit in accordance with generally accepted auditing standards.

Accounting Considerations

.02 Management is responsible for adopting policies and procedures to identify, evaluate, and account for litigation, claims, and assessments as a basis for the preparation of financial statements in conformity with generally accepted accounting principles.

.03 The standards of financial accounting and reporting for loss contingencies, including those arising from litigation, claims, and assessments, are set forth in Financial Accounting Standards Board (FASB) *Accounting Standards Codification* (ASC) 450, *Contingencies*. [Revised, June 2009, to reflect conforming changes necessary due to the issuance of FASB ASC.][2]

Auditing Considerations

.04 With respect to litigation, claims, and assessments, the independent auditor should obtain audit evidence relevant to the following factors:

a. The existence of a condition, situation, or set of circumstances indicating an uncertainty as to the possible loss to an entity arising from litigation, claims, and assessments.

b. The period in which the underlying cause for legal action occurred.

c. The degree of probability of an unfavorable outcome.

d. The amount or range of potential loss.

[Revised, March 2006, to reflect conforming changes necessary due to the issuance of Statement on Auditing Standards No. 105.]

---

[1] This section supersedes the commentary, "Lawyers' Letters," January 1974 (section 1001), and auditing interpretations of section 560 paragraph .12 on lawyers' letters, January 1975 (section 9560 paragraphs .01-.26). It amends section 560 paragraph .12*d* to read as follows: "Inquire of client's legal counsel concerning litigation, claims, and assessments (see section 337)."

[2] Pertinent portions are reprinted in exhibit I (section 337B). Financial Accounting Standards Board (FASB) *Accounting Standards Codification* (ASC) 450, *Contingencies*, also describes the standards of financial accounting and reporting for gain contingencies. The auditor's procedures with respect to gain contingencies are parallel to those described in this SAS for loss contingencies. [Footnote revised, June 2009, to reflect conforming changes necessary due to the issuance of FASB ASC.]

Audit Procedures

.05 Since the events or conditions that should be considered in the financial accounting for and reporting of litigation, claims, and assessments are matters within the direct knowledge and, often, control of management of an entity, management is the primary source of information about such matters. Accordingly, the independent auditor's procedures with respect to litigation, claims, and assessments should include the following:

a. Inquire of and discuss with management the policies and procedures adopted for identifying, evaluating, and accounting for litigation, claims, and assessments.

b. Obtain from management a description and evaluation of litigation, claims, and assessments that existed at the date of the balance sheet being reported on, and during the period from the balance sheet date to the date the information is furnished, including an identification of those matters referred to legal counsel, and obtain assurances from management, ordinarily in writing, that they have disclosed all such matters required to be disclosed by FASB ASC 450.

c. Examine documents in the client's possession concerning litigation, claims, and assessments, including correspondence and invoices from lawyers.

d. Obtain assurance from management, ordinarily in writing, that it has disclosed all unasserted claims that the lawyer has advised them are probable of assertion and must be disclosed in accordance with FASB ASC 450. Also the auditor, with the client's permission, should inform the lawyer that the client has given the auditor this assurance. This client representation may be communicated by the client in the inquiry letter or by the auditor in a separate letter.[3]

[Revised, June 2009, to reflect conforming changes necessary due to the issuance of FASB ASC.]

.06 An auditor ordinarily does not possess legal skills and, therefore, cannot make legal judgments concerning information coming to his attention. Accordingly, the auditor should request the client's management to send a letter of inquiry to those lawyers with whom management consulted concerning litigation, claims, and assessments.

.07 The audit normally includes certain other procedures undertaken for different purposes that might also disclose litigation, claims, and assessments. Examples of such procedures are as follows:

a. Reading minutes of meetings of stockholders, directors, and appropriate committees held during and subsequent to the period being audited.

b. Reading contracts, loan agreements, leases, and correspondence from taxing or other governmental agencies, and similar documents.

---

[3] An example of a separate letter is as follows: We are writing to inform you that (name of company) has represented to us that (except as set forth below and excluding any such matters listed in the letter of audit inquiry) there are no unasserted possible claims that you have advised are probable of assertion and must be disclosed in accordance with FASB ASC 450 in its financial statements at (balance sheet date) and for the (period) then ended. (List unasserted possible claims, if any.) Such a letter should be signed and sent by the auditor. [Footnote revised, June 2009, to reflect conforming changes necessary due to the issuance of FASB ASC.]

c. Obtaining information concerning guarantees from bank confirmation forms.

d. Inspecting other documents for possible guarantees by the client.

Inquiry of a Client's Lawyer[4]

.08 A letter of audit inquiry to the client's lawyer is the auditor's primary means of obtaining corroboration of the information furnished by management concerning litigation, claims, and assessments.[5] Audit evidence obtained from the client's inside general counsel or legal department may provide the auditor with the necessary corroboration. However, audit evidence obtained from inside counsel is not a substitute for information outside counsel refuses to furnish. [Revised, March 2006, to reflect conforming changes necessary due to the issuance of Statement on Auditing Standards No. 105.]

.09 The matters that should be covered in a letter of audit inquiry include, but are not limited to, the following:

a. Identification of the company, including subsidiaries, and the date of the audit.

b. A list prepared by management (or a request by management that the lawyer prepare a list) that describes and evaluates pending or threatened litigation, claims, and assessments with respect to which the lawyer has been engaged and to which he has devoted substantive attention on behalf of the company in the form of legal consultation or representation.

c. A list prepared by management that describes and evaluates unasserted claims and assessments that management considers to be probable of assertion, and that, if asserted, would have at least a reasonable possibility of an unfavorable outcome, with respect to which the lawyer has been engaged and to which he has devoted substantive attention on behalf of the company in the form of legal consultation or representation.

d. As to each matter listed in item *b*, a request that the lawyer either furnish the following information or comment on those matters as to which his views may differ from those stated by management, as appropriate:

(1) A description of the nature of the matter, the progress of the case to date, and the action the company intends to take (for example, to contest the matter vigorously or to seek an out-of-court settlement).

(2) An evaluation of the likelihood of an unfavorable outcome and an estimate, if one can be made, of the amount or range of potential loss.

(3) With respect to a list prepared by management, an identification of the omission of any pending or threatened litigation, claims, and assessments or a statement that the list of such matters is complete.

---

[4] An illustrative inquiry letter to legal counsel is contained in the appendix (section 337A).

[5] It is not intended that the lawyer be requested to undertake a reconsideration of all matters upon which he was consulted during the period under audit for the purpose of determining whether he can form a conclusion regarding the probability of assertion of any possible claim inherent in any of the matters so considered.

e. As to each matter listed in item *c*, a request that the lawyer comment on those matters as to which his views concerning the description or evaluation of the matter may differ from those stated by management.

f. A statement by the client that the client understands that whenever, in the course of performing legal services for the client with respect to a matter recognized to involve an unasserted possible claim or assessment that may call for financial statement disclosure, the lawyer has formed a professional conclusion that the client should disclose or consider disclosure concerning such possible claim or assessment, the lawyer, as a matter of professional responsibility to the client, will so advise the client and will consult with the client concerning the question of such disclosure and the applicable requirements of FASB ASC 450.

g. A request that the lawyer confirm whether the understanding described in item *f* is correct.

h. A request that the lawyer specifically identify the nature of and reasons for any limitation on his response.

Inquiry need not be made concerning matters that are not considered material, provided the client and the auditor have reached an understanding on the limits of materiality for this purpose. [Revised, June 2009, to reflect conforming changes necessary due to the issuance of FASB ASC.]

.10 In special circumstances, the auditor may obtain a response concerning matters covered by the audit inquiry letter in a conference, which offers an opportunity for a more detailed discussion and explanation than a written reply. A conference may be appropriate when the evaluation of the need for accounting for or disclosure of litigation, claims, and assessments involves such matters as the evaluation of the effect of legal advice concerning unsettled points of law, the effect of uncorroborated information, or other complex judgments. The auditor should appropriately document conclusions reached concerning the need for accounting for or disclosure of litigation, claims, and assessments.

.11 In some circumstances, a lawyer may be required by his Code of Professional Responsibility to resign his engagement if his advice concerning financial accounting and reporting for litigation, claims, and assessments is disregarded by the client. When the auditor is aware that a client has changed lawyers or that a lawyer engaged by the client has resigned, the auditor should consider the need for inquiries concerning the reasons the lawyer is no longer associated with the client.

Limitations on the Scope of a Lawyer's Response[6]

.12 A lawyer may appropriately limit his response to matters to which he has given substantive attention in the form of legal consultation or representation. Also, a lawyer's response may be limited to matters that are considered

[6] The American Bar Association has approved a "Statement of Policy Regarding Lawyers' Responses to Auditors' Requests for Information," which explains the concerns of lawyers and the nature of the limitations an auditor is likely to encounter. That Statement of Policy is reprinted as exhibit II (section 337C) for the convenience of readers, but is not an integral part of this Statement.

individually or collectively material to the financial statements, provided the lawyer and auditor have reached an understanding on the limits of materiality for this purpose. Such limitations are not limitations on the scope of the audit.

.13 A lawyer's refusal to furnish the information requested in an inquiry letter either in writing or orally (see paragraphs .09 and .10) would be a limitation on the scope of the audit sufficient to preclude an unqualified opinion (see section 508 paragraph .22 and .23).[7] A lawyer's response to such an inquiry and the procedures set forth in paragraph .05 provide the auditor with sufficient audit evidence to satisfy himself concerning the accounting for and reporting of pending and threatened litigation, claims and assessments. The auditor obtains sufficient audit evidence to satisfy himself concerning reporting for those unasserted claims and assessments required to be disclosed in financial statements from the foregoing procedures and the lawyer's specific acknowledgement of his responsibility to his client in respect of disclosure obligations (see paragraph .09*g*). This approach with respect to unasserted claims and assessments is necessitated by the public interest in protecting the confidentiality of lawyer-client communications. [Revised, March 2006, to reflect conforming changes necessary due to the issuance of Statement on Auditing Standards No. 105.]

Other Limitations on a Lawyer's Response

.14 A lawyer may be unable to respond concerning the likelihood of an unfavorable outcome of litigation, claims, and assessments or the amount or range of potential loss, because of inherent uncertainties. Factors influencing the likelihood of an unfavorable outcome may sometimes not be within a lawyer's competence to judge; historical experience of the entity in similar litigation or the experience of other entities may not be relevant or available; and the amount of the possible loss frequently may vary widely at different stages of litigation. Consequently, a lawyer may not be able to form a conclusion with respect to such matters. In such circumstances, the auditor ordinarily will conclude that the financial statements are affected by an uncertainty concerning the outcome of a future event which is not susceptible of reasonable estimation, and should look to the guidance in section 508 paragraphs .45–.49 to determine the effect, if any, of the lawyer's response on the auditor's report. [Revised, February 1997, to reflect conforming changes necessary due to the issuance of Statement on Auditing Standards No. 79.]

---

[7] A refusal to respond should be distinguished from an inability to form a conclusion with respect to certain matters of judgment (see paragraph .14). Also, lawyers outside the United States sometimes follow practices at variance with those contemplated by this section to the extent that different procedures from those outlined herein may be necessary. In such circumstances, the auditor should exercise judgment in determining whether alternative procedures are adequate to comply with the requirements of this section.

AU Section 337A

Appendix—Illustrative Audit Inquiry Letter to Legal Counsel

Source: SAS No. 12.

Issue date, unless otherwise indicated: January, 1976.

.01 In connection with an audit of our financial statements at (balance sheet date) and for the (period) then ended, management of the Company has prepared, and furnished to our auditors (name and address of auditors), a description and evaluation of certain contingencies, including those set forth below involving matters with respect to which you have been engaged and to which you have devoted substantive attention on behalf of the Company in the form of legal consultation or representation. These contingencies are regarded by management of the Company as material for this purpose (management may indicate a materiality limit if an understanding has been reached with the auditor). Your response should include matters that existed at (balance sheet date) and during the period from that date to the date of your response.

Pending or Threatened Litigation (excluding unasserted claims)

[Ordinarily the information would include the following: (1) the nature of the litigation, (2) the progress of the case to date, (3) how management is responding or intends to respond to the litigation (for example, to contest the case vigorously or to seek an out-of-court settlement), and (4) an evaluation of the likelihood of an unfavorable outcome and an estimate, if one can be made, of the amount or range of potential loss.] Please furnish to our auditors such explanation, if any, that you consider necessary to supplement the foregoing information, including an explanation of those matters as to which your views may differ from those stated and an identification of the omission of any pending or threatened litigation, claims, and assessments or a statement that the list of such matters is complete.

Unasserted Claims and Assessments (considered by management to be probable of assertion, and that, if asserted, would have at least a reasonable possibility of an unfavorable outcome)

[Ordinarily management's information would include the following: (1) the nature of the matter, (2) how management intends to respond if the claim is asserted, and (3) an evaluation of the likelihood of an unfavorable outcome and an estimate, if one can be made, of the amount or range of potential loss.] Please furnish to our auditors such explanation, if any, that you consider necessary to supplement the foregoing information, including an explanation of those matters as to which your views may differ from those stated.

We understand that whenever, in the course of performing legal services for us with respect to a matter recognized to involve an unasserted possible claim or assessment that may call for financial statement disclosure, if you have formed a professional conclusion that we should disclose or consider disclosure concerning such possible claim or assessment, as a matter of professional responsibility to us, you will so advise us and will consult with us concerning the question of such disclosure and the applicable requirements of Financial Accounting Standards Board *Accounting Standards Codification* 450, *Contingencies*. Please specifically confirm to our auditors that our understanding is correct.

Please specifically identify the nature of and reasons for any limitation on your response.

[Revised, June 2009, to reflect conforming changes necessary due to the issuance of FASB ASC.]

AU Section 337B

Exhibit I—Excerpts From Financial Accounting Standards Board Accounting Standards Codification *450,* Contingencies

Source: SAS No. 12.

March, 1975.

The following excerpts are reprinted with the permission of the Financial Accounting Standards Board (FASB).

Overall

Overview and Background

General

450-10-05-4. The Contingencies Topic establishes standards of financial accounting and reporting for loss contingencies and gain contingencies, including standards for disclosures.

450-10-05-5. Resolution of the uncertainty may confirm any of the following:

a. The acquisition of an asset

b. The reduction of a liability

c. The loss or impairment of an asset

d. The incurrence of a liability.

450-10-05-6. Not all uncertainties inherent in the accounting process give rise to contingencies.[1] Estimates are required in financial statements for many ongoing and recurring activities of an entity. The mere fact that an estimate is involved does not of itself constitute the type of uncertainty referred to in the definition of a *loss contingency*[2] or a *gain contingency*.[3] Several examples of situations that are not contingencies are included in Section 450-10-55.

---

[1] According to the Financial Accounting Standards Board (FASB) *Accounting Standards Codification* (ASC) glossary, a *contingency* is "an existing condition, situation, or set of circumstances involving uncertainty as to possible gain or loss (loss contingency) to an entity that will ultimately be resolved when one or more future events occur or fail to occur."

[2] According to the FASB ASC glossary, a *gain contingency* is "an existing condition, situation, or set of circumstances involving uncertainty as to possible gain to an entity that will ultimately be resolved when one or more future events occur or fail to occur."

[3] According to the FASB ASC glossary, a *loss contingency* is "an existing condition, situation, or set of circumstances involving uncertainty as to possible loss to an entity that will ultimately be resolved when one or more future events occur or fail to occur. The term loss is used for convenience to include many charges against income that are commonly referred to as expenses and others that are commonly referred to as losses."

Loss Contingencies

Recognition

General

General Rule

450-20-25-1. When a loss contingency exists, the likelihood that the future event or events will confirm the loss or impairment of an asset or the incurrence of a liability can range from *probable* [4] to *remote*. [5] As indicated in the definition of contingency the term *loss* is used for convenience to include many charges against income that are commonly referred to as expenses and others that are commonly referred to as losses. The Contingencies Topic uses the terms *probable*, *reasonably possible*, [6] and *remote* to identify three areas within that range.

450-20-25-2. An estimated loss from a loss contingency shall be accrued by a charge to income if both of the following conditions are met:

a. Information available prior to issuance of the financial statements indicates that it is probable that an asset had been impaired or a liability had been incurred at the date of the financial statements. Date of the financial statements means the end of the most recent accounting period for which financial statements are being presented. It is implicit in this condition that it must be probable that one or more future events will occur confirming the fact of the loss.

b. The amount of loss can be reasonably estimated.

The purpose of those conditions is to require accrual of losses when they are reasonably estimable and relate to the current or a prior period. Paragraphs 450-20-55-1 through 55-17 and Examples 1–2 (see paragraphs 450-20-55-18 through 55-35) illustrate the application of the conditions. As discussed in paragraph 450-20-50-5, disclosure is preferable to accrual when a reasonable estimate of loss cannot be made. Further, even losses that are reasonably estimable shall not be accrued if it is not probable that an asset has been impaired or a liability has been incurred at the date of an entity's financial statements because those losses relate to a future period rather than the current or a prior period. Attribution of a loss to events or activities of the current or prior periods is an element of asset impairment or liability incurrence.

Disclosure

General

Accruals for Loss Contingencies

450-20-50-1. Disclosure of the nature of an accrual made pursuant to the provisions of paragraph 450-20-25-2, and in some circumstances the amount accrued, may be necessary for the financial statements not to be misleading. Terminology used shall be descriptive of the nature of the accrual, such as estimated liability or liability of an estimated amount. The term *reserve* shall not be used for an accrual made pursuant to paragraph 450-20-25-2; that term is limited to

---

[4] According to the FASB ASC glossary, *probable* is "the future event or events are likely to occur."

[5] According to the FASB ASC glossary, *remote* is "the chance of the future event or events occurring is slight."

[6] According to the FASB ASC glossary, *reasonably possible* is "the chance of the future event or events occurring is more than remote but less than likely."

an amount of unidentified or unsegregated assets held or retained for a specific purpose. Examples 1 (see paragraph 450-20-55-18) and 2, Cases A, B, and D (see paragraphs 450-20-55-23, 450-20-55-27, and 450-20-55-32) illustrate the application of these disclosure standards.

450-20-50-2. If the criteria in paragraph 275-10-50-8 are met, paragraph 275-10-50-9 requires disclosure of an indication that it is at least reasonably possible that a change in an entity's estimate of its probable liability could occur in the near term. Example 3 (see paragraph 450-20-55-36) illustrates this disclosure for an entity involved in litigation.

Unrecognized Contingencies

450-20-50-3. Disclosure of the contingency shall be made if there is at least a reasonable possibility that a loss or an additional loss may have been incurred and either of the following conditions exists:

a. An accrual is not made for a loss contingency because any of the conditions in paragraph 450-20-25-2 are not met.

b. An exposure to loss exists in excess of the amount accrued pursuant to the provisions of paragraph 450-20-30-1.

Examples 1–3 (see paragraphs 450-20-55-18 through 55-37) illustrate the application of these disclosure standards.

450-20-50-4. The disclosure in the preceding paragraph shall include both of the following:

a. The nature of the contingency

b. An estimate of the possible loss or range of loss or a statement that such an estimate cannot be made.

450-20-50-5. Disclosure is preferable to accrual when a reasonable estimate of loss cannot be made. For example, disclosure shall be made of any loss contingency that meets the condition in paragraph 450-20-25-2(a) but that is not accrued because the amount of loss cannot be reasonably estimated (the condition in paragraph 450-20-25-2[b]). Disclosure also shall be made of some loss contingencies that do not meet the condition in paragraph 450-20-25-2(a)—namely, those contingencies for which there is a reasonable possibility that a loss may have been incurred even though information may not indicate that it is probable that an asset had been impaired or a liability had been incurred at the date of the financial statements.

450-20-50-6. Disclosure is not required of a loss contingency involving an unasserted claim or assessment if there has been no manifestation by a potential claimant of an awareness of a possible claim or assessment unless both of the following conditions are met:

a. It is considered probable that a claim will be asserted.

b. There is a reasonable possibility that the outcome will be unfavorable.

450-20-50-7. Disclosure of noninsured or underinsured risks is not required by this Subtopic. However, disclosure in appropriate circumstances is not discouraged.

450-20-50-8. No disclosure about general or unspecified business risks is required by this Subtopic, however, Topic 275 requires disclosure of certain business risks.

Losses Arising After the Date of the Financial Statements

450-20-50-9. Disclosure of a loss, or a loss contingency, arising after the date of an entity's financial statements but before those financial statements are issued, as described in paragraphs 450-20-25-6 through 25-7, may be necessary to keep the financial statements from being misleading if an accrual is not required. If disclosure is deemed necessary, the financial statements shall include both of the following:

a. The nature of the loss or loss contingency

b. An estimate of the amount or range of loss or possible loss or a statement that such an estimate cannot be made.

450-20-50-10. Occasionally, in the case of a loss arising after the date of the financial statements if the amount of asset impairment or liability incurrence can be reasonably estimated, disclosure may best be made by supplementing the historical financial statements with pro forma financial data giving effect to the loss as if it had occurred at the date of the financial statements. It may be desirable to present pro forma statements, usually a balance sheet only, in columnar form on the face of the historical financial statements.

Implementation Guidance and Illustrations

General

Implementation Guidance

Litigation, Claims, and Assessments

450-20-55-10. The following factors should be considered in determining whether accrual and/or disclosure is required with respect to pending or threatened litigation and actual or possible claims and assessments:

a. The period in which the underlying cause (that is, the cause for action) of the pending or threatened litigation or of the actual or possible claim or assessment occurred

b. The degree of probability of an unfavorable outcome

c. The ability to make a reasonable estimate of the amount of loss.

Examples 1 through 2 (see paragraphs 450-20-55-18 through 55-35) illustrate the consideration of these factors in determining whether to accrue or disclose litigation.

Losses Arising Before the Date of the Financial Statements

450-20-55-11. Accrual may be appropriate for litigation, claims, or assessments whose underlying cause is an event occurring on or before the date of an entity's financial statements even if the entity does not become aware of the existence or possibility of the lawsuit, claim, or assessment until after the date of the financial statements. If those financial statements have not been issued, accrual of a loss related to the litigation, claim, or assessment would be required if the probability of loss is such that the condition in paragraph 450-20-25-2(a) is met and the amount of loss can be reasonably estimated.

Assessing Probability of the Incurrence of a Loss

450-20-55-12. If the underlying cause of the litigation, claim, or assessment is an event occurring before the date of an entity's financial statements, the probability of an outcome unfavorable to the entity must be assessed to determine whether the condition in paragraph 450-20-25-2(a) is met. Among the factors that should be considered are the following:

a. The nature of the litigation, claim, or assessment

b. The progress of the case (including progress after the date of the financial statements but before those statements are issued) *c.* The opinions or views of legal counsel and other advisers, although, the fact that legal counsel is unable to express an opinion that the outcome will be favorable to the entity should not necessarily be interpreted to mean that the condition in paragraph 450-20-25-2(a) is met

d. The experience of the entity in similar cases

e. The experience of other entities

f. Any decision of the entity's management as to how the entity intends to respond to the lawsuit, claim, or assessment (for example, a decision to contest the case vigorously or a decision to seek an out-of-court settlement).

450-20-55-13. The filing of a suit or formal assertion of a claim or assessment does not automatically indicate that accrual of a loss may be appropriate. The degree of probability of an unfavorable outcome must be assessed. The condition in paragraph 450-20-25-2(a) would be met if an unfavorable outcome is determined to be probable. Accrual would be inappropriate, but disclosure would be required, if an unfavorable outcome is determined to be reasonably possible but not probable, or if the amount of loss cannot be reasonably estimated.

450-20-55-14. With respect to unasserted claims and assessments, an entity must determine the degree of probability that a suit may be filed or a claim or assessment may be asserted and the possibility of an unfavorable outcome. If an unfavorable outcome is probable and the amount of loss can be reasonably estimated, accrual of a loss is required by paragraph 450-20-25-2. For example:

a. A catastrophe, accident, or other similar physical occurrence predictably engenders claims for redress, and in such circumstances their assertion may be probable.

b. An investigation of an entity by a governmental agency, if enforcement proceedings have been or are likely to be instituted, is often followed by private claims for redress, and the probability of their assertion and the possibility of loss should be considered in each case.

c. An entity may believe there is a possibility that it has infringed on another entity's patent rights, but the entity owning the patent rights has not indicated an intention to take any action and has not even indicated an awareness of the possible infringement. In that case, a judgment must first be made as to whether the assertion of a claim is probable.

450-20-55-15. If the judgment is that assertion is not probable, no accrual or disclosure would be required. On the other hand, if the judgment is that assertion is probable, then a second judgment must be made as to the degree of probability of an unfavorable outcome. The disclosures described in paragraphs 450-20-50-3 through 50-8 would be required in either of the following circumstances:

a. An unfavorable outcome is probable but the amount of loss cannot be reasonably estimated.

b. An unfavorable outcome is reasonably possible but not probable.

Assessing Whether a Loss is Reasonably Estimable

450-20-55-16. As a condition for accrual of a loss contingency, the condition in paragraph 450-20-25-2(b) requires that the amount of loss can be reasonably estimated. In some cases, it may be determined that a loss was incurred because an unfavorable outcome of the litigation, claim, or assessment is probable (thus satisfying the condition in paragraph 450-20-25-2[a]), but the range of possible loss is wide. Examples 1 and 3 (see paragraphs 450-20-55-18 and 450-20-55-36) illustrate the application of the standards in this Subtopic when the range of possible loss is wide.

Losses Arising After the Date of the Financial Statements

450-20-55-17. As a condition for accrual of a loss contingency, the condition in paragraph 450-20-25-2(a) requires that information available prior to the issuance of financial statements indicate that it is probable that an asset had been impaired or a liability had been incurred at the date of the financial statements. Accordingly, accrual would clearly be inappropriate for litigation, claims, or assessments whose underlying cause is an event or condition occurring after the date of financial statements but before those financial statements are issued. For example, an entity would not accrue a suit for damages alleged to have been suffered as a result of an accident that occurred after the date of the financial statements. However, disclosure may be required by paragraphs 450-20-50-9 through 50-10.

Illustrations

Example 1: Litigation Open to Considerable Interpretation

450-20-55-18. An entity may be litigating a dispute with another party. In preparation for the trial, it may determine that, based on recent developments involving one aspect of the litigation, it is probable that it will have to pay $2 million to settle the litigation. Another aspect of the litigation may, however, be open to considerable interpretation, and depending on the interpretation by the court the entity may have to pay an additional $8 million over and above the $2 million.

450-20-55-19. In that case, paragraph 450-20-25-2 requires accrual of the $2 million if that is considered a reasonable estimate of the loss.

450-20-55-20. Paragraphs 450-20-50-1 through 50-2 require disclosure of the nature of the accrual, and depending on the circumstances, may require disclosure of the $2 million that was accrued.

450-20-55-21. Paragraphs 450-20-50-3 through 50-8 require disclosure of the additional exposure to loss if there is a reasonable possibility that the additional amounts will be paid.

[Revised, June 2009, to reflect conforming changes necessary due to the issuance of FASB ASC.]

AU Section 337C

Exhibit II—American Bar Association Statement of Policy Regarding Lawyers' Responses to Auditors' Requests for Information

Note: This document, in the form herein set forth, was approved by the Board of Governors of the American Bar Association in December 1975, which official action permitted its release to lawyers and accountants as the standard recommended by the American Bar Association for the lawyer's response to letters of audit inquiry.

Source: SAS No. 12.

Preamble

The public interest in protecting the confidentiality of lawyer-client communications is fundamental. The American legal, political and economic systems depend heavily upon voluntary compliance with the law and upon ready access to a respected body of professionals able to interpret and advise on the law. The expanding complexity of our laws and governmental regulations increases the need for prompt, specific and unhampered lawyer-client communication. The benefits of such communication and early consultation underlie the strict statutory and ethical obligations of the lawyer to preserve the confidences and secrets of the client, as well as the long-recognized testimonial privilege for lawyer-client communication.

Both the Code of Professional Responsibility and the cases applying the evidentiary privilege recognize that the privilege against disclosure can be knowingly and voluntarily waived by the client. It is equally clear that disclosure to a third party may result in loss of the "confidentiality" essential to maintain the privilege. Disclosure to a third party of the lawyer-client communication on a particular subject may also destroy the privilege as to other communications on that subject. Thus, the mere disclosure by the lawyer to the outside auditor, with due client consent, of the substance of communications between the lawyer and client may significantly impair the client's ability in other contexts to maintain the confidentiality of such communications.

Under the circumstances a policy of audit procedure which requires clients to give consent and authorize lawyers to respond to general inquiries and disclose information to auditors concerning matters which have been communicated in confidence is essentially destructive of free and open communication and early consultation between lawyer and client. The institution of such a policy would inevitably discourage management from discussing potential legal problems with counsel for fear that such discussion might become public and precipitate a loss to or possible liability of the business enterprise and its stockholders that might otherwise never materialize.

It is also recognized that our legal, political and economic systems depend to an important extent on public confidence in published financial statements. To meet this need the accounting profession must adopt and adhere to standards and procedures that will command confidence in the auditing process. It is not, however, believed necessary, or sound public policy, to intrude upon the confidentiality of the lawyer-client relationship in order to command such confidence. On the contrary, the objective of fair disclosure in financial statements is more likely to be better served by maintaining the integrity of the confidential relationship between lawyer and client, thereby strengthening corporate management's confidence in counsel and encouraging its readiness to seek advice of counsel and to act in accordance with counsel's advice.

Consistent with the foregoing public policy considerations, it is believed appropriate to distinguish between, on the one hand, litigation which is pending or which a third party has manifested to the client a present intention to commence and, on the other hand, other contingencies of a legal nature or having legal aspects. As regards the former category, unquestionably the lawyer representing the client in a litigation matter may be the best source for a description of the claim or claims asserted, the client's position (e.g., denial, contest, etc.), and the client's possible exposure in the litigation (to the extent the lawyer is in a position to do so). As to the latter category, it is submitted that, for the reasons set forth above, it is not in the public interest for the lawyer to be required to respond to general inquiries from auditors concerning possible claims.

It is recognized that the disclosure requirements for enterprises subject to the reporting requirements of the Federal securities laws are a major concern of managements and counsel, as well as auditors. It is submitted that compliance therewith is best assured when clients are afforded maximum encouragement, by protecting lawyer-client confidentiality, freely to consult counsel. Likewise, lawyers must be keenly conscious of the importance of their clients being competently advised in these matters.

Statement of Policy

NOW, THEREFORE, BE IT RESOLVED that it is desirable and in the public interest that this Association adopt the following Statement of Policy regarding the appropriate scope of the lawyer's response to the auditor's request, made by the client at the request of the auditor, for information concerning matters referred to the lawyer during the course of his representation of the client:

(1) *Client Consent to Response.* The lawyer may properly respond to the auditor's requests for information concerning loss contingencies (the term and concept established by Statement of Financial Accounting Standards No. 5,* promulgated by the Financial Accounting Standards Board in March 1975 and discussed in Paragraph 5.1 of the accompanying Commentary), to the extent hereinafter set forth, subject to the following:

a. Assuming that the client's initial letter requesting the lawyer to provide information to the auditor is signed by an agent of the client having apparent authority to make such a request, the lawyer may provide to the auditor information requested, without further consent, unless such information discloses a confidence or a secret or requires an evaluation of a claim.

---

* In July 2009, the Financial Accounting Standards Board (FASB) issued FASB *Accounting Standards Codification*™ (ASC) as authoritative. FASB ASC is now the source of authoritative U.S. accounting and reporting standards for nongovernmental entities, in addition to guidance issued by the Securities and Exchange Commission. As of July 1, 2009, all other nongrandfathered, non-SEC accounting literature not included in FASB ASC became nonauthoritative. FASB Statement No. 5, *Accounting for Contingencies*, has been codified as FASB ASC 450, *Contingencies*.

b. In the normal case, the initial request letter does not provide the necessary consent to the disclosure of a confidence or secret or to the evaluation of a claim since that consent may only be given after full disclosure to the client of the legal consequences of such action.

c. Lawyers should bear in mind, in evaluating claims, that an adverse party may assert that any evaluation of potential liability is an admission.

d. In securing the client's consent to the disclosure of confidences or secrets, or the evaluation of claims, the lawyer may wish to have a draft of his letter reviewed and approved by the client before releasing it to the auditor; in such cases, additional explanation would in all probability be necessary so that the legal consequences of the consent are fully disclosed to the client.

(2) *Limitation on Scope of Response.* It is appropriate for the lawyer to set forth in his response, by way of limitation, the scope of his engagement by the client. It is also appropriate for the lawyer to indicate the date as of which information is furnished and to disclaim any undertaking to advise the auditor of changes which may thereafter be brought to the lawyer's attention. *Unless the lawyer's response indicates otherwise, (a) it is properly limited to matters which have been given substantive attention by the lawyer in the form of legal consultation and, where appropriate, legal representation since the beginning of the period or periods being reported upon, and (b) if a law firm or a law department, the auditor may assume that the firm or department has endeavored, to the extent believed necessary by the firm or department, to determine from lawyers currently in the firm or department who have performed services for the client since the beginning of the fiscal period under audit whether such services involved substantive attention in the form of legal consultation concerning those loss contingencies referred to in Paragraph 5(a) below but, beyond that, no review has been made of any of the client's transactions or other matters for the purpose of identifying loss contingencies to be described in the response.*[†]

(3) *Response may be Limited to Material Items.* In response to an auditor's request for disclosure of loss contingencies of a client, it is appropriate for the lawyer's response to indicate that the response is limited to items which are considered individually or collectively material to the presentation of the client's financial statements.

(4) *Limited Responses.* Where the lawyer is limiting his response in accordance with the Statement of Policy, his response should so indicate (see Paragraph 8). If in any other respect the lawyer is not undertaking to respond to or comment on particular aspects of the inquiry when responding to the auditor, he should consider advising the auditor that his response is limited, in order to avoid any inference that the lawyer has responded to all aspects; otherwise, he may be assuming a responsibility which he does not intend.

(5) *Loss Contingencies.* When properly requested by the client, it is appropriate for the lawyer to furnish to the auditor information concerning the following matters if the lawyer has been engaged by the client to represent or advise the client professionally with respect thereto and he has devoted substantive attention to them in the form of legal representation or consultation:

a. *overtly threatened or pending litigation*, whether or not specified by the client;

[†] As contemplated by Paragraph 8 of this Statement of Policy, this sentence is intended to be the subject of incorporation by reference as therein provided.

b. *a contractually assumed obligation* which the client has specifically identified and upon which the client has specifically requested, in the inquiry letter or a supplement thereto, comment to the auditor;

c. *an unasserted possible claim or assessment* which the client has specifically identified and upon which the client has specifically requested, in the inquiry letter or a supplement thereto, comment to the auditor.

With respect to clause (*a*), overtly threatened litigation means that a potential claimant has manifested to the client an awareness of and present intention to assert a possible claim or assessment unless the likelihood of litigation (or of settlement when litigation would normally be avoided) is considered remote. With respect to clause (*c*), where there has been no manifestation by a potential claimant of an awareness of and present intention to assert a possible claim or assessment, consistent with the considerations and concerns outlined in the Preamble and Paragraph 1 hereof, the client should request the lawyer to furnish information to the auditor only if the client has determined that it is probable that a possible claim will be asserted, that there is a reasonable possibility that the outcome (assuming such assertion) will be unfavorable, and that the resulting liability would be material to the financial condition of the client. Examples of such situations might (depending in each case upon the particular circumstances) include the following: (i) a catastrophe, accident or other similar physical occurrence in which the client's involvement is open and notorious, or (ii) an investigation by a government agency where enforcement proceedings have been instituted or where the likelihood that they will not be instituted is remote, under circumstances where assertion of one or more private claims for redress would normally be expected, or (iii) a public disclosure by the client acknowledging (and thus focusing attention upon) the existence of one or more probable claims arising out of an event or circumstance. In assessing whether or not the assertion of a possible claim is probable, it is expected that the client would normally employ, by reason of the inherent uncertainties involved and insufficiency of available data, concepts parallel to those used by the lawyer (discussed below) in assessing whether or not an unfavorable outcome is probable; thus, assertion of a possible claim would be considered probable only when the prospects of its being asserted seem reasonably certain (i.e., supported by extrinsic evidence strong enough to establish a presumption that it will happen) and the prospects of nonassertion seem slight.

It would not be appropriate, however, for the lawyer to be requested to furnish information in response to an inquiry letter or supplement thereto if it appears that (*a*) the client has been required to specify unasserted possible claims without regard to the standard suggested in the preceding paragraph, or (*b*) the client has been required to specify all or substantially all unasserted possible claims as to which legal advice may have been obtained, since, in either case, such a request would be in substance a general inquiry and would be inconsistent with the intent of this Statement of Policy.

The information that lawyers may properly give to the auditor concerning the foregoing matters would include (to the extent appropriate) an identification of the proceedings or matter, the stage of proceedings, the claim(s) asserted, and the position taken by the client.

In view of the inherent uncertainties, the lawyer should normally refrain from expressing judgments as to outcome except in those relatively few clear cases where it appears to the lawyer that an unfavorable outcome is either "probable" or "remote"; for purposes of any such judgment it is appropriate to use the following meanings:

(i) *probable*—an unfavorable outcome for the client is probable if the prospects of the claimant not succeeding are judged to be extremely doubtful and the prospects for success by the client in its defense are judged to be slight.

(ii) *remote*—an unfavorable outcome is remote if the prospects for the client not succeeding in its defense are judged to be extremely doubtful and the prospects of success by the claimant are judged to be slight.

If, in the opinion of the lawyer, considerations within the province of his professional judgment bear on a particular loss contingency to the degree necessary to make an informed judgment, he may in appropriate circumstances communicate to the auditor his view that an unfavorable outcome is "probable" or "remote," applying the above meanings. No inference should be drawn, from the absence of such a judgment, that the client will not prevail.

The lawyer also may be asked to estimate, in dollar terms, the potential amount of loss or range of loss in the event that an unfavorable outcome is not viewed to be "remote." In such a case, the amount or range of potential loss will normally be as inherently impossible to ascertain, with any degree of certainty, as the outcome of the litigation. Therefore, it is appropriate for the lawyer to provide an estimate of the amount or range of potential loss (if the outcome should be unfavorable) only if he believes that the probability of inaccuracy of the estimate of the amount or range of potential loss is slight.

The considerations bearing upon the difficulty in estimating loss (or range of loss) where pending litigation is concerned are obviously even more compelling in the case of unasserted possible claims. In most cases, the lawyer will not be able to provide any such estimate to the auditor.

As indicated in Paragraph 4 hereof, the auditor may assume that all loss contingencies specified by the client in the manner specified in clauses (*b*) and (*c*) above have received comment in the response, unless otherwise therein indicated. The lawyer should not be asked, nor need the lawyer undertake, to furnish information to the auditor concerning loss contingencies except as contemplated by this Paragraph 5.

(6) *Lawyer's Professional Responsibility.* Independent of the scope of his response to the auditor's request for information, the lawyer, depending upon the nature of the matters as to which he is engaged, may have as part of his professional responsibility to his client an obligation to advise the client concerning the need for or advisability of public disclosure of a wide range of events and circumstances. The lawyer has an obligation not knowingly to participate in any violation by the client of the disclosure requirements of the securities laws. In appropriate circumstances, the lawyer also may be required under the Code of Professional Responsibility to resign his engagement if his advice concerning disclosures is disregarded by the client. The auditor may properly assume that whenever, in the course of performing legal services for the client with respect to a matter recognized to involve an unasserted possible claim or assessment which may call for financial statement disclosure, the lawyer has formed a professional conclusion that the client must disclose or consider disclosure concerning such possible claim or assessment, the lawyer, as a matter of professional responsibility to the client, will so advise the client and will consult with the client concerning the question of such disclosure and the applicable requirements[‡] of FAS 5.

---

‡ Under FAS 5, when there has been no manifestation by a potential claimant of an awareness of a possible claim or assessment, disclosure of an unasserted possible claim is required only if the enterprise concludes that (i) it is probable that a claim will be asserted, (ii) there is a reasonable possibility, if the claim is in fact asserted, that the outcome will be unfavorable, and (iii) the liability resulting from such unfavorable outcome would be material to its financial condition.

(7) *Limitation on Use of Response. Unless otherwise stated in the lawyer's response, it shall be solely for the auditor's information in connection with his audit of the financial condition of the client and is not to be quoted in whole or in part or otherwise referred to in any financial statements of the client or related documents, nor is it to be filed with any governmental agency or other person, without the lawyer's prior written consent.*† *Notwithstanding such limitation, the response can properly be furnished to others in compliance with court process or when necessary in order to defend the auditor against a challenge of the audit by the client or a regulatory agency, provided that the lawyer is given written notice of the circumstances at least twenty days before the response is so to be furnished to others, or as long in advance as possible if the situation does not permit such period of notice.*†

(8) *General.* This Statement of Policy, together with the accompanying Commentary (which is an integral part hereof), has been developed for the general guidance of the legal profession. In a particular case, the lawyer may elect to supplement or modify the approach hereby set forth. If desired, this Statement of Policy may be incorporated by reference in the lawyer's response by the following statement: "This response is limited by, and in accordance with, the ABA Statement of Policy Regarding Lawyers' Responses to Auditors' Requests for Information (December 1975); without limiting the generality of the foregoing, the limitations set forth in such Statement on the scope and use of this response (Paragraphs 2 and 7) are specifically incorporated herein by reference, and any description herein of any 'loss contingencies' is qualified in its entirety by Paragraph 5 of the Statement and the accompanying Commentary (which is an integral part of the Statement)."

The accompanying Commentary is an integral part of this Statement of Policy.

Commentary

Paragraph 1 (Client Consent to Response)

In responding to any aspect of an auditor's inquiry letter, the lawyer must be guided by his ethical obligations as set forth in the Code of Professional Responsibility. Under Canon 4 of the Code of Professional Responsibility a lawyer is enjoined to preserve the client's confidences (defined as information protected by the attorney-client privilege under applicable law) and the client's secrets (defined as other information gained in the professional relationship that the client has requested be held inviolate or the disclosure of which would be embarrassing or would be likely to be detrimental to the client). The observance of this ethical obligation, in the context of public policy, "... not only facilitates the full development of facts essential to proper representation of the client but also encourages laymen to seek early legal assistance." (Ethical Consideration 4-1).

The lawyer's ethical obligation therefore includes a much broader range of information than that protected by the attorney-client privilege. As stated in Ethical Consideration 4-4: "The attorney-client privilege is more limited than the ethical obligation of a lawyer to guard the confidences and secrets of his client. This ethical precept, unlike the evidentiary privilege, exists without regard to the nature or source of information or the fact that others share the knowledge."

† See footnote † in paragraph (2) in this section.

In recognition of this ethical obligation, the lawyer should be careful to disclose fully to his client any confidence, secret or evaluation that is to be revealed to another, including the client's auditor, and to satisfy himself that the officer or agent of a corporate client consenting to the disclosure understands the legal consequences thereof and has authority to provide the required consent.

The law in the area of attorney-client privilege and the impact of statements made in letters to auditors upon that privilege has not yet been developed. Based upon cases treating the attorney-client privilege in other contexts, however, certain generalizations can be made with respect to the possible impact of statements in letters to auditors.

It is now generally accepted that a corporation may claim the attorney-client privilege. Whether the privilege extends beyond the control group of the corporation (a concept found in the existing decisional authority), and if so, how far, is yet unresolved.

If a client discloses to a third party a part of any privileged communication he has made to his attorney, there may have been a waiver as to the whole communication; further, it has been suggested that giving accountants *access* to privileged statements made to attorneys may waive any privilege as to those statements. Any disclosure of privileged communications relating to a particular subject matter may have the effect of waiving the privilege on other communications with respect to the same subject matter.

To the extent that the lawyer's knowledge of unasserted possible claims is obtained by means of confidential communications from the client, any disclosure thereof might constitute a waiver as fully as if the communication related to pending claims.

A further difficulty arises with respect to requests for evaluation of either pending or unasserted possible claims. It might be argued that any evaluation of a claim, to the extent based upon a confidential communication with the client, waives any privilege with respect to that claim.

Another danger inherent in a lawyer's placing a value on a claim, or estimating the likely result, is that such a statement might be treated as an admission or might be otherwise prejudicial to the client.

The Statement of Policy has been prepared in the expectation that judicial development of the law in the foregoing areas will be such that useful communication between lawyers and auditors in the manner envisaged in the Statement will not prove prejudicial to clients engaged in or threatened with adversary proceedings. If developments occur contrary to this expectation, appropriate review and revision of the Statement of Policy may be necessary.

Paragraph 2 (Limitation on Scope of Response)

In furnishing information to an auditor, the lawyer can properly limit himself to loss contingencies which he is handling on a substantive basis for the client in the form of legal consultation (advice and other attention to matters not in litigation by the lawyer in his professional capacity) or legal representation (counsel of record or other direct professional responsibility for a matter in litigation). Some auditors' inquiries go further and ask for information on matters of which the lawyer "has knowledge." Lawyers are concerned that such a broad request may be deemed to include information coming from a variety of sources including social contact and third party contacts as well as professional engagement and that the lawyer might be criticized or subjected to liability if some of this information is forgotten at the time of the auditor's request.

It is also believed appropriate to recognize that the lawyer will not necessarily have been authorized to investigate, or have investigated, all legal problems of the client, even when on notice of some facts which might conceivably constitute a legal problem upon exploration and development. Thus, consideration in the form of preliminary or passing advice, or regarding an incomplete or hypothetical state of facts, or where the lawyer has not been requested to give studied attention to the matter in question, would not come within the concept of "substantive attention" and would therefore be excluded. Similarly excluded are matters which may have been mentioned by the client but which are not actually being handled by the lawyer. Paragraph 2 undertakes to deal with these concerns.

Paragraph 2 is also intended to recognize the principle that the appropriate lawyer to respond as to a particular loss contingency is the lawyer having charge of the matter for the client (e.g., the lawyer representing the client in a litigation matter and/or the lawyer having overall charge and supervision of the matter), and that the lawyer not having that kind of role with respect to the matter should not be expected to respond merely because of having become aware of its existence in a general or incidental way.

The internal procedures to be followed by a law firm or law department may vary based on factors such as the scope of the lawyer's engagement and the complexity and magnitude of the client's affairs. Such procedures could, but need not, include use of a docket system to record litigation, consultation with lawyers in the firm or department having principal responsibility for the client's affairs or other procedures which, in light of the cost to the client, are not disproportionate to the anticipated benefit to be derived. Although these procedures may not necessarily identify all matters relevant to the response, the evolution and application of the lawyer's customary procedures should constitute a reasonable basis for the lawyer's response.

As the lawyer's response is limited to matters involving his professional engagement as counsel, such response should not include information concerning the client which the lawyer receives in another role. In particular, a lawyer who is also a director or officer of the client would not include information which he received as a director or officer unless the information was also received (or, absent the dual role, would in the normal course be received) in his capacity as legal counsel in the context of his professional engagement. Where the auditor's request for information is addressed to a law firm as a firm, the law firm may properly assume that its response is not expected to include any information which may have been communicated to the particular individual by reason of his serving in the capacity of director or officer of the client. The question of the individual's duty, in his role as a director or officer, is not here addressed.

Paragraph 3 (Response May Cover only Material Items in Certain Cases)

Paragraph 3 makes it clear that the lawyer may optionally limit his responses to those items which are individually or collectively material to the auditor's inquiry. If the lawyer takes responsibility for making a determination that a matter is not material for the purposes of his response to the audit inquiry, he should make it clear that his response is so limited. The auditor, in such circumstance, should properly be entitled to rely upon the lawyer's response as providing him with the necessary corroboration. It should be emphasized that the employment of inside general counsel by the client should not detract from the acceptability of his response since inside general counsel is as fully bound by the professional obligations and responsibilities contained in the Code of Professional Responsibility as outside counsel. If the audit inquiry sets forth a definition of materiality but the lawyer utilizes a different test of materiality, he should specifically so state. The lawyer may wish to reach an understanding with the auditor concerning the test of materiality to be used in his response, but he need not do so if he assumes responsibility for the criteria used in making materiality determinations. Any such understanding with the auditor should be referred to or set forth in the lawyer's response. In this connection, it is assumed that the test of materiality so agreed upon would not be so low in amount as to result in a disservice to the client and an unreasonable burden on counsel.

Paragraph 4 (Limited Responses)

The Statement of Policy is designed to recognize the obligation of the auditor to complete the procedures considered necessary to satisfy himself as to the fair presentation of the company's financial condition and results, in order to render a report which includes an opinion not qualified because of a limitation on the scope of the audit. In this connection, reference is made to SEC Accounting Series Release No. 90 [Financial Reporting Release No. 1, section 607.01(b)], in which it is stated:

> "A 'subject to' or 'except for' opinion paragraph in which these phrases refer to the scope of the audit, indicating that the accountant has not been able to satisfy himself on some significant element in the financial statements, is not acceptable in certificates filed with the Commission in connection with the public offering of securities. The 'subject to' qualification is appropriate when the reference is to a middle paragraph or to footnotes explaining the status of matters which cannot be resolved at statement date."

Paragraph 5 (Loss Contingencies)

Paragraph 5 of the Statement of Policy summarizes the categories of "loss contingencies" about which the lawyer may furnish information to the auditor. The term loss contingencies and the categories relate to concepts of accounting accrual and disclosure specified for the accounting profession in Statement of Financial Accounting Standards No. 5[*] ("FAS 5") issued by the Financial Accounting Standards Board in March, 1975.

5.1 Accounting Requirements

To understand the significance of the auditor's inquiry and the implications of any response the lawyer may give, the lawyer should be aware of the following accounting concepts and requirements set out in FAS 5:[||]

(a) A "loss contingency" is an existing condition, situation or set of circumstances involving uncertainty as to possible loss to an enterprise that will ultimately be resolved when one or more events occur or fail to occur. Resolutions of the uncertainty may confirm the loss or impairment of an asset or the incurrence of a liability.

(Para. 1)

(b) When a "loss contingency" exists, the likelihood that a future event or events will confirm the loss or impairment of an asset or the incurrence of a liability can range from probable to remote. There are three areas within that range, defined as follows:

---

[*] See footnote * in paragraph (1) in this section.

[||] Citations are to paragraph numbers of FAS 5.

(i) *Probable*—"The future event or events are likely to occur."

(ii) *Reasonably possible*—"The chance of the future event or events occurring is more than remote but less than likely."

(iii) *Remote*—"The chance of the future event or events occurring is slight."

(Para. 3)

(c) *Accrual* in a client's financial statements by a charge to income of the period will be required if *both* the following conditions are met:

(i) "Information available prior to issuance of the financial statements indicates that it is *probable* that an asset had been impaired or a liability had been incurred at the date of the financial statements. It is implicit in this condition that it must be *probable* that one or more future events will occur confirming the fact of the loss." (emphasis added; footnote omitted)

(ii) "The amount of loss can be reasonably estimated."

(Para. 8)

(d) *If there is no accrual* of the loss contingency in the client's financial statements because one of the two conditions outlined in (*c*) above are not met, *disclosure* may be required as provided in the following:

"If no accrual is made for a loss contingency because one or both of the conditions in paragraph 8 are not met, or if an exposure to loss exists in excess of the amount accrued pursuant to the provisions of paragraph 8, *disclosure* of the contingency *shall be made when there is at least a reasonable possibility* that a loss or an additional loss may have been incurred. *The disclosure shall indicate the nature of the contingency and shall give an estimate of the possible loss or range of loss or state that such an estimate cannot be made. Disclosure is not required of* a loss contingency involving *an unasserted claim* or assessment *when there has been no manifestation by potential claimant of an awareness of a possible claim or assessment unless it is considered probable that a claim will be asserted and there is a reasonable possibility that the outcome will be unfavorable*." (emphasis added; footnote omitted)

(Para. 10)

(e) The accounting requirements recognize or specify that (i) the opinions or views of counsel are not the sole source of audit evidence in making determinations about the accounting recognition or treatment to be given to litigation, and (ii) the fact that the lawyer is notable to express an opinion that the outcome will be favorable does not necessarily require an accrual of a loss. Paragraphs 36 and 37 of FAS 5 state as follows:

"If the underlying cause of the litigation, claim, or assessment is an event occurring before the date of an enterprise's financial statements, the probability of an outcome unfavorable to the enterprise must be assessed to determine whether the condition in paragraph 8(*a*) is met. Among the factors that should be considered are the nature of the litigation, claim, or assessment, the progress of the case (including progress after the date of the financial statements but before those statements are issued), the opinions or views of legal counsel and other advisers, the experience of the enterprise in similar cases, the experience of other enterprises, and any decision of the enterprise's management as to how the enterprise intends to respond to the lawsuit, claim, or assessment (for example, a decision to contest the case vigorously or a decision to seek an out-of-court settlement). The fact that legal counsel is unable to express an opinion that the outcome will be favorable to the enterprise should not necessarily be interpreted to mean that the condition for accrual of a loss in paragraph 8(*a*) is met.

"The filing of a suit or formal assertion of a claim or assessment does not automatically indicate that accrual of a loss may be appropriate. The degree of probability of an unfavorable outcome must be assessed. The condition for accrual in paragraph 8(*a*) would be met if an unfavorable outcome is determined to be probable. If an unfavorable outcome is determined to be reasonably possible but not probable, or if the amount of loss cannot be reasonably estimated, accrual would be inappropriate, but disclosure would be required by paragraph 10 of this Statement."

[Revised, March 2006, to reflect conforming changes necessary due to the issuance of Statement on Auditing Standards No. 105.]

(f) Paragraph 38 of FAS 5 focuses on certain examples concerning the determination by the enterprise whether an assertion of an unasserted possible claim may be considered probable:

"With respect to unasserted claims and assessments, an enterprise must determine the degree of probability that a suit may be filed or a claim or assessment may be asserted and the possibility of an unfavorable outcome. For example, a catastrophe, accident, or other similar physical occurrence predictably engenders claims for redress, and in such circumstances their assertion may be probable; similarly, an investigation of an enterprise by a governmental agency, if enforcement proceedings have been or are likely to be instituted, is often followed by private claims for redress, and the probability of their assertion and the possibility of loss should be considered in each case. By way of further example, an enterprise may believe there is a possibility that it has infringed on another enterprise's patent rights, but the enterprise owning the patent rights has not indicated an intention to take any action and has not even indicated an awareness of the possible infringement. In that case, a judgment must first be made as to whether the assertion of a claim is probable. If the judgment is that assertion is not probable, no accrual or disclosure would be required. On the other hand, if the judgment is that assertion is probable, then a second judgment must be made as to the degree of probability of an unfavorable outcome. If an unfavorable outcome is probable and the amount of loss can be reasonably estimated, accrual of a loss is required by paragraph 8. If an unfavorable outcome is probable but the amount of loss cannot be reasonably estimated, accrual would not be appropriate, but disclosure would be required by paragraph 10. If an unfavorable outcome is reasonably possible but not probable, disclosure would be required by paragraph 10."

For a more complete presentation of FAS 5, reference is made to Exhibit I, section 337B, in which are set forth excerpts selected by the AICPA as relevant to a Statement on Auditing Standards, issued by its Auditing Standards Executive Committee, captioned "Inquiry of a Client's Lawyer Concerning Litigation, Claims, and Assessments."

5.2 Lawyer's Response

Concepts of probability inherent in the usage of terms like "probable" or "reasonably possible" or "remote" mean different things in different contexts. Generally, the outcome of, or the loss which may result from, litigation cannot be assessed in any way that is comparable to a statistically or empirically determined concept of "probability" that may be applicable when determining such matters as reserves for warranty obligations or accounts receivable or loan losses when there is a large number of transactions and a substantial body of known historical experience for the enterprise or comparable enterprises. While lawyers are accustomed to counseling clients during the progress of litigation as to the possible amount required for settlement purposes, the estimated risks of the proceedings at particular times and the possible application or establishment of points of law that may be relevant, such advice to the client is not possible at many stages of the litigation and may change dramatically depending upon the development of the proceedings. Lawyers do not generally quantify for clients the "odds" in numerical terms; if they do, the quantification is generally only undertaken in an effort to make meaningful, for limited purposes, a whole host of judgmental factors applicable at a particular time, without any intention to depict "probability" in any statistical, scientific or empirically-grounded sense. Thus, for example, statements that litigation is being defended vigorously and that the client has meritorious defenses do not, and do not purport to, make a statement about the probability of outcome in any measurable sense.

Likewise, the "amount" of loss—that is, the total of costs and damages that ultimately might be assessed against a client—will, in most litigation, be a subject of wide possible variance at most stages; it is the rare case where the amount is precise and where the question is whether the client against which claim is made is liable either for all of it or none of it.

In light of the foregoing considerations, it must be concluded that, as a general rule, it should not be anticipated that meaningful quantifications of "probability" of outcome or amount of damages can be given by lawyers in assessing litigation. To provide content to the definitions set forth in Paragraph 5 of the Statement of Policy, this Commentary amplifies the meanings of the terms under discussion, as follows:

> *"probable"*—An unfavorable outcome is normally "probable" if, but only if, investigation, preparation (including development of the factual data and legal research) and progress of the matter have reached a stage where a judgment can be made, taking all relevant factors into account which may affect the outcome, that it is extremely doubtful that the client will prevail.
>
> *"remote"*—The prospect for an unfavorable outcome appears, at the time, to be slight; i.e., it is extremely doubtful that the client will not prevail. Normally, this would entail the ability to make an unqualified judgment, taking into account all relevant factors which may affect the outcome, that the client may confidently expect to prevail on a motion for summary judgment on all issues due to the clarity of the facts and the law.

In other words, for purposes of the lawyer's response to the request to advise auditors about litigation, an unfavorable outcome will be "probable" only if the chances of the client prevailing appear slight and of the claimant losing appear extremely doubtful; it will be "remote" when the client's chances of losing appear slight and of not winning appear extremely doubtful. It is, therefore, to be anticipated that, in most situations, an unfavorable outcome will be neither "probable" nor "remote" as defined in the Statement of Policy.

The discussion above about the very limited basis for furnishing judgments about the outcome of litigation applies with even more force to a judgment concerning whether or not the assertion of a claim not yet asserted is "probable." That judgment will infrequently be one within the professional competence of lawyers and therefore the lawyer should not undertake such assessment except where such judgment may become meaningful because of the presence of special circumstances, such as catastrophes, investigations and previous public disclosure as cited in Paragraph 5 of the Statement of Policy, or similar extrinsic evidence relevant to such assessment. Moreover, it is unlikely, absent relevant extrinsic evidence, that the client or anyone else will be in a position to make an informed judgment that assertion of a possible claim is "probable" as opposed to "reasonably possible" (in which event disclosure is not required). In light of the legitimate concern that the public interest would not be well served by resolving uncertainties in a way that invites the assertion of claims or otherwise causes unnecessary harm to the client and its stockholders, a decision to treat an unasserted claim as "probable" of assertion should be based only upon compelling judgment.

Consistent with these limitations believed appropriate for the lawyer, he should not represent to the auditor, nor should any inference from his response be drawn, that the unasserted possible claims identified by the client (as contemplated by Paragraph 5(c) of the Statement of Policy) represent all such claims of which the lawyer may be aware or that he necessarily concurs in his client's determination of which unasserted possible claims warrant specification by the client; within proper limits, this determination is one which the client is entitled to make—and should make—and it would be inconsistent with his professional obligations for the lawyer to volunteer information arising from his confidential relationship with his client.

As indicated in Paragraph 5, the lawyer also may be asked to estimate the potential loss (or range) in the event that an unfavorable outcome is not viewed to be "remote." In such a case, the lawyer would provide an estimate only if he believes that the probability of inaccuracy of the estimate of the range or amount is slight. What is meant here is that the estimate of amount of loss presents the same difficulty as assessment of outcome and that the same formulation of "probability" should be used with respect to the determination of estimated loss amounts as should be used with respect to estimating the outcome of the matter.

In special circumstances, with the proper consent of the client, the lawyer may be better able to provide the auditor with information concerning loss contingencies through conferences where there is opportunity for more detailed discussion and interchange. However, the principles set forth in the Statement of Policy and this Commentary are fully applicable to such conferences.

Subsumed throughout this discussion is the ongoing responsibility of the lawyer to assist his client, at the client's request, in complying with the requirements of FAS 5 to the extent such assistance falls within his professional competence. This will continue to involve, to the extent appropriate, privileged discussions with the client to provide a better basis on which the client can make accrual and disclosure determinations in respect of its financial statements.

In addition to the considerations discussed above with respect to the making of any judgment or estimate by the lawyer in his response to the auditor, including with respect to a matter specifically identified by the client, the lawyer should also bear in mind the risk that the furnishing of such a judgment or estimate to any one other than the client might constitute an admission or be otherwise prejudicial to the client's position in its defense against such litigation or claim (see Paragraph 1 of the Statement of Policy and of this Commentary).

Paragraph 6 (Lawyer's Professional Responsibility)

The client must satisfy whatever duties it has relative to timely disclosure, including appropriate disclosure concerning material loss contingencies, and, to the extent such matters are given substantive attention in the form of legal consultation, the lawyer, when his engagement is to advise his client concerning a disclosure obligation, has a responsibility to advise his client concerning its obligations in this regard. Although lawyers who normally confine themselves to a legal specialty such as tax, antitrust, patent or admiralty law, unlike lawyers consulted about SEC or general corporate matters, would not be expected to advise generally concerning the client's disclosure obligations in respect of a matter on which the lawyer is working, the legal specialist should counsel his client with respect to the client's obligations under FAS 5 to the extent contemplated herein. Without regard to legal specialty, the lawyer should be mindful of his professional responsibility to the client described in Paragraph 6 of the Statement of Policy concerning disclosure.

The lawyer's responsibilities with respect to his client's disclosure obligations have been a subject of considerable discussion and there may be, in due course, clarification and further guidance in this regard. In any event, where in the lawyer's view it is clear that (i) the matter is of material importance and seriousness, and (ii) there can be no reasonable doubt that its non-disclosure in the client's financial statements would be a violation of law giving rise to material claims, rejection by the client of his advice to call the matter to the attention of the auditor would almost certainly require the lawyer's withdrawal from employment in accordance with the Code of Professional Responsibility. (See, e.g., Disciplinary Rule 7-102 (A)(3) and (7), and Disciplinary Rule 2-110 (B)(2).) Withdrawal under such circumstances is obviously undesirable and might present serious problems for the client. Accordingly, in the context of financial accounting and reporting for loss contingencies arising from unasserted claims, the standards for which are contained in FAS 5, clients should be urged to disclose to the auditor information concerning an unasserted possible claim or assessment (not otherwise specifically identified by the client) where in the course of the services performed for the client it has become clear to the lawyer that (i) the client has no reasonable basis to conclude that assertion of the claim is not probable (employing the concepts hereby enunciated) and (ii) given the probability of assertion, disclosure of the loss contingency in the client's financial statements is beyond reasonable dispute required.

Paragraph 7 (Limitation on Use of Response)

Some inquiry letters make specific reference to, and one might infer from others, an intention to quote verbatim or include the substance of the lawyer's reply in footnotes to the client's financial statements. Because the client's prospects in pending litigation may shift as a result of interim developments, and because the lawyer should have an opportunity, if quotation is to be made, to review the footnote in full, it would seem prudent to limit the use of the lawyer's reply letter. Paragraph 7 sets out such a limitation.

Paragraph 7 also recognizes that it may be in the client's interest to protect information contained in the lawyer's response to the auditor, if and to the extent possible, against unnecessary further disclosure or use beyond its intended purpose of informing the auditor. For example, the response may contain information which could prejudice efforts to negotiate a favorable settlement of a pending litigation described in the response. The requirement of consent to further disclosure, or of reasonable advance notice where disclosure may be required by court process or necessary in defense of the audit, is designed to give the lawyer an opportunity to consult with the client as to whether consent should be refused or limited or, in the case of legal process or the auditor's defense of the audit, as to whether steps can and should be taken to challenge the necessity of further disclosure or to seek protective measures in connection therewith. It is believed that the suggested standard of twenty days advance notice would normally be a minimum reasonable time for this purpose.

Paragraph 8 (General)

It is reasonable to assume that the Statement of Policy will receive wide distribution and will be readily available to the accounting profession. Specifically, the Statement of Policy has been reprinted as Exhibit II to the Statement on Auditing Standards, "Inquiry of a Client's Lawyer Concerning Litigation, Claims, and Assessments," issued by the Auditing Standards Executive Committee of the American Institute of Certified Public Accountants. Accordingly, the mechanic for its incorporation by reference will facilitate lawyer-auditor communication. The incorporation is intended to include not only limitations, such as those provided by Paragraphs 2 and 7 of the Statement of Policy, but also the explanatory material set forth in this Commentary.

Annex A

[Illustrative forms of letters for full response by outside practitioner or law firm and inside general counsel to the auditor's inquiry letter. These illustrative forms, which are not part of the Statement of Policy, have been prepared by the Committee on Audit Inquiry Responses solely in order to assist those who may wish to have, for reference purposes, a form of response which incorporates the principles of the Statement of Policy and accompanying Commentary. Other forms of response letters will be appropriate depending on the circumstances.]

Illustrative form of letter for use by outside practitioner or law firm:

[Name and Address of Accounting Firm]

Re: [Name of Client] [and Subsidiaries]

Dear Sirs:

By letter date [*insert date of request*] Mr. [*insert name and title of officer signing request*] of [*insert name of client*] [(the "Company") or (together with its subsidiaries, the "Company")] has requested us to furnish you with certain information in connection with your examination of the accounts of the Company as at [*insert fiscal year-end*].

[Insert description of the scope of the lawyer's engagement; the following are sample descriptions:]

While this firm represents the Company on a regular basis, our engagement has been limited to specific matters as to which we were consulted by the Company.

[or]

We call your attention to the fact that this firm has during the past year represented the Company only in connection with certain [*Federal income tax matters*] [*litigation*] [*real estate transactions*] [*describe other specific matters, as appropriate*] and has not been engaged for any other purpose.

Subject to the foregoing and to the last paragraph of this letter, we advise you that since [*insert date of beginning of fiscal period under audit*] we have not been engaged to give substantive attention to, or represent the Company in connection with, [*material*]** loss contingencies coming within the scope of clause (*a*) of Paragraph 5 of the Statement of Policy referred to in the last paragraph of this letter, except as follows:

[Describe litigation and claims which fit the foregoing criteria.]

[If the inquiry letter requests information concerning specified unasserted possible claims or assessments and/or contractually assumed obligations:]

With respect to the matters specifically identified in the Company's letter and upon which comment has been specifically requested, as contemplated by clauses (*b*) or (*c*) of Paragraph 5 of the ABA Statement of Policy, we advise you, subject to the last paragraph of this letter, as follows:

[Insert information as appropriate]

The information set forth herein is [as of the date of this letter] [as of [*insert date*], the date on which we commenced our internal review procedures for purposes of preparing this response], except as otherwise noted, and we disclaim any undertaking to advise you of changes which thereafter may be brought to our attention.

[Insert information with respect to outstanding bills for services and disbursements.]

This response is limited by, and in accordance with, the ABA Statement of Policy Regarding Lawyers' Responses to Auditors' Requests for Information (December 1975); without limiting the generality of the foregoing, the limitations set forth in such Statement on the scope and use of this response (Paragraphs 2 and 7) are specifically incorporated herein by reference, and any description herein of any "loss contingencies" is qualified in its entirety by Paragraph 5 of the Statement and the accompanying Commentary (which is an integral part of the Statement). Consistent with the last sentence of Paragraph 6 of the ABA Statement of Policy and pursuant to the Company's request, this will confirm as correct the Company's understanding as set forth in its audit inquiry letter to us that whenever, in the course of performing legal services for the Company with respect to a matter recognized to involve an unasserted possible claim or assessment that may call for financial statement disclosure, we have formed a professional conclusion that the Company must disclose or consider disclosure concerning such possible claim or assessment, we, as a matter of professional responsibility to the Company, will so advise the Company and will consult with the Company concerning the question of such disclosure and the applicable requirements of Statement of Financial Accounting Standards No. 5. [Describe any other or additional limitation as indicated by Paragraph 4 of the Statement]

Very truly yours,

** ***Note:*** See Paragraph 3 of the Statement of Policy and the accompanying Commentary for guidance where the response is limited to material items.

Illustrative form of letter for use by inside general counsel:

[Name and Address of Accounting Firm]

Re: [Name of Company] [and Subsidiaries]

Dear Sirs:

As General Counsel# of [*insert name of client*] [(the "Company")] [(together with its subsidiaries, the "Company")], I advise you as follows in connection with your examination of the accounts of the Company as at [*insert fiscal year-end*].

I call your attention to the fact that as General Counsel# for the Company I have general supervision of the Company's legal affairs. [*If the general legal supervisory responsibilities of the person signing the letter are limited, set forth here a clear description of those legal matters over which such person exercises general supervision, indicating exceptions to such supervision and situations where primary reliance should be placed on other sources.*] In such capacity, I have reviewed litigation and claims threatened or asserted involving the Company and have consulted with outside legal counsel with respect thereto where I have deemed appropriate.

Subject to the foregoing and to the last paragraph of this letter, I advise you that since [*insert date of beginning of fiscal period under audit*] neither I, nor any of the lawyers over whom I exercise general legal supervision, have given substantive attention to, or represented the Company in connection with, [material]** loss contingencies coming within the scope of clause (*a*) of Paragraph 5 of the Statement of Policy referred to in the last paragraph of this letter, except as follows:

[Describe litigation and claims which fit the foregoing criteria.]

[If information concerning specified unasserted possible claims or assessments and/or contractually assumed obligations is to be supplied:]

With respect to matters which have been specifically identified as contemplated by clauses (*b*) or (*c*) of Paragraph 5 of the ABA Statement of Policy, I advise you, subject to the last paragraph of this letter, as follows:

[Insert information as appropriate]

The information set forth herein is [as of the date of this letter] as of [*insert date*], the date on which we commenced our internal review procedures for purposes of preparing this response], except as otherwise noted, and I disclaim any undertaking to advise you of changes which thereafter may be brought to my attention or to the attention of the lawyers over whom I exercise general legal supervision.

This response is limited by, and in accordance with, the ABA Statement of Policy Regarding Lawyers' Responses to Auditors' Requests for Information (December 1975); without limiting the generality of the foregoing, the limitations set forth in such Statement on the scope and use of this response (Paragraphs 2 and 7) are specifically incorporated herein by reference, and any description herein of any "loss contingencies" is qualified in its entirety by Paragraph 5 of the Statement and the accompanying Commentary (which is an integral part of the Statement). Consistent with the last sentence of Paragraph 6 of the ABA Statement of Policy, this will confirm as correct the Company's understanding that whenever, in the course of performing legal services for the Company with respect to a matter recognized to involve an unasserted

It may be appropriate in some cases for the response to be given by inside counsel other than inside general counsel in which event this letter should be appropriately modified.

** See footnote ** earlier in this section.

possible claim or assessment that may call for financial statement disclosure, I have formed a professional conclusion that the Company must disclose or consider disclosure concerning such possible claim or assessment, I, as a matter of professional responsibility to the Company, will so advise the Company and will consult with the Company concerning the question of such disclosure and the applicable requirements of Statement of Financial Accounting Standards No. 5.* [Describe any other or additional limitation as indicated by Paragraph 4 of the Statement.]

Very truly yours,

____

* See footnote * in paragraph (1) in this section.

AU Section 9337

Inquiry of a Client's Lawyer Concerning Litigation, Claims, and Assessments: Auditing Interpretations of Section 337

1. Specifying Relevant Date in an Audit Inquiry Letter

.01 *Question*—Should the auditor request the client to specify, in his audit inquiry letter to a lawyer prepared in accordance with section 337, *Inquiry of a Client's Lawyer Concerning Litigation, Claims, and Assessments*, the date by which the lawyer's response should be sent to the auditor. Also, should the letter request the lawyer to specify in his response the latest date covered by his review (the "effective date")?

.02 *Interpretation*—Yes. It should be recognized that, to adequately respond to an audit inquiry letter, lawyers will ordinarily employ some internal review procedures which will be facilitated by specifying the earliest acceptable effective date of the response and the latest date by which it should be sent to the auditor. Ordinarily, a two-week period should be allowed between the specified effective date of the lawyer's response and the latest date by which the response should be sent to the auditor. Clearly stating the relevant dates in the letter and specifying these dates to the lawyer in a timely manner will allow the responding lawyer an adequate amount of time to complete his review procedures and assist the auditor in coordinating the timing of the completion of his field work with the latest date covered by the lawyer's review.

.03 Further, the lawyer should be requested to specify the effective date of his response. If the lawyer's response does not specify an effective date, the auditor can assume that the date of the lawyer's response is the effective date.

[Issue Date: March 1977.]

2. Relationship Between Date of Lawyer's Response and Auditor's Report

.04 *Question*—The illustrative form of audit inquiry letter included in the appendix [section 337A] to section 337, *Inquiry of a Client's Lawyer Concerning Litigation, Claims, and Assessments*, requests a response as to matters that existed at the balance sheet date and during the period from that date to the date of the response. What is the relationship between the effective date of the lawyer's response and the date of the auditor's report, which is generally the date of the completion of field work?

.05 *Interpretation*—Section 560 paragraphs .10–.12 indicate that the auditor is concerned with events, which may require adjustments to, or disclosure in, the financial statements, occurring through the date of his or her report. Therefore, the latest date of the period covered by the lawyer's response (the "effective date") should be as close to the date of the auditor's report as is practicable in the circumstances. Consequently, specifying the effective date of the lawyer's response to reasonably approximate the expected date of the auditor's report will in most instances obviate the need for an updated response from the lawyer.

[Issue Date: March 1977; Revised: December 2005.]

3. Form of Audit Inquiry Letter When Client Represents That No Unasserted Claims and Assessments Exist

.06 *Question*—The illustrative audit inquiry letter included in the appendix [section 337A] to section 337, *Inquiry of a Client's Lawyer Concerning Litigation, Claims, and Assessments*, assumes that the client specifies certain unasserted claims and assessments. However, in some cases, clients have stated that there are no such claims or assessments (to be specified to the lawyer for comment) that are probable of assertion and that, if asserted, would have a reasonable possibility of an unfavorable outcome. What appropriate revision to the wording of the letter can be used in such situations?

.07 *Interpretation*—Wording that could be used in an audit inquiry letter, instead of the heading and first paragraph in the section relating to unasserted claims and assessments included in the appendix [section 337A] to section 337, when the client believes that there are no unasserted claims or assessments (to be specified to the lawyer for comment) that are probable of assertion and that, if asserted, would have a reasonable possibility of an unfavorable outcome as specified by Financial Accounting Standards Board *Accounting Standards Codification* 450, *Contingencies*, is as follows:

> *Unasserted claims and assessments*—We have represented to our auditors that there are no unasserted possible claims that you have advised us are probable of assertion and must be disclosed, in accordance with Financial Accounting Standards Board *Accounting Standards Codification* 450, *Contingencies*. (The second paragraph in the section relating to unasserted claims and assessments would not be altered.)

[Issue Date: March 1977; Revised: June 2009.]

4. Documents Subject to Lawyer-Client Privilege

.08 *Question*—Section 337, *Inquiry of a Client's Lawyer Concerning Litigation, Claims, and Assessments*, paragraph .05c, states: "Examine documents in the client's possession concerning litigation, claims, and assessments, including correspondence and invoices from lawyers." Would this include a review of documents at the client's location considered by the lawyer and the client to be subject to the lawyer-client privilege?

.09 *Interpretation*—No. Although ordinarily an auditor would consider the inability to review information that could have a significant bearing on his audit as a scope restriction, in recognition of the public interest in protecting the confidentiality of lawyer-client communications (see section 337 paragraph .13), section 337 paragraph .05(c) is not intended to require an auditor to examine documents that the client identifies as subject to the lawyer-client privilege. In the event of questions concerning the applicability of this privilege, the auditor may request confirmation from the client's counsel that the information is subject to that privilege and that the information was considered by the lawyer in responding to the audit inquiry letter or, if the matters are being handled by another lawyer, an identification of such lawyer for the purpose of sending him an audit inquiry letter.

[Issue Date: March 1977.]

5. Alternative Wording of the Illustrative Audit Inquiry Letter to a Client's Lawyer

.10 *Question*—The appendix [section 337A] of section 337, *Inquiry of a Client's Lawyer Concerning Litigation, Claims, and Assessments*, provides an illustrative audit inquiry letter to legal counsel. That inquiry letter is based on the assumptions that (1) management of the company has prepared and furnished to the auditor and has set forth in the audit inquiry letter a description and evaluation of pending or threatened litigation, claims, and assessments and (2) management has identified and specified for comment in the audit inquiry letter unasserted claims or assessments that are probable of assertion and that, if asserted, would have at least a reasonable possibility of an unfavorable outcome. In many engagements, circumstances may render certain portions of the illustrative letter inappropriate. For instance, many clients ask their lawyers to prepare the list that describes and evaluates pending or threatened litigation, claims, and assessments rather than have management furnish such information. How can the wording of the inquiry letter be modified to recognize circumstances that differ from those assumed in the illustrative letter and to be more specific regarding the timing of the lawyer's response?

.11 *Interpretation*—Section 337 paragraph .09, outlines the matters that should be covered in a letter of audit inquiry. Although section 337 provides an illustrative audit inquiry letter to legal counsel, it should be modified, if necessary, to fit the circumstances. The modified illustrative audit inquiry letter that follows is based on a typical situation: management requests the lawyer to prepare the list that describes and evaluates pending or threatened litigation, claims, and assessments, and also represents that there are no unasserted claims or assessments that are probable of assertion and that, if asserted, would have a reasonable possibility of an unfavorable outcome as specified by Financial Accounting Standards Board (FASB) *Accounting Standards Codification* (ASC) 450, *Contingencies*. It also includes a separate response section with language that clarifies the auditor's expectations regarding the timing of the lawyer's response.

> "In connection with an audit of our financial statements as of (balance-sheet date) and for the (period) then ended, please furnish our auditors, (name and address of auditors), with the information requested below concerning certain contingencies involving matters with respect to which you have devoted substantive attention on behalf of the Company in the form of legal consultation or representation." [When a materiality limit has been established based on an understanding between management and the auditor, the following sentence should be added: This request is limited to contingencies amounting to (amount) individually or items involving lesser amounts that exceed (amount) in the aggregate.]

.12 Pending or Threatened Litigation, Claims, and Assessments

"Regarding pending or threatened litigation, claims, and assessments, please include in your response: (1) the nature of each matter, (2) the progress of each matter to date, (3) how the Company is responding or intends to respond (for example, to contest the case vigorously or seek an out-of-court settlement), and (4) an evaluation of the likelihood of an unfavorable outcome and an estimate, if one can be made, of the amount or range of potential loss."

.13 Unasserted Claims and Assessments

"We have represented to our auditors that there are no unasserted possible claims or assessments that you have advised us are probable of assertion and must be disclosed in accordance with FASB ASC 450.[1] We understand that whenever, in the course of performing legal services for us with respect to a matter recognized to involve an unasserted possible claim or assessment that may call for financial statement disclosure, you have formed a professional conclusion that we should disclose or consider disclosure concerning such possible claim or assessment, as a matter of professional responsibility to us, you will so advise us and will consult with us concerning the question of such disclosure and the applicable requirements of FASB ASC 450. Please specifically confirm to our auditors that our understanding is correct."

.14 Response

"Your response should include matters that existed as of (balance-sheet date) and during the period from that date to the effective date of your response."

"Please specifically identify the nature of and reasons for any limitations on your response."

"Our auditors expect to have the audit completed about (expected completion date). They would appreciate receiving your reply by that date with a specified effective date no earlier than (ordinarily two weeks before expected completion date)."[2]

[Issue Date: June 1983; Revised: June 2009.]

6. Client Has Not Consulted a Lawyer

.15 *Question*—Section 337 paragraph .06 requires an auditor to request that the client's management send a letter of inquiry to those lawyers with whom management has consulted concerning litigation, claims, or assessments. In some instances, management may not have consulted a lawyer. In such circumstances, what should the auditor do to obtain sufficient, appropriate audit evidence regarding litigation, claims, and assessments?

.16 *Interpretation*—Section 337 is expressly limited to inquiry of lawyers with whom management has consulted. If the client has not consulted a lawyer, the auditor normally would rely on the review of internally available information as outlined in section 337 paragraph .05 and .07, and the written

---

[1] A parenthetical statement such as "(excerpts of which can be found in the ABA's *Auditor's Letter Handbook*)" might be added here if the auditor believes that it would be helpful to the lawyer's understanding of the requirements of Financial Accounting Standards Board (FASB) *Accounting Standards Codification* (ASC) 450, *Contingencies*. The *Auditor's Letter Handbook* contains, among other things, a copy of section 337, the ABA's *Statement of Policy Regarding Lawyers' Responses to Auditors' Requests for Information* (section 337C), and excerpts from FASB ASC 450. [Footnote revised, June 2009, to reflect conforming changes necessary due to the issuance of FASB ASC.]

[2] Two auditing interpretations (see Interpretation Nos. 1–2 of section 337 [par. .01–.05]) address relevant dates in an audit inquiry letter and the relationship between the date of the lawyer's response and the audit report date.

representation of management regarding litigation, claims, and assessments as required by section 333, *Management Representations*, paragraph .06*o* and *p*. In those circumstances, the representation regarding litigation, claims, and assessments might be worded as follows:

> We are not aware of any pending or threatened litigation, claims, or assessments or unasserted claims or assessments that are required to be accrued or disclosed in the financial statements in accordance with Financial Accounting Standards Board *Accounting Standards Codification* 450, *Contingencies*, and we have not consulted a lawyer concerning litigation, claims, or assessments.

.17 If information comes to the auditor's attention that may indicate potentially material litigation, claims, and assessments, the auditor should discuss with the client its possible need to consult legal counsel so that the client may evaluate its responsibility under Financial Accounting Standards Board *Accounting Standards Codification* 450, *Contingencies* to accrue or disclose loss contingencies. Depending on the severity of the matter, refusal by the client to consult legal counsel in those circumstances may result in a scope limitation, and the auditor should consider the effect of such a limitation on his audit report.

[Issue Date: June 1983; Revised: January 2004; Revised: March 2006; Revised: June 2009.]

7. Assessment of a Lawyer's Evaluation of the Outcome of Litigation

.18 *Question*—Section 337, *Inquiry of a Client's Lawyer Concerning Litigation, Claims, and Assessments*, paragraph .09*d*(2), states that a letter of audit inquiry should include a request for the lawyer's evaluation of the likelihood of an unfavorable outcome of pending or threatened litigation, claims, and assessments to which he has devoted substantive attention. However, written responses from lawyers vary considerably and may contain evaluation wording that is vague or ambiguous and, thus, of limited use to the auditor. What constitutes a clear response and what should the auditor do if he considers the response unclear?

.19 *Interpretation*—The American Bar Association's *Statement of Policy Regarding Lawyers' Responses to Auditors' Requests for Information* (ABA Statement) is reprinted as exhibit II [section 337C] to section 337. While paragraph 5 of the ABA statement [section 337C] states that the lawyer "may in appropriate circumstances communicate to the auditor his view that an unfavorable outcome is 'probable' or 'remote'," he is not required to use those terms in communicating his evaluation to the auditor. The auditor may find other wording sufficiently clear as long as the terms can be used to classify the outcome of the uncertainty under one of the three probability classifications established in Financial Accounting Standards Board *Accounting Standards Codification* 450, *Contingencies*.[3]

.20 Some examples of evaluations concerning litigation that may be considered to provide sufficient clarity that the likelihood of an unfavorable outcome is "remote" even though they do not use that term are:

- "We are of the opinion that this action will not result in any liability to the company."

---

[3] Financial Accounting Standards Board *Accounting Standards Codification* 450, *Contingencies*, uses the terms *probable*, *reasonably possible*, and *remote* to describe different degrees of likelihood that future events will confirm a loss or an impairment of an asset or incurrence of a liability, and the accounting standards for accrual and disclosure are based on those terms. [Footnote revised, June 2009, to reflect conforming changes necessary due to the issuance of FASB ASC.]

- "It is our opinion that the possible liability to the company in this proceeding is nominal in amount."
- "We believe the company will be able to defend this action successfully."
- "We believe that the plaintiff's case against the company is without merit."
- "Based on the facts known to us, after a full investigation, it is our opinion that no liability will be established against the company in these suits."

.21 Absent any contradictory information obtained by the auditor either in other parts of the lawyer's letter or otherwise, the auditor need not obtain further clarification of evaluations such as the foregoing.

.22 Because of inherent uncertainties described in section 337 paragraph .14 and in the ABA Policy Statement [section 337C], an evaluation furnished by the lawyer may indicate significant uncertainties or stipulations as to whether the client will prevail. The following are examples of lawyers' evaluations that are unclear as to the likelihood of an unfavorable outcome:

- "This action involves unique characteristics wherein authoritative legal precedents do not seem to exist. We believe that the plaintiff will have serious problems establishing the company's liability under the act; nevertheless, if the plaintiff is successful, the award may be substantial."
- "It is our opinion that the company will be able to assert meritorious defenses to this action." (The term "meritorious defenses" indicates that the company's defenses will not be summarily dismissed by the court; it does not necessarily indicate counsel's opinion that the company will prevail.)
- "We believe the action can be settled for less than the damages claimed."
- "We are unable to express an opinion as to the merits of the litigation at this time. The company believes there is absolutely no merit to the litigation." (If client's counsel, with the benefit of all relevant information, is unable to conclude that the likelihood of an unfavorable outcome is "remote," it is unlikely that management would be able to form a judgment to that effect.)
- "In our opinion, the company has a substantial chance of prevailing in this action." (A "substantial chance," a "reasonable opportunity," and similar terms indicate more uncertainty than an opinion that the company will prevail.)

.23 If the auditor is uncertain as to the meaning of the lawyer's evaluation, he should request clarification either in a follow-up letter or a conference with the lawyer and client, appropriately documented. If the lawyer is still unable to give an unequivocal evaluation of the likelihood of an unfavorable outcome in writing or orally, the auditor should look to the guidance in section 508 paragraphs .45–.49 to determine the effect, if any, of the lawyer's response on the auditor's report.

[Issue Date: June 1983; Revised: February 1997; Revised: June 2009.]

8. Use of the Client's Inside Counsel in the Evaluation of Litigation, Claims, and Assessments

.24 Question—Section 337 paragraph .06 requires an auditor to request that the client's management send a letter of inquiry to those lawyers with whom management has consulted concerning litigation, claims, and assessments. Sometimes, the client's inside general counsel or legal department (hereinafter referred to as "inside counsel") is handling litigation, claims, and assessments either exclusive of or in conjunction with outside lawyers. In such circumstances, when does inside counsel's response constitute sufficient, appropriate audit evidence regarding litigation, claims, and assessments?

.25 *Interpretation*—Section 337 paragraph .08 states that "Audit evidence obtained from the client's inside general counsel or legal department may provide the auditor with the necessary corroboration." Inside counsel can range from one lawyer to a large staff, with responsibilities ranging from specific internal matters to a comprehensive coverage of all of the client's legal needs, including litigation with outside parties. Because both inside counsel and outside lawyers are bound by the ABA's Code of Professional Responsibilities, there is no difference in their professional obligations and responsibilities. In some circumstances, outside lawyers, if used at all, may be used only for limited purposes, such as data accumulation or account collection activity. In such circumstances, inside counsel has the primary responsibility for corporate legal matters and is in the best position to know and precisely describe the status of all litigation, claims, and assessments or to corroborate information furnished by management.

.26 Audit inquiry letters should be sent to those lawyers, which may be either inside counsel or outside lawyers, who have the primary responsibility for, and knowledge about, particular litigation, claims, and assessments. If inside counsel in handling litigation, claims, and assessments exclusively, their evaluation and response ordinarily would be considered adequate. Similarly, if both inside counsel and outside lawyers have been involved in the matters, but inside counsel ha s assumed the primary responsibility for the matters, inside counsel's evaluation may well be considered adequate.[4] However, there may be circumstances when litigation, claims, or assessments involving substantial overall participation by outside lawyers are of such significance to the financial statements that the auditor should consider obtaining the outside lawyers' response that they have not formulated a substantive conclusion that differs in any material respect from inside counsel's evaluation, even though inside counsel may have primary responsibility.

.27 If both inside counsel and outside lawyers have devoted substantive attention to a legal matter, but their evaluations of the possible outcome differ, the auditor should discuss the differences with the parties involved. Failure to reach agreement between the lawyers may require the auditor to consider appropriate modification of his audit report.

[Issue Date: June 1983; Revised: March 2006.]

9. Use of Explanatory Language About the Attorney-Client Privilege or the Attorney Work-Product Privilege

.28 *Question*—In some cases, in order to emphasize the preservation of the attorney-client privilege or the attorney work-product privilege, some clients

---

[4] This does not alter the caveat in section 337 paragraph .08 that "evidential matter obtained from inside counsel is not a substitute for information outside counsel refuses to furnish."

have included the following or substantially similar language in the audit inquiry letter to legal counsel:

> We do not intend that either our request to you to provide information to our auditor or your response to our auditor should be construed in any way to constitute a waiver of the attorney-client privilege or the attorney work-product privilege.

For the same reason, some lawyers have included the following or substantially similar language in their response letters to auditors:

> The Company [OR OTHER DEFINED TERM] has advised us that, by making the request set forth in its letter to us, the Company [OR OTHER DEFINED TERM] does not intend to waive the attorney-client privilege with respect to any information which the Company [OR OTHER DEFINED TERM] has furnished to us. Moreover, please be advised that our response to you should not be construed in any way to constitute a waiver of the protection of the attorney work-product privilege with respect to any of our files involving the Company [OR OTHER DEFINED TERM].

Does the explanatory language about the attorney-client privilege or the attorney work-product privilege result in a limitation on the scope of the audit?

.29 *Answer*—No. According to the *Report by the American Bar Association's Subcommittee on Audit Inquiry Responses*, explanatory language similar to the foregoing in the letters of the client or the lawyer is not a limitation on the scope of the lawyer's response. The report states that such language simply makes explicit what has always been implicit, namely, the language states clearly that neither the client nor the lawyer intended a waiver. The report further states that non-inclusion of either or both of the foregoing statements by the client or the lawyer in their respective letters at any time in the past or the future would not constitute an expression of intent to waive the privileges. The *Report by the American Bar Association's Subcommittee on Audit Inquiry Responses* is reprinted in paragraph .30.

.30 Report of the Subcommittee on Audit Inquiry Responses*

Because of a recent court case and other judicial decisions involving lawyers' responses to auditors' requests for information, an area of uncertainty or concern has been brought to the Subcommittee's attention and is the subject of the following comment:

This Committee's report does not modify the ABA Statement of Policy, nor does it constitute an interpretation thereof. The Preamble to the ABA Statement of Policy states as follows:

> Both the Code of Professional Responsibility and the cases applying the evidentiary privilege recognize that the privilege against disclosure can be knowingly and voluntarily waived by the client. It is equally clear that disclosure to a third party may result in loss of the "confidentiality" essential to maintain the privilege. Disclosure to a third party of the lawyer-client communication on a particular subject may also destroy the privilege as to other communications on that subject. Thus, the mere disclosure by the lawyer to the outside auditor, with due client consent, of the substance of communications between the lawyer and client may significantly impair the client's ability in other contexts to maintain the confidentiality of such communications.

---

* "Excerpted from 'Statement of Policy Regarding Lawyers' Responses to Auditors' Requests for Information,' *The Business Lawyer*, vol. 31, no. 3, April 1976, copyright 1976 American Bar Association, reprinted by permission of the American Bar Association."

Under the circumstances a policy of audit procedure which requires clients to give consent and authorize lawyers to respond to general inquiries and disclose information to auditors concerning matters which have been communicated in confidence is essentially destructive of free and open communication and early consultation between lawyer and client. The institution of such a policy would inevitably discourage management from discussing potential legal problems with counsel for fear that such discussion might become public and precipitate a loss to or possible liability of the business enterprise and its stockholders that might otherwise never materialize.

It is also recognized that our legal, political, and economic systems depend to an important extent on public confidence in published financial statements. To meet this need the accounting profession must adopt and adhere to standards and procedures that will command confidence in the auditing process. It is not, however, believed necessary, or sound public policy, to intrude upon the confidentiality of the lawyer-client relationship in order to command such confidence. On the contrary, the objective of fair disclosure in financial statements is more likely to be better served by maintaining the integrity of the confidential relationship between lawyer and client, thereby strengthening corporate management's confidence in counsel and to act in accordance with counsel's advice.

Paragraph (1) of the ABA Statement of Policy provides as follows:

(1) *Client Consent to Response.* The lawyer may properly respond to the auditor's requests for information concerning loss contingencies (the term and concept established by Statement of Financial Accounting Standards No. 5,† promulgated by the Financial Accounting Standards Board in March 1975 and discussed in Paragraph 5.1 of the accompanying commentary), to the extent hereinafter set forth, subject to the following:

(a) Assuming that the client's initial letter requesting the lawyer to provide information to the auditor is signed by an agent of the client having apparent authority to make such a request, the lawyer may provide to the auditor information requested, without further consent, unless such information discloses a confidence or a secret or requires an evaluation of a claim.

(b) In the normal case, the initial request letter does not provide the necessary consent to the disclosure of a confidence or secret or to the evaluation of a claim since that consent may only be given after full disclosure to the client of the legal consequences of such action.

(c) Lawyers should bear in mind, in evaluating claims, that an adverse party may assert that any evaluation of potential liability is an admission.

(d) In securing the client's consent to the disclosure of confidences or secrets, or the evaluation of claims, the lawyer may wish to have a draft of his letter reviewed and approved by the client before releasing it to the auditor; in such cases, additional explanation would in all probability be necessary so that the legal consequences of the consent are fully disclosed to the client.

In order to preserve explicitly the evidentiary privileges, some lawyers have suggested that clients include language in the following or substantially similar form:

---

† In July 2009, the Financial Accounting Standards Board (FASB) issued FASB *Accounting Standards Codification*™ (ASC) as authoritative. FASB ASC is now the source of authoritative U.S. accounting and reporting standards for nongovernmental entities, in addition to guidance issued by the Securities and Exchange Commission. As of July 1, 2009, all other nongrandfathered, non-SEC accounting literature not included in FASB ASC became nonauthoritative. FASB Statement No. 5, *Accounting for Contingencies*, has been codified as FASB ASC 450, *Contingencies*.

> We do not intend that either our request to you to provide information to our auditor or your response to our auditor should be construed in any way to constitute a waiver of the attorney-client privilege or the attorney work-product privilege.

If client's request letter does not contain language similar to that in the preceding paragraph, the lawyer's statement that the client has so advised him or her may be based upon the fact that the client has in fact so advised the lawyer, in writing or orally, in other communications or in discussions.

For the same reason, the response letter from some lawyers also includes language in the following or substantially similar form:

> The Company [OR OTHER DEFINED TERM] has advised us that, by making the request set forth in its letter to us, the Company [OR OTHER DEFINED TERM] does not intend to waive the attorney-client privilege with respect to any information which the Company [OR OTHER DEFINED TERM] has furnished to us. Moreover, please be advised that our response to you should not be construed in any way to constitute a waiver of the protection of the attorney work-product privilege with respect to any of our files involving the Company [OR OTHER DEFINED TERM].

We believe that language similar to the foregoing in letters of the client or the lawyer simply makes explicit what has always been implicit, namely, it expressly states clearly that neither the client nor the lawyer intended a waiver. It follows that non-inclusion of either or both of the foregoing statements by the client or the lawyer in their respective letters at any time in the past or the future would not constitute an expression of intent to waive the privileges.

On the other hand, the inclusion of such language does not necessarily assure the client that, depending on the facts and circumstances, a waiver may not be found by a court of law to have occurred.

We do not believe that the foregoing types of inclusions cause a negative impact upon the public policy considerations described in the Preamble to the ABA Statement of Policy nor do they intrude upon the arrangements between the legal profession and the accounting profession contemplated by the ABA Statement of Policy. Moreover, we do not believe that such language interferes in any way with the standards and procedures of the accounting profession in the auditing process nor should it be construed as a limitation upon the lawyer's reply to the auditors. We have been informed that the Auditing Standards Board of the AICPA has adopted an interpretation of SAS 12 recognizing the propriety of these statements.

Lawyers, in any case, should be encouraged to have their draft letters to auditors reviewed and approved by the client before releasing them to the auditors and may wish to explain to the client the legal consequences of the client's consent to lawyer's response as contemplated by subparagraph 1(*d*) of the Statement of Policy.

December 1989

[Issue Date: February, 1990.]

10. Use of Explanatory Language Concerning Unasserted Possible Claims or Assessments in Lawyers' Responses to Audit Inquiry Letters

.31 *Question*—In order to emphasize the preservation of the attorney-client privilege with respect to unasserted possible claims or assessments, some lawyers include the following or substantially similar language in their responses to audit inquiry letters:

"Please be advised that pursuant to clauses (*b*) and (*c*) of Paragraph 5 of the ABA Statement of Policy [American Bar Association's *Statement of Policy Regarding Lawyers' Responses to Auditors' Requests for Information*] and related Commentary referred to in the last paragraph of this letter, it would be inappropriate for this firm to respond to a general inquiry relating to the existence of unasserted possible claims or assessments involving the Company. We can only furnish information concerning those unasserted possible claims or assessments upon which the Company has specifically requested in writing that we comment. We also cannot comment upon the adequacy of the Company's listing, if any, of unasserted possible claims or assessments or its assertions concerning the advice, if any, about the need to disclose same."

Does the inclusion of this or similar language result in a limitation on the scope of the audit?

.32 *Interpretation*—No. Additional language similar to the foregoing in a letter of a lawyer is not a limitation on the scope of the audit. However, the ABA Statement of Policy [section 337C] and the understanding between the legal and accounting professions assumes that the lawyer, under certain circumstances, will advise and consult with the client concerning the client's obligation to make financial statement disclosure with respect to unasserted possible claims or assessments.[5] Confirmation of this understanding should be included in the lawyer's response.

[Issue Date: January 1997; Revised: June 2009.]

---

[5] See paragraph 6 of the ABA Statement of Policy [section 337C] and its commentary [section 337C]. In addition, Annex A to the ABA Statement of Policy [section 337C] contains the following illustrative language in the lawyers' response letter to the auditors:

> Consistent with the last sentence of Paragraph 6 of the ABA Statement of Policy and pursuant to the Company's request, this will confirm as correct the Company's understanding as set forth in its audit inquiry letter to us that whenever, in the course of performing legal services for the Company with respect to a matter recognized to involve an unasserted possible claim or assessment that may call for financial statement disclosure, we have formed a professional conclusion that the Company must disclose or consider disclosure concerning such possible claim or assessment, we, as a matter of professional responsibility to the Company, will so advise the Company and will consult with the Company concerning the question of such disclosure and the applicable requirements of FASB Statement No. 5, *Accounting for Contingencies*.

[See footnote †.] [Footnote revised, June 2009, to reflect conforming changes necessary due to the issuance of FASB ASC.]

AU Section 339

Audit Documentation

(Supersedes SAS No. 96.)

Source: SAS No. 103.

See section 9339 for interpretations of this section.

Effective for audits of financial statements for periods ending on or after December 15, 2006.

Introduction

.01 The purpose of this section is to establish standards and provide guidance on audit documentation. The exercise of professional judgment is integral in applying the provisions of this section. For example, professional judgment is used in determining the quantity, type, and content of audit documentation consistent with this section.

.02 Other Statement on Auditing Standards contain specific documentation requirements (see appendix A [paragraph .36]). Additionally, specific documentation or document retention requirements may be included in other standards (for example, government auditing standards), laws, and regulations applicable to the engagement.

.03 The auditor must prepare audit documentation in connection with each engagement in sufficient detail to provide a clear understanding of the work performed (including the nature, timing, extent, and results of audit procedures performed), the audit evidence obtained and its source, and the conclusions reached. Audit documentation:

a. Provides the principal support for the representation in the auditor's report that the auditor performed the audit in accordance with generally accepted auditing standards.

b. Provides the principal support for the opinion expressed regarding the financial information or the assertion to the effect that an opinion cannot be expressed.

.04 Audit documentation is an essential element of audit quality. Although documentation alone does not guarantee audit quality, the process of preparing sufficient and appropriate documentation contributes to the quality of an audit.

.05 Audit documentation is the record of audit procedures performed, relevant audit evidence obtained, and conclusions the auditor reached. Audit documentation, also known as working papers or workpapers, may be recorded on paper or on electronic or other media. When transferring or copying paper documentation to another media, the auditor should apply procedures to generate a copy that is faithful in form and content to the original paper document.[1]

---

[1] There may be legal, regulatory, or other reasons to retain the original paper document.

.06 Audit documentation includes, for example, audit programs,[2] analyses, issues memoranda, summaries of significant findings or issues, letters of confirmation and representation, checklists, abstracts or copies of important documents, correspondence (including e-mail) concerning significant findings or issues, and schedules of the work the auditor performed. Abstracts or copies of the entity's records (for example, significant and specific contracts and agreements) should be included as part of the audit documentation if they are needed to enable an experienced auditor to understand the work performed and conclusions reached. The audit documentation for a specific engagement is assembled in an audit file.[3]

.07 The auditor need not retain in audit documentation superseded drafts of working papers or financial statements, notes that reflect incomplete or preliminary thinking, previous copies of documents corrected for typographical or other errors, and duplicates of documents.

.08 In addition to the objectives set out in paragraph .03, audit documentation serves a number of other purposes, including:

- Assisting the audit team to plan and perform the audit;
- Assisting auditors who are new to an engagement and review the prior year's documentation to understand the work performed as an aid in planning and performing the current engagement;
- Assisting members of the audit team responsible for supervision to direct and supervise the audit work, and to review the quality of work performed;
- Demonstrating the accountability of the audit team for its work by documenting the procedures performed, the audit evidence examined, and the conclusions reached;
- Retaining a record of matters of continuing significance to future audits of the same entity;
- Assisting quality control reviewers (for example, internal inspectors) who review documentation to understand how the engagement team reached significant conclusions and whether there is adequate evidential support for those conclusions;
- Enabling an experienced auditor to conduct inspections or peer reviews in accordance with applicable legal, regulatory, or other requirements; and
- Assisting a successor auditor who reviews a predecessor auditor's audit documentation.

.09 For the purposes of this section, *experienced auditor* means an individual (whether internal or external to the firm) who possesses the competencies and skills that would have enabled him or her to perform the audit. These competencies and skills include an understanding of (*a*) audit processes, (*b*) the SASs and applicable legal and regulatory requirements, (*c*) the business environment in which the entity operates, and (*d*) auditing and financial reporting issues relevant to the entity's industry.

---

[2] See paragraph .05 of section 311, *Planning and Supervision*, as amended, for guidance regarding preparation of audit programs.

[3] The audit documentation contained within the audit file may consist of cross-references to documentation for audit engagements with related entities. For example, the documentation for an audit of the financial statements of an employee benefit plan may consist partly of cross-references to the documentation of dual-purpose payroll-related tests performed in connection with the audit of the financial statements of the plan's sponsor.

Form, Content, and Extent of Audit Documentation

.10 The auditor should prepare audit documentation that enables an experienced auditor, having no previous connection to the audit, to understand:

a. The nature, timing, and extent of auditing procedures performed to comply with SASs and applicable legal and regulatory requirements;

b. The results of the audit procedures performed and the audit evidence obtained;

c. The conclusions reached on significant matters; and

d. That the accounting records agree or reconcile with the audited financial statements or other audited information.

.11 The form, content, and extent of audit documentation depend on the circumstances of the engagement and the audit methodology and tools used. Oral explanations on their own do not represent sufficient support for the work the auditor performed or conclusions the auditor reached but may be used by the auditor to clarify or explain information contained in the audit documentation. It is, however, neither necessary nor practicable to document every matter the auditor considers during the audit.

.12 In determining the form, content, and extent of audit documentation, the auditor should consider the following factors:

- The nature of the auditing procedures to be performed;
- The identified risk of material misstatement associated with the assertion, or account or class of transactions, including related disclosures;
- The extent of judgment involved in performing the work and evaluating the results;
- The significance of the audit evidence obtained to the assertion being tested;
- The nature and extent of exceptions identified; and
- The need to document a conclusion or the basis for a conclusion not readily determinable from the documentation of the work performed or evidence obtained.

.13 Certain matters, such as auditor independence and staff training, that are not engagement specific, may be documented either centrally within a firm or in the audit documentation for an audit engagement. Documentation of matters specific to a particular engagement should be included in the audit file for the specific engagement.

Significant Findings or Issues

.14 The auditor should document significant findings or issues, actions taken to address them (including any additional evidence obtained), and the basis for the final conclusions reached. Judging the significance of a finding or issue requires an objective analysis of the facts and circumstances. Significant findings or issues include, but are not limited to, the following:

a. Significant matters involving the selection, application, and consistency of accounting principles with regard to the financial statements, including related disclosures. Such matters include, but are not limited to (*1*) accounting for complex or unusual transactions or (*2*) accounting estimates and uncertainties and, if applicable, the related management assumptions.

b. Results of audit procedures indicating (*1*) that the financial information or disclosures could be materially misstated or (*2*) a need to revise the auditor's previous assessment of the risks of material misstatement and the auditor's responses to those risks.

c. Circumstances that cause the auditor significant difficulty in applying auditing procedures the auditor considered necessary,[4] for example, the lack of responsiveness to confirmation or information requests, or the lack of original documents.

d. Findings that could result in a modification of the auditor's report.

e. Audit adjustments. For purposes of this section, an audit adjustment is a correction of a misstatement of the financial information that is identified by the auditor, whether or not recorded by management, that could, either individually or when aggregated with other misstatements, have a material effect on the company's financial information.

.15 The auditor should document discussions of significant findings or issues with management and others on a timely basis, including responses. The audit documentation should include documentation of the significant findings or issues discussed, and when and with whom the discussions took place. It is not limited to documentation prepared by the auditor but may include other appropriate evidence, such as minutes of meetings prepared by the entity's personnel. Others with whom the auditor may discuss significant findings or issues include those charged with governance;[5] those responsible for the oversight of the financial reporting process; other personnel within the entity, for example, internal audit; and external parties, such as persons providing professional services to the entity.

.16 If the auditor has identified information that contradicts or is inconsistent with the auditor's final conclusions regarding a significant finding or issue, the auditor should document how the auditor addressed the contradiction or inconsistency in forming the conclusion.

.17 The documentation of how the auditor addressed the contradiction or inconsistency, however, does not imply that the auditor needs to retain documentation that is incorrect or superseded (except as required by paragraph .30). The documentation of the contradiction or inconsistency may include, but is not limited to, procedures performed in response to the information, and records documenting consultations on, or resolutions of, differences in professional judgment among members of the engagement team or between the engagement team and others consulted.

Identification of Preparer and Reviewer

.18 In documenting the nature, timing, and extent of audit procedures performed, the auditor should record:

a. Who performed the audit work and the date such work was completed; and

---

[4] See paragraphs .34*b* and .39 of section 380, *The Auditor's Communication With Those Charged With Governance*, for guidance regarding communication with those charged with governance of any serious difficulties encountered in dealing with management related to the performance of the audit. [Footnote revised, February 2008, to reflect conforming changes necessary due to the effective date of Statement on Auditing Standards No. 114.]

[5] The term *those charged with governance* means the person(s) with responsibility for overseeing the strategic direction of the entity and obligations related to the accountability of the entity. This includes overseeing the financial reporting and disclosure process. In some cases, those charged with governance are responsible for approving the financial statements (in other cases, management has this responsibility). For entities with a board of directors, this term encompasses the term *board of directors* or *audit committees* expressed elsewhere in the Statements on Auditing Standards.

b. Who reviewed specific audit documentation and the date of such review.

.19 The requirement to document who reviewed the audit work performed does not imply a need for each specific working paper to include evidence of review. It should be clear from the audit documentation who reviewed specified elements of the audit work performed and when.

Documentation of Specific Items Tested

.20 Audit documentation of procedures performed, including tests of operating effectiveness of controls and substantive tests of details that involve inspection of documents or confirmation should include the identifying characteristics of the specific items tested.

.21 Recording the identifying characteristics serves a number of purposes. For example, it improves the ability of the auditor to supervise and review the work performed and thus demonstrates the accountability of the audit team for its work and facilitates the investigation of exceptions or inconsistencies. Identifying characteristics will vary with the nature of the audit procedure and the subject matter. For example:

- For a detailed test of entity-generated purchase orders, the auditor may identify the documents selected for testing by their dates and unique purchase order numbers.
- For a procedure requiring selection or review of all items over a specific amount from a given population, the auditor may record the scope of the procedure and identify the population (for example, all journal entries over $25,000 from the journal register).
- For a procedure requiring inquiries of specific entity personnel, the auditor may record the dates of the inquiries, the names and job designations of the entity personnel, and the inquiry made.
- For an observation procedure, the auditor may record the process or subject matter being observed, the relevant individuals, their respective responsibilities, and where and when the observation was carried out.
- For a procedure requiring systematic sampling from a population of documents, the auditor may identify the documents selected by recording their source, the starting point, and the sampling interval (for example, a systematic sample of shipping reports was selected from the shipping log for the period from X to Y, starting with report number 14564 and selecting every 250th report from that point).

Documentation of Departures From Statements on Auditing Standards

.22 As required by paragraph .04 of section 150, *Generally Accepted Auditing Standards*, as amended, when, in rare circumstances, the auditor departs from a presumptively mandatory requirement, the auditor must document in the working papers his or her justification for the departure and how the alternative procedures performed in the circumstances were sufficient to achieve the objectives of the presumptively mandatory requirement.

Revisions to Audit Documentation After the Date of the Auditor's Report

.23 The auditor's report should not be dated earlier than the date on which the auditor has obtained sufficient appropriate audit evidence to support the opinion. Among other things, sufficient appropriate audit evidence includes evidence that the audit documentation has been reviewed and that the entity's financial statements, including disclosures, have been prepared and that management has asserted that it has taken responsibility for them. This will ordinarily result in a report date that is close to the date the auditor grants the entity permission to use the auditor's report in connection with the financial statements (report release date).[6] Delays in releasing the report may require the auditor to perform additional procedures to comply with the requirements of section 560, *Subsequent Events*, as amended.

Documentation of New Information

.24 If, as a result of consideration of the procedures performed and the evidence obtained, the auditor concludes that procedures considered necessary at the time of the audit in the circumstances then existing were omitted from the audit of the financial information, the auditor should follow the guidance in section 390, *Consideration of Omitted Procedures After the Report Date*. The audit documentation supporting the auditor's compliance with section 390 should be prepared in accordance with the requirements in this section.

.25 If the auditor subsequently becomes aware of information relating to financial information previously reported on by him or her, but that was not known to him or her at the date of the report, the auditor should follow the guidance in section 561, *Subsequent Discovery of Facts Existing at the Date of the Auditor's Report*, as amended.

.26 In the circumstances described in paragraphs .24–.25, the auditor should make the changes necessary to reflect either the performance of the new audit procedure or the new conclusion reached, including:

- When and by whom such changes were made and (where applicable) reviewed;
- The specific reasons for the changes; and
- The effect, if any, of the changes on the auditor's conclusions.

Changes Resulting From the Process of Assembling and Completing the Audit File

.27 The auditor should complete the assembly of the final audit file on a timely basis, but within 60 days following the report release date (documentation completion date). Statutes, regulations, or the audit firm's quality control policies may specify a shorter period of time in which this assembly process should be completed.

---

[6] In many cases, the report release date will be the date the auditor delivers the audit report to the entity.

.28 At anytime prior to the documentation completion date, the auditor may make changes to the audit documentation to:

a. Complete the documentation and assembly of audit evidence that the auditor has obtained, discussed, and agreed with relevant members of the audit team prior to the date of the auditor's report;

b. Perform routine file-assembling procedures such as deleting or discarding superseded documentation and sorting, collating, and cross-referencing final working papers;

c. Sign off on file completion checklists prior to completing and archiving the audit file; and

d. Add information received after the date of the auditor's report, for example, an original confirmation that was previously faxed.

.29 The report release date should be recorded in the audit documentation.

Changes After the Documentation Completion Date

.30 After the documentation completion date, the auditor must not delete or discard audit documentation before the end of the specified retention period, as discussed in paragraph .32. When the auditor finds it necessary to make an addition (including amendments) to audit documentation after the documentation completion date, the auditor should document the addition in accordance with paragraph .26.

Ownership and Confidentiality of Audit Documentation

.31 Audit documentation is the property of the auditor, and some states recognize this right of ownership in their statutes. The auditor may make available to the entity at the auditor's discretion copies of the audit documentation, provided such disclosure does not undermine the independence or the validity of the audit process.

.32 The auditor should adopt reasonable procedures to retain and access audit documentation for a period of time sufficient to meet the needs of his or her practice and to satisfy any applicable legal or regulatory requirements for records retention. Such retention period, however, should not be shorter than five years from the report release date. Statutes, regulations, or the audit firm's quality control policies may specify a longer retention period.

.33 The auditor has an ethical and, in some situations, a legal obligation to maintain the confidentiality of client information.[7] Because audit documentation often contains confidential client information, the auditor should adopt reasonable procedures to maintain the confidentiality of that information.

.34 Whether audit documentation is in paper, electronic, or other media, the integrity, accessibility, and retrievability of the underlying data may be compromised if the documentation could be altered, added to, or deleted without the auditor's knowledge, or could be permanently lost or damaged. Accordingly, the auditor should apply appropriate and reasonable controls for audit documentation to:

a. Clearly determine when and by whom audit documentation was created, changed, or reviewed;

---

[7] Also, see Rule 301, *Confidential Client Information.*

b. Protect the integrity of the information at all stages of the audit, especially when the information is shared within the audit team or transmitted to other parties via electronic means;

c. Prevent unauthorized changes to the documentation; and

d. Allow access to the documentation by the audit team and other authorized parties as necessary to properly discharge their responsibilities.

Effective Date

.35 This section is effective for audits of financial statements for periods ending on or after December 15, 2006. Earlier application is permitted.

.36

Appendix A

Audit Documentation Requirements in Other Statements on Auditing Standards

A1. Documentation requirements are included in other Statements on Auditing Standards (SASs). This section does not change the requirements in:

a. Paragraph .05*d* of section 337, *Inquiry of a Client's Lawyer Concerning Litigation, Claims, and Assessments*, to document in either the audit inquiry letter or a separate letter to the client's lawyer that the client has assured the auditor that the letter has disclosed all unasserted claims that the lawyer has advised the client are probable of assertion and must be disclosed in accordance with Financial Accounting Standards Board *Accounting Standards Codification* 450, *Contingencies*. Also, this section does not change the requirement in paragraph .10 of section 337 to document the conclusions reached as a result of responses obtained in a conference relating to matters covered by the audit inquiry letter.

b. Paragraph .08 of section 311, *Planning and Supervision*, to establish an understanding with the client regarding the services to be performed for each engagement and to document the understanding through a written communication with the client.

c. Paragraph .19 of section 311 to develop an audit plan in which the auditor documents the audit procedures to be used that, when performed, are expected to reduce audit risk to an acceptably low level. Paragraph .21 of section 311 requires the auditor to document changes to the original audit plan.

d. Paragraph .69 of section 312, *Audit Risk and Materiality in Conducting an Audit*, to document (*a*) the levels of materiality and tolerable misstatement, including any changes thereto, used in the audit and the basis on which those levels were determined; (*b*) a summary of uncorrected misstatements, other than those that are trivial, related to known and likely misstatements; (*c*) the auditor's conclusion as to whether uncorrected misstatements, individually or in aggregate, do or do not cause the financial statements to be materially misstated, and the basis for that conclusion; and (*d*) all known and likely misstatements identified by the auditor during the audit, other than those that are trivial, that have been corrected by management.

e. Paragraph .70 of section 312 to document uncorrected misstatements in a manner that allows the auditor to (*a*) separately consider the effects of known and likely misstatements, including uncorrected misstatements identified in prior periods; (*b*) consider the aggregate effect of misstatements on the financial statements; and (*c*) consider the qualitative factors that are relevant to the auditor's consideration whether misstatements are material.

f. Paragraph .122 of section 314, *Understanding the Entity and its Environment and Assessing the Risks of Material Misstatement*, to document (*a*) the discussion among the audit team regarding the susceptibility of the entity's financial statements to material misstatement due to error or fraud, including how and when the discussion occurred, the subject matter discussed, the audit team members who participated, and significant decisions reached concerning planned responses at the financial statement and relevant assertion levels; (*b*) key elements of the understanding obtained regarding each of the aspects of the entity and its environment identified in paragraph .21, including each of the components of internal control identified in paragraph .41, that assess the risks of material misstatement of the financial statements; the sources of information from which the understanding was obtained; and the risk assessment procedures; (*c*) the assessment of the risks of material misstatement both at the financial statement level and at the relevant assertion level as required by paragraph .102 and the basis for the assessment; and (*d*) the risks identified and related controls evaluated as a result of the requirements in paragraphs .110 and .117.

g. Paragraph .77 of section 318, *Performing Audit Procedures in Response to Assessed Risks and Evaluating the Audit Evidence Obtained*, to document (*a*) the overall responses to address the assessed risks of misstatement at the financial statement level; (*b*) the nature, timing, and extent of the further audit procedures; (*c*) the linkage of those procedures with the assessed risks at the relevant assertion level; (*d*) the results of the audit procedures; and (*e*) the conclusions reached with regard to the use in the current audit of audit evidence about the operating effectiveness of controls that was obtained in a prior audit.

h. Paragraph .02 of section 534, *Reporting on Financial Statements Prepared for Use in Other Countries*, to obtain written representations from management regarding the purpose and uses of financial statements prepared in conformity with the accounting principles of another country.

i. Paragraph .17 of section 317, *Illegal Acts by Clients*, to document oral communications to the audit committee or others with equivalent authority and responsibility regarding illegal acts that come to the auditor's attention.

j. Paragraph .22 of section 329, *Analytical Procedures*, to document (*a*) the expectation, where that expectation is not otherwise readily determinable from the documentation of the work performed, and factors considered in its development; (*b*) the results of the comparison of the expectation to the recorded amounts or ratios developed from recorded amounts; and (*c*) any additional auditing procedures performed in response to significant unexpected differences arising from the analytical procedure and the results of such additional procedures.

k. Paragraph .71 of section 508, *Reports on Audited Financial Statements*, for the predecessor auditor to obtain representation letters from management of the former client and from the successor auditor before reissuing (or consenting to the reissue of) a report previously issued on the financial statements of a prior period.

l. Paragraph .18 of section 341, *The Auditor's Consideration of an Entity's Ability to Continue as a Going Concern*, to document (*a*) the conditions or events that led him or her to believe that there is substantial doubt about the entity's ability to continue as a going concern; (*b*) the work performed in connection with the auditor's evaluation of management's plans; (*c*) the auditor's conclusion as to whether substantial doubt about the entity's ability to continue as a going concern for a reasonable period of time remains or is alleviated; and (*d*) the consideration and effect of that conclusion on the financial statements, disclosures, and the audit report.

m. Paragraph .64 of section 380, *The Auditor's Communication With Those Charged With Governance*, to document any matters that have been communicated orally. When matters have been communicated in writing, the auditor should retain a copy of the communication.

n. Paragraph .29 of section 330, *The Confirmation Process*, to document oral confirmations. Also, when the auditor has not requested confirmations in the examination of accounts receivable, this section does not change the requirement in paragraph .35 of section 330 to document how the auditor overcame this presumption.

o. Paragraphs .39–.42 of section 801, *Compliance Audits*, to document (*a*) the risk assessment procedures performed, including those related to gaining an understanding of internal control over compliance; (*b*) the auditor's responses to the assessed risks of material noncompliance, the procedures performed to test compliance with the applicable compliance requirements, and the results of those procedures, including any tests of controls over compliance; (*c*) materiality levels and the basis on which they were determined; and (*d*) how the auditor complied with the specific governmental audit requirements that are supplementary to GAAS and *Government Auditing Standards*.

p. Section 333, *Management Representations*, to obtain written representations from management.

q. Section 316, *Consideration of Fraud in a Financial Statement Audit*, to document (*a*) the discussion among engagement personnel in planning the audit regarding the susceptibility of the entity's financial statements to material misstatement due to fraud, including how and when the discussion occurred, the audit team members who participated, and the subject matter discussed; (*b*) the procedures performed to obtain information necessary to identify and assess the risks of material misstatement due to fraud; (*c*) specific risks of material misstatement due to fraud that were identified and a description of the auditor's response to those risks; (*d*) if the auditor has not identified in a particular circumstance improper revenue recognition as a risk of material misstatement due to fraud, the reasons supporting the auditor's conclusion; (*e*) the results of the procedures performed to further address the risk of management override of controls; (*f*) other conditions and analytical relationships that caused the auditor to believe that additional auditing procedures or other responses were required and any further responses the auditor concluded were appropriate to address such risks or other conditions; and (*g*) the nature of the communications about fraud made to management, the audit committee, and others.

r. Section 722, *Interim Financial Information*, to prepare documentation in connection with a review of interim financial information, the form and content of which should be designed to meet the circumstances of the particular engagement.

[Revised, May 2006, to reflect conforming changes necessary due to the issuance of Statement on Auditing Standards No. 112; Revised, December 2007, to reflect conforming changes necessary due to the issuance of Statement on Auditing Standards Nos. 107–110 and 114. Revised, February 2008, to reflect conforming changes necessary due to the effective date of Statement on Auditing Standards No. 108. Revised, June 2009, to reflect conforming changes necessary due to the issuance of FASB ASC. Revised, December 2010, to reflect conforming changes necessary due to the issuance of SAS No. 117.]

AU Section 9339

Audit Documentation: Auditing Interpretations of Section 339

1. Providing Access to or Copies of Audit Documentation to a Regulator[1,2]

.01 *Question*—Section 339, *Audit Documentation*, paragraph .33, states that "the auditor has an ethical, and in some situations a legal, obligation to maintain the confidentiality of client information. Because audit documentation often contains confidential client information, the auditor should adopt reasonable procedures to maintain the confidentiality of that information." However, auditors are sometimes required by law, regulation or audit contract,[3] to provide a regulator, or a duly appointed representative, access to audit documentation. For example, a regulator may request access to the audit documentation to fulfill a quality review requirement or to assist in establishing the scope of a regulatory examination. Furthermore, as part of the regulator's review of the audit documentation, the regulator may request copies of all or selected portions of the audit documentation during or after the review. The regulator may intend, or decide, to make copies (or information derived from the audit documentation) available to others, including other governmental agencies, for their particular purposes, with or without the knowledge of the auditor or the client. When a regulator requests the auditor to provide access to (and possibly copies of) audit documentation pursuant to law, regulation or audit contract, what steps should the auditor take?

.02 *Interpretation*—When a regulator requests access to audit documentation pursuant to law, regulation or audit contract, the auditor should take the following steps:

a. Consider advising the client that the regulator has requested access to (and possibly copies of) the audit documentation and that the auditor intends to comply with such request.[4]

---

[1] The term "regulator(s)" includes federal, state and local government officials with legal oversight authority over the entity. Examples of regulators who may request access to audit documentation include, but are not limited to, state insurance and utility regulators, various health care authorities, and federal agencies such as the Federal Deposit Insurance Corporation, the Office of Thrift Supervision, the Department of Housing and Urban Development, the Department of Labor, and the Rural Electrification Administration.

[2] The guidance in this Interpretation does not apply to requests from the Internal Revenue Service, firm practice-monitoring programs to comply with AICPA or state professional requirements such as peer or quality reviews, proceedings relating to alleged ethics violations, or subpoenas.

[3] For situations in which the auditor is not required by law, regulation or audit contract to provide a regulator access to the audit documentation, reference should be made to the guidance in paragraphs .11–.15 of this Interpretation.

[4] The auditor may wish (and in some cases may be required by law, regulation, or audit contract) to confirm in writing with the client that the auditor may be required to provide a regulator access to the audit documentation. Sample language that may be used follows:
"The audit documentation for this engagement is the property of (*name of auditor*) and constitutes confidential information. However, we may be requested to make certain audit documentation available to (*name of regulator*) pursuant to authority given to it by law or regulation. If requested, access to such audit documentation will be provided under the supervision of (*name of auditor*) personnel. Furthermore, upon request, we may provide copies of selected audit documentation to (*name of regulator*). The (*name of regulator*) may intend, or decide, to distribute the copies or information contained therein to others, including other governmental agencies."

b. Make appropriate arrangements with the regulator for the review.

c. Maintain control over the audit documentation, and

d. Consider submitting the letter described in paragraph .05 of this Interpretation to the regulator.

.03 The auditor should make appropriate arrangements with the regulator. These arrangements ordinarily would include the specific details such as the date, time and location of the review. The audit documentation may be made available to a regulator at the offices of the client, the auditor, or a mutually agreed-upon location, so long as the auditor maintains control. Furthermore, the auditor should take appropriate steps to maintain control of the audit documentation. For example, the auditor (or his or her representative) should consider being present when the audit documentation is reviewed by the regulator. Maintaining control of audit documentation is necessary to ensure the continued integrity of the audit documentation and to ensure confidentiality of client information.

.04 Ordinarily, the auditor should not agree to transfer ownership of the audit documentation to a regulator. Furthermore, the auditor should not agree, without client authorization, that the information contained therein about the client may be communicated to or made available to any other party. In this regard, the action of an auditor providing access to, or copies of, the audit documentation shall not constitute transfer of ownership or authorization to make them available to any other party.

.05 An audit performed in accordance with generally accepted auditing standards is not intended to, and does not, satisfy a regulator's oversight responsibilities. To avoid any misunderstanding, prior to allowing a regulator access to the audit documentation, the auditor should consider submitting a letter to the regulator that:

a. Sets forth the auditor's understanding of the purpose for which access is being requested

b. Describes the audit process and the limitations inherent in a financial statement audit

c. Explains the purpose for which the audit documentation was prepared, and that any individual conclusions must be read in the context of the auditor's report on the financial statements

d. States, except when not applicable, that the audit was not planned or conducted in contemplation of the purpose for which access is being granted or to assess the entity's compliance with laws and regulations

e. States that the audit and the audit documentation should not supplant other inquiries and procedures that should be undertaken by the regulator for its purposes

f. Requests confidential treatment under the Freedom of Information Act or similar laws and regulations,[5] when a request for the audit documentation is made, and that written notice be given to the auditor before transmitting any information contained in the audit documentation to others, including other governmental agencies, except when such transfer is required by law or regulation, and

---

[5] The auditor may need to consult the regulations of individual agencies and, if necessary, consult with legal counsel regarding the specific procedures and requirements necessary to gain confidential treatment.

g. States that if any copies are to be provided, they will be identified as "Confidential Treatment Requested by (*name of auditor, address, telephone number*)."

The auditor may wish to obtain a signed acknowledgment copy of the letter as evidence of the regulator's receipt of the letter.

.06 An example of a letter containing the elements described in paragraph .05 of this Interpretation is presented below:

Illustrative Letter to Regulator[6]

(*Date*)

(*Name and Address of Regulatory Agency*)

Your representatives have requested access to our audit documentation in connection with our audit of the December 31, 20XX financial statements of (name of client). It is our understanding that the purpose of your request is (*state purpose: for example, "to facilitate your regulatory examination"*).[7]

Our audit of (*name of client*) December 31, 20XX financial statements was conducted in accordance with auditing standards generally accepted in the United States of America,[8] the objective[9] of which is to form an opinion as to whether the financial statements, which are the responsibility and representations of management, present fairly, in all material respects, the financial position, results of operations and cash flows in conformity with generally accepted accounting principles.[10] Under generally accepted auditing standards, we have the responsibility, within the inherent limitations of the auditing process, to design our audit to provide reasonable assurance that errors and fraud that have a material effect on the financial statements will be detected, and to exercise due care in the conduct of our audit. The concept of selective testing of the data being audited, which involves judgment both as to the number of transactions to be audited and as to the areas to be tested, has been generally accepted as a valid and sufficient basis for an auditor to express an opinion on financial statements. Thus, our audit, based on the concept of selective testing, is subject to the inherent risk that material errors or fraud, if they exist, would not be detected. In addition, an audit does not address the possibility that material errors or fraud may occur in the future. Also, our use of professional judgment and the assessment of materiality for the purpose of our audit means that matters may have existed that would have been assessed differently by you.

---

[6] The auditor should appropriately modify this letter when the audit has been performed in accordance with generally accepted auditing standards and also in accordance with additional auditing requirements specified by a regulatory agency (for example, the requirements specified in *Government Auditing Standards* issued by the Comptroller General of the United States).

[7] If the auditor is not required by law, regulation, or audit contract to provide a regulator access to the audit documentation but otherwise intends to provide such access (see paragraphs .11–.15 of this Interpretation), the letter should include a statement that: "Management of (*name of client*) has authorized us to provide you access to our audit documentation for (*state purpose*)."

[8] Refer to footnote 6.

[9] In an audit performed in accordance with the *Single Audit Act of 1984*, and certain other federal audit requirements, an additional objective of the audit is to assess compliance with laws and regulations applicable to federal financial assistance. Accordingly, in these situations, the above letter should be modified to include the additional objective.

[10] If the financial statements have been prepared in conformity with regulatory accounting practices, the phrase "financial position, results of operations and cash flows in conformity with generally accepted accounting principles" should be replaced with appropriate wording such as, in the case of an insurance company, the "admitted assets, liabilities... of the XYZ Insurance Company in conformity with accounting practices prescribed or permitted by the state of... insurance department."

The audit documentation was prepared for the purpose of providing the principal support for our report on (*name of client*) December 31, 20XX financial statements and to aid in the conduct and supervision of our audit. The audit documentation is the principal record of auditing procedures performed, evidence obtained and conclusions reached in the engagement. The auditing procedures that we performed were limited to those we considered necessary under generally accepted auditing standards[11] to enable us to formulate and express an opinion on the financial statements[12] taken as a whole. Accordingly, we make no representation as to the sufficiency or appropriateness, for your purposes, of either the information contained in our audit documentation or our auditing procedures. In addition, any notations, comments, and individual conclusions appearing on any of the audit documents do not stand alone, and should not be read as an opinion on any individual amounts, accounts, balances or transactions.

Our audit of (*name of client*) December 31, 20XX financial statements was performed for the purpose stated above and has not been planned or conducted in contemplation of your (*state purpose: for example, "regulatory examination"*) or for the purpose of assessing (*name of client*) compliance with laws and regulations.[13] Therefore, items of possible interest to you may not have been specifically addressed. Accordingly, our audit and the audit documentation prepared in connection therewith, should not supplant other inquiries and procedures that should be undertaken by the (*name of regulatory agency*) for the purpose of monitoring and regulating the financial affairs of the (*name of client*). In addition, we have not audited any financial statements of (*name of client*) since (*date of audited balance sheet referred to in the first paragraph above*) nor have we performed any auditing procedures since (*date*), the date of our auditor's report, and significant events or circumstances may have occurred since that date.

The audit documentation constitutes and reflects work performed or evidence obtained by (*name of auditor*) in its capacity as independent auditor for (*name of client*). The documents contain trade secrets and confidential commercial and financial information of our firm and (*name of client*) that is privileged and confidential, and we expressly reserve all rights with respect to disclosures to third parties. Accordingly, we request confidential treatment under the Freedom of Information Act or similar laws and regulations[14] when requests are made for the audit documentation or information contained therein or any documents created by the (*name of regulatory agency*) containing information derived therefrom. We further request that written notice be given to our firm before distribution of the information in the audit documentation (or copies thereof) to others, including other governmental agencies, except when such distribution is required by law or regulation.

[*If it is expected that copies will be requested, add*:

Any copies of our audit documentation we agree to provide you will be identified as "Confidential Treatment Requested by (*name of auditor, address, telephone number*)."]

Firm signature

---

[11] Refer to footnote 6.

[12] Refer to footnote 9.

[13] Refer to footnote 9.

[14] This illustrative paragraph may not in and of itself be sufficient to gain confidential treatment under the rules and regulations of certain regulatory agencies. The auditor should consider tailoring this paragraph to the circumstances after consulting the regulations of each applicable regulatory agency and, if necessary, consult with legal counsel regarding the specific procedures and requirements to gain confidential treatment.

.07 *Question*—A regulator may request access to the audit documentation before the audit has been completed and the report released. May the auditor allow access in such circumstances?

.08 *Interpretation*—When the audit has not been completed, the audit documentation is necessarily incomplete because (*a*) additional information may be added as a result of further tests and review by supervisory personnel and (*b*) any audit results and conclusions reflected in the incomplete audit documentation may change. Accordingly, it is preferable that access be delayed until all auditing procedures have been completed and all internal reviews have been performed. If access is provided prior to completion of the audit, the auditor should consider issuing the letter referred to in paragraph .05 of this Interpretation, appropriately modified, and including additional language along the following lines:

> "We have been engaged to audit in accordance with auditing standards generally accepted in the United States of America the December 31, 20XX, financial statements of XYZ Company, but have not as yet completed our audit. Accordingly, at this time we do not express any opinion on the Company's financial statements. Furthermore, the contents of the audit documentation may change as a result of additional auditing procedures and review of the audit documentation by supervisory personnel of our firm. Accordingly, our audit documentation is incomplete."

Because the audit documentation may change prior to completion of the audit, the auditor ordinarily should not provide copies of the audit documentation until the audit has been completed.

.09 *Question*—Some regulators may engage an independent party, such as another independent public accountant, to perform the audit documentation review on behalf of the regulatory agency. Are there any special precautions the auditor should observe in these circumstances?

.10 *Interpretation*—The auditor should be satisfied that the party engaged by the regulator is subject to the same confidentiality restrictions as the regulatory agency itself. This can be accomplished by obtaining acknowledgment, preferably in writing, from the regulator stating that the third party is acting on behalf of the regulator and agreement from the third party that he or she is subject to the same restrictions on disclosure and use of audit documentation and the information contained therein as the regulator.

.11 *Question*—When a regulator requests the auditor to provide access to (and possibly copies of) audit documentation and the auditor is not otherwise required by law, regulation or audit contract to provide such access, what steps should the auditor take?

.12 *Interpretation*—The auditor should obtain an understanding of the reasons for the regulator's request for access to the audit documentation and may wish to consider consulting with legal counsel regarding the request. If the auditor decides to provide such access, the auditor should obtain the client's consent, preferably in writing, to provide the regulator access to the audit documentation.

.13 Following is an example of language that may be used in the written communication to the client:

> "The audit documentation for this engagement is the property of (*name of auditor*) and constitutes confidential information. However, we have been requested to make certain audit documentation available to (*name of regulator*)

for (*describe the regulator's basis for its request*). Access to such audit documentation will be provided under the supervision of (*name of auditor*) personnel. Furthermore, upon request, we may provide copies of selected audit documentation to (*name of regulator*).

"You have authorized (*name of auditor*) to allow (*name of regulator*) access to the audit documentation in the manner discussed above. Please confirm your agreement to the above by signing below and returning to (*name of auditor, address*)."

Firm signature

____

Agreed and acknowledged:

____

(*Name and title*)

____

(*Date*)

.14 If the client requests to review the audit documentation before allowing the regulator access, the auditor may provide the client with the opportunity to obtain an understanding of the nature of the information about its financial statements contained in the audit documentation that is being made available to the regulator. When a client reviews the audit documentation, the auditor should maintain control of the audit documentation as discussed in paragraph .03 of this Interpretation.

.15 The auditor should also refer to the guidance in paragraphs .03–.10 of this Interpretation which provide guidance on making arrangements with the regulator for access to the audit documentation, maintaining control over the audit documentation and submitting a letter describing various matters to the regulator.

[Issue Date: July, 1994; Revised: June, 1996;
Revised: October, 2000; Revised: January, 2002; Revised: December, 2005.]

AU Section 341

*The Auditor's Consideration of an Entity's Ability to Continue as a Going Concern**

(Supersedes section 340.)

Source: SAS No. 59; SAS No. 64; SAS No. 77; SAS No. 96; SAS No. 113; SAS No. 114.

See section 9341 for interpretations of this section.

Effective for audits of financial statements for periods beginning on or after January 1, 1989, unless otherwise indicated.

.01 This section provides guidance to the auditor in conducting an audit of financial statements in accordance with generally accepted auditing standards with respect to evaluating whether there is substantial doubt about the entity's ability to continue as a going concern.[1,2] Continuation of an entity as a going concern is assumed in financial reporting in the absence of significant information to the contrary. Ordinarily, information that significantly contradicts the going concern assumption relates to the entity's inability to continue to meet its obligations as they become due without substantial disposition of assets outside the ordinary course of business, restructuring of debt, externally forced revisions of its operations, or similar actions.

The Auditor's Responsibility

.02 The auditor has a responsibility to evaluate whether there is substantial doubt about the entity's ability to continue as a going concern for a reasonable period of time, not to exceed one year beyond the date of the financial statements being audited (hereinafter referred to as *a reasonable period of time*). The auditor's evaluation is based on his or her knowledge of relevant conditions and events that exist at or have occurred prior to the date of the auditor's report.

---

* The Financial Accounting Standards Board (FASB) has issued proposed Statement of Financial Accounting Standards *Going Concern* to (*a*) provide guidance on the preparation of financial statements as a going concern and on management's responsibility to evaluate a reporting entity's ability to continue as a going concern and (*b*) require disclosures when either financial statements are not prepared on a going concern basis or there is substantial doubt as to an entity's ability to continue as a going concern. FASB has decided that this guidance also belongs in the accounting literature because it is management's responsibility to assess the ongoing viability of the reporting entity. The proposed statement would amend FASB *Accounting Standards Codification*™ by inserting subtopic 30, *Going Concern*, to topic 205, *Presentation of Financial Statements*. Readers are encouraged to consult FASB ASC for guidance regarding going concern.

[1] This section does not apply to an audit of financial statements based on the assumption of liquidation (for example, when [*a*] an entity is in the process of liquidation, [*b*] the owners have decided to commence dissolution or liquidation, or [*c*] legal proceedings, including bankruptcy, have reached a point at which dissolution or liquidation is probable). See Auditing Interpretation, "Reporting on Financial Statements Prepared on a Liquidation Basis of Accounting" (section 9508.33–.38).

[2] The guidance provided in this section applies to audits of financial statements prepared either in accordance with generally accepted accounting principles or in accordance with a comprehensive basis of accounting other than generally accepted accounting principles. References in this section to generally accepted accounting principles are intended to include a comprehensive basis of accounting other than generally accepted accounting principles (excluding liquidation basis).

Information about such conditions or events is obtained from the application of auditing procedures planned and performed to achieve audit objectives that are related to management's assertions embodied in the financial statements being audited, as described in section 326, *Audit Evidence*. [Revised, March 2006, to reflect conforming changes necessary due to the issuance of Statement on Auditing Standards No. 106. As amended, effective for audits of financial statements for periods ending on or after December 15, 2006, by Statement on Auditing Standards No. 113.]

.03 The auditor should evaluate whether there is substantial doubt about the entity's ability to continue as a going concern for a reasonable period of time in the following manner:

a. The auditor considers whether the results of his procedures performed in planning, gathering audit evidence relative to the various audit objectives, and completing the audit identify conditions and events that, when considered in the aggregate, indicate there could be substantial doubt about the entity's ability to continue as a going concern for a reasonable period of time. It may be necessary to obtain additional information about such conditions and events, as well as the appropriate audit evidence to support information that mitigates the auditor's doubt.

b. If the auditor believes there is substantial doubt about the entity's ability to continue as a going concern for a reasonable period of time, he should (1) obtain information about management's plans that are intended to mitigate the effect of such conditions or events, and (2) assess the likelihood that such plans can be effectively implemented.

c. After the auditor has evaluated management's plans, he concludes whether he has substantial doubt about the entity's ability to continue as a going concern for a reasonable period of time. If the auditor concludes there is substantial doubt, he should (1) consider the adequacy of disclosure about the entity's possible inability to continue as a going concern for a reasonable period of time, and (2) include an explanatory paragraph (following the opinion paragraph) in his audit report to reflect his conclusion. If the auditor concludes that substantial doubt does not exist, he should consider the need for disclosure.

[Revised, March 2006, to reflect conforming changes necessary due to the issuance of Statement on Auditing Standards No. 105.]

.04 The auditor is not responsible for predicting future conditions or events. The fact that the entity may cease to exist as a going concern subsequent to receiving a report from the auditor that does not refer to substantial doubt, even within one year following the date of the financial statements, does not, in itself, indicate inadequate performance by the auditor. Accordingly, the absence of reference to substantial doubt in an auditor's report should not be viewed as providing assurance as to an entity's ability to continue as a going concern.

Audit Procedures

.05 It is not necessary to design audit procedures solely to identify conditions and events that, when considered in the aggregate, indicate there could be substantial doubt about the entity's ability to continue as a going concern for a reasonable period of time. The results of auditing procedures designed and performed to achieve other audit objectives should be sufficient for that purpose.

The following are examples of procedures that may identify such conditions and events:

- Analytical procedures
- Review of subsequent events
- Review of compliance with the terms of debt and loan agreements
- Reading of minutes of meetings of stockholders, board of directors, and important committees of the board
- Inquiry of an entity's legal counsel about litigation, claims, and assessments
- Confirmation with related and third parties of the details of arrangements to provide or maintain financial support

Consideration of Conditions and Events

.06 In performing audit procedures such as those presented in paragraph .05, the auditor may identify information about certain conditions or events that, when considered in the aggregate, indicate there could be substantial doubt about the entity's ability to continue as a going concern for a reasonable period of time. The significance of such conditions and events will depend on the circumstances, and some may have significance only when viewed in conjunction with others. The following are examples of such conditions and events:

- *Negative trends*—for example, recurring operating losses, working capital deficiencies, negative cash flows from operating activities, adverse key financial ratios
- *Other indications of possible financial difficulties*—for example, default on loan or similar agreements, arrearages in dividends, denial of usual trade credit from suppliers, restructuring of debt, noncompliance with statutory capital requirements, need to seek new sources or methods of financing or to dispose of substantial assets
- *Internal matters*—for example, work stoppages or other labor difficulties, substantial dependence on the success of a particular project, uneconomic long-term commitments, need to significantly revise operations
- *External matters that have occurred*—for example, legal proceedings, legislation, or similar matters that might jeopardize an entity's ability to operate; loss of a key franchise, license, or patent; loss of a principal customer or supplier; uninsured or underinsured catastrophe such as a drought, earthquake, or flood

Consideration of Management's Plans

.07 If, after considering the identified conditions and events in the aggregate, the auditor believes there is substantial doubt about the ability of the entity to continue as a going concern for a reasonable period of time, he should consider management's plans for dealing with the adverse effects of the conditions and events. The auditor should obtain information about the plans and consider whether it is likely the adverse effects will be mitigated for a reasonable period of time and that such plans can be effectively implemented.

The auditor's considerations relating to management plans may include the following:

- Plans to dispose of assets
  - — Restrictions on disposal of assets, such as covenants limiting such transactions in loan or similar agreements or encumbrances against assets
  - — Apparent marketability of assets that management plans to sell
  - — Possible direct or indirect effects of disposal of assets
- Plans to borrow money or restructure debt
  - — Availability of debt financing, including existing or committed credit arrangements, such as lines of credit or arrangements for factoring receivables or sale-leaseback of assets
  - — Existing or committed arrangements to restructure or subordinate debt or to guarantee loans to the entity
  - — Possible effects on management's borrowing plans of existing restrictions on additional borrowing or the sufficiency of available collateral
- Plans to reduce or delay expenditures
  - — Apparent feasibility of plans to reduce overhead or administrative expenditures, to postpone maintenance or research and development projects, or to lease rather than purchase assets
  - — Possible direct or indirect effects of reduced or delayed expenditures
- Plans to increase ownership equity
  - — Apparent feasibility of plans to increase ownership equity, including existing or committed arrangements to raise additional capital
  - — Existing or committed arrangements to reduce current dividend requirements or to accelerate cash distributions from affiliates or other investors

.08 When evaluating management's plans, the auditor should identify those elements that are particularly significant to overcoming the adverse effects of the conditions and events and should plan and perform auditing procedures to obtain audit evidence about them. For example, the auditor should consider the adequacy of support regarding the ability to obtain additional financing or the planned disposal of assets. [Revised, March 2006, to reflect conforming changes necessary due to the issuance of Statement on Auditing Standards No. 105.]

.09 When prospective financial information is particularly significant to management's plans, the auditor should request management to provide that information and should consider the adequacy of support for significant assumptions underlying that information. The auditor should give particular attention to assumptions that are—

- Material to the prospective financial information.
- Especially sensitive or susceptible to change.
- Inconsistent with historical trends.

The auditor's consideration should be based on knowledge of the entity, its business, and its management and should include (*a*) reading of the prospective financial information and the underlying assumptions and (*b*) comparing prospective financial information in prior periods with actual results and comparing prospective information for the current period with results achieved to date. If the auditor becomes aware of factors, the effects of which are not reflected in such prospective financial information, he should discuss those factors with management and, if necessary, request revision of the prospective financial information.

Consideration of Financial Statement Effects

.10 When, after considering management's plans, the auditor concludes there is substantial doubt about the entity's ability to continue as a going concern for a reasonable period of time, the auditor should consider the possible effects on the financial statements and the adequacy of the related disclosure. Some of the information that might be disclosed includes—

- Pertinent conditions and events giving rise to the assessment of substantial doubt about the entity's ability to continue as a going concern for a reasonable period of time.
- The possible effects of such conditions and events.
- Management's evaluation of the significance of those conditions and events and any mitigating factors.
- Possible discontinuance of operations.
- Management's plans (including relevant prospective financial information).[3]
- Information about the recoverability or classification of recorded asset amounts or the amounts or classification of liabilities.

.11 When, primarily because of the auditor's consideration of management's plans, he concludes that substantial doubt about the entity's ability to continue as a going concern for a reasonable period of time is alleviated, he should consider the need for disclosure of the principal conditions and events that initially caused him to believe there was substantial doubt. The auditor's consideration of disclosure should include the possible effects of such conditions and events, and any mitigating factors, including management's plans.

Consideration of the Effects on the Auditor's Report

.12 If, after considering identified conditions and events and management's plans, the auditor concludes that substantial doubt about the entity's ability to continue as a going concern for a reasonable period of time remains, the audit report should include an explanatory paragraph (following the opinion paragraph) to reflect that conclusion.[4] The auditor's conclusion about the entity's ability to continue as a going concern should be expressed through the use of the phrase "substantial doubt about its (the entity's) ability to continue as a going concern" [or similar wording that includes the terms substantial doubt *and* going concern] as illustrated in paragraph .13. [As amended, effective for

---

[3] It is not intended that such prospective financial information constitute prospective financial statements meeting the minimum presentation guidelines set forth in AT section 301, *Financial Forecasts and Projections*, nor that the inclusion of such information require any consideration beyond that normally required by generally accepted auditing standards. [Footnote revised, January 2001, to reflect conforming changes necessary due to the issuance of Statement on Standards for Attestation Engagements No. 10.]

[4] The inclusion of an explanatory paragraph (following the opinion paragraph) in the auditor's report contemplated by this section should serve adequately to inform the users of the financial statements. Nothing in this section, however, is intended to preclude an auditor from declining to express an opinion in cases involving uncertainties. If he disclaims an opinion, the uncertainties and their possible effects on the financial statements should be disclosed in an appropriate manner (see paragraph .10), and the auditor's report should give all the substantive reasons for his disclaimer of opinion (see section 508, *Reports on Audited Financial Statements*).

reports issued after December 31, 1990, by Statement on Auditing Standards No. 64.]

.13 An example follows of an explanatory paragraph (following the opinion paragraph) in the auditor's report describing an uncertainty about the entity's ability to continue as a going concern for a reasonable period of time.[5]

> The accompanying financial statements have been prepared assuming that the Company will continue as a going concern. As discussed in Note X to the financial statements, the Company has suffered recurring losses from operations and has a net capital deficiency that raise substantial doubt about its ability to continue as a going concern. Management's plans in regard to these matters are also described in Note X. The financial statements do not include any adjustments that might result from the outcome of this uncertainty.

[As amended, effective for reports issued after December 31, 1990, by Statement on Auditing Standards No. 64.]

.14 If the auditor concludes that the entity's disclosures with respect to the entity's ability to continue as a going concern for a reasonable period of time are inadequate, a departure from generally accepted accounting principles exists. This may result in either a qualified (except for) or an adverse opinion. Reporting guidance for such situations is provided in section 508, *Reports on Audited Financial Statements*.

.15 Substantial doubt about the entity's ability to continue as a going concern for a reasonable period of time that arose in the current period does not imply that a basis for such doubt existed in the prior period and, therefore, should not affect the auditor's report on the financial statements of the prior period that are presented on a comparative basis. When financial statements of one or more prior periods are presented on a comparative basis with financial statements of the current period, reporting guidance is provided in section 508.

.16 If substantial doubt about the entity's ability to continue as a going concern for a reasonable period of time existed at the date of prior period financial statements that are presented on a comparative basis, and that doubt has been removed in the current period, the explanatory paragraph included in the auditor's report (following the opinion paragraph) on the financial statements of the prior period should not be repeated.

Communication With Those Charged With Governance

.17 If, after considering identified conditions and events in the aggregate and after considering management's plans, the auditor concludes that substantial doubt about the entity's ability to continue as a going concern for a reasonable period of time remains, the auditor should communicate with those charged with governance:

a. The nature of the events or conditions identified.

b. The possible effect on the financial statements and the adequacy of related disclosures in the financial statements.

---

[5] In a going-concern explanatory paragraph, the auditor should not use conditional language in expressing a conclusion concerning the existence of substantial doubt about the entity's ability to continue as a going concern. Examples of inappropriate wording in the explanatory paragraph would be, "If the Company continues to suffer recurring losses from operations and continues to have a net capital deficiency, there may be substantial doubt about its ability to continue as a going concern" or "The Company has been unable to renegotiate its expiring credit agreements. Unless the Company is able to obtain financial support, there is substantial doubt about its ability to continue as a going concern." [Footnote added, effective for reports issued after December 15, 1995, by Statement on Auditing Standards No. 77.]

c. The effects on the auditor's report.

[Paragraph added, effective for audits of financial statements for periods beginning on or after December 15, 2006, by Statement on Auditing Standards No. 114.]

Documentation

.18 As stated in paragraph .03 of this section, the auditor considers whether the results of the auditing procedures performed in planning, gathering audit evidence relative to the various audit objectives, and completing the audit identify conditions and events that, when considered in the aggregate, indicate there could be substantial doubt about the entity's ability to continue as a going concern for a reasonable period of time. If, after considering the identified conditions and events in the aggregate, the auditor believes there is substantial doubt about the ability of the entity to continue as a going concern for a reasonable period of time, he or she follows the guidance in paragraphs .07–.16. In connection with that guidance, the auditor should document all of the following:

a. The conditions or events that led him or her to believe that there is substantial doubt about the entity's ability to continue as a going concern for a reasonable period of time.

b. The elements of management's plans that the auditor considered to be particularly significant to overcoming the adverse effects of the conditions or events.

c. The auditing procedures performed and evidence obtained to evaluate the significant elements of management's plans.

d. The auditor's conclusion as to whether substantial doubt about the entity's ability to continue as a going concern for a reasonable period of time remains or is alleviated. If substantial doubt remains, the auditor also should document the possible effects of the conditions or events on the financial statements and the adequacy of the related disclosures. If substantial doubt is alleviated, the auditor also should document the conclusion as to the need for disclosure of the principal conditions and events that initially caused him or her to believe there was substantial doubt.

e. The auditor's conclusion as to whether he or she should include an explanatory paragraph in the audit report. If disclosures with respect to an entity's ability to continue as a going concern are inadequate, the auditor also should document the conclusion as to whether to express a qualified or adverse opinion for the resultant departure from generally accepted accounting principles.

[Paragraph added, effective for audits of financial statements for periods beginning on or after May 15, 2002, by Statement on Auditing Standards No. 96. Revised, March 2006, to reflect conforming changes necessary due to the issuance of Statement on Auditing Standards No. 105. Paragraph renumbered by the issuance of Statement on Auditing Standards No. 114, December 2006.]

Effective Date

.19 This section is effective for audits of financial statements for periods beginning on or after January 1, 1989. Early application of the provisions of this section is permissible. [Paragraph renumbered by the issuance of Statement on Auditing Standards No. 96, January 2002. Paragraph subsequently renumbered by the issuance of Statement on Auditing Standards No. 114, December 2006.]

AU Section 9341

The Auditor's Consideration of an Entity's Ability to Continue as a Going Concern: Auditing Interpretations of Section 341

1. Eliminating a Going-Concern Explanatory Paragraph From a Reissued Report

.01 *Question*—An auditor may be asked to reissue his or her report on financial statements and eliminate the going-concern explanatory paragraph that appeared in the original report. Such requests ordinarily occur after the conditions that gave rise to substantial doubt about the entity's ability to continue as a going concern have been resolved. For example, subsequent to the date of the auditor's original report, an entity might obtain needed financing. In such circumstances, may the auditor reissue his or her report and eliminate the going-concern explanatory paragraph that appeared in the original report?

.02 *Interpretation*—An auditor has no obligation to reissue his or her report.[1] However, if the auditor decides to reissue the report,[2] the auditor should perform the following procedures when determining whether to reissue the report without the going-concern explanatory paragraph that appeared in the original report:

- Audit the event or transaction that prompted the request to reissue the report without the going-concern explanatory paragraph.
- Perform the procedures listed in section 560, *Subsequent Events*, paragraph .12, at or near the date of reissuance.
- Consider the factors described in section 341, *The Auditor's Consideration of an Entity's Ability to Continue as a Going Concern*, paragraphs .06 through .11, based on the conditions and circumstances at the date of reissuance.

The auditor may perform any other procedures that he or she deems necessary in the circumstances. Based on the information that the auditor becomes aware of as a result of performing the procedures mentioned above, the auditor should reassess the going-concern status of the entity.

[Issue Date: August, 1995.]

[2.] Effect of the Year 2000 Issue on the Auditor's Consideration of an Entity's Ability to Continue as a Going Concern

[.03–.27] [Withdrawn July 2000 by the Audit Issues Task Force.]

---

[1] If the auditor decides not to reissue his or her report, the auditor may agree to be engaged to audit the financial statements for a period subsequent to that covered by the original report. This might be the case, for example, if the entity is experiencing profitable operations.

[2] Section 530, *Dating of the Independent Auditor's Report*, paragraph .05, states that an auditor may either "dual-date" or "later-date" his or her reissued report.

AU Section 342

Auditing Accounting Estimates

Source: SAS No. 57; SAS No. 113.

See section 9342 for interpretations of this section.

Effective for audits of financial statements for periods beginning on or after January 1, 1989, unless otherwise indicated.

.01 This section provides guidance to auditors on obtaining and evaluating sufficient appropriate audit evidence to support significant accounting estimates in an audit of financial statements in accordance with generally accepted auditing standards. For purposes of this section, an *accounting estimate* is an approximation of a financial statement element, item, or account. Accounting estimates are often included in historical financial statements because—

a. The measurement of some amounts or the valuation of some accounts is uncertain, pending the outcome of future events.

b. Relevant data concerning events that have already occurred cannot be accumulated on a timely, cost-effective basis.

[Revised, March 2006, to reflect conforming changes necessary due to the issuance of Statement on Auditing Standards No. 105.]

.02 Accounting estimates in historical financial statements measure the effects of past business transactions or events, or the present status of an asset or liability. Examples of accounting estimates include net realizable values of inventory and accounts receivable, property and casualty insurance loss reserves, revenues from contracts accounted for by the percentage-of-completion method, and pension and warranty expenses.[1]

.03 Management is responsible for making the accounting estimates included in the financial statements. Estimates are based on subjective as well as objective factors and, as a result, judgment is required to estimate an amount at the date of the financial statements. Management's judgment is normally based on its knowledge and experience about past and current events and its assumptions about conditions it expects to exist and courses of action it expects to take.

.04 The auditor is responsible for evaluating the reasonableness of accounting estimates made by management in the context of the financial statements taken as a whole. As estimates are based on subjective as well as objective factors, it may be difficult for management to establish controls over them. Even when management's estimation process involves competent personnel using relevant and reliable data, there is potential for bias in the subjective factors. Accordingly, when planning and performing procedures to evaluate accounting estimates, the auditor should consider, with an attitude of professional skepticism, both the subjective and objective factors.

---

[1] Additional examples of accounting estimates included in historical financial statements are presented in paragraph .16.

Developing Accounting Estimates

.05 Management is responsible for establishing a process for preparing accounting estimates. Although the process may not be documented or formally applied, it normally consists of—

a. Identifying situations for which accounting estimates are required.

b. Identifying the relevant factors that may affect the accounting estimate.

c. Accumulating relevant, sufficient, and reliable data on which to base the estimate.

d. Developing assumptions that represent management's judgment of the most likely circumstances and events with respect to the relevant factors.

e. Determining the estimated amount based on the assumptions and other relevant factors.

f. Determining that the accounting estimate is presented in conformity with applicable accounting principles and that disclosure is adequate.

The risk of material misstatement of accounting estimates normally varies with the complexity and subjectivity associated with the process, the availability and reliability of relevant data, the number and significance of assumptions that are made, and the degree of uncertainty associated with the assumptions.

Internal Control Related to Accounting Estimates

.06 An entity's internal control may reduce the likelihood of material misstatements of accounting estimates. Specific relevant aspects of internal control include the following:

a. Management communication of the need for proper accounting estimates

b. Accumulation of relevant, sufficient, and reliable data on which to base an accounting estimate

c. Preparation of the accounting estimate by qualified personnel

d. Adequate review and approval of the accounting estimates by appropriate levels of authority, including—

1. Review of sources of relevant factors
2. Review of development of assumptions
3. Review of reasonableness of assumptions and resulting estimates
4. Consideration of the need to use the work of specialists
5. Consideration of changes in previously established methods to arrive at accounting estimates

e. Comparison of prior accounting estimates with subsequent results to assess the reliability of the process used to develop estimates

f. Consideration by management of whether the resulting accounting estimate is consistent with the operational plans of the entity.

Evaluating Accounting Estimates

.07 The auditor's objective when evaluating accounting estimates is to obtain sufficient appropriate audit evidence to provide reasonable assurance that—

a. All accounting estimates that could be material to the financial statements have been developed.

b. Those accounting estimates are reasonable in the circumstances.

c. The accounting estimates are presented in conformity with applicable accounting principles[2] and are properly disclosed.[3]

[Revised, March 2006, to reflect conforming changes necessary due to the issuance of Statement on Auditing Standards No. 105.]

Identifying Circumstances That Require Accounting Estimates

.08 In evaluating whether management has identified all accounting estimates that could be material to the financial statements, the auditor considers the circumstances of the industry or industries in which the entity operates, its methods of conducting business, new accounting pronouncements, and other external factors. The auditor should consider performing the following procedures:

a. Consider assertions embodied in the financial statements to determine the need for estimates. (See paragraph .16 for examples of accounting estimates included in financial statements.)

b. Evaluate information obtained in performing other procedures, such as—

1. Information about changes made or planned in the entity's business, including changes in operating strategy, and the industry in which the entity operates that may indicate the need to make an accounting estimate (section 311, *Planning and Supervision*).
2. Changes in the methods of accumulating information.
3. Information concerning identified litigation, claims, and assessments (section 337, *Inquiry of a Client's Lawyer Concerning Litigation, Claims, and Assessments*), and other contingencies.
4. Information from reading available minutes of meetings of stockholders, directors, and appropriate committees.
5. Information contained in regulatory or examination reports, supervisory correspondence, and similar materials from applicable regulatory agencies.

c. Inquire of management about the existence of circumstances that may indicate the need to make an accounting estimate.

Evaluating Reasonableness

.09 In evaluating the reasonableness of an estimate, the auditor normally concentrates on key factors and assumptions that are—

a. Significant to the accounting estimate.

b. Sensitive to variations.

c. Deviations from historical patterns.

d. Subjective and susceptible to misstatement and bias.

---

[2] [Footnote deleted, October 2009, to reflect conforming changes necessary due to the withdrawal of SAS No. 69.]

[3] Section 431, *Adequacy of Disclosure in Financial Statements*, discusses the auditor's responsibility to consider whether the financial statements include adequate disclosures of material matters in light of the circumstances and facts of which he is aware.

The auditor normally should consider the historical experience of the entity in making past estimates as well as the auditor's experience in the industry. However, changes in facts, circumstances, or entity's procedures may cause factors different from those considered in the past to become significant to the accounting estimate.[4]

.10 In evaluating reasonableness, the auditor should obtain an understanding of how management developed the estimate. Based on that understanding, the auditor should use one or a combination of the following approaches:

a. Review and test the process used by management to develop the estimate.

b. Develop an independent expectation of the estimate to corroborate the reasonableness of management's estimate.

c. Review subsequent events or transactions occurring prior to the date of the auditor's report.

[As amended, effective for audits of financial statements for periods ending on or after December 15, 2006, by Statement on Auditing Standards No. 113.]

.11 Review and test management's process. In many situations, the auditor assesses the reasonableness of an accounting estimate by performing procedures to test the process used by management to make the estimate. The following are procedures the auditor may consider performing when using this approach:

a. Identify whether there are controls over the preparation of accounting estimates and supporting data that may be useful in the evaluation.

b. Identify the sources of data and factors that management used in forming the assumptions, and consider whether such data and factors are relevant, reliable, and sufficient for the purpose based on information gathered in other audit tests.

c. Consider whether there are additional key factors or alternative assumptions about the factors.

d. Evaluate whether the assumptions are consistent with each other, the supporting data, relevant historical data, and industry data.

e. Analyze historical data used in developing the assumptions to assess whether the data is comparable and consistent with data of the period under audit, and consider whether such data is sufficiently reliable for the purpose.

f. Consider whether changes in the business or industry may cause other factors to become significant to the assumptions.

g. Review available documentation of the assumptions used in developing the accounting estimates and inquire about any other plans, goals, and objectives of the entity, as well as consider their relationship to the assumptions.

h. Consider using the work of a specialist regarding certain assumptions (section 336, *Using the Work of a Specialist*).

i. Test the calculations used by management to translate the assumptions and key factors into the accounting estimate.

---

[4] In addition to other evidential matter about the estimate, in certain instances, the auditor may wish to obtain written representation from management regarding the key factors and assumptions.

.12 *Develop an expectation.* Based on the auditor's understanding of the facts and circumstances, he may independently develop an expectation as to the estimate by using other key factors or alternative assumptions about those factors.

.13 *Review subsequent events or transactions.* Events or transactions sometimes occur subsequent to the date of the balance sheet, but prior to the date of the auditor's report, that are important in identifying and evaluating the reasonableness of accounting estimates or key factors or assumptions used in the preparation of the estimate. In such circumstances, an evaluation of the estimate or of a key factor or assumption may be minimized or unnecessary as the event or transaction can be used by the auditor in evaluating their reasonableness. [As amended, effective for audits of financial statements for periods ending on or after December 15, 2006, by Statement on Auditing Standards No. 113.]

.14 As discussed in section 312, *Audit Risk and Materiality in Conducting an Audit*, paragraph .56, the auditor evaluates the reasonableness of accounting estimates in relationship to the financial statements taken as a whole:

> Because no one accounting estimate can be considered accurate with certainty, the auditor may determine that a difference between an estimated amount best supported by the audit evidence and the estimated amount included in the financial statements may not be significant, and such difference would not be considered to be a likely misstatement. However, if the auditor believes the estimated amount included in the financial statements is unreasonable, he or she should treat the difference between that estimate and the closest reasonable estimate as a likely misstatement.

[Revised, March 2006, to reflect conforming changes necessary due to the issuance of Statement on Auditing Standards No. 107.]

Effective Date

.15 This section is effective for audits of financial statements for periods beginning on or after January 1, 1989. Early application of the provisions of this section is permissible.

.16

Appendix

Examples of Accounting Estimates

The following are examples of accounting estimates that are included in financial statements. The list is presented for information only. It should not be considered all-inclusive.

Receivables:
- Uncollectible receivables
- Allowance for loan losses
- Uncollectible pledges

Inventories:
- Obsolete inventory
- Net realizable value of inventories where future selling prices and future costs are involved
- Losses on purchase commitments

Financial instruments:
- Valuation of securities
- Trading versus investment security classification
- Probability of high correlation of a hedge
- Sales of securities with puts and calls

Productive facilities, natural resources and intangibles:
- Useful lives and residual values
- Depreciation and amortization methods
- Recoverability of costs
- Recoverable reserves

Accruals:
- Property and casualty insurance company loss reserves
- Compensation in stock option plans and deferred plans
- Warranty claims
- Taxes on real and personal property Renegotiation refunds
- Actuarial assumptions in pension costs

Revenues:
- Airline passenger revenue
- Subscription income
- Freight and cargo revenue
- Dues income
- Losses on sales contracts

Contracts:
- Revenue to be earned
- Costs to be incurred
- Percent of completion

Leases:
- Initial direct costs
- Executory costs
- Residual values

Litigation:
- Probability of loss
- Amount of loss

Rates:
- Annual effective tax rate in interim reporting
- Imputed interest rates on receivables and payables
- Gross profit rates under program method of accounting

Other:
- Losses and net realizable value on disposal of segment or restructuring of a business
- Fair values in nonmonetary exchanges
- Interim period costs in interim reporting
- Current values in personal financial statements

AU Section 9342

Auditing Accounting Estimates: Auditing Interpretations of Section 342

1. Performance and Reporting Guidance Related to Fair Value Disclosures

.01 *Question*—Financial Accounting Standards Board (FASB) *Accounting Standards Codification* (ASC) 825, *Financial Instruments*, requires all entities to disclose the fair value of certain financial instruments for which it is practicable to estimate fair value. Some entities may disclose the information required by FASB ASC 825 and also disclose voluntarily the fair value of assets and liabilities not encompassed by FASB ASC 825. What are the auditor's responsibilities in situations in which entities are disclosing required or both required and voluntary fair value financial information?

.02 *Interpretation*—The auditor should determine whether the fair value disclosures represent only those required by FASB ASC 825 or whether additional voluntary fair value information has been disclosed by the entity. When auditing management's estimate of both required and voluntary fair value information, the auditor should obtain sufficient appropriate audit evidence to reasonably assure that

- the valuation principles are acceptable, are being consistently applied, and are supported by the underlying documentation, and
- the method of estimation and significant assumptions used are properly disclosed.

If such assurance cannot be obtained, the auditor should evaluate whether the financial statements are materially affected by the departure from generally accepted accounting principles.

.03 *Required Information Presented.* When an entity discloses in its basic financial statements only information required by FASB ASC 825, the auditor may issue a standard unqualified opinion (assuming no other report modifications are necessary). The auditor may add an emphasis-of-matter paragraph describing the nature and possible range of such fair value information especially when management's best estimate of value is used in the absence of quoted market values and the range of possible values is significant. If the entity has not disclosed required fair value information, the auditor should evaluate whether the financial statements are materially affected by the departure from generally accepted accounting principles.

.04 *Required and Voluntary Information Presented.* When voluntary information is presented in addition to required information the auditor may audit the voluntary information only if both the following conditions exist:

- The measurement and disclosure criteria used to prepare the fair value financial information are reasonable.
- Competent persons using the measurement and disclosure criteria would ordinarily obtain materially similar measurements or disclosures.

In applying this guidance to fair value disclosures, the intention is that another auditor would reach similar conclusions regarding the reasonableness of the valuation or estimation techniques and methods used by the entity.

.05 Voluntary disclosures may supplement required disclosures in such a fashion as to constitute either a complete balance sheet (the fair value of all material items in the balance sheet) or a presentation of less than a complete balance sheet.

.06 When the audited disclosures constitute a complete balance sheet presentation, the auditor should add a paragraph to the report, similar to the following:

> We have also audited in accordance with auditing standards generally accepted in the United States of America the supplemental fair value balance sheet of ABC Company as of December 31, 20XX. As described in Note X, the supplemental fair value balance sheet has been prepared by management to present relevant financial information that is not provided by the historical-cost balance sheets and is not intended to be a presentation in conformity with generally accepted accounting principles. In addition, the supplemental fair value balance sheet does not purport to present the net realizable, liquidation, or market value of ABC Company as a whole. Furthermore, amounts ultimately realized by ABC Company from the disposal of assets may vary significantly from the fair values presented. In our opinion, the supplemental fair value balance sheet referred to above presents fairly, in all material respects, the information set forth therein as described in Note X.

.07 When the audited disclosures do not constitute a complete balance sheet presentation and are located on the face of the financial statements or in the notes, the auditor may issue a standard unqualified opinion and need not mention the disclosures in the report. When the audited disclosures do not constitute a complete balance sheet presentation and are included in a supplemental schedule or exhibit, the auditor should report on the audited disclosures in either (*a*) an explanatory paragraph following the opinion paragraph in the auditor's report on the financial statements or (*b*) in a separate report on the audited disclosures as discussed in paragraph .09 of section 551, *Supplementary Information in Relation to the Financial Statements as a Whole*.

.08 In some situations, the auditor may not be engaged to audit the voluntary information or may be unable to audit it because it does not meet both conditions in paragraph .04 of this interpretation. When the unaudited voluntary disclosures are located on the face of the financial statements, the notes, or in a supplemental schedule to the basic financial statements, the auditor is not required to reference the unaudited information in the auditor's report on the financial statements. However, the auditor may include an other matter paragraph disclaiming an opinion on the unaudited information as discussed in paragraph .A1 of section 550.

[.09] [Paragraph deleted, December 2010, to reflect conforming changes necessary due to the issuance of SAS Nos. 118–120.]

.10 The auditing guidance related to each of these alternatives is presented in the following flowcharts:

AUDITING GUIDANCE FOR FAIR VALUE INFORMATION
Required* Information Only

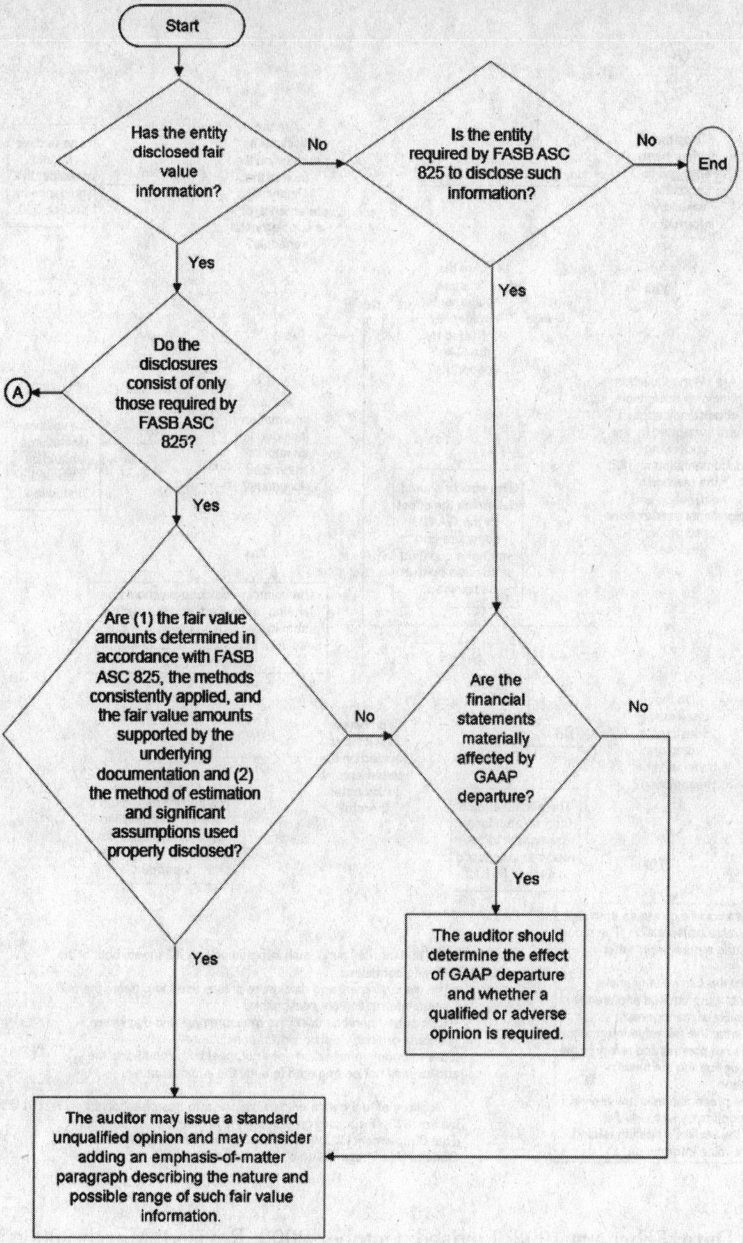

* Required by Financial Accounting Standards Board *Accounting Standards Codification* 825, *Financial Instruments*. [Footnote revised, June 2009, to reflect conforming changes necessary due to the issuance of FASB ASC.]

AUDITING GUIDANCE FOR FAIR VALUE INFORMATION
Required and Voluntary Information

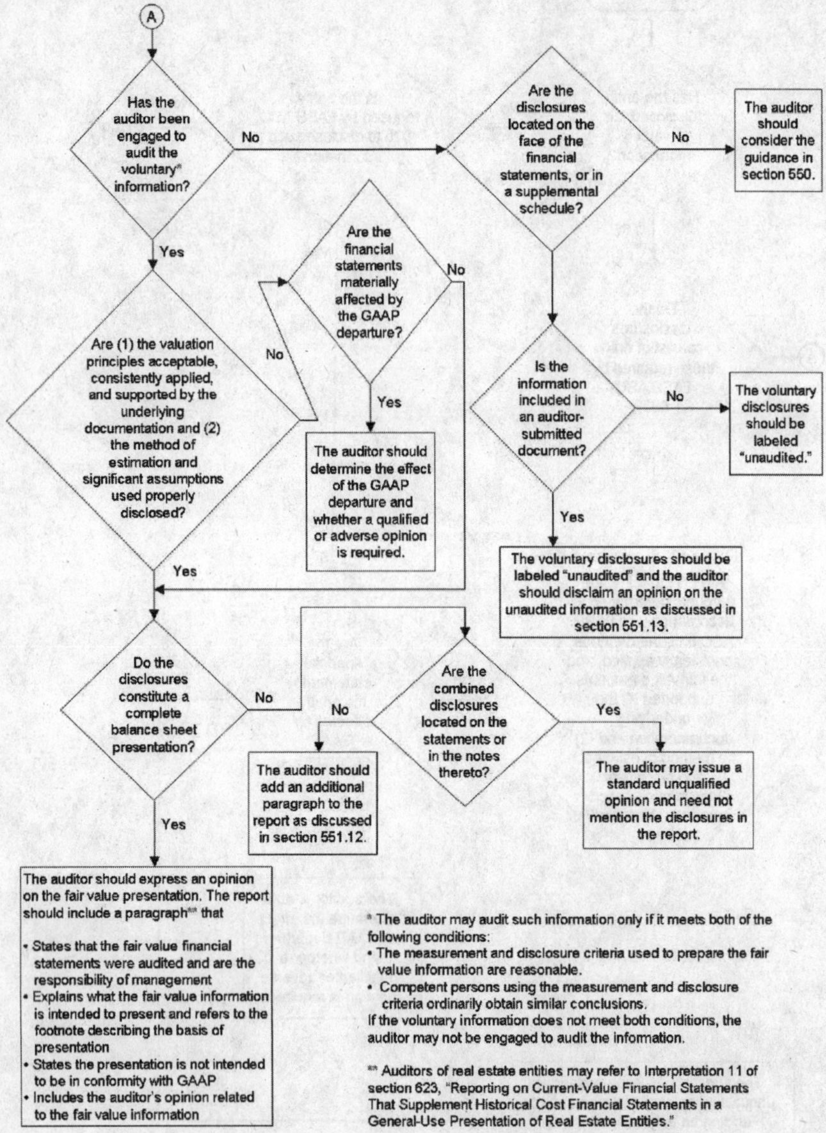

[Issue Date: February 1993; Revised: October 2000; Revised: March 2006; Revised: June 2009; Revised: December 2010.]

AU Section 350

Audit Sampling

(Supersedes SAS No. 1, sections 320A and 320B.)

Source: SAS No. 39; SAS No. 43; SAS No. 45; SAS No. 111.

See section 9350 for interpretations of this section.

Effective for periods ended on or after June 25, 1983, unless otherwise indicated.

.01 Audit sampling is the application of an audit procedure to less than 100 percent of the items within an account balance or class of transactions for the purpose of evaluating some characteristic of the balance or class.[1] This section provides guidance for planning, performing, and evaluating audit samples.

.02 The auditor often is aware of account balances and transactions that may be more likely to contain misstatements.[2] He considers this knowledge in planning his procedures, including audit sampling. The auditor usually will have no special knowledge about other account balances and transactions that, in his judgment, will need to be tested to fulfill his audit objectives. Audit sampling is especially useful in these cases.

.03 There are two general approaches to audit sampling: nonstatistical and statistical. Both approaches require that the auditor use professional judgment in planning, performing, and evaluating a sample and in relating the audit evidence produced by the sample to other audit evidence when forming a conclusion about the related account balance or class of transactions. The guidance in this section applies equally to nonstatistical and statistical sampling. [Revised, March 2006, to reflect conforming changes necessary due to the issuance of Statement on Auditing Standards No. 105.]

.04 The third standard of field work states, "The auditor must obtain sufficient appropriate audit evidence by performing audit procedures to afford a reasonable basis for an opinion regarding the financial statements under audit." Either approach to audit sampling, when properly applied, can provide sufficient audit evidence. [Revised, March 2006, to reflect conforming changes necessary due to the issuance of Statement on Auditing Standards No. 105.]

.05 The sufficiency of audit evidence is related to the design and size of an audit sample, among other factors. The size of a sample necessary to provide sufficient audit evidence depends on both the objectives and the efficiency of the sample. For a given objective, the efficiency of the sample relates to its design; one sample is more efficient than another if it can achieve the same objectives with a smaller sample size. In general, careful design can produce more efficient

---

[1] There may be other reasons for an auditor to examine less than 100 percent of the items comprising an account balance or class of transactions. For example, an auditor may examine only a few transactions from an account balance or class of transactions to (*a*) gain an understanding of the nature of an entity's operations or (*b*) clarify his understanding of the entity's internal control. In such cases, the guidance in this statement is not applicable.

[2] For purposes of this section the use of the term misstatement can include both errors and fraud as appropriate for the design of the sampling application. Errors and fraud are discussed in section 312, *Audit Risk and Materiality in Conducting an Audit*.

samples. [Revised, March 2006, to reflect conforming changes necessary due to the issuance of Statement on Auditing Standards No. 105.]

.06 Evaluating the appropriateness of audit evidence is solely a matter of auditing judgment and is not determined by the design and evaluation of an audit sample. In a strict sense, the sample evaluation relates only to the likelihood that existing monetary misstatements or deviations from prescribed controls are proportionately included in the sample, not to the auditor's treatment of such items. Thus, the choice of nonstatistical or statistical sampling does not directly affect the auditor's decisions about the auditing procedures to be applied, the appropriateness of the audit evidence obtained with respect to individual items in the sample, or the actions that might be taken in light of the nature and cause of particular misstatements. [Revised, March 2006, to reflect conforming changes necessary due to the issuance of Statement on Auditing Standards No. 105.]

Uncertainty and Audit Sampling

.07 Some degree of uncertainty is implicit in the concept of "a reasonable basis for an opinion" referred to in the third standard of field work. The justification for accepting some uncertainty arises from the relationship between such factors as the cost and time required to examine all of the data and the adverse consequences of possible erroneous decisions based on the conclusions resulting from examining only a sample of the data. If these factors do not justify the acceptance of some uncertainty, the only alternative is to examine all of the data. Since this is seldom the case, the basic concept of sampling is well established in auditing practice.

.08 The uncertainty inherent in applying audit procedures is referred to as audit risk. Audit risk includes both uncertainties due to sampling and uncertainties due to factors other than sampling. These aspects of audit risk are sampling risk and nonsampling risk, respectively.[3] [As amended, effective for audits of financial statements for periods beginning on or after December 15, 2006, by Statement on Auditing Standards No. 111.]

[.09] [As amended, effective for audits of financial statements for periods ended after September 30, 1983, by Statement on Auditing Standards No. 45. Paragraph deleted by the issuance of Statement on Auditing Standards No. 111, March 2006.]

.10 Sampling risk arises from the possibility that, when a test of controls or a substantive test is restricted to a sample, the auditor's conclusions may be different from the conclusions he would reach if the test were applied in the same way to all items in the account balance or class of transactions. That is, a particular sample may contain proportionately more or less monetary misstatements or deviations from prescribed controls than exist in the balance or class as a whole. For a sample of a specific design, sampling risk varies inversely with sample size: the smaller the sample size, the greater the sampling risk.

.11 Nonsampling risk includes all the aspects of audit risk that are not due to sampling. An auditor may apply a procedure to all transactions or balances and still fail to detect a material misstatement. Nonsampling risk includes the possibility of selecting audit procedures that are not appropriate to achieve the

[3] See paragraph .22 of section 312, *Audit Risk and Materiality in Conducting an Audit*, for definition of risk of material misstatement. [Footnote added, effective for audits of financial statements for periods beginning on or after December 15, 2006, by Statement on Auditing Standards No. 111.]

specific objective. For example, confirming recorded receivables cannot be relied on to reveal unrecorded receivables. Nonsampling risk also arises because the auditor may fail to recognize misstatements included in documents that he examines, which would make that procedure ineffective even if he were to examine all items. Nonsampling risk can be reduced to a negligible level through such factors as adequate planning and supervision (see section 311, *Planning and Supervision*) and proper conduct of a firm's audit practice (see section 161, *The Relationship of Generally Accepted Auditing Standards to Quality Control Standards*). [As amended, effective for audits of financial statements for periods ended after September 30, 1983, by Statement on Auditing Standards No. 45.]

Sampling Risk

.12 The auditor should apply professional judgment in assessing sampling risk. In performing substantive tests of details the auditor is concerned with two aspects of sampling risk:

- *The risk of incorrect acceptance* is the risk that the sample supports the conclusion that the recorded account balance is not materially misstated when it is materially misstated.
- *The risk of incorrect rejection* is the risk that the sample supports the conclusion that the recorded account balance is materially misstated when it is not materially misstated.

The auditor is also concerned with two aspects of sampling risk in performing tests of controls when sampling is used:

- *The risk of assessing control risk too low* is the risk that the assessed level of control risk based on the sample is less than the true operating effectiveness of the control.
- *The risk of assessing control risk too high* is the risk that the assessed level of control risk based on the sample is greater than the true operating effectiveness of the control.

.13 The risk of incorrect rejection and the risk of assessing control risk too high relate to the efficiency of the audit. For example, if the auditor's evaluation of an audit sample leads him to the initial erroneous conclusion that a balance is materially misstated when it is not, the application of additional audit procedures and consideration of other audit evidence would ordinarily lead the auditor to the correct conclusion. Similarly, if the auditor's evaluation of a sample leads him to unnecessarily assess control risk too high for an assertion, he would ordinarily increase the scope of substantive tests to compensate for the perceived ineffectiveness of the controls. Although the audit may be less efficient in these circumstances, the audit is, nevertheless, effective.

.14 The risk of incorrect acceptance and the risk of assessing control risk too low relate to the effectiveness of an audit in detecting an existing material misstatement. These risks are discussed in the following paragraphs.

Sampling in Substantive Tests of Details

Planning Samples

.15 Planning involves developing a strategy for conducting an audit of financial statements. For general guidance on planning, see section 311, *Planning and Supervision*.

.16 When planning a particular sample for a substantive test of details, the auditor should consider

- The relationship of the sample to the relevant audit objective (see section 326, *Audit Evidence*).
- Preliminary judgments about materiality levels.
- The auditor's allowable risk of incorrect acceptance.
- Characteristics of the population, that is, the items comprising the account balance or class of transactions of interest.

[Revised, March 2006, to reflect conforming changes necessary due to the issuance of Statement on Auditing Standards No. 106.]

.17 When planning a particular sample, the auditor should consider the specific audit objective to be achieved and should determine that the audit procedure, or combination of procedures, to be applied will achieve that objective. The auditor should determine that the population from which he draws the sample is appropriate for the specific audit objective. For example, an auditor would not be able to detect understatements of an account due to omitted items by sampling the recorded items. An appropriate sampling plan for detecting such understatements would involve selecting from a source in which the omitted items are included. To illustrate, subsequent cash disbursements might be sampled to test recorded accounts payable for understatement because of omitted purchases, or shipping documents might be sampled for understatement of sales due to shipments made but not recorded as sales.

.18 Evaluation in monetary terms of the results of a sample for a test of details contributes directly to the auditor's purpose, since such an evaluation can be related to the auditor's judgment of the monetary amount of misstatements that would be material for the test. When planning a sample for a test of details, the auditor should consider how much monetary misstatement in the related account balance or class of transactions may exist when combined with misstatements that may be found in other tests without causing the financial statements to be materially misstated. This maximum monetary misstatement that the auditor is willing to accept for the balance or class is called tolerable misstatement for the sample. Tolerable misstatement is a planning concept and is related to the auditor's determination of materiality for planning the financial statement audit in such a way that tolerable misstatement, combined for all of the tests in the entire audit, does not exceed materiality for the financial statements. This means that auditors should normally set tolerable misstatement for a specific audit procedure at less than financial statement materiality so that when the results of the audit procedures are aggregated, the required overall assurance is attained. [As amended, effective for audits of financial statements for periods beginning on or after December 15, 2006, by Statement on Auditing Standards No. 111.]

.19 The second standard of field work states, "The auditor must obtain a sufficient understanding of the entity and its environment, including its internal control to assess the risk of material misstatement of the financial statements whether due to error or fraud, and to design the nature, timing, and extent of further audit procedures." After assessing and considering the levels of inherent and control risks, the auditor performs substantive tests to restrict detection risk to an acceptable level. As the assessed levels of inherent risk, control risk, and detection risk for other substantive procedures directed toward the same specific audit objective decreases, the auditor's allowable risk of incorrect acceptance for the substantive tests of details increases and, thus, the smaller the required sample size for the substantive tests of details. For example, if inherent and control risks are assessed at the maximum, and no other substantive tests directed toward the same specific audit objectives are performed, the auditor should allow for a low risk of incorrect acceptance for the substantive tests of details.[4] Thus, the auditor would select a larger sample size for the tests of details than if he allowed a higher risk of incorrect acceptance. [Revised, March 2006, to reflect conforming changes necessary due to the issuance of Statement on Auditing Standards No. 105.]

.20 The auditor planning a statistical or nonstatistical sample may use the model in paragraph .26 of section 312, *Audit Risk and Materiality in Conducting an Audit*, to assist in planning the allowable risk of incorrect acceptance for a specific test of details. To do so, the auditor should determine an acceptable audit risk and subjectively quantify his or her judgment of the risk of material misstatement (consisting of inherent risk and control risk), and the risk that substantive analytical procedures and other relevant substantive procedures would fail to detect misstatements that could occur in an assertion equal to tolerable misstatement, given that such misstatements occur and are not detected by the entity's controls. Some levels of these risks are implicit in evaluating audit evidence and reaching conclusions. Auditors using the model might prefer to evaluate these judgment risks explicitly. The relationships between these risks are illustrated in Table 1 of the Appendix [paragraph .48]. [As amended, effective for audits of financial statements for periods beginning on or after December 15, 2006, by Statement on Auditing Standards No. 111.]

.21 As discussed in section 326, the sufficiency of tests of details for a particular account balance or class of transactions is related to the individual importance of the items examined as well as to the potential for material misstatement. When planning a sample for a substantive test of details, the auditor uses his judgment to determine which items, if any, in an account balance or class of transactions should be individually examined and which items, if any, should be subject to sampling. The auditor should examine those items for which, in his judgment, acceptance of some sampling risk is not justified. For example, these may include items for which potential misstatements could individually equal or exceed the tolerable misstatement. Any items that the auditor has decided to examine 100 percent are not part of the items subject to sampling. Other items that, in the auditor's judgment, need to be tested to fulfill the audit objective but need not be examined 100 percent, would be subject to sampling.

.22 The auditor may be able to reduce the required sample size by separating items subject to sampling into relatively homogeneous groups on the basis of some characteristic related to the specific audit objective. For example, common bases for such groupings are the recorded or book value of the items, the nature of controls related to processing the items, and special considerations associated with certain items. An appropriate number of items is then selected from each group.

---

[4] Some auditors prefer to think of risk levels in quantitative terms. For example, in the circumstances described, an auditor might think in terms of a 5 percent risk of incorrect acceptance for the substantive test of details. Risk levels used in sampling applications in other fields are not necessarily relevant in determining appropriate levels for applications in auditing because an audit includes many interrelated tests and sources of evidence. [Footnote renumbered by the issuance of Statement on Auditing Standards No. 111, March 2006.]

.23 To determine the number of items to be selected in a sample for a particular test of details, the auditor should consider the tolerable misstatement and the expected misstatement, the audit risk, the characteristics of the population, the assessed risk of material misstatement (inherent risk and control risk), and the assessed risk for other substantive procedures related to the same assertion. An auditor who applies statistical sampling uses tables or formulas to compute sample size based on these judgments. An auditor who applies nonstatistical sampling uses professional judgment to relate these factors in determining the appropriate sample size. Ordinarily, this would result in a sample size comparable to the sample size resulting from an efficient and effectively designed statistical sample, considering the same sampling parameters.[5] Table 2 in the Appendix [paragraph .48] illustrates the effect these factors may have on sample size. [As amended, effective for audits of financial statements for periods beginning on or after December 15, 2006, by Statement on Auditing Standards No. 111.]

Sample Selection

.24 Sample items should be selected in such a way that the sample can be expected to be representative of the population. Therefore, all items in the population should have an opportunity to be selected. For example, haphazard and random-based selection of items represents two means of obtaining such samples.[6]

Performance and Evaluation

.25 Audit procedures that are appropriate to the particular audit objective should be applied to each sample item. In some circumstances the auditor may not be able to apply the planned audit procedures to selected sample items because, for example, the entity might not be able to locate supporting documentation. The auditor's treatment of unexamined items will depend on their effect on his or her evaluation of the sample. If the auditor's evaluation of the sample results would not be altered by considering those unexamined items to be misstated, it is not necessary to examine the items. However, if considering those unexamined items to be misstated would lead to a conclusion that the balance or class contains material misstatement, the auditor should consider alternative audit procedures that would provide sufficient appropriate audit evidence to form a conclusion. The auditor should also consider whether the reasons for his or her inability to examine the items have implications in relation to assessing risks of material misstatement due to fraud,[7] the assessed level of control risk that he or she expects to be supported, or the degree of reliance on management representations. [As amended, effective for audits of financial statements for periods beginning on or after December 15, 2006, by Statement on Auditing Standards No. 111.]

---

[5] This guidance does not suggest that the auditor using nonstatistical sampling compute a corresponding sample size using statistical theory. [Footnote added, effective for audits of financial statements for periods beginning on or after December 15, 2006, by Statement on Auditing Standards No. 111.]

[6] Random-based selection includes, for example, random sampling, stratified random sampling, sampling with probability proportional to size, and systematic sampling (for example, every hundredth item) with one or more random starts. [Footnote renumbered by the issuance of Statement on Auditing Standards No. 111, March 2006.]

[7] See section 316, *Consideration of Fraud in a Financial Statement Audit*. [Footnote added, effective for audits of financial statements for periods beginning on or after December 15, 2006, by Statement on Auditing Standards No. 111.]

.26 The auditor should project the misstatement results of the sample to the items from which the sample was selected.[8,9] There are several acceptable ways to project misstatements from a sample. For example, an auditor may have selected a sample of every twentieth item (50 items) from a population containing one thousand items. If he discovered overstatements of $3,000 in that sample, the auditor could project a $60,000 overstatement by dividing the amount of misstatement in the sample by the fraction of total items from the population included in the sample. The auditor should add that projection to the misstatements discovered in any items examined 100 percent. This total projected misstatement should be compared with the tolerable misstatement for the account balance or class of transactions, and appropriate consideration should be given to sampling risk. If the total projected misstatement is less than tolerable misstatement for the account balance or class of transactions, the auditor should consider the risk that such a result might be obtained even though the true monetary misstatement for the population exceeds tolerable misstatement. For example, if the tolerable misstatement in an account balance of $1 million is $50,000 and the total projected misstatement based on an appropriate sample (see paragraph .23) is $10,000, he may be reasonably assured that there is an acceptably low sampling risk that the true monetary misstatement for the population exceeds tolerable misstatement. On the other hand, if the total projected misstatement is close to the tolerable misstatement, the auditor may conclude that there is an unacceptably high risk that the actual misstatements in the population exceed the tolerable misstatement. An auditor uses professional judgment in making such evaluations.

.27 In addition to the evaluation of the frequency and amounts of monetary misstatements, consideration should be given to the qualitative aspects of the misstatements. These include (*a*) the nature and cause of misstatements, such as whether they are differences in principle or in application, are errors or are caused by fraud, or are due to misunderstanding of instructions or to carelessness, and (*b*) the possible relationship of the misstatements to other phases of the audit. The discovery of fraud ordinarily requires a broader consideration of possible implications than does the discovery of an error.

.28 If the sample results suggest that the auditor's planning assumptions were incorrect, he should take appropriate action. For example, if monetary misstatements are discovered in a substantive test of details in amounts or frequency that is greater than is consistent with the assessed levels of inherent and control risk, the auditor should alter his risk assessments. The auditor should also consider whether to modify the other audit tests that were designed based upon the inherent and control risk assessments. For example, a large number of misstatements discovered in confirmation of receivables may indicate the need to reconsider the control risk assessment related to the assertions that impacted the design of substantive tests of sales or cash receipts.

.29 The auditor should relate the evaluation of the sample to other relevant audit evidence when forming a conclusion about the related account balance or class of transactions.

---

[8] If the auditor has separated the items subject to sampling into relatively homogeneous groups (see paragraph .22), he separately projects the misstatement results of each group and sums them. [Footnote renumbered by the issuance of Statement on Auditing Standards No. 111, March 2006.]

[9] See section 316, *Consideration of Fraud in a Financial Statement Audit*, paragraphs .75–.78, for a further discussion of the auditor's consideration of differences between the accounting records and the underlying facts and circumstances. This section provides specific guidance on the auditor's consideration of an audit adjustment that is, or may be, fraud. [Footnote revised, January 2004, to reflect conforming changes necessary due to the issuance of Statement on Auditing Standards No. 99. Footnote renumbered by the issuance of Statement on Auditing Standards No. 111, March 2006.]

.30 Projected misstatement results for all audit sampling applications and all known misstatements from nonsampling applications should be considered in the aggregate along with other relevant audit evidence when the auditor evaluates whether the financial statements taken as a whole may be materially misstated.

Sampling in Tests of Controls

Planning Samples

.31 When planning a particular audit sample for a test of controls, the auditor should consider

- The relationship of the sample to the objective of the test of controls.
- The maximum rate of deviations from prescribed controls that would support his planned assessed level of control risk.
- The auditor's allowable risk of assessing control risk too low.
- Characteristics of the population, that is, the items comprising the account balance or class of transactions of interest.

.32 Sampling applies when the auditor needs to decide whether the rate of deviation from a prescribed procedure is no greater than a tolerable rate, for example in testing a matching process or an approval process. However, risk assessment procedures performed to obtain an understanding of internal control do not involve sampling.[10] Sampling concepts also do not apply for some tests of controls. Tests of automated application controls are generally tested only once or a few times when effective (IT) general controls are present, and thus do not rely on the concepts of risk and tolerable deviation as applied in other sampling procedures. Sampling generally is not applicable to analyses of controls for determining the appropriate segregation of duties or other analyses that do not examine documentary evidence of performance. In addition, sampling may not apply to tests of certain documented controls or to analyses of the effectiveness of security and access controls. Sampling also may not apply to some tests directed toward obtaining audit evidence about the operation of the control environment or the accounting system, for example, inquiry or observation of explanation of variances from budgets when the auditor does not desire to estimate the rate of deviation from the prescribed control, or when examining the actions of those charged with governance[11] for assessing their effectiveness. [As amended, effective for audits of financial statements for periods beginning on or after December 15, 2006, by Statement on Auditing Standards No. 111.]

.33 When designing samples for tests of controls the auditor ordinarily should plan to evaluate operating effectiveness in terms of deviations from prescribed controls, as to either the rate of such deviations or the monetary amount of the related transactions.[12] In this context, pertinent controls are

---

[10] The auditor often plans to perform tests of controls concurrently with obtaining an understanding of internal control (see section 318.27) for the purpose of estimating the rate of deviation from the prescribed controls, as to either the rate of such deviations or monetary amount of the related transactions. Sampling, as defined in this section, applies to such tests of controls. [Footnote revised, May 2001, to reflect conforming changes necessary due to the issuance of Statement on Auditing Standards No. 94. Footnote renumbered by the issuance of Statement on Auditing Standards No. 111, March 2006.]

[11] See footnote 4 in section 311, *Planning and Supervision*, for the definition of those charged with governance. [Footnote added, effective for audits of financial statements for periods beginning on or after December 15, 2006, by Statement on Auditing Standards No. 111.]

[12] For simplicity the remainder of this section will refer to only the rate of deviations. [Footnote renumbered by the issuance of Statement on Auditing Standards No. 111, March 2006.]

ones that, had they not been included in the design of internal control would have adversely affected the auditor's planned assessed level of control risk. The auditor's overall assessment of control risk for a particular assertion involves combining judgments about the prescribed controls, the deviations from prescribed controls, and the degree of assurance provided by the sample and other tests of controls.

.34 The auditor should determine the maximum rate of deviations from the prescribed control that he would be willing to accept without altering his planned assessed level of control risk. This is the *tolerable rate*. In determining the tolerable rate, the auditor should consider (*a*) the planned assessed level of control risk, and (*b*) the degree of assurance desired by the audit evidence in the sample. For example, if the auditor plans to assess control risk at a low level, and he desires a high degree of assurance from the audit evidence provided by the sample for tests of controls (i.e., not perform other tests of controls for the assertion), he might decide that a tolerable rate of 5 percent or possibly less would be reasonable. If the auditor either plans to assess control risk at a higher level, or he desires assurance from other tests of controls along with that provided by the sample (such as inquiries of appropriate entity personnel or observation of the application of the policy or procedure), the auditor might decide that a tolerable rate of 10 percent or more is reasonable. [Revised, March 2006, to reflect conforming changes necessary due to the issuance of Statement on Auditing Standards No. 105.]

.35 In assessing the tolerable rate of deviations, the auditor should consider that, while deviations from pertinent controls increase the risk of material misstatements in the accounting records, such deviations do not necessarily result in misstatements. For example, a recorded disbursement that does not show evidence of required approval may nevertheless be a transaction that is properly authorized and recorded. Deviations would result in misstatements in the accounting records only if the deviations and the misstatements occurred on the same transactions. Deviations from pertinent controls at a given rate ordinarily would be expected to result in misstatements at a lower rate.

.36 In some situations, the risk of material misstatement for an assertion may be related to a combination of controls. If a combination of two or more controls is necessary to affect the risk of material misstatement for an assertion, those controls should be regarded as a single procedure, and deviations from any controls in combination should be evaluated on that basis.

.37 Samples taken to test the operating effectiveness of controls are intended to provide a basis for the auditor to conclude whether the controls are being applied as prescribed. When the degree of assurance desired by the audit evidence in the sample is high, the auditor should allow for a low level of sampling risk (that is, the risk of assessing control risk too low). [Revised, March 2006, to reflect conforming changes necessary due to the issuance of Statement on Auditing Standards No. 105.][13]

.38 To determine the number of items to be selected for a particular sample for a test of controls, the auditor should consider the tolerable rate of deviation from the controls being tested, the likely rate of deviations, and the allowable risk of assessing control risk too low. An auditor applies professional judgment to relate these factors in determining the appropriate sample size.

---

[13] The auditor who prefers to think of risk levels in quantitative terms might consider, for example, a 5 percent to 10 percent risk of assessing control risk too low. [Footnote renumbered by the issuance of Statement on Auditing Standards No. 111, March 2006.]

Sample Selection

.39 Sample items should be selected in such a way that the sample can be expected to be representative of the population. Therefore, all items in the population should have an opportunity to be selected. Random-based selection of items represents one means of obtaining such samples. Ideally, the auditor should use a selection method that has the potential for selecting items from the entire period under audit. Section 318.37 provides guidance applicable to the auditor's use of sampling during interim and remaining periods. [Revised, May 2001, to reflect conforming changes necessary due to the issuance of Statement on Auditing Standards No. 94.]

Performance and Evaluation

.40 Auditing procedures that are appropriate to achieve the objective of the test of controls should be applied to each sample item. If the auditor is not able to apply the planned audit procedures or appropriate alternative procedures to selected items, he should consider the reasons for this limitation, and he should ordinarily consider those selected items to be deviations from the prescribed policy or procedure for the purpose of evaluating the sample.

.41 The deviation rate in the sample is the auditor's best estimate of the deviation rate in the population from which it was selected. If the estimated deviation rate is less than the tolerable rate for the population, the auditor should consider the risk that such a result might be obtained even though the true deviation rate for the population exceeds the tolerable rate for the population. For example, if the tolerable rate for a population is 5 percent and no deviations are found in a sample of 60 items, the auditor may conclude that there is an acceptably low sampling risk that the true deviation rate in the population exceeds the tolerable rate of 5 percent. On the other hand, if the sample includes, for example, two or more deviations, the auditor may conclude that there is an unacceptably high sampling risk that the rate of deviations in the population exceeds the tolerable rate of 5 percent. An auditor applies professional judgment in making such an evaluation.

.42 In addition to the evaluation of the frequency of deviations from pertinent procedures, consideration should be given to the qualitative aspects of the deviations. These include (*a*) the nature and cause of the deviations, such as whether they are due to error or fraud, and (*b*) the possible relationship of the deviations to other phases of the audit. The discovery of fraud ordinarily requires a broader consideration of possible implications than does the discovery of an error. [As amended, effective for audits of financial statements for periods beginning on or after December 15, 2006, by Statement on Auditing Standards No. 111.]

.43 If the auditor concludes that the sample results do not support the planned assessed level of control risk for an assertion, he should re-evaluate the nature, timing, and extent of substantive procedures based on a revised consideration of the assessed level of control risk for the relevant financial statement assertions.

Dual-Purpose Samples

.44 In some circumstances the auditor may design a sample that will be used for dual purposes: testing the operating effectiveness of an identified control and testing whether the recorded monetary amount of transactions is correct.[14] In general, an auditor planning to use a dual-purpose sample would have made a preliminary assessment that there is an acceptably low risk that the rate of deviations from the prescribed control in the population exceeds the tolerable rate. For example, an auditor designing a test of control over entries in the voucher register may plan a related substantive procedure at a risk level that anticipates a particular assessed level of control risk. The size of a sample designed for dual purposes should be the larger of the samples that would otherwise have been designed for the two separate purposes.[15] In evaluating such tests, deviations from the prescribed control and monetary misstatements should be evaluated separately using the risk levels applicable for the respective purposes. The absence of monetary misstatements detected in a sample does not necessarily imply that related controls are effective; however, misstatements that the auditor detects by performing substantive procedures should be considered by the auditor as a possible indication of a control failure when assessing the operating effectiveness of related controls. [As amended, effective for audits of financial statements for periods beginning on or after December 15, 2006, by Statement on Auditing Standards No. 111.]

Selecting a Sampling Approach

.45 As discussed in paragraph .04, either a nonstatistical or statistical approach to audit sampling, when properly applied, can provide sufficient audit evidence. [Revised, March 2006, to reflect conforming changes necessary due to the issuance of Statement on Auditing Standards No. 105.]

.46 Statistical sampling helps the auditor (*a*) to design an efficient sample, (*b*) to measure the sufficiency of the audit evidence obtained, and (*c*) to evaluate the sample results. By using statistical theory, the auditor can quantify sampling risk to assist himself in limiting it to a level he considers acceptable. However, statistical sampling involves additional costs of training auditors, designing individual samples to meet the statistical requirements, and selecting the items to be examined. Because either nonstatistical or statistical sampling can provide sufficient audit evidence, the auditor chooses between them after considering their relative cost and effectiveness in the circumstances. [Revised, March 2006, to reflect conforming changes necessary due to the issuance of Statement on Auditing Standards No. 105.]

Effective Date

.47 This section is effective for audits of financial statements for periods ended on or after June 25, 1983. Earlier application is encouraged. [As amended, effective retroactively to June 25, 1982, by Statement on Auditing Standards No. 43.]

---

[14] Section 318, *Performing Audit Procedures in Response to Assessed Risks and Evaluating the Audit Evidence Obtained*, discusses dual-purpose tests in paragraph .33. [Footnote added, effective for audits of financial statements for periods beginning on or after December 15, 2006, by Statement on Auditing Standards No. 111.]

[15] The test requiring the smaller sample size may be selected as a subset of the larger sample. [Footnote added, effective for audits of financial statements for periods beginning on or after December 15, 2006, by Statement on Auditing Standards No. 111.]

.48

Appendix

Relating the Risk of Incorrect Acceptance for a Substantive Test of Details to Other Sources of Audit Assurance

In Table 1 it is assumed, for illustrative purposes, that the auditor has chosen an audit risk (AR) of 5 percent for an assertion. Table 1 incorporates the premise that internal control cannot be expected to be completely effective in detecting aggregate misstatements equal to tolerable misstatement that might occur. The table also illustrates the fact that the risk level for substantive procedures for particular assertions is not an isolated decision. Rather, it is a direct consequence of the auditor's assessments of the risk of material misstatement (RMM) (combined assessments of inherent and control risks), and judgments about the effectiveness of substantive analytical procedures (AP) and other relevant tests of details (TD), and it cannot be properly considered out of this context.[1]

Table 1

Allowable Risk of Incorrect Acceptance (TD) for Various Assessments of RMM and AP; for AR = .05

Auditor's subjective assessment of risk of material misstatement.	Auditor's subjective assessment of risk that substantive analytical procedures and other relevant substantive procedures might fail to detect aggregate misstatements equal to tolerable misstatement.			
RMM	*AP*			
	10%	*30%*	*50%*	*100%*
		TD		
10%	*	*	*	50%
30%	*	55%	33%	16%
50%	*	33%	20%	10%
100%	50%	16%	10%	5%

* The allowable level of AR of 5 percent exceeds the product of RMM and AP, and thus, the planned test of details may not be necessary unless specified by regulation or other Standards (e.g., confirmation or inventory observation procedures).

Note: The table entries for TD are computed from the illustrated model: TD equals AR/(RMM x AP). For example, for RMM = .50, AP = .30, TD = .05/(.50 x .30) or .33 (equals 33%).

---

[1] As amended, effective for audits of financial statements for periods ended after September 30, 1983, by Statement on Auditing Standards No. 45. Footnote deleted by the issuance of Statement on Auditing Standards No. 111, March 2006.]

Table 2

Factors Influencing Sample Sizes for a Test of Details in Sample Planning

Factor	*Conditions leading to* Smaller sample size	*Conditions leading to* Larger sample size	*Related factor for substantive sample planning*
a. Assessment of inherent risk.	Low assessed level of inherent risk.	High assessed level of inherent risk.	Allowable risk of incorrect acceptance.
b. Assessment of control risk.	Low assessed level of control risk.	High assessed level of control risk.	Allowable risk of incorrect acceptance.
c. Assessment of risk for other substantive procedures related to the same assertion (including substantive analytical procedures and other relevant substantive procedures).	Low assessment of risk associated with other relevant substantive procedures.	High assessment of risk associated with other relevant substantive procedures.	Allowable risk of incorrect acceptance.
d. Measure of tolerable misstatement for a specific account.	Larger measure of tolerable misstatement.	Smaller measure of tolerable misstatement.	Tolerable misstatement.
e. Expected size and frequency of misstatements.	Smaller misstatements or lower frequency.	Larger misstatements or higher frequency.	Assessment of population characteristics.
f. Number of items in the population.	Virtually no effect on sample size unless population is very small.		
g. Choice between statistical and nonstatistical sampling	Ordinarily, sample sizes are comparable.		

[As amended, effective for audits of financial statements for periods ended after September 30, 1983, by Statement on Auditing Standards No. 45. As amended, effective for audits of financial statements for periods beginning on or after December 15, 2006, by Statement on Auditing Standards No. 111.]

AU Section 9350

Audit Sampling: Auditing Interpretations of Section 350

1. Applicability

.01 *Question*—Section 350, *Audit Sampling*, paragraph .01, footnote 1, states that there may be reasons other than sampling for an auditor to examine less than 100 percent of the items comprising an account balance or class of transactions. For what reasons might an auditor's examination of less than 100 percent of the items comprising an account balance or class of transactions *not* be considered audit sampling?

.02 *Interpretation*—The auditor's examination of less than 100 percent of the items comprising an account balance or class of transactions would not be considered to be an audit sampling application under the following circumstances.

a. *It is not the auditor's intent to extend the conclusion that he reaches by examining the items to the remainder of the items in the account balance or class.* Audit sampling is defined as the application of an audit procedure to less than 100 percent of the items within an account balance or class of transactions for the purpose of evaluating some characteristic of the balance or class. Thus, if the purpose of the auditor's application of an auditing procedure to less than 100 percent of the items in an account balance or class of transactions is something other than evaluating a trait of the entire balance or class, he is not using audit sampling.

   For example, an auditor might trace several transactions through an entity's accounting system to gain an understanding of the nature of the entity's operations or clarify his understanding of the design of the entity's internal control. In such cases the auditor's intent is to gain a general understanding of the accounting system or other relevant parts of the internal control, rather than the evaluation of a characteristic of all transactions processed. As a result, the auditor is not using audit sampling.

   Occasionally auditors perform procedures such as checking arithmetical calculations or tracing journal entries into ledger accounts on a test basis. When such procedures are applied to less than 100 percent of the arithmetical calculations or ledger postings that affect the financial statements, audit sampling may not be involved if the procedure is not a test to evaluate a characteristic of an account balance or class of transactions, but is intended only to provide limited knowledge that supplements the auditor's other audit evidence regarding a financial statement assertion.

b. *Although he might not be examining all the items in an account balance or class of transactions, the auditor might be examining 100 percent of the items in a given population.* A "population" for audit sampling purposes does not necessarily need to be an entire account balance or class of transactions. For example, in some circumstances, an auditor might examine all of the items that comprise an account balance or class of transactions that exceed a given amount or that have an unusual characteristic and either apply other auditing procedures (e.g., analytical procedures) to those items that do not exceed the given amount or possess the unusual characteristic or apply no auditing procedures to them because of their insignificance. Again, the auditor is not using audit sampling. Rather, he has broken the account balance or class of transactions into two groups. One group is tested 100 percent, the other group is either tested by analytical procedures or considered insignificant. The auditor would be using audit sampling only if he applied an auditing procedure to less than all of the items in the second group to form a conclusion about that group. For the same reason, cutoff tests often do not involve audit sampling applications. In performing cutoff tests auditors often examine all significant transactions for a period surrounding the cutoff date and, as a result, such tests do not involve the application of audit sampling.

c. *The auditor is testing controls that are not documented.* Auditors choose from a variety of methods including inquiry, observation, and examination of documentary evidence in testing controls. For example, observation of a client's physical inventory count procedures is a test that is performed primarily through the auditor's observation of controls over such things as inventory movement, counting procedures and other procedures used by the client to control the count of the inventory. The procedures that the auditor uses to observe the client's physical inventory count generally do not require use of audit sampling. However, audit sampling may be used in certain tests of controls or substantive tests of details of inventory, for example, in tracing selected test counts into inventory records.

d. *The auditor is not performing a substantive test of details.* Substantive tests consist of tests of details of transactions and balances, analytical review and or from a combination of both. In performing substantive tests, audit sampling is generally used only in testing details of transactions and balances.

[Issue Date: January, 1985; Revised: March, 2006.]

AU Section 380

The Auditor's Communication With Those Charged With Governance

(Supersedes SAS No. 61.)

Source: SAS No. 114.

Effective for audits of financial statements for periods beginning on or after December 15, 2006.

.01 This section establishes standards and provides guidance on the auditor's communication with those charged with governance in relation to an audit of financial statements.[1] Although this section applies regardless of an entity's governance structure or size, particular considerations apply where all of those charged with governance are involved in managing an entity. This section does not establish requirements regarding the auditor's communication with an entity's management or owners unless they are also charged with a governance role.

.02 This section has been drafted in terms of an audit of financial statements, but may also be applied, adapted as necessary in the circumstances, to audits of other historical financial information when those charged with governance have a responsibility to oversee the preparation and presentation of the other historical financial information.

.03 For purposes of this section:

a. *Those charged with governance* means the person(s) with responsibility for overseeing the strategic direction of the entity and obligations related to the accountability of the entity. This includes overseeing the financial reporting process. In some cases, those charged with governance are responsible for approving the entity's financial statements (in other cases management has this responsibility). For entities with a board of directors, this term encompasses the term *board of directors* or *audit committee* used elsewhere in generally accepted auditing standards.

b. *Management* means the person(s) responsible for achieving the objectives of the entity and who have the authority to establish policies and make decisions by which those objectives are to be pursued. Management is responsible for the financial statements, including designing, implementing, and maintaining effective internal control over financial reporting.

.04 Recognizing the importance of effective two-way communication to the audit, this section provides a framework for the auditor's communication with those charged with governance and identifies some specific matters to be communicated with them. Additional matters to be communicated are identified

---

[1] The provisions of this section apply to audits of financial statements prepared either in accordance with generally accepted accounting principles or in accordance with a comprehensive basis of accounting other than generally accepted accounting principles. References in this section to generally accepted accounting principles are intended to also refer to other comprehensive bases of accounting when the reference is relevant to the basis of accounting used.

in other Statements on Auditing Standards (see Appendix A [paragraph .66]). Further matters may be communicated by agreement with those charged with governance or management, or in accordance with external requirements.

.05 The auditor must communicate with those charged with governance matters related to the financial statement audit that are, in the auditor's professional judgment, significant and relevant to the responsibilities of those charged with governance in overseeing the financial reporting process.

.06 Clear communication of specific matters in accordance with this section is an integral part of every audit. However, the auditor is not required to perform procedures specifically to identify other significant matters to communicate with those charged with governance.

The Role of Communication

.07 The principal purposes of communication with those charged with governance are to:

a. Communicate clearly with those charged with governance the responsibilities of the auditor in relation to the financial statement audit, and an overview of the scope and timing of the audit.

b. Obtain from those charged with governance information relevant to the audit.

c. Provide those charged with governance with timely observations arising from the audit that are relevant to their responsibilities in overseeing the financial reporting process.

.08 This section focuses primarily on communications from the auditor to those charged with governance. However, effective two-way communication is also very important in assisting:

a. The auditor and those charged with governance in understanding matters related to the audit in context, and in developing a constructive working relationship. This relationship is developed while maintaining the auditor's independence and objectivity.

b. The auditor in obtaining from those charged with governance information relevant to the audit. For example, those charged with governance may assist the auditor in understanding the entity and its environment, in identifying appropriate sources of audit evidence, and in providing information about specific transactions or events.

c. Those charged with governance in fulfilling their responsibility to oversee the financial reporting process, thereby reducing the risks of material misstatement of the financial statements.

.09 Although the auditor is responsible for communicating specific matters in accordance with this section, management also has a responsibility to communicate matters of governance interest to those charged with governance. Communication by the auditor does not relieve management of this responsibility.

Legal Considerations

.10 In certain circumstances, the auditor may be required to report to a regulatory or enforcement body certain matters communicated with those charged with governance. For example, governmental auditing standards require auditors to report fraud, illegal acts, violations of provisions of contracts or grant agreements, and abuse directly to parties outside the audited entity in certain circumstances.

.11 In rare circumstances, laws or regulations may prevent the auditor from communicating certain matters with those charged with governance, or others within the entity. For example, laws or regulations may specifically prohibit a communication, or other action, that might prejudice an investigation by an appropriate authority into an actual or suspected illegal act. In such circumstances, it may be appropriate for the auditor to seek legal advice.

Those Charged With Governance

.12 The auditor should determine the appropriate person(s) within the entity's governance structure with whom to communicate. The appropriate person(s) may vary depending on the matter to be communicated.

.13 Governance structures vary by entity, reflecting influences such as size and ownership characteristics. For example:

- In some entities, those charged with governance hold positions that are an integral part of the entity's legal structure, for example, company directors. For other entities, a body that is not part of the entity may be charged with governance, as with some government agencies.
- In some cases, some or all of those charged with governance also have management responsibilities. In others, those charged with governance and management are different people.

.14 In most entities, governance is the collective responsibility of a governing body, such as a board of directors, a supervisory board, partners, proprietors, a committee of management, trustees, or equivalent persons. In some smaller entities, however, one person may be charged with governance, such as the owner-manager where there are no other owners, or a sole trustee. When governance is a collective responsibility, a subgroup, such as an audit committee or even an individual, may be charged with specific tasks to assist the governing body in meeting its responsibilities.

.15 Such diversity means that it is not possible for this section to specify for all audits the person(s) with whom the auditor is to communicate particular matters. Also, in some cases the appropriate person(s) with whom to communicate may not be clearly identifiable from the engagement circumstances, for example, entities where the governance structure is not formally defined, such as some family-owned entities, some not-for-profit organizations, and some government entities. The auditors understanding of the entity's governance structure and processes obtained in accordance with section 314, *Understanding the Entity and Its Environment and Assessing the Risks of Material Misstatement*, is relevant in deciding with whom to communicate matters.

.16 When the appropriate person(s) with whom to communicate are not clearly identifiable, the auditor and the engaging party should agree on the relevant person(s) within the entity's governance structure with whom the auditor will communicate. When the entity being audited is a component[2] of a group,[3] the appropriate person(s) with whom to communicate is dependent on the nature of the matter to be communicated and the terms of the engagement.

---

[2] *Component* means a head office, parent, division, branch, subsidiary, joint venture, associated company, equity investee, or other entity whose financial information is or should be included in the consolidated financial statements of a group.

[3] *Group* means an entity whose consolidated financial statements include or should include financial information of more than one component.

Communication With the Audit Committee or Other Subgroup of Those Charged With Governance

.17 Audit committees (or similar subgroups with different names) exist in many entities. Although their specific authority and functions may differ, communication with the audit committee, where one exists, is a key element in the auditor's communication with those charged with governance. Good governance principles suggest that:

- The auditor has access to the audit committee as necessary.
- The chair of the audit committee and, when relevant, the other members of the audit committee, meet with the auditor periodically.
- The audit committee meets with the auditor without management present at least annually.

.18 The auditor should evaluate whether communication with a subgroup of those charged with governance, such as the audit committee or an individual, adequately fulfills the auditor's responsibility to communicate with those charged with governance. When considering communicating with a subgroup of those charged with governance, the auditor may take into account such matters as:

- The respective responsibilities of the subgroup and the governing body.
- The nature of the matter to be communicated.
- Relevant legal or regulatory requirements.
- Whether the subgroup (*a*) has the authority to take action in relation to the information communicated and (*b*) can provide further information and explanations the auditor may need.
- Whether the auditor is aware of potential conflicts of interest between the subgroup and other members of the governing body.
- Whether there is also a need to communicate the information, in full or in summary form, to the governing body. This decision may be influenced by the auditor's assessment of how effectively and appropriately the subgroup communicates relevant information with the governing body. The auditor retains the right to communicate with the governing body, a fact the auditor may make explicit in the terms of the engagement.

Communication With Management

.19 Many matters may be discussed with management in the ordinary course of an audit, including matters to be communicated with those charged with governance in accordance with this section. Such discussions recognize management's executive responsibility for the conduct of the entity's operations and, in particular, management's responsibility for the financial statements.

.20 Before communicating matters with those charged with governance, the auditor may discuss them with management unless that is inappropriate. For example, it may not be appropriate to discuss with management questions of management's competence or integrity. In addition to recognizing management's responsibility, these initial discussions may clarify facts and issues, and give management an opportunity to provide further information and explanations. Similarly, when the entity has an internal audit function, the auditor may discuss matters with the internal auditor before communicating with those charged with governance.

When All of Those Charged With Governance Are Involved in Managing the Entity

.21 In some cases, all of those charged with governance are involved in managing the entity. In these cases, if matters required by this section are communicated with person(s) with management responsibilities, and those person(s) also have governance responsibilities, the matters need not be communicated again with those same person(s) in their governance role.

.22 When all of those charged with governance are involved in managing the entity, the auditor should consider whether communication with person(s) with financial reporting responsibilities adequately informs all of those with whom the auditor would otherwise communicate in their governance capacity. (See paragraphs .12 and .18.)

Matters to Be Communicated

.23 The auditor should communicate with those charged with governance:

a. The auditor's responsibilities under generally accepted auditing standards (see paragraphs .26 through .28);

b. An overview of the planned scope and timing of the audit (see paragraphs .29 through .33); and

c. Significant findings from the audit (see paragraphs .34 through .44).

.24 Management's communication of these matters to those charged with governance does not relieve the auditor of the responsibility to also communicate them. However, communication of these matters by management may affect the form or timing of the auditor's communication.

.25 Nothing in this section precludes the auditor from communicating any other matters to those charged with governance.

The Auditor's Responsibilities Under Generally Accepted Auditing Standards

.26 The auditor should communicate with those charged with governance the auditor's responsibilities under generally accepted auditing standards, including that:

a. The auditor is responsible for forming and expressing an opinion about whether the financial statements that have been prepared by management with the oversight of those charged with governance are presented fairly, in all material respects, in conformity with generally accepted accounting principles.

b. The audit of the financial statements does not relieve management or those charged with governance of their responsibilities.

These responsibilities may be communicated through the engagement letter, or other form of contract that records the terms of the engagement, if that letter or contract is provided to those charged with governance.

.27 The auditor may also communicate that:

a. The auditor is responsible for performing the audit in accordance with generally accepted auditing standards and that the audit is designed to obtain reasonable, rather than absolute, assurance about whether the financial statements are free of material misstatement.

b. An audit of financial statements includes consideration of internal control over financial reporting as a basis for designing audit procedures that are appropriate in the circumstances, but not for the purpose of expressing an opinion on the effectiveness of the entity's internal control over financial reporting.

c. The auditor is responsible for communicating significant matters related to the financial statement audit that are, in the auditor's professional judgment, relevant to the responsibilities of those charged with governance in overseeing the financial reporting process. Generally accepted auditing standards do not require the auditor to design procedures for the purpose of identifying other matters to communicate with those charged with governance.

d. When applicable, the auditor is also responsible for communicating particular matters required by laws or regulations, by agreement with the entity or by additional requirements applicable to the engagement.

.28 Section 550, *Other Information in Documents Containing Audited Financial Statements*, addresses the auditor's responsibility in relation to other information in documents containing audited financial statements and the auditor's report thereon.[4] If the entity includes other information in documents containing audited financial statements, the auditor should communicate with those charged with governance the auditor's responsibility with respect to such other information, any procedures performed relating to the other information, and the results. [Revised, December 2010, to reflect conforming changes necessary due to the issuance of SAS Nos. 118–120.]

Planned Scope and Timing of the Audit

.29 The auditor should communicate with those charged with governance an overview of the planned scope and timing of the audit. However, it is important for the auditor not to compromise the effectiveness of the audit, particularly where some or all of those charged with governance are involved in managing the entity. For example, communicating the nature and timing of detailed audit procedures may reduce the effectiveness of those procedures by making them too predictable. Certain factors described in paragraph .53 may be relevant in determining the nature and extent of this communication.

.30 Communication regarding the planned scope and timing of the audit may:

a. Assist those charged with governance in understanding better the consequences of the auditor's work for their oversight activities, discussing with the auditor issues of risk and materiality, and identifying any areas in which they may request the auditor to undertake additional procedures; and

b. Assist the auditor to understand better the entity and its environment.

.31 Matters communicated may include the following:

- How the auditor proposes to address the significant risks of material misstatement, whether due to fraud or error.
- The auditor's approach to internal control relevant to the audit, including, when applicable, whether the auditor will express an opinion on the effectiveness of internal control over financial reporting.

---

[4] [Footnote deleted, December 2010, to reflect conforming changes necessary due to the issuance of SAS Nos. 118–120.]

- The concept of materiality in planning and executing the audit, focusing on the factors considered rather than on specific thresholds or amounts.
- Where the entity has an internal audit function, the extent to which the auditor will use the work of internal audit, and how the external and internal auditors can best work together.

.32 Other planning matters that the auditor may consider discussing with those charged with governance include:

- The views of those charged with governance about:
  - — The appropriate person(s) in the entity's governance structure with whom to communicate.
  - — The allocation of responsibilities between those charged with governance and management.
  - — The entity's objectives and strategies, and the related business risks that may result in material misstatements.
  - — Matters those charged with governance consider warrant particular attention during the audit, and any areas where they request additional procedures to be undertaken.
  - — Significant communications with regulators.
  - — Other matters those charged with governance believe are relevant to the audit of the financial statements.
- The attitudes, awareness, and actions of those charged with governance concerning (*a*) the entity's internal control and its importance in the entity, including how those charged with governance oversee the effectiveness of internal control and (*b*) the detection or the possibility of fraud.
- The actions of those charged with governance in response to developments in financial reporting, laws, accounting standards, corporate governance practices, and other related matters.
- The actions of those charged with governance in response to previous communications with the auditor.

.33 While communication with those charged with governance may assist the auditor in planning the scope and timing of the audit, it does not change the auditor's sole responsibility to determine the overall audit strategy and the audit plan, including the nature, timing, and extent of procedures necessary to obtain sufficient appropriate audit evidence.

Significant Findings From the Audit

.34 The auditor should communicate with those charged with governance the following matters:

a. The auditor's views about qualitative aspects of the entity's significant accounting practices, including accounting policies, accounting estimates, and financial statement disclosures (see paragraphs .37 and .38).

b. Significant difficulties, if any, encountered during the audit (see paragraph .39).

c. Uncorrected misstatements, other than those the auditor believes are trivial, if any (see paragraphs .40 and .41).

d. Disagreements with management, if any, (see paragraph .42).

e. Other findings or issues, if any, arising from the audit that are, in the auditor's professional judgment, significant and relevant to those charged with governance regarding their oversight of the financial reporting process.

.35 Unless all of those charged with governance are involved in managing the entity, the auditor also should communicate:

a. Material, corrected misstatements that were brought to the attention of management as a result of audit procedures. The auditor also may communicate other corrected immaterial misstatements, such as frequently recurring immaterial misstatements that may indicate a particular bias in the preparation of the financial statements.

b. Representations the auditor is requesting from management. The auditor may provide those charged with governance with a copy of management's written representations.

c. Management's consultations with other accountants (see paragraph .43).

d. Significant issues, if any, arising from the audit that were discussed, or the subject of correspondence, with management (see paragraph .44).

.36 The communication of significant findings from the audit may include requesting further information from those charged with governance in order to complete the audit evidence obtained. For example, the auditor may confirm that those charged with governance have the same understanding of the facts and circumstances relevant to specific transactions or events.

Qualitative Aspects of the Entity's Significant Accounting Practices

.37 Generally accepted accounting principles provide for the entity to make accounting estimates and judgments about accounting policies and financial statement disclosures. Open and constructive communication about qualitative aspects of the entity's significant accounting practices may include comment on the acceptability of significant accounting practices. Appendix B [paragraph .67] provides guidance on the matters that may be included in this communication.

.38 The auditor should explain to those charged with governance why the auditor considers a significant accounting practice not to be appropriate and, when considered necessary, request changes. If requested changes are not made, the auditor should inform those charged with governance that the auditor will consider the effect of this on the financial statements of the current and future years, and on the auditor's report.

Significant Difficulties Encountered During the Audit

.39 The auditor should inform those charged with governance of any significant difficulties encountered in dealing with management related to the performance of the audit. Significant difficulties encountered during the audit may include such matters as:

- Significant delays in management providing required information.
- An unnecessarily brief time within which to complete the audit.
- Extensive unexpected effort required to obtain sufficient appropriate audit evidence.
- The unavailability of expected information.

- Restrictions imposed on the auditors by management.
- Management's unwillingness to provide information about management's plans for dealing with the adverse effects of the conditions or events that lead the auditor to believe there is substantial doubt about the entity's ability to continue as a going concern.

In some circumstances, such difficulties may constitute a scope limitation that leads to a modification of the auditor's opinion.

Uncorrected Misstatements

.40 Section 312, *Audit Risk and Materiality in Conducting an Audit*, requires the auditor to accumulate all known and likely misstatements identified during the audit, other than those that the auditor believes are trivial, and communicate them to the appropriate level of management. The auditor should communicate with those charged with governance uncorrected misstatements and the effect that they may have on the opinion in the auditor's report, and request their correction. In communicating the effect that material uncorrected misstatements may have on the opinion in the auditor's report, the auditor should communicate them individually. Where there are a large number of small uncorrected misstatements, the auditor may communicate the number and overall monetary effect of the misstatements, rather than the details of each individual misstatement.

.41 The auditor should discuss with those charged with governance the implications of a failure to correct known and likely misstatements, if any, considering qualitative as well as quantitative considerations, including possible implications in relation to future financial statements. The auditor should also communicate with those charged with governance the effect of uncorrected misstatements related to prior periods on the relevant classes of transactions, account balances or disclosures, and the financial statements as a whole.

Disagreements With Management

.42 The auditor should discuss with those charged with governance any disagreements with management, whether or not satisfactorily resolved, about matters that individually or in the aggregate could be significant to the entity's financial statements or the auditor's report. Disagreements with management may occasionally arise over, among other things, the application of accounting principles to the entity's specific transactions and events and the basis for management's judgments about accounting estimates. Disagreements may also arise regarding the scope of the audit, disclosures to be included in the entity's financial statements, and the wording of the auditor's report. For purposes of this section, disagreements do not include differences of opinion based on incomplete facts or preliminary information that are later resolved.

Management's Consultations With Other Accountants

.43 In some cases, management may decide to consult with other accountants about auditing and accounting matters. When the auditor is aware that such consultation has occurred, the auditor should discuss with those charged with governance his or her views about significant matters that were the subject of such consultation.[5]

---

[5] Circumstances in which the auditor should be informed of such consultations are described in paragraph .07 of section 625, *Reports on the Application of Accounting Principles*.

Significant Issues Discussed, or Subject to Correspondence, With Management

.44 The auditor should communicate with those charged with governance any significant issues that were discussed or were the subject of correspondence with management. Significant issues may include such matters as:

- Business conditions affecting the entity, and business plans and strategies that may affect the risks of material misstatement.
- Discussions or correspondence in connection with the initial or recurring retention of the auditor including, among other matters, any discussions or correspondence regarding the application of accounting principles and auditing standards.

Independence

.45 Generally accepted auditing standards require independence for all audits. Relevant matters to consider in reaching a conclusion about independence include circumstances or relationships that create threats to auditor independence and the related safeguards that have been applied to eliminate those threats or reduce them to an acceptable level.[6]

.46 Although the auditor's report affirms the auditor's independence, in certain situations, particularly for public interest entities,[7] the auditor may determine that it is appropriate to communicate with those charged with governance circumstances or relationships (for example, financial interests, business or family relationships, or nonaudit services provided or expected to be provided) that in the auditor's professional judgment may reasonably be thought to bear on independence and that the auditor gave significant consideration to in reaching the conclusion that independence has not been impaired.

.47 The form and timing of communications regarding independence may be affected by the entity's governance structure and whether a formal subgroup such as an audit committee exists. In situations where all of those charged with governance are involved in managing the entity, the auditor may determine that those charged with governance have been informed of relevant facts regarding the auditor's independence through their management activities or through other means, such as the engagement letter. This is particularly likely where the entity is owner-managed, and the auditor's firm has little involvement with the entity beyond a financial statement audit.

---

[6] Comprehensive guidance on threats to independence and safeguards, including application to specific situations, is set forth in the AICPA's *Conceptual Framework for AICPA Independence Standards* [ET section 100-1].

[7] In addition to entities subject to Securities and Exchange Commission reporting requirements, the *Conceptual Framework for AICPA Independence Standards* [ET section 100-1] considers the following entities to be *public interest entities*: (1) employee benefit and health and welfare plans subject to Employee Retirement Income Security Act audit requirements; (2) governmental retirement plans; (3) entities or programs (including for-profit entities) subject to Single Audit Act OMB Circular A-133 audit requirements and entities or programs subject to similar program oversight; and (4) financial institutions, credit unions, and insurance companies. These entities are public interest entities because their audited financial statements are directly relied upon by significant numbers of stakeholders to make investment, credit, or similar decisions or indirectly relied upon through regulatory oversight (for example, in the case of pension plans, banks, and insurance companies) and, therefore, the potential extent of harm to the public from an audit failure involving one of these entities would generally be significant.

The Communication Process

Establishing a Mutual Understanding

.48 The auditor should communicate with those charged with governance the form, timing, and expected general content of communications. Clear communication of the auditor's responsibilities (paragraphs .26 through .28), an overview of the planned scope and timing of the audit (paragraphs .29 through .33), and the expected general content of communications helps establish the basis for effective two-way communication.

.49 Matters that may also contribute to effective two-way communication include discussion of:

- The purpose of communications. When the purpose is clear, the auditor and those charged with governance are in a better position to have a mutual understanding of relevant issues and the expected actions arising from the communication process.
- The form in which communications will be made.
- The person(s) on the audit team and among those charged with governance who will communicate regarding particular matters.
- The auditor's expectation that communication will be two way, and that those charged with governance will communicate with the auditor matters they consider relevant to the audit. Such matters might include strategic decisions that may significantly affect the nature, timing, and extent of audit procedures; the suspicion or the detection of fraud; or concerns about the integrity or competence of senior management.
- The process for taking action and reporting back on matters communicated by the auditor.
- The process for taking action and reporting back on matters communicated by those charged with governance.

.50 The communication process will vary with the circumstances, including the size and governance structure of the entity, how those charged with governance operate, and the auditor's view of the significance of matters to be communicated. Difficulty in establishing effective two-way communication may indicate that the communication between the auditor and those charged with governance is not adequate for the purpose of the audit (see paragraph .60).

Forms of Communication

.51 The auditor should communicate in writing with those charged with governance significant findings from the audit (see paragraphs .34 and .35) when, in the auditor's professional judgment, oral communication would not be adequate. This communication need not include matters that arose during the course of the audit that were communicated with those charged with governance and satisfactorily resolved. Other communications may be oral or in writing.

.52 Effective communication may involve formal presentations and written reports as well as less formal communications, including discussions. Written communications may include an engagement letter that is provided to those charged with governance.

.53 In addition to the significance of a particular matter, the form of communication (for example, whether to communicate orally or in writing, the extent of detail or summarization in the communication, and whether to communicate in a formal or informal manner) may be affected by such factors as:

- Whether the matter has been satisfactorily resolved.
- Whether management has previously communicated the matter.
- The size, operating structure, control environment, and legal structure of the entity being audited.
- Legal or regulatory requirements that may require a written communication with those charged with governance.
- The expectations of those charged with governance, including arrangements made for periodic meetings or communications with the auditor.
- The amount of ongoing contact and dialogue the auditor has with those charged with governance.
- Whether there have been significant changes in the membership of a governing body.
- In the case of a special purpose financial statement audit, whether the auditor also audits the entity's general purpose financial statements.

.54 When a significant matter is discussed with an individual member of those charged with governance, for example, the chair of an audit committee, it may be appropriate for the auditor to summarize the matter in later communications so that all of those charged with governance have full and balanced information.

.55 When the auditor communicates matters in accordance with this section in writing, the auditor should indicate in the communication that it is intended solely for the information and use of those charged with governance and, if appropriate, management and is not intended to be and should not be used by anyone other than these specified parties.

Timing of Communications

.56 The auditor should communicate with those charged with governance on a sufficiently timely basis to enable those charged with governance to take appropriate action.

.57 The appropriate timing for communications will vary with the circumstances of the engagement. Considerations include the significance and nature of the matter, and the action expected to be taken by those charged with governance. The auditor may consider communicating:

- Planning matters early in the audit engagement and, for an initial engagement, as part of the terms of the engagement.
- Significant difficulties encountered during the audit as soon as practicable if those charged with governance are able to assist the auditor to overcome the difficulties, or if the difficulties are likely to lead to a modified opinion.

.58 Other factors that may be relevant to the timing of communications include:

- The size, operating structure, control environment, and legal structure of the entity being audited.
- Any legal obligation to communicate certain matters within a specified timeframe.

- The expectations of those charged with governance, including arrangements made for periodic meetings or communications with the auditor.

- The time at which the auditor identifies certain matters, for example, timely communication of a material weakness to enable appropriate remedial action to be taken.

- Whether the auditor is auditing both general purpose and special purpose financial statements.

Adequacy of the Communication Process

.59 The auditor should evaluate whether the two-way communication between the auditor and those charged with governance has been adequate for the purpose of the audit. If it has not, the auditor should take appropriate action to address the effectiveness of the communication process. (See paragraph .62.)

.60 As discussed in paragraph .08, effective two-way communication assists both the auditor and those charged with governance. Further, section 314, *Understanding the Entity and Its Environment and Assessing the Risks of Material Misstatement*, identifies participation by those charged with governance, including their interaction with internal audit, if any, and external auditors, as an element of the entity's control environment. Inadequate two-way communication may indicate an unsatisfactory control environment, which will influence the auditor's assessment of the risks of material misstatements.

.61 The auditor need not design specific procedures to support the evaluation required by paragraph .59. Rather, that evaluation may be based on observations resulting from audit procedures performed for other purposes. Such observations may include:

- The appropriateness and timeliness of actions taken by those charged with governance in response to matters communicated by the auditor.

- The apparent openness of those charged with governance in their communications with the auditor.

- The willingness and capacity of those charged with governance to meet with the auditor without management present.

- The apparent ability of those charged with governance to fully comprehend matters communicated by the auditor, such as the extent to which those charged with governance probe issues and question recommendations made to them.

- Difficulty in establishing with those charged with governance a mutual understanding of the form, timing, and expected general content of communications.

- Where all or some of those charged with governance are involved in managing the entity, their apparent awareness of how matters discussed with the auditor affect their broader governance responsibilities, as well as their management responsibilities.

.62 If, in the auditor's judgment, the two-way communication between the auditor and those charged with governance is not adequate, there is a risk the auditor may not have obtained all the audit evidence required to form an opinion on the financial statements. The auditor should consider the effect, if any, on the auditor's assessment of the risks of material misstatements.

.63 The auditor may discuss the situation with those charged with governance. If the situation cannot be resolved, the auditor may take such actions as:

- Modifying the auditor's opinion on the basis of a scope limitation.
- Obtaining legal advice about the consequences of different courses of action.
- Communicating with third parties (for example, a regulator), or a higher authority in the governance structure that is outside the entity, such as the owners of a business (for example, shareholders in a general meeting), or the responsible government agency for certain governmental entities.
- Withdrawing from the engagement.

Documentation

.64 When matters required to be communicated by this section have been communicated orally, the auditor should document them.[8] When matters have been communicated in writing, the auditor should retain a copy of the communication. Documentation of oral communication may include a copy of minutes prepared by the entity if those minutes are an appropriate record of the communication.

Effective Date

.65 This section is effective for audits of financial statements for periods beginning on or after December 15, 2006.

---

[8] Section 339, *Audit Documentation*, requires the auditor to document discussions of significant findings or issues with management and others (including those charged with governance) on a timely basis, including responses. That section also requires that the audit documentation include documentation of the significant findings or issues discussed, and when and with whom the discussions took place.

.66

Appendix A

Requirements to Communicate With Those Charged With Governance in Other Statements on Auditing Standards

A1. Requirements for the auditor to communicate with those charged with governance are included in other Statements on Auditing Standards. This section does not change the requirements in:

a. Paragraph .17 of section 317, *Illegal Acts by Clients*, to communicate with the audit committee or others with equivalent authority and responsibility illegal acts that come to the auditor's attention.

b. Paragraphs .36–.37 of section 801, *Compliance Audits*, for the auditor to communicate (i) in writing to management and those charged with governance identified significant deficiencies and material weakness in internal control over compliance, even in the absence of a governmental audit requirement to report on internal control over compliance; and (ii) to those charged with governance of the entity, the auditor's responsibilities under GAAS, *Government Auditing Standards*, and the governmental audit requirement, an overview of the planned scope and timing of the compliance audit, and significant findings from the compliance audit.

c. Paragraph .22 of section 316, *Consideration of Fraud in a Financial Statement Audit*, to inquire directly of the audit committee (or at least its chair) regarding the audit committee's views about the risks of fraud and whether the audit committee has knowledge of any fraud or suspected fraud affecting the entity.

d. Paragraph .79 of section 316, *Consideration of Fraud in a Financial Statement Audit*, to communicate with those charged with governance fraud involving senior management and fraud (whether caused by senior management or other employees) that causes a material misstatement of the financial statements. In addition, the auditor should reach an understanding with those charged with governance regarding the nature and extent of communications with those charged with governance about misappropriations perpetrated by lower-level employees.

e. Paragraph .20 of section 325, *Communicating Internal Control Related Matters Identified in an Audit*, to communicate in writing to management and those charged with governance control deficiencies identified during an audit that upon evaluation are considered significant deficiencies or material weaknesses.

[Revised, December 2010, to reflect conforming changes necessary due to the issuance of SAS No. 117.]

.67

Appendix B

Qualitative Aspects of Accounting Practices

The communication in accordance with paragraph .34*a* of this section, and discussed in paragraphs .37 and .38, may include such matters as the following:

Accounting Policies

- The appropriateness of the accounting policies to the particular circumstances of the entity, considering the need to balance the cost of providing information with the likely benefit to users of the entity's financial statements. Where acceptable alternative accounting policies exist, the communication may include identification of the financial statement items that are affected by the choice of significant policies as well as information on accounting policies used by similar entities.
- The initial selection of, and changes in, significant accounting policies, including the application of new accounting pronouncements. The communication may include the effect of the timing and method of adoption of a change in accounting policy on the current and future earnings of the entity; and the timing of a change in accounting policies in relation to expected new accounting pronouncements.
- The effect of significant accounting policies in controversial or emerging areas (or those unique to an industry, particularly when there is a lack of authoritative guidance or consensus).
- The effect of the timing of transactions in relation to the period in which they are recorded.

Accounting Estimates

- For items for which estimates are significant, issues discussed in section 342, *Auditing Accounting Estimates,* and section 328, *Auditing Fair Value Measurements and Disclosures*, including, for example:
  - — Management's identification of accounting estimates.
  - — Management's process for making accounting estimates.
  - — Risks of material misstatement.
  - — Indicators of possible management bias.
  - — Disclosure of estimation uncertainty in the financial statements.

Financial Statement Disclosures

- The issues involved, and related judgments made, in formulating particularly sensitive financial statement disclosures (for example, disclosures related to revenue recognition, going concern, subsequent events, and contingency issues).
- The overall neutrality, consistency, and clarity of the disclosures in the financial statements.

Related Matters

- The potential effect on the financial statements of significant risks and exposures, and uncertainties, such as pending litigation, that are disclosed in the financial statements.

- The extent to which the financial statements are affected by unusual transactions including nonrecurring amounts recognized during the period, and the extent to which such transactions are separately disclosed in the financial statements.
- The factors affecting asset and liability carrying values, including the entity's bases for determining useful lives assigned to tangible and intangible assets. The communication may explain how factors affecting carrying values were selected and how alternative selections would have affected the financial statements.
- The selective correction of misstatements, for example, correcting misstatements with the effect of increasing reported earnings, but not those that have the effect of decreasing reported earnings.

AU Section 390

Consideration of Omitted Procedures After the Report Date

Source: SAS No. 46.

Effective, unless otherwise indicated: October 31, 1983.

.01 This section provides guidance on the considerations and procedures to be applied by an auditor who, subsequent to the date of his report on audited financial statements, concludes that one or more auditing procedures considered necessary at the time of the audit in the circumstances then existing were omitted from his audit of the financial statements, but there is no indication that those financial statements are not fairly presented in conformity with generally accepted accounting principles or with another comprehensive basis of accounting.[1] This circumstance should be distinguished from that described in section 561, which applies if an auditor, subsequent to the date of his report on audited financial statements, becomes aware that facts regarding those financial statements may have existed at that date that might have affected his report had he then been aware of them.

.02 Once he has reported on audited financial statements, an auditor has no responsibility to carry out any retrospective review of his work. However, reports and working papers relating to particular engagements may be subjected to post-issuance review in connection with a firm's internal inspection program,[2] peer review, or otherwise, and the omission of a necessary auditing procedure may be disclosed.

.03 A variety of conditions might be encountered in which an auditing procedure considered necessary at the time of the audit in the circumstances then existing has been omitted; therefore, the considerations and procedures described herein necessarily are set forth only in general terms. The period of time during which the auditor considers whether this section applies to the circumstances of a particular engagement and then takes the actions, if any, that are required hereunder may be important. Because of legal implications that may be involved in taking the actions contemplated herein, the auditor would be well advised to consult with his attorney when he encounters the circumstances to which this section may apply, and, with the attorney's advice and assistance, determine an appropriate course of action.

.04 When the auditor concludes that an auditing procedure considered necessary at the time of the audit in the circumstances then existing was omitted from his audit of financial statements, he should assess the importance of the omitted procedure to his present ability to support his previously expressed

---

[1] The provisions of this section are not intended to apply to an engagement in which an auditor's work is at issue in a threatened or pending legal proceeding or regulatory investigation. (A *threatened legal proceeding* means that a potential claimant has manifested to the auditor an awareness of, and present intention to assert, a possible claim.)

[2] See section 161, *The Relationship of Generally Accepted Auditing Standards to Quality Control Standards*, paragraph .02, and related quality control standards regarding the quality control function of inspection.

opinion regarding those financial statements taken as a whole. A review of his working papers, discussion of the circumstances with engagement personnel and others, and a re-evaluation of the overall scope of his audit may be helpful in making this assessment. For example, the results of other procedures that were applied may tend to compensate for the one omitted or make its omission less important. Also, subsequent audits may provide audit evidence in support of the previously expressed opinion.

.05 If the auditor concludes that the omission of a procedure considered necessary at the time of the audit in the circumstances then existing impairs his present ability to support his previously expressed opinion regarding the financial statements taken as a whole, and he believes there are persons currently relying, or likely to rely, on his report, he should promptly undertake to apply the omitted procedure or alternative procedures that would provide a satisfactory basis for his opinion.

.06 When as a result of the subsequent application of the omitted procedure or alternative procedures, the auditor becomes aware that facts regarding the financial statements existed at the date of his report that would have affected that report had he been aware of them, he should be guided by the provisions of section 561.05–.09.

.07 If in the circumstances described in paragraph .05, the auditor is unable to apply the previously omitted procedure or alternative procedures, he should consult his attorney to determine an appropriate course of action concerning his responsibilities to his client, regulatory authorities, if any, having jurisdiction over the client, and persons relying, or likely to rely, on his report.

Effective Date

.08 This section is effective as of October 31, 1983.

AU Section 400

THE FIRST, SECOND, AND THIRD STANDARDS OF REPORTING

TABLE OF CONTENTS

AU Section 410

Adherence to Generally Accepted Accounting Principles

Source: SAS No. 1, section 410; SAS No. 62.

See section 9410 for interpretations of this section.

Issue date, unless otherwise indicated: November, 1972.

.01 The first standard of reporting is:

> The auditor must state in the auditor's report whether the financial statements are presented in accordance with generally accepted accounting principles.

[Revised, November 2006, to reflect conforming changes necessary due to the issuance of SAS No. 113.]

.02 The term *generally accepted accounting principles* as used in reporting standards is construed to include not only accounting principles and practices but also the methods of applying them. The first reporting standard is construed not to require a statement of fact by the auditor but an opinion as to whether the financial statements are presented in conformity with such principles.[1] If limitations on the scope of the audit make it impossible for the auditor to form an opinion as to such conformity, appropriate qualification of his report is required. [Amended by SAS No. 14, effective with respect to engagements to issue special reports on data for periods beginning after December 31, 1976.]

[.03–.04] [Superseded, July 1975, by SAS No. 5, as superseded by section 411, as withdrawn by the Auditing Standards Board.]

---

[1] When an auditor reports on financial statements prepared in accordance with a comprehensive basis of accounting other than generally accepted accounting principles, the first standard of reporting is satisfied by disclosing in the auditor's report that the statements have been prepared in conformity with another comprehensive basis of accounting other than generally accepted accounting principles and by expressing an opinion (or disclaiming an opinion) on whether the financial statements are presented in conformity with the comprehensive basis of accounting used (see section 623, *Special Reports*, paragraphs .02-.10).

AU Section 9410

Adherence to Generally Accepted Accounting Principles: Auditing Interpretations of Section 410

[1.] Accounting Principles Recommended by Trade Associations[1]

[.01–.03] [Withdrawn, August 1982, by Statement on Auditing Standards No. 43.]

[2.] The Impact of FASB Statement No. 2 on Auditor's Report Issued Prior to the Statement's Effective Date[2]

[.04–.12] [Superseded, October 1979, by Interpretation No. 3, paragraphs .13–.18.]

3. The Impact on an Auditor's Report of Accounting Guidance Prior to its Effective Date

.13 *Question*—What is the impact on the auditor's report when (*a*) the auditor is reporting on financial statements issued before the effective date of accounting guidance currently reflected in Financial Accounting Standards Board (FASB) *Accounting Standards Codification*™ (ASC) as "pending content" due to transition and open effective date information, and (*b*) these financial statements will have to be restated in the future because this "pending content" will require retroactive application of its provisions by prior period adjustment?

.14 *Interpretation*—Where the accounting guidance being followed is currently acceptable, the auditor should not qualify his opinion if a company does not adopt the accounting guidance that is currently reflected as "pending content" in FASB ASC due to transition and open effective date information. An example would include the accounting guidance originally issued on research and development costs, which is now reflected in FASB ASC 730, *Research and Development Costs*. This guidance was originally issued in October 1974, but was effective for fiscal years beginning on or after January 1, 1975. This guidance requires companies to expense certain research and development costs in the period they are incurred. Companies that had deferred research and development costs were required to restate their financial statements by prior period adjustment in the period in which this guidance became effective. Deferring research and development costs before this guidance became effective was an acceptable alternative principle under generally accepted accounting principles (GAAP), although this guidance proscribed such treatment for fiscal years beginning on or after January 1, 1975. Other reporting considerations are addressed in the following paragraphs.

.15 Section 508, *Reports on Audited Financial Statements*, paragraph .41 states: "Information essential for a fair presentation in conformity with generally accepted accounting principles should be set forth in the financial statements (which include related notes)." For financial statements that

---

[1] [Footnote deleted.]

2 Originally issued under the title "Effect on the Auditor's Opinion of FASB Statement on Research and Development Costs" (*Journal of Accountancy*, Jan. 1975, p. 74).

are prepared on the basis of accounting principles that are acceptable at the financial-statement date but that will not be acceptable in the future, the auditor should consider whether disclosure of the impending change in principle and the resulting restatement are essential data. If he decides that the matter should be disclosed and it is not, the auditor should express a qualified or adverse opinion as to conformity with GAAP, as required by section 508 paragraph .41.

.16 To evaluate the adequacy of disclosure of the prospective change in principle, the auditor should assess the potential effect on the financial statements. Using the research and development cost example given previously, the effect of the anticipated prior period adjustment to write off previously deferred research and development costs would in some instances be so material that disclosure would be essential for an understanding of the financial statements. In cases such as this, where the estimated impact is so material, disclosure can best be made by supplementing the historical financial statements with pro forma financial data that give effect to the future adjustment as if it had occurred on the date of the balance sheet. (See section 560 paragraph .05.) The pro forma data may be presented in columnar form alongside the historical statements, in the notes to the historical statements, or in separate pro forma statements presented with the historical statements.

.17 The auditor also should consider whether disclosure is needed for other effects that may result upon the required future adoption of an accounting principle. For example, the future adoption of such a principle may result in a reduction to stockholders' equity that may cause the company to be in violation of its debt covenants, which in turn may accelerate the due date for repayment of debt.

.18 Even if the auditor decides that the disclosure of the forthcoming change and its effects are adequate and, consequently, decides not to qualify his opinion, he nevertheless may decide to include an explanatory paragraph in his report if the effects of the change are expected to be unusually material. The explanatory paragraph should not be construed as a qualification of the auditor's opinion; it is intended to highlight circumstances of particular importance and to aid in interpreting the financial statements (see section 508 paragraph .19).

[Issue Date: October 1979; Revised: December 1992; Revised: June 1993; Revised: February 1997; Revised: June 2009.]

AU Section 411

The Meaning of Present Fairly in Conformity With Generally Accepted Accounting Principles

(Supersedes SAS No. 5.)

Source: SAS No. 69; SAS No. 91; SAS No. 93.

See section 9411 for interpretations of this section.

Effective for audits of financial statements for periods ending after March 15, 1992, unless otherwise indicated.

Notice of Withdrawal of Statement on Auditing Standards (SAS) No. 69, *The Meaning of* Present Fairly in Conformity With Generally Accepted Accounting Principles, and Interpretation No. 3, "The Auditor's Consideration of Management's Adoption of Accounting Principles for New Transactions or Events"

The hierarchies of generally accepted accounting principles (GAAP hierarchies) of nongovernmental, state and local, and federal reporting entities have resided in SAS No. 69 in the auditing literature. The Financial Accounting Standards Board (FASB), the Governmental Accounting Standards Board (GASB), and the Federal Accounting Standards Advisory Board (FASAB) have issued the following pronouncements that incorporate their respective GAAP hierarchy into their respective authoritative literature:

- FASB Statement No. 162, *The Hierarchy of Generally Accepted Accounting Principles*, as superseded by FASB Statement No. 168, *The* FASB Accounting Standards Codification™ *and the Hierarchy of Generally Accepted Accounting Principles—a replacement of FASB Statement No. 162*
- GASB Statement No. 55, *The Hierarchy of Generally Accepted Accounting Principles for State and Local Governments*
- Statement of Federal Financial Accounting Standards No. 34, *The Hierarchy of Generally Accepted Accounting Principles, Including the Application of Standards Issued by the Financial Accounting Standards Board*

Therefore, the Auditing Standards Board (ASB) has withdrawn SAS No. 69, *The Meaning of* Present Fairly in Conformity With Generally Accepted Accounting Principles, and its interpretation.

AU Section 9411

The Meaning of Present Fairly in Conformity With Generally Accepted Accounting Principles: *Auditing Interpretations of Section 411*

Notice of Withdrawal of Statement on Auditing Standards (SAS) No. 69, *The Meaning of* Present Fairly in Conformity With Generally Accepted Accounting Principles, and Interpretation No. 3, "The Auditor's Consideration of Management's Adoption of Accounting Principles for New Transactions or Events"

The hierarchies of generally accepted accounting principles (GAAP hierarchies) of nongovernmental, state and local, and federal reporting entities have resided in SAS No. 69 in the auditing literature. The Financial Accounting Standards Board (FASB), the Governmental Accounting Standards Board (GASB), and the Federal Accounting Standards Advisory Board (FASAB) have issued the following pronouncements that incorporate their respective GAAP hierarchy into their respective authoritative literature:

- † FASB Statement No. 162, *The Hierarchy of Generally Accepted Accounting Principles*, as superseded by FASB Statement No. 168, *The* FASB Accounting Standards Codification™ *and the Hierarchy of Generally Accepted Accounting Principles—a replacement of FASB Statement No. 162*
- † GASB Statement No. 55, *The Hierarchy of Generally Accepted Accounting Principles for State and Local Governments*
- † Statement of Federal Financial Accounting Standards No. 34, *The Hierarchy of Generally Accepted Accounting Principles, Including the Application of Standards Issued by the Financial Accounting Standards Board*

Therefore, the Auditing Standards Board (ASB) has withdrawn SAS No. 69, *The Meaning of* Present Fairly in Conformity With Generally Accepted Accounting Principles, and its interpretation.

AU Section 420

*Consistency of Application of Generally Accepted Accounting Principles**

Source: SAS No. 1, section 420; SAS No. 43; SAS No. 88.

See section 9420 for interpretations of this section.

Issue date, unless otherwise indicated: November, 1972.

.01 The second standard of reporting (referred to herein as the consistency standard) is:

> The auditor must identify in the auditor's report those circumstances in which such principles have not been consistently observed in the current period in relation to the preceding period.

[Revised, November 2006, to reflect conforming changes necessary due to the issuance of Statement on Auditing Standards No. 113.]

.02 The objective of the consistency standard is to ensure that if comparability of financial statements between periods has been materially affected by changes in accounting principles, there will be appropriate reporting by the independent auditor regarding such changes.[1] It is also implicit in the objective that such principles have been consistently observed within each period. The auditor's standard report implies that the auditor is satisfied that the comparability of financial statements between periods has not been materially affected by changes in accounting principles and that such principles have been consistently applied between or among periods because either (*a*) no change in accounting principles has occurred, or (*b*) there has been a change in accounting principles or in the method of their application, but the effect of the change on the comparability of the financial statements is not material. In these cases, the auditor would not refer to consistency in his report.

.03 Proper application of the consistency standard by the independent auditor requires an understanding of the relationship of consistency to

---

* This section has not been updated to reflect the issuance of Financial Accounting Standards Board (FASB) Statement No. 154, *Accounting Changes and Error Corrections—a replacement of APB Opinion No. 20 and FASB Statement No. 3*, which supersedes Accounting Principles Board Opinion No. 20, *Accounting Changes*. It is expected to be updated when this section is clarified in accordance with the AICPA Auditing Standards Board's (ASB) Clarity Project. The clarity project is a significant effort that the ASB has undertaken to make U.S. generally accepted auditing standards easier to read, understand, and apply by utilizing established clarity drafting conventions. Once finalized, the effective date of all clarified standards is expected to apply to audits of financial statements for periods beginning on or after December 15, 2010. This date is provisional, but will not be earlier.

In July 2009, FASB approved FASB *Accounting Standards Codification* (ASC), effectively superseding FASB Statement No. 162, *The Hierarchy of Generally Accepted Accounting Principles*, because all of the FASB ASC content carries the same level of authority. FASB ASC is now the source of authoritative U.S. accounting and reporting standards for nongovernmental entities, in addition to guidance issued by the Securities and Exchange Commission (SEC). As of July 1, 2009, all other non-grandfathered, non-SEC accounting literature not included in FASB ASC became nonauthoritative.

As a result of these developments, this section has not been conformed to reflect FASB ASC.

[1] The appropriate form of reporting on a lack of consistency is discussed in section 508, *Reports on Audited Financial Statements*, paragraphs .16–.18. [Footnote added to reflect the conforming changes necessary due to the issuance of Statement on Auditing Standards Nos. 53–62.]

comparability. Although lack of consistency may cause lack of comparability, other factors unrelated to consistency may also cause lack of comparability.[2]

.04 A comparison of the financial statements of an entity between years may be affected by (*a*) accounting changes, (*b*) an error in previously issued financial statements, (*c*) changes in classification, and (*d*) events or transactions substantially different from those accounted for in previously issued statements. Accounting change, as defined in APB Opinion No. 20 [AC section A06], means a change in (1) an accounting principle, (2) an accounting estimate, or (3) the reporting entity (which is a special type of change in accounting principle).

.05 Changes in accounting principle having a material effect on the financial statements require recognition in the independent auditor's report through the addition of an explanatory paragraph (following the opinion paragraph). Other factors affecting comparability in financial statements may require disclosure, but they would not ordinarily be commented upon in the independent auditor's report.

Accounting Changes Affecting Consistency

Change in Accounting Principle

.06 "A change in accounting principle results from adoption of a generally accepted accounting principle different from the one used previously for reporting purposes. The term *accounting principle* includes not only accounting principles and practices but also the methods of applying them."[3] A change in accounting principle includes, for example, a change from the straight-line method to the declining balance method of depreciation for all assets in a class or for all newly acquired assets in a class. The consistency standard is applicable to this type of change and requires recognition in the auditor's report through the addition of an explanatory paragraph. [As modified, effective January 1, 1975, by FASB Statement No. 2 (AC section R50).]

Change in the Reporting Entity

.07 A change in the reporting entity is a special type of change in accounting principle, which results in financial statements that, in effect, are those of a different reporting entity. This type is limited mainly to—

a. Presenting consolidated or combined statements in place of statements of individual companies.

b. Changing specific subsidiaries comprising the group of companies for which consolidated statements are presented.

c. Changing the companies included in combined financial statements.

A business combination accounted for by the pooling of interests method also results in a different reporting entity.[4] [As amended, effective December 1999, by Statement on Auditing Standards No. 88.]

---

[2] For a discussion of comparability of financial statements of a single enterprise, see paragraphs 111 through 119 of FASB Statement of Financial Accounting Concepts No. 2, "Qualitative Characteristics of Accounting Information." [Footnote renumbered to reflect the conforming changes necessary due to the issuance of Statement on Auditing Standards Nos. 53–62. Revised, June, 1993, to reflect conforming changes necessary due to the issuance of Statement of Position 93-3.]

[3] Accounting Principles Board Opinion No. 20, paragraph 7 [AC section A06.105]. [Footnote renumbered to reflect the conforming changes necessary due to the issuance of Statement on Auditing Standards Nos. 53–62.]

[4] APB Opinion No. 20 paragraph .12. [Footnote added, effective December 1999, by Statement on Auditing Standards No. 88.]

.08 A change in the reporting entity resulting from a transaction or event, such as a pooling of interests, or the creation, cessation, or complete or partial purchase or disposition of a subsidiary or other business unit, does not require that an explanatory paragraph about consistency be included in the auditor's report. A change in the reporting entity that does not result from a transaction or event requires recognition in the auditor's report through inclusion of an explanatory paragraph. [Paragraph added, effective December 1999, by Statement on Auditing Standards No. 88.]

.09 When companies have merged or combined in a pooling of interests, appropriate effect of the pooling should be given in the presentation of financial position, results of operations, cash flows, and other historical financial data of the continuing business for the year in which the combination is consummated and, in comparative financial statements, for years prior to the year of pooling, as described in APB Opinion No. 16, *Business Combinations* [AC section B50]. If prior year financial statements, presented in comparison with current year financial statements, are not restated to give appropriate recognition to a pooling of interests, a departure from generally accepted accounting principles has occurred which necessitates that the auditor express a qualified or an adverse opinion as discussed in section 508, *Reports on Audited Financial Statements*, paragraphs .35–.40. Since the inconsistency arises not from a change in the application of an accounting principle in the current year, but from the lack of such application to prior years, an explanatory paragraph (in addition to the modification relating to the departure from generally accepted accounting principles) is not required. [Paragraph added to reflect the conforming changes necessary due to the issuance of Statement on Auditing Standards Nos. 53 through 62. Paragraph renumbered and amended, effective December 1999, by Statement on Auditing Standards No. 88.]

[.10] [Paragraph added to reflect the conforming changes necessary due to the issuance of Statement on Auditing Standards Nos. 53 through 62. Paragraph renumbered and deleted by the issuance of Statement on Auditing Standards No. 88, December 1999.]

[.11] [Paragraph renumbered to reflect the conforming changes necessary due to the issuance of Statement on Auditing Standards Nos. 53 through 62. Paragraph subsequently renumbered and deleted by the issuance of Statement on Auditing Standards No. 88, December 1999.]

Correction of an Error in Principle

.12 A change from an accounting principle that is not generally accepted to one that is generally accepted, including correction of a mistake in the application of a principle, is a correction of an error. Although this type of change in accounting principle should be accounted for as the correction of an error,[5] the change requires recognition in the auditor's report through the addition of an explanatory paragraph. [Paragraph renumbered to reflect the conforming changes necessary due to the issuance of Statement on Auditing Standards Nos. 53 through 62. Paragraph subsequently renumbered by the issuance of Statement on Auditing Standards No. 88, December 1999.][6]

---

[5] See paragraphs 13, 36, and 37 of APB Opinion No. 20 [AC section A35.104-.105]. [Footnote renumbered to reflect the conforming changes necessary due to the issuance of Statement on Auditing Standards Nos. 53 through 62. Footnote subsequently renumbered by the issuance of Statement on Auditing Standards No. 88, December 1999.]

[6] [Footnote deleted to reflect the conforming changes necessary due to the issuance of Statement on Auditing Standards Nos. 53–62. Footnote renumbered by the issuance of Statement on Auditing Standards No. 88, December 1999.]

Change in Principle Inseparable From Change in Estimate

.13 The effect of a change in accounting principle may be inseparable from the effect of a change in estimate.[7] Although the accounting for such a change is the same as that accorded a change only in estimate, a change in principle is involved. Accordingly, this type of change requires recognition in the independent auditor's report through the addition of an explanatory paragraph. [Paragraph renumbered to reflect the conforming changes necessary due to the issuance of Statement on Auditing Standards Nos. 53 through 62. Paragraph subsequently renumbered by the issuance of Statement on Auditing Standards No. 88, December 1999.]

Changes in Presentation of Cash Flows

.14 For purposes of presenting cash flows, FASB Statement No. 95, *Statement of Cash Flows* [AC section C25], states that, "An enterprise shall disclose its policy for determining which items are treated as cash equivalents. Any change to that policy is a change in accounting principle that shall be effected by restating financial statements for earlier years presented for comparative purposes." Accordingly, this type of change in presentation of cash flows requires recognition in the independent auditor's report through the addition of an explanatory paragraph. [Paragraph added to reflect the conforming changes necessary due to the issuance of Statement on Auditing Standards Nos. 53–62. Paragraph renumbered by the issuance of Statement on Auditing Standards No. 88, December 1999.]

Changes Not Affecting Consistency

Change in Accounting Estimate

.15 Accounting estimates (such as service lives and salvage values of depreciable assets and provisions for warranty costs, uncollectible receivables, and inventory obsolescence) are necessary in the preparation of financial statements. Accounting estimates change as new events occur and as additional experience and information are acquired. This type of accounting change is required by altered conditions that affect comparability but do not involve the consistency standard. The independent auditor, in addition to satisfying himself with respect to the conditions giving rise to the change in accounting estimate, should satisfy himself that the change does not include the effect of a change in accounting principle. Provided he is so satisfied, he need not comment on the change in his report.[8] However, an accounting change of this type having a material effect on the financial statements may require disclosure in a note to the financial statements.[9] [Paragraph renumbered to reflect the conforming changes necessary due to the issuance of Statement on Auditing Standards

---

[7] See paragraph 11 of Accounting Principles Board Opinion No. 20 [AC section A06.110]. [Footnote renumbered to reflect the conforming changes necessary due to the issuance of Statement on Auditing Standards Nos. 53 through 62. Footnote subsequently renumbered by the issuance of Statement on Auditing Standards No. 88, December 1999.]

[8] [Footnote deleted. Footnote renumbered to reflect the conforming changes necessary due to the issuance of Statement on Auditing Standards Nos. 53 through 62. Footnote subsequently renumbered by the issuance of Statement on Auditing Standards No. 88, December 1999.]

[9] See paragraph 33 of Accounting Principles Board Opinion No. 20 [AC section A06.132]. [Footnote renumbered to reflect the conforming changes necessary due to the issuance of Statement on Auditing Standards Nos. 53 through 62. Footnote subsequently renumbered by the issuance of Statement on Auditing Standards No. 88, December 1999.]

Nos. 53 through 62. Paragraph subsequently renumbered by the issuance of Statement on Auditing Standards No. 88, December 1999.]

Error Correction Not Involving Principle

.16 Correction of an error in previously issued financial statements resulting from mathematical mistakes, oversight, or misuse of facts that existed at the time the financial statements were originally prepared does not involve the consistency standard if no element of accounting principles or their application is included. Accordingly, the independent auditor need not recognize the correction in his report.[10] [Paragraph renumbered to reflect the conforming changes necessary due to the issuance of Statement on Auditing Standards Nos. 53–62. Paragraph subsequently renumbered by the issuance of Statement on Auditing Standards No. 88, December 1999.]

Changes in Classification and Reclassifications

.17 Classifications in the current financial statements may be different from classifications in the prior year's financial statements. Although changes in classification are usually not of sufficient importance to necessitate disclosure, material changes in classification should be indicated and explained in the financial statements or notes. These changes and material reclassifications made in previously issued financial statements to enhance comparability with current financial statements ordinarily would not need to be referred to in the independent auditor's report. [Paragraph renumbered to reflect the conforming changes necessary due to the issuance of Statement on Auditing Standards Nos. 53–62. Paragraph subsequently renumbered by the issuance of Statement on Auditing Standards No. 88, December 1999.]

Variations in Presentation of Statement of Changes in Financial Position

[.18] [Paragraph renumbered to reflect the conforming changes necessary due to the issuance of Statement on Auditing Standards Nos. 53–62. Paragraph subsequently renumbered by the issuance of Statement on Auditing Standards No. 88.]

Substantially Different Transactions or Events

.19 Accounting principles are adopted when events or transactions first become material in their effect. Such adoption, as well as modification or adoption of an accounting principle necessitated by transactions or events that are clearly different in substance from those previously occurring, do not involve the consistency standard although disclosure in the notes to the financial statements may be required. [Paragraph renumbered by the issuance of Statement on Auditing Standards No. 43, August 1982. Paragraph subsequently renumbered to reflect the conforming changes necessary due to the issuance of Statement on Auditing Standards Nos. 53–62. Paragraph subsequently renumbered by the issuance of Statement on Auditing Standards No. 88, December 1999.]

---

[10] If the independent auditor had previously reported on the financial statements containing the error, he should refer to section 561, *Subsequent Discovery of Facts Existing at the Date of the Auditor's Report*. [Footnote renumbered to reflect the conforming changes necessary due to the issuance of Statement on Auditing Standards Nos. 53–62. Footnote subsequently renumbered by the issuance of Statement on Auditing Standards No. 88, December 1999.]

Changes Expected to Have a Material Future Effect

.20 If an accounting change has no material effect on the financial statements in the current year, but the change is reasonably certain to have substantial effect in later years, the change should be disclosed in the notes to the financial statements whenever the statements of the period of change are presented, but the independent auditor need not recognize the change in his report. [Paragraph renumbered by the issuance of Statement on Auditing Standards No. 43, August 1982. Paragraph subsequently renumbered to reflect the conforming changes necessary due to the issuance of Statement on Auditing Standards Nos. 53–62. Paragraph subsequently renumbered by the issuance of Statement on Auditing Standards No. 88, December 1999.]

Disclosure of Changes Not Affecting Consistency

.21 While the matters do not require the addition of an explanatory paragraph about consistency in the independent auditor's report, the auditor should qualify his opinion as to the disclosure matter if necessary disclosures are not made. (See section 431.) [Paragraph renumbered by the issuance of Statement on Auditing Standards No. 43, August 1982. Paragraph subsequently renumbered to reflect the conforming changes necessary due to the issuance of Statement on Auditing Standards Nos. 53–62. Paragraph subsequently renumbered by the issuance of Statement on Auditing Standards No. 88, December 1999.]

Periods to Which the Consistency Standard Relates

.22 When the independent auditor reports only on the current period, he should obtain sufficient appropriate audit evidence about consistency of the application of accounting principles, regardless of whether financial statements for the preceding period are presented. (The term "current period" means the most recent year, or period of less than one year, upon which the independent auditor is reporting.) When the independent auditor reports on two or more years, he should address the consistency of the application of accounting principles between such years and the consistency of such years with the year prior thereto if such prior year is presented with the financial statements being reported upon. [Paragraph renumbered by the issuance of Statement on Auditing Standards No. 43, August 1982. Paragraph subsequently renumbered to reflect the conforming changes necessary due to the issuance of Statement on Auditing Standards Nos. 53–62. Paragraph subsequently renumbered by the issuance of Statement on Auditing Standards No. 88, December 1999. Revised, March 2008, to reflect conforming changes necessary due to the issuance of Statement on Auditing Standards No. 105.]

Consistency Expression

[.23] [Paragraph renumbered and deleted to reflect the conforming changes necessary due to the issuance of Statement on Auditing Standards Nos. 53–62. Paragraph subsequently renumbered by the issuance of Statement on Auditing Standards No. 88, December 1999.]

First Year Audits

.24 When the independent auditor has not audited the financial statements of a company for the preceding year, he should adopt procedures that are practicable and reasonable in the circumstances to assure himself that the accounting principles employed are consistent between the current and the preceding year. Where adequate records have been maintained by the client, it is usually practicable and reasonable to extend auditing procedures to gather sufficient appropriate audit evidence about consistency. [Paragraph renumbered by the issuance of Statement on Auditing Standards No. 88, December 1999. Revised, March 2008, to reflect conforming changes necessary due to the issuance of Statement on Auditing Standards No. 105.]

.25 Inadequate financial records or limitations imposed by the client may preclude the independent auditor from obtaining sufficient appropriate audit evidence about the consistent application of accounting principles between the current and the prior year, as well as to the amounts of assets or liabilities at the beginning of the current year. Where such amounts could materially affect current operating results, the independent auditor would also be unable to express an opinion on the current year's results of operations and cash flows. [Paragraph renumbered by the issuance of Statement on Auditing Standards No. 88, December 1999. Revised, March 2008, to reflect conforming changes necessary due to the issuance of Statement on Auditing Standards No. 105.]

AU Section 9420

*Consistency of Application of Generally Accepted Accounting Principles: Auditing Interpretations of Section 420**

[1.] The Effect of APB Opinion No. 30 on Consistency[1]

[.01–.10] [Superseded October 1979 by Interpretation No. 5 paragraphs .28–.31.]

2. The Effect of APB Opinion No. 28 on Consistency

.11 *Question*—Independent auditors may be engaged to report on financial information for an annual period and a subsequent interim period. Should the auditor add an explanatory paragraph (following the opinion paragraph) to his report in those circumstances where accounting principles and practices used in preparing the annual financial information have been modified in accordance with APB Opinion No. 28 [AC section I73] in preparing the interim financial statements?

.12 *Interpretation*—No. The auditor should not add an explanatory paragraph to his report because of these modifications. Although the modifications deemed appropriate under Opinion No. 28 [AC section I73] may appear to be changes in the methods of applying accounting principles, they differ from changes in methods that require an explanatory paragraph since the modifications are made in order to recognize a difference in circumstances, that is, a difference between presenting financial information for a year and presenting financial information for only a part of a year.

.13 Section 420, *Consistency of Application of Generally Accepted Accounting Principles*, paragraph .02, states: "The objective of the consistency standard is to ensure that if comparability of financial statements between periods has been materially affected by changes in accounting principles there will be appropriate reporting by the independent auditor regarding such changes." Section 420 paragraph .02 refers to changes in methods that lessen the usefulness

---

* This section has not been updated to reflect the issuance of Financial Accounting Standards Board (FASB) Statement No. 154, *Accounting Changes and Error Corrections—a replacement of APB Opinion No. 20 and FASB Statement No. 3*, which supersedes Accounting Principles Board Opinion No. 20, *Accounting Changes*. It is expected to be updated when this section is clarified in accordance with the AICPA Auditing Standards Board's (ASB) Clarity Project. The clarity project is a significant effort that the ASB has undertaken to make U.S. generally accepted auditing standards easier to read, understand, and apply by utilizing established clarity drafting conventions. Once finalized, the effective date of all clarified standards is expected to apply to audits of financial statements for periods beginning on or after December 15, 2010. This date is provisional, but will not be earlier.

In July 2009, FASB approved FASB *Accounting Standards Codification* (ASC), effectively superseding FASB Statement No. 162, *The Hierarchy of Generally Accepted Accounting Principles*, because all of the FASB ASC content carries the same level of authority. FASB ASC is now the source of authoritative U.S. accounting and reporting standards for nongovernmental entities, in addition to guidance issued by the Securities and Exchange Commission (SEC). As of July 1, 2009, all other non-grandfathered, non-SEC accounting literature not included in FASB ASC became nonauthoritative.

As a result of these developments, this section has not been conformed to reflect FASB ASC.

[1] Originally issued under the title "Reporting on Consistency and Extraordinary Items" (*Journal of Accountancy*, Jan. '74, p. 67).

of financial statements in comparing the financial information of one period with that of an earlier period. Thus, the purpose of an explanatory paragraph about consistency in the auditor's report is to alert readers of the report not to make an unqualified comparison of the financial information for the two periods.

.14 The modifications introduced by Opinion No. 28 [AC section I73], however, do not lessen the comparability of the financial information of an interim period with that of a preceding annual period. On the contrary, those modifications are intended to enhance comparability between the two sets of financial information. As paragraph 10 of Opinion No. 28 [AC section I73.103] states, the modifications are needed "so that the reported results for the interim period may better relate to the results of operations for the annual period."

.15 Thus the modifications introduced by Opinion No. 28 [AC section I73] are not of the type that would require an explanatory paragraph (following the opinion paragraph) in the auditor's report. Independent auditors should, of course, add an explanatory paragraph if changes of the type that lessen comparability are introduced in the interim financial information.

[Issue Date: February 1974.]

3. Impact on the Auditor's Report of FIFO to LIFO Change in Comparative Financial Statements

.16 *Question*—Changing economic conditions have caused some companies to change their inventory pricing methods from the first-in, first-out (FIFO) method to the last in, first out (LIFO) method. When a company presents comparative financial statements and the year of the FIFO to LIFO change is the earliest year both presented and reported on, should the auditor refer to that change in accounting principle in his report?

.17 *Interpretation*—The auditor would not be required to refer in his report to a FIFO to LIFO change in the circumstances described above.

.18 A change in accounting principle usually results in including the cumulative effect of the change in net income of the period of the change. A change in inventory pricing method from FIFO to LIFO, however, is a change in accounting principle that ordinarily does not affect retained earnings at the beginning of the period in which the change was made. (See APB Opinion No. 20, paragraphs 14(d) and 26.)[2]

.19 An example of typical disclosure of a FIFO to LIFO change in the year of the change is as follows:

> "In 1974, the company adopted the last in, first out (LIFO) method of costing inventory. Previously, the first in, first out (FIFO) method of costing inventory was used. Management believes that the LIFO method has the effect of minimizing the impact of price level changes on inventory valuations and generally matches current costs against current revenues in the income statement. The effect of the change was to reduce net income by $xxxx ($.xx per share) from that which would otherwise have been reported. There is no cumulative effect on prior years since the ending inventory as previously reported (1973) is the beginning inventory for LIFO purposes. Accordingly, pro forma results of operations for the prior year had LIFO been followed is not determinable."

.20 Section 420, *Consistency of Application of Generally Accepted Accounting Principles*, paragraph .22 discusses the periods to which the consistency

---

[2] AC section A06.122.

standard relates: "When the independent auditor reports on two or more years, he should address the consistency of the application of accounting principles between such years. . . ." For a FIFO to LIFO change made in the earliest year presented and reported on, there is no inconsistency in the application of accounting principles, and comparability between the earliest year and subsequent years is not affected since no cumulative effect is reported in the year of the change. Consequently, the independent auditor need not refer to the change in inventory pricing methods.

[.21–.23] [Paragraphs deleted to reflect the conforming changes necessary due to the issuance of Statement on Auditing Standards Nos. 53 through 62.]

[Issue Date: January 1975; Amended: April 1989.]

[4.] The Effect of FASB Statement No. 13 on Consistency[3]

[.24–.27] [Withdrawn March 1989 by the Auditing Standards Board.]

[5.] The Effects of Changes in Accounting Principles and Classification on Consistency

[.28–.31] [Withdrawn December 1992 by the Audit Issues Task Force.]

[6.] The Effect of FASB Statement No. 34 on Consistency

[.32–.43] [Withdrawn March 1989 by the Auditing Standards Board.]

[7.] The Effect of FASB Statement No. 31 on Consistency

[.44–.51] [Withdrawn March 1989 by the Auditing Standards Board.]

8. The Effect of Accounting Changes by an Investee on Consistency

.52 *Question*—Does a change in accounting principle by an investee accounted for by the equity method require the auditor to add an explanatory paragraph (following the opinion paragraph) to his report on the financial statements of the investor?

.53 *Interpretation*—Changes in accounting principle affect the comparability of financial statements regardless of whether such changes originate at the investor level or are made solely by an investee.[4] Section 420, *Consistency of Application of Generally Accepted Accounting Principles*, paragraph .02 states: "The objective of the consistency standard is to ensure that if comparability of financial statements between periods has been materially affected by changes in accounting principles there will be appropriate reporting by the independent auditor regarding such changes."

.54 Thus, the auditor would need to add an explanatory paragraph (following the opinion paragraph) to his report when there has been a change in accounting principle by an investee accounted for by the equity method that causes a material lack of comparability in the financial statements of an investor.

[.55–.57] [Paragraphs deleted to reflect the conforming changes necessary due to the issuance of Statement on Auditing Standards Nos. 53 through 62.]

[Issue Date: July 1980; Revised: June 1993.]

---

[3] [Footnote deleted.]

[4] For a discussion of comparability of financial statements of a single enterprise, see paragraphs 111 through 119 of FASB Statement of Financial Accounting Concepts No. 2, "Qualitative Characteristics of Accounting Information."

[9.] The Effect of Adoption of FASB Statement No. 35 on Consistency

[.58–.63] [Withdrawn March 1989 by the Auditing Standards Board.]

10. Change in Presentation of Accumulated Benefit Information in the Financial Statements of a Defined Benefit Pension Plan

.64 *Question*—FASB Statement No. 35, *Accounting and Reporting by Defined Benefit Pension Plans* [AC section Pe5] requires the presentation of information regarding the actuarial present value of accumulated plan benefits and year-to-year changes therein of a defined benefit pension plan but permits certain flexibility in presenting such information. The information may be included on the face of a financial statement (a separate statement or one that combines accumulated benefit information with asset information), or it may be included in the notes to the financial statements. Furthermore, the benefit information may be as of the beginning of the period being reported upon or as of the end of that period. Does a change in the format of presentation of accumulated benefit information or a change in the date as of which such information is presented require the auditor to add an explanatory paragraph (after the opinion paragraph) to his report because of the change?

.65 *Interpretation*—Such changes in the presentation of information regarding accumulated benefits are considered reclassifications or variations in the nature of information presented. Changes such as these that are material should be explained in the financial statements or notes, but these changes ordinarily would not require the auditor to add this explanatory paragraph to his report (see section 420 paragraph .17).

[Issue Date: December 1980.]

[11.] The Effect of the Adoption of FASB Statement No. 36 on Consistency

[.66–.68] [Withdrawn March 1989 by the Auditing Standards Board.]

12. The Effect on the Auditor's Report of an Entity's Adoption of a New Accounting Standard That Does Not Require the Entity to Disclose the Effect of the Change in the Year of Adoption

.69 *Question*—An entity adopts a new accounting standard (for example, Financial Accounting Standards Board Statement of Financial Accounting Standards No. 133, *Accounting for Derivative Instruments and Hedging Activities*) and the standard does not require the entity to disclose, and the entity has not disclosed or determined, the effect of the change in the year of adoption.[5]

.70 Section 420, *Consistency of Application of Generally Accepted Accounting Principles*, paragraph .05 states, in part, that:

> Changes in accounting principle having a *material* [emphasis added] effect on the financial statements require recognition in the independent auditor's report through the addition of an explanatory paragraph (following the opinion paragraph).

.71 If an accounting standard does not require the entity to disclose, and the entity has not disclosed or determined, the effect of the change in accounting principle in the year of adoption, how should the auditor determine materiality for purposes of applying the consistency standard?

---

[5] Accounting Principles Board Opinion (APB) No. 20, *Accounting Changes*, does not apply to initial adoption of an accounting standard that specifies the manner of reporting the accounting change to conform with the conclusions of that standard. See APB No. 20, paragraph 4.

.72 *Interpretation*—According to section 420 paragraph .02, the objective of the second standard of reporting (referred to in section 420 as the *consistency standard*) is to:

> ... ensure that if comparability of financial statements between periods has been materially affected by changes in accounting principles, there will be appropriate reporting by the independent auditor regarding such changes. [Footnote omitted]

When an accounting standard does not require the entity to disclose the effect of the change in accounting principle in the year of adoption, section 420 does not require the auditor to independently determine the effect of that change in the year of adoption. Therefore, to determine whether to add an explanatory paragraph to the audit report for the accounting change resulting from adoption of such an accounting standard, the auditor should consider (*a*) the materiality of the cumulative effect of the change, where the accounting standard specifies that the cumulative effect of the change be recorded as of the beginning of the reporting period, and (*b*) the entity's voluntary disclosure, and the related support, regarding how it believes the change in accounting principle affected the financial statements in the year of adoption, when such disclosure is made. An explanatory paragraph would be required only if the cumulative effect of the change is material or if management discloses that it believes that the effect is or may be material in the year of adoption.

[Issue Date: April 2002.]

AU Section 431

Adequacy of Disclosure in Financial Statements

(Supersedes SAS No. 1, section 430.)

Source: SAS No. 32.

Issue date, unless otherwise indicated: October, 1980.

.01 The third standard of reporting is:

> When the auditor determines that informative disclosures are not reasonably adequate, the auditor must so state in the auditor's report.

[Revised, November 2006, to reflect conforming changes necessary due to the issuance of Statement on Auditing Standards No. 113.]

.02 The presentation of financial statements in conformity with generally accepted accounting principles includes adequate disclosure of material matters. These matters relate to the form, arrangement, and content of the financial statements and their appended notes, including, for example, the terminology used, the amount of detail given, the classification of items in the statements, and the bases of amounts set forth. An independent auditor considers whether a particular matter should be disclosed in light of the circumstances and facts of which he is aware at the time.

.03 If management omits from the financial statements, including the accompanying notes, information that is required by generally accepted accounting principles, the auditor should express a qualified or an adverse opinion and should provide the information in his report, if practicable, unless its omission from the auditor's report is recognized as appropriate by a specific Statement on Auditing Standards.[1] In this context, *practicable* means that the information is reasonably obtainable from management's accounts and records and that providing the information in the report does not require the auditor to assume the position of a preparer of financial information. For example, the auditor would not be expected to prepare a basic financial statement or segment information and include it in his report when management omits such information.

.04 In considering the adequacy of disclosure, and in other aspects of his audit, the auditor uses information received in confidence from the client. Without such confidence, the auditor would find it difficult to obtain information necessary for him to form an opinion on financial statements. Thus, the auditor should not ordinarily make available, without the client's consent, information that is not required to be disclosed in financial statements to comply with generally accepted accounting principles (see AICPA Code of Professional Conduct, Rule 301 [ET section 301.01]).

---

[1] An independent auditor may participate in preparing financial statements, including accompanying notes. The financial statements, including accompanying notes, however, remain the representations of management, and such participation by the auditor does not require him to modify his report (see section 110.03).

AU Section 500
THE FOURTH STANDARD OF REPORTING

TABLE OF CONTENTS

AU Section 504
Association With Financial Statements

(Supersedes SAS No. 1, sections 516, 517, and 518 and SAS No. 15, paragraphs 13–15.)[1]

Source: SAS No. 26; SAS No. 35; SAS No. 72.

See section 9504 for interpretations of this section.

Issue date, unless otherwise indicated: November, 1979.

.01 The fourth standard of reporting is:

> The auditor must either express an opinion regarding the financial statements, taken as a whole, or state that an opinion cannot be expressed, in the auditor's report. When the auditor cannot express an overall opinion, the auditor should state the reasons therefor in the auditor's report. In all cases where an auditor's name is associated with financial statements, the auditor should clearly indicate the character of the auditor's work, if any, and the degree of responsibility the auditor is taking, in the auditor's report.

The objective of the fourth reporting standard is to prevent misinterpretation of the degree of responsibility the accountant assumes when his name is associated with financial statements. [Revised, November 2006, to reflect conforming changes necessary due to the issuance of Statement on Auditing Standards No. 113.]

.02 This section defines *association* as that term is used in the fourth reporting standard. It provides guidance to an accountant associated with the financial statements of a public entity or with a nonpublic entity's financial statements that he has been engaged to audit in accordance with generally accepted auditing standards.[2]

.03 An accountant is associated with financial statements when he has consented to the use of his name in a report, document, or written communication containing the statements.[3] Also, when an accountant submits to his client or others financial statements that he has prepared or assisted in preparing, he is deemed to be associated even though the accountant does not append his name to the statements. Although the accountant may participate in the preparation of financial statements, the statements are representations of management, and the fairness of their presentation in conformity with generally accepted accounting principles is management's responsibility.

---

[1] [Footnote deleted to reflect the conforming changes necessary due to the issuance of Statement on Auditing Standards Nos. 53 through 62.]

[2] For purposes of this section, a public entity is any entity (*a*) whose securities trade in a public market either on a stock exchange (domestic or foreign) or in the over-the-counter market, including securities quoted only locally or regionally, (*b*) that makes a filing with a regulatory agency in preparation for the sale of any class of its securities in a public market, or (*c*) a subsidiary, corporate joint venture, or other entity controlled by an entity covered by (*a*) or (*b*). Statements on Standards for Accounting and Review Services provide guidance in connection with the unaudited financial statements or other unaudited financial information of a nonpublic entity.

[3] However, this section does not apply to data, such as tax returns, prepared solely for submission to taxing authorities.

.04 An accountant may be associated with audited or unaudited financial statements. Financial statements are audited if the accountant has applied auditing procedures sufficient to permit him to report on them as described in section 508, *Reports on Audited Financial Statements*. The unaudited interim financial statements (or financial information) of a public entity are reviewed when the accountant has applied procedures sufficient to permit him to report on them as described in section 722, *Interim Financial Information*.

Disclaimer of Opinion on Unaudited Financial Statements

.05 When an accountant is associated with the financial statements of a public entity, but has not audited or reviewed[4] such statements, the form of report to be issued is as follows:

> The accompanying balance sheet of X Company as of December 31, 19X1, and the related statements of income, retained earnings, and cash flows for the year then ended were not audited by us and, accordingly, we do not express an opinion on them.
>
> (Signature and date)

This disclaimer of opinion is the means by which the accountant complies with the fourth standard of reporting when associated with unaudited financial statements in these circumstances. The disclaimer may accompany the unaudited financial statements or it may be placed directly on them. In addition, each page of the financial statements should be clearly and conspicuously marked as unaudited. When an accountant issues this form of disclaimer of opinion, he has no responsibility to apply any procedures beyond reading the financial statements for obvious material misstatements. Any procedures that may have been applied should not be described, except in the limited circumstances set forth in paragraphs .18–.20. Describing procedures that may have been applied might cause the reader to believe the financial statements have been audited or reviewed.

.06 If the accountant is aware that his name is to be included in a client-prepared written communication of a public entity containing financial statements that have not been audited or reviewed, he should request (*a*) that his name not be included in the communication or (*b*) that the financial statements be marked as unaudited and that there be a notation that he does not express an opinion on them. If the client does not comply, the accountant should advise the client that he has not consented to the use of his name and should consider what other actions might be appropriate.[5]

Disclaimer of Opinion on Unaudited Financial Statements Prepared on a Comprehensive Basis of Accounting

.07 When an accountant is associated with unaudited financial statements of a public entity prepared in accordance with a comprehensive basis of

---

[4] When a public entity does not have its annual financial statements audited, an accountant may be requested to review its annual or interim financial statements. In those circumstances, an accountant may make a review and look to the guidance in Statements on Standards for Accounting and Review Services for the standards and procedures and form of report applicable to such an engagement.

[5] In considering what actions, if any, may be appropriate in the circumstances, the accountant may wish to consult his legal counsel.

accounting other than generally accepted accounting principles, he should follow the guidance provided by paragraph .05, except that he should modify the identification of financial statements in his disclaimer of opinion (see section 623.02-.10, *Special Reports*).[6] For example, a disclaimer of opinion on cash-basis statements might be worded as follows:

> The accompanying statement of assets and liabilities resulting from cash transactions of XYZ Corporation as of December 31, 19X1, and the related statement of revenues collected and expenses paid during the year then ended were not audited by us and, accordingly, we do not express an opinion on them.
>
> (Signature and date)

A note to the financial statements should describe how the basis of presentation differs from generally accepted accounting principles, but the monetary effect of such differences need not be stated.

Disclaimer of Opinion When Not Independent

.08 The second general standard states, "The auditor must maintain independence in mental attitude in all matters relating to the audit." The independent public accountant must be without bias with respect to the client; otherwise, he would lack that impartiality necessary for the dependability of his findings. Whether the accountant is independent is something he must decide as a matter of professional judgment. [Revised, November 2006, to reflect conforming changes necessary due to the issuance of Statement on Auditing Standards No. 113.]

.09 When an accountant is not independent, any procedures he might perform would not be in accordance with generally accepted auditing standards, and he would be precluded from expressing an opinion on such statements. Accordingly, he should disclaim an opinion with respect to the financial statements and should state specifically that he is not independent.

.10 If the financial statements are those of a nonpublic entity, the accountant should look to the guidance in Statements on Standards for Accounting and Review Services. In all other circumstances, regardless of the extent of procedures applied, the accountant should follow the guidance in paragraph .05, except that the disclaimer of opinion should be modified to state specifically that he is not independent. The reasons for lack of independence and any procedures he has performed should not be described; including such matters might confuse the reader concerning the importance of the impairment of independence. An example of such a report is as follows:

> We are not independent with respect to XYZ Company, and the accompanying balance sheet as of December 31, 19X1, and the related statements of income, retained earnings, and cash flows for the year then ended were not audited by us and, accordingly, we do not express an opinion on them.
>
> (Signature and date)

Circumstances Requiring a Modified Disclaimer

.11 If the accountant concludes on the basis of facts known to him that the unaudited financial statements on which he is disclaiming an opinion are not in conformity with generally accepted accounting principles, which include adequate disclosure, he should suggest appropriate revision; failing that, he should describe the departure in his disclaimer of opinion. This description

---

[6] Reference to generally accepted accounting principles in this section includes, where applicable, another comprehensive basis of accounting.

should refer specifically to the nature of the departure and, if practicable, state the effects on the financial statements or include the necessary information for adequate disclosure.

.12 When the effects of the departure on the financial statements are not reasonably determinable, the disclaimer of opinion should so state. When a departure from generally accepted accounting principles involves inadequate disclosure, it may not be practicable for the accountant to include the omitted disclosures in his report. For example, when management has elected to omit substantially all of the disclosures, the accountant should clearly indicate that in his report, but the accountant would not be expected to include such disclosures in his report.

.13 If the client will not agree to revision of the financial statements or will not accept the accountant's disclaimer of opinion with the description of the departure from generally accepted accounting principles, the accountant should refuse to be associated with the statements and, if necessary, withdraw from the engagement.

Reporting on Audited and Unaudited Financial Statements in Comparative Form

.14 When unaudited financial statements are presented in comparative form with audited financial statements in documents filed with the Securities and Exchange Commission, such statements should be clearly marked as "unaudited" but should not be referred to in the auditor's report.

.15 When unaudited financial statements are presented in comparative form with audited financial statements in any other document, the financial statements that have not been audited should be clearly marked to indicate their status and either (*a*) the report on the prior period should be reissued (see section 530.06–.08)[7] or (*b*) the report on the current period should include as a separate paragraph an appropriate description of the responsibility assumed for the financial statements of the prior period (see paragraphs .16 and .17). Either reissuance or reference in a separate paragraph is acceptable; in both circumstances, the accountant should consider the current form and manner of presentation of the financial statements of the prior period in light of the information of which he has become aware during his current engagement.

.16 When the financial statements of the prior period have been audited and the report on the current period is to contain a separate paragraph, it should indicate (*a*) that the financial statements of the prior period were audited previously, (*b*) the date of the previous report, (*c*) the type of opinion expressed previously, (*d*) if the opinion was other than unqualified, the substantive reasons therefor, and (*e*) that no auditing procedures were performed after the date of the previous report. An example of such a separate paragraph is as follows:

> The financial statements for the year ended December 31, 19X1, were audited by us (other accountants) and we (they) expressed an unqualified opinion on them in our (their) report dated March 1, 19X2, but we (they) have not performed any auditing procedures since that date.

.17 When the financial statements of the prior period have not been audited and the report on the current period is to contain a separate paragraph, it should include (*a*) a statement of the service performed in the prior period, (*b*) the date

---

[7] For reissuance of a compilation or review report, see Statements on Standards for Accounting and Review Services.

of the report on that service, (*c*) a description of any material modifications noted in that report, and (*d*) a statement that the service was less in scope than an audit and does not provide the basis for the expression of an opinion on the financial statements taken as a whole. When the financial statements are those of a public entity, the separate paragraph should include a disclaimer of opinion (see paragraph .05) or a description of a review. When the financial statements are those of a nonpublic entity and the financial statements were compiled or reviewed, the separate paragraph should contain an appropriate description of the compilation or review. For example, a separate paragraph describing a review might be worded as follows:

> The 20X1 financial statements were reviewed by us (other accountants) and our (their) report thereon, dated March 1, 20X2, stated we (they) were not aware of any material modifications that should be made to those statements for them to be in conformity with generally accepted accounting principles. However, a review is substantially less in scope than an audit and does not provide a basis for the expression of an opinion on the financial statements taken as a whole.

A separate paragraph describing a compilation might be worded as follows:

> The 19X1 financial statements were compiled by us (other accountants) and our (their) report thereon, dated March 1, 19X2, stated we (they) did not audit or review those financial statements and, accordingly, express no opinion or other form of assurance on them.

Negative Assurance

.18 When an accountant, for whatever reason, disclaims an opinion on financial statements his disclaimer should not be contradicted by the inclusion of expressions of assurance on the absence of knowledge of departures from generally accepted accounting principles except as specifically recognized as appropriate in applicable standards established by the American Institute of Certified Public Accountants.

.19 Negative assurances, for example, are permissible in letters for underwriters in which the independent auditor reports on limited procedures followed with respect to unaudited financial statements or other financial data pertinent to a registration statement filed with the Securities and Exchange Commission (see section 634, *Letters for Underwriters and Certain Other Requesting Parties*[*]).

[.20] [Superseded, February 1993, by Statement on Auditing Standards No. 72.] (See section 634.)

---

[*] [Section 631, formerly 630, changed by the issuance of Statement on Auditing Standards No. 38 (superseded). Section 634, formerly 631, changed by the issuance of Statement on Auditing Standards No. 49 (superseded). Title of section 634 changed, February 1993, to reflect the issuance of Statement on Auditing Standards No. 72.] (See section 634.)

of the report on that service, a description of any material modifications noted in that report, and a statement that the service was less in scope than an audit and does not provide the basis for the expression of an opinion on the financial statements taken as a whole. When the financial statements are those of a public entity, the separate paragraph should include a disclaimer of opinion (see paragraphs .05 and .06) or a description of a review. When the financial statements are those of a nonpublic entity and the financial statements were compiled or reviewed, the separate paragraph should contain an appropriate description of the compilation or review. For example, a separate paragraph describing a review might be worded as follows:

> The 20X1 financial statements were reviewed by us (other accountants) and our (their) report thereon, dated March 1, 20X2, stated we (they) were not aware of any material modifications that should be made to those statements for them to be in conformity with generally accepted accounting principles. However, a review is substantially less in scope than an audit and does not provide a basis for the expression of an opinion on the financial statements taken as a whole.

A separate paragraph describing a compilation might be worded as follows:

> The 20X1 financial statements were compiled by us (other accountants) and our (their) report thereon, dated March 1, 20X2, stated we (they) did not audit or review those financial statements and, accordingly, express no opinion or other form of assurance on them.

Negative Assurance

.18 When an accountant, for whatever reason, disclaims an opinion on financial statements, his disclaimer should not be contradicted by the inclusion of expressions of assurance on the absence of knowledge of departures from generally accepted accounting principles except as specifically recognized as appropriate in applicable standards established by the American Institute of Certified Public Accountants.[*]

.19 Negative assurances, for example, are permissible in letters for underwriters in which the independent auditor reports on limited procedures followed with respect to unaudited financial statements or other financial data pertinent to a registration statement filed with the Securities and Exchange Commission (see section 634, *Letters for Underwriters and Certain Other Requesting Parties*).

.20 [Superseded February 1993 by Statement on Auditing Standards No. 72.] (See section 634.)

[*] Section 631 [illegible] (Statement on Auditing Standards No. 38), which had been superseded [illegible] renumbered [illegible] by the issuance of Statement on Auditing Standards No. 49, was superseded by section 634 [illegible] January 1993 [illegible] Statement on Auditing Standards No. 72 [illegible]

AU Section 9504

Association With Financial Statements: Auditing Interpretations of Section 504

1. Annual Report Disclosure of Unaudited Fourth Quarter Interim Data

.01 *Question*—Financial Accounting Standards Board (FASB) *Accounting Standards Codification* (ASC) 270-10-50-2, which applies to publicly traded companies, states: "If interim financial data and disclosures are not separately reported for the fourth quarter, users of the interim financial information often make inferences about that quarter by subtracting data based on the third quarter interim report from the annual results. In the absence of a separate fourth quarter report or disclosure of the results (as outlined in FASB ASC 270-10-50-1) for that quarter in the annual report, disposals of components of an entity and extraordinary, unusual, or infrequently occurring items recognized in the fourth quarter, as well as the aggregate effect of year-end adjustments that are material to the results of that quarter (see FASB ASC 270-10-05-2 and 270-10-45-10) shall be disclosed in the annual report in a note to the annual financial statements." Does the auditor have an obligation, arising from the disclosure requirements of FASB ASC 270-10-50-2 to audit interim data?

.02 *Interpretation*—No. If the auditor has not been specifically engaged to audit interim information, he does not have an obligation to audit interim data as a result of his audit of the annual financial statements.

.03 Disclosure of fourth quarter adjustments and other disclosures required by FASB ASC 270-10-50-2 would appear in a note to the annual financial statements of a publicly traded company only if fourth quarter data were not separately distributed or did not appear elsewhere in the annual report. Consequently, such disclosures are not essential for a fair presentation of the annual financial statements in conformity with generally accepted accounting principles.

.04 If interim financial data and disclosures are not separately reported (as outlined in FASB ASC 270-10-50-1) for the fourth quarter, the independent auditor, during his audit of the annual financial statements, should inquire as to whether there are fourth quarter items that need to be disclosed in a note to the annual financial statements.

.05 Information on fourth quarter adjustments and similar items that appear in notes to the annual financial statements to comply with FASB ASC 270-10-50-2 would ordinarily not be audited separately and, therefore, the information would be labeled "unaudited" or "not covered by auditor's report."

.06 If a publicly traded company fails to comply with the provisions of FASB ASC 270-10-50-2, the auditor should suggest appropriate revision; failing that, he should call attention in his report to the omission of the information. The auditor need not qualify his opinion on the annual financial statements since the disclosure is not essential for a fair presentation of those statements in conformity with generally accepted accounting principles.

.07 Reference should be made to section 722 for guidance with respect to reviews of interim financial information of SEC registrants or non-SEC registrants that make a filing with a regulatory agency in preparation for a public offering or listing.

[Issue Date: November 1979; Revised: November 2002; Revised: June 2009.]

[2.] Association of the Auditor of an Acquired Company With Unaudited Statements in a Listing Application

[.08–.12] [Deleted May 1980.]

[3.] Association of the Auditor of the Acquiring Company With Unaudited Statements in a Listing Application

[.13–.14] [Deleted May 1980.]

4. Auditor's Identification With Condensed Financial Data

.15 *Question*—Section 150 paragraph .02 states in part: "In all cases where an auditor's name is associated with financial statements, the report should contain a clear-cut indication of the character of the auditor's work, if any, and the degree of responsibility the auditor is taking." Section 504 paragraph .03 states that "An accountant is associated with financial statements when he has consented to the use of his name in a report, document, or written communication containing the statements." Is the auditor "associated" with condensed financial data when he is identified by a financial reporting service as being a company's independent auditor or when his report is reproduced and presented with such data?

.16 *Interpretation*—No. The accountant has not consented to the use of his name when it is published by a financial reporting service. Financial data released to the public by a company and the name of its auditor are public information. Accordingly, neither the auditor nor his client has the ability to require a financial reporting service to withhold publishing such information.

.17 Financial reporting services, such as Dun & Bradstreet and Moody's Investors Service, furnish to subscribers information and ratings concerning commercial enterprises as a basis for credit, insurance, marketing and other business purposes. Those reports frequently include condensed financial data and other data such as payments to trade creditors, loan experience with banks, a brief history of the entity and a description of its operations. Also, as part of its report, the financial service often discloses the names of the officers and directors or principals or owners of the company and the name of the company's auditor.

.18 In the context in which the auditor's name appears, it is doubtful that readers will assume that he has audited the information presented. However, the AICPA has suggested to certain financial reporting services that they identify data as "unaudited" if the data has been extracted from unaudited financial statements. Also, the AICPA has suggested that when summarized financial data is presented together with an auditor's report on complete financial statements (including notes), the financial reporting services state that the auditor's report applies to the complete financial statements which are not presented.

[Issue Date: November, 1979.]

5. Applicability of Guidance on Reporting When Not Independent

.19 *Question*—Section 504 describes the reporting responsibilities of the certified public accountant who has determined that he is not independent with respect to financial statements with which he is associated. That section, however, does not indicate how he should determine whether he is independent. What should the certified public accountant consider in determining whether he is independent? Also, should his consideration be any different for an engagement to prepare unaudited financial statements?

.20 *Interpretation*—Section 504 explains the certified public accountant's reporting responsibilities when he is not independent. However, it does not attempt to explain how the certified public accountant determines whether he is independent because that is a question of professional ethics. Section 220 paragraph .04 states: "The profession has established, through the AICPA Code of Professional Conduct, precepts to guard against the . . . loss of independence." The AICPA, state CPA societies and state boards of accountancy have issued pronouncements to provide the certified public accountant with guidance to aid him in determining whether he is independent.

.21 The certified public accountant should consider the AICPA's Code of Professional Conduct in determining whether he is independent and whether the reporting requirements of section 504 apply. He should also consider the ethical requirements of his state CPA society or state board of accountancy.

.22 Section 504 paragraph .10 states that the reporting guidance applies, *regardless of the extent of procedures applied*, (emphasis added) in all circumstances other than when the financial statements are those of a nonpublic entity.[1] Thus, the accountant's consideration of whether he is independent should be the same whether the financial statements are audited or unaudited.

[Issue Date: November, 1979.]

[6.] Reporting on Solvency

[.23–.35] [Rescinded May 1988 by the issuance of attestation interpretation, "Responding to Requests for Reports on Matters Relating to Solvency."] (See AT section 9101.23–.33.) [Revised, January 2001, to reflect conforming changes necessary due to the issuance of Statement on Standards for Attestation Engagements No. 10.]

---

[1] If the financial statements are those of a nonpublic entity, the accountant should look to the guidance in Statements on Standards for Accounting and Review Services.

AU Section 508*

Reports on Audited Financial Statements

(Supersedes sections 505, 509, 542, 545, and 546.)

Source: SAS No. 58; SAS No. 64; SAS No. 79; SAS No. 85; SAS No. 93; SAS No. 98.

See section 9508 for interpretations of this section.

Effective for reports issued or reissued on or after January 1, 1989, unless otherwise indicated.

Introduction

.01 This section applies to auditors' reports issued in connection with audits[1] of historical financial statements that are intended to present financial position, results of operations, and cash flows in conformity with generally accepted accounting principles. It distinguishes the types of reports, describes the circumstances in which each is appropriate, and provides example reports.

.02 This section does not apply to unaudited financial statements as described in section 504, *Association With Financial Statements*, nor does it apply to reports on incomplete financial information or other special presentations as described in section 623, *Special Reports*.

.03 Justification for the expression of the auditor's opinion rests on the conformity of his or her audit with generally accepted auditing standards and on the findings. Generally accepted auditing standards include four standards of reporting.[2] This section is concerned primarily with the relationship of the fourth reporting standard to the language of the auditor's report.

.04 The fourth standard of reporting is as follows:

> The auditor must either express an opinion regarding the financial statements, taken as a whole, or state that an opinion cannot be expressed, in the auditor's

---

* This section has been revised to reflect the conforming changes necessary due to the issuance of Statement on Auditing Standards No. 93.

[1] An audit, for purposes of this section, is defined as an examination of historical financial statements performed in accordance with generally accepted auditing standards in effect at the time the audit is performed. Generally accepted auditing standards include the ten standards as well as the Statements on Auditing Standards that interpret those standards. In some cases, regulatory authorities may have additional requirements applicable to entities under their jurisdiction and auditors of such entities should consider those requirements.

[2] This section revises the second standard of reporting as follows:

> The report shall identify those circumstances in which such principles have not been consistently observed in the current period in relation to the preceding period.

Previously, the second standard required the auditor's report to state whether accounting principles had been consistently applied. As revised, the second standard requires the auditor to add an explanatory paragraph to his report only if accounting principles have not been applied consistently. (See section 420, *Consistency of Application of Generally Accepted Accounting Principles*.) Paragraphs .17–.19 of this section provide reporting guidance under these circumstances.

report. When the auditor cannot express an overall opinion, the auditor should state the reasons therefor in the auditor's report. In all cases where an auditor's name is associated with financial statements, the auditor should clearly indicate the character of the auditor's work, if any, and the degree of responsibility the auditor is taking, in the auditor's report.

[Revised, November 2006, to reflect conforming changes necessary due to the issuance of Statement on Auditing Standards No. 113.]

.05 The objective of the fourth standard is to prevent misinterpretation of the degree of responsibility the auditor is assuming when his or her name is associated with financial statements. Reference in the fourth reporting standard to the financial statements "taken as a whole" applies equally to a complete set of financial statements and to an individual financial statement (for example, to a balance sheet) for one or more periods presented. (Paragraph .65 discusses the fourth standard of reporting as it applies to comparative financial statements.) The auditor may express an unqualified opinion on one of the financial statements and express a qualified or adverse opinion or disclaim an opinion on another if the circumstances warrant.

.06 The auditor's report is customarily issued in connection with an entity's basic financial statements—balance sheet, statement of income, statement of retained earnings and statement of cash flows. Each financial statement audited should be specifically identified in the introductory paragraph of the auditor's report. If the basic financial statements include a separate statement of changes in stockholders' equity accounts, it should be identified in the introductory paragraph of the report but need not be reported on separately in the opinion paragraph since such changes are part of the presentation of financial position, results of operations, and cash flows.

The Auditor's Standard Report

.07 The auditor's standard report states that the financial statements present fairly, in all material respects, an entity's financial position, results of operations, and cash flows in conformity with generally accepted accounting principles. This conclusion may be expressed only when the auditor has formed such an opinion on the basis of an audit performed in accordance with generally accepted auditing standards.

.08 The auditor's standard report identifies the financial statements audited in an opening (introductory) paragraph, describes the nature of an audit in a scope paragraph, and expresses the auditor's opinion in a separate opinion paragraph. The basic elements of the report are the following:

a. A title that includes the word *independent*[3]

b. A statement that the financial statements identified in the report were audited

c. A statement that the financial statements are the responsibility of the Company's management[4] and that the auditor's responsibility is to express an opinion on the financial statements based on his or her audit

---

[3] This section does not require a title for an auditor's report if the auditor is not independent. See section 504, *Association With Financial Statements*, for guidance on reporting when the auditor is not independent.

[4] In some instances, a document containing the auditor's report may include a statement by management regarding its responsibility for the presentation of the financial statements. Nevertheless, the auditor's report should state that the financial statements are management's responsibility.

d. A statement that the audit was conducted in accordance with generally accepted auditing standards and an identification of the United States of America as the country of origin of those standards (for example, auditing standards generally accepted in the United States of America or U.S. generally accepted auditing standards)

e. A statement that those standards require that the auditor plan and perform the audit to obtain reasonable assurance about whether the financial statements are free of material misstatement

f. A statement that an audit includes—

(1) Examining, on a test basis, evidence supporting the amounts and disclosures in the financial statements

(2) Assessing the accounting principles used and significant estimates made by management

(3) Evaluating the overall financial statement presentation[5]

g. A statement that the auditor believes that his or her audit provides a reasonable basis for his or her opinion

h. An opinion as to whether the financial statements present fairly, in all material respects, the financial position of the Company as of the balance sheet date and the results of its operations and its cash flows for the period then ended in conformity with generally accepted accounting principles. The opinion should include an identification of the United States of America as the country of origin of those accounting principles (for example, accounting principles generally accepted in the United States of America or U.S. generally accepted accounting principles[6])

i. The manual or printed signature of the auditor's firm

j. The date[7] of the audit report

The form of the auditor's standard report on financial statements covering a single year is as follows:

Independent Auditor's Report

We have audited the accompanying balance sheet of X Company as of December 31, 20XX, and the related statements of income, retained earnings, and cash flows for the year then ended. These financial statements are the responsibility of the Company's management. Our responsibility is to express an opinion on these financial statements based on our audit.

---

[5] [Footnote deleted, October 2009, to reflect conforming changes necessary due to the withdrawal of SAS No. 69.]

6 A U.S. auditor also may be engaged to report on the financial statements of a U.S. entity that have been prepared in conformity with accounting principles generally accepted in another country. In those circumstances, the auditor should refer to the guidance in section 534, *Reporting on Financial Statements Prepared for Use in Other Countries.* [Footnote added, effective for reports issued or reissued on or after June 30, 2001 by Statement on Auditing Standards No. 93.]

7 For guidance on dating the auditor's report, see section 530, *Dating of the Independent Auditor's Report.* [Footnote renumbered by the issuance of Statement on Auditing Standards No. 93, October 2000.]

We conducted our audit in accordance with auditing standards generally accepted in the United States of America. Those standards require that we plan and perform the audit to obtain reasonable assurance about whether the financial statements are free of material misstatement. An audit includes examining, on a test basis, evidence supporting the amounts and disclosures in the financial statements. An audit also includes assessing the accounting principles used and significant estimates made by management, as well as evaluating the overall financial statement presentation. We believe that our audit provides a reasonable basis for our opinion.

In our opinion, the financial statements referred to above, present fairly, in all material respects, the financial position of X Company as of [at] December 31, 20XX, and the results of its operations and its cash flows for the year then ended in conformity with accounting principles generally accepted in the United States of America.

[Signature]

[Date]

The form of the auditor's standard report on comparative financial statements[8] is as follows:

Independent Auditor's Report

We have audited the accompanying balance sheets of X Company as of December 31, 20X2 and 20X1, and the related statements of income, retained earnings, and cash flows for the years then ended. These financial statements are the responsibility of the Company's management. Our responsibility is to express an opinion on these financial statements based on our audits.

We conducted our audits in accordance with auditing standards generally accepted in the United States of America. Those standards require that we plan and perform the audit to obtain reasonable assurance about whether the financial statements are free of material misstatement. An audit includes examining, on a test basis, evidence supporting the amounts and disclosures in the financial statements. An audit also includes assessing the accounting principles used and significant estimates made by management, as well as evaluating the overall financial statement presentation. We believe that our audits provide a reasonable basis for our opinion.

In our opinion, the financial statements referred to above, present fairly, in all material respects, the financial position of X Company as of [at] December 31, 20X2 and 20X1, and the results of its operations and its cash flows for the years then ended in conformity with accounting principles generally accepted in the United States of America.

[Signature]

[Date]

[As amended, effective for reports issued or reissued on or after June 30, 2001, by Statement on Auditing Standards No. 93.]

---

[8] If statements of income, retained earnings, and cash flows are presented on a comparative basis for one or more prior periods, but the balance sheet(s) as of the end of one (or more) of the prior period(s) is not presented, the phrase "for the years then ended" should be changed to indicate that the auditor's opinion applies to each period for which statements of income, retained earnings, and cash flows are presented, such as "for each of the three years in the period ended [date of latest balance sheet]." [Footnote renumbered by the issuance of Statement on Auditing Standards No. 93, October 2000.]

.09 The report may be addressed to the company whose financial statements are being audited or to its board of directors or stockholders. A report on the financial statements of an unincorporated entity should be addressed as circumstances dictate, for example, to the partners, to the general partner, or to the proprietor. Occasionally, an auditor is retained to audit the financial statements of a company that is not a client; in such a case, the report is customarily addressed to the client and not to the directors or stockholders of the company whose financial statements are being audited.

.10 This section also discusses the circumstances that may require the auditor to depart from the standard report and provides reporting guidance in such circumstances. This section is organized by type of opinion that the auditor may express in each of the various circumstances presented; this section describes what is meant by the various audit opinions:

- *Unqualified opinion.* An unqualified opinion states that the financial statements present fairly, in all material respects, the financial position, results of operations, and cash flows of the entity in conformity with generally accepted accounting principles. This is the opinion expressed in the standard report discussed in paragraph .08.
- *Explanatory language added to the auditor's standard report.* Certain circumstances, while not affecting the auditor's unqualified opinion on the financial statements, may require that the auditor add an explanatory paragraph (or other explanatory language) to his or her report.
- *Qualified opinion.* A qualified opinion states that, except for the effects of the matter(s) to which the qualification relates, the financial statements present fairly, in all material respects, the financial position, results of operations, and cash flows of the entity in conformity with generally accepted accounting principles.
- *Adverse opinion.* An adverse opinion states that the financial statements do not present fairly the financial position, results of operations, or cash flows of the entity in conformity with generally accepted accounting principles.
- *Disclaimer of opinion.* A disclaimer of opinion states that the auditor does not express an opinion on the financial statements.

These opinions are discussed in greater detail throughout the remainder of this section.

Explanatory Language Added to the Auditor's Standard Report

.11 Certain circumstances, while not affecting the auditor's unqualified opinion, may require that the auditor add an explanatory[9] paragraph (or other explanatory language) to the standard report.[10] These circumstances include:

a. The auditor's opinion is based in part on the report of another auditor (paragraphs .12–.13).

---

[9] Unless otherwise required by the provisions of this section, an explanatory paragraph may precede or follow the opinion paragraph in the auditor's report. [Footnote renumbered by the issuance of Statement on Auditing Standards No. 93, October 2000.]

[10] See footnote 3. [Footnote renumbered by the issuance of Statement on Auditing Standards No. 93, October 2000.]

b. To prevent the financial statements from being misleading because of unusual circumstances, the financial statements contain a departure from an accounting principle promulgated by a body designated by the AICPA Council to establish such principles (paragraphs .14–.15).

c. There is substantial doubt about the entity's ability to continue as a going concern.[11]

d. There has been a material change between periods in accounting principles or in the method of their application (paragraphs .16–.18).

e. Certain circumstances relating to reports on comparative financial statements exist (paragraphs .68–.69 and .72–.74).

f. Selected quarterly financial data required by SEC Regulation S-K has been omitted or has not been reviewed. (See section 722, *Interim Financial Information*, paragraph .50.)

g. When a designated accounting standard setter requires information to accompany the entity's basic financial statements (see paragraphs .07–.09 of section 558, *Required Supplementary Information*).

h. Other information in a document containing audited financial statements is materially inconsistent with information appearing in the financial statements. (See paragraph .11 of section 550, *Other Information in Documents Containing Audited Financial Statements*.)

In addition, the auditor may add an explanatory paragraph to emphasize a matter regarding the financial statements (paragraph .19). [As amended, effective for reports issued or reissued on or after February 29, 1996, by Statement on Auditing Standards No. 79. Revised, November 2002, to reflect conforming changes necessary due to the issuance of Statement on Auditing Standards No. 100. Revised, December 2010, to reflect conforming changes necessary due to the issuance of SAS Nos. 118–120.]

Opinion Based in Part on Report of Another Auditor

.12 When the auditor decides to make reference to the report of another auditor as a basis, in part, for his or her opinion, he or she should disclose this fact in the introductory paragraph of his or her report and should refer to the report of the other auditor in expressing his or her opinion. These references indicate division of responsibility for performance of the audit. (See section 543, *Part of Audit Performed by Other Independent Auditors*.)

.13 An example of a report indicating a division of responsibility follows:

Independent Auditor's Report

We have audited the consolidated balance sheets of ABC Company and subsidiaries as of December 31, 20X2 and 20X1, and the related consolidated statements of income, retained earnings, and cash flows for the years then ended.

---

[11] Section 341A, *The Auditor's Consideration of an Entity's Ability to Continue as a Going Concern*, describes the auditor's responsibility to evaluate whether there is substantial doubt about the entity's ability to continue as a going concern for a reasonable period of time and, when applicable, to consider the adequacy of financial statement disclosure and to include an explanatory paragraph in the report to reflect his or her conclusions. [Footnote renumbered by the issuance of Statement on Auditing Standards No. 93, October 2000.]

> These financial statements are the responsibility of the Company's management. Our responsibility is to express an opinion on these financial statements based on our audits. We did not audit the financial statements of B Company, a wholly-owned subsidiary, which statements reflect total assets of $_____ and $_____ as of December 31, 20X2 and 20X1, respectively, and total revenues of $_____ and $_____ for the years then ended. Those statements were audited by other auditors whose report has been furnished to us, and our opinion, insofar as it relates to the amounts included for B Company, is based solely on the report of the other auditors.
>
> We conducted our audits in accordance with auditing standards generally accepted in the United States of America. Those standards require that we plan and perform the audit to obtain reasonable assurance about whether the financial statements are free of material misstatement. An audit includes examining, on a test basis, evidence supporting the amounts and disclosures in the financial statements. An audit also includes assessing the accounting principles used and significant estimates made by management, as well as evaluating the overall financial statement presentation. We believe that our audits and the report of other auditors provide a reasonable basis for our opinion.
>
> In our opinion, based on our audits and the report of other auditors, the consolidated financial statements referred to above, present fairly, in all material respects, the financial position of ABC Company and subsidiaries as of December 31, 20X2 and 20X1, and the results of their operations and their cash flows for the years then ended in conformity with accounting principles generally accepted in the United States of America.

Departure From a Promulgated Accounting Principle

.14 Rule 203 [ET section 203.01] of the Code of Professional Conduct of the AICPA states:

> A member shall not (1) express an opinion or state affirmatively that the financial statements or other financial data of any entity are presented in conformity with generally accepted accounting principles or (2) state that he or she is not aware of any material modifications that should be made to such statements or data in order for them to be in conformity with generally accepted accounting principles, if such statements or data contain any departure from an accounting principle promulgated by bodies designated by Council to establish such principles that has a material effect on the statements or data taken as a whole. If, however, the statements or data contain such a departure and the member can demonstrate that due to unusual circumstances the financial statements or data would otherwise have been misleading, the member can comply with the rule by describing the departure, its approximate effects, if practicable, and the reasons why compliance with the principle would result in a misleading statement.

.15 When the circumstances contemplated by Rule 203 (ET section 202 paragraph .01) are present, the auditor's report should include, in a separate paragraph or paragraphs, the information required by the rule. In such a case, it is appropriate for the auditor to express an unqualified opinion with respect to the conformity of the financial statements with generally accepted accounting principles unless there are other reasons, not associated with the departure from a promulgated principle, not to do so. [Title of section 411 amended, effective for reports issued or reissued on or after June 30, 2001, by Statement on Auditing Standards No. 93. Revised, October 2009, to reflect conforming changes necessary due to the withdrawal of SAS No. 69.]

Former paragraphs .16–.33 and related footnotes have been deleted and all subsequent paragraphs and footnotes renumbered by the issuance of Statement on Auditing Standards No. 79, effective for reports issued or reissued on or after February 29, 1996.

Lack of Consistency

.16 The auditor's standard report implies that the auditor is satisfied that the comparability of financial statements between periods has not been materially affected by changes in accounting principles and that such principles have been consistently applied between or among periods because either (*a*) no change in accounting principles has occurred, or (*b*) there has been a change in accounting principles or in the method of their application, but the effect of the change on the comparability of the financial statements is not material. In these cases, the auditor should not refer to consistency in the report. If, however, there has been a change in accounting principles or in the method of their application that has a material effect on the comparability of the company's financial statements, the auditor should refer to the change in an explanatory paragraph of the report. Such explanatory paragraph (following the opinion paragraph) should identify the nature of the change and refer the reader to the note in the financial statements that discusses the change in detail. The auditor's concurrence with a change is implicit unless he or she takes exception to the change in expressing his or her opinion as to fair presentation of the financial statements in conformity with generally accepted accounting principles.[12] When there is a change in accounting principles, there are also other matters that the auditor should consider (see paragraphs .50–.57). [Paragraph renumbered by the issuance of Statement on Auditing Standards No. 79, December 1995.]

.17 Following is an example of an appropriate explanatory paragraph:

> As discussed in Note X to the financial statements, the Company changed its method of computing depreciation in 20X2.

[Paragraph renumbered by the issuance of Statement on Auditing Standards No. 79, December 1995.]

.18 The addition of this explanatory paragraph in the auditor's report is required in reports on financial statements of subsequent years as long as the year of the change is presented and reported on.[13] However, if the accounting change is accounted for by retroactive restatement of the financial statements

---

[12] With respect to the method of accounting for the effect of a change in accounting principle, see Financial Accounting Standards Board *Accounting Standards Codification* 250, *Accounting Changes and Error Corrections*. [Footnote renumbered by the issuance of Statement on Auditing Standards No. 79, December 1995. Footnote subsequently renumbered by the issuance of Statement on Auditing Standards No. 93, October 2000. Footnote revised, June 2009, to reflect conforming changes necessary due to the issuance of FASB ASC.]

[13] An exception to this requirement occurs when a change in accounting principle that does not require a cumulative effect adjustment is made at the beginning of the earliest year presented and reported on. That exception is addressed in the auditing interpretation of section 420, *Consistency of Application of Generally Accepted Accounting Principles*, titled "Impact on the Auditor's Report of FIFO to LIFO Change in Comparative Financial Statements," (section 9420.16–.23). [Footnote renumbered by the issuance of Statement on Auditing Standards No. 79, December 1995. Footnote subsequently renumbered by the issuance of Statement on Auditing Standards No. 93, October 2000.]

affected, the additional paragraph is required only in the year of the change since, in subsequent years, all periods presented will be comparable. [Paragraph renumbered by the issuance of Statement on Auditing Standards No. 79, December 1995.]

Emphasis of a Matter

.19 In any report on financial statements, the auditor may emphasize a matter regarding the financial statements. Such explanatory information should be presented in a separate paragraph of the auditor's report. Phrases such as "with the foregoing [following] explanation" should not be used in the opinion paragraph if an emphasis paragraph is included in the auditor's report. Emphasis paragraphs are never required; they may be added solely at the auditor's discretion. Examples of matters the auditor may wish to emphasize are—

- That the entity is a component of a larger business enterprise.
- That the entity has had significant transactions with related parties.
- Unusually important subsequent events.
- Accounting matters, other than those involving a change or changes in accounting principles, affecting the comparability of the financial statements with those of the preceding period.

[Paragraph renumbered and amended, effective for reports issued or reissued on or after February 29, 1996, by the issuance of Statement on Auditing Standards No. 79.]

Departures From Unqualified Opinions

Qualified Opinions

.20 Certain circumstances may require a qualified opinion. A qualified opinion states that, *except for* the effects of the matter to which the qualification relates, the financial statements present fairly, in all material respects, financial position, results of operations, and cash flows in conformity with generally accepted accounting principles. Such an opinion is expressed when—

a. There is a lack of sufficient appropriate audit evidence or there are restrictions on the scope of the audit that have led the auditor to conclude that he or she cannot express an unqualified opinion and he or she has concluded not to disclaim an opinion (paragraphs .22–.34).

b. The auditor believes, on the basis of his or her audit, that the financial statements contain a departure from generally accepted accounting principles, the effect of which is material, and he or she has concluded not to express an adverse opinion (paragraphs .35–.57).

[Paragraph renumbered by the issuance of Statement on Auditing Standards No. 79, December 1995. Revised, March 2006, to reflect conforming changes necessary due to the issuance of Statement on Auditing Standards No. 105.]

.21 When the auditor expresses a qualified opinion, he or she should disclose all of the substantive reasons in one or more separate explanatory paragraph(s) preceding the opinion paragraph of the report. The auditor should also include, in the opinion paragraph, the appropriate qualifying language and a reference to the explanatory paragraph. A qualified opinion should include the word *except* or *exception* in a phrase such as *except for* or *with the exception of*. Phrases such as *subject to* and *with the foregoing explanation* are not clear or forceful enough and should not be used. Since accompanying notes are part of the financial statements, wording such as *fairly presented, in all material respects, when read in conjunction with Note 1* is likely to be misunderstood and should not be used. [Paragraph renumbered by the issuance of Statement on Auditing Standards No. 79, December 1995.]

Scope Limitations

.22 The auditor can determine that he or she is able to express an unqualified opinion only if the audit has been conducted in accordance with generally accepted auditing standards and if he or she has therefore been able to apply all the procedures he considers necessary in the circumstances. Restrictions on the scope of the audit, whether imposed by the client or by circumstances, such as the timing of his or her work, the inability to obtain sufficient appropriate audit evidence, or an inadequacy in the accounting records, may require the auditor to qualify his or her opinion or to disclaim an opinion. In such instances, the reasons for the auditor's qualification of opinion or disclaimer of opinion should be described in the report. [Paragraph renumbered by the issuance of Statement on Auditing Standards No. 79, December 1995. Revised, March 2006, to reflect conforming changes necessary due to the issuance of Statement on Auditing Standards No. 105.]

.23 The auditor's decision to qualify his or her opinion or disclaim an opinion because of a scope limitation depends on his or her assessment of the importance of the omitted procedure(s) to his or her ability to form an opinion on the financial statements being audited. This assessment will be affected by the nature and magnitude of the potential effects of the matters in question and by their significance to the financial statements. If the potential effects relate to many financial statement items, this significance is likely to be greater than if only a limited number of items is involved. [Paragraph renumbered by the issuance of Statement on Auditing Standards No. 79, December 1995.]

.24 Common restrictions on the scope of the audit include those applying to the observation of physical inventories and the confirmation of accounts receivable by direct communication with debtors.[14] Another common scope restriction involves accounting for long-term investments when the auditor has not been able to obtain audited financial statements of an investee. Restrictions on the application of these or other audit procedures to important elements of the financial statements require the auditor to decide whether he or she has examined sufficient appropriate audit evidence to permit him or her to express an unqualified or qualified opinion, or whether he or she should disclaim an opinion. When restrictions that significantly limit the scope of the audit are imposed by the client, ordinarily the auditor should disclaim an opinion on the financial statements. [Paragraph renumbered by the issuance of Statement on

[14] Circumstances such as the timing of the work may make it impossible for the auditor to accomplish these procedures. In this case, if the auditor is able to satisfy himself or herself as to inventories or accounts receivable by applying alternative procedures, there is no significant limitation on the scope of the work, and the report need not include a reference to the omission of the procedures or the use of alternative procedures. It is important to understand, however, that section 331, *Inventories*, states that "it will always be necessary for the auditor to make, or observe, some physical counts of the inventory and apply appropriate tests of intervening transactions." [Footnote renumbered by the issuance of Statement on Auditing Standards No. 79, December 1995. Footnote subsequently renumbered by the issuance of Statement on Auditing Standards No. 93, October 2000.]

Auditing Standards No. 79, December 1995. Revised, March 2006, to reflect conforming changes necessary due to the issuance of Statement on Auditing Standards No. 105.]

.25 When a qualified opinion results from a limitation on the scope of the audit or an insufficiency of audit evidence, the situation should be described in an explanatory paragraph preceding the opinion paragraph and referred to in both the scope and opinion paragraphs of the auditor's report. It is not appropriate for the scope of the audit to be explained in a note to the financial statements, since the description of the audit scope is the responsibility of the auditor and not that of the client. [Paragraph renumbered by the issuance of Statement on Auditing Standards No. 79, December 1995. Revised, March 2006, to reflect conforming changes necessary due to the issuance of Statement on Auditing Standards No. 105.]

.26 When an auditor qualifies his or her opinion because of a scope limitation, the wording in the opinion paragraph should indicate that the qualification pertains to the possible effects on the financial statements and not to the scope limitation itself. Wording such as "In our opinion, except for the abovementioned limitation on the scope of our audit . . ." bases the exception on the restriction itself, rather than on the possible effects on the financial statements and, therefore, is unacceptable. An example of a qualified opinion related to a scope limitation concerning an investment in a foreign affiliate (assuming the effects of the limitation are such that the auditor has concluded that a disclaimer of opinion is not appropriate) follows:

Independent Auditor's Report

[*Same first paragraph as the standard report*]

Except as discussed in the following paragraph, we conducted our audits in accordance with auditing standards generally accepted in the United States of America. Those standards require that we plan and perform the audit to obtain reasonable assurance about whether the financial statements are free of material misstatement. An audit includes examining, on a test basis, evidence supporting the amounts and disclosures in the financial statements. An audit also includes assessing the accounting principles used and significant estimates made by management, as well as evaluating the overall financial statement presentation. We believe that our audits provide a reasonable basis for our opinion.

We were unable to obtain audited financial statements supporting the Company's investment in a foreign affiliate stated at $_____ and $_____ at December 31, 20X2 and 20X1, respectively, or its equity in earnings of that affiliate of $_____ and $_____, which is included in net income for the years then ended as described in Note X to the financial statements; nor were we able to satisfy ourselves as to the carrying value of the investment in the foreign affiliate or the equity in its earnings by other auditing procedures.

In our opinion, except for the effects of such adjustments, if any, as might have been determined to be necessary had we been able to examine evidence regarding the foreign affiliate investment and earnings, the financial statements referred to in the first paragraph above, present fairly, in all material respects, the financial position of X Company as of December 31, 20X2 and 20X1, and the results of its operations and its cash flows for the years then ended in conformity with accounting principles generally accepted in the United States of America.

[Paragraph renumbered by the issuance of Statement on Auditing Standards No. 79, December 1995.]

.27 ***Other scope limitations.*** Sometimes, notes to financial statements may contain unaudited information, such as pro forma calculations or other similar disclosures. If the unaudited information (for example, an investor's share, material in amount, of an investee's earnings recognized on the equity method) is such that it should be subjected to auditing procedures in order for the auditor to form an opinion with respect to the financial statements taken as a whole, the auditor should apply the procedures he or she deems necessary to the unaudited information. If the auditor has not been able to apply the procedures he or she considers necessary, the auditor should qualify his or her opinion or disclaim an opinion because of a limitation on the scope of the audit. [Paragraph renumbered by the issuance of Statement on Auditing Standards No. 79, December 1995.]

.28 If, however, these disclosures are not necessary to fairly present the financial position, operating results, or cash flows on which the auditor is reporting, such disclosures may be identified as *unaudited* or as *not covered by the auditor's report*. For example, the pro forma effects of a business combination or of a subsequent event may be labelled unaudited. Therefore, while the event or transaction giving rise to the disclosures in these circumstances should be audited, the pro forma disclosures of that event or transaction would not be. The auditor should be aware, however, that section 530, *Dating of the Independent Auditor's Report*, states that, if the auditor is aware of a material subsequent event that has occurred after the date of the auditor's report but before issuance of the report that should be disclosed, the auditor's only options are to dual date the report or date the report as of the date of the subsequent event and extend the procedures for review of subsequent events to that date. Labelling the note unaudited is not an acceptable alternative in these circumstances. [Paragraph renumbered by the issuance of Statement on Auditing Standards No. 79, December 1995. Revised, December 2005, to reflect conforming changes necessary due to the issuance of Statement on Auditing Standards No. 103.]

.29 ***Uncertainties and scope limitations.*** A matter involving an uncertainty is one that is expected to be resolved at a future date, at which time conclusive audit evidence concerning its outcome would be expected to become available. Uncertainties include, but are not limited to, contingencies covered by FASB *Accounting Standards Codification* (ASC) 450, *Contingencies*, and matters related to estimates covered by FASB ASC 275, *Risks and Uncertainties*. [Paragraph added, effective for reports issued or reissued on or after February 29, 1996, by Statement on Auditing Standards No. 79. Revised, March 2006, to reflect conforming changes necessary due to the issuance of Statement on Auditing Standards No. 105. Revised, June 2009, to reflect conforming changes necessary due to the issuance of FASB ASC.]

.30 Conclusive audit evidence concerning the ultimate outcome of uncertainties cannot be expected to exist at the time of the audit because the outcome and related audit evidence are prospective. In these circumstances, management is responsible for estimating the effect of future events on the financial statements, or determining that a reasonable estimate cannot be made and making the required disclosures, all in accordance with generally accepted accounting principles, based on management's analysis of existing conditions. An audit includes an assessment of whether the audit evidence is sufficient to support management's analysis. Absence of the existence of information related to the outcome of an uncertainty does not necessarily lead to a conclusion that the audit evidence supporting management's assertion is not sufficient. Rather, the auditor's judgment regarding the sufficiency of the audit evidence is based on the audit evidence that is, or should be, available. If, after considering the existing conditions and available evidence, the auditor concludes that sufficient audit evidence supports management's assertions about the nature of a matter involving an uncertainty and its presentation or disclosure in the financial statements, an unqualified opinion ordinarily is appropriate. [Paragraph added, effective for reports issued or reissued on or after February 29, 1996, by Statement on Auditing Standards No. 79. Revised, March 2006, to reflect conforming changes necessary due to the issuance of Statement on Auditing Standards No. 105.]

.31 If the auditor is unable to obtain sufficient audit evidence to support management's assertions about the nature of a matter involving an uncertainty and its presentation or disclosure in the financial statements, the auditor should consider the need to express a qualified opinion or to disclaim an opinion because of a scope limitation. A qualification or disclaimer of opinion because of a scope limitation is appropriate if sufficient audit evidence related to an uncertainty does or did exist but was not available to the auditor for reasons such as management's record retention policies or a restriction imposed by management. [Paragraph added, effective for reports issued or reissued on or after February 29, 1996, by Statement on Auditing Standards No. 79. Revised, March 2006, to reflect conforming changes necessary due to the issuance of Statement on Auditing Standards No. 105.]

.32 Scope limitations related to uncertainties should be differentiated from situations in which the auditor concludes that the financial statements are materially misstated due to departures from generally accepted accounting principles related to uncertainties. Such departures may be caused by inadequate disclosure concerning the uncertainty, the use of inappropriate accounting principles, or the use of unreasonable accounting estimates. Paragraphs .45–.49 provide guidance to the auditor when financial statements contain departures from generally accepted accounting principles related to uncertainties. [Paragraph added, effective for reports issued or reissued on or after February 29, 1996, by Statement on Auditing Standards No. 79.]

.33 ***Limited reporting engagements.*** The auditor may be asked to report on one basic financial statement and not on the others. For example, he or she may be asked to report on the balance sheet and not on the statements of income, retained earnings or cash flows. These engagements do not involve scope limitations if the auditor's access to information underlying the basic financial statements is not limited and if the auditor applies all the procedures he considers necessary in the circumstances; rather, such engagements involve limited reporting objectives. [Paragraph renumbered by the issuance of Statement on Auditing Standards No. 79, December 1995.]

.34 An auditor may be asked to report on the balance sheet only. In this case, the auditor may express an opinion on the balance sheet only. An example of an unqualified opinion on a balance-sheet-only audit follows (the report assumes that the auditor has been able to satisfy himself or herself regarding the consistency of application of accounting principles):

Independent Auditor's Report

> We have audited the accompanying balance sheet of X Company as of December 31, 20XX. This financial statement is the responsibility of the Company's management. Our responsibility is to express an opinion on this financial statement based on our audit.
>
> We conducted our audit in accordance with auditing standards generally accepted in the United States of America. Those standards require that we plan

and perform the audit to obtain reasonable assurance about whether the balance sheet is free of material misstatement. An audit includes examining, on a test basis, evidence supporting the amounts and disclosures in the balance sheet. An audit also includes assessing the accounting principles used and significant estimates made by management, as well as evaluating the overall balance sheet presentation. We believe that our audit of the balance sheet provides a reasonable basis for our opinion.

In our opinion, the balance sheet referred to above, presents fairly, in all material respects, the financial position of X Company as of December 31, 20XX, in conformity with accounting principles generally accepted in the United States of America.

[Paragraph renumbered by the issuance of Statement on Auditing Standards No. 79, December 1995.]

Departure From a Generally Accepted Accounting Principle

.35 When financial statements are materially affected by a departure from generally accepted accounting principles and the auditor has audited the statements in accordance with generally accepted auditing standards, he or she should express a qualified (paragraphs .36–.57) or an adverse (paragraphs .58–.60) opinion. The basis for such opinion should be stated in the report. [Paragraph renumbered by the issuance of Statement on Auditing Standards No. 79, December 1995.]

.36 In deciding whether the effects of a departure from generally accepted accounting principles are sufficiently material to require either a qualified or adverse opinion, one factor to be considered is the dollar magnitude of such effects. However, the concept of materiality does not depend entirely on relative size; it involves qualitative as well as quantitative judgments. The significance of an item to a particular entity (for example, inventories to a manufacturing company), the pervasiveness of the misstatement (such as whether it affects the amounts and presentation of numerous financial statement items), and the effect of the misstatement on the financial statements taken as a whole are all factors to be considered in making a judgment regarding materiality. [Paragraph renumbered by the issuance of Statement on Auditing Standards No. 79, December 1995.]

.37 When the auditor expresses a qualified opinion, he or she should disclose, in a separate explanatory paragraph(s) preceding the opinion paragraph of the report, all of the substantive reasons that have led him or her to conclude that there has been a departure from generally accepted accounting principles. Furthermore, the opinion paragraph of the report should include the appropriate qualifying language and a reference to the explanatory paragraph(s). [Paragraph renumbered by the issuance of Statement on Auditing Standards No. 79, December 1995.]

.38 The explanatory paragraph(s) should also disclose the principal effects of the subject matter of the qualification on financial position, results of operations, and cash flows, if practicable.[15] If the effects are not reasonably

---

[15] Section 431, *Adequacy of Disclosure in the Financial Statements*, defines *practicable* as ". . . the information is reasonably obtainable from management's accounts and records and that providing the information in the report does not require the auditor to assume the position of a preparer of financial information." For example, if the information can be obtained from the accounts and records without the auditor substantially increasing the effort that would normally be required to complete the audit, the information should be presented in the report. [Footnote renumbered by the issuance of Statement on Auditing Standards No. 79, December 1995. Footnote subsequently renumbered by the issuance of Statement on Auditing Standards No. 93, October 2000.]

determinable, the report should so state. If such disclosures are made in a note to the financial statements, the explanatory paragraph(s) may be shortened by referring to it. [Paragraph renumbered by the issuance of Statement on Auditing Standards No. 79, December 1995.]

.39 An example of a report in which the opinion is qualified because of the use of an accounting principle at variance with generally accepted accounting principles follows (assuming the effects are such that the auditor has concluded that an adverse opinion is not appropriate):

> Independent Auditor's Report
>
> [*Same first and second paragraphs as the standard report*]
>
> The Company has excluded, from property and debt in the accompanying balance sheets, certain lease obligations that, in our opinion, should be capitalized in order to conform with accounting principles generally accepted in the United States of America. If these lease obligations were capitalized, property would be increased by $_____ and $_____, long-term debt by $_____ and $_____, and retained earnings by $_____ and $_____ as of December 31, 20X2 and 20X1, respectively. Additionally, net income would be increased (decreased) by $_____ and $_____ and earnings per share would be increased (decreased) by $_____ and $_____, respectively, for the years then ended.
>
> In our opinion, except for the effects of not capitalizing certain lease obligations as discussed in the preceding paragraph, the financial statements referred to above, present fairly, in all material respects, the financial position of X Company as of December 31, 20X2 and 20X1, and the results of its operations and its cash flows for the years then ended in conformity with accounting principles generally accepted in the United States of America.

[Paragraph renumbered by the issuance of Statement on Auditing Standards No. 79, December 1995.]

.40 If the pertinent facts are disclosed in a note to the financial statements, a separate paragraph (preceding the opinion paragraph) of the auditor's report in the circumstances illustrated in paragraph .39 might read as follows:

> As more fully described in Note X to the financial statements, the Company has excluded certain lease obligations from property and debt in the accompanying balance sheets. In our opinion, accounting principles generally accepted in the United States of America require that such obligations be included in the balance sheets.

[Paragraph renumbered by the issuance of Statement on Auditing Standards No. 79, December 1995.]

.41 ***Inadequate disclosure.*** Information essential for a fair presentation in conformity with generally accepted accounting principles should be set forth in the financial statements (which include the related notes). When such information is set forth elsewhere in a report to shareholders, or in a prospectus, proxy statement, or other similar report, it should be referred to in the financial statements. If the financial statements, including accompanying notes, fail to disclose information that is required by generally accepted accounting principles, the auditor should express a qualified or adverse opinion because of the departure from those principles and should provide the information in the report, if practicable,[16] unless its omission from the auditor's report is recognized as

---

[16] See footnote 15. [Paragraph renumbered by the issuance of Statement on Auditing Standards No. 79, December 1995. Footnote subsequently renumbered by the issuance of Statement on Auditing Standards No. 93, October 2000.]

appropriate by a specific Statement on Auditing Standards. [Paragraph renumbered by the issuance of Statement on Auditing Standards No. 79, December 1995.]

.42 Following is an example of a report qualified for inadequate disclosure (assuming that the auditor has concluded that it is not practicable to present the required information and the effects are such that the auditor has concluded an adverse opinion is not appropriate):

Independent Auditor's Report

[*Same first and second paragraphs as the standard report*]

The Company's financial statements do not disclose [*describe the nature of the omitted information that it is not practicable to present in the auditor's report*]. In our opinion, disclosure of this information is required by accounting principles generally accepted in the United States of America.

In our opinion, except for the omission of the information discussed in the preceding paragraph, . . .

[Paragraph renumbered by the issuance of Statement on Auditing Standards No. 79, December 1995.]

.43 If a company issues financial statements that purport to present financial position and results of operations but omits the related statement of cash flows, the auditor will normally conclude that the omission requires qualification of his opinion. [Paragraph renumbered by the issuance of Statement on Auditing Standards No. 79, December 1995.]

.44 The auditor is not required to prepare a basic financial statement (for example, a statement of cash flows for one or more periods) and include it in the report if the company's management declines to present the statement. Accordingly, in these cases, the auditor should ordinarily qualify the report in the following manner:

Independent Auditor's Report

We have audited the accompanying balance sheets of X Company as of December 31, 20X2 and 20X1, and the related statements of income and retained earnings for the years then ended. These financial statements are the responsibility of the Company's management. Our responsibility is to express an opinion on these financial statements based on our audit.

[*Same second paragraph as the standard report*]

The Company declined to present a statement of cash flows for the years ended December 31, 20X2 and 20X1. Presentation of such statement summarizing the Company's operating, investing, and financing activities is required by accounting principles generally accepted in the United States of America.

In our opinion, except that the omission of a statement of cash flows results in an incomplete presentation as explained in the preceding paragraph, the financial statements referred to above, present fairly, in all material respects, the financial position of X Company as of December 31, 20X2 and 20X1, and the results of its operations for the years then ended in conformity with accounting principles generally accepted in the United States of America.

[Paragraph renumbered by the issuance of Statement on Auditing Standards No. 79, December 1995.]

.45 ***Departures from generally accepted accounting principles involving risks or uncertainties, and materiality considerations.***

Departures from generally accepted accounting principles involving risks or uncertainties generally fall into one of the following categories:

- Inadequate disclosure (paragraphs .46–.47)
- Inappropriate accounting principles (paragraph .48)
- Unreasonable accounting estimates (paragraph .49)

[Paragraph added, effective for reports issued or reissued on or after February 29, 1996, by Statement on Auditing Standards No. 79.]

.46 If the auditor concludes that a matter involving a risk or an uncertainty is not adequately disclosed in the financial statements in conformity with generally accepted accounting principles, the auditor should express a qualified or an adverse opinion. [Paragraph added, effective for reports issued or reissued on or after February 29, 1996, by Statement on Auditing Standards No. 79.]

.47 The auditor should consider materiality in evaluating the adequacy of disclosure of matters involving risks or uncertainties in the financial statements in the context of the financial statements taken as a whole. The auditor's consideration of materiality is a matter of professional judgment and is influenced by his or her perception of the needs of a reasonable person who will rely on the financial statements. Materiality judgments involving risks or uncertainties are made in light of the surrounding circumstances. The auditor evaluates the materiality of reasonably possible losses that may be incurred upon the resolution of uncertainties both individually and in the aggregate. The auditor performs the evaluation of reasonably possible losses without regard to his or her evaluation of the materiality of known and likely misstatements in the financial statements. [Paragraph added, effective for reports issued or reissued on or after February 29, 1996, by Statement on Auditing Standards No. 79.]

.48 In preparing financial statements, management estimates the outcome of certain types of future events. For example, estimates ordinarily are made about the useful lives of depreciable assets, the collectibility of accounts receivable, the realizable value of inventory items, and the provision for product warranties. Paragraphs 10–11 of FASB ASC 310-10-35 and FASB ASC 460-10-25-6 describe situations in which the inability to make a reasonable estimate may raise questions about the appropriateness of the accounting principles used. If, in those or other situations, the auditor concludes that the accounting principles used cause the financial statements to be materially misstated, he or she should express a qualified or an adverse opinion. [Paragraph added, effective for reports issued or reissued on or after February 29, 1996, by Statement on Auditing Standards No. 79. Revised, June 2009, to reflect conforming changes necessary due to the issuance of FASB ASC.]

.49 Usually, the auditor is able to satisfy himself or herself regarding the reasonableness of management's estimate of the effects of future events by considering various types of audit evidence, including the historical experience of the entity. If the auditor concludes that management's estimate is unreasonable (see section 312, *Audit Risk and Materiality*, and section 342, *Auditing Accounting Estimates*) and that its effect is to cause the financial statements to be materially misstated, he or she should express a qualified or an adverse opinion. [Paragraph added, effective for reports issued or reissued on or after February 29, 1996, by Statement on Auditing Standards No. 79. Revised, March 2006, to reflect conforming changes necessary due to the issuance of Statement on Auditing Standards No. 105.]

.50 ***Accounting changes.*** The auditor should evaluate a change in accounting principle to satisfy himself that (*a*) the newly adopted accounting principle is a generally accepted accounting principle, (*b*) the method of accounting for the effect of the change is in conformity with generally accepted accounting principles, and (*c*) management's justification for the change is reasonable. If a change in accounting principle does not meet these conditions, the auditor's report should so indicate, and his opinion should be appropriately qualified as discussed in paragraphs .51–.52. [Paragraph renumbered by the issuance of Statement on Auditing Standards No. 79, December 1995.]

.51 If (*a*) a newly adopted accounting principle is not a generally accepted accounting principle, (*b*) the method of accounting for the effect of the change is not in conformity with generally accepted accounting principles, or (*c*) management has not provided reasonable justification for the change in accounting principle, the auditor should express a qualified opinion or, if the effect of the change is sufficiently material, the auditor should express an adverse opinion on the financial statements. [Paragraph renumbered by the issuance of Statement on Auditing Standards No. 79, December 1995.]

.52 According to FASB ASC 250-10-45-2, a reporting entity shall change an accounting principle only if either of the following apply:

a. The change is required by a newly issued codification update.

b. The entity can justify the use of an allowable alternative accounting principle on the basis that it is preferable.

If management has not provided reasonable justification for the change in accounting principle, the auditor should express an exception to the change having been made without reasonable justification. An example of a report qualified for this reason follows:

Independent Auditor's Report

[*Same first and second paragraphs as the standard report*]

As disclosed in Note X to the financial statements, the Company adopted, in 20X2, the first-in, first-out method of accounting for its inventories, whereas it previously used the last-in, first-out method. Although use of the first-in, first-out method is in conformity with accounting principles generally accepted in the United States of America, in our opinion the Company has not provided reasonable justification for making this change as required by those principles.[17]

In our opinion, except for the change in accounting principle discussed in the preceding paragraph, the financial statements referred to above, present fairly, in all material respects, the financial position of X Company as of December 31, 20X2 and 20X1, and the results of its operations and its cash flows for the years then ended in conformity with accounting principles generally accepted in the United States of America.

[Paragraph renumbered by the issuance of Statement on Auditing Standards No. 79, December 1995. Revised, June 2009, to reflect conforming changes necessary due to the issuance of FASB ASC.]

---

[17] Section 420, *Consistency of Application of Generally Accepted Accounting Principles*, states that a change from an accounting principle that is not generally accepted to one that is generally accepted is a correction of an error and that such a change requires recognition in the auditor's report as to consistency. Therefore, the auditor should add an explanatory paragraph to the report discussing the accounting change.

However, because the middle paragraph included in the example presented contains all of the information required in an explanatory paragraph on consistency, a separate explanatory paragraph (following the opinion paragraph) as required by paragraphs .16–.18 of this section is not necessary in this instance. A separate paragraph that identifies the change in accounting principle would be required if the substance of the disclosure did not fulfill the requirements outlined in these paragraphs. [Footnote renumbered by the issuance of Statement on Auditing Standards No. 79, December 1995. Footnote subsequently renumbered by the issuance of Statement on Auditing Standards No. 93, October 2000.]

.53 Whenever an accounting change results in an auditor expressing a qualified or adverse opinion on the conformity of financial statements with generally accepted accounting principles for the year of change, the auditor should consider the possible effects of that change when reporting on the entity's financial statements for subsequent years, as discussed in paragraphs .54–.57. [Paragraph renumbered by the issuance of Statement on Auditing Standards No. 79, December 1995.]

.54 If the financial statements for the year of such change are presented and reported on with a subsequent year's financial statements, the auditor's report should disclose his or her reservations with respect to the statements for the year of change. [Paragraph renumbered by the issuance of Statement on Auditing Standards No. 79, December 1995.]

.55 If an entity has adopted an accounting principle that is not a generally accepted accounting principle, its continued use might have a material effect on the statements of a subsequent year on which the auditor is reporting. In this situation, the independent auditor should express either a qualified opinion or an adverse opinion, depending on the materiality of the departure in relation to the statements of the subsequent year. [Paragraph renumbered by the issuance of Statement on Auditing Standards No. 79, December 1995.]

.56 If an entity accounts for the effect of a change prospectively when generally accepted accounting principles require restatement or the inclusion of the cumulative effect of the change in the year of change, a subsequent year's financial statements could improperly include a charge or credit that is material to those statements. This situation also requires that the auditor express a qualified or an adverse opinion. [Paragraph renumbered by the issuance of Statement on Auditing Standards No. 79, December 1995.]

.57 If management has not provided reasonable justification for a change in accounting principles, the auditor's opinion should express an exception to the change having been made without reasonable justification, as previously indicated. In addition, the auditor should continue to express his or her exception with respect to the financial statements for the year of change as long as they are presented and reported on. However, the auditor's exception relates to the accounting change and does not affect the status of a newly adopted principle as a generally accepted accounting principle. Accordingly, while expressing an exception for the year of change, the independent auditor's opinion regarding the subsequent years' statements need not express an exception to use of the newly adopted principle. [Paragraph renumbered by the issuance of Statement on Auditing Standards No. 79, December 1995.]

Adverse Opinions

.58 An adverse opinion states that the financial statements do not present fairly the financial position or the results of operations or cash flows in conformity with generally accepted accounting principles. Such an opinion is expressed when, in the auditor's judgment, the financial statements taken as a whole are not presented fairly in conformity with generally accepted accounting principles. [Paragraph renumbered by the issuance of Statement on Auditing Standards No. 79, December 1995.]

.59 When the auditor expresses an adverse opinion, he or she should disclose in a separate explanatory paragraph(s) preceding the opinion paragraph of the report (*a*) all the substantive reasons for his or her adverse opinion, and (*b*) the principal effects of the subject matter of the adverse opinion on financial position, results of operations, and cash flows, if practicable.[18] If the effects are not reasonably determinable, the report should so state.[19] [Paragraph renumbered by the issuance of Statement on Auditing Standards No. 79, December 1995.]

.60 When an adverse opinion is expressed, the opinion paragraph should include a direct reference to a separate paragraph that discloses the basis for the adverse opinion, as shown as follows:

Independent Auditor's Report

[*Same first and second paragraphs as the standard report*]

As discussed in Note X to the financial statements, the Company carries its property, plant and equipment accounts at appraisal values, and provides depreciation on the basis of such values. Further, the Company does not provide for income taxes with respect to differences between financial income and taxable income arising because of the use, for income tax purposes, of the installment method of reporting gross profit from certain types of sales. Accounting principles generally accepted in the United States of America require that property, plant and equipment be stated at an amount not in excess of cost, reduced by depreciation based on such amount, and that deferred income taxes be provided.

Because of the departures from accounting principles generally accepted in the United States of America identified above, as of December 31, 20X2 and 20X1, inventories have been increased $_____ and $_____ by inclusion in manufacturing overhead of depreciation in excess of that based on cost; property, plant and equipment, less accumulated depreciation, is carried at $_____ and $_____ in excess of an amount based on the cost to the Company; and deferred income taxes of $_____ and $_____ have not been recorded; resulting in an increase of $_____ and $_____ in retained earnings and in appraisal surplus of $_____ and $_____, respectively. For the years ended December 31, 20X2 and 20X1, cost of goods sold has been increased $_____ and $_____, respectively, because of the effects of the depreciation accounting referred to above and deferred income taxes of $_____ and $_____ have not been provided, resulting in an increase in net income of $_____ and $_____, respectively.

In our opinion, because of the effects of the matters discussed in the preceding paragraphs, the financial statements referred to above do not present fairly, in conformity with accounting principles generally accepted in the United States of America, the financial position of X Company as of December 31, 20X2 and 20X1, or the results of its operations or its cash flows for the years then ended.

[Paragraph renumbered by the issuance of Statement on Auditing Standards No. 79, December 1995.]

---

[18] See footnote 15. [Footnote renumbered by the issuance of Statement on Auditing Standards No. 79, December 1995. Footnote subsequently renumbered by the issuance of Statement on Auditing Standards No 93, October 2000.]

[19] When the auditor expresses an adverse opinion, he or she should also consider the need for an explanatory paragraph under the circumstances identified in paragraph .11, subsection (*c*), (*d*), and (*e*) of this section. [Footnote renumbered by the issuance of Statement on Auditing Standards No. 79, December 1995. Footnote subsequently renumbered by the issuance of Statement on Auditing Standards No. 93, October 2000.]

Disclaimer of Opinion

.61 A disclaimer of opinion states that the auditor does not express an opinion on the financial statements. An auditor may decline to express an opinion whenever he or she is unable to form or has not formed an opinion as to the fairness of presentation of the financial statements in conformity with generally accepted accounting principles. If the auditor disclaims an opinion, the auditor's report should give all of the substantive reasons for the disclaimer. [Paragraph renumbered and amended, effective for reports issued or reissued on or after February 29, 1996, by the issuance of Statement on Auditing Standards No. 79.]

.62 A disclaimer is appropriate when the auditor has not performed an audit sufficient in scope to enable him or her to form an opinion on the financial statements.[20] A disclaimer of opinion should not be expressed because the auditor believes, on the basis of his or her audit, that there are material departures from generally accepted accounting principles (see paragraphs .35–.57). When disclaiming an opinion because of a scope limitation, the auditor should state in a separate paragraph or paragraphs all of the substantive reasons for the disclaimer. He or she should state that the scope of the audit was not sufficient to warrant the expression of an opinion. The auditor should not identify the procedures that were performed nor include the paragraph describing the characteristics of an audit (that is, the scope paragraph of the auditor's standard report); to do so may tend to overshadow the disclaimer. In addition, the auditor should also disclose any other reservations he or she has regarding fair presentation in conformity with generally accepted accounting principles. [Paragraph renumbered and amended, effective for reports issued or reissued on or after February 29, 1996, by the issuance of Statement on Auditing Standards No. 79.]

.63 An example of a report disclaiming an opinion resulting from an inability to obtain sufficient appropriate audit evidence because of the scope limitation follows:

Independent Auditor's Report

We were engaged to audit the accompanying balance sheets of X Company as of December 31, 20X2 and 20X1, and the related statements of income, retained earnings, and cash flows for the years then ended. These financial statements are the responsibility of the Company's management.[21]

---

[20] If an accountant is engaged to conduct an audit of the financial statements of a nonpublic entity in accordance with generally accepted auditing standards, but is requested to change the engagement to a review or a compilation of the statements, he or she should look to the guidance in paragraphs 46–51 of Statement on Standards for Accounting and Review Services No. 1, *Compilation and Review of Financial Statements* (AR section 100 paragraphs .46–.51]. Section 504, *Association With Financial Statements*, paragraph .05 provides guidance to an accountant who is associated with the financial statements of a public entity, but has not audited such statements. [Footnote renumbered and amended, effective for reports issued or reissued on or after February 29, 1996, by the issuance of Statement on Auditing Standards No. 79. Footnote subsequently renumbered by the issuance of Statement on Auditing Standards No. 93, October 2000. Footnote revised, November 2002, to reflect conforming changes necessary due to the issuance of Statement on Standards for Accounting and Review Services No. 9.]

[21] The wording in the first paragraph of the auditor's standard report is changed in a disclaimer of opinion because of a scope limitation. The first sentence now states that "we were engaged to audit" rather than "we have audited" since, because of the scope limitation, the auditor was not able to perform an audit in accordance with generally accepted auditing standards. In addition, the last sentence of the first paragraph is also deleted, because of the scope limitation, to eliminate the reference to the auditor's responsibility to express an opinion. [Footnote renumbered by the issuance of Statement on Auditing Standards No. 79, December 1995. Footnote subsequently renumbered by the issuance of Statement on Auditing Standards No. 93, October 2000.]

[*Second paragraph of standard report should be omitted*]

The Company did not make a count of its physical inventory in 20X2 or 20X1, stated in the accompanying financial statements at $_____ as of December 31, 20X2, and at $______ as of December 31, 20X1. Further, evidence supporting the cost of property and equipment acquired prior to December 31, 20X1, is no longer available. The Company's records do not permit the application of other auditing procedures to inventories or property and equipment.

Since the Company did not take physical inventories and we were not able to apply other auditing procedures to satisfy ourselves as to inventory quantities and the cost of property and equipment, the scope of our work was not sufficient to enable us to express, and we do not express, an opinion on these financial statements.

[Paragraph renumbered by the issuance of Statement on Auditing Standards No. 79, December 1995. Revised, March 2006, to reflect conforming changes necessary due to the issuance of Statement on Auditing Standards No. 105.]

Piecemeal Opinions

.64 Piecemeal opinions (expressions of opinion as to certain identified items in financial statements) should not be expressed when the auditor has disclaimed an opinion or has expressed an adverse opinion on the financial statements *taken as a whole* because piecemeal opinions tend to overshadow or contradict a disclaimer of opinion or an adverse opinion. [Paragraph renumbered by the issuance of Statement on Auditing Standards No. 79, December 1995.]

Reports on Comparative Financial Statements

.65 The fourth standard of reporting requires that the auditor either express an opinion regarding the financial statements *taken as a whole* or an assertion to the effect that an opinion cannot be expressed, in the auditor's report. Reference in the fourth reporting standard to the financial statements *taken as a whole* applies not only to the financial statements of the current period but also to those of one or more prior periods that are presented on a comparative basis with those of the current period. Therefore, a continuing auditor[22] should update[23] the report on the individual financial statements of the one or more prior periods presented on a comparative basis with those of

---

[22] A *continuing auditor* is one who has audited the financial statements of the current period and of one or more consecutive periods immediately prior to the current period.

If one firm of independent auditors merges with another firm and the new firm becomes the auditor of a former client of one of the former firms, the new firm may accept responsibility and express an opinion on the financial statements for the prior period(s), as well as for those of the current period. In such circumstances, the new firm should follow the guidance in paragraphs .65–.69 and may indicate in its report or signature that a merger took place and may name the firm of independent auditors that was merged with it. If the new firm decides not to express an opinion on the prior-period financial statements, the guidance in paragraphs .70–.74 should be followed. [Footnote renumbered by the issuance of Statement on Auditing Standards No. 79, December 1995. Footnote subsequently renumbered by the issuance of Statement on Auditing Standards No. 93, October 2000.]

[23] An updated report on prior-period financial statements should be distinguished from a reissuance of a previous report (see section 530, *Dating of the Independent Auditor's Report*, paragraphs .06–.08), since in issuing an updated report the continuing auditor considers information that he or she has become aware of during his or her audit of the current-period financial statements (see paragraph .68) and because an updated report is issued in conjunction with the auditor's report on the current-period financial statements. [Footnote renumbered by the issuance of Statement on Auditing Standards No. 79, December 1995. Footnote subsequently renumbered by the issuance of Statement on Auditing Standards No. 93, October 2000.]

the current period.[24] Ordinarily, the auditor's report on comparative financial statements should not be dated earlier than the date on which the auditor has obtained sufficient appropriate audit evidence on which to support the opinion for the most recent audit. (See section 530, *Dating of the Independent Auditor's Report*, paragraph .01.) [Paragraph renumbered by the issuance of Statement on Auditing Standards No. 79, December 1995. As amended, effective September 2002, by Statement on Auditing Standards No. 98. Revised, December 2005, to reflect conforming changes necessary due to the issuance of Statement on Auditing Standards No. 103.]

.66 During the audit of the current-period financial statements, the auditor should be alert for circumstances or events that affect the prior-period financial statements presented (see paragraph .68) or the adequacy of informative disclosures concerning those statements. (See section 431, *Adequacy of Disclosure in Financial Statements*, and FASB ASC 205, *Presentation of Financial Statements*.) In updating his or her report on the prior-period financial statements, the auditor should consider the effects of any such circumstances or events coming to his or her attention. [Paragraph renumbered by the issuance of Statement on Auditing Standards No. 79, December 1995. Revised, June 2009, to reflect conforming changes necessary due to the issuance of FASB ASC.]

Different Reports on Comparative Financial Statements Presented

.67 Since the auditor's report on comparative financial statements applies to the individual financial statements presented, an auditor may express a qualified or adverse opinion, disclaim an opinion, or include an explanatory paragraph with respect to one or more financial statements for one or more periods, while issuing a different report on the other financial statements presented. Following are examples of reports on comparative financial statements (excluding the standard introductory and scope paragraphs, where applicable) with different reports on one or more financial statements presented.

Standard Report on the Prior-Year Financial Statements and a Qualified Opinion on the Current-Year Financial Statements

Independent Auditor's Report

[*Same first and second paragraphs as the standard report*]

The Company has excluded, from property and debt in the accompanying 20X2 balance sheet, certain lease obligations that were entered into in 20X2 which, in our opinion, should be capitalized in order to conform with accounting principles

---

[24] A continuing auditor need not report on the prior-period financial statements if only summarized comparative information of the prior period(s) is presented. For example, entities such as state and local governmental units frequently present total-all-funds information for the prior period(s) rather than information by individual funds because of space limitations or to avoid cumbersome or confusing formats. Also, not-for-profit organizations frequently present certain information for the prior period(s) in total rather than by net asset class. In some circumstances, the client may request the auditor to express an opinion on the prior period(s) as well as the current period. In those circumstances, the auditor should consider whether the information included for the prior period(s) contains sufficient detail to constitute a fair presentation in conformity with generally accepted accounting principles. In most cases, this will necessitate including additional columns or separate detail by fund or net asset class, or the auditor would need to modify his or her report. [Footnote renumbered by the issuance of Statement on Auditing Standards No. 79, December 1995. Footnote subsequently renumbered by the issuance of Statement on Auditing Standards No. 93, October 2000. Revised, April 2002, to reflect conforming changes necessary due to the issuance of FASB Statement No. 117.]

generally accepted in the United States of America. If these lease obligations were capitalized, property would be increased by $_____, long-term debt by $_____, and retained earnings by $_____ as of December 31, 20X2, and net income and earnings per share would be increased (decreased) by $_____ and $_____, respectively, for the year then ended.

In our opinion, except for the effects on the 20X2 financial statements of not capitalizing certain lease obligations as described in the preceding paragraph, the financial statements referred to in the preceding present fairly, in all material respects, the financial position of ABC Company as of December 31, 20X2 and 20X1, and the results of its operations and its cash flows for the years then ended in conformity with accounting principles generally accepted in the United States of America.

Standard Report on the Current-Year Financial Statements With a Disclaimer of Opinion on the Prior-Year Statements of Income, Retained Earnings, and Cash Flows

Independent Auditor's Report

[*Same first paragraph as the standard report*]

Except as explained in the following paragraph, we conducted our audits in accordance with auditing standards generally accepted in the United States of America. Those standards require that we plan and perform our audit to obtain reasonable assurance about whether the financial statements are free of material misstatement. An audit includes examining, on a test basis, evidence supporting the amounts and disclosures in the financial statements. An audit also includes assessing the accounting principles used and significant estimates made by management, as well as evaluating the overall financial statement presentation. We believe that our audits provide a reasonable basis for our opinion.

We did not observe the taking of the physical inventory as of December 31, 20X0, since that date was prior to our appointment as auditors for the Company, and we were unable to satisfy ourselves regarding inventory quantities by means of other auditing procedures. Inventory amounts as of December 31, 20X0, enter into the determination of net income and cash flows for the year ended December 31, 20X1.[25]

Because of the matter discussed in the preceding paragraph, the scope of our work was not sufficient to enable us to express, and we do not express, an opinion on the results of operations and cash flows for the year ended December 31, 20X1.

In our opinion, the balance sheets of ABC Company as of December 31, 20X2 and 20X1, and the related statements of income, retained earnings, and cash flows for the year ended December 31, 20X2, present fairly, in all material respects, the financial position of ABC Company as of December 31, 20X2 and 20X1, and the results of its operations and its cash flows for the year ended December 31, 20X2, in conformity with accounting principles generally accepted in the United States of America.

---

[25] It is assumed that the independent auditor has been able to satisfy himself or herself as to the consistency of application of generally accepted accounting principles. See section 420, *Consistency of Application of Generally Accepted Accounting Principles*, for a discussion of consistency. [Footnote renumbered by the issuance of Statement on Auditing Standards No. 79, December 1995; the former footnote 29 has been deleted and subsequent footnotes renumbered by the issuance of Statement on Auditing Standards No. 79, December 1995. Footnote subsequently renumbered by the issuance of Statement on Auditing Standards No. 93, October 2000.]

[Paragraph renumbered by the issuance of Statement on Auditing Standards No. 79, December 1995.]

Opinion on Prior-Period Financial Statements Different From the Opinion Previously Expressed

.68 If, during the current audit, an auditor becomes aware of circumstances or events that affect the financial statements of a prior period, he or she should consider such matters when updating his or her report on the financial statements of the prior period. For example, if an auditor has previously qualified his or her opinion or expressed an adverse opinion on financial statements of a prior period because of a departure from generally accepted accounting principles, and the prior-period financial statements are restated in the current period to conform with generally accepted accounting principles, the auditor's updated report on the financial statements of the prior period should indicate that the statements have been restated and should express an unqualified opinion with respect to the restated financial statements. [Paragraph renumbered by the issuance of Statement on Auditing Standards No. 79, December 1995.]

.69 If, in an updated report, the opinion is different from the opinion previously expressed on the financial statements of a prior period, the auditor should disclose all the substantive reasons for the different opinion in a separate explanatory paragraph(s) preceding the opinion paragraph of his or her report.[fn 29] The explanatory paragraph(s) should disclose (*a*) the date of the auditor's previous report, (*b*) the type of opinion previously expressed, (*c*) the circumstances or events that caused the auditor to express a different opinion, and (*d*) that the auditor's updated opinion on the financial statements of the prior period is different from his or her previous opinion on those statements. The following is an example of an explanatory paragraph that may be appropriate when an auditor issues an updated report on the financial statements of a prior period that contains an opinion different from the opinion previously expressed:

<u>Independent Auditor's Report</u>

[*Same first and second paragraphs as the standard report*]

In our report dated March 1, 20X2, we expressed an opinion that the 20X1 financial statements did not fairly present financial position, results of operations, and cash flows in conformity with accounting principles generally accepted in the United States of America because of two departures from such principles: (1) the Company carried its property, plant, and equipment at appraisal values, and provided for depreciation on the basis of such values, and (2) the Company did not provide for deferred income taxes with respect to differences between income for financial reporting purposes and taxable income. As described in Note X, the Company has changed its method of accounting for these items and restated its 20X1 financial statements to conform with accounting principles generally accepted in the United States of America. Accordingly, our present opinion on the 20X1 financial statements, as presented herein, is different from that expressed in our previous report.[26]

In our opinion, the financial statements referred to above, present fairly, in all material respects, the financial position of X Company as of December 31, 20X2 and 20X1, and the results of its operations and its cash flows for the years

---

[26] See footnote 17. [Footnote renumbered by the issuance of Statement on Auditing Standards No. 79, December 1995. Footnote subsequently renumbered by the issuance of Statement on Auditing Standards No. 93, October 2000.]

then ended in conformity with accounting principles generally accepted in the United States of America.

[Paragraph renumbered by the issuance of Statement on Auditing Standards No. 79, December 1995.]

Report of Predecessor Auditor

.70 A predecessor auditor ordinarily would be in a position to reissue his or her report on the financial statements of a prior period at the request of a former client if he or she is able to make satisfactory arrangements with the former client to perform this service and if he or she performs the procedures described in paragraph .71.[27] [Paragraph renumbered by the issuance of Statement on Auditing Standards No. 79, December 1995.]

Predecessor Auditor's Report Reissued

.71 Before reissuing (or consenting to the reuse of) a report previously issued on the financial statements of a prior period, when those financial statements are to be presented on a comparative basis with audited financial statements of a subsequent period, a predecessor auditor should consider whether his or her previous report on those statements is still appropriate. Either the current form or manner of presentation of the financial statements of the prior period or one or more subsequent events might make a predecessor auditor's previous report inappropriate. Consequently, a predecessor auditor should (*a*) read the financial statements of the current period, (*b*) compare the prior-period financial statements that he or she reported on with the financial statements to be presented for comparative purposes, and (*c*) obtain representation letters from management of the former client and from the successor auditor. The representation letter from management of the former client should state (*a*) whether any information has come to management's attention that would cause them to believe that any of the previous representations should be modified, and (*b*) whether any events have occurred subsequent to the balance-sheet date of the latest prior-period financial statements reported on by the predecessor auditor that would require adjustment to or disclosure in those financial statements.[28] The representation letter from the successor auditor should state whether the successor's audit revealed any matters that, in the successor's opinion, might have a material effect on, or require disclosure in, the financial statements reported on by the predecessor auditor. Also, the predecessor auditor may wish to consider the matters described in section 543, *Part of Audit Performed by Other Independent Auditors*, paragraphs .10–.12. However, the predecessor auditor should not refer in his or her reissued report to the report or work of the successor auditor. [Paragraph renumbered by the issuance of Statement on Auditing Standards No. 79, December 1995. As amended, effective for reports reissued on or after June 30, 1998, by Statement on Auditing Standards No. 85.]

.72 A predecessor auditor who has agreed to reissue his or her report may become aware of events or transactions occurring subsequent to the date of his

---

[27] It is recognized that there may be reasons why a predecessor auditor's report may not be reissued and this section does not address the various situations that could arise. [Footnote renumbered by the issuance of Statement on Auditing Standards No. 79, December 1995. Footnote subsequently renumbered by the issuance of Statement on Auditing Standards No. 93, October 2000.]

[28] See section 333, *Management Representations*, appendix C (paragraph .18), "Illustrative Updating Management Representation Letter." [Footnote added, effective for reports reissued on or after June 30, 1998, by Statement on Auditing Standards No. 85. Footnote renumbered by the issuance of Statement on Auditing Standards No. 93, October 2000.]

or her previous report on the financial statements of a prior period that may affect his or her previous report (for example, the successor auditor might indicate in the response that certain matters have had a material effect on the prior-period financial statements reported on by the predecessor auditor). In such circumstances, the predecessor auditor should make inquiries and perform other procedures that he or she considers necessary (for example, reviewing the working papers of the successor auditor as they relate to the matters affecting the prior-period financial statements). The auditor should then decide, on the basis of the audit evidence obtained, whether to revise the report. If a predecessor auditor concludes that the report should be revised, he or she should follow the guidance in paragraphs .68–.69 and .73 of this section. [Paragraph renumbered by the issuance of Statement on Auditing Standards No. 79, December 1995. Revised, March 2006, to reflect conforming changes necessary due to the issuance of Statement on Auditing Standards No. 105.]

.73 A predecessor auditor's knowledge of the current affairs of his former client is obviously limited in the absence of a continuing relationship. Consequently, when reissuing the report on prior-period financial statements, a predecessor auditor should use the date of his or her previous report to avoid any implication that he or she has examined any records, transactions, or events after that date. If the predecessor auditor revises the report or if the financial statements are restated, he or she should dual-date the report. (See section 530, *Dating of the Independent Auditor's Report*, paragraph .05.) [Paragraph renumbered by the issuance of Statement on Auditing Standards No. 79, December 1995.]

Predecessor Auditor's Report Not Presented

.74 If the financial statements of a prior period have been audited by a predecessor auditor whose report is not presented, the successor auditor should indicate in the introductory paragraph of his or her report (*a*) that the financial statements of the prior period were audited by another auditor,[29] (*b*) the date of his or her report, (*c*) the type of report issued by the predecessor auditor, and (*d*) if the report was other than a standard report, the substantive reasons therefore.[30] An example of a successor auditor's report when the predecessor auditor's report is not presented is shown as follows:

Independent Auditor's Report

We have audited the balance sheet of ABC Company as of December 31, 20X2, and the related statements of income, retained earnings, and cash flows for the year then ended. These financial statements are the responsibility of the Company's management. Our responsibility is to express an opinion on these financial statements based on our audit. The financial statements of ABC Company as of December 31, 20X1, were audited by other auditors whose report dated March 31, 20X2, expressed an unqualified opinion on those statements.

---

[29] The successor auditor should not name the predecessor auditor in his or her report; however, the successor auditor may name the predecessor auditor if the predecessor auditor's practice was acquired by, or merged with, that of the successor auditor. [Footnote renumbered by the issuance of Statement on Auditing Standards No. 79, December 1995. Footnote subsequently renumbered by the issuance of Statement on Auditing Standards No. 85, November 1997. Footnote subsequently renumbered by the issuance of Statement on Auditing Standards No. 93, October 2000.]

[30] If the predecessor's report was issued before the effective date of this section and contained an uncertainties explanatory paragraph, a successor auditor's report issued or reissued after the effective date hereof should not make reference to the predecessor's previously required explanatory paragraph. [Footnote added, effective for reports issued or reissued on or after February 29, 1996, by Statement on Auditing Standards No. 79. Footnote renumbered by the issuance of Statement on Auditing Standards No. 85, November 1997. Footnote subsequently renumbered by the issuance of Statement on Auditing Standards No. 93, October 2000.]

> [*Same second paragraph as the standard report*]
>
> In our opinion, the 20X2 financial statements referred to above, present fairly, in all material respects, the financial position of ABC Company as of December 31, 20X2, and the results of its operations and its cash flows for the year then ended in conformity with accounting principles generally accepted in the United States of America.

If the predecessor auditor's report was other than a standard report, the successor auditor should describe the nature of and reasons for the explanatory paragraph added to the predecessor's report or the opinion qualification. Following is an illustration of the wording that may be included in the successor auditor's report:

> . . . were audited by other auditors whose report dated March 1, 20X2, on those statements included an explanatory paragraph that described the change in the Company's method of computing depreciation discussed in Note X to the financial statements.

If the financial statements have been restated, the introductory paragraph should indicate that a predecessor auditor reported on the financial statements of the prior period before restatement. In addition, if the successor auditor is engaged to audit and applies sufficient procedures to satisfy himself or herself as to the appropriateness of the restatement adjustments, he or she may also include the following paragraph in his report:

> We also audited the adjustments described in Note X that were applied to restate the 20X1 financial statements. In our opinion, such adjustments are appropriate and have been properly applied.

[As amended, effective for reports issued after December 31, 1990, by Statement on Auditing Standards No. 64. Paragraph renumbered and amended, effective for reports issued or reissued on or after February 29, 1996, by the issuance of Statement on Auditing Standards No. 79.]

Effective Date and Transition

.75 This section is effective for reports issued or reissued on or after February 29, 1996. Earlier application of the provisions of this section is permissible. [Paragraph renumbered and amended, effective for reports issued or reissued on or after February 29, 1996, by the issuance of Statement on Auditing Standards No. 79.]

.76 An auditor who previously included an uncertainties explanatory paragraph in a report should not repeat that paragraph and is not required to include an emphasis paragraph related to the uncertainty in a reissuance of that report or in a report on subsequent periods' financial statements, even if the uncertainty has not been resolved. If the auditor decides to include an emphasis paragraph related to the uncertainty, the paragraph may include an explanation of the change in reporting standards.[31] [Paragraph renumbered and amended, effective for reports issued or reissued on or after February 29, 1996, by the issuance of Statement on Auditing Standards No. 79.]

---

[31] [Footnote renumbered and deleted by the issuance of Statement on Auditing Standards No. 79, December 1995. Footnote subsequently renumbered by the issuance of Statement on Auditing Standards No. 85, November 1997. Footnote subsequently renumbered by the issuance of Statement on Auditing Standards No. 93, October 2000.]

AU Section 9508

Reports on Audited Financial Statements: Auditing Interpretations of Section 508

1. Report of an Outside Inventory-Taking Firm as an Alternative Procedure for Observing Inventories

.01 *Question*—Section 508, *Reports on Audited Financial Statements*, paragraph .24 states that "Common restrictions on the scope of the audit include those applying to the observation of physical inventories and the confirmation of accounts receivable by direct communication with debtors. . . ." A footnote to that paragraph states: "Circumstances such as the timing of the work may make it impossible for the auditor to accomplish these procedures. In this case, if the auditor is able to satisfy himself or herself as to inventories or accounts receivable by applying alternative procedures, there is no significant limitation on the scope of the work, and the report need not include reference to the omission of the procedures or to the use of alternative procedures." Outside firms of nonaccountants specializing in the taking of physical inventories are used at times by some companies, such as retail stores, hospitals, and automobile dealers, to count, list, price and subsequently compute the total dollar amount of inventory on hand at the date of the physical count. Would obtaining the report of an outside inventory-taking firm be an acceptable alternative procedure to the independent auditor's own observation of physical inventories?

.02 *Interpretation*—Sufficient appropriate audit evidence for inventories is discussed in section 331, *Inventories*, paragraphs .09–.12. Paragraph .09 of section 331 states that ". . . it is ordinarily necessary for the independent auditor to be present at the time of count and, by suitable observation, tests, and inquiries, satisfy himself respecting the effectiveness of the methods of inventory-taking and the measure of reliance which may be placed upon the client's representations about the quantities and physical condition of the inventories."

.03 Section 331 paragraphs .10–.11 discuss two variations of that procedure when the client has well-kept perpetual records that are checked periodically by comparisons with physical counts or when the client uses statistical sampling to determine inventories. In such instances, the auditor may vary the timing and extent of his observation of physical counts, but he "must be present to observe such counts as he deems necessary and must satisfy himself as to the effectiveness of the counting procedures used."

.04 Section 331 paragraph .12 deals with circumstances in which the auditor has not satisfied himself or herself as to inventories in the possession of the client through procedures described in section 331 paragraphs .09–.11. In those circumstances, the general requirement for satisfactory alternative procedures is that ". . . tests of the accounting records alone will not be sufficient for him to become satisfied as to quantities; it will always be necessary for the auditor to make, or observe, some physical counts of the inventory and apply appropriate tests of intervening transactions."

.05 The fact that the inventory is counted by an outside inventory firm of nonaccountants is not, by itself, a satisfactory substitute for the auditor's own observation or taking of some physical counts. The auditor's concern, in this respect, is to satisfy himself as to the effectiveness of the counting procedures used. If the client engages an outside inventory firm to take the physical inventory, the auditor's primary concern would be to evaluate the effectiveness of the procedures used by the outside firm and his auditing procedures would be applied accordingly.

.06 Thus, the auditor would examine the outside firm's program, observe its procedures and controls, make or observe some physical counts of the inventory, recompute calculations of the submitted inventory on a test basis and apply appropriate tests to the intervening transactions. The independent auditor ordinarily may reduce the extent of the work on the physical count of inventory because of the work of an outside inventory firm, but any restriction on the auditor's judgment concerning the extent of his or her contact with the inventory would be a scope restriction.

[Issue Date: July 1975; Revised: October 2000; Revised: March 2006.]

[2.] Reporting on Comparative Financial Statements of Nonprofit Organizations

[.07–.10] [Superseded by Statement on Auditing Standards (SAS) No. 15, effective for periods ending after June 30, 1977.]

[3.] Reporting on Loss Contingencies

[.11–.14] [Superseded by SAS No. 58, effective for reports issued or reissued on or after January 1, 1989.] (See section 508.)

[4.] Reports on Consolidated Financial Statements That Include Supplementary Consolidating Information

[.15–.20] [Superseded December 31, 1980, by SAS No. 29, as superseded by SAS Nos. 118 and 119.]

[5.] Disclosures of Subsequent Events

[.21–.24] [Superseded by SAS No. 58, effective for reports issued or reissued on or after January 1, 1989.] (See section 508.)

[6.] The Materiality of Uncertainties

[.25–.28] [Superseded by SAS No. 58, effective for reports issued or reissued on or after January 1, 1989.] (See section 508.)

[7.] Reporting on an Uncertainty

[.29–.32] [Withdrawn, August 1982, by SAS No. 43.]

8. Reporting on Financial Statements Prepared on a Liquidation Basis of Accounting

.33 *Question*—Footnote †† of Statement of Position (SOP) 93-3, *Rescission of Accounting Principles Board Statements* (AICPA, *Technical Practice Aids*, ACC sec. 10,560), states that an enterprise is not viewed as a going concern if liquidation appears imminent. How should the auditor report on financial statements that are prepared on a liquidation basis of accounting for an entity in liquidation or for which liquidation appears imminent?

.34 *Answer*—A liquidation basis of accounting may be considered generally accepted accounting principles GAAP for entities in liquidation or for which liquidation appears imminent. Therefore, the auditor should issue an unqualified opinion on such financial statements, provided that the liquidation basis of accounting has been properly applied, and that adequate disclosures are made in the financial statements.

.35 Typically, the financial statements of entities that adopt a liquidation basis of accounting are presented along with financial statements of a period prior to adoption of a liquidation basis that were prepared on the basis of GAAP for going concerns. In such circumstances, the auditor's report ordinarily should include an explanatory paragraph that states that the entity has changed the basis of accounting used to determine the amounts at which assets and liabilities are carried from the going concern basis to a liquidation basis.

.36 Examples of auditor's reports with such an explanatory paragraph follow.

Report on Single Year Financial Statements in Year of Adoption of Liquidation Basis

"We have audited the statement of net assets in liquidation of XYZ Company as of December 31, 20X2, and the related statement of changes in net assets in liquidation for the period from April 26, 20X2 to December 31, 20X2. In addition, we have audited the statements of income, retained earnings, and cash flows for the period from January 1, 20X2 to April 25, 20X2. These financial statements are the responsibility of the Company's management. Our responsibility is to express an opinion on these financial statements based on our audit.

"We conducted our audit in accordance with auditing standards generally accepted in the United States of America. Those standards require that we plan and perform the audit to obtain reasonable assurance about whether the financial statements are free of material misstatement. An audit includes examining, on a test basis, evidence supporting the amounts and disclosures in the financial statements. An audit also includes assessing the accounting principles used and significant estimates made by management, as well as evaluating the overall financial statement presentation. We believe that our audit provides a reasonable basis for our opinion.

"As described in Note X to the financial statements, the stockholders of XYZ Company approved a plan of liquidation on April 25, 20X2, and the company commenced liquidation shortly thereafter. As a result, the company has changed its basis of accounting for periods subsequent to April 25, 20X2 from the going-concern basis to a liquidation basis.

"In our opinion, the financial statements referred to above present fairly, in all material respects, the net assets in liquidation of XYZ Company as of December 31, 20X2, the changes in its net assets in liquidation for the period from April 26, 20X2 to December 31, 20X2, and the results of its operations and its cash flows for the period from January 1, 20X2 to April 25, 20X2, in conformity with accounting principles generally accepted in the United States of America applied on the bases described in the preceding paragraph."

Report on Comparative Financial Statements in Year of Adoption of Liquidation Basis

"We have audited the balance sheet of XYZ Company as of December 31, 20X1, the related statements of income, retained earnings, and cash flows for the year then ended, and the statements of income, retained earnings, and cash flows for the period from January 1, 20X2 to April 25, 20X2. In addition, we have audited the statement of net assets in liquidation as of December 31, 20X2, and the related statement of changes in net assets in liquidation for the period from April 26, 20X2 to December 31, 20X2. These financial statements are the responsibility of the Company's management. Our responsibility is to express an opinion on these financial statements based on our audits.

"We conducted our audits in accordance with auditing standards generally accepted in the United States of America. Those standards require that we plan and perform the audit to obtain reasonable assurance about whether the financial statements are free of material misstatements. An audit includes examining, on a test basis, evidence supporting the amounts and disclosures in the financial statements. An audit also includes assessing the accounting principles used and significant estimates made by management, as well as evaluating the overall financial statement presentation. We believe that our audits provide a reasonable basis for our opinion.

"As described in Note X to the financial statements, the stockholders of XYZ Company approved a plan of liquidation on April 25, 20X2, and the company commenced liquidation shortly thereafter. As a result, the company has changed its basis of accounting for periods subsequent to April 25, 20X2 from the going-concern basis to a liquidation basis.

"In our opinion, the financial statements referred to above present fairly, in all material respects, the financial position of XYZ Company as of December 31, 20X1, the results of its operations and its cash flows for the year then ended and for the period from January 1, 20X2 to April 25, 20X2, its net assets in liquidation as of December 31, 20X2, and the changes in its net assets in liquidation for the period from April 26, 20X2 to December 31, 20X2, in conformity with accounting principles generally accepted in the United States of America applied on the bases described in the preceding paragraph."

.37 The auditor may, in subsequent years, continue to include an explanatory paragraph in his report to emphasize that the financial statements are presented on a liquidation basis of accounting.

[.38] [Paragraph deleted to reflect conforming changes necessary due to the issuance of SAS No. 79.]

[Issue Date: December 1984; Revised: June 1993; Revised: February 1997; Revised: October 2000; Revised: June 2009.]

[9.] Quantifying Departures From Generally Accepted Accounting Principles

[.39–.43] [Superseded by SAS No. 58, effective for reports issued or reissued on or after January 1, 1989.] (See section 508.)

[10.] Updated Reports Resulting From the Retroactive Suspension of Earnings per Share and Segment Information Disclosure Requirements

[.44–.48] [Withdrawn, March 1989, by the Auditing Standards Board (ASB).]

[11.] Restating Financial Statements Reported on by a Predecessor Auditor

[.49–.50] [Superseded by SAS No. 84, effective with respect to acceptance of an engagement after March 31, 1998.] (See section 315, *Communications Between Predecessor and Successor Auditors*.)

12. Reference in Auditor's Standard Report to Management's Report

.51 *Question*—One of the basic elements of the auditor's standard report is a statement that the financial statements are the responsibility of the Company's management. That statement is required in the auditor's report even when a document containing the auditor's report includes a statement by management regarding its responsibility for the presentation of the financial statements. When an annual shareholders' report (or other client-prepared document that includes audited financial statements) contains a management report that states the financial statements are the responsibility of management, is it permissible for the auditor's report to include a reference to the management report?

.52 *Interpretation*—No. The statement about management's responsibilities for the financial statements required by section 508, *Reports on Audited Financial Statements*, should not be further elaborated upon in the auditor's standard report or referenced to management's report. Such modifications to the standard auditor's report may lead users to erroneously believe that the auditor is providing assurances about representations made by management about their responsibility for financial reporting, internal controls and other matters that might be discussed in the management report.

[Issue Date: January 1989.]

[13.] Reference to Country of Origin in the Auditor's Standard Report

[.53–.55] [Withdrawn October 2000 by SAS No. 93.]

14. Reporting on Audits Conducted in Accordance With Auditing Standards Generally Accepted in the United States of America and in Accordance With International Standards on Auditing

.56 *Question*—Section 508 states that a basic element of the auditor's report is a statement that the audit was conducted in accordance with generally accepted auditing standards (GAAS) and an identification of the United States of America as the country of origin of those standards. If the auditor conducts the audit in accordance with standards generally accepted in the United States of America and in accordance with the International Standards on Auditing (ISA) promulgated by the International Auditing and Assurance Standards Board (IAASB), may the auditor so indicate in the auditor's report?

.57 *Interpretation*—Yes. Section 508 requires that the auditor indicate in the auditor's report that the audit was conducted in accordance with GAAS and an identification of the United States of America as the country of origin of those standards; however, section 508 does not prohibit the auditor from indicating that the audit also was conducted in accordance with another set of auditing standards. If the audit also was conducted in accordance with the ISAs, in their entirety, the auditor may so indicate in the auditor's report. To determine whether an audit was conducted in accordance with the ISAs, it is necessary to consider the text of the ISA in their entirety, including the basic principles and essential procedures together with the related guidance included in the ISA.[1]

.58 When reporting on an audit performed in accordance with auditing standards generally accepted in the United States of America and ISA, the auditor should comply with reporting standards generally accepted in the United States of America.

.59 An example of reporting on an audit conducted in accordance with auditing standards generally accepted in the United States and in accordance with ISA follows:

> We conducted our audit in accordance with auditing standards generally accepted in the United States of America and in accordance with International Standards on Auditing. Those standards require that we plan and perform the audit to obtain reasonable assurance about whether the financial statements are free of material misstatement. An audit includes examining, on a test basis, evidence supporting the amounts and disclosures in the financial statements. An audit also includes assessing the accounting principles used and significant estimates made by management, as well as evaluating the overall financial statement presentation. We believe that our audit provides a reasonable basis for our opinion.

[Issue Date: March 2002; Revised: May 2008.]

15. Reporting as Successor Auditor When Prior-Period Audited Financial Statements Were Audited by a Predecessor Auditor Who Has Ceased Operations[2]

.60 *Question*—If the prior-period financial statements audited by a predecessor auditor who has ceased operations are presented for comparative purposes with current-period audited financial statements, how is the successor auditor's report affected?

.61 *Interpretation*—If the prior-period audited financial statements are *unchanged*, pursuant to section 508 paragraph .74, the successor auditor should indicate in the introductory paragraph of his or her report (*a*) that the financial statements of the prior period were audited by another auditor, (*b*) the date of the predecessor auditor's report, (*c*) the type of report issued by the predecessor auditor, and (*d*) if the report was other than a standard report, the substantive reasons therefor. The successor auditor ordinarily also should indicate that the other auditor has ceased operations. Footnote 29 of section 508 indicates that the successor auditor should not name the predecessor auditor in the report. An example of the reference that would be added to the introductory paragraph of the successor auditor's report is presented as follows:

> The financial statements of ABC Company as of December 31, 20X1, and for the year then ended were audited by other auditors who have ceased operations. Those auditors expressed an unqualified opinion on those financial statements in their report dated March 31, 20X2.

A reference to the predecessor auditor's report should be included even if the predecessor auditor's report on the prior-period financial statements is

[1] [Footnote deleted, November 2010, due to the removal of AU appendix B.]

2 A firm is considered to have ceased operations when it no longer issues audit opinions either in its own name or in the name of a successor firm. A firm may cease operations with respect to public entities and still issue audit opinions with respect to nonpublic entities.

reprinted and accompanies the successor auditor's report, because reprinting does not constitute reissuance of the predecessor auditor's report.

.62 If the prior-period financial statements *have been restated*, and the entity does not file annual financial statements with the Securities and Exchange Commission (SEC), the successor auditor should follow the guidance in paragraph .61, indicating that the predecessor auditor reported on such financial statements before restatement.

.63 When the prior-period financial statements have been restated, the successor auditor may be engaged either to reaudit the prior-period financial statements or to audit only the restatement adjustments. If the successor auditor is engaged to audit only the restatement adjustments and applies sufficient procedures to satisfy himself or herself as to the appropriateness of the restatement adjustments, the successor auditor may report on the restatement adjustments using the guidance in section 508 paragraph .74. (The auditor also may use the guidance on alternative language contained in paragraph .71.) In determining the nature, timing and extent of procedures, the successor auditor should consider that a predecessor auditor who has ceased operations cannot perform the procedures to evaluate the appropriateness of the restatement adjustments as described in section 561, *Subsequent Discovery of Facts Existing at the Date of the Auditor's Report*.

.64 If the successor auditor neither performs a reaudit of the prior-period financial statements nor audits only the restatement adjustments, the note to the financial statements describing the restatement adjustments should be marked "Unaudited." Depending on the nature and extent of the restatement adjustments, it may be appropriate for the prior-period financial statements to be marked "Unaudited."

.65 If the entity files annual financial statements with the SEC, the SEC staff has indicated (specifically with respect to Arthur Andersen LLP) that, in annual reports (on Form 10-K and to shareholders), the predecessor auditor's latest signed and dated report on the prior-period financial statements should be reprinted with a legend indicating (*a*) that the report is a copy of the previously issued report and (*b*) that the predecessor auditor has not reissued the report.[3]

.66 The successor auditor should refer to the predecessor auditor's report in his or her report, as described in paragraph .61, and, if the prior-period financial statements *have been restated*, indicate that the predecessor auditor reported on such financial statements before restatement.

.67 SEC rules require that annual and, in some instances, other financial statements be audited. To satisfy the SEC audit requirement when the prior-period financial statements have been restated, the successor auditor may be engaged either to reaudit the prior-period financial statements or to audit only the restatement adjustments. A successor auditor who is engaged to audit only the restatement adjustments is not required to perform procedures to identify all adjustments to the financial statements that may be appropriate.[4]

---

[3] See Securities and Exchange Commission (SEC) Release No. 33-8070, *Requirements for Arthur Andersen LLP Auditing Clients*.

[4] However, a successor auditor who identifies other adjustments that may be appropriate to the prior-period financial statements, either in the course of auditing the restatement adjustments or in the audit of current-period financial statements, should consider their effect on the prior-period financial statements. See section 315, *Communications Between Predecessor and Successor Auditors*. Section 561, *Subsequent Discovery of Facts Existing at the Date of the Auditor's Report*, provides further guidance that may be useful to a successor auditor who either reaudits the prior-period financial statements or audits only the restatement adjustments.

.68 In some cases, prior-period financial statement disclosures may be revised in a manner that does not involve restating amounts in the prior-period financial statements, but rather involves the addition of disclosures. In such cases, the successor auditor may be engaged to perform audit procedures to satisfy himself or herself as to the appropriateness of the additional disclosures. Financial statements that have been revised are considered to be restated for the purposes of this interpretation.

.69 Some revisions may be sufficiently inconsequential such that audit procedures by the successor auditor would be unnecessary and the reference to the predecessor auditor's report on the prior-period financial statements would not indicate that the predecessor auditor reported on such financial statements before restatement. For example, inconsequential revisions might include conforming editorial modifications to footnote disclosures or reclassifications made for comparative purposes in the financial statements.[5]

.70 When the successor auditor is engaged to audit only the restatement adjustments, the procedures performed will vary significantly depending on the nature of adjustment. In some instances, the successor auditor may determine that conducting a reaudit of the prior-period financial statements is necessary based on the nature of the restatement adjustments. Examples of restatement adjustments whose nature indicates that a reaudit ordinarily is necessary (particularly with respect to entities that file financial statements with the SEC) include, but are not limited to:

- corrections of an error.
- reflection of a change in reporting entity.
- retroactive accounting changes (*a*) with significant impact on previously reported amounts or (*b*) that affect previously reported net income or net assets.
- reporting discontinued operations.
- changes affecting previously reported net income or net assets.

.71 If the successor auditor is engaged to audit only the restatement adjustments and applies sufficient procedures to satisfy himself or herself as to the appropriateness of the restatement adjustments, the successor auditor may report on the restatement adjustments using the guidance in section 508 paragraph .74. Alternatively, the successor auditor may wish to make it clear that he or she did not audit, review, or apply other procedures to the prior-period financial statements beyond the procedures applied to the restatement adjustments. Accordingly, he or she may include the following paragraph in his or her report:

> As discussed above, the financial statements of ABC Company as of December 31, 20X1, and for the year then ended were audited by other auditors who have ceased operations. As described in Note X, these financial statements have been restated [revised]. We audited the adjustments described in Note X that were applied to restate [revise] the 20X1 financial statements. In our opinion, such adjustments are appropriate and have been properly applied. However, we were not engaged to audit, review, or apply any procedures to the 20X1 financial statements of the Company other than with respect to such adjustments and, accordingly, we do not express an opinion or any other form of assurance on the 20X1 financial statements taken as a whole.

---

[5] If reclassifications result in material changes to prior-period financial statements, they should be disclosed and the successor auditor would, at a minimum, need to perform audit procedures on the related restatement adjustments.

.72 If the auditor wishes to identify the procedures performed in his or her report, he or she may include in his or her report a paragraph similar to the following example:

Restatement Adjustments for Changes in Segment Composition

As discussed above, the financial statements of ABC Company as of December 31, 20X1, and for the year then ended were audited by other auditors who have ceased operations. As described in Note X, the Company changed the composition of its reportable segments in 20X2, and the amounts in the 20X1 financial statements relating to reportable segments have been restated to conform to the 20X2 composition of reportable segments. We audited the adjustments that were applied to restate the disclosures for reportable segments reflected in the 20X1 financial statements. Our procedures included (*a*) agreeing the adjusted amounts of segment revenues, operating income and assets to the Company's underlying records obtained from management, and (*b*) testing the mathematical accuracy of the reconciliations of segment amounts to the consolidated financial statements. In our opinion, such adjustments are appropriate and have been properly applied. However, we were not engaged to audit, review, or apply any procedures to the 20X1 financial statements of the Company other than with respect to such adjustments and, accordingly, we do not express an opinion or any other form of assurance on the 20X1 financial statements taken as a whole.

[.73] [Paragraph deleted due to the passage of time, June 2009.]

.74 *Question*—If the prior-period financial statements audited by a predecessor auditor who has ceased operations have been subsequently restated, but the successor auditor has not yet completed an audit of current-period financial statements, can the successor auditor report on the restatement adjustments pursuant to section 508 paragraph .74?

.75 *Interpretation*—No. Section 508 paragraph .74 is only applicable when the prior-period financial statements are presented for comparative purposes with current-period audited financial statements. If the prior-period financial statements have been restated, and the successor auditor is requested to report on those financial statements without also reporting on current-period audited financial statements, the successor auditor would need to reaudit the prior-period financial statements in order to report on them.

[Issue Date: November 2002; Revised: June 2009.]

16. Effect on Auditor's Report of Omission of Schedule of Investments by Investment Partnerships That Are Exempt From Securities and Exchange Commission Registration Under the Investment Company Act of 1940

.76 *Question*—Financial Accounting Standards Board (FASB) *Accounting Standards Codification* (ASC) 946, *Financial Services—Investment Companies*, addresses financial statement presentation and disclosure requirements for investment partnerships that are exempt from SEC registration under the Investment Company Act of 1940 (the 1940 act). FASB ASC 946-210-50 specifically describes information that should be disclosed in a Schedule of Investments. FASB ASC 946-210-50-6 states that the financial statements of an investment partnership that is exempt from SEC registration under the Investment Company Act of 1940, should, at a minimum, include a condensed schedule of investments in securities owned by the partnership at the close of the most recent period. Such a schedule shall do all of the following:

a. Categorize investments by all of the following:

(1) Type (such as common stocks, preferred stocks, convertible securities, fixed-income securities, government securities, options purchased, options written, warrants, futures, loan participations, short sales, other investment companies, and so forth)

(2) Country or geographic region, except for derivative instruments for which the underlying is not a security (see [a][4])

(3) Industry, except for derivative instruments for which the underlying is not a security (see [a][4])

(4) For derivative instruments for which the underlying is not a security, by broad category of underlying (for example, grains and feeds, fibers and textiles, foreign currency, or equity indexes) in place of the categories in (a)(2) and (a)(3)

b. Report the percent of net assets that each such category represents and the total value and cost for each category in (a)(1) and (a)(2)

c. Disclose the name, shares or principal amount, value, and type of both of the following:

(1) Each investment (including short sales) constituting more than 5 percent of net assets, except for derivative instruments (see [e]); in applying the 5 percent test, total long and total short positions in any one issuer should be considered separately

(2) All investments in any one issuer aggregating more than 5 percent of net assets, except for derivative instruments (see [e]); in applying the 5 percent test, total long and total short positions in any one issuer shall be considered separately

d. Aggregate other investments (each of which is 5 percent or less of net assets) without specifically identifying the issuers of such investments, and categorize them in accordance with the guidance in (a); in applying the 5 percent test, total long and total short positions in any one issuer shall be considered separately

e. Disclose the number of contracts, range of expiration dates, and cumulative appreciation (depreciation) for open futures contracts of a particular underlying (such as wheat, cotton, specified equity index, or U.S. Treasury Bonds), regardless of exchange, delivery location, or delivery date, if cumulative appreciation (depreciation) on the open contracts exceeds 5 percent of net assets; in applying the 5 percent test, total long and total short positions in any one issuer shall be considered separately

f. Disclose the range of expiration dates and fair value for all other derivative instruments of a particular underlying (such as foreign currency, wheat, specified equity index, or U.S. Treasury Bonds) regardless of counterparty, exchange, or delivery date, if fair value exceeds 5 percent of net assets; in applying the 5 percent test, total long and total short positions in any one issuer shall be considered separately

g. Provide both of the following additional qualitative descriptions for each investment in another nonregistered investment partnership whose fair value constitutes more than 5 percent of net assets:

(1) The investment objective

(2) Restrictions on redemption (that is, liquidity provisions)

.77 Section 508 paragraph .41 addresses the effect of inadequate disclosure of information essential for fair presentation of the financial statements on the auditor's report. It states:

> If the financial statements, including accompanying notes, fail to disclose information that is required by GAAP, the auditor should express a qualified or adverse opinion because of the departure from those principles and should provide the information in the report, if practicable, unless its omission from the auditor's report is recognized as appropriate by a specific SAS.

.78 Section 508 paragraph .42 provides an example of a report qualified for inadequate disclosure (assuming that the auditor has concluded that it is not practicable to present the required information and the effects are such that the auditor has concluded an adverse opinion is not appropriate) as follows:

Independent Auditor's Report

> [*Same first and second paragraphs as the standard report*]
>
> The Company's financial statements do not disclose [*describe the nature of the omitted information that it is not practicable to present in the auditor's report*]. In our opinion, disclosure of this information is required by accounting principles generally accepted in the United States of America.
>
> In our opinion, except for the omission of the information discussed in the preceding paragraph, . . .

.79 FASB ASC 946 does not make it clear how the guidance in section 508 paragraphs .41–.42 should be applied to reports on financial statements of investment partnerships that are exempt from SEC registration and that do not include all the investment information required in the Schedule of Investments as required by FASB ASC 946. For example, if the financial statements did not disclose each of the required items for each investment, the guidance in section 508 paragraph .41 indicates the auditor should, if practicable, include the missing information (for example, the Schedule of Investments or information about individual investments) in the auditor's report. However, the example in section 508 paragraph .42 provides that the auditor would disclose the nature of the missing information, rather than the actual information, in the auditor's report.

.80 In applying section 508 paragraphs .41–.42 to an auditor's report on financial statements of an investment partnership that is exempt from SEC registration and that does not include the required Schedule of Investments information required by FASB ASC 946-210-50-6, is it sufficient for the auditor to describe "the nature of the omitted disclosures" in his or her report expressing a qualified (or adverse) opinion?

.81 *Interpretation*—No. The example in section 508 paragraph .42 does not change the requirement in section 508 paragraph .41 for the auditor to issue a qualified or adverse opinion and also to provide the missing information, if practicable. If the investment disclosures required by FASB ASC 946 are not included in the financial statements and it is practicable for the auditor to determine them or any portion thereof, the auditor should include the information in his or her report expressing the qualified or adverse opinion.

.82 Footnote 15 of section 508 indicates that it is practicable to provide the missing information if "the information is reasonably obtainable from management's accounts and records and ... providing the information in the report does not require the auditor to assume the position of a preparer of financial information." Ordinarily, it would be practicable for the auditor to obtain and present the information about investments constituting more than 5 percent of net assets called for by section (*b*) of the disclosure requirement described in paragraph .76. However, due to the need to categorize the investments for the purpose of preparing the schedule called for by section (*a*) of the disclosure requirement described in paragraph .76, the auditor might be in the position of preparer of financial information and, therefore, would not include the schedule in his or her report. In rare cases, the Schedule of Investments information may be so limited that the auditor may conclude that disclosure of the entire schedule is practicable.

.83 Following is an illustration of a report that expresses a qualified opinion because the Schedule of Investments fails to disclose investments constituting more than 5 percent of net assets, but in all other respects conforms to the requirements of FASB ASC 946:

Independent Auditor's Report

[*Same first and second paragraphs as the standard report*]

The Schedule of Investments included in the Partnership's financial statements does not disclose required information about the following investments, each constituting more than 5 percent of the Partnership's total net assets, at December 31, 20X2:

- Amalgamated Buggy Whips, Inc., 10,000 shares of common stock—fair value $3,280,000 (Consumer nondurable goods)
- Paper Airplane Corp., 6.25% Cv. Deb. due 20XX, $4.5 million par value—fair value $4,875,000 (Aviation)

In our opinion, disclosure of this information is required by accounting principles generally accepted in the United States of America.

In our opinion, except for the omission of the information discussed in the preceding paragraph, the financial statements and financial highlights referred to above present fairly, . . .

.84 An illustration of an adverse opinion relating to failure to present the entire Schedule of Investments and all of the related required information follows.[6] This illustration assumes that the auditor has concluded that it is not practicable to present all of the required information. In such circumstances, the auditor presents in his or her report the missing information, where it is practicable to do so, and describes the nature of the missing information where it is not practicable to present the information in the report:

Independent Auditor's Report

[*Same first and second paragraphs as the standard report*]

The Partnership has declined to prepare and present a Schedule of Investments and the related information as of December 31, 20X2. Accounting principles generally accepted in the United States of America require presentation of this Schedule and the related information. Presentation of this Schedule would have disclosed required information about the following investments, each constituting more than 5 percent of the Partnership's total net assets, at December 31, 20X2:

- Amalgamated Buggy Whips, Inc., 10,000 shares of common stock—fair value $3,280,000 (Consumer nondurable goods)[7]

[6] Section 508 paragraph .36 discusses the factors the auditor considers in deciding whether to issue a qualified opinion or an adverse opinion.

[7] In the absence of a Schedule of Investments containing categorizations by type, country or geographic region, and industry, such categorizations should be provided only if readily ascertainable from management's accounts and records. The auditor should not assign such categorizations if management has not done so.

- Paper Airplane Corp., 6.25% Cv. Deb. due 20XX, $4.5 million par value—fair value $4,875,000 (Aviation)

In addition, presentation of the Schedule of Investments would have disclosed [*describe the nature of the information that it is not practicable to present in the auditor's report*].

In our opinion, because the omission of a Schedule of Investments results in an incomplete presentation as explained in the preceding paragraph, the financial statements and financial highlights referred to above do not present fairly, . . .

[Issue Date: April 9, 2003; Revised: June 2009.]

17. Clarification in the Audit Report of the Extent of Testing of Internal Control Over Financial Reporting in Accordance With Generally Accepted Auditing Standards

.85 *Question*—Auditing standards established by the ASB of the AICPA are in effect and are enforceable[8] for audits of entities that are not *issuers*, as that term is defined by the Sarbanes-Oxley Act of 2002 (the act) or whose audit is not prescribed by the rules of the SEC. For purposes of this interpretation, these entities are referred to as *nonissuers*.[9]

.86 Section 314, *Understanding the Entity and Its Environment and Assessing the Risks of Material Misstatement*, provides guidance on the auditor's consideration of internal control in an audit of a nonissuer's financial statements in accordance with GAAS. That consideration is intended to provide the auditor a sufficient understanding of internal control to plan the audit and to determine the nature, timing, and extent of tests to be performed. The scope of the auditor's procedures required under section 314 is considerably less than that required for an attestation of internal control pursuant to Section 404(b) of the act.

.87 To clarify that an audit performed in accordance with GAAS does not require the same level of testing and reporting on internal control over financial reporting as an audit of an issuer when Section 404(b) of the act is applicable, may the auditor expand his or her audit report to indicate that the purpose and extent of the auditor's testing of internal control over financial reporting was to determine the auditor's procedures and was not sufficient to express an opinion on the effectiveness of internal control over financial reporting?

---

[8] The AICPA governing council designated the Public Company Accounting Oversight Board (PCAOB) as the body, pursuant to Rule 201, *General Standards* (ET sec. 201 par. .01), and Rule 202, *Compliance With Standards* (ET sec. 202 par. .01) of the AICPA's Code of Professional Conduct, with the authority to promulgate auditing and related attestation standards, quality control, ethics, independence and other standards relating to the preparation and issuance of audit reports for issuers, as defined by the Sarbanes-Oxley Act of 2002. The council also designated the Auditing Standards Board (ASB), pursuant to Rules 201 and 202 (ET sec. 201 par. .01 and ET sec. 202 par. .01), as the body with the authority to promulgate auditing, attestation, and quality control standards and procedures for all other entities.

[9] In a report issued on the audit of the financial statements of a subsidiary, investee, or other type of affiliate of an issuer, that is not itself an issuer, the auditor should refer to the audit as having been performed in accordance with generally accepted auditing standards (GAAS) if the report will not be filed with the SEC. For example, a subsidiary of an issuer may be subject to certain regulations that require an audit be performed in accordance with *Government Auditing Standards* (the Yellow Book). In this example, the auditor's report of the nonissuer should refer to GAAS and generally accepted government auditing standards.

.88 *Interpretation*—Yes. An auditor may add such language to the auditor's standard report. An example of additional language[10] that may be included in the auditor's report to indicate this matter follows:

Independent Auditor's Report

[*Same first paragraph as the standard report*]

We conducted our audit in accordance with auditing standards generally accepted in the United States of America. Those standards require that we plan and perform the audit to obtain reasonable assurance about whether the financial statements are free of material misstatement. *An audit includes consideration of internal control over financial reporting as a basis for designing audit procedures that are appropriate in the circumstances, but not for the purpose of expressing an opinion on the effectiveness of the Company's internal control over financial reporting. Accordingly, we express no such opinion.* An audit also includes examining, on a test basis, evidence supporting the amounts and disclosures in the financial statements, assessing the accounting principles used and significant estimates made by management, as well as evaluating the overall financial statement presentation. We believe that our audit provides a reasonable basis for our opinion.

[*Same opinion paragraph as the standard report*]

[Issue Date: June 2004; Revised: March 2006.]

18. Reference to PCAOB Standards in an Audit Report on a Nonissuer[11]

.89 *Question*—Auditing Standard No. 1, *References in Auditors' Reports to the Standards of the Public Company Accounting Oversight Board* (AICPA, *PCAOB Standards and Related Rules*, Auditing Standards), directs auditors to state in the auditor's report that the engagement was conducted in accordance with "the standards of the Public Company Accounting Oversight Board (United States)" whenever the auditor has performed the engagement in accordance with Public Company Accounting Oversight Board (PCAOB) standards. Additionally, the release accompanying the standard states that "nothing in the Board's rules would preclude an accounting firm from conducting an audit of a company that is not an issuer in accordance with the Board's standards and so stating in its audit report. This is true regardless of whether or not the accounting firm performing the audit is registered with the Board."

.90 If an auditor is engaged to perform an audit of a nonissuer in accordance with PCAOB standards, which standards are applicable and how should the auditor report?

.91 *Interpretation*—Section 508 requires the auditor to indicate in the auditor's report that the audit was conducted in accordance with GAAS and an identification of the United States of America as the country of origin of those standards. However, an auditor may indicate that the audit was also conducted in accordance with another set of auditing standards. If the auditor conducted

---

[10] The additional language related to internal control should not be used when reporting on the audit of financial statements of a nonissuer that engages its auditor to examine (or audit) and report on the effectiveness of internal control over financial reporting either voluntarily or to comply with regulatory requirements.

[11] In a report issued on the audit of the financial statements of a subsidiary, investee, or other type of affiliate of an issuer, that is not itself an issuer, the auditor should refer to the audit as having been performed in accordance with GAAS if the report will not be filed with the SEC. For example, a subsidiary of an issuer may be subject to certain regulations that require an audit be performed in accordance with *Government Auditing Standards* (the Yellow Book). In this example, the auditor's report of the nonissuer should refer to GAAS and generally accepted government auditing standards.

the audit in accordance with GAAS *and* the auditing standards of the PCAOB, the auditor may indicate in the auditor's report that the audit was conducted in accordance with both sets of standards.

.92 Following is an example of additional language that may be included [12] in the auditor's report to indicate that an audit was conducted in accordance with both GAAS and the PCAOB's auditing standards, and to clarify that the purpose and extent of the auditor's testing of internal control over financial reporting was to determine the auditor's procedures and was not sufficient to express an opinion on the effectiveness of internal control. To clarify the source of GAAS in a dual reference reporting situation, the auditor may indicate that the audit was conducted in accordance with GAAS as established by the ASB:

Independent Auditor's Report

[*Same first paragraph as the standard report*]

We conducted our audit in accordance with *generally accepted auditing standards as established by the Auditing Standards Board (United States) and in accordance with the auditing standards of the Public Company Accounting Oversight Board (United States).* Those standards require that we plan and perform the audit to obtain reasonable assurance about whether the financial statements are free of material misstatement. *The Company is not required to have, nor were we engaged to perform, an audit of its internal control over financial reporting. Our audit included consideration of internal control over financial reporting as a basis for designing audit procedures that are appropriate in the circumstances, but not for the purpose of expressing an opinion on the effectiveness of the Company's internal control over financial reporting. Accordingly we express no such opinion.* An audit also includes examining, on a test basis, evidence supporting the amounts and disclosures in the financial statements, assessing the accounting principles used and significant estimates made by management, as well as evaluating the overall financial statement presentation. We believe that our audit provides a reasonable basis for our opinion.

[*Same opinion paragraph as the standard report*]

[Issue Date: June 2004.]

19. Financial Statements Prepared in Conformity With International Financial Reporting Standards as Issued by the International Accounting Standards Board

.93 *Question*—Section 508 provides guidance regarding auditors' reports issued in connection with audits of historical financial statements prepared in conformity with GAAP. May an independent auditor apply the guidance in section 508 when engaged to report on financial statements presented in conformity with International Financial Reporting Standards (IFRS) as issued by the International Accounting Standards Board (IASB)?

---

[12] This example includes the illustrative language from paragraph .88. Because the PCAOB's Auditing Standard No. 5, *An Audit of Internal Control Over Financial Reporting That Is Integrated with An Audit of Financial Statements* (AICPA, *PCAOB Standards and Related Rules*, Auditing Standards), requires an audit of internal control for certain entities that are subject to Section 404(a) of the act, an audit of a nonissuer performed under PCAOB auditing standards does not require an audit of internal control unless otherwise required by a regulator with jurisdiction over the nonissuer. The additional language related to internal control should not be used when reporting on the audit of financial statements of a nonissuer that engages its auditor to examine (or audit) and report on the effectiveness of internal control over financial reporting either voluntarily or to comply with regulatory requirements.

.94 *Interpretation*—Yes. Because the IASB has been designated by the council of the AICPA as the body to establish international financial reporting standards for both private and public entities pursuant to Rule 202 (ET sec. 202 par. .01) and Rule 203, *Accounting Principles* (ET sec. 203 par. .01), of the AICPA Code of Professional Conduct and as of May 18, 2008, an auditor may report on general purpose financial statements presented in conformity with IFRS as issued by the IASB. When the auditor reports on financial statements prepared in conformity with IFRS, the auditor would refer, in the auditor's report, to IFRS rather than U.S. GAAP.

.95 An example of the opinion paragraph follows:

> In our opinion, the financial statements referred to above present fairly, in all material respects, the financial position of X Entity as of [at] December 31, 20X2 and 20X1, and the results of its operations, comprehensive income, changes in equity and its cash flows for the years then ended in conformity with International Financial Reporting Standards as issued by the International Accounting Standards Board.

.96 An entity may prepare financial statements in conformity with a jurisdictional variation of IFRS such that the entity's financial statements do not contain an explicit and unreserved statement of compliance with IFRS as issued by the IASB. Because the council of the AICPA has not designated bodies other than the IASB to establish international financial reporting standards, section 534, *Reporting on Financial Statements Prepared for Use in Other Countries*, applies to such financial statements prepared for use outside the United States, and paragraphs .14–.15 of section 534 and paragraphs .35–.60 of section 508 apply to financial statements prepared for more than limited distribution in the United States.

.97 If financial statements are presented in conformity with both IFRS as issued by the IASB and a jurisdictional variation of IFRS (for example, financial statements prepared in conformity with IFRS as issued by the IASB and with IFRS as endorsed by the European Union), an auditor may follow the guidance as described above.

[Issue Date: May 2008.]

AU Section 530

Dating of the Independent Auditor's Report

Source: SAS No. 1, section 530; SAS No. 29; SAS No. 98; SAS No. 103.

Issue date, unless otherwise indicated: November, 1972.

.01 The auditor's report should not be dated earlier than the date on which the auditor has obtained sufficient appropriate audit evidence[1] to support the opinion. Paragraph .05 describes the procedure to be followed when a subsequent event occurring after the date of the auditor's report is disclosed in the financial statements. [As amended, effective for audits of financial statements for periods ending on or after December 15, 2006, by Statement on Auditing Standards No. 103.]

.02 The auditor has no responsibility to make any inquiry or carry out any auditing procedures for the period after the date of his report.[2] However, with respect to filings under the Securities Act of 1933, reference should be made to section 711.10–.13.[*]

Events Occurring After Completion of Field Work But Before Issuance of Report

.03 In case a subsequent event of the type requiring adjustment of the financial statements (as discussed in section 560.03) occurs after the date of the independent auditor's report but before the issuance of the related financial statements, and the event comes to the attention of the auditor, the financial statements should be adjusted or the auditor should qualify his or her opinion.[3] When the adjustment is made without disclosure of the event, the report ordinarily should be dated in accordance with paragraph .01. However, if the financial statements are adjusted and disclosure of the event is made, or if no adjustment is made and the auditor qualifies his or her opinion,[4] the procedures set forth in paragraph .05 should be followed. [As amended, effective September 2002, by Statement on Auditing Standards No. 98.]

.04 In case a subsequent event of the type requiring disclosure (as discussed in section 560.05) occurs after the date of the auditor's report but before the issuance of the related financial statements, and the event comes to the attention of the auditor, it should be disclosed in a note to the financial statements

---

[1] Among other things, sufficient appropriate audit evidence includes evidence that the audit documentation has been reviewed and that the entity's financial statements, including disclosures, have been prepared and that management has asserted that they have taken responsibility for them. [Footnote added, effective for audits of financial statements for periods ending on or after December 15, 2006, by Statement on Auditing Standards No. 103.]

[2] See section 561 regarding procedures to be followed by the auditor who, subsequent to the date of his report upon audited financial statements, becomes aware that facts may have existed at that date which might have affected his report had he then been aware of such facts. [Footnote renumbered, by the issuance of Statement on Auditing Standards No. 103, December 2005.]

[*] Section number revised, April 1981, by the issuance of Statement on Auditing Standards No. 37.

[3] In some cases, a disclaimer of opinion or an adverse opinion may be appropriate. [Footnote renumbered, by the issuance of Statement on Auditing Standards No. 103, December 2005.]

[4] Ibid. [Footnote renumbered, by the issuance of Statement on Auditing Standards No. 103, December 2005.]

or the auditor should qualify his or her opinion.[5] If disclosure of the event is made, either in a note or in the auditor's report, the auditor would date the report as set forth in the following paragraph. [As amended, effective September 2002, by Statement on Auditing Standards No. 98.]

.05 The independent auditor has two methods available for dating the report when a subsequent event disclosed in the financial statements occurs after the original date of the auditor's report but before the issuance of the related financial statements. The auditor may use "dual dating," for example, "February 16, 20_, except for Note _, as to which the date is March 1, 20_," or may date the report as of the later date. In the former instance, the responsibility for events occurring subsequent to the original report date is limited to the specific event referred to in the note (or otherwise disclosed). In the latter instance, the independent auditor's responsibility for subsequent events extends to the date of the report and, accordingly, the procedures outlined in section 560.12 generally should be extended to that date. [As amended, effective September 2002, by Statement on Auditing Standards No. 98. As amended, effective for audits of financial statements for periods ending on or after December 15, 2006, by Statement on Auditing Standards No. 103.]

Reissuance of the Independent Auditor's Report

.06 An independent auditor may reissue his or her report on financial statements contained in annual reports filed with the Securities and Exchange Commission or other regulatory agencies or in a document that contains information in addition to the client's basic financial statements subsequent to the date of his or her original report on the basic financial statements. An independent auditor may also be requested by his or her client to furnish additional copies of a previously issued report. Use of the original report date in a reissued report removes any implication that records, transactions, or events after that date have been examined or reviewed. In such cases, the independent auditor has no responsibility to make further investigation or inquiry as to events which may have occurred during the period between the original report date and the date of the release of additional reports. However, see section 711[*] as to an auditor's responsibility when his or her report is included in a registration statement filed under the Securities Act of 1933 and see section 508.70–.73, for the predecessor auditor's responsibility when reissuing or consenting to the reuse of a report previously issued on the financial statements of a prior period. [As modified, effective December 31, 1980, by SAS No. 29. Revised, December 2010, to reflect conforming changes necessary due to the issuance of SAS Nos. 118–120.]

.07 In some cases, it may not be desirable for the independent auditor to reissue his report in the circumstances described in paragraph .06 because he has become aware of an event that occurred subsequent to the date of his original report that requires adjustment or disclosure in the financial statements. In such cases, adjustment with disclosure or disclosure alone should be made as described in section 560.08. The independent auditor should consider the effect of these matters on his opinion and he should date his report in accordance with the procedures described in paragraph .05.

---

[5] Ibid. [Footnote renumbered, by the issuance of Statement on Auditing Standards No. 103, December 2005.]

[*] See footnote * in paragraph .02.

.08 However, if an event of the type requiring disclosure only (as discussed in section 560.05 and .08) occurs between the date of the independent auditor's original report and the date of the reissuance of such report, and if the event comes to the attention of the independent auditor, the event may be disclosed in a separate note to the financial statements captioned somewhat as follows:

Event (Unaudited) Subsequent to the Date of the
Independent Auditor's Report

Under these circumstances, the report of the independent auditor would carry the same date used in the original report.

AU Section 532

Restricting the Use of an Auditor's Report

Source: SAS No. 87.

Effective for reports issued after December 31, 1998, unless otherwise indicated.

Introduction and Applicability

.01 This section provides guidance to auditors on restricting the use of reports issued pursuant to Statements on Auditing Standards (SASs).[1] This section—

- Defines the terms *general use* and *restricted use.*
- Describes the circumstances in which the use of auditors' reports should be restricted.
- Specifies the language to be used in auditors' reports that are restricted as to use.

The reporting guidance in paragraph .19 of this section is not applicable to reports issued under section 634, *Letters for Underwriters and Certain Other Requesting Parties.* [Revised, August 2011, to reflect conforming changes necessary due to the issuance of SSAE No. 16.]

General-Use and Restricted-Use Reports

.02 The term *general use* applies to auditors' reports that are not restricted to specified parties. Auditors' reports on financial statements prepared in conformity with generally accepted accounting principles or certain comprehensive bases of accounting other than generally accepted accounting principles[2] ordinarily are not restricted as to use.[3, 4]

.03 The term *restricted use* applies to auditors' reports intended only for specified parties. The need for restriction on the use of a report may result from a number of circumstances, including the purpose of the report, the nature of the procedures applied in its preparation, the basis of or assumptions used in its preparation, the extent to which the procedures performed generally are known or understood, and the potential for the report to be misunderstood when taken out of the context in which it was intended to be used.

---

[1] Throughout this section, the term *accountant* may be used interchangeably with the term *auditor*. The term accountant refers to a person possessing the professional qualifications required to practice as an independent auditor. See section 110, *Responsibilities and Functions of the Independent Auditor*, paragraphs .04 and .05.

[2] Section 623, *Special Reports*, paragraph .04, defines a comprehensive basis of accounting other than generally accepted accounting principles.

[3] However, see section 623.05*f* for restrictions on the use of reports on financial statements prepared in conformity with the requirements of the financial reporting provisions of a governmental regulatory agency.

[4] Nothing in this section precludes an auditor from restricting the use of any report.

.04 An auditor should restrict the use of a report in the following circumstances.

a. The subject matter of the auditor's report or the presentation being reported on is based on measurement or disclosure criteria contained in contractual agreements or regulatory provisions that are not in conformity with generally accepted accounting principles or an other comprehensive basis of accounting (OCBOA). (See paragraph .05.)

b. The auditor's report is issued as a by-product of a financial statement audit and is based on the results of procedures designed to enable the auditor to express an opinion on the financial statements taken as a whole, not to provide assurance on the specific subject matter of the report. (See paragraphs .07 through 11.)

[Revised, October 2000, to reflect conforming changes necessary due to the issuance of Statement on Auditing Standards No. 93.]

Reporting on Subject Matter or Presentations Based on Measurement or Disclosure Criteria Contained in Contractual Agreements or Regulatory Provisions

.05 Reports on subject matter or presentations based on measurement or disclosure criteria contained in contractual agreements or regulatory provisions that are not in conformity with generally accepted accounting principles or an OCBOA are restricted as to use because the basis, assumptions, or purpose of such presentations (contained in such agreements or regulatory provisions) are developed for and directed only to the parties to the agreement or regulatory agency responsible for the provisions.

Reporting When Specified Parties Accept Responsibility for the Sufficiency of the Procedures Performed

[.06] [Paragraph deleted to reflect conforming changes necessary due to the issuance of Statement on Auditing Standards No. 93.]

Reporting as a By-Product of a Financial Statement Audit

.07 An auditor may issue certain reports on matters coming to his or her attention during the course of an audit of financial statements. Such reports include but are not limited to reports issued pursuant to the following:

- Section 325, *Communicating Internal Control Related Matters Identified in an Audit*
- Section 380, *The Auditor's Communication With Those Charged With Governance*
- Paragraphs .19 through .21 of section 623, *Special Reports*, for reporting on compliance with aspects of contractual agreements or regulatory requirements related to audited financial statements

[Revised, May 2006, to reflect conforming changes necessary due to the issuance of Statement on Auditing Standards No. 112. Revised, April 2007, to reflect conforming changes necessary due to the issuance of Statement on Auditing Standards No. 114.]

.08 Reports issued pursuant to the aforementioned auditing standards are based on the results of procedures designed to enable an auditor to express an opinion on the financial statements taken as a whole, not to provide assurance on the specific subject matter of the report. These reports are by-products of an audit of financial statements and are referred to as by-product reports in this section.

.09 Because the issuance of the by-product report is not the primary objective of the engagement, an audit generally includes only limited procedures directed toward the subject matter of the by-product report. Accordingly, because of the potential for misinterpretation or misunderstanding of the limited degree of assurance associated with a by-product report, the use of such reports should be restricted. For example, a report issued under section 325 should be restricted because the purpose of the engagement is to report on an entity's financial statements, not to provide assurance on its internal control.

.10 An auditor may issue a by-product report in connection with other engagements conducted in accordance with generally accepted auditing standards, such as an engagement to express an opinion on one or more specified elements, accounts, or items of a financial statement.

.11 In consideration of the foregoing, the use of by-product reports should be restricted to management, those charged with governance, others within the organization, and any specified governmental authorities, when communicating internal control related matters identified in an audit (see section 325); those charged with governance and, if appropriate, management when communicating with those charged with governance (see section 380), and, in the case of reports on compliance with aspects of contractual agreements, to the parties to the contract or agreement (see section 623). [Revised, May 2006, to reflect conforming changes necessary due to the issuance of Statement on Auditing Standards No. 112. Revised, April 2007, to reflect conforming changes necessary due to the issuance of Statement on Auditing Standards No. 114.]

Combined Reports Covering Both Restricted-Use and General-Use Subject Matter or Presentations

.12 If an auditor issues a single combined report covering both (*a*) subject matter or presentations that require a restriction on use to specified parties and (*b*) subject matter or presentations that ordinarily do not require such a restriction, the use of such a single combined report should be restricted to the specified parties.

Inclusion of a Separate Restricted-Use Report in the Same Document With a General-Use Report

.13 In some instances, a separate restricted-use report may be included in a document that also contains a general-use report.[5] The inclusion of a separate restricted-use report in a document that contains a general-use report does

[5] Such a requirement exists in audits performed in accordance with U.S. Office of Management and Budget Circular A-133, *Audits of States, Local Governments, and Non-Profit Organizations*, and U.S. General Accounting Office, *Government Auditing Standards*.

not affect the intended use of either report. The restricted-use report remains restricted as to use, and the general-use report continues to be for general use.

Adding Other Specified Parties

.14 Subsequent to the completion of an engagement resulting in a restricted-use report, or in the course of such an engagement, an auditor may be asked to consider adding other parties as specified parties.

.15 As noted in paragraph .11 of this section, the use of by-product reports should be restricted to management, those charged with governance, others within the organization, and any specified governmental authorities, when communicating internal control related matters identified in an audit (see section 325); those charged with governance and, if appropriate, management when communicating with those charged with governance (see section 380), and, in the case of reports on compliance with aspects of contractual agreements, to the parties to the contract or agreement. An auditor should not agree to add other parties as specified parties of a by-product report. [Revised, May 2006, to reflect conforming changes necessary due to the issuance of Statement on Auditing Standards No. 112. Revised, April 2007, to reflect conforming changes necessary due to the issuance of Statement on Auditing Standards No. 114.]

.16 If an auditor is reporting on subject matter or a presentation based on measurement or disclosure criteria contained in contractual agreements or regulatory provisions, as described in paragraph .05 of this section, the auditor may agree to add other parties as specified parties based on the auditor's consideration of factors such as the identity of the other parties and the intended use of the report. If the auditor agrees to add other parties as specified parties, the auditor should obtain affirmative acknowledgment, ordinarily in writing, from the other parties of their understanding of the nature of the engagement, the measurement or disclosure criteria used in the engagement, and the related report. If the other parties are added after the auditor has issued his or her report, the report may be reissued or the auditor may provide other written acknowledgment that the other parties have been added as specified parties. If the report is reissued, the report date should not be changed. If the auditor provides written acknowledgment that the other parties have been added as specified parties, such written acknowledgment ordinarily should state that no procedures have been performed subsequent to the date of the report.

[.17] [Paragraph deleted to reflect conforming changes necessary due to the issuance of Statement on Auditing Standards No. 93.]

Limiting the Distribution of Reports

.18 Because of the reasons presented in paragraph .03 of this section, an auditor should consider informing his or her client that restricted-use reports are not intended for distribution to nonspecified parties, regardless of whether they are included in a document containing a separate general-use report.[6;7] However, an auditor is not responsible for controlling a client's distribution of restricted-use reports. Accordingly, a restricted-use report should alert readers

---

[6] In some cases, restricted-use reports filed with regulatory agencies are required by law or regulation to be made available to the public as a matter of public record. Also, a regulatory agency as part of its oversight responsibility for an entity may require access to restricted-use reports in which they are not named as a specified party.

[7] This section does not preclude an auditor, in connection with establishing the terms of the engagement, from reaching an understanding with the client that the intended use of the report will be restricted, and from obtaining the client's agreement that the client and the specified parties will not distribute the report to parties other than those identified in the report.

to the restriction on the use of the report by indicating that the report is not intended to be and should not be used by anyone other than the specified parties.

Report Language—Restricted Use

.19 An auditor's report that is restricted as to use should contain a separate paragraph at the end of the report that includes the following elements:

a. A statement indicating that the report is intended solely for the information and use of the specified parties

b. An identification of the specified parties to whom use is restricted

c. A statement that the report is not intended to be and should not be used by anyone other than the specified parties

An example of such a paragraph is the following:

> This report is intended solely for the information and use of [*the specified parties*][8] and is not intended to be and should not be used by anyone other than these specified parties.

Effective Date

.20 This section is effective for reports issued after December 31, 1998. Early application of the provisions of this section is permitted.

---

8 The report may list the specified parties or refer the reader to the specified parties listed elsewhere in the report. For reports on engagements performed in accordance with U.S. Office of Management and Budget Circular A-133, *Audits of States, Local Governments, and Non-Profit Organizations*, the specified parties may be identified as "federal awarding agencies and pass-through entities."

AU Section 534

Reporting on Financial Statements Prepared for Use in Other Countries

Source: SAS No. 51.

See section 9534 for interpretations of this section.

Effective for audits of financial statements for periods beginning after July 31, 1986, unless otherwise indicated.

.01 This section provides guidance for an independent auditor practicing in the United States who is engaged to report on the financial statements of a U.S. entity that have been prepared in conformity with accounting principles generally accepted in another country for use outside the United States.[1] A "U.S. entity" is an entity that is either organized or domiciled in the United States.

Purpose and Use of Financial Statements

.02 A U.S. entity ordinarily prepares financial statements for use in the United States in conformity with accounting principles generally accepted in the United States, but it may also prepare financial statements that are intended for use outside the United States and are prepared in conformity with accounting principles generally accepted in another country. For example, the financial statements of a U.S. entity may be prepared for inclusion in the consolidated financial statements of a non-U.S. parent. A U.S. entity may also have non-U.S. investors or may decide to raise capital in another country. Before reporting on financial statements prepared in conformity with the accounting principles of another country, the auditor should have a clear understanding of, and obtain written representations from management regarding, the purpose and uses of such financial statements. If the auditor uses the standard report of another country, and the financial statements will have general distribution in that country, he should consider whether any additional legal responsibilities are involved.

General and Fieldwork Standards

.03 When auditing the financial statements of a U.S. entity prepared in conformity with accounting principles generally accepted in another country, the auditor should perform the procedures that are necessary to comply with the general and fieldwork standards of U.S. generally accepted auditing standards (GAAS).

---

[1] See paragraph .07, however, for a discussion of financial statements prepared in conformity with accounting principles generally accepted in another country for limited distribution in the United States.

.04 The auditing procedures generally performed under U.S. GAAS may need to be modified, however. The assertions embodied in financial statements prepared in conformity with accounting principles generally accepted in another country may differ from those prepared in conformity with U.S. generally accepted accounting principles. For example, accounting principles generally accepted in another country may require that certain assets be revalued to adjust for the effects of inflation—in which case, the auditor should perform procedures to test the revaluation adjustments. On the other hand, another country's accounting principles may not require or permit recognition of deferred taxes; consequently, procedures for testing deferred tax balances would not be applicable. As another example, the accounting principles of some countries do not require or permit disclosure of related party transactions. Determining that such transactions are properly disclosed, therefore, would not be an audit objective in such cases. Other objectives, however, would remain relevant—such as identifying related parties in order to fully understand the business purpose, nature, and extent of the transactions and their effects on the financial statements.

.05 The auditor should understand the accounting principles generally accepted in the other country. Such knowledge may be obtained by reading the statutes or professional literature (or codifications thereof) that establish or describe the accounting principles generally accepted in the other country. Application of accounting principles to a particular situation often requires practical experience; the auditor should consider, therefore, consulting with persons having such expertise in the accounting principles of the other country. If the accounting principles of another country are not established with sufficient authority or by general acceptance, or a broad range of practices is acceptable, the auditor may nevertheless be able to report on financial statements for use in such countries if, in the auditor's judgment, the client's principles and practices are appropriate in the circumstances and are disclosed in a clear and comprehensive manner. In determining the appropriateness of the accounting principles used, the auditor may consider, for example, International Accounting Standards established by the International Accounting Standards Committee.

Compliance With Auditing Standards of Another Country

.06 In those circumstances in which the auditor is requested to apply the auditing standards of another country when reporting on financial statements prepared in conformity with accounting principles generally accepted in that country, the auditor should comply with the general and fieldwork standards of that country as well as with those standards in U.S. GAAS. This may require the auditor to perform certain procedures required by auditing standards of the other country in addition to those required by U.S. GAAS. The auditor will need to read the statutes or professional literature, or codifications thereof, that establish or describe the auditing standards generally accepted in the other country. He should understand, however, that such statutes or professional literature may not be a complete description of auditing practices and, therefore, should consider consulting with persons having expertise in the auditing standards of the other country.

Reporting Standards

.07 If financial statements prepared in conformity with accounting principles generally accepted in another country are prepared for use only outside the United States, the auditor may report using either (*a*) a U.S.-style report modified to report on the accounting principles of another country (see paragraphs .09 and .10) or (*b*) if appropriate, the report form of the other country (see paragraphs .11 and .12). This is not intended to preclude limited distribution of the financial statements to parties (such as banks, institutional investors, and other knowledgeable parties that may choose to rely on the report) within the United States that deal directly with the entity, if the financial statements are to be used in a manner that permits such parties to discuss differences from U.S. accounting and reporting practices and their significance with the entity.

.08 Financial statements prepared in conformity with accounting principles generally accepted in another country ordinarily are not useful to U.S. users. Therefore, if financial statements are needed for use both in another country and within the United States, the auditor may report on two sets of financial statements for the entity—one prepared in conformity with accounting principles generally accepted in another country for use outside the United States, and the other prepared in accordance with accounting principles generally accepted in the United States (see paragraph .13). If dual statements are not prepared, or for some other reason the financial statements prepared in conformity with accounting principles generally accepted in another country will have more than limited distribution in the United States, the auditor should report on them using the U.S. standard form of report, modified as appropriate for departures from accounting principles generally accepted in the United States (see paragraph .14).

Use Only Outside the United States

.09 A U.S.-style report modified to report on financial statements prepared in conformity with accounting principles generally accepted in another country that are intended for use only outside the United States should include—

a. A title that includes the word "independent."[2]

b. A statement that the financial statements identified in the report were audited.

c. A statement that refers to the note to the financial statements that describes the basis of presentation of the financial statements on which the auditor is reporting, including identification of the nationality of the accounting principles.

d. A statement that the financial statements are the responsibility of the Company's management[3] and that the auditor's responsibility is to express an opinion on the financial statements based on his audit.

---

[2] This statement does not require a title for an auditor's report if the auditor is not independent. See section 504, *Association With Financial Statements*, for guidance on reporting when the auditor is not independent. [Footnote added to reflect conforming changes necessary due to the issuance of Statement on Auditing Standards Nos. 53 through 62.]

[3] In some instances, a document containing the auditor's report may include a statement by management regarding its responsibility for the presentation of the financial statements. Nevertheless, the auditor's report should state that the financial statements are management's responsibility. [Footnote added to reflect conforming changes necessary due to the issuance of Statement on Auditing Standards Nos. 53 through 62.]

e. A statement that the audit was conducted in accordance with auditing standards generally accepted in the United States of America (and, if appropriate, with the auditing standards of the other country).

f. A statement that U.S. standards require that the auditor plan and perform the audit to obtain reasonable assurance about whether the financial statements are free of material misstatement.

g. A statement that an audit includes:

(1) Examining, on a test basis, evidence supporting the amounts and disclosures in the financial statements,

(2) Assessing the accounting principles used and significant estimates made by management, and

(3) Evaluating the overall financial statement presentation.[4]

h. A statement that the auditor believes that his audit provides a reasonable basis for his opinion.

i. A paragraph that expresses the auditor's opinion on whether the financial statements are presented fairly, in all material respects, in conformity with the basis of accounting described. If the auditor concludes that the financial statements are not fairly presented on the basis of accounting described, all substantive reasons for that conclusion should be disclosed in an additional explanatory paragraph (preceding the opinion paragraph) of the report, and the opinion paragraph should include appropriate modifying language as well as a reference to the explanatory paragraph.

j. If the auditor is auditing comparative financial statements and the described basis of accounting has not been applied in a manner consistent with that of the preceding period and the change has had a material effect on the comparability of the financial statements, the auditor should add an explanatory paragraph to his report (following the opinion paragraph) that describes the change in accounting principle and refers to the note to the financial statements that discusses the change and its effect on the financial statements.

k. The manual or printed signature of the auditor's firm.

l. Date.[5]

[As amended to reflect conforming changes necessary due to the issuance of Statement on Auditing Standards Nos. 53 through 62. Revised, October 2000, to reflect conforming changes necessary due to the issuance of Statement on Auditing Standards No. 93.]

---

[4] [Footnote added to reflect conforming changes necessary due to the issuance of Statement on Auditing Standards Nos. 53 through 62. Title of section 411 amended, effective for reports issued or reissued on or after June 30, 2001, by Statement on Auditing Standards No. 93. Footnote deleted, October 2009, to reflect conforming changes necessary due to the withdrawal of SAS No. 69.]

[5] For guidance on dating the independent auditor's report, see section 530, *Dating of the Independent Auditor's Report*. [Footnote added to reflect conforming changes necessary due to the issuance of Statement on Auditing Standards Nos. 53 through 62.]

.10 The following is an illustration of such a report:

Independent Auditor's Report

We have audited the accompanying balance sheet of International Company as of December 31, 20XX and the related statements of income, retained earnings, and cash flows for the year then ended which, as described in Note X, have been prepared on the basis of accounting principles generally accepted in [*name of country*]. These financial statements are the responsibility of the Company's management. Our responsibility is to express an opinion on these financial statements based on our audit.

We conducted our audit in accordance with auditing standards generally accepted in the United States of America (and in [*name of country*]). U.S. standards require that we plan and perform the audit to obtain reasonable assurance about whether the financial statements are free of material misstatement. An audit includes examining, on a test basis, evidence supporting the amounts and disclosures in the financial statements. An audit also includes assessing the accounting principles used and significant estimates made by management, as well as evaluating the overall financial statement presentation. We believe that our audit provides a reasonable basis for our opinion.

In our opinion, the financial statements referred to above present fairly, in all material respects, the financial position of International Company as of [*at*] December 31, 20XX, and the results of its operations and its cash flows for the year then ended in conformity with accounting principles generally accepted in [*name of country*].

[As amended to reflect conforming changes necessary due to the issuance of Statement on Auditing Standards Nos. 53 through 62. Revised, October 2000, to reflect conforming changes necessary due to the issuance of Statement on Auditing Standards No. 93.]

.11 The independent auditor may also use the auditor's standard report of another country, provided that—

a. Such a report would be used by auditors in the other country in similar circumstances.

b. The auditor understands, and is in a position to make, the attestations contained in such a report (see paragraph .12).

The auditor should consider whether the standard report of another country or the financial statements may be misunderstood because they resemble those prepared in conformity with U.S. standards. When the auditor believes there is a risk of misunderstanding, he should identify the other country in the report.

.12 When the auditor uses the standard report of the other country, the auditor should comply with the reporting standards of that country. The auditor should recognize that the standard report used in another country, even when it appears similar to that used in the United States, may convey a different meaning and entail a different responsibility on the part of the auditor due to custom or culture. Use of a standard report of another country may also require the auditor to provide explicit or implicit assurance of statutory compliance or otherwise require understanding of local law. When using the auditor's standard report of another country, the auditor needs to understand applicable legal responsibilities, in addition to the auditing standards and the accounting principles generally accepted in the other country. Accordingly, depending on the nature and extent of the auditor's knowledge and experience, he should consider consulting with persons having expertise in the audit reporting practices of the other country to attain the understanding needed to issue that country's standard report.

.13 A U.S. entity that prepares financial statements in conformity with U.S. generally accepted accounting principles also may prepare financial statements in conformity with accounting principles generally accepted in another country for use outside the United States. In such circumstances, the auditor may report on the financial statements that are in conformity with accounting principles of the other country by following the guidance in paragraphs .09 and .10. The auditor may wish to include, in one or both of the reports, a statement that another report has been issued on the financial statements for the entity that have been prepared in accordance with accounting principles generally accepted in another country. The auditor may also wish to reference any note describing significant differences between the accounting principles used and U.S. GAAP. An example of such a statement follows.

> We also have reported separately on the financial statements of International Company for the same period presented in accordance with accounting principles generally accepted in [*name of country*]. (The significant differences between the accounting principles accepted in [*name of country*] and those generally accepted in the United States are summarized in Note X.)

Use in the United States

.14 If the auditor is requested to report on the fair presentation of financial statements, prepared in conformity with the accounting principles generally accepted in another country, that will have more than limited distribution in the United States, he should use the U.S. standard form of report (see section 508, *Reports on Audited Financial Statements*, paragraph .08), modified as appropriate (see section 508.35-.57), because of departures from accounting principles generally accepted in the United States.[6] The auditor may also, in a separate paragraph to the report, express an opinion on whether the financial statements are presented in conformity with accounting principles generally accepted in another country.

.15 The auditor may also report on the same set of financial statements, prepared in conformity with accounting principles generally accepted in another country, that will have more than limited distribution in the United States by using both the standard report of the other country or a U.S.-style report (described in paragraph .09) for distribution outside the United States, and a U.S. form of report (described in paragraph .14) for distribution in the United States.

Effective Date

.16 This section is effective for audits of financial statements for periods beginning after July 31, 1986.

---

[6] This section does not apply to reports on financial statements of U.S. subsidiaries of foreign registrants presented in SEC filings of foreign parent companies where the subsidiaries' financial statements have been prepared on the basis of accounting principles used by the parent company. [Footnote renumbered to reflect the conforming changes necessary due to the issuance of Statement on Auditing Standards Nos. 53 through 62.]

AU Section 9534

Reporting on Financial Statements Prepared for Use in Other Countries: Auditing Interpretations of Section 534

[1.] Financial Statements for General Use Only Outside of the United States in Accordance With International Accounting Standards and International Standards on Auditing

[.01–.04] [Withdrawn, May 2008, by the Audit Issues Task Force.][1]

2. Financial Statements Prepared in Conformity With International Financial Reporting Standards as Issued by the International Accounting Standards Board

.05 *Question*—Section 534, *Reporting on Financial Statements Prepared for Use in Other Countries* provides guidance for the independent auditor practicing in the United States who is engaged to report on the financial statements of a U.S. entity[2] for use outside of the United States in conformity with accounting principles generally accepted in another country. Does the guidance in section 534 apply to the financial statements of a U.S. entity presented in conformity with the International Financial Reporting Standards (IFRS) as issued by the International Accounting Standards Board (IASB)?

.06 *Interpretation*—No. The IASB has been designated by the council of the AICPA as the body to establish international financial reporting standards for both private and public entities pursuant to Rule 202, *Compliance With Standards* [ET section 202 paragraph.01], and Rule 203, *Accounting Principles* [ET section 203 paragraph .01], of the AICPA Code of Professional Conduct and as of May 18, 2008. Accordingly, section 534 is not applicable to financial statements prepared in conformity with IFRS as issued by the IASB. When the auditor reports on financial statements of a U.S. entity prepared in conformity with IFRS as issued by the IASB, the auditor would refer to section 508, *Reports on Audited Financial Statements*.[3]

.07 An entity may prepare financial statements in conformity with a jurisdictional variation of IFRS such that the entity's financial statements do not contain an explicit and unreserved statement of compliance with IFRS as issued by the IASB. Because the council of the AICPA has not designated bodies other than the IASB to establish IFRS, Section 534 applies to such financial statements prepared for use outside the United States, and paragraphs .14–.15 of section 534 and paragraphs .35–.37 of section 508 apply to financial statements prepared for more than limited distribution in the United States.

---

[1] [Footnote deleted.]

[2] A U.S. entity is an entity that is either organized or domiciled in the United States.

[3] Also see Auditing Interpretation No. 19, "Financial Statements Prepared in Conformity With International Financial Reporting Standards as Issued by the International Accounting Standards Board," of section 508, *Reports on Audited Financial Statements* [section 9508 paragraph .93].

.08 If financial statements are presented in conformity with both IFRS as issued by the IASB and a jurisdictional variation of IFRS (for example, financial statements prepared in conformity with IFRS as issued by the IASB and with IFRS as endorsed by the European Union), an auditor may follow the guidance in section 508 (and in paragraphs .93–.94 of Auditing Interpretation No. 19, "Financial Statements Prepared in Conformity With International Financial Reporting Standards as Issued by the International Accounting Standards Board," of section 508 [section 9508 paragraphs .93–.94]).

[Issue Date: May, 2008.]

3. Financial Statements Audited in Accordance With International Standards on Auditing

.09 *Question*—May a U.S. auditor perform an audit of financial statements of a U.S. entity in accordance with the International Standards on Auditing (ISA)? The financial statements subject to audit may be prepared in conformity with IFRS, accounting principles generally accepted in the United States, or accounting principles generally accepted in another country.

.10 *Interpretation*—Yes. In such an engagement where the financial statements are for use outside the United States, the auditor should follow the guidance in section 534 in planning and performing the engagement. Section 534 requires the U.S. auditor, in these circumstances, to comply with the general and fieldwork standards of U.S. generally accepted auditing standards as well as any additional requirements of the ISA. When the financial statements are intended for general use only outside of the United States, the auditor may use either a U.S. style report [section 534 paragraph .09] or the report form set forth in the ISA.

.11 When the financial statements are intended for use in the United States, section 534 would not be applicable; however, section 508 would apply. Also see paragraph .56 of Auditing Interpretation No. 14, "Reporting on Audits Conducted in Accordance With Auditing Standards Generally Accepted in the United States of America and in Accordance With International Standards on Auditing," of section 508 [section 9508 paragraph .56].

[Issue Date: May, 2008.]

AU Section 543

Part of Audit Performed by Other Independent Auditors

Source: SAS No. 1, section 543; SAS No. 64.

See section 9543 for interpretations of this section.

Issue date, unless otherwise indicated: November, 1972.

.01 This section provides guidance on the professional judgments the independent auditor makes in deciding (*a*) whether he may serve as principal auditor and use the work and reports of other independent auditors who have audited the financial statements of one or more subsidiaries, divisions, branches, components, or investments included in the financial statements presented and (*b*) the form and content of the principal auditor's report in these circumstances.[1] Nothing in this section should be construed to require or imply that an auditor, in deciding whether he may properly serve as principal auditor without himself auditing particular subsidiaries, divisions, branches, components, or investments of his client, should make that decision on any basis other than his judgment regarding the professional considerations as discussed in paragraphs .02 and .10; nor should an auditor state or imply that a report that makes reference to another auditor is inferior in professional standing to a report without such a reference. [As modified, September 1981, by the Auditing Standards Board.]

Principal Auditor's Course of Action

.02 The auditor considering whether he may serve as principal auditor may have performed all but a relatively minor portion of the work, or significant parts of the audit may have been performed by other auditors. In the latter case, he must decide whether his own participation is sufficient to enable him to serve as the principal auditor and to report as such on the financial statements. In deciding this question, the auditor should consider, among other things, the materiality of the portion of the financial statements he has audited in comparison with the portion audited by other auditors, the extent of his knowledge of the overall financial statements, and the importance of the components he audited in relation to the enterprise as a whole. [As modified, September 1981, by the Auditing Standards Board.]

.03 If the auditor decides that it is appropriate for him to serve as the principal auditor, he must then decide whether to make reference in his report[2] to the audit performed by another auditor. If the principal auditor decides to assume responsibility for the work of the other auditor insofar as

---

[1] Section 315 applies if an auditor uses the work of a predecessor auditor in expressing an opinion on financial statements.

[2] See paragraph .09 for example of appropriate reporting when reference is made to the audit of other auditors.

that work relates to the principal auditor's expression of an opinion on the financial statements taken as a whole, no reference should be made to the other auditor's work or report. On the other hand, if the principal auditor decides not to assume that responsibility, his report should make reference to the audit of the other auditor and should indicate clearly the division of responsibility between himself and the other auditor in expressing his opinion on the financial statements. Regardless of the principal auditor's decision, the other auditor remains responsible for the performance of his own work and for his own report.

Decision Not to Make Reference

.04 If the principal auditor is able to satisfy himself as to the independence and professional reputation of the other auditor (see paragraph .10) and takes steps he considers appropriate to satisfy himself as to the audit performed by the other auditor (see paragraph .12), he may be able to express an opinion on the financial statements taken as a whole without making reference in his report to the audit of the other auditor. If the principal auditor decides to take this position, he should not state in his report that part of the audit was made by another auditor because to do so may cause a reader to misinterpret the degree of responsibility being assumed.

.05 Ordinarily, the principal auditor would be able to adopt this position when:

a. Part of the audit is performed by another independent auditor which is an associated or correspondent firm and whose work is acceptable to the principal auditor based on his knowledge of the professional standards and competence of that firm; or

b. The other auditor was retained by the principal auditor and the work was performed under the principal auditor's guidance and control; or

c. The principal auditor, whether or not he selected the other auditor, nevertheless takes steps he considers necessary to satisfy himself as to the audit performed by the other auditor and accordingly is satisfied as to the reasonableness of the accounts for the purpose of inclusion in the financial statements on which he is expressing his opinion; or

d. The portion of the financial statements audited by the other auditor is not material to the financial statements covered by the principal auditor's opinion.

Decision to Make Reference

.06 On the other hand, the principal auditor may decide to make reference to the audit of the other auditor when he expresses his opinion on the financial statements. In some situations, it may be impracticable for the principal auditor to review the other auditor's work or to use other procedures which in the judgment of the principal auditor would be necessary for him to satisfy himself as to the audit performed by the other auditor. Also, if the financial statements of a component audited by another auditor are material in relation to the total, the principal auditor may decide, regardless of any other considerations, to make reference in his report to the audit of the other auditor.

.07 When the principal auditor decides that he will make reference to the audit of the other auditor, his report should indicate clearly, in both the introductory, scope and opinion paragraphs, the division of responsibility as between that portion of the financial statements covered by his own audit and that covered by the audit of the other auditor. The report should disclose the magnitude of the portion of the financial statements audited by the other auditor. This may be done by stating the dollar amounts or percentages of one or more of the following: total assets, total revenues, or other appropriate criteria, whichever most clearly reveals the portion of the financial statements audited by the other auditor. The other auditor may be named but only with his express permission and provided his report is presented together with that of the principal auditor.[3]

.08 Reference in the report of the principal auditor to the fact that part of the audit was made by another auditor is not to be construed as a qualification of the opinion but rather as an indication of the divided responsibility between the auditors who conducted the audits of various components of the overall financial statements. [As modified, September 1981, by the Auditing Standards Board.]

.09 An example of appropriate reporting by the principal auditor indicating the division of responsibility when he makes reference to the audit of the other auditor follows:

Independent Auditor's Report

We have audited the consolidated balance sheet of X Company and subsidiaries as of December 31, 20...., and the related consolidated statements of income and retained earnings and cash flows for the year then ended. These financial statements are the responsibility of the Company's management. Our responsibility is to express an opinion on these financial statements based on our audits. We did not audit the financial statements of B Company, a wholly-owned subsidiary, which statements reflect total assets and revenues constituting 20 percent and 22 percent, respectively, of the related consolidated totals. Those statements were audited by other auditors whose report has been furnished to us, and our opinion, insofar as it relates to the amounts included for B Company, is based solely on the report of the other auditors.

We conducted our audit in accordance with auditing standards generally accepted in the United States of America. Those standards require that we plan and perform the audit to obtain reasonable assurance about whether the financial statements are free of material misstatement. An audit includes examining, on a test basis, evidence supporting the amounts and disclosures in the financial statements. An audit also includes assessing the accounting principles used and significant estimates made by management, as well as evaluating the overall financial statement presentation. We believe that our audit and the report of the other auditors provide a reasonable basis for our opinion.

In our opinion, based on our audit and the report of the other auditors, the consolidated financial statements referred to above present fairly, in all material respects, the financial position of X Company as of [*at*] December 31, 20...., and the results of its operations and its cash flows for the year then ended in conformity with accounting principles generally accepted in the United States of America.

---

[3] As to filings with the Securities and Exchange Commission, see Rule 2-05 of Regulation S-X.

When two or more auditors in addition to the principal auditor participate in the audit, the percentages covered by the other auditors may be stated in the aggregate. [Revised, April 1998, to reflect conforming changes necessary due to the issuance of Statement on Auditing Standards Nos. 53 through 62. Revised, October 2000, to reflect conforming changes necessary due to the issuance of Statement on Auditing Standards No. 93.]

Procedures Applicable to Both Methods of Reporting

.10 Whether or not the principal auditor decides to make reference to the audit of the other auditor, he should make inquiries concerning the professional reputation and independence of the other auditor. He also should adopt appropriate measures to assure the coordination of his activities with those of the other auditor in order to achieve a proper review of matters affecting the consolidating or combining of accounts in the financial statements. These inquiries and other measures may include procedures such as the following:

a. Make inquiries as to the professional reputation and standing of the other auditor to one or more of the following:

(i) The American Institute of Certified Public Accountants,[4] the applicable state society of certified public accountants and/or the local chapter, or in the case of a foreign auditor, his corresponding professional organization.

(ii) Other practitioners.

(iii) Bankers and other credit grantors.

(iv) Other appropriate sources.

b. Obtain a representation from the other auditor that he is independent under the requirements of the American Institute of Certified Public Accountants and, if appropriate, the requirements of the Securities and Exchange Commission (SEC).[4a]

c. Ascertain through communication with the other auditor:

(i) That he is aware that the financial statements of the component which he is to audit are to be included in the financial statements on which the principal auditor will report and that the other auditor's report thereon will be relied upon (and, where applicable, referred to) by the principal auditor.

---

[4] The AICPA Professional Ethics Division can respond to inquiries about whether individuals are members of the American Institute of Certified Public Accountants and whether complaints against members have been adjudicated by the Joint Trial Board. The division cannot respond to inquiries about public accounting firms or provide information about letters of required corrective action issued by the division or pending disciplinary proceedings or investigations. The AICPA Division for CPA Firms can respond to inquiries about whether specific public accounting firms are members of either the Private Companies Practice Section (PCPS) or the SEC Practice Section (SECPS), and can indicate whether a firm had a peer review in compliance with the Section's membership requirements and whether any sanctions against the firm have been publicly announced. In addition, the division will supply copies of peer-review reports that have been accepted by the applicable section of the division and information submitted by member firms on applications for membership and annual updates. The AICPA Practice Monitoring staff or the appropriate state CPA society can respond to inquiries as to whether specific public accounting firms are enrolled in the AICPA Peer Review Program and can indicate whether a firm had a peer review in compliance with the AICPA *Standards for Performing and Reporting on Peer Reviews* [PR section 100]. [As amended by the Auditing Standards Board, June 1990.]

[4a] [Footnote deleted, December 2001, to acknowledge the dissolution of the Independence Standard Board.]

(ii) That he or she is familiar with accounting principles generally accepted in the United States of America and with the generally accepted auditing standards promulgated by the American Institute of Certified Public Accountants and will conduct his or her audit and will report in accordance therewith.

(iii) That he has knowledge of the relevant financial reporting requirements for statements and schedules to be filed with regulatory agencies such as the Securities and Exchange Commission, if appropriate.

(iv) That a review will be made of matters affecting elimination of intercompany transactions and accounts and, if appropriate in the circumstances, the uniformity of accounting practices among the components included in the financial statements.

(Inquiries as to matters under *a*, and *c* (ii) and (iii) ordinarily would be unnecessary if the principal auditor already knows the professional reputation and standing of the other auditor and if the other auditor's primary place of practice is in the United States.) [As modified, September 1981, by the Auditing Standards Board. Revised, October 2000, to reflect conforming changes necessary due to the issuance of Statement on Auditing Standards No. 93.]

.11 If the results of inquiries and procedures by the principal auditor with respect to matters described in paragraph .10 lead him to the conclusion that he can neither assume responsibility for the work of the other auditor insofar as that work relates to the principal auditor's expression of an opinion on the financial statements taken as a whole, nor report in the manner set forth in paragraph .09, he should appropriately qualify his opinion or disclaim an opinion on the financial statements taken as a whole. His reasons therefor should be stated, and the magnitude of the portion of the financial statements to which his qualification extends should be disclosed.

Additional Procedures Under Decision Not to Make Reference

.12 When the principal auditor decides not to make reference to the audit of the other auditor, in addition to satisfying himself as to the matters described in paragraph .10, he should also consider whether to perform one or more of the following procedures:

a. Visit the other auditor and discuss the audit procedures followed and results thereof.

b. Review the audit programs of the other auditor. In some cases, it may be appropriate to issue instructions to the other auditor as to the scope of his audit work.

c. Review the working papers of the other auditor, including the understanding of internal control and the assessment of control risk.

.13 In some circumstances the principal auditor may consider it appropriate to participate in discussions regarding the accounts with management personnel of the component whose financial statements are being audited by other auditors and/or to make supplemental tests of such accounts. The determination of the extent of additional procedures, if any, to be applied rests with the principal auditor alone in the exercise of his professional judgment and in no way constitutes a reflection on the adequacy of the other auditor's work. Because the principal auditor in this case assumes responsibility for his opinion on the financial statements on which he is reporting without making reference to the audit performed by the other auditor, his judgment must govern as to the extent of procedures to be undertaken.

Long-Term Investments

.14 With respect to investments accounted for under the equity method, the auditor who uses another auditor's report for the purpose of reporting on the investor's equity in underlying net assets and its share of earnings or losses and other transactions of the investee is in the position of a principal auditor using the work and reports of other auditors. Under these circumstances, the auditor may decide that it would be appropriate to refer to the work and report of the other auditor in his report on the financial statements of the investor. (See paragraphs .06-.11.) When the work and reports of other auditors constitute a major element of evidence with respect to investments accounted for under the cost method, the auditor may be in a position analogous to that of a principal auditor.

Other Auditor's Report Departs From Standard Report

.15 If the report of the other auditor is other than a standard report, the principal auditor should decide whether the reason for the departure from the standard report is of such nature and significance in relation to the financial statements on which the principal auditor is reporting that it would require recognition in his own report. If the reason for the departure is not material in relation to such financial statements and the other auditor's report is not presented, the principal auditor need not make reference in his report to such departure. If the other auditor's report is presented, the principal auditor may wish to make reference to such departure and its disposition.

Restated Financial Statements of Prior Years Following a Pooling of Interests

.16 Following a pooling-of-interests transaction, an auditor may be asked to report on restated financial statements for one or more prior years when other auditors have audited one or more of the entities included in such financial statements. In some of these situations the auditor may decide that he has not audited a sufficient portion of the financial statements for such prior year or years to enable him to serve as principal auditor (see paragraph .02). Also, in such cases, it often is not possible or it may not be appropriate or necessary for the auditor to satisfy himself with respect to the restated financial statements. In these circumstances it may be appropriate for him to express his opinion solely with respect to the combining of such statements; however, no opinion should be expressed unless the auditor has audited the statements of at least one of the entities included in the restatement for at least the latest period presented. The following is an illustration of appropriate reporting on such combination that can be presented in an additional paragraph of the auditor's report following the standard introductory, scope and opinion paragraphs covering the consolidated financial statements for the current year: *

> We previously audited and reported on the consolidated statements of income and cash flows of XYZ Company and subsidiaries for the year ended December 31, 19X1, prior to their restatement for the 19X2 pooling of interests. The contribution of XYZ Company and subsidiaries to revenues and net income represented ..... percent and ..... percent of the respective restated totals. Separate financial statements of the other companies included in the 19X1 restated consolidated statements of income and cash flows were audited and reported on separately by other auditors. We also audited the combination of the accompanying consolidated statements of income and cash flows for the year ended December 31, 19X1, after restatement for the 19X2 pooling of interests; in our opinion, such consolidated statements have been properly combined on the basis described in Note A of notes to consolidated financial statements.

[As modified, October 1980, by the Auditing Standards Board. As amended, effective for reports issued after December 31, 1990, by Statement on Auditing Standards No. 64.]

.17 In reporting on restated financial statements as described in the preceding paragraph, the auditor does not assume responsibility for the work of other auditors nor the responsibility for expressing an opinion on the restated financial statements taken as a whole. He should apply procedures which will enable him to express an opinion only as to proper combination of the financial statements. These procedures include testing the combination for clerical accuracy and the methods used to combine the restated financial statements for conformity with generally accepted accounting principles. For example, the auditor should make inquiries and apply procedures regarding such matters as the following:

a. Elimination of intercompany transactions and accounts.

b. Combining adjustments and reclassifications.

c. Adjustments to treat like items in a comparable manner, if appropriate.

d. The manner and extent of presentation of disclosure matters in the restated financial statements and notes thereto.

The auditor should also consider the application of procedures contained in paragraph .10. [As modified, October 1980, by the Auditing Standards Board.]

Predecessor Auditor

[.18] [Superseded by Statement on Auditing Standards No. 7, effective November 30, 1975, as superseded by Statement on Auditing Standards No. 84, effective with respect to acceptance of an engagement after March 31, 1998.] (See section 315.)

---

* If restated consolidated balance sheets are also presented, the auditor may also express his opinion with respect to the combination of the consolidated balance sheets.

AU Section 9543

Part of Audit Performed by Other Independent Auditors: Auditing Interpretations of Section 543

1. Specific Procedures Performed by the Other Auditor at the Principal Auditor's Request

.01 *Question*—An independent auditor is auditing the financial statements of a component[1] in accordance with generally accepted auditing standards and is issuing a report to his client that will also be used by another independent auditor who is acting as a principal auditor.[2] The principal auditor requests the other auditor to perform specific procedures, for example, to furnish or test amounts to be eliminated in consolidation, such as intercompany profits, or to read other information in documents containing audited financial statements. In those circumstances, who is responsible to determine the extent of the procedures to be performed?

.02 *Interpretation*—Section 543, *Part of Audit Performed by Other Independent Auditors*, paragraph .10, states that the principal auditor "should adopt appropriate measures to assure the coordination of his activities with those of the other auditor in order to achieve a proper review of matters affecting the consolidating or combining of accounts in the financial statements." Section 543.10*c*(iv) further states that those measures may include procedures such as ascertaining through communication with the other auditor "that a review will be made of matters affecting elimination of intercompany transactions and accounts."

.03 Thus, when the principal auditor requests the other auditor to perform procedures, the principal auditor is responsible for determining the extent of the procedures to be performed. The principal auditor should provide specific instructions on procedures to be performed, materiality considerations for that purpose, and other information that may be necessary in the circumstances. The other auditor should perform the requested procedures in accordance with the principal auditor's instructions and report the findings solely for the use of the principal auditor.

[Issue Date: April, 1979; Revised: November 1996.]

2. Inquiries of the Principal Auditor by the Other Auditor

.04 *Question*—Section 543, *Part of Audit Performed by Other Independent Auditors*, gives guidance to a principal auditor on making inquiries of the other auditor. Section 543.03 also states that "the other auditor remains responsible for the performance of his own work and for his own report." Should the other auditor also make inquiries of the principal auditor to fulfill that responsibility?

---

[1] For the purposes of this interpretation, the entities whose separate financial statements collectively comprise the consolidated or other financial statements are referred to as components.

[2] See section 543 for the definition of a principal auditor. For the purposes of this interpretation, the auditor whose work is used by a principal auditor is referred to as the other auditor.

.05 *Interpretation*—Section 334, *Related Parties*, states that there may be inquiry of the principal auditor regarding related parties. In addition, before issuing his report, the other auditor should consider whether he should inquire of the principal auditor as to matters that may be significant to his own audit.

.06 The other auditor's consideration of whether to make the inquiry should be based on factors such as his awareness that there are transactions or relationships which are unusual or complex between the component he is auditing and the component the principal auditor is auditing, or his knowledge that in the past matters relating to his audit have arisen that were known to the principal auditor but not to him.

.07 If the other auditor believes inquiry is appropriate he may furnish the principal auditor with a draft of the financial statements expected to be issued and of his report solely for the purpose of aiding the principal auditor to respond to the inquiry. The inquiry would concern transactions, adjustments, or other matters that have come to the principal auditor's attention that he believes require adjustment to or disclosure in the financial statements of the component being audited by the other auditor. Also, the other auditor should inquire about any relevant limitation on the scope of the audit performed by the principal auditor.

[Issue Date: April, 1979.]

3. Form of Inquiries of the Principal Auditor Made by the Other Auditor

.08 *Question*—In those circumstances when the other auditor believes an inquiry of the principal auditor is appropriate, what form should the inquiry take and when should it be made?

.09 *Interpretation*—The other auditor's inquiry ordinarily should be in writing. It should indicate whether the response should be in writing, and should specify the date as of which the principal auditor should respond. Ordinarily, that date should be near the anticipated date of the other auditor's report. An example of a written inquiry from the other auditor is as follows:

> "We are auditing the financial statements of (name of client) as of (date) and for the (period of audit) for the purpose of expressing an opinion as to whether the financial statements present fairly, in all material respects, the financial position, results of operations, and cash flows of (name of client) in conformity with generally accepted accounting principles.
>
> A draft of the financial statements referred to above and a draft of our report are enclosed solely to aid you in responding to this inquiry. Please provide us (in writing) (orally) with the following information in connection with your current examination of the consolidated financial statements of (name of parent company):
>
> 1. Transactions or other matters (including adjustments made during consolidation or contemplated at the date of your reply) that have come to your attention that you believe require adjustment to or disclosure in the financial statements of (name of client) being audited by us.
>
> 2. Any limitation on the scope of your audit that is related to the financial statements of (name of client) being audited by us, or that limits your ability to provide us with the information requested in this inquiry.

Please make your response as of a date near (expected date of the other auditor's report)."

.10 The principal auditor's reply will often be made as of a date when his audit is still in progress; however, the other auditor should expect that ordinarily the response should satisfy his need for information. However, there may be instances when the principal auditor's response explains that it is limited because his audit has not progressed to a point that enables him to provide a response that satisfies the other auditor's need for information. If the principal auditor's response is limited in that manner, the other auditor should consider whether to apply acceptable alternative procedures, delay the issuance of his report until the principal auditor can respond, or qualify his opinion or disclaim an opinion for a limitation on the scope of his audit.

[Issue Date: April, 1979]

4. Form of Principal Auditor's Response to Inquiries from Other Auditors

.11 *Question*—An independent auditor acting in the capacity of a principal auditor may receive an inquiry from another independent auditor performing the audit of the financial statements of a component concerning transactions, adjustments, or limitations on his audit.[3] What should be the form of the principal auditor's response?

.12 *Interpretation*—The principal auditor should respond promptly to the other auditor's inquiry, based on his audit, and if applicable, on his reading of the draft financial statements and report furnished by the other auditor. His response may be written or oral, as requested by the other auditor. However, the principal auditor's response ordinarily should be in writing if it contains information that may have a significant effect on the other auditor's audit.

.13 The principal auditor should identify the stage of completion of his audit as of the date of his reply. He should also indicate that no audit procedures were performed for the purpose of identifying matters that would not affect his audit and report, and therefore, not all the information requested would necessarily be revealed. If the principal auditor has been furnished with a draft of the financial statements being audited by the other auditor and a draft of his report, the principal auditor should state that he has read the draft only to aid him in making his reply.

.14 An example of a written response from the principal auditor is as follows:

"This letter is furnished to you in response to your request that we provide you with certain information in connection with your audit of the financial statements of (name of component), a (subsidiary, division, branch or investment) of Parent Company for the year ended (date).

We are in the process of performing an audit of the consolidated financial statements of Parent Company for the year ended (date) (but have not completed our work as of this date). The objective of our audit is to enable us to express an opinion on the consolidated financial statements of Parent Company and, accordingly, we have performed no procedures directed toward identifying matters that would not affect our audit or our report. However, solely for the purpose of responding to your inquiry, we have read the draft of the financial statements of (name of component) as of (date) and for the (period of audit) and the draft of your report on them, included with your inquiry dated (date of inquiry).

---

[3] See section 9543.04-.07, "Inquiries of the Principal Auditor by the Other Auditor," above.

Based solely on the work we have performed (to date) in connection with our audit of the consolidated financial statements, which would not necessarily reveal all or any of the matters covered in your inquiry, we advise you that:

1. No transactions or other matters (including adjustments made during consolidation or contemplated at this date) have come to our attention that we believe require adjustment to or disclosure in the financial statements of (name of component) being audited by you.

2. No limitation has been placed by Parent Company on the scope of our audit that, to our knowledge, is related to the financial statements of (name of component) being audited by you, that has limited our ability to provide you with the information requested in your inquiry."

[Issue Date: April, 1979.]

5. Procedures of the Principal Auditor

.15 *Question*—What steps, if any, should the principal auditor take in responding to an inquiry such as that described in section 9543.11?

.16 *Interpretation*—The principal auditor's response should ordinarily be made by the auditor with final responsibility for the engagement. He should take those steps that he considers reasonable under the circumstances to be informed of known matters pertinent to the other auditor's inquiry. For example, the auditor with final responsibility may inquire of principal assistants[4] responsible for various aspects of the engagement or he may direct assistants to bring to his attention any significant matters of which they become aware during the audit. The principal auditor is not required to perform any procedures directed toward identifying matters that would not affect his audit or his report.

.17 If between the date of his response and the completion of his audit, the principal auditor becomes aware of information that he would have included in his response to the other auditor's inquiry had he been aware of it, the principal auditor should promptly communicate such information to the other auditor.[5]

[Issue Date: April, 1979.]

6. Application of Additional Procedures Concerning the Audit Performed by the Other Auditor

.18 *Question*—If a principal auditor decides not to make reference to the audit of another auditor, section 543 requires him to consider whether to apply procedures to obtain information about the adequacy of the audit performed by the other auditor. In making a decision about (*a*) whether to apply one or more of the procedures listed in section 543.12 and (*b*), if applicable, the extent of those procedures, may the principal auditor consider his knowledge of the other auditor's compliance with quality control policies and procedures?

.19 *Interpretation*—Yes. The principal auditor's judgment about the extent of additional procedures, if any, to be applied in the circumstances may be affected by various factors including his knowledge of the other auditor's quality

---

[4] See section 311, *Planning and Supervision*, for the definition of "assistants."

[5] See section 561, *Subsequent Discovery of Facts Existing at the Date of the Auditor's Report*, concerning procedures to be followed by the other auditor if he receives the information after the issuance of his report.

control policies and procedures that provide the other auditor with reasonable assurance of conformity with generally accepted auditing standards in his audit engagements.

.20 Other factors that the principal auditor may wish to consider in making that decision include his previous experience with the other auditor, the materiality of the portion of the financial statements audited by the other auditor, the control exercised by the principal auditor over the conduct of the audit performed by the other auditor, and the results of the principal auditor's other procedures that may indicate whether additional audit evidence is necessary.

[Issue Date: December, 1981; Revised: March, 2006.]

[7.] Reporting on Financial Statements Presented on a Comprehensive Annual Financial Report of a Governmental Entity When One Fund Has Been Audited by Another Auditor

[.21–.24] [Withdrawn December, 1992 by the Audit Issues Task Force.][6-7]

[6-7] [Footnotes deleted.]

AU Section 544

Lack of Conformity With Generally Accepted Accounting Principles

Source: SAS No. 1, section 544; SAS No. 2; SAS No. 62; SAS No. 77.

Issue date, unless otherwise indicated: November, 1972.

[.01] [Superseded by Statement on Auditing Standards No. 2, effective December 31, 1974.]

Regulated Companies

.02 The basic postulates and broad principles of accounting comprehended in the term "generally accepted accounting principles" which pertain to business enterprises in general apply also to companies whose accounting practices are prescribed by governmental regulatory authorities or commissions. (For example, public utilities and insurance companies.) Accordingly, the first reporting standard is equally applicable to opinions on financial statements of such regulated companies presented for purposes other than filings with their respective supervisory agencies; and material variances from generally accepted accounting principles, and their effects, should be dealt with in the independent auditor's report in the same manner followed for companies which are not regulated.[1] Ordinarily, this will require either a qualified or an adverse opinion on such statements. An adverse opinion may be accompanied by an opinion on supplementary data which are presented in conformity with generally accepted accounting principles. [As amended, effective periods ending on or after December 31, 1974, by Statement on Auditing Standards No. 2. As amended by Statement on Auditing Standards No. 62, effective for reports issued on or after July 1, 1989.]

.03 It should be recognized, however, that appropriate differences exist with respect to the application of generally accepted accounting principles as between regulated and nonregulated businesses because of the effect in regulated businesses of the rate-making process, a phenomenon not present in nonregulated businesses (Financial Accounting Standards Board *Accounting Standards Codification* 980, *Regulated Operations*). Such differences usually concern mainly the time at which various items enter into the determination of net income in accordance with the principle of matching costs and revenues. It should also be recognized that accounting requirements not directly related to the rate-making process commonly are imposed on regulated businesses and

---

[1] When reporting on financial statements of a regulated entity that are prepared in accordance with the requirements of financial reporting provisions of a government regulatory agency to whose jurisdiction the entity is subject, the auditor may report on the financial statements as being prepared in accordance with a comprehensive basis of accounting other than generally accepted accounting principles (see section 623, *Special Reports* paragraphs .02 and .10). Reports of this nature, however, should be issued only if the financial statements are intended solely for filing with one or more regulatory agencies to whose jurisdiction the entity is subject. [As amended, effective for audits of financial statements for periods ended on or after December 31, 1996, by Statement on Auditing Standards No. 77.]

that the imposition of such accounting requirements does not necessarily mean that they conform with generally accepted accounting principles. [Revised, June 2009, to reflect conforming changes necessary due to the issuance of FASB ASC.]

.04 When financial statements of a regulated entity are prepared in accordance with a basis of accounting prescribed by one or more regulatory agencies or the financial reporting provisions of another agency, the independent auditor may also be requested to report on their fair presentation in conformity with such prescribed basis of accounting in presentations for distribution in other than filings with the entity's regulatory agency. In those circumstances, the auditor should use the standard form of report (see section 508, *Reports on Audited Financial Statements*, paragraph .08), modified as appropriate (see paragraphs .35–.60 of section 508) because of the departures from generally accepted accounting principles, and then, in an additional paragraph to the report, express an opinion on whether the financial statements are presented in conformity with the prescribed basis of accounting. [As amended by Statement on Auditing Standards No. 62, effective for reports issued on or after July 1, 1989. As amended, effective for audits of financial statements for periods ended on or after December 31, 1996, by Statement on Auditing Standards No. 77.]

AU Section 9544

Lack of Conformity With Generally Accepted Accounting Principles: Auditing Interpretations of Section 544

[1.] Auditors' Reports Solely for Purposes of Filing With Insurance Regulatory Agencies

[.01–.09] [Superseded October, 1979.]

[2.] Reports on Filings Other Than With the Regulatory Agency on Financial Statements Prepared Using FHLBB Accounting Practices—Savings and Loan Associations

[.10–.14] [Withdrawn March, 1989.]

AU Section 550

Other Information in Documents Containing Audited Financial Statements

(Supersedes SAS Nos. 8 and 29 and portions of SAS Nos. 52 and 98.)

Source: SAS No. 118.

Effective for audits of financial statements for periods beginning on or after December 15, 2010. Early application is permitted.

Introduction

Scope of This Section

.01 This section addresses the auditor's responsibility in relation to other information in documents containing audited financial statements and the auditor's report thereon. In the absence of any separate requirement in the particular circumstances of the engagement, the auditor's opinion on the financial statements does not cover other information, and the auditor has no responsibility for determining whether such information is properly stated. This section establishes the requirement for the auditor to read the other information of which the auditor is aware because the credibility of the audited financial statements may be undermined by material inconsistencies between the audited financial statements and other information. (Ref: par. .A1–.A2)

.02 In this section, *documents containing audited financial statements* refers to annual reports (or similar documents) that are issued to owners (or similar stakeholders) and annual reports of governments and organizations for charitable or philanthropic purposes that are available to the public that contain audited financial statements and the auditor's report thereon. This section also may be applied, adapted as necessary in the circumstances, to other documents to which the auditor, at management's request, devotes attention. (Ref: par. .A3–.A5)

Effective Date

.03 This section is effective for audits of financial statements for periods beginning on or after December 15, 2010. Early application is permitted.

Objective

.04 The objective of the auditor is to respond appropriately when the auditor becomes aware that documents containing audited financial statements and the auditor's report thereon include other information that could undermine the credibility of those financial statements and the auditor's report.

Definitions

.05 For purposes of generally accepted auditing standards (GAAS), the following terms have the meanings attributed as follows:

Other information. Financial and nonfinancial information (other than the financial statements and the auditor's report thereon) that is included in a document containing audited financial statements and the auditor's report thereon, excluding required supplementary information.[1]

Inconsistency. Other information that conflicts with information contained in the audited financial statements. A material inconsistency may raise doubt about the audit conclusions drawn from audit evidence previously obtained and, possibly, about the basis for the auditor's opinion on the financial statements.

Misstatement of fact. Other information that is unrelated to matters appearing in the audited financial statements that is incorrectly stated or presented. A material misstatement of fact may undermine the credibility of the document containing audited financial statements.

Requirements

Reading Other Information

.06 The auditor should read the other information of which the auditor is aware in order to identify material inconsistencies, if any, with the audited financial statements.

.07 The auditor should make appropriate arrangements with management or those charged with governance to obtain the other information prior to the report release date.[2] If it is not possible to obtain all of the other information prior to the report release date, the auditor should read such other information as soon as practicable. (Ref: par. .A6)

.08 The auditor should communicate with those charged with governance the auditor's responsibility with respect to the other information, any procedures performed relating to the other information, and the results.

Material Inconsistencies

.09 If, on reading the other information, the auditor identifies a material inconsistency, the auditor should determine whether the audited financial statements or the other information needs to be revised.

Material Inconsistencies Identified in Other Information Obtained Prior to the Report Release Date

.10 When the auditor identifies a material inconsistency prior to the report release date that requires revision of the audited financial statements and management refuses to make the revision, the auditor should modify the auditor's opinion in accordance with section 508, *Reports on Audited Financial Statements*.

.11 When the auditor identifies a material inconsistency prior to the report release date that requires revision of the other information and management refuses to make the revision, the auditor should communicate this matter to those charged with governance and

---

[1] *Required supplementary information* is defined in paragraph .04 of section 558, *Required Supplementary Information*.

[2] See paragraph .23 of section 339, *Audit Documentation*, for the definition of *report release date*.

a. include in the auditor's report an explanatory paragraph describing the material inconsistency, in accordance with paragraph .11 of section 508;

b. withhold the auditor's report; or

c. when withdrawal is possible under applicable law or regulation, withdraw from the engagement.

(Ref: par. .A7–.A8)

Material Inconsistencies Identified in Other Information Obtained Subsequent to the Report Release Date

.12 When revision of the audited financial statements is necessary as a result of a material inconsistency with other information and the auditor's report on the financial statements has already been released, the auditor should apply the relevant requirements in section 561, *Subsequent Discovery of Facts Existing at the Date of the Auditor's Report*.

.13 When revision of the other information is necessary after the report release date and management agrees to make the revision, the auditor should carry out the procedures necessary under the circumstances. (Ref: par. .A9)

.14 When revision of the other information is necessary after the report release date but management refuses to make the revision, the auditor should notify those charged with governance of the auditor's concerns regarding the other information and take any further appropriate action. (Ref: par. .A10)

Material Misstatements of Fact

.15 If, on reading the other information for the purpose of identifying material inconsistencies, the auditor becomes aware of an apparent material misstatement of fact, the auditor should discuss the matter with management. (Ref: par. .A11)

.16 When, following such discussions, the auditor still considers that there is an apparent material misstatement of fact, the auditor should request management to consult with a qualified third party, such as the entity's legal counsel, and the auditor should consider the advice received by the entity in determining whether such matter is a material misstatement of fact.

.17 When the auditor concludes that there is a material misstatement of fact in the other information that management refuses to correct, the auditor should notify those charged with governance of the auditor's concerns regarding the other information and take any further appropriate action. (Ref: par. .A12)

Application and Other Explanatory Material

Scope of This Section (Ref: par. .01–.02)

.A1 This section also addresses other information for which a designated accounting standard setter[3] has issued standards or guidance regarding the format to be used and content to be included when such information is voluntarily presented in a document containing the audited financial statements and the auditor's report thereon. The auditor's responsibility for other information presented in a document containing audited financial statements that is required to be included by a designated accounting standard setter is addressed in section 558, *Required Supplementary Information*.

.A2 The auditor is not required to reference the other information in the auditor's report on the financial statements. However, the auditor may include an explanatory paragraph disclaiming an opinion on the other information. For example, an auditor may choose to include a disclaimer on the other information when the auditor believes that the auditor could be associated with the information and the user may infer a level of assurance that is not intended. Exhibit A, "Example of an Explanatory Paragraph to Disclaim an Opinion on Other Information," has an example of how an auditor may word such a disclaimer of opinion on other information.

.A3 Other information may comprise the following:

- A report by management or those charged with governance on operations
- Financial summaries or highlights
- Employment data
- Planned capital expenditures
- Financial ratios
- Names of officers and directors
- Selected quarterly data

.A4 For purposes of GAAS, other information does not encompass, for example, the following:

- A press release or similar memorandum or cover letter accompanying the document containing audited financial statements and the auditor's report thereon
- Information contained in analyst briefings
- Information contained on the entity's website

Considerations Specific to Governmental Entities (Ref: par. .02)

.A5 The term *annual reports of governments* is intended to include comprehensive annual reports or other annual financial reports that include the government's financial statements and the auditor's report thereon.

---

[3] *Designated accounting standard setter* is defined in paragraph .04 of section 558.

Reading Other Information (Ref: par. .07)

.A6 Obtaining the other information prior to the report release date enables the auditor to resolve possible material inconsistencies and apparent material misstatements of fact with management on a timely basis. An agreement with management regarding when other information will be available may be helpful. The auditor may delay the release of the auditor's report until management provides the other information to the auditor.

Material Inconsistencies

Material Inconsistencies Identified in Other Information Obtained Prior to the Report Release Date (Ref: par. .11)

.A7 When management refuses to revise the other information, the auditor may base any decision on what further action to take on advice from the auditor's legal counsel.

Considerations Specific to Governmental Entities (Ref: par. .11)

.A8 In audits of governmental entities, withdrawal from the engagement or withholding the auditor's report may not be options. In such cases, the auditor may issue a report to those charged with governance and the appropriate statutory body, if applicable, giving details of the inconsistency.

Material Inconsistencies Identified in Other Information Obtained Subsequent to the Report Release Date (Ref: par. .13–.14)

.A9 When revision of other information is necessary after the report release date and management agrees to make the revision, the auditor's procedures may include reviewing the steps taken by management to ensure that individuals in receipt of the previously issued financial statements, the auditor's report thereon, and the other information are informed of the need for revision.

.A10 When revision of other information is necessary after the report release date but management refuses to make the revision, appropriate further actions by the auditor may include obtaining advice from the auditor's legal counsel.

Material Misstatements of Fact (Ref: par. .15–.17)

.A11 When discussing an apparent material misstatement of fact with management, the auditor may not be able to evaluate the validity of some disclosures included within the other information and management's responses to the auditor's inquiries and may conclude that valid differences of judgment or opinion exist.

.A12 When the auditor concludes that there is a material misstatement of fact that management refuses to correct, appropriate further actions by the auditor may include obtaining advice from the auditor's legal counsel, withholding the auditor's report if such report has not been released, or withdrawing from the engagement.

.A13

Exhibit A: Example of an Explanatory Paragraph to Disclaim an Opinion on Other Information

The following is an example of an explanatory paragraph that the auditor may use to disclaim an opinion on other information:

> Our audit was conducted for the purpose of forming an opinion on the basic financial statements as a whole. The [*identify the other information*] is presented for purposes of additional analysis and is not a required part of the basic financial statements. Such information has not been subjected to the auditing procedures applied in the audit of the basic financial statements, and accordingly, we do not express an opinion or provide any assurance on it.

.A14

Exhibit B: Comparison of Section 550, *Other Information in Documents Containing Audited Financial Statements*, With International Standard on Auditing 720, *The Auditor's Responsibility in Relation to Other Information in Documents Containing Audited Financial Statements*

This analysis was prepared by the Audit and Attest Standards staff to highlight substantive differences between section 550, *Other Information in Documents Containing Audited Financial Statements*, and International Standard on Auditing (ISA) 720, *The Auditor's Responsibility in Relation to Other Information in Documents Containing Audited Financial Statements*, and the rationale therefore. This analysis is not authoritative and is prepared for informational purposes only. It has not been acted on or reviewed by the Auditing Standards Board (ASB).

This section clarifies that the auditor's objective is to respond appropriately (in paragraph .04), and the requirement is to read the other information (in paragraph .06) when the auditor becomes aware that documents containing audited financial statements and the auditor's report thereon include other information that could undermine the credibility of those financial statements and the auditor's report. The objective in ISA 720 and the corresponding requirement are not specifically limited to documents of which the auditor is aware. However, the ISA states that *documents containing audited financial statements* refers to annual reports (or similar documents) that are issued to owners (or similar stakeholders) containing audited financial statements and the auditor's report thereon. The ISA further states that it may be applied, adapted as necessary in the circumstances, to other documents containing audited financial statements. The ASB believes that the language added to this section limiting the auditor's responsibilities clarifies the intent of the objective and the requirement in the ISA and is appropriate in the U.S. legal environment.

This section applies the requirements in paragraphs .07 and .10–.14 to the report release date, but ISA 720 applies the corresponding requirements to the date of the auditor's report. The ASB determined that the report release date, as defined in auditing standards generally accepted in the United States, is more appropriate in the U.S. environment.

The ASB has made various changes to the language throughout this section, in comparison with ISA 720. The changes to this section include the following:

- In paragraph .01, clarifying that *auditor's opinion* is the opinion on the financial statements.
- In paragraph .02, adding clarifying language that documents containing audited financial statements refer to "annual reports of governments and organizations for charitable or philanthropic purposes that are available to the public" and that this section also applies to "other documents to which the auditor, at management's request, devotes attention."

- In paragraph .05
  - — deleting the phrase *either by law, regulation or custom* from the definition of *other information* to avoid confusion with required supplementary information.
  - — replacing *contradicts* with *conflicts with* to better define the term *inconsistency*.
- In paragraph .11, adding the word *explanatory* to clarify the report modification.
- In paragraph .16, adding the wording "by the entity in determining whether such matter is a material misstatement of fact" to clarify that the advice is received by the entity.

Such changes have been made to make this section easier to read and apply. The ASB believes that such changes will not create differences between the application of ISA 720 and the application of this section.

AU Section 551

Supplementary Information in Relation to the Financial Statements as a Whole

(With SAS No. 118, supersedes former section 551, *Reporting on Information Accompanying the Basic Financial Statements in Auditor-Submitted Documents.*)

Source: SAS No. 119.

Effective for audits of financial statements for periods beginning on or after December 15, 2010. Early application is permitted.

Introduction

Scope of This Section

.01 This section addresses the auditor's responsibility when engaged to report on whether supplementary information is fairly stated, in all material respects, in relation to the financial statements as a whole. The information covered by this section is presented outside the basic financial statements and is not considered necessary for the financial statements to be fairly presented in accordance with the applicable financial reporting framework. This section also may be applied, with the report wording adapted as necessary, when an auditor has been engaged to report on whether required supplementary information [1] is fairly stated, in all material respects, in relation to the financial statements as a whole. (Ref: par. .A1–.A6)

Effective Date

.02 This section is effective for audits of financial statements for periods beginning on or after December 15, 2010. Early application is permitted.

Objective

.03 The objective of the auditor, when engaged to report on supplementary information in relation to the financial statements as a whole, is

a. to evaluate the presentation of the supplementary information in relation to the financial statements as a whole and

b. to report on whether the supplementary information is fairly stated, in all material respects, in relation to the financial statements as a whole.

Definition

.04 For purposes of generally accepted auditing standards, *supplementary information* is defined as information presented outside the basic financial

---

[1] *Required supplementary information* is defined in paragraph .04 of section 558, *Required Supplementary Information.*

statements, excluding required supplementary information that is not considered necessary for the financial statements to be fairly presented in accordance with the applicable financial reporting framework. Such information may be presented in a document containing the audited financial statements or separate from the financial statements. (Ref: par. .A7–.A8)

Requirements

Procedures to Determine Whether Supplementary Information Is Fairly Stated, in All Material Respects, in Relation to the Financial Statements as a Whole (Ref: par. .A9–.A15)

.05 In order to opine on whether supplementary information is fairly stated, in all material respects, in relation to the financial statements as a whole, the auditor should determine that all of the following conditions are met:

a. The supplementary information was derived from, and relates directly to, the underlying accounting and other records used to prepare the financial statements.

b. The supplementary information relates to the same period as the financial statements.

c. The financial statements were audited, and the auditor served as the principal auditor in that engagement.

d. Neither an adverse opinion nor a disclaimer of opinion was issued on the financial statements. (Paragraph .11 addresses reporting while not opining on supplementary information when the report on the financial statements contains an adverse opinion or a disclaimer of opinion.)

e. The supplementary information will accompany the entity's audited financial statements, or such audited financial statements will be made readily available by the entity. (Ref: par. .A9)

.06 The auditor should obtain the agreement of management that it acknowledges and understands its responsibility

a. for the preparation of the supplementary information in accordance with the applicable criteria.

b. to provide the auditor with the written representations described in paragraph .07(g).

c. to include the auditor's report on the supplementary information in any document that contains the supplementary information and that indicates that the auditor has reported on such supplementary information.

d. to present the supplementary information with the audited financial statements or, if the supplementary information will not be presented with the audited financial statements, to make the audited financial statements readily available to the intended users of the supplementary information no later than the date of issuance by the entity of the supplementary information and the auditor's report thereon. (Ref: par. .A9)

.07 In addition to the procedures performed during the audit of the financial statements, in order to opine on whether supplementary information is fairly stated, in all material respects, in relation to the financial statements as a whole, the auditor should perform the following procedures using the same materiality level used in the audit of the financial statements:

a. Inquire of management about the purpose of the supplementary information and the criteria used by management to prepare the supplementary information, such as an applicable financial reporting framework, criteria established by a regulator, a contractual agreement, or other requirements

b. Determine whether the form and content of the supplementary information complies with the applicable criteria

c. Obtain an understanding about the methods of preparing the supplementary information and determine whether the methods of preparing the supplementary information have changed from those used in the prior period and, if the methods have changed, the reasons for such changes

d. Compare and reconcile the supplementary information to the underlying accounting and other records used in preparing the financial statements or to the financial statements themselves

e. Inquire of management about any significant assumptions or interpretations underlying the measurement or presentation of the supplementary information

f. Evaluate the appropriateness and completeness of the supplementary information, considering the results of the procedures performed and other knowledge obtained during the audit of the financial statements (Ref: par. .A13)

g. Obtain written representations from management

i. that it acknowledges its responsibility for the presentation of the supplementary information in accordance with the applicable criteria;

ii. that it believes the supplementary information, including its form and content, is fairly presented in accordance with the applicable criteria;

iii. that the methods of measurement or presentation have not changed from those used in the prior period or, if the methods of measurement or presentation have changed, the reasons for such changes;

iv. about any significant assumptions or interpretations underlying the measurement or presentation of the supplementary information; and

v. that when the supplementary information is not presented with the audited financial statements, management will make the audited financial statements readily available to the intended users of the supplementary information no later than the date of issuance by the entity of the supplementary information and the auditor's report thereon. (Ref: par. .A9)

.08 The auditor has no responsibility for the consideration of subsequent events with respect to the supplementary information. However, if information comes to the auditor's attention prior to the release of the auditor's report on the financial statements regarding subsequent events that affect the financial statements, the auditor should apply the relevant requirements in section 560, *Subsequent Events*. If information comes to the auditor's attention subsequent to the release of the auditor's report on the financial statements regarding facts that may have existed at that date, which might have affected the report had the auditor been aware of such facts, the auditor should apply the relevant requirements in section 561, *Subsequent Discovery of Facts Existing at the Date of the Auditor's Report*.

Reporting

.09 When the entity presents the supplementary information with the financial statements, the auditor should report on the supplementary information in either (1) an explanatory paragraph following the opinion paragraph in the auditor's report on the financial statements or (2) in a separate report on the supplementary information. The explanatory paragraph or separate report should include the following elements:

a. A statement that the audit was conducted for the purpose of forming an opinion on the financial statements as a whole

b. A statement that the supplementary information is presented for purposes of additional analysis and is not a required part of the financial statements

c. A statement that the supplementary information is the responsibility of management and was derived from, and relates directly to, the underlying accounting and other records used to prepare the financial statements

d. A statement that the supplementary information has been subjected to the auditing procedures applied in the audit of the financial statements and certain additional procedures, including comparing and reconciling such information directly to the underlying accounting and other records used to prepare the financial statements or to the financial statements themselves and other additional procedures, in accordance with auditing standards generally accepted in the United States of America

e. If the auditor issues an unqualified opinion on the financial statements and the auditor has concluded that the supplementary information is fairly stated, in all material respects, in relation to the financial statements as a whole, a statement that, in the auditor's opinion, the supplementary information is fairly stated, in all material respects, in relation to the financial statements as a whole

f. If the auditor issues a qualified opinion on the financial statements and the qualification has an effect on the supplementary information, a statement that, in the auditor's opinion, except for the effects on the supplementary information of (refer to the paragraph in the auditor's report explaining the qualification), such information is fairly stated, in all material respects, in relation to the financial statements as a whole

.10 When the audited financial statements are not presented with the supplementary information, the auditor should report on the supplementary information in a separate report. When reporting separately on the supplementary information, the report should include, in addition to the elements in paragraph .09, a reference to the report on the financial statements, the date of that report, the nature of the opinion expressed on the financial statements, and any report modifications. (Ref: par. .A16)

.11 When the auditor's report on the audited financial statements contains an adverse opinion or a disclaimer of opinion and the auditor has been engaged to report on whether supplementary information is fairly stated, in all material respects, in relation to such financial statements as a whole, the auditor is precluded from expressing an opinion on the supplementary information. When permitted by law or regulation, the auditor may withdraw from the engagement to report on the supplementary information. If the auditor does not withdraw, the auditor's report on the supplementary information should state that because of the significance of the matter disclosed in the auditor's report, it is inappropriate to, and the auditor does not, express an opinion on the supplementary information.

.12 The date of the auditor's report on the supplementary information in relation to the financial statements as a whole should not be earlier than the date on which the auditor completed the procedures required in paragraph .07.

.13 If the auditor concludes, on the basis of the procedures performed, that the supplementary information is materially misstated in relation to the financial statements as a whole, the auditor should discuss the matter with management and propose appropriate revision of the supplementary information. If management does not revise the supplementary information, the auditor should either

a. modify the auditor's opinion on the supplementary information and describe the misstatement in the auditor's report or

b. if a separate report is being issued on the supplementary information, withhold the auditor's report on the supplementary information.

Application and Other Explanatory Material

Scope of This Section (Ref: par. .01)

.A1 The auditor's responsibility for information that a designated accounting standard setter[2] requires to accompany an entity's basic financial statements is addressed in section 558, *Required Supplementary Information*.

.A2 The auditor's responsibility for financial and nonfinancial information (other than the financial statements and the auditor's report thereon) that is included in a document containing audited financial statements and the auditor's report thereon, excluding required supplementary information, is addressed in section 550, *Other Information in Documents Containing Audited Financial Statements*.

.A3 The supplementary information need not be presented with the audited financial statements in order for the auditor to express an opinion on whether such supplementary information is fairly stated, in all material respects, in relation to the financial statements as a whole. However, in accordance with paragraph .10, if the supplementary information is not presented with the audited financial statements, the auditor's report on the supplementary information is required to make reference to the auditor's report on the financial statements.

.A4 The auditor may be engaged to express an opinion on specified elements, accounts, or items of financial statements for the purpose of a separate presentation, in accordance with paragraphs .11–.18 of section 623, *Special Reports*. In such an engagement, the auditor's procedures are designed to provide the auditor with reasonable assurance that the supplementary information is not misstated by an amount that would be material to the information itself. An engagement to examine the supplementary information or an assertion related to the supplementary information also may be performed in accordance with AT section 101, *Attest Engagements*.

.A5 Although an auditor has no obligation to apply auditing procedures to supplementary information presented outside the basic financial statements, the auditor may choose to modify or redirect certain of the procedures to be applied in the audit of the basic financial statements so that the auditor may express an opinion on the supplementary information in relation to the financial statements as a whole.

.A6 Management may include nonaccounting information and accounting information that is not directly related to the basic financial statements in a document containing the basic financial statements. Ordinarily, such information would not have been subjected to the auditing procedures applied in the audit of the basic financial statements, and accordingly, the auditor would be unable to opine on the information in relation to the financial statements as a whole. In some circumstances, however, such information may have been obtained or derived from accounting records that have been tested by the auditor (for example, number of units produced related to royalties under a license agreement or number of employees related to a given payroll period). Accordingly, the auditor may be in a position to express an opinion on such information in relation to the financial statements as a whole.

---

[2] *Designated accounting standard setter* is defined in paragraph .04 of section 558.

Definitions (Ref: par. .04)

.A7 Supplementary information includes additional details or explanations of items in or related to the basic financial statements, consolidating information, historical summaries of items extracted from the basic financial statements, statistical data, and other material, some of which may be from sources outside the accounting system or outside the entity.

.A8 Supplementary information may be prepared in accordance with an applicable financial reporting framework, by regulatory or contractual requirements, in accordance with management's criteria, or in accordance with other requirements.

Procedures to Determine Whether Supplementary Information Is Fairly Stated, in All Material Respects, in Relation to the Financial Statements as a Whole (Ref: par. .05–.08)

The Meaning of Readily Available (Ref: par. .05(e), .06(d), and .07(f))

.A9 Audited financial statements are deemed to be readily available if a third party user can obtain the audited financial statements without any further action by the entity. For example, financial statements on an entity's website may be considered readily available, but being available upon request is not considered readily available.

Procedures Performed on Supplementary Information (Ref: par. .07)

.A10 When engaged to report on supplementary information in relation to the financial statements as a whole, the auditor need not apply procedures as extensive as would be necessary to express an opinion on the information on a stand-alone basis.

.A11 With respect to the supplementary information, the auditor is not required to obtain a separate understanding of the entity's internal control or to assess fraud risk.

.A12 The auditor may consider materiality in determining which information to compare and reconcile to the underlying accounting and other records used in preparing the financial statements or to the financial statements themselves.

.A13 In evaluating the appropriateness and completeness of the supplementary information as required by paragraph 07(f), the auditor may consider testing accounting or other records through observation or examination of source documents or other procedures ordinarily performed in an audit of the financial statements.

.A14 The auditor may consider whether it is appropriate to address the supplementary information in procedures that the auditor performs in auditing the financial statements, including, but not limited to, the following:

a. Obtaining an updating representation letter, in accordance with section 333, *Management Representations*

b. Performing subsequent events procedures, in accordance with section 560 *c.* Sending a letter of audit inquiry to the client's lawyer specifically regarding the information contained in the supplementary information, in accordance with section 337, *Inquiry of a Client's Lawyer Concerning Litigation, Claims, and Assessments*

Considerations Specific to Audits of Governmental Entities

.A15 For most state and local governments, the auditor's report on the financial statements includes multiple opinions to address individual reporting units or aggregation of reporting units of the governmental entity. Accordingly, materiality is considered by the auditor for each opinion unit. However, in the context of this section, the auditor's opinion on the supplementary information is in relation to the financial statements as a whole. Accordingly, in this situation, materiality is considered at a level that represents the entire governmental entity.

Reporting (Ref: par. .09–.13)

.A16 The auditor may consider restricting the use of a separate report on supplementary information to the appropriate specified parties, in accordance with section 532, *Restricting the Use of an Auditor's Report*, to avoid potential misinterpretation or misunderstanding of the supplementary information that is not presented with the financial statements.

.A17

Exhibit: Illustrative Reporting Examples

The following is an example of an explanatory paragraph that the auditor may use when engaged to report on supplementary information in relation to the financial statements as a whole and the auditor is issuing an unqualified opinion on the financial statements and the auditor has concluded that the supplementary information is fairly stated, in all material respects, in relation to the financial statements as a whole:

> Our audit was conducted for the purpose of forming an opinion on the financial statements as a whole. The [*identify accompanying supplementary information*] is presented for purposes of additional analysis and is not a required part of the financial statements. Such information is the responsibility of management and was derived from and relates directly to the underlying accounting and other records used to prepare the financial statements. The information has been subjected to the auditing procedures applied in the audit of the financial statements and certain additional procedures, including comparing and reconciling such information directly to the underlying accounting and other records used to prepare the financial statements or to the financial statements themselves, and other additional procedures in accordance with auditing standards generally accepted in the United States of America. In our opinion, the information is fairly stated in all material respects in relation to the financial statements as a whole.

The following is an example of an explanatory paragraph that the auditor may use when engaged to report on supplementary information in relation to the financial statements as a whole and the auditor is issuing a qualified opinion on the financial statements and a qualified opinion on the supplementary information:

> Our audit was conducted for the purpose of forming an opinion on the financial statements as a whole. The [*identify accompanying supplementary information*] is presented for purposes of additional analysis and is not a required part of the financial statements. Such information is the responsibility of management and was derived from and relates directly to the underlying accounting and other records used to prepare the financial statements. The information has been subjected to the auditing procedures applied in the audit of the financial statements and certain additional procedures, including comparing and reconciling such information directly to the underlying accounting and other records used to prepare the financial statements or to the financial statements themselves, and other additional procedures in accordance with auditing standards generally accepted in the United States of America. In our opinion, except for the effect on the supplementary information of [*describe reason for qualification of the auditor's opinion on the financial statements and reference the explanatory paragraph*], the information is fairly stated in all material respects in relation to the financial statements as a whole.

The following is an example of an explanatory paragraph that the auditor may use when engaged to report on supplementary information in relation to the financial statements as a whole and the auditor is disclaiming an opinion on the financial statements:

> We were engaged for the purpose of forming an opinion on the basic financial statements as a whole. The [*identify accompanying supplementary information*] is presented for the purposes of additional analysis

> and is not a required part of the financial statements. Because of the significance of the matter described above [the auditor may describe the basis for the disclaimer of opinion], it is inappropriate to and we do not express an opinion on the supplementary information referred to above.

The following is an example of an explanatory paragraph that the auditor may use when engaged to report on supplementary information in relation to the financial statements as a whole and the auditor is issuing an adverse opinion on the financial statements:

> Our audit was conducted for the purpose of forming an opinion on the financial statements as a whole. The [*identify accompanying supplementary information*] is presented for the purposes of additional analysis and is not a required part of the financial statements. Because of the significance of the matter described above [the auditor may describe the basis for the adverse opinion], it is inappropriate to and we do not express an opinion on the supplementary information referred to above.

The following are reporting examples that the auditor may use when reporting separately on supplementary information in relation to the financial statements as a whole.

The following may be used when the auditor has issued an unqualified opinion on the financial statements and an unqualified opinion on the supplementary information:

> We have audited the financial statements of XYZ Entity as of and for the year ended June 30, 20X1, and have issued our report thereon dated [*date of the auditor's report on the financial statements*] which contained an unqualified opinion on those financial statements. Our audit was performed for the purpose of forming an opinion on the financial statements as a whole. The [*identify supplementary information*] is presented for the purposes of additional analysis and is not a required part of the financial statements. Such information is the responsibility of management and was derived from and relates directly to the underlying accounting and other records used to prepare the financial statements. The information has been subjected to the auditing procedures applied in the audit of the financial statements and certain additional procedures, including comparing and reconciling such information directly to the underlying accounting and other records used to prepare the financial statements or to the financial statements themselves, and other additional procedures in accordance with auditing standards generally accepted in the United States of America. In our opinion, the information is fairly stated in all material respects in relation to the financial statements as a whole.

The following may be used when the auditor has issued a qualified opinion on the financial statements and a qualified opinion on the supplementary information:

> We have audited the financial statements of XYZ Entity as of and for the year ended June 30, 20X1, and have issued our report thereon dated [*date of the auditor's report on the financial statements, the nature of the opinion expressed on the financial statements, and a description of the report modifications*]. Our audit was performed for the purpose of forming an opinion on the financial statements as a whole. The [*identify supplementary information*] is presented for the purposes of additional analysis and is not a required part of the financial statements. Such information is the responsibility of management

and was derived from and relates directly to the underlying accounting and other records used to prepare the financial statements. The information has been subjected to the auditing procedures applied in the audit of the financial statements and certain additional procedures, including comparing and reconciling such information directly to the underlying accounting and other records used to prepare the financial statements or to the financial statements themselves, and other additional procedures in accordance with auditing standards generally accepted in the United States of America. In our opinion, except for the effect on the accompanying information of the qualified opinion on the financial statements as described above, the information is fairly stated in all material respects in relation to the financial statements as a whole.

The following may be used when the auditor has disclaimed an opinion on the financial statements:

> We were engaged to audit the financial statements of XYZ Entity as of and for the year ended June 30, 20X1, and have issued our report thereon dated [*date of the auditor's report on the financial statements*]. However, the scope of our audit of the financial statements was not sufficient to enable us to express an opinion because [*describe reasons*] and accordingly we did not express an opinion on such financial statements. The [*identify the supplementary information*] is presented for purposes of additional analysis and is not a required part of the basic financial statements. Because of the significance of the matter discussed above, it is inappropriate to and we do not express an opinion on the supplementary information referred to above.

The following may be used when the auditor has issued an adverse opinion on the financial statements:

> We have audited the financial statements of XYZ Entity as of and for the year ended June 30, 20X1, and have issued our report thereon dated [*date of the auditor's report on the financial statements*] which stated that the financial statements are not presented fairly in accordance with [*identify the applicable financial reporting framework (for example, accounting principles generally accepted in the United States of America [GAAP])*] because [*describe reasons*]. The [*identify the supplementary information*] is presented for purposes of additional analysis and is not a required part of the basic financial statements. Because of the significance of the matter discussed above, it is inappropriate to and we do not express an opinion on the supplementary information referred to above.

AU Section 9551

Supplementary Information in Relation to the Financial Statements as a Whole: Auditing Interpretations of Section 551

1. Dating the Auditor's Report on Supplementary Information

.01 *Question*—In accordance with paragraph .12 of section 551, *Supplementary Information in Relation to the Financial Statements as a Whole*, the auditor's report on supplementary information should not be dated earlier than the date on which the auditor completed the procedures required by paragraph .07 of section 551. When the auditor completes those procedures subsequent to the date of the auditor's report on the audited financial statements, the auditor is not required to obtain additional evidence with respect to the audited financial statements. When reporting on the supplementary information (either in a separate report or in an explanatory paragraph within the auditor's report on the financial statements) after the date of the auditor's report on the financial statements, how may an auditor make it clear that no additional procedures were performed on the audited financial statements subsequent to the date of the auditor's report on those financial statements?

.02 *Interpretation*—Although not required, an auditor may

a. when issuing a separate report on the supplementary information, include in such report a statement that the auditor has not performed any auditing procedures with respect to the audited financial statements subsequent to the date of the auditor's report on those audited financial statements (see paragraph .03 of this interpretation), or

b. when reissuing a report on the audited financial statements to include an explanatory paragraph to report on the supplementary information, include two report dates to indicate that the date of reporting on the supplementary information is as of a later date (see paragraph .04 of this interpretation).

.03 The following illustrative separate report on supplementary information includes additional language intended to make it clear that no procedures were performed subsequent to the date of the auditor's report on the audited financial statements.

<u>Independent Auditor's Report on [*Identify Supplementary Information*]</u>

[*Appropriate Addressee*]

We have audited the financial statements of XYZ Entity as of and for the year ended June 30, 20X1, and have issued our report thereon dated [*date of the auditor's report on the financial statements, for example, "September 15, 20X1"*], which contained an unqualified opinion on those financial statements. Our audit was performed for the purpose of forming an opinion on the financial statements as a whole. *We have not performed any procedures with respect to the audited financial statements subsequent to* [*date of the auditor's report on the financial statements, for example, "September 15, 20X1"*].

The [*identify supplementary information*] is presented for the purposes of additional analysis and is not a required part of the financial statements. Such information is the responsibility of management and was derived from and relates directly to the underlying accounting and other records used to prepare the financial statements. The information has been subjected to the auditing procedures applied in the audit of the financial statements and certain additional procedures, including comparing and reconciling such information directly to the underlying accounting and other records used to prepare the financial statements or to the financial statements themselves, and other additional procedures in accordance with auditing standards generally accepted in the United States of America. In our opinion, the information is fairly stated in all material respects in relation to the financial statements as a whole.

[*Auditor's signature*]

[*Auditor's city and state*]

December 1, 20X1 [*Date of the auditor's report on the supplementary information—not to be earlier than the date on which the auditor completed the procedures required by paragraph .07 of section 551*]

.04 The following illustrative report on the audited financial statements includes an explanatory paragraph to report on supplementary information subsequent to the date of the report on the audited financial statements. For this illustration, March 31, 20X2, is the original date of the report on the audited financial statements.

Independent Auditor's Report

[*Appropriate Addressee*]

We have audited the accompanying consolidated balance sheets of ABC Company and its subsidiaries as of December 31, 20X1 and 20X0, and the related consolidated statements of income, changes in stockholders' equity and cash flows for the years then ended. These financial statements are the responsibility of the Company's management. Our responsibility is to express an opinion on these consolidated financial statements based on our audits.

We conducted our audits in accordance with auditing standards generally accepted in the United States of America. Those standards require that we plan and perform the audit to obtain reasonable assurance about whether the consolidated financial statements are free from material misstatement. An audit includes examining, on a test basis, evidence supporting the amounts and disclosures in the consolidated financial statements. An audit also includes assessing the accounting principles used and significant estimates made by management, as well as evaluating the overall consolidated financial statements presentation. We believe that our audits provide a reasonable basis for our opinion.

In our opinion, the consolidated financial statements referred to above present fairly, in all material respects, the financial position of ABC Company and its subsidiaries as of December 31, 20X1 and 20X0, and the results of their operations and their cash flows for the years then ended in accordance with accounting principles generally accepted in the United States of America.

Report on [*Identify Supplementary Information*]

Our audit was conducted for the purpose of forming an opinion on the financial statements as a whole. The [*identify accompanying supplementary information*] is presented for purposes of additional analysis and is not a required part of the financial statements. Such information is the responsibility of management and was derived from and relates directly to the underlying accounting and other records used to prepare the financial statements. The information has been subjected to the auditing procedures applied in the audit of the financial statements and certain additional procedures, including comparing and reconciling such information directly to the underlying accounting and other records used to prepare the financial statements or to the financial statements themselves, and other additional procedures in accordance with auditing standards generally accepted in the United States of America. In our opinion, the information is fairly stated in all material respects in relation to the financial statements as a whole.

[*Auditor's signature*]

[*Auditor's city and state*]

March 31, 20X2, except for our report on the supplementary information for which the date is June 1, 20X2 [*Date of the auditor's report on the audited financial statements, with a later date used for the paragraph labeled "Report on [*identify supplementary information*]," which is as of a date not earlier than the date on which the auditor completed the procedures required by paragraph .07 of section 551*]

[Issue Date: July 2011; Revised: October 2011.]

AU Section 552

Reporting on Condensed Financial Statements and Selected Financial Data[*]

Source: SAS No. 42; SAS No. 71.

Effective for reports issued or reissued on or after January 1, 1989, on condensed financial statements or selected financial data unless otherwise indicated.

.01 This section provides guidance on reporting in a client-prepared document on—

a. Condensed financial statements (either for an annual or an interim period) that are derived from audited financial statements of a public entity[1] that is required to file, at least annually, complete audited financial statements with a regulatory agency.

b. Selected financial data that are derived from audited financial statements of either a public or a nonpublic entity and that are presented in a document that includes audited financial statements (or, with respect to a public entity, that incorporates audited financial statements by reference to information filed with a regulatory agency).

Guidance on reporting on condensed financial statements or selected financial data that accompany audited financial statements in a document that contains audited financial statements and the auditor's report thereon is provided in section 550, *Other Information in Documents Containing Audited Financial Statements*. [Revised, December 2010, to reflect conforming changes necessary due to the issuance of SAS Nos. 118–120.]

.02 In reporting on condensed financial statements or selected financial data in circumstances other than those described in paragraph .01, the auditor should follow the guidance in section 508, *Reports on Audited Financial Statements*, paragraphs .41 through .44, section 623, *Special Reports*, or other applicable Statements on Auditing Standards.[2]

Condensed Financial Statements

.03 Condensed financial statements are presented in considerably less detail than complete financial statements that are intended to present financial position, results of operations, and cash flows in conformity with generally

---

[*] This section has been revised to reflect the conforming changes necessary due to the issuance of Statement on Auditing Standards Nos. 53 through 62.

[1] *Public entity* is defined in section 504, *Association With Financial Statements*, footnote 2.

[2] An auditor who has audited and reported on complete financial statements of a nonpublic entity may subsequently be requested to compile financial statements for the same period that omit substantially all disclosures required by generally accepted accounting principles. Reporting on comparative financial statements in those circumstances is described in SSARS No. 2, paragraphs 29 and 30 [AR section 200.29 and .30].

accepted accounting principles. For this reason, they should be read in conjunction with the entity's most recent complete financial statements that include all the disclosures required by generally accepted accounting principles.

.04 An auditor may be engaged to report on condensed financial statements that are derived from audited financial statements. Because condensed financial statements do not constitute a fair presentation of financial position, results of operations, and cash flows in conformity with generally accepted accounting principles, an auditor should not report on condensed financial statements in the same manner as he reported on the complete financial statements from which they are derived. To do so might lead users to assume, erroneously, that the condensed financial statements include all the disclosures necessary for complete financial statements. For the same reason, it is desirable that the condensed financial statements be so marked.

.05 In the circumstances described in paragraph .01*a*,[3] the auditor's report on condensed financial statements that are derived from financial statements that he has audited should indicate (*a*) that the auditor has audited and expressed an opinion on the complete financial statements, (*b*) the date of the auditor's report on the complete financial statements,[4] (*c*) the type of opinion expressed, and (*d*) whether, in the auditor's opinion, the information set forth in the condensed financial statements is fairly stated in all material respects in relation to the complete financial statements from which it has been derived.[5]

.06 The following is an example of wording that an auditor may use in the circumstances described in paragraph .01*a* to report on condensed financial statements that are derived from financial statements that he or she has audited and on which he or she has issued a standard report:

Independent Auditor's Report

> We have audited, in accordance with auditing standards generally accepted in the United States of America, the consolidated balance sheet of X Company and subsidiaries as of December 31, 20X0, and the related consolidated statements of income, retained earnings, and cash flows for the year then ended (not presented herein); and in our report dated February 15, 20X1, we expressed an unqualified opinion on those consolidated financial statements.

---

[3] SEC regulations require certain registrants to include in filings, as a supplementary schedule to the consolidated financial statements, condensed financial information of the parent company. The auditor should report on such condensed financial information in the same manner as he reports on other supplementary schedules.

[4] Reference to the date of the original report removes any implication that records, transactions, or events after that date have been examined. The auditor does not have a responsibility to investigate or inquire further into events that may have occurred during the period between the date of the report on the complete financial statements and the date of the report on the condensed financial statements. (However, see section 711, *Filings Under Federal Securities Statutes*, regarding the auditor's responsibility when his report is included in a registration statement filed under the Securities Act of 1933.)

[5] If the auditor's opinion on the complete financial statements was other than unqualified, the report should describe the nature of, and the reasons for, the qualification. The auditor should also consider the effect that any modification of the report on the complete financial statements might have on the report on the condensed financial statements or selected financial data. For example, if the auditor's report on the complete financial statements referred to another auditor or included an explanatory paragraph because of a material uncertainty, a going concern matter, or an inconsistency in the application of accounting principles, the report on the condensed financial statements should state that fact. However, no reference to the inconsistency is necessary if a change in accounting referred to in the auditor's report on the complete financial statements does not affect the comparability of the information being presented.

In our opinion, the information set forth in the accompanying condensed consolidated financial statements is fairly stated, in all material respects, in relation to the consolidated financial statements from which it has been derived.

[Revised, October 2000, to reflect conforming changes necessary due to the issuance of Statement on Auditing Standards No. 93.]

.07 A client might make a statement in a client-prepared document that names the auditor and also states that condensed financial statements have been derived from audited financial statements. Such a statement does not, in itself, require the auditor to report on the condensed financial statements, provided that they are included in a document that contains audited financial statements (or that incorporates such statements by reference to information filed with a regulatory agency). However, if such a statement is made in a client-prepared document of a public entity that is required to file, at least annually, complete audited financial statements with a regulatory agency and that document does not include audited financial statements (or does not incorporate such statements by reference to information filed with a regulatory agency),[6] the auditor should request that the client either (*a*) not include the auditor's name in the document or (*b*), include the auditor's report on the condensed financial statements, as described in paragraph .05. If the client will neither delete the reference to the auditor nor allow the appropriate report to be included, the auditor should advise the client that he does not consent to either the use of his name or the reference to him, and he should consider what other actions might be appropriate.[7]

---

[6] If such a statement is made in a client-prepared document that does not include audited financial statements and the client is not a public entity that is required to file complete audited financial statements with a regulatory agency (at least annually), the auditor would ordinarily express an adverse opinion on the condensed financial statements because of inadequate disclosure. (See section 508, *Reports on Audited Financial Statements*, paragraphs .41 through .44.) The auditor would not be expected to provide the disclosure in his report. The following is an example of an auditor's report on condensed financial statements in such circumstances when the auditor had previously audited and reported on the complete financial statements:

Independent Auditor's Report

We have audited the consolidated balance sheet of X Company and subsidiaries as of December 31, 20X0, and the related earnings, and cash flows for the year then ended (not presented herein). These financial statements are the responsibility of the Company's management. Our responsibility is to express an opinion on these financial statements based on our audit.

We conducted our audit in accordance with auditing standards generally accepted in the United States of America. Those standards require that we plan and perform the audit to obtain reasonable assurance about whether the financial statements are free of material misstatement. An audit includes examining, on a test basis, evidence supporting the amounts and disclosures in the financial statements. An audit also includes assessing the accounting principles used and significant estimates made by management, as well as evaluating the overall financial statement presentation. We believe that our audit provides a reasonable basis for our opinion.

The condensed consolidated balance sheet as of December 31, 20X0, and the related condensed statements of income, retained earnings, and cash flows for the year then ended, presented on pages xx-xx, are presented as a summary and therefore do not include all of the disclosures required by accounting principles generally accepted in the United States of America.

In our opinion, because of the significance of the omission of the information referred to in the preceding paragraph, the condensed consolidated financial statements referred to above do not present fairly, in conformity with accounting principles generally accepted in the United States of America, the financial position of X Company and subsidiaries as of December 31, 20X0, or the results of its operations or its cash flows for the year then ended.

[Footnote revised, October 2000, to reflect conforming changes necessary due to the issuance of Statement on Auditing Standards No. 93.]

[7] In considering what other actions, if any, may be appropriate in these circumstances, the auditor may wish to consult his legal counsel.

.08 Condensed financial statements derived from audited financial statements of a public entity may be presented on a comparative basis with interim financial information as of a subsequent date that is accompanied by the auditor's review report. In that case, the auditor should report on the condensed financial statements of each period in a manner appropriate for the type of service provided for each period. The following is an example of a review report on a condensed balance sheet as of March 31, 19X1, and the related condensed statements of income and cash flows for the three-month periods ended March 31, 19X1 and 19X0, together with a report on a condensed balance sheet derived from audited financial statements as of December 31, 19X0, included in Form 10-Q:[8]

> We have reviewed the condensed consolidated balance sheet of ABC Company and subsidiaries as of March 31, 19X1, and the related condensed consolidated statements of income and cash flows for the three-month periods ended March 31, 19X1 and 19X0. These financial statements are the responsibility of the company's management.
>
> We conducted our review in accordance with standards established by the American Institute of Certified Public Accountants. A review of interim financial information consists principally of applying analytical procedures to financial data and making inquiries of persons responsible for financial and accounting matters. It is substantially less in scope than an audit conducted in accordance with generally accepted auditing standards, the objective of which is the expression of an opinion regarding the financial statements taken as a whole. Accordingly, we do not express such an opinion.
>
> Based on our review, we are not aware of any material modifications that should be made to the condensed consolidated financial statements referred to above for them to be in conformity with generally accepted accounting principles.
>
> We have previously audited, in accordance with auditing standards generally accepted in the United States of America, the consolidated balance sheet as of December 31, 20X0, and the related consolidated statements of income, retained earnings, and cash flows for the year then ended (not presented herein); and in our report dated February 15, 20X1, we expressed an unqualified opinion on those consolidated financial statements. In our opinion, the information set forth in the accompanying condensed consolidated balance sheet as of December 31, 20X0, is fairly stated, in all material respects, in relation to the consolidated balance sheet from which it has been derived.

[Revised, May 1992, to reflect the conforming changes necessary due to the issuance of Statement on Auditing Standards No. 71. Revised, October 2000,

---

[8] Regulation S-X specifies that the following financial information should be provided in filings on Form 10-Q:

a. An interim balance sheet as of the end of the most recent fiscal quarter and a balance sheet (which may be condensed to the same extent as the interim balance sheet) as of the end of the preceding fiscal year.

b. Interim condensed statements of income for the most recent fiscal quarter, for the period between the end of the preceding fiscal year and the end of the most recent fiscal quarter, and for the corresponding periods of the preceding fiscal year.

c. Interim condensed cash flow statements for the period between the end of the preceding fiscal year and the end of the most recent fiscal quarter and for the corresponding period for the preceding fiscal year.

The Securities and Exchange Commission requires a registrant to engage an independent accountant to review the registrant's interim financial information before the registrant files its interim financial information on Form 10-Q or Form 10-QSB. If the auditor has made a review of interim financial information, he may agree to the reference to his name and the inclusion of his review report in a Form 10-Q. (See section 722, *Interim Financial Information*, paragraph .03.) [Footnote revised, November 2002, to reflect conforming changes necessary due to the issuance of Statement on Auditing Standards No. 100.]

to reflect conforming changes necessary due to the issuance of Statement on Auditing Standards No. 93.]

Selected Financial Data

.09 An auditor may be engaged to report on selected financial data that are included in a client-prepared document that contains audited financial statements (or, with respect to a public entity, that incorporates such statements by reference to information filed with a regulatory agency). Selected financial data are not a required part of the basic financial statements, and the entity's management is responsible for determining the specific selected financial data to be presented.[9] If the auditor is engaged to report on the selected financial data, his report should be limited to data that are derived from audited financial statements (which may include data that are calculated from amounts presented in the financial statements, such as working capital). If the selected financial data that management presents include both data derived from audited financial statements and other information (such as number of employees or square footage of facilities), the auditor's report should specifically identify the data on which he is reporting. The report should indicate (*a*) that the auditor has audited and expressed an opinion on the complete financial statements, (*b*) the type of opinion expressed,[10] and (*c*) whether, in the auditor's opinion, the information set forth in the selected financial data is fairly stated in all material respects in relation to the complete financial statements from which it has been derived.[11] If the selected financial data for any of the years presented are derived from financial statements that were audited by another independent auditor, the report on the selected financial data should state that fact, and the auditor should not express an opinion on that data.

.10 The following is an example of an auditor's report that includes an additional paragraph because he is also engaged to report on selected financial data for a five-year period ended December 31, 19X5, in a client-prepared document that includes audited financial statements:

Independent Auditor's Report

We have audited the consolidated balance sheets of ABC Company and subsidiaries as of December 31, 19X5 and 19X4, and the related consolidated statements of income, retained earnings, and cash flows for each of the three years in the period ended December 31, 19X5. These financial statements are the responsibility of the Company's management. Our responsibility is to express an opinion on these financial statements based on our audit.

We conducted our audits in accordance with auditing standards generally accepted in the United States of America. Those standards require that we plan and perform the audit to obtain reasonable assurance about whether the financial statements are free of material misstatement. An audit includes examining, on a test basis, evidence supporting the amounts and disclosures in the

---

[9] Under regulations of the SEC, certain reports must include, for each of the last five fiscal years, selected financial data in accordance with regulation S-K, including net sales or operating revenues, income or loss from continuing operations, income or loss from continuing operations per common share, total assets, long-term obligations and redeemable preferred stock and cash dividends declared per common share. Registrants may include additional items that they believe may be useful. There is no SEC requirement for the auditor to report on selected financial data.

[10] See footnote 5.

[11] Nothing in this section is intended to preclude an auditor from expressing an opinion on one or more specified elements, accounts, or items of a financial statement, providing the provisions of section 623, *Special Reports*, are observed.

financial statements. An audit also includes assessing the accounting principles used and significant estimates made by management, as well as evaluating the overall financial statement presentation. We believe that our audits provided a reasonable basis for our opinion.

In our opinion, the consolidated financial statements referred to above present fairly, in all material respects, the financial position of the ABC Company and subsidiaries as of December 31, 20X5 and 20X4, and the results of their operations and their cash flows for each of the three years in the period ended December 31, 20X5, in conformity with accounting principles generally accepted in the United States of America.

We have also previously audited, in accordance with auditing standards generally accepted in the United States of America, the consolidated balance sheets as of December 31, 20X3, 20X2, and 20X1, and the related statements of income, retained earnings, and cash flows for the years ended December 31, 20X2, and 20X1 (none of which are presented herein); and we expressed unqualified opinions on those consolidated financial statements. In our opinion, the information set forth in the selected financial data for each of the five years in the period ended December 31, 20X5, appearing on page xx, is fairly stated, in all material respects, in relation to the consolidated financial statements from which it has been derived.

[Revised, October 2000, to reflect conforming changes necessary due to the issuance of Statement on Auditing Standards No. 93.]

.11 In introductory material regarding the selected financial data included in a client-prepared document, an entity might name the independent auditor and state that the data are derived from financial statements that he audited. Such a statement does not, in itself, require the auditor to report on the selected financial data, provided that the selected financial data are presented in a document that contains audited financial statements (or, with respect to a public entity, that incorporates such statements by reference to information filed with a regulatory agency). If such a statement is made in a document that does not include (or incorporate by reference) audited financial statements, the auditor should request that neither his name nor reference to him be associated with the information, or he should disclaim an opinion on the selected financial data and request that the disclaimer be included in the document. If the client does not comply, the auditor should advise the client that he does not consent to either the use of his name or the reference to him, and he should consider what other actions might be appropriate.[12]

Effective Date

.12 This section is effective for reports issued or reissued on or after January 1, 1989. Earlier application of the provision of this section is permissible.

---

[12] See footnote 7.

AU Section 558

Required Supplementary Information

(Supersedes portions of SAS Nos. 52 and 98.)

Source: SAS No. 120.

Effective for audits of financial statements for periods beginning on or after December 15, 2010. Early application is permitted.

Introduction

Scope of This Section

.01 This section addresses the auditor's responsibility with respect to information that a designated accounting standard setter requires to accompany an entity's basic financial statements (hereinafter referred to as *required supplementary information*). In the absence of any separate requirement in the particular circumstances of the engagement, the auditor's opinion on the basic financial statements does not cover required supplementary information. (Ref: par. .A1)

Effective Date

.02 This section is effective for audits of financial statements for periods beginning on or after December 15, 2010. Early application is permitted.

Objective

.03 The objectives of the auditor when a designated accounting standard setter requires information to accompany an entity's basic financial statements are to perform specified procedures in order to

a. describe, in the auditor's report, whether required supplementary information is presented and

b. communicate therein when some or all of the required supplementary information has not been presented in accordance with guidelines established by a designated accounting standard setter or when the auditor has identified material modifications that should be made to the required supplementary information for it to be in accordance with guidelines established by the designated accounting standard setter.

Definitions

.04 For purposes of generally accepted auditing standards, the following terms have the meanings attributed as follows:

Required supplementary information. Information that a designated accounting standard setter requires to accompany an entity's basic financial statements. Required supplementary information is not part of the basic financial statements; however, a designated accounting standard setter considers the information to be an essential part of financial reporting for placing the basic financial statements in an appropriate operational, economic, or historical context. In addition, authoritative guidelines for the methods of measurement and presentation of the information have been established.

Designated accounting standard setter. A body designated by the AICPA council to establish GAAP pursuant to Rule 202, *Compliance With Standards* (ET sec. 202 par. .01), and Rule 203, *Accounting Principles* (ET sec. 203 par. .01). The bodies designated by the council to establish professional standards with respect to financial accounting and reporting principles pursuant to Rules 202 and 203 are the Financial Accounting Standards Board, the Governmental Accounting Standards Board, the Federal Accounting Standards Advisory Board, and the International Accounting Standards Board.

Basic financial statements. Financial statements presented in accordance with an applicable financial reporting framework as established by a designated accounting standard setter, excluding required supplementary information.

Applicable financial reporting framework. The financial reporting framework adopted by management and, when appropriate, those charged with governance in the preparation of the financial statements that is acceptable in view of the nature of the entity and the objective of the financial statements, or that is required by law or regulation.

Prescribed guidelines. The authoritative guidelines established by the designated accounting standard setter for the methods of measurement and presentation of the required supplementary information.

Requirements

Procedures

.05 The auditor should apply the following procedures to required supplementary information:

a. Inquire of management about the methods of preparing the information, including (1) whether it has been measured and presented in accordance with prescribed guidelines, (2) whether methods of measurement or presentation have been changed from those used in the prior period and the reasons for any such changes, and (3) whether there were any significant assumptions or interpretations underlying the measurement or presentation of the information

b. Compare the information for consistency with (1) management's responses to the foregoing inquiries, (2) the basic financial statements, and (3) other knowledge obtained during the audit of the basic financial statements

c. Obtain written representations from management (1) that it acknowledges its responsibility for the required supplementary information; (2) about whether the required supplementary information is measured and presented in accordance with prescribed guidelines; (3) about whether the methods of measurement or presentation have changed from those used in the prior period and, if so, the reasons for such changes; and (4) about any significant assumptions or interpretations underlying the measurement or presentation of the required supplementary information [1]

.06 If the auditor is unable to complete the procedures in paragraph .05, the auditor should consider whether management contributed to the auditor's inability to complete the procedures. If the auditor concludes that the inability to complete the procedures was due to significant difficulties encountered in dealing with management, the auditor should inform those charged with governance.[2]

Reporting

.07 The auditor should include an explanatory paragraph in the auditor's report on the financial statements to refer to the required supplementary information. The explanatory paragraph should be included after the opinion paragraph and should include language to explain the following circumstances, as applicable:

a. The required supplementary information is included, and the auditor has applied the procedures in paragraph .05 of this section.

b. The required supplementary information is omitted.

c. Some required supplementary information is missing and some is presented in accordance with the prescribed guidelines.

d. The auditor has identified material departures from the prescribed guidelines.

e. The auditor is unable to complete the procedures in paragraph .05 of this section.

f. The auditor has unresolved doubts about whether the required supplementary information is presented in accordance with prescribed guidelines.

.08 If the entity has presented all or some of the required supplementary information, the explanatory paragraph referred to in paragraph .07 should include the following elements:

a. A statement that [*identify the applicable financial reporting framework (for example, accounting principles generally accepted in the United States of America)*] require that the [*identify the required supplementary information*] be presented to supplement the basic financial statements

b. A statement that such information, although not a part of the basic financial statements, is required by [*identify designated accounting standard setter*], who considers it to be an essential part of financial reporting for placing the basic financial statements in an appropriate operational, economic, or historical context

c. If the auditor is able to complete the procedures in paragraph .05 of this section,

i. a statement that the auditor has applied certain limited procedures to the required supplementary information in

---

[1] See section 333, *Management Representations*, for additional requirements and guidance with respect to obtaining written representations from management as part of an audit of financial statements performed in accordance with generally accepted auditing standards.

[2] See paragraph .39 of section 380, *The Auditor's Communication With Those Charged With Governance*, for additional guidance when the auditor encounters significant difficulties in dealing with management during the audit.

accordance with auditing standards generally accepted in the United States of America, which consisted of inquiries of management about the methods of preparing the information and comparing the information for consistency with management's responses to the auditor's inquiries, the basic financial statements, and other knowledge the auditor obtained during the audit of the basic financial statements

ii. a statement that the auditor does not express an opinion or provide any assurance on the information because the limited procedures do not provide the auditor with sufficient evidence to express an opinion or provide any assurance

d. If the auditor is unable to complete the procedures in paragraph .05 of this section,

i. a statement that the auditor was unable to apply certain limited procedures to the required supplementary information in accordance with auditing standards generally accepted in the United States because [*state the reasons*]

ii. a statement that the auditor does not express an opinion or provide any assurance on the information

e. If some of the required supplementary information is omitted,

i. a statement that management has omitted [*description of the missing required supplementary information*] that [*identify the applicable financial reporting framework (for example, accounting principles generally accepted in the United States of America)*] require to be presented to supplement the basic financial statements

ii. a statement that such missing information, although not a part of the basic financial statements, is required by [*identify designated accounting standard setter*], who considers it to be an essential part of financial reporting for placing the basic financial statements in an appropriate operational, economic, or historical context

iii. a statement that the auditor's opinion on the basic financial statements is not affected by the missing information

f. If the measurement or presentation of the required supplementary information departs materially from the prescribed guidelines, a statement that although the auditor's opinion on the basic financial statements is not affected, material departures from prescribed guidelines exist [*describe the material departures from the applicable financial reporting framework*]

g. If the auditor has unresolved doubts about whether the required supplementary information is measured or presented in accordance with prescribed guidelines, a statement that although the auditor's opinion on the basic financial statements is not affected, the results of the limited procedures have raised doubts about whether material modifications should be made to the required supplementary information for it to be presented in accordance with guidelines established by [*identify designated accounting standard setter*]

(Ref: par. .A2)

.09 If all of the required supplementary information is omitted, the explanatory paragraph should include the following elements:

a. A statement that management has omitted [*description of the missing required supplementary information*] that [*identify the applicable financial reporting framework (for example, accounting principles generally accepted in the United States of America)*] require to be presented to supplement the basic financial statements

b. A statement that such missing information, although not a part of the basic financial statements, is required by [*identify designated accounting standard setter*], who considers it to be an essential part of financial reporting for placing the basic financial statements in an appropriate operational, economic, or historical context

c. A statement that the auditor's opinion on the basic financial statements is not affected by the missing information

Application and Other Explanatory Material

Scope of This Section (Ref: par. .01)

.A1 The auditor's responsibility for financial and nonfinancial information (other than the financial statements and the auditor's report thereon) that is included in a document containing audited financial statements and the auditor's report thereon but that is not required by a designated accounting standard setter is addressed in section 550, *Other Information in Documents Containing Audited Financial Statements*.

Reporting (Ref: par. .07–.09)

.A2 Because the required supplementary information accompanies the basic financial statements, the auditor's report on the financial statements includes a discussion of the responsibility taken by the auditor on that information. However, because the required supplementary information is not part of the basic financial statements, the auditor's opinion on the fairness of presentation of such financial statements in accordance with the applicable financial reporting framework is not affected by the presentation by the entity of the required supplementary information or the failure to present some or all of such required supplementary information. Furthermore, if the required supplementary information is omitted by the entity, the auditor does not have a responsibility to present that information.

.A3

Exhibit: Examples of Explanatory Paragraphs When Reporting on Required Supplementary Information

The Required Supplementary Information Is Included, the Auditor Has Applied the Specified Procedures, and No Material Departures From Prescribed Guidelines Have Been Identified

[*Identify the applicable financial reporting framework (for example, accounting principles generally accepted in the United States of America)*] require that the [*identify the required supplementary information*] on page XX be presented to supplement the basic financial statements. Such information, although not a part of the basic financial statements, is required by [*identify designated accounting standard setter*] who considers it to be an essential part of financial reporting for placing the basic financial statements in an appropriate operational, economic, or historical context. We have applied certain limited procedures to the required supplementary information in accordance with auditing standards generally accepted in the United States of America, which consisted of inquiries of management about the methods of preparing the information and comparing the information for consistency with management's responses to our inquiries, the basic financial statements, and other knowledge we obtained during our audit of the basic financial statements. We do not express an opinion or provide any assurance on the information because the limited procedures do not provide us with sufficient evidence to express an opinion or provide any assurance.

All Required Supplementary Information Omitted

Management has omitted [*describe the missing required supplementary information*] that [*identify the applicable financial reporting framework (for example, accounting principles generally accepted in the United States of America)*] require to be presented to supplement the basic financial statements. Such missing information, although not a part of the basic financial statements, is required by [*identify designated accounting standard setter*] who considers it to be an essential part of financial reporting for placing the basic financial statements in an appropriate operational, economic, or historical context. Our opinion on the basic financial statements is not affected by this missing information.

Some Required Supplementary Information Is Omitted and Some Is Presented in Accordance With the Prescribed Guidelines

[*Identify the applicable financial reporting framework (for example, accounting principles generally accepted in the United States of America)*] require that [*identify the included supplementary information*] be presented to supplement the basic financial statements. Such information, although not a part of the basic financial statements, is required by [*identify designated accounting standard setter*] who considers it to be an essential part of financial reporting for placing the basic financial statements in an appropriate operational, economic, or historical context. We have applied certain limited procedures to the required supplementary information in accordance with auditing standards generally accepted in the United States of America, which consisted of inquiries of management about the methods of preparing the information and comparing the information for consistency with management's responses to our inquiries, the basic financial statements, and other knowledge we obtained during our audit of the basic financial statements. We do not express an opinion or provide any assurance on the information because the limited procedures do not provide us with evidence sufficient to express an opinion or provide any assurance.

Management has omitted [*describe the missing required supplementary information*] that [*identify the applicable financial reporting framework*] require to be presented to supplement the basic financial statements. Such missing information, although not a part of the basic financial statements, is required by [*identify designated accounting standard* setter] who considers it to be an essential part of financial reporting for placing the basic financial statements in an appropriate operational, economic, or historical context. Our opinion on the basic financial statements is not affected by this missing information.

Material Departures From Prescribed Guidelines Identified

[*Identify the applicable financial reporting framework (for example, accounting principles generally accepted in the United States of America)*] require that the [*identify the supplementary information*] on page XX be presented to supplement the basic financial statements. Such information, although not a part of the basic financial statements, is required by [*identify designated accounting standard setter*] who considers it to be an essential part of financial reporting for placing the basic financial statements in an appropriate operational, economic, or historical context. We have applied certain limited procedures to the required supplementary information in accordance with auditing standards generally accepted in the United States of America, which consisted of inquiries of management about the methods of preparing the information and comparing the information for consistency with management's responses to our inquiries, the basic financial statements, and other knowledge we obtained during our audit of the basic financial statements. Although our opinion on the basic financial statements is not affected, the following material departures from the prescribed guidelines exist [*identify the required supplementary information and describe the material departures from the prescribed guidelines*]. We do not express an opinion or provide any assurance on the information.

Specified Procedures Not Completed

[*Identify the applicable financial reporting framework (for example, accounting principles generally accepted in the United States of America)*] require that the [*identify the supplementary information*] on page XX be presented to supplement the basic financial statements. Such information, although not a part of the basic financial statements, is required by [*identify designated accounting standard setter*] who considers it to be an essential part of financial reporting for placing the basic financial statements in an appropriate operational, economic, or historical context. We were unable to apply certain limited procedures to the required supplementary information in accordance with auditing standards generally accepted in the United States of America because [*state the reasons*]. We do not express an opinion or provide any assurance on the information.

Unresolved Doubts About Whether the Required Supplementary Information Is in Accordance With Prescribed Guidelines

[*Identify the applicable financial reporting framework (for example, accounting principles generally accepted in the United States of America)*] require that the [*identify the supplementary information*] on page XX be presented to supplement the basic financial statements. Such information, although not a part of the basic financial statements, is required by [*identify designated accounting standard setter*] who considers it to be an essential part of financial reporting for placing the basic financial statements in an appropriate operational, economic, or historical context. We have applied certain limited procedures to the required supplementary information in accordance with auditing standards generally accepted in the United States of America, which consisted of inquiries of management about the methods of preparing the information and comparing the information for consistency with management's responses to our inquiries, the basic financial statements, and other knowledge we obtained during our audit of the basic financial statements. We do not express an opinion or provide any assurance on the information because the limited procedures do not provide us with sufficient evidence to express an opinion or provide any assurance. Although our opinion on the basic financial statements is not affected, the results of the limited procedures have raised doubts about whether material modifications should be made to the required supplementary information for it to be presented in accordance with guidelines established by [*identify designated accounting standard setter*]. [*The auditor may consider including in the report the reason(s) he or she was unable to resolve his or her doubts.*]

AU Section 560

Subsequent Events

Source: SAS No. 1, section 560; SAS No. 12; SAS No. 98; SAS No. 113.

Issue date, unless otherwise indicated: November, 1972.

.01 An independent auditor's report ordinarily is issued in connection with historical financial statements that purport to present financial position at a stated date and results of operations and cash flows for a period ended on that date. However, events or transactions sometimes occur subsequent to the balance-sheet date, but prior to the issuance of the financial statements, that have a material effect on the financial statements and therefore require adjustment or disclosure in the statements. These occurrences hereinafter are referred to as "subsequent events." [As amended, effective September 2002, by Statement on Auditing Standards No. 98.]

.02 Two types of subsequent events require consideration by management and evaluation by the independent auditor.

.03 The first type consists of those events that provide additional evidence with respect to conditions that existed at the date of the balance sheet and affect the estimates inherent in the process of preparing financial statements. All information that becomes available prior to the issuance of the financial statements should be used by management in its evaluation of the conditions on which the estimates were based. The financial statements should be adjusted for any changes in estimates resulting from the use of such evidence.

.04 Identifying events that require adjustment of the financial statements under the criteria stated above calls for the exercise of judgment and knowledge of the facts and circumstances. For example, a loss on an uncollectible trade account receivable as a result of a customer's deteriorating financial condition leading to bankruptcy subsequent to the balance-sheet date would be indicative of conditions existing at the balance-sheet date, thereby calling for adjustment of the financial statements before their issuance. On the other hand, a similar loss resulting from a customer's major casualty such as a fire or flood subsequent to the balance-sheet date would not be indicative of conditions existing at the balance-sheet date and adjustment of the financial statements would not be appropriate. The settlement of litigation for an amount different from the liability recorded in the accounts would require adjustment of the financial statements if the events, such as personal injury or patent infringement, that gave rise to the litigation had taken place prior to the balance-sheet date.

.05 The second type consists of those events that provide evidence with respect to conditions that did not exist at the date of the balance sheet being reported on but arose subsequent to that date. These events should not result in adjustment of the financial statements.[1] Some of these events, however, may be of such a nature that disclosure of them is required to keep the financial statements from being misleading. Occasionally such an event may be so significant that disclosure can best be made by supplementing the historical

---

[1] This paragraph is not intended to preclude giving effect in the balance sheet, with appropriate disclosure, to stock dividends or stock splits or reverse splits consummated after the balance-sheet date but before issuance of the financial statements.

financial statements with pro forma financial data giving effect to the event as if it had occurred on the date of the balance sheet. It may be desirable to present pro forma statements, usually a balance sheet only, in columnar form on the face of the historical statements.

.06 Examples of events of the second type that require disclosure to the financial statements (but should not result in adjustment) are:

a. Sale of a bond or capital stock issue.

b. Purchase of a business.

c. Settlement of litigation when the event giving rise to the claim took place subsequent to the balance-sheet date.

d. Loss of plant or inventories as a result of fire or flood.

e. Losses on receivables resulting from conditions (such as a customer's major casualty) arising subsequent to the balance-sheet date.

.07 Subsequent events affecting the realization of assets such as receivables and inventories or the settlement of estimated liabilities ordinarily will require adjustment of the financial statements (see paragraph .03) because such events typically represent the culmination of conditions that existed over a relatively long period of time. Subsequent events such as changes in the quoted market prices of securities ordinarily should not result in adjustment of the financial statements (see paragraph .05) because such changes typically reflect a concurrent evaluation of new conditions.

.08 When financial statements are reissued, for example, in reports filed with the Securities and Exchange Commission or other regulatory agencies, events that require disclosure in the reissued financial statements to keep them from being misleading may have occurred subsequent to the original issuance of the financial statements. Events occurring between the time of original issuance and reissuance of financial statements should not result in adjustment of the financial statements[2] unless the adjustment meets the criteria for the correction of an error or the criteria for prior period adjustments set forth in Financial Accounting Standards Board *Accounting Standards Codification* 250, *Accounting Changes and Error Corrections*. Similarly, financial statements reissued in comparative form with financial statements of subsequent periods should not be adjusted for events occurring subsequent to the original issuance unless the adjustment meets the criteria stated above. [Revised, June 2009, to reflect conforming changes necessary due to the issuance of FASB ASC.]

.09 Occasionally, a subsequent event of the second type has such a material impact on the entity that the auditor may wish to include in his report an explanatory paragraph directing the reader's attention to the event and its effects. (See section 508 paragraph .19.)

Auditing Procedures in the Subsequent Period

.10 There is a period after the balance-sheet date with which the auditor must be concerned in completing various phases of his audit. This period is known as the "subsequent period" and is considered to extend to the date of the auditor's report. Its duration will depend upon the practical requirements of each audit and may vary from a relatively short period to one of several months. Also, all auditing procedures are not carried out at the same time and some phases of an audit will be performed during the subsequent period,

---

[2] However, see paragraph .05 as to the desirability of presenting pro forma financial statements to supplement the historical financial statements in certain circumstances.

whereas other phases will be substantially completed on or before the balance-sheet date. As an audit approaches completion, the auditor will be concentrating on the unresolved auditing and reporting matters and he is not expected to be conducting a continuing review of those matters to which he has previously applied auditing procedures and reached satisfaction.

.11 Certain specific procedures are applied to transactions occurring after the balance-sheet date such as (*a*) the examination of data to assure that proper cutoffs have been made and (*b*) the examination of data which provide information to aid the auditor in his evaluation of the assets and liabilities as of the balance-sheet date.

.12 In addition, the independent auditor should perform other auditing procedures with respect to the period after the balance-sheet date for the purpose of ascertaining the occurrence of subsequent events that may require adjustment or disclosure essential to a fair presentation of the financial statements in conformity with generally accepted accounting principles. These procedures should be performed at or near the date of the auditor's report. The auditor generally should:

a. Read the latest available interim financial statements; compare them with the financial statements being reported upon; and make any other comparisons considered appropriate in the circumstances. In order to make these procedures as meaningful as possible for the purpose expressed above, the auditor should inquire of officers and other executives having responsibility for financial and accounting matters as to whether the interim statements have been prepared on the same basis as that used for the statements under audit.

b. Inquire of and discuss with officers and other executives having responsibility for financial and accounting matters (limited where appropriate to major locations) as to:

(i) Whether any substantial contingent liabilities or commitments existed at the date of the balance sheet being reported on or at the date of inquiry.

(ii) Whether there was any significant change in the capital stock, long-term debt, or working capital to the date of inquiry.

(iii) The current status of items, in the financial statements being reported on, that were accounted for on the basis of tentative, preliminary, or inconclusive data.

(iv) Whether any unusual adjustments had been made during the period from the balance-sheet date to the date of inquiry.

c. Read the available minutes of meetings of stockholders, directors, and appropriate committees; as to meetings for which minutes are not available, inquire about matters dealt with at such meetings.

d. Inquire of client's legal counsel concerning litigation, claims, and assessments. [As amended, January 1976, by Statement on Auditing Standards No. 12.] (See section 337.)

e. Obtain a letter of representations, dated as of the date of the auditor's report, from appropriate officials, generally the chief executive officer, chief financial officer, or others with equivalent positions in the entity, as to whether any events have occurred subsequent to the date of the financial statements being reported on by the independent auditor that in the officer's opinion would require adjustment or disclosure in these statements. The auditor may elect to have the client include representations as to significant matters disclosed to the auditor in his or her performance of the procedures in subparagraphs (*a*) to (*d*) above and (*f*) below. (See section 333, *Management Representations*.)

f. Make such additional inquiries or perform such procedures as he considers necessary and appropriate to dispose of questions that arise in carrying out the foregoing procedures, inquiries, and discussions.

[As amended, effective for audits of financial statements for periods ending on or after December 15, 2006, by Statement on Auditing Standards No. 113.]

AU Section 9560

Subsequent Events: Auditing Interpretations of Section 560

[1.–4.] Lawyers' Letters

[.01–.26] [Superseded January, 1976.]

AU Section 561

Subsequent Discovery of Facts Existing at the Date of the Auditor's Report

Source: SAS No. 1, section 561; SAS No. 98.

See section 9561 for interpretations of this section.

Issue date, unless otherwise indicated: November, 1972.

.01 The procedures described in this section should be followed by the auditor who, subsequent to the date of the report upon audited financial statements, becomes aware that facts may have existed at that date which might have affected the report had he or she then been aware of such facts.[1] [As amended, effective September 2002, by Statement on Auditing Standards No. 98.]

.02 Because of the variety of conditions which might be encountered, some of these procedures are necessarily set out only in general terms; the specific actions to be taken in a particular case may vary somewhat in the light of the circumstances. The auditor would be well advised to consult with an attorney when he or she encounters the circumstances to which this section may apply because of legal implications that may be involved in actions contemplated herein, including, for example, the possible effect of state statutes regarding confidentiality of auditor-client communications. [As amended, effective September 2002, by Statement on Auditing Standards No. 98.]

.03 After the date of the report, the auditor has no obligation[2] to make any further or continuing inquiry or perform any other auditing procedures with respect to the audited financial statements covered by that report, unless new information which may affect the report comes to his or her attention. [As amended, effective September 2002, by Statement on Auditing Standards No. 98.]

.04 When the auditor becomes aware of information which relates to financial statements previously reported on by him, but which was not known to him at the date of his report, and which is of such a nature and from such a source that he would have investigated it had it come to his attention during the course of his audit, he should, as soon as practicable, undertake to determine whether the information is reliable and whether the facts existed at the date of his report. In this connection, the auditor should discuss the matter with his client at whatever management levels he deems appropriate, including the board of directors, and request cooperation in whatever investigation may be necessary.

---

[1] If the financial statements have not yet been issued, see the guidance found in section 560, *Subsequent Events*. [Footnote added, effective September 2002, by Statement on Auditing Standards No. 98.]

[2] However, see paragraphs .10–.13 of section 711 as to an auditor's obligation with respect to audited financial statements included in registration statements filed under the Securities Act of 1933 between the date of the auditor's report and the effective date of the registration statement. [Footnote revised by the issuance of Statement on Auditing Standards No. 37, April 1981. Footnote renumbered by the issuance of Statement on Auditing Standards No. 98, September 2002.]

.05 When the subsequently discovered information is found both to be reliable and to have existed at the date of the auditor's report, the auditor should take action in accordance with the procedures set out in subsequent paragraphs if the nature and effect of the matter are such that (*a*) his report would have been affected if the information had been known to him at the date of his report and had not been reflected in the financial statements and (*b*) he believes there are persons currently relying or likely to rely on the financial statements who would attach importance to the information. With respect to (*b*), consideration should be given, among other things, to the time elapsed since the financial statements were issued.

.06 When the auditor has concluded, after considering (*a*) and (*b*) in paragraph .05, that action should be taken to prevent future reliance on his report, he should advise his client to make appropriate disclosure of the newly discovered facts and their impact on the financial statements to persons who are known to be currently relying or who are likely to rely on the financial statements and the related auditor's report. When the client undertakes to make appropriate disclosure, the method used and the disclosure made will depend on the circumstances.

a. If the effect on the financial statements or auditor's report of the subsequently discovered information can promptly be determined, disclosure should consist of issuing, as soon as practicable, revised financial statements and auditor's report. The reasons for the revision usually should be described in a note to the financial statements and referred to in the auditor's report. Generally, only the most recently issued audited financial statements would need to be revised, even though the revision resulted from events that had occurred in prior years.[3]

b. When issuance of financial statements accompanied by the auditor's report for a subsequent period is imminent, so that disclosure is not delayed, appropriate disclosure of the revision can be made in such statements instead of reissuing the earlier statements pursuant to subparagraph (*a*).[4]

c. When the effect on the financial statements of the subsequently discovered information cannot be determined without a prolonged investigation, the issuance of revised financial statements and auditor's report would necessarily be delayed. In this circumstance, when it appears that the information will require a revision of the statements, appropriate disclosure would consist of notification by the client to persons who are known to be relying or who are likely to rely on the financial statements and the related report that they should not be relied upon, and that revised financial statements and auditor's report will be issued upon completion of an investigation. If applicable, the client should be advised to discuss with the Securities and Exchange Commission, stock exchanges, and appropriate regulatory agencies the disclosure to be made or other measures to be taken in the circumstances.

---

[3] See paragraphs 7–10 of Financial Accounting Standards Board *Accounting Standards Codification* 250-10-50 regarding disclosure of adjustments applicable to prior periods. [Footnote renumbered by the issuance of Statement on Auditing Standards No. 98, September 2002. Footnote revised, June 2009, to reflect conforming changes necessary due to the issuance of FASB ASC.]

[4] Ibid. [Footnote renumbered by the issuance of Statement on Auditing Standards No. 98, September 2002.]

.07 The auditor should take whatever steps he deems necessary to satisfy himself that the client has made the disclosures specified in paragraph .06.

.08 If the client refuses to make the disclosures specified in paragraph .06, the auditor should notify each member of the board of directors of such refusal and of the fact that, in the absence of disclosure by the client, the auditor will take steps as outlined as follows to prevent future reliance upon his report. The steps that can appropriately be taken will depend upon the degree of certainty of the auditor's knowledge that there are persons who are currently relying or who will rely on the financial statements and the auditor's report, and who would attach importance to the information, and the auditor's ability as a practical matter to communicate with them. Unless the auditor's attorney recommends a different course of action, the auditor should take the following steps to the extent applicable:

a. Notification to the client that the auditor's report must no longer be associated with the financial statements.

b. Notification to regulatory agencies having jurisdiction over the client that the auditor's report should no longer be relied upon.

c. Notification to each person known to the auditor to be relying on the financial statements that his report should no longer be relied upon. In many instances, it will not be practicable for the auditor to give appropriate individual notification to stockholders or investors at large, whose identities ordinarily are unknown to him; notification to a regulatory agency having jurisdiction over the client will usually be the only practicable way for the auditor to provide appropriate disclosure. Such notification should be accompanied by a request that the agency take whatever steps it may deem appropriate to accomplish the necessary disclosure. The Securities and Exchange Commission and the stock exchanges are appropriate agencies for this purpose as to corporations within their jurisdictions.

.09 The following guidelines should govern the content of any disclosure made by the auditor in accordance with paragraph .08 to persons other than his client:

a. If the auditor has been able to make a satisfactory investigation of the information and has determined that the information is reliable:

(i) The disclosure should describe the effect the subsequently acquired information would have had on the auditor's report if it had been known to him at the date of his report and had not been reflected in the financial statements. The disclosure should include a description of the nature of the subsequently acquired information and of its effect on the financial statements.

(ii) The information disclosed should be as precise and factual as possible and should not go beyond that which is reasonably necessary to accomplish the purpose mentioned in the preceding subparagraph (*i*). Comments concerning the conduct or motives of any person should be avoided.

b. If the client has not cooperated and as a result the auditor is unable to conduct a satisfactory investigation of the information, his disclosure need not detail the specific information but can merely indicate that information has come to his attention which his client has not cooperated in attempting to substantiate and that, if the information is true, the auditor believes that his report must no longer be relied upon or be associated with the financial statements. No such disclosure should be made unless the auditor believes that the financial statements are likely to be misleading and that his report should not be relied on.

.10 The concepts embodied in this section are not limited solely to corporations but apply in all cases where financial statements have been audited and reported on by independent auditors.

AU Section 9561

Subsequent Discovery of Facts Existing at the Date of the Auditor's Report: Auditing Interpretations of Section 561

1. Auditor Association With Subsequently Discovered Information When the Auditor Has Resigned or Been Discharged

.01 *Question*—New information may come to an auditor's attention subsequent to the date of his report on audited financial statements that might affect the previously issued audit report. Is the auditor's responsibility with respect to that information different if the auditor has resigned or been discharged prior to undertaking or completing his investigation than if he were the continuing auditor?

.02 *Interpretation*—No. Section 561, *Subsequent Discovery of Facts Existing at the Date of the Auditor's Report*, requires the auditor to undertake to determine whether the information is reliable and whether the facts existed at the date of his report. This undertaking must be performed even when the auditor has resigned or been discharged.

[Issue Date: February, 1989.]

AU Section 600

OTHER TYPES OF REPORTS

TABLE OF CONTENTS

AU Section 622

Engagements to Apply Agreed-Upon Procedures to Specified Elements, Accounts, or Items of a Financial Statement

(Supersedes SAS No. 35.)

Source: SAS No. 75; SAS No. 87; SAS No. 93.

Notice of Withdrawal of Statement on Auditing Standards (SAS) No. 75, *Engagements to Apply Agreed-Upon Procedures to Specified Elements, Accounts, or Items of a Financial Statement* and Auditing Interpretation No. 1, "Applying Agreed-Upon Procedures to All, or Substantially All, of the Elements, Accounts, or Items of a Financial Statement"

The Auditing Standards Board (ASB) has withdrawn SAS No. 75, *Engagements to Apply Agreed-Upon Procedures to Specified Elements, Accounts, or Items of a Financial Statement*, and its interpretation in order to consolidate the guidance applicable to agreed-upon procedures engagements in professional standards. For guidance relating to performing and reporting on agreed-upon procedures engagements, practitioners should refer to AT section 201, *Agreed-Upon Procedures Engagements*.

AU Section 622

Engagements to Apply Agreed-Upon Procedures to Specified Elements, Accounts, or Items of a Financial Statement

(Supersedes SAS No. 35.)

Source: SAS No. 75; SAS No. 87; SAS No. 93.

Notice of Withdrawal of Statement on Auditing Standards (SAS) No. 75, *Engagements to Apply Agreed-Upon Procedures to Specified Elements, Accounts, or Items of a Financial Statement*, and Auditing Interpretation No. 1, "Applying Agreed-Upon Procedures to All or Substantially All of the Elements, Accounts, or Items of a Financial Statement"

The Auditing Standards Board (ASB) has withdrawn SAS No. 75, *Engagements to Apply Agreed-Upon Procedures to Specified Elements, Accounts, or Items of a Financial Statement*, and its interpretation in order to consolidate the guidance applicable to agreed-upon procedures engagements in professional standards. For guidance relating to performing and reporting on agreed-upon procedures engagements, practitioners should refer to AT section 201, *Agreed-Upon Procedures Engagements*.

AU Section 9622

Engagements to Apply Agreed-Upon Procedures to Specified Elements, Accounts, or Items of a Financial Statement: Auditing Interpretations of Section 622

[1.] Applying Agreed-Upon Procedures to All, or Substantially All, of the Elements, Accounts, or Items of a Financial Statement

[.01–.02]

Notice of Withdrawal of Statement on Auditing Standards (SAS) No. 75, *Engagements to Apply Agreed-Upon Procedures to Specified Elements, Accounts, or Items of a Financial Statement* and Auditing Interpretation No. 1, "Applying Agreed-Upon Procedures to All, or Substantially All, of the Elements, Accounts, or Items of a Financial Statement"

The Auditing Standards Board (ASB) has withdrawn SAS No. 75, *Engagements to Apply Agreed-Upon Procedures to Specified Elements, Accounts, or Items of a Financial Statement*, and its interpretation in order to consolidate the guidance applicable to agreed-upon procedures engagements in professional standards. For guidance relating to performing and reporting on agreed-upon procedures engagements, practitioners should refer to AT section 201, *Agreed-Upon Procedures Engagements*.

AU Section 623

Special Reports

(Supersedes section 621.)

Source: SAS No. 62; SAS No. 77.

See section 9623 for interpretations of this section.

Effective for reports issued on or after July 1, 1989, unless otherwise indicated.

Introduction

.01 This section applies to auditors' reports issued in connection with the following:

a. Financial statements that are prepared in conformity with a comprehensive basis of accounting other than generally accepted accounting principles (paragraphs .02 through .10)

b. Specified elements, accounts, or items of a financial statement (paragraphs .11 through .18)

c. Compliance with aspects of contractual agreements or regulatory requirements related to audited financial statements (paragraphs .19 through .21)

d. Financial presentations to comply with contractual agreements or regulatory provisions (paragraphs .22 through .30)

e. Financial information presented in prescribed forms or schedules that require a prescribed form of auditor's reports (paragraphs .32 and .33)

Financial Statements Prepared in Conformity With a Comprehensive Basis of Accounting Other Than Generally Accepted Accounting Principles

.02 Generally accepted auditing standards are applicable when an auditor conducts an audit of and reports on any financial statement. A financial statement may be, for example, that of a corporation, a consolidated group of corporations, a combined group of affiliated entities, a not-for-profit organization, a governmental unit, an estate or trust, a partnership, a proprietorship, a segment of any of these, or an individual. The term *financial statement* refers to a presentation of financial data, including accompanying notes, derived from accounting records and intended to communicate an entity's economic resources or obligations at a point in time or the changes therein for a period of time in conformity with a comprehensive basis of accounting. For reporting purposes, the independent auditor should consider each of the following types of financial presentations to be a financial statement:

a. Balance sheet

b. Statement of income or statement of operations

c. Statement of retained earnings

d. Statement of cash flows

e. Statement of changes in owners' equity

f. Statement of assets and liabilities that does not include owners' equity accounts

g. Statement of revenue and expenses

h. Summary of operations

i. Statement of operations by product lines

j. Statement of cash receipts and disbursements

.03 An independent auditor's judgment concerning the overall presentation of financial statements should be applied within an identifiable framework. Normally, the framework is provided by generally accepted accounting principles, and the auditor's judgment in forming an opinion is applied accordingly. In some circumstances, however, a comprehensive basis of accounting other than generally accepted accounting principles may be used. [Title of section 411 amended, effective for reports issued or reissued on or after June 30, 2001, by Statement on Auditing Standards No. 93. Revised, October 2009, to reflect conforming changes necessary due to the withdrawal of SAS No. 69.]

.04 For purposes of this section, a comprehensive basis of accounting other than generally accepted accounting principles is one of the following—

a. A basis of accounting that the reporting entity uses to comply with the requirements or financial reporting provisions of a governmental regulatory agency to whose jurisdiction the entity is subject. An example is a basis of accounting insurance companies use pursuant to the rules of a state insurance commission.

b. A basis of accounting that the reporting entity uses or expects to use to file its income tax return for the period covered by the financial statements.

c. The cash receipts and disbursements basis of accounting, and modifications of the cash basis having substantial support, such as recording depreciation on fixed assets or accruing income taxes.

d. A definite set of criteria having substantial support that is applied to all material items appearing in financial statements, such as the price-level basis of accounting.

Unless one of the foregoing descriptions applies, reporting under the provisions of paragraph .05 is not permitted.

Reporting on Financial Statements Prepared in Conformity With an Other Comprehensive Basis of Accounting (OCBOA)

.05 When reporting on financial statements prepared in conformity with a comprehensive basis of accounting other than generally accepted accounting principles, as defined in paragraph .04, an independent auditor should include in the report—

a. A title that includes the word *independent*.[1]

b. A paragraph that—

(1) States that the financial statements identified in the report were audited.

(2) States that the financial statements are the responsibility of the Company's management[2] and that the auditor is responsible for expressing an opinion on the financial statements based on the audit.

c. A paragraph that—

(1) States that the audit was conducted in accordance with generally accepted auditing standards and includes an identification of the United States of America as the country of origin of those standards (for example, auditing standards generally accepted in the United States of America or U.S. generally accepted auditing standards).

(2) States that those standards require that the auditor plan and perform the audit to obtain reasonable assurance about whether the financial statements are free of material misstatement.

(3) States that an audit includes—

(a) Examining, on a test basis, evidence supporting the amounts and disclosures in the financial statements,

(b) Assessing the accounting principles used and significant estimates made by management, and

(c) Evaluating the overall financial statement presentation (see paragraph .09).

(4) States that the auditor believes that his or her audit provides a reasonable basis for the opinion.

d. A paragraph that—

(1) States the basis of presentation and refers to the note to the financial statements that describes the basis (see paragraphs .09 and .10).

(2) States that the basis of presentation is a comprehensive basis of accounting other than generally accepted accounting principles.

e. A paragraph that expresses the auditor's opinion (or disclaims an opinion) on whether the financial statements are presented fairly, in

---

[1] This section does not require a title for an auditor's report if the auditor is not independent. See section 504, *Association With Financial Statements*, for guidance on reporting when the auditor is not independent.

[2] In some instances, a document containing the auditor's report may include a statement by management regarding its responsibility for the presentation of the financial statements. Nevertheless, the auditor's report should state that the financial statements are management's responsibility. However, the statement about management's responsibility should not be further elaborated upon in the auditor's standard report or referenced to management's report.

all material respects, in conformity with the basis of accounting described. If the auditor concludes that the financial statements are not presented fairly on the basis of accounting described or if there has been a limitation on the scope of the audit, he or she should disclose all the substantive reasons for the conclusion in an explanatory paragraph(s) (preceding the opinion paragraph) of the report and should include in the opinion paragraph the appropriate modifying language and a reference to such explanatory paragraph(s).[3]

f. If the financial statements are prepared in conformity with the requirements or financial reporting provisions of a governmental regulatory agency (see paragraph .04*a*), a separate paragraph at the end of the report stating that the report is intended solely for the information and use of those within the entity and the regulatory agencies to whose jurisdiction the entity is subject, and is not intended to be and should not be used by anyone other than these specified parties. Such a paragraph is appropriate even though by law or regulation the auditor's report may be made a matter of public record.[4] The auditor may use this form of report only if the financial statements and report are intended solely for use by those within the entity and one or more regulatory agencies to whose jurisdiction the entity is subject.[5]

g. The manual or printed signature of the auditor's firm.

h. The date.[6]

[As amended, effective for audits of financial statements for periods ended on or after December 31, 1996, by Statement on Auditing Standards No. 77. Revised, October 2000, to reflect conforming changes necessary due to the issuance of Statement on Auditing Standards No. 93.]

.06 Unless the financial statements meet the conditions for presentation in conformity with a "comprehensive basis of accounting other than generally accepted accounting principles" as defined in paragraph .04, the auditor should use the standard form of report (see section 508, *Reports on Audited Financial Statements*, paragraph .08) modified as appropriate because of the departures from generally accepted accounting principles.

.07 Terms such as *balance sheet*, *statement of financial position*, *statement of income*, *statement of operations*, and *statement of cash flows*, or similar

---

[3] Paragraph .31 discusses other circumstances that may require that the auditor add additional explanatory language to the special report.

[4] Public record, for purposes of auditor's reports on financial statements of a regulated entity that are prepared in accordance with the financial reporting provisions of a government regulatory agency, includes circumstances in which specific requests must be made by the public to obtain access to or copies of the report. In contrast, the auditor would be precluded from using this form of report in circumstances in which the entity distributes the financial statements to parties other than the regulatory agency either voluntarily or upon specific request. [Footnote added, effective for audits of financial statements for periods ended on or after December 31, 1996, by Statement on Auditing Standards No. 77.]

[5] If the financial statements and report are intended for use by parties other than those within the entity and one or more regulatory agencies to whose jurisdiction the entity is subject, the auditor should follow the guidance in section 544, *Lack of Conformity With Generally Accepted Accounting Principles*. [Footnote renumbered and amended, effective for audits of financial statements for periods ended on or after December 31, 1996, by the issuance of Statement on Auditing Standards No. 77.]

[6] For guidance on dating the auditor's report, see section 530, *Dating of the Independent Auditor's Report*. [Footnote renumbered by the issuance of Statement on Auditing Standards No. 77, November 1995.]

unmodified titles are generally understood to be applicable only to financial statements that are intended to present financial position, results of operations, or cash flows in conformity with generally accepted accounting principles. Consequently, the auditor should consider whether the financial statements that he or she is reporting on are suitably titled. For example, cash basis financial statements might be titled *statement of assets and liabilities arising from cash transactions*, or *statement of revenue collected and expenses paid*, and a financial statement prepared on a statutory or regulatory basis might be titled *statement of income—statutory basis*. If the auditor believes that the financial statements are not suitably titled, the auditor should disclose his or her reservations in an explanatory paragraph of the report and qualify the opinion.

.08 Following are illustrations of reports on financial statements prepared in conformity with a comprehensive basis of accounting other than generally accepted accounting principles.[7]

Financial Statements Prepared on a Basis Prescribed by a Regulatory Agency Solely for Filing With That Agency

Independent Auditor's Report

We have audited the accompanying statements of admitted assets, liabilities, and surplus—statutory basis of XYZ Insurance Company as of December 31, 20X2 and 20X1, and the related statements of income and cash flows—statutory basis and changes in surplus—statutory basis for the years then ended. These financial statements are the responsibility of the Company's management. Our responsibility is to express an opinion on these financial statements based on our audits.

We conducted our audits in accordance with auditing standards generally accepted in the United States of America. Those standards require that we plan and perform the audit to obtain reasonable assurance about whether the financial statements are free of material misstatement. An audit includes examining, on a test basis, evidence supporting the amounts and disclosures in the financial statements. An audit also includes assessing the accounting principles used and significant estimates made by management, as well as evaluating the overall financial statement presentation. We believe that our audits provide a reasonable basis for our opinion.

As described in Note X, these financial statements were prepared in conformity with the accounting practices prescribed or permitted by the Insurance Department of [*State*], which is a comprehensive basis of accounting other than generally accepted accounting principles.

In our opinion, the financial statements referred to above present fairly, in all material respects, the admitted assets, liabilities, and surplus of XYZ Insurance Company as of December 31, 20X2 and 20X1, and the results of its operations and its cash flows for the years then ended, on the basis of accounting described in Note X.

This report is intended solely for the information and use of the board of directors and management of XYZ Insurance Company and [*name of regulatory agency*] and is not intended to be and should not be used by anyone other than these specified parties.

---

[7] [Footnote deleted to reflect conforming changes necessary due to the issuance of Statement on Auditing Standards No. 87.]

Financial Statements Prepared on the Entity's Income Tax Basis

Independent Auditor's Report

We have audited the accompanying statements of assets, liabilities, and capital—income tax basis of ABC Partnership as of December 31, 20X2 and 20X1, and the related statements of revenue and expenses—income tax basis and of changes in partners' capital accounts—income tax basis for the years then ended. These financial statements are the responsibility of the Partnership's management. Our responsibility is to express an opinion on these financial statements based on our audits.

We conducted our audits in accordance with auditing standards generally accepted in the United States of America. Those standards require that we plan and perform the audit to obtain reasonable assurance about whether the financial statements are free of material misstatement. An audit includes examining, on a test basis, evidence supporting the amounts and disclosures in the financial statements. An audit also includes assessing the accounting principles used and significant estimates made by management, as well as evaluating the overall financial statement presentation. We believe that our audits provide a reasonable basis for our opinion.

As described in Note X, these financial statements were prepared on the basis of accounting the Partnership uses for income tax purposes, which is a comprehensive basis of accounting other than generally accepted accounting principles.

In our opinion, the financial statements referred to above present fairly, in all material respects, the assets, liabilities, and capital of ABC Partnership as of [*at*] December 31, 20X2 and 20X1, and its revenue and expenses and changes in partners' capital accounts for the years then ended, on the basis of accounting described in Note X.

Financial Statements Prepared on the Cash Basis

Independent Auditor's Report

We have audited the accompanying statements of assets and liabilities arising from cash transactions of XYZ Company as of December 31, 20X2 and 20X1, and the related statements of revenue collected and expenses paid for the years then ended. These financial statements are the responsibility of the Company's management. Our responsibility is to express an opinion on these financial statements based on our audits.

We conducted our audits in accordance with auditing standards generally accepted in the United States of America. Those standards require that we plan and perform the audit to obtain reasonable assurance about whether the financial statements are free of material misstatement. An audit includes examining, on a test basis, evidence supporting the amounts and disclosures in the financial statements. An audit also includes assessing the accounting principles used and significant estimates made by management, as well as evaluating the overall financial statement presentation. We believe that our audits provide a reasonable basis for our opinion.

As described in Note X, these financial statements were prepared on the basis of cash receipts and disbursements, which is a comprehensive basis of accounting other than generally accepted accounting principles.

In our opinion, the financial statements referred to above present fairly, in all material respects, the assets and liabilities arising from cash transactions of XYZ Company as of December 31, 20X2 and 20X1, and its revenue collected and expenses paid during the years then ended, on the basis of accounting described in Note X.

[Revised, October 2000, to reflect conforming changes necessary to reflect the issuance of Statement on Auditing Standards No. 93.]

Evaluating the Adequacy of Disclosure in Financial Statements Prepared in Conformity With an Other Comprehensive Basis of Accounting

.09 When reporting on financial statements prepared on a comprehensive basis of accounting other than generally accepted accounting principles, the auditor should consider whether the financial statements (including the accompanying notes) include all informative disclosures that are appropriate for the basis of accounting used. The auditor should apply essentially the same criteria to financial statements prepared on an other comprehensive basis of accounting as he or she does to financial statements prepared in conformity with generally accepted accounting principles. Therefore, the auditor's opinion should be based on his or her judgment regarding whether the financial statements, including the related notes, are informative of matters that may affect their use, understanding, and interpretation. [Title of section 411 amended, effective for reports issued or reissued on or after June 30, 2001, by Statement on Auditing Standards No. 93. Revised, October 2009, to reflect conforming changes necessary due to the withdrawal of SAS No. 69.]

.10 Financial statements prepared on an other comprehensive basis of accounting should include, in the accompanying notes, a summary of significant accounting policies that discusses the basis of presentation and describes how that basis differs from generally accepted accounting principles. However, the effects of the differences between generally accepted accounting principles and the basis of presentation of the financial statements that the auditor is reporting on need not be quantified. In addition, when the financial statements contain items that are the same as, or similar to, those in financial statements prepared in conformity with generally accepted accounting principles, similar informative disclosures are appropriate. For example, financial statements prepared on an income tax basis or a modified cash basis of accounting usually reflect depreciation, long-term debt and owners' equity. Thus, the informative disclosures for depreciation, long-term debt and owners' equity in such financial statements should be comparable to those in financial statements prepared in conformity with generally accepted accounting principles. When evaluating the adequacy of disclosures, the auditor should also consider disclosures related to matters that are not specifically identified on the face of the financial statements, such as (*a*) related party transactions, (*b*) restrictions on assets and owners' equity, (*c*) subsequent events, and (*d*) uncertainties.

Specified Elements, Accounts, or Items of a Financial Statement

.11 An independent auditor may be requested to express an opinion on one or more specified elements, accounts, or items of a financial statement. In such an engagement, the specified element(s), account(s), or item(s) may be presented in the report or in a document accompanying the report. Examples of one or more specified elements, accounts, or items of a financial statement that an auditor may report on based on an audit made in accordance with generally accepted auditing standards include rentals, royalties, a profit participation, or a provision for income taxes.[8]

.12 When expressing an opinion on one or more specified elements, accounts, or items of a financial statement, the auditor should plan and perform the audit and prepare his or her report with a view to the purpose of the engagement. With the exception of the first standard of reporting, the ten generally accepted auditing standards are applicable to any engagement to express an opinion on one or more specified elements, accounts, or items of a financial statement. The first standard of reporting, which requires the auditor to state in the auditor's report whether the financial statements are presented in conformity with generally accepted accounting principles, is applicable only when the specified elements, accounts, or items of a financial statement are intended to be presented in conformity with generally accepted accounting principles. [Revised, November 2006, to reflect conforming changes necessary due to the issuance of Statement on Auditing Standards No. 113.]

.13 An engagement to express an opinion on one or more specified elements, accounts, or items of a financial statement may be undertaken as a separate engagement or in conjunction with an audit of financial statements. In either case, an auditor expresses an opinion on each of the specified elements, accounts, or items encompassed by the auditor's report; therefore, the measurement of materiality must be related to each individual element, account, or item reported on rather than to the aggregate thereof or to the financial statements taken as a whole. Consequently, an audit of a specified element, account, or item for purposes of reporting thereon is usually more extensive than if the same information were being considered in conjunction with an audit of financial statements taken as a whole. Also, many financial statement elements are interrelated, for example, sales and receivables; inventory and payables; and buildings and equipment and depreciation. The auditor should be satisfied that elements, accounts, or items that are interrelated with those on which he or she has been engaged to express an opinion have been considered in expressing an opinion.

.14 The auditor should not express an opinion on specified elements, accounts, or items included in financial statements on which he or she has expressed an adverse opinion or disclaimed an opinion based on an audit, if such reporting would be tantamount to expressing a piecemeal opinion on the financial statements (see section 508, *Reports on Audited Financial Statements*, paragraph .64). However, an auditor would be able to express an opinion on one or more specified elements, accounts, or items of a financial statement provided that the matters to be reported on and the related scope of the audit were not intended to and did not encompass so many elements, accounts, or items as to constitute a major portion of the financial statements. For example, it may be appropriate for an auditor to express an opinion on an entity's accounts receivable balance even if the auditor has disclaimed an opinion on the financial statements taken as a whole. However, the report on the specified element, account, or item should be presented separately from the report on the financial statements of the entity.

---

[8] See AT section 201, *Agreed-Upon Procedures Engagements*, for guidance when reporting on the results of applying agreed-upon procedures to one or more specified elements, accounts, or items of a financial statement. See AT section 101, *Attest Engagements*, for guidance when reporting on a review of one or more specified elements, accounts, or items of a financial statement. [Footnote renumbered by the issuance of Statement on Auditing Standards No. 77, November 1995. Footnote revised, January 2001, to reflect conforming changes necessary due to the issuance of Statement on Standards for Attestation Engagements No. 10.]

Reports on One or More Specified Elements, Accounts, or Items of a Financial Statement

.15 When an independent auditor is engaged to express an opinion on one or more specified elements, accounts, or items of a financial statement, the report should include—

a. A title that includes the word *independent*.[9]

b. A paragraph that—

(1) States that the specified elements, accounts, or items identified in the report were audited. If the audit was made in conjunction with an audit of the company's financial statements, the paragraph should so state and indicate the date of the auditor's report on those financial statements. Furthermore, any departure from the standard report on those statements should also be disclosed if considered relevant to the presentation of the specified element, account or item.

(2) States that the specified elements, accounts, or items are the responsibility of the Company's management and that the auditor is responsible for expressing an opinion on the specified elements, accounts or items based on the audit.

c. A paragraph that—

(1) States that the audit was conducted in accordance with generally accepted auditing standards and includes an identification of the United States of America as the country of origin of those standards (for example, auditing standards generally accepted in the United States of America or U.S. generally accepted auditing standards).

(2) States that those standards require that the auditor plan and perform the audit to obtain reasonable assurance about whether the specified elements, accounts, or items are free of material misstatement.

(3) States that an audit includes—

(a) Examining, on a test basis, evidence supporting the amounts and disclosures in the presentation of the specified elements, accounts, or items,

(b) Assessing the accounting principles used and significant estimates made by management, and

(c) Evaluating the overall presentation of the specified elements, accounts, or items.

(4) States that the auditor believes that his or her audit provides a reasonable basis for the auditor's opinion.

d. A paragraph[10] that—

(1) Describes the basis on which the specified elements, accounts, or items are presented (see paragraphs .09 and .10) and, when

---

[9] See footnote 1. [Footnote renumbered by the issuance of Statement on Auditing Standards No. 77, November 1995.]

[10] Alternatively, this requirement can be met by incorporating the description in the introductory paragraph discussed in paragraph .15*b above*. [Footnote renumbered by the issuance of Statement on Auditing Standards No. 77, November 1995.]

applicable, any agreements specifying such basis if the presentation is not prepared in conformity with generally accepted accounting principles.[11] If the presentation is prepared in conformity with generally accepted accounting principles, the paragraph should include an identification of the United States of America as the country of origin of those accounting principles (for example, accounting principles generally accepted in the United States of America or U.S. generally accepted accounting principles).

(2) If considered necessary, includes a description and the source of significant interpretations, if any, made by the Company's management, relating to the provisions of a relevant agreement.

e. A paragraph that expresses the auditor's opinion (or disclaims an opinion) on whether the specified elements, accounts, or items are fairly presented, in all material respects, in conformity with the basis of accounting described. If the auditor concludes that the specified elements, accounts, or items are not presented fairly on the basis of accounting described or if there has been a limitation on the scope of the audit, the auditor should disclose all the substantive reasons for that conclusion in an explanatory paragraph(s) (preceding the opinion paragraph) of the report and should include in the opinion paragraph appropriate modifying language and a reference to such explanatory paragraph(s).[12]

f. If the specified element, account, or item is prepared to comply with the requirements or financial reporting provisions of a contract or agreement that results in a presentation that is not in conformity with either generally accepted accounting principles or an other comprehensive basis of accounting, a separate paragraph at the end of the report stating that the report is intended solely for the information and use of those within the entity and the parties to the contract or agreement,[13] and is not intended to be and should not be used by anyone other than these specified parties. Such a restriction on the use of the report is necessary because the basis, assumptions, or purpose of the presentation (contained in the contract or agreement) is developed for and directed only to the parties to the contract or agreement.

g. The manual or printed signature of the auditor's firm.

h. The date.[14]

When expressing an opinion on one or more specified elements, accounts, or items of a financial statement, the auditor, to provide more information as to

---

[11] When the specified element, account, or item is presented in conformity with an other comprehensive basis of accounting, see paragraph .05*d*(2). [Footnote renumbered by the issuance of Statement on Auditing Standards No. 77, November 1995.]

[12] Paragraph 31 discusses other circumstances that may require that the auditor add additional explanatory language to the special report. [Footnote renumbered by the issuance of Statement on Auditing Standards No. 77, November 1995.]

[13] If the presentation is prepared on a basis prescribed by a governmental regulatory agency (which is also OCBOA), the auditor should restrict the distribution of the report on such presentation. See paragraph .05*f* for further reporting guidance in this situation. [Footnote renumbered by the issuance of Statement on Auditing Standards No. 77, November 1995.]

[14] See footnote 6. [Footnote renumbered by the issuance of Statement on Auditing Standards No. 77, November 1995.]

the scope of the audit, may wish to describe in a separate paragraph certain other auditing procedures applied. However, no modification in the content of paragraph .15*c* above should be made. [Revised, October 2000, to reflect conforming changes necessary due to the issuance of Statement on Auditing Standards No. 93.]

.16 If a specified element, account, or item is, or is based upon, an entity's net income or stockholders' equity or the equivalent thereof, the auditor should have audited the complete financial statements to express an opinion on the specified element, account, or item.

.17 The auditor should consider the effect that any departure, including additional explanatory language because of the circumstances discussed in section 508, *Reports on Audited Financial Statements*, paragraph .11, from the standard report on the audited financial statements might have on the report on a specified element, account, or item thereof.

.18 Following are illustrations of reports expressing an opinion on one or more specified elements, accounts, or items of a financial statement.

Report Relating to Accounts Receivable

Independent Auditor's Report

We have audited the accompanying schedule of accounts receivable of ABC Company as of December 31, 20X2. This schedule is the responsibility of the Company's management. Our responsibility is to express an opinion on this schedule based on our audit.

We conducted our audit in accordance with auditing standards generally accepted in the United States of America. Those standards require that we plan and perform the audit to obtain reasonable assurance about whether the schedule of accounts receivable is free of material misstatement. An audit includes examining, on a test basis, evidence supporting the amounts and disclosures in the schedule of accounts receivable. An audit also includes assessing the accounting principles used and significant estimates made by management, as well as evaluating the overall schedule presentation. We believe that our audit provides a reasonable basis for our opinion.

In our opinion, the schedule of accounts receivable referred to above presents fairly, in all material respects, the accounts receivable of ABC Company as of December 31, 20X2, in conformity with accounting principles generally accepted in the United States of America.[15]

Report Relating to Amount of Sales for the Purpose of Computing Rental

Independent Auditor's Report

We have audited the accompanying schedule of gross sales (as defined in the lease agreement dated March 4, 20XX, between ABC Company, as lessor, and XYZ Stores Corporation, as lessee) of XYZ Stores Corporation at its Main Street store, [*City*], [*State*], for the year ended December 31, 20X2. This schedule is the responsibility of XYZ Stores Corporation's management. Our responsibility is to express an opinion on this schedule based on our audit.

---

[15] Since this presentation was prepared in conformity with generally accepted accounting principles, the report need not be restricted. [Footnote renumbered by the issuance of Statement on Auditing Standards No. 77, November 1995.]

We conducted our audit in accordance with auditing standards generally accepted in the United States of America. Those standards require that we plan and perform the audit to obtain reasonable assurance about whether the schedule of gross sales is free of material misstatement. An audit includes examining, on a test basis, evidence supporting the amounts and disclosures in the schedule of gross sales. An audit also includes assessing the accounting principles used and significant estimates made by management, as well as evaluating the overall schedule presentation. We believe that our audit provides a reasonable basis for our opinion.

In our opinion, the schedule of gross sales referred to above presents fairly, in all material respects, the gross sales of XYZ Stores Corporation at its Main Street store, [*City*], [*State*], for the year ended December 31, 20X2, as defined in the lease agreement referred to in the first paragraph.

This report is intended solely for the information and use of the boards of directors and managements of XYZ Stores Corporation and ABC Company and is not intended to be and should not be used by anyone other than these specified parties.

Report Relating to Royalties

Independent Auditor's Report

We have audited the accompanying schedule of royalties applicable to engine production of the Q Division of XYZ Corporation for the year ended December 31, 20X2, under the terms of a license agreement dated May 14, 20XX, between ABC Company and XYZ Corporation. This schedule is the responsibility of XYZ Corporation's management. Our responsibility is to express an opinion on this schedule based on our audit.

We conducted our audit in accordance with auditing standards generally accepted in the United States of America. Those standards require that we plan and perform the audit to obtain reasonable assurance about whether the schedule of royalties is free of material misstatement. An audit includes examining, on a test basis, evidence supporting the amounts and disclosures in the schedule of royalties. An audit also includes assessing the accounting principles used and significant estimates made by management, as well as evaluating the overall schedule presentation. We believe that our audit provides a reasonable basis for our opinion.

We have been informed that, under XYZ Corporation's interpretation of the agreement referred to in the first paragraph, royalties were based on the number of engines produced after giving effect to a reduction for production retirements that were scrapped, but without a reduction for field returns that were scrapped, even though the field returns were replaced with new engines without charge to customers.

In our opinion, the schedule of royalties referred to above presents fairly, in all material respects, the number of engines produced by the Q Division of XYZ Corporation during the year ended December 31, 20X2, and the amount of royalties applicable thereto, under the license agreement referred to above.

This report is intended solely for the information and use of the boards of directors and managements of XYZ Corporation and ABC Company and is not intended to be and should not be used by anyone other than these specified parties.

Report on a Profit Participation[16]

Independent Auditor's Report

We have audited, in accordance with auditing standards generally accepted in the United States of America, the financial statements of XYZ Company for the year ended December 31, 20X1, and have issued our report thereon dated March 10, 20X2. We have also audited XYZ Company's schedule of John Smith's profit participation for the year ended December 31, 20X1. This schedule is the responsibility of the Company's management. Our responsibility is to express an opinion on this schedule based on our audit.

We conducted our audit of the schedule in accordance with auditing standards generally accepted in the United States of America. Those standards require that we plan and perform the audit to obtain reasonable assurance about whether the schedule of profit participation is free of material misstatement. An audit includes examining, on a test basis, evidence supporting the amounts and disclosures in the schedule. An audit also includes assessing the accounting principles used and significant estimates made by management, as well as evaluating the overall schedule presentation. We believe that our audit provides a reasonable basis for our opinion.

We have been informed that the documents that govern the determination of John Smith's profit participation are (*a*) the employment agreement between John Smith and XYZ Company dated February 1, 20X0, (*b*) the production and distribution agreement between XYZ Company and Television Network Incorporated dated March 1, 20X0, and (*c*) the studio facilities agreement between XYZ Company and QRX Studios dated April 1, 20X0, as amended November 1, 20X0.

In our opinion, the schedule of profit participation referred to above presents fairly, in all material respects, John Smith's participation in the profits of XYZ Company for the year ended December 31, 20X1, in accordance with the provisions of the agreements referred to above.

This report is intended solely for the information and use of the boards of directors and managements of XYZ Company and John Smith and is not intended to be and should not be used by anyone other than these specified parties.

Report on Federal and State Income Taxes Included in Financial Statements[17]

Independent Auditor's Report

We have audited, in accordance with auditing standards generally accepted in the United States of America, the financial statements of XYZ Company, Inc., for the year ended June 30, 20XX, and have issued our report thereon dated August 15, 20XX. We have also audited the current and deferred provision for the Company's federal and state income taxes for the year ended June 30, 20XX, included in those financial statements, and the related asset and liability tax accounts as of June 30, 20XX. This income tax information is the responsibility of the Company's management. Our responsibility is to express an opinion on it based on our audit.

[16] See paragraph .16. [Footnote renumbered by the issuance of Statement on Auditing Standards No. 77, November 1995.]

[17] See paragraph .16. [Footnote renumbered by the issuance of Statement on Auditing Standards No. 77, November 1995.]

We conducted our audit of the income tax information in accordance with auditing standards generally accepted in the United States of America. Those standards require that we plan and perform the audit to obtain reasonable assurance about whether the federal and state income tax accounts are free of material misstatement. An audit includes examining, on a test basis, evidence supporting the amounts and disclosures related to the federal and state income tax accounts. An audit also includes assessing the accounting principles used and significant estimates made by management, as well as evaluating the overall presentation of the federal and state income tax accounts. We believe that our audit provides a reasonable basis for our opinion.

In our opinion, the Company has paid or, in all material respects, made adequate provision in the financial statements referred to above for the payment of all federal and state income taxes and for related deferred income taxes that could be reasonably estimated at the time of our audit of the financial statements of XYZ Company, Inc., for the year ended June 30, 20XX.

[Revised, October 2000, to reflect conforming changes necessary due to the issuance of Statement on Auditing Standards No. 93.]

Compliance With Aspects of Contractual Agreements or Regulatory Requirements Related to Audited Financial Statements

.19 Entities may be required by contractual agreements, such as certain bond indentures and loan agreements, or by regulatory agencies to furnish compliance reports by independent auditors.[18] For example, loan agreements often impose on borrowers a variety of obligations involving matters such as payments into sinking funds, payments of interest, maintenance of current ratios, and restrictions of dividend payments. They usually also require the borrower to furnish annual financial statements that have been audited by an independent auditor. In some instances, the lenders or their trustees may request assurance from the independent auditor that the borrower has complied with certain covenants of the agreement relating to accounting matters. The independent auditor may satisfy this request by giving negative assurance relative to the applicable covenants based on the audit of the financial statements. This assurance may be given in a separate report or in one or more paragraphs of the auditor's report accompanying the financial statements. Such assurance, however, should not be given unless the auditor has audited the financial statements to which the contractual agreements or regulatory requirements relate and should not extend to covenants that relate to matters that have not been subjected to the audit procedures applied in the audit of the financial statements.[19] In addition, such assurance should not be given if the auditor has

---

[18] When the auditor is engaged to test compliance with laws and regulations in accordance with *Government Auditing Standards* issued by the Comptroller General of the United States (Yellow Book) and that engagement also requires the auditor to comply with generally accepted auditing standards and a law or regulation that requires the auditor to express an opinion on compliance, he or she should follow the requirements and guidance contained in section 801, *Compliance Audits*. However, absent all three requirements, the auditor needs to determine the appropriate audit or attestation section to follow. Paragraphs .01, .03, and .A1–.A2 of section 801 provide additional guidance. [Footnote renumbered by the issuance of Statement on Auditing Standards No. 77, November 1995. Footnote revised, December 2010, to reflect conforming changes necessary due to the issuance of SAS No. 117.]

[19] When the auditor is engaged to provide assurance on compliance with contractual agreements or regulatory provisions that relate to matters that have not been subjected to the audit procedures applied in the audit of the financial statements, the auditor should refer to the guidance in AT section 601, *Compliance Attestation*. [Footnote renumbered by the issuance of Statement on Auditing

(continued)

expressed an adverse opinion or disclaimed an opinion on the financial statements to which these covenants relate.

.20 When an auditor's report on compliance with contractual agreements or regulatory provisions is being given in a separate report, the report should include—

a. A title that includes the word *independent*.[20]

b. A paragraph that states the financial statements were audited in accordance with generally accepted auditing standards and includes an identification of the United States of America as the country of origin of those standards (for example, auditing standards generally accepted in the United States of America or U.S. generally accepted auditing standards) and the date of the auditor's report on those financial statements. Furthermore, any departure from the standard report on those statements should also be disclosed.

c. A paragraph that includes a reference to the specific covenants or paragraphs of the agreement, provides negative assurance relative to compliance with the applicable covenants of the agreement insofar as they relate to accounting matters, and specifies that the negative assurance is being given in connection with the audit of the financial statements. The auditor should ordinarily state that the audit was not directed primarily toward obtaining knowledge regarding compliance.

d. A paragraph that includes a description and the source of significant interpretations, if any, made by the Company's management relating to the provisions of a relevant agreement.

e. A separate paragraph at the end of the report stating that the report is intended solely for the information and use of those within the entity and the parties to the contract or agreement or the regulatory agency with which the report is being filed, and is not intended to be and should not be used by anyone other than these specified parties. Such a restriction on the use of the report is necessary because the basis, assumptions, or purpose of such presentations (contained in such contracts, agreements, or regulatory provisions) are developed for and directed only to the parties to the contract or agreement, or regulatory agency responsible for the provisions.

f. The manual or printed signature of the auditor's firm.

g. The date.[21]

[Revised, October 2000, to reflect conforming changes necessary due to the issuance of Statement on Auditing Standards No. 93.]

.21 When an auditor's report on compliance with contractual agreements or regulatory provisions is included in the report that expresses the auditor's opinion on the financial statements, the auditor should include a paragraph, after the opinion paragraph, that provides negative assurance relative to

(footnote continued)

Standards No. 77, November 1995. Footnote revised, February 1997, to reflect conforming changes necessary due to the issuance of Statement on Standards for Attestation Engagements No. 3. Footnote revised, January 2001, to reflect conforming changes necessary due to the issuance of Statement on Standards for Attestation Engagements No. 10.]

[20] See footnote 1. [Footnote renumbered by the issuance of Statement on Auditing Standards No. 77, November 1995.]

[21] See footnote 6. [Footnote renumbered by the issuance of Statement on Auditing Standards No. 77, November 1995.]

compliance with the applicable covenants of the agreement, insofar as they relate to accounting matters, and that specifies the negative assurance is being given in connection with the audit of the financial statements. The auditor should also ordinarily state that the audit was not directed primarily toward obtaining knowledge regarding compliance. In addition, the report should include a paragraph that includes a description and source of any significant interpretations made by the entity's management as discussed in paragraph .20*d* as well as a paragraph that restricts the use of the report to the specified parties as discussed in paragraph .20*e*. Following are examples of reports that might be issued:

Report on Compliance With Contractual Provisions Given in a Separate Report[22]

Independent Auditor's Report

We have audited, in accordance with auditing standards generally accepted in the United States of America, the balance sheet of XYZ Company as of December 31, 20X2, and the related statement of income, retained earnings, and cash flows for the year then ended, and have issued our report thereon dated February 16, 20X3.

In connection with our audit, nothing came to our attention that caused us to believe that the Company failed to comply with the terms, covenants, provisions, or conditions of sections XX to XX, inclusive, of the Indenture dated July 21, 20X0, with ABC Bank insofar as they relate to accounting matters. However, our audit was not directed primarily toward obtaining knowledge of such noncompliance.

This report is intended solely for the information and use of the boards of directors and management of XYZ Company and ABC Bank and is not intended to be and should not be used by anyone other than these specified parties.

Report on Compliance With Regulatory Requirements Given in a Separate Report When the Auditor's Report on the Financial Statements Included an Explanatory Paragraph Because of an Uncertainty

Independent Auditor's Report

We have audited, in accordance with auditing standards generally accepted in the United States of America, the balance sheet of XYZ Company as of December 31, 20X2, and the related statement of income, retained earnings, and cash flows for the year then ended, and have issued our report thereon dated March 5, 20X3, which included an explanatory paragraph that described the litigation discussed in Note X of those statements.

In connection with our audit, nothing came to our attention that caused us to believe that the Company failed to comply with the accounting provisions in sections (1), (2) and (3) of the [*name of state regulatory agency*]. However, our audit was not directed primarily toward obtaining knowledge of such noncompliance.

---

[22] When the auditor's report on compliance with contractual agreements or regulatory provisions is included in the report that expresses the auditor's opinion on the financial statements, the last two paragraphs of this report are examples of the paragraphs that should follow the opinion paragraph of the auditor's report on the financial statements. [Footnote renumbered by the issuance of Statement on Auditing Standards No. 77, November 1995.]

This report is intended solely for the information and use of the board of directors and managements of XYZ Company and the [*name of state regulatory agency*] and is not intended to be and should not be used by anyone other than these specified parties.

[Revised, October 2000, to reflect conforming changes necessary due to the issuance of Statement on Auditing Standards No. 93.]

Special-Purpose Financial Presentations to Comply With Contractual Agreements or Regulatory Provisions

.22 An auditor is sometimes asked to report on special-purpose financial statements prepared to comply with a contractual agreement[23] or regulatory provisions. In most circumstances, these types of presentations are intended solely for the use of the parties to the agreement, regulatory bodies, or other specified parties. This section discusses reporting on these types of presentations, which include the following:

a. A special-purpose financial presentation prepared in compliance with a contractual agreement or regulatory provision that does not constitute a complete presentation of the entity's assets, liabilities, revenues and expenses, but is otherwise prepared in conformity with generally accepted accounting principles or an other comprehensive basis of accounting (paragraphs .23 through .26).

b. A special-purpose financial presentation (may be a complete set of financial statements or a single financial statement) prepared on a basis of accounting prescribed in an agreement that does not result in a presentation in conformity with generally accepted accounting principles or an other comprehensive basis of accounting (paragraphs .27 through .30).

Financial Statements Prepared on a Basis of Accounting Prescribed in a Contractual Agreement or Regulatory Provision That Results in an Incomplete Presentation But One That is Otherwise in Conformity With Generally Accepted Accounting Principles or an Other Comprehensive Basis of Accounting

.23 A governmental agency may require a schedule of gross income and certain expenses of an entity's real estate operation in which income and expenses are measured in conformity with generally accepted accounting principles, but expenses are defined to exclude certain items such as interest, depreciation, and income taxes. Such a schedule may also present the excess of gross income over defined expenses. Also, a buy-sell agreement may specify a schedule of gross assets and liabilities of the entity measured in conformity with generally accepted accounting principles, but limited to the assets to be sold and liabilities to be transferred pursuant to the agreement.

.24 Paragraph .02 of this section defines the term *financial statement* and includes a list of financial presentations that an auditor should consider to be financial statements for reporting purposes. The concept of specified elements,

---

[23] A contractual agreement as discussed in this section is an agreement between the client and one or more third parties other than the auditor. [Footnote renumbered by the issuance of Statement on Auditing Standards No. 77, November 1995.]

accounts, or items of a financial statement discussed in paragraphs .11 through .18, on the other hand, refers to accounting information that is part of, but significantly less than, a financial statement. The financial presentations described above and similar presentations should generally be regarded as financial statements, even though, as indicated above, certain items may be excluded. Thus, when the auditor is asked to report on these types of presentations, the measurement of materiality for purposes of expressing an opinion should be related to the presentations taken as a whole (see section 312, *Audit Risk and Materiality in Conducting an Audit*). Further, the presentations should differ from complete financial statements only to the extent necessary to meet special purposes for which they were prepared. In addition, when these financial presentations contain items that are the same as, or similar to, those contained in a full set of financial statements prepared in conformity with generally accepted accounting principles, similar informative disclosures are appropriate (see paragraphs .09 and .10). The auditor should also be satisfied that the financial statements presented are suitably titled to avoid any implication that the special-purpose financial statements on which he or she is reporting are intended to present financial position, results of operations, or cash flows.

.25 When the auditor is asked to report on financial statements prepared on a basis of accounting prescribed in a contractual agreement or regulatory provision that results in an incomplete presentation but one that is otherwise in conformity with generally accepted accounting principles or an other comprehensive basis of accounting, the auditor's report should include—

a. A title that includes the word *independent*.[24]

b. A paragraph that—

(1) States that the financial statements identified in the report were audited.

(2) States that the financial statements are the responsibility of the Company's management[25] and that the auditor is responsible for expressing an opinion on the financial statements based on the audit.[26]

c. A paragraph that—

(1) States that the audit was conducted in accordance with generally accepted auditing standards and includes an identification of the United States of America as the country of origin of those standards (for example, auditing standards generally accepted in the United States of America or U.S. generally accepted auditing standards).

(2) States that those standards require that the auditor plan and perform the audit to obtain reasonable assurance about whether the financial statements are free of material misstatement.

---

[24] See footnote 1. [Footnote renumbered by the issuance of Statement on Auditing Standards No. 77, November 1995.]

[25] Sometimes the auditor's client may not be the person responsible for the financial statements on which the auditor is reporting. For example, when the auditor is engaged by the buyer to report on the seller's financial statements prepared in conformity with a buy-sell agreement, the person responsible for the financial statements may be the seller's management. In this case, the wording of this statement should be changed to clearly identify the party that is responsible for the financial statements reported on. [Footnote renumbered by the issuance of Statement on Auditing Standards No. 77, November 1995.]

[26] See footnote 2. [Footnote renumbered by the issuance of Statement on Auditing Standards No. 77, November 1995.]

(3) States that an audit includes—

(a) Examining, on a test basis, evidence supporting the amounts and disclosures in the financial statements,

(b) Assessing the accounting principles used and significant estimates made by management, and

(c) Evaluating the overall financial statement presentation.

(4) States that the auditor believes that the audit provides a reasonable basis for his or her opinion.

d. A paragraph that—

(1) Explains what the presentation is intended to present and refers to the note to the special-purpose financial statements that describes the basis of presentation (see paragraphs .09 and .10).

(2) If the basis of presentation is in conformity with generally accepted accounting principles, states that the presentation is not intended to be a complete presentation of the entity's assets, liabilities, revenues and expenses.[27]

e. A paragraph that expresses the auditor's opinion (or disclaims an opinion) related to the fair presentation, in all material respects, of the information the presentation is intended to present in conformity with generally accepted accounting principles or an other comprehensive basis of accounting. If the presentation is prepared in conformity with generally accepted accounting principles, the paragraph should include an identification of the United States of America as the country of origin of those accounting principles (for example, accounting principles generally accepted in the United States of America or U.S. generally accepted accounting principles). If the auditor concludes that the information the presentation is intended to present is not presented fairly on the basis of accounting described or if there has been a limitation on the scope of the audit, the auditor should disclose all the substantive reasons for that conclusion in an explanatory paragraph(s) (preceding the opinion paragraph) of the report and should include in the opinion paragraph appropriate modifying language and a reference to such explanatory paragraph(s).[28]

f. A separate paragraph at the end of the report stating that the report is intended solely for the information and use of those within the entity, the parties to the contract or agreement, the regulatory agency with which the report is being filed, or those with whom the entity is negotiating directly, and is not intended to be and should not be used by anyone other than these specified parties. However, such a paragraph is not appropriate if the report and related financial presentation are to be filed with a regulatory agency, such as the Securities and Exchange Commission, and are to be included in a document (such as a prospectus) that is distributed to the general public.

---

27 If the basis of presentation is an other comprehensive basis of accounting, the paragraph should state that the basis of presentation is a comprehensive basis of accounting other than generally accepted accounting principles and that it is not intended to be a complete presentation of the entity's assets, liabilities, revenues and expenses on the basis described. [Footnote renumbered by the issuance of Statement on Auditing Standards No. 77, November 1995.]

28 Paragraph .31 discusses other circumstances that may require that the auditor add additional explanatory language to the special report. [Footnote renumbered by the issuance of Statement on Auditing Standards No. 77, November 1995.]

g. The manual or printed signature of the auditor's firm.

h. The date.[29]

[Revised, October 2000, to reflect conforming changes necessary due to the issuance of Statement on Auditing Standards No. 93.]

.26 The following examples illustrate reports expressing an opinion on such special-purpose financial statements:

Report on a Schedule of Gross Income and Certain Expenses to Meet a Regulatory Requirement and to Be Included in a Document Distributed to the General Public

Independent Auditor's Report

We have audited the accompanying Historical Summaries of Gross Income and Direct Operating Expenses of ABC Apartments, City, State (Historical Summaries), for each of the three years in the period ended December 31, 20XX. These Historical Summaries are the responsibility of the Apartments' management. Our responsibility is to express an opinion on the Historical Summaries based on our audits.

We conducted our audits in accordance with auditing standards generally accepted in the United States of America. Those standards require that we plan and perform the audit to obtain reasonable assurance about whether the Historical Summaries are free of material misstatement. An audit includes examining, on a test basis, evidence supporting the amounts and disclosures in the Historical Summaries. An audit also includes assessing the accounting principles used and significant estimates made by management, as well as evaluating the overall presentation of the Historical Summaries. We believe that our audits provide a reasonable basis for our opinion.

The accompanying Historical Summaries were prepared for the purpose of complying with the rules and regulations of the Securities and Exchange Commission (for inclusion in the registration statement on Form S-11 of DEF Corporation) as described in Note X and are not intended to be a complete presentation of the Apartments' revenues and expenses.

In our opinion, the Historical Summaries referred to above present fairly, in all material respects, the gross income and direct operating expenses described in Note X of ABC Apartments for each of the three years in the period ended December 31, 20XX, in conformity with accounting principles generally accepted in the United States of America.

Report on a Statement of Assets Sold and Liabilities Transferred to Comply With a Contractual Agreement

Independent Auditor's Report

We have audited the accompanying statement of net assets sold of ABC Company as of June 8, 20XX. This statement of net assets sold is the responsibility of ABC Company's management. Our responsibility is to express an opinion on the statement of net assets sold based on our audit.

---

[29] See footnote 6. [Footnote renumbered by the issuance of Statement on Auditing Standards No. 77, November 1995.]

We conducted our audit in accordance with auditing standards generally accepted in the United States of America. Those standards require that we plan and perform the audit to obtain reasonable assurance about whether the statement of net assets sold is free of material misstatement. An audit includes examining, on a test basis, evidence supporting the amounts and disclosures in the statement. An audit also includes assessing the accounting principles used and significant estimates made by management, as well as evaluating the overall presentation of the statement of net assets sold. We believe that our audit provides a reasonable basis for our opinion.

The accompanying statement was prepared to present the net assets of ABC Company sold to XYZ Corporation pursuant to the purchase agreement described in Note X, and is not intended to be a complete presentation of ABC Company's assets and liabilities.

In our opinion, the accompanying statement of net assets sold presents fairly, in all material respects, the net assets of ABC Company as of June 8, 20XX sold pursuant to the purchase agreement referred to in Note X, in conformity with accounting principles generally accepted in the United States of America.

This report is intended solely for the information and use of the boards of directors and managements of ABC Company and XYZ Corporation and is not intended to be and should not be used by anyone other than these specified parties.

[Revised, October 2000, to reflect conforming changes necessary due to the issuance of Statement on Auditing Standards No. 93.]

Financial Statements Prepared on a Basis of Accounting Prescribed in an Agreement That Results in a Presentation That is not in Conformity With Generally Accepted Accounting Principles or an Other Comprehensive Basis of Accounting

.27 The auditor may be asked to report on special-purpose financial statements prepared in conformity with a basis of accounting that departs from generally accepted accounting principles or an other comprehensive basis of accounting. A loan agreement, for example, may require the borrower to prepare consolidated financial statements in which assets, such as inventory, are presented on a basis that is not in conformity with generally accepted accounting principles or an other comprehensive basis of accounting. An acquisition agreement may require the financial statements of the entity being acquired (or a segment of it) to be prepared in conformity with generally accepted accounting principles except for certain assets, such as receivables, inventories, and properties for which a valuation basis is specified in the agreement.

.28 Financial statements prepared under a basis of accounting as discussed above are not considered to be prepared in conformity with a "comprehensive basis of accounting" as contemplated by paragraph .04 of this section because the criteria used to prepare such financial statements do not meet the requirement of being "criteria having substantial support," even though the criteria are definite.

.29 When an auditor is asked to report on these types of financial presentations, the report should include—

a. A title that includes the word *independent*.[30]

---

[30] See footnote 1. [Footnote renumbered by the issuance of Statement on Auditing Standards No. 77, November 1995.]

b. A paragraph that—

(1) States that the special-purpose financial statements identified in the report were audited.

(2) States that the financial statements are the responsibility of the Company's management[31] and that the auditor is responsible for expressing an opinion on the financial statements based on the audit.[32]

c. A paragraph that—

(1) States that the audit was conducted in accordance with generally accepted auditing standards and includes an identification of the United States of America as the country of origin of those standards (for example, auditing standards generally accepted in the United States of America or U.S. generally accepted auditing standards).

(2) States that those standards require that the auditor plan and perform the audit to obtain reasonable assurance about whether the financial statements are free of material misstatement.

(3) States that an audit includes—

(*a*) Examining, on a test basis, evidence supporting the amounts and disclosures in the financial statements,

(*b*) Assessing the accounting principles used and significant estimates made by management, and

(*c*) Evaluating the overall financial statement presentation.

(4) States that the auditor believes that the audit provides a reasonable basis for the auditor's opinion.

d. A paragraph that—

(1) Explains what the presentation is intended to present and refers to the note to the special-purpose financial statements that describes the basis of presentation (see paragraphs .09 and .10).

(2) States that the presentation is not intended to be a presentation in conformity with generally accepted accounting principles.

e. A paragraph that includes a description and the source of significant interpretations, if any, made by the Company's management relating to the provisions of a relevant agreement.

f. A paragraph that expresses the auditor's opinion (or disclaims an opinion) related to the fair presentation, in all material respects, of the information the presentation is intended to present on the basis of accounting specified. If the auditor concludes that the information the presentation is intended to present is not presented fairly on the basis of accounting described or if there has been a limitation on the scope of the audit, the auditor should disclose all the substantive reasons for that conclusion in an explanatory paragraph(s) (preceding

---

[31] See footnote 25. [Footnote renumbered by the issuance of Statement on Auditing Standards No. 77, November 1995.]

[32] See footnote 2. [Footnote renumbered by the issuance of Statement on Auditing Standards No. 77, November 1995.]

the opinion paragraph) of the report and should include in the opinion paragraph appropriate modifying language and a reference to such explanatory paragraph(s).[33]

g. A separate paragraph at the end of the report stating that the report is intended solely for the information and use of those within the entity, the parties to the contract or agreement, the regulatory agency with which the report is being filed, or those with whom the entity is negotiating directly, and is not intended to be and should not be used by anyone other than these specified parties. For example, if the financial statements have been prepared for the specified purpose of obtaining bank financing, the report's use should be restricted to the various banks with whom the entity is negotiating the proposed financing.

h. The manual or printed signature of the auditor's firm.

i. The date.[34]

[Revised, October 2000, to reflect conforming changes necessary due to the issuance of Statement on Auditing Standards No. 93.]

.30 The following example illustrates reporting on special-purpose financial statements that have been prepared pursuant to a loan agreement:

Report on Financial Statements Prepared Pursuant to a Loan Agreement That Results in a Presentation not in Conformity With Generally Accepted Accounting Principles or an Other Comprehensive Basis of Accounting

Independent Auditor's Report

We have audited the special-purpose statement of assets and liabilities of ABC Company as of December 31, 20X2 and 20X1, and the related special-purpose statements of revenues and expenses and of cash flows for the years then ended. These financial statements are the responsibility of the Company's management. Our responsibility is to express an opinion on these financial statements based on our audits.

We conducted our audits in accordance with auditing standards generally accepted in the United States of America. Those standards require that we plan and perform the audit to obtain reasonable assurance about whether the financial statements are free of material misstatement. An audit includes examining, on a test basis, evidence supporting the amounts and disclosures in the financial statements. An audit also includes assessing the accounting principles used and significant estimates made by management, as well as evaluating the overall financial statement presentation. We believe that our audits provide a reasonable basis for our opinion.

The accompanying special-purpose financial statements were prepared for the purpose of complying with Section 4 of a loan agreement between DEF Bank and the Company as discussed in Note X, and are not intended to be a presentation in conformity with generally accepted accounting principles.

---

[33] Paragraph .31 discusses other circumstances that may require that the auditor add additional explanatory language to the special report. [Footnote renumbered by the issuance of Statement on Auditing Standards No. 77, November 1995.]

[34] See footnote 6. [Footnote renumbered by the issuance of Statement on Auditing Standards No. 77, November 1995.]

In our opinion, the special-purpose financial statements referred to above present fairly, in all material respects, the assets and liabilities of ABC Company at December 31, 20X2 and 20X1, and the revenues, expenses and cash flows for the years then ended, on the basis of accounting described in Note X.

This report is intended solely for the information and use of the boards of directors and management of ABC Company and DEF Bank and is not intended to be and should not be used by anyone other than these specified parties.

[Revised, October 2000, to reflect conforming changes necessary due to the issuance of Statement on Auditing Standards No. 93.]

Circumstances Requiring Explanatory Language in an Auditor's Special Report

.31 Certain circumstances, while not affecting the auditor's unqualified opinion, may require that the auditor add additional explanatory language to the special report. These circumstances include the following:

a. *Lack of Consistency in Accounting Principles.* If there has been a change in accounting principles or in the method of their application,[35] the auditor should add an explanatory paragraph to the report (following the opinion paragraph) that describes the change and refers to the note to the financial presentation (or specified elements, accounts, or items thereof) that discusses the change and its effect thereon[36] if the accounting change is considered relevant to the presentation. Guidance on reporting in this situation is contained in section 508, *Reports on Audited Financial Statements*, paragraphs .16 through .18.[37–38]

b. *Going Concern Uncertainties.* If the auditor has substantial doubt about the entity's ability to continue as a going concern for a reasonable period of time not to exceed one year beyond the date of the financial statement, the auditor should add an explanatory paragraph after the opinion paragraph of the report only if the auditor's substantial doubt is relevant to the presentation.[39]

c. *Other Auditors.* When the auditor decides to make reference to the report of another auditor as a basis, in part, for his or her opinion, the auditor should disclose that fact in the introductory paragraph

---

[35] When financial statements (or specified elements, accounts, or items thereof) have been prepared in conformity with generally accepted accounting principles in prior years, and the entity changes its method of presentation in the current year by preparing its financial statements in conformity with an other comprehensive basis of accounting, the auditor need not follow the reporting guidance in this subparagraph. However, the auditor may wish to add an explanatory paragraph to the report to highlight (1) a difference in the basis of presentation from that used in prior years or (2) that another report has been issued on the entity's financial statements prepared in conformity with another basis of presentation (for example, when cash basis financial statements are issued in addition to GAAP financial statements). [Footnote renumbered by the issuance of Statement on Auditing Standards No. 77, November 1995.]

[36] A change in the tax law is not considered to be a change in accounting principle for which the auditor would need to add an explanatory paragraph, although disclosure may be necessary. [Footnote renumbered by the issuance of Statement on Auditing Standards No. 77, November 1995.]

[37–38] [Footnotes deleted to reflect conforming changes necessary due to the issuance of Statement on Auditing Standards No. 79.]

[39] See section 341A, *The Auditor's Consideration of an Entity's Ability to Continue as a Going Concern*, for a report example when the auditor has substantial doubt about the entity's ability to continue as a going concern. [Footnote renumbered by the issuance of Statement on Auditing Standards No. 77, November 1995.]

of the report and should refer to the report of the other auditors in expressing his or her opinion. Guidance on reporting in this situation is contained in section 508, *Reports on Audited Financial Statements*, paragraphs .12 and .13.

d. *Comparative Financial Statements (or Specified Elements, Accounts, or Items Thereof).* If the auditor expresses an opinion on prior-period financial statements (or specified elements, accounts, or items thereof) that is different from the opinion he or she previously expressed on that same information, the auditor should disclose all of the substantive reasons for the different opinion in a separate explanatory paragraph preceding the opinion paragraph of the report. Guidance on reporting in this situation is contained in section 508, *Reports on Audited Financial Statements*, paragraphs .68 and .69.

As in reports on financial statements prepared in conformity with generally accepted accounting principles, the auditor may add an explanatory paragraph to emphasize a matter regarding the financial statements (or specified elements, accounts, or items thereof). [Revised, February 1997, to reflect conforming changes necessary due to the issuance of Statement on Auditing Standards No. 79.]

Financial Information Presented in Prescribed Forms or Schedules

.32 Printed forms or schedules designed or adopted by the bodies with which they are to be filed often prescribe the wording of an auditor's report. Many of these forms are not acceptable to independent auditors because the prescribed form of auditor's report does not conform to the applicable professional reporting standards. For example, the prescribed language of the report may call for statements by the auditor that are not consistent with the auditor's function or responsibility.

.33 Some report forms can be made acceptable by inserting additional wording; others can be made acceptable only by complete revision. When a printed report form calls upon an independent auditor to make a statement that he or she is not justified in making, the auditor should reword the form or attach a separate report. In those situations, the reporting provisions of paragraph .05 may be appropriate.

Effective Date

.34 This section is effective for reports issued on or after July 1, 1989. Early application of the provisions of this section is permissible.

AU Section 9623

Special Reports: Auditing Interpretations of Section 623

[1.] Auditor's Report Under Employee Retirement Income Security Act of 1974

[.01–.08] [Withdrawn February 1983.]

[2.] Reports on Elements, Accounts, or Items of a Financial Statement That Are Presented in Conformity with GAAP

[.09–.10] [Withdrawn March 1989, by SAS No. 62.] (See section 623.)

[3.] Compliance With the Foreign Corrupt Practices Act of 1977

[.11–.14] [Transferred to section 9642; Deleted October 1993.] [Revised, January 2001, to reflect conforming changes necessary due to the issuance of Statement on Standards for Attestation Engagements No. 10; Revised, January 2009, to reflect conforming changes necessary due to the issuance of Statement on Standards for Attestation Engagements No. 15.]

[4.] Reports on Engagements Solely to Meet State Regulatory Examination Requirements

[.15–.16] [Deleted April 1981 by SAS No. 35, as superseded by SAS No. 75, as superseded by SAS No. 93.] (See section 622.) [Revised, October 2000, to reflect conforming changes necessary due to the issuance of Statement on Auditing Standards No. 93.]

[5.] Financial Statements Prepared in Accordance with Accounting Practices Specified in an Agreement

[.17–.25] [Withdrawn March 1989 by SAS No. 62.] (See section 623.)

[6.] Reporting on Special-Purpose Financial Presentations[3–4]

[.26–.31] [Withdrawn March 1989 by SAS No. 62.] (See section 623.)

[7.] Understanding of Agreed-Upon Procedures

[.32–.33] [Deleted April 1981 by SAS No. 35, as superseded by SAS No. 75, as superseded by SAS No. 93.] (See section 622.) [Revised, October 2000, to reflect conforming changes necessary due to the issuance of Statement on Auditing Standards No. 93.]

[8.] Adequacy of Disclosure in Financial Statements Prepared on a Comprehensive Basis of Accounting Other Than Generally Accepted Accounting Principles

[.34–.39] [Withdrawn March 1989 by SAS No. 62.] (See section 623.)

[3–4] [Footnote deleted.]

9. Auditors' Special Reports on Property and Liability Insurance Companies' Loss Reserves

.40 *Question*—The instructions to the statutory annual statement to be filed by property and liability insurance companies with state regulatory agencies include the following:

> If a company is required by its domiciliary commissioner, there is to be submitted to the commissioner as an addendum to the Annual Statement by April 1 of the subsequent year a statement of a qualified loss reserve specialist setting forth his or her opinion relating to loss and loss adjustment expense reserves.
>
> The term "qualified loss reserve specialist" includes an independent auditor who has competency in loss reserve evaluation.

.41 If an independent auditor who has made an audit of the insurance company's financial statements in accordance with generally accepted auditing standards is engaged to express a separate opinion on the company's loss and loss adjustment expense reserves for the purpose of compliance with the above instruction, what form of report should be used by the independent auditor?

.42 *Interpretation*—Section 623 paragraphs .11–.18 provide guidance on auditors' reports expressing an opinion on one or more specified elements, accounts, or items of a financial statement. Following are illustrations of the auditor's report expressing an opinion on a company's loss and loss adjustment expense reserves and the schedule of liabilities for losses and loss adjustment expenses that would accompany the report.[5]

Illustrative report

Board of Directors

X Insurance Company

We are members of the American Institute of Certified Public Accountants (AICPA) and are the independent public accountants of X Insurance Company. We acknowledge our responsibility under the AICPA's Code of Professional Conduct to undertake only those engagements which we can complete with professional competence.

We have audited the financial statements prepared in conformity with accounting principles generally accepted in the United States of America [*or prepared in conformity with accounting practices prescribed or permitted by the Insurance Department of the State of..........*] of X Insurance Company as of December 31, 20X0, and have issued our report thereon dated March 1, 19X1. In the course of our audit, we have audited the estimated liabilities for unpaid losses and unpaid loss adjustment expenses of X Insurance Company as of December 31, 20X0, as set forth in the accompanying schedule including consideration of the assumptions and methods relating to the estimation of such liabilities.

In our opinion, the accompanying schedule presents fairly, in all material respects, the estimated unpaid losses and unpaid loss adjustment expenses of X Insurance Company that could be reasonably estimated at December 31, 20X0, in conformity with accounting practices prescribed or permitted by the Insurance Department of the State of .... on a basis consistent with that of the preceding year.

---

[5] If a significant period of time has elapsed between the date of the report on the financial statements and the date he is reporting on the loss and loss adjustment expense reserves, the auditor may wish to include the following paragraph after the opinion paragraph: Because we have not audited any financial statements of X Insurance Company as of any date or for any period subsequent to December 31, 20X0, we have no knowledge of the effects, if any, on the liability for unpaid losses and unpaid loss adjustment expenses of events that may have occurred subsequent to the date of our audit.

This report is intended solely for the information and use of the board of directors and management of X Insurance Company and [*the state regulatory agencies to whose jurisdiction the entity is subject*] and is not intended to be and should not be used by anyone other than these specified parties.

Signature
Date

X Insurance Company
Schedule of Liabilities for Losses and Loss Adjustment Expenses
December 31, 19X0

Liability for losses	$xx,xxx,xxx
Liability for loss adjustment expenses	x,xxx,xxx
Total	$xx,xxx,xxx

Note 1—Basis of presentation

The above schedule has been prepared in conformity with accounting practices prescribed or permitted by the Insurance Department of the State of .... (Significant differences between statutory practices and generally accepted accounting principles for the calculation of the above amounts should be described but the monetary effect of any such differences need not be stated.)

Losses and loss adjustment expenses are provided for when incurred in accordance with the applicable requirements of the insurance laws [and/or regulations] of the State of .... Such provisions include (1) individual case estimates for reported losses, (2) estimates received from other insurers with respect to reinsurance assumed, (3) estimates for unreported losses based on past experience modified for current trends, and (4) estimates of expenses for investigating and settling claims.

Note 2—Reinsurance

The Company reinsures certain portions of its liability insurance coverages to limit the amount of loss on individual claims and purchases catastrophe insurance to protect against aggregate single occurrence losses. Certain portions of property insurance are reinsured on a quota share basis.

The liability for losses and the liability for loss adjustment expenses were reduced by $xxx,xxx and $xxx,xxx, respectively, for reinsurance ceded to other companies.

Contingent liability exists with respect to reinsurance which would become an actual liability in the event the reinsuring companies, or any of them, might be unable to meet their obligations to the Company under existing reinsurance agreements.

.43 *Question*—The instructions to the statutory annual statement also include the following:

> If there has been any material change in the assumptions and/or methods from those previously employed, that change should be described in the statement of opinion by inserting a phrase such as:
>
> A material change in assumptions (and/or methods) was made during the past year, but such change accords with accepted loss reserving standards.

A brief description of the change should follow.

.44 In what circumstances is it appropriate for the independent auditor to modify his special report on loss and loss adjustment expense reserves for material changes in assumptions and/or methods?

.45 *Interpretation*—Section 420 paragraph .06 states that changes in accounting principles and methods of applying them affect consistency and require the addition of an explanatory paragraph (following the opinion paragraph) in the auditor's report on the audited financial statements. Section 623 paragraph .16 states that, if applicable, any departures from the auditor's standard report on the related financial statements should be indicated in the special report on an element, account, or item of a financial statement.

.46 Section 420 paragraph .16 states that a change in accounting estimate is not a change affecting consistency requiring recognition in the auditor's report. However, such changes in estimates that are disclosed in the financial statements on which the auditor has reported should also be disclosed in the notes to the schedule of liabilities for unpaid losses and unpaid loss adjustment expenses accompanying the auditor's special report. (See Financial Accounting Standards Board (FASB) *Accounting Standards Codification* (ASC) 250-10-50-4.)

[Issue Date: May 1981; Revised: February 1999; Revised: October 2000; Revised: June 2009.]

10. Reports on the Financial Statements Included in Internal Revenue Form 990, "Return of Organizations Exempt from Income Tax"

.47 *Question*—Internal Revenue Form 990, "Return of Organizations Exempt from Income Tax," may be used as a uniform annual report by charitable organizations in some states for reporting to both state and federal governments. Many states require an auditor's opinion on whether the financial statements included in the report[6] are presented fairly in conformity with generally accepted accounting principles. Ordinarily, financial statements included in a Form 990 used by a charitable organization as a uniform annual report may be expected to contain certain material departures from the accounting principles in FASB ASC 954, *Health Care Entities*, and FASB ASC 958, *Not-for-Profit Entities*.

.48 In most states the report is used primarily to satisfy statutory requirements, but regulatory authorities make the financial statements and the accompanying auditor's report a matter of public record. In some situations, however, there may be public distribution of the report. What should be the form of the auditor's report in each of the above situations?

.49 *Interpretation*—In both situations, the auditor should first consider whether the financial statements (including appropriate notes to financial statements) are in conformity with generally accepted accounting principles. If they are, the auditor can express an unqualified opinion.

.50 If the financial statements are not in conformity with generally accepted accounting principles, the auditor should consider the distribution of the report to determine whether it is appropriate to issue a special report (as illustrated in section 623, *Special Reports*, paragraph .08, for reporting on financial statements prepared in accordance with the requirements or financial reporting provisions of a government regulatory agency).

.51 Section 623 permits this type of special report only if the financial statements and report are intended solely for use by those within the entity and one or more regulatory agencies to whose jurisdiction the entity is subject.

---

[6] As used in this interpretation, the report refers to a Form 990 report by a charitable organization in a filing with a government agency.

However, section 623 makes this form of reporting appropriate, even though by law or regulation the accountant's report may be made a matter of public record.[7]

.52 The following example illustrates a report expressing an opinion on such special purpose financial statements:

Independent Auditor's Report

We have audited the balance sheet (Part IV) of XYZ Charity as of December 31, 20XX, and the related statement of revenue, expenses and changes in net assets (Part I) and statement of functional expenses (Part II) for the year then ended included in the accompanying Internal Revenue Service Form 990. These financial statements are the responsibility of Charity's management. Our responsibility is to express an opinion on these financial statements based on our audit.

We conducted our audit in accordance with auditing standards generally accepted in the United States of America. Those standards require that we plan and perform the audit to obtain reasonable assurance about whether the financial statements are free of material misstatement. An audit includes examining, on a test basis, evidence supporting the amounts and disclosures in the financial statements. An audit also includes assessing the accounting principles used and significant estimates made by management, as well as evaluating the overall financial statement presentation. We believe that our audit provides a reasonable basis for our opinion.

As described in Note X, these financial statements were prepared in conformity with the accounting practices prescribed by the Internal Revenue Service and the Office of the State of ......, which is a comprehensive basis of accounting other than generally accepted accounting principles.

In our opinion, the financial statements referred to above present fairly, in all material respects, the assets, liabilities and fund balances of XYZ Charity as of December 31, 19XX and its revenue and expenses and changes in fund balances for the year then ended on the basis of accounting described in Note X.[8]

Our audit was made for the purpose of forming an opinion on the above financial statements taken as a whole. The accompanying information on pages ...... to ...... is presented for purposes of additional analysis and is not a required part of the above financial statements. Such information, except for that portion marked "unaudited," on which we express no opinion, has been subjected to the auditing procedures applied in the audit of the above financial statements; and, in our opinion, the information is fairly stated in all material respects in relation to the financial statements taken as a whole.

This report is intended solely for the information and use of the board of directors and management of XYZ Charity, the Internal Revenue Service, and the Office of the State of ...... and is not intended to be and should not be used by anyone other than these specified parties.

[*Signature*]

[*Date*]

---

[7] *Public record*, for purposes of auditors' reports in states with filing requirements for exempt organizations, includes circumstances in which specific requests must be made by the public to obtain access to or copies of the report, notwithstanding the fact that some states may advertise or require the exempt organization to advertise the availability of Form 990. In contrast, *public distribution*, for purposes of auditors' reports in state filings on various Forms 990 dealing with exempt organizations, includes circumstances in which the regulatory agency or the exempt organization, either because of regulatory requirements or voluntarily, distributes copies of Form 990 to contributors or others without receiving a specific request for such distribution.

[8] [Footnote deleted.]

.53 If there is public distribution[9] of the report, because the law requires it or otherwise (copies of Form 990 are distributed to contributors or others without receiving a specific request for such distribution) and the financial statements included in it are not in conformity with generally accepted accounting principles, a special report (as illustrated in section 623 paragraph .08) is not appropriate. In such cases, the auditor should express a qualified or adverse opinion and disclose the effects on the financial statements of the departures from generally accepted accounting principles if the effects are reasonably determinable. If the effects are not reasonably determinable, the report should so state.

[.54] [Paragraph deleted to reflect conforming changes necessary due to the issuance of Statement on Auditing Standards No. 87.]

[Issue Date: December 1991; Revised: February 1997; Revised: February 1999; Revised: October 2000; Revised: June 2009.]

11. Reporting on Current-Value Financial Statements That Supplement Historical-Cost Financial Statements in Presentations of Real Estate Entities

.55 *Question*—A real estate entity presents current-value financial statements[10] to supplement historical-cost financial statements. May an auditor accept an engagement to report on current-value financial statements that supplement historical-cost financial statements, and if so, how should the auditor report?

.56 *Interpretation*—An auditor may accept an engagement to report on current-value financial statements that supplement historical-cost financial statements of a real estate entity only if the auditor believes the following two conditions exist—

- the measurement and disclosure criteria used to prepare the current-value financial statements are reasonable, and
- competent persons using the measurement and disclosure criteria would ordinarily obtain materially similar measurements or disclosures.

.57 If these conditions are satisfied, an auditor may report on such current-value financial statements in a manner similar to that discussed in section 623, *Special Reports*, paragraph .29. However, because the current-value financial statements only supplement the historical-cost financial statements and are not presented as a stand-alone presentation, it is not necessary to restrict the use of the auditor's report on the presentation as required by that paragraph.

---

[9] Auditors should consider whether there is a public distribution requirement by reference to the relevant state law. However, at this time (April 1982), most state laws do not contain a public distribution requirement and a special report is ordinarily appropriate. For example, the laws of New York, New Jersey and Connecticut do not presently require public distribution as defined by this interpretation.

[10] Generally accepted accounting principles require the use of current-value accounting for financial statements of certain types of entities (for example, investment companies, employee benefit plans, personal financial statements, and mutual and common trust funds). This interpretation does not apply to reports on current-value financial statements of such entities. The auditor engaged to report on current-value financial statements of such entities should follow the guidance in section 508, *Reports on Audited Financial Statements*, and applicable industry guidance. [Footnote revised, June 2009, to reflect conforming changes necessary due to the issuance of recent authoritative literature.]

.58 The following is an example of a report an auditor might issue when reporting on current-value financial statements that supplement historical-cost financial statements of a real estate entity:

Independent Auditor's Report

We have audited the accompanying historical-cost balance sheets of X Company as of December 31, 20X3 and 20X2, and the related historical-cost statements of income, shareholders' equity and cash flows for each of the three years in the period ended December 31, 20X3. We also have audited the supplemental current-value balance sheets of X Company as of December 31, 20X3 and 20X2, and the related supplemental current-value statements of income and shareholders' equity for each of the three years in the period ended December 31, 20X3. These financial statements are the responsibility of the Company's management. Our responsibility is to express an opinion on these financial statements based on our audits.

We conducted our audits in accordance with auditing standards generally accepted in the United States of America. Those standards require that we plan and perform the audit to obtain reasonable assurance about whether the financial statements are free of material misstatement. An audit includes examining, on a test basis, evidence supporting the amounts and disclosures in the financial statements. An audit also includes assessing the accounting principles used and significant estimates made by management, as well as evaluating the overall financial statement presentation. We believe that our audits provide a reasonable basis for our opinion.

In our opinion, the historical-cost financial statements referred to above present fairly, in all material respects, the financial position of X Company as of December 31, 20X3 and 20X2, and the results of its operations and its cash flows for each of the three years in the period ended December 31, 20X3, in conformity with accounting principles generally accepted in the United States of America.

As described in Note 1, the supplemental current-value financial statements have been prepared by management to present relevant financial information that is not provided by the historical-cost financial statements and are not intended to be a presentation in conformity with generally accepted accounting principles. In addition, the supplemental current-value financial statements do not purport to present the net realizable, liquidation, or market value of the Company as a whole. Furthermore, amounts ultimately realized by the Company from the disposal of properties may vary significantly from the current values presented.

In our opinion, the supplemental current-value financial statements referred to above present fairly, in all material respects, the information set forth in them on the basis of accounting described in Note 1.

[*Signature*]

[*Date*]

.59 The auditor should also consider the adequacy of disclosures relating to the current value financial statements. Such disclosures should describe the accounting policies applied and such matters as the basis of presentation, nature of the reporting entity's properties, status of construction-in-process, valuation bases used for each classification of assets and liabilities, and sources of valuation. These matters should be disclosed in the notes in a sufficiently clear and comprehensive manner that enables a knowledgeable reader to understand the current-value financial statements.

[Issue Date: July 1990; Revised: February 1999; Revised: October 2000.]

12. Evaluation of the Appropriateness of Informative Disclosures in Insurance Enterprises' Financial Statements Prepared on a Statutory Basis[11]

.60 *Question*—Insurance enterprises issue financial statements prepared in accordance with accounting practices prescribed or permitted by insurance regulators (a "statutory basis") in addition to, or instead of, financial statements prepared in accordance with generally accepted accounting principles (GAAP). Effective January 1, 2001, most states are expected to adopt a comprehensively updated *Accounting Practices and Procedures Manual*, as revised by the National Association of Insurance Commissioners' (NAIC's) Codification project. The updated *Accounting Practices and Procedures Manual*, along with any subsequent revisions, is referred to as the revised Manual. The revised Manual contains extensive disclosure requirements. As a result, after a state adopts the revised Manual, its statutory basis of accounting will include informative disclosures appropriate for that basis of accounting. The NAIC Annual Statement Instructions prescribe the financial statements to be included in the annual audited financial report. Some states may not adopt the revised Manual or may adopt it with significant departures. How should auditors evaluate whether informative disclosures in financial statements prepared on a statutory basis are appropriate?[12] [As amended, effective for annual financial statements for fiscal years ending on or after December 15, 2001, and complete sets of interim financial statements for periods beginning on or after that date and audits of those financial statements, by Statement of Position 01-5.]

.61 *Interpretation*—Financial statements prepared on a statutory basis are financial statements prepared on a comprehensive basis of accounting other than GAAP according to section 623, *Special Reports*, paragraph .04. Section 623 paragraph .09 states that "When reporting on financial statements prepared on a comprehensive basis of accounting other than generally accepted accounting principles, the auditor should consider whether the financial statements (including the accompanying notes) include all informative disclosures that are appropriate for the basis of accounting used. The auditor should apply essentially the same criteria to financial statements prepared on an other comprehensive basis of accounting as he or she does to financial statements prepared in conformity with generally accepted accounting principles. Therefore, the auditor's opinion should be based on his or her judgment regarding whether the financial statements, including the related notes, are informative of matters that may affect their use, understanding, and interpretation. [Title of section 411 amended, effective for reports issued or reissued on or after June 30, 2001, by Statement on Auditing Standards No. 93. As amended, effective for annual financial statements for fiscal years ending on or after December 15, 2001, and complete sets of interim financial statements for periods beginning

---

[11] Interpretation No. 14, "Evaluating the Adequacy of Disclosure and Presentation in Financial Statements Prepared in Conformity With an Other Comprehensive Basis of Accounting (OCBOA)" (paragraphs .90–.95), provides interpretive guidance applicable to all OCBOA presentations. This interpretation provides additional guidance regarding the appropriateness of informative disclosures in insurance enterprises' financial statements prepared on a statutory basis. [Footnote added by the revision of Interpretations No. 12 and No. 14, January 2005.]

[12] It is possible for one of three different situations to occur: The state adopted the revised Manual without significant departures, adopted the revised Manual with significant departures, or has not yet adopted the revised Manual. [Footnote added, effective for annual financial statements for fiscal years ending on or after December 15, 2001, and complete sets of interim financial statements for periods beginning on or after that date and audits of those financial statements, by Statement of Position 01-5. Footnote renumbered by the revision of Interpretations No. 12 and No. 14, January 2005.]

on or after that date and audits of those financial statements, by Statement of Position 01-5. Revised, October 2009, to reflect conforming changes necessary due to the withdrawal of SAS No. 69.]

.62 Section 623 paragraph .02 states that generally accepted auditing standards apply when an auditor conducts an audit of and reports on financial statements prepared on an other comprehensive basis of accounting. Thus, in accordance with the third standard of reporting, "When the auditor determines that informative disclosures are not reasonably adequate, the auditor must so state in the report."

.63 *Question*—What types of items or matters should auditors consider in evaluating whether informative disclosures are reasonably adequate?

.64 *Interpretation*—Section 623 paragraph .09 and .10 indicates that financial statements prepared on a comprehensive basis of accounting other than GAAP should include "all informative disclosures that are appropriate for the basis of accounting used." That includes a summary of significant accounting policies that discusses the basis of presentation and describes how that basis differs from GAAP. The provisions of the preamble of the revised Manual that states, "GAAP pronouncements do not become part of Statutory Accounting Principles until and unless adopted by the NAIC," do not negate the requirements of section 623 paragraph .10, which also states that when "the financial statements [prepared on an other comprehensive basis of accounting] contain items that are the same as, or similar to, those in financial statements prepared in conformity with generally accepted accounting principles, similar informative disclosures are appropriate." [As amended, effective for annual financial statements for fiscal years ending on or after December 15, 2001, and complete sets of interim financial statements for periods beginning on or after that date and audits of those financial statements, by Statement of Position 01-5.]

[.65–.66] [Paragraphs deleted by the issuance of Statement of Position 01-5, December 2001.]

.67 *Question*—How does the auditor evaluate whether "similar informative disclosures" are appropriate for—

a. Items and transactions that are accounted for essentially the same or in a similar manner under a statutory basis as under GAAP?

b. Items and transactions that are accounted for differently under a statutory basis than under GAAP?

c. Items and transactions that are accounted for differently under requirements of the state of domicile than under the revised Manual?

[As amended, effective for annual financial statements for fiscal years ending on or after December 15, 2001, and complete sets of interim financial statements for periods beginning on or after that date and audits of those financial statements, by Statement of Position 01-5.]

.68 *Interpretation*—Disclosures in statutory basis financial statements for items and transactions that are accounted for essentially the same or in a similar manner under the statutory basis as under GAAP should be the same as, or similar to, the disclosures required by GAAP unless the revised Manual specifically states the NAIC Codification rejected the GAAP disclosures.[13] Disclosures

---

[13] The provisions of the preamble of the revised Manual that states, "GAAP pronouncements do not become part of Statutory Accounting Principles until and unless adopted by the NAIC" or any other explicit rejection of a GAAP disclosure does not negate the requirements of section 623 paragraph .10. [Footnote added by the revision of Interpretations No. 12 and No. 14, January 2005.]

should also include those required by the revised Manual. [As amended, effective for annual financial statements for fiscal years ending on or after December 15, 2001, and complete sets of interim financial statements for periods beginning on or after that date and audits of those financial statements, by Statement of Position 01-5.]

[.69] [Paragraph deleted by the issuance of Statement of Position 01-5, December 2001.]

.70 Disclosures in statutory basis financial statements for items or transactions that are accounted for differently under the statutory basis than under GAAP, but in accordance with the revised Manual, should be the disclosures required by the revised Manual. [As amended, effective for annual financial statements for fiscal years ending on or after December 15, 2001, and complete sets of interim financial statements for periods beginning on or after that date and audits of those financial statements, by Statement of Position 01-5.]

.71 If the accounting required by the state of domicile for an item or transaction differs from the accounting set forth in the revised Manual for that item or transaction, but it is in accordance with GAAP or superseded GAAP, the disclosures in statutory basis financial statements for that item or transaction should be the applicable GAAP disclosures for the GAAP or superseded GAAP. If the accounting required by the state of domicile for an item or transaction differs from the accounting set forth in the revised Manual, GAAP or superseded GAAP, sufficient relevant disclosures should be made. [As amended, effective for annual financial statements for fiscal years ending on or after December 15, 2001, and complete sets of interim financial statements for periods beginning on or after that date and audits of those financial statements, by Statement of Position 01-5.]

[.72–.76] [Paragraphs deleted by the issuance of Statement of Position 01-5, December 2001.]

.77 When evaluating the adequacy of disclosures, the auditor should also consider disclosures related to matters that are not specifically identified on the face of the financial statements, such as (*a*) related party transactions, (*b*) restrictions on assets and owners' equity, (*c*) subsequent events, and (*d*) uncertainties. Other matters should be disclosed if such disclosures are necessary to keep the financial statements from being misleading.

[.78–.79] [Paragraphs deleted to reflect conforming changes necessary due to the issuance of FASB Statement No. 120, *Accounting and Reporting by Mutual Life Insurance Enterprises and by Insurance Enterprises for Certain Long-Duration Participating Contracts*, and FASB Interpretation No. 40, *Applicability of Generally Accepted Accounting Principles to Mutual Life Insurance and Other Enterprises*.]

[.80–.81] [Paragraphs deleted by the revision of Interpretation Nos. 12 and 14, January 2005.]

[Issue Date: December 1991; Revised: February 1997; Amended: December 2001; Revised: January 2005; Revised: November 2006.]

13. Reporting on a Special-Purpose Financial Statement That Results in an Incomplete Presentation But Is Otherwise in Conformity With Generally Accepted Accounting Principles

.82 *Question*—An auditor may be requested to report on a special-purpose financial statement that results in an incomplete presentation but otherwise is in conformity with generally accepted accounting principles. For example, an entity wishing to sell a division or product line may prepare an offering memorandum that includes a special-purpose financial statement that presents certain assets and liabilities, revenues and expenses relating to the division or product line being sold. Section 623, *Special Reports*, paragraph .22 states that the auditor may report on a special-purpose financial statement prepared to comply with a contractual agreement. Does an offering memorandum (not including a filing with a regulatory agency) constitute a contractual agreement for purposes of issuing an auditor's report under this section? [Paragraph renumbered by the issuance of Statement of Position 01-5, December 2001.]

.83 *Interpretation*—No. An offering memorandum generally is a document providing information as the basis for negotiating an offer to sell certain assets or businesses or to raise funds. Normally, parties to an agreement or other specified parties for whom the special-purpose financial presentation is intended have not been identified. Accordingly, the auditor should follow the reporting guidance in section 508, *Reports on Audited Financial Statements*, paragraphs .35–.44 and .58–.60. [Paragraph renumbered by the issuance of Statement of Position 01-5, December 2001.]

.84 *Question*—Does an agreement between a client and one or more third parties other than the auditor to prepare financial statements using a special-purpose presentation constitute a contractual agreement for purposes of issuing an auditor's report under this section? [Paragraph renumbered by the issuance of Statement of Position 01-5, December 2001.]

.85 *Interpretation*—Yes. In such cases, the auditor should follow the guidance in section 623 paragraphs .22–.26, and use of the auditor's report should be restricted to those within the entity, to the parties to the contract or agreement or to those with whom the entity is negotiating directly.

.86 If there is no such agreement, the auditor should follow the guidance in section 508 paragraphs .35–.44 and .58–.60. [Paragraph renumbered by the issuance of Statement of Position 01-5, December 2001.]

[.87–.89] [Paragraphs deleted to reflect conforming changes necessary due to the issuance of Statement on Auditing Standards No. 87. Paragraphs renumbered by the issuance of Statement of Position 01-5, December 2001.]

[Issue Date: May 1995; Revised: February 1999.]

14. Evaluating the Adequacy of Disclosure and Presentation in Financial Statements Prepared in Conformity With an Other Comprehensive Basis of Accounting (OCBOA)[14]

.90 *Question*—Section 623, *Special Reports*, paragraph .10, requires that financial statements prepared on a comprehensive basis of accounting other than generally accepted accounting principles (GAAP) include a summary of significant accounting policies that discusses the basis of presentation and describes how that basis differs from GAAP. It also states that when such financial statements contain items that are the same as, or similar to, those in statements prepared in conformity with GAAP, "similar informative disclosures are appropriate." To illustrate how to apply that statement, section 623 paragraphs .10

[14] While this interpretation provides guidance applicable to all OCBOA presentations, Interpretation No. 12 (paragraphs .60–.81) provides additional interpretive guidance regarding the appropriateness of informative disclosures in insurance enterprises' financial statements prepared on a statutory basis. [Footnote added by the revision of Interpretations No. 12 and No. 14, January 2005.]

says that the disclosures for depreciation, long-term debt, and owners' equity should be "comparable to" those in financial statements prepared in conformity with GAAP. That paragraph then states that the auditor "should also consider" the need for disclosure of matters that are not specifically identified on the face of the statements, such as (*a*) related party transactions, (*b*) restrictions on assets and owners' equity, (*c*) subsequent events, and (*d*) uncertainties. How should the guidance in section 623 paragraph .10 be applied in evaluating the adequacy of disclosure in financial statements prepared in conformity with an other comprehensive basis of accounting (OCBOA)? [Paragraph renumbered by the issuance of Statement of Position 01-5, December 2001.]

.91 *Interpretation*—The discussion of the basis of presentation may be brief; for example: "The accompanying financial statements present financial results on the accrual basis of accounting used for federal income tax reporting." Only the primary differences from GAAP need to be described. To illustrate, assume that several items are accounted for differently than they would be under GAAP, but that only the differences in depreciation calculations are significant. In that situation, a brief description of the depreciation differences is all that would be necessary, and the remaining differences need not be described. Quantifying differences is not required. [Paragraph renumbered by the issuance of Statement of Position 01-5, December 2001.]

.92 If OCBOA financial statements contain elements, accounts, or items for which GAAP would require disclosure, the statements should either provide the relevant disclosure that would be required for those items in a GAAP presentation or provide information that communicates the substance of that disclosure. That may result in substituting qualitative information for some of the quantitative information required for GAAP presentations. For example, disclosing the repayment terms of significant long-term borrowings may sufficiently communicate information about future principal reduction without providing the summary of principal reduction during each of the next five years that would be required for a GAAP presentation. Similarly, disclosing estimated percentages of revenues, rather than amounts that GAAP presentations would require, may sufficiently convey the significance of sales or leasing to related parties. GAAP disclosure requirements that are not relevant to the measurement of the element, account, or item need not be considered. To illustrate:

a. The fair value information that FASB ASC 320, *Investments—Debt and Equity Securities*, would require disclosing for debt and equity securities reported in GAAP presentations would not be relevant when the basis of presentation does not adjust the cost of such securities to their fair value.

b. The information based on actuarial calculations that FASB ASC 715, *Compensation—Retirement Benefits*, would require disclosing for contributions to defined benefit plans reported in GAAP presentations would not be relevant in income tax or cash basis financial statements.

[Paragraph renumbered by the issuance of Statement of Position 01-5, December 2001.]

.93 If GAAP sets forth requirements that apply to the presentation of financial statements, the OCBOA financial statements should either comply with those requirements or provide information that communicates the substance of those requirements. The substance of GAAP presentation requirements may be communicated using qualitative information and without modifying the financial statement format. For example:

a. Information about the effects of accounting changes, discontinued operations, and extraordinary items could be disclosed in a note to the financial statements without following the GAAP presentation requirements in the statement of results of operations, using those terms, or disclosing net-of-tax effects.

b. Instead of showing expenses by their functional classifications, the income tax basis statement of activities of a trade organization could present expenses according to their natural classifications, and a note to the statement could use estimated percentages to communicate information about expenses incurred by the major program and supporting services. A voluntary health and welfare organization could take such an approach instead of presenting the matrix of natural and functional expense classifications that would be required for a GAAP presentation, or, if information has been gathered for the Form 990 matrix required for such organizations, it could be presented either in the form of a separate statement or in a note to the financial statements.

c. Instead of showing the amounts of, and changes in, the unrestricted and temporarily and permanently restricted classes of net assets, which would be required for a GAAP presentation, the income tax basis statement of financial position of a voluntary health and welfare organization could report total net assets or fund balances, the related statement of activities could report changes in those totals, and a note to the financial statements could provide information, using estimated or actual amounts or percentages, about the restrictions on those amounts and on any deferred restricted amounts, describe the major restrictions, and provide information about significant changes in restricted amounts.

[Paragraph renumbered by the issuance of Statement of Position 01-5, December 2001.]

.94 Presentations using OCBOA often include a presentation consisting entirely or mainly of cash receipts and disbursements. Such presentations need not conform with the requirements for a statement of cash flows that would be included in a GAAP presentation. While a statement of cash flows is not required, if a presentation of cash receipts and disbursements is presented in a format similar to a statement of cash flows or if the entity chooses to present such a statement, for example in a presentation on the accrual basis of accounting used for federal income tax reporting, the statement should either conform to the requirements for a GAAP presentation or communicate their substance. As an example, the statement of cash flows might disclose noncash acquisitions through captions on its face. [Paragraph renumbered by the issuance of Statement of Position 01-5, December 2001.]

.95 If GAAP would require disclosure of other matters, the auditor should consider the need for that same disclosure or disclosure that communicates the substance of those requirements. Some examples are contingent liabilities, going concern considerations, and significant risks and uncertainties. However, the disclosures need not include information that is not relevant to the basis of accounting. To illustrate, the general information about the use of estimates that is required to be disclosed in GAAP presentations by FASB ASC 275, *Risks and Uncertainties*, would not be relevant in a presentation that has no estimates, such as one based on cash receipts and disbursements. [Paragraph renumbered by the issuance of Statement of Position 01-5, December 2001.]

[Issue Date: January 1998; Revised: January 2005; Revised: June 2009.]

15. Auditor Reports on Regulatory Accounting or Presentation When the Regulated Entity Distributes the Financial Statements to Parties Other Than the Regulatory Agency Either Voluntarily or Upon Specific Request

.96 *Question*—Occasionally, certain state and local governmental entities, as well as other regulated entities, prepare their financial statements in conformity with the requirements or financial reporting provisions of a governmental regulatory agency. If the financial statements and report are intended for use by parties other than those within the entity and one or more regulatory agencies to whose jurisdiction the entity is subject or the financial statements and report are distributed by the entity to parties other than the regulatory agencies to whose jurisdiction the entity is subject, either voluntarily or upon specific request, what report should the auditor issue?

.97 *Interpretation*—Section 623.05*f*, footnote 4, states in part that the auditor is precluded from using the form of report set forth in section 623 "in circumstances in which the entity distributes the financial statements to parties other than the regulatory agency either voluntarily or upon specific request." Footnote 5 states further that the auditor should follow the guidance in section 544, *Lack of Conformity With Generally Accepted Accounting Principles*, if the financial statements and report are intended for use by parties other than those within the entity and one or more regulatory agencies to whose jurisdiction the entity is subject. Section 544 paragraph .04, in turn, states in those circumstances [referring to circumstances in which the financial statements and reports will be used by parties or distributed by the entity to parties other than the regulatory agencies to whose jurisdiction the entity is subject] the auditor should use the standard form of report modified as appropriate because of the departures from generally accepted accounting principles and then in an additional paragraph express an opinion on whether the financial statements are presented in conformity with the regulatory basis of accounting.

The following is an illustration of a report prepared on a regulatory basis of accounting prescribed by a regulatory agency, to whose jurisdiction an entity is subject, that requires a presentation of cash and unencumbered cash, cash receipts and disbursements, and budgetary comparisons and the financial statements are not prepared solely for filing with that agency:

<u>Independent Auditor's Report</u>

> We have audited the accompanying statement of cash and unencumbered cash; cash receipts and disbursements; and disbursements—budget and actual for each fund of City of Example, Any State, as of and for the year ended June 30, 20XX. These financial statements are the responsibility of City's management. Our responsibility is to express an opinion on these financial statements based on our audit.
>
> We conducted our audit in accordance with auditing standards generally accepted in the United States of America. Those standards require that we plan and perform the audit to obtain reasonable assurance about whether the financial statements are free of material misstatement. An audit includes examining, on a test basis, evidence supporting the amounts and disclosures in the financial statements. An audit also includes assessing the accounting principles used and significant estimates made by management, as well as evaluating the overall financial statement presentation. We believe that our audit provides a reasonable basis for our opinion.

As described more fully in Note X, City has prepared these financial statements using accounting practices prescribed or permitted by [*name of regulatory agency*], which practices differ from accounting principles generally accepted in the United States of America. The effects on the financial statements of the variances between these regulatory accounting practices and accounting principles generally accepted in the United States of America, although not reasonably determinable, are presumed to be material.

In our opinion, because of the effects of the matter discussed in the preceding paragraph, the financial statements referred to above do not present fairly, in conformity with accounting principles generally accepted in the United States of America, the financial position of each fund of City as of June 30, 20XX, or changes in financial position or cash flows[15] thereof for the year then ended.

In our opinion, the financial statements referred to above present fairly, in all material respects, the cash and unencumbered cash balances of each fund of City as of June 30, 20XX, and their respective cash receipts and disbursements, and budgetary results for the year then ended, on the basis of accounting described in Note X.

[*Signature*]

[*Date*]

.98 If the auditor issues a report in accordance with section 623 paragraph .05(f), nothing precludes the auditor, in connection with establishing the terms of the engagement, from reaching an understanding with the client that the intended use of the report will be restricted, and from obtaining the client's agreement that the client and the specified parties will not distribute the report to parties other than those identified in the report.

[Issue Date: January 2005.]

---

[15] Reference to cash flows would not be needed if the entity, under generally accepted accounting principles, is not required to present a statement of cash flows.

AU Section 625

Reports on the Application of Accounting Principles

Source: SAS No. 50; SAS No. 97.

See section 9625 for interpretations of this section.

Issue date, unless otherwise indicated: July, 1986.

Introduction

.01 There may be differing interpretations as to whether and, if so, how existing accounting principles apply to new transactions and financial products.[1] Management and others often consult with accountants on the application of accounting principles to those transactions and products, or to increase their knowledge of specific financial reporting issues.[2] Such consultations often provide relevant information and insights not otherwise available. [As amended, effective for written reports issued or oral advice provided on or after June 30, 2002, by Statement on Auditing Standards No. 97.]

.02 For purposes of this section, reporting accountant refers to an accountant in public practice[3] who prepares a written report[4] or provides oral advice on the application of accounting principles to specified transactions involving facts and circumstances of a specific entity, or the type of opinion that may be rendered on a specific entity's financial statements. Continuing accountant refers to an accountant who has been engaged to report on the financial statements of a specific entity.[5] [Paragraph added, effective for written reports issued or oral advice provided on or after June 30, 2002, by Statement on Auditing Standards No. 97.]

.03 This section provides guidance that a reporting accountant, either in connection with a proposal to obtain a new client or otherwise, should apply when preparing a written report on—

a. The application of accounting principles to specified transactions, either completed or proposed, involving facts and circumstances of a specific entity ("specific transactions").

b. The type of opinion that may be rendered on a specific entity's financial statements.

---

[1] Accounting principles include generally accepted accounting principles and other comprehensive bases of accounting. See section 623, *Special Reports*, paragraph .04 for a description of other comprehensive bases of accounting.

[2] [Footnote deleted by the issuance of Statement on Auditing Standards No. 97, June 2002.]

[3] See ET section 92.29 of the AICPA Code of Professional Conduct for a definition of "practice of public accounting."

[4] Written report, for purposes of this section, includes any written communication that expresses a conclusion on the appropriate accounting principle(s) to be applied or the type of opinion that may be rendered on an entity's financial statements. [Footnote added, effective for written reports issued or oral advice provided on or after June 30, 2002, by Statement on Auditing Standards No. 97.]

[5] An accountant engaged by the entity to perform services other than reporting on the entity's financial statements is not considered to be a continuing accountant. [Footnote added, effective for written reports issued or oral advice provided on or after June 30, 2002, by Statement on Auditing Standards No. 97.]

This section also applies to oral advice that the reporting accountant concludes is intended to be used by a principal to the transaction as an important factor considered in reaching a decision on the application of accounting principles to a specific transaction, or the type of opinion that may be rendered on a specific entity's financial statements. [Paragraph renumbered and amended, effective for written reports issued or oral advice provided on or after June 30, 2002, by Statement on Auditing Standards No. 97.]

.04 Because of the nature of a transaction not involving facts or circumstances of a specific entity ("hypothetical transaction"), a reporting accountant cannot know, for example, whether the continuing accountant has reached a different conclusion on the application of accounting principles for the same or a similar transaction, or how the specific entity has accounted for similar transactions in the past. Therefore an accountant should not undertake an engagement to provide a written report on the application of accounting principles to a hypothetical transaction. [Paragraph added, effective for written reports issued or oral advice provided on or after June 30, 2002, by Statement on Auditing Standards No. 97.]

.05 This section does not apply to a continuing accountant with respect to the specific entity whose financial statements he or she has been engaged to report on, to engagements either to assist in litigation involving accounting matters or to provide expert testimony in connection with such litigation, or to professional advice provided to another accountant in public practice. [Paragraph renumbered and amended, effective for written reports issued or oral advice provided on or after June 30, 2002, by Statement on Auditing Standards No. 97.]

.06 This section also does not apply to communications such as position papers prepared by an accountant for the purpose of presenting views on an issue involving the application of accounting principles or the type of opinion that may be rendered. Position papers include newsletters, articles, speeches and texts thereof, lectures and other forms of public presentations, and letters for the public record to professional and governmental standard-setting bodies. However, if communications of the type discussed in this paragraph are intended to provide guidance on the application of accounting principles to a specific transaction, or on the type of opinion that may be rendered on a specific entity's financial statements, the provisions of this section should be followed. [Paragraph renumbered and amended, effective for written reports issued or oral advice provided on or after June 30, 2002, by Statement on Auditing Standards No. 97.]

Performance Standards

.07 The reporting accountant should exercise due professional care in performing the engagement and should have adequate technical training and proficiency. The reporting accountant should also plan the engagement adequately, supervise the work of assistants, if any, and accumulate sufficient information to provide a reasonable basis for the professional judgment described in the report. The reporting accountant should consider the circumstances under which the written report or oral advice is requested, the purpose of the request, and the intended use of the written report or oral advice. [Paragraph renumbered and amended, effective for written reports issued or oral advice provided on or after June 30, 2002, by Statement on Auditing Standards No. 97.]

.08 To aid in forming a judgment, the reporting accountant should perform the following procedures: (*a*) obtain an understanding of the form and substance of the transaction(s); (*b*) review applicable generally accepted accounting principles; (*c*) if appropriate, consult with other professionals or experts; and (*d*) if appropriate, perform research or other procedures to ascertain and consider the existence of creditable precedents or analogies. [Paragraph renumbered by the issuance of Statement on Auditing Standards No. 97, June 2002. Revised, October 2009, to reflect conforming changes necessary due to the withdrawal of SAS No. 69.]

.09 When evaluating accounting principles that relate to a specific transaction or determining the type of opinion that may be rendered on a specific entity's financial statements, the reporting accountant should consult with the continuing accountant of the entity to ascertain all the available facts relevant to forming a professional judgment. The continuing accountant may provide information not otherwise available to the reporting accountant regarding, for example, the following: the form and substance of the transaction; how management has applied accounting principles to similar transactions; whether the method of accounting recommended by the continuing accountant is disputed by management; or whether the continuing accountant has reached a different conclusion on the application of accounting principles or the type of opinion that may be rendered on the entity's financial statements. The reporting accountant should explain to the entity's management the need to consult with the continuing accountant, request permission to do so, and request the entity's management to authorize the continuing accountant to respond fully to the reporting accountant's inquiries. The responsibilities of an entity's continuing accountant to respond to inquiries by the reporting accountant are the same as the responsibilities of a predecessor auditor to respond to inquiries by a successor auditor. See section 315, *Communications Between Predecessor and Successor Auditors*, paragraph .10. [Paragraph renumbered and amended, effective for written reports issued or oral advice provided on or after June 30, 2002, by Statement on Auditing Standards No. 97.]

Reporting Standards

.10 The accountant's written report should be addressed to the requesting entity (for example, management or the board of directors of the entity), and should ordinarily include the following:[6]

a. A brief description of the nature of the engagement and a statement that the engagement was performed in accordance with applicable AICPA standards.

b. Identification of the specific entity, a description of the transaction(s), a statement of the relevant facts, circumstances, and assumptions, and a statement about the source of the information.

c. A statement describing the appropriate accounting principle(s) (including the country of origin) to be applied or type of opinion that may be rendered on the entity's financial statements, and, if appropriate, a description of the reasons for the reporting accountant's conclusion.

d. A statement that the responsibility for the proper accounting treatment rests with the preparers of the financial statements, who should consult with their continuing accountant.

---

[6] Although the reporting standards in this section apply only to written reports, accountants may find this guidance useful in providing oral advice. [Footnote renumbered and amended, effective for written reports issued or oral advice provided on or after June 30, 2002, by Statement on Auditing Standards No. 97.]

e. A statement that any difference in the facts, circumstances, or assumptions presented may change the report.

f. A separate paragraph at the end of the report that includes the following elements:[7]

- A statement indicating that the report is intended solely for the information and use of the specified parties;
- An identification of the specified parties to whom use is restricted; and
- A statement that the report is not intended to be and should not be used by anyone other than the specified parties.

[Paragraph renumbered and amended, effective for written reports issued or oral advice provided on or after June 30, 2002, by Statement on Auditing Standards No. 97.]

.11 The following is an illustration of sections of the report described in paragraph .10.

Introduction

We have been engaged to report on the appropriate application of accounting principles generally accepted in [*country of origin of such principles*] to the specific transaction described below. This report is being issued to ABC Company for assistance in evaluating accounting principles for the described specific transaction. Our engagement has been conducted in accordance with standards established by the American Institute of Certified Public Accountants.

Description of Transaction

The facts, circumstances, and assumptions relevant to the specific transaction as provided to us by the management of ABC Company are as follows:

Appropriate Accounting Principles

[*Text discussing generally accepted accounting principles*]

Concluding Comments

The ultimate responsibility for the decision on the appropriate application of accounting principles generally accepted in [*country of origin of such principles*] for an actual transaction rests with the preparers of financial statements, who should consult with their continuing accountant. Our judgment on the appropriate application of accounting principles generally accepted in [*country of origin of such principles*] for the described specific transaction is based solely on the facts provided to us as described above; should these facts and circumstances differ, our conclusion may change.

Restricted Use

This report is intended solely for the information and use of the board of directors and management of ABC Company and is not intended to be and should not be used by anyone other than these specified parties.

[Paragraph renumbered and amended, effective for written reports issued or oral advice provided on or after June 30, 2002, by Statement on Auditing Standards No. 97.]

---

[7] See section 532, *Restricting the Use of an Auditor's Report*. Although restricted, this is not intended to preclude distribution of the report to the continuing accountant. [Footnote added, effective for written reports issued or oral advice provided on or after June 30, 2002, by Statement on Auditing Standards No. 97.]

AU Section 9625

Reports on the Application of Accounting Principles: Auditing Interpretations of Section 625

1. Requirement to Consult With the Continuing Accountant

.01 *Question*—Section 625, *Reports on the Application of Accounting Principles*, provides guidance to a reporting accountant when asked to provide a written report or oral advice on (*a*) the application of accounting principles to specified transactions, either completed or proposed, involving facts and circumstances of a specific entity or (*b*) the type of opinion that may be rendered on a specific entity's financial statements.

.02 Section 625 paragraph .02 refers to a reporting accountant as an accountant in public practice. Footnote 3 to that paragraph states: "See ET section 92.29 of the AICPA Code of Professional Conduct for a definition of 'practice of public accounting.'"

.03 Section 625 paragraph .09 states in part:

> When evaluating accounting principles that relate to a specific transaction or determining the type of opinion that may be rendered on a specific entity's financial statements, the reporting accountant should consult with the continuing accountant of the entity to ascertain all the available facts relevant to forming a professional judgment. The continuing accountant may provide information not otherwise available to the reporting accountant regarding, for example, the following: the form and substance of the transaction; how management has applied accounting principles to similar transactions; whether the method of accounting recommended by the continuing accountant is disputed by management; or whether the continuing accountant has reached a different conclusion on the application of accounting principles or the type of opinion that may be rendered on the entity's financial statements.

.04 In today's environment, primarily driven by independence concerns, a nonissuer may engage an accountant in public practice (or his or her firm), other than the entity's independent auditor, as an advisory accountant[1] to assist management in certain recurring accounting or reporting functions (for example, bookkeeping or assistance in preparing financial statements or notes, performing fair value impairment tests, or assistance in preparing regulatory filings). In this capacity, an advisory accountant may be frequently asked to provide advice on the application of accounting principles or to assist management to formulate its accounting positions prior to discussing such positions with its auditor. In these situations, an advisory accountant is not engaged to provide a second opinion and would generally be in a position to have full access to management and have full knowledge of the form and substance of the transaction, how management has applied similar transactions in the past, and whether this method of accounting has been discussed with the continuing auditor.

---

[1] The term *advisory accountant* is used in this interpretation rather than the term "reporting accountant" to distinguish the fact that an accountant in this capacity is not engaged to provide a second opinion and is typically engaged to provide accounting and reporting advice on a recurring basis.

.05 When an accountant in public practice, acting in the capacity of an advisory accountant, has been engaged by a nonissuer to assist management with recurring accounting matters and is asked to provide advice (not a second opinion) on the application of accounting principles to specified transactions, either completed or proposed, based on the specific facts and circumstances of the client, and the advisory accountant has full access to management and full knowledge of the form and substance of the transaction, is he or she still required to consult with the continuing accountant?

.06 *Answer*—Section 625 was issued to provide guidance to a reporting accountant when engaged to provide a "second opinion" on the application of accounting principles to a specific transaction or transactions. In those cases, the reporting accountant may not have been provided all the relevant facts by management or he or she may not have full knowledge of the form and substance of the transaction in order to form a "second opinion." To help eliminate this issue, section 625 states that the reporting accountant should consult with the continuing accountant so the continuing accountant has an opportunity to convey relevant facts and circumstances that the reporting accountant may not have.

.07 An advisory accountant may be able to overcome the presumptive requirement[2] of section 625 paragraph .09 to consult with the continuing accountant when he or she believes, due to the facts and circumstances of the engagement, that he or she is not being asked to provide a second opinion and that he or she has obtained all relevant information from management to provide written or oral guidance regarding the application of accounting principles to that client's specified transactions.

.08 An important distinction to consider in overcoming the presumptive requirement to consult with the continuing accountant is the nature of the engagement and whether the services are recurring as contrasted to periodic. A recurring engagement may constitute the effective outsourcing of certain controllership or other financial reporting functions that would typically not be indicative of opinion shopping and would typically allow the advisory accountant to have complete access to management. A member in public practice engaged in the capacity of an advisory accountant nonetheless should be alert to any instances in which the nonissuer attempts to use the advisory accountant to "opinion shop." The advisory accountant should establish an understanding with the client that includes the substance of section 625 paragraph .10(*d*)[3] and that the client, along with the advisory accountant will notify the continuing accountant and members of any governance body (such as audit committee) of the arrangement.

.09 The advisory accountant should document his or her conclusion that consultation with the continuing accountant was not considered necessary under the circumstances. Additionally, the advisory accountant should comply with the other requirements of section 625, including section 625 paragraph .08, which requires the accountant to (*a*) obtain an understanding of the form and substance of the transaction(s); (*b*) review applicable generally accepted

---

[2] The ability to overcome this presumption would apply only to the application of accounting principles. If the advisory accountant was asked to provide oral advice or a written report on the type of opinion that may be rendered by the continuing accountant, the advisory accountant would not have the ability to obtain all relevant information and, therefore, the requirements of section 625 paragraph .09 to consult with the continuing accountant would apply.

[3] The advisory accountant's understanding would include a statement that the responsibility for the proper accounting treatment rests with management, who should consult with their continuing accountant.

accounting principles; (*c*) if appropriate, consult with other professionals or experts; and (*d*) if appropriate, perform research or other procedures to ascertain and consider the existence of creditable precedents or analogies.

[Issue Date: January, 2005.]

AU Section 634

Letters for Underwriters and Certain Other Requesting Parties

(Supersedes SAS No. 49.)

Source: SAS No. 72; SAS No. 76; SAS No. 86.

See section 9634 for interpretations of this section.

Effective for comfort letters issued on or after June 30, 1993, unless otherwise indicated.

Introduction

.01 This section[1] provides guidance to accountants for performing and reporting on the results of engagements to issue letters for underwriters and certain other requesting parties described in and meeting the requirements of paragraph .03, .04, or .05 (commonly referred to as "comfort letters") in connection with financial statements and financial statement schedules contained in registration statements filed with the Securities and Exchange Commission (SEC) under the Securities Act of 1933 (the act) and other securities offerings. In paragraph .09, this section also provides guidance to accountants for performing and reporting on the results of engagements to issue letters for certain requesting parties, other than underwriters or other parties with a due diligence defense under Section 11 of the act, that are described in, but do not meet the requirements of, paragraph .03, .04, or .05. [As amended, effective for letters issued pursuant to paragraph .09 of this section after April 30, 1996, by Statement on Auditing Standards No. 76.]

.02 The service of accountants providing letters for underwriters developed following enactment of the act. Section 11 of the act provides that underwriters, among others, could be liable if any part of a registration statement contains material omissions or misstatements. The act also provides for an affirmative defense for underwriters if it can be demonstrated that, after a reasonable investigation, the underwriter has reasonable grounds to believe that there were no material omissions or misstatements. Consequently, underwriters request accountants to assist them in developing a record of reasonable investigation. An accountant issuing a comfort letter is one of a number of procedures that may be used to establish that an underwriter has conducted a reasonable investigation.

Applicability

.03 Accountants may provide a comfort letter to underwriters,[2] or to other parties with a statutory due diligence defense under Section 11 of the act, in connection with financial statements and financial statement schedules included

---

[1] [Footnote deleted by the issuance of Statement on Auditing Standards No. 76, September 1995.]

[2] The term *underwriter* is defined in Section 2 of the act as "any person who has purchased from an issuer with a view to, or offers or sells for an issuer in connection with, the distribution of any security, or participates or has a participation in the direct or indirect participation in any such

(continued)

(incorporated by reference) in registration statements filed with the SEC under the act. A comfort letter may be addressed to parties with a statutory due diligence defense under Section 11 of the act, other than a named underwriter, only when a law firm or attorney for the requesting party issues a written opinion to the accountants that states that such party has a due diligence defense under Section 11 of the act.[3] An attorney's letter indicating that a party "may" be deemed to be an underwriter or has liability substantially equivalent to that of an underwriter under the securities laws would not meet this requirement. If the requesting party, in a securities offering registered pursuant to the act, other than a named underwriter (such as a selling shareholder or sales agent) cannot provide such a letter, he or she must provide the representation letter described in paragraphs .06–.07 for the accountants to provide them with a comfort letter.

.04 Accountants may also issue a comfort letter to a broker-dealer or other financial intermediary, acting as principal or agent in an offering or a placement of securities, in connection with the following types of securities offerings:

- Foreign offerings, including Regulation S, Eurodollar, and other offshore offerings
- Transactions that are exempt from the registration requirements of Section 5 of the act, including those pursuant to Regulation A, Regulation D, and Rule 144A
- Offerings of securities issued or backed by governmental, municipal, banking, tax-exempt, or other entities that are exempt from registration under the act

In these situations the accountants may provide a comfort letter to a broker-dealer or other financial intermediary in connection with a securities offering only if the broker-dealer or other financial intermediary provides in writing the representations described in paragraphs .06–.07.

.05 Accountants may also issue a comfort letter in connection with acquisition transactions (for example, cross-comfort letters in a typical Form S-4 or merger proxy situation) in which there is an exchange of stock and such comfort letters are requested by the buyer or seller, or both, as long as the representation letter described in paragraphs .06–.07 is provided. An accountants' report on a preliminary investigation in connection with a proposed transaction (for example, a merger, an acquisition, or a financing) is not covered by this section; accountants should refer to the guidance in AT section 201, *Agreed-Upon Procedures Engagements*. [Revised, January 2001, to reflect conforming changes necessary due to the issuance of Statement on Standards for Attestation Engagements No. 10.]

.06 The required elements of the representation letter from a broker-dealer or other financial intermediary, or of other requesting parties described in paragraphs .03 and .05, are as follows:

(footnote continued)

undertaking or participates or has a participation in the direct or indirect underwriting of any such undertaking; but such term shall not include a person whose interest is limited to a commission from an underwriter or dealer not in excess of the usual and customary distributors' or sellers' commission. As used in this paragraph, the term *issuer* shall include, in addition to an issuer, any person directly or indirectly controlling or controlled by the issuer, or any person under direct or indirect common control with the issuer."

[3] This section is not intended to preclude accountants from providing to the client's board of directors, when appropriate, a letter addressed to the board of directors similar in content to a comfort letter. See Interpretation No. 1, "Letters to Directors Relating to Annual Reports on Form 10-K", of section 634 (sec. 9634 par. .01-.09).

- The letter should be addressed to the accountants.
- The letter should contain the following:

  "This review process, applied to the information relating to the issuer, is (will be) substantially consistent[4] with the due diligence review process that we would perform if this placement of securities (or issuance of securities in an acquisition transaction) were being registered pursuant to the Securities Act of 1933 (the act). We are knowledgeable with respect to the due diligence review process that would be performed if this placement of securities were being registered pursuant to the act."[5]

- The letter should be signed by the requesting party.

.07 An example of a letter, setting forth the required elements specified in paragraph .06, from a party requesting a comfort letter follows:

> [*Date*]
>
> Dear ABC Accountants:
>
> [*Name of financial intermediary*], as principal or agent, in the placement of [*identify securities*] to be issued by [*name of issuer*], will be reviewing certain information relating to [*issuer*] that will be included (incorporated by reference) in the document [*if appropriate, the document should be identified*], which may be delivered to investors and utilized by them as a basis for their investment decision. This review process, applied to the information relating to the issuer, is (will be) substantially consistent with the due diligence review process that we would perform if this placement of securities[6] were being registered pursuant to the Securities Act of 1933 (the act). We are knowledgeable with respect to the due diligence review process that would be performed if this placement of securities were being registered pursuant to the act. We hereby request that you deliver to us a "comfort" letter concerning the financial statements of the issuer and certain statistical and other data included in the offering document. We will contact you to identify the procedures we wish you to follow and the form we wish the comfort letter to take.
>
> Very truly yours,
>
> [*Name of Financial Intermediary*]

.08 When one of the parties identified in paragraphs .03, .04, and .05 requests a comfort letter and has provided the accountants with the representation letter described above, the accountants should refer in the comfort letter to the requesting party's representations (see example P [paragraph .64]).

---

[4] It is recognized that what is "substantially consistent" may vary from situation to situation and may not be the same as that done in a registered offering of the same securities for the same issuer; whether the procedures being, or to be, followed will be "substantially consistent" will be determined by the requesting party on a case-by-case basis.

[5] If a nonunderwriter requests a comfort letter in connection with a securities offering pursuant to the act, the wording of the representation letter should be revised as follows:

> "This review process . . . is substantially consistent with the due diligence review process that an underwriter would perform in connection with this placement of securities. We are knowledgeable with respect to the due diligence review process that an underwriter would perform in connection with a placement of securities registered pursuant to the Securities Act of 1933."

[6] In an acquisition of securities, this sentence could be reworded to refer to "issuance of securities." See paragraph .05.

.09 When one of the parties identified in paragraphs .03, .04, or .05, other than an underwriter or other party with a due diligence defense under Section 11 of the act, requests a comfort letter but does not provide the representation letter described in paragraphs .06–.07, accountants should not provide a comfort letter but may provide another form of letter. In such a letter, the accountants should not provide negative assurance on the financial statements as a whole, or on any of the specified elements, accounts, or items thereof. The other guidance in this section is applicable to performing procedures in connection with a letter and on the form of the letter (see paragraphs .36–.43 and .54–.60). example Q in the appendix [paragraph .64] provides an example of a letter issued in such a situation. Any such letter should include the following statements:

a. It should be understood that we have no responsibility for establishing (and did not establish) the scope and nature of the procedures enumerated in the paragraphs above; rather, the procedures enumerated therein are those the requesting party asked us to perform. Accordingly, we make no representations regarding questions of legal interpretation[7] or regarding the sufficiency for your purposes of the procedures enumerated in the preceding paragraphs; also, such procedures would not necessarily reveal any material misstatement of the amounts or percentages listed above as set forth in the offering circular. Further, we have addressed ourselves solely to the foregoing data and make no representations regarding the adequacy of disclosures or whether any material facts have been omitted. This letter relates only to the financial statement items specified above and does not extend to any financial statement of the company taken as a whole.

b. The foregoing procedures do not constitute an audit conducted in accordance with generally accepted auditing standards. Had we performed additional procedures or had we conducted an audit or a review of the company's [*give dates of any interim financial statements*] consolidated financial statements in accordance with standards established by the American Institute of Certified Public Accountants, other matters might have come to our attention that would have been reported to you.

c. These procedures should not be taken to supplant any additional inquiries or procedures that you would undertake in your consideration of the proposed offering.

d. This letter is solely for your information and to assist you in your inquiries in connection with the offering of the securities covered by the offering circular, and it is not to be used, circulated, quoted, or otherwise referred to for any other purpose, including but not limited to the registration, purchase, or sale of securities, nor is it to be filed with or referred to in whole or in part in the offering document or any other document, except that reference may be made to it in any list of closing documents pertaining to the offering of the securities covered by the offering document.

---

[7] If this letter is requested in connection with a secured debt offering, the accountants should also refer to the Interpretation No. 2, "Responding to Requests for Reports on Matters Relating to Solvency," of AT section 101 (AT sec. 9101 par. .23–.33) for inclusion of additional statements. [Footnote added, effective for letters issued pursuant to paragraph .09 of this section after April 30, 1996, by Statement on Auditing Standards No. 76. Footnote revised, January 2001, to reflect conforming changes necessary due to the issuance of Statement on Standards for Attestation Engagements No. 10.]

e. We have no responsibility to update this letter for events and circumstances occurring after [*cutoff date*].

[As amended, effective for letters issued pursuant to this paragraph after April 30, 1996, by Statement on Auditing Standards No. 76.]

.10 When a party other than those described in paragraphs .03, .04, or .05 requests a comfort letter, the accountants should not provide that party with a comfort letter or the letter described in paragraph .09 or example Q [paragraph .64]. The accountants may instead provide that party with a report on agreed-upon procedures and should refer to AT section 201, *Agreed-Upon Procedures Engagements*, for guidance. [Paragraph added, effective for letters issued pursuant to paragraph .09 of this section after April 30, 1996, by Statement on Auditing Standards No. 76. Revised, January 2001, to reflect conforming changes necessary due to the issuance of Statement on Standards for Attestation Engagements No. 10.]

General

.11 The services of independent accountants include audits of financial statements and financial statement schedules included (incorporated by reference) in registration statements filed with the SEC under the act. In connection with this type of service, accountants are often called upon to confer with clients, underwriters, and their respective counsel concerning the accounting and auditing requirements of the act and the SEC and to perform other services. One of these other services is the issuance of letters for underwriters, which generally address the subjects described in paragraph .22. [Paragraph renumbered by the issuance of Statement on Auditing Standards No. 76, September 1995.]

.12 Much of the uncertainty, and consequent risk of misunderstanding, with regard to the nature and scope of comfort letters has arisen from a lack of recognition of the necessarily limited nature of the comments that accountants can properly make with respect to financial information, in a registration statement or other offering document (hereafter referred to as a registration statement), that has not been audited in accordance with generally accepted auditing standards and, accordingly, is not covered by their opinion. In requesting comfort letters, underwriters are generally seeking assistance on matters of importance to them. They wish to perform a "reasonable investigation" of financial and accounting data not "expertized"[8] (that is, covered by a report of independent accountants, who consent to be named as experts, based on an audit performed in accordance with generally accepted auditing standards) as a defense against possible claims under section 11 of the act.[9] What constitutes a reasonable investigation of unaudited financial information sufficient to satisfy an underwriter's purposes has never been authoritatively established. Consequently, only the underwriter can determine what is sufficient for his or her purposes. Accountants will normally be willing to

---

[8] See the Interpretation No. 2, "Consenting to Be Named as an Expert in an Offering Document in Connection With Securities Offerings Other Than Those Registered Under the Securities Act of 1933," of section 711, *Filings Under Federal Securities Statutes* (AT sec. 9711 par. .12-.15). [Footnote renumbered by the issuance of Statement on Auditing Standards No. 76, September 1995.]

[9] See section 711 for a discussion of certain responsibilities of accountants that result from the inclusion of their reports in registration statements. [Footnote renumbered by the issuance of Statement on Auditing Standards No. 76, September 1995.]

assist the underwriter, but the assistance accountants can provide by way of comfort letters is subject to limitations. One limitation is that independent accountants can properly comment in their professional capacity only on matters to which their professional expertise is substantially relevant. Another limitation is that procedures short of an audit, such as those contemplated in a comfort letter, provide the accountants with a basis for expressing, at the most, negative assurance.[10] Such limited procedures may bring to the accountants' attention significant matters affecting the financial information, but they do not provide assurance that the accountants will become aware of any or all significant matters that would be disclosed in an audit. Accordingly, there is necessarily a risk that the accountants may have provided negative assurance of the absence of conditions or matters that may prove to have existed. [Paragraph renumbered by the issuance of Statement on Auditing Standards No. 76, September 1995.]

.13 This section deals with several different kinds of matters. First, it addresses whether, in a number of areas involving professional standards, it is proper for independent accountants, acting in their professional capacity, to comment in a comfort letter on specified matters, and, if so, the form such a comment should take. Second, practical suggestions are offered on which form of comfort letter is suitable in a given circumstance, procedural matters, the dating of letters, and what steps may be taken when information that may require special mention in a letter comes to the accountants' attention.[11] Third, it suggests ways of reducing or avoiding the uncertainties, described in the preceding paragraph, regarding the nature and extent of accountants' responsibilities in connection with a comfort letter. Accountants who have been requested to follow a course other than what has been recommended, with regard to points not involving professional standards, would do well to consult their legal counsel. [Paragraph renumbered by the issuance of Statement on Auditing Standards No. 76, September 1995.]

.14 Comfort letters are not required under the act, and copies are not filed with the SEC. It is nonetheless a common condition of an underwriting agreement in connection with the offering for sale of securities registered with the SEC under the act that the accountants are to furnish a comfort letter. Some underwriters do not make the receipt of a comfort letter a condition of the underwriting agreement or purchase agreement (hereafter referred to as the underwriting agreement) but nevertheless ask for such a letter.[12]

---

[10] Negative assurance consists of a statement by accountants that, as a result of performing specified procedures, nothing came to their attention that caused them to believe that specified matters do not meet a specified standard (for example, that nothing came to their attention that caused them to believe that any material modifications should be made to the unaudited financial statements or unaudited condensed financial statements for them to be in conformity with generally accepted accounting principles). [Footnote renumbered by the issuance of Statement on Auditing Standards No. 76, September 1995.]

[11] It is important to note that although the illustrations in this section describe procedures that may be followed by accountants as a basis for their comments in comfort letters, this section does not necessarily prescribe such procedures. [Footnote renumbered by the issuance of Statement on Auditing Standards No. 76, September 1995.]

[12] Except when the context otherwise requires, the word underwriter (or certain other requesting parties, as described in paragraphs .03, .04, and .05), as used in this section refers to the managing, or lead, underwriter, who typically negotiates the underwriting agreement for a group of underwriters whose exact composition is not determined until shortly before a registration statement becomes effective. In competitive bidding situations in which legal counsel for the underwriters acts as the underwriters' representative prior to opening and acceptance of the bid, the accountants should carry out the discussions and other communications contemplated by this section with the legal counsel until the underwriter is selected. [Footnote renumbered by the issuance of Statement on Auditing Standards No. 76, September 1995.]

[Paragraph renumbered by the issuance of Statement on Auditing Standards No. 76, September 1995.]

.15 The accountants should suggest to the underwriter that they meet together with the client to discuss the procedures to be followed in connection with a comfort letter; during this meeting, the accountants may describe procedures that are frequently followed (see the examples in the appendix [paragraph .64]). Because of the accountants' knowledge of the client, such a meeting may substantially assist the underwriter in reaching a decision about procedures to be followed by the accountants. However, any discussion of procedures should be accompanied by a clear statement that the accountants cannot furnish any assurance regarding the sufficiency of the procedures for the underwriter's purposes, and the appropriate way of expressing this is shown in paragraph 4 of example A [paragraph .64]. [Paragraph renumbered by the issuance of Statement on Auditing Standards No. 76, September 1995.]

.16 Because the underwriter will expect the accountants to furnish a comfort letter of a scope to be specified in the underwriting agreement, a draft of that agreement should be furnished to the accountants so that they can indicate whether they will be able to furnish a letter in acceptable form. It is desirable practice for the accountants, promptly after they have received the draft of the agreement (or have been informed that a letter covering specified matters, although not a condition of the agreement, will nonetheless be requested), to prepare a draft of the form of the letter they expect to furnish. To the extent possible, the draft should deal with all matters to be covered in the final letter and should use exactly the same terms as those to be used in the final letter (subject, of course, to the understanding that the comments in the final letter cannot be determined until the procedures underlying it have been performed). The draft letter should be identified as a draft to avoid giving the impression that the procedures described therein have been performed. This practice of furnishing a draft letter at an early point permits the accountants to make clear to the client and the underwriter what they may expect the accountants to furnish. Thus furnished with a draft letter, the underwriter is afforded the opportunity to discuss further with the accountants the procedures that the accountants have indicated they expect to follow and to request any additional procedures that the underwriter may desire. If the additional procedures pertain to matters relevant to the accountants' professional competence, the accountants would ordinarily be willing to perform them, and it is desirable for them to furnish the underwriter with an appropriately revised draft letter. The accountants may reasonably assume that the underwriter, by indicating his or her acceptance of the draft comfort letter, and subsequently, by accepting the letter in final form, considers the procedures described sufficient for his or her purposes. It is important, therefore, that the procedures[13] to be followed by the accountants be clearly set out in the comfort letter, in both draft and final form, so that there will be no misunderstanding about the basis on which the accountants' comments have been made and so that the underwriter can decide whether the procedures performed are sufficient for his or her purposes. For reasons explained in paragraph .12, statements or implications that the accountants are carrying out such procedures as they consider necessary should be avoided, since this may lead to misunderstanding about the responsibility

---

[13] When the accountants have been requested to provide negative assurance on interim financial information or capsule financial information and the procedures required for an SAS No. 100 (section 722) review have been performed, those procedures need not be specified. See paragraphs .37–.41. [Footnote renumbered by the issuance of Statement on Auditing Standards No. 76, September 1995. Footnote revised, January 2006, to reflect conforming changes necessary due to the issuance of Statement on Auditing Standards No. 100.]

for the sufficiency of the procedures for the underwriter's purposes. The following is a suggested form of legend that may be placed on the draft letter for identification and explanation of its purposes and limitations.

> This draft is furnished solely for the purpose of indicating the form of letter that we would expect to be able to furnish [*name of underwriter*] in response to their request, the matters expected to be covered in the letter, and the nature of the procedures that we would expect to carry out with respect to such matters. Based on our discussions with [*name of underwriter*], it is our understanding that the procedures outlined in this draft letter are those they wish us to follow.[14] Unless [*name of underwriter*] informs us otherwise, we shall assume that there are no additional procedures they wish us to follow. The text of the letter itself will depend, of course, on the results of the procedures, which we would not expect to complete until shortly before the letter is given and in no event before the cutoff date indicated therein.

[Paragraph renumbered by the issuance of Statement on Auditing Standards No. 76, September 1995.]

.17 Comfort letters are occasionally requested from more than one accountant (for example, in connection with registration statements to be used in the subsequent sale of shares issued in recently effected mergers and from predecessor auditors). At the earliest practicable date, the client should advise any other accountants who may be involved about any letter that may be required from them and should arrange for them to receive a draft of the underwriting agreement so that they may make arrangements at an early date for the preparation of a draft of their letter (a copy of which should be furnished to the principal accountants) and for the performance of their procedures. In addition, the underwriter may wish to meet with the other accountants for the purposes discussed in paragraph .15. [Paragraph renumbered by the issuance of Statement on Auditing Standards No. 76, September 1995.]

.18 There may be situations in which more than one accountant is involved in the audit of the financial statements of a business and in which the reports of more than one accountant appear in the registration statement. For example, certain significant divisions, branches, or subsidiaries may be audited by other accountants. The principal accountants (that is, those who report on the consolidated financial statements and, consequently, are asked to give a comfort letter with regard to information expressed on a consolidated basis) should read the letters of the other accountants reporting on significant units. Such letters should contain statements similar to those contained in the comfort letter prepared by the principal accountants, including statements about their independence. The principal accountants should state in their comfort letters that (*a*) reading letters of the other accountants was one of the procedures followed, and (*b*) the procedures performed by the principal accountants (other than reading the letters of the other accountants) relate solely to companies audited by the principal accountants and to the consolidated financial statements. [Paragraph renumbered by the issuance of Statement on Auditing Standards No. 76, September 1995.]

.19 Regulations under the act permit companies, in certain circumstances, to register a designated amount of securities for continuous or delayed offerings

---

[14] In the absence of any discussions with the underwriter, the accountants should outline in the draft letter those procedures specified in the underwriting agreement that they are willing to perform. In that event, the sentence to which this footnote refers should be revised as follows: "In the absence of any discussions with [*name of underwriter*], we have set out in this draft letter those procedures referred to in the draft underwriting agreement (of which we have been furnished a copy) that we are willing to follow." [Footnote renumbered by the issuance of Statement on Auditing Standards No. 76, September 1995.]

during an extended period by filing one "shelf" registration statement. At the effective date of a shelf registration statement, the registrant may not have selected an underwriter (see footnote 12). A client or the legal counsel designated to represent the underwriting group might, however, ask the accountants to issue a comfort letter at the effective date of a shelf registration statement to expedite the due diligence activities of the underwriter when he or she is subsequently designated and to avoid later corrections of financial information included in an effective prospectus. However, as stated in paragraph .12, only the underwriter can determine the procedures that will be sufficient for his or her purposes. Under these circumstances, therefore, the accountants should not agree to furnish a comfort letter addressed to the client, legal counsel or a nonspecific addressee such as "any or all underwriters to be selected." The accountants may agree to furnish the client or legal counsel for the underwriting group with a draft comfort letter describing the procedures that the accountants have performed and the comments the accountants are willing to express as a result of those procedures. The draft comfort letter should include a legend, such as the following, describing the letter's purpose and limitations:

> This draft describes the procedures that we have performed and represents a letter we would be prepared to sign as of the effective date of the registration statement if the managing underwriter had been chosen at that date and requested such a letter. Based on our discussions with [*name of client or legal counsel*], the procedures set forth are similar to those that experience indicates underwriters often request in such circumstances. The text of the final letter will depend, of course, on whether the managing underwriter who is selected requests that other procedures be performed to meet his or her needs and whether the managing underwriter requests that any of the procedures be updated to the date of issuance of the signed letter.

A signed comfort letter may be issued to the underwriter selected for the portion of the issue then being offered when the underwriting agreement for an offering is signed and on each closing date. [Paragraph renumbered by the issuance of Statement on Auditing Standards No. 76, September 1995.]

.20 Accountants, when issuing a letter under the guidance provided in this section, may not issue any additional letters or reports, under any other section, to the underwriter or the other requesting parties identified in paragraphs .03, .04, and .05 (hereinafter referred to as the underwriter) in connection with the offering or placement of securities, in which the accountants comment on items for which commenting is otherwise precluded by this section. [Paragraph renumbered by the issuance of Statement on Auditing Standards No. 76, September 1995. As amended, effective for comfort letters issued on or after June 30, 1998, by Statement on Auditing Standards No. 86.]

.21 While the guidance in this section generally addresses comfort letters issued in connection with securities offerings registered pursuant to the act, it also provides guidance on comfort letters issued in other securities transactions. However, the guidance that specifically refers to compliance of the information commented on with SEC rules and regulations, such as compliance with Regulation S-X[15] or S-K,[16] generally applies only to comfort letters issued

---

[15] Regulation S-X, "Form and Content of and Requirements for Financial Statements, Securities Act of 1933, Securities Exchange Act of 1934, Public Utility Holding Company Act of 1935, Investment Company Act of 1940, and Energy Policy and Conservation Act of 1975." [Footnote renumbered by the issuance of Statement on Auditing Standards No. 76, September 1995.]

[16] Regulation S-K, "Standard Instructions for Filing Forms Under Securities Act of 1933, Securities Exchange Act of 1934 and Energy Policy and Conservation Act of 1975." [Footnote renumbered by the issuance of Statement on Auditing Standards No. 76, September 1995.]

in connection with securities offerings registered pursuant to the act. [Paragraph renumbered by the issuance of Statement on Auditing Standards No. 76, September 1995.]

Guidance on the Format and Contents of Comfort Letters

.22 This section (paragraphs .22–.62) provides guidance on the format and possible contents of a typical comfort letter. It addresses how the comfort letter should be dated, to whom it may be addressed, and the contents of the introductory paragraph of the comfort letter. Further, it addresses the subjects that may be covered in a comfort letter:

a. The independence of the accountants (paragraphs .31 and .32)

b. Whether the audited financial statements and financial statement schedules included (incorporated by reference) in the registration statement comply as to form in all material respects with the applicable accounting requirements of the act and the related rules and regulations adopted by the SEC (paragraphs .33 and .34)

c. Unaudited financial statements, condensed interim financial information, capsule financial information, pro forma financial information, financial forecasts, management's discussion and analysis (MD&A), and changes in selected financial statement items during a period subsequent to the date and period of the latest financial statements included (incorporated by reference) in the registration statement (paragraphs .29 and .35–.53)

d. Tables, statistics, and other financial information included (incorporated by reference) in the registration statement (paragraphs .54–.62)

e. Negative assurance as to whether certain nonfinancial statement information, included (incorporated by reference) in the registration statement complies as to form in all material respects with Regulation S-K (paragraph .57)

[Paragraph renumbered by the issuance of Statement on Auditing Standards No. 76, September 1995. As amended, effective for comfort letters issued on or after June 30, 1998, by Statement on Auditing Standards No. 86.]

Dating

.23 The letter ordinarily is dated on or shortly before the effective date (that is, the date on which the registration statement becomes effective). On rare occasions, letters have been requested to be dated at or shortly before the filing date (that is, the date on which the registration statement is first filed with the SEC). The underwriting agreement ordinarily specifies the date, often referred to as the "cutoff date," to which certain procedures described in the letter are to relate (for example, a date five days before the date of the letter). The letter should state that the inquiries and other procedures described in the letter did not cover the period from the cutoff date to the date of the letter. [Paragraph renumbered by the issuance of Statement on Auditing Standards No. 76, September 1995.]

.24 An additional letter may also be dated at or shortly before the closing date (that is, the date on which the issuer or selling security holder delivers the securities to the underwriter in exchange for the proceeds of the offering). If more than one letter is requested, it will be necessary to carry out the specified procedures and inquiries as of the cutoff date for each letter. Although comments contained in an earlier letter may, on occasion, be incorporated by reference in a subsequent letter (see example C [paragraph .64]), any subsequent letter should relate only to information in the registration statement as most recently amended. [Paragraph renumbered by the issuance of Statement on Auditing Standards No. 76, September 1995.]

Addressee

.25 The letter should not be addressed or given to any parties other than the client and the named underwriters,[17] broker-dealer, financial intermediary or buyer or seller. The appropriate addressee is the intermediary who has negotiated the agreement with the client, and with whom the accountants will deal in discussions regarding the scope and sufficiency of the letter. When a comfort letter is furnished to other accountants, it should be addressed in accordance with the guidance in this paragraph and copies should be furnished to the principal accountants and their client. [Paragraph renumbered by the issuance of Statement on Auditing Standards No. 76, September 1995.]

Introductory Paragraph

.26 It is desirable to include an introductory paragraph similar to the following:

> We have audited the [*identify the financial statements and financial statement schedules*] included (incorporated by reference) in the registration statement (no. 33-00000) on Form _______ filed by the company under the Securities Act of 1933 (the act); our reports with respect thereto are also included (incorporated by reference) in that registration statement. The registration statement, as amended as of _______, is herein referred to as the registration statement.

[Paragraph renumbered by the issuance of Statement on Auditing Standards No. 76, September 1995.]

.27 When the report on the audited financial statements and financial statement schedules included (incorporated by reference) in the registration statement departs from the standard report, for instance, where one or more explanatory paragraphs or a paragraph to emphasize a matter regarding the financial statements have been added to the report, the accountants should refer[18] to that fact in the comfort letter and discuss the subject matter of the paragraph.[19] In those rare instances in which the SEC accepts a qualified opinion on historical financial statements, the accountants should refer to the qualification in the opening paragraph of the comfort letter and discuss the subject matter of the qualification. (See also paragraph .35*f*.) [Paragraph renumbered by the issuance of Statement on Auditing Standards No. 76, September 1995.]

---

[17] An example of an appropriate form of address for this purpose is "The Blank Company and XYZ & Company, as Representative of the Several Underwriters." [Footnote renumbered by the issuance of Statement on Auditing Standards No. 76, September 1995.]

[18] The accountants may also refer in the opening paragraph to expansions of their report that do not affect their opinion on the basic financial statements, for example, expansions of their report regarding (*a*) interim financial information accompanying or included in the notes to audited financial statements (see section 722 paragraph .50) or (*b*) required supplementary information described in section 558, *Required Supplementary Information*, paragraphs .08–.11. See paragraph .30 of this section. [Footnote renumbered by the issuance of Statement on Auditing Standards No. 76, September 1995. Footnote revised, September 2002, to reflect conforming changes necessary due to the issuance of Statement on Auditing Standards No. 98. Footnote revised, November 2002, to reflect conforming changes necessary due to the issuance of Statement on Auditing Standards No. 100.]

[19] The accountants need not refer to or discuss explanatory paragraphs covering consistency of application of accounting principles. [Footnote renumbered by the issuance of Statement on Auditing Standards No. 76, September 1995.]

.28 The underwriter occasionally requests the accountants to repeat in the comfort letter their report on the audited financial statements included (incorporated by reference) in the registration statement. Because of the special significance of the date of the accountants' report, the accountants should not repeat their opinion.[20] The underwriter sometimes requests negative assurance regarding the accountants' report. Because accountants have a statutory responsibility with respect to their opinion as of the effective date of a registration statement, and because the additional significance, if any, of negative assurance is unclear and such assurance may therefore give rise to misunderstanding, accountants should not give such negative assurance. Furthermore, the accountants should not give negative assurance with respect to financial statements and financial statement schedules that have been audited and are reported on in the registration statement by other accountants. [Paragraph renumbered by the issuance of Statement on Auditing Standards No. 76, September 1995.]

.29 The accountants may refer in the introductory paragraphs of the comfort letter to the fact that they have issued reports on—[21]

a. Condensed financial statements that are derived from audited financial statements (see section 552, *Reporting on Condensed Financial Statements and Selected Financial Data*).

b. Selected financial data (see section 552).

c. Interim financial information (see section 722).

d. Pro forma financial information (see AT section 401, *Reporting on Pro Forma Financial Information*).

e. A financial forecast (see AT section 301, *Financial Forecasts and Projections*).

f. Management's discussion and analysis (see AT section 701, *Management's Discussion and Analysis*).

Such a reference should be to the accountants' reports that were previously issued, and if the reports are not included (incorporated by reference) in the registration statement, they may be attached to the comfort letter.[22] In referring to previously issued reports, the accountants should not repeat their reports in the comfort letter or otherwise imply that they are reporting as of the date of the comfort letter or that they assume responsibility for the sufficiency of the procedures for the underwriter's purposes. However, for certain information on which they have reported, the accountants may agree to comment regarding compliance with rules and regulations adopted by the SEC (see paragraphs .33 and .34). Accountants should not mention in a comfort letter reports issued in accordance with section 325, *Communicating Internal Control Related Matters Identified in an Audit*, or any restricted use reports issued to a client in connection with procedures performed on the client's internal control in accordance with AT section 501A, *Reporting on an Entity's Internal Control Over*

---

[20] See section 530, *Dating of the Independent Auditor's Report*, paragraphs .03–.08. [Footnote renumbered by the issuance of Statement on Auditing Standards No. 76, September 1995.]

[21] Except for a review report on management's discussion and analysis (MD&A), the accountants should not refer to or attach to the comfort letter any restricted use report, such as a report on agreed-upon procedures. [Footnote renumbered by the issuance of Statement on Auditing Standards No. 76, September 1995. As amended, effective for comfort letters issued on or after June 30, 1998, by Statement on Auditing Standards No. 86.]

[22] When the accountant does not perform a review or an examination of MD&A or does not attach or refer to a report on MD&A, the accountant may perform agreed-upon procedures with respect to items in MD&A, subject to controls over financial reporting (see paragraph .55). [Footnote added, effective for comfort letters issued on or after June 30, 1998, by Statement on Auditing Standards No. 86.]

Financial Reporting. [Paragraph renumbered by the issuance of Statement on Auditing Standards No. 76, September 1995. As amended, effective for comfort letters issued on or after June 30, 1998, by Statement on Auditing Standards No. 86. Revised, January 2001, to reflect conforming changes necessary due to the issuance of Statement on Standards for Attestation Engagements No. 10. Revised, May 2006, to reflect conforming changes necessary due to the issuance of Statement on Auditing Standards No. 112.]

.30 An underwriter may also request that the accountants comment in their comfort letter on (*a*) unaudited interim financial information required by item 302(a) of Regulation S-K, to which section 722 pertains or (*b*) required supplementary information, to which section 558, *Required Supplementary Information*, pertains. Section 558, and in certain instances section 722, provide that the accountant should expand the standard report on the audited financial statements to refer to such information. Such expansions of the accountants' standard report in the registration statement would ordinarily be referred to in the opening paragraph of the comfort letter (see also paragraph .35f). Additional comments on such unaudited information are therefore unnecessary. However, if the underwriter requests that the accountants perform procedures with regard to such information in addition to those performed in connection with their review or audit as prescribed by sections 722 and 558, the accountants may do so and report their findings. [Paragraph renumbered, September 1995, by the issuance of SAS No. 76. Revised, December 2010, to reflect conforming changes necessary due to the issuance of SAS Nos. 118–120.]

Independence

.31 It is customary in conjunction with SEC filings for the underwriting agreement to provide for the accountants to make a statement in the letter concerning their independence. This may be done substantially as follows:

> We are independent certified public accountants with respect to The Blank Company, Inc., within the meaning of the act and the applicable rules and regulations thereunder adopted by the SEC.

Regulation S-K requires disclosure in the prospectus and registration statement of interests of named experts (including independent accountants) in the registrant. Regulation S-X precludes accountants who report on financial statements included (incorporated by reference) in a registration statement from having interests of the type requiring disclosure in the prospectus or registration statement. Therefore, if the accountants make a statement in a comfort letter that they are independent within the meaning of the act and the applicable rules and regulations thereunder adopted by the SEC, any additional comments on independence would be unnecessary.[22a] In a non-SEC filing, the accountants may refer to the AICPA's *Code of Professional Conduct* (ET section 101). This may be done substantially as follows:

> We are independent certified public accountants with respect to The Blank Company, Inc., under rule 101 of the AICPA's *Code of Professional Conduct* and its interpretations and rulings.

[Paragraph renumbered by the issuance of Statement on Auditing Standards No. 76, September 1995.]

[22a] The SEC, in Financial Reporting Release No. 50 dated February 18, 1998, recognized the establishment of the Independence Standards Board (ISB) and indicated that the SEC intends to look to the ISB as the private sector body responsible for establishing independence standards and interpretations for auditors of public entities. [Footnote added, June 1999, to acknowledge the SEC's recognition of the ISB.]

.32 When comfort letters are requested from more than one accountant (see paragraphs .17–.18), each accountant must, of course, be sure he or she is independent within the meaning of the act and the applicable rules and regulations thereunder adopted by the SEC. The accountants for previously nonaffiliated companies recently acquired by the registrant would not be required to have been independent with respect to the company whose shares are being registered. In such a case, the accountants should modify the wording suggested in paragraph .31 and make a statement regarding their independence along the following lines.

> As of [*insert date of the accountants' most recent report on the financial statements of their client*] and during the period covered by the financial statements on which we reported, we were independent certified public accountants with respect to [*insert the name of their client*] within the meaning of the act and the applicable rules and regulations thereunder adopted by the SEC.

[Paragraph renumbered by the issuance of Statement on Auditing Standards No. 76, September 1995.]

Compliance With SEC Requirements

.33 The accountants may be requested to express an opinion on whether the financial statements covered by their report comply as to form with the pertinent accounting requirements adopted by the SEC.[23] This may be done substantially as follows:

> In our opinion [*include phrase "except as disclosed in the registration statement," if applicable*], the [*identify the financial statements and financial statement schedules*] audited by us and included (incorporated by reference) in the registration statement comply as to form in all material respects with the applicable accounting requirements of the act and the related rules and regulations adopted by the SEC.[24]

If there is a material departure from the pertinent rules and regulations adopted by the SEC, the departure should be disclosed in the letter.[25] An appropriate manner of doing this is shown in example K [paragraph .64].

[23] The phrase rules and regulations adopted by the SEC is used because accountants should not be expected to be familiar with, or express assurances on compliance with, informal positions of the SEC staff. [Footnote renumbered by the issuance of Statement on Auditing Standards No. 76, September 1995. Footnote subsequently renumbered and amended, effective for comfort letters issued on or after June 30, 1998, by Statement on Auditing Standards No. 86.]

[24] Certain financial statements may be incorporated in a registration statement under the act by reference to filings under the Securities Exchange Act of 1934 (the 1934 Act). In those circumstances, the accountants may refer to whether the audited financial statements and financial statement schedules included (incorporated by reference) in the registration statement comply as to form in all material respects with the applicable accounting requirements of the 1934 Act and the related rules and regulations adopted by the SEC (see example B [paragraph .64]). However, the accountants should not refer to compliance with the provisions of the 1934 Act regarding internal accounting control. See AT section 501A, *Reporting on an Entity's Internal Control Over Financial Reporting*, paragraph .82. [Footnote renumbered by the issuance of Statement on Auditing Standards No. 76, September 1995. Footnote subsequently renumbered and amended, effective for comfort letters issued on or after June 30, 1998, by Statement on Auditing Standards No. 86. Footnote revised, January 2001, to reflect conforming changes necessary due to the issuance of Statement on Standards for Attestation Engagements No. 10.]

[25] Departures from rules and regulations adopted by the SEC that require mention in a comfort letter ordinarily do not affect fair presentation in conformity with generally accepted accounting principles; however, if they do, the accountants will, of course, mention these departures in expressing their opinion and in consenting to the use of their report in the registration statement. If departures from rules and regulations adopted by the SEC that require mention in a comfort letter either are not disclosed in the registration statement or have not been agreed to by representatives of the SEC, the accountants should carefully consider whether a consent to the use of their report in the registration statement should be issued. [Footnote renumbered by the issuance of Statement on Auditing Standards No. 76, September 1995. Footnote subsequently renumbered and amended, effective for comfort letters issued on or after June 30, 1998, by Statement on Auditing Standards No. 86.]

[Paragraph renumbered by the issuance of Statement on Auditing Standards No. 76, September 1995.]

.34 Accountants may provide positive assurance on compliance as to form with requirements under the rules and regulations adopted by the SEC only with respect to those rules and regulations applicable to the form and content of financial statements and financial statement schedules that they have audited. Accountants are limited to providing negative assurance on compliance as to form when the financial statements or financial statement schedules have not been audited. (For guidance in commenting on compliance as to form, see paragraph .37 regarding unaudited condensed interim financial information, paragraph .42 regarding pro forma financial information, paragraph .44 regarding a forecast, and paragraph .57 regarding Regulation S-K items.[26]) [Paragraph renumbered by the issuance of Statement on Auditing Standards No. 76, September 1995.]

Commenting in a Comfort Letter on Information Other Than Audited Financial Statements

General

.35 Comments included in the letter will often concern (*a*) unaudited condensed interim financial information (see paragraphs .36–.38),[27] (*b*) capsule financial information (see paragraphs .36 and .39–.41), (*c*) pro forma financial information (see paragraphs .42–.43), (*d*) financial forecasts (see paragraphs .36 and .44), and (*e*) changes in capital stock, increases in long-term debt, and decreases in other specified financial statement items (see paragraphs .36 and .45–.53). For commenting on these matters, the following guidance is important:

a. As explained in paragraph .16, the agreed-upon procedures performed by the accountants should be set forth in the letter, except that when the accountants have been requested to provide negative assurance on interim financial information or capsule financial information, the procedures involved in an SAS No. 100 [section 722] review need not be specified (see paragraphs .37–.41 of this section and paragraph 4 of example A [paragraph .64]).

b. To avoid any misunderstanding about the responsibility for the sufficiency of the agreed-upon procedures for the underwriter's purposes, the accountants should not make any statements, or imply that they have applied procedures that they have determined to be necessary or sufficient for the underwriter's purposes. If the accountants state that they have performed an SAS No. 100 [section 722] review, this does not imply that those procedures are sufficient for the underwriter's purposes. The underwriter may ask the accountants to perform additional

---

[26] Accountants should not comment in a comfort letter on compliance as to form of MD&A with rules and regulations adopted by the SEC; accountants may agree to examine or review MD&A in accordance with AT section 701. [Footnote added, effective for comfort letters issued on or after June 30, 1998, by Statement on Auditing Standards No. 86. Footnote revised, January 2001, to reflect conforming changes necessary due to the issuance of Statement on Standards for Attestation Engagements No. 10.]

[27] The SEC requirements specify condensed financial statements. However, the guidance in paragraphs .37 and .38 also applies to complete financial statements. For purposes of this section, interim financial statements may be for a twelve-month period ending on a date other than the entity's normal year end. [Footnote renumbered by the issuance of Statement on Auditing Standards No. 76, September 1995. Footnote subsequently renumbered by the issuance of Statement on Auditing Standards No. 86, March 1998.]

procedures. For example, if the underwriter requests the accountants to apply additional procedures and specifies items of financial information to be reviewed and the materiality level for changes in those items that would necessitate further inquiry by the accountants, the accountants may perform those procedures and should describe them in their letter. Descriptions of procedures in the comfort letter should include descriptions of the criteria specified by the underwriter.

c. Terms of uncertain meaning (such as *general review*, *limited review*, *reconcile*, *check*, or *test*) should not be used in describing the work, unless the procedures comprehended by these terms are described in the comfort letter.

d. The procedures performed with respect to interim periods may not disclose changes in capital stock, increases in long-term debt or decreases in the specified financial statement items, inconsistencies in the application of generally accepted accounting principles, instances of noncompliance as to form with accounting requirements of the SEC, or other matters about which negative assurance is requested. An appropriate manner of making this clear is shown in the last three sentences in paragraph 4 of example A [paragraph .64].

e. Matters to be covered by the letter should be made clear in the meetings with the underwriter and should be identified in the underwriting agreement and in the draft comfort letter. Since there is no way of anticipating other matters that would be of interest to an underwriter, accountants should not make a general statement in a comfort letter that, as a result of carrying out the specified procedures, nothing else has come to their attention that would be of interest to the underwriter.

f. When the report on the audited financial statements and financial statement schedules in the registration statement departs from the auditor's standard report, and the comfort letter includes negative assurance with respect to subsequent unaudited condensed interim financial information included (incorporated by reference) in the registration statement or with respect to an absence of specified subsequent changes, increases, or decreases, the accountant should consider the effect thereon of the subject matter of the qualification, explanatory paragraph(s), or paragraph(s) emphasizing a matter regarding the financial statements. The accountant should also follow the guidance in paragraph .27. An illustration of how this type of situation may be dealt with is shown in example I [paragraph .64].

[Paragraph renumbered by the issuance of Statement on Auditing Standards No. 76, September 1995. Revised, January 2006, to reflect conforming changes necessary due to the issuance of Statement on Auditing Standards No. 100.]

Knowledge of Internal Control

.36 The accountants should not comment in a comfort letter on (*a*) unaudited condensed interim financial information, (*b*) capsule financial information, (*c*) a financial forecast when historical financial statements provide a basis for one or more significant assumptions for the forecast, or (*d*) changes in capital stock, increases in long-term debt and decreases in selected financial statement items, unless they have obtained knowledge of a client's internal control as it relates to the preparation of both annual and interim financial information. Knowledge of the client's internal control over financial reporting includes knowledge of the control environment, risk assessment, control activities, information and communication, and monitoring. Sufficient knowledge of a client's internal control as it relates to the preparation of annual financial information ordinarily would have been acquired, and may have been acquired with respect to interim financial information, by the accountants who have audited a client's financial statements for one or more periods. When the accountants have not audited the most recent annual financial statements, and thus have not acquired sufficient knowledge of the entity's internal control, the accountants should perform procedures to obtain that knowledge. [Paragraph renumbered by the issuance of Statement on Auditing Standards No. 76, September 1995. Revised, February 1997, to reflect conforming changes necessary due to the issuance of Statement on Auditing Standards No. 78.]

Unaudited Condensed Interim Financial Information

.37 Comments concerning the unaudited condensed interim financial information[28] included (incorporated by reference) in the registration statement provide negative assurance as to whether (*a*) any material modifications should be made to the unaudited condensed interim financial information for it to be in conformity with generally accepted accounting principles and (*b*) the unaudited condensed interim financial information complies as to form in all material respects with the applicable accounting requirements of the act and the related rules and regulations adopted by the SEC. Accountants may comment in the form of negative assurance only when they have conducted a review of the interim financial information in accordance with section 722. The accountants may (*a*) state in the comfort letter that they have performed the procedures identified in section 722 for a review of interim financial information (see paragraphs 4a and 5a of example A [paragraph .64] or (*b*) if the accountants have issued a report on the review, they may mention that fact in the comfort letter. If it is mentioned in the comfort letter, the accountants should attach the review report to the letter unless the review report is already included (incorporated by reference) in the registration statement. When the accountants have not conducted a review in accordance with section 722, the accountants may not comment in the form of negative assurance and are, therefore, limited to reporting procedures performed and findings obtained (see example O [paragraph .64]). [Paragraph renumbered by the issuance of Statement on Auditing Standards No. 76, September 1995.]

.38 The letter should specifically identify any unaudited condensed interim financial information and should state that the accountants have not audited the condensed interim financial information in accordance with generally accepted auditing standards and do not express an opinion concerning such information. An appropriate manner of making this clear is shown in paragraph 3 of example A [paragraph .64]. [Paragraph renumbered by the issuance of Statement on Auditing Standards No. 76, September 1995.]

Capsule Financial Information

.39 In some registration statements, the information shown in the audited financial statements or unaudited condensed interim financial information is supplemented by unaudited summarized interim information for subsequent periods (commonly called "capsule financial information"). This capsule financial information (either in narrative or tabular form) often is provided for the most recent interim period and for the corresponding period of the prior year. With regard to selected capsule financial information, the accountants—

---

[28] When accountants are engaged to perform procedures on interim financial information, they may have additional responsibilities under certain circumstances. The accountants should refer to section 722 for guidance. [Footnote renumbered by the issuance of Statement on Auditing Standards No. 76, September 1995. Footnote subsequently renumbered by the issuance of Statement on Auditing Standards No. 86, March 1998.]

a. May give negative assurance with regard to conformity with generally accepted accounting principles and may refer to whether the dollar amounts were determined on a basis substantially consistent with that of the corresponding amounts in the audited financial statements if (1) the selected capsule financial information is presented in accordance with the minimum disclosure requirements of Financial Accounting Standards Board (FASB) *Accounting Standards Codification* (ASC) 270-10-50-1 and (2) the accountants have performed a SAS No. 100 [section 722] review of the financial statements underlying the capsule financial information. If those conditions have not been met, the accountants are limited to reporting procedures performed and findings obtained.

b. May give negative assurance as to whether the dollar amounts were determined on a basis substantially consistent with that of the corresponding amounts in the audited financial statements if the selected capsule financial information is more limited than the minimum disclosures described in FASB ASC 270-10-50-1 (see example L [paragraph .64]), as long as the accountants have performed a SAS No. 100 [section 722] review of the financial statements underlying the capsule financial information. If a SAS No. 100 [section 722] review has not been performed, the accountants are limited to reporting procedures performed and findings obtained.

[Paragraph renumbered by the issuance of Statement on Auditing Standards No. 76, September 1995. Revised, January 2006, to reflect conforming changes necessary due to the issuance of Statement on Auditing Standards No. 100. Revised, June 2009, to reflect conforming changes necessary due to the issuance of FASB ASC.]

.40 The underwriter occasionally asks the accountants to give negative assurance with respect to the unaudited interim financial statements or unaudited condensed interim financial information (see paragraph .37 and the interim financial information requirements of Regulation S-X) that underlie the capsule financial information and asks the accountants to state that the capsule financial information agrees with amounts set forth in such statements. Paragraphs 4*b* and 5*b* in example L [paragraph .64] provide an example of the accountants' comments in these circumstances. [Paragraph renumbered by the issuance of Statement on Auditing Standards No. 76, September 1995.]

.41 The underwriter might ask the accountants to give negative assurance on the unaudited condensed interim financial information, or information extracted therefrom, for a monthly period ending after the latest financial statements included (incorporated by reference) in the registration statement. In those cases, the guidance in paragraph .37 is applicable. The unaudited condensed interim financial information should be attached to the comfort letter so that it is clear what financial information is being referred to; if the client requests, the unaudited condensed interim financial information may be attached only to the copy of the letter intended for the managing underwriter. [Paragraph renumbered by the issuance of Statement on Auditing Standards No. 76, September 1995.]

Pro Forma Financial Information

.42 Accountants should not comment in a comfort letter on pro forma financial information unless they have an appropriate level of knowledge of the accounting and financial reporting practices of the entity (or, in the case of a business combination, of a significant constituent part of the combined entity). This would ordinarily have been obtained by the accountants auditing or reviewing historical financial statements of the entity for the most recent annual or interim period for which the pro forma financial information is presented. Accountants should not give negative assurance in a comfort letter on the application of pro forma adjustments to historical amounts, the compilation of pro forma financial information, whether the pro forma financial information complies as to form in all material respects with the applicable accounting requirements of rule 11-02 of Regulation S-X or otherwise provide negative assurance with respect to pro forma financial information unless they have obtained the required knowledge described above and they have performed an audit of the annual financial statements, or an SAS No. 100 [section 722] review of the interim financial statements, of the entity (or, in the case of a business combination, of a significant constituent part of the combined entity) to which the pro forma adjustments were applied. In the case of a business combination, the historical financial statements of each constituent part of the combined entity on which the pro forma financial information is based should be audited or reviewed. [Paragraph renumbered by the issuance of Statement on Auditing Standards No. 76, September 1995. Revised, January 2006, to reflect conforming changes necessary due to the issuance of Statement on Auditing Standards No. 100.]

.43 If the accountants have obtained the required knowledge as described in paragraph .36, but have not met the requirements for giving negative assurance, the accountants are limited to reporting procedures performed and findings obtained. (See example O [paragraph .64].) The accountants should comply with the relevant guidance on reporting the results of agreed-upon procedures in AT section 201. [Paragraph renumbered by the issuance of Statement on Auditing Standards No. 76, September 1995. Revised, January 2001, to reflect conforming changes necessary due to the issuance of Statement on Standards for Attestation Engagements No. 10.]

Financial Forecasts

.44 For accountants to perform agreed-upon procedures on a financial forecast and comment thereon in a comfort letter, they should obtain the knowledge described in paragraph .36 and then perform procedures prescribed in AT section 301 paragraph .69, for reporting on compilation of a forecast. Having performed these procedures, they should follow the guidance in AT section 301 paragraphs .18–.19 regarding reports on compilations of prospective financial information and should attach their report[29] thereon to the comfort letter.[30] Then they can perform additional procedures and report their findings in the comfort letter (see examples E and O [paragraph .64]). Accountants may not

[29] For purposes of issuing a comfort letter, if the forecast is included in the registration statement, the forecast must be accompanied by an indication that the accountants have not examined the forecast and therefore do not express an opinion on it. If a compilation report on the forecast has been issued in connection with the comfort letter, the report need not be included in the registration statement. [Footnote renumbered by the issuance of Statement on Auditing Standards No. 76, September 1995. Footnote subsequently renumbered by the issuance of Statement on Auditing Standards No. 86, March 1998.]

[30] When a client's securities are subject to regulation by the SEC, the accountants should be aware of the SEC's views regarding independence when agreeing to perform a compilation of a forecast. Independence may be deemed to be impaired when services include preparation or assembly of financial forecasts. The SEC generally will not question the accountants' independence, however, when services are limited to issuing a report on a forecast as a result of performing the procedures stated in paragraph 5 of AT section 301 paragraph .69. [Footnote renumbered by the issuance of Statement on Auditing Standards No. 76, September 1995. Footnote subsequently renumbered by the issuance of Statement on Auditing Standards No. 86, March 1998. Footnote revised, January 2001, to reflect conforming changes necessary due to the issuance of Statement on Standards for Attestation Engagements No. 10.]

provide negative assurance on the results of procedures performed. Further, accountants may not provide negative assurance with respect to compliance of the forecast with rule 11-03 of Regulation S-X unless they have performed an examination of the forecast in accordance with AT section 301. [Paragraph renumbered by the issuance of Statement on Auditing Standards No. 76, September 1995. Revised, January 2001, to reflect conforming changes necessary due to the issuance of Statement on Standards for Attestation Engagements No. 10.]

Subsequent Changes

.45 Comments regarding subsequent changes typically relate to whether there has been any change in capital stock, increase in long-term debt or decreases in other specified financial statement items during a period, known as the "change period," subsequent to the date and period of the latest financial statements included (incorporated by reference) in the registration statement (see paragraph .50). These comments would also address such matters as subsequent changes in the amounts of (*a*) net current assets or stockholders' equity and (*b*) net sales and the total and per-share amounts of income before extraordinary items and of net income. The accountants ordinarily will be requested to read minutes and make inquiries of company officials relating to the whole of the change period.[31] For the period between the date of the latest financial statements made available and the cutoff date, the accountants must base their comments solely on the limited procedures actually performed with respect to that period (which, in most cases, will be limited to the reading of minutes and the inquiries of company officials referred to in the preceding sentence), and their comfort letter should make this clear (see paragraph 6 of example A [paragraph .64]). [Paragraph renumbered by the issuance of Statement on Auditing Standards No. 76, September 1995.]

.46 If the underwriter requests negative assurance as to subsequent changes in specified financial statement items as of a date less than 135 days from the end of the most recent period for which the accountants have performed an audit or a review, the accountants may provide such negative assurance in the comfort letter. For instance—

- When the accountants have audited the December 31, 19X6, financial statements, the accountants may provide negative assurance on increases and decreases of specified financial statement items as of any date up to May 14 (135 days subsequent to December 31).
- When the accountants have audited the December 31, 19X6, financial statements and have also conducted an SAS No. 100 [section 722] review of the interim financial information as of and for the quarter ended March 31, 19X7, the accountants may provide negative assurance as to increases and decreases of specified financial statement items as of any date up to August 14, 19X7 (135 days subsequent to March 31).

An appropriate manner of expressing negative assurance regarding subsequent changes is shown in paragraphs 5*b* and 6 of example A [paragraph .64], if there has been no decrease and in example M [paragraph .64], if there has been a decrease. [Paragraph renumbered by the issuance of Statement on Auditing Standards No. 76, September 1995. Revised, January 2006, to reflect conforming changes necessary due to the issuance of Statement on Auditing Standards No. 100.]

---

[31] The answers to these inquiries generally should be supported by appropriate written representations of the company officials. [Footnote renumbered by the issuance of Statement on Auditing Standards No. 76, September 1995. Footnote subsequently renumbered by the issuance of Statement on Auditing Standards No. 86, March 1998.]

.47 However, if the underwriter requests negative assurance as to subsequent changes in specified financial statement items as of a date 135 days or more subsequent to the end of the most recent period for which the accountants have performed an audit or a review, the accountants may not provide negative assurance but are limited to reporting procedures performed and findings obtained (see example O [paragraph .64]). [Paragraph renumbered by the issuance of Statement on Auditing Standards No. 76, September 1995.]

.48 In order that comments on subsequent changes be unambiguous and their determination be within accountants' professional expertise, the comments should not relate to "adverse changes," since that term has not acquired any clearly understood meaning. If there has been a change in an accounting principle during the change period, the accountants should note that fact in the letter. [Paragraph renumbered by the issuance of Statement on Auditing Standards No. 76, September 1995.]

.49 Comments on the occurrence of changes in capital stock, increases in long-term debt, and decreases in other specified financial statement items are limited to changes, increases, or decreases not disclosed in the registration statement. Accordingly, the phrase "except for changes, increases, or decreases that the registration statement discloses have occurred or may occur" should be included in the letter when it has come to the accountants' attention that a change, increase, or decrease has occurred during the change period, and the amount of such change, increase, or decrease is disclosed in the registration statement. This phrase need not be included in the letter when no changes, increases, or decreases in the specified financial statement items are disclosed in the registration statement. [Paragraph renumbered by the issuance of Statement on Auditing Standards No. 76, September 1995.]

.50 ***Change period.*** In the context of a comfort letter, a decrease occurs when the amount of a financial statement item at the cutoff date or for the change period (as if financial statements had been prepared at that date and for that period) is less than the amount of the same item at a specified earlier date or for a specified earlier period. With respect to the items mentioned in paragraph .45, the term *decrease* means (*a*) any combination of changes in amounts of current assets and current liabilities that results in decreased net current assets, (*b*) any combination of changes in amounts of assets and liabilities that results in decreased stockholders' equity, (*c*) decreased net sales, and (*d*) any combination of changes in amounts of sales, expenses and outstanding shares that results in decreased total and per-share amounts of income before extraordinary items and of net income (including, in each instance, a greater loss or other negative amount). The change period for which the accountants give negative assurance in the comfort letter ends on the cutoff date (see paragraph .23) and ordinarily begins, for balance sheet items, immediately after the date of the latest balance sheet in the registration statement and, for income statement items, immediately after the latest period for which such items are presented in the registration statement. The comparison relates to the entire period and not to portions of that period. A decrease during one part of the period may be offset by an equal or larger increase in another part of the period; however, because there was no decrease for the period as a whole, the comfort letter would not report the decrease occurring during one part of the period (see, however, paragraph .62). [Paragraph renumbered by the issuance of Statement on Auditing Standards No. 76, September 1995.]

.51 The underwriting agreement usually specifies the dates as of which, and periods for which, data at the cutoff date and data for the change period are to be compared. For balance sheet items, the comparison date is normally that of the latest balance sheet included (incorporated by reference) in the registration statement (that is, immediately prior to the beginning of the change period). For income statement items, the comparison period or periods might be one or more of the following: (*a*) the corresponding period of the preceding year, (*b*) a period of corresponding length immediately preceding the change period, (*c*) a proportionate part of the preceding fiscal year, or (*d*) any other period of corresponding length chosen by the underwriter. Whether or not specified in the underwriting agreement, the date and period used in comparison should be identified in the comfort letter in both draft and final form so that there is no misunderstanding about the matters being compared and so that the underwriter can determine whether the comparison period is suitable for his or her purposes. [Paragraph renumbered by the issuance of Statement on Auditing Standards No. 76, September 1995.]

.52 The underwriter occasionally requests that the change period begin immediately after the date of the latest audited balance sheet (which is, ordinarily, also the closing date of the latest audited statement of income) in the registration statement, even though the registration statement includes a more recent unaudited condensed balance sheet and condensed statement of income. The use of the earlier date may defeat the underwriter's purpose, since it is possible that an increase in one of the items referred to in paragraph .45 occurring between the dates of the latest audited and unaudited balance sheets included (incorporated by reference) in the registration statement might more than offset a decrease occurring after the latter date. A similar situation might arise in the comparison of income statement items. In these circumstances, the decrease occurring after the date of the latest unaudited condensed interim financial statements included (incorporated by reference) in the registration statement would not be reported in the comfort letter. It is desirable for the accountants to explain the foregoing considerations to the underwriter; however, if the underwriter nonetheless requests the use of a change period or periods other than those described in paragraph .50, the accountants may use the period or periods requested. [Paragraph renumbered by the issuance of Statement on Auditing Standards No. 76, September 1995.]

.53 When other accountants are involved and their letters do not disclose matters that affect the negative assurance given, an appropriate manner of expressing these comments is shown in example J [paragraph .64]. When appropriate, the principal accountants may comment that there were no decreases in the consolidated financial statement items despite the possibility that decreases have been mentioned by the other accountants. In such a case, the principal accountants could make a statement that "nothing came to our attention regarding the consolidated financial statements as a result of the specified procedures (which, so far as the related company was concerned, consisted solely of reading the other accountants' letter) that caused us to believe that...." [Paragraph renumbered by the issuance of Statement on Auditing Standards No. 76, September 1995.]

Tables, Statistics, and Other Financial Information

.54 The underwriting agreement sometimes calls for a comfort letter that includes comments on tables, statistics, and other financial information appearing in the registration statement. [Paragraph renumbered by the issuance of Statement on Auditing Standards No. 76, September 1995.]

.55 The accountants should refrain from commenting on certain matters in a comfort letter. Except as indicated in the next sentence, they should comment only with respect to information (*a*) that is expressed in dollars (or percentages derived from such dollar amounts) and that has been obtained from accounting records that are subject to the entity's controls over financial reporting or (*b*) that has been derived directly from such accounting records by analysis or computation. The accountants may also comment on quantitative information that has been obtained from an accounting record if the information is subject to the same controls over financial reporting as the dollar amounts. The accountants should not comment on matters merely because they happen to be present and are capable of reading, counting, measuring, or performing other functions that might be applicable. Examples of matters that, unless subjected to the entity's controls over financial reporting (which is not ordinarily the case), should not be commented on by the accountants include the square footage of facilities, number of employees (except as related to a given payroll period), and backlog information.[32] The accountants should not comment on tables, statistics, and other financial information relating to an unaudited period unless (*a*) they have performed an audit of the client's financial statements for a period including or immediately prior to the unaudited period or have completed an audit for a later period or (*b*) they have otherwise obtained knowledge of the client's internal control as provided for in paragraph .36 herein. In addition, the accountants should not comment on information subject to legal interpretation, such as beneficial share ownership. [Paragraph renumbered by the issuance of Statement on Auditing Standards No. 76, September 1995. As amended, effective for comfort letters issued on or after June 30, 1998, by Statement on Auditing Standards No. 86.]

.56 As with comments relating to financial statement information, it is important that the procedures followed by the accountants with respect to other information be clearly set out in the comfort letter, in both draft and final form, so that there will be no misunderstanding about the basis of the comments on the information. Further, so that there will be no implication that the accountants are furnishing any assurance with respect to the sufficiency of the procedures for the underwriter's intended purpose, the comfort letter should contain a statement to this effect. An appropriate way of expressing this is shown in paragraph 10 of example F [paragraph .64] (see also paragraph .16 of this section). [Paragraph renumbered by the issuance of Statement on Auditing Standards No. 76, September 1995.]

.57 Certain financial information in registration statements is included because of specific requirements of Regulation S-K. Accountants may comment as to whether this information is in conformity with the disclosure requirements of Regulation S-K if the following conditions are met:

a. The information is derived from the accounting records subject to the entity's controls over financial reporting, or has been derived directly from such accounting records by analysis or computation.

b. This information is capable of evaluation against reasonable criteria that have been established by the SEC.

---

[32] Accountants generally will be unable to comment on nonfinancial data presented in MD&A. However, when the accountants have conducted an examination or a review of MD&A in accordance with AT section 701, they may agree to trace nonfinancial data presented outside MD&A to similar data included in the MD&A presentation. When the accountant does not perform a review or an examination of MD&A or does not attach or refer to a report on MD&A, the accountant may perform agreed-upon procedures with respect to items in MD&A subject to controls over financial reporting. [Footnote added, effective for comfort letters issued on or after June 30, 1998, by Statement on Auditing Standards No. 86. Footnote revised, January 2001, to reflect conforming changes necessary due to the issuance of Statement on Standards for Attestation Engagements No. 10.]

The following are the disclosure requirements of Regulation S-K[33] that generally meet these conditions:

- Item 301, "Selected Financial Data"
- Item 302, "Supplementary Financial Information"
- Item 402, "Executive Compensation"
- Item 503(d), "Ratio of Earnings to Fixed Charges"

Accountants may not give positive assurance on conformity with the disclosure requirements of Regulation S-K; they are limited to giving negative assurance, since this information is not given in the form of financial statements and generally has not been audited by the accountants. Even with respect to the abovementioned items, there may be situations in which it would be inappropriate to provide negative assurance with respect to conformity of this information with Regulation S-K because conditions (*a*) and (*b*) above have not been met. Since information relevant to Regulation S-K disclosure requirements other than those noted previously is generally not derived from the accounting records subject to the entity's controls over financial reporting, it is not appropriate for the accountants to comment on conformity of this information with Regulation S-K. The accountants' inability to comment on conformity with Regulation S-K does not preclude accountants from performing procedures and reporting findings with respect to this information. [Paragraph renumbered by the issuance of Statement on Auditing Standards No. 76, September 1995.]

.58 To avoid ambiguity, the specific information commented on in the letter should be identified by reference to specific captions, tables, page numbers, paragraphs, or sentences. Descriptions of the procedures followed and the findings obtained may be stated individually for each item of specific information commented on. Alternatively, if the procedures and findings are adequately described, some or all of the descriptions may be grouped or summarized, as long as the applicability of the descriptions to items in the registration statement is clear and the descriptions do not imply that the accountants assume responsibility for the adequacy of the procedures. It would also be appropriate to present a matrix listing the financial information and common procedures employed and indicating the procedures applied to the specific items. Another presentation that could be used identifies procedures performed with specified symbols and identifies items to which those procedures have been applied directly on a copy of the prospectus which is attached to the comfort letter. (See examples F, G, and H [paragraph .64]). [Paragraph renumbered by the issuance of Statement on Auditing Standards No. 76, September 1995.]

.59 Comments in the comfort letter concerning tables, statistics, and other financial information included (incorporated by reference) in the registration statement should be made in the form of a description of the procedures followed; the findings (ordinarily expressed in terms of agreement between items compared); and in some cases, as described below, statements with respect to the acceptability of methods of allocation used in deriving the figures commented on. Whether comments on the allocation of income or expense items between categories of sales (such as military and commercial sales) may appropriately be

---

[33] Accountants should not comment in a comfort letter on compliance as to form of MD&A with rules and regulations adopted by the SEC; accountants may agree to examine or review MD&A in accordance with AT section 701. [Footnote added, effective for comfort letters issued on or after June 30, 1998, by Statement on Auditing Standards No. 86. Footnote revised, January 2001, to reflect conforming changes necessary due to the issuance of Statement on Standards for Attestation Engagements No. 10.]

made will depend on the extent to which such allocation is made in, or can be derived directly by analysis or computation from, the client's accounting records. In any event, such comments, if made, should make clear that such allocations are to a substantial extent arbitrary, that the method of allocation used is not the only acceptable one, and that other acceptable methods of allocation might produce significantly different results. Furthermore, no comments should be made regarding segment information (or the appropriateness of allocations made to derive segment information) included in financial statements, since the accountants' report encompasses that information.[34] Appropriate ways of expressing comments on tables, statistics, and other financial information are shown in examples F, G, and H [paragraph .64]. [Paragraph renumbered by the issuance of Statement on Auditing Standards No. 76, September 1995. Revised, June 2009, to reflect conforming changes necessary due to the issuance of recent authoritative literature.]

.60 In comments concerning tables, statistics, and other financial information, the expression "presents fairly" (or a variation of it) should not be used. That expression, when used by independent accountants, ordinarily relates to presentations of financial statements and should not be used in commenting on other types of information. Except with respect to requirements for financial statements and certain Regulation S-K items discussed in paragraph .57, the question of what constitutes appropriate information for compliance with the requirements of a particular item of the registration statement form is a matter of legal interpretation outside the competence of accountants. Consequently, the letter should state that the accountants make no representations regarding any matter of legal interpretation. Since the accountants will not be in a position to make any representations about the completeness or adequacy of disclosure or about the adequacy of the procedures followed, the letter should so state. It should point out, as well, that such procedures would not necessarily disclose material misstatements or omissions in the information to which the comments relate. An appropriate manner of expressing the comments is shown in examples F, G, and H [paragraph .64]. [Paragraph renumbered by the issuance of Statement on Auditing Standards No. 76, September 1995.]

Concluding Paragraph

.61 In order to avoid misunderstanding of the purpose and intended use of the comfort letter, it is desirable that the letter conclude with a paragraph along the following lines:

> This letter is solely for the information of the addressees and to assist the underwriters[35] in conducting and documenting their investigation of the affairs of the company in connection with the offering of the securities covered by the registration statement, and it is not to be used, circulated, quoted, or otherwise referred to within or without the underwriting group for any other purpose, including, but not limited to, the registration, purchase, or sale of securities,

---

[34] See paragraph .30 regarding requests by an underwriter for comments on interim financial information required by item 302(*a*) of Regulation S-K and required supplementary information described in section 558A. [Footnote renumbered by the issuance of Statement on Auditing Standards No. 76, September 1995. Footnote subsequently renumbered by the issuance of Statement on Auditing Standards No. 86, March 1998.]

[35] See paragraph .30 regarding requests by an underwriter for comments on (*a*) interim financial information required by item 302(*a*) of Regulation S-K and (*b*) required supplementary information described in section 558. [Footnote renumbered by the issuance of Statement on Auditing Standards No. 76, September 1995. Footnote subsequently renumbered by the issuance of Statement on Auditing Standards No. 86, March 1998.]

> nor is it to be filed with or referred to in whole or in part in the registration statement or any other document, except that reference may be made to it in the underwriting agreement or in any list of closing documents pertaining to the offering of the securities covered by the registration statement.

[Paragraph renumbered by the issuance of Statement on Auditing Standards No. 76, September 1995.]

Disclosure of Subsequently Discovered Matters

.62 Accountants who discover matters that may require mention in the final comfort letter but that are not mentioned in the draft letter that has been furnished to the underwriter, such as changes, increases, or decreases in specified items not disclosed in the registration statement (see paragraphs .45 and .49), will naturally want to discuss them with their client so that consideration can be given to whether disclosure should be made in the registration statement. If disclosure is not to be made, the accountants should inform the client that the matters will be mentioned in the comfort letter and should suggest that the underwriter be informed promptly. It is recommended that the accountants be present when the client and the underwriter discuss such matters. [Paragraph renumbered by the issuance of Statement on Auditing Standards No. 76, September 1995.]

Effective Date

.63 This section is effective for comfort letters issued on or after June 30, 1993. Early application of this section is encouraged. [Paragraph renumbered by the issuance of Statement on Auditing Standards No. 76, September 1995.]

.64

Appendix

Examples

1. The contents of comfort letters vary, depending on the extent of the information in the registration statement and the wishes of the underwriter or other requesting party. Shelf registration statements may have several closing dates and different underwriters. Descriptions of procedures and findings regarding interim financial statements, tables, statistics, or other financial information that is incorporated by reference from previous 1934 Act filings may have to be repeated in several comfort letters. To avoid restating these descriptions in each comfort letter, accountants may initially issue the comments in a format (such as an appendix) that can be referred to in, and attached to, subsequently issued comfort letters.

Example A: Typical Comfort Letter

2. A typical comfort letter includes—

a. A statement regarding the independence of the accountants (paragraphs .31–.32).

b. An opinion regarding whether the audited financial statements and financial statement schedules included (incorporated by reference) in the registration statement comply as to form in all material respects with the applicable accounting requirements of the act and related rules and regulations adopted by the SEC (paragraphs .33–.34).

c. Negative assurance on whether—

1. The unaudited condensed interim financial information included (incorporated by reference) in the registration statement (paragraph .37) complies as to form in all material respects with the applicable accounting requirements of the act and the related rules and regulations adopted by the SEC.
2. Any material modifications should be made to the unaudited condensed consolidated financial statements included (incorporated by reference) in the registration statement for them to be in conformity with generally accepted accounting principles.

d. Negative assurance on whether, during a specified period following the date of the latest financial statements in the registration statement and prospectus, there has been any change in capital stock, increase in long-term debt or any decrease in other specified financial statement items (paragraphs .45–.53).

Example A is a letter covering all these items. Letters that cover some of the items may be developed by omitting inapplicable portions of example A.

Example A assumes the following circumstances.[1] The prospectus (part I of the registration statement) includes audited consolidated balance sheets as of December 31, 19X5 and 19X4, and audited consolidated statements of income, retained earnings (stockholders' equity), and cash flows for each of the three

---

[1] The example includes financial statements required by SEC regulations to be included in the filing. If additional financial information is covered by the comfort letter, appropriate modifications should be made.

years in the period ended December 31, 19X5. Part I also includes an unaudited condensed consolidated balance sheet as of March 31, 19X6, and unaudited condensed consolidated statements of income, retained earnings (stockholders' equity), and cash flows for the three-month periods ended March 31, 19X6 and 19X5, reviewed in accordance with section 722 but not previously reported on by the accountants. Part II of the registration statement includes audited consolidated financial statement schedules for the three years ended December 31, 19X5. The cutoff date is June 23, 19X6, and the letter is dated June 28, 19X6. The effective date is June 28, 19X6.

Each of the comments in the letter is in response to a requirement of the underwriting agreement. For purposes of example A, the income statement items of the current interim period are to be compared with those of the corresponding period of the preceding year.

June 28, 19X6

[*Addressee*]

Dear Sirs:

We have audited the consolidated balance sheets of The Blank Company, Inc. (the company) and subsidiaries as of December 31, 19X5 and 19X4, and the consolidated statements of income, retained earnings (stockholders' equity), and cash flows for each of the three years in the period ended December 31, 19X5, and the related financial statement schedules all included in the registration statement (no. 33-00000) on Form S-1 filed by the company under the Securities Act of 1933 (the act); our reports with respect thereto are also included in that registration statement. The registration statement, as amended on June 28, 19X6, is herein referred to as the registration statement.[2]

In connection with the registration statement—

1. We are independent certified public accountants with respect to the company within the meaning of the act and the applicable rules and regulations thereunder adopted by the SEC.

2. In our opinion [*include the phrase "except as disclosed in the registration statement," if applicable*], the consolidated financial statements and financial statement schedules audited by us and included in the registration statement comply as to form in all material respects with the applicable accounting requirements of the act and the related rules and regulations adopted by the SEC.

3. We have not audited any financial statements of the company as of any date or for any period subsequent to December 31, 19X5; although we have conducted an audit for the year ended December 31, 19X5, the purpose (and therefore the scope) of the audit was to enable us to express our opinion on the consolidated financial statements as of December 31, 19X5, and for the year then ended, but not on the financial statements for any interim period within that year. Therefore, we are unable to and do not express any opinion on the

---

[2] The example assumes that the accountants have not previously reported on the interim financial information. If the accountants have previously reported on the interim financial information, they may refer to that fact in the introductory paragraph of the comfort letter as follows:

> Also, we have reviewed the unaudited condensed consolidated financial statements as of March 31, 19X6 and 19X5, and for the three-month periods then ended, as indicated in our report dated May 15, 19X6, which is included (incorporated by reference) in the registration statement.

The report may be attached to the comfort letter (see paragraph .29). The accountants may agree to comment in the comment letter on whether the interim financial information complies as to form in all material respects with the applicable accounting requirements of the rules and regulations adopted by the SEC.

unaudited condensed consolidated balance sheet as of March 31, 19X6, and the unaudited condensed consolidated statements of income, retained earnings (stockholders' equity), and cash flows for the three-month periods ended March 31, 19X6 and 19X5, included in the registration statement, or on the financial position, results of operations, or cash flows as of any date or for any period subsequent to December 31, 19X5.

4. For purposes of this letter we have read the 19X6 minutes of meetings of the stockholders, the board of directors, and [*include other appropriate committees, if any*] of the company and its subsidiaries as set forth in the minute books at June 23, 19X6, officials of the company having advised us that the minutes of all such meetings[3] through that date were set forth therein; we have carried out other procedures to June 23, 19X6, as follows (our work did not extend to the period from June 24, 19X6, to June 28, 19X6, inclusive):

a. With respect to the three-month periods ended March 31, 19X6 and 19X5, we have—

(i) Performed the procedures specified by the American Institute of Certified Public Accountants for a review of interim financial information as described in SAS No. 100, *Interim Financial Information*, on the unaudited condensed consolidated balance sheet as of March 31, 19X6, and unaudited condensed consolidated statements of income, retained earnings (stockholders' equity), and cash flows for the three-month periods ended March 31, 19X6 and 19X5, included in the registration statement.

(ii) Inquired of certain officials of the company who have responsibility for financial and accounting matters whether the unaudited condensed consolidated financial statements referred to in *a*(i) comply as to form in all material respects with the applicable accounting requirements of the act and the related rules and regulations adopted by the SEC.

b. With respect to the period from April 1, 19X6, to May 31, 19X6, we have—

(i) Read the unaudited consolidated financial statements[4] of the company and subsidiaries for April and May of both 19X5 and 19X6 furnished us by the company, officials of the company having advised us that no such financial statements as of any date or for any period subsequent to May 31, 19X6, were available.

(ii) Inquired of certain officials of the company who have responsibility for financial and accounting matters whether the unaudited consolidated financial statements referred to in *b*(i) are stated on a basis substantially consistent with that of the audited consolidated financial statements included in the registration statement.

The foregoing procedures do not constitute an audit conducted in accordance with generally accepted auditing standards. Also, they would not necessarily reveal matters of significance with respect to the comments in the following paragraph. Accordingly, we make no representations regarding the sufficiency of the foregoing procedures for your purposes.

---

[3] The accountants should discuss with the secretary those meetings for which minutes have not been approved. The letter should be modified to identify specifically the unapproved minutes of meetings that the accountants have discussed with the secretary.

[4] If the interim financial information is incomplete, a sentence similar to the following should be added: "The financial information for April and May is incomplete in that it omits the statements of cash flows and other disclosures."

5. Nothing came to our attention as a result of the foregoing procedures, however, that caused us[5] to believe that—

a. (i) Any material modifications should be made to the unaudited condensed consolidated financial statements described in 4*a*(i), included in the registration statement, for them to be in conformity with generally accepted accounting principles.[6]

(ii) The unaudited condensed consolidated financial statements described in 4*a*(i) do not comply as to form in all material respects with the applicable accounting requirements of the act and the related rules and regulations adopted by the SEC.

b. (i) At May 31, 19X6, there was any change in the capital stock, increase in long-term debt, or decrease in consolidated net current assets or stockholders' equity of the consolidated companies as compared with amounts shown in the March 31, 19X6, unaudited condensed consolidated balance sheet included in the registration statement, or

(ii) for the period from April 1, 19X6, to May 31, 19X6, there were any decreases, as compared to the corresponding period in the preceding year, in consolidated net sales or in the total or per-share amounts of income before extraordinary items or of net income, except in all instances for changes, increases, or decreases that the registration statement discloses have occurred or may occur.

6. As mentioned in 4*b*, company officials have advised us that no consolidated financial statements as of any date or for any period subsequent to May 31, 19X6, are available; accordingly, the procedures carried out by us with respect to changes in financial statement items after May 31, 19X6, have, of necessity, been even more limited than those with respect to the periods referred to in 4. We have inquired of certain officials of the company who have responsibility for financial and accounting matters whether (*a*) at June 23, 19X6, there was any change in the capital stock, increase in long-term debt or any decreases in consolidated net current assets or stockholders' equity of the consolidated companies as compared with amounts shown on the March 31, 19X6, unaudited condensed consolidated balance sheet included in the registration statement or (*b*) for the period from April 1, 19X6, to June 23, 19X6, there were any decreases, as compared with the corresponding period in the preceding year, in consolidated net sales or in the total or per-share amounts of income before extraordinary items or of net income. On the basis of these inquiries and our reading of the minutes as described in 4, nothing came to our attention that caused us to believe that there was any such change, increase, or decrease, except in all instances for changes, increases, or decreases that the registration statement discloses have occurred or may occur.

7. This letter is solely for the information of the addressees and to assist the underwriters in conducting and documenting their investigation of the affairs of the company in connection with the offering of the securities covered by the registration statement, and it is not to be used, circulated, quoted, or otherwise referred to within or without the underwriting group for any purpose, including but not limited to the registration, purchase, or sale of securities, nor is it to be filed with or referred to in whole or in part in the registration statement or any other document, except that reference may be made to it in the underwriting

---

[5] If there has been a change in accounting principle during the interim period, a reference to that change should be included herein.

[6] Section 722 does not require the accountants to modify the report on a review of interim financial information for a lack of consistency in the application of accounting principles provided that the interim financial information appropriately discloses such matters.

agreement or in any list of closing documents pertaining to the offering of the securities covered by the registration statement.

Example B: Letter When a Short-Form Registration Statement Is Filed Incorporating Previously Filed Forms 10-K and 10-Q by Reference

3. Example B is applicable when a registrant uses a short-form registration statement (Form S-2 or S-3) which, by reference, incorporates previously filed Forms 10-K and 10-Q. It assumes that the short-form registration statement and prospectus include the Form 10-K for the year ended December 31, 19X5, and Form 10-Q for the quarter ended March 31, 19X6, which have been incorporated by reference. In addition to the information presented below, the letter would also contain paragraphs 6 and 7 of the typical letter in example A. A Form S-2 registration statement will often both incorporate and include the registrant's financial statements. In such situations, the language in the following example should be appropriately modified to refer to such information as being both incorporated and included.

June 28, 19X6

[*Addressee*]

Dear Sirs:

We have audited the consolidated balance sheets of The Blank Company, Inc. (the company) and subsidiaries as of December 31, 19X5 and 19X4, and the consolidated statements of income, retained earnings (stockholders' equity), and cash flows for each of the three years in the period ended December 31, 19X5, and the related financial statement schedules, all included (incorporated by reference) in the company's annual report on Form 10-K for the year ended December 31, 19X5, and incorporated by reference in the registration statement (no. 33-00000) on Form S-3 filed by the company under the Securities Act of 1933 (the act); our report with respect thereto is also incorporated by reference in that registration statement. The registration statement, as amended on June 28, 19X6, is herein referred to as the registration statement.

In connection with the registration statement—

1. We are independent certified public accountants with respect to the company within the meaning of the act and the applicable rules and regulations thereunder adopted by the SEC.

2. In our opinion, the consolidated financial statements and financial statement schedules audited by us and incorporated by reference in the registration statement comply as to form in all material respects with the applicable accounting requirements of the act and the Securities Exchange Act of 1934 and the related rules and regulations adopted by the SEC.

3. We have not audited any financial statements of the company as of any date or for any period subsequent to December 31, 19X5; although we have conducted an audit for the year ended December 31, 19X5, the purpose (and therefore the scope) of the audit was to enable us to express our opinion on the consolidated financial statements as of December 31, 19X5, and for the year then ended, but not on the consolidated financial statements for any interim period within that year. Therefore, we are unable to and do not express any opinion on the unaudited condensed consolidated balance sheet as of March 31, 19X6, and the unaudited condensed consolidated statements of income, retained earnings (stockholders' equity), and cash flows for the three-month periods ended March 31, 19X6 and 19X5, included in the company's quarterly

report on Form 10-Q for the quarter ended March 31, 19X6, incorporated by reference in the registration statement, or on the financial position, results of operations, or cash flows as of any date or for any period subsequent to December 31, 19X5.

4. For purposes of this letter, we have read the 19X6 minutes of the meetings of the stockholders, the board of directors, and [*include other appropriate committees, if any*] of the company and its subsidiaries as set forth in the minute books at June 23, 19X6, officials of the company having advised us that the minutes of all such meetings[7] through that date were set forth therein; we have carried out other procedures to June 23, 19X6, as follows (our work did not extend to the period from June 24, 19X6, to June 28, 19X6, inclusive):

a. With respect to the three-month periods ended March 31, 19X6 and 19X5, we have—

(i) Performed the procedures specified by the American Institute of Certified Public Accountants for a review of interim financial information as described in SAS No. 100, *Interim Financial Information*, on the unaudited condensed consolidated financial statements for these periods, described in 3, included in the company's quarterly report on Form 10-Q for the quarter ended March 31, 19X6, incorporated by reference in the registration statement.

(ii) Inquired of certain officials of the company who have responsibility for financial and accounting matters whether the unaudited condensed consolidated financial statements referred to in *a*(i) comply as to form in all material respects with the applicable accounting requirements of the Securities Exchange Act of 1934 as it applies to Form 10-Q and the related rules and regulations adopted by the SEC.

b. With respect to the period from April 1, 19X6, to May 31, 19X6, we have—

(i) Read the unaudited consolidated financial statements[8] of the company and subsidiaries for April and May of both 19X5 and 19X6 furnished us by the company, officials of the company having advised us that no such financial statements as of any date or for any period subsequent to May 31, 19X6, were available.

(ii) Inquired of certain officials of the company who have responsibility for financial and accounting matters whether the unaudited consolidated financial statements referred to in *b*(i) are stated on a basis substantially consistent with that of the audited consolidated financial statements incorporated by reference in the registration statement.

The foregoing procedures do not constitute an audit conducted in accordance with generally accepted auditing standards. Also, they would not necessarily reveal matters of significance with respect to the comments in the following paragraph. Accordingly, we make no representations about the sufficiency of the foregoing procedures for your purposes.

5. Nothing came to our attention as a result of the foregoing procedures, however, that caused us to believe that—

a. (i) Any material modifications should be made to the unaudited condensed consolidated financial statements described in 3, incorporated by reference in the registration statement, for them to be in conformity with generally accepted accounting principles.

---

[7] See footnote 3 of the appendix.

[8] See footnote 4 of the appendix.

(ii) The unaudited condensed consolidated financial statements described in 3 do not comply as to form in all material respects with the applicable accounting requirements of the Securities Exchange Act of 1934 as it applies to Form 10-Q and the related rules and regulations adopted by the SEC.

b. (i) At May 31, 19X6, there was any change in the capital stock, increase in long-term debt, or any decreases in consolidated net current assets or stockholders' equity of the consolidated companies as compared with amounts shown in the March 31, 19X6 unaudited condensed consolidated balance sheet incorporated by reference in the registration statement or

(ii) for the period from April 1, 19X6, to May 31, 19X6, there were any decreases, as compared with the corresponding period in the preceding year, in consolidated net sales or in the total or per-share amounts of income before extraordinary items or of net income, except in all instances for changes, increases, or decreases that the registration statement discloses have occurred or may occur.

Example C: Letter Reaffirming Comments in Example A as of a Later Date

4. If more than one comfort letter is requested, the later letter may, in appropriate situations, refer to information appearing in the earlier letter without repeating such information (see paragraph .24 and paragraph 1 of the appendix). Example C reaffirms and updates the information in example A.

July 25, 19X6

[*Addressee*]

Dear Sirs:

We refer to our letter of June 28, 19X6, relating to the registration statement (no. 33-00000) of The Blank Company, Inc. (the company). We reaffirm as of the date hereof (and as though made on the date hereof) all statements made in that letter except that, for the purposes of this letter—

a. The registration statement to which this letter relates is as amended on July 13, 19X6 [*effective date*].

b. The reading of minutes described in paragraph 4 of that letter has been carried out through July 20, 19X6 [*the new cutoff date*].

c. The procedures and inquiries covered in paragraph 4 of that letter were carried out to July 20, 19X6 [*the new cutoff date*] (our work did not extend to the period from July 21, 19X6, to July 25, 19X6 [*date of letter*], inclusive).

d. The period covered in paragraph 4*b* of that letter is changed to the period from April 1, 19X6, to June 30, 19X6, officials of the company having advised us that no such financial statements as of any date or for any period subsequent to June 30, 19X6, were available.

e. The references to May 31, 19X6, in paragraph 5*b* of that letter are changed to June 30, 19X6.

f. The references to May 31, 19X6, and June 23, 19X6, in paragraph 6 of that letter are changed to June 30, 19X6, and July 20, 19X6, respectively.

This letter is solely for the information of the addressees and to assist the underwriters in conducting and documenting their investigation of the affairs of the company in connection with the offering of the securities covered by the registration statement, and it is not to be used, circulated, quoted, or otherwise referred to within the underwriting group for any other purpose, including but not limited to the registration, purchase, or sale of securities, nor is it to be filed with or referred to in whole or in part in the registration statement or any other document, except that reference may be made to it in the underwriting agreement or any list of closing documents pertaining to the offering of the securities covered by the registration statement.

Example D: Comments on Pro Forma Financial Information

5. Example D is applicable when the accountants are asked to comment on (*a*) whether the pro forma financial information included in a registration statement complies as to form in all material respects with the applicable accounting requirements of rule 11-02 of Regulation S-X, and (*b*) the application of pro forma adjustments to historical amounts in the compilation of the pro forma financial information (see paragraphs .42 and .43). The material in this example is intended to be inserted between paragraphs 6 and 7 in example A. The accountants have audited the December 31, 19X5, financial statements and have conducted an SAS No. 100 [section 722] review of the March 31, 19X6, interim financial information of the acquiring company. Other accountants conducted a review of the March 31, 19X6, interim financial information of XYZ Company, the company being acquired. The example assumes that the accountants have not previously reported on the pro forma financial information. If the accountants did previously report on the pro forma financial information, they may refer in the introductory paragraph of the comfort letter to the fact that they have issued a report, and the report may be attached to the comfort letter (see paragraph .29). In that circumstance, therefore, the procedures in 7*b*(i) and 7c ordinarily would not be performed, and the accountants should not separately comment on the application of pro forma adjustments to historical financial information, since that assurance is encompassed in the accountants' report on pro forma financial information. The accountants may, however, agree to comment on compliance as to form with the applicable accounting requirements of rule 11-02 of Regulation S-X.

7. At your request, we have—

a. Read the unaudited pro forma condensed consolidated balance sheet as of March 31, 19X6, and the unaudited pro forma condensed consolidated statements of income for the year ended December 31, 19X5, and the three-month period ended March 31, 19X6, included in the registration statement.

b. Inquired of certain officials of the company and of XYZ Company (the company being acquired) who have responsibility for financial and accounting matters about—

(i) The basis for their determination of the pro forma adjustments, and

(ii) Whether the unaudited pro forma condensed consolidated financial statements referred to in 7a comply as to form in all material respects with the applicable accounting requirements of rule 11-02 of Regulation S-X.

c. Proved the arithmetic accuracy of the application of the pro forma adjustments to the historical amounts in the unaudited pro forma condensed consolidated financial statements.

The foregoing procedures are substantially less in scope than an examination, the objective of which is the expression of an opinion on management's assumptions, the pro forma adjustments, and the application of those adjustments to historical financial information. Accordingly, we do not express such an opinion. The foregoing procedures would not necessarily reveal matters of significance with respect to the comments in the following paragraph. Accordingly, we make no representation about the sufficiency of such procedures for your purposes.

8. Nothing came to our attention as a result of the procedures specified in paragraph 7, however, that caused us to believe that the unaudited pro forma condensed consolidated financial statements referred to in 7*a* included in the registration statement do not comply as to form in all material respects with the applicable accounting requirements of rule 11-02 of Regulation S-X and that the pro forma adjustments have not been properly applied to the historical amounts in the compilation of those statements. Had we performed additional procedures or had we made an examination of the pro forma condensed consolidated financial statements, other matters might have come to our attention that would have been reported to you.

Example E: Comments on a Financial Forecast

6. Example E is applicable when accountants are asked to comment on a financial forecast (see paragraph .44). The material in this example is intended to be inserted between paragraphs 6 and 7 in example A. The example assumes that the accountants have previously reported on the compilation of the financial forecast and that the report is attached to the letter (see paragraph .29 and example O).

7. At your request, we performed the following procedure with respect to the forecasted consolidated balance sheet and consolidated statements of income and cash flows as of December 31, 19X6, and for the year then ending. With respect to forecasted rental income, we compared the occupancy statistics about expected demand for rental of the housing units to statistics for existing comparable properties and found them to be the same.

8. Because the procedure described above does not constitute an examination of prospective financial statements in accordance with standards established by the American Institute of Certified Public Accountants, we do not express an opinion on whether the prospective financial statements are presented in conformity with AICPA presentation guidelines or on whether the underlying assumptions provide a reasonable basis for the presentation.

Had we performed additional procedures or had we made an examination of the forecast in accordance with standards established by the American Institute of Certified Public Accountants, matters might have come to our attention that would have been reported to you. Furthermore, there will usually be differences between the forecasted and actual results, because events and circumstances frequently do not occur as expected, and those differences may be material.

Example F: Comments on Tables, Statistics, and Other Financial Information—Complete Description of Procedures and Findings

7. Example F is applicable when the accountants are asked to comment on tables, statistics, or other compilations of information appearing in a registration statement (paragraphs .54–.60). Each of the comments is in response to a specific request. The paragraphs in example F are intended to follow paragraph 6 in example A.

7. For purposes of this letter, we have also read the following, set forth in the registration statement on the indicated pages.[9]

Item	*Page*	*Description*
a	4	"Capitalization." The amounts under the captions "Amount Outstanding as of June 15, 19X6" and "As Adjusted." The related notes, except the following in Note 2: "See 'Transactions With Interested Persons.' From the proceeds of this offering the company intends to prepay $900,000 on these notes, pro rata. See 'Use of Proceeds.'"
b	13	"History and Business—Sales and Marketing." The table following the first paragraph.
c	22	"Executive Compensation—19X5 Compensation."[10]
d	33	"Selected Financial Data."

8. Our audit of the consolidated financial statements for the periods referred to in the introductory paragraph of this letter comprised audit tests and procedures deemed necessary for the purpose of expressing an opinion on such financial statements taken as a whole. For none of the periods referred to therein, or any other period, did we perform audit tests for the purpose of expressing an opinion on individual balances of accounts or summaries of selected transactions such as those enumerated above, and, accordingly, we express no opinion thereon.

9. However, for purposes of this letter we have performed the following additional procedures, which were applied as indicated with respect to the items enumerated above.

Item in 7	*Procedures and Findings*
a	We compared the amounts and numbers of shares listed under the caption "Amount Outstanding as of June 15, 19X6" with the balances in the appropriate accounts in the company's general ledger at May 31, 19X6 (the latest date for which posting had been made), and found them to be in agreement. We were informed by company officials who have responsibility for financial and accounting matters that there have been no changes in such amounts and numbers of shares between May 31, 19X6, and June 15, 19X6. We compared the amounts and numbers of shares listed under the caption "Amount Outstanding as of June 15, 19X6," adjusted for the issuance of the debentures to be offered by means of the registration statement and for the proposed use of a portion of the proceeds thereof to prepay portions of certain notes, as described under "Use of Proceeds," with the amounts and numbers of shares shown under the caption "As Adjusted" and found such amounts and numbers of shares to be in agreement. (However, we make no comments regarding the reasonableness of the "Use of Proceeds" or whether such use will actually take place.) We compared the description of the securities and the information (except certain information in Note 2, referred to in 7) included in the notes to the table with the corresponding descriptions and information in the company's consolidated financial statements,

[9] In some cases it may be considered desirable to combine in one paragraph the substance of paragraphs 7 and 9. This may be done by expanding the identification of items in paragraph 9 to provide the identification information contained in paragraph 7. In such cases, the introductory sentences in paragraphs 7 and 9 and the text of paragraph 8 might be combined as follows: "For purposes of this letter, we have also read the following information and have performed the additional procedures stated below with respect to such information. Our audit of the consolidated financial statements. . ."

[10] In some cases the company or the underwriter may request that the independent accountants report on "selected financial data" as described in section 552, *Reporting on Condensed Financial Statements and Selected Financial Data*. When the accountants report on this data and the report is included in the registration statement, separate comments should not be included in the comfort letter (see paragraph .30).

Item in 7	Procedures and Findings
	including the notes thereto included in the registration statement, and found such description and information to be in agreement.
b	We compared the amounts of military sales, commercial sales, and total sales shown in the registration statement with the balances in the appropriate accounts in the company's accounting records for the respective fiscal years and for the unaudited interim periods and found them to be in agreement. We proved the arithmetic accuracy of the percentages of such amounts of military sales and commercial sales to total sales for the respective fiscal years and for the unaudited interim periods. We compared such computed percentages with the corresponding percentages appearing in the registration statement and found them to be in agreement.
c	We compared the dollar amounts of compensation (salary, bonus, and other compensation) for each individual listed in the table "Annual Compensation" with the corresponding amounts shown by the individual employee earnings records for the year 19X5 and found them to be in agreement. We compared the dollar amount of aggregate executive officers' cash compensation on page 22 with the corresponding amount shown in an analysis prepared by the company and found the amounts to be in agreement. We traced every item over $10,000 on the analysis to the individual employee records for 19X5. We compared the dollar amounts shown under the heading of "Long-Term Compensation" on page 24 for each listed individual and the aggregate amounts for executive officers with corresponding amounts shown in an analysis prepared by the company and found such amounts to be in agreement.
	We compared the executive compensation information with the requirements of item 402 of Regulation S-K. We also inquired of certain officials of the company who have responsibility for financial and accounting matters whether the executive compensation information conforms in all material respects with the disclosure requirements of item 402 of Regulation S-K. Nothing came to our attention as a result of the foregoing procedures that caused us to believe that this information does not conform in all material respects with the disclosure requirements of item 402 of Regulation S-K.
d	We compared the amounts of net sales, income from continuing operations, income from continuing operations per common share, and cash dividends declared per common share for the years ended December 31, 19X5, 19X4, and 19X3, with the respective amounts in the consolidated financial statements on pages 27 and 28 and the amounts for the years ended December 31, 19X2, and 19X1, with the respective amounts in the consolidated financial statements included in the company's annual reports to stockholders for 19X2 and 19X1 and found them to be in agreement.
	We compared the amounts of total assets, long-term obligations, and redeemable preferred stock at December 31, 19X5 and 19X4, with the respective amounts in the consolidated financial statements on pages 27 and 28 and the amounts at December 31, 19X3, and 19X2, and 19X1 with the corresponding amounts in the consolidated financial statements included in the company's annual reports to stockholders for 19X3, 19X2, and 19X1 and found them to be in agreement.
	We compared the information included under the heading "Selected Financial Data" with the requirements of item 301 of Regulation S-K. We also inquired of certain officials of the company who have responsibility for financial and accounting matters whether this information conforms in all material respects with the disclosure requirements of item 301 of Regulation S-K. Nothing came to our attention as a result of the foregoing procedures that caused us to believe that this information does not conform in all material respects with the disclosure requirements of item 301 of Regulation S-K.

10. It should be understood that we make no representations regarding questions of legal interpretation or regarding the sufficiency for your purposes of the procedures enumerated in the preceding paragraph; also, such procedures would not necessarily reveal any material misstatement of the amounts or percentages listed above. Further, we have addressed ourselves solely to the foregoing data as set forth in the registration statement and make no representations regarding the adequacy of disclosure or regarding whether any material facts have been omitted.

11. This letter is solely for the information of the addressees and to assist the underwriters in conducting and documenting their investigation of the affairs of the company in connection with the offering of the securities covered by the registration statement, and it is not to be used, circulated, quoted, or otherwise referred to within or without the underwriting group for any other purpose, including but not limited to the registration, purchase, or sale of securities, nor is it to be filed with or referred to in whole or in part in the registration statement or any other document, except that reference may be made to it in the underwriting agreement or in any list of closing documents pertaining to the offering of the securities covered by the registration statement.

Example G: Comments on Tables, Statistics, and Other Financial Information—Summarized Description of Procedures and Findings Regarding Tables, Statistics, and Other Financial Information

8. Example G illustrates, in paragraph 9*a*, a method of summarizing the descriptions of procedures and findings regarding tables, statistics, and other financial information in order to avoid repetition in the comfort letter. The summarization of the descriptions is permitted by paragraph .58. Each of the comments is in response to a specific request. The paragraphs in example G are intended to follow paragraph 6 in example A.[11]

7. For purposes of this letter, we have also read the following, set forth in the registration statement on the indicated pages.

Item	Page	Description
a	4	"Capitalization." The amounts under the captions "Amount Outstanding as of June 15, 19X6" and "As Adjusted." The related notes, except the following in Note 2: "See 'Transactions With Interested Persons.' From the proceeds of this offering the company intends to prepay $900,000 on these notes, pro rata. See 'Use of Proceeds.'"
b	13	"History and Business—Sales and Marketing." The table following the first paragraph.
c	22	"Executive Compensation—19X5 Compensation."
d	33	"Selected Financial Data."[12]

8. Our audit of the consolidated financial statements for the periods referred to in the introductory paragraph of this letter comprised audit tests and procedures deemed necessary for the purpose of expressing an opinion on such financial statements taken as a whole. For none of the periods referred to therein, or

[11] Other methods of summarizing the descriptions may also be appropriately used. For example, the letter may present a matrix listing the financial information and common procedures employed and indicating the procedures applied to specific items.

[12] See footnote 10 of the appendix.

any other period, did we perform audit tests for the purpose of expressing an opinion on individual balances of accounts or summaries of selected transactions such as those enumerated above, and, accordingly, we express no opinion thereon.

9. However, for purposes of this letter and with respect to the items enumerated in 7 above—

a. Except for item 7*a*, we have (i) compared the dollar amounts either with the amounts in the audited consolidated financial statements described in the introductory paragraph of this letter or, for prior years, included in the company's annual report to stockholders for the years 19X1, 19X2, and 19X3, or with amounts in the unaudited consolidated financial statements described in paragraph 3 to the extent such amounts are included in or can be derived from such statements and found them to be in agreement; (ii) compared the amounts of military sales, commercial sales, and total sales and the dollar amounts of compensation for each listed individual with amounts in the company's accounting records and found them to be in agreement; (iii) compared other dollar amounts with amounts shown in analyses prepared by the company and found them to be in agreement; and (iv) proved the arithmetic accuracy of the percentages based on the data in the above-mentioned financial statements, accounting records, and analyses.

We compared the information in items 7*c* and 7*d* with the disclosure requirements of Regulation S-K. We also inquired of certain officials of the company who have responsibility for financial and accounting matters whether this information conforms in all material respects with the disclosure requirements of Regulation S-K. Nothing came to our attention as a result of the foregoing procedures that caused us to believe that this information does not conform in all material respects with the disclosure requirements of items 402 and 301, respectively, of Regulation S-K.

b. With respect to item 7*a*, we compared the amounts and numbers of shares listed under the caption "Amount Outstanding as of June 15, 19X6" with the balances in the appropriate accounts in the company's general ledger at May 31, 19X6 (the latest date for which postings had been made), and found them to be in agreement. We were informed by officials of the company who have responsibility for financial and accounting matters that there had been no changes in such amounts and numbers of shares between May 31, 19X6, and June 15, 19X6. We compared the amounts and numbers of shares listed under the caption "Amount Outstanding as of June 15, 19X6" adjusted for the issuance of the debentures to be offered by means of the registration statement and for the proposed use of a portion of the proceeds thereof to prepay portions of certain notes, as described under "Use of Proceeds," with the amounts and numbers of shares shown under the caption "As Adjusted" and found such amounts and numbers of shares to be in agreement. (However, we make no comments regarding the reasonableness of "Use of Proceeds" or whether such use will actually take place.) We compared the description of the securities and the information (except certain information in Note 2, referred to in 7) included in the notes to the table with the corresponding descriptions and information in the company's consolidated financial statements, including the notes thereto, included in the registration statement and found such descriptions and information to be in agreement.

10. It should be understood that we make no representations regarding questions of legal interpretation or regarding the sufficiency for your purposes of the procedures enumerated in the preceding paragraph; also, such procedures would not necessarily reveal any material misstatement of the amounts

or percentages listed above. Further, we have addressed ourselves solely to the foregoing data as set forth in the registration statement and make no representations regarding the adequacy of disclosure or regarding whether any material facts have been omitted.

11. This letter is solely for the information of the addressees and to assist the underwriters in conducting and documenting their investigation of the affairs of the company in connection with the offering of the securities covered by the registration statement, and it is not to be used, circulated, quoted, or otherwise referred to within or without the underwriting group for any other purpose, including but not limited to the registration, purchase, or sale of securities, nor is it to be filed with or referred to in whole or in part in the registration statement or any other document, except that reference may be made to it in the underwriting agreement or in any list of closing documents pertaining to the offering of the securities covered by the registration statement.

Example H: Comments on Tables, Statistics, and Other Financial Information: Descriptions of Procedures and Findings Regarding Tables, Statistics, and Other Financial Information—Attached Registration Statement (or Selected Pages) Identifies With Designated Symbols Items to Which Procedures Were Applied

9. This example illustrates an alternate format which could facilitate reporting when the accountant is requested to perform procedures on numerous statistics included in a registration statement. This format is permitted by paragraph .58. Each of the comments is in response to a specific request. The paragraph in example H is intended to follow paragraph 6 in example A.

7. For purposes of this letter, we have also read the items identified by you on the attached copy of the registration statement (prospectus), and have performed the following procedures, which were applied as indicated with respect to the symbols explained below:

- ✓ (looped) Compared the amount with the XYZ (Predecessor Company) financial statements for the period indicated and found them to be in agreement.
- ✓ (crossed) Compared the amount with the XYZ (Predecessor Company) financial statements for the period indicated contained in the registration statement and found them to be in agreement.
- ✓ Compared the amount with ABC Company's financial statements for the period indicated contained in the registration statement and found them to be in agreement.
- ⦸ Compared with a schedule or report prepared by the Company and found them to be in agreement.

The letter would also contain paragraphs 8, 10, and 11 of the letter in example F.

[*The following is an extract from a registration statement that illustrates how an accountant can document procedures performed on numerous statistics included in the registration statement.*]

The following summary is qualified in its entirety by the financial statements and detailed information appearing elsewhere in this Prospectus.

The Company

ABC Company (the "Company") designs, constructs, sells, and finances single-family homes for the entry-level and move-up homebuyer. The Company and its predecessor have built and delivered more single-family homes in the metropolitan area than any other homebuilder for each of the last five years. The Company delivered 1,000 homes in the year ending December 31, 19X5, and at December 31, 19X5, had 500 homes[13] under contract with an aggregate sales price of approximately $45,000,000. The Company's wholly owned mortgage banking subsidiary, which commenced operations in March 19X5, currently originates a substantial portion of the mortgages for homes sold by the Company.

The Company typically does not engage in land development without related homebuilding operations and limits speculative building. The Company purchases only that land which it is prepared to begin developing immediately for home production. A substantial portion of the Company's homes are under contract for sale before construction commences.

The DEF area has been among the top five markets in the country in housing starts for each of the last five years, with more than 90,000 single-family starts during that period. During the same period, the DEF metropolitan area has experienced increases in population, personal income, and employment at rates above the national average. The Company is a major competitive factor in three of the seven market areas, and is expanding significantly in a fourth area.

The Offering

Stock Offered by the Company.	750,000 shares of Common Stock—$.01 par value (the Common Stock")
Common Stock to Be Outstanding.	3,250,000 shares
Use of Proceeds.	To repay indebtedness incurred for the acquisition of the Company.
Proposed NASDAQ Symbol.	ABC

Assumes no exercise of the Underwriters' overallotment option. See "Underwriting".

Summary Financial Information
(In thousands, except per-share data)

Income Statement Data	*XYZ (Predecessor Company) Year Ended December 31,*				*ABC Company Year Ended December 31,*
	19X1	*19X2*	*19X3*	*19X4*	*19X5*
Revenue from home sales	$106,603	$88,970	$104,110	$115,837	$131,032
Gross profit from sales	15,980	21,138	23,774	17,099	22,407
Income from home building net of tax	490	3,473	7,029	1,000	3,425
Earnings per share	—	—	—	—	$ 1.37

[13] See paragraph .55.

Example I: Alternate Wording When Accountants' Report on Audited Financial Statements Contains an Explanatory Paragraph

10. Example I is applicable when the accountants' report on the audited financial statements included in the registration statement contains an explanatory paragraph regarding a matter that would also affect the unaudited condensed consolidated interim financial statements included in the registration statement. The introductory paragraph of example A would be revised as follows:

> Our reports with respect thereto (which contain an explanatory paragraph that describes a lawsuit to which the Company is a defendant, discussed in note 8 to the consolidated financial statements) are also included in the registration statement.

The matter described in the explanatory paragraph should also be evaluated to determine whether it also requires mention in the comments on the unaudited condensed consolidated interim financial information (paragraph 5b of example A). If it is concluded that mention of such a matter in the comments on unaudited condensed consolidated financial statements is appropriate, a sentence should be added at the end of paragraph 5*b* in example A:

> Reference should be made to the introductory paragraph of this letter which states that our audit report covering the consolidated financial statements as of and for the year ended December 31, 19X5, includes an explanatory paragraph that describes a lawsuit to which the company is a defendant, discussed in note 8 to the consolidated financial statements.

Example J: Alternate Wording When More Than One Accountant Is Involved

11. Example J applies when more than one accountant is involved in the audit of the financial statements of a business and the principal accountants have obtained a copy of the comfort letter of the other accountants (see paragraph .18). Example J consists of an addition to paragraph 4*c*, a substitution for the applicable part of paragraph 5, and an addition to paragraph 6 of example A.

> [*4*]c. We have read the letter dated ______ of [*the other accountants*] with regard to [*the related company*].
>
> 5. Nothing came to our attention as a result of the foregoing procedures (which, so far as [*the related company*] is concerned, consisted solely of reading the letter referred to in 4*c*), however, that caused us to believe that....
>
> 6. . . .On the basis of these inquiries and our reading of the minutes and the letter dated ______ of [*the other accountants*] with regard to [*the related company*], as described in 4, nothing came to our attention that caused us to believe that there was any such change, increase, or decrease, except in all instances for changes, increases, or decreases that the registration statement discloses have occurred or may occur.

Example K: Alternate Wording When the SEC Has Agreed to a Departure From Its Accounting Requirements

12. Example K is applicable when (*a*) there is a departure from the applicable accounting requirements of the act and the related rules and regulations adopted by the SEC and (*b*) representatives of the SEC have agreed to the departure. Paragraph 2 of example A would be revised to read as follows:

2. In our opinion [*include the phrase "except as disclosed in the registration statement," if applicable*], the consolidated financial statements and financial statement schedules audited by us and included (incorporated by reference) in the registration statement comply as to form in all material respects with the applicable accounting requirements of the act and the related rules and regulations adopted by the SEC; however, as agreed to by representatives of the SEC, separate financial statements and financial statement schedules of ABC Company (an equity investee) as required by rule 3-09 of Regulation S-X have been omitted.

Example L: Alternate Wording When Recent Earnings Data Are Presented in Capsule Form

13. Example L is applicable when (*a*) the statement of income in the registration statement is supplemented by later information regarding sales and earnings (capsule financial information), (*b*) the accountants are asked to comment on that information (paragraphs .39–.41), and (*c*) the accountants have conducted a review in accordance with section 722 of the financial statements from which the capsule financial information is derived. The same facts exist as in example A, except for the following:

a. Sales, net income (no extraordinary items), and earnings per share for the six-month periods ended June 30, 19X6 and 19X5 (both unaudited), are included in capsule form more limited than that specified by Financial Accounting Standards Board *Accounting Standards Codification* 270, *Interim Reporting*.

b. No financial statements later than those for June 19X6 are available.

c. The letter is dated July 25, 19X6, and the cutoff date is July 20, 19X6.

Paragraphs 4, 5, and 6 of example A should be revised to read as follows:

4. For purposes of this letter we have read the 19X6 minutes of the meetings of the stockholders, the board of directors, and [*include other appropriate committees, if any*] of the company and its subsidiaries as set forth in the minute books at July 20, 19X6, officials of the company having advised us that the minutes of all such meetings[14] through that date were set forth therein; we have carried out other procedures to July 20, 19X6, as follows (our work did not extend to the period from July 21, 19X6, to July 25, 19X6, inclusive):

a. With respect to the three-month periods ended March 31, 19X6 and 19X5, we have—

(i) Performed the procedures specified by the American Institute of Certified Public Accountants for a review of interim financial information as described in SAS No. 100, *Interim Financial Information*, on the unaudited condensed consolidated balance sheet as of March 31, 19X6, and the unaudited condensed consolidated statements of income, retained earnings (stockholders' equity), and cash flows for the three-month periods ended March 31, 19X6 and 19X5, included in the registration statement.

(ii) Inquired of certain officials of the company who have responsibility for financial and accounting matters whether the unaudited condensed consolidated financial statements referred to in (i) comply as to form in all material respects with the applicable accounting requirements of the act and the related rules and regulations adopted by the SEC.

---

14 See footnote 3 of the appendix.

b. With respect to the six-month periods ended June 30, 19X6 and 19X5, we have—

(i) Read the unaudited amounts for sales, net income, and earnings per share for the six-month periods ended June 30, 19X6 and 19X5, as set forth in paragraph [*identify location*].

(ii) Performed the procedures specified by the American Institute of Certified Public Accountants for a review of financial information as described in SAS No. 100, *Interim Financial Information*, on the unaudited condensed consolidated balance sheet as of June 30, 19X6 and the unaudited condensed consolidated statements of income, retained earnings (stockholders' equity), and cash flows for the six-month periods ended June 30, 19X6 and 19X5 from which the unaudited amounts referred to in *b*(i) are derived.

(iii) Inquired of certain officials of the company who have responsibility for financial and accounting matters whether the unaudited amounts referred to in (i) are stated on a basis substantially consistent with that of the corresponding amounts in the audited consolidated statements of income.

The foregoing procedures do not constitute an audit conducted in accordance with generally accepted auditing standards. Also, they would not necessarily reveal matters of significance with respect to the comments in the following paragraph. Accordingly, we make no representations regarding the sufficiency of the foregoing procedures for your purposes.

5. Nothing came to our attention as a result of the foregoing procedures, however, that caused us to believe that—

a. (i) Any material modifications should be made to the unaudited condensed consolidated financial statements described in 4*a*(i), included in the registration statement, for them to be in conformity with generally accepted accounting principles.

(ii) The unaudited condensed consolidated financial statements described in 4*a*(i) do not comply as to form in all material respects with the applicable accounting requirements of the act and the related rules and regulations adopted by the SEC.

b. (i) The unaudited amounts for sales, net income and earnings per share for the six-month periods ended June 30, 19X6 and 19X5, referred to in 4*b*(i) do not agree with the amounts set forth in the unaudited consolidated financial statements for those same periods.

(ii) The unaudited amounts referred to in *b*(i) were not determined on a basis substantially consistent with that of the corresponding amounts in the audited consolidated statements of income.

c. At June 30, 19X6, there was any change in the capital stock, increase in long-term debt or any decreases in consolidated net current assets or stockholders' equity of the consolidated companies as compared with amounts shown in the March 31, 19X6, unaudited condensed consolidated balance sheet included in the registration statement, except in all instances for changes, increases, or decreases that the registration statement discloses have occurred or may occur.

6. Company officials have advised us that no consolidated financial statements as of any date or for any period subsequent to June 30, 19X6, are available; accordingly, the procedures carried out by us with respect to changes in financial statement items after June 30, 19X6, have been, of necessity, even more limited than those with respect to the periods referred to in 4. We have inquired of certain officials of the company who have responsibility for financial and accounting matters regarding whether (*a*) at July 20, 19X6, there was

any change in the capital stock, increase in long-term debt or any decreases in consolidated net current assets or stockholders' equity of the consolidated companies as compared with amounts shown on the March 31, 19X6 unaudited condensed consolidated balance sheet included in the registration statement; or (*b*) for the period from July 1, 19X6, to July 20, 19X6, there were any decreases, as compared with the corresponding period in the preceding year, in consolidated net sales or in the total or per-share amounts of income before extraordinary items or of net income. On the basis of these inquiries and our reading of the minutes as described in 4, nothing came to our attention that caused us to believe that there was any such change, increase, or decrease, except in all instances for changes, increases, or decreases that the registration statement discloses have occurred or may occur.

[Revised, June 2009, to reflect conforming changes necessary due to the issuance of FASB ASC.]

Example M: Alternate Wording When Accountants Are Aware of a Decrease in a Specified Financial Statement Item

14. Example M covers a situation in which accountants are aware of a decrease in a financial statement item on which they are requested to comment (see paragraphs .45–.53). The same facts exist as in example A, except for the decrease covered in the following change in paragraph 5*b*.

a. (i) At May 31, 19X6, there was any change in the capital stock, increase in long-term debt or any decrease in consolidated stockholders' equity of the consolidated companies as compared with amounts shown in the March 31, 19X6, unaudited condensed consolidated balance sheet included in the registration statement, or (ii) for the period from April 1, 19X6, to May 31, 19X6, there were any decreases, as compared with the corresponding period in the preceding year, in consolidated net sales or the total or per-share amounts of income before extraordinary items or of net income, except in all instances for changes, increases, or decreases that the registration statement discloses have occurred or may occur and except that the unaudited consolidated balance sheet as of May 31, 19X6, which we were furnished by the company, showed a decrease from March 31, 19X6, in consolidated net current assets as follows (in thousands of dollars):

	Current Assets	*Current Liabilities*	*Net Current Assets*
March 31, 19X6	$4,251	$1,356	$2,895
May 31, 19X6	3,986	1,732	2,254

6. As mentioned in 4*b*, company officials have advised us that no consolidated financial statements as of any date or for any period subsequent to May 31, 19X6, are available; accordingly, the procedures carried out by us with respect to changes in financial statement items after May 31, 19X6, have been, of necessity, even more limited than those with respect to the periods referred to in 4. We have inquired of certain officials of the company who have responsibility for financial and accounting matters regarding whether (*a*) there was any change at June 23, 19X6, in the capital stock, increase in long-term debt or any decreases in consolidated net current assets or stockholders' equity of the consolidated companies as compared with amounts shown on the March 31, 19X6, unaudited condensed consolidated balance sheet included in the registration statement; or (*b*) for the period from April 1, 19X6, to June 23, 19X6, there were any decreases, as compared with the corresponding period in the preceding year, in consolidated net sales or in the total or per-share amounts of income before extraordinary items or of net income. On the basis of these

inquiries and our reading of the minutes as described in 4, nothing came to our attention that caused us to believe that there was any such change, increase, or decrease, except in all instances for changes, increases, or decreases that the registration statement discloses have occurred or may occur and except as described in the following sentence. We have been informed by officials of the company that there continues to be a decrease in net current assets that is estimated to be approximately the same amount as set forth in 5*b* [*or whatever other disclosure fits the circumstances*].

Example N: Alternate Wording of the Letter for Companies That Are Permitted to Present Interim Earnings Data for a Twelve-Month Period

15. Certain types of companies are permitted to include earnings data for a twelve-month period to the date of the latest balance sheet furnished in lieu of earnings data for both the interim period between the end of the latest fiscal year and the date of the latest balance sheet and the corresponding period of the preceding fiscal year. The following would be substituted for the applicable part of paragraph 3 of example A.

3. . . .was to enable us to express our opinion on the financial statements as of December 31, 19X5, and for the year then ended, but not on the financial statements for any period included in part within that year. Therefore, we are unable to and do not express any opinion on the unaudited condensed consolidated balance sheet as of March 31, 19X6, and the related unaudited condensed consolidated statements of income, retained earnings (stockholders' equity), and cash flows for the twelve months then ended included in the registration statement. . . .

Example O: Alternate Wording When the Procedures That the Underwriter Has Requested the Accountant to Perform on Interim Financial Information Are Less Than an SAS No. 100 Review

16. The example assumes that the underwriter has asked the accountants to perform specified procedures on the interim financial information and report thereon in the comfort letter. The letter is dated June 28, 19X6; procedures were performed through June 23, 19X6, the cutoff date. Since an SAS No. 100 [section 722] review was not performed on the interim financial information as of March 31, 19X6 and for the quarter then ended, the accountants are limited to reporting procedures performed and findings obtained on the interim financial information. In addition to the information presented below, the letter would also contain paragraph 7 of the typical comfort letter in example A.

June 28, 19X6

[*Addressee*]

Dear Sirs:

We have audited the consolidated balance sheets of The Blank Company, Inc. (the company) and the subsidiaries as of December 31, 19X5 and 19X4, and the consolidated statements of income, retained earnings (stockholders' equity), and cash flows for each of the three years in the period ended December 31, 19X5 and the related financial statement schedules all included in the registration statement (no. 33-00000) on Form S-1 filed by the company under the Securities Act of 1933 (the act); our reports with respect thereto are included in that registration statement. The registration statement, as amended on June 28, 19X6, is herein referred to as the registration statement.

Also, we have compiled the forecasted balance sheet and consolidated statements of income, retained earnings (stockholders' equity), and cash flows as of December 31, 19X6 and for the year then ending, attached to the registration statement, as indicated in our report dated May 15, 19X6, which is attached.

In connection with the registration statement—

1. We are independent certified public accountants with respect to the company within the meaning of the act and the applicable rules and regulations thereunder adopted by the SEC.

2. In our opinion [*include the phrase "except as disclosed in the registration statement," if applicable*], the consolidated financial statements and financial statement schedules audited by us and included in the registration statement comply as to form in all material respects with the applicable accounting requirements of the act and the related rules and regulations adopted by the SEC.

3. We have not audited any financial statements of the company as of any date or for any period subsequent to December 31, 19X5; although we have conducted an audit for the year ended December 31, 19X5, the purpose (and therefore the scope) of the audit was to enable us to express our opinion on the consolidated financial statements as of December 31, 19X5, and for the year then ended, but not on the financial statements for any interim period within that year. Therefore, we are unable to and do not express any opinion on the unaudited condensed consolidated balance sheet as of March 31, 19X6, and the unaudited condensed consolidated statements of income, retained earnings (stockholders' equity), and cash flows for the three-month periods ended March 31, 19X6 and 19X5, included in the registration statement, or on the financial position, results of operations, or cash flows as of any date or for any period subsequent to December 31, 19X5.

4. For purposes of this letter, we have read the 19X6 minutes of meetings of the stockholders, the board of directors, and [*include other appropriate committees, if any*] of the company as set forth in the minute books at June 23, 19X6, officials of the company having advised us that the minutes of all such meetings[15] through that date were set forth therein; we have carried out other procedures to June 23, 19X6, as follows (our work did not extend to the period from June 24, 19X6, to June 28, 19X6, inclusive):

a. With respect to the three-month periods ended March 31, 19X6 and 19X5, we have—

(i) Read the unaudited condensed consolidated balance sheet as of March 31, 19X6, and unaudited condensed consolidated statements of income, retained earnings (stockholders' equity), and cash flows for the three-month periods ended March 31, 19X6 and 19X5, included in the registration statement, and agreed the amounts contained therein with the company's accounting records as of March 31, 19X6 and 19X5, and for the three-month periods then ended.

(ii) Inquired of certain officials of the company who have responsibility for financial and accounting matters whether the unaudited condensed consolidated financial statements referred to in *a*(i): (1) are in conformity with generally accepted accounting principles[16] applied on a basis substantially consistent with that of the audited consolidated financial statements included in the registration statement, and (2) comply as to form in all material respects with the applicable accounting requirements of the act and the related rules and regulations adopted by the SEC. Those officials

---

[15] See footnote 3 of the appendix.

[16] See footnote 5 of the appendix.

stated that the unaudited condensed consolidated financial statements (1) are in conformity with generally accepted accounting principles applied on a basis substantially consistent with that of the audited financial statements, and (2) comply as to form in all material respects with the applicable accounting requirements of the act and the related rules and regulations adopted by the SEC.

b. With respect to the period from April 1, 19X6, to May 31, 19X6, we have—

(i) Read the unaudited condensed consolidated financial statements of the company[17] for April and May of both 19X5 and 19X6 furnished us by the company, and agreed the amounts contained therein to the company's accounting records. Officials of the company have advised us that no such financial statements as of any date or for any period subsequent to May 31, 19X6, were available.

(ii) Inquired of certain officials of the company who have responsibility for financial and accounting matters whether (1) the unaudited financial statements referred to in *b*(i) are stated on a basis substantially consistent with that of the audited consolidated financial statements included in the registration statement, (2) at May 31, 19X6, there was any change in the capital stock, increase in long-term debt or any decrease in consolidated net current assets or stockholders' equity of the consolidated companies as compared with amounts shown in the March 31, 19X6 unaudited condensed consolidated balance sheet included in the registration statement, and (3) for the period from April 1, 19X6, to May 31, 19X6, there were any decreases, as compared with the corresponding period in the preceding year, in consolidated net sales or in the total or per-share amounts of income before extraordinary items or of net income.

Those officials stated that (1) the unaudited consolidated financial statements referred to in 4*b*(i) are stated on a basis substantially consistent with that of the audited consolidated financial statements included in the registration statement, (2) at May 31, 19X6, there was no change in the capital stock, no increase in long-term debt, and no decrease in net current assets or stockholders' equity of the consolidated companies as compared with amounts shown in the March 31, 19X6, unaudited condensed consolidated balance sheet included in the registration statement, and (3) there were no decreases for the period from April 1, 19X6, to May 31, 19X6, as compared with the corresponding period in the preceding year, in consolidated net sales or in the total or per-share amounts of income before extraordinary items or of net income.

c. As mentioned in 4*b*(i), company officials have advised us that no financial statements as of any date or for any period subsequent to May 31, 19X6, are available; accordingly, the procedures carried out by us with respect to changes in financial statement items after May 31, 19X6, have, of necessity, been even more limited than those with respect to the periods referred to in 4*a* and 4*b*. We have inquired of certain officials of the company who have responsibility for financial and accounting matters whether (*a*) at June 23, 19X6, there was any change in the capital stock, increase in long-term debt or any decreases in consolidated net current assets or stockholders' equity of the consolidated companies as compared with amounts shown on the March 31, 19X6, unaudited condensed balance sheet included in the registration statement, or (*b*) for the period from April 1, 19X6, to June 23, 19X6, there were any decreases, as compared with the corresponding

[17] See footnote 4 of the appendix.

period in the preceding year, in consolidated net sales or in the total or per-share amounts of income before extraordinary items or of net income. Those officials stated that (1) at June 23, 19X6, there was no change in the capital stock, no increase in long-term debt and no decreases in consolidated net current assets or stockholders' equity of the consolidated companies as compared with amounts shown on the March 31, 19X6, unaudited condensed consolidated balance sheet, and (2) for the period from April 1, 19X6, to June 23, 19X6, there were no decreases, as compared with the corresponding period in the preceding year, in consolidated net sales or in the total or per-share amounts of income before extraordinary items or of net income.

The foregoing procedures do not constitute an audit conducted in accordance with generally accepted auditing standards. We make no representations regarding the sufficiency of the foregoing procedures for your purposes. Had we performed additional procedures or had we conducted an audit or a review, other matters might have come to our attention that would have been reported to you.

5. At your request, we also performed the following procedures:

a. Read the unaudited pro forma condensed consolidated balance sheet as of March 31, 19X6, and the unaudited pro forma condensed consolidated statements of income for the year ended December 31, 19X5, and the three-month period ended March 31, 19X6, included in the registration statement.

b. Inquired of certain officials of the company and of XYZ Company (the company being acquired) who have responsibility for financial and accounting matters as to whether all significant assumptions regarding the business combination had been reflected in the pro forma adjustments and whether the unaudited pro forma condensed consolidated financial statements referred to in (*a*) comply as to form in all material respects with the applicable accounting requirements of rule 11-02 of Regulation S-X.

Those officials referred to above stated, in response to our inquiries, that all significant assumptions regarding the business combination had been reflected in the pro forma adjustments and that the unaudited pro forma condensed consolidated financial statements referred to in (*a*) comply as to form in all material respects with the applicable accounting requirements of rule 11-02 of Regulation S-X.

c. Compared the historical financial information for the company included on page 20 in the registration statement with historical financial information for the company on page 12 and found them to be in agreement.

We also compared the financial information included on page 20 of the registration statement with the historical information for XYZ Company on page 13 and found them to be in agreement.

d. Proved the arithmetic accuracy of the application of the pro forma adjustments to the historical amounts in the unaudited pro forma condensed consolidated financial statements.

The foregoing procedures are less in scope than an examination, the objective of which is the expression of an opinion on management's assumptions, the pro forma adjustments, and the application of those adjustments to historical financial information. Accordingly, we do not express such an opinion. We make no representation about the sufficiency of the foregoing procedures for your purposes. Had we performed additional procedures or had we made an examination of the pro forma financial information, other matters might have come to our attention that would have been reported to you.

6. At your request, we performed the following procedures with respect to the forecasted consolidated balance sheet and consolidated statements of income and cash flows as of December 31, 19X6, and for the year then ending. With respect to forecasted rental income, we compared the occupancy statistics about expected demand for rental of the housing units to statistics for existing comparable properties and found them to be the same.

Because the procedures described above do not constitute an examination of prospective financial statements in accordance with standards established by the American Institute of Certified Public Accountants, we do not express an opinion on whether the prospective financial statements are presented in conformity with AICPA presentation guidelines or on whether the underlying assumptions provide a reasonable basis for the presentation. Furthermore, there will usually be differences between the forecasted and actual results, because events and circumstances frequently do not occur as expected, and those differences may be material. We make no representations about the sufficiency of such procedures for your purposes. Had we performed additional procedures or had we made an examination of the forecast in accordance with standards established by the AICPA, matters might have come to our attention that would have been reported to you.

Example P: A Typical Comfort Letter in a Non-1933 Act Offering, Including the Required Underwriter Representations

.17. Example P is applicable when a comfort letter is issued in a non-1933 Act offering. The underwriter has given the accountants a letter including the representations regarding their due diligence review process, as described in paragraphs .06 and .07, and the comfort letter refers to those representations. In addition, the example assumes that the accountants were unable, or were not requested, to perform an SAS No. 100 [section 722] review of a subsequent interim period and therefore no negative assurance has been given. See paragraph .47.

November 30, 19X5

[*Addressee*]

Dear Sirs:

We have audited the balance sheets of Example City, Any State Utility System as of June 30, 19X5 and 19X4, and the statements of revenues, expenses, and changes in retained earnings and cash flows for the years then ended, included in the Official Statement for $30,000,000 of Example City, Any State Utility System Revenue Bonds due November 30, 19Z5. Our report with respect thereto is included in the Official Statement. This Official Statement, dated November 30, 19X5, is herein referred to as the Official Statement.

This letter is being furnished in reliance upon your representation to us that—

a. You are knowledgeable with respect to the due diligence review process that would be performed if this placement of securities were being registered pursuant to the Securities Act of 1933 (the act).

b. In connection with the offering of revenue bonds, the review process you have performed is substantially consistent with the due diligence review process that you would have performed if this placement of securities were being registered pursuant to the act.

In connection with the Official Statement—

1. We are independent certified public accountants with respect to Example City, Any State and its Utility System under rule 101 of the AICPA's *Code of Professional Conduct*, and its interpretations and rulings.

2. We have not audited any financial statements of Example City, Any State Utility System as of any date or for any period subsequent to June 30, 19X5;

although we have conducted an audit for the year ended June 30, 19X5, the purpose (and therefore the scope) of the audit was to enable us to express our opinion on the financial statements as of June 30, 19X5, and for the year then ended, but not on the financial statements for any interim period within that year. Therefore, we are unable to and do not express any opinion on the financial position, results of operations, or cash flows as of any date or for any period subsequent to June 30, 19X5, for the Example City, Any State Utility System.

3. For purposes of this letter we have read the 19X5 minutes of the meetings of the City Council of Example City, Any State as set forth in the minutes books as of November 25, 19X5, the City Clerk of Example City having advised us that the minutes of all such meetings[18] through that date were set forth therein.

4. With respect to the period subsequent to June 30, 19X5, we have carried out other procedures to November 25, 19X5, as follows (our work did not extend to the period from November 26, 19X5, to November 30, 19X5, inclusive):

- We have inquired of, and received assurance from, city officials who have responsibility for financial and accounting matters, that no financial statements as of any date or for any period subsequent to June 30, 19X5, are available.
- We have inquired of those officials regarding whether (*a*) at November 25, 19X5, there was any increase in long-term debt or any decrease in net current assets of Example City, Any State Utility System as compared with amounts shown on the June 30, 19X5, balance sheet, included in the Official Statement, or (*b*) for the period from July 1, 19X5, to November 25, 19X5, there were any decreases, as compared with the corresponding period in the preceding year, in total operating revenues, income from operations or net income. Those officials stated that (1) at November 25, 19X5, there was no increase in long-term debt and no decrease in net current assets of the Example City, Any State Utility System as compared with amounts shown in the June 30, 19X5, balance sheet; and (2) there were no decreases for the period from July 1, 19X5, to November 25, 19X5, as compared with the corresponding period in the preceding year, in total operating revenues, income from operations, or net income, except in all instances for changes, increases, or decreases that the Official Statement discloses have occurred or may occur.

5. For accounting data pertaining to the years 19X3–19X5, inclusive, shown on page 11 of the Official Statement, we have (i) for data shown in the audited financial statements, compared such data with the audited financial statements of the Example City, Any State Utility System for 19X3–19X5 and found them to be in agreement; and (ii) for data not directly shown in the audited financial statements, compared such data with the general ledger and accounting records of the Utility System from which such information was derived, and found them to be in agreement.

6. The procedures enumerated in the preceding paragraphs do not constitute an audit conducted in accordance with generally accepted auditing standards. Accordingly, we make no representations regarding the sufficiency of the foregoing procedures for your purposes.

7. This letter is solely for the information of the addressees and to assist the underwriters in conducting and documenting their investigation of the affairs of the Example City, Any State Utility System in connection with the offering of securities covered by the Official Statement, and it is not to be used, circulated, quoted, or otherwise referred to for any other purpose, including but not limited

[18] See footnote 3 of paragraph .03.

to the purchase or sale of securities, nor is it to be filed with or referred to in whole or in part in the Official Statement or any other document, except that reference may be made to it in the Purchase Contract or in any list of closing documents pertaining to the offering of securities covered by the Official Statement.

Example Q: Letter to a Requesting Party That Has Not Provided the Representation Letter Described in Paragraphs .06 and .07

18. This example assumes that these procedures are being performed at the request of the placement agent on information included in an offering circular in connection with a private placement of unsecured notes with two insurance companies.[19] The letter is dated June 30, 19X6; procedures were performed through June 25, 19X6, the cutoff date. The statements in paragraphs 5–9 of the example should be included in any letter issued pursuant to paragraph .09.[20]

June 30, 19X6

[*Addressee*]

Dear Sirs:

We have audited the consolidated balance sheets of The Blank Company, Inc. (the company) and subsidiaries as of December 31, 19X5 and 19X4, and the consolidated statements of income, retained earnings (stockholders' equity), and cash flows for each of the three years in the period ended December 31, 19X5, included in the offering circular for $30,000,000 of notes due June 30, 20X6. Our report with respect thereto is included in the offering circular. The offering circular dated June 30, 19X6, is herein referred to as the offering circular.

We are independent certified public accountants with respect to the company under rule 101 of the AICPA's Code of Professional Conduct, and its interpretations and rulings.[21]

We have not audited any financial statements of the company as of any date or for any period subsequent to December 31, 19X5; although we have conducted an audit for the year ended December 31, 19X5, the purpose (and, therefore, the scope) of the audit was to enable us to express our opinion on the consolidated financial statements as of December 31, 19X5, and for the year then ended, but not on the financial statements for any interim period within that year. Therefore, we are unable to and do not express any opinion on the unaudited condensed consolidated balance sheet as of March 31, 19X6, and the unaudited condensed consolidated statements of income, retained earnings (stockholders'

[19] This same example could be used in conjunction with a municipal bond offering in which the accountant has not received the representation letter described in paragraphs .06 and .07. [Footnote added, effective for letters issued pursuant to paragraph .09 of this section after April 30, 1996, by Statement on Auditing Standards No. 76.]

[20] This example may also be used in connection with a filing under the Securities Act of 1933 (the act) when a party other than a named underwriter (for example, a selling shareholder) has not provided the accountant with the representation letter described in paragraphs .06 and .07. In such a situation, this example may be modified to include the accountant's comments on independence and compliance as to form of the audited financial statements and financial statement schedules with the applicable accounting requirements of the act and the related rules and regulations adopted by the SEC. Example paragraph 1*a*(ii) may include an inquiry, and the response of company officials, on compliance as to form of the unaudited condensed interim financial statements. [Footnote added, effective for letters issued pursuant to paragraph .09 of this section after April 30, 1996, by Statement on Auditing Standards No. 76.]

[21] See paragraphs .31 and .32 for guidance in commenting on independence. [Footnote added, effective for letters issued pursuant to paragraph .09 of this section after April 30, 1996, by Statement on Auditing Standards No. 76.]

equity), and cash flows for the three-month periods ended March 31, 19X6 and 19X5, included in the offering circular, or on the financial position, results of operations, or cash flows as of any date or for any period subsequent to December 31, 19X5.

1. At your request, we have read the 19X6 minutes of meetings of the stockholders, the board of directors, and [*include other appropriate committees, if any*] of the company as set forth in the minute books at June 25, 19X6, officials of the company having advised us that the minutes of all such meetings[22] through that date were set forth therein; we have carried out other procedures to June 25, 19X6 (our work did not extend to the period from June 26, 19X6, to June 30, 19X6, inclusive), as follows:

a. With respect to the three-month periods ended March 31, 19X6 and 19X5, we have—

(i) Read the unaudited condensed consolidated balance sheet as of March 31, 19X6, and the unaudited condensed consolidated statements of income, retained earnings (stockholders' equity), and cash flows[23, 24] of the company for the three-month periods ended March 31, 19X6 and 19X5, included in the offering circular, and agreed the amounts contained therein with the company's accounting records as of March 31, 19X6 and 19X5, and for the three-month periods then ended.

(ii) Inquired of certain officials of the company who have responsibility for financial and accounting matters whether the unaudited condensed consolidated financial statements referred to in *a*(i) are in conformity with generally accepted accounting principles applied on a basis substantially consistent with that of the audited consolidated financial statements included in the offering circular. Those officials stated that the unaudited condensed consolidated financial statements are in conformity with generally accepted accounting principles applied on a basis substantially consistent with that of the audited consolidated financial statements.

b. With respect to the period from April 1, 19X6, to May 31, 19X6, we have—

(i) Read the unaudited condensed consolidated financial statements of the company for April and May of both 19X5 and 19X6, furnished us by the company, and agreed the amounts contained therein with the company's accounting records. Officials of the company have advised us that no financial statements as of any date or for any period subsequent to May 31, 19X6, were available.

(ii) Inquired of certain officials of the company who have responsibility for financial and accounting matters whether (1) the unaudited condensed consolidated financial statements referred to in *b*(i) are stated on a basis substantially consistent with that of the audited consolidated financial statements included in the offering circular, (2) at May 31, 19X6, there was any change in the capital stock, increase in long-term debt or any decrease in consolidated net current assets or stockholders' equity of the consolidated companies

---

[22] See footnote 3 of the appendix. [Footnote added, effective for letters issued pursuant to paragraph .09 of this section after April 30, 1996, by Statement on Auditing Standards No. 76.]

[23] See footnotes 4 and 5 of the appendix. [Footnote added, effective for letters issued pursuant to paragraph .09 of this section after April 30, 1996, by Statement on Auditing Standards No. 76.]

[24] Generally, accountants should recognize that the criteria for summarized financial information have not been established for entities other than SEC registrants. [Footnote added, effective for letters issued pursuant to paragraph .09 of this section after April 30, 1996, by Statement on Auditing Standards No. 76.]

as compared with amounts shown in the March 31, 19X6, unaudited condensed consolidated balance sheet included in the offering circular, and (3) for the period from April 1, 19X6, to May 31, 19X6, there were any decreases, as compared with the corresponding period in the preceding year, in consolidated net sales or in the total or per-share amounts of income before extraordinary items or of net income.

Those officials stated that (1) the unaudited condensed consolidated financial statements referred to in *b*(ii) are stated on a basis substantially consistent with that of the audited consolidated financial statements included in the offering circular, (2) at May 31, 19X6, there was no change in the capital stock, no increase in long-term debt, and no decrease in consolidated net current assets or stockholders' equity of the consolidated companies as compared with amounts shown in the March 31, 19X6, unaudited condensed consolidated balance sheet included in the offering circular, and (3) there were no decreases for the period from April 1, 19X6, to May 31, 19X6, as compared with the corresponding period in the preceding year, in consolidated net sales or in the total or per-share amounts of income before extraordinary items or of net income.

c. As mentioned in 1*b*, company officials have advised us that no financial statements as of any date or for any period subsequent to May 31, 19X6, are available; accordingly, the procedures carried out by us with respect to changes in financial statement items after May 31, 19X6, have, of necessity, been even more limited than those with respect to the periods referred to in 1*a* and 1*b*. We have inquired of certain officials of the company who have responsibility for financial and accounting matters whether (i) at June 25, 19X6, there was any change in the capital stock, increase in long-term debt, or any decreases in consolidated net current assets or stockholders' equity of the consolidated companies as compared with amounts shown on the March 31, 19X6, unaudited condensed consolidated balance sheet included in the offering circular or (ii) for the period from April 1, 19X6, to June 25, 19X6, there were any decreases, as compared with the corresponding period in the preceding year, in consolidated net sales or in the total or per-share amounts of income before extraordinary items or of net income.

Those officials referred to above stated that (i) at June 25, 19X6, there was no change in the capital stock, no increase in long-term debt, and no decreases in consolidated net current assets or stockholders' equity of the consolidated companies as compared with amounts shown on the March 31, 19X6, unaudited condensed consolidated balance sheet, and (ii) there were no decreases for the period from April 1, 19X6, to June 25, 19X6, as compared with the corresponding period in the preceding year, in consolidated net sales or in the total or per-share amounts of income before extraordinary items or of net income.

2. At your request, we have read the following items in the offering circular on the indicated pages.[25]

---

[25] In some cases it may be considered desirable to combine in one paragraph the substance of paragraphs 2 and 4. This may be done by expanding the identification of terms in paragraph 4 to provide the identification information contained in paragraph 2. In such cases the introductory sentences in paragraphs 2 and 4 and the text of paragraph 3 might be combined as follows: "At your request, we have also read the following information and have performed the additional procedures stated below with respect to such information. Our audit of the consolidated financial statements...." [Footnote added, effective for letters issued pursuant to paragraph .09 of this section after April 30, 1996, by Statement on Auditing Standards No. 76.]

Item	*Page*	*Description*
a	13	"History and Business—Sales and Marketing." The table following the first paragraph.
b	22	"Executive Compensation—19X5 Compensation."
c	33	"Selected Financial Data."[26]

3. Our audits of the consolidated financial statements for the periods referred to in the introductory paragraph of this letter comprised audit tests and procedures deemed necessary for the purpose of expressing an opinion on such financial statements taken as a whole. For none of the periods referred to therein, nor for any other period, did we perform audit tests for the purpose of expressing an opinion on individual balances of accounts or summaries of selected transactions such as those enumerated above, and, accordingly, we express no opinion thereon.

4. However, at your request, we have performed the following additional procedures, which were applied as indicated with respect to the items enumerated above.

Item in 2	*Procedures and Findings*
a	We compare the amounts of military sales, commercial sales, and total sales shown in the registration statement with the balances in the appropriate accounts in the company's accounting records for the respective fiscal years and for the unaudited interim periods and found them to be in agreement. We proved the arithmetic accuracy of the percentages of such amounts of military sales and commercial sales to total sales for the respective fiscal years and for the unaudited interim periods. We compared such computed percentages with the corresponding percentages appearing in the registration statement and found them to be in agreement.
b	We compared the dollar amounts of compensation (salary, bonus, and other compensation) for each individual listed in the table "Annual Compensation" with the corresponding amounts shown by the individual employee earnings records for the year 19X5 and found them to be in agreement. We compared the dollar amounts shown under the heading of "Long-Term Compensation" on page 24 for each listed individual and the aggregate amounts for executive officers with corresponding amounts shown in an analysis prepared by the company and found such amounts to be in agreement.
c	We compared the amounts of net sales, income from continuing operations, income from continuing operations per common share, and cash dividends declared per common share for the years ended December 31, 19X5, 19X4, and 19X3, with the respective amounts in the consolidated financial statements on pages 27 and 28 and the amounts for the years ended December 31, 19X2, and 19X1, with the respective amounts in the consolidated financial statements included in the company's annual reports to stockholders for 19X2 and 19X1 and found them to be in agreement. We compared the amounts of total assets, long-term obligations, and redeemable preferred stock at December 31, 19X5 and 19X4, with the respective amounts in the consolidated financial statements on pages 27 and 28 and the amounts at December 31, 19X3, and 19X2, and 19X1 with the corresponding amounts in the consolidated financial statements included in the company's annual reports to stockholders for 19X3, 19X2, and 19X1 and found them to be in agreement.

[26] See footnote 10 of the appendix. [Footnote added, effective for letters issued pursuant to paragraph .09 of this section after April 30, 1996, by Statement on Auditing Standards No. 76.]

5. It should be understood that we have no responsibility for establishing (and did not establish) the scope and nature of the procedures enumerated in paragraphs 1–4 above; rather, the procedures enumerated therein are those the requesting party asked us to perform. Accordingly, we make no representations regarding questions of legal interpretation[27] or regarding the sufficiency for your purposes of the procedures enumerated in the preceding paragraphs; also, such procedures would not necessarily reveal any material misstatement of the amounts or percentages listed above as set forth in the offering circular. Further, we have addressed ourselves solely to the foregoing data and make no representations regarding the adequacy of disclosures or whether any material facts have been omitted. This letter relates only to the financial statement items specified above and does not extend to any financial statement of the company taken as a whole.

6. The foregoing procedures do not constitute an audit conducted in accordance with generally accepted auditing standards. Had we performed additional procedures or had we conducted an audit or a review of the company's March 31, April 30, or May 31, 19X6 and 19X5, condensed consolidated financial statements in accordance with standards established by the American Institute of Certified Public Accountants, other matters might have come to our attention that would have been reported to you.

7. These procedures should not be taken to supplant any additional inquiries or procedures that you would undertake in your consideration of the proposed offering.

8. This letter is solely for your information and to assist you in your inquiries in connection with the offering of the securities covered by the offering circular, and it is not to be used, circulated, quoted, or otherwise referred to for any other purpose, including but not limited to the registration, purchase, or sale of securities, nor is it to be filed with or referred to in whole or in part in the offering document or any other document, except that reference may be made to it in any list of closing documents pertaining to the offering of the securities covered by the offering document.

9. We have no responsibility to update this letter for events and circumstances occurring after June 25, 19X6.

Example R: Comfort Letter That Includes Reference to Examination of Annual MD&A and Review of Interim MD&A

19. This example assumes the following circumstances.[28] The prospectus (part I of the registration statement) includes audited consolidated balance sheets as of December 31, 19X5 and 19X4, and audited consolidated statements of income, retained earnings (stockholders' equity), and cash flows for each of the three years in the period ended December 31, 19X5. Part I also includes an unaudited condensed consolidated balance sheet as of March 31, 19X6, and unaudited condensed consolidated statements of income, retained earnings (stockholders' equity), and cash flows for the three-month periods ended March 31, 19X6 and 19X5. Part II of the registration statement includes audited consolidated financial statement schedules for the three years ended

---

[27] See footnote 7 to paragraph .09. [Footnote added, effective for letters issued pursuant to paragraph .09 of this section after April 30, 1996, by Statement on Auditing Standards No. 76.]

[28] The example includes financial statements required by SEC regulations to be included in the filing. If additional financial information is covered by the comfort letter, appropriate modifications should be made. [Footnote added, effective for comfort letters issued on or after June 30, 1998, by Statement on Auditing Standards No. 86.]

December 31, 19X5. The accountants have examined the company's management's discussion and analysis (MD&A) for the year ended December 31, 19X5, in accordance with AT section 701; the accountants have also performed reviews of the company's unaudited condensed consolidated financial statements, referred to above, in accordance with section 722, and the company's MD&A for the three-month period ended March 31, 19X6, in accordance with AT section 701. The accountant's reports on the examination and review of MD&A have been previously issued, but not distributed publicly; none of these reports is included in the registration statement. The cutoff date is June 23, 19X6, and the letter is dated June 28, 19X6. The effective date is June 28, 19X6.

Each of the comments in the letter is in response to a requirement of the underwriting agreement. For purposes of example R, the income statement items of the current interim period are to be compared with those of the corresponding period of the preceding year.

June 28, 19X6

[*Addressee*]

Dear Sirs:

We have audited the consolidated balance sheets of The Blank Company, Inc. (the company) and subsidiaries as of December 31, 19X5 and 19X4, and the consolidated statements of income, retained earnings (stockholders' equity), and cash flows for each of the three years in the period ended December 31, 19X5, and the related financial statement schedules, all included in the registration statement (no. 33-00000) on Form S-1 filed by the company under the Securities Act of 1933 (the act); our reports with respect thereto are also included in that registration statement. The registration statement, as amended on June 28, 19X6, is herein referred to as the registration statement. Also, we have examined[29] the company's Management's Discussion and Analysis for the year ended December 31, 19X5, included in the registration statement, as indicated in our report dated March 28, 19X6; our report with respect thereto is attached.[30] We have also reviewed the unaudited condensed consolidated financial statements as of March 31, 19X6 and 19X5, and for the three-month periods then ended, included in the registration statement, as indicated in our report dated May 15, 19X6, and have also reviewed the company's Management's Discussion and Analysis for the three-month period ended March 31, 19X6, included in the registration statement, as indicated in our report dated May 15, 19X6; our reports with respect thereto are attached.[31]

In connection with the registration statement—

1. We are independent certified public accountants with respect to the company within the meaning of the act and the applicable rules and regulations thereunder adopted by the SEC.

2. In our opinion [*include the phrase "except as disclosed in the registration statement," if applicable*], the consolidated financial statements and financial statement schedules audited by us and included in the registration statement comply as to form in all material respects with the applicable accounting requirements of the act and the related rules and regulations adopted by the SEC.

---

[29] If the accountant has performed a review of the company's annual MD&A, the opening paragraph of the comfort letter should be revised accordingly. [Footnote added, effective for comfort letters issued on or after June 30, 1998, by Statement on Auditing Standards No. 86.]

[30] The accountant has elected to attach the previously issued reports to the comfort letter (see paragraph .29). [Footnote added, effective for comfort letters issued on or after June 30, 1998, by Statement on Auditing Standards No. 86.]

[31] See footnote 30 of the appendix. [Footnote added, effective for comfort letters issued on or after June 30, 1998, by Statement on Auditing Standards No. 86.]

3. We have not audited any financial statements of the company as of any date or for any period subsequent to December 31, 19X5; although we have conducted an audit for the year ended December 31, 19X5, the purpose (and therefore the scope) of the audit was to enable us to express our opinion on the consolidated financial statements as of December 31, 19X5, and for the year then ended, but not on the financial statements for any interim period within that year. Therefore, we are unable to and do not express any opinion on the unaudited condensed consolidated balance sheet as of March 31, 19X6, and the unaudited condensed consolidated statements of income, retained earnings (stockholders' equity), and cash flows for the three-month periods ended March 1, 19X6 and 19X5, included in the registration statement, or on the financial position, results of operations, or cash flows as of any date or for any period subsequent to December 31, 19X5.

4. We have not examined any management's discussion and analysis of the company as of or for any period subsequent to December 31, 19X5; although we have made an examination of the company's Management's Discussion and Analysis for the year ended December 31, 19X5, included in the company's registration statement, the purpose (and therefore the scope) of the examination was to enable us to express our opinion on such Management's Discussion and Analysis, but not on the management's discussion and analysis for any interim period within that year. Therefore, we are unable to and do not express any opinion on the Management's Discussion and Analysis for the three-month period ended March 31, 19X6, included in the registration statement, or for any period subsequent to March 31, 19X6.

5. For purposes of this letter we have read the 19X6 minutes of meetings of the stockholders, the board of directors, and [*include other appropriate committees, if any*] of the company and its subsidiaries as set forth in the minute books at June 23, 19X6, officials of the company having advised us that the minutes of all such meetings[32] through that date were set forth therein; we have carried out other procedures to June 23, 19X6, as follows (our work did not extend to the period from June 24, 19X6, to June 28, 19X6, inclusive):

a. With respect to the three-month periods ended March 31, 19X6 and 19X5, we have inquired of certain officials of the company who have responsibility for financial and accounting matters whether the unaudited condensed consolidated balance sheet as of March 31, 19X6, and the unaudited condensed consolidated statements of income, retained earnings (stockholders' equity), and cash flows for the three-month periods ended March 31, 19X6 and 19X5, included in the registration statement, comply as to form in all material respects with the applicable accounting requirements of the act and the related rules and regulations adopted by the SEC.

b. With respect to the period from April 1, 19X6, to May 31, 19X6, we have—

(i) Read the unaudited consolidated financial statements[33] of the company and subsidiaries for April and May of both 19X5 and 19X6 furnished to us by the company, officials of the company having advised us that no such financial statements as of any date or for any period subsequent to May 31, 19X6, were available.

---

[32] See footnote 3 of the appendix. [Footnote added, effective for comfort letters issued on or after June 30, 1998, by Statement on Auditing Standards No. 86.]

[33] See footnote 4 of the appendix. [Footnote added, effective for comfort letters issued on or after June 30, 1998, by Statement on Auditing Standards No. 86.]

(ii) Inquired of certain officials of the company who have responsibility for financial and accounting matters whether the unaudited consolidated financial statements referred to in item b(i) are stated on a basis substantially consistent with that of the audited consolidated financial statements included in the registration statement.

The foregoing procedures do not constitute an audit of financial statements conducted in accordance with generally accepted auditing standards. Also, they would not necessarily reveal matters of significance with respect to the comments in the following paragraph. Accordingly, we make no representations regarding the sufficiency of the foregoing procedures for your purposes.

6. Nothing came to our attention as a result of the foregoing procedures, however, that caused us[34] to believe that—

a. The unaudited condensed consolidated financial statements described in item 5*a* do not comply as to form in all material respects with the applicable accounting requirements of the act and the related rules and regulations adopted by the SEC.

b. (i) At May 31, 19X6, there was any change in the capital stock, increase in long-term debt, or decrease in consolidated net current assets or stockholders' equity of the consolidated companies as compared with amounts shown in the March 31, 19X6, unaudited condensed consolidated balance sheet included in the registration statement, or

(ii) For the period from April 1, 19X6, to May 31, 19X6, there were any decreases, as compared to the corresponding period in the preceding year, in consolidated net sales or in the total or per-share amounts of income before extraordinary items or of net income, except in all instances for changes, increases, or decreases that the registration statement discloses have occurred or may occur.

7. As mentioned in item 5*b*, company officials have advised us that no consolidated financial statements as of any date or for any period subsequent to May 31, 19X6, are available; accordingly, the procedures carried out by us with respect to changes in financial statement items after May 31, 19X6, have, of necessity, been even more limited than those with respect to the periods referred to in item 5. We have inquired of certain officials of the company who have responsibility for financial and accounting matters whether (*a*) at June 23, 19X6, there was any change in the capital stock, increase in long-term debt or any decreases in consolidated net current assets or stockholders' equity of the consolidated companies as compared with amounts shown on the March 31, 19X6, unaudited condensed consolidated balance sheet included in the registration statement or (*b*) for the period from April 1, 19X6, to June 23, 19X6, there were any decreases, as compared with the corresponding period in the preceding year, in consolidated net sales or in the total or per-share amounts of income before extraordinary items or of net income. On the basis of these inquiries and our reading of the minutes as described in item 5, nothing came to our attention that caused us to believe that there was any such change, increase, or decrease, except in all instances for changes, increases, or decreases that the registration statement discloses have occurred or may occur.

---

[34] See footnote 5 of the appendix. [Footnote added, effective for comfort letters issued on or after June 30, 1998, by Statement on Auditing Standards No. 86.]

8. This letter is solely for the information of the addressees and to assist the underwriters in conducting and documenting their investigation of the affairs of the company in connection with the offering of the securities covered by the registration statement, and it is not to be used, circulated, quoted, or otherwise referred to within or without the underwriting group for any purpose, including but not limited to the registration, purchase, or sale of securities, nor is it to be filed with or referred to in whole or in part in the registration statement or any other document, except that reference may be made to it in the underwriting agreement or in any list of closing documents pertaining to the offering of the securities covered by the registration statement.

[Paragraph renumbered and amended, effective for letters issued pursuant to paragraph .09 of this section after April 30, 1996, by the issuance of Statement on Auditing Standards No. 76. As amended, effective for comfort letters issued on or after June 30, 1998, by Statement on Auditing Standards No. 86. Revised, January 2001, to reflect conforming changes necessary due to the issuance of Statement on Standards for Attestation Engagements No. 10. Revised, January 2006, to reflect conforming changes necessary due to the issuance of Statement on Auditing Standards No. 100.]

AU Section 9634

Letters for Underwriters and Certain Other Requesting Parties: Auditing Interpretations of Section 634

1. Letters to Directors Relating to Annual Reports on Form 10-K[*]

.01 *Question*—Annual reports to the Securities and Exchange Commission (SEC) on Form 10-K must be signed by at least a majority of the registrant's board of directors. In reviewing the Form 10-K, directors may seek the involvement of the registrant's independent auditors and other professionals.

.02 What types of services could the auditor perform at the request of the board of directors in connection with the Form 10-K? For example, is it permissible for the auditor to comment on compliance of the registrant's Form 10-K with the requirements of the various SEC rules and regulations?[1]

.03 *Interpretation*—The auditor can express an opinion to the board of directors on whether the financial statements and financial statement schedules audited comply as to form with the applicable accounting requirements of the Securities Exchange Act of 1934 and the related rules and regulations thereunder adopted by the SEC (see section 634 paragraph .33).[2]

.04 The auditor may affirm to the board of directors that under generally accepted auditing standards the auditor is required to read the information in addition to audited financial statements contained in the Form 10-K, for the purpose of considering whether such information may be materially inconsistent with information appearing in the financial statements (see section 550). However, the report to the board of directors should state that the auditor has no obligation to perform any procedures to corroborate such information.

.05 In addition, the auditor could perform, at the request of the board of directors, specified procedures and report the results of those procedures concerning various information contained in the Form 10-K such as tables, statistics and other financial information. There should be a clear understanding with the board as to the nature, extent and limitations of the procedures to be performed and as to the kind of report to be issued. Although the guidance provided in section 634 is intended primarily for auditors issuing a letter to underwriters and certain other requesting parties in connection with an offering of securities, the guidance in section 634 paragraphs .54–.60 would also be applicable when the auditor is asked to furnish a letter to the board of directors in connection with the filing of Form 10-K under the Securities Exchange Act of 1934.[3] The types of information on which auditors may comment are described in section 634 paragraph .55. The auditor should comment only on that information if

---

[*] [Footnote deleted June 1993, by the issuance of Statement on Auditing Standards No. 72.]

[1] [Footnote deleted June 1993, by the issuance of Statement on Auditing Standards No. 72.]

[2] The auditor should not provide any assurance on compliance with the provisions of the Securities Exchange Act of 1934 regarding controls. [Revised, January 2009, to reflect conforming changes necessary due to the issuance of Statement on Standards for Attestation Engagements No. 15.]

[3] Section 634 paragraph .12 states in part: "Accountants will normally be willing to assist the underwriter but the assistance accountants can provide by way of comfort letters is subject to limitations. One limitation is that independent accountants can properly comment in their professional capacity only on matters to which his professional expertise is substantially relevant."

the criteria in section 634 paragraphs .55 and .57 have been met. The comments should be made in the form of description of procedures performed and findings obtained, ordinarily expressed in terms of agreement between items compared.

.06 Certain financial information in Form 10-K is included because of specific requirements of Regulation S-K. The auditor may comment as to whether this information is in conformity with the disclosure requirements of Regulation S-K if the conditions in section 634 paragraph .57 are met. Section 634 paragraph .57 identifies the disclosure requirements of Regulation S-K that generally meet those conditions. The auditor is limited to giving negative assurance, since this information is not given in the form of financial statements and generally has not been audited by the accountants. (See section 634 paragraph .57.)

.07 The auditor should not comment on matters that are primarily subjective or judgmental in nature such as those included in Item 7 of Form 10-K, "Management's Discussion and Analysis of Financial Condition and Results of Operations." For example, changes between periods in gross profit ratios may be caused by factors that are not necessarily within the expertise of auditors. However, the auditor can comment on specific changes in comparative amounts that are included in management's discussion if the amounts used to compute such changes are obtained from the financial statements or accounting records as discussed in section 634 paragraph .55, but cannot comment with respect to the appropriateness of the explanations.

.08 There are no criteria by which to measure the sufficiency of the procedures performed by the accountants for the directors' purposes. Ordinarily the auditor should discuss with the directors or the audit committee the procedures to be performed and may suggest procedures that might be meaningful in the circumstances. However, the auditor should clearly indicate to the board of directors that the auditor cannot make any representations as to whether the agreed-upon procedures are sufficient for the directors' purposes.

.09 It should not ordinarily be necessary for the auditor to reaffirm the auditor's independence to the board of directors. If such a representation is requested, however, the auditor may include in the letter a statement similar to that described in section 634 paragraph .31.

[Issue Date: April, 1981; Modified: May, 1981;
Revised: June, 1993; Revised: January, 2001.]

[2.] Negative Assurance on Unaudited Condensed Interim Financial Statements Attached to Comfort Letters

[.10–.12] [Deleted April 1993 by Statement on Auditing Standards No. 72.]

3. Commenting in a Comfort Letter on Quantitative Disclosures About Market Risk Made in Accordance With Item 305 of Regulation S-K

.13 *Introduction*—Regulation S-K Item 305, *Quantitative and Qualitative Disclosures About Market Risk*, requires certain quantitative and qualitative disclosures with respect to derivative financial instruments, generally as defined in Financial Accounting Standards Board *Accounting Standards Codification* glossary.

.14 In addition to qualitative (i.e., descriptive) disclosures, Item 305 requires quantitative disclosures that may be presented in the form of a tabular presentation, sensitivity analysis, or value-at-risk disclosures. Disclosures generally include a combination of historical and fair value data and the hypothetical effects on such data of assumed changes in interest rates, foreign currency exchange rates, commodity prices and other relevant market rates. The quantitative and qualitative information required by Item 305 should be disclosed outside the financial statements and related notes thereto.

.15 *Question*—May an accountant provide positive or negative assurance on conformity with Item 305 of Regulation S-K?

.16 *Interpretation*—Section 634, *Letters for Underwriters and Certain Other Requesting Parties*, paragraph .57, states that accountants may not give positive assurance on conformity of information with the disclosure requirements of Regulation S-K since this information is not in the form of financial statements and generally has not been audited by the accountants. Accountants may provide negative assurance on conformity with Regulation S-K only if the following conditions are met:

a. The information is derived from the accounting records subject to the entity's controls over financial reporting, or has been derived directly from such accounting records by analysis or computation.

b. This information is capable of evaluation against reasonable criteria that have been established by the SEC.

Although some information needed to comply with Item 305 is derived from the accounting records, registrants must also provide a substantial amount of information that is not derived from accounting records subject to the entity's controls over financial reporting. As a result, accountants should not provide negative assurance on conformity with Item 305 of Regulation S-K.

.17 *Question*—May an accountant otherwise provide comments in a comfort letter on items disclosed by registrants in accordance with Item 305 of Regulation S-K?

.18 *Interpretation*—Section 634 paragraph .55 states that accountants should comment only with respect to information—

a. That is expressed in dollars (or percentages derived from such dollar amounts) and that has been obtained from accounting records that are subject to the entity's controls over financial reporting or

b. That has been derived directly from such accounting records by analysis or computation.

As a result, accountants should not comment on the Item 305 qualitative disclosures.

.19 The three alternative forms of quantitative disclosures under Item 305 reflect hypothetical effects on market-risk-sensitive instruments and result in differing presentations. The forward-looking information used to prepare these presentations may be substantially removed from the accounting records that are subject to the entity's controls over financial reporting. Further, section 634 paragraph .55 also states that "the accountants should not comment on matters merely because they happen to be present and are capable of reading, counting, measuring, or performing other functions that might be applicable." Accordingly, an accountant's ability to comment on these disclosures is largely dependent upon the degree to which the forward-looking information used to prepare these disclosures is linked to such accounting records.

.20 The tabular presentation includes the fair values of market-risk-sensitive instruments and contract terms to determine the future cash flows from those instruments that are categorized by expected maturity dates. This approach may require the use of yield curves and implied forward rates to determine expected maturity dates, as well as assumptions regarding prepayments and weighted average interest rates.

.21 The term *sensitivity analysis* describes a general class of models that are designed to assess the risk of loss in market-risk-sensitive instruments, based upon hypothetical changes in market rates or prices. Sensitivity analysis does not refer to any one, specific model and may include duration analysis or other "sensitivity" measures. The disclosures are dependent upon assumptions about theoretical future market conditions and, therefore, are not derived from the accounting records.

.22 The term *value at risk* describes a general class of models that provide a probabilistic assessment of the risk of loss in market-risk-sensitive instruments over a selected period of time, with a selected likelihood of occurrences based upon selected confidence intervals. Value-at-risk disclosures are extremely aggregated and, in addition to the assumptions made for sensitivity analyses, may include additional assumptions regarding correlation between asset classes and future market volatilities. As a result, these disclosures are not derived from the accounting records.

.23 Of the three disclosure alternatives, the tabular presentation contains the most limited number of assumptions and least complex mathematical calculations. Furthermore, certain information, such as contractual terms, included in a tabular presentation is derived from the accounting records. Accordingly, accountants may perform limited procedures related to tabular presentations to the extent that such information is derived from the accounting records.

.24 The modeling techniques and underlying assumptions utilized for sensitivity analysis and value-at-risk disclosures generally will be highly complex. The resultant disclosures may be substantially different from the basic historical financial input derived directly from the accounting records. Due to the hypothetical and forward-looking nature of these disclosures and the potentially limited usefulness of any procedures that may be performed, accountants should not agree to make any comments or perform any procedures related to sensitivity analysis or value-at-risk disclosures.

.25 When performing procedures related to tabular presentation disclosures, the accountant will need to consider whether the entity's documentation of its contractual positions in derivatives, commodities and other financial instruments is subject to the entity's controls over financial reporting and whether it provides a complete record of the entity's market-risk-sensitive instruments. In addition, the accountant should disclaim as to the reasonableness of the assumptions underlying the disclosures.

.26 Item 305 requires registrants to stratify financial instruments according to market risk category, i.e., interest rate risk, foreign exchange risk, and equity price risk. Item 305 stipulates that, if an instrument is at risk in more than one category, the instrument should be included in the disclosures for each applicable category. In reporting findings from agreed-upon procedures relating to market risk categories, the accountant should not provide any findings that the company's stratifications are complete or comply as to form with Item 305 requirements and should disclaim with respect to the company's determination of market risk categories.

.27 Item 305 encourages registrants to provide quantitative and qualitative information about market risk in terms of, among other things, the magnitude of actual past market movements and estimates of possible near-term market movements. Accountants should not agree to perform any procedures related to such market data.

.28 The accountant should establish a clear understanding with the underwriter as to the limitations of the procedures to be performed with respect to the market risk disclosures. Further, accountants should consider the need to utilize a specialist in performing procedures related to those disclosures.

.29 The following examples, based upon example H of section 634 paragraph .64, provide very simplified procedures, findings and limitations related to Item 305 tabular presentation disclosures. In practice, the procedures generally will be substantially more complex.

Symbol	Procedures and Findings
p	Compared with a schedule prepared by the Company from its accounting records. We (*a*) compared the amounts on the schedule to corresponding amounts appearing in the accounting records and found such amounts to be in agreement and (*b*) determined that the schedule was mathematically correct. However, we make no comment as to the appropriateness or completeness of the Company's classification of its market-risk-sensitive instruments into market risk categories, nor as to its determination of the expected maturity dates or amounts. (Note: This is an example of procedures related to tabular presentations of face amounts, carrying amounts, fair values and notional amounts which stratify such amounts as to interest rate risk.)
›	Compared with a schedule prepared by the Company from its accounting records to calculate weighted average fixed interest rates and weighted average fixed pay and receive rates, and found such percentages to be in agreement. We (*a*) compared the amounts on the schedule to corresponding amounts appearing in the accounting records and found such amounts to be in agreement and (*b*) determined that the schedule was mathematically correct. However, we make no comment as to the appropriateness of the Company's methodology in calculating weighted average fixed rates.
	(Note: It may be necessary to provide a more complete description of the procedures performed in other circumstances.)
	We make no comment as to the appropriateness or completeness of the Company's determination of the Regulation S-K requirements for quantitative and qualitative disclosures about market risks or with respect to the reasonableness of the assumptions underlying the disclosures.

[*The following is an extract from a registration statement that illustrates how an accountant can document procedures performed on a tabular presentation of market risk disclosures made in accordance with Item 305 of Regulation S-K.*]

INTEREST RATE SENSITIVITY

The table that follows provides information about the Company's derivative financial instruments and other financial instruments that are sensitive to changes in interest rates, including interest rate swaps and debt obligations. For debt obligations, the table presents principal cash flows and related weighted average interest rates by expected maturity dates. For interest rate swaps, the table presents notional amounts and weighted average interest rates by expected maturity dates. Notional amounts are used to calculate the contractual payments to be exchanged under the contract. Weighted average variable rates are based on implied forward rates in the yield curve at the reporting date. The information is presented in U.S. dollar equivalents, which is the Company's reporting currency. The instrument's actual cash flows are denominated in both U.S. dollars ($US) and German deutschmarks (DM), as indicated in parentheses.

	Expected maturity dates						
	19X2[4]	*19X3*[4]	*19X4*[4]	*19X5*[4]	*There-after*[4]	*Total*	*Fair Value*
Liabilities	*($US equivalent in millions)*						
Long-Term Debt:							
Fixed Rate ($US)	$XXX	$XXX	$XXX	$XXX	$XXX	$XXX[p]	$XXX[p]
Average interest rate	XX%	XX%	XX%	XX%	XX%	XX%›	
Fixed Rate (DM)	XXX	XXX	XXX	XXX	XXX	XXX[p]	XXX[p]
Average interest rate	XX%	XX%	XX%	XX%	XX%	XX%›	
Variable Rate ($US)	XXX	XXX	XXX	XXX	XXX	XXX[p]	XXX[p]
Average interest rate	XX%	XX%	XX%	XX%	XX%	XX%[4]	
Interest Rate Derivatives	*($US equivalent in millions)*						
Interest Rate Swaps:							
Variable to Fixed ($US)	*$XXX*	*$XXX*	*$XXX*	*$XXX*	*$XXX*	*$XXX*[p]	*$XXX*[p]
Average pay rate-fixed	*XX%*	*XX%*	*XX%*	*XX%*	*XX%*	*XX%*›	
Average receive rate-variable	*XX%*	*XX%*	*XX%*	*XX%*	*XX%*	*XX%*[4]	
Fixed to Variable ($US)	*XXX*	*XXX*	*XXX*	*XXX*	*XXX*	*XXX*[p]	*XXX*[p]
Average pay rate-variable	*XX%*	*XX%*	*XX%*	*XX%*	*XX%*	*XX%*[4]	
Average receive rate-fixed	*XX%*	*XX%*	*XX%*	*XX%*	*XX%*	*XX%*›	

[Issue Date: August 1998; Revised: June 2009.]

---

[4] No findings should be expressed on amounts in these columns because these disclosures include either management's expectations of future cash flows or the use of implied forward rates applied to such expected cash flows. Accordingly, such information does not meet the criteria of seciton 634 paragraph .55.

AU Section 9642

Reporting on Internal Accounting Control: Auditing Interpretations of SAS No. 30

Many of the interpretations in this section were based on the concepts in Statement on Auditing Standards (SAS) No. 30, *Reporting on Internal Accounting Control*. SAS No. 30 was superseded in May 1993 by the issuance of Statement on Standards for Attestation Engagements (SSAE) No. 2, *Reporting on an Entity's Internal Control Over Financial Reporting*. Subsequently, SSAE No. 2 was superseded by SSAE No. 10, *Attestation Standards: Revision and Recodification*, which was issued in January 2001. The AICPA's Auditing Standards Board decided at its October 1993 meeting to delete these interpretations. Notes have been included below to indicate where current guidance may be found in AICPA literature.

[1.] Pre-Award Surveys[*]

[.01–.03] [Deleted October 1993.] (See the guidance provided in attest interpretation No. 7 of SSAE No. 1 (AT section 9101.59–.69). [Revised, January 2001, to reflect conforming changes necessary due to the issuance of Statement on Standards for Attestation Engagements No. 10; Revised, January 2009, to reflect conforming changes necessary due to the issuance of Statement on Standards for Attestation Engagements No. 15.]

[2.] Award Survey Made in Conjunction With an Audit

[.04–.05] [Deleted October 1993.] (See the guidance provided in attest interpretation No. 7 of SSAE No. 1 (AT section 9101.59–.69). [Revised, January 2001, to reflect conforming changes necessary due to the issuance of Statement on Standards for Attestation Engagements No. 10; Revised, January 2009, to reflect conforming changes necessary due to the issuance of Statement on Standards for Attestation Engagements No. 15.]

[3.] Reporting on Matters Not Covered by Government-Established Criteria

[.06–.07] [Deleted October 1993. Revised, January 2001, to reflect conforming changes necessary due to the issuance of Statement on Standards for Attestation Engagements No. 10.]

[4.] Limited Scope

[.08–.09] [Deleted October 1993.] (See the guidance provided in SSAE No. 15 paragraphs 117–121 (AT section 501.117–.121).) [Revised, January 2001, to reflect conforming changes necessary due to the issuance of Statement on Standards for Attestation Engagements No. 10; Revised, January 2009, to reflect

[*] [Footnote deleted, October 1993.]

conforming changes necessary due to the issuance of Statement on Standards for Attestation Engagements No. 15.]

[5.] Compliance With the Foreign Corrupt Practices Act of 1977

[.10–.13] [Deleted October 1993.]) [Revised, January 2001, to reflect conforming changes necessary due to the issuance of Statement on Standards for Attestation Engagements No. 10; Revised, January 2009, to reflect conforming changes necessary due to the issuance of Statement on Standards for Attestation Engagements No. 15.]

[6.] Reports on Internal Accounting Control of Trust Departments of Banks

[.14–.17] [Deleted October 1993.] (See the guidance provided in SSAE No. 15, paragraphs 117–121 (AT section 501.117–.121.) [Revised, January 2001, to reflect conforming changes necessary due to the issuance of Statement on Standards for Attestation Engagements No. 10; Revised, January 2009, to reflect conforming changes necessary due to the issuance of Statement on Standards for Attestation Engagements No. 15.]

[7.] Report Required by U.S. General Accounting Office[1-7]

[.18–.25] [Superseded by Statement on Auditing Standards No. 60, effective for audits of financial statements for periods beginning on or after January 1, 1989.]

[8.] Form of Report on Internal Accounting Control Based Solely on a Study and Evaluation Made as Part of an Audit[8-10]

[.26–.32] [Superseded by Statement on Auditing Standards No. 60, effective for audits of financial statements for periods beginning on or after January 1, 1989.]

[9.] Reporting on Internal Accounting Control Based Solely on an Audit When a Minimum Study and Evaluation Is Made

[.33–.34] [Superseded by Statement on Auditing Standards No. 60, effective for audits of financial statements for periods beginning on or after January 1, 1989.]

[10.] Report Required by U.S. General Accounting Office Based on a Financial and Compliance Audit When a Study and Evaluation Does Not Extend Beyond the Preliminary Review Phase[11-15]

[.35–.36] [Superseded by Statement on Auditing Standards No. 60, effective for audits of financial statements for periods beginning on or after January 1, 1989.]

[1-7] [Superseded by Statement on Auditing Standards No. 60, effective for audits of financial statements for periods beginning on or after January 1, 1989.]

[8-10] [Superseded by Statement on Auditing Standards No. 60, effective for audits of financial statements for periods beginning on or after January 1, 1989.]

[11-15] [Superseded by Statement on Auditing Standards No. 60, effective for audits of financial statements for periods beginning on or after January 1, 1989.]

[11.] Restricted Purpose Report Required by Law to Be Made Available to the Public[16]

[.37–.38] [Superseded by Statement on Auditing Standards No. 60, effective for audits of financial statements for periods beginning on or after January 1, 1989.]

[12.] Reporting on Internal Accounting Control "Compliance With the Currency and Foreign Transactions Reporting Act"[*]

[.39–.41] [Deleted October 1993.]

---

[16] [Superseded by Statement on Auditing Standards No. 60, effective for audits of financial statements for periods beginning on or after January 1, 1989.]

[*] See footnote [*] in paragraphs [.01–.03].

[11.] Restricted Purpose Report Required by Law to Be Made Available to the Public[6]

[.37–.38] [Superseded by Statement on Auditing Standards No. 60, effective for audits of financial statements for periods beginning on or after January 1, 1989.]

[12.] Reporting on Internal Accounting Control Compliance With the Currency and Foreign Transactions Reporting Act[7]

[.39–.41] [Deleted October, 1982.]

---

[6] Superseded by Statement on Auditing Standards No. 60, effective for audits of financial statements for periods beginning on or after January 1, 1989.

[7] See footnote 6, in paragraph .36 (title).

AU Section 700
SPECIAL TOPICS

TABLE OF CONTENTS

AU Section 711*

Filings Under Federal Securities Statutes

Source: SAS No. 37.

See section 9711 for interpretations of this section.

Issue date, unless otherwise indicated: April, 1981.

.01 As in the case of financial statements used for other purposes, management has the responsibility for the financial representations contained in documents filed under the federal securities statutes. In this connection the Securities and Exchange Commission has said:

> The fundamental and primary responsibility for the accuracy of information filed with the Commission and disseminated among the investors rests upon management. Management does not discharge its obligations in this respect by the employment of independent public accountants, however reputable. Accountants' certificates are required not as a substitute for management's accounting of its stewardship, but as a check upon the accounting.[1]

.02 When an independent accountant's report is included in registration statements, proxy statements, or periodic reports filed under the federal securities statutes, the accountant's responsibility, generally, is in substance no different from that involved in other types of reporting. However, the nature and extent of this responsibility are specified in some detail in these statutes and in the related rules and regulations. For example, section 11(*a*) of the Securities Act of 1933, as amended, imposes responsibility for false or misleading statements in an effective registration statement, or for omissions that render statements made in such a document misleading, on

> every accountant, engineer, or appraiser, or any person whose profession gives authority to a statement made by him, who has with his consent been named as having prepared or certified any part of the registration statement, or as having prepared or certified any report or valuation which is used in connection with the registration statement, report, or valuation, which purports to have been prepared or certified by him.

.03 Section 11 also makes specific mention of the independent accountant's responsibility as an expert when his report is included in a registration statement filed under that act.[2] Section 11(*b*) states, in part, that no person shall be liable as provided therein if that person sustains the burden of proof that

> as regards any part of the registration statement purporting to be made upon his authority as an expert or purporting to be a copy of or extract from a report or valuation of himself as an expert, (i) he had, after reasonable investigation,

---

* ***Note:*** This section supersedes Statement on Auditing Standards No. 1, section 710, *Filings Under Federal Securities Statutes*. The changes provide guidance for the accountant whose report based on a review of interim financial information is presented, or incorporated by reference, in a filing under the Securities Act of 1933.

[1] 4 S. E. C. 721 (1939).

[2] Under rules of the Securities and Exchange Commission, a report based on a review of interim financial information is not a report by the accountant under section 11 (see paragraph .06).

> reasonable ground to believe and did believe, at the time such part of the registration statement became effective, that the statements therein were true and that there was no omission to state a material fact required to be stated therein or necessary to make the statements therein not misleading, or (ii) such part of the registration statement did not fairly represent his statement as an expert or was not a fair copy of or extract from his report or valuation as an expert....

Section 11 further provides that, in determining what constitutes reasonable investigation and reasonable ground to believe, "the standard of reasonableness shall be that required of a prudent man in the management of his own property."

.04 This discussion of the independent accountant's responsibilities in connection with filings under the federal securities statutes is not intended to offer legal interpretations and is based on an understanding of the meaning of the statutes as they relate to accounting principles and auditing standards and procedures. The discussion is subject to any judicial interpretations that may be issued.

.05 Because a registration statement under the Securities Act of 1933 speaks as of its effective date, the independent accountant whose report is included in such a registration statement has a statutory responsibility that is determined in the light of the circumstances on that date. This aspect of responsibility is peculiar to reports used for this purpose (see paragraphs .10 through .12).

.06 Under rules of the Securities and Exchange Commission, an independent accountant's report based on a review of interim financial information is not a report by the accountant within the meaning of section 11. Thus, the accountant does not have a similar statutory responsibility for such reports as of the effective date of the registration statement (see paragraph .13).

.07 The other federal securities statutes, while not containing so detailed an exposition, do impose responsibility, under certain conditions, on persons making false or misleading statements with respect to any material fact in applications, reports, or other documents filed under the statute.

.08 In filings under the Securities Act of 1933, a statement frequently is made in the prospectus (sometimes included in a section of the prospectus called the *experts section*) that certain information is included in the registration statement in reliance upon the report of certain named experts. The independent accountant should read the relevant section of the prospectus to make sure that his name is not being used in a way that indicates that his responsibility is greater than he intends. The experts section should be so worded that there is no implication that the financial statements have been prepared by the independent accountant or that they are not the direct representations of management.

.09 The Securities and Exchange Commission requires that, when an independent accountant's report based on a review of interim financial information is presented or incorporated by reference in a registration statement, a prospectus that includes a statement about the independent accountant's involvement should clarify that his review report is not a "report" or "part" of the registration statement within the meaning of sections 7 and 11 of the Securities Act of 1933. In this respect, wording such as the following in a prospectus would ordinarily be considered a satisfactory description for the accountant's purposes of the status of his review report that was included in a Form 10-Q filing that was later incorporated by reference in a registration statement.[3]

---

[3] A similar description of the status of the accountant's report would also ordinarily be satisfactory for the accountant's purposes when the accountant's review report is presented in the registration statement rather than incorporated by reference. In that case, the description in the prospectus would specifically refer to that report in the registration statement.

Independent Public Accountants

The consolidated balance sheets as of December 31, 19X2 and 19X1, and the consolidated statements of income, retained earnings, and cash flows for each of the three years in the period ended December 31, 19X2, incorporated by reference in this prospectus, have been included herein in reliance on the report of _______ independent public accountants, given on the authority of that firm as experts in auditing and accounting.

With respect to the unaudited interim financial information for the periods ended March 31, 19X3 and 19X2, incorporated by reference in this prospectus, the independent public accountants have reported that they have applied limited procedures in accordance with professional standards for a review of such information. However, their separate report included in the company's quarterly report on Form 10-Q for the quarter ended March 31, 19X3, and incorporated by reference herein, states that they did not audit and they do not express an opinion on that interim financial information. Accordingly, the degree of reliance on their report on such information should be restricted in light of the limited nature of the review procedures applied. The accountants are not subject to the liability provisions of section 11 of the Securities Act of 1933 for their report on the unaudited interim financial information because that report is not a "report" or a "part" of the registration statement prepared or certified by the accountants within the meaning of sections 7 and 11 of the act.

The independent accountant should also read other sections of the prospectus to make sure that his name is not being used in a way that indicates that his responsibility is greater than he intends.

Subsequent Events Procedures in 1933 Act Filings

.10 To sustain the burden of proof that he has made a "reasonable investigation" (see paragraph .03), as required under the Securities Act of 1933, an auditor should extend his procedures with respect to subsequent events from the date of his audit report up to the effective date or as close thereto as is reasonable and practicable in the circumstances. In this connection, he should arrange with his client to be kept advised of the progress of the registration proceedings so that his review of subsequent events can be completed by the effective date. The likelihood that the auditor will discover subsequent events necessarily decreases following the completion of field work, and, as a practical matter, after that time the independent auditor may rely, for the most part, on inquiries of responsible officials and employees. In addition to performing the procedures outlined in section 560.12, at or near the effective date, the auditor generally should

a. Read the entire prospectus and other pertinent portions of the registration statement.

b. Inquire of and obtain written representations from officers and other executives responsible for financial and accounting matters (limited where appropriate to major locations) about whether any events have occurred, other than those reflected or disclosed in the registration statement, that, in the officers' or other executives' opinion, have a material effect on the audited financial statements included therein or that should be disclosed in order to keep those statements from being misleading.

.11 A registration statement filed with the Securities and Exchange Commission may contain the reports of two or more independent auditors on their audits of the financial statements for different periods. An auditor who has audited the financial statements for prior periods but has not audited the financial statements for the most recent audited period included in the registration statement has a responsibility relating to events subsequent to the date of the prior-period financial statements, and extending to the effective date, that bear materially on the prior-period financial statements on which he reported. Generally, he should

a. Read pertinent portions of the prospectus and of the registration statement.

b. Obtain a letter of representation from the successor independent auditor regarding whether his audit (including his procedures with respect to subsequent events) revealed any matters that, in his opinion, might have a material effect on the financial statements reported on by the predecessor auditor or would require disclosure in the notes thereto.

The auditor should make inquiries and perform other procedures that he considers necessary to satisfy himself regarding the appropriateness of any adjustment or disclosure affecting the prior-period financial statements covered by his report (see section 508).

Response to Subsequent Events and Subsequently Discovered Facts

.12 If, subsequent to the date of his report on audited financial statements, the auditor (including a predecessor auditor) (*a*) discovers, in performing the procedures described in paragraphs .10 and .11 above, subsequent events that require adjustment or disclosure in the financial statements or (*b*) becomes aware that facts may have existed at the date of his report that might have affected his report had he then been aware of those facts, he should follow the guidance in sections 560 and 561. If the financial statements are appropriately adjusted or the required additional disclosure is made, the auditor should follow the guidance in section 530.05, .07, and .08 with respect to dating his report. If the client refuses to make appropriate adjustment or disclosure in the financial statements for a subsequent event or subsequently discovered facts, the auditor should follow the procedures in section 561.08 and .09. In such circumstances, the auditor should also consider, probably with the advice of his legal counsel, withholding his consent to the use of his report on the audited financial statements in the registration statement.

.13 If an accountant concludes on the basis of facts known to him that unaudited financial statements or unaudited interim financial information presented or incorporated by reference in a registration statement are not in conformity with generally accepted accounting principles, he should insist on appropriate revision. Failing that,

a. If the accountant has reported on a review of such interim financial information and the subsequently discovered facts are such that they would have affected his report had they been known to him at the date of his report, he should refer to section 561, because certain provisions of that section may be relevant to his consideration of those matters (see section 722.46).

b. If the accountant has not reported on a review of the unaudited financial statements or interim financial information, he should modify his report on the audited financial statements to describe the departure from generally accepted accounting principles contained in the unaudited financial statements or interim financial information.

In either case, the accountant should also consider, probably with the advice of his legal counsel, withholding his consent to the use of his report on the audited financial statements in the registration statement. [Revised, November 2002, to reflect conforming changes necessary due to the issuance of Statement on Auditing Standards No. 100.]

b. If the accountant has not reported on a review of the unaudited interim financial statements or interim financial information, he should modify his report on the audited financial statements to describe the departure from generally accepted accounting principles contained in the unaudited financial statements or interim financial information.

In either case, the accountant should also consider, probably with the advice of his legal counsel, withholding his consent to the use of his report on the audited financial statements in the registration statement. [Revised, November 1980, to reflect conforming changes necessary due to the issuance of Statement on Auditing Standards No. 10.]

AU Section 9711

Filings Under Federal Securities Statutes: Auditing Interpretations of Section 711

1. Subsequent Events Procedures for Shelf Registration Statements Updated after the Original Effective Date

.01 *Question*—Rule 415 of Regulation C under the Securities Act of 1933 (1933 Act) permits companies to register a designated amount of securities for continuous or delayed offerings by filing one "shelf" registration statement with the SEC. Under this rule, a registrant can register an amount of securities it reasonably expects to offer and sell within the next two years, generally without the later need to prepare and file a new prospectus and registration statement for each sale.

.02 A Rule 415 shelf registration statement can be updated after its original effective date by—

a. The filing of a post-effective amendment,

b. The incorporation by reference of subsequently filed material, or

c. The addition of a supplemental prospectus (sometimes referred to as a "sticker").

.03 Section 711, *Filings Under Federal Securities Statutes*, paragraph .05, states, "Because a registration statement under the Securities Act of 1933 speaks as of its effective date, the independent accountant whose report is included in such a registration statement has a statutory responsibility that is determined in the light of the circumstances on that date." The independent accountant's statutory responsibility regarding information covered by his report and included in a registration statement is specified in Section 11 of the 1933 Act. Section 11(b)(3)(B) states that the accountant will not be held liable if he can sustain a burden of proof that "he had, after reasonable investigation, reasonable ground to believe and did believe, at the time such part of the registration statement became effective, that the statements therein were true and that there was no omission to state a material fact required to be stated therein or necessary to make the statements therein not misleading." To sustain the burden of proof that he has made a "reasonable investigation" as of the effective date, the accountant performs subsequent events procedures (as described in section 711.10 and .11) to a date as close to the effective date of the registration statement as is reasonable and practicable in the circumstances.

.04 In connection with Rule 415 shelf registrations, under what circumstances does the independent accountant have a responsibility to perform subsequent events procedures after the original effective date of the registration statement?

.05 *Interpretation*—As discussed in more detail below, in general, the accountant should perform the subsequent events procedures described in section 711.10 and .11, when either:

a. A post-effective amendment to the shelf registration statement, as defined by SEC rules, is filed pursuant to Item 512(a) of Regulation S-K,[1] or

b. A 1934 Act filing that includes or amends audited financial statements is incorporated by reference into the shelf registration statement.

.06 When a post-effective amendment is filed pursuant to the registrant's undertaking required by Item 512 of Regulation S-K, a shelf registration statement is considered to have a new effective date because Item 512(a)(2) of Regulation S-K states, ". . . for the purpose of determining any liability under the Securities Act of 1933, each such post-effective amendment shall be deemed to be a new registration statement. . . ." Accordingly, in such cases, the accountant should perform subsequent events procedures to a date as close to the new effective date of the registration statement as is reasonable and practicable in the circumstances.

.07 Item 512(b) of Regulation S-K states that for purposes of determining any liability under the Securities Act of 1933 each filing of a registrant's annual report (Form 10-K) and each filing of an employee benefit plan annual report (Form 11-K) that is incorporated by reference into a shelf registration statement is deemed to be a new registration statement relating to the securities offering. Accordingly, when a Form 10-K or Form 11-K is incorporated by reference into a shelf registration statement, the accountant should perform subsequent events procedures to a date as close to the date of the filing of the Form 10-K or Form 11-K as is reasonable and practicable in the circumstances and date his consent as of that date.

.08 In many circumstances, a Form 10-Q, Form 8-K, or other 1934 Act filing can be incorporated by reference into a shelf registration statement (sometimes this occurs automatically—for example, in a Form S-3 or Form S-8) without the need for a post-effective amendment. In those circumstances, the accountant has no responsibility to perform subsequent events procedures unless the filing includes or amends audited financial statements—for example, a Form 8-K that includes audited financial statements of an acquired company. In these latter circumstances, when the filing is incorporated into a registration statement, SEC rules require a currently dated consent of the accountant who audited those statements, and that accountant should perform subsequent events procedures to a date as close to the date of the incorporation by reference of the related material as is reasonable and practicable in the circumstances.[2]

.09 In addition, an accountant's report on a review of interim financial information contained in a Form 10-Q may also include his report on the information presented in the condensed year-end balance sheet that has also been included in the form and has been derived from the latest audited annual balance sheet. (See section 552, *Reporting on Condensed Financial Statements and Selected Financial Data*, paragraph .08.) When the Form 10-Q is incorporated

---

[1] Item 512(a) of Regulation S-K provides that the registrant is required to undertake to file a post-effective amendment to a shelf registration statement to (*a*) file updated financial statements pursuant to section 10(*a*)(3) of the Securities Act of 1933, (*b*) reflect a "fundamental change" in the information in the registration statement arising from facts or events occurring after the effective date of the registration statement or previous post-effective amendments, or (*c*) include new material information regarding the plan of distribution.

[2] Typically in such cases, the affected audited financial statements are not those of the registrant, and accordingly, there would be no requirement for the registrant's auditor to update his subsequent events procedures with respect to the registrant's financial statements.

by reference into the shelf registration (which may occur automatically), the report on the year-end condensed balance sheet may be considered a report of an "expert." Because it is not clear what the accountant's responsibility is in those circumstances, the accountant should perform subsequent events procedures (as described in section 711.10 and .11) to a date as close to the date of the incorporation by reference of the Form 10-Q as is reasonable and practicable in the circumstances.

.10 One of the subsequent events procedures described in section 711 is to "read the entire prospectus and other pertinent portions of the registration statement." The reading of the entire prospectus (including any supplemental prospectuses and documents incorporated by reference—such as Form 10-Ks, 10-Qs, and 8-Ks) and the other procedures described in section 711.10 and .11, help assure that the accountant has fulfilled his statutory responsibilities under the 1933 Act to perform a "reasonable investigation."

.11 When a shelf registration statement is updated by a supplemental prospectus (or "sticker"), the effective date of the registration statement is considered to be unchanged since the supplemental prospectus does not constitute an amendment to the registration statement, and, consequently, no posteffective amendment has been filed. Accordingly, an accountant has no responsibility to update his performance of subsequent events procedures through the date of the supplemental prospectus or sticker. The accountant, however, may nevertheless become aware that facts may have existed at the date of his report that might have affected his report had he then been aware of those facts. Section 711.12 and .13, provide guidance on the accountant's response to subsequent events and subsequently discovered facts.

[Issue Date: May, 1983.]

2. Consenting to be Named as an Expert in an Offering Document in Connection With Securities Offerings Other Than Those Registered Under the Securities Act of 1933

.12 *Question*—Should the auditor consent to be named, or referred to, as an expert in an offering document in connection with securities offerings other than those registered under the Securities Act of 1933 (the Act)?

.13 *Interpretation*—No. The term "expert" has a specific statutory meaning under the Act.[3] The act states that anyone who purchases a security registered under the Act may sue specified persons if the registration statement contains an untrue statement or omits to state a material fact. Those persons who may be sued include "every accountant, engineer, or appraiser, or any person whose profession gives authority to a statement made by him, who has with his consent been named as having prepared or certified any part of the registration statement." These persons are typically referred to as "experts." Auditors sign a statement, known as a consent, in which they agree to be identified as experts in a section of the registration statement.

.14 Outside the 1933 Act arena, however, the term "expert" is typically undefined and the auditor's responsibility, as a result of the use of that term, is also undefined.

---

[3] If the term "expert" is defined under applicable state law, for instance, the accountant may agree to be named as an expert in an offering document in an intra-state securities offering. The accountant may also agree to be named as an expert, as that term is used by the Office of Thrift Supervision (OTS), in securities offering documents which are subject to the jurisdiction of the OTS.

.15 When a client wishes to make reference to the auditor's role in an offering document in connection with a securities offering that is not registered under the Act, the caption "Independent Auditors" should be used to title that section of the document; the caption "Experts" should not be used, nor should the auditors be referred to as experts anywhere in the document. The following paragraph should be used to describe the auditors role.

Independent Auditors

> The financial statements as of December 31, 19XX and for the year then ended, included in this offering circular, have been audited by ABC, independent auditors, as stated in their report(s) appearing herein.

If the client refuses to delete from the offering document the reference to the auditors as experts, the auditor should not permit inclusion of the auditor's report in the offering document.

[Issue Date: June, 1992; Amended: March, 1995.]

3. Consenting to the Use of an Audit Report in an Offering Document in Securities Offerings Other Than One Registered Under the Securities Act of 1933

.16 *Question*—May the auditor consent to the use of his or her audit report in an offering document other than one registered under the Securities Act of 1933?

.17 *Interpretation*—When an auditor's report is included in an offering document other than one registered under the Securities Act of 1933, it is not usually necessary for the accountant to provide a consent. If the accountant is requested to provide a consent, he or she may do so. The following is example language the accountant might use:

> We agree to the inclusion in this offering circular of our report, dated February 5, 19XX, on our audit of the financial statements of [name of entity].

[Issue Date: June, 1992.]

AU Section 722

Interim Financial Information

(Supersedes SAS No. 71.)

Source: SAS No. 100; SAS No. 116; SAS No. 121.

Effective for interim periods beginning after December 15, 2002, unless otherwise indicated.

Introduction

.01 The purpose of this section is to establish standards and provide guidance on the nature, timing, and extent of the procedures to be performed by an independent accountant when conducting a review of *interim financial information* (as that term is defined in paragraph .02 of this section) when the conditions in paragraph .05 are met. The three general standards discussed in section 150, *Generally Accepted Auditing Standards*, paragraph .02, are applicable to a review of interim financial information conducted in accordance with this section. This section provides guidance on the application of the field work and reporting standards to a review of interim financial information, to the extent those standards are relevant. [Revised, January 2009, to reflect conforming changes necessary due to the issuance of SAS No. 116. As amended, effective for reviews of interim financial information for interim periods beginning after December 15, 2009, by SAS No. 116.]

.02 For purposes of this section, the term *interim financial information* means financial information or statements covering a period less than a full year or for a 12-month period ending on a date other than the entity's fiscal year end. Interim financial information may be condensed or in the form of a complete set of financial statements. Additionally, the term *applicable financial reporting framework* means a set of criteria used to determine measurement, recognition, presentation, and disclosure of all material items appearing in the financial statements; for example, accounting principles generally accepted in the United States of America (also known as U.S. GAAP), International Financial Reporting Standards (IFRS) issued by the International Accounting Standards Board (IASB), or comprehensive bases of accounting other than GAAP. [Revised, January 2009, to reflect conforming changes necessary due to the issuance of SAS No. 116. As amended, effective for reviews of interim financial information for interim periods beginning after December 15, 2009, by SAS No. 116.]

.03 An entity may be required or otherwise desire to engage an independent accountant to perform a review of the entity's interim financial information.[1] Although this section generally does not require an accountant to issue a written report on a review of interim financial information, an accountant's review report should accompany the interim financial information if, in a report; document; or written communication containing the reviewed interim financial information, the entity states that the interim financial information has been reviewed by an independent public accountant or makes other reference to the accountant's association. In other situations, the accountant may determine it

---

[1] [Footnote deleted, January 2009, to reflect conforming changes necessary due to the issuance of SAS No. 116.]

appropriate to issue a written report to address the risk that a user of interim financial information may associate the accountant with the interim financial information and, in the absence of a review report, inappropriately assume a higher level of assurance than that obtained. Paragraphs .37–.46 of this section provide reporting guidance for a review of interim financial information. [Revised, January 2009, to reflect conforming changes necessary due to the issuance of SAS No. 116. As amended, effective for reviews of interim financial information for interim periods beginning after December 15, 2009, by SAS No. 116.]

.04 Section 315, *Communications Between Predecessor and Successor Auditors*, requires a successor auditor to contact the entity's predecessor auditor and make inquiries of the predecessor auditor in deciding whether to accept appointment as an entity's independent auditor. Such inquiries should be completed before accepting an engagement to perform an initial review of an entity's interim financial information.

Applicability

.05 An accountant may conduct, in accordance with this section, a review of interim financial information[3];[4] if

a. the entity's latest annual financial statements have been audited by the accountant or a predecessor;

b. the accountant has been engaged to audit the entity's current year financial statements, or the accountant audited the entity's latest annual financial statements and expects to be engaged to audit the current year financial statements;*

---

[3] [Footnote deleted, January 2009, to reflect conforming changes necessary due to the issuance of SAS No. 116.]

[4] [Footnote deleted, January 2009, to reflect conforming changes necessary due to the issuance of SAS No. 116.]

* In February 2011, the Auditing Standards Board issued Statement on Auditing Standards (SAS) No. 121, *Revised Applicability of Statement on Auditing Standards No. 100,* Interim Financial Information. SAS No. 121 is effective for interim reviews of interim financial information for periods beginning after December 15, 2011, with early application permitted. SAS No. 121 revises the conditions in paragraph .05 of this section as follows (new language is shown in boldface italics; deleted language is shown by strikethrough):

An accountant may conduct, in accordance with this section, a review of interim financial information[3] [4] if

a. the entity's latest annual financial statements have been audited by the accountant or a predecessor;

b. the accountant ***either***

i. has been engaged to audit the entity's current year financial statements, or

ii. ~~the accountant~~ audited the entity's latest annual financial statements and***, when it is expected that the current year financial statements will be audited,*** ~~expects to be engaged~~ ***the appointment of another accountant*** to audit the current year financial statements ***is not effective prior to the beginning of the period covered by the review***;

c. the ~~client~~ ***entity*** prepares its interim financial information in accordance with the same financial reporting framework as that used to prepare the annual financial statements; and

d. ~~if~~ ***when*** the interim financial information is condensed information, all of the following conditions are met:

i. The condensed interim financial information purports to conform with an appropriate financial reporting framework, which includes appropriate form and content of interim financial statements; for example, Financial Accounting Standards Board (FASB) *Accounting Standards Codification* (ASC) 270, *Interim Reporting*, and Article 10 of SEC Regulation S-X with respect to accounting principles generally accepted in the United

(continued)

c. the client prepares its interim financial information in accordance with the same financial reporting framework as that used to prepare the annual financial statements; and

d. if the interim financial information is condensed information, all of the following conditions are met:

i. The condensed interim financial information purports to conform with an appropriate financial reporting framework, which includes appropriate form and content of interim financial statements; for example, Financial Accounting Standards Board (FASB) *Accounting Standards Codification* (ASC) 270, *Interim Reporting*, and Article 10 of SEC Regulation S-X with respect to accounting principles generally accepted in the United States of America[5] or International Accounting Standard 34, *Interim Financial Reporting*, with respect to IFRS issued by the IASB may be appropriate financial reporting frameworks for interim financial information.

ii. The condensed interim financial information includes a note that the financial information does not represent complete financial statements and should be read in conjunction with the entity's latest annual audited financial statements.

iii. The condensed interim financial information accompanies the entity's latest audited annual financial statements or such audited annual financial statements are made readily available by the entity. The financial statements are deemed to be readily available if a third party user can obtain the financial statements without any further action by the entity (for example, financial statements on an entity's website may be considered readily available, but being available upon request is not considered readily available).

(footnote continued)

States of America[5] or International Accounting Standard 34, *Interim Financial Reporting*, with respect to IFRS issued by the IASB may be appropriate financial reporting frameworks for interim financial information.

ii. The condensed interim financial information includes a note that the financial information does not represent complete financial statements and should be read in conjunction with the entity's latest annual audited financial statements.

iii. The condensed interim financial information accompanies the entity's latest audited annual financial statements or such audited annual financial statements are made readily available by the entity. The financial statements are deemed to be readily available if a third party user can obtain the financial statements without any further action by the entity (for example, financial statements on an entity's website may be considered readily available, but being available upon request is not considered readily available).

[5] Financial Accounting Standards Board (FASB) *Accounting Standards Codification* (ASC) 270, *Interim Reporting*, outlines the application of U.S. generally accepted accounting principles (GAAP) to the determination of income when interim financial information is presented, provides for the use of estimated effective income tax rates, and specifies certain disclosure requirements for summarized interim financial information issued by public companies. In addition to FASB ASC 270, other FASB ASC guidance also includes disclosure requirements for interim financial information. [Footnote revised, January 2009, to reflect conforming changes necessary due to the issuance of SAS No. 116. Footnote revised, June 2009, to reflect conforming changes necessary due to the issuance of FASB ASC. As amended, effective for reviews of interim financial information for interim periods beginning after December 15, 2009, by SAS No. 116.]

[Revised, January 2009, to reflect conforming changes necessary due to the issuance of SAS No. 116. Revised, June 2009, to reflect conforming changes necessary due to the issuance of FASB ASC. As amended, effective for reviews of interim financial information for interim periods beginning after December 15, 2009, by SAS No. 116.]

[.06] [Deleted, January 2009, to reflect conforming changes necessary due to the issuance of SAS No. 116.]

Objective of a Review of Interim Financial Information

.07 The objective of a review of interim financial information pursuant to this section is to provide the accountant with a basis for communicating whether he or she is aware of any material modifications that should be made to the interim financial information for it to conform with the applicable financial reporting framework. The objective of a review of interim financial information differs significantly from that of an audit conducted in accordance with generally accepted auditing standards. A review of interim financial information does not provide a basis for expressing an opinion about whether the interim financial information is presented fairly, in all material respects, in conformity with the applicable financial reporting framework. A review consists principally of performing analytical procedures and making inquiries of persons responsible for financial and accounting matters, and does not contemplate (*a*) tests of accounting records through inspection, observation, or confirmation; (*b*) tests of controls to evaluate their effectiveness; (*c*) the obtainment of corroborating evidence in response to inquiries; or (*d*) the performance of certain other procedures ordinarily performed in an audit. A review may bring to the accountant's attention significant matters affecting the interim financial information, but it does not provide assurance that the accountant will become aware of all significant matters that would be identified in an audit. Paragraph .22 of this section provides guidance to the accountant if he or she becomes aware of information that leads him or her to believe that the interim financial information may not be in conformity with the applicable financial reporting framework. [Revised, January 2009, to reflect conforming changes necessary due to the issuance of SAS No. 116. As amended, effective for reviews of interim financial information for interim periods beginning after December 15, 2009, by SAS No. 116.]

Establishing an Understanding With the Client

.08 The accountant should establish an understanding with the client regarding the services to be performed in an engagement to review interim financial information [6] and should document the understanding through a written communication with the client. Such an understanding reduces the risk that either the accountant or the client may misinterpret the needs or expectations of the other party. The understanding should include the objectives of the engagement, the limitations of the engagement, management's responsibilities, and the accountant's responsibilities. The understanding should also include the expected form of the communication upon completion of the engagement (that is, whether as a written or oral report). Additionally, prior to accepting the engagement, the accountant should, through inquiry and, if applicable, information obtained during the course of the previous or current annual audit or during other engagements, assess management's ability to acknowledge their responsibility to establish and maintain controls that are sufficient to provide a

---

[6] See paragraph .28 of QC section 10B, *A Firm's System of Quality Control*. [Footnote amended due to the issuance of SQCS No. 7, December 2008.]

reasonable basis for the preparation of reliable interim financial information in accordance with the applicable financial reporting framework. If management does not have the ability to make such an acknowledgement of its responsibility, the independent accountant should not accept the engagement. [Revised, January 2009, to reflect conforming changes necessary due to the issuance of SAS No. 116. As amended, effective for reviews of interim financial information for interim periods beginning after December 15, 2009, by SAS No. 116.]

.09 An understanding with the client regarding a review of interim financial information generally includes the following matters.

Objectives of the engagement

- The objective of a review of interim financial information is to provide the accountant with a basis for communicating whether he or she is aware of any material modifications that should be made to the interim financial information for it to conform with the applicable financial reporting framework.[7]
- A review includes obtaining sufficient knowledge of the entity's business and its internal control as it relates to the preparation of both annual and interim financial information to
  — identify the types of potential material misstatements in the interim financial information and consider the likelihood of their occurrence.
  — select the inquiries and analytical procedures that will provide the accountant with a basis for communicating whether the accountant is aware of any material modifications that should be made to the interim financial information for it to conform with the applicable financial reporting framework.

Limitations of the engagement

- A review does not provide a basis for expressing an opinion about whether the financial information is presented fairly, in all material respects, in conformity with the applicable financial reporting framework.
- A review does not provide assurance that the accountant will become aware of all significant matters that would be identified in an audit.
- A review is not designed to provide assurance on internal control or to identify significant deficiencies and material weaknesses in internal control; however, the accountant is responsible for communicating to management and those charged with governance any significant deficiencies or material weaknesses in internal control that the accountant identified.

Management's responsibilities

- Management is responsible for
  — the entity's interim financial information.
  — establishing and maintaining effective internal control over financial reporting.

---

[7] Paragraph .05 of this section addresses the selection of the applicable financial reporting framework for interim financial information. [Footnote added, January 2009, to reflect conforming changes necessary due to the issuance of SAS No. 116. As amended, effective for reviews of interim financial information for interim periods beginning after December 15, 2009, by SAS No. 116.]

— identifying and ensuring that the entity complies with the laws and regulations applicable to its activities.
— making all financial records and related information available to the accountant.
— providing the accountant, at the conclusion of the engagement, with a letter confirming certain representations made during the review.
— adjusting the interim financial information to correct material misstatements. Although a review of interim financial information is not designed to obtain reasonable assurance that the interim financial information is free from material misstatement, management also is responsible for affirming in its representation letter to the accountant that the effects of any uncorrected misstatements aggregated by the accountant during the current engagement and pertaining to the current-year period(s) under review are immaterial, both individually and in the aggregate, to the interim financial information taken as a whole.

The accountant's responsibilities

- The accountant is responsible for conducting the review in accordance with standards established by the AICPA. A review of interim financial information consists principally of performing analytical procedures and making inquiries of persons responsible for financial and accounting matters. It is substantially less in scope than an audit conducted in accordance with auditing standards generally accepted in the United States of America, the objective of which is the expression of an opinion regarding the financial information taken as a whole. Accordingly, the accountant will not express an opinion on the interim financial information.

Expected form of the communication

- A description of the expected form of the accountant's communication upon completion of the engagement, (that is, whether as a written or oral report) and a statement that if the entity states in any report, document, or written communication containing the interim financial information that the information has been reviewed by the accountant or makes other reference to the accountant's association, that the accountant's review report will be included in the document.

[Revised, May 2006, to reflect conforming changes necessary due to the issuance of SAS No. 112. Revised, January 2009, to reflect conforming changes necessary due to the issuance of SAS No. 116. As amended, effective for reviews of interim financial information for interim periods beginning after December 15, 2009, by SAS No. 116.]

The Accountant's Knowledge of the Entity's Business and Its Internal Control

.10 To perform a review of interim financial information, the accountant should have sufficient knowledge of the entity's business and its internal control[8] as they relate to the preparation of both annual and interim financial information to

[8] Paragraph .08 establishes a presumptively mandatory requirement that the accountant assess, through inquiry and, if applicable, information obtained during the course of the previous or current

(continued)

- identify the types of potential material misstatements in the interim financial information and consider the likelihood of their occurrence.
- select the inquiries and analytical procedures that will provide the accountant with a basis for communicating whether he or she is aware of any material modifications that should be made to the interim financial information for it to conform with the applicable financial reporting framework.

[Revised, January 2009, to reflect conforming changes necessary due to the issuance of SAS No. 116. As amended, effective for reviews of interim financial information for interim periods beginning after December 15, 2009, by SAS No. 116.]

.11 In planning a review of interim financial information, the accountant should perform procedures to update his or her knowledge of the entity's business and its internal control to (*a*) aid in the determination of the inquiries to be made and the analytical procedures to be performed and (*b*) identify particular events, transactions, or assertions to which the inquiries may be directed or analytical procedures applied. Such procedures should include

- reading documentation of the preceding year's audit and of reviews of prior interim period(s) of the current year and corresponding interim period(s) of the prior year to the extent necessary, based on the accountant's judgment, to enable the accountant to identify matters that may affect the current-period interim financial information. In reading such documents, the accountant should specifically consider the nature of any (*a*) corrected material misstatements; (*b*) matters identified in any summary of uncorrected misstatements;[9] (*c*) identified risks of material misstatement due to fraud, including the risk of management override of controls; and (*d*) significant financial accounting and reporting matters that may be of continuing significance, such as significant deficiencies and material weaknesses.
- reading the most recent annual and comparable prior interim period financial information.
- considering the results of any audit procedures performed with respect to the current year's financial statements.
- inquiring of management about changes in the entity's business activities.
- inquiring of management about whether significant changes in internal control, as it relates to the preparation of interim financial information, have occurred subsequent to the preceding annual audit or

---

(footnote continued)

annual audit or during other engagements, management's ability to acknowledge their responsibility to establish and maintain controls that are sufficient to provide a reasonable basis for the preparation of reliable interim financial information in accordance with the applicable financial reporting framework as a precondition to performing a review under this section. [Footnote added, January 2009, to reflect conforming changes necessary due to the issuance of SAS No. 116. As amended, effective for reviews of interim financial information for interim periods beginning after December 15, 2009, by SAS No. 116.]

[9] Section 312, *Audit Risk and Materiality in Conducting an Audit*, paragraphs .69 and .70, requires the auditor to document the nature and effect of misstatements that the auditor aggregates as well as the auditor's conclusion as to whether such misstatements, individually or in the aggregate, cause the audited financial statements to be materially misstated. Paragraphs .25 and .26 of this section describe the accountant's consideration of such misstatements in a review of interim financial information. [Footnote revised, March 2006, to reflect conforming changes necessary due to the issuance of SAS No. 107. Footnote renumbered, January 2009, to reflect conforming changes necessary due to the issuance of SAS No. 116. As amended, effective for reviews of interim financial information for interim periods beginning after December 15, 2009, by SAS No. 116.]

prior review of interim financial information, including changes in the entity's policies, procedures, and personnel, as well as the nature and extent of such changes.

[Revised, January 2009, to reflect conforming changes necessary due to the issuance of SAS No. 116. As amended, effective for reviews of interim financial information for interim periods beginning after December 15, 2009, by SAS No. 116.]

.12 In an initial review of interim financial information, the accountant should perform procedures that will enable him or her to obtain sufficient knowledge of the entity's business and its internal control to address the objective discussed in paragraph .07 of this section. As part of the procedures to obtain this knowledge, the accountant performing an initial review of interim financial information makes inquiries of the predecessor accountant and reviews the predecessor accountant's documentation for the preceding annual audit and for any prior interim periods in the current year that have been reviewed by the predecessor accountant if the predecessor accountant permits access to such documentation.[10] In doing so, the accountant should specifically consider the nature of any (*a*) corrected material misstatements; (*b*) matters identified in any summary of uncorrected misstatements; (*c*) identified risks of material misstatement due to fraud, including the risk of management override of controls; and (*d*) significant financial accounting and reporting matters that may be of continuing significance, such as significant deficiencies or material weaknesses. However, the inquiries made and analytical procedures performed or other procedures performed in the initial review and the conclusions reached are solely the responsibility of the successor accountant. If the successor accountant is reporting on the review, the successor accountant should not make reference to the report or work of the predecessor accountant as the basis, in part, for the successor accountant's own report. If the predecessor accountant does not respond to the successor accountant's inquiries, or does not allow the successor accountant to review the predecessor accountant's documentation, the successor accountant should use alternative procedures to obtain knowledge of the matters discussed in this paragraph. [Revised, January 2009, to reflect conforming changes necessary due to the issuance of SAS No. 116. As amended, effective for reviews of interim financial information for interim periods beginning after December 15, 2009, by SAS No. 116.]

.13 The accountant who has audited the entity's financial statements for one or more annual periods would have acquired sufficient knowledge of an entity's internal control as it relates to the preparation of annual financial information and may have acquired such knowledge with respect to interim financial information. If the accountant has not audited the most recent annual financial statements, the accountant should perform procedures to obtain such knowledge. Knowledge of an entity's internal control, as it relates to the preparation of both annual and interim financial information, includes knowledge of the relevant aspects of the control environment, the entity's risk assessment process, control activities, information and communication, and monitoring, as those terms are defined in section 314, *Understanding the Entity and Its Environment and Assessing the Risks of Material Misstatement*. Internal control over the preparation of interim financial information may differ from internal control over the preparation of annual financial statements because certain accounting principles and practices used for interim financial information may

---

[10] The accountant also may consider reviewing the predecessor accountant's documentation related to reviews of interim period(s) in the prior year. [Footnote renumbered, January 2009, to reflect conforming changes necessary due to the issuance of SAS No. 116. As amended, effective for reviews of interim financial information for interim periods beginning after December 15, 2009, by SAS No. 116.]

differ from those used for the preparation of annual financial statements, for example, the use of estimated effective income tax rates for the preparation of interim financial information, which is prescribed by FASB ASC 270. [Revised, March 2006, to reflect conforming changes necessary due to the issuance of SAS No. 109. Revised, June 2009, to reflect conforming changes necessary due to the issuance of FASB ASC.]

.14 A restriction on the scope of the review may be imposed if the entity's internal control appears to contain deficiencies so significant that it would be impracticable for the accountant, based on his or her judgment, to effectively perform review procedures that would provide a basis for communicating whether he or she is aware of any material modifications that should be made to the interim financial information for it to conform with the applicable financial reporting framework.[11] [Revised, January 2009, to reflect conforming changes necessary due to the issuance of SAS No. 116. As amended, effective for reviews of interim financial information for interim periods beginning after December 15, 2009, by SAS No. 116.]

Analytical Procedures, Inquiries, and Other Review Procedures

.15 Procedures for conducting a review of interim financial information generally are limited to analytical procedures, inquiries, and other procedures that address significant accounting and disclosure matters relating to the interim financial information to be reported. The accountant performs these procedures to obtain a basis for communicating whether he or she is aware of any material modifications that should be made to the interim financial information for it to conform with the applicable financial reporting framework. The specific inquiries made and the analytical and other procedures performed should be tailored to the engagement based on the accountant's knowledge of the entity's business and its internal control. The accountant's knowledge of an entity's business and its internal control influences the inquiries made and analytical procedures performed. For example, if the accountant becomes aware of a significant change in the entity's control activities at a particular location, the accountant may consider (*a*) making additional inquiries, such as whether management monitored the changes and considered whether they were operating as intended, (*b*) employing analytical procedures with a more precise expectation, or (*c*) both. [Revised, January 2009, to reflect conforming changes necessary due to the issuance of SAS No. 116. As amended, effective for reviews of interim financial information for interim periods beginning after December 15, 2009, by SAS No. 116.]

.16 *Analytical procedures and related inquiries.* The accountant should apply analytical procedures to the interim financial information to identify and provide a basis for inquiry about the relationships and individual items that appear to be unusual and that may indicate a material misstatement. Analytical procedures, for the purposes of this section, should include

- comparing the interim financial information with comparable information for the immediately preceding interim period, if applicable, and with the corresponding period(s) in the previous year, giving consideration to knowledge about changes in the entity's business and specific transactions.

---

[11] See paragraph .28 of this section. [Footnote renumbered, January 2009, to reflect conforming changes necessary due to the issuance of SAS No. 116. As amended, effective for reviews of interim financial information for interim periods beginning after December 15, 2009, by SAS No. 116.]

- considering plausible relationships among both financial and, where relevant, nonfinancial information. The accountant also may wish to consider information developed and used by the entity, for example, information in a director's information package or in a senior committee's briefing materials.
- comparing recorded amounts, or ratios developed from recorded amounts, to expectations developed by the accountant. The accountant develops such expectations by identifying and using plausible relationships that are reasonably expected to exist based on the accountant's understanding of the entity and the industry in which the entity operates (see paragraph .17 of this section).
- comparing disaggregated revenue data, for example, comparing revenue reported by month and by product line or operating segment during the current interim period with that of comparable prior periods.

See appendix A [paragraph .54] of this section for examples of analytical procedures an accountant may consider performing when conducting a review of interim financial information. The accountant may find the guidance in section 329, *Analytical Procedures*, useful in conducting a review of interim financial information. [Revised, January 2009, to reflect conforming changes necessary due to the issuance of SAS No. 116. As amended, effective for reviews of interim financial information for interim periods beginning after December 15, 2009, by SAS No. 116.]

.17 Expectations developed by the accountant in performing analytical procedures in connection with a review of interim financial information ordinarily are less precise than those developed in an audit. Also, in a review the accountant ordinarily is not required to corroborate management's responses with other evidence. However, the accountant should consider the reasonableness and consistency of management's responses in light of the results of other review procedures and the accountant's knowledge of the entity's business and its internal control.[12]

.18 *Inquiries and other review procedures.* The following are inquiries the accountant should make and other review procedures the accountant should perform when conducting a review of interim financial information:

a. Reading the available minutes of meetings of stockholders, directors, and appropriate committees, and inquiring about matters dealt with at meetings for which minutes are not available, to identify matters that may affect the interim financial information.

b. Obtaining reports from other accountants, if any, who have been engaged to perform a review of the interim financial information of significant components of the reporting entity, its subsidiaries, or its other investees, or inquiring of those accountants if reports have not been issued.[13]

c. Inquiring of members of management who have responsibility for financial and accounting matters concerning

---

[12] See paragraph .22 of this section. [Footnote renumbered, January 2009, to reflect conforming changes necessary due to the issuance of SAS No. 116. As amended, effective for reviews of interim financial information for interim periods beginning after December 15, 2009, by SAS No. 116.]

[13] In these circumstances, the accountant ordinarily is in a position similar to that of an auditor who acts as principal auditor (see section 543, *Part of Audit Performed by Other Independent Auditors*) and makes use of the work or reports of other auditors in the course of an audit of financial statements. [Footnote renumbered, January 2009, to reflect conforming changes necessary due to the issuance of SAS No. 116. As amended, effective for reviews of interim financial information for interim periods beginning after December 15, 2009, by SAS No. 116.]

i. whether the interim financial information has been prepared in conformity with the applicable financial reporting framework consistently applied.

ii. unusual or complex situations that may have an effect on the interim financial information. (See appendix B [paragraph .55] of this section for examples of unusual or complex situations about which the accountant ordinarily would inquire of management.)

iii. significant transactions occurring or recognized in the last several days of the interim period.

iv. the status of uncorrected misstatements identified during the previous audit and interim review (that is, whether adjustments had been recorded subsequent to the prior audit or interim period and, if so, the amounts recorded and period in which such adjustments were recorded).

v. matters about which questions have arisen in the course of applying the review procedures.

vi. events subsequent to the date of the interim financial information that could have a material effect on the presentation of such information.

vii. their knowledge of any fraud or suspected fraud affecting the entity involving (1) management, (2) employees who have significant roles in internal control, or (3) others where the fraud could have a material effect on the financial information.

viii. whether they are aware of allegations of fraud or suspected fraud affecting the entity, for example, received in communications from employees, former employees, analysts, regulators, short sellers, or others.

ix. significant journal entries and other adjustments.

x. communications from regulatory agencies.

xi. significant deficiencies, including material weaknesses, in the design or operation of internal control as it relates to the preparation of both annual and interim financial information.

d. Obtaining evidence that the interim financial information agrees or reconciles with the accounting records. For example, the accountant may compare the interim financial information to (1) the accounting records, such as the general ledger; (2) a consolidating schedule derived from the accounting records; or (3) other supporting data in the entity's records. In addition, the accountant should consider inquiring of management as to the reliability of the records to which the interim financial information was compared or reconciled.

e. Reading the interim financial information to consider whether, based on the results of the review procedures performed and other information that has come to the accountant's attention, the information to be reported conforms with the applicable financial reporting framework.

f. Reading other information in documents containing the interim financial information[14] to consider whether such information or the manner

[14] The accountant may consider section 550, *Other Information in Documents Containing Audited Financial Statements*, which provides guidance for the auditor's consideration of other information included in such documents. [Footnote added, January 2009, to reflect conforming changes necessary due to the issuance of SAS No. 116. As amended, effective for reviews of interim financial information for interim periods beginning after December 15, 2009, by SAS No. 116.]

of its presentation is materially inconsistent with the interim financial information.[15] If the accountant concludes that there is a material inconsistency, or becomes aware of information that he or she believes is a material misstatement of fact, the action taken will depend on his or her judgment in the particular circumstances.

[Revised, January 2009, to reflect conforming changes necessary due to the issuance of SAS No. 116. As amended, effective for reviews of interim financial information for interim periods beginning after December 15, 2009, by SAS No. 116.]

.19 Many of the aforementioned review procedures can be performed before or simultaneously with the entity's preparation of the interim financial information. For example, it may be practicable to update the understanding of the entity's internal control and begin reading applicable minutes before the end of an interim period. Performing some of the review procedures earlier in the interim period also permits early identification and consideration of significant accounting matters affecting the interim financial information.

.20 *Inquiry concerning litigation, claims, and assessments*. A review of interim financial information does not contemplate obtaining corroborating evidence for responses to inquiries concerning litigation, claims, and assessments (see paragraph .07 of this section). Consequently, it ordinarily is not necessary to send an inquiry letter to an entity's lawyer concerning litigation, claims, and assessments. However, if information comes to the accountant's attention that leads him or her to question whether the interim financial information departs from the applicable financial reporting framework[16] with respect to litigation, claims, or assessments, and the accountant believes the entity's lawyer may have information concerning that question, an inquiry of the lawyer concerning the specific question is appropriate. [Revised, January 2009, to reflect conforming changes necessary due to the issuance of SAS No. 116. As amended, effective for reviews of interim financial information for interim periods beginning after December 15, 2009, by SAS No. 116.]

.21 *Inquiry concerning an entity's ability to continue as a going concern.* A review of interim financial information is not designed to identify conditions or events that may indicate substantial doubt about an entity's ability to continue as a going concern. However, such conditions or events may have existed at the date of prior-period financial statements.[17] In addition, in the course of performing review procedures on the current-period interim financial information, the

---

[15] The principal accountant also may request other accountants involved in the engagement, if any, to read the other information. [Footnote renumbered, January 2009, to reflect conforming changes necessary due to the issuance of SAS No. 116. As amended, effective for reviews of interim financial information for interim periods beginning after December 15, 2009, by SAS No. 116.]

[16] For example, in accordance with FASB ASC 270 and Article 10 of Regulation S-X, contingencies and other uncertainties that could be expected to affect the fairness of the presentation of financial data at an interim date should be disclosed in interim financial information in the same manner required for annual financial statements. Such disclosures should be repeated in interim financial information and annual financial statements until the contingencies have been removed, resolved, or become immaterial. The significance of a contingency or uncertainty should be judged in relation to annual financial statements. [Footnote revised and renumbered, January 2009, to reflect conforming changes necessary due to the issuance of SAS No. 116. Footnote revised, June 2009, to reflect conforming changes necessary due to the issuance of FASB ASC. As amended, effective for reviews of interim financial information for interim periods beginning after December 15, 2009, by SAS No. 116.]

[17] For purposes of this section, "conditions or events that existed at the date of prior-period financial statements" include (*a*) substantial doubt about the entity's ability to continue as a going concern that existed at the preceding year end, regardless of whether the substantial doubt was alleviated by the auditor's consideration of management's plans, or (*b*) conditions and events disclosed in the immediately preceding interim period. [Footnote renumbered, January 2009, to reflect conforming changes necessary due to the issuance of SAS No. 116. As amended, effective for reviews of interim financial information for interim periods beginning after December 15, 2009, by SAS No. 116.]

accountant may become aware of conditions or events that might be indicative of the entity's possible inability to continue as a going concern. In either case, the accountant should (*a*) inquire of management as to its plans for dealing with the adverse effects of the conditions and events and (*b*) consider the adequacy of the disclosure about such matters in the interim financial information.[18] It ordinarily is not necessary for the accountant to obtain evidence in support of the information that mitigates the effects of the conditions and events.

.22 *Extension of interim review procedures.* If, in performing a review of interim financial information, the accountant becomes aware of information that leads him or her to believe that the interim financial information may not be in conformity with the applicable financial reporting framework in all material respects, the accountant should make additional inquiries or perform other procedures that the accountant considers appropriate to provide a basis for communicating whether he or she is aware of any material modifications that should be made to the interim financial information. For example, if the accountant's interim review procedures lead him or her to question whether a significant sales transaction is recorded in conformity with the applicable financial reporting framework, the accountant should perform additional procedures, such as discussing the terms of the transaction with senior marketing and accounting personnel, reading the sales contract, or both, to resolve his or her questions. [Revised, January 2009, to reflect conforming changes necessary due to the issuance of SAS No. 116. As amended, effective for reviews of interim financial information for interim periods beginning after December 15, 2009, by SAS No. 116.]

.23 *Coordination with the audit.* The accountant performing the review of interim financial information ordinarily will also be engaged to perform an audit of the annual financial statements of the entity. Certain auditing procedures associated with the annual audit may be performed concurrently with the review of interim financial information. For example, information gained from reading the minutes of meetings of the board of directors in connection with the review also may be used for the annual audit. Also, there may be significant or unusual transactions occurring during the interim period under review for which the auditing procedures that would need to be performed for purposes of the audit of the annual financial statements could be performed, to the extent practicable, at the time of the interim review, for example, business combinations, restructurings, or significant revenue transactions. [Revised, January 2009, to reflect conforming changes necessary due to the issuance of SAS No. 116. As amended, effective for reviews of interim financial information for interim periods beginning after December 15, 2009, by SAS No. 116.]

Written Representations From Management

.24 Written representations from management should be obtained for all interim financial information presented and for all periods covered by the review. Specific representations should relate to the following matters:[19]

---

[18] Information that might be disclosed is set forth in section 341, *The Auditor's Consideration of an Entity's Ability to Continue as a Going Concern*, paragraph .10. If the accountant determines that the disclosure about the entity's possible inability to continue as a going concern is inadequate, a departure from generally accepted accounting principles exists. [Footnote revised and renumbered, January 2009, to reflect conforming changes necessary due to the issuance of SAS No. 116. As amended, effective for reviews of interim financial information for interim periods beginning after December 15, 2009, by SAS No. 116.]

[19] For additional guidance regarding written management representations, see section 333, *Management Representations*, paragraphs .08–.12. [Footnote renumbered, January 2009, to reflect

(continued)

Interim Financial Information

a. Management's acknowledgement of its responsibility for the fair presentation of the interim financial information in conformity with the applicable financial reporting framework.

b. Management's belief that the interim financial information has been prepared and presented in conformity with the applicable financial reporting framework applicable to interim financial information.

Internal Control

c. Management's acknowledgement of its responsibility to establish and maintain controls that are sufficient to provide a reasonable basis for the preparation of reliable interim financial information in accordance with the applicable financial reporting framework.

d. Disclosure of all significant deficiencies and material weaknesses in the design or operation of internal control as it relates to the preparation of both annual and interim financial information.

e. Acknowledgment of management's responsibility for the design and implementation of programs and controls to prevent and detect fraud.

f. Knowledge of fraud or suspected fraud affecting the entity involving (1) management, (2) employees who have significant roles in internal control, or (3) others where the fraud could have a material effect on the interim financial information.

g. Knowledge of any allegations of fraud or suspected fraud affecting the entity received in communications from employees, former employees, analysts, regulators, short sellers, or others.

Completeness of Information

h. Availability of all financial records and related data.

i. Completeness and availability of all minutes of meetings of stockholders, directors, and committees of directors or summaries of actions of recent meetings for which minutes have not yet been prepared.

j. Communications with regulatory agencies concerning noncompliance with or deficiencies in financial reporting practices.

k. Absence of unrecorded transactions.

Recognition, Measurement, and Disclosure

l. Management's belief that the effects of any uncorrected financial statement misstatements aggregated by the accountant during the current review engagement and pertaining to the interim period(s) in the current year are immaterial, both individually and in the aggregate, to the interim financial information as a whole. (A summary of such items should be included in or attached to the letter.)[20]

m. Plans or intentions that may materially affect the carrying value or classification of assets or liabilities.

(footnote continued)

conforming changes necessary due to the issuance of SAS No. 116. As amended, effective for reviews of interim financial information for interim periods beginning after December 15, 2009, by SAS No. 116.]

[20] If a summary of uncorrected misstatements is unnecessary because there were no uncorrected misstatements identified, this representation should be eliminated. [Footnote renumbered, January 2009, to reflect conforming changes necessary due to the issuance of SAS No. 116. As amended, effective for reviews of interim financial information for interim periods beginning after December 15, 2009, by SAS No. 116.]

n. Information concerning related-party transactions and amounts receivable from or payable to related parties.

o. Guarantees, whether written or oral, under which the entity is contingently liable.

p. Significant estimates and material concentrations known to management that are required to be disclosed in accordance with FASB ASC 275, *Risks and Uncertainties*.

q. Violations or possible violations of laws or regulations whose effects should be considered for disclosure in the interim financial information or as a basis for recording a loss contingency.

r. Unasserted claims or assessments that are probable of assertion and must be disclosed in accordance with FASB ASC 450, *Contingencies*.

s. Other liabilities or gain or loss contingencies that are required to be accrued or disclosed by FASB ASC 450.

t. Satisfactory title to all owned assets, liens or encumbrances on such assets, and assets pledged as collateral.

u. Compliance with aspects of contractual agreements that may affect the interim financial information.

Subsequent Events

v. Information concerning subsequent events.

The representation letter ordinarily should be tailored to include additional representations from management related to matters specific to the entity's business or industry. Appendix C [paragraph .56] of this section presents illustrative representation letters. [Revised, January 2009, to reflect conforming changes necessary due to the issuance of SAS No. 116. Revised, June 2009, to reflect conforming changes necessary due to the issuance of FASB ASC. As amended, effective for reviews of interim financial information for interim periods beginning after December 15, 2009, by SAS No. 116.]

Evaluating the Results of Interim Review Procedures

.25 A review of interim financial information is not designed to obtain reasonable assurance that the interim financial information is free of material misstatement. However, based on the review procedures performed, the accountant may become aware of *likely misstatements*. In the context of an interim review, a likely misstatement is the accountant's best estimate of the total misstatement in the account balances or classes of transactions on which he or she has performed review procedures. The accountant should accumulate for further evaluation likely misstatements identified in performing the review procedures. The accountant may designate an amount below which misstatements need not be accumulated, based on his or her professional judgment. However, the accountant should recognize that aggregated misstatements of relatively small amounts could have a material effect on the interim financial information.

.26 Misstatements identified by the accountant or brought to the accountant's attention, including inadequate disclosure,[21] should be evaluated individually and in the aggregate to determine whether material modification

[21] For example, Rule 10-01 of Regulation S-X states

> The interim financial information shall include disclosures either on the face of the financial statements or in accompanying footnotes sufficient so as to make the interim information presented not misleading. Registrants may presume that users of the interim financial information have read or have access to the audited financial

(continued)

should be made to the interim financial information for it to conform with the applicable financial reporting framework.[22] The accountant should use his or her professional judgment in evaluating the materiality of any likely misstatements that the entity has not corrected. The accountant should consider matters such as (*a*) the nature, cause (if known), and amount of the misstatements; (*b*) whether the misstatements originated in the preceding year or interim periods of the current year; (*c*) materiality judgments made in conjunction with the current or prior year's annual audit; and (*d*) the potential effect of the misstatements on future interim or annual periods.[23] [Revised, January 2009, to reflect conforming changes necessary due to the issuance of SAS No. 116. As amended, effective for reviews of interim financial information for interim periods beginning after December 15, 2009, by SAS No. 116.]

.27 When evaluating whether uncorrected likely misstatements, individually or in the aggregate, are material, the accountant also should (*a*) consider the appropriateness of offsetting a misstatement of an estimated amount with a misstatement of an item capable of precise measurement and (*b*) recognize that an accumulation of immaterial misstatements in the balance sheet could contribute to material misstatements in future periods.

.28 When an accountant is unable to perform the procedures he or she considers necessary to achieve the objective of a review of interim financial information, or the client does not provide the accountant with the written representations the accountant believes are necessary, the review will be incomplete.

(footnote continued)

statements for the preceding fiscal year and that the adequacy of additional disclosure needed for a fair presentation, except in regard to material contingencies, may be determined in that context. Accordingly, footnote disclosure which would substantially duplicate the disclosure contained in the most recent annual report to security holders or latest audited financial statements, such as a statement of significant accounting policies and practices, details of accounts which have not changed significantly in amount or composition since the end of the most recently completed fiscal year, and detailed disclosures prescribed by Rule 4-08 of this Regulation, may be omitted. However, disclosure shall be provided where events subsequent to the end of the most recent fiscal year have occurred which have a material impact on the registrant. Disclosures should encompass for example, significant changes since the end of the most recently completed fiscal year in such items as: accounting principles and practices; estimates inherent in the preparation of the financial statements; status of long-term contracts; capitalization including significant new borrowings or modification of existing financing arrangements; and the reporting entity resulting from business combinations or dispositions. Notwithstanding the above, where material contingencies exist, disclosure of such matters shall be provided even though a significant change since year end may not have occurred.

[Footnote revised and renumbered, January 2009, to reflect conforming changes necessary due to the issuance of SAS No. 116. As amended, effective for reviews of interim financial information for interim periods beginning after December 15, 2009, by SAS No. 116.]

[22] FASB ASC 270 describes the applicability of generally accepted accounting principles to interim financial information and indicates the types of disclosures necessary to report on a meaningful basis for a period of less than a full year. FASB ASC 270-10-45-16 provides guidance on assessing materiality in interim periods. For example, FASB ASC 270-10-45-16 states, "In determining materiality for the purpose of reporting the correction of an error, amounts shall be related to the estimated income for the full fiscal year and also to the effect on the trend of earnings." [Footnote revised and renumbered, January 2009, to reflect conforming changes necessary due to the issuance of SAS No. 116. Footnote revised, June 2009, to reflect conforming changes necessary due to the issuance of FASB ASC. As amended, effective for reviews of interim financial information for interim periods beginning after December 15, 2009, by SAS No. 116.]

[23] Section 312 paragraph .60 provides guidance with respect to the auditor's qualitative considerations in evaluating whether the misstatements are material. [Footnote revised, March 2006, to reflect conforming changes necessary due to the issuance of SAS No. 107. Footnote revised and renumbered, January 2009, to reflect conforming changes necessary due to the issuance of SAS No. 116. As amended, effective for reviews of interim financial information for interim periods beginning after December 15, 2009, by SAS No. 116.]

An incomplete review is not an adequate basis for issuing a review report. If the accountant cannot complete the review, the accountant should communicate that information in accordance with the guidance in paragraphs .29–.31 of this section. Nevertheless, if the accountant has become aware of material modifications that should be made to the interim financial information for it to conform with the applicable financial reporting framework, such matters should be communicated pursuant to paragraphs .29–.31 of this section. [Revised, January 2009, to reflect conforming changes necessary due to the issuance of SAS No. 116. As amended, effective for reviews of interim financial information for interim periods beginning after December 15, 2009, by SAS No. 116.]

Communications to Management and Those Charged With Governance

.29 As a result of conducting a review of interim financial information, the accountant may become aware of matters that cause him or her to believe that (*a*) material modification should be made to the interim financial information for it to conform with the applicable financial reporting framework or (*b*) that the entity issued the interim financial information before the completion of the review, in those circumstances in which a review is required. In such circumstances, the accountant should communicate the matter(s) to the appropriate level of management as soon as practicable. [Revised, January 2009, to reflect conforming changes necessary due to the issuance of SAS No. 116. As amended, effective for reviews of interim financial information for interim periods beginning after December 15, 2009, by SAS No. 116.]

.30 If, in the accountant's judgment, management does not respond appropriately to the accountant's communication within a reasonable period of time, the accountant should inform those charged with governance of the matters as soon as practicable. This communication may be oral or written. If information is communicated orally, the accountant should document the communication. [Revised, April 2007, to reflect conforming changes necessary due to the issuance of SAS No. 114.]

.31 If, in the accountant's judgment, those charged with governance do not respond appropriately to the accountant's communication within a reasonable period of time, the accountant should evaluate whether to resign from the engagement to review the interim financial information and as the entity's auditor. The accountant may wish to consult with his or her attorney when making these evaluations. [Revised, April 2007, to reflect conforming changes necessary due to the issuance of SAS No. 114.]

.32 When conducting a review of interim financial information, the accountant may become aware of fraud or possible illegal acts. If the matter involves fraud, it should be brought to the attention of the appropriate level of management. If the fraud involves senior management or results in a material misstatement of the interim financial information, the accountant should communicate the matter directly to those charged with governance as described in section 316, *Consideration of Fraud in a Financial Statement Audit*, paragraphs .79–.82. If the matter involves possible illegal acts, the accountant should assure himself or herself that those charged with governance are adequately informed, unless the matter is clearly inconsequential.[24] (See section 317, *Illegal Acts by*

---

[24] The accountant may have additional communication responsibilities pursuant to section 317, *Illegal Acts by Clients*, and section 316, *Consideration of Fraud in a Financial Statement Audit*. [Footnote revised and renumbered, January 2009, to reflect conforming changes necessary due to the issuance of SAS No. 116. As amended, effective for reviews of interim financial information for interim periods beginning after December 15, 2009, by SAS No. 116.]

Clients, paragraph .17.) [Revised, April 2007, to reflect conforming changes necessary due to the issuance of SAS No. 114. Revised, January 2009, to reflect conforming changes necessary due to the issuance of SAS No. 116. As amended, effective for reviews of interim financial information for interim periods beginning after December 15, 2009, by SAS No. 116.]

.33 When conducting a review of interim financial information, the accountant may become aware of significant deficiencies or material weaknesses in internal control as it relates to the preparation of annual and interim financial information that should be communicated to management and those charged with governance. Section 325, *Communicating Internal Control Related Matters Identified in an Audit*, defines *significant deficiency* as a deficiency, or combination of deficiencies, in internal control over financial reporting, that is less severe than a material weakness, yet important enough to merit attention by those charged with governance.[25] Section 325 defines *material weakness* as a deficiency, or combination of deficiencies, in internal control over financial reporting, such that there is a reasonable possibility that a material misstatement of the entity's financial statements will not be prevented, or detected and corrected on a timely basis. A reasonable possibility exists when the likelihood of the event is either reasonably possible or probable as those terms are used in FASB ASC 450. The accountant also may wish to submit recommendations related to other matters that come to the accountant's attention. [26] [Revised, May 2006, to reflect conforming changes necessary due to the issuance of SAS No. 112. Revised, January 2009, to reflect conforming changes necessary due to the issuance of SAS No. 116. Revised, June 2009, to reflect conforming changes necessary due to the issuance of FASB ASC. As amended, effective for reviews of interim financial information for interim periods beginning after December 15, 2009, by SAS No. 116.]

.34 When conducting a review of interim financial information, the accountant also should determine whether any of the matters described in section 380, *The Auditor's Communication With Those Charged With Governance*, as they relate to the interim financial information, have been identified. If such matters have been identified, the accountant should communicate them to those charged with governance. For example, the accountant should communicate with those charged with governance about a change in a significant accounting policy affecting the interim financial information; about adjustments that, either individually or in the aggregate, could have a significant effect on the entity's financial reporting process; and about uncorrected misstatements aggregated by the accountant that were determined by management to be immaterial, both individually and in the aggregate, to the interim financial information taken as a whole. [27] [Revised, April 2007, to reflect conforming changes necessary due

---

[25] [Footnote deleted, January 2009, to reflect conforming changes necessary due to the issuance of SAS No. 116.]

[26] Section 325, *Communicating Internal Control Related Matters Identified in an Audit*, provides guidance on communicating significant deficiencies and material weaknesses in internal control. [Footnote renumbered and revised, May 2006, to reflect conforming changes necessary due to the issuance of SAS No. 112. Footnote renumbered, January 2009, to reflect conforming changes necessary due to the issuance of SAS No. 116. As amended, effective for reviews of interim financial information for interim periods beginning after December 15, 2009, by SAS No. 116.]

[27] The presentation to those charged with governance should be similar to the summary of uncorrected misstatements included in or attached to the management representation letter that is described in paragraph .24*l* of this section. [Footnote renumbered to reflect conforming changes necessary due to the issuance of SAS No. 112. Footnote revised, April 2007, to reflect conforming changes necessary due to the issuance of SAS No. 114. Footnote revised and renumbered, January 2009, to reflect conforming changes necessary due to the issuance of SAS No. 116. As amended, effective for reviews of interim financial information for interim periods beginning after December 15, 2009, by SAS No. 116.]

to the issuance of SAS No. 114. Revised, January 2009, to reflect conforming changes necessary due to the issuance of SAS No. 116. As amended, effective for reviews of interim financial information for interim periods beginning after December 15, 2009, by SAS No. 116.]

.35 The objective of a review of interim financial information differs significantly from that of an audit. Therefore, any communication the accountant may make about the quality, not just the acceptability, of the entity's accounting principles as applied to its interim financial reporting generally would be limited to the effect of significant events, transactions, and changes in accounting estimates that the accountant considered when conducting the review of interim financial information. Further, interim review procedures do not provide assurance that the accountant will become aware of all matters that might affect the accountant's judgments about the quality of the entity's accounting principles that would be identified as a result of an audit.

.36 If the accountant has identified matters to be communicated to those charged with governance, the accountant should attempt to make such communications with those charged with governance, or at least the chair of its audit committee (or a similar subgroup with a different name), on a sufficiently timely basis to enable those charged with governance to take appropriate action. The communications may be oral or written. If information is communicated orally, the accountant should document the communications. [Revised, April 2007, to reflect conforming changes necessary due to the issuance of SAS No. 114. Revised, January 2009, to reflect conforming changes necessary due to the issuance of SAS No. 116. As amended, effective for reviews of interim financial information for interim periods beginning after December 15, 2009, by SAS No. 116.]

The Accountant's Report on a Review of Interim Financial Information[28]

Form of Accountant's Review Report

.37 Pursuant to paragraph .03 of this standard, an accountant is not required to issue a report on a review of interim financial information; however, if the accountant is engaged to issue a written report or, based upon the guidance in paragraph .03, determines to issue a written report, the accountant's review report accompanying interim financial information should consist of the following:

a. A title that includes the word *independent*.

b. A statement that the interim financial information identified in the report was reviewed.

c. A statement that the interim financial information is the responsibility of the entity's management.

d. A statement that the review of interim financial information was conducted in accordance with standards established by the AICPA.

e. A description of the procedures for a review of interim financial information.

f. A statement that a review of interim financial information is substantially less in scope than an audit conducted in accordance with auditing standards generally accepted in the United States, the objective of

[28] [Footnote deleted, January 2009, to reflect conforming changes necessary due to the issuance of SAS No. 116.]

which is an expression of an opinion regarding the financial information taken as a whole, and accordingly, no such opinion is expressed.

g. A statement about whether the accountant is aware of any material modifications that should be made to the accompanying interim financial information for it to conform with the applicable financial reporting framework. The statement should include an identification of the country of origin of those accounting principles (for example, accounting principles generally accepted in the United States of America or U.S. generally accepted accounting principles).

h. The manual or printed signature of the accountant's firm.

i. The date of the review report. (Generally, the report should be dated as of the date of completion of the review procedures.[29])

In addition, each page of the interim financial information should be clearly marked as unaudited.

.38 The following is an example of a review report:[30]

Independent Accountant's Report

We have reviewed the accompanying [*describe the interim financial information or statements reviewed*] of ABC Company and consolidated subsidiaries as of September 30, 20X1, and for the three-month and nine-month periods then ended. This interim financial information is the responsibility of the company's management.

We conducted our review in accordance with standards established by the American Institute of Certified Public Accountants. A review of interim financial information consists principally of applying analytical procedures and making inquiries of persons responsible for financial and accounting matters. It is substantially less in scope than an audit conducted in accordance with auditing standards generally accepted in the United States, the objective of which is the expression of an opinion regarding the financial information taken as a whole. Accordingly, we do not express such an opinion.

Based on our review, we are not aware of any material modifications that should be made to the accompanying interim financial information for it to be in conformity with [*identify the applicable financial reporting framework; for example, accounting principles generally accepted in the United States of America*].

[*Signature*]

[*Date*]

[Revised, January 2009, to reflect conforming changes necessary due to the issuance of SAS No. 116. As amended, effective for reviews of interim financial

---

[29] Other reporting issues related to the dating of reports or subsequent events are similar to those encountered in an audit of financial statements. See sections 530, *Dating of the Independent Auditor's Report*, and 560, *Subsequent Events*. [Footnote renumbered to reflect conforming changes necessary due to the issuance of SAS No. 112. Footnote renumbered, January 2009, to reflect conforming changes necessary due to the issuance of SAS No. 116. As amended, effective for reviews of interim financial information for interim periods beginning after December 15, 2009, by SAS No. 116.]

[30] If interim financial information of a prior period is presented with that of the current period and the accountant has conducted a review of that information, the accountant should report on his or her review of the prior period. An example of the first sentence of such a report follows: "We have reviewed ... of ABC Company and consolidated subsidiaries as of September 30, 20X1 and 20X2, and for the three-month and nine-month periods then ended...." [Footnote renumbered to reflect conforming changes necessary due to the issuance of SAS No. 112. Footnote renumbered, January 2009, to reflect conforming changes necessary due to the issuance of SAS No. 116. As amended, effective for reviews of interim financial information for interim periods beginning after December 15, 2009, by SAS No. 116.]

information for interim periods beginning after December 15, 2009, by SAS No. 116.]

.39 An accountant may be engaged to report on a review of comparative interim financial information.[31] The following is an example of a review report on a condensed balance sheet as of March 31, 20X1, the related condensed statements of income and cash flows for the three-month periods ended March 31, 20X1 and 20X0, and a condensed balance sheet derived from audited financial statements as of December 31, 20X0.[32]

Independent Accountant's Report

We have reviewed the condensed consolidated balance sheet of ABC Company and subsidiaries as of March 31, 20X1, and the related condensed consolidated statements of income and cash flows for the three-month periods ended March 31, 20X1 and 20X0. This condensed financial information is the responsibility of the company's management.

We conducted our reviews in accordance with standards established by the American Institute of Certified Public Accountants. A review of interim financial information consists principally of applying analytical procedures and making inquiries of persons responsible for financial and accounting matters. It is substantially less in scope than an audit conducted in accordance with auditing standards generally accepted in the United States, the objective of which is the expression of an opinion regarding the financial information taken as a whole. Accordingly, we do not express such an opinion.

Based on our reviews, we are not aware of any material modifications that should be made to the condensed financial information referred to above for them to be in conformity with [*identify the applicable financial reporting framework; for example, accounting principles generally accepted in the United States of America*].

We have previously audited, in accordance with auditing standards generally accepted in the United States of America, the consolidated balance sheet of ABC Company and subsidiaries as of December 31, 20X0, and the related consolidated statements of income, retained earnings, and cash flows for the year then ended (not presented herein); and in our report dated February 15, 20X1, we expressed an unqualified opinion on those consolidated financial statements. In our opinion, the information set forth in the accompanying condensed consolidated balance sheet as of December 31, 20X0, is fairly stated, in all material respects, in relation to the consolidated balance sheet from which it has been derived.[33]

[*Signature*]

[*Date*]

---

[31] As interim financial reporting is intended to be an update to year end reporting, balance sheet information as of the most recent year end ordinarily would be presented for comparative purposes with the corresponding information as of the latest interim period. Likewise, the comparative presentation for income statement and cash flow information presented for the current interim period would be that of the corresponding interim period of the prior year. [Footnote added, January 2009, to reflect conforming changes necessary due to the issuance of SAS No. 116. As amended, effective for reviews of interim financial information for interim periods beginning after December 15, 2009, by SAS No. 116.]

[32] [Footnote deleted, January 2009, to reflect conforming changes necessary due to the issuance of SAS No. 116.]

[33] If the auditor's report on the preceding year-end financial statements was other than unqualified, referred to other auditors, or included an explanatory paragraph because of a going-concern matter or an inconsistency in the application of accounting principles, the last paragraph of the illustrative report in paragraph .39 should be appropriately modified. [Footnote renumbered to reflect

(continued)

[Revised, January 2009, to reflect conforming changes necessary due to the issuance of SAS No. 116. As amended, effective for reviews of interim financial information for interim periods beginning after December 15, 2009, by SAS No. 116.]

.40 The accountant may use and make reference to another accountant's review report on the interim financial information of a significant component of a reporting entity. This reference indicates a division of responsibility for performing the review.[34] The following is an example of report including such a reference:

Independent Accountant's Report

We have reviewed the accompanying [*describe the interim financial information or statements reviewed*] of ABC Company and consolidated subsidiaries as of September 30, 20X1, and for the three-month and nine-month periods then ended. This interim financial information is the responsibility of the company's management.

We were furnished with the report of other accountants on their review of the interim financial information of DEF subsidiary, whose total assets as of September 30, 20X1, and whose revenues for the three-month and nine-month periods then ended, constituted 15 percent, 20 percent, and 22 percent, respectively, of the related consolidated totals.

We conducted our review in accordance with standards established by the American Institute of Certified Public Accountants. A review of interim financial information consists principally of applying analytical procedures and making inquiries of persons responsible for financial and accounting matters. It is substantially less in scope than an audit conducted in accordance with auditing standards generally accepted in the United States, the objective of which is the expression of an opinion regarding the financial information taken as a whole. Accordingly, we do not express such an opinion.

Based on our review and the report of other accountants, we are not aware of any material modifications that should be made to the accompanying interim financial information for it to be in conformity with [*identify the applicable financial reporting framework; for example, accounting principles generally accepted in the United States of America*].

[*Signature*]

[*Date*]

[Revised, January 2009, to reflect conforming changes necessary due to the issuance of SAS No. 116. As amended, effective for reviews of interim financial information for interim periods beginning after December 15, 2009, by SAS No. 116.]

(footnote continued)

conforming changes necessary due to the issuance of SAS No. 112. Footnote revised and renumbered, January 2009, to reflect conforming changes necessary due to the issuance of SAS No. 116. As amended, effective for reviews of interim financial information for interim periods beginning after December 15, 2009, by SAS No. 116.]

[34] See section 543, *Part of Audit Performed by Other Independent Auditors*. [Footnote renumbered to reflect conforming changes necessary due to the issuance of SAS No. 112. Footnote revised and renumbered, January 2009, to reflect conforming changes necessary due to the issuance of SAS No. 116. As amended, effective for reviews of interim financial information for interim periods beginning after December 15, 2009, by SAS No. 116.]

Modification of the Accountant's Review Report

.41 The accountant's report on a review of interim financial information should be modified for departures from the applicable financial reporting framework,[35] which include inadequate disclosure and changes in accounting principle that are not in conformity with the applicable financial reporting framework. The existence of substantial doubt about the entity's ability to continue as a going concern or a lack of consistency in the application of accounting principles affecting the interim financial information would not require the accountant to add an additional paragraph to the report, provided that the interim financial information appropriately discloses such matters. Although not required, the accountant may wish to emphasize such matters in a separate explanatory paragraph of the report. See paragraphs .44–.45 of this section for examples of paragraphs that address matters related to an entity's ability to continue as a going concern. [Revised, January 2009, to reflect conforming changes necessary due to the issuance of SAS No. 116. As amended, effective for reviews of interim financial information for interim periods beginning after December 15, 2009, by SAS No. 116.]

.42 *Departure from the applicable financial reporting framework.* If the accountant becomes aware that the interim financial information is materially affected by a departure from the applicable financial reporting framework, he or she should modify the report. The modification should describe the nature of the departure and, if practicable, should state the effects on the interim financial information. Following is an example of such a modification of the accountant's report.

> [*Explanatory paragraph*]
>
> Based on information furnished to us by management, we believe that the company has excluded from property and debt in the accompanying balance sheet certain lease obligations that we believe should be capitalized to conform with [*identify the applicable financial reporting framework; for example, accounting principles generally accepted in the United States of America*]. This information indicates that if these lease obligations were capitalized at September 30, 20X1, property would be increased by $____, long-term debt by $____, and net income and earnings per share would be increased (decreased) by $_____, $_____, $_____, and $_____, respectively, for the three-month and nine-month periods then ended.
>
> [*Concluding paragraph*]
>
> Based on our review, with the exception of the matter(s) described in the preceding paragraph(s), we are not aware of any material modifications that should be made to the accompanying interim financial information for it to be in conformity with [*identify the applicable financial reporting framework; for example, accounting principles generally accepted in the United States of America*].

[Revised, January 2009, to reflect conforming changes necessary due to the issuance of SAS No. 116. As amended, effective for reviews of interim financial information for interim periods beginning after December 15, 2009, by SAS No. 116.]

---

[35] If the circumstances contemplated by Rule 203, *Accounting Principles* [ET sec. 203 par. 01], are present, the accountant should refer to the guidance in section 508, *Reports on Audited Financial Statements*, paragraph .15. [Footnote renumbered to reflect conforming changes necessary due to the issuance of SAS No. 112. Footnote revised and renumbered, January 2009, to reflect conforming changes necessary due to the issuance of SAS No. 116. As amended, effective for reviews of interim financial information for interim periods beginning after December 15, 2009, by SAS No. 116.]

.43 *Inadequate disclosure*. The information necessary for adequate disclosure is influenced by the form and context in which the interim financial information is presented. For example, the disclosures considered necessary for interim financial information presented in accordance with the minimum disclosure requirements of FASB ASC 270-10-50-1, which is applicable to summarized financial statements of public companies, are considerably less extensive than those necessary for annual financial statements that present financial position, results of operations, and cash flows in conformity with the applicable financial reporting framework.[36] If information that the accountant believes is necessary for adequate disclosure in conformity with the applicable financial reporting framework[37] is not included in the interim financial information, the accountant should modify the report and, if practicable, include the necessary information in the report. The following is an example of such a modification of the accountant's report:

> [*Explanatory paragraph*]
>
> Management has informed us that the company is presently defending a claim regarding [*describe the nature of the loss contingency*] and that the extent of the company's liability, if any, and the effect on the accompanying information is not determinable at this time. The information fails to disclose these matters, which we believe are required to be disclosed in conformity with [*identify the applicable financial reporting framework; for example, accounting principles generally accepted in the United States of America*].
>
> [*Concluding paragraph*]
>
> Based on our review, with the exception of the matter(s) described in the preceding paragraph(s), we are not aware of any material modifications that should be made to the accompanying interim financial information for it to be in conformity with [*identify the applicable financial reporting framework; for example, accounting principles generally accepted in the United States of America*].

[Revised, January 2009, to reflect conforming changes necessary due to the issuance of SAS No. 116. Revised, June 2009, to reflect conforming changes necessary due to the issuance of FASB ASC. As amended, effective for reviews of interim financial information for interim periods beginning after December 15, 2009, by SAS No. 116.]

.44 *Going-concern paragraph was included in the prior year's audit report; conditions giving rise to the paragraph continue to exist.* If (*a*) the auditor's report for the prior year end contained an explanatory paragraph indicating the existence of substantial doubt about the entity's ability to continue as a

---

[36] For example, FASB ASC 270-10-50-3 states that "there is a presumption that users of summarized interim financial data will have read the latest published annual report, including the financial disclosures required by generally accepted accounting principles and management's commentary concerning the annual financial results, and that the summarized interim data will be viewed in that context." See footnote 21 of this section for additional disclosure requirements. [Footnote renumbered to reflect conforming changes necessary due to the issuance of SAS No. 112. Footnote revised and renumbered, January 2009, to reflect conforming changes necessary due to the issuance of SAS No. 116. Footnote revised, June 2009, to reflect conforming changes necessary due to the issuance of FASB ASC. As amended, effective for reviews of interim financial information for interim periods beginning after December 15, 2009, by SAS No. 116.]

[37] Such disclosures include those set forth in section 341A, *The Auditor's Consideration of an Entity's Ability to Continue as a Going Concern*, paragraph .10. If the accountant determines that disclosure about the entity's possible inability to continue as a going concern is inadequate, a departure from generally accepted accounting principles exists. [Footnote renumbered to reflect conforming changes necessary due to the issuance of SAS No. 112. Footnote renumbered, January 2009, to reflect conforming changes necessary due to the issuance of SAS No. 116. As amended, effective for reviews of interim financial information for interim periods beginning after December 15, 2009, by SAS No. 116.]

going concern, (*b*) the conditions that raised such doubt continued to exist as of the interim reporting date covered by the review, and (*c*) there is adequate and appropriate disclosure about these conditions in the interim financial information, the accountant is not required to modify his or her report. However, the accountant may add an explanatory paragraph to the review report, after the concluding paragraph, emphasizing the matter disclosed in the audited financial statements and the interim financial information. The following is an example of such a paragraph.

> Note 4 of the Company's audited financial statements as of December 31, 20X1, and for the year then ended discloses that the Company was unable to renew its line of credit or obtain alternative financing at December 31, 20X1. Our auditor's report on those financial statements includes an explanatory paragraph referring to the matters in Note 4 of those financial statements and indicating that these matters raised substantial doubt about the Company's ability to continue as a going concern. As indicated in Note 3 of the Company's unaudited interim financial information as of March 31, 20X2, and for the three months then ended, the Company was still unable to renew its line of credit or obtain alternative financing as of March 31, 20X2. The accompanying interim financial information does not include any adjustments that might result from the outcome of this uncertainty.

[Revised, January 2009, to reflect conforming changes necessary due to the issuance of SAS No. 116. As amended, effective for reviews of interim financial information for interim periods beginning after December 15, 2009, by SAS No. 116.]

.45 *Going-concern paragraph was not included in the prior year's audit report; conditions or events exist as of the interim reporting date covered by the review that might be indicative of the entity's possible inability to continue as a going concern.* If (*a*) conditions or events exist as of the interim reporting date covered by the review that might be indicative of the entity's possible inability to continue as a going concern, and (*b*) there is adequate and appropriate disclosure about these conditions or events in the interim financial information, the accountant is not required to modify his or her report. However, the accountant may add an explanatory paragraph to the review report, after the concluding paragraph, emphasizing the matter disclosed in the interim financial information. The following is an example of such a paragraph.

> As indicated in note 3, certain conditions indicate that the Company may be unable to continue as a going concern. The accompanying interim financial information does not include any adjustments that might result from the outcome of this uncertainty.

Subsequent Discovery of Facts Existing at the Date of the Accountant's Report or Completion of the Interim Review Procedures

.46 Subsequent to the date of the accountant's review report or the completion of the interim review procedures, if a report is not issued, the accountant may become aware that facts existed at the date of the review report (or the completion of the review procedures) that might have affected the accountant's report (or conclusion, if a report is not issued) had he or she then been aware of those matters. Because of the variety of conditions that might be encountered, the specific actions to be taken by the accountant in a particular case may vary with the circumstances. In any event, the accountant should consider the guidance in section 561, *Subsequent Discovery of Facts Existing at the Date of the Auditor's Report*.

Client's Representation Concerning a Review of Interim Financial Information

.47 If a client represents in a report, document, or written communication containing the reviewed interim financial information that the accountant has reviewed the interim financial information, the accountant should advise the entity that his or her review report must be included in the report, document, or written communication. If the client will not agree to include the accountant's review report, the accountant should perform the following procedures:

- Request that the accountant's name be neither associated with the interim financial information nor referred to in the document.
- If the client does not comply with the request, advise the client that the accountant will not permit either the use of his or her name or reference to him or her.
- Communicate the client's noncompliance with the request to those charged with governance.
- When appropriate, recommend that the client consult with its legal counsel about the application of relevant laws and regulations to the circumstances.
- Consider what other actions might be appropriate.[38]

[Revised, January 2009, to reflect conforming changes necessary due to the issuance of SAS No. 116. As amended, effective for reviews of interim financial information for interim periods beginning after December 15, 2009, by SAS No. 116.]

.48 If a client represents in a document filed with a regulatory agency or issued to stockholders or third parties that the accountant has reviewed the interim financial information included in the document, and the accountant has been unable to complete the review of the interim financial information, the accountant should refer to paragraphs .28 and .47 of this section for guidance.

[Revised, January 2009, to reflect conforming changes necessary due to the issuance of SAS No. 116. As amended, effective for reviews of interim financial information for interim periods beginning after December 15, 2009, by SAS No. 116.]

Interim Financial Information Accompanying Audited Financial Statements

.49 Interim financial information may be presented as supplementary information outside audited financial statements. In such circumstances, each page of the interim financial information should be clearly marked as unaudited. If management chooses or is required to present interim financial information in a note to the audited financial statements, the information also should be clearly marked as unaudited.

.50 The auditor ordinarily need not modify his or her report on the audited financial statements to refer to his or her having performed a review in

---

[38] In considering what actions, if any, may be appropriate in these circumstances, the accountant should consider consulting his or her legal counsel. [Footnote renumbered to reflect conforming changes necessary due to the issuance of SAS No. 112. Footnote renumbered, January 2009, to reflect conforming changes necessary due to the issuance of SAS No. 116. As amended, effective for reviews of interim financial information for interim periods beginning after December 15, 2009, by SAS No. 116.]

accordance with this section or to refer to the interim financial information accompanying the audited financial statements because the interim financial information has not been audited and is not required for the audited financial statements to be fairly stated in conformity with the applicable financial reporting framework. The auditor's report on the audited financial statements should, however, be modified in the following circumstances:

a. The interim financial information included in a note to the financial statements, including information that has been reviewed in accordance with this section, is not appropriately marked as unaudited. (In these circumstances the auditor should disclaim an opinion on the interim financial information.)

b. The interim financial information accompanying audited financial statements does not appear to be presented in conformity with the applicable financial reporting framework (see paragraphs .42–.43 of this section). However, the auditor need not modify his or her report on the audited financial statements if his or her separate review report, which refers to those circumstances, is presented with the information.

[Revised, January 2009, to reflect conforming changes necessary due to the issuance of SAS No. 116. As amended, effective for reviews of interim financial information for interim periods beginning after December 15, 2009, by SAS No. 116.]

Documentation

.51 The accountant should prepare documentation in connection with a review of interim financial information, the form and content of which should be designed to meet the circumstances of the particular engagement. Documentation is the principal record of the review procedures performed and the conclusions reached by the accountant in performing the review.[39] Examples of documentation are review programs, analyses, memoranda, and letters of representation. Documentation may be in paper or electronic form, or other media. The quantity, type, and content of the documentation are matters of the accountant's professional judgment.

.52 Because of the different circumstances in individual engagements, it is not possible to specify the form or content of the documentation the accountant should prepare. However, the documentation should include any findings or issues that in the accountant's judgment are significant, for example, the results of review procedures that indicate that the interim financial information could be materially misstated, including actions taken to address such findings, and the basis for the final conclusions reached. In addition, the documentation should (*a*) enable members of the engagement team with supervision and review responsibilities to understand the nature, timing, extent, and results of the review procedures performed; (*b*) identify the engagement team member(s) who performed and reviewed the work; and (*c*) identify the evidence the accountant obtained in support of the conclusion that the interim financial information being reviewed agreed or reconciled with the accounting records (see paragraph .18*d* of this section).

---

[39] However, an accountant would not be precluded from supporting his or her conclusions by other means in addition to the review documentation. [Footnote renumbered to reflect conforming changes necessary due to the issuance of SAS No. 112. Footnote revised and renumbered, January 2009, to reflect conforming changes necessary due to the issuance of SAS No. 116. As amended, effective for reviews of interim financial information for interim periods beginning after December 15, 2009, by SAS No. 116.]

Effective Date

.53 This section is effective for reviews of interim financial information for interim periods beginning after December 15, 2009. Earlier application of the provisions of this section is permitted. [Revised, January 2009, to reflect conforming changes necessary due to the issuance of SAS No. 116. As amended, effective for reviews of interim financial information for interim periods beginning after December 15, 2009, by SAS No. 116.]

.54

Appendix A

Analytical Procedures the Accountant May Consider Performing When Conducting a Review of Interim Financial Information

A1. Analytical procedures are designed to identify relationships and individual items that appear to be unusual and that may reflect a material misstatement of the interim financial information. These procedures may consist of comparing interim financial information with prior period information, actual interim results with anticipated results (such as budgets or forecasts), and recorded amounts or ratios with expectations developed by the accountant. Examples of analytical procedures an accountant may consider performing in a review of interim financial information include

- comparing current interim financial information with anticipated results, such as budgets or forecasts (for example, comparing tax balances and the relationship between the provision for income taxes and pretax income in the current interim financial information with corresponding information in (*a*) budgets, using expected rates, and (*b*) financial information for prior periods).[1]
- comparing current interim financial information with relevant nonfinancial information.
- comparing ratios and indicators for the current interim period with expectations based on prior periods, for example, performing gross profit analysis by product line and operating segment using elements of the current interim financial information and comparing the results with corresponding information for prior periods. Examples of key ratios and indicators are the current ratio, receivable turnover or days' sales outstanding, inventory turnover, depreciation to average fixed assets, debt to equity, gross profit percentage, net income percentage, and plant operating rates.
- comparing ratios and indicators for the current interim period with those of entities in the same industry.
- comparing relationships among elements in the current interim financial information with corresponding relationships in the interim financial information of prior periods, for example, expense by type as a percentage of sales, assets by type as a percentage of total assets, and percentage of change in sales to percentage of change in receivables.
- comparing disaggregated data. The following are examples of how data may be disaggregated:
  - — By period, for example, financial statement items disaggregated into quarterly, monthly, or weekly amounts.

---

[1] The accountant should exercise caution when comparing and evaluating current interim financial information with budgets, forecasts, or other anticipated results because of the inherent lack of precision in estimating the future and susceptibility of such information to manipulation and misstatement by management to reflect desired interim results.

— By product line or operating segment.

— By location, for example, subsidiary, division, or branch.

A2. Analytical procedures may include such statistical techniques as trend analysis or regression analysis and may be performed manually or with the use of computer-assisted techniques.

.55

Appendix B

Unusual or Complex Situations to Be Considered by the Accountant When Conducting a Review of Interim Financial Information

B1. The following are examples of situations about which the accountant would ordinarily inquire of management:

- Business combinations
- New or complex revenue recognition methods
- Impairment of assets
- Disposal of a segment of a business
- Use of derivative instruments and hedging activities
- Sales and transfers that may call into question the classification of investments in securities, including management's intent and ability with respect to the remaining securities classified as held to maturity
- Computation of earnings per share in a complex capital structure
- Adoption of new stock compensation plans or changes to existing plans
- Restructuring charges taken in the current and prior quarters
- Significant, unusual, or infrequently occurring transactions
- Changes in litigation or contingencies
- Changes in major contracts with customers or suppliers
- Application of new accounting principles
- Changes in accounting principles or the methods of applying them
- Trends and developments affecting accounting estimates,[1] such as allowances for bad debts and excess or obsolete inventories, provisions for warranties and employee benefits, and realization of unearned income and deferred charges
- Compliance with debt covenants
- Changes in related parties or significant new related-party transactions
- Material off-balance-sheet transactions, special-purpose entities, and other equity investments
- Unique terms for debt or capital stock that could affect classification

[1] The accountant may wish to refer to the guidance in section 342, *Auditing Accounting Estimates*, paragraphs .05–.06.

.56

Appendix C

Illustrative Management Representation Letters for a Review of Interim Financial Information

C1. The following illustrative management representation letters, which relate to a review of interim financial information prepared in conformity with an applicable financial reporting framework, are presented for illustrative purposes only. The first letter is designed to be used in conjunction with the representation letter provided by management in connection with the audit of the financial statements of the prior year. The second illustrative representation letter may be used independently of any other representation letter.

C2. The introductory paragraph of the letters should specify the financial information and periods covered by the accountant's report, for example, "condensed balance sheets of XYZ Company as of June 30, 20X1 and 20X2, and the related condensed statements of income and retained earnings and cash flows for the three-month and nine-month periods then ended." The written representations to be obtained should be based on the circumstances of the engagement and the nature and basis of presentation of the interim financial information being reviewed. Appendix B, "Additional Illustrative Representations," of section 333, *Management Representations*, presents examples of such representations. Illustrative representations for specialized industries are presented in AICPA Audit and Accounting Guides.

C3. If matters exist that should be disclosed to the accountant, they should be indicated by modifying the related representation. For example, if an event subsequent to the date of the balance sheet has been disclosed in the interim financial information, the final paragraph could be modified as follows: "To the best of our knowledge and belief, except as discussed in note X to the interim financial information, no events have occurred. . . ." In appropriate circumstances, item 10 of the second illustrative representation letter could be modified as follows: "The company has no plans or intentions that may materially affect the carrying value or classification of assets and liabilities, except for our plans to dispose of segment A, as disclosed in note X to the interim financial information, which are discussed in the minutes of the June 7, 20X2, meeting of the board of directors (or disclosed to you at our meeting on June 15, 20X2)." Similarly, if management has received a communication regarding an allegation of fraud or suspected fraud, item 7 of the first illustrative representation letter and item 9 of the second illustrative representation letter could be modified as follows: "Except for the allegation discussed in the minutes of the December 7, 20X1, meeting of the board of directors (or disclosed to you at our meeting on October 15, 20X1), we have no knowledge of any allegations of fraud or suspected fraud affecting the company received in communications from employees, former employees, analysts, regulators, short sellers, or others."

C4. The qualitative discussion of materiality used in the illustrative letters is adapted from the Financial Accounting Standards Board Statement of Financial Accounting Concepts No. 2, *Qualitative Characteristics of Accounting Information*.

C5. Certain terms are used in the illustrative letters that are described elsewhere in authoritative literature. Examples are *fraud*, in section 316, *Consideration of Fraud in a Financial Statement Audit*, and *related parties*, in section 334, *Related Parties*, footnote 1). To avoid misunderstanding concerning the meaning of such terms, the accountant may wish to furnish those definitions to management or request that the definitions be included in the written representations.

C6. The illustrative letters assume that management and the accountant have reached an understanding on the limits of materiality for purposes of the written representations. However, it should be noted that a materiality limit would not apply for certain representations, as explained in section 333 paragraph .08.

1. Illustrative Short-Form Representation Letter for a Review of Interim Financial Information

[*This representation letter is to be used in conjunction with the representation letter for the audit of the financial statements of the prior year. Management confirms the representations made in the representation letter for the audit of the financial statements of the prior year end as they apply to the interim financial information, and makes additional representations that may be needed for the interim financial information.*]

[*Date*]

To [*Independent Accountant*]:

We are providing this letter in connection with your review of the [*identification of interim financial information*] of [*name of entity*] as of [*dates*] and for the [*periods*] for the purpose of determining whether any material modifications should be made to the [*consolidated*] interim financial information for it to conform with [*identify the applicable financial reporting framework; for example, accounting principles generally accepted in the United States of America, including, if appropriate, an indication as to the appropriate form and content of interim financial information (for example, Article 10 of SEC Regulation S-X)*]. We confirm that we are responsible for the fair presentation of the [*consolidated*] interim financial information in conformity with [*identify the applicable financial reporting framework; for example, generally accepted accounting principles*] and that we are responsible for establishing and maintaining controls that are sufficient to provide a reasonable basis for the preparation of reliable interim financial information in accordance with [*identify the applicable financial reporting framework; for example, generally accepted accounting principles*].

Certain representations in this letter are described as being limited to matters that are material. Items are considered material, regardless of size, if they involve an omission or misstatement of accounting information that, in the light of surrounding circumstances, makes it probable that the judgment of a reasonable person relying on the information would be changed or influenced by the omission or misstatement.

We confirm, to the best of our knowledge and belief, [*as of (date of accountant's report or completion of review),*] the following representations made to you during your review:

1. The interim financial information referred to above has been prepared and presented in conformity with [*identify the applicable financial reporting framework; for example, generally accepted accounting principles*] applicable to interim financial information.

2. We have made available to you

   a. all financial records and related data.

b. all minutes of the meetings of stockholders, directors, and committees of directors, or summaries of actions of recent meetings for which minutes have not yet been prepared. All significant board and committee actions are included in the summaries.

3. We believe that the effects of any uncorrected financial statement misstatements aggregated by you during the current review engagement and pertaining to the interim period(s) in the current year, as summarized in the accompanying schedule, are immaterial, both individually and in the aggregate, to the interim financial information taken as a whole.[1]
4. There are no significant deficiencies or material weaknesses in the design or operation of internal controls as it relates to the preparation of both annual and interim financial information.
5. We acknowledge our responsibility for the design and implementation of programs and controls to prevent and detect fraud.
6. We have no knowledge of any fraud or suspected fraud affecting the company involving
   a. management;
   b. employees who have significant roles in internal control; or
   c. others where the fraud could have a material effect on the interim financial information.
7. We have no knowledge of any allegations of fraud or suspected fraud affecting the company received in communications from employees, former employees, analysts, regulators, short sellers, or others.
8. We have reviewed our representation letter to you dated [*date of representation letter relating to most recent audit*] with respect to the audited financial statements for the year ended [*prior year-end date*]. We believe that representations A, B, and C within that representation letter do not apply to the interim financial information referred to above. We now confirm those representations 1 through X, as they apply to the interim financial information referred to above, and incorporate them herein, with the following changes:

[*Indicate any changes.*]

9. [*Add any representations related to new accounting or auditing standards that are being implemented for the first time.*]

To the best of our knowledge and belief, no events have occurred subsequent to the balance-sheet date and through the date of this letter that would require adjustment to or disclosure in the aforementioned interim financial information.

____

[*Name of chief executive officer and title*]

____

[*Name of chief financial officer and title*]

____

[*Name of chief accounting officer and title*]

[1] If a summary of uncorrected misstatements is unnecessary because no uncorrected misstatements were identified, this representation should be eliminated.

2. Illustrative Representation Letter for a Review of Interim Financial Information

[*This representation letter is similar in detail to the management-representation letter used for the audit of the financial statements of the prior year and thus need not refer to the written management representations received in the most recent audit.*]

[*Date*]

To [*Independent Accountant*]:

We are providing this letter in connection with your review of the [*identification of interim financial information*] of [*name of entity*] as of [*dates*] and for the [*periods*] for the purpose of determining whether any material modifications should be made to the [*consolidated*] interim financial information for it to conform with [*identify the applicable financial reporting framework; for example, accounting principles generally accepted in the United States of America, including, if appropriate, an indication as to the appropriate form and content of interim financial information (for example, Article 10 of SEC Regulation S-X)*]. We confirm that we are responsible for the fair presentation of the [*consolidated*] interim financial information in conformity with [*identify the applicable financial reporting framework; for example, generally accepted accounting principles*] and that we are responsible for establishing and maintaining controls that are sufficient to provide a reasonable basis for the preparation of reliable interim financial information in accordance with [*identify the applicable financial reporting framework; for example, generally accepted accounting principles*].

Certain representations in this letter are described as being limited to matters that are material. Items are considered material, regardless of size, if they involve an omission or misstatement of accounting information that, in the light of surrounding circumstances, makes it probable that the judgment of a reasonable person relying on the information would be changed or influenced by the omission or misstatement.

We confirm, to the best of our knowledge and belief, [*as of* (*date of accountant's report or the completion of the review*)], the following representations made to you during your review:

1. The interim financial information referred to above has been prepared and presented in conformity with [*identify the applicable financial reporting framework; for example, generally accepted accounting principles*] applicable to interim financial information.
2. We have made available to you
   a. all financial records and related data.
   b. all minutes of the meetings of stockholders, directors, and committees of directors, or summaries of actions of recent meetings for which minutes have not yet been prepared. All significant board and committee actions are included in the summaries.
3. There have been no communications from regulatory agencies concerning noncompliance with or deficiencies in financial reporting practices.
4. There are no material transactions that have not been properly recorded in the accounting records underlying the interim financial information.
5. We believe that the effects of any uncorrected financial statement misstatements aggregated by you during the current review engagement

and pertaining to the interim period(s) in the current year, as summarized in the accompanying schedule, are immaterial, both individually and in the aggregate, to the interim financial information taken as a whole.[2]

6. There are no significant deficiencies or material weaknesses in the design or operation of internal control as it relates to the preparation of both annual and interim financial information.

7. We acknowledge our responsibility for the design and implementation of programs and controls to prevent and detect fraud.

8. We have no knowledge of any fraud or suspected fraud affecting the company involving

   a. management;

   b. employees who have significant roles in internal control; or

   c. others where the fraud could have a material effect on the interim financial information.

9. We have no knowledge of any allegations of fraud or suspected fraud affecting the company received in communications from employees, former employees, analysts, regulators, short sellers, or others.

10. The company has no plans or intentions that may materially affect the carrying value or classification of assets and liabilities.

11. The following have been properly recorded or disclosed in the interim financial information:

   a. Related-party transactions, including sales, purchases, loans, transfers, leasing arrangements, and guarantees, and amounts receivable from or payable to related parties.

   b. Guarantees, whether written or oral, under which the company is contingently liable.

   c. Significant estimates and material concentrations known to management that are required to be disclosed in accordance with Financial Accounting Standards Board (FASB) *Accounting Standards Codification* (ASC) 275, *Risks and Uncertainties*. [*Significant estimates are estimates at the balance sheet date that could change materially within the next year. Concentrations refer to volumes of business, revenues, available sources of supply, or markets or geographic areas for which events could occur that would significantly disrupt normal finances within the next year.*]

12. There are no

   a. violations or possible violations of laws or regulations whose effects should be considered for disclosure in the interim financial information or as a basis for recording a loss contingency.

   b. unasserted claims or assessments that are probable of assertion and must be disclosed in accordance with FASB ASC 450, *Contingencies*.

   c. other liabilities or gain or loss contingencies that are required to be accrued or disclosed by FASB ASC 450.

---

[2] If a summary of uncorrected misstatements is unnecessary because no uncorrected misstatements were identified, this representation should be eliminated.

13. The company has satisfactory title to all owned assets, and there are no liens or encumbrances on such assets; nor has any asset been pledged as collateral.
14. The company has complied with all aspects of contractual agreements that would have a material effect on the interim financial information in the event of noncompliance.
15. [*Add additional representations that are unique to the entity's business or industry. See section 333,* Management Representations, *paragraph .17).*]
16. [*Add any representations related to new accounting or auditing standards that are being implemented for the first time.*]

To the best of our knowledge and belief, no events have occurred subsequent to the balance-sheet date and through the date of this letter that would require adjustment to or disclosure in the aforementioned interim financial information.

____

[*Name of chief executive officer and title*]

____

[*Name of chief financial officer and title*]

____

[*Name of chief accounting officer and title*]

[Revised, January 2009, to reflect conforming changes necessary due to the issuance of SAS No. 116. Revised, June 2009, to reflect conforming changes necessary due to the issuance of FASB ASC. As amended, effective for reviews of interim financial information for interim periods beginning after December 15, 2009, by SAS No. 116.]

AU Section 800

COMPLIANCE AUDITING

TABLE OF CONTENTS

AU Section 801

Compliance Audits

(Supersedes SAS No. 74.)

Source: SAS No. 117.

Effective for compliance audits for fiscal periods ending on or after June 15, 2010. Earlier application is permitted.

Introduction and Applicability

.01 Governments frequently establish governmental audit requirements for entities to undergo an audit of their compliance with applicable compliance requirements. This section is applicable when an auditor is engaged, or required by law or regulation, to perform a compliance audit in accordance with all of the following:

- Generally accepted auditing standards (GAAS)
- The standards for financial audits under *Government Auditing Standards*
- A governmental audit requirement that requires an auditor to express an opinion on compliance (Ref: par. .A1–.A2)

.02 This section addresses the application of GAAS to a compliance audit. Compliance audits usually are performed in conjunction with a financial statement audit. This section does not apply to the financial statement audit component of such engagements. Although certain AU sections are not applicable to a compliance audit, as identified in the appendix of this section, all AU sections other than section 801 are applicable to the audit of financial statements performed in conjunction with a compliance audit.

.03 This section is not applicable when the governmental audit requirement calls for an examination, in accordance with Statements on Standards for Attestation Engagements, of an entity's compliance with specified requirements or an examination of an entity's internal control over compliance. AT section 601, *Compliance Attestation*, is applicable to these engagements. If the entity is required to undergo a compliance audit and an examination of internal control over compliance, this section is applicable to performing and reporting on the compliance audit, and AT section 601 is applicable to performing and reporting on the examination of internal control over compliance. (Ref: par. .A2)

.04 Sections 100–700 and 900 address audits of financial statements, as well as other kinds of engagements. Sections 100–300 and 500 generally can be adapted to the objectives of a compliance audit. However, with certain exceptions, sections 400, 600, 700, and 900 generally cannot be adapted to a compliance audit because they address the auditor's report on an audit of financial statements and other topics that are not applicable to a compliance audit.

.05 The AU sections that are not applicable to a compliance audit are listed in the appendix of this section. All of the other AU sections are applicable to a compliance audit. However, the auditor is not required, in planning and performing a compliance audit, to make a literal translation of each procedure that might be performed in a financial statement audit, but rather to obtain sufficient appropriate audit evidence to support the auditor's opinion on compliance.

.06 Some AU sections can be adapted and applied to a compliance audit with relative ease, for example, by simply replacing the word *misstatement* with the word *noncompliance*. Other AU sections are more difficult to adapt and apply and entail additional modification. For that reason, this section provides more specific guidance on how to adapt and apply certain AU sections to a compliance audit.

.07 *Government Auditing Standards* and governmental audit requirements contain certain standards and requirements that are supplementary to those in GAAS, as well as guidance on how to apply those standards and requirements.

Management's Responsibilities

.08 A compliance audit is based on the premise that management is responsible for the entity's compliance with compliance requirements. Management's responsibility for the entity's compliance with compliance requirements includes the following:

a. Identifying the entity's government programs and understanding and complying with the compliance requirements

b. Establishing and maintaining effective controls that provide reasonable assurance that the entity administers government programs in compliance with the compliance requirements

c. Evaluating and monitoring the entity's compliance with the compliance requirements

d. Taking corrective action when instances of noncompliance are identified, including corrective action on audit findings of the compliance audit

Effective Date

.09 The provisions of this section are effective for compliance audits for fiscal periods ending on or after June 15, 2010. Earlier application is permitted.

Objectives (Ref: par. .A3)

.10 The auditor's objectives in a compliance audit are to

a. obtain sufficient appropriate audit evidence to form an opinion and report at the level specified in the governmental audit requirement on whether the entity complied in all material respects with the applicable compliance requirements; and

b. identify audit and reporting requirements specified in the governmental audit requirement that are supplementary to GAAS and *Government Auditing Standards*, if any, and perform procedures to address those requirements.

Definitions

.11 For the purpose of adapting GAAS to a compliance audit, the following terms have the meanings attributed as follows:

Applicable compliance requirements. Compliance requirements that are subject to the compliance audit.

Audit findings. The matters that are required to be reported by the auditor in accordance with the governmental audit requirement.

Audit risk of noncompliance. The risk that the auditor expresses an inappropriate audit opinion on the entity's compliance when material noncompliance exists. Audit risk of noncompliance is a function of the risks of material noncompliance and detection risk of noncompliance.

Compliance audit. A program-specific audit or an organization-wide audit of an entity's compliance with applicable compliance requirements.

Compliance requirements. Laws, regulations, rules, and provisions of contracts or grant agreements applicable to government programs with which the entity is required to comply.

Deficiency in internal control over compliance. A deficiency in internal control over compliance exists when the design or operation of a control over compliance does not allow management or employees, in the normal course of performing their assigned functions, to prevent, or detect and correct, noncompliance on a timely basis.

> A deficiency in *design* exists when a control necessary to meet the control objective is missing or an existing control is not properly designed so that, even if the control operates as designed, the control objective would not be met.
>
> A deficiency in *operation* exists when a properly designed control does not operate as designed or the person performing the control does not possess the necessary authority or competence to perform the control effectively.

Detection risk of noncompliance. The risk that the procedures performed by the auditor to reduce audit risk of noncompliance to an acceptably low level will not detect noncompliance that exists and that could be material, either individually or when aggregated with other instances of noncompliance.

Governmental audit requirement. A government requirement established by law, regulation, rule, or provision of contracts or grant agreements requiring that an entity undergo an audit of its compliance with applicable compliance requirements related to one or more government programs that the entity administers. (Ref: par. .A4)

Government Auditing Standards. Standards and guidance issued by the Comptroller General of the United States, U.S. Government Accountability Office for financial audits, attestation engagements, and performance audits. *Government Auditing Standards* also is known as generally accepted government auditing standards (GAGAS) or the Yellow Book.

Government program. The means by which governmental entities achieve their objectives. For example, one of the objectives of the U.S. Department of Agriculture is to provide nutrition to individuals in need. Examples of government programs designed to achieve that objective are the Supplemental Nutrition Assistance Program and the National School Lunch Program. Government programs that are relevant to this section are those in which a grantor or pass-through entity provides an award to another entity, usually in the form of a grant, contract, or other agreement. Not all government programs provide cash assistance; sometimes noncash assistance is provided (for example, a loan guarantee, commodities, or property).

Grantor. A government agency from which funding for the government program originates.

Known questioned costs. Questioned costs specifically identified by the auditor. Known questioned costs are a subset of likely questioned costs.

Likely questioned costs. The auditor's best estimate of total questioned costs, not just the known questioned costs. Likely questioned costs are developed by extrapolating from audit evidence obtained, for example, by projecting known questioned costs identified in an audit sample to the entire population from which the sample was drawn.

Material noncompliance. In the absence of a definition of material noncompliance in the governmental audit requirement, a failure to follow compliance requirements or a violation of prohibitions included in the applicable compliance requirements that results in noncompliance that is quantitatively or qualitatively material, either individually or when aggregated with other noncompliance, to the affected government program.

Material weakness in internal control over compliance. A deficiency, or combination of deficiencies, in internal control over compliance, such that there is a reasonable possibility that material noncompliance with a compliance requirement will not be prevented, or detected and corrected, on a timely basis. In this section, a reasonable possibility exists when the likelihood of the event is either reasonably possible or probable as defined as follows:

> **Reasonably possible.** The chance of the future event or events occurring is more than remote but less than likely.
>
> **Remote.** The chance of the future event or events occurring is slight.
>
> **Probable.** The future event or events are likely to occur.

Organization-wide audit. An audit of an entity's financial statements and an audit of its compliance with the applicable compliance requirements as they relate to one or more government programs that the entity administers.

Pass-through entity. An entity that receives an award from a grantor or other entity and distributes all or part of it to another entity to administer a government program.

Program-specific audit. An audit of an entity's compliance with applicable compliance requirements as they relate to one government program that the entity administers. The compliance audit portion of a program-specific audit is performed in conjunction with either an audit of the entity's or the program's financial statements.

Questioned costs. Costs that are questioned by the auditor because (1) of a violation or possible violation of the applicable compliance requirements, (2) the costs are not supported by adequate documentation, or (3) the incurred costs appear unreasonable and do not reflect the actions that a prudent person would take in the circumstances.

Risk of material noncompliance. The risk that material noncompliance exists prior to the audit. This consists of two components, described as follows:

> **Inherent risk of noncompliance.** The susceptibility of a compliance requirement to noncompliance that could be material, either individually or when aggregated with other instances of noncompliance, before consideration of any related controls over compliance.
>
> **Control risk of noncompliance.** The risk that noncompliance with a compliance requirement that could occur and that could be material, either individually or when aggregated with other instances of noncompliance, will not be

prevented, or detected and corrected, on a timely basis by the entity's internal control over compliance.

Significant deficiency in internal control over compliance. A deficiency, or a combination of deficiencies, in internal control over compliance that is less severe than a material weakness in internal control over compliance, yet important enough to merit attention by those charged with governance.

Requirements

Adapting and Applying the AU Sections to a Compliance Audit (Ref: par. .A5 and .A38)

.12 When performing a compliance audit, the auditor, using professional judgment, should adapt and apply the AU sections to the objectives of a compliance audit, except for the AU sections listed in the appendix of this section.

Establishing Materiality Levels (Ref: par. .A6–.A8)

.13 The auditor should establish and apply materiality levels for the compliance audit based on the governmental audit requirement.

Identifying Government Programs and Applicable Compliance Requirements (Ref: par. .A9–.A11)

.14 As discussed in paragraph .08, a compliance audit is based on the premise that management is responsible for identifying the entity's government programs and understanding and complying with the compliance requirements. The auditor should determine which of those government programs and compliance requirements to test (that is, the applicable compliance requirements) in accordance with the governmental audit requirement.

Performing Risk Assessment Procedures (Ref: par. .A12–.A15)

.15 For each of the government programs and applicable compliance requirements selected for testing, the auditor should perform risk assessment procedures to obtain a sufficient understanding of the applicable compliance requirements and the entity's internal control over compliance with the applicable compliance requirements.[1]

.16 In performing risk assessment procedures, the auditor should inquire of management about whether there are findings and recommendations in reports or other written communications resulting from previous audits, attestation engagements, and internal or external monitoring that directly relate to the objectives of the compliance audit. The auditor should gain an understanding of management's response to findings and recommendations that could have a material effect on the entity's compliance with the applicable compliance requirements (for example, taking corrective action). The auditor should use this information to assess risk and determine the nature, timing, and extent of the audit procedures for the compliance audit, including determining the extent to which testing the implementation of any corrective actions is applicable to the audit objectives.

---

[1] See paragraphs .01–.08, .10–.43, .46–.82, and .87–.101 of section 314, *Understanding the Entity and Its Environment and Assessing the Risks of Material Misstatement*.

Assessing the Risks of Material Noncompliance (Ref: par. .A16–.A18)

.17 The auditor should assess the risks of material noncompliance whether due to fraud or error for each applicable compliance requirement and should consider whether any of those risks are pervasive to the entity's compliance because they may affect the entity's compliance with many compliance requirements.[2]

Performing Further Audit Procedures in Response to Assessed Risks

.18 If the auditor identifies risks of material noncompliance that are pervasive to the entity's compliance, the auditor should develop an overall response to such risks. (Ref: par. .A19)

.19 The auditor should design and perform further audit procedures, including tests of details (which may include tests of transactions) to obtain sufficient appropriate audit evidence about the entity's compliance with each of the applicable compliance requirements in response to the assessed risks of material noncompliance. Risk assessment procedures, tests of controls, and analytical procedures alone are not sufficient to address a risk of material noncompliance. (Ref: par. .A20–.A23)

.20 The auditor should design and perform further audit procedures in response to the assessed risks of material noncompliance. These procedures should include performing tests of controls over compliance if

- the auditor's risk assessment includes an expectation of the operating effectiveness of controls over compliance related to the applicable compliance requirements;
- substantive procedures alone do not provide sufficient appropriate audit evidence; or
- such tests of controls over compliance are required by the governmental audit requirement.

If any of the conditions in this paragraph are met, the auditor should test the operating effectiveness of controls over each applicable compliance requirement to which the conditions apply in each compliance audit. (Ref: par. .A24–.A25)

Supplementary Audit Requirements

.21 The auditor should determine whether audit requirements are specified in the governmental audit requirement that are supplementary to GAAS and *Government Auditing Standards* and perform procedures to address those requirements, if any. (Ref: par. .A26)

.22 In instances where audit guidance provided by a governmental agency for the performance of compliance audits has not been updated for, or otherwise conflicts with, current GAAS or *Government Auditing Standards,* the auditor should comply with the most current applicable GAAS and *Government Auditing Standards* instead of the outdated or conflicting guidance. (Ref: par. .A27)

---

[2] See paragraphs .103–.121 of section 314.

Written Representations

.23 The auditor should request from management written representations [3] that are tailored to the entity and the governmental audit requirement: (Ref: par. .A28)

a. acknowledging management's responsibility for understanding and complying with the compliance requirements;

b. acknowledging management's responsibility for establishing and maintaining controls that provide reasonable assurance that the entity administers government programs in accordance with the compliance requirements;

c. stating that management has identified and disclosed to the auditor all of its government programs and related activities subject to the governmental audit requirement;

d. stating that management has made available to the auditor all contracts and grant agreements, including amendments, if any, and any other correspondence relevant to the programs and related activities subject to the governmental audit requirement;

e. stating that management has disclosed to the auditor all known noncompliance with the applicable compliance requirements or stating that there was no such noncompliance;

f. stating whether management believes that the entity has complied with the applicable compliance requirements (except for noncompliance it has disclosed to the auditor);

g. stating that management has made available to the auditor all documentation related to compliance with the applicable compliance requirements;

h. identifying management's interpretation of any applicable compliance requirements that are subject to varying interpretations;

i. stating that management has disclosed to the auditor any communications from grantors and pass-through entities concerning possible noncompliance with the applicable compliance requirements, including communications received from the end of the period covered by the compliance audit to the date of the auditor's report;

j. stating that management has disclosed to the auditor the findings received and related corrective actions taken for previous audits, attestation engagements, and internal or external monitoring that directly relate to the objectives of the compliance audit, including findings received and corrective actions taken from the end of the period covered by the compliance audit to the date of the auditor's report;

k. stating that management has disclosed to the auditor all known noncompliance with the applicable compliance requirements subsequent to the period covered by the auditor's report or stating that there were no such known instances; and

l. stating that management is responsible for taking corrective action on audit findings of the compliance audit.

---

[3] See section 333, *Management Representations*.

.24 If the auditor determines that it is necessary to obtain additional representations related to the entity's compliance with the applicable compliance requirements, the auditor should request such additional representations.

Subsequent Events

.25 The auditor should perform audit procedures up to the date of the auditor's report to obtain sufficient appropriate audit evidence that all subsequent events related to the entity's compliance during the period covered by the auditor's report on compliance have been identified. (Ref: par. .A29)

.26 The auditor should take into account the auditor's risk assessment in determining the nature and extent of such audit procedures, which should include, but are not limited to, inquiring of management about and considering

- relevant internal auditors' reports issued during the subsequent period.
- other auditors' reports identifying noncompliance that were issued during the subsequent period.
- reports from grantors and pass-through entities on the entity's noncompliance that were issued during the subsequent period.
- information about the entity's noncompliance obtained through other professional engagements performed for that entity.

.27 The auditor has no obligation to perform any audit procedures related to the entity's compliance during the period subsequent to the period covered by the auditor's report. However, if before the report release date, the auditor becomes aware of noncompliance in the period subsequent to the period covered by the auditor's report that is of such a nature and significance that its disclosure is needed to prevent report users from being misled, the auditor should discuss the matter with management and, if appropriate, those charged with governance, and should include an explanatory paragraph in his or her report describing the nature of the noncompliance. (Ref: par. .A30)

Evaluating the Sufficiency and Appropriateness of the Audit Evidence and Forming an Opinion (Ref: par. .A31–.A32)

.28 The auditor should evaluate the sufficiency and appropriateness of the audit evidence obtained.[4]

.29 The auditor should form an opinion, at the level specified by the governmental audit requirement, on whether the entity complied in all material respects with the applicable compliance requirements, and report appropriately. In forming an opinion, the auditor should evaluate likely questioned costs, not just known questioned costs, as well as other material noncompliance that, by its nature, may not result in questioned costs.

Reporting

Report on Compliance Only

.30 The auditor's report on compliance should include the following elements:

a. A title that includes the word *independent*

---

[4] See paragraphs .70–.76 of section 318, *Performing Audit Procedures in Response to Assessed Risks and Evaluating the Audit Evidence Obtained.*

b. Identification of the one or more government programs covered by the compliance audit or reference to a separate schedule containing that information

c. Identification of the applicable compliance requirements or a reference to where they can be found

d. Identification of the period covered by the report

e. A statement that compliance with the applicable compliance requirements is the responsibility of the entity's management

f. A statement that the auditor's responsibility is to express an opinion on the entity's compliance with the applicable compliance requirements based on the compliance audit

g. A statement that the compliance audit was conducted in accordance with auditing standards generally accepted in the United States of America, the standards applicable to financial audits contained in *Government Auditing Standards*, and the governmental audit requirement

h. A statement that the compliance audit included examining, on a test basis, evidence about the entity's compliance with those requirements and performing such other procedures as the auditor considered necessary in the circumstances

i. A statement that the auditor believes the compliance audit provides a reasonable basis for his or her opinion

j. A statement that the compliance audit does not provide a legal determination of the entity's compliance

k. The auditor's opinion, at the level specified by the governmental audit requirement, on whether the entity complied, in all material respects, with the applicable compliance requirements

l. If noncompliance that results in an opinion modification is identified, a description of such noncompliance, or a reference to a description of such noncompliance in an accompanying schedule (Ref: par. .A34)

m. If other noncompliance that is required to be reported by the governmental audit requirement is identified (that is, noncompliance that does not result in an opinion modification), a description of such noncompliance or a reference to a description of such noncompliance in an accompanying schedule (Ref: par. .A34)

n. If the criteria used to evaluate compliance are

i. established or determined by contractual agreement or regulatory provisions that are developed solely for the parties to the agreement or regulatory agency responsible for the provisions or

ii. available only to the specified parties,

a separate paragraph at the end of the report that includes (1) a statement indicating that the report is intended solely for the information and use of the specified parties (2) an identification of the specified parties to whom use is restricted, and (3) a statement that the report is not intended to be and should not be used by anyone other than the specified parties (Ref: par. .A33)

o. The manual or printed signature of the auditor's firm

p. The date of the auditor's report

Combined Report on Compliance and Internal Control Over Compliance

.31 If the governmental audit requirement requires the auditor to report on internal control over compliance and the auditor combines the auditor's report on compliance with a report on internal control over compliance, the following should be added to the report elements listed in paragraph .30:

a. A statement that management is responsible for establishing and maintaining effective internal control over compliance with the requirements of laws, regulations, rules, and provisions of contracts or grant agreements applicable to government programs.

b. A statement that in planning and performing the compliance audit, the auditor considered the entity's internal control over compliance with the applicable compliance requirements to determine the auditing procedures for the purpose of expressing an opinion on compliance, but not for the purpose of expressing an opinion on the effectiveness of internal control over compliance.

c. A statement that the auditor is not expressing an opinion on internal control over compliance.

d. A statement that the auditor's consideration of the entity's internal control over compliance was not designed to identify all deficiencies in internal control that might be significant deficiencies or material weaknesses in internal control over compliance.

e. The definition of *deficiency in internal control over compliance* and *material weakness in internal control over compliance.*

f. A description of any identified material weaknesses in internal control over compliance or a reference to an accompanying schedule containing such a description.

g. If significant deficiencies in internal control over compliance were identified, the definition of *significant deficiency in internal control over compliance* and a description of the deficiencies or a reference to an accompanying schedule containing such a description.

h. If no material weaknesses in internal control over compliance were identified, a statement to that effect.

i. The restricted use paragraph described in paragraph .30(n). The restricted use paragraph should be included in all combined reports on the entity's compliance and internal control over compliance.

A combined report on compliance and internal control over compliance is presented in the exhibit of this section.

Separate Report on Internal Control Over Compliance

.32 If the governmental audit requirement requires the auditor to report on internal control over compliance and the auditor chooses to issue a separate report on internal control over compliance, the auditor should include in that separate report the elements in paragraph .31(a)–(i) and the following additional elements:

a. A title that includes the word *independent*

b. A statement that the auditor audited the entity's compliance with applicable compliance requirements pertaining to [*identify the government program(s) and the period audited*] and a reference to the auditor's report on compliance *c.* A statement that the compliance audit was conducted in accordance with auditing standards generally accepted in the United States of America, the standards applicable to financial audits contained in *Government Auditing Standards*, and the governmental audit requirement

d. The manual or printed signature of the auditor's firm

e. The date of the auditor's report

.33 The auditor should report noncompliance as well as other matters that are required to be reported by the governmental audit requirement in the manner specified by the governmental audit requirement. If the other matters required to be reported by the governmental audit requirement are not appropriate for the auditor to report on, the auditor should follow paragraph .38. (Ref: par. .A34)

.34 The auditor should modify his or her opinion on compliance in accordance with section 508, *Reports on Audited Financial Statements*, if any of the following conditions exist:

a. The compliance audit identifies noncompliance with the applicable compliance requirements that the auditor believes has a material effect on the entity's compliance.

b. A restriction on the scope of the compliance audit.

.35 The auditor should modify the report described in paragraphs .30 and .32 when the auditor makes reference to the report of another auditor as the basis, in part, for the auditor's report.

.36 In the absence of a governmental audit requirement to report on internal control over compliance, the auditor should, nevertheless, communicate in writing to management and those charged with governance identified significant deficiencies and material weakness in internal control over compliance.[5] (Ref: par. .A35–.A36)

.37 The auditor also should communicate to those charged with governance of the entity the auditor's responsibilities under GAAS, *Government Auditing Standards*, and the governmental audit requirement, an overview of the planned scope and timing of the compliance audit, and significant findings from the compliance audit.[6]

.38 Printed forms, schedules, or reports designed or adopted by government agencies with which they are to be filed sometimes contain prescribed wording. If a printed form, schedule, or report requires the auditor to make a statement that he or she has no basis to make, the auditor should accordingly reword the form, schedule, or report or attach an appropriately worded separate report. (Ref: par. .A37)

Documentation (Ref: par. .A38)

.39 The auditor should document the risk assessment procedures performed, including those related to gaining an understanding of internal control over compliance.[7]

.40 The auditor should document his or her responses to the assessed risks of material noncompliance, the procedures performed to test compliance with

---

[5] See section 325, *Communicating Internal Control Related Matters Identified in an Audit.*

[6] See section 380, *The Auditor's Communication With Those Charged With Governance.*

[7] See paragraphs .122–.123 of section 314.

the applicable compliance requirements, and the results of those procedures, including any tests of controls over compliance.[8]

.41 The auditor should document materiality levels and the basis on which they were determined.

.42 The auditor should document how he or she complied with the specific governmental audit requirements that are supplementary to GAAS and *Government Auditing Standards*.

Reissuance of the Compliance Report (Ref: par. .A39–.A40)

.43 If an auditor reissues his or her report, the reissued report should include an explanatory paragraph stating that the report is replacing a previously issued report and describing the reasons why the report is being reissued, and any changes from the previously issued report. If additional procedures are performed to obtain sufficient appropriate audit evidence for all of the government programs being reported on, the auditor's report date should be updated to reflect the date the auditor obtained sufficient appropriate audit evidence regarding the events that caused the auditor to perform the new procedures. If, however, additional procedures are performed to obtain sufficient appropriate audit evidence for only some of the government programs being reported on, the auditor should dual date the report with the updated report date reflecting the date the auditor obtained sufficient appropriate audit evidence regarding the government programs affected by the circumstances and referencing the government programs for which additional audit procedures have been performed. Reissuance of an auditor-prepared document required by the governmental audit requirement that is incorporated by reference into the auditor's report is considered to be a reissuance of the report.

---

[8] See paragraph .77 of section 318.

Application Guidance and Explanatory Material

Introduction and Applicability

.A1 An example of an engagement to which this section is applicable is an audit performed in accordance with the provisions of Office of Management and Budget (OMB) Circular A-133, *Audits of States, Local Governments and Non-Profit Organizations*. This section is applicable because OMB Circular A-133 is a governmental audit requirement that requires the auditor to perform a compliance audit in accordance with both GAAS and *Government Auditing Standards* and to express an opinion on compliance. Another example is a department specific requirement such as the U.S. Department of Housing and Urban Development *Audit Requirements Related to Entities Such As Public Housing Agencies, Nonprofit and For-Profit Housing Projects, and Certain Lenders*. An example of an engagement to which this section is not applicable is an engagement performed to satisfy a law or regulation requiring the entity to have an auditor determine whether the entity has spent transportation excise tax monies in accordance with the specific purposes outlined in the law or regulation, but not requiring that the audit be performed in accordance with both GAAS and *Government Auditing Standards*. Such an engagement could be performed under AT section 601; AT section 101, *Attest Engagements*; or AT section 201, *Agreed-Upon Procedures Engagements*, depending on the requirements of the government. Law or regulation will not always indicate which standards to follow. In such cases, auditor judgment will be needed to determine, based on the circumstances, the appropriate standards to follow. (Ref: par. .01)

.A2 An example of a governmental audit requirement that calls for an examination of an entity's compliance with specified requirements in accordance with AT section 601 is the U.S. Department of Education's audit guide *Audits of Federal Student Financial Assistance Programs at Participating Institutions and Institution Servicers*. (Ref: par. .01 and .03)

Objectives and Definitions

.A3 Most governmental audit requirements specify that the auditor's opinion on compliance is at the program level. However, some governmental audit requirements may specify a different level (for example, at the applicable compliance requirement level). (Ref: par. .10)

.A4 Governmental audit requirements also may set forth specific supplementary requirements of the compliance audit (for example, procedures to be performed by the auditor, documentation requirements, the form of reporting, and continuing professional education requirements with which the auditor is required to comply. (Ref: par. .11, definition of *governmental audit requirement*)

Adapting and Applying the AU Sections to a Compliance Audit (Ref: par. .12)

.A5 AU sections often identify audit procedures and contain examples that are specific to a financial statement audit. The auditor is not expected to adapt or apply all such procedures to the compliance audit, only those that, in the auditor's professional judgment, are relevant and necessary to meet the objectives of the compliance audit.

Establishing Materiality Levels (Ref: par. .13)

.A6 In a compliance audit, the auditor's purpose for establishing materiality levels is to

a. determine the nature and extent of risk assessment procedures.

b. identify and assess the risks of material noncompliance.

c. determine the nature, timing, and extent of further audit procedures.

d. evaluate whether the entity complied with the applicable compliance requirements.

e. report findings of noncompliance and other matters required to be reported by the governmental audit requirement.

.A7 Generally, for all of the purposes identified in paragraph .A6, the auditor's consideration of materiality is in relation to the government program taken as a whole. However, the governmental audit requirement may specify a different level of materiality for one or more of these purposes. For example, for purposes of reporting findings of noncompliance, OMB Circular A-133 requires that noncompliance that is material in relation to one of the 14 types of compliance requirements identified in the OMB *Compliance Supplement* (*Compliance Supplement*) be reported. (See paragraph .A10 for further information about the *Compliance Supplement*.)

.A8 Because the governmental audit requirement usually is established by the grantors and the auditor's report on compliance is primarily for their use, the auditor's determination of materiality usually is influenced by the needs of the grantors. However, in a compliance audit, the auditor's judgment about matters that are material to users of the auditor's report also is based on consideration of the needs of users as a group, including grantors.

Identifying Government Programs and Applicable Compliance Requirements (Ref: par. .14)

.A9 Some governmental audit requirements specifically identify the applicable compliance requirements. Other governmental audit requirements provide a framework for the auditor to determine the applicable compliance requirements. For example, the *Compliance Supplement* provides such a framework for OMB Circular A-133 audits.

.A10 The following are some of the sources an auditor may consult when identifying and obtaining an understanding of the applicable compliance requirements:

a. The *Compliance Supplement*, which is issued by OMB, and used in OMB Circular A-133 audits, contains the compliance requirements that typically are applicable to federal government programs, as well as suggested audit procedures when compliance requirements are applicable and have a direct and material effect on the entity's compliance. Part 7 of the *Compliance Supplement* provides guidance for identifying compliance requirements for programs not included therein.

b. The applicable program-specific audit guide issued by the grantor agency, which contains the compliance requirements pertaining to the government program and suggested audit procedures to test for compliance with the applicable compliance requirements.

.A11 The following are procedures the auditor may perform to identify and obtain an understanding of the applicable compliance requirements if the *Compliance Supplement* or a program-specific audit guide is not applicable:

a. Reading laws, regulations, rules, and provisions of contracts or grant agreements that pertain to the government program

b. Making inquiries of management and other knowledgeable entity personnel (for example, the chief financial officer, internal auditors, legal counsel, compliance officers, or grant or contract administrators)

c. Making inquiries of appropriate individuals outside the entity, such as

   i. the office of the federal, state, or local program official or auditor, or other appropriate audit oversight organizations or regulators, about the laws and regulations applicable to entities within their jurisdiction, including statutes and uniform reporting requirements

   ii. a third-party specialist, such as an attorney

d. Reading the minutes of meetings of the governing board of the entity being audited

e. Reading audit documentation about the applicable compliance requirements prepared during prior years' audits or other engagements

f. Discussing the applicable compliance requirements with auditors who performed prior years' audits or other engagements

The procedures listed in this paragraph also may assist the auditor in obtaining a further understanding of the applicable compliance requirements even when the *Compliance Supplement* or program-specific audit guide is applicable.

Performing Risk Assessment Procedures (Ref: par. .15–.16)

.A12 Obtaining an understanding of the government program, the applicable compliance requirements, and the entity's internal control over compliance establishes a frame of reference within which the auditor plans the compliance audit and exercises professional judgment about assessing risks of material noncompliance and responding to those risks throughout the compliance audit.

.A13 The nature and extent of the risk assessment procedures the auditor performs may vary from entity to entity and are influenced by factors such as the following:

- The newness and complexity of the applicable compliance requirements
- The auditor's knowledge of the entity's internal control over compliance with the applicable compliance requirements obtained in previous audits or other professional engagements
- The nature of the applicable compliance requirements
- The services provided by the entity and how they are affected by external factors
- The level of oversight by the grantor or pass-through entity
- How management addresses findings

.A14 Performing risk assessment procedures to obtain an understanding of the entity's internal control over compliance includes an evaluation of the design of controls and whether the controls have been implemented. Internal control consists of the following five interrelated components: the control environment, the entity's risk assessment, information and communication systems, control activities, and monitoring.[9] Paragraphs .14, .67–.101, and appendix B of section 314, *Understanding the Entity and Its Environment and Assessing the Risks of Material Misstatement*, contain a detailed discussion of these components.

.A15 The auditor's procedures described in paragraph .16, related to understanding how management has responded to findings and recommendations that could have a material effect on the entity's compliance with the applicable compliance requirements, are performed to assist the auditor in understanding whether management responded appropriately to such findings. Examples of external monitoring include regulatory reviews, program reviews by government agencies or pass-through entities, and grantor reviews. Examples of internal monitoring include reports prepared by the internal audit function and internal quality assessments.

Assessing the Risks of Material Noncompliance (Ref: par. .17)

.A16 Factors the auditor may consider in assessing the risks of material noncompliance are as follows:

- The complexity of the applicable compliance requirements
- The susceptibility of the applicable compliance requirements to noncompliance
- The length of time the entity has been subject to the applicable compliance requirements
- The auditor's observations about how the entity has complied with the applicable compliance requirements in prior years
- The potential effect on the entity of noncompliance with the applicable compliance requirements
- The degree of judgment involved in adhering to the compliance requirements
- The auditor's assessment of the risks of material misstatement in the financial statement audit

.A17 In assessing the risks of material noncompliance, the auditor may evaluate inherent risk of noncompliance and control risk of noncompliance individually or in combination.

.A18 Examples of situations in which there may be a risk of material noncompliance that is pervasive to the entity's noncompliance are as follows:

- An entity that is experiencing financial difficulty and for which there is an increased risk that grant funds will be diverted for unauthorized purposes
- An entity that has a history of poor recordkeeping for its government programs

---

[9] See paragraph .41 of section 314.

Performing Further Audit Procedures in Response to Assessed Risks

.A19 Paragraphs .04–.06 of section 318, *Performing Audit Procedures in Response to Assessed Risks and Evaluating the Audit Evidence Obtained*, provide guidance that may be adapted when developing an overall response to the risks of material noncompliance. (Ref: par. .18)

.A20 A compliance audit includes designing procedures to detect both intentional and unintentional material noncompliance. The auditor can obtain reasonable, but not absolute, assurance about the entity's compliance because of factors such as the need for judgment, the use of sampling, the inherent limitations of internal control over compliance with applicable compliance requirements, and the fact that much of the evidence available to the auditor is persuasive rather than conclusive in nature. Also, procedures that are effective for detecting noncompliance that is unintentional may be ineffective for detecting noncompliance that is intentional and concealed through collusion between entity personnel and a third party or among management or employees of the entity. Therefore, the subsequent discovery that material noncompliance with applicable compliance requirements exists does not, in and of itself, evidence inadequate planning, performance, or judgment on the part of the auditor. (Ref: par. .19)

.A21 An auditor may decide to use audit sampling to obtain sufficient appropriate audit evidence in a compliance audit. Section 350, *Audit Sampling*, discusses the factors to be considered in planning, designing, and evaluating audit samples, including sampling for tests of controls. In addition, the AICPA Audit Guide Government Auditing Standards *and Circular A-133 Audits* contains guidance on sampling in the context of a compliance audit. (Ref: par. .19)

.A22 To test for compliance with applicable laws and regulations, tests of details (including tests of transactions) may be performed in the following areas:

- Grant disbursements or expenditures
- Eligibility files
- Cost allocation plans
- Periodic reports filed with grantor agencies (Ref: par. .19)

.A23 The use of analytical procedures to gather substantive evidence is generally less effective in a compliance audit than it is in a financial statement audit. However, substantive analytical procedures may contribute some evidence when performed in addition to tests of transactions and other auditing procedures necessary to provide the auditor with sufficient appropriate audit evidence. (Ref: par. .19)

.A24 Paragraphs .07–.39 and .46–.67 of section 318 provide guidance related to designing and performing further audit procedures in response to the assessed risks of material noncompliance. Paragraphs .40–.45 of section 318, which address the use of audit evidence about the operating effectiveness of controls obtained in prior audits, are not applicable to a compliance audit. (Ref: par. .20)

.A25 Some governmental audit requirements, for example, OMB Circular A-133, require tests of the operating effectiveness of controls identified as likely to be effective, even if the auditor believes that such testing would be inefficient. (Ref: par. .20)

Supplementary Audit Requirements

.A26 Examples of supplementary audit requirements are the requirements in OMB Circular A-133 for the auditor to

- perform specified procedures to identify major programs.
- follow up on prior audit findings and perform procedures to assess the reasonableness of the summary schedule of prior audit findings. (Ref: par. .21)

.A27 When there is conflicting guidance, the auditor may decide to consult with the government agency responsible for establishing audit guidance or that provides the funding. (Ref: par. .22)

Written Representations

.A28 In some cases, management may include qualifying language in the written representations to the effect that representations are made to the best of management's knowledge and belief. However, such qualifying language is not appropriate for the representations in paragraphs .23(a), .23(b), and .23(l). (Ref: par. .23)

Subsequent Events

.A29 Two types of subsequent events may occur. The first type consists of events that provide additional evidence with respect to conditions that existed at the end of the reporting period that affect the entity's compliance during the reporting period. The second type consists of events of noncompliance that did not exist at the end of the reporting period but arose subsequent to the reporting period. (Ref: par. .25)

.A30 An example of a matter of noncompliance that may occur subsequent to the period being audited but before the report release date that may warrant disclosure to prevent report users from being misled is the discovery of noncompliance in the subsequent period of such magnitude that it caused the grantor to stop funding the program. (Ref: par. .27)

Evaluating the Sufficiency and Appropriateness of the Audit Evidence and Forming an Opinion (Ref: par. .28–.29)

.A31 In determining whether an entity has materially complied with the applicable compliance requirements, the auditor may consider the following factors:

a. The frequency of noncompliance with the applicable compliance requirements identified during the compliance audit

b. The nature of the noncompliance with the applicable compliance requirements identified

c. The adequacy of the entity's system for monitoring compliance with the applicable compliance requirements and the possible effect of any noncompliance on the entity

d. Whether any identified noncompliance with the applicable compliance requirements resulted in likely questioned costs that are material to the government program

.A32 The auditor's evaluation of whether the entity materially complied with applicable compliance requirements includes consideration of noncompliance identified by the auditor, regardless of whether the entity corrected the noncompliance after the auditor brought it to management's attention.

Reporting

.A33 Nothing precludes the auditor from restricting the use of any report to intended users.[10] (Ref: par. .30(n))

.A34 If the report is a matter of public record or available for public inspection, removing personally identifiable information in the compliance audit report and findings of noncompliance will reduce the likelihood of sensitive information being disclosed. (Ref: par. .30(l)–(m) and .33)

.A35 When the auditor communicates significant deficiencies or material weaknesses in internal control over compliance to management and those charged with governance, *Government Auditing Standards* also requires the auditor to obtain a response from the responsible officials, preferably in writing, concerning their views on the findings, conclusions, and recommendations included in the auditor's report on internal control over compliance and include a copy of any written response in the auditor's report.[11] (Ref: par. .36)

.A36 If such a written response is included in a document containing the auditor's written communication to management and those charged with governance concerning identified significant deficiencies or material weaknesses in internal control over compliance, the auditor may add a paragraph to his or her written communication disclaiming an opinion on such information. Following is an example of such a paragraph:

> ABC Agency's written response to the significant deficiencies [*and material weaknesses*] in internal control over compliance identified in our compliance audit was not subjected to the auditing procedures applied in the compliance audit of ABC Agency's compliance and, accordingly, we express no opinion on it. (Ref: par. .36)

.A37 If the auditor is submitting a reworded form, schedule, or report or appropriately worded separate report, the auditor may include a separate communication to the agency explaining why the auditor's report was modified. (Ref: par. .38)

Documentation (Ref: par. .12 and .39–.42)

.A38 The auditor is not expected to prepare specific documentation of how the auditor adapted and applied each of the applicable AU sections to the objectives of a compliance audit. The documentation of the audit strategy, audit plan, and work performed cumulatively demonstrate whether the auditor has complied with the requirement in paragraph .12.

Reissuance of the Compliance Report (Ref: par. .43)

.A39 The following are examples of situations in which the auditor might reissue the compliance report:

---

10 Footnote 4 of section 532, *Restricting the Use of an Auditor's Report*.

11 Paragraphs 5.32–.38 of *Government Auditing Standards*.

- A quality control review performed by a governmental agency indicates that the auditor did not test an applicable compliance requirement.
- The discovery subsequent to the date of the compliance report that the entity had another government program that was required to be tested.

.A40 An example of an auditor-prepared document required by a governmental audit requirement that is incorporated by reference in the auditor's report is the schedule of findings and questioned costs in a compliance audit under OMB Circular A-133.

.A41

Appendix: AU Sections That Are Not Applicable to Compliance Audits[1]

The following sections are not applicable to a compliance audit performed under section 801 either because (*a*) they are not relevant to a compliance audit environment, (*b*) the procedures and guidance would not contribute to meeting the objectives of a compliance audit, or (*c*) the subject matter is specifically covered in section 801. However, nothing precludes an auditor from applying these sections if the auditor believes they will provide appropriate audit evidence in the specific circumstances to support the auditor's opinion on compliance.

AU Sections That Do Not Apply to Compliance Audits
Paragraph .01 of section 110, *Responsibilities and Functions of the Independent Auditor*
Standards of reporting in paragraph .02 of section 150, *Generally Accepted Auditing Standards*
Paragraphs .09, .44–.45, .83–.86, and .102 of section 314, *Understanding the Entity and Its Environment and Assessing the Risks of Material Misstatement*
Paragraphs .12–.13 and .21–.22 of section 315, *Communications Between Predecessor and Successor Auditors*
Section 317, *Illegal Acts by Clients*
Paragraphs .40–.45, .52, .68–.69, and the appendix of section 318, *Performing Audit Procedures in Response to Assessed Risks and Evaluating the Audit Evidence Obtained*
Paragraphs .22–.62 of section 324, *Service Organizations*
Paragraphs .14–.19 of section 326, *Audit Evidence*
Section 328, *Auditing Fair Value Measurements and Disclosures*
Section 330, *The Confirmation Process*
Section 331, *Inventories*
Section 332, *Auditing Derivative Instruments, Hedging Activities, and Investments in Securities*
Paragraph .12 of section 333, *Management Representations*
Section 334, *Related Parties*
Section 337, *Inquiry of a Client's Lawyer Concerning Litigation, Claims, and Assessments*
Section 341, *The Auditor's Consideration of an Entity's Ability to Continue as a Going Concern*
Section 342, *Auditing Accounting Estimates*
Section 410, *Adherence to Generally Accepted Accounting Principles*
Section 420, *Consistency of Application of Generally Accepted Accounting Principles*
Section 431, *Adequacy of Disclosure in Financial Statements*
Section 504, *Association With Financial Statements*

[1] As part of its clarity project, the Auditing Standards Board is revising Statements on Auditing Standards, which will result in conforming changes to the affected references to AU sections in this appendix.

AU Sections That Do Not Apply to Compliance Audits
Paragraphs .05, .08–.09, .11(b)–(h), .14–.18, .27–.28, .33–.34, .38, .41–.57, and .64–.76 of section 508, *Reports on Audited Financial Statements*
Section 534, *Reporting on Financial Statements Prepared for Use in Other Countries*
Paragraphs .14 and .16 of section 543, *Part of Audit Performed by Other Independent Auditors*
Section 544, *Lack of Conformity With Generally Accepted Accounting Principles*
Section 550, *Other Information in Documents Containing Audited Financial Statements*
Section 551, *Supplementary Information in Relation to the Financial Statements as a Whole*
Section 552, *Reporting on Condensed Financial Statements and Selected Financial Data*
Section 558, *Required Supplementary Information*
Section 560, *Subsequent Events*
Section 623, *Special Reports*
Section 625, *Reports on the Application of Accounting Principles*
Section 634, *Letters for Underwriters and Certain Other Requesting Parties*
Section 711, *Filings Under Federal Securities Statutes*
Section 722, *Interim Financial Information*
Section 901, *Public Warehouses—Controls and Auditing Procedures for Goods Held*

[Revised, August 2011, to reflect conforming changes necessary due to the issuance of SSAE No. 16.]

.A42

Exhibit: Illustrative Combined Report on Compliance With Applicable Requirements and Internal Control Over Compliance—*(Unqualified Opinion on Compliance; No Material Weaknesses or Significant Deficiencies in Internal Control Over Compliance Identified)*

The following is an illustrative combined report on compliance with applicable requirements and internal control over compliance that contains the elements in paragraphs .30–.31. This illustrative report contains an unqualified opinion on compliance with no material weaknesses or significant deficiencies in internal control over compliance identified. The AICPA Audit Guide Government Auditing Standards *and Circular A-133 Audits* contains illustrative language for other types of reports, including reports containing qualified or adverse opinions on compliance with either material weaknesses in internal control over compliance, significant deficiencies in internal control over compliance, or both identified.

Independent Auditor's Report

[*Addressee*]

Compliance

We have audited Example Entity's compliance with the [*identify the applicable compliance requirements or refer to the document that describes the applicable compliance requirements*] applicable to Example Entity's [*identify the government program(s) audited or refer to a separate schedule that identifies the program(s)*] for the year ended June 30, 20X1. Compliance with the requirements referred to above is the responsibility of Example Entity's management. Our responsibility is to express an opinion on Example Entity's compliance based on our audit.

We conducted our audit of compliance in accordance with auditing standards generally accepted in the United States of America; the standards applicable to financial audits contained in *Government Auditing Standards* [1] issued by the Comptroller General of the United States; and [*insert the name of the governmental audit requirement or program-specific audit guide*]. Those standards and [*insert the name of the governmental audit requirement or program-specific audit guide*] require that we plan and perform the audit to obtain reasonable assurance about whether noncompliance with the compliance requirements referred to above that could have a material effect on [*identify the government program(s) audited or refer to a separate schedule that identifies the program(s)*] occurred. An audit includes examining, on a test basis, evidence about Example Entity's compliance with those requirements and performing such other procedures as we considered necessary in the circumstances. We believe that our audit provides a reasonable basis for our opinion. Our audit does not provide a legal determination of Example Entity's compliance with those requirements.

In our opinion, Example Entity complied, in all material respects, with the compliance requirements referred to above that are applicable to [*identify the government program(s) audited*] for the year ended June 30, 20X1.

---

[1] The standards applicable to financial audits are in chapters 1–5 of *Government Auditing Standards*.

Internal Control Over Compliance

Management of Example Entity is responsible for establishing and maintaining effective internal control over compliance with the compliance requirements referred to above. In planning and performing our audit, we considered Example Entity's internal control over compliance to determine the auditing procedures for the purpose of expressing our opinion on compliance, but not for the purpose of expressing an opinion on the effectiveness of internal control over compliance. Accordingly, we do not express an opinion on the effectiveness of Example Entity's internal control over compliance.

A *deficiency in internal control over compliance* exists when the design or operation of a control does not allow management or employees, in the normal course of performing their assigned functions, to prevent, or detect and correct, noncompliance on a timely basis. A *material weakness* in internal control over compliance is a deficiency, or combination of deficiencies in internal control over compliance, such that there is a reasonable possibility that material noncompliance with a compliance requirement will not be prevented, or detected and corrected, on a timely basis.

Our consideration of internal control over compliance was for the limited purpose described in the first paragraph of this section and was not designed to identify all deficiencies in internal control that might be deficiencies, significant deficiencies, or material weaknesses in internal control over compliance. We did not identify any deficiencies in internal control over compliance that we consider to be material weaknesses, as defined above.

This report is intended solely for the information and use of management, [*identify the body or individuals charged with governance*], others within the entity, [*identify the legislative or regulatory body*], and [*identify the grantor agency(ies)*] and is not intended to be and should not be used by anyone other than these specified parties.

[*Signature*]

[*Date*]

AU Section 900

SPECIAL REPORTS OF THE COMMITTEE ON AUDITING PROCEDURE

TABLE OF CONTENTS

AU Section 901

Public Warehouses—Controls and Auditing Procedures for Goods Held *

Source: SAS No. 1, section 901; SAS No. 43.

Issue date, unless otherwise indicated: November, 1972.

Introduction

.01 This section discusses controls of a public warehouse, the procedures of its independent auditor with respect to goods in the warehouse's custody, and auditing procedures performed by the independent auditor of the owner of goods in the warehouse.[1] [As amended, effective after August 31, 1982, by Statement on Auditing Standards No. 43.]

General Considerations

.02 The management of a business has the responsibility for the proper recording of transactions in its books of account, for the safeguarding of its assets, and for the substantial accuracy and adequacy of its financial statements. The independent auditor is not an insurer or guarantor; his responsibility is to express a professional opinion on the financial statements he has audited.[2] [Paragraph renumbered by the issuance of Statement on Auditing Standards No. 43, August 1982.]

Summary of Recommendations

.03 The Committee recommends that the independent auditor of the warehouseman:

a. Obtain an understanding of controls, relating to the accountability for and the custody of all goods placed in the warehouse and perform tests of controls to evaluate their effectiveness.

b. Test the warehouseman's records relating to accountability for all goods placed in his custody.

c. Test the warehouseman's accountability under recorded outstanding warehouse receipts.

d. Observe physical counts of the goods in custody, wherever practicable and reasonable, and reconcile his tests of such counts with records of goods stored.

---

* Title revised, February 1997, to reflect conforming changes necessary due to the issuance of Statement on Auditing Standards No. 78.

[1] This section reports the conclusions of a 1966 study of the AICPA Committee on Auditing Procedure on the accountability of warehousemen for goods stored in public warehouses. [Footnote renumbered by the issuance of Statement on Auditing Standards No. 43, August 1982.]

[2] See section 110.

e. Confirm accountability (to the extent considered necessary) by direct communication with the holders of warehouse receipts.

The independent auditor should apply such other procedures as he considers necessary in the circumstances. [Paragraph renumbered by the issuance of Statement on Auditing Standards No. 43, August 1982. Paragraph subsequently renumbered by the issuance of Statement on Auditing Standards No. 48, July 1984.]

.04 Warehousing activities are diverse because the warehoused goods are diverse, the purposes of placing goods in custody are varied, and the scope of operations of warehouses is not uniform. The independent auditor has the responsibility to exercise his judgment in determining what procedures, including those recommended in this report, are necessary in the circumstances to afford a reasonable basis for his opinion on the financial statements.[3] [Paragraph renumbered by the issuance of Statement on Auditing Standards No. 43, August 1982.]

.05 The following sections of this report describe those aspects of warehousing operations of primary concern to independent auditors, suggest elements of internal control for warehousemen, and offer the Committee's recommendations as to procedures of the independent auditor. [Paragraph renumbered by the issuance of Statement on Auditing Standards No. 43, August 1982.]

Public Warehouse Operations

Types of Warehouses

.06 A warehouse may be described as a facility operated by a warehouseman whose business is the maintaining of effective custody of goods for others. [Paragraph renumbered by the issuance of Statement on Auditing Standards No. 43, August 1982.]

.07 Warehouses may be classified functionally as terminal warehouses or field warehouses:

Terminal Warehouse. The principal economic function of a terminal warehouse is to furnish storage. It may, however, perform other functions, including packaging and billing. It may be used to store a wide variety of goods or only a particular type of commodity.

Field Warehouse. A field warehouse is established in space leased by the warehouseman on the premises of the owner of the goods or the premises of a customer of the owner. In most circumstances all or most of the personnel at the warehouse location are employed by the warehouseman from among the employees of the owner (or customer), usually from among those who previously have been responsible for custody and handling of the goods. Field warehousing is essentially a financing arrangement, rather than a storage operation. The warehouse is established to permit the warehouseman to take and maintain custody of goods and issue warehouse receipts to be used as collateral for a loan or other form of credit.

Warehouses may be classified also by types of goods stored. Foods and other perishable products may be stored in refrigerated warehouses, constructed and equipped to meet controlled temperature and special handling requirements. Certain bulk commodities, such as various agricultural products and chemicals,

---

[3] See section 326.

are stored in commodity warehouses; these warehouses often are designed and equipped to store only one commodity, and fungible goods frequently are commingled without regard to ownership. A wide variety of goods, usually not requiring special storage facilities, is stored in general merchandise warehouses. Some warehouses confine their activities to storing furniture, other household goods, and personal effects. [Paragraph renumbered by the issuance of Statement on Auditing Standards No. 43, August 1982.]

Warehouse Receipts

.08 A basic document in warehousing is the warehouse receipt. Article 7 of the Uniform Commercial Code regulates the issuance of warehouse receipts, prescribes certain terms that must be contained in such receipts, provides for their negotiation and transfer, and establishes the rights of receipt holders. [Paragraph renumbered by the issuance of Statement on Auditing Standards No. 43, August 1982.]

.09 Warehouse receipts may be in negotiable form or non-negotiable form and may be used as evidence of collateral for loans or other forms of credit. Goods represented by a negotiable warehouse receipt may be released only upon surrender of the receipt to the warehouseman for cancellation or endorsement, whereas goods represented by a non-negotiable receipt may be released upon valid instructions without the need for surrender of the receipt. Other important ways in which the two kinds of receipts differ concern the manner in which the right of possession to the goods they represent may be transferred from one party to another and the rights acquired by bona fide purchasers of the receipts. [Paragraph renumbered by the issuance of Statement on Auditing Standards No. 43, August 1982.]

.10 Since goods covered by non-negotiable receipts may be released without surrender of the receipts, such outstanding receipts are not necessarily an indication of accountability on the part of the warehouseman or of evidence of ownership by the depositor. Since goods are frequently withdrawn piecemeal, the warehouseman's accountability at any given time is for the quantity of goods for which receipts have been issued minus the quantities released against properly authorized withdrawals. [Paragraph renumbered by the issuance of Statement on Auditing Standards No. 43, August 1982.]

.11 Article 7 of the Uniform Commercial Code, in addition to provisions with respect to the issuance and contents of warehouse receipts, contains provisions with respect to, among other things, the storage and release of warehoused goods, the standard of care to be exercised by the warehouseman, warehouseman's liability, and liens for the warehouseman's charges and expenses and the manner in which they may be enforced. [Paragraph renumbered by the issuance of Statement on Auditing Standards No. 43, August 1982.]

Government Regulation

.12 There are various other statutes and regulations, applicable in special situations, relating to the rights and duties of warehousemen and the operation of warehouses. Among the more important are (*a*) the United States Warehouse Act and the regulations adopted thereunder by the Department of Agriculture, providing for licensing and regulation of warehouses storing certain agricultural commodities, (*b*) the regulations adopted by commodity exchanges licensed under the United States Commodity Exchange Act, providing for issuance and registration of receipts and licensing and regulation of warehouses, and (*c*) the Internal Revenue Code and the Tariff Act of 1930, and regulations adopted thereunder, relating respectively to United States Revenue Bonded Warehouses and United States Customs Bonded Warehouses, providing for licensing, bonding, and regulation of such warehouses. In addition, there are statutes and regulations in various states relating to licensing, bonding, insurance, and other matters. [Paragraph renumbered by the issuance of Statement on Auditing Standards No. 43, August 1982.]

The Warehouseman

Controls

.13 Goods held in custody for others are not owned by the warehouseman and, therefore, do not appear as assets in his financial statements. Similarly, the related custodial responsibility does not appear as a liability. However, as in other businesses, the warehouseman is exposed to the risk of loss or claims for damage stemming from faulty performance of his operating functions. Faulty performance may take the form of loss or improper release of goods, improper issuance of warehouse receipts, failure to maintain effective custody of goods so that lenders' preferential liens are lost, and other forms. [Paragraph renumbered by the issuance of Statement on Auditing Standards No. 43, August 1982.]

.14 The recommendation herein that the independent auditor of the warehouseman obtain an understanding of relevant controls and perform tests of controls to evaluate their effectiveness is based upon the important relationship of such controls to the custodial responsibilities of the warehouseman, which are not reflected in his financial statements. Significant unrecorded liabilities may arise if these custodial responsibilities are not discharged properly. [Paragraph renumbered by the issuance of Statement on Auditing Standards No. 43, August 1982. Revised, April 1989, to reflect conforming changes necessary due to the issuance of Statement on Auditing Standards Nos. 53 through 62.]

.15 Whether and to what extent the suggested controls that follow may be applicable to a particular warehouse operation will depend on the nature of the operation, of the goods stored, and of the warehouseman's organization. Appropriate segregation of duties in the performance of the respective operating functions should be emphasized.

Receiving, Storing, and Delivering Goods

Receipts should be issued for all goods admitted into storage.

Receiving clerks should prepare reports as to all goods received. The receiving report should be compared with quantities shown on bills of lading or other documents received from the owner or other outside sources by an employee independent of receiving, storing, and shipping.

Goods received should be inspected, counted, weighed, measured, or graded in accordance with applicable requirements. There should be a periodic check of the accuracy of any mechanical facilities used for these purposes.

Unless commingling is unavoidable, such as with fungible goods, goods should be stored so that each lot is segregated and identified with the pertinent warehouse receipt. The warehouse office records should show the location of the goods represented by each outstanding receipt.

Instructions should be issued that goods may be released only on proper authorization which, in the case of negotiable receipts, includes surrender of the receipt.

Access to the storage area should be limited to those employees whose duties require it, and the custody of keys should be controlled.

Periodic statements to customers should identify the goods held and request that discrepancies be reported to a specified employee who is not connected with receiving, storing, and delivery of goods.

The stored goods should be physically counted or tested periodically, and quantities agreed to the records by an employee independent of the storage function; the extent to which this is done may depend on the nature of the goods, the rate of turnover, and the effectiveness of other internal control structure policies and procedures.

Where the goods held are perishable, a regular schedule for inspection of condition should be established.

Protective devices such as burglar alarms, fire alarms, sprinkler systems, and temperature and humidity controls should be inspected regularly.

Goods should be released from the warehouse only on the basis of written instructions received from an authorized employee who does not have access to the goods.

Counts of goods released as made by stock clerks should be independently checked by shipping clerks or others and the two counts should be compared before the goods are released.

Warehouse Receipts

Prenumbered receipt forms should be used, and procedures established for accounting for all forms used and for cancellation of negotiable receipts when goods have been delivered.

Unused forms should be safeguarded against theft or misuse and their custody assigned to a responsible employee who is not authorized to prepare or sign receipts.

Receipt forms should be furnished only to authorized persons, and in a quantity limited to the number required for current use.

The signer of receipts should ascertain that the receipts are supported by receiving records or other underlying documents.

Receipts should be prepared and completed in a manner designed to prevent alteration.

Authorized signers should be a limited number of responsible employees.

Insurance

The adequacy, as to both type and amount, of insurance coverage carried by the warehouseman should be reviewed at appropriate intervals.

[Paragraph renumbered by the issuance of Statement on Auditing Standards No. 43, August 1982.]

Additional Controls for Field Warehouses

.16 As indicated earlier, the purpose of field warehousing differs from terminal warehousing. Operating requirements also may differ because a field warehouseman may operate at a large number of locations. [Paragraph renumbered by the issuance of Statement on Auditing Standards No. 43, August 1982.]

.17 In field warehousing, controls are applied at two points: the field location and the warehouseman's central office. At the field location, the controls as to receipt, storage, and delivery of goods and issuance of warehouse receipts generally will comprise the controls suggested above, with such variations as may be appropriate in light of the requirements, and available personnel, at the respective locations. Only non-negotiable warehouse receipts should be issued from field locations, and the receipt forms should be furnished to the field locations by the central office in quantities limited to current requirements. [Paragraph renumbered by the issuance of Statement on Auditing Standards No. 43, August 1982.]

.18 The central office should investigate and approve the field warehousing arrangements, and exercise control as to custody and release of goods and issuance of receipts at the field locations. Controls suggested for the central office are the following:

Consideration of the business reputation and financial standing of the depositor.

Preparation of a field warehouse contract in accordance with the particular requirements of the depositor and the lender.

Determination that the leased warehouse premises meet the physical requirements for segregation and effective custody of goods.

Satisfaction as to legal matters relative to the lease of the warehouse premises.

Investigation and bonding of the employees at the field locations.

Providing employees at field locations with written instructions covering their duties and responsibilities.

Maintenance of inventory records at the central office showing the quantity (and stated value, where applicable) of goods represented by each outstanding warehouse receipt.

Examination of the field warehouse by representatives of the central office. These examinations would include inspection of the facilities, observation as to adherence to prescribed procedures, physical counts or tests of goods in custody and reconcilement of quantities to records at the central office and at field locations, accounting for all receipt forms furnished to the field locations, and confirmation (on a test basis, where appropriate) of outstanding warehouse receipts with the registered holders.

[Paragraph renumbered by the issuance of Statement on Auditing Standards No. 43, August 1982.]

Procedures of the Independent Auditor

.19 The Committee recommends that the independent auditor of the warehouseman:

a. Obtain an understanding of controls, relating to the accountability for and the custody of all goods placed in the warehouse and perform tests of controls to evaluate their effectiveness.

b. Test the warehouseman's records relating to accountability for all goods placed in his custody.

c. Test the warehouseman's accountability under recorded outstanding warehouse receipts.

d. Observe physical counts of the goods in custody, wherever practicable and reasonable, and reconcile his tests of such counts with records of goods stored.

e. Confirm accountability (to the extent considered necessary) by direct communication with the holders of warehouse receipts.

The independent auditor should apply such other procedures as he considers necessary in the circumstances. [Paragraph renumbered by the issuance of Statement on Auditing Standards No. 43, August 1982.]

.20 The auditor's procedures relating to accountability might include, on a test basis, comparison of documentary evidence of goods received and delivered with warehouse receipts records, accounting for issued and unissued warehouse receipts by number, and comparison of the records of goods stored with billings for storage. In some circumstances, the auditor may consider it necessary to obtain confirmation from the printer as to the serial numbers of receipt forms supplied. [Paragraph renumbered by the issuance of Statement on Auditing Standards No. 43, August 1982.]

.21 In the case of a field warehouseman where goods are stored at many scattered locations, the independent auditor may satisfy himself that the warehouseman's physical count procedures are adequate by observing the procedures at certain selected locations. The amount of testing required will be dependent upon the effectiveness of both design and operation of controls. [Paragraph renumbered by the issuance of Statement on Auditing Standards No. 43, August 1982.]

.22 The confirmation of negotiable receipts with holders may be impracticable, since the identity of the holders usually is not known to the warehouseman. Confirmation with the depositor to whom the outstanding receipt was originally issued, however, would be audit evidence of the accountability for certain designated goods. It should be recognized, too, that as to both negotiable and non-negotiable receipts, confirmation may not be conclusive in the light of the possibility of issued but unrecorded receipts. In some circumstances, it may be desirable to request confirmations from former depositors who are not currently holders of record. [Paragraph renumbered by the issuance of Statement on Auditing Standards No. 43, August 1982.]

.23 The independent auditor should review the nature and extent of the warehouseman's insurance coverage and the adequacy of any reserves for losses under damage claims. [Paragraph renumbered by the issuance of Statement on Auditing Standards No. 43, August 1982.]

Controls and Auditing Procedures for Owner's Goods Stored in Public Warehouses

.24 The following paragraphs provide guidance on the controls for the owner of the goods and on the auditing procedures to be employed by his independent auditor. [As amended, effective after August 31, 1982, by Statement on Auditing Standards No. 43.]

Controls

.25 The controls of the owner should be designed to provide reasonable safeguards over his goods in a warehouseman's custody. Ordinarily, the controls should include an investigation of the warehouseman before the goods are placed in custody, and a continuing evaluation of the warehouseman's performance in maintaining custody of the goods. [Paragraph renumbered by the issuance of Statement on Auditing Standards No. 43, August 1982.]

.26 Among the suggested controls that may be comprehended in an investigation of the warehouseman before the goods are placed in his custody are the following:

Consideration of the business reputation and financial standing of the warehouseman.

Inspection of the physical facilities.

Inquiries as to the warehouseman's controls and whether the warehouseman holds goods for his own account.

Inquiries as to type and adequacy of the warehouseman's insurance.

Inquiries as to government or other licensing and bonding requirements and the nature, extent, and results of any inspection by government or other agencies.

Review of the warehouseman's financial statements and related reports of independent auditors.

[Paragraph renumbered by the issuance of Statement on Auditing Standards No. 43, August 1982.]

.27 After the goods are placed in the warehouse, suggested controls that may be applied periodically by the owner in evaluating the warehouseman's performance in maintaining custody of goods include the following:

Review and update the information developed from the investigation described above.

Physical counts (or test counts) of the goods, wherever practicable and reasonable (may not be practicable in the case of fungible goods).

Reconcilement of quantities shown on statements received from the warehouseman with the owner's records.

In addition, he should review his own insurance, if any, on goods in the custody of the warehouseman.

[Paragraph renumbered by the issuance of Statement on Auditing Standards No. 43, August 1982.]

Procedures of the Independent Auditor

.28 Section 331.14 describes the procedures that the auditor should apply if inventories are held in public warehouses. [As amended, effective after August 31, 1982, by Statement on Auditing Standards No. 43.]

AU APPENDIXES

TABLE OF CONTENTS

AU Appendix A
Historical Background

In 1917, the American Institute of Certified Public Accountants, then known as the American Institute of Accountants, at the request of the Federal Trade Commission, prepared "a memorandum on balance-sheet audits," which the Federal Trade Commission approved and transmitted to the Federal Reserve Board.

The Federal Reserve Board, after giving the memorandum its provisional endorsement, published it in the *Federal Reserve Bulletin* of April 1917; reprints were widely disseminated for the consideration of "banks, bankers, banking associations; merchants, manufacturers, and associations of manufacturers; auditors, accountants, and associations of accountants" in pamphlet form with the title of "Uniform Accounting: a Tentative Proposal Submitted by the Federal Reserve Board."

In 1918, it was reissued under the same sponsorship, with a new title "Approved Methods for the Preparation of Balance-Sheet Statements." There was practically no change from 1917 except that, as indicated by the respective titles and corresponding change in the preface, instead of the objective of "a uniform system of accounting to be adopted by manufacturing and merchandising concerns," the new objective was "the preparation of balance-sheet statements" for the same businesses.

In 1929, a special committee of the Institute undertook revision of the earlier pamphlet in the light of the experience of the past decade; again under the auspices of the Federal Reserve Board, the revised pamphlet was issued in 1929 as "Verification of Financial Statements."

The preface of the 1929 pamphlet spoke of its predecessors as having been criticized, on the one hand, by some accountants for being "more comprehensive than their conception of the so-called balance-sheet audit," and, on the other hand, by other accountants because "the procedure would not bring out all the desired information." This recognition of opposing views evidenced the growing realization of the impracticability of uniform procedures to fit the variety of situations encountered in practice. Of significance is the appearance in the opening paragraph of "General Instructions" in the 1929 publication of the statement:

> The extent of the verification will be determined by the conditions in each concern. In some cases, the auditor may find it necessary to verify a substantial portion or all of the transactions recorded upon the books. In others, where the system of internal check is good, tests only may suffice. The responsibility for the extent of the work required must be assumed by the auditor.

Between 1932 and 1934, there was correspondence, dealing with both accounting and auditing matters, between the Institute's special committee on cooperation with stock exchanges and the committee on stock list of the New York Stock Exchange. The views expressed were an important development in the recognition of the position of accountancy in finance and business. The series of letters was published in 1934 under the title *Audits of Corporate Accounts*.

In 1936, a committee of the Institute prepared and published a further revision of the earlier pamphlets under the title of "Examination of Financial Statements by Independent Public Accountants." The Institute availed itself of the views of persons outside the ranks of the profession whose opinions would be helpful, but the authority behind and responsibility for the publication of the pamphlet rested wholly with the Institute as the authoritative representative of a profession that had by that time become well established in the business community.

In the 1936 revision, aside from the very briefly noted "Modifications of Program for Larger or Smaller Companies," the detailed procedures were restrictively stated to be an "outline of examination of financial statements of a small or moderate size company." Moreover, the nature and extent of such examinations were based on the purpose of the examination, the required detail to be reported on, the type of business, and, most important of all, the system of internal control; variations in the extent of the examination were specifically related to "the size of the organization and the personnel employed" and were said to be "essentially a matter of judgment which must be exercised by the accountant."

It is possible from the foregoing narrative to trace the development of the profession's view of an audit based on the experience of three decades. The succession of titles is illustrative. The earliest ambition for "uniform accounting" was quickly realized to be unattainable, and the same listed procedures were related instead to "balance-sheet statements." Then, with the gradually greater emphasis on periodic earnings, the earlier restrictive consideration of the balance sheet was superseded in the 1929 title, "Verification of Financial Statements," by according the income statement at least equal status. When in turn the 1936 revision was undertaken, there was a growing realization that, with the complexity of modern business and the need of the independent auditor to rely on testing, such a word as "verification" was not an accurate portrayal of the independent auditor's function. Accordingly, the bulletin of that year was stated to cover an "examination" of financial statements.

Statements on Auditing Procedure

The Committee on Auditing Procedure had its beginning on January 30, 1939, when the executive committee of the Institute authorized the appointment of a small committee "to examine into auditing procedure and other related questions in the light of recent public discussion."

On May 9 of that year, the report "Extensions of Auditing Procedure" of this special committee was adopted by the Council of the Institute and authority given for its publication and distribution, and in the same year the bylaws were amended to create a standing Committee on Auditing Procedure.

In 1941, the executive committee authorized the issuance to Institute members, in pamphlet form, of the Statements on Auditing Procedure, prepared by the Committee on Auditing Procedure, previously published only in *The Journal of Accountancy*.

The Statements on Auditing Procedure were designed to guide the independent auditor in the exercise of his judgment in the application of auditing procedures. In no sense were they intended to take the place of auditing textbooks; by their very nature textbooks must deal in a general way with the description of procedures and refinement of detail rather than the variety of circumstances encountered in practice that require the independent auditor to exercise his judgment.

Largely to meet this need, the Institute began the series of Statements on Auditing Procedure. The first of these presented the report of the original special committee, as modified and approved, at the Institute's annual meeting on September 19, 1939, and issued under the title of "Extensions of Auditing Procedure."

Statement No. 1 presented conclusions drawn from the experience and tradition of the profession which largely furnished the foundation for the Committee's present structural outline of auditing standards; the other Statements on Auditing Procedure appropriately fit into that structural outline.

The "Codification of Statements on Auditing Procedure" was issued by the Committee on Auditing Procedure in 1951 to consolidate the features of the first 24 pronouncements, which were of continuing usefulness.

When the Securities and Exchange Commission (SEC) adopted the requirement that a representation on compliance with generally accepted auditing standards be included in the independent auditor's report on financial statements filed with the SEC, it became apparent that a pronouncement was needed to define these standards. Accordingly, the Committee on Auditing Procedure undertook a special study of auditing standards (as distinguished from auditing procedures) and submitted a report that was published in October 1947 under the title "Tentative Statement of Auditing Standards—Their Generally Accepted Significance and Scope." The recommendations of this brochure ceased to be tentative when, at the September 1948 meeting, the membership of the Institute approved the summarized statement of auditing standards.

In 1954 the tentative brochure was replaced by the booklet *Generally Accepted Auditing Standards—Their Significance and Scope*, which was issued as a special report of the Committee on Auditing Procedure. This pronouncement also gave recognition to the approval of Statement on Auditing Procedure No. 23 (Revised), *Clarification of Accountant's Report When Opinion Is Omitted* (1949) and the issuance of the codification (1951).

Statement on Auditing Procedure No. 33 was issued in 1963 as a consolidation of, and a replacement for, the following pronouncements of the Committee on Auditing Procedure: *Internal Control* (1949), *Generally Accepted Auditing Standards* (1954), *Codification of Statements on Auditing Procedure* (1951), and Statements on Auditing Procedure Nos. 25–32, which were issued between 1951 and 1963. Statement No. 33 was a codification of earlier committee pronouncements that the committee believed to be of continuing interest to the independent auditor.

Statements on Auditing Standards

After issuance of Statement on Auditing Procedure No. 33, 21 additional Statements on Auditing Procedure, Nos. 34–54, were issued by the Committee on Auditing Procedure. In November 1972, these pronouncements were codified in Statement on Auditing Standards (SAS) No. 1, *Codification of Auditing Standards and Procedures*. Also, in 1972, the name of the committee was changed to the Auditing Standards Executive Committee to recognize its role as the AICPA's senior technical committee charged with interpreting generally accepted auditing standards.

The Auditing Standards Executive Committee issued 22 additional statements through No. 23. These statements were incorporated in this publication, which provides a continuous codification of SASs.

Creation of the Auditing Standards Board

As a result of the recommendations of the Commission on Auditors' Responsibilities, an independent study group appointed by the AICPA, a special committee was formed to study the structure of the AICPA's auditing standard-setting activity. In May 1978, the AICPA Council adopted the recommendations of that committee to restructure the Committee. Accordingly, in October 1978 the Auditing Standards Board (ASB) was formed as the successor to prior senior technical committees on auditing matters. The ASB was given the following charge:

> The AICPA Auditing Standards Board shall be responsible for the promulgation of auditing standards and procedures to be observed by members of the AICPA in accordance with the Institute's rules of conduct.
>
> The board shall be alert to new opportunities for auditors to serve the public, both by the assumption of new responsibilities and by improved ways of meeting old ones, and shall as expeditiously as possible develop standards and procedures that will enable the auditor to assume those responsibilities.
>
> Auditing standards and procedures promulgated by the board shall—
>
> *a.* Define the nature and extent of the auditor's responsibilities.
>
> *b.* Provide guidance to the auditor in carrying out his duties, enabling him to express an opinion on the reliability of the representations on which he is reporting.
>
> *c.* Make special provision, where appropriate, to meet the needs of small enterprises.
>
> *d.* Have regard to the costs which they impose on society in relation to the benefits reasonably expected to be derived from the audit function.
>
> The Auditing Standards Board shall provide auditors with all possible guidance in the implementation of its pronouncements, by means of interpretations of its statements, by the issuance of guidelines, and by any other means available to it.

Changes Created by Sarbanes-Oxley Act of 2002

AICPA members who perform auditing and other related professional services have been required to comply with SASs promulgated by the AICPA ASB. These standards constitute what is known as generally accepted auditing standards (GAAS). Prior to Sarbanes-Oxley, the ASB's auditing standards have applied to audits of all entities. However, as a result of the passage of the Sarbanes-Oxley Act of 2002, auditing rules and related professional practice standards to be used in the performance of and reporting on audits of the financial statements of public companies (or issuers) are to be established by the Public Company Accounting Oversight Board (PCAOB). Accordingly, public accounting firms auditing issuers are now required to be registered with the PCAOB and to adhere to all PCAOB rules and standards in those audits. In 2003, the PCAOB adopted the then-existing Audit and Attest Standards as its interim auditing standards.

The preparation and issuance of audit reports for those entities not subject to the Sarbanes-Oxley Act or the rules of the SEC (hereinafter referred to as nonissuers) continue to be governed by GAAS promulgated by the ASB.

The Reconstituted ASB

In February 2004, the AICPA's Board of Directors unanimously recommended that the AICPA's Governing Council take the following action at its meeting in May 2004:

- Designate the PCAOB as a body with the authority to promulgate auditing and related attestation standards, quality control, ethics, independence, and other standards relating to the preparation and issuance of audit reports for issuers.

- Amend the ASB's current designation to recognize the ASB as a body with the authority to promulgate auditing, attestation, and quality control standards relating to the preparation and issuance of audit reports for non-issuers only.

As a result of this action, the ASB was reconstituted and its jurisdiction amended by AICPA Council to recognize the ASB as a body with the authority to promulgate auditing, attestation and quality control standards relating to the preparation and issuance of audit and attestation reports for nonissuers.

U.S. Auditing Standards—AICPA (Clarified)

In October 2011, the ASB issued SAS No. 122, *Statements on Auditing Standards: Clarification and Recodification*, which was the culmination of a multi-year Clarity Project to clarify the SASs and converge them with the International Standards on Auditing. Beginning with SAS No. 122, all new SASs are now included in the section *U.S. Auditing Standards—AICPA (Clarified)*. SAS No. 122 is effective for audits of financial statements for periods ending on or after December 15, 2012. Refer to individual AU-C sections for specific effective date language.

The AU-C foreword discusses SAS No. 122 and the Clarity Project.

AU Appendix B

[*Reserved.*]

AU Appendix C

[*Reserved.*]

AU Appendix D

AICPA Audit and Accounting Guides and Statements of Position

Audit and Accounting Guides

Airlines

Analytical Procedures

Assessing and Responding to Audit Risk in a Financial Statement Audit

Audit Sampling

Auditing Derivative Instruments, Hedging Activities, and Investments in Securities

Auditing Revenue in Certain Industries

Brokers and Dealers in Securities

Compilation and Review Engagements

Construction Contractors

Depository and Lending Institutions: Banks and Savings Institutions, Credit Unions, Finance Companies and Mortgage Companies

Employee Benefit Plans

Entities With Oil and Gas Producing Activities

Gaming

Government Auditing Standards *and Circular A-133 Audits*

Health Care Entities

Investment Companies

Life and Health Insurance Entities

Not-for-Profit Entities

Property and Liability Insurance Entities

Prospective Financial Information

Reporting on Controls at a Service Organization Relevant to Security, Availability, Processing Integrity, Confidentiality, or Privacy (SOC 2)

Service Organizations: Applying SSAE No. 16, Reporting on Controls at a Service Organization *(SOC 1)*

State and Local Governments

Statements of Position—Auditing and Attestation

Auditing Property / Casualty Insurance Entities' Statutory Financial Statements— Applying Certain Requirements of the NAIC Annual Statement Instructions	*10/92*
Guidance to Practitioners in Conducting and Reporting on an Agreed-Upon Procedures Engagement to Assist Management in Evaluating the Effectiveness of Its Corporate Compliance Program	*5/99*
Auditing Health Care Third-Party Revenues and Related Receivables	*3/00*

(continued)

Statements of Position—Auditing and Attestation—continued

Performing Agreed-Upon Procedures Engagements That Address Internal Control Over Derivative Transactions as Required by the New York State Insurance Law	*6/01*
Performing Agreed-Upon Procedures Engagements That Address Annual Claims Prompt Payment Reports as Required by the New Jersey Administrative Code	*5/02*
Attest Engagements on Greenhouse Gas Emissions Information	*9/03*
Auditing the Statement of Social Insurance	*11/04*
Reporting Pursuant to the Global Investment Performance Standards	*04/06*
Attestation Engagements That Address Specified Compliance Control Objectives and Related Controls at Entities That Provide Services to Investment Companies, Investment Advisers, or Other Service Providers	*10/07*
Performing Agreed-Upon Procedures Engagements That Address the Completeness, Accuracy, or Consistency of XBRL-Tagged Data	*4/09*

AU Appendix E

Schedule of Changes in Statements on Auditing Standards

Section	*Paragraph*	*Changes*	*Date of Change*
110	.02	New paragraph added by issuance of Statement on Auditing Standards (SAS) No. 82	January 1998
110	.03	Amended by SAS No. 78	February 1997
110	.06–.09	Superseded by SAS No. 16	January 1977
150		Superseded by SAS No. 95	December 2001
150	.02	Amended by SAS No. 105	March 2006
150	.02	Amended by SAS No. 113	November 2006
150	.04	Amended by SAS No. 102	December 2005
150	.04	Amended by SAS No. 113	November 2006
150	.05	Amended by SAS No. 98	September 2002
160	.25	Superseded by SAS No. 25	November 1979
161		Headnote amended by SAS No. 98	September 2002
161	.02	Amended by SAS No. 98	September 2002
161	.03	Amended by SAS No. 98	September 2002
210	.05	Amended by SAS No. 5	July 1975
230		Title amended by SAS No. 82	February 1997
230	.01–.03	Amended by SAS No. 82	January 1998
230	.04	Amended by SAS No. 41	April 1982
230	.04	Amended by SAS No. 82	January 1998
230	.05–.10	New paragraphs added by issuance of SAS No. 82	January 1998
230	.10	Amended by SAS No. 104	March 2006
230	.11–.12	New paragraphs added by issuance of SAS No. 82	January 1998
230	.12	Amended by SAS No. 99	October 2002
230	.13	New paragraph added by issuance of SAS No. 82	January 1998
310		Superseded by SAS No. 108	March 2006
310		Deleted by SAS No. 108	January 2008
311		Superseded by SAS No. 108	March 2006
311	.25	Amended by SAS No. 114	December 2006
312		Superseded by SAS No. 107	March 2006
313		Superseded by SAS No. 110	March 2006
313		Deleted by SAS No. 110	January 2008
315		Superseded by SAS No. 84	October 1997
315	.02	Amended by SAS No. 93	October 2000
315	.12	Amended by SAS No. 93	October 2000
316		Superseded by SAS No. 99	October 2002
316	.35	Amended by SAS No. 113	November 2006
316	.46	Amended by SAS No. 113	November 2006
318		Superseded by SAS No. 56	April 1988

(continued)

Section	*Paragraph*	*Changes*	*Date of Change*
319		Superseded by SAS No. 109 and SAS No. 110	March 2006
319		Deleted by SAS Nos. 109 and 110	January 2008
320		Superseded by SAS No. 55	April 1988
320A		Superseded by SAS No. 39	June 1981
320B		Superseded by SAS No. 39	June 1981
321		Superseded by SAS No. 48	July 1984
322		Superseded by SAS No. 65	April 1991
323		Superseded by SAS No. 60	April 1988
324		Superseded by SAS No. 70	May 1992
324		Title amended by SAS No. 88	December 1999
324	.03	Amended by SAS No. 88	December 1999
324	.06	Amended by SAS No. 88	December 1999
324	.07	Amended by SAS No. 78	February 1997
324	.07	Amended by SAS No. 88	December 1999
324	.08	Deleted by SAS No. 88	December 1999
324	.09–.10	Amended by SAS No. 88	December 1999
324	.26	Amended by SAS No. 78	February 1997
324	.42	Amended by SAS No. 78	February 1997
324	.57–.60	New paragraphs added by issuance of SAS No. 98	September 2002
324	.61	Amended by SAS No. 98	September 2002
325		Superseded by SAS No. 115	September 2008
326		Superseded by SAS No. 106	March 2006
327		Superseded by SAS No. 53	April 1988
328		Superseded by SAS No. 54	April 1988
328	.41	Amended by SAS No. 113	November 2006
329	.22	New paragraph added by issuance of SAS No. 96	January 2002
331		Title amended by SAS No. 67	November 1991
331	.01	Amended by SAS No. 67	November 1991
331	.03–.08	Superseded by SAS No. 67	November 1991
331	.14	Amended by SAS No. 43	August 1982
331	.15	Amended by SAS No. 2	December 1974
332		Superseded by SAS No. 92	September 2000
333		Superseded by SAS No. 85	November 1997
333	.06	Amended by SAS No. 89	December 1999
333	.06	Amended by SAS No. 99	October 2002
333	.09	Amended by SAS No. 113	November 2006
333	.16	Amended by SAS No. 89	December 1999
333	.16	Amended by SAS No. 99	October 2002
335		Superseded by SAS No. 45	August 1983
336		Superseded by SAS No. 73	July 1994
338		Superseded by SAS No. 41	April 1982
339		Superseded by SAS No. 103	December 2005
340		Superseded by SAS No. 59	April 1988
341	.02	Amended by SAS No. 113	November 2006
341	.12	Amended by SAS No. 64	December 1990
341	.13	Amended by SAS No. 64	December 1990
341	.13	Amended by SAS No. 77	November 1995
341	.17	New paragraph added by issuance of SAS No. 114	December 2006

Section	*Paragraph*	*Changes*	*Date of Change*
341	.18	New paragraph added by issuance of SAS No. 96	January 2002
342	.10	Amended by SAS No. 113	November 2006
342	.13	Amended by SAS No. 113	November 2006
350	.08	Amended by SAS No. 111	March 2006
350	.09	Amended by SAS No. 45	August 1983
350	.09	Deleted by SAS No. 111	March 2006
350	.11	Amended by SAS No. 45	August 1983
350	.18	Amended by SAS No. 111	March 2006
350	.20	Amended by SAS No. 111	March 2006
350	.23	Amended by SAS No. 111	March 2006
350	.25	Amended by SAS No. 111	March 2006
350	.32	Amended by SAS No. 111	March 2006
350	.42	Amended by SAS No. 111	March 2006
350	.44	Amended by SAS No. 111	March 2006
350	.47	Amended by SAS No. 43	June 1982
350	.48	Amended by SAS No. 45	August 1983
350	.48	Amended by SAS No. 111	March 2006
380		Superseded by SAS No. 114	December 2006
380	.68	Deleted by SAS No. 114	January 2008
410	.02	Amended by SAS No. 14	December 1976
410	.03–.04	Superseded by SAS No. 5	July 1975
411		Superseded by SAS No. 69	January 1992
411		Title amended by SAS No. 93	October 2000
411	.01	Amended by SAS No. 93	October 2000
411	.14–.15	New paragraphs added by issuance of SAS No. 91	April 2000
411	.18	Amended by SAS No. 91	April 2000
411		Withdrawn by the Auditing Standards Board	September 2009
420	.07	Amended by SAS No. 88	December 1999
420	.08	New paragraph added by issuance of SAS No. 88	December 1999
420	.09	Added[1]	April 1989
420	.09	Amended by SAS No. 88	December 1999
420	.10	Added[1]	April 1989
420	.10–.11	Deleted by SAS No. 88	December 1999
420	.14	Added[1]	April 1989
420	.18	Deleted[1]	April 1989
420	.23	Deleted[1]	April 1989
430		Superseded by SAS No. 32	October 1980
435[2]		Rescinded by the Auditing Standards Board	April 1998
504	.20	Superseded by SAS No. 72	March 1993
505		Superseded by SAS No. 58	April 1988
508	.08	Amended by SAS No. 93	October 2000
508	.11	Amended by SAS No. 79	December 1995
508	.16–.33	Deleted by SAS No. 79	December 1995
508	.19	Amended by SAS No. 79	December 1995
508	.29–.32	New paragraphs added by issuance of SAS No. 79	December 1995

(continued)

Section	Paragraph	Changes	Date of Change
508	.45–.49	New paragraphs added by issuance of SAS No. 79	December 1995
508	.61–.62	Amended by SAS No. 79	December 1995
508	.65	Amended by SAS No. 98	September 2002
508	.71	Amended by SAS No. 85	June 1998
508	.74	Amended by SAS No. 64	December 1990
508	.74–.76	Amended by SAS No. 79	December 1995
509		Superseded by SAS No. 58	April 1988
510		Superseded by SAS No. 2	December 1974
511		Superseded by SAS No. 2	December 1974
512		Superseded by SAS No. 2	December 1974
513		Superseded by SAS No. 2	December 1974
514		Superseded by SAS No. 2	December 1974
515		Superseded by SAS No. 2	December 1974
516		Superseded by SAS No. 26	November 1979
517		Superseded by SAS No. 26	November 1979
518		Superseded by SAS No. 26	November 1979
519		Superseded by SAS No. 24	March 1979
530	.01	Amended by SAS No. 103	December 2005
530	.03–.04	Amended by SAS No. 98	September 2002
530	.05	Amended by SAS No. 98	September 2002
530	.05	Amended by SAS No. 103	December 2005
532	.06	Deleted by SAS No. 93	October 2000
532	.17	Deleted by SAS No. 93	October 2000
535		Superseded by SAS No. 2	December 1974
540		Superseded by SAS No. 2	December 1974
541		Superseded by SAS No. 2	December 1974
542		Superseded by SAS No. 58	April 1988
543	.10	Amended by the Auditing Standards Board	June 1990
543	.16	Amended by SAS No. 64	December 1990
543	.18	Superseded by SAS No. 7	November 1975
544	.01	Superseded by SAS No. 2	December 1974
544	.02	Amended by SAS No. 2	December 1974
544	.02	Amended by SAS No. 14	December 1976
544	.02	Amended by SAS No. 62	April 1989
544	.02	Amended by SAS No. 77	November 1995
544	.04	Amended by SAS No. 62	April 1989
544	.04	Amended by SAS No. 77	November 1995
545		Superseded by SAS No. 58	April 1988
546		Superseded by SAS No. 58	April 1988
547		Superseded by SAS No. 2	December 1974
550	.07	New paragraph added by issuance of SAS No. 98	September 2002
550		Superseded by SAS No. 118	February 2010
551	.15	Amended by SAS No. 52	April 1988
551	.15	Amended by SAS No. 98	September 2002
551	.16	New paragraph added by issuance of SAS No. 98	September 2002
551		Superseded by SAS No. 119	February 2010
553		Superseded by SAS No. 52	April 1988
554		Superseded by SAS No. 52	April 1988
555		Superseded by SAS No. 45	August 1983
556		Superseded by SAS No. 52	April 1988

Section	*Paragraph*	*Changes*	*Date of Change*
557		Superseded by SAS No. 52	April 1988
558	.02	Amended by SAS No. 98	September 2002
558	.08	Amended by SAS No. 98	September 2002
558	.09	New paragraph added by issuance of SAS No. 98	September 2002
558	.10–.11	Amended by SAS No. 98	September 2002
558		Superseded by SAS No. 120	February 2010
560	.01	Amended by SAS No. 98	September 2002
560	.01	Amended by SAS No. 98	September 2002
560	.12	Amended by SAS No. 12	January 1976
560	.12	Amended by SAS No. 113	November 2006
561	.01–.03	Amended by SAS No. 98	September 2002
610		Superseded by SAS No. 29	December 1980
620		Superseded by SAS No. 14	December 1976
621		Superseded by SAS No. 63	April 1989
622[3]		Withdrawn by SAS No. 93	October 2000
623	.05	Amended by SAS No. 77	November 1995
625	.01	Amended by SAS No. 97	June 2002
625	.02	New paragraph added by issuance of SAS No. 97	June 2002
625	.03	Amended by SAS No. 97	June 2002
625	.04	New paragraph added by issuance of SAS No. 97	June 2002
625	.05–.07	Amended by SAS No. 97	June 2002
625	.09–.11	Amended by SAS No. 97	June 2002
630		Superseded by SAS No. 38	April 1981
631		Superseded by SAS No. 49	September 1984
634		Superseded by SAS No. 72	March 1993
634	.01	Amended by SAS No. 76	September 1995
634	.09	Amended by SAS No. 76	September 1995
634	.10	New paragraph added by issuance of SAS No. 76	September 1995
634	.20	Amended by SAS No. 86	June 1998
634	.22	Amended by SAS No. 86	June 1998
634	.29	Amended by SAS No. 86	June 1998
634	.33–.34	Amended by SAS No. 86	June 1998
634	.55	Amended by SAS No. 86	June 1998
634	.57	Amended by SAS No. 86	June 1998
634	.64	Amended by SAS No. 76	September 1995
634	.64	Amended by SAS No. 86	June 1998
640		Superseded by SAS No. 30	July 1980
641		Superseded by SAS No. 30	July 1980
642		Superseded by SSAE 2	June 1993
710		Superseded by SAS No. 37	April 1981
720		Superseded by SAS No. 24	March 1979
721		Superseded by SAS No. 36	April 1981
722		Superseded by SAS No. 100	November 2002
722		Amended by SAS No. 116	January 2009
722	.05	Amended by SAS No. 121	February 2011
730		Withdrawn by the Auditing Standards Board	April 1981
801		Superseded by SAS No. 74	February 1995
801	.01	Amended by SAS No. 75	September 1995

(continued)

Section	Paragraph	Changes	Date of Change
801		Superseded by SAS No. 117	December 2009
901	.01	Amended by SAS No. 43	August 1982
901	.02–.05	Deleted by SAS No. 43	August 1982
901	.24	Amended by SAS No. 43	August 1982
901	.28	Amended by SAS No. 43	August 1982

[1] Paragraphs reflect the conforming changes necessary due to the issuance of Statement on Auditing Standards (SAS) Nos. 53–62.

[2] The Auditing Standards Board (ASB) rescinded SAS No. 21, *Segment Information*, effective for audits of financial statements to which Financial Accounting Standards Board (FASB) Statement No. 131, *Disclosures about Segments of an Enterprise and Related Information*, has been applied. FASB Statement No. 131 became effective for fiscal years beginning after December 15, 1997.

[3] The ASB has withdrawn SAS No. 75 and its auditing interpretation, effective for audits of financial statements for periods ending on or after June 30, 2001, in order to consolidate the guidance applicable to agreed-upon procedures engagements in professional standards. For guidance relating to performing and reporting on agreed-upon procedures engagements, practitioners should refer to AT section 201, *Agreed-Upon Procedures Engagements*.

AU Appendix F

Other Auditing Publications

This listing identifies *other auditing publications* published by the AICPA that have been reviewed by the AICPA Audit and Attest Standards staff and are therefore presumed to be appropriate as defined in section 150, *Generally Accepted Auditing Standards*, paragraphs .07–.08. Products may be obtained through www.cpa2biz.com.

Auditing Practice Releases

(available in hard copy)

- The Information Technology Age: Evidential Matter in the Electronic Environment (1997)
- Confirmation of Accounts Receivable (1995)

AICPA *Technical Practice Aids* Accounting and Auditing Publications Technical Questions and Answers (TISs)

(available in hard copy)

- TIS section 8000, *Audit Field Work*
- TIS section 9000, *Auditors' Reports*

Current AICPA Audit Risk Alerts

Communicating Internal Control Related Matters in an Audit—Understanding SAS No. 115

Compilation and Review Developments

Employee Benefit Plans Industry Developments

Financial Institutions Industry Developments: Including Depository and Lending Institutions and Brokers and Dealers in Securities

General Accounting and Auditing Developments

Government Auditing Standards *and Circular A-133 Developments*

Health Care Industry Developments

Independence and Ethics Developments

Insurance Industry Developments

Investment Companies Industry Developments

Not-for-Profit Entities Industry Developments

Real Estate and Construction Industry Developments

Service Organizations: New Reporting Options

State and Local Governmental Developments

Understanding the New Auditing Standards Related to Risk Assessment

Other Publications

Accounting and Auditing for Related Parties and Related Party Transactions Toolkit

Alternative Investments—Audit Considerations (available for download at www.aicpa.org/interestareas/frc/auditattest/fieldwork/pages/alternative_investments.aspx)

Auditing Recipients of Federal Awards: Practical Guidance for Applying OMB Circular A-133

Audits of Futures Commission Merchants, Introducing Brokers, and Commodity Pools

Fraud Detection in a GAAS Audit

Applying OCBOA in State and Local Governmental Financial Statements

Auditing Governmental Financial Statements: Programs and Other Practice Aids

Auditing Multiemployer Plans

SAS No. 70 Reports and Employee Benefit Plans

AU TOPICAL INDEX

References are to AU section and paragraph numbers.
Section numbers in the 9000 series refer to Auditing Interpretations.

A

References are to AU section and paragraph numbers.

References are to AU section and paragraph numbers.

References are to AU section and paragraph numbers.

References are to AU section and paragraph numbers.

References are to AU section and paragraph numbers.

References are to AU section and paragraph numbers.

References are to AU section and paragraph numbers.

References are to AU section and paragraph numbers.

P

References are to AU section and paragraph numbers.

References are to AU section and paragraph numbers.

References are to AU section and paragraph numbers.

References are to AU section and paragraph numbers.

References are to AU section and paragraph numbers.

U

References are to AU section and paragraph numbers.

AT Section

STATEMENTS ON STANDARDS FOR ATTESTATION ENGAGEMENTS

TABLE OF CONTENTS

AT CROSS-REFERENCES TO SSAEs

Statements on Standards for Attestation Engagements*

No.	Date Issued	Title	Section
1	Mar. 1986	Attestation Standards [Revised and recodified by SSAE No. 10; see AT sections 101, 301, and 401]	
1	Dec. 1987	Attest Services Related to MAS Engagements [Revised and recodified by SSAE No. 10; see AT sections 101, 301, and 401]	
1	Oct. 1985	Financial Forecasts and Projections [Revised and recodified by SSAE No. 10; see AT sections 101, 301, and 401]	
1	Sept. 1988	Reporting on Pro Forma Financial Information [Revised and recodified by SSAE No. 10; see AT sections 101, 301, and 401]	
2	May 1993	Reporting on an Entity's Internal Control Over Financial Reporting [Revised and recodified by SSAE No. 10; subsequently superseded by SSAE No. 15, see AT section 501]	
3	Dec. 1993	Compliance Attestation [Revised and recodified by SSAE No. 10; see AT section 601]	
4	Sept. 1995	Agreed-Upon Procedures Engagements [Revised and recodified by SSAE No. 10; see AT section 201]	
5	Nov. 1995	Amendment to Statement on Standards for Attestation Engagements No. 1, *Attestation Standards* [Revised and recodified by SSAE No. 10; see AT section 101]	
6	Dec. 1995	Reporting on an Entity's Internal Control Over Financial Reporting: An Amendment to Statement on Standards for Attestation Engagements No. 2 [Revised and recodified by SSAE No. 10]	
7	Oct. 1997	Establishing an Understanding With the Client [Revised and recodified by SSAE No. 10; see AT section 101]	

(continued)

* Pronouncements in effect are indicated in **boldface** type.

Statements on Standards for Attestation Engagements—continued

No.	Date Issued	Title	Section
8	Mar. 1998	Management's Discussion and Analysis [Revised and recodified by SSAE No. 10; see AT section 701]	
9	Jan. 1999	Amendments to Statement on Standards for Attestation Engagements Nos. 1, 2, and 3 [Revised and recodified by SSAE No. 10; see AT sections 101 and 601]	
10	**Jan. 2001**	**Attestation Standards: Revision and Recodification**[1]	
11	**Jan. 2002**	**Attest Documentation**[2]	
12	**Sept. 2002**	**Amendment to Statement on Standards for Attestation Engagements No. 10, *Attestation Standards: Revision and Recodification***[3]	
13	**Dec. 2005**	**Defining Professional Requirements in Statements on Standards for Attestation Engagements**	20
14	**Nov. 2006**	**SSAE Hierarchy**	50
15	**Sept. 2008**	**An Examination of an Entity's Internal Control Over Financial Reporting That Is Integrated With an Audit of Its Financial Statements**	501
16	**April 2010**	**Reporting on Controls at a Service Organization**	801
17	**Dec. 2010**	**Reporting on Compiled Prospective Financial Statements When the Practitioner's Independence Is Impaired**[4]	

[1] SSAE No. 10 has been integrated within AT sections 101, 201, 301, 401, 601, and 701.

[2] SSAE No. 11 has been integrated within AT sections 101.100–[.108], 201[.27–.30], 301[.17], and 301[.32].

[3] SSAE No. 12 has been integrated within AT sections 101.17–.18.

[4] SSAE No. 17 has been integrated within AT section 301.23.

Sources of Sections in Current Text

AT Section	*Contents*	*Source*
20	Defining Professional Requirements in Statements on Standards for Attestation Engagements	SSAE No. 13
50	SSAE Hierarchy	SSAE No. 14
101	Attest Engagements	SSAE No. 10
201	Agreed-Upon Procedures Engagements	SSAE No. 10
301	Financial Forecasts and Projections	SSAE No. 10
401	Reporting on Pro Forma Financial Information	SSAE No. 10
501	An Examination of an Entity's Internal Control Over Financial Reporting That Is Integrated With an Audit of Its Financial Statements	SSAE No. 15
601	Compliance Attestation	SSAE No. 10
701	Management's Discussion and Analysis	SSAE No. 10
801	Reporting on Controls at a Service Organization	SSAE No. 16

ATTESTATION STANDARDS

Introduction

The accompanying "attestation standards" provide guidance and establish a broad framework for a variety of attest services increasingly demanded of the accounting profession. The standards and related interpretive commentary are designed to provide professional guidelines that will enhance both consistency and quality in the performance of such services.

For years, attest services generally were limited to expressing a positive opinion on historical financial statements on the basis of an audit in accordance with generally accepted auditing standards (GAAS). However, certified public accountants increasingly have been requested to provide, and have been providing, assurance on representations other than historical financial statements and in forms other than the positive opinion. In responding to these needs, certified public accountants have been able to generally apply the basic concepts underlying GAAS to these attest services. As the range of attest services has grown, however, it has become increasingly difficult to do so.

Consequently, the main objective of adopting these attestation standards and the related interpretive commentary is to provide a general framework for and set reasonable boundaries around the attest function. As such, the standards and commentary (*a*) provide useful and necessary guidance to certified public accountants engaged to perform new and evolving attest services and (*b*) guide AICPA standard-setting bodies in establishing, if deemed necessary, interpretive standards for such services.

The attestation standards are a natural extension of the ten generally accepted auditing standards. Like the auditing standards, the attestation standards deal with the need for technical competence, independence in mental attitude, due professional care, adequate planning and supervision, sufficient evidence, and appropriate reporting; however, they are much broader in scope. (The eleven attestation standards are listed below.) Such standards apply to a growing array of attest services. These services include, for example, reports on descriptions of systems of internal control; on descriptions of computer software; on compliance with statutory, regulatory, and contractual requirements; on investment performance statistics; and on information supplementary to financial statements. Thus, the standards have been developed to be responsive to a changing environment and the demands of society.

These attestation standards apply only to attest services rendered by a certified public accountant in the practice of public accounting—that is, a practitioner as defined in footnote 1 of paragraph .01.

The attestation standards do not supersede any of the existing standards in Statements on Auditing Standards (SASs) and Statements on Standards for Accounting and Review Services (SSARSs). Therefore, the practitioner who is engaged to perform an engagement subject to these existing standards should follow such standards.

Attestation Standards

General Standards

1. The practitioner must have adequate technical training and proficiency to perform in the attestation engagement.
2. The practitioner must have adequate knowledge of the subject matter.
3. The practitioner must have reason to believe that the subject matter is capable of evaluation against criteria that are suitable and available to users.
4. The practitioner must maintain independence in mental attitude in all matters relating to the engagement.
5. The practitioner must exercise due professional care in the planning and performance of the engagement and the preparation of the report.

Standards of Fieldwork

1. The practitioner must adequately plan the work and must properly supervise any assistants.
2. The practitioner must obtain sufficient evidence to provide a reasonable basis for the conclusion that is expressed in the report.

Standards of Reporting

1. The practitioner must identify the subject matter or the assertion being reported on and state the character of the engagement in the report.
2. The practitioner must state the practitioner's conclusion about the subject matter or the assertion in relation to the criteria against which the subject matter was evaluated.
3. The practitioner must state all of the practitioner's significant reservations about the engagement, the subject matter, and, if applicable, the assertion related thereto in the report.
4. The practitioner must state in the report that the report is intended solely for the information and use of the specified parties under the following circumstances:
   - When the criteria used to evaluate the subject matter are determined by the practitioner to be appropriate only for a limited number of parties who either participated in their establishment or can be presumed to have an adequate understanding of the criteria
   - When the criteria used to evaluate the subject matter are available only to specified parties
   - When reporting on subject matter and a written assertion has not been provided by the responsible party
   - When the report is on an attestation engagement to apply agreed-upon procedures to the subject matter

[As amended, effective for attest reports issued on or after June 30, 1999, by Statement on Standards for Attestation Engagements No. 9. As amended, effective when the subject matter or assertion is as of or for a period ending on or after June 1, 2001, by Statement on Standards for Attestation Engagements No. 10. Revised, December 2006, to reflect conforming changes necessary due to the issuance of Statement on Standards for Attestation Engagements No. 14.]

Introduction

AT Section

STATEMENTS ON STANDARDS FOR ATTESTATION ENGAGEMENTS

The following is a Codification of currently effective Statements on Standards for Attestation Engagements (SSAEs) and related Attestation Interpretations. Statements on Standards for Attestation Engagements are issued by senior technical bodies of the AICPA designated to issue pronouncements on attestation matters. Rule 202, Compliance With Standards, *of the AICPA Code of Professional Conduct requires an AICPA member who performs an attest engagement (a practitioner) to comply with such pronouncements. A practitioner is required to comply with an unconditional requirement in all cases in which the circumstances exist to which the unconditional requirement applies. A practitioner is also required to comply with a presumptively mandatory requirement in all cases in which the circumstances exist to which the presumptively mandatory requirement applies; however, in rare circumstances, the practitioner may depart from a presumptively mandatory requirement provided the practitioner documents his or her justification for the departure and how the alternative procedures performed in the circumstances were sufficient to achieve the objectives of the presumptively mandatory requirement.*

Attestation Interpretations are recommendations on the application of SSAEs in specific circumstances, including engagements for entities in specialized industries, issued under the authority of AICPA senior technical bodies. An interpretation is not as authoritative as a pronouncement; however, if a practitioner does not apply an attestation interpretation, the practitioner should be prepared to explain how he or she complied with the SSAE provisions addressed by such attestation interpretation. The specific terms used to define professional requirements in the SSAEs are not intended to apply to interpretations because interpretations are not attestation standards. It is the Auditing Standards Board's intention to make conforming changes to the interpretations over the next several years to remove any language that would imply a professional requirement where none exists.

TABLE OF CONTENTS

Section		Paragraph

Section | Paragraph

AT Section 20

Defining Professional Requirements in Statements on Standards for Attestation Engagements

Source: SSAE No. 13.

Effective December 2005.

Introduction

.01 This section sets forth the meaning of certain terms used in Statements on Standards for Attestation Engagements (SSAEs) issued by the Auditing Standards Board in describing the professional requirements imposed on practitioners.

Professional Requirements

.02 SSAEs contain professional requirements together with related guidance in the form of explanatory material. Practitioners have a responsibility to consider the entire text of an SSAE in carrying out their work on an engagement and in understanding and applying the professional requirements of the relevant SSAEs.

.03 Not every paragraph of an SSAE carries a professional requirement that the practitioner is expected to fulfill. Rather, the professional requirements are communicated by the language and the meaning of the words used in the SSAEs.

.04 SSAEs use two categories of professional requirements, identified by specific terms, to describe the degree of responsibility they impose on practitioners, as follows:

- *Unconditional requirements.* The practitioner is required to comply with an unconditional requirement in all cases in which the circumstances exist to which the unconditional requirement applies. SSAEs use the words *must* or *is required* to indicate an unconditional requirement.
- *Presumptively mandatory requirements.* The practitioner is also required to comply with a presumptively mandatory requirement in all cases in which the circumstances exist to which the presumptively mandatory requirement applies; however, in rare circumstances, the practitioner may depart from a presumptively mandatory requirement provided the practitioner documents his or her justification for the departure and how the alternative procedures performed in the circumstances were sufficient to achieve the objectives of the presumptively mandatory requirement. SSAEs use the word *should* to indicate a presumptively mandatory requirement.

If an SSAE provides that a procedure or action is one that the practitioner "should consider," the consideration of the procedure or action is presumptively required, whereas carrying out the procedure or action is not. The professional requirements of an SSAE are to be understood and applied in the context of the explanatory material that provides guidance for their application.

Explanatory Material

.05 Explanatory material is defined as the text within an SSAE (excluding any related appendixes or interpretations[1]) that may:

- Provide further explanation and guidance on the professional requirements; or
- Identify and describe other procedures or actions relating to the activities of the practitioner.

.06 Explanatory material that provides further explanation and guidance on the professional requirements is intended to be descriptive rather than imperative. That is, it explains the objective of the professional requirements (where not otherwise self-evident); it explains why the practitioner might consider or employ particular procedures, depending on the circumstances; and it provides additional information for the practitioner to consider in exercising professional judgment in performing the engagement.

.07 Explanatory material that identifies and describes other procedures or actions relating to the activities of the practitioner is not intended to impose a professional requirement for the practitioner to perform the suggested procedures or actions. Rather, these procedures or actions require the practitioner's attention and understanding; how and whether the practitioner carries out such procedures or actions in the engagement depends on the exercise of professional judgment in the circumstances consistent with the objective of the standard. The words *may*, *might*, and *could* are used to describe these actions and procedures.

Application

.08 The provisions of this section are effective upon issuance.[2]

[1] Interpretive publications differ from explanatory material. Interpretive publications, for example, interpretations of the Statements on Standards for Attestation Engagements (SSAEs), appendixes to the SSAEs and AICPA auditing Statements of Position, are issued under the authority of the Auditing Standards Board (ASB). In contrast, explanatory material is always contained within the standards sections of the SSAE and is meant to be more descriptive in nature.

[2] The specific terms used to define professional requirements in this attestation standard are not intended to apply to any interpretive publications issued under the authority of the ASB, for example, interpretations of the SSAEs, or appendixes to the SSAEs, since interpretive publications are not attestation standards. (See footnote 1.) It is the ASB's intention to make conforming changes to the interpretive publications over the next several years to remove any language that would imply a professional requirement where none exists. It is the ASB's intention that such language would only be used in the standards sections of the SSAEs.

AT Section 50

SSAE Hierarchy

Source: SSAE No. 14.

Effective when the subject matter or assertion is as of or for a period ending on or after December 15, 2006.

.01 A practitioner plans, conducts, and reports the results of an attestation engagement in accordance with attestation standards. Attestation standards provide a measure of quality and the objectives to be achieved in the attestation engagement. Attestation procedures differ from attestation standards. Attestation procedures are acts that the practitioner performs during the course of the attestation engagement to comply with the attestation standards.

Attestation Standards

.02 The general, fieldwork, and reporting standards (the 11 attestation standards) approved and adopted by the membership of the AICPA, as amended by the AICPA Auditing Standards Board (ASB), are as follows:

General Standards

1. The practitioner must have adequate technical training and proficiency to perform the attestation engagement.
2. The practitioner must have adequate knowledge of the subject matter.
3. The practitioner must have reason to believe that the subject matter is capable of evaluation against criteria that are suitable and available to users.
4. The practitioner must maintain independence in mental attitude in all matters relating to the engagement.
5. The practitioner must exercise due professional care in the planning and performance of the engagement and the preparation of the report.

Standards of Fieldwork

1. The practitioner must adequately plan the work and must properly supervise any assistants.
2. The practitioner must obtain sufficient evidence to provide a reasonable basis for the conclusion that is expressed in the report.

Standards of Reporting[1]

1. The practitioner must identify the subject matter or the assertion being reported on and state the character of the engagement in the report.
2. The practitioner must state the practitioner's conclusion about the subject matter or the assertion in relation to the criteria against which the subject matter was evaluated in the report.
3. The practitioner must state all of the practitioner's significant reservations about the engagement, the subject matter, and, if applicable, the assertion related thereto in the report.

---

[1] The reporting standards apply only when the practitioner issues a report.

4. The practitioner must state in the report that the report is intended solely for the information and use of the specified parties under the following circumstances:
   - When the criteria used to evaluate the subject matter are determined by the practitioner to be appropriate only for a limited number of parties who either participated in their establishment or can be presumed to have an adequate understanding of the criteria.
   - When the criteria used to evaluate the subject matter are available only to specified parties.
   - When reporting on subject matter and a written assertion has not been provided by the responsible party.
   - When the report is on an attestation engagement to apply agreed-upon procedures to the subject matter.

Footnote 1 is also to be added to the heading *Standards of Reporting* preceding paragraph .63 of section 101, *Attest Engagements*.

.03 Statements on Standards for Attestation Engagements (SSAEs) are issued by senior technical bodies of the AICPA designated to issue pronouncements on attestation matters. Rule 202, *Compliance With Standards* [ET section 202.01], of the AICPA Code of Professional Conduct requires an AICPA member who performs an attestation engagement (the practitioner) to comply with such pronouncements.[2] SSAEs are developed and issued through a due process that includes deliberation in meetings open to the public, public exposure of proposed SSAEs, and a formal vote. The SSAEs are codified within the framework of the 11 attestation standards.

.04 The nature of the 11 attestation standards and the SSAEs requires the practitioner to exercise professional judgment in applying them. When, in rare circumstances, the practitioner departs from a presumptively mandatory requirement, the practitioner must document in the working papers his or her justification for the departure and how the alternative procedures performed in the circumstances were sufficient to achieve the objectives of the presumptively mandatory requirement.[3]

Attestation Interpretations

.05 Attestation interpretations consist of Interpretations of the SSAEs, appendixes to the SSAEs,[4] attestation guidance included in AICPA Audit and Accounting Guides, and AICPA attestation Statements of Position. Attestation interpretations are recommendations on the application of SSAEs in specific circumstances, including engagements for entities in specialized industries, issued under the authority of the AICPA senior technical bodies.

.06 The practitioner should be aware of and consider attestation interpretations applicable to the attestation engagement. If the practitioner does not apply the attestation guidance included in an applicable attestation interpretation, the practitioner should be prepared to explain how he or she complied with the SSAE provisions addressed by such attestation guidance.

---

[2] In certain engagements, the practitioner also may be subject to other attestation requirements, such as *Government Auditing Standards* issued by the comptroller general of the United States.

[3] The term *presumptively mandatory requirement* is defined in section 20, *Defining Professional Requirements in Statements on Standards for Attestation Engagements*.

[4] Appendixes to Statements on Standards for Attestation Engagements (SSAEs) referred to in paragraph .05 of this section do not include previously issued appendixes to original pronouncements that, when adopted, modified other SSAEs.

Other Attestation Publications

.07 Other attestation publications include AICPA attestation publications not referred to above; attestation articles in the *Journal of Accountancy* and other professional journals; attestation articles in the AICPA *CPA Letter*; continuing professional education programs and other instruction materials, textbooks, guide books, attest programs, and checklists; and other attestation publications from state CPA societies, other organizations, and individuals.[5] Other attestation publications have no authoritative status; however, they may help the practitioner understand and apply the SSAEs.

.08 A practitioner may apply the attestation guidance included in an other attestation publication if he or she is satisfied that, in his or her judgment, it is both relevant to the circumstances of the attestation engagement, and appropriate. In determining whether an other attestation publication is appropriate, the practitioner may wish to consider the degree to which the publication is recognized as being helpful in understanding and applying SSAEs and the degree to which the issuer or author is recognized as an authority in attestation matters. Other attestation publications published by the AICPA that have been reviewed by the AICPA Audit and Attest Standards Staff are presumed to be appropriate.

.09 This section is effective when the subject matter or assertion is as of or for a period ending on or after December 15, 2006.

---

[5] The practitioner is not expected to be aware of the full body of other attestation publications.

AT Section 101

Attest Engagements

Source: SSAE No. 10; SSAE No. 11; SSAE No. 12; SSAE No. 14.

See section 9101 for interpretations of this section.

Effective when the subject matter or assertion is as of or for a period ending on or after June 1, 2001, unless otherwise indicated.

Applicability

.01 This section applies to engagements, except for those services discussed in paragraph .04, in which a certified public accountant in the practice of public accounting[1] (hereinafter referred to as a *practitioner*) is engaged to issue or does issue an examination, a review, or an agreed-upon procedures report on subject matter, or an assertion about the subject matter (hereafter referred to as *the assertion*), that is the responsibility of another party.[2]

.02 This section establishes a framework for attest[3] engagements performed by practitioners and for the ongoing development of related standards. For certain subject matter, specific attestation standards have been developed to provide additional requirements for engagement performance and reporting.

.03 When a practitioner undertakes an attest engagement for the benefit of a government body or agency and agrees to follow specified government standards, guides, procedures, statutes, rules, and regulations, the practitioner is obliged to follow those governmental requirements as well as the applicable attestation standards.

.04 Professional services provided by practitioners that are not covered by this SSAE include the following:

a. Services performed in accordance with Statements on Auditing Standards (SASs)

b. Services performed in accordance with Statements on Standards for Accounting and Review Services (SSARSs)

c. Services performed in accordance with the Statement on Standards for Consulting Services (SSCS), such as engagements in which the practitioner's role is solely to assist the client (for example, acting as the company accountant in preparing information other than financial statements), or engagements in which a practitioner is engaged to testify as an expert witness in accounting, auditing, taxation, or other matters, given certain stipulated facts

---

[1] For a definition of the term *practice of public accounting*, see *Definitions* [ET section 92.29].

[2] See section 301, *Financial Forecasts and Projections*,paragraph .02, for additional guidance on applicability when engaged to provide an attest service on a financial forecast or projection.

[3] The term *attest* and its variants, such as *attesting* and *attestation,* are used in a number of state accountancy laws, and in regulations issued by state boards of accountancy under such laws, for different purposes and with different meanings from those intended by this section. Consequently, the definition of *attest engagements* set out in paragraph .01, and the attendant meaning of *attest* and *attestation* as used throughout the section, should not be understood as defining these terms and similar terms, as they are used in any law or regulation, nor as embodying a common understanding of the terms which may also be reflected in such laws or regulations.

d. Engagements in which the practitioner is engaged to advocate a client's position—for example, tax matters being reviewed by the Internal Revenue Service

e. Tax engagements in which a practitioner is engaged to prepare tax returns or provide tax advice

.05 An attest engagement may be part of a larger engagement, for example, a feasibility study or business acquisition study may also include an examination of prospective financial information. In such circumstances, these standards apply only to the attest portion of the engagement.

.06 Any professional service resulting in the expression of assurance must be performed under AICPA professional standards that provide for the expression of such assurance. Reports issued by a practitioner in connection with other professional standards should be written to be clearly distinguishable from and not to be confused with attest reports. For example, a practitioner performing an engagement which is intended solely to assist an organization in improving its controls over the privacy of client data should not issue a report as a result of that engagement expressing assurance as to the effectiveness of such controls. Additionally, a report that merely excludes the words, " ...was conducted in accordance with attestation standards established by the American Institute of Certified Public Accountants..." but is otherwise similar to an examination, a review or an agreed-upon procedures attest report may be inferred to be an attest report.

Definitions and Underlying Concepts

Subject Matter

.07 The subject matter of an attest engagement may take many forms, including the following:

a. Historical or prospective performance or condition (for example, historical or prospective financial information, performance measurements, and backlog data)

b. Physical characteristics (for example, narrative descriptions, square footage of facilities)

c. Historical events (for example, the price of a market basket of goods on a certain date)

d. Analyses (for example, break-even analyses)

e. Systems and processes (for example, internal control)

f. Behavior (for example, corporate governance, compliance with laws and regulations, and human resource practices)

The subject matter may be as of a point in time or for a period of time.

Assertion

.08 An assertion is any declaration or set of declarations about whether the subject matter is based on or in conformity with the criteria selected.

.09 A practitioner may report on a written assertion or may report directly on the subject matter. In either case, the practitioner should ordinarily obtain a written assertion in an examination or a review engagement. A written assertion may be presented to a practitioner in a number of ways, such as in a narrative description, within a schedule, or as part of a representation letter appropriately identifying what is being presented and the point in time or period of time covered.

.10 When a written assertion has not been obtained, a practitioner may still report on the subject matter; however, the form of the report will vary depending on the circumstances and its use should be restricted.[4] In this section, see paragraphs .58 and .60 on gathering sufficient evidence and paragraphs .73 to .75 and .78 to .80 for reporting guidance.

Responsible Party

.11 The *responsible party* is defined as the person or persons, either as individuals or representatives of the entity, responsible for the subject matter. If the nature of the subject matter is such that no such party exists, a party who has a reasonable basis for making a written assertion about the subject matter may provide such an assertion (hereinafter referred to as the *responsible party*).

.12 The practitioner may be engaged to gather information to enable the responsible party to evaluate the subject matter in connection with providing a written assertion. Regardless of the procedures performed by the practitioner, the responsible party must accept responsibility for its assertion and the subject matter and must not base its assertion solely on the practitioner's procedures.[5]

.13 Because the practitioner's role in an attest engagement is that of an *attester*, the practitioner should not take on the role of the responsible party in an attest engagement. Therefore, the need to clearly identify a responsible party is a prerequisite for an attest engagement. A practitioner may accept an engagement to perform an examination, a review or an agreed-upon procedures engagement on subject matter or an assertion related thereto provided that one of the following conditions is met.

a. The party wishing to engage the practitioner is responsible for the subject matter, or has a reasonable basis for providing a written assertion about the subject matter if the nature of the subject matter is such that a responsible party does not otherwise exist.

b. The party wishing to engage the practitioner is not responsible for the subject matter but is able to provide the practitioner, or have a third party who is responsible for the subject matter provide the practitioner, with evidence of the third party's responsibility for the subject matter.

.14 The practitioner should obtain written acknowledgment or other evidence of the responsible party's responsibility for the subject matter, or the written assertion, as it relates to the objective of the engagement. The responsible party can acknowledge that responsibility in a number of ways, for example, in an engagement letter, a representation letter, or the presentation of the subject matter, including the notes thereto, or the written assertion. If the practitioner is not able to directly obtain written acknowledgment, the practitioner should obtain other evidence of the responsible party's responsibility for the subject matter (for example, by reference to legislation, a regulation, or a contract).

---

[4] When the practitioner is unable to perform the inquiry and analytical or other procedures that he or she considers necessary to achieve the limited assurance contemplated by a review, or when the client is the responsible party and does not provide the practitioner with a written assertion, the review will be incomplete. A review that is incomplete is not an adequate basis for issuing a review report and, accordingly, the practitioner should withdraw from the engagement.

[5] See paragraph .112 regarding the practitioner's assistance in developing subject matter or criteria.

Applicability to Agreed-Upon Procedures Engagements

.15 An agreed-upon procedures attest engagement is one in which a practitioner is engaged to issue a report of findings based on specific procedures performed on subject matter. The general, fieldwork, and reporting standards for attest engagements set forth in this section are applicable to agreed-upon procedures engagements. Because the application of these standards to agreed-upon procedures engagements is discussed in section 201, *Agreed-Upon Procedures Engagements*, such engagements are not discussed further in this section.

The Relationship of Attestation Standards to Quality Control Standards

.16 The practitioner is responsible for compliance with the American Institute of Certified Public Accountants' (AICPA's) Statements on Standards for Attestation Engagements (SSAEs) in an attest engagement. Rule 202, *Compliance With Standards*, of the Code of Professional Conduct [ET section 202.01], requires members to comply with such standards when conducting professional services.

.17 A firm of practitioners has a responsibility to adopt a system of quality control in the conduct of a firm's attest practice.[6] Thus, a firm should establish quality control policies and procedures to provide it with reasonable assurance that its personnel comply with the attestation standards in its attest engagements. The nature and extent of a firm's quality control policies and procedures depend on factors such as its size, the degree of operating autonomy allowed its personnel and its practice offices, the nature of its practice, its organization, and appropriate cost-benefit considerations. [As amended, effective September 2002, by SSAE No. 12.]

.18 Attestation standards relate to the conduct of individual attest engagements; quality control standards relate to the conduct of a firm's attest practice as a whole. Thus, attestation standards and quality control standards are related and the quality control policies and procedures that a firm adopts may affect both the conduct of individual attest engagements and the conduct of a firm's attest practice as a whole. However, deficiencies in or instances of noncompliance with a firm's quality control policies and procedures do not, in and of themselves, indicate that a particular engagement was not performed in accordance with attestation standards. [As amended, effective September 2002, by Statement on Standards for Attestation Engagements No. 12.]

General Standards

Training and Proficiency

.19 The first general standard is—*The practitioner must have adequate technical training and proficiency to perform the attestation engagement.* [As amended, effective when the subject matter or assertion is as of or for a period

---

[6] The elements of a system of quality control are identified in Statement on Quality Control Standards (SQCS) No. 7, *A Firm's System of Quality Control* [QC section 10B]. A system of quality control consists of policies designed to provide the firm with reasonable assurance that the firm and its personnel comply with professional standards and applicable legal and regulatory requirements and that reports issued by the firm are appropriate in the circumstances, and the procedures necessary to implement and monitor compliance with those policies. [As amended, effective September 2002, by SSAE No. 12. Footnote amended due to the issuance of SQCS No. 7, December 2008.]

ending on or after December 15, 2006, by Statement on Standards for Attestation Engagements No. 14.]

.20 Performing attest services is different from preparing and presenting subject matter or an assertion. The latter involves collecting, classifying, summarizing, and communicating information; this usually entails reducing a mass of detailed data to a manageable and understandable form. On the other hand, performing attest services involves gathering evidence to support the subject matter or the assertion and objectively assessing the measurements and communications of the responsible party. Thus, attest services are analytical, critical, investigative, and are concerned with the basis and support for the subject matter or the assertion.

Adequate Knowledge of Subject Matter

.21 The second general standard is—*The practitioner must have adequate knowledge of the subject matter.* [As amended, effective when the subject matter or assertion is as of or for a period ending on or after December 15, 2006, by Statement on Standards for Attestation Engagements No. 14.]

.22 A practitioner may obtain adequate knowledge of the subject matter through formal or continuing education, including self-study, or through practical experience. However, this standard does not necessarily require a practitioner to personally acquire all of the necessary knowledge in the subject matter to be qualified to express a conclusion. This knowledge requirement may be met, in part, through the use of one or more specialists on a particular attest engagement if the practitioner has sufficient knowledge of the subject matter (*a*) to communicate to the specialist the objectives of the work and (*b*) to evaluate the specialist's work to determine if the objectives were achieved.

Suitability and Availability of Criteria

.23 The third general standard is—*The practitioner must have reason to believe that the subject matter is capable of evaluation against criteria that are suitable and available to users.* [As amended, effective when the subject matter or assertion is as of or for a period ending on or after December 15, 2006, by Statement on Standards for Attestation Engagements No. 14.]

Suitability of Criteria

.24 Criteria are the standards or benchmarks used to measure and present the subject matter and against which the practitioner evaluates the subject matter.* Suitable criteria must have each of the following attributes:

- *Objectivity*—Criteria should be free from bias.
- *Measurability*—Criteria should permit reasonably consistent measurements, qualitative or quantitative, of subject matter.
- *Completeness*—Criteria should be sufficiently complete so that those relevant factors that would alter a conclusion about subject matter are not omitted.
- *Relevance*—Criteria should be relevant to the subject matter.

.25 Criteria that are established or developed by groups composed of experts that follow due process procedures, including exposure of the proposed

---

* An example of suitable criteria are the Trust Services criteria (includes WebTrust and SysTrust) developed by the AICPA's Assurance Services Executive Committee. These criteria may be used when the subject matter of the engagement is the security, availability, processing integrity, or confidentiality of a system or an entity's privacy. The Trust Services criteria are presented in TSP sections 100 and 200 of the AICPA's *Technical Practice Aids*. [Footnote added by the Assurance Services Executive Committee, January 2003. Footnote revised, May 2006, to reflect conforming changes necessary due to the issuance of Generally Accepted Privacy Principles.]

criteria for public comment, ordinarily should be considered suitable. Criteria promulgated by a body designated by the AICPA Governing Council under the AICPA Code of Professional Conduct are, by definition, considered to be suitable.

.26 Criteria may be established or developed by the client, the responsible party, industry associations, or other groups that do not follow due process procedures or do not as clearly represent. the public interest. To determine whether these criteria are suitable, the practitioner should evaluate them based on the attributes described in paragraph .24.

.27 Regardless of who establishes or develops the criteria, the responsible party or the client is responsible for selecting the criteria and the client is responsible for determining that such criteria are appropriate for its purposes.

.28 The use of suitable criteria does not presume that all persons or groups would be expected to select the same criteria in evaluating the same subject matter. There may be more than one set of suitable criteria for a given subject matter. For example, in an engagement to express assurance about customer satisfaction, a responsible party may select as a criterion for customer satisfaction that all customer complaints are resolved to the satisfaction of the customer. In other cases, another responsible party may select a different criterion, such as the number of repeat purchases in the three months following the initial purchase.

.29 In evaluating the measurability attribute as described in paragraph .24, the practitioner should consider whether the criteria are sufficiently precise to permit people having competence in and using the same measurement criterion to be able to ordinarily obtain materially similar measurements. Consequently, practitioners should not perform an engagement when the criteria are so subjective or vague that reasonably consistent measurements, qualitative or quantitative, of subject matter cannot ordinarily be obtained. However, practitioners will not always reach the same conclusion because such evaluations often require the exercise of considerable professional judgment.

.30 For the purpose of assessing whether the use of particular criteria can be expected to yield reasonably consistent measurement and evaluation, consideration should be given to the nature of the subject matter. For example, *soft information*, such as forecasts or projections, would be expected to have a wider range of reasonable estimates than *hard* data, such as the calculated investment performance of a defined portfolio of managed investment products.

.31 Some criteria may be appropriate for only a limited number of parties who either participated in their establishment or can be presumed to have an adequate understanding of the criteria. For instance, criteria set forth in a lease agreement for override payments may be appropriate only for reporting to the parties to the agreement because of the likelihood that such criteria would be misunderstood or misinterpreted by parties other than those who have specifically agreed to the criteria. Such criteria can be agreed upon directly by the parties or through a designated representative. If a practitioner determines that such criteria are appropriate only for a limited number of parties, the use of the report should be restricted to those specified parties who either participated in their establishment or can be presumed to have an adequate understanding of the criteria.

.32 The third general standard in paragraph .23 applies equally regardless of the level of the attest service to be provided. Consequently, it is inappropriate to perform a review engagement if the practitioner concludes that an examination cannot be performed because competent persons using the same criteria would not be able to obtain materially similar evaluations.

Availability of Criteria

.33 The criteria should be available to users in one or more of the following ways:

a. Available publicly

b. Available to all users through inclusion in a clear manner in the presentation of the subject matter or in the assertion

c. Available to all users through inclusion in a clear manner in the practitioner's report

d. Well understood by most users, although not formally available (for example, "The distance between points A and B is twenty feet;" the criterion of distance measured in feet is considered to be well understood)

e. Available only to specified parties; for example, terms of a contract or criteria issued by an industry association that are available only to those in the industry

.34 If criteria are only available to specified parties, the practitioner's report should be restricted to those parties who have access to the criteria as described in paragraphs .78 and .80.

Independence

.35 The fourth general standard is—*The practitioner must maintain independence in mental attitude in all matters relating to the engagement.*[7] [As amended, effective when the subject matter or assertion is as of or for a period ending on or after December 15, 2006, by Statement on Standards for Attestation Engagements No. 14.]

.36 The practitioner should maintain the intellectual honesty and impartiality necessary to reach an unbiased conclusion about the subject matter or the assertion. This is a cornerstone of the attest function.

.37 In the final analysis, independence in mental attitude means objective consideration of facts, unbiased judgments, and honest neutrality on the part of the practitioner in forming and expressing conclusions. It implies not the attitude of an advocate or an adversary but an impartiality that recognizes an obligation for fairness. Independence in mental attitude presumes an undeviating concern for an unbiased conclusion about the subject matter or an assertion no matter what the subject matter or the assertion may be.

.38 The profession has established, through the AICPA's Code of Professional Conduct, precepts to guard against the *presumption* of loss of independence. Presumption is stressed because the possession of intrinsic independence is a matter of personal quality rather than of rules that formulate certain objective tests. Insofar as these precepts have been incorporated in the profession's code, they have the force of professional law for the independent practitioner.

---

[7] The practitioner performing an attest engagement should be *independent* pursuant to Rule 101, *Independence*, of the Code of Professional Conduct [ET section 101.01]. Interpretation No. 11, "Independence and the Performance of Professional Services Under the Statements on Standards for Attestation Engagements and Statement on Auditing Standards No. 75, *Engagements to Apply Agreed-Upon Procedures to Specified Elements, Accounts, or Items of a Financial Statement*," [ET section 101.13], to rule 101 [ET section 101.01] provides guidance about its application to certain attest engagements.

Due Professional Care

.39 The fifth general standard is—*The practitioner must exercise due professional care in the planning and performance of the engagement and the preparation of the report.* [As amended, effective when the subject matter or assertion is as of or for a period ending on or after December 15, 2006, by Statement on Standards for Attestation Engagements No. 14.]

.40 Due professional care imposes a responsibility on each practitioner involved with the engagement to observe each of the attestation standards. Exercise of due professional care requires critical review at every level of supervision of the work done and the judgment exercised by those assisting in the engagement, including the preparation of the report.

.41 *Cooley on Torts*, a legal treatise, describes the obligation for due care as follows:

> Every man who offers his services to another and is employed assumes the duty to exercise in the employment such skill as he possesses with reasonable care and diligence. In all these employments where peculiar skill is requisite, if one offers his services, he is understood as holding himself out to the public as possessing the degree of skill commonly possessed by others in the same employment, and if his pretentions are unfounded, he commits a species of fraud upon every man who employs him in reliance on his public profession. But no man, whether skilled or unskilled, undertakes that the task he assumes shall be performed successfully, and without fault or error; he undertakes for good faith and integrity, but not for infallibility, and he is liable to his employer for negligence, bad faith, or dishonesty, but not for losses consequent upon mere errors of judgment.[8]

Standards of Fieldwork

Planning and Supervision

.42 The first standard of fieldwork is—*The practitioner must adequately plan the work and must properly supervise any assistants.* [As amended, effective when the subject matter or assertion is as of or for a period ending on or after December 15, 2006, by Statement on Standards for Attestation Engagements No. 14.]

.43 Proper planning and supervision contribute to the effectiveness of attest procedures. Proper planning directly influences the selection of appropriate procedures and the timeliness of their application, and proper supervision helps ensure that planned procedures are appropriately applied.

.44 Planning an attest engagement involves developing an overall strategy for the expected conduct and scope of the engagement. To develop such a strategy, practitioners need to have sufficient knowledge to enable them to understand adequately the events, transactions, and practices that, in their judgment, have a significant effect on the subject matter or the assertion.

.45 Factors to be considered by the practitioner in planning an attest engagement include the following:

a. The criteria to be used

---

[8] D. Haggard, *Cooley on Torts*, 472 (4th ed., 1932).

b. Preliminary judgments about attestation risk[9] and materiality for attest purposes

c. The nature of the subject matter or the items within the assertion that are likely to require revision or adjustment

d. Conditions that may require extension or modification of attest procedures

e. The nature of the report expected to be issued

.46 The practitioner should establish an understanding with the client regarding the services to be performed for each engagement.[10] Such an understanding reduces the risk that either the practitioner or the client may misinterpret the needs or expectations of the other party. For example, it reduces the risk that the client may inappropriately rely on the practitioner to protect the entity against certain risks or to perform certain functions that are the client's responsibility. The understanding should include the objectives of the engagement, management's responsibilities, the practitioner's responsibilities, and limitations of the engagement. The practitioner should document the understanding in the working papers, preferably through a written communication with the client. If the practitioner believes an understanding with the client has not been established, he or she should decline to accept or perform the engagement.

.47 The nature, extent, and timing of planning will vary with the nature and complexity of the subject matter or the assertion and the practitioner's prior experience with management. As part of the planning process, the practitioner should consider the nature, extent, and timing of the work to be performed to accomplish the objectives of the attest engagement. Nevertheless, as the attest engagement progresses, changed conditions may make it necessary to modify planned procedures.

.48 Supervision involves directing the efforts of assistants who participate in accomplishing the objectives of the attest engagement and determining whether those objectives were accomplished. Elements of supervision include instructing assistants, staying informed of significant problems encountered, reviewing the work performed, and dealing with differences of opinion among personnel. The extent of supervision appropriate in a given instance depends on many factors, including the nature and complexity of the subject matter and the qualifications of the persons performing the work.

.49 Assistants should be informed of their responsibilities, including the objectives of the procedures that they are to perform and matters that may affect the nature, extent, and timing of such procedures. The practitioner with final responsibility for the engagement should direct assistants to bring to his or her attention significant questions raised during the attest engagement so that their significance may be assessed.

.50 The work performed by each assistant should be reviewed to determine whether it was adequately performed and to evaluate whether the results are consistent with the conclusion to be presented in the practitioner's report.

---

[9] *Attestation risk* is the risk that the practitioner may unknowingly fail to appropriately modify his or her attest report on the subject matter or an assertion that is materially misstated. It consists of (*a*) the risk (consisting of *inherent risk* and *control risk*) that the subject matter or assertion contains deviations or misstatements that could be material and (*b*) the risk that the practitioner will not detect such deviations or misstatements (*detection risk*).

[10] See SQCS No. 7 paragraph 28 (QC sec. 10B). [Footnote amended due to the issuance of SQCS No. 7, December 2008.]

Obtaining Sufficient Evidence

.51 The second standard of fieldwork is—*The practitioner must obtain sufficient evidence to provide a reasonable basis for the conclusion that is expressed in the report.* [As amended, effective when the subject matter or assertion is as of or for a period ending on or after December 15, 2006, by Statement on Standards for Attestation Engagements No. 14.]

.52 Selecting and applying procedures that will accumulate evidence that is sufficient in the circumstances to provide a reasonable basis for the level of assurance to be expressed in the attest report requires the careful exercise of professional judgment. A broad array of available procedures may be applied in an attest engagement. In establishing a proper combination of procedures to appropriately restrict attestation risk, the practitioner should consider the following presumptions, bearing in mind that they are not mutually exclusive and may be subject to important exceptions.

a. Evidence obtained from independent sources outside an entity provides greater assurance about the subject matter or the assertion than evidence secured solely from within the entity.

b. Information obtained from the independent attester's direct personal knowledge (such as through physical examination, observation, computation, operating tests, or inspection) is more persuasive than information obtained indirectly.

c. The more effective the controls over the subject matter, the more assurance they provide about the subject matter or the assertion.

.53 Thus, in the hierarchy of available attest procedures, those that involve search and verification (for example, inspection, confirmation, or observation), particularly when using independent sources outside the entity, are generally more effective in restricting attestation risk than those involving internal inquiries and comparisons of internal information (for example, analytical procedures and discussions with individuals responsible for the subject matter or the assertion). On the other hand, the latter are generally less costly to apply.

.54 In an attest engagement designed to provide a high level of assurance (referred to as an *examination*), the practitioner's objective is to accumulate sufficient evidence to restrict attestation risk to a level that is, in the practitioner's professional judgment, appropriately low for the high level of assurance that may be imparted by his or her report. In such an engagement, a practitioner should select from all available procedures—that is, procedures that assess inherent and control risk and restrict detection risk—any combination that can restrict attestation risk to such an appropriately low level.

.55 In an attest engagement designed to provide a moderate level of assurance (referred to as a *review*), the objective is to accumulate sufficient evidence to restrict attestation risk to a moderate level. To accomplish this, the types of procedures performed generally are limited to inquiries and analytical procedures (rather than also including search and verification procedures).

.56 Nevertheless, there will be circumstances in which inquiry and analytical procedures (*a*) cannot be performed, (*b*) are deemed less efficient than other procedures, or (*c*) yield evidence indicating that the subject matter or the assertion may be incomplete or inaccurate. In the first circumstance, the practitioner should perform other procedures that he or she believes can provide him or her with a level of assurance equivalent to that which inquiries and analytical procedures would have provided. In the second circumstance, the practitioner may perform other procedures that he or she believes would be more efficient to provide him or her with a level of assurance equivalent to that which inquiries and analytical procedures would provide. In the third circumstance, the practitioner should perform additional procedures.

.57 The extent to which attestation procedures will be performed should be based on the level of assurance to be provided and the practitioner's consideration of (*a*) the nature and materiality of the information to be tested to the subject matter or the assertion taken as a whole, (*b*) the likelihood of misstatements, (*c*) knowledge obtained during current and previous engagements, (*d*) the responsible party's competence in the subject matter, (*e*) the extent to which the information is affected by the asserter's judgment, and (*f*) inadequacies in the responsible party's underlying data.

.58 As part of the attestation procedures, the practitioner considers the written assertion ordinarily provided by the responsible party. If a written assertion cannot be obtained from the responsible party, the practitioner should consider the effects on his or her ability to obtain sufficient evidence to form a conclusion about the subject matter. When the practitioner's client is the responsible party, a failure to obtain a written assertion should result in the practitioner concluding that a scope limitation exists.[11] When the practitioner's client is not the responsible party and a written assertion is not provided, the practitioner may be able to conclude that he or she has sufficient evidence to form a conclusion about the subject matter.

Representation Letter

.59 During an attest engagement, the responsible party makes many representations to the practitioner, both oral and written, in response to specific inquiries or through the presentation of subject matter or an assertion. Such representations from the responsible party are part of the evidential matter the practitioner obtains.

.60 Written representations from the responsible party ordinarily confirm representations explicitly or implicitly given to the practitioner, indicate and document the continuing appropriateness of such representations, and reduce the possibility of misunderstanding concerning the matters that are the subject of the representations. Accordingly, in an examination or a review engagement, a practitioner should consider obtaining a representation letter from the responsible party. Examples of matters that might appear in such a representation letter include the following:[12]

a. A statement acknowledging responsibility for the subject matter and, when applicable, the assertion

b. A statement acknowledging responsibility for selecting the criteria, where applicable

---

[11] When the client is the responsible party, it is presumed that the client will be capable of providing the practitioner with a written assertion regarding the subject matter. Failure to provide the written assertion in this circumstance is a client-imposed limitation on the practitioner's evidence-gathering efforts. In an examination, the practitioner should modify the report for the scope limitation. In a review engagement, such a scope limitation results in an incomplete review and the practitioner should withdraw from the engagement.

[12] Specific written representations will depend on the circumstances of the engagement (for example, whether the client is the responsible party) and the nature of the subject matter and the criteria. For example, when the client is not the responsible party but has selected the criteria, the practitioner might obtain the representation regarding responsibility for selection of the criteria from the client rather than the responsible party (see paragraph .61).

c. A statement acknowledging responsibility for determining that such criteria are appropriate for its purposes, where the responsible party is the client

d. The assertion about the subject matter based on the criteria selected

e. A statement that all known matters contradicting the assertion and any communication from regulatory agencies affecting the subject matter or the assertion have been disclosed to the practitioner

f. Availability of all records relevant to the subject matter

g. A statement that any known events subsequent to the period (or point in time) of the subject matter being reported on that would have a material effect on the subject matter (or, if applicable, the assertion) have been disclosed to the practitioner

h. Other matters as the practitioner deems appropriate

.61 When the client is not the responsible party, the practitioner should consider obtaining a letter of written representations from the client as part of the attest engagement. Examples of matters that might appear in such a representation letter include the following:

a. A statement that any known events subsequent to the period (or point in time) of the subject matter being reported on that would have a material effect on the subject matter (or, if applicable, the assertion) have been disclosed to the practitioner

b. A statement acknowledging the client's responsibility for selecting the criteria, where applicable

c. A statement acknowledging the client's responsibility for determining that such criteria are appropriate for its purposes

d. Other matters as the practitioner deems appropriate

.62 If the responsible party or the client refuses to furnish all written representations that the practitioner deems necessary, the practitioner should consider the effects of such a refusal on his or her ability to issue a conclusion about the subject matter. If the practitioner believes that the representation letter is necessary to obtain sufficient evidence to issue a report, the responsible party's or the client's refusal to furnish such evidence in the form of written representations constitutes a limitation on the scope of an examination sufficient to preclude an unqualified opinion and is ordinarily sufficient to cause the practitioner to disclaim an opinion or withdraw from an examination engagement. However, based on the nature of the representations not obtained or the circumstances of the refusal, the practitioner may conclude, in an examination engagement, that a qualified opinion is appropriate. Further, the practitioner should consider the effects of the refusal on his or her ability to rely on other representations. When a scope limitation exists in a review engagement, the practitioner should withdraw from the engagement. (See paragraph .75.)

Standards of Reporting[13]

.63 The first standard of reporting is—*The practitioner must identify the subject matter or the assertion being reported on and state the character of the engagement in the report.* [As amended, effective when the subject matter or assertion is as of or for a period ending on or after December 15, 2006, by Statement on Standards for Attestation Engagements No. 14.]

---

[13] The reporting standards apply only when the practitioner issues a report. [Footnote added, effective when the subject matter or assertion is as of or for a period ending on or after December 15, 2006, by Statement on Standards for Attestation Engagements No. 14.]

.64 The practitioner who accepts an attest engagement should issue a report on the subject matter or the assertion or withdraw from the attest engagement. If the practitioner is reporting on the assertion, the assertion should be bound with or accompany the practitioner's report or the assertion should be clearly stated in the practitioner's report.[14]

.65 The statement of the character of an attest engagement includes the following two elements: (*a*) a description of the nature and scope of the work performed and (*b*) a reference to the professional standards governing the engagement. The terms *examination* and *review* should be used to describe engagements to provide, respectively, a high level and a moderate level of assurance. The reference to professional standards should be accomplished by referring to "attestation standards established by the American Institute of Certified Public Accountants."

.66 The second standard of reporting is—*The practitioner must state the practitioner's conclusion about the subject matter or the assertion in relation to the criteria against which the subject matter was evaluated in the report.* However, if conditions exist that, individually or in combination, result in one or more material misstatements or deviations from the criteria, the practitioner should modify the report and, to most effectively communicate with the reader of the report, should ordinarily express his or her conclusion directly on the subject matter,[15] not on the assertion. [As amended, effective when the subject matter or assertion is as of or for a period ending on or after December 15, 2006, by Statement on Standards for Attestation Engagements No. 14.]

.67 The practitioner should consider the concept of materiality in applying this standard. In expressing a conclusion, the practitioner should consider an omission or a misstatement to be material if the omission or misstatement—individually or when aggregated with others—is such that a reasonable person would be influenced by the omission or misstatement. The practitioner should consider both qualitative and quantitative aspects of omissions and misstatements.

.68 The term *general use* applies to attest reports that are not restricted to specified parties. General-use attest reports should be limited to two levels of assurance: one based on a restriction of attestation risk to an appropriately low level (an *examination*) and the other based on a restriction of attestation risk to a moderate level (a *review*). In an engagement to achieve a high level of assurance (an *examination*), the practitioner's conclusion should be expressed in the form of an opinion. When attestation risk has been restricted only to a moderate level (a *review*), the conclusion should be expressed in the form of negative assurance.

.69 A practitioner may report on subject matter or an assertion at multiple dates or covering multiple periods during which criteria have changed (for example, a report on comparative information). In those circumstances, the practitioner should determine whether the criteria are clearly stated or described for each of the dates or periods, and whether the changes have been adequately disclosed.

---

[14] The use of a "hot link" within the practitioner's report to management's assertion, such as might be used in a WebTrust[SM] report, would meet this requirement. [Footnote renumbered by the issuance of Statement on Standards for Attestation Engagements No. 14, November 2006.]

[15] Specific standards may require that the practitioner express his or her conclusion directly on the subject matter. For example, if management states in its assertion that a material weakness exists in the entity's internal control over financial reporting, the practitioner should state his or her opinion directly on the effectiveness of internal control, not on management's assertion related thereto. [Footnote renumbered by the issuance of Statement on Standards for Attestation Engagements No. 14, November 2006.]

.70 If the criteria used for the subject matter for the current date or period differ from those criteria used for the subject matter for a preceding date or period and the subject matter for the prior date or period is not presented, the practitioner should consider whether the changes in criteria are likely to be significant to users of the report. If so, the practitioner should determine whether the criteria are clearly stated or described and the fact that the criteria have changed is disclosed. (See paragraphs .76 and .77.)

.71 The third standard of reporting is—*The practitioner must state all of the practitioner's significant reservations about the engagement, the subject matter, and, if applicable, the assertion related thereto in the report.* [As amended, effective when the subject matter or assertion is as of or for a period ending on or after December 15, 2006, by Statement on Standards for Attestation Engagements No. 14.]

.72 *Reservations about the engagement* refers to any unresolved problem that the practitioner had in complying with these attestation standards, interpretive standards, or the specific procedures agreed to by the specified parties. The practitioner should not express an unqualified conclusion unless the engagement has been conducted in accordance with the attestation standards. Such standards will not have been complied with if the practitioner has been unable to apply all the procedures that he or she considers necessary in the circumstances.

.73 Restrictions on the scope of an engagement, whether imposed by the client or by such other circumstances as the timing of the work or the inability to obtain sufficient evidence, may require the practitioner to qualify the assurance provided, to disclaim any assurance, or to withdraw from the engagement. For example, if the practitioner's client is the responsible party, a failure to obtain a written assertion should result in the practitioner concluding that a scope limitation exists. (See paragraph .58.)

.74 The practitioner's decision to provide a qualified opinion, to disclaim an opinion, or to withdraw because of a scope limitation in an examination engagement depends on an assessment of the effect of the omitted procedure(s) on his or her ability to express assurance. This assessment will be affected by the nature and magnitude of the potential effects of the matters in question, and by their significance to the subject matter or the assertion. If the potential effects are pervasive to the subject matter or the assertion, a disclaimer or withdrawal is more likely to be appropriate. When restrictions that significantly limit the scope of the engagement are imposed by the client or the responsible party, the practitioner generally should disclaim an opinion or withdraw from the engagement. The reasons for a qualification or disclaimer should be described in the practitioner's report.

.75 In a review engagement, when the practitioner is unable to perform the inquiry and analytical or other procedures he or she considers necessary to achieve the limited assurance contemplated by a review, or when the client is the responsible party and does not provide the practitioner with a written assertion, the review will be incomplete. A review that is incomplete is not an adequate basis for issuing a review report and, accordingly, the practitioner should withdraw from the engagement.

.76 *Reservations about the subject matter or the assertion* refers to any unresolved reservation about the assertion or about the conformity of the subject matter with the criteria, including the adequacy of the disclosure of material matters. They can result in either a qualified or an adverse opinion, depending on the materiality of the departure from the criteria against which the subject matter or the assertion was evaluated, or a modified conclusion in a review engagement.

.77 Reservations about the subject matter or the assertion may relate to the measurement, form, arrangement, content, or underlying judgments and assumptions applicable to the subject matter or the assertion and its appended notes, including, for example, the terminology used, the amount of detail given, the classification of items, and the bases of amounts set forth. The practitioner considers whether a particular reservation should affect the report given the circumstances and facts of which he or she is aware at the time.

.78 The fourth standard of reporting is—*The practitioner must state in the report that the report is intended solely for the information and use of the specified parties under the following circumstances:*

- *When the criteria used to evaluate the subject matter are determined by the practitioner to be appropriate only for a limited number of parties who either participated in their establishment or can be presumed to have an adequate understanding of the criteria*
- *When the criteria used to evaluate the subject matter are available only to specified parties*
- *When reporting on subject matter and a written assertion has not been provided by the responsible party*
- *When the report is on an attestation engagement to apply agreed-upon procedures to the subject matter*

[As amended, effective when the subject matter or assertion is as of or for a period ending on or after December 15, 2006, by Statement on Standards for Attestation Engagements No. 14.]

.79 The need for restriction on the use of a report may result from a number of circumstances, including the purpose of the report, the criteria used in preparation of the subject matter, the extent to which the procedures performed are known or understood, and the potential for the report to be misunderstood when taken out of the context in which it was intended to be used. A practitioner should consider informing his or her client that restricted-use reports are not intended for distribution to nonspecified parties, regardless of whether they are included in a document containing a separate general-use report.[16, 17] However, a practitioner is not responsible for controlling a client's distribution of restricted-use reports. Accordingly, a restricted-use report should alert readers to the restriction on the use of the report by indicating that the report is not intended to be and should not be used by anyone other than the specified parties.

.80 An attest report that is restricted as to use should contain a separate paragraph at the end of the report that includes the following elements:

a. A statement indicating that the report is intended solely for the information and use of the specified parties

---

[16] In some cases, restricted-use reports filed with regulatory agencies are required by law or regulation to be made available to the public as a matter of public record. Also, a regulatory agency as part of its oversight responsibility for an entity may require access to restricted-use reports in which they are not named as a specified party. [Footnote renumbered by the issuance of Statement on Standards for Attestation Engagements No. 14, November 2006.]

[17] This section does not preclude the practitioner, in connection with establishing the terms of the engagement, from reaching an understanding with the client that the intended use of the report will be restricted, and from obtaining the client's agreement that the client and the specified parties will not distribute the report to parties other than those identified in the report. [Footnote renumbered by the issuance of Statement on Standards for Attestation Engagements No. 14, November 2006.]

b. An identification of the specified parties to whom use is restricted

c. A statement that the report is not intended to be and should not be used by anyone other than the specified parties

An example of such a paragraph is the following.

> This report is intended solely for the information and use of [*the specified parties*] and is not intended to be and should not be used by anyone other than these specified parties.

.81 Other attestation standards may specify situations that require restricted reports such as the following:

a. A review report on management's discussion and analysis

b. A report on prospective financial information when the report is intended for use by the responsible party alone, or by the responsible party and third parties with whom the responsible party is negotiating directly, as described in section 301, *Financial Forecasts and Projections*, paragraph .10.

Furthermore, nothing in this section precludes a practitioner from restricting the use of any report.

.82 If a practitioner issues a single combined report covering both (*a*) subject matter or presentations that require a restriction on use to specified parties and (*b*) subject matter or presentations that ordinarily do not require such a restriction, the use of such a single combined report should be restricted to the specified parties.

.83 In some instances, a separate restricted-use report may be included in a document that also contains a general-use report. The inclusion of a separate restricted-use report in a document that contains a general-use report does not affect the intended use of either report. The restricted-use report remains restricted as to use, and the general-use report continues to be for general use.

Examination Reports

.84 When expressing an opinion, the practitioner should clearly state whether, in his or her opinion, (*a*) the subject matter is based on (or in conformity with) the criteria in all material respects or (*b*) the assertion is presented (or fairly stated), in all material respects, based on the criteria. Reports expressing an opinion may be qualified or modified for some aspect of the subject matter, the assertion or the engagement (see the third reporting standard). However, as stated in paragraph .66, if conditions exist that, individually or in combination, result in one or more material misstatements or deviations from the criteria, the practitioner should modify the report and, to most effectively communicate with the reader of the report, should ordinarily express his or her conclusion directly on the subject matter, not on the assertion. In addition, such reports may emphasize certain matters relating to the attest engagement, the subject matter, or the assertion. The form of the practitioner's report will depend on whether the practitioner opines on the subject matter or the assertion.

.85 The practitioner's examination report on subject matter should include the following:

a. A title that includes the word *independent*

b. An identification of the subject matter and the responsible party

c. A statement that the subject matter is the responsibility of the responsible party *d.* A statement that the practitioner's responsibility is to express an opinion on the subject matter based on his or her examination

e. A statement that the examination was conducted in accordance with attestation standards established by the American Institute of Certified Public Accountants, and, accordingly, included procedures that the practitioner considered necessary in the circumstances

f. A statement that the practitioner believes the examination provides a reasonable basis for his or her opinion

g. The practitioner's opinion on whether the subject matter is based on (or in conformity with) the criteria in all material respects

h. A statement restricting the use of the report to specified parties under the following circumstances (see paragraphs .78 to .83):

(1) When the criteria used to evaluate the subject matter are determined by the practitioner to be appropriate only for a limited number of parties who either participated in their establishment or can be presumed to have an adequate understanding of the criteria

(2) When the criteria used to evaluate the subject matter are available only to the specified parties

(3) When a written assertion has not been provided by the responsible party (The practitioner should also include a statement to that effect in the introductory paragraph of the report.)

i. The manual or printed signature of the practitioner's firm

j. The date of the examination report

Appendix A [paragraph .114], *Examination Reports*, includes a standard examination report on subject matter. (See Example 1.)

.86 The practitioner's examination report on an assertion should include the following:

a. A title that includes the word *independent*

b. An identification of the assertion and the responsible party (When the assertion does not accompany the practitioner's report, the first paragraph of the report should also contain a statement of the assertion.)

c. A statement that the assertion is the responsibility of the responsible party

d. A statement that the practitioner's responsibility is to express an opinion on the assertion based on his or her examination

e. A statement that the examination was conducted in accordance with attestation standards established by the American Institute of Certified Public Accountants, and, accordingly, included procedures that the practitioner considered necessary in the circumstances

f. A statement that the practitioner believes the examination provides a reasonable basis for his or her opinion

g. The practitioner's opinion on whether the assertion is presented (or fairly stated), in all material respects, based on the criteria (However, see paragraph .66.)

h. A statement restricting the use of the report to specified parties under the following circumstances (see paragraphs .78 to .83):

(1) When the criteria used to evaluate the subject matter are determined by the practitioner to be appropriate only for a limited number of parties who either participated in their establishment

or can be presumed to have an adequate understanding of the criteria

(2) When the criteria used to evaluate the subject matter are available only to the specified parties

i. The manual or printed signature of the practitioner's firm

j. The date of the examination report

Appendix A [paragraph .114] includes a standard examination report on an assertion. (See Example 2.)

.87 Nothing precludes the practitioner from examining an assertion but opining directly on the subject matter. (See Appendix A [paragraph .114], Example 3.)

Review Reports

.88 In a review report, the practitioner's conclusion should state whether any information came to the practitioner's attention on the basis of the work performed that indicates that (*a*) the subject matter is not based on (or in conformity with) the criteria or (*b*) the assertion is not presented (or fairly stated) in all material respects based on the criteria. (As discussed more fully in the commentary to the third reporting standard, if the subject matter or the assertion is not modified to correct for any such information that comes to the practitioner's attention, such information should be described in the practitioner's report.)

.89 The practitioner's review report on subject matter should include the following:

a. A title that includes the word *independent*

b. An identification of the subject matter and the responsible party

c. A statement that the subject matter is the responsibility of the responsible party

d. A statement that the review was conducted in accordance with attestation standards established by the American Institute of Certified Public Accountants

e. A statement that a review is substantially less in scope than an examination, the objective of which is an expression of opinion on the subject matter, and accordingly, no such opinion is expressed

f. A statement about whether the practitioner is aware of any material modifications that should be made to the subject matter in order for it to be based on (or in conformity with), in all material respects, the criteria, other than those modifications, if any, indicated in his or her report

g. A statement restricting the use of the report to specified parties under the following circumstances (see paragraphs .78 to .83):

(1) When the criteria used to evaluate the subject matter are determined by the practitioner to be appropriate only for a limited number of parties who either participated in their establishment or can be presumed to have an adequate understanding of the criteria

(2) When the criteria used to evaluate the subject matter are available only to the specified parties

(3) When a written assertion has not been provided by the responsible party and the responsible party is not the client (The practitioner should also include a statement to that effect in the introductory paragraph of the report.)

h. The manual or printed signature of the practitioner's firm

i. The date of the review report

Appendix B [paragraph .115] *Review Reports*, includes a standard review report on subject matter. (See Example 1.) Appendix B [paragraph .115] also includes a review report on subject matter that is the responsibility of a party other than client; the report is restricted as to use because a written assertion has not been provided by the responsible party. (See Example 2.)

.90 The practitioner's review report on an assertion should include the following:

a. A title that includes the word *independent*

b. An identification of the assertion and the responsible party (When the assertion does not accompany the practitioner's report, the first paragraph of the report should also contain a statement of the assertion.)

c. A statement that the assertion is the responsibility of the responsible party

d. A statement that the review was conducted in accordance with attestation standards established by the American Institute of Certified Public Accountants

e. A statement that a review is substantially less in scope than an examination, the objective of which is an expression of opinion on the assertion, and accordingly, no such opinion is expressed

f. A statement about whether the practitioner is aware of any material modifications that should be made to the assertion in order for it to be presented (or fairly stated), in all material respects, based on (or in conformity with) the criteria, other than those modifications, if any, indicated in his or her report (However, see paragraph .66.)

g. A statement restricting the use of the report to specified parties under the following circumstances (see paragraphs .78 to .83):

(1) When the criteria used to evaluate the subject matter are determined by the practitioner to be appropriate only for a limited number of parties who either participated in their establishment or can be presumed to have an adequate understanding of the criteria

(2) When the criteria used to evaluate the subject matter are available only to the specified parties

h. The manual or printed signature of the practitioner's firm

i. The date of the review report

Appendix B [paragraph .115] includes a review report on an assertion that is restricted as to use because the criteria are available only to the specified parties. (See Example 3.)

Other Information in a Client-Prepared Document Containing the Practitioner's Attest Report[18]

.91 A client may publish various documents that contain information (hereinafter referred to as *other information*) in addition to the practitioner's attest report on subject matter (or on an assertion related thereto). Paragraphs .92 to .94 provide guidance to the practitioner when the other information is contained in (*a*) annual reports to holders of securities or beneficial interests, annual reports of organizations for charitable or philanthropic purposes distributed to the public, and annual reports filed with regulatory authorities under the Securities Exchange Act of 1934 or (*b*) other documents to which the practitioner, at the client's request, devotes attention. These paragraphs are not applicable when an attest report appears in a registration statement filed under the Securities Act of 1933. (See AU section 634, *Letters for Underwriters and Certain Other Requesting Parties*, and AU section 711, *Filings Under Federal Securities Statutes*.) Also, these paragraphs are not applicable to other information on which the practitioner or another practitioner is engaged to issue an opinion.

.92 The practitioner's responsibility with respect to other information in such a document does not extend beyond the information identified in his or her report, and the practitioner has no obligation to perform any procedures to corroborate any other information contained in the document. However, the practitioner should read the other information not covered by the practitioner's report or by the report of the other practitioner and consider whether it, or the manner of its presentation, is materially inconsistent with the information appearing in the practitioner's report. If the practitioner believes that the other information is inconsistent with the information appearing in the practitioner's report, he or she should consider whether the practitioner's report requires revision. If the practitioner concludes that the report does not require revision, he or she should request the client to revise the other information. If the other information is not revised to eliminate the material inconsistency, the practitioner should consider other actions, such as revising his or her report to include an explanatory paragraph describing the material inconsistency, withholding the use of his or her report in the document, or withdrawing from the engagement.

.93 If, while reading the other information for the reasons set forth in paragraph .92, the practitioner becomes aware of information that he or she believes is a material misstatement of fact that is not a material inconsistency as described in paragraph .92, he or she should discuss the matter with the client. In connection with this discussion, the practitioner should consider that he or she may not have the expertise to assess the validity of the statement, that there may be no standards by which to assess its presentation, and that there may be valid differences of judgment or opinion. If the practitioner concludes he or she has a valid basis for concern, the practitioner should propose that the client consult with some other party whose advice may be useful, such as the entity's legal counsel.

---

[18] Such guidance pertains only to other information in a client-prepared document. The practitioner has no responsibility to read information contained in documents of nonclients. Further, the practitioner is not required to read information contained in electronic sites, or to consider the consistency of other information in electronic sites with the original documents since electronic sites are a means of distributing information and are not "documents" as that term is used in this section. Practitioners may be asked by their clients to render attest services with respect to information in electronic sites, in which case, other attest standards may apply to those services. [Footnote renumbered by the issuance of Statement on Standards for Attestation Engagements No. 14, November 2006.]

.94 If, after discussing the matter, the practitioner concludes that a material misstatement of fact remains, the action taken will depend on his or her judgment in the circumstances. The practitioner should consider steps such as notifying the client's management and audit committee in writing of his or her views concerning the information and consulting his or her legal counsel about further action appropriate in the circumstances.[19]

Consideration of Subsequent Events in an Attest Engagement

.95 Events or transactions sometimes occur subsequent to the point in time or period of time of the subject matter being tested but prior to the date of the practitioner's report that have a material effect on the subject matter and therefore require adjustment or disclosure in the presentation of the subject matter or assertion. These occurrences are referred to as *subsequent events.* In performing an attest engagement, a practitioner should consider information about subsequent events that comes to his or her attention. Two types of subsequent events require consideration by the practitioner.

.96 The first type consists of events that provide additional information with respect to conditions that existed at the point in time or during the period of time of the subject matter being tested. This information should be used by the practitioner in considering whether the subject matter is presented in conformity with the criteria and may affect the presentation of the subject matter, the assertion, or the practitioner's report.

.97 The second type consists of those events that provide information with respect to conditions that arose subsequent to the point in time or period of time of the subject matter being tested that are of such a nature and significance that their disclosure is necessary to keep the subject matter from being misleading. This type of information will not normally affect the practitioner's report if the information is appropriately disclosed.

.98 While the practitioner has no responsibility to detect subsequent events, the practitioner should inquire of the responsible party (and his or her client if the client is not the responsible party) as to whether they are aware of any subsequent events, through the date of the practitioner's report, that would have a material effect on the subject matter or assertion.[20] If the practitioner has decided to obtain a representation letter, the letter ordinarily would include a representation concerning subsequent events. (See paragraphs .60 and .61.)

.99 The practitioner has no responsibility to keep informed of events subsequent to the date of his or her report; however, the practitioner may later become aware of conditions that existed at that date that might have affected

---

[19] If the client does not have an audit committee, the practitioner should communicate with individuals whose authority and responsibility are equivalent to those of an audit committee, such as the board of directors, the board of trustees, an owner in a owner-managed entity, or those who engaged the practitioner. [Footnote renumbered by the issuance of Statement on Standards for Attestation Engagements No. 14, November 2006.]

[20] For certain subject matter, specific subsequent event standards have been developed to provide additional requirements for engagement performance and reporting. Additionally, a practitioner engaged to examine the design or effectiveness of internal control over items not covered by section 501, *An Examination of an Entity's Internal Control Over Financial Reporting That Is Integrated With an Audit of Its Financial Statements*, or section 601, *Compliance Attestation*, should consider the subsequent events guidance set forth in sections 501.129–.134 and 601.50–.52. [Footnote renumbered by the issuance of Statement on Standards for Attestation Engagements No. 14, November 2006.]

the practitioner's report had he or she been aware of them. In such circumstances, the practitioner may wish to consider the guidance in AU section 561, *Subsequent Discovery of Facts Existing at the Date of the Auditor's Report*.

Attest Documentation[21]

.100 The practitioner should prepare and maintain attest documentation, the form and content of which should be designed to meet the circumstances of the particular attest engagement.[22] Attest documentation is the principal record of attest procedures applied, information obtained, and conclusions or findings reached by the practitioner in the engagement. The quantity, type, and content of attest documentation are matters of the practitioner's professional judgment. [As amended, effective for attest engagements when the subject matter or assertion is as of or for a period ending on or after December 15, 2002, by Statement on Standards for Attestation Engagements No. 11.]

.101 Attest documentation serves mainly to:

a. Provide the principal support for the practitioner's report, including the representation regarding observance of the standards of fieldwork, which is implicit in the reference in the report to attestation standards.[23]

b. Aid the practitioner in the conduct and supervision of the attest engagement.

For examinations of prospective financial statements, attest documentation ordinarily should indicate that the process by which the entity develops its prospective financial statements was considered in determining the scope of the examination. [Paragraph added, effective for attest engagements when the subject matter or assertion is as of or for a period ending on or after December 15, 2002, by Statement on Standards for Attestation Engagements No. 11.]

.102 Examples of attest documentation are work programs, analyses, memoranda, letters of confirmation and representation, abstracts or copies of entity documents, and schedules or commentaries prepared or obtained by the practitioner. Attest documentation may be in paper form, electronic form, or other media. [Paragraph renumbered and amended, effective for attest engagements when the subject matter or assertion is as of or for a period ending on or after December 15, 2002, by Statement on Standards for Attestation Engagements No. 11.]

.103 Attest documentation should be sufficient to (*a*) enable members of the engagement team with supervision and review responsibilities to understand the nature, timing, extent, and results of attest procedures performed,

---

[21] *Attest documentation* also may be referred to as *working papers*. [Footnote added, effective for attest engagements when the subject matter or assertion is as of or for a period ending on or after December 15, 2002, by Statement on Standards for Attestation Engagements No. 11. Footnote renumbered by the issuance of Statement on Standards for Attestation Engagements No. 14, November 2006.]

[22] [Footnote renumbered and deleted by the issuance of Statement on Standards for Attestation Engagements No. 11, January 2002. Footnote subsequently renumbered by the issuance of Statement on Standards for Attestation Engagements No. 14, November 2006.]

[23] However, there is no intention to imply that the practitioner would be precluded from supporting his or her report by other means in addition to attest documentation. [Footnote added, effective for attest engagements when the subject matter or assertion is as of or for a period ending on or after December 15, 2002, by Statement on Standards for Attestation Engagements No. 11. Footnote renumbered by the issuance of Statement on Standards for Attestation Engagements No. 14, November 2006.]

and the information obtained[24] and (*b*) indicate the engagement team member(s) who performed and reviewed the work. [Paragraph added, effective for attest engagements when the subject matter or assertion is as of or for a period ending on or after December 15, 2002, by Statement on Standards for Attestation Engagements No. 11.]

.104 Attest documentation is the property of the practitioner, and some states recognize this right of ownership in their statutes. The practitioner should adopt reasonable procedures to retain attest documentation for a period of time sufficient to meet the needs of his or her practice and to satisfy any applicable legal or regulatory requirements for records retention.[25, [26]] [Paragraph renumbered and amended, effective for attest engagements when the subject matter or assertion is as of or for a period ending on or after December 15, 2002, by Statement on Standards for Attestation Engagements No. 11.]

.105 The practitioner has an ethical, and in some situations a legal, obligation to maintain the confidentiality of client information or information of the responsible party.[27] Because attest documentation often contains confidential information, the practitioner should adopt reasonable procedures to maintain the confidentiality of that information.[†] [Paragraph added, effective for attest engagements when the subject matter or assertion is as of or for a period ending on or after December 15, 2002, by Statement on Standards for Attestation Engagements No. 11.]

.106 The practitioner also should adopt reasonable procedures to prevent unauthorized access to attest documentation. [Paragraph added, effective for attest engagements when the subject matter or assertion is as of or for a period ending on or after December 15, 2002, by Statement on Standards for Attestation Engagements No. 11.]

.107 Certain attest documentation may sometimes serve as a useful reference source for the client, but it should not be regarded as a part of, or a substitute for, the client's records. [Paragraph renumbered and amended, effective for attest engagements when the subject matter or assertion is as of or for a period ending on or after December 15, 2002, by Statement on Standards for Attestation Engagements No. 11.]

---

[24] A firm of practitioners has a responsibility to adopt a system of quality control policies and procedures to provide the firm with reasonable assurance that its personnel comply with applicable professional standards, including attestation standards, and the firm's standards of quality in conducting individual attest engagements. Review of attest documentation and discussions with engagement team members are among the procedures a firm performs when monitoring compliance with the quality control policies and procedures that it has established. (Also, see paragraphs .17 and .18.) [Footnote added, effective for attest engagements when the subject matter or assertion is as of or for a period ending on or after December 15, 2002, by Statement on Standards for Attestation Engagements No. 11. Footnote renumbered by the issuance of Statement on Standards for Attestation Engagements No. 14, November 2006.]

[25] The procedures should enable the practitioner to access electronic attest documentation throughout the retention period. [Footnote added, effective for attest engagements when the subject matter or assertion is as of or for a period ending on or after December 15, 2002, by Statement on Standards for Attestation Engagements No. 11. Footnote renumbered by the issuance of Statement on Standards for Attestation Engagements No. 14, November 2006.]

[[26]] [Footnote renumbered and deleted by the issuance of Statement on Standards for Attestation Engagements No. 11, January 2002. Footnote subsequently renumbered by the issuance of Statement on Standards for Attestation Engagements No. 14, November 2006.]

[27] Also, see Rule 301, *Confidential Client Information*, of the AICPA's Code of Professional Conduct [ET section 301.01]. [Footnote added, effective for attest engagements when the subject matter or assertion is as of or for a period ending on or after December 15, 2002, by Statement on Standards for Attestation Engagements No. 11. Footnote renumbered by the issuance of Statement on Standards for Attestation Engagements No. 14, November 2006.]

[†] ***Note:*** See the Attest Interpretation, "Providing Access to or Copies of Attest Documentation to a Regulator" (section 9101.43–.46).

[.108] [Paragraph renumbered and deleted by the issuance of Statement on Standards for Attestation Engagements No. 11, January 2002.]

Attest Services Related to Consulting Service Engagements

Attest Services as Part of a Consulting Service Engagement

.109 When a practitioner provides an attest service (as defined in this section) as part of a consulting service engagement, this SSAE applies only to the attest service. The SSCS applies to the balance of the consulting service engagement. [Paragraph renumbered by the issuance of Statement on Standards for Attestation Engagements No. 11, January 2002.]

.110 When the practitioner determines that an attest service is to be provided as part of a consulting service engagement, the practitioner should inform the client of the relevant differences between the two types of services and obtain concurrence that the attest service is to be performed in accordance with the appropriate professional requirements. The practitioner should take such actions because the professional requirements for an attest service differ from those for a consulting service engagement. [Paragraph renumbered by the issuance of Statement on Standards for Attestation Engagements No. 11, January 2002.]

.111 The practitioner should issue separate reports on the attest engagement and the consulting service engagement and, if presented in a common binder, the report on the attest engagement or service should be clearly identified and segregated from the report on the consulting service engagement. [Paragraph renumbered by the issuance of Statement on Standards for Attestation Engagements No. 11, January 2002.]

Subject Matter, Assertions, Criteria, and Evidence

.112 An attest service may involve subject matter, an assertion, criteria, or evidential matter developed during a concurrent or prior consulting service engagement. Subject matter or an assertion developed with the practitioner's advice and assistance as the result of such consulting services engagement may be the subject of an attest engagement, provided the responsible party accepts and acknowledges responsibility for the subject matter or assertion. (See paragraph .12.) Criteria developed with the practitioner's assistance may be used to evaluate subject matter in an attest engagement, provided such criteria meet the requirements of this section. Relevant information obtained in the course of a concurrent or prior consulting service engagement may be used as evidential matter in an attest engagement, provided the information satisfies the requirements of this section. [Paragraph renumbered by the issuance of Statement on Standards for Attestation Engagements No. 11, January 2002.]

Effective Date

.113 This section is effective when the subject matter or assertion is as of or for a period ending on or after June 1, 2001. Early application is permitted. [Paragraph renumbered by the issuance of Statement on Standards for Attestation Engagements No. 11, January 2002.]

.114

Appendix A

Examination Reports

Example 1

This is a standard examination report on subject matter for general use. This report pertains to subject matter for which suitable criteria exist and are available to all users through inclusion in a clear manner in the presentation of the subject matter. (See paragraphs .78 to .83 for guidance on restricting the use of the report when criteria are available only to specified parties; see Example 4 for an illustration of such a report.) A written assertion has been obtained from the responsible party.

Independent Accountant's Report

We have examined the [*identify the subject matter—for example, the accompanying schedule of investment returns of XYZ Company for the year ended December 31, 20XX*]. XYZ Company's management is responsible for the schedule of investment returns. Our responsibility is to express an opinion based on our examination.

Our examination was conducted in accordance with attestation standards established by the American Institute of Certified Public Accountants and, accordingly, included examining, on a test basis, evidence supporting [*identify the subject matter—for example, XYZ Company's schedule of investment returns*] and performing such other procedures as we considered necessary in the circumstances. We believe that our examination provides a reasonable basis for our opinion.

[*Additional paragraph(s) may be added to emphasize certain matters relating to the attest engagement or the subject matter.*]

In our opinion, the schedule referred to above presents, in all material respects, [*identify the subject matter—for example, the investment returns of XYZ Company for the year ended December 31, 20XX*] based on [*identify criteria—for example, the ABC criteria set forth in Note 1*].

[*Signature*]

[*Date*]

Example 2

This report is a standard examination report on an assertion for general use. The report pertains to subject matter for which suitable criteria exist and are available to all users through inclusion in a clear manner in the presentation of the subject matter. (See paragraphs .78 to .83 for guidance on restricting the use of the report when criteria are available only to specified parties.) A written assertion has been obtained from the responsible party.

Independent Accountant's Report

We have examined management's assertion that [*identify the assertion—for example, the accompanying schedule of investment returns of XYZ Company for the year ended December 31, 20XX is presented in accordance with ABC criteria set forth in Note 1*]. XYZ Company's management is responsible for the assertion. Our responsibility is to express an opinion on the assertion based on our examination.

Our examination was conducted in accordance with attestation standards established by the American Institute of Certified Public Accountants and, accordingly, included examining, on a test basis, evidence supporting management's assertion and performing such other procedures as we considered necessary in the circumstances. We believe that our examination provides a reasonable basis for our opinion.

[*Additional paragraph(s) may be added to emphasize certain matters relating to the attest engagement or the assertion.*]

In our opinion, management's assertion referred to above is fairly stated, in all material respects, based on [*identify established or stated criteria—for example, the ABC criteria set forth in Note 1*].

[*Signature*]

[*Date*]

Example 3

This is an examination report for general use; the introductory paragraph states the practitioner has examined management's assertion but the practitioner opines directly on the subject matter (see paragraph .87). The report pertains to subject matter for which suitable criteria exist and are available to all users through inclusion in a clear manner in the presentation of the subject matter. (See paragraphs .78 to .83 for guidance on restricting the use of the report when criteria are available only to specified parties.) A written assertion has been obtained from the responsible party.

Independent Accountant's Report

We have examined management's assertion that [*identify the assertion—for example, the accompanying schedule of investment returns of XYZ Company for the year ended December 31, 20XX is presented in accordance with the ABC criteria set forth in Note 1*]. XYZ Company's management is responsible for the assertion. Our responsibility is to express an opinion based on our examination.

Our examination was conducted in accordance with attestation standards established by the American Institute of Certified Public Accountants and, accordingly, included examining, on a test basis, evidence supporting [*identify the subject matter—for example, XYZ Company's schedule of investment returns*] and performing such other procedures as we considered necessary in the circumstances. We believe that our examination provides a reasonable basis for our opinion.

[*Additional paragraph(s) may be added to emphasize certain matters relating to the attest engagement or the assertion.*]

In our opinion, the schedule referred to above, presents, in all material respects, [*identify the subject matter—for example, the investment returns of XYZ Company for the year ended December 31, 20XX*] based on [*identify criteria—for example, the ABC criteria set forth in Note 1*].

[*Signature*]

[*Date*]

Example 4

This is an examination report on subject matter. Although suitable criteria exist, use of the report is restricted because the criteria are available only to specified parties. (See paragraph .34.) A written assertion has been obtained from the responsible party.

Independent Accountant's Report

We have examined the accompanying schedule of investment returns of XYZ Company for the year ended December 31, 20XX. XYZ Company's management is responsible for the schedule of investment returns. Our responsibility is to express an opinion based on our examination.

Our examination was conducted in accordance with attestation standards established by the American Institute of Certified Public Accountants and, accordingly, included examining, on a test basis, evidence supporting [*identify the subject matter—for example, XYZ Company's schedule of investment returns*] and performing such other procedures as we considered necessary in the circumstances. We believe that our examination provides a reasonable basis for our opinion.

[*Additional paragraph(s) may be added to emphasize certain matters relating to the attest engagement or the assertion.*]

In our opinion, the schedule referred to above, presents, in all material respects, [*identify the subject matter—for example, the investment returns of XYZ Company for the year ended December 31, 20XX*] based on the ABC criteria referred to in the investment management agreement between XYZ Company and DEF Investment Managers, Ltd., dated November 15, 20X1.

This report is intended solely for the information and use of XYZ Company and [*identify other specified parties—for example, DEF Investment Managers, Ltd.*] and is not intended to be and should not be used by anyone other than these specified parties.

[*Signature*]

[*Date*]

Example 5

This is an examination report with a qualified opinion because conditions exist that, individually or in combination, result in one or more material misstatements or deviations from the criteria; the report is for general use. The report pertains to subject matter for which suitable criteria exist and are available to all users through inclusion in a clear manner in the presentation of the subject matter. (See paragraphs .78 to .83 for guidance on restricting the use of the report when criteria are available only to specified parties.) A written assertion has been obtained from the responsible party.

Independent Accountant's Report

We have examined the accompanying schedule of investment returns of XYZ Company for the year ended December 31, 20XX. XYZ Company's management is responsible for the schedule of investment returns. Our responsibility is to express an opinion based on our examination.

Our examination was conducted in accordance with attestation standards established by the American Institute of Certified Public Accountants and, accordingly, included examining, on a test basis, evidence supporting [*identify the subject matter—for example, XYZ Company's schedule of investment returns*] and performing such other procedures as we considered necessary in the circumstances. We believe that our examination provides a reasonable basis for our opinion.

Our examination disclosed the following [*describe condition(s) that, individually or in the aggregate, resulted in a material misstatement or deviation from the criteria*].

In our opinion, except for the material misstatement [*or deviation from the criteria*] described in the preceding paragraph, the schedule referred to above, presents, in all material respects, [*identify the subject matter—for example, the investment returns of XYZ Company for the year ended December 31, 20XX*] based on [*identify criteria—for example, the ABC criteria set forth in Note 1*].

[*Signature*]

[*Date*]

Example 6

This is an examination report that contains a disclaimer of opinion because of a scope restriction. (See paragraph .74 for reporting guidance when there is a scope restriction.) The report pertains to subject matter for which suitable criteria exist and are available to all users through inclusion in a clear manner in the presentation of the subject matter.

Independent Accountant's Report

We were engaged to examine the accompanying schedule of investment returns of XYZ Company for the year ended December 31, 20XX. XYZ Company's management is responsible for the schedule of investment returns.

[*Scope paragraph should be omitted.*]

[*Include paragraph to describe scope restrictions.*]

Because of the restriction on the scope of our examination discussed in the preceding paragraph, the scope of our work was not sufficient to enable us to express, and we do not express, an opinion on whether the schedule referred to above presents, in all material respects, [*identify the subject matter—for example, the investment returns of XYZ Company for the year ended December 31, 20XX*] based on [*identify criteria—for example, the ABC criteria set forth in Note 1*].

[*Signature*]

[*Date*]

Example 7

This is an examination report on subject matter that is the responsibility of a party other than the client. The report is restricted as to use since a written assertion has not been provided by the responsible party. (See paragraph .78.) The subject matter pertains to criteria that are suitable and are available to the client.

Independent Accountant's Report

To the Board of Directors

DEF Company:

We have examined the [*identify the subject matter—for example, the accompanying schedule of investment returns of XYZ Company for the year ended December 31, 20XX*]. XYZ Company's management is responsible for the schedule of investment returns. XYZ management did not provide us a written assertion about their schedule of investment returns for the year ended December 31, 20XX. Our responsibility is to express an opinion based on our examination.

Our examination was conducted in accordance with attestation standards established by the American Institute of Certified Public Accountants and, accordingly, included examining, on a test basis, evidence supporting [*identify the subject matter—for example, XYZ Company's schedule of investment returns*] and performing such other procedures as we considered necessary in the circumstances. We believe that our examination provides a reasonable basis for our opinion.

[*Additional paragraph(s) may be added to emphasize certain matters relating to the attest engagement or the subject matter.*]

In our opinion, the schedule referred to above presents, in all material respects, [*identify the subject matter—for example, the investment returns of XYZ Company for the year ended December 31, 20XX*] based on [*identify criteria—for example, the ABC criteria set forth in Note 1*].

This report is intended solely for the information and use of the management and board of directors of DEF Company and is not intended to be and should not be used by anyone other than these specified parties.

[*Signature*]

[*Date*]

[Paragraph renumbered by the issuance of Statement on Standards for Attestation Engagements No. 11, January 2002.]

.115

Appendix B

Review Reports

Example 1

This is a standard review report on subject matter for general use. The report pertains to subject matter for which suitable criteria exist and are available to all users through inclusion in a clear manner in the presentation of the subject matter. (See paragraphs .78 to .83 for guidance on restricting the use of the report when criteria are available only to specified parties.) A written assertion has been obtained from the responsible party.

Independent Accountant's Report

We have reviewed the [*identify the subject matter—for example, the accompanying schedule of investment returns of XYZ Company for the year ended December 31, 20XX*]. XYZ Company's management is responsible for the schedule of investment returns.

Our review was conducted in accordance with attestation standards established by the American Institute of Certified Public Accountants. A review is substantially less in scope than an examination, the objective of which is the expression of an opinion on [*identify the subject matter—for example, XYZ Company's schedule of investment returns*]. Accordingly, we do not express such an opinion.

[*Additional paragraph(s) may be added to emphasize certain matters relating to the attest engagement or the subject matter.*]

Based on our review, nothing came to our attention that caused us to believe that the [*identify the subject matter—for example, schedule of investment returns of XYZ Company for the year ended December 31, 20XX*] is not presented, in all material respects, in conformity with [*identify the criteria—for example, the ABC criteria set forth in Note 1*].

[*Signature*]

[*Date*]

Example 2

This is a review report on subject matter that is the responsibility of a party other than the client. This review report is restricted as to use since a written assertion has not been provided by the responsible party. (See paragraph .78.) The subject matter pertains to criteria that are suitable and are available to the client.

Independent Accountant's Report

To the Board of Directors

DEF Company:

We have reviewed [*identify the subject matter—for example, the accompanying schedule of investment returns of XYZ Company for the year ended December 31, 20XX*]. XYZ Company's management is responsible for the schedule of investment returns. XYZ Company's management did not provide us a written assertion about their schedule of investment returns for the year ended December 31, 20XX.

Our review was conducted in accordance with attestation standards established by the American Institute of Certified Public Accountants. A review is substantially less in scope than an examination, the objective of which is the expression of an opinion on [*identify the subject matter—for example, XYZ Company's schedule of investment returns*]. Accordingly, we do not express such an opinion.

[*Additional paragraph(s) may be added to emphasize certain matters relating to the attest engagement or the subject matter.*]

Based on our review, nothing came to our attention that caused us to believe that [*identify the subject matter—for example, the schedule of investment returns of XYZ Company for the year ended December 31, 20XX*] is not presented, in all material respects, in conformity with [*identify the criteria—for example, the ABC criteria set forth in Note 1*].

This report is intended solely for the information and use of the management and board of directors of DEF Company and is not intended to be and should not be used by anyone other than these specified parties.

[*Signature*]

[*Date*]

Example 3

This is a review report on an assertion. Although suitable criteria exist for the subject matter, the report is restricted as to use since the criteria are available only to specified parties; if the criteria are available as described in paragraph .33 (*a*) to (*d*), the paragraph restricting the use of the report would be omitted. A written assertion has been obtained from the responsible party.

Independent Accountant's Report

We have reviewed management's assertion that [*identify the assertion—for example, the accompanying schedule of investment returns of XYZ Company for the year ended December 31, 20XX is presented in accordance with the ABC criteria referred to in Note 1*]. XYZ Company's management is responsible for the assertion.

Our review was conducted in accordance with attestation standards established by the American Institute of Certified Public Accountants. A review is substantially less in scope than an examination, the objective of which is the expression of an opinion on management's assertion. Accordingly, we do not express such an opinion.

[*Additional paragraph(s) may be added to emphasize certain matters relating to the attest engagement or the assertion.*]

Based on our review, nothing came to our attention that caused us to believe that management's assertion referred to above is not fairly stated, in all material respects, based on [*identify the criteria—for example, the ABC criteria referred to in the investment management agreement between XYZ Company and DEF Investment Managers, Ltd., dated November 15, 20X1*].

This report is intended solely for the information and use of XYZ Company and [*identify other specified parties—for example, DEF Investment Managers, Ltd.*] and is not intended to be and should not be used by anyone other than these specified parties.

[*Signature*]

[*Date*]

[Paragraph renumbered by the issuance of Statement on Standards for Attestation Engagements No. 11, January 2002.]

Based on our review, nothing came to our attention that caused us to believe that [identify the assertion—for example, XYZ Company's assertion that the investment performance statistics of XYZ Company for the year ended December 31, 20XX is presented in accordance with the criteria established by the ABC Group] is not fairly stated, in all material respects, based on [identify established or stated criteria—for example, the ABC criteria set forth in Note 1].

AT Section 9101

Attest Engagements: Attest Engagements Interpretations of Section 101

1. Defense Industry Questionnaire on Business Ethics and Conduct[1]

.01 *Question*—Certain defense contractors have made a commitment to adopt and implement six principles of business ethics and conduct contained in the *Defense Industry Initiatives on Business Ethics and Conduct* (initiatives). One of those principles concerns defense contractors' public accountability for their commitment to the initiatives. That public accountability begins by the contractor completing an annual *Public Accountability Questionnaire* (questionnaire).

.02 Each of the participating signatory companies (signatories) completes a questionnaire concerning certain policies, procedures, and programs that were to have been in place during the reporting period. The public accountability process requires signatories to perform internal audits and to provide officer certifications as to whether the responses to the questionnaire are current and accurate.

.03 Alternatively, a defense contractor may request its independent public accountant (practitioner) to examine or review its responses to the questionnaire for the purpose of expressing a conclusion about the appropriateness of those responses in a report. Would such an engagement be an attest engagement under section 101, *Attest Engagements*?

.04 *Interpretation*—Section 101 states that the attestation standards apply when a CPA in the practice of public accounting is engaged to issue or does issue an examination, a review, or an agreed-upon procedures report on subject matter, or an assertion about the subject matter that is the responsibility of another party. When a practitioner is engaged by a defense contractor to provide an examination or a review report on the contractor's written responses to the questionnaire, such an engagement involves subject matter that is the responsibility of the defense contractor. Consequently, section 101 applies to such engagements.

.05 *Question*—Paragraph .23 of section 101 specifies that "the practitioner must have reason to believe that the subject matter is capable of evaluation against criteria that are suitable and available to users." What are the criteria against which such subject matter is to be evaluated and are such criteria suitable and available?

.06 *Interpretation*—The criteria for evaluating the defense contractor's responses are set forth primarily in the questionnaire and the instructions thereto. The suitability of those criteria should be evaluated by assessing whether the criteria meet the characteristics discussed in paragraph .24 of section 101.

.07 The criteria set forth in the questionnaire and its instructions will, when properly followed, be suitable. Although these should provide suitable

[1] Information regarding the Defense Industry Initiative on Business Ethics and Conduct (DII) is available at DII's website www.dii.org.

criteria, the questionnaire and its instructions are not generally available. Therefore, the practitioner's report should normally be restricted. The availability requirement can be met if the defense contractor attaches the criteria to the presentation.

.08 *Question*—What is the nature of the procedures that should be applied to the questionnaire responses?

.09 *Interpretation*—The objective of the procedures performed in either an examination or a review engagement is to obtain evidential matter that the defense contractor has designed and placed in operation policies and programs in a manner that supports the signatory's responses to each of the questions on the questionnaire and that the policies and programs operated during the period covered by the questionnaire. The objective does not include providing assurance about whether the defense contractor's policies and programs operated effectively to ensure compliance with the defense contractor's code of business ethics and conduct on the part of individual employees or about whether the defense contractor and its employees have complied with federal procurement laws. In an examination, the evidential matter should be sufficient to limit attestation risk to a level that is appropriately low for the high degree of assurance imparted by an examination report. In a review, this evidential matter should be sufficient to limit attestation risk to a moderate level.

.10 Examination procedures include obtaining evidential matter by reading relevant policies and programs, making inquiries of appropriate defense contractor personnel, inspecting documents and records, confirming defense contractor assertions with its employees or others, and observing activities. In an examination it will be necessary for a practitioner's procedures to go beyond simply reading relevant policies and programs and making inquiries of appropriate defense contractor personnel. Alternatively, review procedures are generally limited to reading relevant policies and procedures and making inquiries of appropriate defense contractor personnel. When applying examination or review procedures, the practitioner should assess the appropriateness (including the comprehensiveness) of the policies and programs supporting the signatory's responses to each of the questions on the questionnaire.

.11 A particular defense contractor's policies and programs may vary from those of other defense contractors. As a result, evidential matter obtained from the procedures performed cannot be evaluated solely on a quantitative basis. Consequently, it is not practicable to establish only quantitative guidelines for determining the nature or extent of the evidential matter that is necessary to provide the assurance required in either an examination or a review. The qualitative aspects should also be considered.

.12 In determining the nature, timing, and extent of examination or review procedures, the practitioner should consider information obtained in the performance of other services for the defense contractor, for example, the audit of the defense contractor's financial statements. For multi-location defense contractors, whether policies and programs operated during the period should be evaluated for both the defense contractor's headquarters and for selected defense contracting locations. The practitioner may consider using the work of the defense contractor's internal auditors. The guidance in AU section 322, *The Auditor's Consideration of the Internal Audit Function in an Audit of Financial Statements*, may be useful in that consideration.

.13 Examination procedures, and in some instances review procedures, may require access to information involving specific instances of actual or alleged noncompliance with laws. An inability to obtain access to such information because of restrictions imposed by a defense contractor (for example, to protect attorney-client privilege) may constitute a scope limitation. Section 101 paragraphs .73–.75 provide guidance in such situations. The practitioner should assess the effect of the inability to obtain access to such information on his or her ability to form a conclusion about whether the related policy or program operated during the period. If the defense contractor's reasons for not permitting access to the information are reasonable (for example, the information is the subject of litigation or a governmental investigation) and have been approved by an executive officer of the defense contractor, the occurrences of restricted access to information are few in number, and the practitioner has access to other information about that specific instance or about other instances that is sufficient to permit a conclusion to be formed about whether the related policy or program operated during the period, the practitioner ordinarily would conclude that it is not necessary to disclaim assurance.

.14 If the practitioner's scope of work has been restricted with respect to one or more questions, the practitioner should consider the implications of that restriction on the practitioner's ability to form a conclusion about other questions. In addition, as the nature or number of questions on which the defense contractor has imposed scope limitations increases in significance, the practitioner should consider whether to withdraw from the engagement.

.15 *Question*—What is the form of report that should be issued to meet the requirements of section 101?

.16 *Interpretation*—The standards of reporting in section 101 provide guidance about report content and wording and the circumstances that may require report modification. Appendix A and appendix B provide illustrative reports appropriate for various circumstances. Section 101 paragraph .66 permits the practitioner to report directly on the subject matter or on management's assertion. In either case, the practitioner should ordinarily obtain a written assertion. An illustrative defense contractor assertion is also presented in appendix A and appendix B.

.17 The engagements addressed in this interpretation do not include providing assurance about whether the defense contractor's policies and programs operated effectively to ensure compliance with the defense contractor's code of business ethics and conduct on the part of individual employees or about whether the defense contractor and its employees have complied with federal procurement laws. The practitioner's report should explicitly disclaim an opinion on the extent of such compliance.

.18 Because variations in individual performance and interpretation will affect the operation of the defense contractor's policies and programs during the period, adherence to all such policies and programs in every case may not be possible. In determining whether a reservation about a response in the questionnaire is sufficiently significant to result in an opinion modified for an exception to that response, the practitioner should consider the nature, causes, patterns, and pervasiveness of the instances in which the policies and programs did not operate as designed and their implications for that response in the questionnaire.

.19 When scope limitations have precluded the practitioner from forming an opinion on the responses to one or more questions, the practitioner's report should describe all such scope restrictions. If the defense contractor imposed such a scope limitation after the practitioner had begun performing procedures, that fact should be stated in the report.

.20 A defense contractor may request the practitioner to communicate to management, the board of directors, or one of its committees, either orally or in writing, conditions noted that do not constitute significant reservations about the answers to the questionnaire but that might nevertheless be of value to management. Agreed-upon arrangements between the practitioner and the defense contractor to communicate conditions noted may include, for example, the reporting of matters of less significance than those contemplated by the criteria, the existence of conditions specified by the defense contractor, the results of further investigation of matters noted to identify underlying causes, or suggestions for improvements in various policies or programs. Under these arrangements, the practitioner may be requested to visit specific locations, assess the effectiveness of specific policies or programs, or undertake specific procedures not otherwise planned. In addition, the practitioner is not precluded from communicating matters believed to be of value, even if no specific request has been made.

.21

Appendix A

Illustrative Defense Contractor Assertions and Examination Reports

Defense Industry Questionnaire on Business Ethics and Conduct

Illustration 1: Unqualified Opinion Unrestricted With Criteria Attached to the Presentation

Defense Contractor Assertion

Statement of Responses to the Defense Industry Questionnaire on *Business Ethics and Conduct for the period from _______ to _______.*

The affirmative responses in the accompanying *Questionnaire on Business Ethics and Conduct with Responses by the XYZ Company for the period from _______ to _______* are based on policies and programs in operation for that period and are appropriately presented in conformity with the criteria set forth in the *Defense Industry Initiatives on Business Ethics and Conduct*, including the Questionnaire.

Attachments:

Defense Industry Initiatives on Business Ethics and Conduct

Instructions and Questionnaire on Business Ethics and Conduct with Responses by the XYZ Company for the period from _______ to _______.

Examination Report

Independent Accountant's Report

To the Board of Directors of the XYZ Company

We have examined the XYZ Company's *Statement of Responses to the Defense Industry Questionnaire on Business Ethics and Conduct for the period from _______ to _______*, and the Questionnaire and responses attached thereto. XYZ Company's management is responsible for its responses to the Questionnaire. Our responsibility is to express an opinion based on our examination.

Our examination was conducted in accordance with attestation standards established by the American Institute of Certified Public Accountants and, accordingly, included examining, on a test basis, evidence as to whether XYZ Company had policies and programs in operation during that period that support the affirmative responses to the *Questionnaire* and performing such other procedures as we considered necessary in the circumstances. We believe that our examination provides a reasonable basis for our opinion. Our examination procedures were not designed, however, to evaluate whether the aforementioned policies and programs operated effectively to ensure compliance with the Company's *Code of Business Ethics and Conduct* on the part of individual employees or to evaluate the extent to which the Company or its employees have complied with federal procurement laws, and we do not express an opinion or any other form of assurance thereon.

In our opinion, the affirmative responses in the Questionnaire accompanying the *Statement of Responses to the Defense Industry Questionnaire on Business Ethics and Conduct for the period from _______ to _______* referred to above are appropriately presented in conformity with the criteria set forth in the *Defense Industry Initiatives on Business Ethics and Conduct*, including the Questionnaire.

Illustration 2: Unqualified Opinion; Report Modified for Negative Responses to Defense Contractor Assertion; Use of the Report is Restricted Because Criteria are Available Only to Specified Parties

Defense Contractor Assertion

Statement of Responses to the Defense Industry Questionnaire on *Business Ethics and Conduct for the period from _______ to _______.*

The affirmative responses in the accompanying *Questionnaire on Business Ethics and Conduct with Responses by the XYZ Company for the period from _______ to _______* are based on policies and programs in operation for that period and are appropriately presented in conformity with the criteria set forth in the *Defense Industry Initiatives on Business Ethics and Conduct*, including the Questionnaire. Negative responses indicate that the Company did not have policies and programs in operation during that period with respect to those areas.

Attachments: None

(The responses could include an explanation of negative responses if the defense contractor so desired.)

Examination Report

Independent Accountant's Report

To the Board of Directors of the XYZ Company

We have examined the XYZ Company's *Statement of Responses to the Defense Industry Questionnaire on Business Ethics and Conduct for the period from _______ to _______.* XYZ Company's management is responsible for its responses to the Questionnaire. Our responsibility is to express an opinion based on our examination.

[*Standard Scope Paragraph*]

In our opinion, the affirmative responses in the Questionnaire referred to above are appropriately presented in conformity with the criteria set forth in the *Defense Industry Initiatives on Business Ethics and Conduct*, including the Questionnaire. The negative responses to Questions _______ and _______ in the Questionnaire indicate that the Company did not have policies and programs in operation during the period with respect to those areas.

This report is intended solely for the information and use of the XYZ Company and [*identify other specified parties—for example,* the Defense Industry Initiative] and is not intended to be and should not be used by anyone other than these specified parties.

Illustration 3: Opinion Modified for Exception on Certain Response

Defense Contractor Assertion

Statement of Responses to the Defense Industry Questionnaire on *Business Ethics and Conduct for the period from _______ to _______*.

The affirmative responses in the accompanying *Questionnaire on Business Ethics and Conduct with Responses by the XYZ Company for the period from _______ to _______*, are based on policies and programs in operation for that period and are appropriately presented in conformity with the criteria set forth in the *Defense Industry Initiatives on Business Ethics and Conduct*, including the Questionnaire.

Attachments:

Defense Industry Initiatives on Business Ethics and Conduct

Questionnaire on Business Ethics and Conduct with Responses by the XYZ Company for the period from _______ to _______.

Examination Report

Independent Accountant's Report

To the Board of Directors of the XYZ Company

[*Standard Introductory and Scope Paragraphs*]

Management believes that an appropriate mechanism exists for informing employees of the results of any follow-up into their charges of violations of the Company's Code of Business Ethics and Conduct, and has accordingly answered Question 12 in the affirmative. That mechanism consists principally of distributing newspaper articles and press releases of violations of federal procurement laws that have been voluntarily reported to the appropriate governmental agencies. We do not believe that such a mechanism is sufficient, inasmuch as it does not provide follow-up information on violations reported by employees that are not deemed reportable to a governmental agency. Consequently, in our opinion, the affirmative response to Question 12 in the Questionnaire is not appropriately presented in conformity with the criteria set forth in the *Defense Industry Initiatives on Business Ethics and Conduct*, including the Questionnaire.

In our opinion, except for the response to Question 12 as discussed in the preceding paragraph, the affirmative responses in the Questionnaire accompanying the *Statement of Responses to the Defense Industry Questionnaire on Business Ethics and Conduct for the period from _______ to _______* referred to above are appropriately presented in conformity with the criteria set forth in the Defense Industry Initiatives on Business Ethics and Conduct, including the Questionnaire.

Illustration 4: Opinion Modified for Exception on a Certain Response; Report also Modified for Negative Responses

Defense Contractor Assertion

Statement of Responses to the *Defense Industry Questionnaire on Business Ethics and Conduct for the period from _______ to _______*.

The affirmative responses in the accompanying *Questionnaire on Business Ethics and Conduct with Responses by the XYZ Company for the period from _______ to _______* are based on policies and programs in operation for that period and are appropriately presented in conformity with the criteria set forth in the *Defense Industry Initiatives on Business Ethics and Conduct*, including the Questionnaire. Negative responses indicate that the Company did not have policies and programs in operation during that period with respect to those areas.

Attachments:

Defense Industry Initiatives on Business Ethics and Conduct

Questionnaire on Business Ethics and Conduct with Responses by the XYZ Company for the period from _______ to _______.

(The responses could include an explanation of negative responses if the defense contractor so desired.)

Examination Report

Independent Accountant's Report

To the Board of Directors of the XYZ Company

[*Standard Introductory and Scope Paragraphs*]

Management believes that an appropriate mechanism exists for letting employees know of the results of any follow-up into their charges of violations of the Company's Code of Business Ethics and Conduct, and has accordingly answered Question 12 in the affirmative. That mechanism consists principally of distributing newspaper articles and press releases of violations of federal procurement laws that have been voluntarily reported to the appropriate governmental agencies. We do not believe that such a mechanism is sufficient, inasmuch as it does not provide follow-up information on violations reported by employees that are not deemed reportable to a governmental agency. Consequently, in our opinion, the affirmative response to Question 12 in the Questionnaire is not appropriately presented in conformity with the criteria set forth in the Defense Industry Initiatives on Business Ethics and Conduct, including the Questionnaire.

In our opinion, except for the response to Question 12 as discussed in the preceding paragraph, the affirmative responses in the Questionnaire accompanying the *Statement of Responses to the Defense Industry Questionnaire on Business Ethics and Conduct for the period from _______ to _______* referred to above are appropriately presented in conformity with the criteria set forth in the *Defense Industry Initiatives on Business Ethics and Conduct*, including the Questionnaire. The negative responses to Questions _______ and _______ in the Questionnaire indicate that the Company did not have policies and programs in operation during the period with respect to those areas.

Illustration 5: Opinion Disclaimed on Certain Responses Because of Scope Restrictions Imposed by Client

Defense Contractor Assertion

Statement of Responses to the Defense Industry Questionnaire on *Business Ethics and Conduct for the period from _______ to _______.*

The affirmative responses in the accompanying *Questionnaire on Business Ethics and Conduct with Responses by the XYZ Company for the period from _______ to _______* are based on policies and programs in operation for that period and are appropriately presented in conformity with the criteria set forth in the *Defense Industry Initiatives on Business Ethics and Conduct*, including the Questionnaire.

Attachments:

Defense Industry Initiatives on Business Ethics and Conduct

Questionnaire on Business Ethics and Conduct with Responses by the XYZ Company for the period from _______ to _______.

Examination Report

Independent Accountant's Report

To the Board of Directors of the XYZ Company

[*Standard Introductory Paragraph*]

Except as described below, our examination was conducted in accordance with attestation standards established by the American Institute of Certified Public Accountants and, accordingly, included examining, on a test basis, evidence as to whether XYZ Company had policies and programs in operation during that period that support the affirmative responses to the *Questionnaire*. We believe that our examination provides a reasonable basis for our opinion. Our examination procedures were not designed, however, to evaluate whether the aforementioned policies and programs operated effectively to ensure compliance with the Company's *Code of Business Ethics and Conduct* on the part of individual employees or to evaluate the extent to which the Company or its employees have complied with federal procurement laws, and we do not express an opinion or any other form of assurance thereon.

We were not permitted to read relevant documents and files or interview appropriate employees to determine that the affirmative answers to Questions 6, 7, and 8 are appropriate. The nature of those questions precluded us from satisfying ourselves as to the appropriateness of those answers by means of other examination procedures.

In our opinion, the affirmative responses to Questions 1 through 5 and 9 through 17 in the Questionnaire accompanying the *Statement of Responses to the Defense Industry Questionnaire on Business Ethics and Conduct for the period from _______ to _______* referred to above are appropriately presented in conformity with the criteria set forth in the *Defense Industry Initiatives on Business Ethics and Conduct*, including the Questionnaire. Because of the matters discussed in the preceding paragraph, the scope of our work was not sufficient to express, and we do not express, an opinion on the appropriateness of the affirmative responses to Questions 6, 7, and 8 in the Questionnaire.

.22

Appendix B

Illustrative Defense Contractor Assertion and Review Report Restricted Because Criteria Are Available Only To Specified Parties

Defense Industry Questionnaire on Business Ethics and Conduct

Defense Contractor Assertion

Statement of Responses to the Defense Industry Questionnaire on *Business Ethics and Conduct for the period from _______ to _______.*

The affirmative responses in the accompanying *Questionnaire on Business Ethics and Conduct with Responses by the XYZ Company for the period from _______ to _______* are based on policies and programs in operation during that period and are appropriately presented in conformity with the criteria set forth in the *Defense Industry Initiatives on Business Ethics and Conduct*, including the Questionnaire.

Attachments: None

Review Report

Independent Accountant's Report

To the Board of Directors of the XYZ Company

We have reviewed the XYZ Company's *Statement of Responses to the Defense Industry Questionnaire on Business Ethics and Conduct for the period from _______ to _______*. XYZ Company's management is responsible for the Statement of Responses to the Defense Industry Questionnaire on Business Ethics.

Our review was conducted in accordance with attestation standards established by the American Institute of Certified Public Accountants. A review is substantially less in scope than an examination, the objective of which is the expression of an opinion on the affirmative responses in the Questionnaire. Accordingly, we do not express such an opinion. Additionally, our review was not designed to evaluate whether the aforementioned policies and programs operated effectively to ensure compliance with the Company's *Code of Business Ethics and Conduct* on the part of individual employees or to evaluate the extent to which the Company or its employees have complied with federal procurement laws and we do not express an opinion or any other form of assurance thereon.

Based on our review, nothing came to our attention that caused us to believe that the affirmative responses in the Questionnaire referred to above are not appropriately presented in conformity with the criteria set forth in the *Defense Industry Initiatives on Business Ethics and Conduct*, including the Questionnaire.

This report is intended solely for the information and use of the XYZ Company and [*identify other specified parties—for example,* the Defense Industry Initiative] and is not intended to be and should not be used by anyone other than these specified parties.

[Issue Date: August 1987; Amended: February 1989;
Modified: May 1989; Revised: January 2001; November 2006.]

2. Responding to Requests for Reports on Matters Relating to Solvency

.23 *Question*—Lenders, as a requisite to the closing of certain secured financings in connection with leveraged buyouts, recapitalizations and certain other financial transactions, have sometimes requested written assurance from an accountant regarding the prospective borrower's solvency and related matters.[2] The lender is concerned that such financings not be considered to include a fraudulent conveyance or transfer under the Federal Bankruptcy Code[3] or the relevant state fraudulent conveyance or transfer statute.[4] If the financing is subsequently determined to have included a fraudulent conveyance or transfer, repayment obligations and security interests may be set aside or subordinated to the claims of other creditors.

.24 May a practitioner provide assurance concerning *matters relating to solvency* as hereinafter defined?

.25 *Interpretation*—No. For reasons set forth subsequently, a practitioner should not provide any form of assurance, through examination, review, or agreed-upon procedures engagements, that an entity

- is not insolvent at the time the debt is incurred or would not be rendered insolvent thereby.
- does not have unreasonably small capital.
- has the ability to pay its debts as they mature.

---

[2] Although this interpretation describes requests from secured lenders and summarizes the potential effects of fraudulent conveyance or transfer laws upon such lenders, the interpretation is not limited to requests from lenders. All requests for assurance on matters relating to solvency are governed by this interpretation.

[3] Section 548 of the Federal Bankruptcy Code defines *fraudulent transfers and obligations* as follows:

> The trustee may avoid any transfer of an interest of the debtor in property or any obligation incurred by the debtor, that was made or incurred on or within one year before the date of the filing of the petition, if the debtor voluntarily or involuntarily—
>
> (1) made such transfer or incurred such obligation with actual intent to hinder, delay, or defraud any entity to which the debtor was or became, on or after the date that such transfer occurred or such obligation was incurred, indebted; or
>
> (2)(A) received less than a reasonably equivalent value in exchange for such transfer or obligation; and
>
> (2)(B)(i) was insolvent on the date that such transfer was made or such obligation was incurred, or became insolvent as a result of such transfer or obligation;
>
> (2)(B)(ii) was engaged in business or a transaction, or was about to engage in business or a transaction, for which any property remaining with the debtor was an unreasonably small capital; or
>
> (2)(B)(iii) intended to incur, or believed that the debtor would incur, debts that would be beyond the debtor's ability to pay as such debts matured. (Bankruptcy Law Reporter, 3 vols. [Chicago: Commerce Clearing House, 1986], vol. 1, 1339).

[4] State fraudulent conveyance or transfer statutes such as the Uniform Fraudulent Conveyance Act and the Uniform Fraudulent Transfer Act reflect substantially similar provisions. These state laws may be employed absent a declaration of bankruptcy or by a bankruptcy trustee under Section 544(1) of the Federal Bankruptcy Code. Although the statute of limitations varies from state to state, in some states financing transactions may be vulnerable to challenge for up to six years from closing.

In the context of particular transactions other terms are sometimes used or defined by the parties as equivalents of or substitutes for the terms listed above (for example, *fair salable value of assets exceeds liabilities*). These terms, and those matters listed previously, are hereinafter referred to as *matters relating to solvency*. The prohibition extends to providing assurance concerning all such terms.

.26 The third general attestation standard states that the practitioner must have reason to believe that the subject matter is capable of evaluation against criteria that are suitable and available to users. Suitable criteria must have each of the following attributes:

- *Objectivity*—Criteria should be free from bias.
- *Measurability*—Criteria should permit reasonably consistent measurements, qualitative or quantitative, of subject matter.
- *Completeness*—Criteria should be sufficiently complete so those relevant factors that would alter a conclusion about subject matter are not omitted.
- *Relevance*—Criteria should be relevant to the subject matter.

In addition, the second general attestation standard states that the practitioner must have adequate knowledge of the subject matter.

.27 The matters relating to solvency mentioned in paragraph .23 are subject to legal interpretation under, and varying legal definition in, the Federal Bankruptcy Code and various state fraudulent conveyance and transfer statutes. Because these matters are not clearly defined in an accounting sense, and are therefore subject to varying interpretations, they do not provide the practitioner with suitable criteria required to evaluate the subject matter or an assertion under the third general attestation standard. In addition, lenders are concerned with legal issues on matters relating to solvency and the practitioner is generally unable to evaluate or provide assurance on these matters of legal interpretation. Therefore, practitioners are precluded from giving any form of assurance on matters relating to solvency or any financial presentation of matters relating to solvency.

.28 Under existing AICPA standards, the practitioner may provide a client with various professional services that may be useful to the client in connection with a financing. These services include the following:

- Audit of historical financial statements
- Review of historical financial information (a review in accordance with AU section 722, *Interim Financial Information*, of interim financial information, or in accordance with AR section 100, *Compilation and Review of Financial Statements*)
- Examination or review of pro forma financial information (section 401, *Reporting on Pro Forma Financial Information*)
- Examination or compilation of prospective financial information (section 301, *Financial Forecasts and Projections*)

.29 In addition, under existing AICPA attestation standards (section 201, *Agreed-Upon Procedures Engagements*), the practitioner can provide the client and lender with an agreed-upon procedures report. In such an engagement, a client and lender may request that specified procedures be applied to various financial presentations, such as historical financial information, pro forma financial information, and prospective financial information, which can be useful to a client or lender in connection with a financing.

.30 The practitioner should be aware that certain of the services described in paragraph .28 require that the practitioner have an appropriate level of knowledge of the entity's accounting and financial reporting practices and its internal control. This has ordinarily been obtained by the practitioner auditing historical financial statements of the entity for the most recent annual period or by otherwise obtaining an equivalent knowledge base. When considering acceptance of an engagement relating to a financing, the practitioner should consider whether he or she can perform these services without an equivalent knowledge base.

.31 A report on agreed-upon procedures should not provide any assurances on matters relating to solvency or any financial presentation of matters relating to solvency (for example, fair salable value of assets less liabilities or fair salable value of assets less liabilities, contingent liabilities, and other commitments). A practitioner's report on the results of applying agreed-upon procedures should contain the report elements set forth in paragraph .31 of section 201 (or paragraph .55 of section 301 if applying agreed upon procedures to prospective financial information). The practitioner's report on the results of applying agreed-upon procedures should state that

- the service has been requested in connection with a financing (no reference should be made to any solvency provisions in the financing agreement).
- no representations are provided regarding questions of legal interpretation.
- no assurance is provided concerning the borrower's (*a*) solvency, (*b*) adequacy of capital, or (*c*) ability to pay its debts.
- the procedures should not be taken to supplant any additional inquiries and procedures that the lender should undertake in its consideration of the proposed financing.
- where applicable, an audit of recent historical financial statements has previously been performed and that no audit of any historical financial statements for a subsequent period has been performed. In addition, if any services have been performed pursuant to paragraph .28, they may be referred to.

.32 The report ordinarily is dated at or shortly before the closing date. The financing agreement ordinarily specifies the date, often referred to as the cutoff date, to which the report is to relate (for example, a date three business days before the date of the report). The report should state that the inquiries and other procedures carried out in connection with the report did not cover the period from the cutoff date to the date of the report.

.33 The practitioner might consider furnishing the client with a draft of the agreed-upon procedures report. The draft report should deal with all matters expected to be covered in the terms expected to be used in the final report. The draft report should be identified as a draft in order to avoid giving the impression that the procedures described therein have been performed. This practice of furnishing a draft report at an early point permits the practitioner to make clear to the client and lender what they may expect the accountant to furnish and gives them an opportunity to change the financing agreement or the agreed-upon procedures if they so desire.

[Issue Date: May 1988; Amended: February 1993;
Revised: January 2001; November 2006.]

3. Applicability of Attestation Standards to Litigation Services

.34 *Question*—Section 101 paragraph .04 provides an example of a litigation service provided by practitioners that would not be considered an attest engagement as defined by section 101. When does section 101 not apply to litigation service engagements?

.35 *Interpretation*—Section 101 does not apply to litigation services that involve pending or potential formal legal or regulatory proceedings before a *trier of fact*[5] in connection with the resolution of a dispute between two or more parties in any of the following circumstances when the

a. practitioner has not been engaged to issue and does not issue an examination, a review, or an agreed-upon procedures report on subject matter, or an assertion about the subject matter that is the responsibility of another party.

b. service comprises being an expert witness.

c. service comprises being a trier of fact or acting on behalf of one.

d. practitioner's work under the rules of the proceedings is subject to detailed analysis and challenge by each party to the dispute.

e. practitioner is engaged by an attorney to do work that will be protected by the attorney's work product privilege and such work is not intended to be used for other purposes.

When performing such litigation services, the practitioner should comply with Rule 201, *General Standards* (ET sec. 201 par. .01) of the AICPA Code of Professional Conduct.

.36 *Question*—When does section 101 apply to litigation service engagements?

.37 *Interpretation*—Section 101 applies to litigation service engagements only when the practitioner is engaged to issue or does issue an examination, a review, or an agreed-upon procedures report on subject matter, or an assertion about the subject matter, that is the responsibility of another party.

.38 *Question*—Paragraph .04(c) of section 101 provides the following example of litigation service engagements that are not considered attest engagements: "Services performed in accordance with the Statement on Standards for Consulting Services, such as.... engagements in which a practitioner is engaged to testify as an expert witness in accounting, auditing, taxation, or other matters, given certain stipulated facts."

What does the term *stipulated facts* as used in section 101 paragraph .04(c) mean?

.39 *Interpretation*—The term *stipulated facts* as used in section 101 paragraph .04(c) means facts or assumptions that are specified by one or more parties to a dispute to serve as the basis for the development of an expert opinion. It is not used in its typical legal sense of facts agreed to by all parties involved in a dispute.

.40 *Question*—Does Interpretation No. 2, "Responding to Requests for Reports on Matters Relating to Solvency," of section 101 (AR sec. 9101 par. .23–.33), prohibit a practitioner from providing expert testimony, as described in section 101 paragraph .04(c) before a trier of fact on matters relating to solvency?

---

[5] A *trier of fact* in this section means a court, regulatory body, or government authority; their agents; a grand jury; or an arbitrator or mediator of the dispute.

.41 *Interpretation*—No. Matters relating to solvency mentioned in paragraph .25 are subject to legal interpretation under, and varying legal definition in, the Federal Bankruptcy Code and various state fraudulent conveyance and transfer statutes. Because these matters are not clearly defined in an accounting sense, and therefore subject to varying interpretations, they do not provide the practitioner with the suitable criteria required to evaluate the assertion. Thus, Interpretation No. 2 (paragraphs .23–.33) prohibits a practitioner from providing any form of assurance in reporting upon examination, review, or agreed-upon procedures engagements about matters relating to solvency (as defined in paragraph .25).

.42 However, a practitioner who is involved with pending or potential formal legal or regulatory proceedings before a trier of fact in connection with the resolution of a dispute between two or more parties may provide an expert opinion or consulting advice about matters relating to solvency. The prohibition in paragraphs .23–.33 does not apply in such engagements because as part of the legal or regulatory proceedings, each party to the dispute has the opportunity to analyze and challenge the legal definition and interpretation of the matters relating to solvency and the criteria the practitioner uses to evaluate matters related to solvency. Such services are not intended to be used by others who do not have the opportunity to analyze and challenge such definitions and interpretations.

[Issue Date: July 1990; Revised: January 2001.]

4. Providing Access to or Copies of Attest Documentation to a Regulator

.43 *Question*—Interpretation No. 1, "Providing Access to or Copies of Audit Documentation to a Regulator," of AU section 339, *Audit Documentation* (AU sec. 9339 par. .01–.15), contains guidance relating to providing access to or copies of audit documentation to a regulator. Is this guidance applicable to an attest engagement when a regulator requests access to or copies of the attest documentation?

.44 *Interpretation*—Yes. The guidance in Interpretation No. 1 (AU sec. 9339 par. .01–.15) is applicable in these circumstances; however, the letter to a regulator should be tailored to meet the individual engagement characteristics or the purpose of the regulatory request, for example, a quality control review. Illustrative letters for an examination engagement performed in accordance with section 601, *Compliance Attestation*, and an agreed-upon procedures engagement performed in accordance with section 201, follow.

.45 Illustrative letter for examination engagement:

Illustrative Letter to Regulator[6]

[*Date*]

[*Name and Address of Regulatory Agency*]

Your representatives have requested access to our attest documentation in connection with our engagement to examine (*identify the subject matter examined*

[6] The practitioner should appropriately modify this letter when the engagement has been conducted in accordance with Statements on Standards for Attestation Engagements (SSAE) and also in accordance with additional attest requirements specified by a regulatory agency (for example, the requirements specified in *Government Auditing Standards* issued by the Comptroller General of the United States).

or restate management's assertion). It is our understanding that the purpose of your request is (*state purpose*: for example, "to facilitate your regulatory examination").[7]

Our examination was conducted in accordance with attestation standards[8] established by the American Institute of Certified Public Accountants, the objective of which is to form an opinion as to whether the subject matter (or management's assertion) is fairly stated, in all material respects, based on (*identify criteria*). Under these standards, we have the responsibility to plan and perform our examination to provide a reasonable basis for our opinion and to exercise due professional care in the performance of our examination. Our examination is subject to the inherent risk that material noncompliance, if it exists, would not be detected. In addition, our examination does not address the possibility that material noncompliance may occur in the future. Also, our use of professional judgment and the assessments of attestation risk and materiality for the purpose of our examination means that matters may have existed that would have been assessed differently by you. Our examination does not provide a legal determination on (*name of entity*)'s compliance with specified requirements.

The attest documentation was prepared for the purpose of providing the principal support for our opinion on (*name of entity*)'s compliance and to aid in the performance and supervision of our examination. The attest documentation is the principal record of attest procedures performed, information obtained, and conclusions reached in the examination. The procedures that we performed were limited to those we considered necessary under attestation standards[9] established by the American Institute of Certified Public Accountants to provide us with reasonable basis for our opinion. Accordingly, we make no representation as to the sufficiency or appropriateness, for your purposes, of either the procedures or information in our attest documentation. In addition, any notations, comments, and individual conclusions appearing on any of the attest documentation do not stand alone and should not be read as an opinion on any part of management's assertion or the related subject matter.

Our examination was conducted for the purpose stated above and was not planned or performed in contemplation of your (*state purpose*: for example, "regulatory examination"). Therefore, items of possible interest to you may not have been specifically addressed. Accordingly, our examination, and the attest documentation prepared in connection therewith, should not supplant other inquiries and procedures that should be undertaken by the (*name of regulatory agency*) for the purpose of monitoring and regulating (*name of entity*). In addition, we have not performed any procedures since the date of our report with respect to the subject matter (*or management's assertion related thereto*), and significant events or circumstances may have occurred since that date.

The attest documentation constitutes and reflects work performed or information obtained by us in the course of our examination. The documents contain trade secrets and confidential commercial and financial information of our firm and (*name of entity*) that is privileged and confidential, and we expressly reserve all rights with respect to disclosures to third parties. Accordingly, we request confidential treatment under the Freedom of Information Act or similar laws and regulations when requests are made for the attest documentation or

---

[7] If the practitioner is not required by law, regulation, or engagement contract to provide a regulator access to the attest documentation but otherwise intends to provide such access (see Interpretation No. 1, "Providing Access to or Copies of Audit Documentation to a Regulator," of AU section 339, *Audit Documentation* [AU sec. 9339 par. .11–.15]), the letter should include a statement that: "Management of (*name of entity*) has authorized us to provide you access to our attest documentation for (*state purpose*)."

[8] Refer to footnote 6.

[9] Refer to footnote 6.

information contained therein or any documents created by the (*name of regulatory agency*) containing information derived there from. We further request that written notice be given to our firm before distribution of the information in the attest documentation (or copies thereof) to others, including other governmental agencies, except when such distribution is required by law or regulation.[10]

[*If it is expected that copies will be requested, add the following*:

Any copies of our attest documentation we agree to provide you will contain a legend "Confidential Treatment Requested by (*name of practitioner, address, telephone number*)."]

[*Firm signature*]

.46 Example letter for agreed-upon procedures engagements:

Illustrative Letter to Regulator[11]

[*Date*]

[*Name and Address of Regulatory Agency*]

Your representatives have requested access to our attest documentation in connection with our engagement to perform agreed-upon procedures on (*identify the subject matter or management's assertion*). It is our understanding that the purpose of your request is (*state purpose:* for example, "to facilitate your regulatory examinations").[12]

Our agreed-upon procedures engagement was conducted in accordance with attestation standards[13] established by the American Institute of Certified Public Accountants. Under these standards, we have the responsibility to perform the agreed-upon procedures to provide a reasonable basis for the findings expressed in our report. We were not engaged to, and did not, perform an examination, the objective of which would be to form an opinion on (*identify the subject matter or management's assertion*). Our engagement is subject to the inherent risk that material misstatement of (*identify the subject matter or management's assertion*), if it exists, would not be detected. (*The practitioner may add the following:* "In addition, our engagement does not address the possibility that material misstatement of (*identify the subject matter or management's assertion*) may occur in the future.") The procedures that we performed were limited to those agreed to by the specified users, and the sufficiency of these procedures is solely the responsibility of the specified users of the report. Further, our engagement does not provide a legal determination on (*name of entity*)'s compliance with specified requirements.

The attest documentation was prepared to document agreed-upon procedures applied, information obtained, and findings reached in the engagement. Accordingly, we make no representation, for your purposes, as to the sufficiency

---

[10] This illustrative paragraph may not in and of itself be sufficient to gain confidential treatment under the rules and regulations of certain regulatory agencies. The practitioner should consider tailoring this paragraph to the circumstances after consulting the regulations of each applicable regulatory agency and, if necessary, consult with legal counsel regarding the specific procedures and requirements necessary to gain confidential treatment.

[11] The practitioner should appropriately modify this letter when the engagement has been conducted in accordance with the SSAEs and also in accordance with additional attest requirements specified by a regulatory agency (for example, the requirements specified in *Government Auditing Standards* issued by the Comptroller General of the United States).

[12] If the practitioner is not required by law, regulation or engagement contract to provide a regulator access to the attest documentation but otherwise intends to provide such access (see Interpretation No. 1 of AU section 339 [AU sec. 9339 par. .11–.15]) the letter should include a statement that: "Management of (*name of entity*) has authorized us to provide you access to our attest documentation for (*state purpose*)."

[13] Refer to footnote 6.

or appropriateness of the information in our attest documentation. In addition, any notations, comments, and individual findings appearing on any of the attest documentation should not be read as an opinion on management's assertion or the related subject matter, or any part thereof.

Our engagement was performed for the purpose stated above and was not performed in contemplation of your (*state purpose*: for example, "regulatory examination"). Therefore, items of possible interest to you may not have been specifically addressed. Accordingly, our engagement, and the attest documentation prepared in connection therewith, should not supplant other inquiries and procedures that should be undertaken by the (*name of regulatory agency*) for the purpose of monitoring and regulating (*name of client*). In addition, we have not performed any procedures since the date of our report with respect to the subject matter or management's assertion related thereto, and significant events or circumstances may have occurred since that date.

The attest documentation constitutes and reflects procedures performed or information obtained by us in the course of our engagement. The documents contain trade secrets and confidential commercial and financial information of our firm and (*name of client*) that is privileged and confidential, and we expressly reserve all rights with respect to disclosures to third parties. Accordingly, we request confidential treatment under the Freedom of Information Act or similar laws and regulations when requests are made for the attest documentation or information contained therein or any documents created by the (*name of regulatory agency*) containing information derived therefrom. We further request that written notice be given to our firm before distribution of the information in the attest documentation (or copies thereof) to others, including other governmental agencies, except when such distribution is required by law or regulation.[14]

[*If it is expected that copies will be requested, add the following:*

Any copies of our attest documentation we agree to provide you will contain a legend "Confidential Treatment Requested by (*name of practitioner, address, telephone number*)."]

[*Firm signature*]

[Issue Date: May 1996; Revised: January 2001; January 2002.]

5. Attest Engagements on Financial Information[15] Included in eXtensible Business Reporting Language Instance Documents

.47 *Question*—What is eXtensible Business Reporting Language (XBRL) and an XBRL Instance Document?

.48 *Interpretation*—XBRL, the business reporting aspect of the Extensible Markup Language (XML), is a freely licensable open technology standard, which makes it possible to store and transfer data along with the complex hierarchies, data processing rules, and descriptions that enable analysis and

---

[14] This illustrative paragraph may not in and of itself be sufficient to gain confidential treatment under the rules and regulations of certain regulatory agencies. The practitioner should consider tailoring this paragraph to the circumstances after consulting the regulations of each applicable regulatory agency and, if necessary, consult with legal counsel regarding the specific procedures and requirements necessary to gain confidential treatment.

[15] Financial information includes data presented in audited or reviewed financial statements or other financial information (for example, management discussion and analysis).

distribution.[16] An entity may make its financial information available in the form of an XBRL Instance Document (instance document). An *instance document* is essentially a machine-readable format of financial information (that is, a computer can read the data, search for information, or perform calculations). Through the XBRL tagging process, a mapping of the financial information is created that enables a user to extract specific information, facilitating analysis. For example, XBRL would enable a user to use a software tool to automatically extract certain financial line items and automatically import those amounts into a worksheet calculating financial ratios.

.49 The instance document consists of various data points and their corresponding XBRL tags (that describe the financial information) and may include references to other items such as a PDF (Adobe Acrobat) version of financial information. Hence, an instance document is a stand-alone document that may be published using a website, e-mail, and other electronic distribution means.

.50 *Question*—What are the practitioner's considerations when the practitioner has been engaged to examine and report on whether the instance document accurately reflects the financial information?

.51 *Interpretation*—The third general attestation standard states that the practitioner shall perform the engagement only if he or she has reason to believe that the subject matter is capable of evaluation against criteria that are suitable and available to users. Two related criteria, XBRL taxonomies and XBRL International Technical Specifications, meet the available and suitable attributes under the attestation standards because a panel of experts developed the criteria and followed due process procedures that included exposure of the proposed criteria for public comment. The entity has the ability to extend the XBRL taxonomy by creating its own entity extension taxonomy. The entity may also create one or more custom entity taxonomies (for example, for a unique industry that is not yet represented by an XBRL taxonomy). Because neither the XBRL entity extension nor the custom taxonomy typically undergoes due process procedures when developed, the practitioner should evaluate whether the XBRL entity extension or custom taxonomy represents suitable and available criteria as described in paragraphs .24–.34 of section 101.

.52 The practitioner should perform procedures he or she believes are necessary to obtain sufficient evidential matter to form an opinion. Example procedures the practitioner should consider performing include the following:

- Compare the rendered[17] instance document to the financial information.
- Trace and agree the instance document's tagged information to the financial information.
- Test that the financial information is appropriately tagged and included in the instance document.
- Test for consistency of tagging (for example, an entity may use one taxonomy tag for one year and then switch to a different tag for the same financial information the following year. In this case, the financial information for both years should use the same tag).

---

[16] The eXtensible Business Reporting Language (XBRL) tags and their relationship to other XBRL tags are represented in a taxonomy. The XBRL taxonomy is needed for a full rendering of the XBRL Instance Document.

[17] A rendered instance document converts the machine-readable format to a human readable version through a software tool.

- Test that the entity extension or custom taxonomy meets the XBRL International Technical Specification (for example, through the use of a validation tool).

.53 When the client is the responsible party, the client will provide the practitioner with a written assertion regarding the subject matter. An example of a written assertion follows:

We assert that the accompanying XBRL Instance Document accurately reflects the data presented in the financial statements of XYZ Company as of December 31, 20XX, and for the year then ended in conformity with [*identify the criteria—for example, specify XBRL taxonomy, such as "XBRL U.S. Consumer and Industrial Taxonomy," and where applicable, the company extension taxonomy, such as "XYZ Company's extension taxonomy" and the XBRL International Technical Specifications (specify version)*].

.54 The practitioner should identify in his or her report whether the underlying financial information has been audited or reviewed, and should refer to the report of such audit or review.[18] If the underlying information has not been audited or reviewed, the practitioner should disclaim an opinion on the underlying information. Any information in the Instance Document that is not covered by the practitioner's report should clearly be identified as such.

.55 Report Examples

Example 1: Reporting on the Subject Matter

Independent Accountant's Report

We have examined the accompanying XBRL Instance Document of XYZ Company, which reflects the data presented in the financial statements of XYZ Company as of December 31, 20XX, and for the year then ended [*optional to include the location of the financial statements, such as "included in the Company's Form 10-K for the year ended December 31, 20XX"*]. XYZ Company's management is responsible for the XBRL Instance Document. Our responsibility is to express an opinion based on our examination.

We have also audited, in accordance with auditing standards generally accepted in the United States of America, the financial statements of XYZ Company as of December 31, 20XX, and for the year then ended, and in our report dated [*Month*] XX, 20XX, we expressed an unqualified opinion on those financial statements.[19,20]

Our examination was conducted in accordance with attestation standards established by the American Institute of Certified Public Accountants and,

---

[18] When no audit or review report has been issued, no reference to a report is required.

[19] If the financial statements have been reviewed, the sentence would read: "We have also reviewed, in accordance with [*standards established by the American Institute of Certified Public Accountants*] [*Statements on Standards for Accounting and Review Services issued by the American Institute of Certified Public Accountants*], the financial statements of XYZ Company as of March 31, 20XX, and for the three months then ended, the objective of which was the expression of limited assurance on such financial statements, and issued our report thereon dated [*Month*] XX, 20XX, [*describe any modifications of such report*]."

If the financial information has not been audited or reviewed, no reference to a report is required. The sentence would read: "We were not engaged to and did not conduct an audit or review of the [*identify information*], the objectives of which would have been the expression of an opinion or limited assurance on such [*identify information*]. Accordingly, we do not express an opinion or any other assurance on [*it*] [*them*]."

[20] If the audit opinion on the related financial statements is other than unqualified, the practitioner should disclose that fact, and any substantive reasons therefore.

accordingly, included examining, on a test basis, evidence supporting the XBRL Instance Document and performing such other procedures as we considered necessary in the circumstances. We believe that our examination provides a reasonable basis for our opinion.

In our opinion, the XBRL Instance Document of XYZ Company referred to above accurately reflects, in all material respects, the data presented in the financial statements in conformity with [*identify the criteria—for example, specific XBRL taxonomy, such as the "XBRL U.S. Consumer and Industrial Taxonomy," and where applicable, the company extension taxonomy, such as "XYZ Company's extension taxonomy," and the XBRL International Technical Specifications 2.0*].

[*Signature*]

[*Date*]

Example 2: Reporting on Management's Assertions

Independent Accountant's Report

We have examined management's assertion that [*identify the assertion—for example, the accompanying XBRL Instance Document accurately reflects the data presented in the financial statements of XYZ Company as of December 31, 20XX, and for the year then ended in conformity with (identify the criteria—for example, specific XBRL taxonomy, such as the "XBRL U.S. Consumer and Industrial Taxonomy," and where applicable, the company extension taxonomy, such as "XYZ Company's extension taxonomy," and the XBRL International Technical Specifications 2.0)*]. XYZ Company's management is responsible for the assertion. Our responsibility is to express an opinion on the assertion based on our examination.

We have also audited, in accordance with auditing standards generally accepted in the United States of America, the financial statements of XYZ Company as of December 31, 20XX, and for the year then ended, and in our report dated [*Month*] XX, 20XX, we expressed an unqualified opinion on those financial statements.

Our examination was conducted in accordance with attestation standards established by the American Institute of Certified Public Accountants and, accordingly, included examining, on a test basis, evidence supporting the XBRL Instance Document and performing such other procedures as we considered necessary in the circumstances. We believe that our examination provides a reasonable basis for our opinion.

In our opinion, management's assertion referred to above is fairly stated, in all material respects, in conformity with [*identify the criteria—for example, specific XBRL taxonomy, such as the "XBRL U.S. Consumer and Industrial Taxonomy," and where applicable, the company extension taxonomy, such as "XYZ Company's extension taxonomy," and the XBRL International Technical Specifications 2.0*].

[*Signature*]

[*Date*]

[Issue Date: September 2003.]

6. Reporting on Attestation Engagements Performed in Accordance With *Government Auditing Standards*[21]

.56 *Question*—In July 2007, the U.S. Government Accountability Office issued its 2007 revised *Government Auditing Standards* (commonly referred to as the Yellow Book). Chapter 6 of the revised Yellow Book sets forth general fieldwork and reporting standards for attestation engagements performed pursuant to generally accepted government auditing standards (GAGAS). Practitioners performing attestation engagements under GAGAS are also required to follow the general standards set forth in chapter 3 of the Yellow Book. For attestation engagements performed pursuant to GAGAS, paragraph 6.31 of the Yellow Book prescribes additional reporting standards[22] that go beyond the standards of reporting set forth in section 101 paragraphs .63–.90. When a practitioner performs an attestation examination in accordance with GAGAS, how should the report be modified?

.57 *Interpretation*—The practitioner should modify the scope paragraph of the attestation report to indicate that the examination or review was "conducted in accordance with attestation standards established by the American Institute of Certified Public Accountants and the standards applicable to attestation engagements contained in *Government Auditing Standards* issued by the Comptroller General of the United States."

.58 Additionally, GAGAS require the practitioner's attestation report to disclose any matters that are set forth in paragraph 6.31 of the revised Yellow Book. Paragraphs 6.42–.43 of the revised Yellow Book set forth the reporting elements that the practitioner should use, to the extent possible, in reporting a finding. The following illustration is a standard examination report modified to make reference to a schedule of findings when any of the matters set forth in paragraph 6.31 have been identified. This report pertains to subject matter for which suitable criteria exist and are available to all users through inclusion in a clear manner in the presentation of the subject matter. A written assertion has been obtained from the responsible party. Although the following illustrative report modifications would comply with the Yellow Book requirement, this illustration is not intended to preclude a practitioner from complying with these additional Yellow Book reporting requirements in other ways.

Independent Accountant's Report

We have examined [*identify the subject matter—for example, the accompanying schedule of performance measures of XYZ Agency for the year ended December 31, 20XX*]. XYZ Agency's management is responsible for the [*identify the subject matter—for example, schedule of performance measures*]. Our responsibility is to express an opinion based on our examination.

Our examination was conducted in accordance with attestation standards established by the American Institute of Certified Public Accountants and the

---

[21] Although separate interpretations for other AT sections have not been issued to deal with attestation engagements performed in accordance with *Government Auditing Standards*, a practitioner may use this guidance to help him or her appropriately modify an attest report pursuant to other AT sections.

[22] Paragraph 6.31 of the Yellow Book sets forth the additional reporting requirements: (*a*) reporting auditors' compliance with generally accepted government auditing standards, (*b*) reporting deficiencies in internal control, fraud, illegal acts, violations of provisions of contracts or grant agreements, and abuse, (*c*) reporting views of responsible officials, (*d*) reporting confidential or sensitive information, and (*e*) distributing reports. [Footnote revised: January 2008, to reflect conforming changes necessary due to the issuance of the 2007 revised *Government Auditing Standards*.]

standards applicable to attestation engagements contained in *Government Auditing Standards* issued by the Comptroller General of the United States and, accordingly, included examining, on a test basis, evidence supporting [*identify the subject matter—for example, XYZ Agency's schedule of performance measures*] and performing such other procedures as we considered necessary in the circumstances. We believe that our examination provides a reasonable basis for our opinion.

[*Additional paragraph(s) may be added to emphasize certain matters relating to the attest engagement or the subject matter.*]

In our opinion, the schedule referred to above presents, in all material respects, [*identify the subject matter—for example, the performance measures of XYZ Agency for the year ended December 31, 20XX*], in conformity with [*identify criteria—for example, the criteria set forth in Note 1*].

[*When any of the matters set forth in paragraph 6.31 of the Yellow Book have been identified the following paragraph would be added.*]

In accordance with *Government Auditing Standards*, we are required to report significant deficiencies in internal control, identifying those considered to be material weaknesses, violations of provisions of contracts or grant agreements, and abuse that could have material effect on [*identify the subject matter—for example, XYZ Agency's schedule of performance measures*][23] and any fraud and illegal acts that are more than inconsequential that come to our attention during our examination. We are also required to obtain the views of management on those matters. We performed our examination to express an opinion on whether [*identify the subject matter—for example, XYZ Agency's schedule of performance measures*] is presented in accordance with the criteria described above and not for the purpose of expressing an opinion on the internal control over [*identify the subject matter—for example, reporting of performance measures*] or on compliance and other matters; accordingly, we express no such opinions. Our examination disclosed certain findings that are required to be reported under *Government Auditing Standards* and those findings, along with the views of management, are described in the attached Schedule of Findings.[24]

[*Signature*]

[*Date*]

---

[23] Note that paragraph 6.37 of *Government Auditing Standards* states that when auditors detect violations of provisions of contracts or grant agreements or abuse that have an effect on the subject matter that is less than material but more than inconsequential, they should communicate those findings in writing to entity officials. [Footnote added: January 2008, to reflect conforming changes necessary due to the issuance of the 2007 revised *Government Auditing Standards*.]

[24] [Footnote renumbered and deleted to reflect conforming changes necessary due to the issuance of the 2007 revised *Government Auditing Standards*.]

Illustrative Schedule of Findings

XYZ Agency
Schedule of Findings[25]
Year Ended December 31, 20XX

Finding No. 1

Criteria

Condition

Cause

Effect or Potential Effect

Management's Response

Finding No. 2

Criteria

Condition

Cause

Effect or Potential Effect

Management's Response

[Issue Date: December 2004; Revised: January 2008.]

[25] Refer to paragraphs 6.42–.43 of the Yellow Book regarding the content of the schedule of findings. [Footnote renumbered and revised: January 2008, to reflect conforming changes necessary due to the issuance of the 2007 revised *Government Auditing Standards*.]

7. Reporting on the Design of Internal Control

.59 *Question*—A practitioner may be asked to report on the suitability[26] of the design of an entity's internal control over financial reporting (internal control) for preventing or detecting and correcting material misstatements of the entity's financial statements on a timely basis. Such requests may be made by, for example,

- an entity applying for a government grant or contract that is required to submit a written preaward survey by management about the suitability of the design of the entity's internal control or a portion of the entity's internal control, together with a practitioner's report thereon.
- a new casino applying for a license to operate that is required by a regulatory agency to submit a practitioner's report on whether the entity's internal control *that it plans to implement* is suitably designed to provide reasonable assurance that the control objectives specified in the regulatory agency's regulations would be achieved. (In this situation the casino would not yet have begun operations, and audited financial statements or financial data relevant to the period covered by the engagement may not exist.)

May a practitioner report on the suitability of the design of an entity's internal control based on the risk assessment procedures the auditor performs to obtain a sufficient understanding of the entity and its environment, including its internal control, in an audit of the entity's financial statements?

.60 *Interpretation*—No. In a financial statement audit, the purpose of the auditor's understanding of the entity and its environment, including its internal control, is to enable the auditor to assess the risk of material misstatement of the financial statements whether due to error or fraud, and to design the nature, timing, and extent of further audit procedures. The understanding obtained in a financial statement audit does not provide the practitioner with a sufficient basis to report on the suitability of the design of an entity's internal control or any portion thereof.

.61 *Question*—How may a practitioner report on the suitability of the design of an entity's internal control or a portion thereof?

.62 *Interpretation*—The practitioner may perform an examination under section 101, or apply agreed-upon procedures under section 201, to management's written assertion about the suitability of the design of the entity's internal control. Footnote 4 of section 501, *An Examination of an Entity's Internal Control Over Financial Reporting That is Integrated With an Audit of Its Financial Statements*, states that although section 501 does not directly apply when an auditor is engaged to examine the suitability of design of an entity's internal control, it may be useful in planning and performing such engagements. Paragraphs .57–.59 of section 501 discuss how the auditor evaluates the design effectiveness of controls.

.63 When the engagement involves the application of agreed-upon procedures to a written assertion about the suitability of the design of an entity's internal control over compliance with specified requirements, the practitioner should also follow the provisions of paragraphs .09 and .11–.29 of section 601.

---

[26] In this interpretation, the *suitability of the design of internal control* means the same thing as the *design effectiveness of an entity's internal control.*

.64 The following is an illustrative report a practitioner may issue when reporting on the suitability of the design of an entity's internal control that has been implemented. The report may be modified, as appropriate, to fit the particular circumstances.

Independent Accountant's Report

[*Introductory paragraph*]

We have examined the suitability of the design of W Company's internal control over financial reporting to prevent or detect and correct material misstatements in its financial statements on a timely basis as of December 31, 20XX, based on [*identify criteria*].[27] W Company's management is responsible for the suitable design of internal control over financial reporting. Our responsibility is to express an opinion on the design of internal control based on our examination.

[*Scope paragraph*]

Our examination was conducted in accordance with attestation standards established by the American Institute of Certified Public Accountants and, accordingly, included obtaining an understanding of internal control over financial reporting, evaluating the design of internal control, and performing such other procedures as we considered necessary in the circumstances. We believe that our examination provides a reasonable basis for our opinion. We were not engaged to examine and report on the operating effectiveness of W Company's internal control over financial reporting as of December 31, 20XX, and, accordingly, we express no opinion on operating effectiveness.

[*Inherent limitations paragraph*]

Because of its inherent limitations, internal control over financial reporting may not prevent or detect and correct misstatements. Also, projections of any evaluation of effectiveness to future periods are subject to the risk that controls may become inadequate because of changes in conditions, or that the degree of compliance with the policies or procedures may deteriorate.

[*Opinion paragraph*]

In our opinion, W Company's internal control over financial reporting was suitably designed, in all material respects, to prevent or detect and correct material misstatements in the financial statements on a timely basis as of December 31, 20XX, based on [*identify criteria*].

[*Signature*]

[*Date*]

.65 When reporting on the suitability of the design of an entity's internal control that has not yet been implemented, the practitioner would be unable to confirm that the controls have been implemented and should disclose that information in the practitioner's report. In those circumstances, the practitioner should modify (1) the scope paragraph of the illustrative report in paragraph .64 to inform readers that the controls identified in the report have not yet been implemented and (2) the inherent limitations paragraph to reflect the related risk. Following are modified illustrative report paragraphs for use when controls have not yet been implemented. (New language is shown in boldface italics. Deleted language is shown in strikethrough.)

---

[27] This report assumes that the control criteria are both suitable and available to users as discussed in section 101 paragraphs .23–.33. Therefore, the use of this report is not restricted.

Our examination was conducted in accordance with attestation standards established by the American Institute of Certified Public Accountants and, accordingly, included obtaining an understanding of internal control over financial reporting, evaluating the design of internal control, and performing such other procedures as we considered necessary in the circumstances. We believe that our examination provides a reasonable basis for our opinion. ***Because operations had not begun as of December 31, 20XX, we could not confirm that the specified controls were implemented. Accordingly, our report solely addresses the suitability of the design of the Company's internal control and does not address whether the controls were implemented. Furthermore, because the specified controls have not yet been implemented, we were unable to test, and did not test,*** the operating effectiveness of W Company's internal control over financial reporting as of December 31, 20XX, and, accordingly, we express no opinion on operating effectiveness.

[*Inherent limitations paragraph*]

Because of its inherent limitations, internal control over financial reporting may not prevent or detect and correct misstatements. Also, projections of any evaluation of effectiveness to future periods are subject to the risk that controls ***may not be implemented as intended when operations begin or*** may become inadequate because of changes in conditions~~, or that the degree of compliance with the policies or procedures may deteriorate~~.

.66 *Question*—A practitioner may be asked to sign a prescribed form developed by the party to whom the form is to be submitted regarding the design of an entity's internal control. What are the practitioner's responsibilities when requested to sign such a form if it includes language that is not consistent with the practitioner's function or responsibility or with the reporting requirements of professional standards?

.67 *Interpretation*—Paragraphs .32–.33 of AU section 623, *Special Reports*, address such situations in the context of an audit of financial statements and indicate that the auditor should either revise the prescribed form or attach a separate report that conforms with the auditor's function or responsibility and professional standards. When reporting on the suitability of the design of an entity's internal control under section 101, the practitioner's report should contain all of the elements in either paragraphs .85 or .86, as applicable, which can be accomplished by either revising the prescribed form or attaching a separate report in place of the prescribed form.

.68 *Question*—An entity may be required to submit a practitioner's report about an entity's *ability* to establish suitably designed internal control (or its assertion thereon). May a practitioner issue such a report based on (*a*) the risk assessment procedures related to existing internal control that the auditor performs in an audit of an entity's financial statements or (*b*) the performance of an attest engagement?

.69 *Interpretation*—No. Neither the risk assessment procedures the auditor performs in an audit of an entity's financial statements nor the performance of an attest engagement provide the practitioner with a basis for issuing a report on the *ability* of an entity to establish suitably designed internal control. There are no suitable criteria for evaluating an entity's ability to establish suitably designed internal control. The requesting party may be willing to accept a report of the practitioner on a consulting service. The practitioner may include in the consulting service report

a. a statement that the practitioner is unable to perform an attest engagement that addresses the entity's ability to establish suitably designed internal control because there are no suitable criteria for evaluating the entity's ability to do so;

b. a description of the nature and scope of the practitioner's services; and

c. the practitioner's findings.

The practitioner may refer to the guidance in CS section 100, *Consulting Services: Definitions and Standards.*

[Issue Date: December 2008.]

8. Including a Description of Tests of Controls or Other Procedures, and the Results Thereof, in an Examination Report

.70 *Question*—Section 801, *Reporting on Controls at a Service Organization*, addresses examination engagements undertaken by a service auditor to report on controls at organizations that provide services to user entities when those controls are likely to be relevant to user entities' internal control over financial reporting (ICFR). For a type 2 report resulting from such an examination engagement, section 801 provides for a separate section of the report that includes a description of the service auditor's tests of controls likely to be relevant to user entities' ICFR and the results of those tests. This information is intended for user auditors who may need detailed information about the results of such tests of controls to determine how the results affect a particular user entity's financial statements.

.71 Paragraph .02 of section 801 refers the practitioner to section 101, when a practitioner is engaged to examine and report on controls at a service organization other than those likely to be relevant to user entities' ICFR (for example, controls at a service provider that are relevant to user entities' compliance with laws or regulations or controls at a service provider that are relevant to the privacy of user entities' information).[28] If a practitioner performs an examination engagement under section 101, may the practitioner's examination report include, in a separate section, a description of tests of controls or other procedures performed in support of the practitioner's opinion resulting from such an engagement?

.72 *Interpretation*—Nothing in section 101 precludes a practitioner from including in a separate section of his or her examination report a description of tests of controls or other procedures performed and the results thereof. However, in some cases, such a description may overshadow the practitioner's overall opinion or may cause report users to misunderstand the opinion. Therefore, the circumstances of the particular engagement are relevant to the practitioner's consideration regarding whether to include a description of tests of controls or other procedures performed, and the results thereof, in a separate section of the practitioner's examination report. In determining whether to include such a description in the practitioner's examination report, the following considerations are relevant:

- Whether there has been a request for such information and whether the specified parties making the request have an appropriate business need or reasonable basis for requesting the information (for example, the specified parties are required to maintain

[28] As indicated in paragraph A2 of section 801, *Reporting on Controls at a Service Organization*, paragraph .02 of section 801 is not intended to permit a report that combines reporting on a service organization's controls likely to be relevant to user entities' internal control over financial reporting (ICFR) with reporting on controls that are not likely to be relevant to user entities' ICFR.

and monitor controls that either encompass or are dependent on controls that are the subject of the examination and, therefore, need information about the tests of controls to enable them to have a basis for concluding that they have met the requirements applicable to them)

- Whether the specified parties have an understanding of the nature and subject matter of the engagement and experience in using the information in such reports
- Whether including such a description in the examination report is likely to cause report users to misunderstand the opinion
- Whether the practitioner's tests of controls or other procedures performed directly relate to the subject matter of the engagement

Paragraph .79 of section 101 states, "The need for restriction on the use of a report may result from a number of circumstances, including the purpose of the report, the criteria used in preparation of the subject matter, the extent to which the procedures performed are known or understood, and the potential for the report to be misunderstood when taken out of the context in which it was intended to be used." The addition of a description of tests of controls or other procedures performed, and the results thereof, in a separate section of an examination report may increase the need for use of the report to be restricted to specified parties.

[Issue Date: July 2010.]

and monitoring controls [illegible] provide no [illegible] controls [illegible] the examination and, therefore, need more information about the tests of controls to enable them to [illegible] conclusion that they have met the requirements applicable to them

- Whether the specified parties have a reasonable understanding of the nature and [illegible] of the engagement and experience in using the information in such reports
- Whether including such a description in the examination report is likely to cause report users to misunderstand the opinion
- Whether the practitioner's tests of controls or other procedures performed [illegible] relate to the subject matter of the engagement

Paragraph 98 See section [illegible] [illegible] report may result from a number of circumstances, including the purpose of the report, the criteria used in preparation of the subject matter, the extent to which the procedures performed are known or understood, and the potential for the report to be misunderstood when taken out of the context in which it was intended to be used. The addition of a description of tests of controls or other procedures performed and the results thereof in a separate section of an examination report may increase the potential for the report to be restricted to specified parties.

[Issue Date: January 2017.]

AT Section 201

Agreed-Upon Procedures Engagements

Source: SSAE No. 10; SSAE No. 11.

Effective when the subject matter or assertion is as of or for a period ending on or after June 1, 2001, unless otherwise indicated.

Introduction and Applicability

.01 This section sets forth attestation standards and provides guidance to a practitioner concerning performance and reporting in all agreed-upon procedures engagements, except as noted in paragraph .02. A practitioner also should refer to the following sections of this Statement on Standards for Attestation Engagements (SSAE), which provide additional guidance for certain types of agreed-upon procedures engagements:

a. Section 301, *Financial Forecasts and Projections*

b. Section 601, *Compliance Attestation*

.02 This section does not apply to the following:[1]

a. Situations in which an auditor reports on specified compliance requirements based solely on an audit of financial statements, as addressed in AU section 623, *Special Reports*, paragraphs .19–.21

b. Engagements for which the objective is to report in accordance with AU section 801, *Compliance Audits*, unless the terms of the engagement specify that the engagement be performed pursuant to SSAEs

c. Engagements covered by AU section 634, *Letters for Underwriters and Certain Other Requesting Parties*

d. Certain professional services that would not be considered as falling under this section as described in section 101, *Attest Engagements*, paragraph .04.

[Revised, December 2010, to reflect conforming changes necessary due to the issuance of SAS No. 117. Revised, August 2011, to reflect conforming changes necessary due to the issuance of SSAE No. 16.]

Agreed-Upon Procedures Engagements

.03 An agreed-upon procedures engagement is one in which a practitioner is engaged by a client to issue a report of findings based on specific procedures performed on subject matter. The client engages the practitioner to assist specified parties in evaluating subject matter or an assertion as a result of a need or needs of the specified parties.[2] Because the specified parties require that

---

[1] The Attest Interpretation, "Responding to Requests for Reports on Matters Relating to Solvency" (section 9101.23–.33), prohibits the performance of any attest engagements concerning matters of solvency or insolvency.

[2] See paragraphs .08 and .09 for a discussion of subject matter and assertion.

findings be independently derived, the services of a practitioner are obtained to perform procedures and report his or her findings. The specified parties and the practitioner agree upon the procedures to be performed by the practitioner that the specified parties believe are appropriate. Because the needs of the specified parties may vary widely, the nature, timing, and extent of the agreed-upon procedures may vary as well; consequently, the specified parties assume responsibility for the sufficiency of the procedures since they best understand their own needs. In an engagement performed under this section, the practitioner does not perform an examination or a review, as discussed in section 101, and does not provide an opinion or negative assurance.[3] (See paragraph .24.) Instead, the practitioner's report on agreed-upon procedures should be in the form of procedures and findings. (See paragraph .31.)

.04 As a consequence of the role of the specified parties in agreeing upon the procedures performed or to be performed, a practitioner's report on such engagements should clearly indicate that its use is restricted to those specified parties.[4] Those specified parties, including the client, are hereinafter referred to as *specified parties.*

Standards

.05 The general, fieldwork, and reporting standards for attestation engagements as established in section 50, *SSAE Hierarchy*, together with interpretive guidance regarding their application as addressed throughout this section, should be followed by the practitioner in performing and reporting on agreed-upon procedures engagements. [Revised, November 2006, to reflect conforming changes necessary due to the issuance of Statement on Standards for Attestation Engagements No. 14.]

Conditions for Engagement Performance

.06 The practitioner may perform an agreed-upon procedures attest engagement provided that—

a. The practitioner is independent.

b. One of the following conditions is met.

(1) The party wishing to engage the practitioner is responsible for the subject matter, or has a reasonable basis for providing a written assertion about the subject matter when the nature of the subject matter is such that a responsible party does not otherwise exist.

(2) The party wishing to engage the practitioner is not responsible for the subject matter but is able to provide the practitioner, or have a third party who is responsible for the subject matter provide the practitioner with evidence of the third party's responsibility for the subject matter.

c. The practitioner and the specified parties agree upon the procedures performed or to be performed by the practitioner.

---

[3] For guidance on expressing an opinion on specified elements, accounts, or items of a financial statement based on an audit, see AU section 623.11–.18.

[4] See section 101.78–.83 for additional guidance regarding restricted-use reports.

d. The specified parties take responsibility for the sufficiency of the agreed-upon procedures for their purposes.

e. The specific subject matter to which the procedures are to be applied is subject to reasonably consistent measurement.

f. Criteria to be used in the determination of findings are agreed upon between the practitioner and the specified parties.

g. The procedures to be applied to the specific subject matter are expected to result in reasonably consistent findings using the criteria.

h. Evidential matter related to the specific subject matter to which the procedures are applied is expected to exist to provide a reasonable basis for expressing the findings in the practitioner's report.

i. Where applicable, the practitioner and the specified parties agree on any materiality limits for reporting purposes. (See paragraph .25.)

j. Use of the report is restricted to the specified parties.

k. For agreed-upon procedures engagements on prospective financial information, the prospective financial statements include a summary of significant assumptions. (See section 301.52.)

Agreement on and Sufficiency of Procedures

.07 To satisfy the requirements that the practitioner and the specified parties agree upon the procedures performed or to be performed and that the specified parties take responsibility for the sufficiency of the agreed-upon procedures for their purposes, ordinarily the practitioner should communicate directly with and obtain affirmative acknowledgment from each of the specified parties. For example, this may be accomplished by meeting with the specified parties or by distributing a draft of the anticipated report or a copy of an engagement letter to the specified parties and obtaining their agreement. If the practitioner is not able to communicate directly with all of the specified parties, the practitioner may satisfy these requirements by applying any one or more of the following or similar procedures.

- Compare the procedures to be applied to written requirements of the specified parties.
- Discuss the procedures to be applied with appropriate representatives of the specified parties involved.
- Review relevant contracts with or correspondence from the specified parties.

The practitioner should not report on an engagement when specified parties do not agree upon the procedures performed or to be performed and do not take responsibility for the sufficiency of the procedures for their purposes. (See paragraph .36 for guidance on satisfying these requirements when the practitioner is requested to add other parties as specified parties after the date of completion of the agreed-upon procedures.)

Subject Matter and Related Assertions

.08 The subject matter of an agreed-upon procedures engagement may take many different forms and may be at a point in time or covering a period of time. In an agreed-upon procedures engagement, it is the specific subject matter to which the agreed-upon procedures are to be applied using the criteria selected. Even though the procedures are agreed upon between the practitioner and the specified parties, the subject matter and the criteria must meet the conditions set forth in the third general standard. (See section 101.23 and .24.) The criteria against which the specific subject matter needs to be measured may be recited within the procedures enumerated or referred to in the practitioner's report.

.09 An assertion is any declaration or set of declarations about whether the subject matter is based on or in conformity with the criteria selected. A written assertion is generally not required in an agreed-upon procedures engagement unless specifically required by another attest standard (for example, see section 601.11). If, however, the practitioner requests the responsible party to provide an assertion, the assertion may be presented in a representation letter or another written communication from the responsible party, such as in a statement, narrative description, or schedule appropriately identifying what is being presented and the point in time or the period of time covered.

Establishing an Understanding With the Client

.10 The practitioner should establish an understanding with the client regarding the services to be performed. When the practitioner documents the understanding through a written communication with the client (an *engagement letter*), such communication should be addressed to the client, and in some circumstances also to all specified parties. Matters that might be included in such an understanding include the following:

- The nature of the engagement
- Identification of the subject matter (or the assertion related thereto), the responsible party, and the criteria to be used
- Identification of specified parties (See paragraph .36.)
- Specified parties' acknowledgment of their responsibility for the sufficiency of the procedures
- Responsibilities of the practitioner (See paragraphs .12 to .14 and .40.)
- Reference to attestation standards established by the American Institute of Certified Public Accountants (AICPA)
- Agreement on procedures by enumerating (or referring to) the procedures (See paragraphs .15 to .18.)
- Disclaimers expected to be included in the practitioner's report
- Use restrictions
- Assistance to be provided to the practitioner (See paragraphs .22 and .23.)
- Involvement of a specialist (See paragraphs .19 to .21.)
- Agreed-upon materiality limits (See paragraph .25.)

Nature, Timing, and Extent of Procedures

Responsibility of the Specified Parties

.11 Specified parties are responsible for the sufficiency (nature, timing, and extent) of the agreed-upon procedures because they best understand their own needs. The specified parties assume the risk that such procedures might be insufficient for their purposes. In addition, the specified parties assume the risk that they might misunderstand or otherwise inappropriately use findings properly reported by the practitioner.

Practitioner's Responsibility

.12 The responsibility of the practitioner is to carry out the procedures and report the findings in accordance with the general, fieldwork, and reporting standards as discussed and interpreted in this section. The practitioner assumes the risk that misapplication of the procedures may result in inappropriate findings being reported. Furthermore, the practitioner assumes the risk that appropriate findings may not be reported or may be reported inaccurately. The practitioner's risks can be reduced through adequate planning and supervision and due professional care in performing the procedures, determining the findings, and preparing the report.

.13 The practitioner should have adequate knowledge in the specific subject matter to which the agreed-upon procedures are to be applied. He or she may obtain such knowledge through formal or continuing education, practical experience, or consultation with others.[5]

.14 The practitioner has no responsibility to determine the differences between the agreed-upon procedures to be performed and the procedures that the practitioner would have determined to be necessary had he or she been engaged to perform another form of attest engagement. The procedures that the practitioner agrees to perform pursuant to an agreed-upon procedures engagement may be more or less extensive than the procedures that the practitioner would determine to be necessary had he or she been engaged to perform another form of engagement.

Procedures to Be Performed

.15 The procedures that the practitioner and specified parties agree upon may be as limited or as extensive as the specified parties desire. However, mere reading of an assertion or specified information about the subject matter does not constitute a procedure sufficient to permit a practitioner to report on the results of applying agreed-upon procedures. In some circumstances, the procedures agreed upon evolve or are modified over the course of the engagement. In general, there is flexibility in determining the procedures as long as the specified parties acknowledge responsibility for the sufficiency of such procedures for their purposes. Matters that should be agreed upon include the nature, timing, and extent of the procedures.

---

[5] Section 601.19 and .20 provide guidance about obtaining an understanding of certain requirements in an agreed-upon procedures engagement on compliance.

.16 The practitioner should not agree to perform procedures that are overly subjective and thus possibly open to varying interpretations. Terms of uncertain meaning (such as general review, limited review, check, or test) should not be used in describing the procedures unless such terms are defined within the agreed-upon procedures. The practitioner should obtain evidential matter from applying the agreed-upon procedures to provide a reasonable basis for the finding or findings expressed in his or her report, but need not perform additional procedures outside the scope of the engagement to gather additional evidential matter.

.17 Examples of appropriate procedures include the following:

- Execution of a sampling application after agreeing on relevant parameters
- Inspection of specified documents evidencing certain types of transactions or detailed attributes thereof
- Confirmation of specific information with third parties
- Comparison of documents, schedules, or analyses with certain specified attributes
- Performance of specific procedures on work performed by others (including the work of internal auditors—see paragraphs .22 and .23)
- Performance of mathematical computations

.18 Examples of inappropriate procedures include the following:

- Mere reading of the work performed by others solely to describe their findings
- Evaluating the competency or objectivity of another party
- Obtaining an understanding about a particular subject
- Interpreting documents outside the scope of the practitioner's professional expertise

Involvement of a Specialist[6]

.19 The practitioner's education and experience enable him or her to be knowledgeable about business matters in general, but he or she is not expected to have the expertise of a person trained for or qualified to engage in the practice of another profession or occupation. In certain circumstances, it may be appropriate to involve a specialist to assist the practitioner in the performance of one or more procedures. The following are examples.

- An attorney might provide assistance concerning the interpretation of legal terminology involving laws, regulations, rules, contracts, or grants.
- A medical specialist might provide assistance in understanding the characteristics of diagnosis codes documented in patient medical records.
- An environmental engineer might provide assistance in interpreting environmental remedial action regulatory directives that may affect

[6] A *specialist* is a person (or firm) possessing skill or knowledge in a particular field other than the attest function. As used herein, a specialist does not include a person employed by the practitioner's firm who participates in the attest engagement.

the agreed-upon procedures applied to an environmental liabilities account in a financial statement.

- A geologist might provide assistance in distinguishing between varying physical characteristics of a generic minerals group related to information to which the agreed-upon procedures are applied.

.20 The practitioner and the specified parties should explicitly agree to the involvement of the specialist in assisting a practitioner in the performance of an agreed-upon procedures engagement. This agreement may be reached when obtaining agreement on the procedures performed or to be performed and acknowledgment of responsibility for the sufficiency of the procedures, as discussed in paragraph .07. The practitioner's report should describe the nature of the assistance provided by the specialist.

.21 A practitioner may agree to apply procedures to the report or work product of a specialist that does not constitute assistance by the specialist to the practitioner in an agreed-upon procedures engagement. For example, the practitioner may make reference to information contained in a report of a specialist in describing an agreed-upon procedure. However, it is inappropriate for the practitioner to agree to merely read the specialist's report solely to describe or repeat the findings, or to take responsibility for all or a portion of any procedures performed by a specialist or the specialist's work product.

Internal Auditors and Other Personnel

.22 The agreed-upon procedures to be enumerated or referred to in the practitioner's report are to be performed entirely by the practitioner except as discussed in paragraphs .19 to .21.[7] However, internal auditors or other personnel may prepare schedules and accumulate data or provide other information for the practitioner's use in performing the agreed-upon procedures. Also, internal auditors may perform and report separately on procedures that they have carried out. Such procedures may be similar to those that a practitioner may perform under this section.

.23 A practitioner may agree to perform procedures on information documented in the working papers of internal auditors. For example, the practitioner may agree to—

- Repeat all or some of the procedures.
- Determine whether the internal auditors' working papers contain documentation of procedures performed and whether the findings documented in the working papers are presented in a report by the internal auditors.

However, it is inappropriate for the practitioner to—

- Agree to merely read the internal auditors' report solely to describe or repeat their findings.
- Take responsibility for all or a portion of any procedures performed by internal auditors by reporting those findings as the practitioner's own.
- Report in any manner that implies shared responsibility for the procedures with the internal auditors.

---

[7] AU section 322, *The Auditor's Consideration of the Internal Audit Function in an Audit of Financial Statements*, does not apply to agreed-upon procedures engagements.

Findings

.24 A practitioner should present the results of applying agreed-upon procedures to specific subject matter in the form of findings. The practitioner should not provide negative assurance about whether the subject matter or the assertion is fairly stated based on the criteria. For example, the practitioner should not include a statement in his or her report that "nothing came to my attention that caused me to believe that the [*identify subject matter*] is not presented based on [or the assertion is not fairly stated based on] [*identify criteria*]."

.25 The practitioner should report all findings from application of the agreed-upon procedures. The concept of materiality does not apply to findings to be reported in an agreed-upon procedures engagement unless the definition of materiality is agreed to by the specified parties. Any agreed-upon materiality limits should be described in the practitioner's report.

.26 The practitioner should avoid vague or ambiguous language in reporting findings. Examples of appropriate and inappropriate descriptions of findings resulting from the application of certain agreed-upon procedures follow.

Procedures Agreed Upon	***Appropriate Description of Findings***	***Inappropriate Description of Findings***
Inspect the shipment dates for a sample (agreed-upon) of specified shipping documents, and determine whether any such dates were subsequent to December 31, 20XX.	No shipment dates shown on the sample of shipping documents were subsequent to December 31, 20XX.	Nothing came to my attention as a result of applying that procedure.
Calculate the number of blocks of streets paved during the year ended September 30, 20XX, shown on contractors' certificates of project completion; compare the resultant number to the number in an identified chart of performance statistics.	The number of blocks of streets paved in the chart of performance statistics was Y blocks more than the number calculated from the contractors' certificates of project completion.	The number of blocks of streets paved approximated the number of blocks included in the chart of performance statistics.
Calculate the rate of return on a specified investment (according to an agreed-upon formula) and verify that the resultant percentage agrees to the percentage in an identified schedule.	No exceptions were found as a result of applying the procedure.	The resultant percentage approximated the predetermined percentage in the identified schedule.

Procedures Agreed Upon	*Appropriate Description of Findings*	*Inappropriate Description of Findings*
Inspect the quality standards classification codes in identified performance test documents for products produced during a specified period; compare such codes to those shown in an identified computer printout.	All classification codes inspected in the identified documents were the same as those shown in the computer printout except for the following: [*List all exceptions.*]	All classification codes appeared to comply with such performance documents.
Trace all outstanding checks appearing on a bank reconciliation as of a certain date to checks cleared in the bank statement of the subsequent month.	All outstanding checks appearing on the bank reconciliation were cleared in the subsequent month's bank statement except for the following: [*List all exceptions.*]	Nothing came to my attention as a result of applying the procedure.
Compare the amounts of the invoices included in the "over ninety days" column shown in an identified schedule of aged accounts receivable of a specific customer as of a certain date to the amount and invoice date shown on the outstanding invoice and determine whether or not the invoice dates precede the date indicated on the schedule by more than ninety days.	All outstanding invoice amounts agreed with the amounts shown on the schedule in the "over ninety days" column, and the dates shown on such invoices preceded the date indicated on the schedule by more than ninety days.	The outstanding invoice amounts agreed within approximation of the amounts shown on the schedule in the "over ninety days" column, and nothing came to our attention that the dates shown on such invoices preceded the date indicated on the schedule by more than ninety days.

Working Papers

[.27–.30] [Paragraphs deleted by the issuance of Statement on Standards for Attestation Engagements No. 11, January 2002.][8–9]

[8–9] [Footnotes deleted by the issuance of Statement on Standards for Attestation Engagements No. 11, January 2002.]

Reporting

Required Elements

.31 The practitioner's report on agreed-upon procedures should be in the form of procedures and findings. The practitioner's report should contain the following elements:

a. A title that includes the word *independent*

b. Identification of the specified parties (See paragraph .36.)

c. Identification of the subject matter[10] (or the written assertion related thereto) and the character of the engagement

d. Identification of the responsible party

e. A statement that the subject matter is the responsibility of the responsible party

f. A statement that the procedures performed were those agreed to by the specified parties identified in the report

g. A statement that the agreed-upon procedures engagement was conducted in accordance with attestation standards established by the AICPA

h. A statement that the sufficiency of the procedures is solely the responsibility of the specified parties and a disclaimer of responsibility for the sufficiency of those procedures

i. A list of the procedures performed (or reference thereto) and related findings (The practitioner should not provide negative assurance—see paragraph .24.)

j. Where applicable, a description of any agreed-upon materiality limits (See paragraph .25.)

k. A statement that the practitioner was not engaged to and did not conduct an examination[11, 12] of the subject matter, the objective of which would be the expression of an opinion, a disclaimer of opinion on the subject matter, and a statement that if the practitioner

---

[10] In some agreed-upon procedures engagements, the practitioner may be asked to apply agreed-upon procedures to more than one subject matter or assertion. In these engagements, the practitioner may issue one report that refers to all subject matter covered or assertions presented. (For example, see section 601.28.)

[11] If the practitioner also wishes to refer to a review, alternate wording would be as follows.

> A statement that the practitioner was not engaged to and did not conduct an examination or a review of the subject matter, the objectives of which would be the expression of an opinion or limited assurance, a disclaimer of opinion on the subject matter, and a statement that if the practitioner had performed additional procedures, other matters might have come to his or her attention that would have been reported.

[12] If the subject matter consists of elements, accounts, or items of a financial statement, this statement may be worded as follows.

> We were not engaged to and did not conduct an audit [*or a review*], the objective of which would be the expression of an opinion [*or limited assurance*] on the [*identify elements, accounts, or items of a financial statement*]. Accordingly, we do not express such an opinion [*or limited assurance*].

Alternatively, the wording may be the following.

> These agreed-upon procedures do not constitute an audit [*or a review*] of financial statements or any part thereof, the objective of which is the expression of opinion [or limited assurance] on the financial statements or a part thereof.

had performed additional procedures, other matters might have come to his or her attention that would have been reported[13]

l. A statement of restrictions on the use of the report because it is intended to be used solely by the specified parties[14]

m. Where applicable, reservations or restrictions concerning procedures or findings as discussed in paragraphs .33, .35, .39, and .40

n. For an agreed-upon procedures engagement on prospective financial information, all items included in section 301.55

o. Where applicable, a description of the nature of the assistance provided by a specialist as discussed in paragraphs .19 through .21

p. The manual or printed signature of the practitioner's firm

q. The date of the report

Illustrative Report

.32 The following is an illustration of an agreed-upon procedures report.

Independent Accountant's Report
on Applying Agreed-Upon Procedures

To the Audit Committees and Managements of ABC Inc. and XYZ Fund:

We have performed the procedures enumerated below, which were agreed to by the audit committees and managements of ABC Inc. and XYZ Fund, solely to assist you in evaluating the accompanying Statement of Investment Performance Statistics of XYZ Fund (prepared in accordance with the criteria specified therein) for the year ended December 31, 20X1. XYZ Fund's management is responsible for the statement of investment performance statistics. This agreed-upon procedures engagement was conducted in accordance with attestation standards established by the American Institute of Certified Public Accountants. The sufficiency of these procedures is solely the responsibility of those parties specified in this report. Consequently, we make no representation regarding the sufficiency of the procedures described below either for the purpose for which this report has been requested or for any other purpose.

[*Include paragraphs to enumerate procedures and findings.*]

---

[13] When the practitioner consents to the inclusion of his or her report on an agreed-upon procedures engagement in a document or written communication containing the entity's financial statements, he or she should refer to AU section 504, *Association With Financial Statements*, or to Statement on Standards for Accounting and Review Services (SSARS) No. 1, *Compilation and Review of Financial Statements* [AR section 100], as appropriate, for guidance on his or her responsibility pertaining to the financial statements.

The practitioner should follow (*a*) AU section 504.04 when the financial statements of a public or nonpublic entity are audited (or reviewed in accordance with AU section 722, *Interim Financial Information*, or (*b*) AU section 504.05 when the financial statements of a public entity are unaudited. The practitioner should follow SSARS No. 1, paragraph 3 [AR section 100.03] when (*a*) the financial statements of a nonpublic entity are reviewed or compiled or (*b*) the financial statements of a nonpublic entity are *not* reviewed or compiled and are not submitted by the accountant, as defined in SSARS No. 1, paragraph 1 [AR section 100.01]. (See section 101.82 and .83 for guidance when the practitioner combines or includes in a document a restricted-use report with a general-use report.) [Footnote revised, November 2002, to reflect conforming changes necessary due to the issuance of Statement on Standards for Accounting and Review Services No. 9.]

[14] The purpose of the restriction on the use of the practitioner's report on applying agreed-upon procedures is to restrict its use to only those parties that have agreed upon the procedures performed and taken responsibility for the sufficiency of the procedures. Paragraph .36 describes the process for adding parties who were not originally contemplated in the agreed-upon procedures engagement.

We were not engaged to and did not conduct an examination, the objective of which would be the expression of an opinion on the accompanying Statement of Investment Performance Statistics of XYZ Fund. Accordingly, we do not express such an opinion. Had we performed additional procedures, other matters might have come to our attention that would have been reported to you.

This report is intended solely for the information and use of the audit committees and managements of ABC Inc. and XYZ Fund,[15] and is not intended to be and should not be used by anyone other than these specified parties.

[*Signature*]

[*Date*]

Explanatory Language

.33 The practitioner also may include explanatory language about matters such as the following:

- Disclosure of stipulated facts, assumptions, or interpretations (including the source thereof) used in the application of agreed-upon procedures (For example, see section 601.26.)
- Description of the condition of records, controls, or data to which the procedures were applied
- Explanation that the practitioner has no responsibility to update his or her report
- Explanation of sampling risk

Dating of Report

.34 The date of completion of the agreed-upon procedures should be used as the date of the practitioner's report.

Restrictions on the Performance of Procedures

.35 When circumstances impose restrictions on the performance of the agreed-upon procedures, the practitioner should attempt to obtain agreement from the specified parties for modification of the agreed-upon procedures. When such agreement cannot be obtained (for example, when the agreed-upon procedures are published by a regulatory agency that will not modify the procedures), the practitioner should describe any restrictions on the performance of procedures in his or her report or withdraw from the engagement.

Adding Specified Parties (Nonparticipant Parties)

.36 Subsequent to the completion of the agreed-upon procedures engagement, a practitioner may be requested to consider the addition of another party as a specified party (*a nonparticipant party*). The practitioner may agree to add a nonparticipant party as a specified party, based on consideration of such factors as the identity of the nonparticipant party and the intended use of the report.[16] If the practitioner does agree to add the nonparticipant party, he or

---

[15] The report may list the specified parties or refer the reader to the specified parties listed elsewhere in the report.

[16] When considering whether to add a nonparticipant party, the guidance in AU section 530, *Dating of the Independent Auditor's Report*, paragraphs .06 and .07, may be helpful.

she should obtain affirmative acknowledgment, normally in writing, from the nonparticipant party agreeing to the procedures performed and of its taking responsibility for the sufficiency of the procedures. If the nonparticipant party is added after the practitioner has issued his or her report, the report may be reissued or the practitioner may provide other written acknowledgment that the nonparticipant party has been added as a specified party. If the report is reissued, the report date should not be changed. If the practitioner provides written acknowledgment that the nonparticipant party has been added as a specified party, such written acknowledgment ordinarily should state that no procedures have been performed subsequent to the date of the report.

Written Representations

.37 A practitioner may find a representation letter to be a useful and practical means of obtaining representations from the responsible party. The need for such a letter may depend on the nature of the engagement and the specified parties. For example, section 601.68 requires a practitioner to obtain written representations from the responsible party in an agreed-upon procedures engagement related to compliance with specified requirements.

.38 Examples of matters that might appear in a representation letter from the responsible party include the following:

a. A statement acknowledging responsibility for the subject matter and, when applicable, the assertion

b. A statement acknowledging responsibility for selecting the criteria and for determining that such criteria are appropriate for their purposes

c. The assertion about the subject matter based on the criteria selected

d. A statement that all known matters contradicting the subject matter or the assertion and any communication from regulatory agencies affecting the subject matter or the assertion has been disclosed to the practitioner

e. Availability of all records relevant to the subject matter and the agreed-upon procedures

f. Other matters as the practitioner deems appropriate

.39 The responsible party's refusal to furnish written representations determined by the practitioner to be appropriate for the engagement constitutes a limitation on the performance of the engagement. In such circumstances, the practitioner should do one of the following.

a. Disclose in his or her report the inability to obtain representations from the responsible party.

b. Withdraw from the engagement.[17]

c. Change the engagement to another form of engagement.

---

[17] For an agreed-upon procedures engagement performed pursuant to section 601, management's refusal to furnish all required representations also constitutes a limitation on the scope of the engagement that requires the practitioner to withdraw from the engagement.

Knowledge of Matters Outside Agreed-Upon Procedures

.40 The practitioner need not perform procedures beyond the agreed-upon procedures. However, in connection with the application of agreed-upon procedures, if matters come to the practitioner's attention by other means that significantly contradict the subject matter (or written assertion related thereto) referred to in the practitioner's report, the practitioner should include this matter in his or her report.[18] For example, if, during the course of applying agreed-upon procedures regarding an entity's internal control, the practitioner becomes aware of a material weakness by means other than performance of the agreed-upon procedure, the practitioner should include this matter in his or her report.

Change to an Agreed-Upon Procedures Engagement From Another Form of Engagement

.41 A practitioner who has been engaged to perform another form of attest engagement or a nonattest service engagement may, before the engagement's completion, be requested to change the engagement to an agreed-upon procedures engagement under this section. A request to change the engagement may result from a change in circumstances affecting the client's requirements, a misunderstanding about the nature of the original services or the alternative services originally available, or a restriction on the performance of the original engagement, whether imposed by the client or caused by circumstances.

.42 Before a practitioner who was engaged to perform another form of engagement agrees to change the engagement to an agreed-upon procedures engagement, he or she should consider the following:

a. The possibility that certain procedures performed as part of another type of engagement are not appropriate for inclusion in an agreed-upon procedures engagement

b. The reason given for the request, particularly the implications of a restriction on the scope of the original engagement or the matters to be reported

c. The additional effort required to complete the original engagement

d. If applicable, the reasons for changing from a general-use report to a restricted-use report

.43 If the specified parties acknowledge agreement to the procedures performed or to be performed and assume responsibility for the sufficiency of the procedures to be included in the agreed-upon procedures engagement, either of the following would be considered a reasonable basis for requesting a change in the engagement—

a. A change in circumstances that requires another form of engagement

b. A misunderstanding concerning the nature of the original engagement or the available alternatives

---

[18] If the practitioner has performed (or has been engaged to perform) an audit of the entity's financial statements to which an element, account, or item of a financial statement relates and the auditor's report on such financial statements includes a departure from a standard report [see AU section 508, *Reports on Audited Financial Statements*], he or she should consider including a reference to the auditor's report and the departure from the standard report in his or her agreed-upon procedures report.

.44 In all circumstances, if the original engagement procedures are substantially complete or the effort to complete such procedures is relatively insignificant, the practitioner should consider the propriety of accepting a change in the engagement.

.45 If the practitioner concludes, based on his or her professional judgment, that there is reasonable justification to change the engagement, and provided he or she complies with the standards applicable to agreed-upon procedures engagements, the practitioner should issue an appropriate agreed-upon procedures report. The report should not include reference to either the original engagement or performance limitations that resulted in the changed engagement. (See paragraph .40.)

Combined Reports Covering Both Restricted-Use and General-Use Subject Matter or Presentations

.46 When a practitioner performs services pursuant to an engagement to apply agreed-upon procedures to specific subject matter as part of or in addition to another form of service, this section applies only to those services described herein; other Standards would apply to the other services. Other services may include an audit, review, or compilation of a financial statement, another attest service performed pursuant to the SSAEs, or a nonattest service.[19] Reports on applying agreed-upon procedures to specific subject matter may be combined with reports on such other services, provided the types of services can be clearly distinguished and the applicable Standards for each service are followed. See section 101.82 and .83, regarding restricting the use of the combined report.

Effective Date

.47 This section is effective when the subject matter or assertion is as of or for a period ending on or after June 1, 2001. Early application is permitted.

---

[19] See section 101.105–.107 for requirements relating to attest services provided as part of a consulting service engagement.

.48

Appendix

Additional Illustrative Reports

The following are additional illustrations of reporting on applying agreed-upon procedures to elements, accounts, or items of a financial statement.

1. Report in Connection With a Proposed Acquisition

Independent Accountant's Report
on Applying Agreed-Upon Procedures

To the Board of Directors and Management of X Company:

We have performed the procedures enumerated below, which were agreed to by the Board of Directors and Management of X Company, solely to assist you in connection with the proposed acquisition of Y Company as of December 31, 20XX. Y Company is responsible for its cash and accounts receivable records. This agreed-upon procedures engagement was conducted in accordance with attestation standards established by the American Institute of Certified Public Accountants. The sufficiency of these procedures is solely the responsibility of the parties specified in this report. Consequently, we make no representation regarding the sufficiency of the procedures described below either for the purpose for which this report has been requested or for any other purpose.

The procedures and the associated findings are as follows:

Cash

1. We obtained confirmation of the cash on deposit from the following banks, and we agreed the confirmed balance to the amount shown on the bank reconciliations maintained by Y Company. We mathematically checked the bank reconciliations and compared the resultant cash balances per book to the respective general ledger account balances.

Bank	*General Ledger Account Balances as of December 31, 20XX*
ABC National Bank	$ 5,000
DEF State Bank	3,776
XYZ Trust Company regular account	86,912
XYZ Trust Company payroll account	5,000
	$110,688

We found no exceptions as a result of the procedures.

Accounts Receivable

2. We added the individual customer account balances shown in an aged trial balance of accounts receivable (identified as Exhibit A) and compared the resultant total with the balance in the general ledger account.

   We found no difference.

3. We compared the individual customer account balances shown in the aged trial balance of accounts receivable (Exhibit A) as of December 31, 19XX, to the balances shown in the accounts receivable subsidiary ledger.

   We found no exceptions as a result of the comparisons.

4. We traced the aging (according to invoice dates) for 50 customer account balances shown in Exhibit A to the details of outstanding invoices in the accounts receivable subsidiary ledger. The balances selected for tracing were determined by starting at the eighth item and selecting every fifteenth item thereafter.

   We found no exceptions in the aging of the amounts of the 50 customer account balances selected. The sample size traced was 9.8 percent of the aggregate amount of the customer account balances.

5. We mailed confirmations directly to the customers representing the 150 largest customer account balances selected from the accounts receivable trial balance, and we received responses as indicated below. We also traced the items constituting the outstanding customer account balance to invoices and supporting shipping documents for customers from which there was no reply. As agreed, any individual differences in a customer account balance of less than $300 were to be considered minor, and no further procedures were performed.

   Of the 150 customer balances confirmed, we received responses from 140 customers; 10 customers did not reply. No exceptions were identified in 120 of the confirmations received. The differences disclosed in the remaining 20 confirmation replies were either minor in amount (as defined above) or were reconciled to the customer account balance without proposed adjustment thereto. A summary of the confirmation results according to the respective aging categories is as follows.

	Accounts Receivable December 31, 20XX		
Aging Categories	*Customer Account Balances*	*Confirmations Requested*	*Confirmations Received*
Current	$156,000	$ 76,000	$ 65,000
Past due:			
Less than one month:	60,000	30,000	19,000
One to three months	36,000	18,000	10,000
Over three months	48,000	48,000	8,000
	$300,000	$172,000	$102,000

We were not engaged to and did not conduct an audit, the objective of which would be the expression of an opinion on cash and accounts receivable. Accordingly, we do not express such an opinion. Had we performed additional procedures, other matters might have come to our attention that would have been reported to you.

This report is intended solely for the information and use of the board of directors and management of X Company and is not intended to be and should not be used by anyone other than these specified parties.

[*Signature*]

[*Date*]

2. Report in Connection With Claims of Creditors

Independent Accountant's Report
on Applying Agreed-Upon Procedures

To the Trustee of XYZ Company:

We have performed the procedures described below, which were agreed to by the Trustee of XYZ Company, with respect to the claims of creditors solely to assist you in determining the validity of claims of XYZ Company as of May 31, 20XX, as set forth in the accompanying Schedule A. XYZ Company is responsible for maintaining records of claims submitted by creditors of XYZ Company. This agreed-upon procedures engagement was conducted in accordance with attestation standards established by the American Institute of Certified Public Accountants. The sufficiency of these procedures is solely the responsibility of the party specified in this report. Consequently, we make no representation regarding the sufficiency of the procedures described below either for the purpose for which this report has been requested or for any other purpose.

The procedures and associated findings are as follows:

1. Compare the total of the trial balance of accounts payable at May 31, 20XX, prepared by XYZ Company, to the balance in the related general ledger account.

The total of the accounts payable trial balance agreed with the balance in the related general ledger account.

2. Compare the amounts for claims received from creditors (as shown in claim documents provided by XYZ Company) to the respective amounts shown in the trial balance of accounts payable. Using the data included in the claims documents and in XYZ Company's accounts payable detail records, reconcile any differences found to the accounts payable trial balance.

All differences noted are presented in column 3 of Schedule A. Except for those amounts shown in column 4 of Schedule A, all such differences were reconciled.

3. Obtain the documentation submitted by creditors in support of the amounts claimed and compare it to the following documentation in XYZ Company's files: invoices, receiving reports, and other evidence of receipt of goods or services.

No exceptions were found as a result of these comparisons.

We were not engaged to and did not conduct an audit, the objective of which would be the expression of an opinion on the claims of creditors set forth in the accompanying Schedule A. Accordingly, we do not express such an opinion. Had we performed additional procedures, other matters might have come to our attention that would have been reported to you.

This report is intended solely for the information and use of the Trustee of XYZ Company and is not intended to be and should not be used by anyone other than this specified party.

[*Signature*]

[*Date*]

AT Section 301

Financial Forecasts and Projections

Source: SSAE No. 10; SSAE No. 11; SSAE No. 17.

Effective when the date of the practitioner's report is on or after June 1, 2001, unless otherwise indicated.

Introduction

.01 This section sets forth standards and provides guidance to practitioners who are engaged to issue or do issue examination (paragraphs .29–.50), compilation (paragraphs .12–.28), or agreed-upon procedures reports (paragraphs .51–.56) on prospective financial statements.

.02 Whenever a practitioner (*a*) submits, to his or her client or others, prospective financial statements that he or she has assembled, or assisted in assembling, that are or reasonably might be expected to be used by another (third) party[1] or (*b*) reports on prospective financial statements that are, or reasonably might be expected to be used by another (third) party, the practitioner should perform one of the engagements described in the preceding paragraph. In deciding whether the prospective financial statements are or reasonably might be expected to be used by a third party, the practitioner may rely on either the written or oral representation of the responsible party, unless information comes to his or her attention that contradicts the responsible party's representation. If such third-party use of the prospective financial statements is not reasonably expected, the provisions of this section are not applicable unless the practitioner has been engaged to examine, compile, or apply agreed-upon procedures to the prospective financial statements.

.03 This section also provides standards for a practitioner who is engaged to examine, compile, or apply agreed-upon procedures to partial presentations. A partial presentation is a presentation of prospective financial information that excludes one or more of the items required for prospective financial statements as described in appendix A [paragraph .68], "Minimum Presentation Guidelines."

.04 The practitioner who has been engaged to or does compile, examine, or apply agreed-upon procedures to a partial presentation should perform the engagement in accordance with the guidance in paragraphs .12–.28 for compilations, .29–.50 for examinations, and .51–.56 for agreed-upon procedures, respectively, modified to reflect the nature of the presentation as discussed in paragraphs .03, .57, and .58.

.05 This section does not provide standards or procedures for engagements involving prospective financial statements used solely in connection with litigation support services. A practitioner may, however, look to these standards because they provide helpful guidance for many aspects of such engagements and may be referred to as useful guidance in such engagements. Litigation support services are engagements involving pending or potential formal legal proceedings before a trier of fact in connection with the resolution

---

[1] However, paragraph .59 permits an exception to this for certain types of budgets.

of a dispute between two or more parties, for example, when a practitioner acts as an expert witness. This exception is provided because, among other things, the practitioner's work in such proceedings is ordinarily subject to detailed analysis and challenge by each party to the dispute. This exception does not apply, however, if either of the following occur.

a. The practitioner is specifically engaged to issue or does issue an examination, a compilation, or an agreed-upon procedures report on prospective financial statements.

b. The prospective financial statements are for use by third parties who, under the rules of the proceedings, do not have the opportunity for analysis and challenge by each party to a dispute in a legal proceeding.

For example, creditors may not have such opportunities when prospective financial statements are submitted to them to secure their agreement to a plan of reorganization.

.06 In reporting on prospective financial statements, the practitioner may be called on to assist the responsible party in identifying assumptions, gathering information, or assembling the statements.[2] The responsible party is nonetheless responsible for the preparation and presentation of the prospective financial statements because the prospective financial statements are dependent on the actions, plans, and assumptions of the responsible party, and only it can take responsibility for the assumptions. Accordingly, the practitioner's engagement should not be characterized in his or her report or in the document containing his or her report as including "preparation" of the prospective financial statements. A practitioner may be engaged to prepare a financial analysis of a potential project where the engagement includes obtaining the information, making appropriate assumptions, and assembling the presentation. Such an analysis is not and should not be characterized as a forecast or projection and would not be appropriate for general use. However, if the responsible party reviewed and adopted the assumptions and presentation, or based its assumptions and presentation on the analysis, the practitioner could perform one of the engagements described in this section and issue a report appropriate for general use.

.07 The concept of materiality affects the application of this section to prospective financial statements as materiality affects the application of generally accepted auditing standards (GAAS) to historical financial statements. Materiality is a concept that is judged in light of the expected range of reasonableness of the information; therefore, users should not expect prospective information (information about events that have not yet occurred) to be as precise as historical information.

Definitions

.08 For the purposes of this section the following definitions apply.

a. *Prospective financial statements*—Either financial forecasts or financial projections including the summaries of significant assumptions and accounting policies. Although prospective financial statements

[2] Some of these services may not be appropriate if the practitioner is to be named as the person reporting on an examination in a filing with the Securities and Exchange Commission (SEC). SEC Release Nos. 33-5992 and 34-15305, "Disclosure of Projections of Future Economic Performance," state that for prospective financial statements filed with the commission, "a person should not be named as an outside reviewer if he actively assisted in the preparation of the projection."

may cover a period that has partially expired, statements for periods that have completely expired are not considered to be prospective financial statements. Pro forma financial statements and partial presentations are not considered to be prospective financial statements.[3]

b. *Partial presentation*—A presentation of prospective financial information that excludes one or more of the items required for prospective financial statements as described in appendix A (paragraph .68), "Minimum Presentation Guidelines." Partial presentations are not ordinarily appropriate for general use; accordingly, partial presentations should be restricted for use by specified parties who will be negotiating directly with the responsible party.

c. *Financial forecast*—Prospective financial statements that present, to the best of the responsible party's knowledge and belief, an entity's expected financial position, results of operations, and cash flows. A financial forecast is based on the responsible party's assumptions reflecting the conditions it expects to exist and the course of action it expects to take. A financial forecast may be expressed in specific monetary amounts as a single point estimate of forecasted results or as a range, where the responsible party selects key assumptions to form a range within which it reasonably expects, to the best of its knowledge and belief, the item or items subject to the assumptions to actually fall. When a forecast contains a range, the range is not selected in a biased or misleading manner, for example, a range in which one end is significantly less expected than the other. Minimum presentation guidelines for prospective financial statements are set forth in appendix A (paragraph .68).

d. *Financial projection*—Prospective financial statements that present, to the best of the responsible party's knowledge and belief, given one or more hypothetical assumptions, an entity's expected financial position, results of operations, and cash flows. A financial projection is sometimes prepared to present one or more hypothetical courses of action for evaluation, as in response to a question such as, "What would happen if . . . ?" A financial projection is based on the responsible party's assumptions reflecting conditions it expects would exist and the course of action it expects would be taken, given one or more hypothetical assumptions. A projection, like a forecast, may contain a range. Minimum presentation guidelines for prospective financial statements are set forth in appendix A (paragraph .68).

e. *Entity*—Any unit, existing or to be formed, for which financial statements could be prepared in accordance with generally accepted accounting principles (GAAP) or another comprehensive basis of accounting.[4] For example, an entity can be an individual, partnership, corporation, trust, estate, association, or governmental unit.

f. *Hypothetical assumption*—An assumption used in a financial projection to present a condition or course of action that is not necessarily expected to occur, but is consistent with the purpose of the projection.

---

[3] The objective of pro forma financial information is to show what the significant effects on the historical financial information might have been had a consummated or proposed transaction (or event) occurred at an earlier date. Although the transaction in question may be prospective, this section does not apply to such presentations because they are essentially historical financial statements and do not purport to be prospective financial statements. See section 401, *Reporting on Pro Forma Financial Information*.

[4] AU section 623, *Special Reports*, discusses comprehensive bases of accounting other than GAAP.

g. *Responsible party*—The person or persons who are responsible for the assumptions underlying the prospective financial statements. The responsible party usually is management, but it can be persons outside of the entity who do not currently have the authority to direct operations (for example, a party considering acquiring the entity).

h. *Assembly*—The manual or computer processing of mathematical or other clerical functions related to the presentation of the prospective financial statements. Assembly does not refer to the mere reproduction and collation of such statements or to the responsible party's use of the practitioner's computer processing hardware or software.

i. *Key factors*—The significant matters on which an entity's future results are expected to depend. Such factors are basic to the entity's operations and thus encompass matters that affect, among other things, the entity's sales, production, service, and financing activities. Key factors serve as a foundation for prospective financial statements and are the bases for the assumptions.

Uses of Prospective Financial Statements

.09 Prospective financial statements are for either *general use* or *limited use*. *General use* of prospective financial statements refers to the use of the statements by persons with whom the responsible party is not negotiating directly, for example, in an offering statement of an entity's debt or equity interests. Because recipients of prospective financial statements distributed for general use are unable to ask the responsible party directly about the presentation, the presentation most useful to them is one that portrays, to the best of the responsible party's knowledge and belief, the expected results. Thus, only a financial forecast is appropriate for general use.

.10 *Limited use* of prospective financial statements refers to the use of prospective financial statements by the responsible party alone or by the responsible party and third parties with whom the responsible party is negotiating directly. Examples include use in negotiations for a bank loan, submission to a regulatory agency, and use solely within the entity. Third-party recipients of prospective financial statements intended for limited use can ask questions of the responsible party and negotiate terms directly with it. Any type of prospective financial statements that would be useful in the circumstances would normally be appropriate for limited use. Thus, the presentation may be a financial forecast or a financial projection.

.11 Because a financial projection is not appropriate for general use, a practitioner should not consent to the use of his or her name in conjunction with a financial projection that he or she believes will be distributed to those who will not be negotiating directly with the responsible party, for example, in an offering statement of an entity's debt or equity interests, unless the projection is used to supplement a financial forecast.

Compilation of Prospective Financial Statements

.12 A compilation of prospective financial statements is a professional service that involves the following:

a. Assembling, to the extent necessary, the prospective financial statements based on the responsible party's assumptions *b.* Performing the required compilation procedures,[5] including reading the prospective financial statements with their summaries of significant assumptions and accounting policies, and considering whether they appear to be presented in conformity with AICPA presentation guidelines[6] and not obviously inappropriate

c. Issuing a compilation report

.13 A compilation is not intended to provide assurance on the prospective financial statements or the assumptions underlying such statements. Because of the limited nature of the practitioner's procedures, a compilation does not provide assurance that the practitioner will become aware of significant matters that might be disclosed by more extensive procedures, for example, those performed in an examination of prospective financial statements.

.14 The summary of significant assumptions is essential to the reader's understanding of prospective financial statements. Accordingly, the practitioner should not compile prospective financial statements that exclude disclosure of the summary of significant assumptions. Also, the practitioner should not compile a financial projection that excludes either (*a*) an identification of the hypothetical assumptions or (*b*) a description of the limitations on the usefulness of the presentation.

.15 The following standards apply to a compilation of prospective financial statements and to the resulting report.

a. The compilation should be performed by a person or persons having adequate technical training and proficiency to compile prospective financial statements.

b. Due professional care should be exercised in the performance of the compilation and the preparation of the report.

c. The work should be adequately planned, and assistants, if any, should be properly supervised.

d. Applicable compilation procedures should be performed as a basis for reporting on the compiled prospective financial statements. (See appendix B [paragraph .69], "Training and Proficiency, Planning and Procedures Applicable to Compilations," for the procedures to be performed.)

e. The report based on the practitioner's compilation of prospective financial statements should conform to the applicable guidance in paragraphs .18–.28.

.16 The practitioner should consider, after applying the procedures specified in paragraph .69, whether representations or other information he or she has received appear to be obviously inappropriate, incomplete, or otherwise misleading, and if so, the practitioner should attempt to obtain additional or revised information. If he or she does not receive such information, the practitioner should ordinarily withdraw from the compilation engagement.[7] (Note that the

---

[5] See appendix B (paragraph .69), subparagraph 5, for the required procedures.

[6] AICPA presentation guidelines are detailed in AICPA Guide *Prospective Financial Information*.

[7] The practitioner need not withdraw from the engagement if the effect of such information on the prospective financial statement does not appear to be material.

omission of disclosures, other than those relating to significant assumptions, would not require the practitioner to withdraw. See paragraph .26.)

Working Papers

[.17] [Paragraph deleted by the issuance of Statement on Standards for Attestation Engagements No. 11, January 2002.]

Reports on Compiled Prospective Financial Statements

.18 The practitioner's standard report on a compilation of prospective financial statements should include the following:

a. An identification of the prospective financial statements presented by the responsible party

b. A statement that the practitioner has compiled the prospective financial statements in accordance with attestation standards established by the American Institute of Certified Public Accountants

c. A statement that a compilation is limited in scope and does not enable the practitioner to express an opinion or any other form of assurance on the prospective financial statements or the assumptions

d. A caveat that the prospective results may not be achieved

e. A statement that the practitioner assumes no responsibility to update the report for events and circumstances occurring after the date of the report

f. The manual or printed signature of the practitioner's firm

g. The date of the compilation report

.19 The following is the form of the practitioner's standard report on the compilation of a forecast that does not contain a range.[8]

> We have compiled the accompanying forecasted balance sheet, statements of income, retained earnings, and cash flows of XYZ Company as of December 31, 20XX, and for the year then ending, in accordance with attestation standards established by the American Institute of Certified Public Accountants.[9]
>
> A compilation is limited to presenting in the form of a forecast information that is the representation of management[10] and does not include evaluation of the support for the assumptions underlying the forecast. We have not examined the forecast and, accordingly, do not express an opinion or any other form of

---

[8] The forms of reports provided in this section are appropriate whether the presentation is based on GAAP or on another comprehensive basis of accounting.

[9] When the presentation is summarized as discussed in appendix A (paragraph .68), this sentence might read, "We have compiled the accompanying summarized forecast of XYZ Company as of December 31, 20XX, and for the year then ending in accordance with attestation standards established by the American Institute of Certified Public Accountants."

[10] If the responsible party is other than management, the references to management in the standard reports provided in this section should be changed to refer to the party who assumes responsibility for the assumptions.

assurance on the accompanying statements or assumptions. Furthermore, there will usually be differences between the forecasted and actual results, because events and circumstances frequently do not occur as expected, and those differences may be material. We have no responsibility to update this report for events and circumstances occurring after the date of this report.

[*Signature*]

[*Date*]

.20 When the presentation is a projection, the practitioner's compilation report should include the report elements set forth in paragraph .18. Additionally, the report should include a statement describing the special purpose for which the projection was prepared as well as a separate paragraph that restricts the use of the report because it is intended to be used solely by the specified parties. The following is the form of the practitioner's standard report on a compilation of a projection that does not contain a range.

We have compiled the accompanying projected balance sheet, statements of income, retained earnings, and cash flows of XYZ Company as of December 31, 20XX, and for the year then ending, in accordance with attestation standards established by the American Institute of Certified Public Accountants.[11] The accompanying projection was prepared for [*state special purpose, for example, "the purpose of negotiating a loan to expand XYZ Company's plant"*].

A compilation is limited to presenting in the form of a projection information that is the representation of management and does not include evaluation of the support for the assumptions underlying the projection. We have not examined the projection and, accordingly, do not express an opinion or any other form of assurance on the accompanying statements or assumptions. Furthermore, even if [*describe hypothetical assumption, for example, "the loan is granted and the plant is expanded,"*] there will usually be differences between the projected and actual results, because events and circumstances frequently do not occur as expected, and those differences may be material. We have no responsibility to update this report for events and circumstances occurring after the date of this report.

The accompanying projection and this report are intended solely for the information and use of [*identify specified parties, for example, "XYZ Company and DEF Bank"*] and is not intended to be and should not be used by anyone other than these specified parties.

[*Signature*]

[*Date*]

.21 When the prospective financial statements contain a range, the practitioner's standard report should also include a separate paragraph that states that the responsible party has elected to portray the expected results of one or more assumptions as a range. The following is an example of the separate paragraph to be added to the practitioner's report when he or she compiles prospective financial statements, in this case a forecast, that contain a range.

As described in the summary of significant assumptions, management of XYZ Company has elected to portray forecasted [*describe financial statement element*

---

[11] When the presentation is summarized as discussed in appendix A (paragraph .68), this sentence might read as follows.

We have compiled the accompanying summarized projection of XYZ Company as of December 31, 20XX, and for the year then ending in accordance with attestation standards established by the American Institute of Certified Public Accountants.

or elements for which the expected results of one or more assumptions fall within a range, and identify the assumptions expected to fall within a range, for example, "revenue at the amounts of $X,XXX and $Y,YYY, which is predicated upon occupancy rates of XX percent and YY percent of available apartments,"] rather than as a single point estimate. Accordingly, the accompanying forecast presents forecasted financial position, results of operations, and cash flows [*describe one or more assumptions expected to fall within a range, for example, "at such occupancy rates."*] However, there is no assurance that the actual results will fall within the range of [*describe one or more assumptions expected to fall within a range, for example, "occupancy rates"*] presented.

.22 The date of completion of the practitioner's compilation procedures should be used as the date of the report.

.23 A practitioner may compile prospective financial statements for an entity with respect to which he or she is not independent.[12] In such circumstances, the practitioner's report should be modified to indicate his or her lack of independence in a separate paragraph of the practitioner's report. An example of such a disclosure would be

We are not independent with respect to XYZ Company.

The practitioner is not precluded from disclosing a description about the reason(s) that his or her independence is impaired. The following are examples of descriptions the practitioner may use:

a. We are not independent with respect to XYZ Company as of and for the year ended [*or ending, as applicable*] December 31, 20XX, because a member of the engagement team had a direct financial interest in XYZ Company.

b. We are not independent with respect to XYZ Company as of and for the year ended [*or ending, as applicable*] December 31, 20XX, because an immediate family member of one of the members of the engagement team was employed by XYZ Company.

c. We are not independent with respect to XYZ Company as of and for the year ended [*or ending, as applicable*] December 31, 20XX, because we performed certain accounting services (the practitioner may include a specific description of those services) that impaired our independence.

If the accountant elects to disclose a description about the reasons his or her independence is impaired, the accountant should ensure that all reasons are included in the description.

[As amended, effective for compilations of prospective financial statements for periods ending on or after December 15, 2010, by SSAE No. 17.]

.24 Prospective financial statements may be included in a document that also contains historical financial statements and the practitioner's report thereon.[13] In addition, the historical financial statements that appear in the

---

[12] In making a judgment about whether he or she is independent, the practitioner should be guided by the AICPA Code of Professional Conduct. [Footnote amended, effective for compilations of prospective financial statements for periods ending on or after December 15, 2010, by SSAE No. 17.]

[13] The practitioner's responsibility with respect to those historical financial statements upon which he or she is not engaged to perform a professional service is described in AU section 504, *Association With Financial Statements*, in the case of public entities, and Statement on Standards for Accounting and Review Services (SSARS) No. 1, *Compilation and Review of Financial Statements*, paragraph 3 (AR sec. 100 par. .03), in the case of nonpublic entities. [Footnote revised, November 2002, to reflect conforming changes necessary due to the issuance of Statement on Standards for Accounting and Review Services No. 9.]

document may be summarized and presented with the prospective financial statements for comparative purposes.[14] An example of the reference to the practitioner's report on the historical financial statements when he or she audited, reviewed, or compiled those statements is presented below.

[*Concluding sentence of last paragraph*]

> The historical financial statements for the year ended December 31, 20XX, [*from which the historical data are derived*] and our report thereon are set forth on pages XX-XX of this document.

.25 In some circumstances, a practitioner may wish to expand his or her report to emphasize a matter regarding the prospective financial statements. Such information may be presented in a separate paragraph of the practitioner's report. However, the practitioner should exercise care that emphasizing such a matter does not give the impression that he or she is expressing assurance or expanding the degree of responsibility he or she is taking with respect to such information.[15] For example, the practitioner should not include statements in his or her compilation report about the mathematical accuracy of the statements or their conformity with presentation guidelines.

Modifications of the Standard Compilation Report

.26 An entity may request a practitioner to compile prospective financial statements that contain presentation deficiencies or omit disclosures other than those relating to significant assumptions. The practitioner may compile such prospective financial statements provided the deficiency or omission is clearly indicated in his or her report and is not, to his or her knowledge, undertaken with the intention of misleading those who might reasonably be expected to use such statements.

.27 Notwithstanding the preceding, if the compiled prospective financial statements are presented on a comprehensive basis of accounting other than GAAP and do not include disclosure of the basis of accounting used, the basis should be disclosed in the practitioner's report.

.28 The following is an example of a paragraph that should be added to a report on compiled prospective financial statements, in this case a financial forecast, in which the summary of significant accounting policies has been omitted.

> Management has elected to omit the summary of significant accounting policies required by the guidelines for presentation of a forecast established by the American Institute of Certified Public Accountants. If the omitted disclosures were included in the forecast, they might influence the user's conclusions about the Company's financial position, results of operations, and cash flows for the forecast period. Accordingly, this forecast is not designed for those who are not informed about such matters.

Examination of Prospective Financial Statements

.29 An examination of prospective financial statements is a professional service that involves—

---

[14] AU section 552, *Reporting on Condensed Financial Statements and Selected Financial Data*, discusses the practitioner's report where summarized financial statements are derived from audited statements that are not included in the same document.

[15] However, the practitioner may provide assurance on tax matters in order to comply with the requirements of regulations governing practice before the Internal Revenue Service (IRS) contained in 31 CFR pt. 10 (Treasury Department Circular No. 230).

a. Evaluating the preparation of the prospective financial statements.

b. Evaluating the support underlying the assumptions.

c. Evaluating the presentation of the prospective financial statements for conformity with AICPA presentation guidelines.[16]

d. Issuing an examination report.

.30 As a result of his or her examination, the practitioner has a basis for reporting on whether, in his or her opinion—

a. The prospective financial statements are presented in conformity with AICPA guidelines.

b. The assumptions provide a reasonable basis for the responsible party's forecast, or whether the assumptions provide a reasonable basis for the responsible party's projection given the hypothetical assumptions.

.31 The practitioner should follow the general, fieldwork, and reporting standards for attestation engagements established in section 50, *SSAE Hierarchy*, and further explained in section 101, *Attest Engagements*, in performing an examination of prospective financial statements and reporting thereon. (See paragraph .70 for standards concerning such technical training and proficiency, planning the examination engagement, and the types of procedures a practitioner should perform to obtain sufficient evidence for his or her examination report.) [Revised, November 2006, to reflect conforming changes necessary due to the issuance of Statement on Standards for Attestation Engagements No. 14.]

Working Papers

[.32] [Paragraph deleted by the issuance of Statement on Standards for Attestation Engagements No. 11, January 2002.]

Reports on Examined Prospective Financial Statements

.33 The practitioner's standard report on an examination of prospective financial statements should include the following:

a. A title that includes the word *independent*

b. An identification of the prospective financial statements presented

c. An identification of the responsible party and a statement that the prospective financial statements are the responsibility of the responsible party

d. A statement that the practitioner's responsibility is to express an opinion on the prospective financial statements based on his or her examination

e. A statement that the examination of the prospective financial statements was conducted in accordance with attestation standards established by the American Institute of Certified Public Accountants and, accordingly, included such procedures as the practitioner considered necessary in the circumstances

f. A statement that the practitioner believes that the examination provides a reasonable basis for his or her opinion

---

[16] AICPA presentation guidelines are detailed in AICPA Guide *Prospective Financial Information*.

g. The practitioner's opinion that the prospective financial statements are presented in conformity with AICPA presentation guidelines and that the underlying assumptions provide a reasonable basis for the forecast or a reasonable basis for the projection given the hypothetical assumptions[17]

h. A caveat that the prospective results may not be achieved

i. A statement that the practitioner assumes no responsibility to update the report for events and circumstances occurring after the date of the report

j. The manual or printed signature of the practitioner's firm

k. The date of the examination report

.34 The following is the form of the practitioner's standard report on an examination of a forecast that does not contain a range.

Independent Accountant's Report

We have examined the accompanying forecasted balance sheet, statements of income, retained earnings, and cash flows of XYZ Company as of December 31, 20XX, and for the year then ending.[18] XYZ Company's management is responsible for the forecast. Our responsibility is to express an opinion on the forecast based on our examination.

Our examination was conducted in accordance with attestation standards established by the American Institute of Certified Public Accountants and, accordingly, included such procedures as we considered necessary to evaluate both the assumptions used by management and the preparation and presentation of the forecast. We believe that our examination provides a reasonable basis for our opinion.

In our opinion, the accompanying forecast is presented in conformity with guidelines for presentation of a forecast established by the American Institute of Certified Public Accountants, and the underlying assumptions provide a reasonable basis for management's forecast. However, there will usually be differences between the forecasted and actual results, because events and circumstances frequently do not occur as expected, and those differences may be material. We have no responsibility to update this report for events and circumstances occurring after the date of this report.

[*Signature*]

[*Date*]

.35 When a practitioner examines a projection, his or her opinion regarding the assumptions should be conditioned on the hypothetical assumptions; that is, he or she should express an opinion on whether the assumptions provide a reasonable basis for the projection given the hypothetical assumptions. The practitioner's examination report on a projection should include the report elements set forth in paragraph .33. Additionally, the report should include a statement describing the special purpose for which the projection was prepared as well a separate paragraph that restricts the use of the report because it is intended to be used solely by specified parties. The following is the form of the

---

17 The practitioner's report need not comment on the consistency of the application of accounting principles as long as the presentation of any change in accounting principles is in conformity with AICPA presentation guidelines as detailed in AICPA Guide *Prospective Financial Information*.

18 When the presentation is summarized as discussed in appendix A (paragraph .68), this sentence might read, "We have examined the accompanying summarized forecast of XYZ Company as of December 31, 20XX, and for the year then ending."

practitioner's standard report on an examination of a projection that does not contain a range.

Independent Accountant's Report

We have examined the accompanying projected balance sheet, statements of income, retained earnings, and cash flows of XYZ Company as of December 31, 20XX, and for the year then ending.[19] XYZ Company's management is responsible for the projection, which was prepared for [*state special purpose, for example, "the purpose of negotiating a loan to expand XYZ Company's plant"*]. Our responsibility is to express an opinion on the projection based on our examination.

Our examination was conducted in accordance with attestation standards established by the American Institute of Certified Public Accountants and, accordingly, included such procedures as we considered necessary to evaluate both the assumptions used by management and the preparation and presentation of the projection. We believe that our examination provides a reasonable basis for our opinion.

In our opinion, the accompanying projection is presented in conformity with guidelines for presentation of a projection established by the American Institute of Certified Public Accountants, and the underlying assumptions provide a reasonable basis for management's projection [*describe the hypothetical assumption, for example, "assuming the granting of the requested loan for the purpose of expanding XYZ Company's plant as described in the summary of significant assumptions."*] However, even if [*describe hypothetical assumption, for example, "the loan is granted and the plant is expanded,"*], there will usually be differences between the projected and actual results, because events and circumstances frequently do not occur as expected, and those differences may be material. We have no responsibility to update this report for events and circumstances occurring after the date of this report.

The accompanying projection and this report are intended solely for the information and use of [*identify specified parties, for example, "XYZ Company and DEF National Bank"*] and is not intended to be and should not be used by anyone other than these specified parties.

[*Signature*]

[*Date*]

.36 When the prospective financial statements contain a range, the practitioner's standard report should also include a separate paragraph that states that the responsible party has elected to portray the expected results of one or more assumptions as a range. The following is an example of the separate paragraph to be added to the practitioner's report when he or she examines prospective financial statements, in this case a forecast, that contain a range.

As described in the summary of significant assumptions, management of XYZ Company has elected to portray forecasted [*describe financial statement element or elements for which the expected results of one or more assumptions fall within a range, and identify assumptions expected to fall within a range, for example, "revenue at the amounts of $X,XXX and $Y,YYY, which is predicated upon occupancy rates of XX percent and YY percent of available apartments,"*] rather than as a single point estimate. Accordingly, the accompanying forecast presents forecasted financial position, results of operations, and cash flows [*describe one or more assumptions expected to fall within a range, for example, "at*

---

[19] When the presentation is summarized as discussed in appendix A (paragraph .68), this sentence might read, "We have examined the accompanying summarized projection of XYZ Company as of December 31, 20XX, and for the year then ending."

such occupancy rates."] However, there is no assurance that the actual results will fall within the range of [*describe one or more assumptions expected to fall within a range, for example, "occupancy rates"*] presented.

.37 The date of completion of the practitioner's examination procedures should be used as the date of the report.

Modifications to the Practitioner's Opinion[20]

.38 The following circumstances result in the following types of modified practitioner's report involving the practitioner's opinion.

a. If, in the practitioner's opinion, the prospective financial statements depart from AICPA presentation guidelines, he or she should express a qualified opinion (see paragraph .39) or an adverse opinion. (See paragraph .41.)[21] However, if the presentation departs from the presentation guidelines because it fails to disclose assumptions that appear to be significant, the practitioner should express an adverse opinion. (See paragraphs .41 and .42.)

b. If the practitioner believes that one or more significant assumptions do not provide a reasonable basis for the forecast, or a reasonable basis for the projection given the hypothetical assumptions, he or she should express an adverse opinion. (See paragraph .41.)

c. If the practitioner's examination is affected by conditions that preclude application of one or more procedures he or she considers necessary in the circumstances, he or she should disclaim an opinion and describe the scope limitation in his or her report. (See paragraph .43.)

.39 *Qualified Opinion*. In a qualified opinion, the practitioner should state, in a separate paragraph, all substantive reasons for modifying his or her opinion and describe the departure from AICPA presentation guidelines. His or her opinion should include the words "except" or "exception" as the qualifying language and should refer to the separate explanatory paragraph. The following is an example of an examination report on a forecast that is at variance with AICPA guidelines for presentation of a financial forecast.

Independent Accountant's Report

We have examined the accompanying forecasted balance sheet, statements of income, retained earnings, and cash flows of XYZ Company as of December 31, 20XX, and for the year then ending. XYZ Company's management is responsible for the forecast. Our responsibility is to express an opinion on the forecast based on our examination.

Our examination was conducted in accordance with attestation standards established by the American Institute of Certified Public Accountants and, accordingly, included such procedures as we considered necessary to evaluate both the assumptions used by management and the preparation and presentation of the forecast. We believe that our examination provides a reasonable basis for our opinion.

---

[20] Paragraphs .38–.44 describe circumstances in which the practitioner's standard report on prospective financial statements may require modification. The guidance for modifying the practitioner's standard report is generally applicable to partial presentations. Also, depending on the nature of the presentation, the practitioner may decide to disclose that the partial presentation is not intended to be a presentation of financial position, results of operations, or cash flows. Illustrative reports on partial presentations may be found in AICPA Guide *Prospective Financial Information*.

[21] However, the practitioner may issue the standard examination report on a financial forecast filed with the SEC that meets the presentation requirements of article XI of Regulation S-X.

The forecast does not disclose significant accounting policies. Disclosure of such policies is required by guidelines for presentation of a forecast established by the American Institute of Certified Public Accountants.

In our opinion, except for the omission of the disclosure of the significant accounting policies as discussed in the preceding paragraph, the accompanying forecast is presented in conformity with guidelines for a presentation of a forecast established by the American Institute of Certified Public Accountants and the underlying assumptions provide a reasonable basis for management's forecast. However, there will usually be differences between the forecasted and actual results, because events and circumstances frequently do not occur as expected, and those differences may be material. We have no responsibility to update this report for events and circumstances occurring after the date of this report.

[Signature]

[Date]

.40 Because of the nature, sensitivity, and interrelationship of prospective information, a reader would find a practitioner's report qualified for a measurement departure,[22] the reasonableness of the underlying assumptions, or a scope limitation difficult to interpret. Accordingly, the practitioner should not express his or her opinion about these items with language such as "except for . . ." or "subject to the effects of. . . ." Rather, when a measurement departure, an unreasonable assumption, or a limitation on the scope of the practitioner's examination has led him or her to conclude that he or she cannot issue an unqualified opinion, he or she should issue the appropriate type of modified opinion described in paragraphs .41–.44.

.41 *Adverse Opinion.* In an adverse opinion the practitioner should state, in a separate paragraph, all of the substantive reasons for his or her adverse opinion. His or her opinion should state that the presentation is not in conformity with presentation guidelines and should refer to the explanatory paragraph. When applicable, his or her opinion paragraph should also state that, in the practitioner's opinion, the assumptions do not provide a reasonable basis for the prospective financial statements. An example of an adverse opinion on an examination of prospective financial statements is set forth below. In this case, a financial forecast was examined and the practitioner's opinion was that a significant assumption was unreasonable. The example should be revised as appropriate for a different type of presentation or if the adverse opinion is issued because the statements do not conform to the presentation guidelines.

Independent Accountant's Report

We have examined the accompanying forecasted balance sheet, statements of income, retained earnings, and cash flows of XYZ Company as of December 31, 20XX, and for the year then ending. XYZ Company's management is responsible for the forecast. Our responsibility is to express an opinion on the forecast based on our examination.

Our examination was conducted in accordance with attestation standards established by the American Institute of Certified Public Accountants and, accordingly, included such procedures as we considered necessary to evaluate

[22] An example of a measurement departure is the failure to capitalize a capital lease in a forecast where the historical financial statements for the prospective period are expected to be presented in conformity with GAAP.

both the assumptions used by management and the preparation and presentation of the forecast. We believe that our examination provides a reasonable basis for our opinion.

As discussed under the caption "Sales" in the summary of significant forecast assumptions, the forecasted sales include, among other things, revenue from the Company's federal defense contracts continuing at the current level. The Company's present federal defense contracts will expire in March 20XX. No new contracts have been signed and no negotiations are under way for new federal defense contracts. Furthermore, the federal government has entered into contracts with another company to supply the items being manufactured under the Company's present contracts.

In our opinion, the accompanying forecast is not presented in conformity with guidelines for presentation of a financial forecast established by the American Institute of Certified Public Accountants because management's assumptions, as discussed in the preceding paragraph, do not provide a reasonable basis for management's forecast. We have no responsibility to update this report for events or circumstances occurring after the date of this report.

[*Signature*]

[*Date*]

.42 If the presentation, including the summary of significant assumptions, fails to disclose assumptions that, at the time, appear to be significant, the practitioner should describe the assumptions in his or her report and express an adverse opinion. The practitioner should not examine a presentation that omits all disclosures of assumptions. Also, the practitioner should not examine a financial projection that omits (*a*) an identification of the hypothetical assumptions or (*b*) a description of the limitations on the usefulness of the presentation.

.43 *Disclaimer of Opinion.* In a disclaimer of opinion, the practitioner's report should indicate, in a separate paragraph, the respects in which the examination did not comply with standards for an examination. The practitioner should state that the scope of the examination was not sufficient to enable him or her to express an opinion with respect to the presentation or the underlying assumptions, and his or her disclaimer of opinion should include a direct reference to the explanatory paragraph. The following is an example of a report on an examination of prospective financial statements, in this case a financial forecast, for which a significant assumption could not be evaluated.

Independent Accountant's Report

We were engaged to examine the accompanying forecasted balance sheet, statements of income, retained earnings, and cash flows of XYZ Company as of December 31, 20XX, and for the year then ending. XYZ Company's management is responsible for the forecast.

As discussed under the caption "Income From Investee" in the summary of significant forecast assumptions, the forecast includes income from an equity investee constituting 23 percent of forecasted net income, which is management's estimate of the Company's share of the investee's income to be accrued for 20XX. The investee has not prepared a forecast for the year ending December 31, 20XX, and we were therefore unable to obtain suitable support for this assumption.

Because, as described in the preceding paragraph, we are unable to evaluate management's assumption regarding income from an equity investee and other assumptions that depend thereon, the scope of our work was not sufficient to express, and we do not express, an opinion with respect to the presentation of or the assumptions underlying the accompanying forecast. We have no responsibility to update this report for events and circumstances occurring after the date of this report.

[Signature]

[Date]

.44 When there is a scope limitation and the practitioner also believes there are material departures from the presentation guidelines, those departures should be described in the practitioner's report.

Other Modifications to the Standard Examination Report

.45 The circumstances described below, although not necessarily resulting in modifications to the practitioner's opinion, would result in the following types of modifications to the standard examination report.

.46 *Emphasis of a Matter.* In some circumstances, the practitioner may wish to emphasize a matter regarding the prospective financial statements but nevertheless intends to express an unqualified opinion. The practitioner may present other information and comments he or she wishes to include, such as explanatory comments or other informative material, in a separate paragraph of his or her report.

.47 *Evaluation Based in Part on a Report of Another Practitioner.* When more than one practitioner is involved in the examination, the guidance provided for that situation in connection with examinations of historical financial statements is generally applicable. When the principal practitioner decides to refer to the report of another practitioner as a basis, in part, for his or her own opinion, he or she should disclose that fact in stating the scope of the examination and should refer to the report of the other practitioner in expressing his or her opinion. Such a reference indicates the division of responsibility for the performance of the examination.

.48 *Comparative Historical Financial Information.* Prospective financial statements may be included in a document that also contains historical financial statements and a practitioner's report thereon.[23] In addition, the historical financial statements that appear in the document may be summarized and presented with the prospective financial statements for comparative purposes.[24] An example of the reference to the practitioner's report on the historical financial statements when he or she audited, reviewed, or compiled those statements is presented in paragraph .24.

.49 *Reporting When the Examination Is Part of a Larger Engagement.* When the practitioner's examination of prospective financial statements is part of a larger engagement, for example, a financial feasibility study or business acquisition study, it is appropriate to expand the report on the examination of the prospective financial statements to describe the entire engagement.

---

[23] The practitioner's responsibility with respect to those historical financial statements upon which he or she is not engaged to perform a professional service is described in AU section 504, in the case of public entities, and SSARS No. 1, paragraph 3 (AR sec. 100 par. .03), in the case of nonpublic entities. [Footnote revised, November 2002, to reflect conforming changes necessary due to the issuance of Statement on Standards for Accounting and Review Services No. 9.]

[24] AU section 552 discusses the practitioner's report for summarized financial statements derived from audited financial statements that are not included in the same document.

.50 The following is a report that might be issued when a practitioner chooses to expand his or her report on a financial feasibility study.[25]

Independent Accountant's Report

a. The Board of Directors
Example Hospital
Example, Texas

b. We have prepared a financial feasibility study of Example Hospital's (the Hospital's) plans to expand and renovate its facilities. The study was undertaken to evaluate the ability of the Hospital to meet its operating expenses, working capital needs, and other financial requirements, including the debt service requirements associated with the proposed $25,000,000 [*legal title of bonds*] issue, at an assumed average annual interest rate of 10.0 percent during the five years ending December 31, 20X6.

c. The proposed capital improvements program (the Program) consists of a new two-level addition, which is to provide fifty additional medical-surgical beds, increasing the complement to 275 beds. In addition, various administrative and support service areas in the present facilities are to be remodeled. The Hospital administration anticipates that construction is to begin June 30, 20X2, and to be completed by December 31, 20X3.

d. The estimated total cost of the Program is approximately $30,000,000. It is assumed that the $25,000,000 of revenue bonds that the Example Hospital Finance Authority proposes to issue would be the primary source of funds for the Program. The responsibility for payment of debt service on the bonds is solely that of the Hospital. Other necessary funds to finance the Program are assumed to be provided from the Hospital's funds, from a local fund drive, and from interest earned on funds held by the bond trustee during the construction period.

e. Our procedures included analysis of the following:

- Program history, objectives, timing, and financing
- The future demand for the Hospital's services, including consideration of the following:
  - — Economic and demographic characteristics of the Hospital's defined service area
  - — Locations, capacities, and competitive information pertaining to other existing and planned area hospitals
  - — Physician support for the Hospital and its programs
  - — Historical utilization levels
- Planning agency applications and approvals
- Construction and equipment costs, debt service requirements, and estimated financing costs

[25] Although the entity referred to in the report is a hospital, the form of report is also applicable to other entities such as hotels or stadiums. Also, although the illustrated report format and language should not be departed from in any significant way, the language used should be tailored to fit the circumstances that are unique to a particular engagement (for example, the description of the proposed capital improvement program, paragraph *c*; the proposed financing of the program, paragraphs *b* and *d*; the specific procedures applied by the practitioner, paragraph *e*; and any explanatory comments included in emphasis-of-a-matter paragraphs, paragraph *i*, which deals with general matter; and paragraph *j*, which deals with specific matters).

- Staffing patterns and other operating considerations
- Third-party reimbursement policy and history
- Revenue/expense/volume relationships

f. We also participated in gathering other information, assisted management in identifying and formulating its assumptions, and assembled the accompanying financial forecast based on those assumptions.

g. The accompanying financial forecast for the annual periods ending December 31, 20X2, through 20X6, is based on assumptions that were provided by or reviewed with and approved by management. The financial forecast includes the following:

- Balance sheets
- Statements of operations
- Statements of cash flows
- Statements of changes in net assets

h. We have examined the financial forecast. Example Hospital's management is responsible for the forecast. Our responsibility is to express an opinion on the forecast based on our examination. Our examination was conducted in accordance with attestation standards established by the American Institute of Certified Public Accountants and, accordingly, included such procedures as we considered necessary to evaluate both the assumptions used by management and the preparation and presentation of the forecast. We believe that our examination provides a reasonable basis for our opinion.

i. Legislation and regulations at all levels of government have affected and may continue to affect revenues and expenses of hospitals. The financial forecast is based on legislation and regulations currently in effect. If future legislation or regulations related to hospital operations are enacted, such legislation or regulations could have a material effect on future operations.

j. The interest rate, principal payments, Program costs, and other financing assumptions are described in the section entitled "Summary of Significant Forecast Assumptions and Rationale." If actual interest rates, principal payments, and funding requirements are different from those assumed, the amount of the bond issue and debt service requirements would need to be adjusted accordingly from those indicated in the forecast. If such interest rates, principal payments, and funding requirements are lower than those assumed, such adjustments would not adversely affect the forecast.

k. Our conclusions are presented below.

- In our opinion, the accompanying financial forecast is presented in conformity with guidelines for presentation of a financial forecast established by the American Institute of Certified Public Accountants.
- In our opinion, the underlying assumptions provide a reasonable basis for management's forecast. However, there will usually be differences between the forecasted and actual results, because events and circumstances frequently do not occur as expected, and those differences may be material.

- The accompanying financial forecast indicates that sufficient funds could be generated to meet the Hospital's operating expenses, working capital needs, and other financial requirements, including the debt service requirements associated with the proposed $25,000,000 bond issue, during the forecast periods. However, the achievement of any financial forecast is dependent on future events, the occurrence of which cannot be assured.

l. We have no responsibility to update this report for events and circumstances occurring after the date of this report.

[*Signature*]

[*Date*]

Applying Agreed-Upon Procedures to Prospective Financial Statements

.51 The practitioner who accepts an engagement to apply agreed-upon procedures to prospective financial statements should follow the general, fieldwork, and reporting standards for attest engagements established in section 50, *SSAE Hierarchy*, and the guidance set forth herein and in section 201, *Agreed-Upon Procedures Engagements*. [Revised, November 2006, to reflect conforming changes necessary due to the issuance of Statement on Standards for Attestation Engagements No. 14.]

.52 A practitioner may perform an agreed-upon procedures attest engagement on prospective financial statements[26] provided the following conditions are met.

a. The practitioner is independent.

b. The practitioner and the specified parties agree upon the procedures performed or to be performed by the practitioner.

c. The specified parties take responsibility for the sufficiency of the agreed-upon procedures for their purposes.

d. The prospective financial statements include a summary of significant assumptions.

e. The prospective financial statements to which the procedures are to be applied are subject to reasonably consistent evaluation against criteria that are suitable and available to the specified parties.

f. Criteria to be used in the determination of findings are agreed upon between the practitioner and the specified parties.[27]

g. The procedures to be applied to the prospective financial statements are expected to result in reasonably consistent findings using the criteria.

h. Evidential matter related to the prospective financial statements to which the procedures are applied is expected to exist to provide a reasonable basis for expressing the findings in the practitioner's report.

---

[26] Practitioners should follow the guidance in AU section 634, *Letters for Underwriters and Certain Other Requesting Parties*, when requested to perform agreed-upon procedures on a forecast and report thereon in a letter for an underwriter.

[27] For example, accounting principles and other presentation criteria as discussed in chapter 8, *Presentation Guidelines*, of AICPA Guide *Prospective Financial Information*.

i. Where applicable, the practitioner and the specified users agree on any agreed-upon materiality limits for reporting purposes. (See section 201.25.)

j. Use of the report is to be restricted to the specified parties.[28]

.53 Generally, the practitioner's procedures may be as limited or as extensive as the specified parties desire, as long as the specified parties take responsibility for their sufficiency. However, mere reading of prospective financial statements does not constitute a procedure sufficient to permit a practitioner to report on the results of applying agreed-upon procedures to such statements. (See section 201.15.)

.54 To satisfy the requirements that the practitioner and the specified parties agree upon the procedures performed or to be performed and that the specified parties take responsibility for the sufficiency of the agreed-upon procedures for their purposes, ordinarily the practitioner should communicate directly with and obtain affirmative acknowledgment from each of the specified parties. For example, this may be accomplished by meeting with the specified parties or by distributing a draft of the anticipated report or a copy of an engagement letter to the specified parties and obtaining their agreement. If the practitioner is not able to communicate directly with all of the specified parties, the practitioner may satisfy these requirements by applying any one or more of the following or similar procedures:

- Compare the procedures to be applied to written requirements of the specified parties.
- Discuss the procedures to be applied with appropriate representatives of the specified parties involved.
- Review relevant contracts with or correspondence from the specified parties.

The practitioner should not report on an engagement when specified parties do not agree upon the procedures performed or to be performed and do not take responsibility for the sufficiency of the procedures for their purposes. (See section 201.36 for guidance on satisfying these requirements when the practitioner is requested to add other parties as specified parties after the date of completion of the agreed-upon procedures.)

Reports on the Results of Applying Agreed-Upon Procedures

.55 The practitioner's report on the results of applying agreed-upon procedures should be in the form of procedures and findings. The practitioner's report should contain the following elements:

a. A title that includes the word *independent*

b. Identification of the specified parties

c. Reference to the prospective financial statements covered by the practitioner's report and the character of the engagement

d. A statement that the procedures performed were those agreed to by the specified parties identified in the report

---

[28] In some cases, restricted-use reports filed with regulatory agencies are required by law or regulation to be made available to the public as a matter of public record. Also, a regulatory agency as part of its oversight responsibility for an entity may require access to restricted-use reports in which they are not named as a specified party. (See section 101.79.)

e. Identification of the responsible party and a statement that the prospective financial statements are the responsibility of the responsible party

f. A statement that the agreed-upon procedures engagement was conducted in accordance with attestation standards established by the American Institute of Certified Public Accountants

g. A statement that the sufficiency of the procedures is solely the responsibility of the specified parties and a disclaimer of responsibility for the sufficiency of those procedures

h. A list of the procedures performed (or reference thereto) and related findings (The practitioner should not provide negative assurance—see section 201.24.)

i. Where applicable, a description of any agreed-upon materiality limits (See section 201.25.)

j. A statement that the practitioner was not engaged to and did not conduct an examination of prospective financial statements; a disclaimer of opinion on whether the presentation of the prospective financial statements is in conformity with AICPA presentation guidelines and on whether the underlying assumptions provide a reasonable basis for the forecast, or a reasonable basis for the projection given the hypothetical assumptions; and a statement that if the practitioner had performed additional procedures, other matters might have come to his or her attention that would have been reported

k. A statement of restrictions on the use of the report because it is intended to be used solely by the specified parties

l. Where applicable, reservations or restrictions concerning procedures or findings as discussed in section 201.33, .35, .39, and .40

m. A caveat that the prospective results may not be achieved

n. A statement that the practitioner assumes no responsibility to update the report for events and circumstances occurring after the date of the report

o. Where applicable, a description of the nature of the assistance provided by a specialist as discussed in section 201.19–.21

p. The manual or printed signature of the practitioner's firm

q. The date of the report

.56 The following illustrates a report on applying agreed-upon procedures to the prospective financial statements. (See section 201.)

Independent Accountant's Report
on Applying Agreed-Upon Procedures

Board of Directors—XYZ Corporation

Board of Directors—ABC Company

At your request, we have performed certain agreed-upon procedures, as enumerated below, with respect to the forecasted balance sheet and the related forecasted statements of income, retained earnings, and cash flows of DEF Company, a subsidiary of ABC Company, as of December 31, 20XX, and for the year then ending. These procedures, which were agreed to by the Boards of

Directors of XYZ Corporation and ABC Company, were performed solely to assist you in evaluating the forecast in connection with the proposed sale of DEF Company to XYZ Corporation. DEF Company's management is responsible for the forecast.

This agreed-upon procedures engagement was conducted in accordance with attestation standards established by the American Institute of Certified Public Accountants. The sufficiency of these procedures is solely the responsibility of the specified parties. Consequently, we make no representation regarding the sufficiency of the procedures described below either for the purpose for which this report has been requested or for any other purpose.

[*Include paragraphs to enumerate procedures and findings.*]

We were not engaged to and did not conduct an examination, the objective of which would be the expression of an opinion on the accompanying prospective financial statements. Accordingly, we do not express an opinion on whether the prospective financial statements are presented in conformity with AICPA presentation guidelines or on whether the underlying assumptions provide a reasonable basis for the presentation. Had we performed additional procedures, other matters might have come to our attention that would have been reported to you. Furthermore, there will usually be differences between the forecasted and actual results, because events and circumstances frequently do not occur as expected, and those differences may be material. We have no responsibility to update this report for events and circumstances occurring after the date of this report.

This report is intended solely for the information and use of the Boards of Directors of ABC Company and XYZ Corporation and is not intended to be and should not be used by anyone other than these specified parties.

[*Signature*]

[*Date*]

Partial Presentations

.57 The practitioner's procedures on a partial presentation may be affected by the nature of the information presented. Many elements of prospective financial statements are interrelated. The practitioner should give appropriate consideration to whether key factors affecting elements, accounts, or items that are interrelated with those in the partial presentation he or she has been engaged to examine or compile have been considered, including key factors that may not necessarily be obvious to the partial presentation (for example, productive capacity relative to a sales forecast), and whether all significant assumptions have been disclosed. The practitioner may find it necessary for the scope of the examination or compilation of some partial presentations to be similar to that for the examination or compilation of a presentation of prospective financial statements. For example, the scope of a practitioner's procedures when he or she examines forecasted results of operations would likely be similar to that of procedures used for the examination of prospective financial statements since the practitioner would most likely need to consider the interrelationships of all accounts in the examination of results of operations.

.58 Because partial presentations are generally appropriate only for limited use, reports on partial presentations of both forecasted and projected information should include a description of any limitations on the usefulness of the presentation.

Other Information

.59 When a practitioner's compilation, review, or audit report on historical financial statements is included in a practitioner-submitted document containing prospective financial statements, the practitioner should either examine, compile, or apply agreed-upon procedures to the prospective financial statements and report accordingly, unless the following occur.

a. The prospective financial statements are labeled as a "budget."

b. The budget does not extend beyond the end of the current fiscal year.

c. The budget is presented with interim historical financial statements for the current year.

In such circumstances, the practitioner need not examine, compile, or apply agreed-upon procedures to the budget; however, he or she should report on it and—

a. Indicate that he or she did not examine or compile the budget.

b. Disclaim an opinion or any other form of assurance on the budget.

In addition, the budgeted information may omit the summaries of significant assumptions and accounting policies required by the guidelines for presentation of prospective financial statements established by the AICPA, provided such omission is not, to the practitioner's knowledge, undertaken with the intention of misleading those who might reasonably be expected to use such budgeted information, and is disclosed in the practitioner's report. The following is the form of the standard paragraphs to be added to the practitioner's report in this circumstance when the summaries of significant assumptions and accounting policies have been omitted.

> The accompanying budgeted balance sheet, statements of income, retained earnings, and cash flows of XYZ Company as of December 31, 20XX, and for the six months then ending, have not been compiled or examined by us, and, accordingly, we do not express an opinion or any other form of assurance on them.
>
> Management has elected to omit the summaries of significant assumptions and accounting policies required under established guidelines for presentation of prospective financial statements. If the omitted summaries were included in the budgeted information, they might influence the user's conclusions about the company's budgeted information. Accordingly, this budgeted information is not designed for those who are not informed about such matters.

.60 When the practitioner's compilation, review, or audit report on historical financial statements is included in a client-prepared document containing prospective financial statements, the practitioner should not consent to the use of his or her name in the document unless:

a. He or she has examined, compiled, or applied agreed-upon procedures to the prospective financial statements and his or her report accompanies them.

b. The prospective financial statements are accompanied by an indication by the responsible party or the practitioner that the practitioner has not performed such a service on the prospective financial statements and that the practitioner assumes no responsibility for them.

c. Another practitioner has examined, compiled, or applied agreed-upon procedures to the prospective financial statements and his or her report is included in the document.

In addition, if the practitioner has audited the historical financial statements and the prospective financial statements that he or she did not examine, compile, or apply agreed-upon procedures to are included in a document containing the audited historical financial statements and the auditor's report thereon,[29] he or she should refer to AU section 550, *Other Information in Documents Containing Audited Financial Statements*. [Revised, December 2010, to reflect conforming changes necessary due to the issuance of SAS Nos. 118–120.]

.61 The practitioner whose report on prospective financial statements is included in a client-prepared document containing historical financial statements should not consent to the use of his or her name in the document unless:

a. He or she has compiled, reviewed, or audited the historical financial statements and his or her report accompanies them.

b. The historical financial statements are accompanied by an indication by the responsible party or the practitioner that the practitioner has not performed such a service on the historical financial statements and that the practitioner assumes no responsibility for them.

c. Another practitioner has compiled, reviewed, or audited the historical financial statements and his or her report is included in the document.

.62 An entity may publish various documents that contain information other than historical financial statements in addition to the compiled or examined prospective financial statements and the practitioner's report thereon. The practitioner's responsibility with respect to information in such a document does not extend beyond the financial information identified in the report, and he or she has no obligation to perform any procedures to corroborate other information contained in the document. However, the practitioner should read the other information and consider whether such information, or the manner of its presentation, is materially inconsistent with the information, or manner of its presentation, appearing in the prospective financial statements.

.63 If the practitioner examines prospective financial statements included in a document containing inconsistent information, he or she might not be able to conclude that there is adequate support for each significant assumption. The practitioner should consider whether the prospective financial statements, his or her report, or both require revision. Depending on the conclusion he or she reaches, the practitioner should consider other actions that may be appropriate, such as issuing an adverse opinion, disclaiming an opinion because of a scope limitation, withholding the use of his or her report in the document, or withdrawing from the engagement.

.64 If the practitioner compiles the prospective financial statements included in the document containing inconsistent information, he or she should attempt to obtain additional or revised information. If he or she does not receive such information, the practitioner should withhold the use of his or her report or withdraw from the compilation engagement.

.65 If, while reading the other information appearing in the document containing the examined or compiled prospective financial statements, as

---

[29] AU section 550 applies only to such prospective financial statements contained in (*a*) annual reports (or similar documents) that are issued to owners (or similar stakeholders) and annual reports of governments and organizations for charitable or philanthropic purposes that are available to the public that contain audited financial statements and the auditor's report thereon. AU section 550 also may be applied, adapted as necessary in the circumstances, to other documents to which the auditor, at management's request, devotes attention. AU section 550 does not apply when the historical financial statements and report appear in a registration statement filed under the Securities Act of 1933 (in which case, see AU section 711, *Filings Under Federal Securities Statutes*). [Footnote revised, December 2010, to reflect conforming changes necessary due to the issuance of SAS Nos. 118–120.]

described in the preceding paragraphs, the practitioner becomes aware of information that he or she believes is a material misstatement of fact that is not an inconsistent statement, he or she should discuss the matter with the responsible party. In connection with this discussion, the practitioner should consider that he or she may not have the expertise to assess the validity of the statement made, that there may be no standards by which to assess its presentation, and that there may be valid differences of judgment or opinion. If the practitioner concludes that he or she has a valid basis for concern, he or she should propose that the responsible party consult with some other party whose advice might be useful, such as the entity's legal counsel.

.66 If, after discussing the matter as described in paragraph .65, the practitioner concludes that a material misstatement of fact remains, the action he or she takes will depend on his or her judgment in the particular circumstances. The practitioner should consider steps such as notifying the responsible party in writing of his or her views concerning the information and consulting his or her legal counsel about further appropriate action in the circumstances.

Effective Date

.67 This section is effective when the date of the practitioner's report is on or after June 1, 2001. Early application is permitted.

.68

Appendix A

Minimum Presentation Guidelines*

1. Prospective information presented in the format of historical financial statements facilitates comparisons with financial position, results of operations, and cash flows of prior periods, as well as those actually achieved for the prospective period. Accordingly, prospective financial statements preferably should be in the format of the historical financial statements that would be issued for the period(s) covered unless there is an agreement between the responsible party and potential users specifying another format. Prospective financial statements may take the form of complete basic financial statements[1] or may be limited to the following minimum items (where such items would be presented for historical financial statements for the period).[2]

a. Sales or gross revenues

b. Gross profit or cost of sales

c. Unusual or infrequently occurring items

d. Provision for income taxes

e. Discontinued operations or extraordinary items

f. Income from continuing operations

g. Net income

h. Basic and diluted earnings per share

i. Significant changes in financial position[3]

j. A description of what the responsible party intends the prospective financial statements to present, a statement that the assumptions are based on the responsible party's judgment at the time the prospective information was prepared, and a caveat that the prospective results may not be achieved

---

* ***Note:*** This appendix describes the minimum items that constitute a presentation of a financial forecast or a financial projection, as specified in AICPA Guide *Prospective Financial Information*. Complete presentation guidelines for entities that choose to issue prospective financial statements, together with illustrative presentations, are included in the Guide. The guide also prescribes presentation guidelines for partial presentations.

[1] The details of each statement may be summarized or condensed so that only the major items in each are presented. The usual footnotes associated with historical financial statements need not be included as such. However, significant assumptions and accounting policies should be disclosed.

[2] Similar types of financial information should be presented for entities for which these terms do not describe operations. Further, similar items should be presented if a comprehensive basis of accounting other than GAAP is used to present the prospective financial statements. For example, if the cash basis were used, item a would be cash receipts.

[3] The responsible party should disclose significant cash flows and other significant changes in balance sheet accounts during the period. However, neither a balance sheet nor a statement of cash flows, as described in Financial Accounting Standards Board (FASB) *Accounting Standards Codification* (ASC) 230, *Statement of Cash Flows*, is required. Furthermore, none of the specific captions or disclosures required by FASB ASC 230 is required. Significant changes disclosed will depend on the circumstances; however, such disclosures will often include cash flows from operations. See AICPA Guide *Prospective Financial Information*exhibits 9.07 and 9.11 for illustrations of alternate methods of presenting significant cash flows. [Footnote revised, June 2009, to reflect conforming changes necessary due to the issuance of FASB ASC.]

k. Summary of significant assumptions

l. Summary of significant accounting policies

2. A presentation that omits one or more of the applicable minimum items *a–i* is a partial presentation, which would not ordinarily be appropriate for general use. If an omitted applicable minimum item is derivable from the information presented, the presentation would not be deemed to be a partial presentation. A presentation that contains the applicable minimum items *a–i*, but omits items *j–l*, is subject to all of the provisions of this section applicable to complete presentations.

.69

Appendix B

Training and Proficiency, Planning, and Procedures Applicable to Compilations

Training and Proficiency

1. The practitioner should be familiar with the guidelines for the preparation and presentation of prospective financial statements. The guidelines are contained in AICPA Guide *Prospective Financial Information*.

2. The practitioner should possess or obtain a level of knowledge of the industry and the accounting principles and practices of the industry in which the entity operates or will operate that will enable him or her to compile prospective financial statements that are in appropriate form for an entity operating in that industry.

Planning the Compilation Engagement

3. To compile the prospective financial statements of an existing entity, the practitioner should obtain a general knowledge of the nature of the entity's business transactions and the key factors upon which its future financial results appear to depend. He or she should also obtain an understanding of the accounting principles and practices of the entity to determine whether they are comparable to those used within the industry in which the entity operates.

4. To compile the prospective financial statements of a proposed entity, the practitioner should obtain knowledge of the proposed operations and the key factors upon which its future results appear to depend and that have affected the performance of entities in the same industry.

Compilation Procedures

5. In a compilation of prospective financial statements the practitioner should perform the following, where applicable.

a. Establish an understanding with the client regarding the services to be performed. The understanding should include the objectives of the engagement, the client's responsibilities, the practitioner's responsibilities, and limitations of the engagement. The practitioner should document the understanding in the working papers, preferably through a written communication with the client. If the practitioner believes an understanding with the client has not been established, he or she should decline to accept or perform the engagement.

b. Inquire about the accounting principles used in the preparation of the prospective financial statements.

(1) For existing entities, compare the accounting principles used to those used in the preparation of previous historical financial statements and inquire whether such principles are the same as those expected to be used in the historical financial statements covering the prospective period.

(2) For entities to be formed or entities formed that have not commenced operations, compare specialized industry accounting principles used, if any, to those typically used in the industry. Inquire whether the accounting principles used for the prospective financial statements are those that are expected to be used when or if the entity commences operations.

c. Ask how the responsible party identifies the key factors and develops its assumptions.

d. List, or obtain a list of the responsible party's significant assumptions providing the basis for the prospective financial statements and consider whether there are any obvious omissions in light of the key factors upon which the prospective results of the entity appear to depend.

e. Consider whether there appear to be any obvious internal inconsistencies in the assumptions.

f. Perform or test the mathematical accuracy of the computations that translate the assumptions into prospective financial statements.

g. Read the prospective financial statements, including the summary of significant assumptions, and consider whether—

(1) The statements, including the disclosures of assumptions and accounting policies, appear to be not presented in conformity with the AICPA presentation guidelines for prospective financial statements.[1]

(2) The statements, including the summary of significant assumptions, appear to be not obviously inappropriate in relation to the practitioner's knowledge of the entity and its industry and, for the following:

(a) *Financial forecast*, the expected conditions and course of action in the prospective period

(b) *Financial projection*, the purpose of the presentation

h. If a significant part of the prospective period has expired, inquire about the results of operations or significant portions of the operations (such as sales volume), and significant changes in financial position, and consider their effect in relation to the prospective financial statements. If historical financial statements have been prepared for the expired portion of the period, the practitioner should read such statements and consider those results in relation to the prospective financial statements.

i. Confirm his or her understanding of the statements (including assumptions) by obtaining written representations from the responsible party. Because the amounts reflected in the statements are not supported by historical books and records but rather by assumptions, the practitioner should obtain representations in which the responsible party indicates its responsibility for the assumptions. The representations should be signed by the responsible party at the highest

[1] Presentation guidelines for entities that issue prospective financial statements are set forth and illustrated in AICPA Guide *Prospective Financial Information*.

level of authority who the practitioner believes is responsible for and knowledgeable, directly or through others, about matters covered by the representations.

(1) For a *financial forecast*, the representations should include the responsible party's assertion that the financial forecast presents, to the best of its knowledge and belief, the expected financial position, results of operations, and cash flows for the forecast period and that the forecast reflects the responsible party's judgment, based on present circumstances, of the expected conditions and its expected course of action. The representations should also include a statement that the forecast is presented in conformity with guidelines for presentation of a forecast established by the American Institute of Certified Public Accountants. The representations should also include a statement that the assumptions on which the forecast is based are reasonable. If the forecast contains a range, the representation should also include a statement that, to the best of the responsible party's knowledge and belief, the item or items subject to the assumption are expected to actually fall within the range and that the range was not selected in a biased or misleading manner.

(2) For a *financial projection*, the representations should include the responsible party's assertion that the financial projection presents, to the best of its knowledge and belief, the expected financial position, results of operations, and cash flows for the projection period given the hypothetical assumptions, and that the projection reflects its judgment, based on present circumstances, of expected conditions and its expected course of action given the occurrence of the hypothetical events. The representations should also (*i*) identify the hypothetical assumptions and describe the limitations on the usefulness of the presentation, (*ii*) state that the assumptions are appropriate, (*iii*) indicate if the hypothetical assumptions are improbable, and (*iv*) if the projection contains a range, include a statement that, to the best of the responsible party's knowledge and belief, given the hypothetical assumptions, the item or items subject to the assumption are expected to actually fall within the range and that the range was not selected in a biased or misleading manner. The representations should also include a statement that the projection is presented in conformity with guidelines for presentation of a projection established by the American Institute of Certified Public Accountants.

j. Consider, after applying the preceding procedures, whether he or she has received representations or other information that appears to be obviously inappropriate, incomplete, or otherwise misleading and, if so, attempt to obtain additional or revised information. If he or she does not receive such information, the practitioner should ordinarily withdraw from the compilation engagement.[2] (Note that the omission of disclosures, other than those relating to significant assumptions, would not require the practitioner to withdraw; see paragraph .26.)

---

[2] The practitioner need not withdraw from the engagement if the effect of such information on the prospective financial statements does not appear to be material.

.70

Appendix C

Training and Proficiency, Planning, and Procedures Applicable to Examinations

Training and Proficiency

1. The practitioner should be familiar with the guidelines for the preparation and presentation of prospective financial statements. The guidelines are contained in AICPA Guide *Prospective Financial Information*.

2. The practitioner should possess or obtain a level of knowledge of the industry and the accounting principles and practices of the industry in which the entity operates or will operate that will enable him or her to examine prospective financial statements that are in appropriate form for an entity operating in that industry.

Planning an Examination Engagement

3. Planning the examination engagement involves developing an overall strategy for the expected scope and conduct of the engagement. To develop such a strategy, the practitioner needs to have sufficient knowledge to enable him or her to adequately understand the events, transactions, and practices that, in his or her judgment, may have a significant effect on the prospective financial statements.

4. Factors to be considered by the practitioner in planning the examination include the following:

a. The accounting principles to be used and the type of presentation

b. The anticipated level of attestation risk related to the prospective financial statements[1]

c. Preliminary judgments about materiality levels

d. Items within the prospective financial statements that are likely to require revision or adjustment

e. Conditions that may require extension or modification of the practitioner's examination procedures

f. Knowledge of the entity's business and its industry

g. The responsible party's experience in preparing prospective financial statements

h. The length of the period covered by the prospective financial statements

i. The process by which the responsible party develops its prospective financial statements

---

[1] *Attestation* risk is the risk that the practitioner may unknowingly fail to appropriately modify his or her examination report on prospective financial statements that are materially misstated, that is, that are not presented in conformity with AICPA presentation guidelines or have assumptions that do not provide a reasonable basis for management's forecast, or management's projection given the hypothetical assumptions. It consists of (*a*) the risk (consisting of *inherent risk* and *control risk*) that the prospective financial statements contain errors that could be material and (*b*) the risk (*detection risk*) that the practitioner will not detect such errors.

5. The practitioner should obtain knowledge of the entity's business, accounting principles, and the key factors upon which its future financial results appear to depend. The practitioner should focus on areas such as the following:

a. The availability and cost of resources needed to operate (Principal items usually include raw materials, labor, short-term and long-term financing, and plant and equipment.)

b. The nature and condition of markets in which the entity sells its goods or services, including final consumer markets if the entity sells to intermediate markets

c. Factors specific to the industry, including competitive conditions, sensitivity to economic conditions, accounting policies, specific regulatory requirements, and technology

d. Patterns of past performance for the entity or comparable entities, including trends in revenue and costs, turnover of assets, uses and capacities of physical facilities, and management policies

Examination Procedures

6. The practitioner should establish an understanding with the responsible party regarding the services to be performed. The understanding should include the objectives of the engagement, the responsible party's responsibilities, the practitioner's responsibilities, and limitations of the engagement. The practitioner should document the understanding in the working papers, preferably through a written communication with the responsible party. If the practitioner believes an understanding with the responsible party has not been established, he or she should decline to accept or perform the engagement. If the responsible party is different than the client, the practitioner should establish the understanding with both the client and the responsible party, and the understanding also should include the client's responsibilities.

7. The practitioner's objective in an examination of prospective financial statements is to accumulate sufficient evidence to restrict attestation risk to a level that is, in his or her professional judgment, appropriate for the level of assurance that may be imparted by his or her examination report. In a report on an examination of prospective financial statements, the practitioner provides assurance only about whether the prospective financial statements are presented in conformity with AICPA presentation guidelines and whether the assumptions provide a reasonable basis for management's forecast, or a reasonable basis for management's projection given the hypothetical assumptions. He or she does not provide assurance about the achievability of the prospective results because events and circumstances frequently do not occur as expected and achievement of the prospective results is dependent on the actions, plans, and assumptions of the responsible party.

8. In his or her examination of prospective financial statements, the practitioner should select from all available procedures—that is, procedures that assess inherent and control risk and restrict detection risk—any combination that can restrict attestation risk to such an appropriate level. The extent to which examination procedures will be performed should be based on the practitioner's consideration of the following:

a. The nature and materiality of the information to the prospective financial statements taken as a whole

b. The likelihood of misstatements

c. Knowledge obtained during current and previous engagements

d. The responsible party's competence with respect to prospective financial statements

e. The extent to which the prospective financial statements are affected by the responsible party's judgment, for example, its judgment in selecting the assumptions used to prepare the prospective financial statements

f. The adequacy of the responsible party's underlying data

9. The practitioner should perform those procedures he or she considers necessary in the circumstances to report on whether the assumptions provide a reasonable basis for the following.

a. *Financial forecast.* The practitioner can form an opinion that the assumptions provide a reasonable basis for the forecast if the responsible party represents that the presentation reflects, to the best of its knowledge and belief, its estimate of expected financial position, results of operations, and cash flows for the prospective period[2] and the practitioner concludes, based on his or her examination, (*i*) that the responsible party has explicitly identified all factors expected to materially affect the operations of the entity during the prospective period and has developed appropriate assumptions with respect to such factors[3] and (*ii*) that the assumptions are suitably supported.

b. *Financial projection given the hypothetical assumptions.* The practitioner can form an opinion that the assumptions provide a reasonable basis for the financial projection given the hypothetical assumptions if the responsible party represents that the presentation reflects, to the best of its knowledge and belief, expected financial position, results of operations, and cash flows for the prospective period given the hypothetical assumptions[4] and the practitioner concludes, based on his or her examination, that:

(1) The responsible party has explicitly identified all factors that would materially affect the operations of the entity during the prospective period if the hypothetical assumptions were to materialize and has developed appropriate assumptions with respect to such factors and

(2) The other assumptions are suitably supported given the hypothetical assumptions. However, as the number and significance of the hypothetical assumptions increase, the practitioner may not be able to satisfy himself or herself about the presentation as a whole by obtaining support for the remaining assumptions.

10. The practitioner should evaluate the support for the assumptions.

a. *Financial forecast*—The practitioner can conclude that assumptions are suitably supported if the preponderance of information supports each significant assumption.

---

[2] If the forecast contains a range, the representation should also include a statement that, to the best of the responsible party's knowledge and belief, the item or items subject to the assumption are expected to actually fall within the range and that the range was not selected in a biased or misleading manner.

[3] An attempt to list all assumptions is inherently not feasible. Frequently, basic assumptions that have enormous potential impact are considered to be implicit, such as conditions of peace and absence of natural disasters.

[4] If the projection contains a range, the representation should also include a statement that, to the best of the responsible party's knowledge and belief, given the hypothetical assumptions, the item or items subject to the assumption are expected to actually fall within the range and that the range was not selected in a biased or misleading manner.

b. *Financial projection*—In evaluating support for assumptions other than hypothetical assumptions, the practitioner can conclude that they are suitably supported if the preponderance of information supports each significant assumption given the hypothetical assumptions. The practitioner need not obtain support for the hypothetical assumptions, although he or she should consider whether they are consistent with the purpose of the presentation.

11. In evaluating the support for assumptions, the practitioner should consider—

a. Whether sufficient pertinent sources of information about the assumptions have been considered. Examples of external sources the practitioner might consider are government publications, industry publications, economic forecasts, existing or proposed legislation, and reports of changing technology. Examples of internal sources are budgets, labor agreements, patents, royalty agreements and records, sales backlog records, debt agreements, and actions of the board of directors involving entity plans.

b. Whether the assumptions are consistent with the sources from which they are derived.

c. Whether the assumptions are consistent with each other.

d. Whether the historical financial information and other data used in developing the assumptions are sufficiently reliable for that purpose. Reliability can be assessed by inquiry and analytical or other procedures, some of which may have been completed in past audits or reviews of the historical financial statements. If historical financial statements have been prepared for an expired part of the prospective period, the practitioner should consider the historical data in relation to the prospective results for the same period, where applicable. If the prospective financial statements incorporate such historical financial results and that period is significant to the presentation, the practitioner should make a review of the historical information in conformity with the applicable standards for a review.[5]

e. Whether the historical financial information and other data used in developing the assumptions are comparable over the periods specified or whether the effects of any lack of comparability were considered in developing the assumptions.

f. Whether the logical arguments or theory, considered with the data supporting the assumptions, are reasonable.

12. In evaluating the preparation and presentation of the prospective financial statements, the practitioner should perform procedures that will provide reasonable assurance as to the following.

---

[5] If the entity is an SEC registrant or non-SEC registrant that makes a filing with a regulatory agency in preparation for a public offering or listing, the practitioner should perform the procedures in AU section 722, *Interim Financial Information*, paragraphs .13–.19. If the entity is nonpublic, the practitioner should perform the procedures in SSARS No. 1, *Compilation and Review of Financial Statements*, as amended, paragraphs 24–37 [AR section 100.24–.37]. [Footnote revised, November 2002, to reflect conforming changes necessary due to the issuance of Statement on Auditing Standards No. 100 and Statement on Standards for Accounting and Review Services No. 9. Footnote revised, May 2004, to reflect the conforming changes necessary due to the issuance of Statement on Standards for Accounting and Review Services No. 10.]

a. The presentation reflects the identified assumptions.

b. The computations made to translate the assumptions into prospective amounts are mathematically accurate.

c. The assumptions are internally consistent.

d. Accounting principles used in the—

(1) Financial forecast are consistent with the accounting principles expected to be used in the historical financial statements covering the prospective period and those used in the most recent historical financial statements, if any.

(2) Financial projection are consistent with the accounting principles expected to be used in the prospective period and those used in the most recent historical financial statements, if any, or that they are consistent with the purpose of the presentation.[6]

e. The presentation of the prospective financial statements follows the AICPA guidelines applicable for such statements.[7]

f. The assumptions have been adequately disclosed based on AICPA presentation guidelines for prospective financial statements.

13. The practitioner should consider whether the prospective financial statements, including related disclosures, should be revised because of any of the following:

a. Mathematical errors

b. Unreasonable or internally inconsistent assumptions

c. Inappropriate or incomplete presentation

d. Inadequate disclosure

14. The practitioner should obtain written representations from the responsible party acknowledging its responsibility for both the presentation and the underlying assumptions. The representations should be signed by the responsible party at the highest level of authority who the practitioner believes is responsible for and knowledgeable, directly or through others in the organization, about the matters covered by the representations. Paragraph .69, subparagraph 5*i* describes the specific representations to be obtained for a financial forecast and a financial projection. See paragraph .43 for guidance on the form of report to be rendered if the practitioner is not able to obtain the required representations.

---

[6] The accounting principles used in a financial projection need not be those expected to be used in the historical financial statements for the prospective period if use of different principles is consistent with the purpose of the presentation.

[7] Presentation guidelines for entities that issue prospective financial statements are set forth and illustrated in AICPA Guide *Prospective Financial Information*.

AT Section 401

Reporting on Pro Forma Financial Information

Source: SSAE No. 10.

Effective when the presentation of pro forma financial information is as of or for a period ending on or after June 1, 2001. Earlier application is permitted.

Introduction

.01 This section provides guidance to a practitioner who is engaged to issue or does issue an examination or a review report on pro forma financial information. Such an engagement should comply with the general and fieldwork standards established in section 50, *SSAE Hierarchy*, and the specific performance and reporting standards set forth in this section.[1] [Revised, November 2006, to reflect conforming changes necessary due to the issuance of Statement on Standards for Attestation Engagements No. 14.]

.02 When pro forma financial information is presented outside the basic financial statements but within the same document, and the practitioner is not engaged to report on the pro forma financial information, the practitioner's responsibilities are described in AU section 550, *Other Information in Documents Containing Audited Financial Statements*, and AU section 711, *Filings Under Federal Securities Statutes*.

.03 This section does not apply in those circumstances when, for purposes of a more meaningful presentation, a transaction consummated after the balance-sheet date is reflected in the historical financial statements (such as a revision of debt maturities or a revision of earnings per share calculations for a stock split).[2]

Presentation of Pro Forma Financial Information

.04 The objective of pro forma financial information is to show what the significant effects on historical financial information might have been had a consummated or proposed transaction (or event) occurred at an earlier date. Pro forma financial information is commonly used to show the effects of transactions such as the following:

- Business combination
- Change in capitalization

---

[1] AU section 634, *Letters for Underwriters and Certain Other Requesting Parties*, paragraphs .03–.05, identify certain parties who may request a letter. When one of those parties requests a letter or asks the practitioner to perform agreed-upon procedures on pro forma financial information in connection with an offering, the practitioner should follow the guidance in AU section 634 paragraphs .03, .10, .36, .42, and .43.

[2] In certain circumstances, generally accepted accounting principles (GAAP) may require the presentation of pro forma financial information in the financial statements or the accompanying notes. That information includes, for example, pro forma financial information required by Financial Accounting Standards Board (FASB) *Accounting Standards Codification* (ASC) 805, *Business Combinations*; FASB ASC 250, *Accounting Changes and Error Corrections*; or, in some cases, pro forma financial information relating to subsequent events; see AU section 560, *Subsequent Events*, paragraph .05. For guidance in reporting on audited financial statements that include pro forma financial information for a business combination or subsequent event, see AU section 508, *Reports on Audited Financial Statements*, paragraph .28. [Footnote revised, June 2009, to reflect conforming changes necessary due to the issuance of FASB ASC.]

- Disposition of a significant portion of the business
- Change in the form of business organization or status as an autonomous entity
- Proposed sale of securities and the application of the proceeds

.05 This objective is achieved primarily by applying pro forma adjustments to historical financial information. Pro forma adjustments should be based on management's assumptions and give effect to all significant effects directly attributable to the transaction (or event).

.06 Pro forma financial information should be labeled as such to distinguish it from historical financial information. This presentation should describe the transaction (or event) that is reflected in the pro forma financial information, the source of the historical financial information on which it is based, the significant assumptions used in developing the pro forma adjustments, and any significant uncertainties about those assumptions. The presentation also should indicate that the pro forma financial information should be read in conjunction with related historical financial information and that the pro forma financial information is not necessarily indicative of the results (such as financial position and results of operations, as applicable) that would have been attained had the transaction (or event) actually taken place earlier.[3]

Conditions for Reporting

.07 The practitioner may agree to report on an examination or a review of pro forma financial information if the following conditions are met.

a. The document that contains the pro forma financial information includes (or incorporates by reference) complete historical financial statements of the entity for the most recent year (or for the preceding year if financial statements for the most recent year are not yet available) and, if pro forma financial information is presented for an interim period, the document also includes (or incorporates by reference) historical interim financial information for that period (which may be presented in condensed form).[4] In the case of a business combination, the document should include (or incorporate by reference) the appropriate historical financial information for the significant constituent parts of the combined entity.

b. The historical financial statements of the entity (or, in the case of a business combination, of each significant constituent part of the combined entity) on which the pro forma financial information is based have been audited or reviewed.[5] The practitioner's attestation

---

[3] For further guidance on the presentation of pro forma financial information included in filings with the Securities and Exchange Commission (SEC), see Article 11 of Regulation S-X.

[4] For pro forma financial information included in an SEC Form 8-K, historical financial information previously included in an SEC filing would meet this requirement. Interim historical financial information may be presented as a column in the pro forma financial information.

[5] The practitioner's audit or review report should be included (or incorporated by reference) in the document containing the pro forma financial information. The review may be that as defined in AU section 722, *Interim Financial Information*, for SEC registrants or non-SEC registrants that make a filing with a regulatory agency in preparation for a public offering or listing, or as defined in Statement on Standards for Accounting and Review Services (SSARS) No. 1, *Compilation and Review of Financial Statements* (AR sec. 100), for nonpublic companies. [Footnote revised, November 2002, to reflect conforming changes necessary due to the issuance of Statement on Auditing Standards No. 100.]

risk relating to the pro forma financial information is affected by the scope of the engagement providing the practitioner with assurance about the underlying historical financial information to which the pro forma adjustments are applied. Therefore, the level of assurance given by the practitioner on the pro forma financial information, as of a particular date or for a particular period, should be limited to the level of assurance provided on the historical financial statements (or, in the case of a business combination, the lowest level of assurance provided on the underlying historical financial statements of any significant constituent part of the combined entity). For example, if the underlying historical financial statements of each constituent part of the combined entity have been audited at year-end and reviewed at an interim date, the practitioner may perform an examination or a review of the pro forma financial information at year-end but is limited to performing a review of the pro forma financial information at the interim date.

c. The practitioner who is reporting on the pro forma financial information should have an appropriate level of knowledge of the accounting and financial reporting practices of each significant constituent part of the combined entity. This would ordinarily have been obtained by the practitioner auditing or reviewing historical financial statements of each entity for the most recent annual or interim period for which the pro forma financial information is presented. If another practitioner has performed such an audit or a review, the need, by a practitioner reporting on the pro forma financial information, for an understanding of the entity's accounting and financial reporting practices is not diminished, and that practitioner should consider whether, under the particular circumstances, he or she can acquire sufficient knowledge of these matters to perform the procedures necessary to report on the pro forma financial information.

Practitioner's Objective

.08 The objective of the practitioner's examination procedures applied to pro forma financial information is to provide reasonable assurance as to whether—

- Management's assumptions provide a reasonable basis for presenting the significant effects directly attributable to the underlying transaction (or event).
- The related pro forma adjustments give appropriate effect to those assumptions.
- The pro forma column reflects the proper application of those adjustments to the historical financial statements.

.09 The objective of the practitioner's review procedures applied to pro forma financial information is to provide negative assurance as to whether any information came to the practitioner's attention to cause him or her to believe that—

- Management's assumptions do not provide a reasonable basis for presenting the significant effects directly attributable to the underlying transaction (or event).
- The related pro forma adjustments do not give appropriate effect to those assumptions.

- The pro forma column does not reflect the proper application of those adjustments to the historical financial statements.

Procedures

.10 Other than the procedures applied to the historical financial statements,[6] the procedures the practitioner should apply to the assumptions and pro forma adjustments for either an examination or a review engagement are as follows.

a. Obtain an understanding of the underlying transaction (or event), for example, by reading relevant contracts and minutes of meetings of the board of directors and by making inquiries of appropriate officials of the entity, and, in cases, of the entity acquired or to be acquired.

b. Obtain a level of knowledge of each constituent part of the combined entity in a business combination that will enable the practitioner to perform the required procedures. Procedures to obtain this knowledge may include communicating with other practitioners who have audited or reviewed the historical financial information on which the pro forma financial information is based. Matters that may be considered include accounting principles and financial reporting practices followed, transactions between the entities, and material contingencies.

c. Discuss with management their assumptions regarding the effects of the transaction (or event).

d. Evaluate whether pro forma adjustments are included for all significant effects directly attributable to the transaction (or event).

e. Obtain sufficient evidence in support of such adjustments. The evidence required to support the level of assurance given is a matter of professional judgment. The practitioner typically would obtain more evidence in an examination engagement than in a review engagement. Examples of evidence that the practitioner might consider obtaining are purchase, merger or exchange agreements, appraisal reports, debt agreements, employment agreements, actions of the board of directors, and existing or proposed legislation or regulatory actions.

f. Evaluate whether management's assumptions that underlie the pro forma adjustments are presented in a sufficiently clear and comprehensive manner. Also, evaluate whether the pro forma adjustments are consistent with each other and with the data used to develop them.

g. Determine that computations of pro forma adjustments are mathematically correct and that the pro forma column reflects the proper application of those adjustments to the historical financial statements.

h. Obtain written representations from management concerning their—

- Responsibility for the assumptions used in determining the pro forma adjustments

[6] See paragraph .07*b*.

- Assertion that the assumptions provide a reasonable basis for presenting all of the significant effects directly attributable to the transaction (or event), that the related pro forma adjustments give appropriate effect to those assumptions, and that the pro forma column reflects the proper application of those adjustments to the historical financial statements

- Assertion that the significant effects directly attributable to the transaction (or event) are appropriately disclosed in the pro forma financial information

i. Read the pro forma financial information and evaluate whether—

- The underlying transaction (or event), the pro forma adjustments, the significant assumptions and the significant uncertainties, if any, about those assumptions have been appropriately described.

- The source of the historical financial information on which the pro forma financial information is based has been appropriately identified.

Reporting on Pro Forma Financial Information

.11 The practitioner's report on pro forma financial information should be dated as of the completion of the appropriate procedures. The practitioner's report on pro forma financial information may be added to the practitioner's report on historical financial information, or it may appear separately. If the reports are combined and the date of completion of the procedures for the examination or review of the pro forma financial information is after the date of completion of the fieldwork for the audit or review of the historical financial information, the combined report should be dual-dated. (For example, "February 15, 20X2, except for the paragraphs regarding pro forma financial information as to which the date is March 20, 20X2.")

.12 A practitioner's examination report on pro forma financial information should include the following:

a. A title that includes the word *independent*

b. An identification of the pro forma financial information

c. A reference to the financial statements from which the historical financial information is derived and a statement that such financial statements were audited (The report on pro forma financial information should refer to any modification in the practitioner's report on the historical financial information.)

d. An identification of the responsible party and a statement that the responsible party is responsible for the pro forma financial information

e. A statement that the practitioner's responsibility is to express an opinion on the pro forma financial information based on his or her examination *f.* A statement that the examination of the pro forma financial information was conducted in accordance with attestation standards established by the American Institute of Certified Public Accountants and, accordingly, included such procedures as the practitioner considered necessary in the circumstances

g. A statement that the practitioner believes that the examination provides a reasonable basis for his or her opinion

h. A separate paragraph explaining the objective of pro forma financial information and its limitations

i. The practitioner's opinion as to whether management's assumptions provide a reasonable basis for presenting the significant effects directly attributable to the transaction (or event), whether the related pro forma adjustments give appropriate effect to those assumptions, and whether the pro forma column reflects the proper application of those adjustments to the historical financial statements (see paragraphs .18 and .20)

j. The manual or printed signature of the practitioner's firm

k. The date of the examination report

.13 A practitioner's review report on pro forma financial information should include the following:

a. A title that includes the word *independent*

b. An identification of the pro forma financial information

c. A reference to the financial statements from which the historical financial information is derived and a statement as to whether such financial statements were audited or reviewed (The report on pro forma financial information should refer to any modification in the practitioner's report on the historical financial information.)

d. An identification of the responsible party and a statement that the responsible party is responsible for the pro forma financial information

e. A statement that the review of the pro forma financial information was conducted in accordance with attestation standards established by the American Institute of Certified Public Accountants

f. A statement that a review is substantially less in scope than an examination, the objective of which is the expression of an opinion on the pro forma financial information and, accordingly, the practitioner does not express such an opinion

g. A separate paragraph explaining the objective of pro forma financial information and its limitations

h. The practitioner's conclusion as to whether any information came to the practitioner's attention to cause him or her to believe that management's assumptions do not provide a reasonable basis for presenting the significant effects directly attributable to the transaction (or event), or that the related pro forma adjustments do not give appropriate effect to those assumptions, or that the pro forma column does not reflect the proper application of those adjustments to the historical financial statements (See paragraphs .19 and .20.)

i. The manual or printed signature of the practitioner's firm

j. The date of the review report

.14 Nothing precludes the practitioner from restricting the use of the report (see section 101.78–.83).

.15 Because a pooling-of-interests business combination is accounted for by combining historical amounts retroactively, pro forma adjustments for a proposed transaction generally affect only the equity section of the pro forma condensed balance sheet. Further, because of the requirements of Financial Accounting Standards Board *Accounting Standards Codification* 805, *Business Combinations*, a business combination effected as a pooling of interests would not ordinarily involve a choice of assumptions by management. Accordingly, a report on a proposed pooling transaction need not address management's assumptions unless the pro forma financial information includes adjustments to conform the accounting principles of the combining entities. (See paragraph .21.) [Revised, June 2009, to reflect conforming changes necessary due to the issuance of FASB ASC.]

.16 Restrictions on the scope of the engagement (see section 101.73–.75), reservations about the propriety of the assumptions and the conformity of the presentation with those assumptions (including adequate disclosure of significant matters), or other reservations may require the practitioner to qualify the opinion, disclaim an opinion, or withdraw from the engagement.[7] The practitioner should disclose all substantive reasons for any report modifications. Uncertainty as to whether the transaction (or event) will be consummated would not ordinarily require a report modification. (See paragraph .22.)

Effective Date

.17 This section is effective when the presentation of pro forma financial information is as of or for a period ending on or after June 1, 2001. Early application is permitted.

[7] See section 101.76 and .77.

.18

Appendix A

Report on Examination of Pro Forma Financial Information

Independent Accountant's Report

We have examined the pro forma adjustments reflecting the transaction [*or event*] described in Note 1 and the application of those adjustments to the historical amounts in [*the assembly of*][8] the accompanying pro forma financial condensed balance sheet of X Company as of December 31, 20X1, and the pro forma condensed statement of income for the year then ended. The historical condensed financial statements are derived from the historical financial statements of X Company, which were audited by us, and of Y Company, which were audited by other accountants,[9] appearing elsewhere herein [*or incorporated by reference*].[10] Such pro forma adjustments are based upon management's assumptions described in Note 2. X Company's management is responsible for the pro forma financial information. Our responsibility is to express an opinion on the pro forma financial information based on our examination.

Our examination was conducted in accordance with attestation standards established by the American Institute of Certified Public Accountants and, accordingly, included such procedures as we considered necessary in the circumstances. We believe that our examination provides a reasonable basis for our opinion.

The objective of this pro forma financial information is to show what the significant effects on the historical financial information might have been had the transaction [*or event*] occurred at an earlier date. However, the pro forma condensed financial statements are not necessarily indicative of the results of operations or related effects on financial position that would have been attained had the above-mentioned transaction [*or event*] actually occurred earlier.

[*Additional paragraph(s) may be added to emphasize certain matters relating to the attest engagement or the subject matter.*]

In our opinion, management's assumptions provide a reasonable basis for presenting the significant effects directly attributable to the above-mentioned transaction [*or event*] described in Note 1, the related pro forma adjustments give appropriate effect to those assumptions, and the pro forma column reflects the proper application of those adjustments to the historical financial statement amounts in the pro forma condensed balance sheet as of December 31, 20X1, and the pro forma condensed statement of income for the year then ended.

[*Signature*]

[*Date*]

---

[8] This wording is appropriate when one column of pro forma financial information is presented without separate columns of historical financial information and pro forma adjustments.

[9] If either accountant's report includes an explanatory paragraph or is other than unqualified, that fact should be referred to within this report.

[10] If the option in footnote 4 to paragraph .07*a* is followed, the report should be appropriately modified.

.19

Appendix B

Report on Review of Pro Forma Financial Information

Independent Accountant's Report

We have reviewed the pro forma adjustments reflecting the transaction [*or event*] described in Note 1 and the application of those adjustments to the historical amounts in [*the assembly of*][11] the accompanying pro forma condensed balance sheet of X Company as of March 31, 20X2, and the pro forma condensed statement of income for the three months then ended. These historical condensed financial statements are derived from the historical unaudited financial statements of X Company, which were reviewed by us, and of Y Company, which were reviewed by other accountants,[12, 13] appearing elsewhere herein [*or incorporated by reference*].[14] Such pro forma adjustments are based on management's assumptions as described in Note 2. X Company's management is responsible for the pro forma financial information.

Our review was conducted in accordance with attestation standards established by the American Institute of Certified Public Accountants. A review is substantially less in scope than an examination, the objective of which is the expression of an opinion on management's assumptions, the pro forma adjustments and the application of those adjustments to historical financial information. Accordingly, we do not express such an opinion.

The objective of this pro forma financial information is to show what the significant effects on the historical financial information might have been had the transaction [*or event*] occurred at an earlier date. However, the pro forma condensed financial statements are not necessarily indicative of the results of operations or related effects on financial position that would have been attained had the above-mentioned transaction [*or event*] actually occurred earlier.

[*Additional paragraph(s) may be added to emphasize certain matters relating to the attest engagement or the subject matter.*]

Based on our review, nothing came to our attention that caused us to believe that management's assumptions do not provide a reasonable basis for presenting the significant effects directly attributable to the above-mentioned transaction [*or event*] described in Note 1, that the related pro forma adjustments do not give

---

[11] This wording is appropriate when one column of pro forma financial information is presented without separate columns of historical financial information and pro forma adjustments.

[12] If either accountant's report includes an explanatory paragraph or is modified, that fact should be referred to within this report.

[13] Where one set of historical financial statements is audited and the other set is reviewed, wording similar to the following would be appropriate:

> The historical condensed financial statements are derived from the historical financial statements of X Company, which were audited by us, and of Y Company, which were reviewed by other accountants, appearing elsewhere herein [*or incorporated by reference*].

[14] If the option in footnote 4 to paragraph .07*a* is followed, the report should be appropriately modified.

appropriate effect to those assumptions, or that the pro forma column does not reflect the proper application of those adjustments to the historical financial statement amounts in the pro forma condensed balance sheet as of March 31, 20X2, and the pro forma condensed statement of income for the three months then ended.

[*Signature*]

[*Date*]

.20

Appendix C

Report on Examination of Pro Forma Financial Information at Year-End With a Review of Pro Forma Financial Information for a Subsequent Interim Date

Independent Accountant's Report

We have examined the pro forma adjustments reflecting the transaction [*or event*] described in Note 1 and the application of those adjustments to the historical amounts in [*the assembly of*][15] the accompanying pro forma financial condensed balance sheet of X Company as of December 31, 20X1, and the pro forma condensed statement of income for the year then ended. The historical condensed financial statements are derived from the historical financial statements of X Company, which were audited by us, and of Y Company, which were audited by other accountants,[16] appearing elsewhere herein [*or incorporated by reference*].[17] Such pro forma adjustments are based upon management's assumptions described in Note 2. X Company's management is responsible for the pro forma financial information. Our responsibility is to express an opinion on the pro forma financial information based on our examination.

Our examination was conducted in accordance with attestation standards established by the American Institute of Certified Public Accountants and, accordingly, included such procedures as we considered necessary in the circumstances. We believe that our examination provides a reasonable basis for our opinion.

In addition, we have reviewed the pro forma adjustments and the application of those adjustments to the historical amounts in [*the assembly of*][15] the accompanying pro forma condensed balance sheet of X Company as of March 31, 20X2, and the pro forma condensed statement of income for the three months then ended. The historical condensed financial statements are derived from the historical financial statements of X Company, which were reviewed by us, and of Y Company, which were reviewed by other accountants,[18] appearing elsewhere herein [*or incorporated by reference*].[19] Such pro forma adjustments are based upon management's assumptions as described in Note 2. Our review

---

[15] This wording is appropriate when one column of pro forma financial information is presented without separate columns of historical financial information and pro forma adjustments.

[16] If either accountant's report includes an explanatory paragraph or is other than unqualified, that fact should be referred to within this report.

[17] If the option in footnote 4 to paragraph .07*a* is followed, the report should be appropriately modified.

[18] Where one set of historical financial statements is audited and the other set is reviewed, wording similar to the following would be appropriate:

> The historical condensed financial statements are derived from the historical financial statements of X Company, which were audited by us, and of Y Company, which were reviewed by other accountants, appearing elsewhere herein [*or incorporated by reference*].

[19] If the option in footnote 4 to paragraph .07*a* is followed, the report should be appropriately modified.

was conducted in accordance with attestation standards established by the American Institute of Certified Public Accountants. A review is substantially less in scope than an examination, the objective of which is the expression of an opinion on management's assumptions, the pro forma adjustments, and the application of those adjustments to historical financial information. Accordingly, we do not express such an opinion on the pro forma adjustments or the application of such adjustments to the pro forma condensed balance sheet as of March 31, 20X2, and the pro forma condensed statement of income for the three months then ended.

The objective of this pro forma financial information is to show what the significant effects on the historical financial information might have been had the transactions [*or event*] occurred at an earlier date. However, the pro forma condensed financial statements are not necessarily indicative of the results of operations or related effects on financial position that would have been attained had the above-mentioned transaction [*or event*] actually occurred earlier.

[*Additional paragraph(s) may be added to emphasize certain matters relating to the attest engagements or the subject matter.*]

In our opinion, management's assumptions provide a reasonable basis for presenting the significant effects directly attributable to the above-mentioned transaction [*or event*] described in Note 1, the related pro forma adjustments give appropriate effect to those assumptions, and the pro forma column reflects the proper application of those adjustments to the historical financial statement amounts in the pro forma condensed balance sheet as of December 31, 20X1, and the pro forma condensed statement of income for the year then ended.

Based on our review, nothing came to our attention that caused us to believe that management's assumptions do not provide a reasonable basis for presenting the significant effects directly attributable to the above-mentioned transaction [*or event*] described in Note 1, that the related pro forma adjustments do not give appropriate effect to those assumptions, or that the pro forma column does not reflect the proper application of those adjustments to the historical financial statement amounts in the pro forma condensed balance sheet as of March 31, 20X2, and the pro forma condensed statement of income for the three months then ended.

[*Signature*]

[*Date*]

.21

Appendix D

Report on Examination of Pro Forma Financial Information Giving Effect to a Business Combination to Be Accounted for as a Pooling of Interests[20]

Independent Accountant's Report

We have examined the pro forma adjustments reflecting the proposed business combination to be accounted for as a pooling of interests described in Note 1 and the application of those adjustments to the historical amounts in the accompanying pro forma condensed balance sheet of X Company as of December 31, 20X1, and the pro forma condensed statements of income for each of three years in the period then ended. These historical condensed financial statements are derived from the historical financial statements of X Company, which were audited by us,[21] and of Y Company, which were audited by other accountants, appearing elsewhere herein [*or incorporated by reference*].[22] Such pro forma adjustments are based upon management's assumptions described in Note 2. X Company's management is responsible for the pro forma financial information. Our responsibility is to express an opinion on the pro forma financial information based on our examination.

Our examination was conducted in accordance with attestation standards established by the American Institute of Certified Public Accountants and, accordingly, included such procedures as we considered necessary in the circumstances. We believe that our examination provides a reasonable basis for our opinion.

The objective of this pro forma financial information is to show what the significant effects on the historical financial information might have been had the transactions [*or event*] occurred at an earlier date.

[*Additional paragraph(s) may be added to emphasize certain matters relating to the attest engagement or the subject matter.*]

In our opinion, the accompanying condensed pro forma financial statements of X Company as of December 31, 20X1, and for each of the three years in the period then ended give appropriate effect to the pro forma adjustments necessary to reflect the proposed business combination on a pooling of interests basis as described in Note 1 and the pro forma column reflects the proper application of those adjustments to the historical financial statements.

[*Signature*]

[*Date*]

---

[20] See paragraph .15 for a discussion of the form of the opinion on pro forma financial information in a pooling of interests business combination.

[21] If either accountant's report includes an explanatory paragraph or is other than unqualified, that fact should be referred to within this report.

[22] If the option in footnote 4 to paragraph .07*a* is followed, the report should be appropriately modified.

.22

Appendix E

Other Example Reports

An example of a report qualified because of a scope limitation follows.

Independent Accountant's Report

We have examined the pro forma adjustments reflecting the transaction [*or event*] described in Note 1 and the application of those adjustments to the historical amounts in [*the assembly of*][23] the accompanying pro forma condensed balance sheet of X Company as of December 31, 20X1, and the pro forma condensed statement of income for the year then ended. The historical condensed financial statements are derived from the historical financial statements of X Company, which were audited by us, and of Y Company, which were audited by other accountants,[24] appearing elsewhere herein [*or incorporated by reference*].[25] Such pro forma adjustments are based upon management's assumptions described in Note 2. X Company's management is responsible for the pro forma financial information. Our responsibility is to express an opinion on the pro forma financial information based on our examination.

Except as described below, our examination was conducted in accordance with attestation standards established by the American Institute of Certified Public Accountants and, accordingly, included such procedures as we considered necessary in the circumstances. We believe that our examination provides a reasonable basis for our opinion.

We are unable to perform the examination procedures we considered necessary with respect to assumptions relating to the proposed loan described in Adjustment E in Note 2.

[*Same paragraph as third paragraph in examination report in paragraph .18*]

In our opinion, except for the effects of such changes, if any, as might have been determined to be necessary had we been able to satisfy ourselves as to the assumptions relating to the proposed loan, management's assumptions provide a reasonable basis for presenting the significant effects directly attributable to the above-mentioned transaction [*or event*] described in Note 1, the related pro forma adjustments give appropriate effect to those assumptions, and the pro forma column reflects the proper application of those adjustments to the historical financial statement amounts in the pro forma condensed balance sheet as of December 31, 20X1, and the pro forma condensed statement of income for the year then ended.

[*Signature*]

[*Date*]

---

[23] This wording is appropriate when one column of pro forma financial information is presented without separate columns of historical financial information and pro forma adjustments.

[24] If either accountant's report includes an explanatory paragraph or is other than unqualified, that fact should be referred to within this report.

[25] If the option in footnote 4 to paragraph .07*a* is followed, the report should be appropriately modified.

An example of a report qualified for reservations about the propriety of assumptions on an acquisition transaction follows:

[*Same first three paragraphs as examination report in paragraph .18*]

As discussed in Note 2 to the pro forma financial statements, the pro forma adjustments reflect management's assumption that X Division of the acquired company will be sold. The net assets of this division are reflected at their historical carrying amount; generally accepted accounting principles require these net assets to be recorded at estimated net realizable value.

In our opinion, except for inappropriate valuation of the net assets of X Division, management's assumptions described in Note 2 provide a reasonable basis for presenting the significant effects directly attributable to the above-mentioned transaction [*or event*] described in Note 1, the related pro forma adjustments give appropriate effect to those assumptions, and the pro forma column reflects the proper application of those adjustments to the historical financial statement amounts in the pro forma condensed balance sheet as of December 31, 20X1, and the pro forma condensed statement of income for the year then ended.

[*Signature*]

[*Date*]

An example of a disclaimer of opinion because of a scope limitation follows:

Independent Accountant's Report

We were engaged to examine the pro forma adjustments reflecting the transaction [*or event*] described in Note 1 and the application of those adjustments to the historical amounts in [*the assembly of*][26] the accompanying pro forma financial condensed balance sheet of X Company as of December 31, 20X1, and the pro forma condensed statement of income for the year then ended. The historical condensed financial statements are derived from the historical financial statements of X Company, which were audited by us, and of Y Company, which were audited by other accountants,[27] appearing elsewhere herein [*or incorporated by reference*].[28] Such pro forma adjustments are based upon management's assumptions described in Note 2. X Company's management is responsible for the pro forma financial information.

As discussed in Note 2 to the pro forma financial statements, the pro forma adjustments reflect management's assumptions that the elimination of duplicate facilities would have resulted in a 30 percent reduction in operating costs. Management could not supply us with sufficient evidence to support this assertion.

[*Same paragraph as third paragraph in examination report in paragraph .18*]

Since we were unable to evaluate management's assumptions regarding the reduction in operating costs and other assumptions related thereto, the scope of our work was not sufficient to express and, therefore, we do not express an

---

[26] This wording is appropriate when one column of pro forma financial information is presented without separate columns of historical financial information and pro forma adjustments.

[27] If either accountant's report includes an explanatory paragraph or is other than unqualified, that fact should be referred to within this report.

[28] If the option in footnote 4 to paragraph .07*a* is followed, the report should be appropriately modified.

opinion on the pro forma adjustments, management's underlying assumptions regarding those adjustments and the application of those adjustments to the historical financial statement amounts in the pro forma condensed financial statement amounts in the pro forma condensed balance sheet as of December 31, 20X1, and the pro forma condensed statement of income for the year then ended.

[*Signature*]

[*Date*]

AT Section 501

An Examination of an Entity's Internal Control Over Financial Reporting That Is Integrated With an Audit of Its Financial Statements

Source: SSAE No. 15.

See section 9501 for interpretations of this section.

Effective when the subject matter or assertion is as of or for a period ending on or after December 15, 2008. Earlier application is permitted.

Applicability

.01 This section establishes requirements and provides guidance that applies when a practitioner[1] is engaged to perform an examination of the design and operating effectiveness of an entity's internal control over financial reporting (*examination of internal control*)[2] that is integrated with an audit of financial statements (*integrated audit*).[3]

.02 Ordinarily, the auditor will be engaged to examine the effectiveness of the entity's internal control over financial reporting (hereinafter referred to as *internal control*) as of the end of the entity's fiscal year; however, management may select a different date. If the auditor is engaged to examine the effectiveness of an entity's internal control at a date different from the end of the entity's fiscal year, the examination should, nevertheless, be integrated with a financial statement audit (see paragraphs .18–.19).

.03 An auditor may be engaged to examine the effectiveness of an entity's internal control for a period of time. In that circumstance, the guidance in this section should be modified accordingly, and the examination of internal control should be integrated with an audit of financial statements that covers the same period of time.

.04 This section does not provide guidance for the following:

a. Engagements to examine the suitability of design of an entity's internal control. Such engagements may be developed and performed under AT section 101, *Attest Engagements*[4]

---

[1] In this section, the *practitioner* is referred to as the *auditor* because the examination of internal control is integrated with an audit of financial statements, and an examination provides the same level of assurance as an audit.

[2] In this section, the phrase *examination of internal control* means an engagement to report directly on internal control or on management's assertion thereon. The performance guidance in this section applies equally to either reporting alternative.

[3] Certain regulatory bodies require the examination of internal control and the audit of the financial statements to be performed by the same auditor. There are difficulties inherent in integrating the examination of internal control and the audit of the financial statements to meet the requirements of this section when the audit of the financial statements is performed by a different auditor. In such circumstances, the requirements of this section, nevertheless, apply.

[4] Although this section does not apply when an auditor is engaged to examine the suitability of design of an entity's internal control, it may be useful in planning and performing such engagements.

b. Engagements to examine controls over the effectiveness and efficiency of operations. Such engagements may be developed and performed under AT section 101.

c. Engagements to examine controls over compliance with laws and regulations. See AT section 601, *Compliance Attestation*.

d. Engagements to report on controls at a service organization. See AT section 801, *Reporting on Controls at a Service Organization*.

e. Engagements to perform agreed-upon procedures on controls. See AT section 201, *Agreed-Upon Procedures Engagements*.

[Revised, August 2011, to reflect conforming changes necessary due to the issuance of SSAE No. 16.]

.05 The auditor may be requested to perform certain nonattest services related to the entity's internal control in addition to the examination of internal control. The auditor should determine whether to perform such nonattest services after considering relevant ethical requirements.

.06 An auditor should not accept an engagement to review an entity's internal control or a written assertion thereon.

Definitions and Underlying Concepts

.07 For purposes of this section, the terms listed below are defined as follows:

Control objective. The aim or purpose of specified controls. Control objectives ordinarily address the risks that the controls are intended to mitigate. In the context of internal control, a control objective generally relates to a relevant assertion for a significant account or disclosure and addresses the risk that the controls in a specific area will not provide reasonable assurance that a misstatement or omission in that relevant assertion is prevented, or detected and corrected on a timely basis.

Deficiency. A deficiency in internal control exists when the design or operation of a control does not allow management or employees, in the normal course of performing their assigned functions, to prevent, or detect and correct misstatements on a timely basis. A deficiency in design exists when (*a*) a control necessary to meet the control objective is missing or (*b*) an existing control is not properly designed so that, even if the control operates as designed, the control objective would not be met. A deficiency in operation exists when a properly designed control does not operate as designed, or when the person performing the control does not possess the necessary authority or competence to perform the control effectively.

Detective control. A control that has the objective of detecting and correcting errors or fraud that has already occurred that could result in a misstatement of the financial statements.

Financial statements and related disclosures. An entity's financial statements and notes to the financial statements as presented in accordance with the applicable financial reporting framework.[5] References to financial statements and related disclosures do not extend to the preparation of other financial information presented outside an entity's basic financial statements and notes.

---

[5] The applicable financial reporting framework is the accounting framework used for preparing and presenting the financial statements, such as generally accepted accounting principles (GAAP), International Financial Reporting Standards (IFRSs) as issued by the International Accounting Standards Board, or an other comprehensive basis of accounting (OCBOA), as described in AU section 623, *Special Reports*.

Internal control over financial reporting.[6] A process effected by those charged with governance,[7] management, and other personnel, designed to provide reasonable assurance regarding the preparation of reliable financial statements in accordance with the applicable financial reporting framework and includes those policies and procedures that[8]

i. pertain to the maintenance of records that, in reasonable detail, accurately and fairly reflect the transactions and dispositions of the assets of the entity;
ii. provide reasonable assurance that transactions are recorded as necessary to permit preparation of financial statements in accordance with the applicable financial reporting framework, and that receipts and expenditures of the entity are being made only in accordance with authorizations of management and those charged with governance; and
iii. provide reasonable assurance regarding prevention, or timely detection and correction of unauthorized acquisition, use, or disposition of the entity's assets that could have a material effect on the financial statements.

Internal control has inherent limitations. Internal control is a process that involves human diligence and compliance and is subject to lapses in judgment and breakdowns resulting from human failures. Internal control also can be circumvented by collusion or improper management override. Because of such limitations, there is a risk that material misstatements will not be prevented, or detected and corrected on a timely basis by internal control. However, these inherent limitations are known aspects of the financial reporting process.

Management's assertion. Management's conclusion about the effectiveness of the entity's internal control that is included in management's report on internal control.

Material weakness. A deficiency, or a combination of deficiencies, in internal control such that there is a reasonable possibility[9] that a material misstatement of the entity's financial statements will not be prevented, or detected and corrected on a timely basis.

Preventive control. A control that has the objective of preventing errors or fraud that could result in a misstatement of the financial statements.

---

[6] For insured depository institutions (IDIs) subject to the internal control reporting requirements of Section 112 of the Federal Deposit Insurance Corporation Improvement Act (FDICIA), internal control includes controls over the preparation of the IDI's financial statements and related disclosures in accordance with GAAP and with the instructions to the *Consolidated Financial Statements for Bank Holding Companies*. Internal control also includes controls over the preparation of the IDI's financial statements and related disclosures in accordance with GAAP and controls over the preparation of schedules equivalent to the basic financial statements in accordance with the Federal Financial Institutions Examination Council Instructions for Consolidated Reports of Condition and Income (call report instructions) or with the Office of Thrift Supervision Instructions for Thrift Financial Reports (TFR instructions).

[7] The term *those charged with governance* is defined in paragraph .03 of AU section 380, *The Auditor's Communication With Those Charged With Governance*, as "... the person(s) with responsibility for overseeing the strategic direction of the entity and obligations related to the accountability of the entity. This includes overseeing the financial reporting process. In some cases, those charged with governance are responsible for approving the entity's financial statements (in other cases management has this responsibility). For entities with a board of directors, this term encompasses the term *board of directors* or *audit committee* used elsewhere in generally accepted auditing standards."

[8] The auditor's procedures performed as part of the integrated audit are not part of an entity's internal control.

[9] In this section, a reasonable possibility exists when the likelihood of the event is either *reasonably possible* or *probable*, as those terms are defined in Financial Accounting Standards Board *Accounting Standards Codification* glossary. [Footnote revised, June 2009, to reflect conforming changes necessary due to the issuance of FASB ASC.]

Relevant assertion. A financial statement assertion[10] that has a reasonable possibility of containing a misstatement or misstatements that would cause the financial statements to be materially misstated. The determination of whether an assertion is a relevant assertion is made without regard to the effect of controls.

Significant account or disclosure. An account balance or disclosure that has a reasonable possibility that it could contain a misstatement that, individually or when aggregated with others, has a material effect on the financial statements, considering the risks of both overstatement and understatement. The determination of whether an account balance or disclosure is a significant account or disclosure is made without regard to the effect of controls.

Significant deficiency. A deficiency, or a combination of deficiencies, in internal control that is less severe than a material weakness, yet important enough to merit attention by those charged with governance.

.08 Effective internal control provides reasonable assurance regarding the reliability of financial reporting and the preparation of financial statements for external purposes. If one or more material weaknesses exist, the entity's internal control cannot be considered effective.

.09 The auditor's objective in an examination of internal control is to form an opinion on the effectiveness of the entity's internal control. Because an entity's internal control cannot be considered effective if one or more material weaknesses exist, to form a basis for expressing an opinion, the auditor should plan and perform the examination to obtain sufficient appropriate evidence to obtain reasonable assurance[11] about whether material weaknesses exist as of the date specified in management's assertion. A material weakness in internal control may exist even when financial statements are not materially misstated. The auditor is not required to search for deficiencies that, individually or in combination, are less severe than a material weakness.

.10 An auditor engaged to perform an examination of internal control should comply with the general, fieldwork, and reporting standards in AT section 101, and the specific performance and reporting requirements set forth in this section. In this section, the subject matter is the effectiveness of internal control, and the responsible party usually is management of the entity. Accordingly, the term *management* is used in this section to refer to the responsible party.

.11 The auditor should use the same suitable and available control criteria[12] to perform his or her examination of internal control as management uses for its evaluation of the effectiveness of the entity's internal control.

---

[10] The financial statement assertions are described in AU section 326, *Audit Evidence*. The auditor may use the financial statement assertions as they are described in AU section 326 or express them differently, provided aspects described in AU section 326 have been covered, and the auditor has selected and tested controls over the identified risks in each significant account and disclosure.

[11] The high, but not absolute, level of assurance that is intended to be obtained by the auditor is expressed in the auditor's report as obtaining reasonable assurance about whether effective internal control over financial reporting was maintained in all material respects as of the date specified in management's assertion. See paragraph .54 of AT section 101, *Attest Engagements*, and AU section 230, *Due Professional Care in the Performance of Work*.

[12] According to paragraph .23 of AT section 101 "[t]he third general attestation standard is—*The auditor must have reason to believe that the subject matter is capable of evaluation against criteria that are suitable and available to users.*" The Committee of Sponsoring Organizations of the Treadway Commission's (COSO) report *Internal Control—Integrated Framework* provides suitable and available criteria against which management may evaluate and report on the effectiveness of the entity's

(continued)

.12 An auditor may perform an examination of internal control only if the following conditions are met:

a. Management accepts responsibility for the effectiveness of the entity's internal control.

b. Management evaluates the effectiveness of the entity's internal control using suitable and available criteria.

c. Management supports its assertion about the effectiveness of the entity's internal control with sufficient appropriate evidence (see discussion beginning at paragraph .14).

d. Management provides its assertion about the effectiveness of the entity's internal control in a report that accompanies the auditor's report (see paragraph .95).

.13 Management's refusal to furnish a written assertion should cause the auditor to withdraw from the engagement. However, if law or regulation does not allow the auditor to withdraw from the engagement and management refuses to furnish a written assertion, the auditor should disclaim an opinion on internal control.[13]

Evidence Supporting Management's Assertion

.14 Management is responsible for identifying and documenting the controls and the control objectives that they were designed to achieve. Such documentation serves as a basis for management's assertion. Documentation of the design of controls, including changes to those controls, is evidence that controls upon which management's assertion is based are

- identified.
- capable of being communicated to those responsible for their performance.
- capable of being monitored and evaluated by the entity.

.15 Management's documentation may take various forms, for example, entity policy manuals, accounting manuals, narrative memoranda, flowcharts, decision tables, procedural write-ups, or completed questionnaires. No one, particular form of documentation is prescribed, and the extent of documentation may vary depending upon the size and complexity of the entity and the entity's monitoring activities.

.16 Management's monitoring activities also may provide evidence of the design and operating effectiveness of internal control in support of management's assertion. Monitoring of controls is a process to assess the effectiveness of internal control performance over time. It involves assessing the effectiveness of controls on a timely basis, identifying and reporting deficiencies to appropriate individuals within the organization, and taking necessary corrective actions. Management accomplishes monitoring of controls through ongoing activities, separate evaluations, or a combination of the two.

(footnote continued)

internal control. *Internal Control—Integrated Framework* describes an entity's internal control as consisting of five components: control environment, risk assessment, control activities, information and communication, and monitoring. See AU section 314, *Understanding the Entity and Its Environment and Assessing the Risks of Material Misstatement*, for a discussion of these components. If management selects another framework, see paragraphs .23–.34 of AT section 101 for guidance on evaluating the suitability and availability of criteria.

[13] See paragraphs .117–.121 when disclaiming an opinion, including the requirement for the auditor's report to include a description of any material weaknesses identified.

.17 Ongoing monitoring activities are often built into the normal recurring activities of an entity and include regular management and supervisory activities. The greater the degree and effectiveness of ongoing monitoring, the less need for separate evaluations. Usually, some combination of ongoing monitoring and separate evaluations will ensure that internal control maintains its effectiveness over time.

Integrating the Examination With the Financial Statement Audit

.18 The examination of internal control should be integrated with an audit of financial statements. Although the objectives of the engagements are not the same, the auditor should plan and perform the integrated audit to achieve the objectives of both engagements simultaneously. The auditor should design tests of controls

- to obtain sufficient appropriate evidence to support the auditor's opinion on internal control as of the period-end; and
- to obtain sufficient appropriate evidence to support the auditor's control risk assessments for purposes of the audit of financial statements.

.19 The date specified in management's assertion (the as-of date of the examination) should correspond to the balance sheet date (or period ending date) of the period covered by the financial statements (see paragraph .02).

.20 Obtaining sufficient appropriate evidence to support the operating effectiveness of controls for purposes of the financial statement audit ordinarily allows the auditor to modify the substantive procedures that otherwise would have been necessary to opine on the financial statements. (Integration is described further beginning at paragraph .159.)

.21 In some circumstances, particularly in some audits of smaller, less complex entities, the auditor might choose not to test the operating effectiveness of controls for purposes of the audit of the financial statements. In such circumstances, the auditor's tests of the operating effectiveness of controls would be performed principally for the purpose of supporting his or her opinion on whether the entity's internal control is effective as of period-end. The auditor should consider the results of the financial statement auditing procedures in determining his or her risk assessments and the testing necessary to conclude on the operating effectiveness of a control.

Planning the Examination

.22 The auditor should plan the examination of internal control. Evaluating whether the following matters are important to the entity's financial statements and internal control and, if so, how they may affect the auditor's procedures, may assist the auditor in planning the examination:

- Knowledge of the entity's internal control obtained during other engagements performed by the auditor or, if applicable, during a review of a predecessor auditor's working papers
- Matters affecting the industry in which the entity operates, such as financial reporting practices, economic conditions, laws and regulations, and technological changes
- Matters relating to the entity's business, including its organization, operating characteristics, and capital structure

- The extent of recent changes, if any, in the entity, its operations, or its internal control
- The auditor's preliminary judgments about materiality, risk, and other factors relating to the determination of material weaknesses
- Deficiencies previously communicated to those charged with governance or management
- Legal or regulatory matters of which the entity is aware
- The type and extent of available evidence related to the effectiveness of the entity's internal control
- Preliminary judgments about the effectiveness of internal control
- Public information about the entity relevant to the evaluation of the likelihood of material financial statement misstatements and the effectiveness of the entity's internal control
- Knowledge about risks related to the entity evaluated as part of the auditor's client acceptance and retention evaluation
- The relative complexity of the entity's operations

Role of Risk Assessment

.23 Risk assessment underlies the entire examination process described by this section, including the determination of significant accounts and disclosures and relevant assertions, the selection of controls to test, and the determination of the evidence necessary to conclude on the effectiveness of a given control. When performing an examination of internal control that is integrated with an audit of financial statements, the same risk assessment process supports both engagements.[14]

.24 The auditor should focus more attention on the areas of highest risk. A direct relationship exists between the degree of risk that a material weakness could exist in a particular area of the entity's internal control and the amount of attention that would be devoted to that area. In addition, an entity's internal control is less likely to prevent, or detect and correct a misstatement caused by fraud than a misstatement caused by error. It is not necessary to test controls that, even if deficient, would not present a reasonable possibility of material misstatement to the financial statements.

Scaling the Examination

.25 The size and complexity of the entity, its business processes, and business units may affect the way in which the entity achieves many of its control objectives. Many smaller entities have less complex operations. Additionally, some larger, complex entities may have less complex units or processes. Factors that might indicate less complex operations include fewer business lines; less complex business processes and financial reporting systems; more centralized accounting functions; extensive involvement by senior management in the day-to-day activities of the business; and fewer levels of management, each with a wide span of control. Accordingly, a smaller, less complex entity, or even a larger, less complex entity might achieve its control objectives differently from a more complex entity.

---

[14] The risk assessment procedures performed in connection with a financial statement audit are described in AU section 314.

.26 The size and complexity of the organization, its business processes, and business units also may affect the auditor's risk assessment and the determination of the necessary procedures and the controls necessary to address those risks. Scaling is most effective as a natural extension of the risk-based approach and applicable to examinations of all entities.

Addressing the Risk of Fraud

.27 When planning and performing the examination of internal control, the auditor should incorporate the results of the fraud risk assessment performed in the financial statement audit. As part of identifying and testing entity-level controls, as discussed beginning at paragraph .37, and selecting other controls to test, as discussed beginning at paragraph .54, the auditor should evaluate whether the entity's controls sufficiently address identified risks of material misstatement due to fraud[15] and the risk of management override of other controls. Controls that might address these risks include

- controls over significant, unusual transactions, particularly those that result in late or unusual journal entries;
- controls over journal entries and adjustments made in the period-end financial reporting process;
- controls over related party transactions;
- controls related to significant management estimates; and
- controls that mitigate incentives for, and pressures on, management to falsify or inappropriately manage financial results.

.28 If the auditor identifies deficiencies in controls designed to prevent, or detect and correct misstatements caused by fraud during the examination of internal control, he or she should take into account those deficiencies when developing his or her response to risks of material misstatement during the financial statement audit, as provided in AU section 316, *Consideration of Fraud in a Financial Statement Audit*, paragraphs .44–.45.

Using the Work of Others

.29 The auditor should evaluate the extent to which he or she will use the work of others to reduce the work the auditor might otherwise perform himself or herself.

.30 AU section 322, *The Auditor's Consideration of the Internal Audit Function in an Audit of Financial Statements*, applies in an integrated audit. For purposes of the examination of internal control, however, the auditor may use the work performed by, or receive direct assistance from, internal auditors, entity personnel (in addition to internal auditors), and third parties working under the direction of management or those charged with governance that provide evidence about the effectiveness of internal control. In an integrated audit, the auditor also may use this work to obtain evidence supporting the assessment of control risk for purposes of the financial statement audit.

.31 The auditor should obtain an understanding of the work of others sufficient to identify those activities related to the effectiveness of internal control that are relevant to planning the examination of internal control. The extent

---

[15] See paragraphs .19–.42 of AU section 316, *Consideration of Fraud in a Financial Statement Audit*, regarding identifying risks that may result in material misstatement due to fraud.

of the procedures necessary to obtain this understanding will vary, depending on the nature of those activities.

.32 The auditor should assess the competence and objectivity of the persons whose work the auditor plans to use to determine the extent to which the auditor may use their work. The higher the degree of competence and objectivity, the greater use the auditor may make of the work. The auditor should apply paragraphs .09–.11 of AU section 322 to assess the competence and objectivity of internal auditors. The auditor should apply the principles underlying those paragraphs to assess the competence and objectivity of persons other than internal auditors whose work the auditor plans to use.

.33 For purposes of using the work of others, competence means the attainment and maintenance of a level of understanding, knowledge, and skills that enables that person to perform ably the tasks assigned to them, and objectivity means the ability to perform those tasks impartially and with intellectual honesty. To assess competence, the auditor should evaluate factors about the person's qualifications and ability to perform the work that the auditor plans to use. To assess objectivity, the auditor should evaluate whether factors are present that either inhibit or promote a person's ability to perform with the necessary degree of objectivity the work that the auditor plans to use. The effect of the work of others on the auditor's work also depends on the relationship between the risk associated with a control and the competence and objectivity of those who performed the work. As the risk associated with a control decreases, the necessary level of competence and objectivity decreases as well. In higher risk areas (for example, controls that address specific fraud risks), use of the work of others would be limited, if it could be used at all.

.34 The extent to which the auditor may use the work of others also depends, in part, on the risk associated with the control being tested (see paragraph .62). As the risk associated with a control increases, the need for the auditor to perform his or her own work on the control increases.

Materiality

.35 In planning and performing the examination of internal control, the auditor should use the same materiality used in planning and performing the audit of the entity's financial statements.[16]

Using a Top-Down Approach

.36 The auditor should use a top-down approach[17] to the examination of internal control to select the controls to test. A top-down approach involves

- beginning at the financial statement level;
- using the auditor's understanding of the overall risks to internal control;
- focusing on entity-level controls;
- working down to significant accounts and disclosures and their relevant assertions;

---

[16] See AU section 312, *Audit Risk and Materiality in Conducting an Audit*, which provides additional explanation of materiality.

[17] The top-down approach describes the auditor's sequential thought process in identifying risks and the controls to test, not necessarily the order in which the auditor will perform the examination procedures.

- directing attention to accounts, disclosures, and assertions that present a reasonable possibility of material misstatement to the financial statements and related disclosures;
- verifying the auditor's understanding of the risks in the entity's processes; and
- selecting controls for testing that sufficiently address the assessed risk of material misstatement to each relevant assertion.

Identifying Entity-Level Controls

.37 The auditor should test those entity-level controls that are important to his or her conclusion about whether the entity has effective internal control. The auditor's evaluation of entity-level controls can result in increasing or decreasing the testing that he or she otherwise would have performed on other controls.

.38 Entity-level controls include

- controls related to the control environment;
- controls over management override;[18]
- the entity's risk assessment process;
- centralized processing and controls, including shared service environments;
- controls to monitor results of operations;
- controls to monitor other controls, including activities of the internal audit function, those charged with governance, and self-assessment programs;
- controls over the period-end financial reporting process; and
- programs and controls that address significant business control and risk management practices.

.39 Entity-level controls vary in nature and precision:

- Some entity-level controls, such as certain control environment controls, have an important but indirect effect on the likelihood that a misstatement will be prevented, or detected and corrected on a timely basis. These controls might affect the other controls that the auditor selects for testing and the nature, timing, and extent of procedures the auditor performs on other controls.
- Some entity-level controls monitor the effectiveness of other controls. Such controls might be designed to identify possible breakdowns in lower level controls, but not at a level of precision that would, by themselves, sufficiently address the assessed risk that material misstatements to a relevant assertion will be prevented, or detected and corrected on a timely basis. These controls, when operating effectively, might allow the auditor to reduce the testing of other controls.

---

[18] Controls over management override are important to effective internal control for all entities and may be particularly important at smaller, less complex entities because of the increased involvement of senior management in performing controls and in the period-end financial reporting process. For smaller, less complex entities, the controls that address the risk of management override might be different from those at a larger entity. For example, a smaller, less complex entity might rely on more detailed oversight by those charged with governance that focuses on the risk of management override.

- Some entity-level controls might be designed to operate at a level of precision that would adequately prevent, or detect and correct on a timely basis misstatements to one or more relevant assertions. If an entity-level control sufficiently addresses the assessed risk of material misstatement, the auditor need not test additional controls relating to that risk.

Control Environment

.40 Because of its importance to effective internal control, the auditor should evaluate the control environment at the entity. When evaluating the control environment, the auditor should apply paragraphs .67–.75 of AU section 314, *Understanding the Entity and Its Environment and Assessing the Risks of Material Misstatement*. As part of evaluating the control environment, the auditor should assess

- whether management's philosophy and operating style promote effective internal control;
- whether sound integrity and ethical values, particularly of top management, are developed and understood; and
- whether those charged with governance understand and exercise oversight responsibility over financial reporting and internal control.

Period-End Financial Reporting Process

.41 Because of its importance to financial reporting and to the integrated audit, the auditor should evaluate the period-end financial reporting process.[19] The period-end financial reporting process includes the following:

- Procedures used to enter transaction totals into the general ledger
- Procedures related to the selection and application of accounting policies
- Procedures used to initiate, authorize, record, and process journal entries in the general ledger
- Procedures used to record recurring and nonrecurring adjustments to the financial statements
- Procedures for preparing financial statements and related disclosures

.42 As part of evaluating the period-end financial reporting process, the auditor should assess

- the inputs, procedures performed, and outputs of the processes the entity uses to produce its financial statements;
- the extent of IT involvement in the period-end financial reporting process;
- who participates from management;
- the locations involved in the period-end financial reporting process;
- the types of adjusting and consolidating entries; and
- the nature and extent of the oversight of the process by management and those charged with governance.

---

[19] Because the annual period-end financial reporting process normally occurs after the as-of date of management's assertion, those controls usually cannot be tested until after the as-of date.

Identifying Significant Accounts and Disclosures and Their Relevant Assertions

.43 The auditor should identify significant accounts and disclosures and their relevant assertions. To identify significant accounts and disclosures and their relevant assertions, the auditor should evaluate the qualitative and quantitative risk factors related to the financial statement line items and disclosures. Risk factors relevant to the identification of significant accounts and disclosures and their relevant assertions include

- size and composition of the account;
- susceptibility to misstatement due to errors or fraud;
- volume of activity, complexity, and homogeneity of the individual transactions processed through the account or reflected in the disclosure;
- nature of the account, class of transactions, or disclosure;
- accounting and reporting complexities associated with the account, class of transactions, or disclosure;
- exposure to losses in the account;
- possibility of significant contingent liabilities arising from the activities reflected in the account or disclosure;
- existence of related party transactions in the account; and
- changes from the prior period in the account, class of transactions, or disclosure characteristics.

.44 As part of identifying significant accounts and disclosures and their relevant assertions, the auditor also should determine the likely sources of potential misstatements that would cause the financial statements to be materially misstated. The auditor might determine the likely sources of potential misstatements by asking himself or herself "what could go wrong?" within a given significant account or disclosure.

.45 The risk factors that the auditor should evaluate in the identification of significant accounts and disclosures and their relevant assertions are the same in the examination of internal control as in the audit of the financial statements; accordingly, significant accounts and disclosures and their relevant assertions are the same in an integrated audit.[20]

.46 The components of a potential significant account or disclosure might be subject to significantly different risks. If so, different controls might be necessary to adequately address those risks.

.47 When an entity has multiple locations or business units, the auditor should identify significant accounts and disclosures and their relevant assertions based on the consolidated financial statements.

Understanding Likely Sources of Misstatement

.48 To further understand the likely sources of potential misstatements, and as a part of selecting the controls to test, the auditor should achieve the following objectives:

---

[20] The risk assessment procedures performed in connection with a financial statement audit are described in AU section 314.

- Understand the flow of transactions related to the relevant assertions, including how these transactions are initiated, authorized, processed, and recorded
- Identify the points within the entity's processes at which a misstatement, including a misstatement due to fraud, could arise that, individually or in combination with other misstatements, would be material (for example, points at which information is initiated, transferred, or otherwise modified)
- Identify the controls that management has implemented to address these potential misstatements
- Identify the controls that management has implemented over the prevention, or timely detection and correction of unauthorized acquisition, use, or disposition of the entity's assets that could result in a material misstatement of the financial statements

.49 Because of the degree of judgment required, the auditor should either perform the procedures that achieve the objectives in paragraph .48 himself or herself or supervise the work of others who provide direct assistance to the auditor, as described in AU section 322.

.50 The auditor also should understand how IT affects the entity's flow of transactions. The auditor should apply paragraphs .57–.63 of AU section 314, which discuss the effect of IT on internal control and the risks to assess.

.51 The identification of risks and controls within IT is not a separate evaluation. Instead, it is an integral part of the top-down approach used to identify likely sources of misstatement and the controls to test, as well as to assess risk and allocate audit effort.

Performing Walkthroughs

.52 Performing walkthroughs will frequently be the most effective way of achieving the objectives in paragraph .48. A walkthrough involves following a transaction from origination through the entity's processes, including information systems, until it is reflected in the entity's financial records, using the same documents and IT that entity personnel use. Walkthrough procedures may include a combination of inquiry, observation, inspection of relevant documentation, recalculation, and control reperformance.

.53 A walkthrough includes questioning the entity's personnel about their understanding of what is required by the entity's prescribed procedures and controls at the points at which important processing procedures occur. These probing questions, combined with the other walkthrough procedures, allow the auditor to gain a sufficient understanding of the process and to be able to identify important points at which a necessary control is missing or not designed effectively. Additionally, probing questions that go beyond a narrow focus on the single transaction used as the basis for the walkthrough may provide an understanding of the different types of significant transactions handled by the process.

Selecting Controls to Test

.54 The auditor should test those controls that are important to the auditor's conclusion about whether the entity's controls sufficiently address the assessed risk of material misstatement to each relevant assertion.

.55 There might be more than one control that addresses the assessed risk of material misstatement to a particular relevant assertion; conversely, one control might address the assessed risk of material misstatement to more than one relevant assertion. It may not be necessary to test all controls related to a relevant assertion nor necessary to test redundant controls, unless redundancy is, itself, a control objective.

.56 The decision concerning whether a control would be selected for testing depends on which controls, individually or in combination, sufficiently address the assessed risk of material misstatement to a given relevant assertion rather than on how the control is labeled (for example, entity-level control, transaction-level control, control activity, monitoring control, preventive control, or detective control).

Testing Controls

Evaluating Design Effectiveness

.57 The auditor should evaluate the design effectiveness of controls by determining whether the entity's controls, if they are applied as prescribed by persons possessing the necessary authority and competence to perform the control effectively, satisfy the entity's control objectives, and can effectively prevent, or detect and correct misstatements caused by errors or fraud that could result in material misstatements in the financial statements.

.58 A smaller, less complex entity might achieve its control objectives in a different manner from a larger, more complex organization. For example, a smaller, less complex entity might have fewer employees in the accounting function, limiting opportunities to segregate duties and leading the entity to implement alternative controls to achieve its control objectives. In such circumstances, the auditor should evaluate whether those alternative controls are effective.

.59 Procedures performed to evaluate design effectiveness may include a mix of inquiry of appropriate personnel, observation of the entity's operations, and inspection of relevant documentation. Walkthroughs that include these procedures ordinarily are sufficient to evaluate design effectiveness.

Testing Operating Effectiveness

.60 The auditor should test the operating effectiveness of a control by determining whether the control is operating as designed and whether the person performing the control possesses the necessary authority and competence to perform the control effectively.[21]

.61 Procedures performed to test operating effectiveness may include a mix of inquiry of appropriate personnel, observation of the entity's operations, inspection of relevant documentation, recalculation, and reperformance of the control.

---

[21] In some situations, particularly in smaller, less complex entities, an entity might use a third party to provide assistance with certain financial reporting functions. When assessing the competence of personnel responsible for an entity's financial reporting and associated controls, the auditor may take into account the combined competence of entity personnel and other parties that assist with functions related to financial reporting.

Relationship of Risk to the Evidence to Be Obtained

.62 For each control selected for testing, the evidence necessary to persuade the auditor that the control is effective depends upon the risk associated with the control. The risk associated with a control consists of the risk that the control might not be effective and, if not effective, the risk that a material weakness exists. As the risk associated with the control being tested increases, the evidence that the auditor should obtain also increases.

.63 Although the auditor should obtain evidence about the effectiveness of controls for each relevant assertion, he or she is not responsible for obtaining sufficient appropriate evidence to support an opinion about the effectiveness of each individual control. Rather, the auditor's objective is to express an opinion on the entity's internal control overall. This allows the auditor to vary the evidence obtained regarding the effectiveness of individual controls selected for testing based on the risk associated with the individual control.

.64 Factors that affect the risk associated with a control may include

- the nature and materiality of misstatements that the control is intended to prevent, or detect and correct;
- the inherent risk associated with the related account(s) and assertion(s);
- whether there have been changes in the volume or nature of transactions that might adversely affect control design or operating effectiveness;
- whether the account has a history of errors;
- the effectiveness of entity-level controls, especially controls that monitor other controls;
- the nature of the control and the frequency with which it operates;
- the degree to which the control relies on the effectiveness of other controls (for example, the control environment or IT general controls);
- the competence of the personnel who perform the control or monitor its performance and whether there have been changes in key personnel who perform the control or monitor its performance;
- whether the control relies on performance by an individual or is automated (that is, an automated control would generally be expected to be lower risk if relevant IT general controls are effective);[22] and
- the complexity of the control and the significance of the judgments that would be made in connection with its operation.[23]

.65 When the auditor identifies control deviations, he or she should determine the effect of the deviations on his or her assessment of the risk associated with the control being tested and the evidence to be obtained, as well as on the operating effectiveness of the control.

---

[22] A smaller, less complex entity or business unit with simple business processes and centralized accounting operations might have relatively simple information systems that make greater use of off-the-shelf packaged software without modification. In the areas in which off-the-shelf software is used, the auditor's testing of IT controls might focus on the application controls built into the prepackaged software that management relies on to achieve its control objectives and the IT general controls that are important to the effective operation of those application controls.

[23] Generally, a conclusion that a control is not operating effectively can be supported by less evidence than is necessary to support a conclusion that a control is operating effectively.

.66 Because effective internal control cannot and does not provide absolute assurance of achieving the entity's control objectives, an individual control does not necessarily have to operate without any deviation to be considered effective.

.67 The evidence provided by the auditor's tests of the effectiveness of controls depends upon the mix of the nature, timing, and extent of the auditor's procedures. Further, for an individual control, different combinations of the nature, timing, and extent of testing may provide sufficient appropriate evidence in relation to the risk associated with the control.

.68 Walkthroughs may include a combination of inquiry of appropriate personnel, observation of the entity's operations, inspection of relevant documentation, recalculation, and reperformance of the control and might provide sufficient appropriate evidence of operating effectiveness, depending on the risk associated with the control being tested, the specific procedures performed as part of the walkthrough, and the results of those procedures.

Nature of Tests of Controls

.69 Some types of tests, by their nature, produce greater evidence of the effectiveness of controls than other tests. The following tests that the auditor might perform are presented in order of the evidence that they ordinarily would produce, from least to most: inquiry, observation, inspection of relevant documentation, recalculation, and reperformance of a control. Inquiry alone, however, does not provide sufficient appropriate evidence to support a conclusion about the effectiveness of a control.

.70 The nature of the tests of effectiveness that will provide sufficient appropriate evidence depends, to a large degree, on the nature of the control to be tested, including whether the operation of the control results in documentary evidence of its operation. Documentary evidence of the operation of some controls, such as management's philosophy and operating style, might not exist.

.71 A smaller, less complex entity or unit might have less formal documentation regarding the operation of its controls. In those situations, testing controls through inquiry combined with other procedures, such as observation of activities, inspection of less formal documentation, recalculation, or reperformance of certain controls, might provide sufficient appropriate evidence about whether the control is effective.

Timing and Extent of Tests of Controls

.72 Testing controls over a longer period of time provides more evidence of the effectiveness of controls than testing over a shorter period of time. Further, testing performed closer to the date of management's assertion provides more evidence than testing performed earlier in the year. The auditor should balance performing the tests of controls closer to the as-of date with the need to test controls over a sufficient period of time to obtain sufficient appropriate evidence of operating effectiveness.

.73 Prior to the date specified in management's assertion, management might implement changes to the entity's controls to make them more effective or efficient or to address deficiencies. If the auditor determines that the new controls achieve the related objectives of the control criteria and have been in effect for a sufficient period to permit the auditor to assess their design and operating effectiveness by performing tests of controls, he or she will not need to test the design and operating effectiveness of the superseded controls for purposes of expressing an opinion on internal control. If the operating effectiveness of the superseded controls is important to the auditor's control risk assessment in the financial statement audit, the auditor should test the design and operating effectiveness of those superseded controls, as appropriate. (Integration is discussed beginning at paragraph .159.)

.74 The more extensively a control is tested, the greater the evidence obtained from that test.

Rollforward Procedures

.75 When the auditor reports on the effectiveness of controls as of a specific date and obtains evidence about the operating effectiveness of controls at an interim date, he or she should determine what additional evidence concerning the operation of the controls for the remaining period is necessary.

.76 The additional evidence that is necessary to update the results of testing from an interim date to the entity's period-end depends on the following factors:[24]

- The specific control tested prior to the as-of date, including the risks associated with the control, the nature of the control, and the results of those tests
- The sufficiency of the evidence of operating effectiveness obtained at an interim date
- The length of the remaining period
- The possibility that there have been any significant changes in internal control subsequent to the interim date

Special Considerations for Subsequent Years' Examinations

.77 In subsequent years' examinations, the auditor should incorporate knowledge obtained during past examinations he or she performed of the entity's internal control into the decision making process for determining the nature, timing, and extent of testing necessary. This decision making process is described in paragraphs .62–.76.

.78 Factors that affect the risk associated with a control in subsequent years' examinations include those in paragraph .64 and the following:

- The nature, timing, and extent of procedures performed in previous examinations
- The results of the previous years' testing of the control
- Whether there have been changes in the control or the process in which it operates since the previous examination

.79 After taking into account the risk factors identified in paragraphs .64 and .78, the additional information available in subsequent years' examinations might permit the auditor to assess the risk as lower than in the initial year. This, in turn, might permit the auditor to reduce testing in subsequent years.

.80 The auditor also may use a benchmarking strategy for automated application controls in subsequent years' examinations. Benchmarking is described further beginning at paragraph .153.

.81 In addition, the auditor should vary the nature, timing, and extent of testing of controls from period to period to introduce unpredictability into the testing and respond to changes in circumstances. For this reason, the auditor

---

[24] In some circumstances, such as when evaluation of these factors indicates a low risk that the controls are no longer effective during the rollforward period, inquiry alone might be sufficient as a rollforward procedure.

might test controls at a different interim period, increase or reduce the number and types of tests performed, or change the combination of procedures used.

Evaluating Identified Deficiencies

.82 The auditor should evaluate the severity of each deficiency to determine whether the deficiency, individually or in combination, is a material weakness as of the date of management's assertion.

.83 The severity of a deficiency depends on

- the magnitude of the potential misstatement resulting from the deficiency or deficiencies; and
- whether there is a reasonable possibility that the entity's controls will fail to prevent, or detect and correct a misstatement of an account balance or disclosure.

The severity of a deficiency does not depend on whether a misstatement actually occurred.

.84 Factors that affect the magnitude of the misstatement that might result from a deficiency or deficiencies include, but are not limited to, the following:

- The financial statement amounts or total of transactions exposed to the deficiency
- The volume of activity (in the current period or expected in future periods) in the account or class of transactions exposed to the deficiency

.85 In evaluating the magnitude of the potential misstatement, the maximum amount by which an account balance or total of transactions can be overstated is generally the recorded amount, whereas understatements could be larger.

.86 Risk factors affect whether there is a reasonable possibility that a deficiency, or a combination of deficiencies, will result in a misstatement of an account balance or disclosure. The factors include, but are not limited to, the following:

- The nature of the financial statement accounts, classes of transactions, disclosures, and assertions involved
- The susceptibility of the related asset or liability to loss or fraud
- The subjectivity, complexity, or extent of judgment required to determine the amount involved
- The interaction or relationship of the control with other controls
- The interaction among the deficiencies
- The possible future consequences of the deficiency

.87 The evaluation of whether a deficiency presents a reasonable possibility of misstatement may be made without quantifying the probability of occurrence as a specific percentage or range. Also, in many cases, the probability of a small misstatement will be greater than the probability of a large misstatement.

.88 Multiple deficiencies that affect the same significant account or disclosure, relevant assertion, or component of internal control increase the likelihood of material misstatement and may, in combination, constitute a material weakness, even though such deficiencies individually may be less severe. Therefore, the auditor should determine whether deficiencies that affect the same significant account or disclosure, relevant assertion, or component of internal control collectively result in a material weakness.

.89 Multiple deficiencies that affect the same significant account or disclosure, relevant assertion, or component of internal control also may collectively result in a significant deficiency.

.90 A compensating control can limit the severity of a deficiency and prevent it from being a material weakness. Although compensating controls can mitigate the effects of a deficiency, they do not eliminate the deficiency. The auditor should evaluate the effect of compensating controls when determining whether a deficiency or combination of deficiencies is a material weakness. To have a mitigating effect, the compensating control should operate at a level of precision that would prevent, or detect and correct a material misstatement. The auditor should test the operating effectiveness of compensating controls.

Indicators of Material Weaknesses

.91 Indicators of material weaknesses in internal control include

- identification of fraud, whether or not material, on the part of senior management;
- restatement of previously issued financial statements to reflect the correction of a material misstatement due to error or fraud;
- identification by the auditor of a material misstatement of financial statements under audit in circumstances that indicate that the misstatement would not have been detected and corrected by the entity's internal control; and
- ineffective oversight of the entity's financial reporting and internal control by those charged with governance.

.92 If the auditor determines that a deficiency, or a combination of deficiencies, is not a material weakness, he or she should consider whether prudent officials, having knowledge of the same facts and circumstances, would likely reach the same conclusion.

Concluding Procedures

Forming an Opinion

.93 The auditor should form an opinion on the effectiveness of internal control by evaluating evidence obtained from all sources, including the auditor's testing of controls, misstatements detected during the financial statement audit, and any identified deficiencies.

.94 As part of this evaluation, the auditor should review reports issued during the year by internal audit (or similar functions) that address controls related to internal control and evaluate deficiencies identified in those reports.

.95 After forming an opinion on the effectiveness of the entity's internal control, the auditor should evaluate management's report to determine whether it appropriately contains the following:

- A statement regarding management's responsibility for internal control
- A description of the subject matter of the examination (for example, controls over the preparation of the entity's financial statements in accordance with generally accepted accounting principles [GAAP])

- An identification of the criteria against which internal control is measured (for example, criteria established in the Committee of Sponsoring Organizations of the Treadway Commission's *Internal Control—Integrated Framework*)
- Management's assertion about the effectiveness of internal control
- A description of the material weaknesses, if any
- The date as of which management's assertion is made

.96 If the auditor determines that any required element of management's report is incomplete or improperly presented, the auditor should request management to revise its report. If management does not revise its report, the auditor should apply paragraph .116. If management refuses to furnish a report, the auditor should apply paragraph .13.

Obtaining Written Representations

.97 In an examination of internal control, the auditor should obtain written representations from management

a. acknowledging management's responsibility for establishing and maintaining effective internal control;

b. stating that management has performed an evaluation of the effectiveness of the entity's internal control and specifying the control criteria;

c. stating that management did not use the auditor's procedures performed during the integrated audit as part of the basis for management's assertion;

d. stating management's assertion about the effectiveness of the entity's internal control based on the control criteria as of a specified date;

e. stating that management has disclosed to the auditor all deficiencies in the design or operation of internal control, including separately disclosing to the auditor all such deficiencies that it believes to be significant deficiencies or material weaknesses in internal control;

f. describing any fraud resulting in a material misstatement to the entity's financial statements and any other fraud that does not result in a material misstatement to the entity's financial statements, but involves senior management or management or other employees who have a significant role in the entity's internal control;

g. stating whether the significant deficiencies and material weaknesses identified and communicated to management and those charged with governance during previous engagements pursuant to paragraph .100 have been resolved and specifically identifying any that have not; and

h. stating whether there were, subsequent to the date being reported on, any changes in internal control or other factors that might significantly affect internal control, including any corrective actions taken by management with regard to significant deficiencies and material weaknesses.

.98 The failure to obtain written representations from management, including management's refusal to furnish them, constitutes a limitation on the scope of the examination.[25] The auditor should evaluate the effects of management's refusal on his or her ability to rely on other representations, such as those obtained in the audit of the entity's financial statements.

[25] See paragraph .117 when the scope of the engagement has been restricted.

.99 The auditor should apply AU section 333, *Management Representations*, as it relates to matters such as who should sign the letter, the period to be covered by the letter, and when to obtain an updated letter.

Communicating Certain Matters

.100 Deficiencies identified during the integrated audit that, upon evaluation, are considered significant deficiencies or material weaknesses should be communicated, in writing, to management and those charged with governance as a part of each integrated audit, including significant deficiencies and material weaknesses that were previously communicated to management and those charged with governance and have not yet been remediated. Significant deficiencies and material weaknesses that previously were communicated and have not yet been remediated may be communicated, in writing, by referring to the previously issued written communication and the date of that communication.

.101 If the auditor concludes that the oversight of the entity's financial reporting and internal control by the audit committee (or similar subgroups with different names) is ineffective, the auditor should communicate that conclusion, in writing, to the board of directors or other similar governing body if one exists.

.102 The written communications referred to in paragraphs .100–.101 should be made by the report release date,[26] which is the date the auditor grants the entity permission to use the auditor's report. For a governmental entity, the auditor is not required to make the written communications by the report release date, if such written communications would be publicly available prior to management's report on internal control, the entity's financial statements, and the auditor's report thereon. In that circumstance, the written communications should be made as soon as practicable, but no later than 60 days following the report release date.

.103 Because of the importance of timely communication, the auditor may choose to communicate significant matters during the course of the integrated audit. If the communication is made during the integrated audit, the form of interim communication would be affected by the relative significance of the identified deficiencies and the urgency for corrective follow-up action. Such early communication is not required to be in writing. However, regardless of how the early communication is delivered, the auditor should communicate all significant deficiencies and material weaknesses in writing to management and those charged with governance in accordance with paragraphs .100–.102, even if the significant deficiencies or material weaknesses were remediated during the examination.

.104 The auditor also should communicate to management, in writing, all deficiencies (those deficiencies that are not material weaknesses or significant deficiencies) identified during the integrated audit on a timely basis, but no later than 60 days following the report release date, and inform those charged with governance when such a communication was made. In making the written communication referred to in this paragraph, the auditor is not required to communicate those deficiencies that are not material weaknesses or significant deficiencies that were included in previous written communications, whether those communications were made by the auditor, internal auditors, or others within the organization.

---

[26] See paragraph .23 of AU section 339, *Audit Documentation*, for additional guidance related to the report release date.

.105 The auditor is not required to perform procedures that are sufficient to identify all deficiencies; rather, the auditor communicates deficiencies of which he or she is aware.

.106 Because the integrated audit does not provide the auditor with assurance that he or she has identified all deficiencies less severe than a material weakness, the auditor should not issue a report stating that no such deficiencies were identified during the integrated audit. Also, because the auditor's objective in an examination of internal control is to form an opinion on the effectiveness of the entity's internal control, the auditor should not issue a report indicating that no material weaknesses were identified during the integrated audit.

Reporting on Internal Control

.107 The auditor's report on the examination of internal control should include the following elements:[27]

a. A title that includes the word *independent*

b. A statement that management is responsible for maintaining effective internal control and for evaluating the effectiveness of internal control

c. An identification of management's assertion on internal control that accompanies the auditor's report, including a reference to management's report

d. A statement that the auditor's responsibility is to express an opinion on the entity's internal control (or on management's assertion)[28] based on his or her examination[29]

e. A statement that the examination was conducted in accordance with attestation standards established by the American Institute of Certified Public Accountants

f. A statement that such standards require that the auditor plan and perform the examination to obtain reasonable assurance about whether effective internal control was maintained in all material respects

g. A statement that an examination includes obtaining an understanding of internal control, assessing the risk that a material weakness exists, testing and evaluating the design and operating effectiveness of internal control based on the assessed risk, and performing such other procedures as the auditor considers necessary in the circumstances

h. A statement that the auditor believes the examination provides a reasonable basis for his or her opinion

i. A definition of internal control (the auditor should use the same description of the entity's internal control as management uses in its report)

j. A paragraph stating that, because of inherent limitations, internal control may not prevent, or detect and correct misstatements and that projections of any evaluation of effectiveness to future periods are subject to the risk that controls may become inadequate because of changes in conditions, or that the degree of compliance with the policies or procedures may deteriorate

---

[27] Report modifications are discussed further beginning at paragraph .115.

[28] The auditor may report directly on the entity's internal control or on management's written assertion, except as described in paragraph .112.

[29] Because the examination of internal control is integrated with the audit of the financial statements and an examination provides the same level of assurance as an audit, the auditor may refer to the examination of internal control as an audit in his or her report or other communications.

k. The auditor's opinion on whether the entity maintained, in all material respects, effective internal control as of the specified date, based on the control criteria; or, the auditor's opinion on whether management's assertion about the effectiveness of the entity's internal control as of the specified date is fairly stated, in all material respects, based on the control criteria

l. The manual or printed signature of the auditor's firm

m. The date of the report

Separate or Combined Reports

.108 The auditor may choose to issue a combined report (that is, one report containing both an opinion on the financial statements and an opinion on internal control) or separate reports on the entity's financial statements and on internal control.

.109 If the auditor issues a separate report on internal control, he or she should add the following paragraph to the auditor's report on the financial statements:

> We also have examined [*or audited*][30] in accordance with attestation standards established by the American Institute of Certified Public Accountants, [*company name*]'s internal control over financial reporting as of December 31, 20X8, based on [*identify control criteria*] and our report dated [*date of report, which should be the same as the date of the report on the financial statements*] expressed [*include nature of opinion*].

The auditor also should add the following paragraph to the report on internal control:

> We also have audited, in accordance with auditing standards generally accepted in the United States of America, the [*identify financial statements*] of [*company name*] and our report dated [*date of report, which should be the same as the date of the report on internal control*] expressed [*include nature of opinion*].

Report Date

.110 The auditor should date the report no earlier than the date on which the auditor has obtained sufficient appropriate evidence to support the auditor's opinion. Because the examination of internal control is integrated with the audit of the financial statements, the dates of the reports should be the same.

Adverse Opinions

.111 Paragraphs .82–.92 describe the evaluation of deficiencies. If there are deficiencies that, individually or in combination, result in one or more material weaknesses as of the date specified in management's assertion, the auditor should express an adverse opinion on the entity's internal control, unless there is a restriction on the scope of the engagement.[31]

.112 When internal control is not effective because one or more material weaknesses exist, the auditor is prohibited from expressing an opinion on management's assertion and should report directly on the effectiveness of internal control. In addition, the auditor's report should include

---

[30] See footnote 29.

[31] See paragraph .117 when the scope of the engagement has been restricted.

- the definition of a material weakness.
- a statement that one or more material weaknesses have been identified and an identification of the material weaknesses described in management's assertion. The auditor's report need only refer to the material weaknesses described in management's report and need not include a description of each material weakness, provided each material weakness is included and fairly presented in all material respects in management's report, as described in the following paragraph.

.113 If one or more material weaknesses have not been included in management's report accompanying the auditor's report, the auditor's report should be modified to state that one or more material weaknesses have been identified but not included in management's report. Additionally, the auditor's report should include a description of each material weakness not included in management's report, which should provide the users of the report with specific information about the nature of each material weakness and its actual and potential effect on the presentation of the entity's financial statements issued during the existence of the weakness. In this case, the auditor also should communicate, in writing, to those charged with governance that one or more material weaknesses were not disclosed or identified as a material weakness in management's report. If one or more material weaknesses have been included in management's report but the auditor concludes that the disclosure of such material weaknesses is not fairly presented in all material respects, the auditor's report should describe this conclusion as well as the information necessary to fairly describe each material weakness.

.114 The auditor should determine the effect an adverse opinion on internal control has on his or her opinion on the financial statements. Additionally, the auditor should disclose whether his or her opinion on the financial statements was affected by the material weaknesses.[32]

Report Modifications

.115 The auditor should modify his or her report if any of the following conditions exist:

a. Elements of management's report are incomplete or improperly presented.

b. There is a restriction on the scope of the engagement.

c. The auditor decides to refer to the report of another auditor as the basis, in part, for the auditor's own report.

d. There is other information contained in management's report.

Elements of Management's Report Are Incomplete or Improperly Presented

.116 If the auditor determines that any required element of management's report (see paragraph .95) is incomplete or improperly presented and management does not revise its report, the auditor should modify his or her report to include an explanatory paragraph describing the reasons for this determination. If the auditor determines that the required disclosure about one or more

---

[32] If the auditor issues a separate report on internal control in this circumstance, the disclosure required by this paragraph may be combined with the report language described in paragraph .109. The auditor may present the combined language either as a separate paragraph or as part of the paragraph that identifies the material weakness.

material weaknesses is not fairly presented in all material respects, the auditor should apply paragraph .113.

Scope Limitations

.117 The auditor may express an opinion on the entity's internal control only if the auditor has been able to apply the procedures necessary in the circumstances. If there are restrictions on the scope of the engagement, the auditor should withdraw from the engagement or disclaim an opinion.

.118 When disclaiming an opinion because of a scope limitation, the auditor should state that he or she does not express an opinion on the effectiveness of internal control and, in a separate paragraph or paragraphs, the substantive reasons for the disclaimer. The auditor should not identify the procedures that were performed nor include the statements describing the characteristics of an examination of internal control (paragraph .107[d–h]); to do so might overshadow the disclaimer.

.119 When the auditor plans to disclaim an opinion and the limited procedures performed by the auditor caused the auditor to conclude that one or more material weaknesses exist, the auditor's report also should include

- the definition of a material weakness.
- a description of any material weaknesses identified in the entity's internal control. This description should address the requirements in paragraph .112 and should provide the users of the report with specific information about the nature of any material weakness and its actual and potential effect on the presentation of the entity's financial statements issued during the existence of the weakness. The auditor also should apply the requirements in paragraph .114.

.120 The auditor may issue a report disclaiming an opinion on internal control as soon as the auditor concludes that a scope limitation will prevent the auditor from obtaining the reasonable assurance necessary to express an opinion.[33] The auditor is not required to perform any additional work prior to issuing a disclaimer when the auditor concludes that he or she will not be able to obtain sufficient appropriate evidence to express an opinion.

.121 If the auditor concludes that he or she cannot express an opinion because there has been a limitation on the scope of the examination, the auditor should communicate, in writing, to management and those charged with governance that the examination of internal control cannot be satisfactorily completed.

Opinion Based, in Part, on the Report of Another Auditor

.122 When another auditor has examined the internal control of one or more subsidiaries, divisions, branches, or components of the entity, the auditor should determine whether he or she may serve as the principal auditor and use the work and reports of another auditor as a basis, in part, for his or her opinion. AU section 543, *Part of Audit Performed by Other Independent Auditors*, establishes requirements and provides guidance on the auditor's decision of whether to serve as the principal auditor of the financial statements. The auditor should

[33] In this case, in following paragraph .110 regarding dating the report, the report date is the date that the auditor has obtained sufficient appropriate evidence to support the representations in the report.

apply paragraphs .02–.03 of AU section 543 in deciding whether he or she may serve as the principal auditor of the examination of internal control.

.123 When serving as the principal auditor of internal control, the auditor should decide whether to make reference in his or her report on internal control to the examination of internal control performed by the other auditor. In these circumstances, the decision is based on factors analogous to those of the auditor who uses the work and reports of other independent auditors when reporting on an entity's financial statements as described in AU section 543.

.124 The decision about whether to make reference to another auditor in the report on the examination of internal control might differ from the corresponding decision as it relates to the audit of the financial statements. For example, the audit report on the financial statements may make reference to the audit of a significant equity investment performed by another independent auditor, but the report on internal control might not make a similar reference because management's assertion ordinarily would not extend to controls at the equity method investee.[34]

.125 When the principal auditor decides to make reference to the report of the other auditor as a basis, in part, for his or her opinion on the entity's internal control, the principal auditor should refer to the report of the other auditor when describing the scope of the examination and when expressing the opinion. Whether the other auditor's opinion is expressed on management's assertion or on internal control does not affect the determination of whether the principal auditor's opinion is expressed on management's assertion or on internal control.

Management's Report Contains Additional Information

.126 Management's report accompanying the auditor's report may contain information in addition to the elements described in paragraph .95 that are subject to the auditor's evaluation.[35] If management's report could reasonably be viewed by users of the report as including such additional information, the auditor should disclaim an opinion on the information.

.127 The auditor may use the following sample language as the last paragraph of the auditor's report to disclaim an opinion on such additional information:

> We do not express an opinion or any other form of assurance on [*describe additional information, such as management's cost-benefit statement*].

.128 If the auditor believes that management's additional information contains a material misstatement of fact, he or she should apply the guidance in paragraphs .92–.94 of AT section 101 and take appropriate action. If the auditor concludes that a material misstatement of fact remains, the auditor should notify management and those charged with governance, in writing, of the auditor's views concerning the information. AU section 317, *Illegal Acts by Clients*, also may require the auditor to take additional action.

---

[34] See paragraph .140 for further discussion of the evaluation of the controls for an equity method investment.

[35] An entity may publish various documents that contain information in addition to management's report and the auditor's report on internal control. Paragraphs .91–.94 of AT section 101 provide guidance to the auditor in these circumstances. If management makes the types of disclosures described in paragraph .126 outside its report and includes them elsewhere within a document that includes the auditor's report, the auditor would not need to disclaim an opinion on such information. However, in that situation, the auditor's responsibilities are the same as those described in paragraph .128, if the auditor believes that the additional information contains a material misstatement of fact.

Subsequent Events

.129 Changes in internal control or other factors that might significantly affect internal control might occur subsequent to the date as of which internal control is being examined but before the date of the auditor's report. The auditor should inquire of management whether there were any such changes or factors and obtain written representations from management relating to such matters, as described in paragraph .97.

.130 To obtain additional information about changes in internal control or other factors that might significantly affect the effectiveness of the entity's internal control, the auditor should inquire about and examine, for this subsequent period, the following:

- Relevant internal audit (or similar functions, such as loan review in a financial institution) reports issued during the subsequent period
- Independent auditor reports (if other than the auditor's) of deficiencies
- Regulatory agency reports on the entity's internal control
- Information about the effectiveness of the entity's internal control obtained through other engagements

.131 The auditor might inquire about and examine other documents for the subsequent period. Paragraphs .01–.09 of AU section 560, *Subsequent Events*, establish requirements and provide guidance on subsequent events for a financial statement audit that also may be helpful to the auditor performing an examination of internal control.

.132 If, subsequent to the date as of which internal control is being examined but before the date of the auditor's report, the auditor obtains knowledge about a material weakness that existed as of the date specified in management's assertion, the auditor should report directly on internal control and issue an adverse opinion, as required by paragraph .111. The auditor should also follow paragraph .116 if management's assertion states that internal control is effective. If the auditor is unable to determine the effect of the matter on the effectiveness of the entity's internal control as of the date specified in management's assertion, the auditor should disclaim an opinion. As described in paragraph .126, the auditor should disclaim an opinion on management's disclosures about corrective actions taken by the entity, if any.

.133 The auditor may obtain knowledge about conditions that did not exist at the date specified in management's assertion but arose subsequent to that date and before the release of the auditor's report. If a subsequent event of this type has a material effect on the entity's internal control, the auditor should include in his or her report an explanatory paragraph describing the event and its effects or directing the reader's attention to the event and its effects as disclosed in management's report.

.134 The auditor has no responsibility to keep informed of events subsequent to the date of his or her report; however, after the release of the report on internal control, the auditor may become aware of conditions that existed at the report date that might have affected the auditor's opinion had he or she been aware of them. The evaluation of such subsequent information is similar to the evaluation of information discovered subsequent to the date of the report on an audit of financial statements, as described in AU section 561, *Subsequent Discovery of Facts Existing at the Date of the Auditor's Report*.

Special Topics

Entities With Multiple Locations

.135 In determining the locations or business units at which to perform tests of controls, the auditor should assess the risk of material misstatement to the financial statements associated with the location or business unit and correlate the amount of attention devoted to the location or business unit with the degree of risk. The auditor may eliminate from further consideration locations or business units that, individually or when aggregated with others, do not present a reasonable possibility of material misstatement to the entity's consolidated financial statements.

.136 In assessing and responding to risk, the auditor should test controls over specific risks that present a reasonable possibility of material misstatement to the entity's consolidated financial statements. In lower risk locations or business units, the auditor first might evaluate whether testing entity-level controls, including controls in place to provide assurance that appropriate controls exist throughout the organization, provides the auditor with sufficient appropriate evidence.

.137 In determining the locations or business units at which to perform tests of controls, the auditor may take into account work performed by others on behalf of management. For example, if the internal auditors' planned procedures include relevant audit work at various locations, the auditor may coordinate work with the internal auditors and reduce the number of locations or business units at which the auditor would otherwise need to perform examination procedures.

.138 In applying the requirement in paragraph .81 regarding special considerations for subsequent years' examinations, the auditor should vary the nature, timing, and extent of testing of controls at locations or business units from year to year.

Special Situations

.139 The scope of the examination should include entities that are acquired on or before the date of management's assertion and operations that are accounted for as discontinued operations on the date of management's assertion that are reported in accordance with the applicable financial reporting framework in the entity's financial statements.

.140 For equity method investments, the scope of the examination should include controls over the reporting in accordance with the applicable financial reporting framework, in the entity's financial statements, of the entity's portion of the investees' income or loss, the investment balance, adjustments to the income or loss and investment balance, and related disclosures. The examination ordinarily would not extend to controls at the equity method investee.

.141 In situations in which a regulator allows management to limit its assertion by excluding certain entities, the auditor may limit the examination in the same manner. In these situations, the auditor's opinion would not be affected by a scope limitation. However, the auditor should include, either in an additional explanatory paragraph or as part of the scope paragraph in his or her report, a disclosure similar to management's regarding the exclusion of an entity from the scope of both management's assertion and the auditor's examination of internal control. Additionally, the auditor should evaluate the reasonableness of management's conclusion that the situation meets the criteria of the regulator's allowed exclusion and the appropriateness of any required disclosure related to such a limitation. If the auditor believes that management's disclosure about the limitation requires modification, the auditor should communicate the matter to the appropriate level of management. If, in the auditor's judgment, management does not respond appropriately to the auditor's communication within a reasonable period of time, the auditor should inform those charged with governance of the matter as soon as practicable. If management and those charged with governance do not respond appropriately, the auditor should modify his or her report on the examination of internal control to include an explanatory paragraph describing the reasons why the auditor believes management's disclosure requires modification.

Use of Service Organizations

.142 AU section 324 [36] applies to the audit of financial statements of an entity that obtains services from another organization that are part of the entity's information and communication systems. The auditor may apply the relevant concepts described in AU section 324 to the examination of internal control.

.143 Paragraph .03 of AU section 324 describes the situation in which a service organization's services are part of an entity's information and communication systems. If the service organization's services are part of an entity's information and communication systems, as described therein, then they are part of the information and communication component of the entity's internal control. When the service organization's services are part of the entity's internal control, the auditor should consider the activities of the service organization when determining the evidence required to support his or her opinion.

.144 The auditor should perform the procedures in paragraphs .07–.16 of AU section 324 with respect to the activities performed by the service organization. These procedures include

a. obtaining an understanding of the controls at the service organization that are relevant to the entity's internal control and the controls at the user organization over the activities of the service organization; and

b. obtaining evidence that the controls that are relevant to the auditor's opinion are operating effectively.

.145 Evidence that the controls that are relevant to the auditor's opinion on internal control are operating effectively may be obtained by following the procedures described in paragraph .12 of AU section 324. These procedures include one or more of the following:

a. Obtaining a service auditor's report on management's description of a service organization's system and the suitability of the design and operating effectiveness of controls, which includes a description of the service auditor's tests of controls and results (a type 2 report), [37] or a report on the application of agreed-upon procedures that describes relevant tests of controls. If the evidence regarding operating effectiveness of controls

---

[36] AU section 324, *Service Organizations*, contains the requirements and application guidance for auditors of the financial statements of entities that use a service organization (user auditors). [Footnote added, August 2011, to reflect conforming changes necessary due to the issuance of SSAE No. 16.]

[37] A report on management's description of a service organization's system and the suitability of the design of controls (a type 1 report) does not include a description of the service auditor's tests of controls and results of those tests or the service auditor's opinion on the operating effectiveness of controls and therefore does not provide evidence of the operating effectiveness of controls. Type 1 and type 2 reports are defined in paragraph .07 of AT section 801, *Reporting on Controls at a Service Organization*. [Footnote revised and renumbered, August 2011, to reflect conforming changes necessary due to the issuance of SSAE No. 16.]

comes from an agreed-upon procedures report rather than a type 2 service auditor's report issued pursuant to AT section 801, the auditor should evaluate whether the agreed-upon procedures report provides sufficient appropriate evidence in the same manner described in paragraph .146.

b. Performing tests of the user organization's controls over the activities of the service organization (for example, testing the user organization's independent reperformance of selected items processed by the service organization or testing the user organization's reconciliation of output reports with source documents).

c. Performing tests of controls at the service organization.

[Revised, August 2011, to reflect conforming changes necessary due to the issuance of SSAE No. 16.]

.146 If a service auditor's type 2 report is available, the auditor may evaluate whether this report provides sufficient appropriate evidence to support his or her opinion on internal control. In evaluating whether such a service auditor's report provides sufficient appropriate evidence, the auditor should assess the following factors: [38]

- The time period covered by the tests of controls and its relation to the as-of date of management's assertion
- The scope of the examination and applications covered, the controls tested, and the way in which tested controls relate to the entity's controls
- The results of those tests of controls and the service auditor's opinion on the operating effectiveness of the controls

[Revised, August 2011, to reflect conforming changes necessary due to the issuance of SSAE No. 16.]

.147 If the service auditor's type 2 report contains a statement indicating that the control objectives stated in the description can be achieved only if complementary user entity controls are suitably designed and operating effectively, along with the controls at the service organization, the auditor should evaluate whether the entity is applying the necessary controls. [Revised, August 2011, to reflect conforming changes necessary due to the issuance of SSAE No. 16.]

.148 In determining whether the type 2 service auditor's report provides sufficient appropriate evidence to support the auditor's opinion on internal control, the auditor should make inquiries concerning the service auditor's reputation, competence, and independence. Appropriate sources of information concerning the professional reputation of the service auditor are discussed in paragraph .10(*a*) of AU section 543. [Revised, August 2011, to reflect conforming changes necessary due to the issuance of SSAE No. 16.]

.149 When a significant period of time has elapsed between the time period covered by the tests of controls in the service auditor's report and the date specified in management's assertion, additional procedures should be performed. The auditor should inquire of management to determine whether management has identified any changes in the service organization's controls subsequent to the period covered by the service auditor's report (such as changes

---

[38] These factors are similar to factors the auditor would consider in determining whether the report provides sufficient appropriate evidence to support the auditor's assessed level of control risk in an audit of the financial statements, as described in paragraph .16 of AU section 324. [Footnote renumbered, August 2011, to reflect conforming changes necessary due to the issuance of SSAE No. 16.]

communicated to management from the service organization, changes in personnel at the service organization with whom management interacts, changes in reports or other data received from the service organization, changes in contracts or service level agreements with the service organization, or errors identified in the service organization's processing). If management has identified such changes, the auditor should evaluate the effect of such changes on the effectiveness of the entity's internal control. The auditor also should evaluate whether the results of other procedures he or she performed indicate that there have been changes in the controls at the service organization.

.150 As risk increases, the need for the auditor to obtain additional evidence increases. Accordingly, the auditor should determine whether to obtain additional evidence about the operating effectiveness of controls at the service organization based on the procedures performed by management or the auditor and the results of those procedures and on an evaluation of the following risk factors:

- The elapsed time between the time period covered by the tests of controls in the service auditor's report and the date specified in management's assertion
- The significance of the activities of the service organization
- Whether there are errors that have been identified in the service organization's processing
- The nature and significance of any changes in the service organization's controls identified by management or the auditor

.151 If the auditor concludes that additional evidence about the operating effectiveness of controls at the service organization is required, the auditor's additional procedures might include

- evaluating procedures performed by management and the results of those procedures.
- contacting the service organization, through the user organization, to obtain specific information.
- requesting that a service auditor be engaged to perform procedures that will supply the necessary information.
- visiting the service organization and performing such procedures.

.152 The auditor should not refer to the service auditor's report when expressing an opinion on internal control.

Benchmarking of Automated Controls

.153 Entirely automated application controls are generally less susceptible to breakdowns due to human failure. This feature may allow the auditor to use a benchmarking strategy.

.154 If general controls over program changes, access to programs, and computer operations are effective and continue to be tested, and if the auditor verifies that the automated application control has not changed since the auditor established a baseline (that is, last tested the application control), the auditor may conclude that the automated application control continues to be effective without repeating the prior year's specific tests of the operation of the automated application control. The nature and extent of the evidence that the auditor should obtain to verify that the control has not changed may vary depending on the circumstances, including the strength of the entity's program change controls.

.155 The consistent and effective functioning of the automated application controls may be dependent upon the related files, tables, data, and parameters. For example, an automated application for calculating interest income might be dependent on the continued integrity of a rate table used by the automated calculation.

.156 To determine whether to use a benchmarking strategy, the auditor should assess the following risk factors. As these factors indicate lower risk, the control being evaluated might be well-suited for benchmarking. As these factors indicate increased risk, the control being evaluated is less suited for benchmarking. These factors are

- the extent to which the application control can be matched to a defined program within an application.
- the extent to which the application is stable (that is, there are few changes from period to period).
- the availability and reliability of a report of the compilation dates of the programs placed in production. (This information may be used as evidence that controls within the program have not changed.)

.157 Benchmarking automated application controls can be especially effective for entities using purchased software when the possibility of program changes is remote (for example, when the vendor does not allow access or modification to the source code).

.158 After a period of time, the length of which depends upon the circumstances, the baseline of the operation of an automated application control should be reestablished. To determine when to reestablish a baseline, the auditor should evaluate the following factors:

- The effectiveness of the IT control environment, including controls over application and system software acquisition and maintenance, access controls, and computer operations.
- The auditor's understanding of the nature of changes, if any, on the specific programs that contain the controls.
- The nature and timing of other related tests.
- The consequences of errors associated with the application control that was benchmarked.
- Whether the control is sensitive to other business factors that may have changed. For example, an automated control may have been designed with the assumption that only positive amounts will exist in a file. Such a control would no longer be effective if negative amounts (credits) begin to be posted to the account.

Integration With the Financial Statement Audit

Tests of Controls in an Examination of Internal Control

.159 The objective of the tests of controls in an examination of internal control is to obtain evidence about the effectiveness of controls to support the auditor's opinion on the entity's internal control. The auditor's opinion relates to the effectiveness of the entity's internal control as of a point in time and taken as a whole.

.160 To express an opinion on internal control as of a point in time, the auditor should obtain evidence that internal control has operated effectively for a sufficient period of time, which may be less than the entire period (ordinarily one year) covered by the entity's financial statements. To express an opinion on internal control taken as a whole, the auditor should obtain evidence about the effectiveness of selected controls over all relevant assertions. This entails testing the design and operating effectiveness of controls ordinarily not tested when expressing an opinion only on the financial statements.

.161 When concluding on the effectiveness of internal control for purposes of expressing an opinion on internal control, the auditor should incorporate the results of any additional tests of controls performed to achieve the objective related to expressing an opinion on the financial statements, as discussed in the following section.

Tests of Controls in an Audit of Financial Statements

.162 To express an opinion on the financial statements, the auditor ordinarily performs tests of controls and substantive procedures. Tests of controls are performed when the auditor's risk assessment includes an expectation of the operating effectiveness of controls or when substantive procedures alone do not provide sufficient appropriate audit evidence at the relevant assertion level.[39] Tests of controls are designed to obtain sufficient appropriate audit evidence that the controls are operating effectively throughout the period of reliance.[40] However, the auditor is not required to test controls for all relevant assertions and, for a variety of reasons, the auditor may choose not to do so.

.163 When concluding on the effectiveness of controls for the purpose of the financial statement audit, the auditor also should evaluate the results of any additional tests of controls performed by the auditor to achieve the objective related to expressing an opinion on the entity's internal control, as discussed in paragraph .160. Consideration of these results may cause the auditor to alter the nature, timing, and extent of substantive procedures and to plan and perform further tests of controls, particularly in response to identified deficiencies.

Effect of Tests of Controls on Substantive Procedures

.164 If, during the examination of internal control, the auditor identifies a deficiency, he or she should determine the effect of the deficiency, if any, on the nature, timing, and extent of substantive procedures to be performed to reduce audit risk in the audit of the financial statements to an appropriately low level.

.165 Regardless of the assessed risk of material misstatement in connection with the audit of the financial statements, the auditor should perform substantive procedures for all relevant assertions related to each material class of transactions, account balance, and disclosure.[41] Performing procedures to express an opinion on internal control does not diminish this requirement. [Footnote renumbered, August 2011, to reflect conforming changes necessary due to the issuance of SSAE No. 16.]

Effect of Substantive Procedures on Conclusions About the Operating Effectiveness of Controls

.166 In an examination of internal control, the auditor should evaluate the effect of the findings of the substantive procedures performed in the audit of

---

[39] See paragraph .23 of AU section 318, *Performing Audit Procedures in Response to Assessed Risks and Evaluating the Audit Evidence Obtained*. [Footnote renumbered, August 2011, to reflect conforming changes necessary due to the issuance of SSAE No. 16.]

[40] See paragraph .46 of AU section 318. [Footnote renumbered, August 2011, to reflect conforming changes necessary due to the issuance of SSAE No. 16.]

[41] See paragraphs .09 and .51 of AU section 318. [Footnote renumbered, August 2011, to reflect conforming changes necessary due to the issuance of SSAE No. 16.]

financial statements on the effectiveness of internal control. This evaluation should include, at a minimum

- the risk assessments in connection with the selection and application of substantive procedures, especially those related to fraud.
- findings with respect to illegal acts and related party transactions.
- indications of management bias in making accounting estimates and in selecting accounting principles.
- misstatements detected by substantive procedures. The extent of such misstatements might alter the auditor's judgment about the effectiveness of controls.

.167 To obtain evidence about whether a selected control is effective, the control should be tested directly; the operating effectiveness of a control cannot be inferred from the absence of misstatements detected by substantive procedures. The absence of misstatements detected by substantive procedures, however, may affect the auditor's risk assessments in determining the testing necessary to conclude on the operating effectiveness of a control.

Effective Date

.168 This section is effective for integrated audits for periods ending on or after December 15, 2008. Earlier implementation is permitted.

.169

Exhibit A—Illustrative Reports

1. The following illustrate the report elements described in this section. These illustrative reports refer to an examination; however, the auditor may refer to the examination of internal control as an audit.[1]

2. Report modifications are discussed beginning at paragraph .115 of this section.

Example 1: Unqualified Opinion on Internal Control

3. The following is an illustrative report expressing an unqualified opinion directly on internal control.

Independent Auditor's Report

[*Introductory paragraph*]

We have examined W Company's internal control over financial reporting as of December 31, 20XX, based on [*identify criteria*].[2] W Company's management is responsible for maintaining effective internal control over financial reporting, and for its assertion of the effectiveness of internal control over financial reporting, included in the accompanying [*title of management's report*]. Our responsibility is to express an opinion on W Company's internal control over financial reporting based on our examination.

[*Scope paragraph*]

We conducted our examination in accordance with attestation standards established by the American Institute of Certified Public Accountants. Those standards require that we plan and perform the examination to obtain reasonable assurance about whether effective internal control over financial reporting was maintained in all material respects. Our examination included obtaining an understanding of internal control over financial reporting, assessing the risk that a material weakness exists, and testing and evaluating the design and operating effectiveness of internal control based on the assessed risk. Our examination also included performing such other procedures as we considered necessary in the circumstances. We believe that our examination provides a reasonable basis for our opinion.

[*Definition paragraph*]

An entity's internal control over financial reporting is a process effected by those charged with governance, management, and other personnel, designed to provide reasonable assurance regarding the preparation of reliable financial statements in accordance with [*applicable financial reporting framework, such as accounting principles generally accepted in the United States of America*]. An entity's internal control over financial reporting includes those policies and procedures that (1) pertain to the maintenance of records that, in reasonable detail, accurately and fairly reflect the transactions and dispositions of the assets of the entity; (2) provide reasonable assurance that transactions are recorded as

---

[1] Because the examination of internal control is integrated with the audit of the financial statements and an examination provides the same level of assurance as an audit, the auditor may refer to the examination of internal control as an audit in his or her report or other communications.

[2] For example, the following may be used to identify the criteria: "criteria established in *Internal Control—Integrated Framework* issued by the Committee of Sponsoring Organizations of the Treadway Commission (COSO)."

necessary to permit preparation of financial statements in accordance with [*applicable financial reporting framework, such as accounting principles generally accepted in the United States of America*], and that receipts and expenditures of the entity are being made only in accordance with authorizations of management and those charged with governance; and (3) provide reasonable assurance regarding prevention, or timely detection and correction of unauthorized acquisition, use, or disposition of the entity's assets that could have a material effect on the financial statements.

[*Inherent limitations paragraph*]

Because of its inherent limitations, internal control over financial reporting may not prevent, or detect and correct misstatements. Also, projections of any evaluation of effectiveness to future periods are subject to the risk that controls may become inadequate because of changes in conditions, or that the degree of compliance with the policies or procedures may deteriorate.

[*Opinion paragraph*]

In our opinion, W Company maintained, in all material respects, effective internal control over financial reporting as of December 31, 20XX, based on [*identify criteria*].

[*Audit of financial statements paragraph*]

We also have audited, in accordance with auditing standards generally accepted in the United States of America, the [*identify financial statements*] of W Company and our report dated [*date of report, which should be the same as the date of the report on the examination of internal control*] expressed [*include nature of opinion*].

[*Signature*]

[*Date*]

Example 2: Unqualified Opinion on Management's Assertion

4. The following is an illustrative report expressing an unqualified opinion on management's assertion.

<u>Independent Auditor's Report</u>

[*Introductory paragraph*]

We have examined management's assertion, included in the accompanying [*title of management report*], that W Company maintained effective internal control over financial reporting as of December 31, 20XX based on [*identify criteria*].[3] W Company's management is responsible for maintaining effective internal control over financial reporting, and for its assertion of the effectiveness of internal control over financial reporting, included in the accompanying [*title of management's report*]. Our responsibility is to express an opinion on management's assertion based on our examination.

[*Scope paragraph*]

We conducted our examination in accordance with attestation standards established by the American Institute of Certified Public Accountants. Those standards require that we plan and perform the examination to obtain reasonable

[3] See footnote 2 of this exhibit.

assurance about whether effective internal control over financial reporting was maintained in all material respects. Our examination included obtaining an understanding of internal control over financial reporting, assessing the risk that a material weakness exists, and testing and evaluating the design and operating effectiveness of internal control based on the assessed risk. Our examination also included performing such other procedures as we considered necessary in the circumstances. We believe that our examination provides a reasonable basis for our opinion.

[*Definition paragraph*]

An entity's internal control over financial reporting is a process effected by those charged with governance, management, and other personnel, designed to provide reasonable assurance regarding the preparation of reliable financial statements in accordance with [*applicable financial reporting framework, such as accounting principles generally accepted in the United States of America*]. An entity's internal control over financial reporting includes those policies and procedures that (1) pertain to the maintenance of records that, in reasonable detail, accurately and fairly reflect the transactions and dispositions of the assets of the entity; (2) provide reasonable assurance that transactions are recorded as necessary to permit preparation of financial statements in accordance with [*applicable financial reporting framework, such as accounting principles generally accepted in the United States of America*], and that receipts and expenditures of the entity are being made only in accordance with authorizations of management and those charged with governance; and (3) provide reasonable assurance regarding prevention, or timely detection and correction of unauthorized acquisition, use, or disposition of the entity's assets that could have a material effect on the financial statements.

[*Inherent limitations paragraph*]

Because of its inherent limitations, internal control over financial reporting may not prevent, or detect and correct misstatements. Also, projections of any evaluation of effectiveness to future periods are subject to the risk that controls may become inadequate because of changes in conditions, or that the degree of compliance with the policies or procedures may deteriorate.

[*Opinion paragraph*]

In our opinion, management's assertion that W Company maintained effective internal control over financial reporting as of December 31, 20XX is fairly stated, in all material respects, based on [*identify criteria*].

[*Audit of financial statements paragraph*]

We also have audited, in accordance with auditing standards generally accepted in the United States of America, the [*identify financial statements*] of W Company and our report dated [*date of report, which should be the same as the date of the report on the examination of internal control*] expressed [*include nature of opinion*].

[*Signature*]

[*Date*]

Example 3: Adverse Opinion on Internal Control

5. The following is an illustrative report expressing an adverse opinion on internal control. In this example, the opinion on the financial statements is not affected by the adverse opinion on internal control.

Independent Auditor's Report

[*Introductory paragraph*]

We have examined W Company's internal control over financial reporting as of December 31, 20XX, based on [*identify criteria*].[4] W Company's management is responsible for maintaining effective internal control over financial reporting, and for its assertion of the effectiveness of internal control over financial reporting, included in the accompanying [*title of management's report*]. Our responsibility is to express an opinion on W Company's internal control over financial reporting based on our examination.

[*Scope paragraph*]

We conducted our examination in accordance with attestation standards established by the American Institute of Certified Public Accountants. Those standards require that we plan and perform the examination to obtain reasonable assurance about whether effective internal control over financial reporting was maintained in all material respects. Our examination included obtaining an understanding of internal control over financial reporting, assessing the risk that a material weakness exists, and testing and evaluating the design and operating effectiveness of internal control based on the assessed risk. Our examination also included performing such other procedures as we considered necessary in the circumstances. We believe that our examination provides a reasonable basis for our opinion.

[*Definition paragraph*]

An entity's internal control over financial reporting is a process effected by those charged with governance, management, and other personnel, designed to provide reasonable assurance regarding the preparation of reliable financial statements in accordance with [*applicable financial reporting framework, such as accounting principles generally accepted in the United States of America*]. An entity's internal control over financial reporting includes those policies and procedures that (1) pertain to the maintenance of records that, in reasonable detail, accurately and fairly reflect the transactions and dispositions of the assets of the entity; (2) provide reasonable assurance that transactions are recorded as necessary to permit preparation of financial statements in accordance with [*applicable financial reporting framework, such as accounting principles generally accepted in the United States of America*], and that receipts and expenditures of the entity are being made only in accordance with authorizations of management and those charged with governance; and (3) provide reasonable assurance regarding prevention, or timely detection and correction of unauthorized acquisition, use, or disposition of the entity's assets that could have a material effect on the financial statements.

[*Inherent limitations paragraph*]

Because of its inherent limitations, internal control over financial reporting may not prevent, or detect and correct misstatements. Also, projections of any evaluation of effectiveness to future periods are subject to the risk that controls may become inadequate because of changes in conditions, or that the degree of compliance with the policies or procedures may deteriorate.

[*Explanatory paragraph*]

A material weakness is a deficiency, or a combination of deficiencies, in internal control over financial reporting, such that there is a reasonable possibility

[4] See footnote 2 of this exhibit.

that a material misstatement of the entity's financial statements will not be prevented, or detected and corrected on a timely basis. The following material weakness has been identified and included in the accompanying [*title of management's report*].

[*Identify the material weakness described in management's report.*][5]

[*Opinion paragraph*]

In our opinion, because of the effect of the material weakness described above on the achievement of the objectives of the control criteria, W Company has not maintained effective internal control over financial reporting as of December 31, 20XX, based on [*identify criteria*].

[*Audit of financial statements paragraph*]

We also have audited, in accordance with auditing standards generally accepted in the United States of America, the [*identify financial statements*] of W Company. We considered the material weakness identified above in determining the nature, timing, and extent of audit tests applied in our audit of the 20XX financial statements, and this report does not affect our report dated [*date of report, which should be the same as the date of the report on the examination of internal control*], which expressed [*include nature of opinion*].

[*Signature*]

[*Date*]

Example 4: Disclaimer of Opinion on Internal Control

6. The following is an illustrative report expressing a disclaimer of opinion on internal control. In this example, the auditor is applying paragraph .119 of this section because a material weakness was identified during the limited procedures performed by the auditor.

Independent Auditor's Report

[*Introductory paragraph*]

We were engaged to examine W Company's internal control over financial reporting as of December 31, 20XX, based on [*identify criteria*].[6] W Company's management is responsible for maintaining effective internal control over financial reporting, and for its assertion of the effectiveness of internal control over financial reporting, included in the accompanying [*title of management's report*].

[*Paragraph that describes the substantive reasons for the scope limitation*] Accordingly, we were unable to perform auditing procedures necessary to form an opinion on W Company's internal control over financial reporting as of December 31, 20XX.

[*Definition paragraph*]

An entity's internal control over financial reporting is a process effected by those charged with governance, management, and other personnel, designed

---

[5] See paragraphs .111–.114 of this section for specific reporting requirements. The auditor's report need only refer to the material weaknesses described in management's report and need not include a description of each material weakness, provided each material weakness is included and fairly presented in all material respects in management's report.

[6] See footnote 2 of this exhibit.

to provide reasonable assurance regarding the preparation of reliable financial statements in accordance with [*applicable financial reporting framework, such as accounting principles generally accepted in the United States of America*]. An entity's internal control over financial reporting includes those policies and procedures that (1) pertain to the maintenance of records that, in reasonable detail, accurately and fairly reflect the transactions and dispositions of the assets of the entity; (2) provide reasonable assurance that transactions are recorded as necessary to permit preparation of financial statements in accordance with [*applicable financial reporting framework, such as accounting principles generally accepted in the United States of America*], and that receipts and expenditures of the entity are being made only in accordance with authorizations of management and those charged with governance; and (3) provide reasonable assurance regarding prevention, or timely detection and correction of unauthorized acquisition, use, or disposition of the entity's assets that could have a material effect on the financial statements.

[*Inherent limitations paragraph*]

Because of its inherent limitations, internal control over financial reporting may not prevent, or detect and correct misstatements. Also, projections of any evaluation of effectiveness to future periods are subject to the risk that controls may become inadequate because of changes in conditions, or that the degree of compliance with the policies or procedures may deteriorate.

[*Explanatory paragraph*]

A material weakness is a deficiency, or a combination of deficiencies, in internal control over financial reporting, such that there is a reasonable possibility that a material misstatement of the entity's financial statements will not be prevented, or detected and corrected on a timely basis. If one or more material weaknesses exist, an entity's internal control over financial reporting cannot be considered effective. The following material weakness has been identified and included in the accompanying [*title of management's report*].

[*Identify the material weakness described in management's report and include a description of the material weakness, including its nature and its actual and potential effect on the presentation of the entity's financial statements issued during the existence of the material weakness.*]

[*Opinion paragraph*]

Because of the limitation on the scope of our audit described in the second paragraph, the scope of our work was not sufficient to enable us to express, and we do not express, an opinion on the effectiveness W Company's internal control over financial reporting.

[*Audit of financial statements paragraph*]

We have audited, in accordance with auditing standards generally accepted in the United States of America, the [*identify financial statements*] of W Company and our report dated [*date of report*] expressed [*include nature of opinion*]. We considered the material weakness identified above in determining the nature, timing, and extent of audit tests applied in our audit of the 20XX financial statements, and this report does not affect such report on the financial statements.

[*Signature*]

[*Date*]

Example 5: Unqualified Opinion on Internal Control Based, in Part, on the Report of Another Auditor

7. The following is an illustrative report expressing an unqualified opinion on internal control when the auditor decides to refer to the report of another auditor as the basis, in part, for the auditor's own report.

Independent Auditor's Report

[*Introductory paragraph*]

We have examined W Company's internal control over financial reporting as of December 31, 20XX, based on [*identify criteria*].[7] W Company's management is responsible for maintaining effective internal control over financial reporting, and for its assertion of the effectiveness of internal control over financial reporting, included in the accompanying [*title of management's report*]. Our responsibility is to express an opinion on W Company's internal control over financial reporting based on our examination. We did not examine the effectiveness of internal control over financial reporting of B Company, a wholly owned subsidiary, whose financial statements reflect total assets and revenues constituting 20 percent and 30 percent, respectively, of the related consolidated financial statement amounts as of and for the year ended December 31, 20XX. The effectiveness of B Company's internal control over financial reporting was examined by other auditors whose report has been furnished to us, and our opinion, insofar as it relates to the effectiveness of B Company's internal control over financial reporting, is based solely on the report of the other auditors.

[*Scope paragraph*]

We conducted our examination in accordance with attestation standards established by the American Institute of Certified Public Accountants. Those standards require that we plan and perform the examination to obtain reasonable assurance about whether effective internal control over financial reporting was maintained in all material respects. Our examination included obtaining an understanding of internal control over financial reporting, assessing the risk that a material weakness exists, and testing and evaluating the design and operating effectiveness of internal control based on the assessed risk. Our examination also included performing such other procedures as we considered necessary in the circumstances. We believe that our examination and the report of the other auditors provide a reasonable basis for our opinion.

[*Definition paragraph*]

An entity's internal control over financial reporting is a process effected by those charged with governance, management, and other personnel, designed to provide reasonable assurance regarding the preparation of reliable financial statements in accordance with [*applicable financial reporting framework, such as accounting principles generally accepted in the United States of America*]. An entity's internal control over financial reporting includes those policies and procedures that (1) pertain to the maintenance of records that, in reasonable detail, accurately and fairly reflect the transactions and dispositions of the assets of the entity; (2) provide reasonable assurance that transactions are recorded as necessary to permit preparation of financial statements in accordance with [*applicable financial reporting framework, such as accounting principles generally accepted in the United States of America*], and that receipts and expenditures of the entity are being made only in accordance with authorizations of management and those charged with governance; and (3) provide reasonable assurance

---

[7] See footnote 2 of this exhibit.

regarding prevention, or timely detection and correction of unauthorized acquisition, use, or disposition of the entity's assets that could have a material effect on the financial statements.

[*Inherent limitations paragraph*]

Because of its inherent limitations, internal control over financial reporting may not prevent, or detect and correct misstatements. Also, projections of any evaluation of effectiveness to future periods are subject to the risk that controls may become inadequate because of changes in conditions, or that the degree of compliance with the policies or procedures may deteriorate.

[*Opinion paragraph*]

In our opinion, based on our examination and the report of the other auditors, W Company maintained, in all material respects, effective internal control over financial reporting as of December 31, 20XX, based on [*identify criteria*].[8]

[*Audit of financial statements paragraph*]

We also have audited, in accordance with auditing standards generally accepted in the United States of America, the [*identify financial statements*] of W Company and our report dated [*date of report, which should be the same as the date of the report on the examination of internal control*] expressed [*include nature of opinion*].

[*Signature*]

[*Date*]

Example 6: Combined Report Expressing an Unqualified Opinion on Internal Control and on the Financial Statements

8. The following is an illustrative combined report expressing an unqualified opinion directly on internal control and on the financial statements. This report refers to the examination of internal control as an audit.[9]

Independent Auditor's Report

[*Introductory paragraph*]

We have audited the accompanying balance sheet of W Company as of December 31, 20XX, and the related statements of income, retained earnings, and cash flows for the year then ended. We also have audited W Company's internal control over financial reporting as of December 31, 20XX, based on [*identify criteria*].[10] W. Company's management is responsible for these financial statements, for maintaining effective internal control over financial reporting, and for its assertion of the effectiveness of internal control over financial reporting, included in the accompanying [*title of management's report*]. Our responsibility is to express an opinion on these financial statements and an opinion on W Company's internal control over financial reporting based on our audits.

[*Scope paragraph*]

We conducted our audit of the financial statements in accordance with auditing standards generally accepted in the United States of America and our audit of

---

[8] As discussed in paragraph .125 of this section, whether the other auditor's opinion is expressed on management's assertion or on internal control does not affect the determination of whether the principal auditor's opinion is expressed on management's assertion or on internal control.

[9] See footnote 1 of this exhibit.

[10] See footnote 2 of this exhibit.

internal control over financial reporting in accordance with attestation standards established by the American Institute of Certified Public Accountants. Those standards require that we plan and perform the audits to obtain reasonable assurance about whether the financial statements are free of material misstatement and whether effective internal control over financial reporting was maintained in all material respects. Our audit of the financial statements included examining, on a test basis, evidence supporting the amounts and disclosures in the financial statements, assessing the accounting principles used and significant estimates made by management, as well as evaluating the overall financial statement presentation. Our audit of internal control over financial reporting included obtaining an understanding of internal control over financial reporting, assessing the risk that a material weakness exists, and testing and evaluating the design and operating effectiveness of internal control based on the assessed risk. Our audits also included performing such other procedures as we considered necessary in the circumstances. We believe that our audits provide a reasonable basis for our opinions.

[*Definition paragraph*]

An entity's internal control over financial reporting is a process effected by those charged with governance, management, and other personnel, designed to provide reasonable assurance regarding the preparation of reliable financial statements in accordance with [*applicable financial reporting framework, such as accounting principles generally accepted in the United States of America*]. An entity's internal control over financial reporting includes those policies and procedures that (1) pertain to the maintenance of records that, in reasonable detail, accurately and fairly reflect the transactions and dispositions of the assets of the entity; (2) provide reasonable assurance that transactions are recorded as necessary to permit preparation of financial statements in accordance with [*applicable financial reporting framework, such as accounting principles generally accepted in the United States of America*], and that receipts and expenditures of the entity are being made only in accordance with authorizations of management and those charged with governance; and (3) provide reasonable assurance regarding prevention, or timely detection and correction of unauthorized acquisition, use, or disposition of the entity's assets that could have a material effect on the financial statements.

[*Inherent limitations paragraph*]

Because of its inherent limitations, internal control over financial reporting may not prevent, or detect and correct misstatements. Also, projections of any evaluation of effectiveness to future periods are subject to the risk that controls may become inadequate because of changes in conditions, or that the degree of compliance with the policies or procedures may deteriorate.

[*Opinion paragraph*]

In our opinion, the financial statements referred to above present fairly, in all material respects, the financial position of W Company as of December 31, 20XX, and the results of its operations and its cash flows for the year then ended in conformity with accounting principles generally accepted in the United States of America. Also in our opinion, W Company maintained, in all material respects, effective internal control over financial reporting as of December 31, 20XX, based on [*identify criteria*].

[*Signature*]

[*Date*]

.170

Exhibit B—Illustrative Communication of Significant Deficiencies and Material Weaknesses

1. The following is an illustrative written communication of significant deficiencies and material weaknesses.

> In connection with our audit of W Company's (the "Company") financial statements as of December 31, 20XX and for the year then ended, and our audit of the Company's internal control over financial reporting as of December 31, 20XX ("integrated audit"), the standards established by the American Institute of Certified Public Accountants require that we advise you of the following internal control matters identified during our integrated audit.
>
> Our responsibility is to plan and perform our integrated audit to obtain reasonable assurance about whether the financial statements are free of material misstatement, whether caused by error or fraud, and whether effective internal control over financial reporting was maintained in all material respects (that is, whether material weaknesses exist as of the date specified in management's assertion). The integrated audit is not designed to detect deficiencies that, individually or in combination, are less severe than a material weakness. However, we are responsible for communicating to management and those charged with governance significant deficiencies and material weaknesses identified during the integrated audit. We are also responsible for communicating to management deficiencies that are of a lesser magnitude than a significant deficiency, unless previously communicated, and inform those charged with governance when such a communication was made.
>
> A deficiency in internal control over financial reporting exists when the design or operation of a control does not allow management or employees, in the normal course of performing their assigned functions, to prevent, or detect and correct misstatements on a timely basis. [*A material weakness is a deficiency, or a combination of deficiencies, in internal control over financial reporting, such that there is a reasonable possibility that a material misstatement of the Company's financial statements will not be prevented, or detected and corrected on a timely basis. We believe the following deficiencies constitute material weaknesses:*]
>
> [*Describe the material weaknesses that were identified during the integrated audit. The auditor may separately identify those material weaknesses that exist as of the date of management's assertion by referring to the auditor's report.*]
>
> [*A significant deficiency is a deficiency, or a combination of deficiencies, in internal control over financial reporting that is less severe than a material weakness, yet important enough to merit attention by those charged with governance. We consider the following deficiencies to be significant deficiencies:*]
>
> [*Describe the significant deficiencies that were identified during the integrated audit.*]
>
> This communication is intended solely for the information and use of management, [*identify the body or individuals charged with governance*], others within the organization, and [*identify any specified governmental authorities*] and is not intended to be and should not be used by anyone other than these specified parties.

.171

Exhibit C—Reporting Under Section 112 of the Federal Deposit Insurance Corporation Improvement Act (FDICIA)

1. In Financial Institution Letter (FIL) 86-94, *Additional Guidance Concerning Annual Audits, Audit Committees and Reporting Requirements*, issued December 23, 1994, the Federal Deposit Insurance Corporation (FDIC) provided guidance on the meaning of the term *financial reporting* for purposes of compliance by insured depository institutions (IDIs) with Section 112 of the Federal Deposit Insurance Corporation Improvement Act (FDICIA) (Section 36 of the Federal Deposit Insurance Act, 12.U.S.C. 1831m), and its implementing regulation, 12 CFR Part 363. The FDIC indicated that financial reporting, at a minimum, includes financial statements prepared in accordance with generally accepted accounting principles (GAAP) and the schedules equivalent to the basic financial statements that are included in the IDI's appropriate regulatory report (for example, Schedules RC, RI, and RI-A in the Consolidated Reports of Condition and Income [Call Report]). Accordingly, to comply with FDICIA and Part 363, management of the IDI (or a parent holding company)[1] and the auditor should identify and test controls over the preparation of GAAP-based financial statements as well as the schedules equivalent to the basic financial statements that are included in the IDI's (or its holding company's) appropriate regulatory report. Further, both management and the auditor should include in their report on the IDI's (or its holding company's) internal control a specific description indicating that the scope of internal control included controls over the preparation of the IDI's (or its holding company's) GAAP-based financial statements as well as the schedules equivalent to the basic financial statements that are included in the IDI's (or its holding company's) appropriate regulatory report.

2. In accordance with paragraph .107 of this section, the auditor's report should include a definition of internal control (the auditor should use the same description of the entity's internal control as management uses in its report). The following is an illustrative definition paragraph that may be used when an IDI that is a bank (which is not subject to Section 404 of the Sarbanes-Oxley Act of 2002) elects to report on controls for FDICIA purposes at the bank holding company level:

> An entity's internal control over financial reporting is a process effected by those charged with governance, management, and other personnel, designed to provide reasonable assurance regarding the preparation of reliable financial statements in accordance with accounting principles generally accepted in the United States of America. Because management's assessment and our examination were conducted to meet the reporting requirements of Section 112 of the Federal Deposit Insurance Corporation Improvement Act (FDICIA), our examination of [*Holding Company's*] internal control over financial reporting included controls over the preparation of financial statements in accordance with accounting principles generally accepted in the United States of America and with the instructions to the Consolidated Financial Statements for Bank

[1] See Financial Institution Letter (FIL) 86-94 for further discussion of reporting at the holding company level for Federal Deposit Insurance Corporation Improvement Act purposes and the application of holding company reporting as it relates to controls over the preparation of "regulatory reports."

Holding Companies (Form FR Y-9C).[2] An entity's internal control over financial reporting includes those policies and procedures that (1) pertain to the maintenance of records that, in reasonable detail, accurately and fairly reflect the transactions and dispositions of the assets of the entity; (2) provide reasonable assurance that transactions are recorded as necessary to permit preparation of financial statements in accordance with accounting principles generally accepted in the United States of America, and that receipts and expenditures of the entity are being made only in accordance with authorizations of management and those charged with governance; and (3) provide reasonable assurance regarding prevention, or timely detection and correction of unauthorized acquisition, use, or disposition of the entity's assets that could have a material effect on the financial statements.

[2] This sentence would be modified if the insured depository institution (IDI) reports at the institution level rather than at the bank holding company level to refer to the Federal Financial Institutions Examination Council Instructions for Consolidated Reports of Condition and Income or the Office of Thrift Supervision Instructions for Thrift Financial Reports instead of to the Form FR Y-9C. This sentence would also be modified if the IDI reports at a holding company level and employs another approach to reporting on controls over the preparation of regulatory reports as permitted by FIL 86-94.

.172

Exhibit D—Illustrative Management Report

1. The following is an illustrative management report containing the reporting elements described in paragraph .95 of this section:

Management's Report on Internal Control Over Financial Reporting

W Company's internal control over financial reporting is a process effected by those charged with governance, management, and other personnel, designed to provide reasonable assurance regarding the preparation of reliable financial statements in accordance with [*applicable financial reporting framework, such as accounting principles generally accepted in the United States of America*]. An entity's internal control over financial reporting includes those policies and procedures that (1) pertain to the maintenance of records that, in reasonable detail, accurately and fairly reflect the transactions and dispositions of the assets of the entity; (2) provide reasonable assurance that transactions are recorded as necessary to permit preparation of financial statements in accordance with [*applicable financial reporting framework, such as accounting principles generally accepted in the United States of America*], and that receipts and expenditures of the entity are being made only in accordance with authorizations of management and those charged with governance; and (3) provide reasonable assurance regarding prevention, or timely detection and correction of unauthorized acquisition, use, or disposition of the entity's assets that could have a material effect on the financial statements.

Management is responsible for establishing and maintaining effective internal control over financial reporting. Management assessed the effectiveness of W Company's internal control over financial reporting as of December 31, 20XX, based on the framework set forth by the Committee of Sponsoring Organizations of the Treadway Commission in *Internal Control—Integrated Framework*. Based on that assessment, management concluded that, as of December 31, 20XX, W Company's internal control over financial reporting is effective based on the criteria established in *Internal Control—Integrated Framework*.

W Company

Report signers, if applicable

Date

.172

Exhibit D—Illustrative Management Report

.172 The following is an illustrative management report containing the reporting elements described in paragraph .10 of this section.

Management's Report on Internal Control Over Financial Reporting

W Company's internal control over financial reporting is a process effected by those charged with governance, management, and other personnel, designed to provide reasonable assurance regarding the preparation of reliable financial statements in accordance with [*applicable financial reporting framework, such as accounting principles generally accepted in the United States of America*]. An entity's internal control over financial reporting includes those policies and procedures that (1) pertain to the maintenance of records that, in reasonable detail, accurately and fairly reflect the transactions and dispositions of the assets of the entity; (2) provide reasonable assurance that transactions are recorded as necessary to permit preparation of financial statements in accordance with [*applicable financial reporting framework, such as accounting principles generally accepted in the United States of America*], and that receipts and expenditures of the entity are being made only in accordance with authorizations of management and those charged with governance; and (3) provide reasonable assurance regarding prevention, or timely detection and correction of unauthorized acquisition, use, or disposition of the entity's assets that could have a material effect on the financial statements.

Management is responsible for establishing and maintaining effective internal control over financial reporting. Management assessed the effectiveness of W Company's internal control over financial reporting as of December 31, 20XX, based on the framework set forth by the Committee of Sponsoring Organizations of the Treadway Commission in *Internal Control—Integrated Framework*. Based on that assessment, management concluded that, as of December 31, 20XX, W Company's internal control over financial reporting is effective based on the criteria established in *Internal Control—Integrated Framework*.

W Company

[*Report signers, if applicable*]

[*Date*]

AT Section 9501

An Examination of an Entity's Internal Control Over Financial Reporting That Is Integrated With an Audit of Its Financial Statements: Attest Engagements Interpretations of Section 501

1. Reporting Under Section 112 of the Federal Deposit Insurance Corporation Improvement Act

.01 *Question*—For purposes of compliance by insured depository institutions (IDIs) with Section 112 of the Federal Deposit Insurance Corporation Improvement Act (FDICIA) (Section 36, Independent Annual Audits of Insured Depository Institutions, of the Federal Deposit Insurance Act [*Banks and Banking, U.S. Code* Title 12, Section 1831m]) and its implementing regulation, Title 12 U.S. *Code of Federal Regulations* (CFR) Part 363, an IDI that is a subsidiary of a holding company may use the consolidated holding company's financial statements to satisfy the audited financial statements requirement of 12 CFR 363, provided certain criteria are met.[1] For some IDIs, however, an examination of internal control over financial reporting is required at the IDI level. Paragraph .18 of AT section 501, *An Examination of an Entity's Internal Control Over Financial Reporting That Is Integrated With an Audit of Its Financial Statements* (AICPA, *Professional Standards*, vol. 1), requires that an examination of internal control over financial reporting (internal control) be integrated with an audit of financial statements. For IDIs that require an examination of internal control at the IDI level, can the auditor meet the integrated audit requirement when the IDI does not prepare financial statements for external distribution? If so, how can the auditor report on the effectiveness of the IDI's internal control over financial reporting?

.02 *Interpretation*—To comply with the integrated audit requirement in AT section 501, when the IDI uses the consolidated holding company's financial statements to satisfy the audited financial statements requirement of 12 CFR 363, the auditor would be required to perform procedures necessary to obtain sufficient appropriate audit evidence to enable the auditor to express an opinion on the IDI's financial statements and on its internal control over financial reporting. When the IDI does not prepare financial statements for external distribution, "financial statements" for this purpose may consist of the IDI's financial information in a reporting package or equivalent schedules and analyses that include the IDI information necessary for the preparation of the holding company's consolidated financial statements, including disclosures. The measurement of materiality is determined based on the IDI's financial information rather than the consolidated holding company's financial statements.[2]

---

[1] Refer to Section 36 of the Federal Deposit Insurance Act (FDI Act), Section 363.1: Scope and Definitions, for the requirements pertaining to compliance by subsidiaries of holding companies.

[2] See paragraph .11 of AU section 312, *Audit Risk and Materiality in Conducting an Audit* (AICPA, *Professional Standards*, vol. 1).

If the auditor is unable to apply the procedures necessary to obtain sufficient appropriate audit evidence with respect to the IDI's financial information, the auditor is required by paragraph .117 of AT section 501 to withdraw from the engagement or disclaim an opinion on the effectiveness of the IDI's internal control over financial reporting.

.03 As indicated in exhibit C, "Reporting Under Section 112 of the Federal Deposit Insurance Corporation Improvement Act (FDICIA)," of AT section 501, the FDIC indicated that financial reporting, at a minimum, includes financial statements prepared in accordance with generally accepted accounting principles (GAAP) and the schedules equivalent to the basic financial statements that are included in the IDI's appropriate regulatory report (for example, Schedules RC, RI, and RI-A in the Consolidated Reports of Condition and Income [call report]). When the IDI does not prepare financial statements for external distribution, the auditor is, nevertheless, required by paragraph .41 of AT section 501 to evaluate the IDI's period-end financial reporting process. This process includes, among other things, the IDI's procedures for preparing financial information for purposes of the consolidated holding company's financial statements, which are prepared in accordance with GAAP, and the schedules equivalent to the basic financial statements that are included in the IDI's appropriate regulatory report.

.04 The period-end financial reporting process may occur either at the IDI or the holding company, or both. The organizational structure, including where the controls relevant to the IDI's financial information operate, may affect how the auditor evaluates this process. For example,

a. when the period-end financial reporting process occurs at the holding company and the IDI comprises substantially all of the consolidated total assets, there may be no distinguishable difference between the IDI's and its holding company's process for purposes of the integrated audit. This is because the auditor's risk assessment, including the determination of significant accounts and disclosures and relevant assertions, the selection of controls to test, and the determination of the evidence necessary to conclude on the effectiveness of a given control, would likely be the same for the IDI and the holding company.[3] In this circumstance, the period-end financial reporting process of the holding company would be, in effect, the period-end financial reporting process of the IDI and, therefore, would be included in the scope of the integrated audit of the IDI.

b. when the period-end financial reporting process occurs at the holding company and the IDI does not comprise substantially all of the consolidated total assets, the IDI's financial reporting process may be sufficient for the auditor to meet the requirement in paragraph .41 of AT section 501, if the necessary GAAP information is prepared by the IDI or the holding company, and the process can be evaluated by the auditor. The auditor may determine that the IDI's preparation of the IDI's appropriate regulatory report, together with other financial information at the IDI level that is incorporated into the consolidated holding company's financial statements, is sufficient for this purpose. In this circumstance,

---

[3] See paragraph .23 of AT section 501, *An Examination of an Entity's Internal Control Over Financial Reporting That Is Integrated With an Audit of Its Financial Statements* (AICPA, *Professional Standards*, vol. 1).

both the period-end financial reporting process of the holding company, as it relates to the financial information of the IDI, and the period-end financial reporting process of the IDI, with respect to the preparation of the schedules equivalent to the basic financial statements that are included in the IDI's appropriate regulatory report, would be included in the scope of the integrated audit of the IDI.

.05 The illustrative reports in exhibit A, "Illustrative Reports," of AT section 501 may be used to report on the effectiveness of the IDI's internal control over financial reporting. Because 12 CFR 363 does not require the auditor to issue a separate auditor's report on the IDI's financial statements, the requirement in paragraph .109 of AT section 501 to add a paragraph to the internal control report that references the financial statement audit will not apply when the auditor does not issue a separate auditor's report on the IDI's financial statements. In accordance with paragraph .107 of AT section 501, the auditor's report on internal control is required to include a definition of *internal control* that uses the same description of internal control as management uses in its report. The following is an illustrative definition paragraph that may be used when an IDI that is not subject to Section 404 of the Sarbanes-Oxley Act of 2002 elects to report on controls for FDICIA purposes at the IDI level, and the IDI uses the consolidated holding company's financial statements to satisfy the audited financial statements requirement of 12 CFR 363:

> An entity's internal control over financial reporting is a process effected by those charged with governance, management, and other personnel, designed to provide reasonable assurance regarding the preparation of reliable financial statements in accordance with generally accepted accounting principles. Because management's assessment and our examination were conducted to meet the reporting requirements of Section 112 of the Federal Deposit Insurance Corporation Improvement Act (FDICIA), our examination of [*IDI's*] internal control over financial reporting included controls over the preparation of financial information for purposes of [*consolidated holding company's*] financial statements in accordance with accounting principles generally accepted in the United States of America and controls over the preparation of schedules equivalent to basic financial statements in accordance with the Federal Financial Institutions Examination Council Instructions for Consolidated Reports of Condition and Income (call report instructions). An entity's internal control over financial reporting includes those policies and procedures that (1) pertain to the maintenance of records that, in reasonable detail, accurately and fairly reflect the transactions and dispositions of the assets of the entity; (2) provide reasonable assurance that transactions are recorded as necessary to permit preparation of financial statements in accordance with generally accepted accounting principles, and that receipts and expenditures of the entity are being made only in accordance with authorizations of management and those charged with governance; and (3) provide reasonable assurance regarding prevention, or timely detection and correction of unauthorized acquisition, use, or disposition of the entity's assets that could have a material effect on the financial statements.

.06 Management may evaluate and report on the effectiveness of the IDI's internal control based on the Committee of Sponsoring Organizations of the Treadway Commission's (COSO) report, *Internal Control—Integrated Framework*. Because COSO establishes control objectives relating to the preparation of reliable "published" financial statements, the COSO criteria, as modified for purposes of reporting under Section 112 of FDICIA, is appropriate only for the IDI and its regulatory agencies.

Accordingly, the report is required to be restricted as to use.[4] An example of such a restriction is as follows:

> This report is intended solely for the information and use of management, [*identify the body or individuals charged with governance*], others within the organization, the Federal Deposit Insurance Corporation and [*other federal bank regulatory agency*] and is not intended to be and should not be used by anyone other than these specified parties.

.07 Likewise, the auditor's report and management's assertion refer to the modified COSO criteria. For example, the following may be used to identify the criteria: "criteria established in *Internal Control—Integrated Framework* issued by the Committee of Sponsoring Organizations of the Treadway Commission (COSO) as modified for the express purpose of meeting the regulatory requirements of Section 112 of the Federal Deposit Insurance Corporation Improvement Act (FDICIA)."

[Issue Date: September 2010.]

---

[4] Paragraph .78 of AT section 101, *Attest Engagements* (AICPA, *Professional Standards*, vol. 1), requires the report to be restricted as to use "when the criteria used to evaluate the subject matter are determined by the practitioner to be appropriate only for a limited number of parties who either participated in their establishment or can be presumed to have an adequate understanding of the criteria." Although reports on internal control issued in accordance with this interpretation are required to be restricted as to use, Section 36 of the FDI Act and Title 12 U.S. *Code of Federal Regulations* Part 363 require that these reports be available for public inspection.

AT Section 601

Compliance Attestation

Source: SSAE No. 10.

Effective when the subject matter or assertion is as of or for a period ending on or after June 1, 2001. Earlier application is permitted.

Introduction and Applicability

.01 This section provides guidance for engagements related to either (*a*) an entity's compliance with requirements of specified laws, regulations, rules, contracts, or grants or (*b*) the effectiveness of an entity's internal control over compliance with specified requirements.[1] Compliance requirements may be either financial or nonfinancial in nature. An attest engagement conducted in accordance with this section should comply with the general, fieldwork, and reporting standards established in section 50, *SSAE Hierarchy*, and the specific standards set forth in this section. [Revised, November 2006, to reflect conforming changes necessary due to the issuance of Statement on Standards for Attestation Engagements No. 14.]

.02 This section does not—

a. Affect the auditor's responsibility in an audit of financial statements performed in accordance with generally accepted auditing standards (GAAS).

b. Apply to situations in which an auditor reports on specified compliance requirements based solely on an audit of financial statements, as addressed in AU section 623, *Special Reports*, paragraphs .19 through .21.

c. Apply to engagements for which the objective is to report in accordance with AU section 801, *Compliance Audits*, unless the terms of the engagement specify an attest report under this section.

d. Apply to engagements covered by AU section 634, *Letters for Underwriters and Certain Other Requesting Parties*.

e. Apply to the report that encompasses internal control over compliance for a broker or dealer in securities as required by rule 17a-5 of the Securities Exchange Act of 1934 (the 1934 Act).[2]

[Revised, December 2010, to reflect conforming changes necessary due to the issuance of SAS No. 117.]

---

[1] Throughout this section—

a. An entity's compliance with requirements of specified laws, regulations, rules, contracts, or grants is referred to as *compliance with specified requirements*.

b. An entity's internal control over compliance with specified requirements is referred to as its *internal control over compliance*. The internal control addressed in this section may include parts of but is not the same as internal control over financial reporting.

[2] An example of this report is contained in AICPA Audit and Accounting Guide *Brokers and Dealers in Securities*.

.03 A report issued in accordance with the provisions of this section does not provide a legal determination of an entity's compliance with specified requirements. However, such a report may be useful to legal counsel or others in making such determinations.

Scope of Services

.04 The practitioner may be engaged to perform agreed-upon procedures to assist users in evaluating the following subject matter (or assertions related thereto)—

a. The entity's compliance with specified requirements

b. The effectiveness of the entity's internal control over compliance[3]

c. Both the entity's compliance with specified requirements and the effectiveness of the entity's internal control over compliance

The practitioner also may be engaged to examine the entity's compliance with specified requirements or a written assertion thereon.

.05 An important consideration in determining the type of engagement to be performed is expectations by users of the practitioner's report. Since the users decide the procedures to be performed in an agreed-upon procedures engagement, it often will be in the best interests of the practitioner and users (including the client) to have an agreed-upon procedures engagement rather than an examination engagement. When deciding whether to accept an examination engagement, the practitioner should consider the risks discussed in paragraphs .31 through .35.

.06 A practitioner may be engaged to examine the effectiveness of the entity's internal control over compliance or an assertion thereon. However, in accordance with section 50, the practitioner cannot accept an engagement unless he or she has reason to believe that the subject matter is capable of reasonably consistent evaluation against criteria that are suitable and available to users.[4] If a practitioner determines that such criteria do exist for internal control over compliance, he or she should perform the engagement in accordance with

---

[3] An entity's internal control over compliance is the process by which management obtains reasonable assurance of compliance with specified requirements. Although the comprehensive internal control may include a wide variety of objectives and related policies and procedures, only some of these may be relevant to an entity's compliance with specified requirements. (See footnote 1b.) The components of internal control over compliance vary based on the nature of the compliance requirements. For example, internal control over compliance with a capital requirement would generally include accounting procedures, whereas internal control over compliance with a requirement to practice nondiscriminatory hiring may not include accounting procedures.

[4] Criteria issued by regulatory agencies and other groups composed of experts that follow due-process procedures, including exposure of the proposed criteria for public comment, ordinarily should be considered suitable criteria for this purpose. For example, the Committee of Sponsoring Organizations (COSO) of the Treadway Commission's Report, *Internal Control—Integrated Framework*, provides suitable criteria against which management may evaluate and report on the effectiveness of the entity's internal control. However, more detailed criteria relative to specific compliance requirements may have to be developed and an appropriate threshold for measuring the severity of control deficiencies needs to be developed in order to apply the concepts of the COSO report to internal control over compliance.

Criteria established by a regulatory agency that does not follow such due-process procedures also may be considered suitable criteria for use by the regulatory agency. The practitioner should determine whether such criteria are suitable for general use reporting by evaluating them against the attributes in section 101.24. If the practitioner determines that such criteria are suitable for general use reporting, those criteria should also be available to users as discussed in section 101.33.

If the practitioner concludes that the criteria are appropriate only for a limited number of parties or are available only to specified parties, the practitioner's report shall state that the use of the report is restricted to those parties specified in the report. (See section 101.30, .34, and .78–.83.)

section 101, *Attest Engagements*. Additionally, section 501, *An Examination of an Entity's Internal Control Over Financial Reporting That Is Integrated With an Audit of Its Financial Statements*, may be helpful to a practitioner in such an engagement. [Revised, November 2006, to reflect conforming changes necessary due to the issuance of Statement on Standards for Attestation Engagements No. 14.]

.07 A practitioner should not accept an engagement to perform a review, as defined in section 101.55, of an entity's compliance with specified requirements or about the effectiveness of an entity's internal control over compliance or an assertion thereon.

.08 The practitioner may be engaged to provide other types of services in connection with the entity's compliance with specified requirements or the entity's internal control over compliance. For example, management may engage the practitioner to provide recommendations on how to improve the entity's compliance or related internal control. A practitioner engaged to provide such nonattest services should refer to the guidance in CS section 100, *Consulting Services: Definitions and Standards*.

Conditions for Engagement Performance

.09 A practitioner may perform an agreed-upon procedures engagement related to an entity's compliance with specified requirements or the effectiveness of internal control over compliance if the following conditions are met.

a. The responsible party accepts responsibility for the entity's compliance with specified requirements and the effectiveness of the entity's internal control over compliance.

b. The responsible party evaluates the entity's compliance with specified requirements or the effectiveness of the entity's internal control over compliance.

See also section 201, *Agreed-Upon Procedures Engagements*.

.10 A practitioner may perform an examination engagement related to an entity's compliance with specified requirements if the following conditions are met.

a. The responsible party accepts responsibility for the entity's compliance with specified requirements and the effectiveness of the entity's internal control over compliance.

b. The responsible party evaluates the entity's compliance with specified requirements.

c. Sufficient evidential matter exists or could be developed to support management's evaluation.

.11 As part of engagement performance, the practitioner should obtain from the responsible party a written assertion about compliance with specified requirements or internal control over compliance. The responsible party may present its written assertion in either of the following:

a. A separate report that will accompany the practitioner's report

b. A representation letter to the practitioner

.12 The responsible party's written assertion about compliance with specified requirements or internal control over compliance may take many forms. Throughout this section, for example, the phrase "responsible party's assertion that W Company complied with [*specify compliance requirement*] as of [*date*]," illustrates such an assertion. Other phrases may also be used. However, a practitioner should not accept an assertion that is so subjective (for example, "very effective" internal control over compliance) that people having competence in and using the same or similar criteria would not ordinarily be able to arrive at similar conclusions.

.13 Regardless of whether the practitioner's client is the responsible party, the responsible party's refusal to furnish a written assertion as part of an examination engagement should cause the practitioner to withdraw from the engagement. However, an exception is provided if an examination of an entity's compliance with specified requirements is required by law or regulation. In that instance, the practitioner should disclaim an opinion on compliance unless he or she obtains evidential matter that warrants expressing an adverse opinion. If the practitioner expresses an adverse opinion and the responsible party does not provide an assertion, the practitioner's report should be restricted as to use. (See section 101.78–.81.) If, as part of an agreed-upon procedures engagement, the practitioner's client is the responsible party, a refusal by that party to provide an assertion requires the practitioner to withdraw from the engagement. However, withdrawal is not required if the engagement is required by law or regulation. If, in an agreed-upon procedures engagement, the practitioner's client is not the responsible party, the practitioner is not required to withdraw but should consider the effects of the responsible party's refusal on the engagement and his or her report.

.14 Additionally, at the beginning of the engagement, the practitioner may want to consider discussing with the client and the responsible party the need for the responsible party to provide the practitioner with a written representation letter at the conclusion of the examination engagement or an agreed-upon procedures engagement in which the client is the responsible party. In that letter, the responsible party will be asked to provide, among other possible items, an acknowledgment of their responsibility for establishing and maintaining effective internal control over compliance and their assertion stating their evaluation of the entity's compliance with specified requirements. The responsible party's refusal to furnish these representations (see paragraphs .68 through .70) will constitute a limitation on the scope of the engagement.

Responsible Party

.15 The responsible party is responsible for ensuring that the entity complies with the requirements applicable to its activities. That responsibility encompasses the following.

a. Identify applicable compliance requirements.

b. Establish and maintain internal control to provide reasonable assurance that the entity complies with those requirements.

c. Evaluate and monitor the entity's compliance.

d. Specify reports that satisfy legal, regulatory, or contractual requirements.

The responsible party's evaluation may include documentation such as accounting or statistical data, entity policy manuals, accounting manuals, narrative memoranda, procedural write-ups, flowcharts, completed questionnaires, or internal auditors' reports. The form and extent of documentation will vary depending on the nature of the compliance requirements and the size and complexity of the entity. The responsible party may engage the practitioner to gather information to assist it in evaluating the entity's compliance. Regardless of the procedures performed by the practitioner, the responsible party must accept responsibility for its assertion and must not base such assertion solely on the practitioner's procedures.

Agreed-Upon Procedures Engagement

.16 The objective of the practitioner's agreed-upon procedures is to present specific findings to assist users in evaluating an entity's compliance with specified requirements or the effectiveness of an entity's internal control over compliance based on procedures agreed upon by the users of the report. A practitioner engaged to perform agreed-upon procedures on an entity's compliance with specified requirements or about the effectiveness of an entity's internal control over compliance should follow the guidance set forth herein and in section 201.

.17 The practitioner's procedures generally may be as limited or as extensive as the specified users desire, as long as the specified users (*a*) agree upon the procedures performed or to be performed and (*b*) take responsibility for the sufficiency of the agreed-upon procedures for their purposes. (See section 201.15.)

.18 To satisfy the requirements that the practitioner and the specified users agree upon the procedures performed or to be performed and that the specified users take responsibility for the sufficiency of the agreed-upon procedures for their purposes, ordinarily the practitioner should communicate directly with and obtain affirmative acknowledgment from each of the specified users. For example, this may be accomplished by meeting with the specified users or by distributing a draft of the anticipated report or a copy of an engagement letter to the specified users and obtaining their agreement. If the practitioner is not able to communicate directly with all of the specified users, the practitioner may satisfy these requirements by applying any one or more of the following or similar procedures.

- Compare the procedures to be applied to written requirements of the specified users.
- Discuss the procedures to be applied with appropriate representatives of the specified users involved.
- Review relevant contracts with or correspondence from the specified users.

The practitioner should not report on an engagement when specified users do not agree upon the procedures performed or to be performed and do not take responsibility for the sufficiency of the procedures for their purposes. See section 201.36 for guidance on satisfying these requirements when the practitioner is requested to add other parties as specified parties after the date of completion of the agreed-upon procedures.

.19 In an engagement to perform agreed-upon procedures on an entity's compliance with specified requirements or about the effectiveness of an entity's internal control over compliance, the practitioner is required to perform only the procedures that have been agreed to by users.[5] However, prior to performing such procedures, the practitioner should obtain an understanding of the specified compliance requirements, as discussed in paragraph .20. (See section 201.)

.20 To obtain an understanding of the specified compliance requirements, a practitioner should consider the following:

a. Laws, regulations, rules, contracts, and grants that pertain to the specified compliance requirements, including published requirements

b. Knowledge about the specified compliance requirements obtained through prior engagements and regulatory reports

c. Knowledge about the specified compliance requirements obtained through discussions with appropriate individuals within the entity (for example, the chief financial officer, internal auditors, legal counsel, compliance officer, or grant or contract administrators)

d. Knowledge about the specified compliance requirements obtained through discussions with appropriate individuals outside the entity (for example, a regulator or a third-party specialist)

.21 When circumstances impose restrictions on the scope of an agreed-upon procedures engagement, the practitioner should attempt to obtain agreement from the users for modification of the agreed-upon procedures. When such agreement cannot be obtained (for example, when the agreed-upon procedures are published by a regulatory agency that will not modify the procedures), the practitioner should describe such restrictions in his or her report or withdraw from the engagement.

.22 The practitioner has no obligation to perform procedures beyond the agreed-upon procedures. However, if noncompliance comes to the practitioner's attention by other means, such information ordinarily should be included in his or her report.

.23 The practitioner may become aware of noncompliance that occurs subsequent to the period addressed by the practitioner's report but before the date of the practitioner's report. The practitioner should consider including information regarding such noncompliance in his or her report. However, the practitioner has no responsibility to perform procedures to detect such noncompliance other than obtaining the responsible party's representation about noncompliance in the subsequent period, as described in paragraph .68.

.24 The practitioner's report on agreed-upon procedures on an entity's compliance with specified requirements (or the effectiveness of an entity's internal control over compliance) should be in the form of procedures and findings. The practitioner's report should contain the following elements:

a. A title that includes the word *independent*

b. Identification of the specified parties

c. Identification of the subject matter of the engagement (or management's assertion thereon), including the period or point in time addressed and a reference to the character of the engagement[6]

---

[5] AU section 322, *The Auditor's Consideration of the Internal Audit Function in an Audit of Financial Statements*, does not apply to agreed-upon procedures engagements.

[6] Generally, management's assertion about compliance with specified requirements will address a *period* of time, whereas an assertion about internal control over compliance will address a *point* in time.

d. An identification of the responsible party

e. A statement that the subject matter is the responsibility of the responsible party

f. A statement that the procedures, which were agreed to by the specified parties identified in the report, were performed to assist the specified parties in evaluating the entity's compliance with specified requirements or the effectiveness of its internal control over compliance

g. A statement that the agreed-upon procedures engagement was conducted in accordance with attestation standards established by the American Institute of Certified Public Accountants

h. A statement that the sufficiency of the procedures is solely the responsibility of the specified parties and a disclaimer of responsibility for the sufficiency of those procedures

i. A list of the procedures performed (or reference thereto) and related findings (The practitioner should not provide negative assurance. See section 201.24.)

j. Where applicable, a description of any agreed-upon materiality limits (See section 201.25.)

k. A statement that the practitioner was not engaged to and did not conduct an examination of the entity's compliance with specified requirements (or the effectiveness of an entity's internal control over compliance), a disclaimer of opinion thereon, and a statement that if the practitioner had performed additional procedures, other matters might have come to his or her attention that would have been reported

l. A statement restricting the use of the report to the specified parties

m. Where applicable, reservations or restrictions concerning procedures or findings as discussed in section 201.33, .35, .39, and .40

n. Where applicable, a description of the nature of the assistance provided by the specialist as discussed in section 201.19–.21

o. The manual or printed signature of the practitioner's firm

p. The date of the report

.25 The following is an illustration of an agreed-upon procedures report on an entity's compliance with specified requirements in which the procedures and findings are enumerated rather than referenced.

<u>Independent Accountant's Report on Applying Agreed-Upon Procedures</u>

We have performed the procedures enumerated below, which were agreed to by [*list specified parties*], solely to assist the specified parties in evaluating [*name of entity*]'s compliance with [*list specified requirements*] during the [*period*] ended [*date*].[7] Management is responsible for [*name of entity*]'s compliance with those requirements. This agreed-upon procedures engagement

---

[7] If the agreed-upon procedures have been published by a third-party user (for example, a regulator in regulatory policies or a lender in a debt agreement), this sentence might begin, "We have performed the procedures included in [*title of publication or other document*] and enumerated below, which were agreed to by [*list specified parties*], solely to assist the specified parties in evaluating ...."

was conducted in accordance with attestation standards established by the American Institute of Certified Public Accountants. The sufficiency of these procedures is solely the responsibility of those parties specified in this report. Consequently, we make no representation regarding the sufficiency of the procedures described below either for the purpose for which this report has been requested or for any other purpose.

[*Include paragraphs to enumerate procedures and findings.*]

We were not engaged to and did not conduct an examination, the objective of which would be the expression of an opinion on compliance. Accordingly, we do not express such an opinion. Had we performed additional procedures, other matters might have come to our attention that would have been reported to you.

This report is intended solely for the information and use of [*list or refer to specified parties*] and is not intended to be and should not be used by anyone other than these specified parties.

[*Signature*]

[*Date*]

.26 Evaluating compliance with certain requirements may require interpretation of the laws, regulations, rules, contracts, or grants that establish those requirements. In such situations, the practitioner should consider whether he or she is provided with the suitable criteria required to evaluate an assertion under the third general attestation standard. If these interpretations are significant, the practitioner may include a paragraph stating the description and the source of interpretations made by the entity's management. An example of such a paragraph, which should precede the procedures and findings paragraph(s), follows.

We have been informed that, under [*name of entity*]'s interpretation of [*identify the compliance requirement*], [*explain the nature and source of the relevant interpretation*].

.27 The following is an illustration of an agreed-upon procedures report on the effectiveness of an entity's internal control over compliance in which the procedures and findings are enumerated rather than referenced.

Independent Accountant's Report on Applying Agreed-Upon Procedures

We have performed the procedures enumerated below, which were agreed to by [*list specified parties*], solely to assist the specified parties in evaluating the effectiveness of [*name of entity*]'s internal control over compliance with [*list specified requirements*] as of [*date*].[8] Management is responsible for [*name of entity*]'s internal control over compliance with those requirements. This agreed-upon procedures engagement was conducted in accordance with attestation standards established by the American Institute of Certified Public Accountants. The sufficiency of these procedures is solely the responsibility of those parties specified in this report. Consequently, we make no representation regarding the sufficiency of the procedures described below either for the purpose for which this report has been requested or for any other purpose.

---

[8] If the agreed-upon procedures have been published by a third-party user (for example, a regulator in regulatory policies or a lender in a debt agreement), this sentence might begin, "We have performed the procedures included in [*title of publication or other document*] and enumerated below, which were agreed to by [*list specified parties*], solely to assist the specified parties in evaluating the effectiveness of [*name of entity*]'s internal control over compliance ...."

[*Include paragraphs to enumerate procedures and findings.*]

We were not engaged to and did not conduct an examination, the objective of which would be the expression of an opinion on the effectiveness of internal control over compliance. Accordingly, we do not express such an opinion. Had we performed additional procedures, other matters might have come to our attention that would have been reported to you.

This report is intended solely for the information and use of [*list or refer to specified parties*] and is not intended to be and should not be used by anyone other than these specified parties.

[*Signature*]

[*Date*]

.28 In some agreed-upon procedures engagements, procedures may relate to both compliance with specified requirements and the effectiveness of internal control over compliance. In these engagements, the practitioner may issue one report that addresses both. For example, the first sentence of the introductory paragraph would state the following.

We have performed the procedures enumerated below, which were agreed to by [*list users of report*], solely to assist the users in evaluating [*name of entity*]'s compliance with [*list specified requirements*] during the [*period*] ended [*date*] and the effectiveness of [*name of entity*]'s internal control over compliance with the aforementioned compliance requirements as of [*date*].

.29 The date of completion of the agreed-upon procedures should be used as the date of the practitioner's report.

Examination Engagement

.30 The objective of the practitioner's examination procedures applied to an entity's compliance with specified requirements is to express an opinion on an entity's compliance (or assertion related thereto), based on the specified criteria. To express such an opinion, the practitioner accumulates sufficient evidence about the entity's compliance with specified requirements, thereby restricting attestation risk to an appropriately low level.

Attestation Risk

.31 In an engagement to examine compliance with specified requirements, the practitioner seeks to obtain reasonable assurance that the entity complied, in all material respects, based on the specified criteria. This includes designing the examination to detect both intentional and unintentional material noncompliance. Absolute assurance is not attainable because of factors such as the need for judgment, the use of sampling, and the inherent limitations of internal control over compliance and because much of the evidence available to the practitioner is persuasive rather than conclusive in nature. Also, procedures that are effective for detecting noncompliance that is unintentional may be ineffective for detecting noncompliance that is intentional and concealed through collusion between personnel of the entity and a third party or among management or employees of the entity. Therefore, the subsequent discovery that material noncompliance exists does not, in and of itself, evidence inadequate planning, performance, or judgment on the part of the practitioner.

.32 Attestation risk is the risk that the practitioner may unknowingly fail to modify appropriately his or her opinion. It is composed of inherent risk, control risk, and detection risk. For purposes of a compliance examination, these components are defined as follows:

a. *Inherent risk*—The risk that material noncompliance with specified requirements could occur, assuming there are no related controls

b. *Control risk*—The risk that material noncompliance that could occur will not be prevented or detected on a timely basis by the entity's controls

c. *Detection risk*—The risk that the practitioner's procedures will lead him or her to conclude that material noncompliance does not exist when, in fact, such noncompliance does exist

Inherent Risk

.33 In assessing inherent risk, the practitioner should consider factors affecting risk similar to those an auditor would consider when planning an audit of financial statements. Such factors are discussed in AU section 316, *Consideration of Fraud in a Financial Statement Audit*, paragraph .85 (Appendix). In addition, the practitioner should consider factors relevant to compliance engagements, such as the following:

- The complexity of the specified compliance requirements
- The length of time the entity has been subject to the specified compliance requirements
- Prior experience with the entity's compliance
- The potential impact of noncompliance

[Revised, January 2004, to reflect conforming changes necessary due to the issuance of Statement on Auditing Standards No. 99.]

Control Risk

.34 The practitioner should assess control risk as discussed in paragraphs .45 and .46. Assessing control risk contributes to the practitioner's evaluation of the risk that material noncompliance exists. The process of assessing control risk (together with assessing inherent risk) provides evidential matter about the risk that such noncompliance may exist. The practitioner uses this evidential matter as part of the reasonable basis for his or her opinion.

Detection Risk

.35 In determining an acceptable level of detection risk, the practitioner assesses inherent risk and control risk and considers the extent to which he or she seeks to restrict attestation risk. As assessed inherent risk or control risk decreases, the acceptable level of detection risk increases. Accordingly, the practitioner may alter the nature, timing, and extent of compliance tests performed based on the assessments of inherent risk and control risk.

Materiality

.36 In an examination of an entity's compliance with specified requirements, the practitioner's consideration of materiality differs from that of an audit of financial statements in accordance with GAAS. In an examination of an entity's compliance with specified requirements, the practitioner's consideration of materiality is affected by (*a*) the nature of the compliance requirements, which may or may not be quantifiable in monetary terms, (*b*) the nature and frequency of noncompliance identified with appropriate consideration of sampling risk, and (*c*) qualitative considerations, including the needs and expectations of the report's users.

.37 In a number of situations, the terms of the engagement may provide for a supplemental report of all or certain noncompliance discovered. Such terms should not change the practitioner's judgments about materiality in planning and performing the engagement or in forming an opinion on an entity's compliance with specified requirements or on the responsible party's assertion about such compliance.

Performing an Examination Engagement

.38 The practitioner should exercise (*a*) due care in planning, performing, and evaluating the results of his or her examination procedures and (*b*) the proper degree of professional skepticism to achieve reasonable assurance that material noncompliance will be detected.

.39 In an examination of the entity's compliance with specified requirements, the practitioner should—

a. Obtain an understanding of the specified compliance requirements. (See paragraph .40.)

b. Plan the engagement. (See paragraphs .41 through .44.)

c. Consider relevant portions of the entity's internal control over compliance. (See paragraphs .45 through .47.)

d. Obtain sufficient evidence including testing compliance with specified requirements. (See paragraphs .48 and .49.)

e. Consider subsequent events. (See paragraphs .50 through .52.)

f. Form an opinion about whether the entity complied, in all material respects, with specified requirements (or whether the responsible party's assertion about such compliance is fairly stated in all material respects), based on the specified criteria. (See paragraph .53.)

Obtaining an Understanding of the Specified Compliance Requirements

.40 A practitioner should obtain an understanding of the specified compliance requirements. To obtain such an understanding, a practitioner should consider the following:

a. Laws, regulations, rules, contracts, and grants that pertain to the specified compliance requirements, including published requirements

b. Knowledge about the specified compliance requirements obtained through prior engagements and regulatory reports

c. Knowledge about the specified compliance requirements obtained through discussions with appropriate individuals within the entity (for example, the chief financial officer, internal auditors, legal counsel, compliance officer, or grant or contract administrators)

d. Knowledge about the specified compliance requirements obtained through discussions with appropriate individuals outside the entity (for example, a regulator or third-party specialist)

Planning the Engagement

General Considerations

.41 Planning an engagement to examine an entity's compliance with specified requirements involves developing an overall strategy for the expected conduct and scope of the engagement. The practitioner should consider the planning matters discussed in section 101.42–.47.

Multiple Components

.42 In an engagement to examine an entity's compliance with specified requirements when the entity has operations in several components (for example, locations, branches, subsidiaries, or programs), the practitioner may determine that it is not necessary to test compliance with requirements at every component. In making such a determination and in selecting the components to be tested, the practitioner should consider factors such as the following:

a. The degree to which the specified compliance requirements apply at the component level

b. Judgments about materiality

c. The degree of centralization of records

d. The effectiveness of the control environment, particularly management's direct control over the exercise of authority delegated to others and its ability to supervise activities at various locations effectively

e. The nature and extent of operations conducted at the various components

f. The similarity of operations over compliance for different components

Using the Work of a Specialist

.43 In some compliance engagements, the nature of the specified compliance requirements may require specialized skill or knowledge in a particular field other than accounting or auditing. In such cases, the practitioner may use the work of a specialist and should follow the relevant performance and reporting guidance in AU section 336, *Using the Work of a Specialist*.

Internal Audit Function

.44 Another factor the practitioner should consider when planning the engagement is whether the entity has an internal audit function and the extent to which internal auditors are involved in monitoring compliance with the specified requirements. A practitioner should consider the guidance in AU section 322, *The Auditor's Consideration of the Internal Audit Function in an Audit of Financial Statements*, when addressing the competence and objectivity of internal auditors, the nature, timing, and extent of work to be performed, and other related matters.

Consideration of Internal Control Over Compliance

.45 The practitioner should obtain an understanding of relevant portions of internal control over compliance sufficient to plan the engagement and to assess control risk for compliance with specified requirements. In planning the examination, such knowledge should be used to identify types of potential noncompliance, to consider factors that affect the risk of material noncompliance, and to design appropriate tests of compliance.

.46 A practitioner generally obtains an understanding of the design of specific controls by performing the following:

a. Inquiries of appropriate management, supervisory, and staff personnel

b. Inspection of the entity's documents

c. Observation of the entity's activities and operations

The nature and extent of procedures a practitioner performs vary from entity to entity and are influenced by factors such as the following:

- The newness and complexity of the specified requirements
- The practitioner's knowledge of internal control over compliance obtained in previous professional engagements
- The nature of the specified compliance requirements
- An understanding of the industry in which the entity operates
- Judgments about materiality

When seeking to assess control risk below the maximum, the practitioner should perform tests of controls to obtain evidence to support the assessed level of control risk.

.47 During the course of an examination engagement, the practitioner may become aware of significant deficiencies or material weaknesses in the design or operation of internal control over compliance that could adversely affect the entity's ability to comply with specified requirements. A practitioner's responsibility to communicate these deficiencies in an examination of an entity's compliance with specified requirements is similar to the auditor's responsibility described in AU section 325, *Communicating Internal Control Related Matters Identified in an Audit*. If, in a multiple-party arrangement, the practitioner's client is not the responsible party, the practitioner has no responsibility to communicate significant deficiencies or material weaknesses to the responsible party. For example, if the practitioner is engaged by his or her client to examine the compliance of another entity, the practitioner has no obligation to communicate any significant deficiencies or material weaknesses that he or she becomes aware of to the other entity. However, the practitioner is not precluded from making such a communication. [Revised, May 2006, to reflect conforming changes necessary due to the issuance of Statement on Auditing Standards No. 112. Revised, January 2010, to reflect conforming changes necessary due to the issuance of SAS No. 115.]

Obtaining Sufficient Evidence

.48 The practitioner should apply procedures to provide reasonable assurance of detecting material noncompliance. Determining these procedures and evaluating the sufficiency of the evidence obtained are matters of professional judgment. When exercising such judgment, practitioners should consider the guidance contained in section 101.51–.54 and AU section 350, *Audit Sampling*.

.49 For engagements involving compliance with regulatory requirements, the practitioner's procedures should include reviewing reports of significant examinations and related communications between regulatory agencies and the entity and, when appropriate, making inquiries of the regulatory agencies, including inquiries about examinations in progress.

Consideration of Subsequent Events

.50 The practitioner's consideration of subsequent events in an examination of an entity's compliance with specified requirements is similar to the auditor's consideration of subsequent events in a financial statement audit, as outlined in AU section 560, *Subsequent Events*. The practitioner should consider information about such events that comes to his or her attention after the end of the period addressed by the practitioner's report and prior to the issuance of his or her report.

.51 Two types of subsequent events require consideration by the responsible party and evaluation by the practitioner. The first consists of events that provide additional information about the entity's compliance during the period addressed by the practitioner's report and may affect the practitioner's report. For the period from the end of the reporting period (or point in time) to the date of the practitioner's report, the practitioner should perform procedures to identify such events that provide additional information about compliance during the reporting period. Such procedures should include but may not be limited to inquiring about and considering the following information:

- Relevant internal auditors' reports issued during the subsequent period
- Other practitioners' reports identifying noncompliance, issued during the subsequent period
- Regulatory agencies' reports on the entity's noncompliance, issued during the subsequent period
- Information about the entity's noncompliance, obtained through other professional engagements for that entity

.52 The second type consists of noncompliance that occurs subsequent to the period being reported on but before the date of the practitioner's report. The practitioner has no responsibility to detect such noncompliance. However, should the practitioner become aware of such noncompliance, it may be of such a nature and significance that disclosure of it is required to keep users from being misled. In such cases, the practitioner should include in his or her report an explanatory paragraph describing the nature of the noncompliance.

Forming an Opinion

.53 In evaluating whether the entity has complied in all material respects (or whether the responsible party's assertion about such compliance is stated fairly in all material respects), the practitioner should consider (*a*) the nature and frequency of the noncompliance identified and (*b*) whether such noncompliance is material relative to the nature of the compliance requirements, as discussed in paragraph .36.

Reporting

.54 The practitioner may examine and report directly on an entity's compliance (see paragraphs .55 and .56) or he or she may examine and report on the responsible party's written assertion (see paragraphs .57, .58, and .61), except as described in paragraph .64.

.55 The practitioner's examination report on compliance, which is ordinarily addressed to the entity, should include the following:

a. A title that includes the word *independent*

b. Identification of the specified compliance requirements, including the period covered, and of the responsible party[9]

c. A statement that compliance with the specified requirements is the responsibility of the entity's management

d. A statement that the practitioner's responsibility is to express an opinion on the entity's compliance with those requirements based on his or her examination

e. A statement that the examination was conducted in accordance with attestation standards established by the American Institute of Certified Public Accountants and, accordingly, included examining, on a test basis, evidence about the entity's compliance with those requirements and performing such other procedures as the practitioner considered necessary in the circumstances

f. A statement that the practitioner believes the examination provides a reasonable basis for his or her opinion

g. A statement that the examination does not provide a legal determination on the entity's compliance

h. The practitioner's opinion on whether the entity complied, in all material respects, with specified requirements based on the specified criteria[10] (See paragraph .64 for reporting on material noncompliance.)

i. A statement restricting the use of the report to the specified parties (see the fourth reporting standard)[11] under the following circumstances (See also paragraph .13.):

- When the criteria used to evaluate compliance are determined by the practitioner to be appropriate only for a limited number of parties who either participated in their establishment or can be presumed to have an adequate understanding of the criteria.
- When the criteria used to evaluate compliance are available only to the specified parties

j. The manual or printed signature of the practitioner's firm

k. The date of the examination report

.56 The following is the form of report a practitioner should use when he or she is expressing an opinion on an entity's compliance with specified requirements during a period of time.

---

[9] A practitioner also may be engaged to report on an entity's compliance with specified requirements as of point in time. In this case, the illustrative reports in this section should be adapted as appropriate.

[10] Frequently, criteria will be contained in the compliance requirements, in which case it is not necessary to repeat the criteria in the practitioner's report; however, if the criteria are not included in the compliance requirement, the practitioner's report should identify the criteria. For example, if a compliance requirement is to "maintain $25,000 in capital," it would not be necessary to identify the $25,000 in the report; however, if the requirement is to "maintain adequate capital," the practitioner should identify the criteria used to define *adequate*.

[11] In certain situations, however, criteria that have been specified by management and other report users may be suitable for general use.

Independent Accountant's Report

[Introductory paragraph]

We have examined [*name of entity*]'s compliance with [*list specified compliance requirements*] during the [*period*] ended [*date*]. Management is responsible for [*name of entity*]'s compliance with those requirements. Our responsibility is to express an opinion on [*name of entity*]'s compliance based on our examination.

[Scope paragraph]

Our examination was conducted in accordance with attestation standards established by the American Institute of Certified Public Accountants and, accordingly, included examining, on a test basis, evidence about [*name of entity*]'s compliance with those requirements and performing such other procedures as we considered necessary in the circumstances. We believe that our examination provides a reasonable basis for our opinion. Our examination does not provide a legal determination on [*name of entity*]'s compliance with specified requirements.

[Opinion paragraph]

In our opinion, [*name of entity*] complied, in all material respects, with the aforementioned requirements for the year ended December 31, 20XX.[12]

[*Signature*]

[*Date*]

.57 The practitioner's examination report on an entity's assertion about compliance with specified requirements, which is ordinarily addressed to the entity, should include the following:

a. A title that includes the word *independent*

b. Identification of the responsible party's assertion about the entity's compliance with specified requirements, including the period covered by the responsible party's assertion, and of the responsible party (When the responsible party's assertion does not accompany the practitioner's report, the first paragraph of the report should also contain a statement of the responsible party's assertion.)[13]

c. A statement that compliance with the requirements is the responsibility of the entity's management

d. A statement that the practitioner's responsibility is to express an opinion on the responsible party's assertion on the entity's compliance with those requirements based on his or her examination

e. A statement that the examination was conducted in accordance with attestation standards established by the American Institute of Certified Public Accountants and, accordingly, included examining, on a test basis, evidence about the entity's compliance with those requirements and performing such other procedures as the practitioner considered necessary in the circumstances

[12] If it is necessary to identify criteria (see footnote 10), the criteria should be identified in the opinion paragraph (for example, "... in all material respects, based on the criteria set forth in Attachment 1").

[13] A practitioner also may be engaged to report on the responsible party's assertion about an entity's compliance with specified requirements as of a point in time. In this case, the illustrative reports in this section should be adapted as appropriate.

f. A statement that the practitioner believes the examination provides a reasonable basis for his or her opinion

g. A statement that the examination does not provide a legal determination on the entity's compliance

h. The practitioner's opinion on whether the responsible party's assertion about compliance with specified requirements is fairly stated in all material respects based on the specified criteria[14] (See paragraph .64 for reporting on material noncompliance.)

i. A statement restricting the use of the report to the specified parties (see the fourth reporting standard)[15, 16] under the following circumstances:

- When the criteria used to evaluate compliance are determined by the practitioner to be appropriate only for a limited number of parties who either participated in their establishment or can be presumed to have an adequate understanding of the criteria

- When the criteria used to evaluate compliance are available only to the specified parties

j. The manual or printed signature of the practitioner's firm

k. The date of the examination report

.58 The following is the form of report that a practitioner should use when expressing an opinion on management's assertion about compliance with specified requirements.

Independent Accountant's Report

[*Introductory paragraph*]

We have examined management's assertion, included in the accompanying [*title of management report*], that [*name of entity*] complied with [*list specified compliance requirements*] during the [*period*] ended [*date*].[17, 18] Management is responsible for [*name of entity*]'s compliance with those requirements. Our responsibility is to express an opinion on management's assertion about [*name of entity*]'s compliance based on our examination.

[*Standard scope paragraph*]

[*Opinion paragraph*]

---

[14] Frequently, criteria will be contained in the compliance requirements, in which case it is not necessary to repeat the criteria in the practitioner's report; however, if the criteria are not included in the compliance requirement, the practitioner's report should identify the criteria. For example, if a compliance requirement is to "maintain $25,000 in capital," it would not be necessary to identify the $25,000 in the report; however, if the requirement is to "maintain adequate capital," the practitioner should identify the criteria used to define *adequate.*

[15] Although a practitioner's report may be appropriate for general use, the practitioner is not precluded from restricting the use of the report.

[16] In certain situations, however, criteria that have been specified by management and other report users may be suitable for general use.

[17] The practitioner should identify the management report examined by reference to the report title used by management in its report. Further, he or she should use the same description of compliance requirements as management uses in its report.

[18] If management's assertion is stated in the practitioner's report and does not accompany the practitioner's report, the phrase "included in the accompanying [*title of management report*]" would be omitted.

> In our opinion, management's assertion that [*name of entity*] complied with the aforementioned requirements during the [*period*] ended [*date*] is fairly stated, in all material respects.[19]
>
> [*Signature*]
>
> [*Date*]

.59 Evaluating compliance with certain requirements may require interpretation of the laws, regulations, rules, contracts, or grants that establish those requirements. In such situations, the practitioner should consider whether he or she is provided with the suitable criteria required to evaluate compliance under the third general attestation standard. If these interpretations are significant, the practitioner may include a paragraph stating the description and the source of interpretations made by the entity's management. The following is an example of such a paragraph, which should directly follow the scope paragraph:

> We have been informed that, under [*name of entity*]'s interpretation of [*identify the compliance requirement*], [*explain the source and nature of the relevant interpretation*].

.60 The date of completion of the examination procedures should be used as the date of the practitioner's report.

.61 Nothing precludes the practitioner from examining an assertion but opining directly on compliance.

.62 Section 101.78–.83 provide guidance on restricting the use of an attest report. Nothing in this section precludes the practitioner from restricting the use of the report. For example, if the practitioner is asked by a client to examine another entity's compliance with certain regulations, he or she may want to restrict the use of the report to the client since the practitioner has no control over how the report may be used by the other entity.

Report Modifications

.63 The practitioner should modify the standard report described in paragraphs .55 and .57, if any of the following conditions exist.

- There is material noncompliance with specified requirements (paragraphs .64 through .67).
- There is a restriction on the scope of the engagement.[20]
- The practitioner decides to refer to the report of another practitioner as the basis, in part, for the practitioner's report.[21]

Material Noncompliance

.64 When an examination of an entity's compliance with specified requirements discloses noncompliance with the applicable requirements that the practitioner believes have a material effect on the entity's compliance, the practitioner should modify the report and, to most effectively communicate with the reader of the report, should state his or her opinion on the entity's specified compliance requirements, not on the responsible party's assertion.

---

[19] If it is necessary to identify criteria (see footnote 10), the criteria should be identified in the opinion paragraph (for example, "...in all material respects, based on the criteria set forth in Attachment 1").

[20] The practitioner should refer to section 101.73 and .74 for guidance on scope restrictions.

[21] The practitioner should refer to section 501.122–.125 for guidance on an opinion based in part on the report of another practitioner and adapt such guidance to the standard reports in this section.

.65 The following is the form of report, modified with explanatory language, that a practitioner should use when he or she has concluded that a qualified opinion is appropriate under the circumstances. It has been assumed that the practitioner has determined that the specified compliance requirements are both suitable for general use and available to users as discussed in section 101.23–.33, and, therefore, that a restricted use paragraph is not required.

<u>Independent Accountant's Report</u>

[Introductory paragraph]

We have examined [*name of entity*]'s compliance with [*list specified compliance requirements*] for the [*period*] ended [*date*]. Management is responsible for compliance with those requirements. Our responsibility is to express an opinion on [*name of entity*]'s compliance based on our examination.

[Standard scope paragraph]

[Explanatory paragraph]

Our examination disclosed the following material noncompliance with [*type of compliance requirement*] applicable to [*name of entity*] during the [*period*] ended [*date*]. [*Describe noncompliance.*]

[Opinion paragraph]

In our opinion, except for the material noncompliance described in the third paragraph, [*name of entity*] complied, in all material respects, with the aforementioned requirements for the [*period*] ended [*date*].

[Signature]

[Date]

.66 The following is the form of report, modified with explanatory language, that a practitioner should use when he or she concludes that an adverse opinion is appropriate in the circumstances. The practitioner has determined that the specified compliance requirements are both suitable for general use and available to users as discussed in section 101.23–.33.

<u>Independent Accountant's Report</u>

[Introductory paragraph]

We have examined [*name of entity*]'s compliance with [*list specified compliance requirements*] for the [*period*] ended [*date*]. Management is responsible for compliance with those requirements. Our responsibility is to express an opinion on [*name of entity*]'s compliance based on our examination.

[Standard scope paragraph]

[Explanatory paragraph]

Our examination disclosed the following material noncompliance with [*type of compliance requirement*] applicable to [*name of entity*] during the [*period*] ended [*date*]. [*Describe noncompliance.*]

[Opinion paragraph]

In our opinion, because of the effect of the noncompliance described in the third paragraph, [*name of entity*] has not complied with the aforementioned requirements for the [*period*] ended [*date*].

[Signature]

[Date]

.67 If the practitioner's report on his or her examination of the entity's compliance with specified requirements is included in a document that also includes his or her audit report on the entity's financial statements, the following sentence should be included in the paragraph of an examination report that describes material noncompliance.

> These conditions were considered in determining the nature, timing, and extent of audit tests applied in our audit of the 20XX financial statements, and this report does not affect our report dated [*date of report*] on those financial statements.

The practitioner also may include the preceding sentence when the two reports are not included within the same document.

Representation Letter

.68 In an examination engagement or an agreed-upon procedures engagement, the practitioner should obtain written representations from the responsible party—[22]

a. Acknowledging the responsible party's responsibility for complying with the specified requirements.

b. Acknowledging the responsible party's responsibility for establishing and maintaining effective internal control over compliance.

c. Stating that the responsible party has performed an evaluation of (1) the entity's compliance with specified requirements or (2) the entity's controls for ensuring compliance and detecting noncompliance with requirements, as applicable.

d. Stating the responsible party's assertion about the entity's compliance with the specified requirements or about the effectiveness of internal control over compliance, as applicable, based on the stated or established criteria.

e. Stating that the responsible party has disclosed to the practitioner all known noncompliance.

f. State that the responsible party has made available all documentation related to compliance with the specified requirements.

g. Stating the responsible party's interpretation of any compliance requirements that have varying interpretations.

h. State that the responsible party has disclosed any communications from regulatory agencies, internal auditors, and other practitioners concerning possible noncompliance with the specified requirements, including communications received between the end of the period addressed in the written assertion and the date of the practitioner's report.

i. Stating that the responsible party has disclosed any known noncompliance occurring subsequent to the period for which, or date as of which, the responsible party selects to make its assertion.

---

[22] AU section 333, *Management Representations*, paragraph .09, provides guidance on the date as of which the representation letter should be signed and who should sign it.

.69 The responsible party's refusal to furnish all appropriate written representations in an examination engagement constitutes a limitation on the scope of the engagement sufficient to preclude an unqualified opinion and is ordinarily sufficient to cause the practitioner to disclaim an opinion or withdraw from the engagement. However, based on the nature of the representations not obtained or the circumstances of the refusal, the practitioner may conclude in an examination engagement that a qualified opinion is appropriate. When the practitioner is performing agreed-upon procedures and the practitioner's client is the responsible party, the responsible party's refusal to furnish all appropriate written representations constitutes a limitation on the scope of the engagement sufficient to cause the practitioner to withdraw. When the practitioner's client is not the responsible party, the practitioner is not required to withdraw but should consider the effects of the responsible party's refusal on his or her report. Further, the practitioner should consider the effects of the responsible party's refusal on his or her ability to rely on other representations of the responsible party.

.70 When the practitioner's client is not the responsible party, the practitioner may also want to obtain written representations from the client. For example, when a practitioner's client has entered into a contract with a third party (responsible party) and the practitioner is engaged to examine the responsible party's compliance with that contract, the practitioner may want to obtain written representations from his or her client as to their knowledge of any noncompliance.

Other Information in a Client-Prepared Document Containing Management's Assertion About the Entity's Compliance With Specified Requirements or the Effectiveness of the Internal Control Over Compliance

.71 An entity may publish various documents that contain information (referred to as *other information*) in addition to the practitioner's attest report on either (*a*) the entity's compliance with specified requirements or (*b*) the effectiveness of the entity's internal control over compliance or written assertion thereon. Section 101.91–.94 provide guidance to the practitioner if the other information is contained in either of the following:

a. Annual reports to holders of securities or beneficial interests, annual reports of organizations for charitable or philanthropic purposes distributed to the public, and annual reports filed with regulatory authorities under the 1934 Act

b. Other documents to which the practitioner, at the client's request, devotes attention

Effective Date

.72 This section is effective when the subject matter or assertion is as of or for a period ending on or after June 1, 2001. Early application is permitted.

AT Section 701

Management's Discussion and Analysis

Source: SSAE No. 10.

Effective when management's discussion and analysis is for a period ending on or after June 1, 2001. Earlier application is permitted.

General

.01 This section sets forth attestation standards and provides guidance to a practitioner concerning the performance of an attest engagement[1] with respect to management's discussion and analysis (MD&A) prepared pursuant to the rules and regulations adopted by the Securities and Exchange Commission (SEC), which are presented in annual reports to shareholders and in other documents.[2]

Applicability

.02 This section is applicable to the following levels of service when a practitioner is engaged by (*a*) a public[3] entity that prepares MD&A in accordance with the rules and regulations adopted by the SEC (see paragraph .04) or (*b*) a nonpublic entity that prepares an MD&A presentation and whose management provides a written assertion that the presentation has been prepared using the rules and regulations adopted by the SEC:[4]

- An examination of an MD&A presentation
- A review of an MD&A presentation for an annual period, an interim period, or a combined annual and interim period[5]

---

[1] Section 101, *Attest Engagements*, paragraph .01, defines an attest engagement as one in which a practitioner "is engaged to issue or does issue an examination, a review, or an agreed-upon procedures report on subject matter, or an assertion about the subject matter (hereafter referred to as the *assertion*), that is the responsibility of another party."

[2] Because this section provides guidance specific to attest engagements concerning MD&A presentations, a practitioner should not perform a compliance attestation engagement under section 601, *Compliance Attestation*, with respect to an MD&A presentation.

[3] For purposes of this section, a public entity is any entity (*a*) whose securities trade in a public market either on a stock exchange (domestic or foreign) or in the over-the-counter (OTC) market, including securities quoted only locally or regionally, (*b*) that makes a filing with a regulatory agency in preparation for the sale of any class of its securities in a public market, or (*c*) a subsidiary, corporate joint venture, or other entity controlled by an entity covered by (*a*) or (*b*).

[4] Such assertion may be made by any of the following:
(*a*) Including a statement in the body of the MD&A presentation that it has been prepared using the rules and regulations adopted by the SEC.
(*b*) Providing a separate written assertion to accompany the MD&A presentation.
(*c*) Providing a written assertion in a representation letter to the practitioner.

[5] As discussed in paragraph .85*k*, a review report is not intended to be filed with the SEC as a report under the Securities Act of 1933 (the 1993 Act) or the Securities Exchange Act of 1934 (the 1934 Act) and, accordingly, the review report should contain a statement of restrictions on the use of the report to specified parties if the entity is (*a*) a public entity or (*b*) a nonpublic entity that is making or has made an offering of securities and it appears that the securities may subsequently be registered or subject to a filing with the SEC or other regulatory agency.

A practitioner[6] engaged to examine or review MD&A and report thereon should comply with the general, fieldwork, and reporting standards established in section 50, *SSAE Hierarchy*, and the specific standards set forth in this section. A practitioner engaged to perform agreed-upon procedures on MD&A should follow the guidance set forth in section 201, Agreed-Upon Procedures Engagements.[7] [Revised, November 2006, to reflect conforming changes necessary due to the issuance of Statement on Standards for Attestation Engagements No. 14.]

.03 This section does not—

a. Change the auditor's responsibility in an audit of financial statements performed in accordance with generally accepted auditing standards (GAAS).

b. Apply to situations in which the practitioner is requested to provide management with recommendations to improve the MD&A rather than to provide assurance. A practitioner engaged to provide such nonattest services should refer to CS section 100, *Consulting Services: Definitions and Standards*.

c. Apply to situations in which the practitioner is engaged to provide attest services with respect to an MD&A presentation that is prepared based on criteria other than the rules and regulations adopted by the SEC. A practitioner engaged to perform an examination or a review based upon such criteria should refer to the guidance in section 101, or to section 201 if engaged to perform an agreed-upon procedures engagement.[8]

.04 The requirements for MD&A have changed periodically since the first requirement was adopted by the SEC in 1974. As of the date of issuance of this SSAE, the rules and regulations for MD&A adopted by the SEC are found in Item 303 of Regulation S-K, as interpreted by Financial Reporting Release (FRR) No. 36, *Management's Discussion and Analysis of Financial Condition and Results of Operations; Certain Investment Company Disclosures* (Chapter 5 of the "Codification of Financial Reporting Policies"); Item 303 of Regulation S-B for small business issuers; and Item 9 of Form 20-F for Foreign Private Issuers.[9] Item 303 of Regulation S-K, as interpreted by FRR No. 36, Item 303 of Regulation S-B for small business issuers, and Item 9 of Form 20-F for Foreign Private Issuers, provide the relevant rules and regulations adopted by

---

[6] In this section, the terms *practitioner* or *accountant* generally refer to a person engaged to perform an attest service on MD&A. The term *accountant* may also refer to a person engaged to review financial statements. The term *auditor* refers to a person engaged to audit financial statements. As this section includes certain requirements for the practitioner to have audited or performed a Statement on Auditing Standards (SAS) No. 71 review of financial statements (AU section 722, *Interim Financial Information*), the terms *auditor, practitioner*, or *accountant* may refer, in this section, to the same person.

[7] Practitioners should follow guidance in AU section 634, *Letters for Underwriters and Certain Other Requesting Parties*, when requested to perform agreed-upon procedures on MD&A and report thereon in a letter for an underwriter.

[8] The guidance in this section may be helpful when performing an engagement to provide attest services with respect to an MD&A presentation that is based on criteria other than the rules and regulations adopted by the SEC. Such other criteria would have to be suitable and available as discussed in section 101.23–.33.

[9] The SEC staff from time to time issues guidance related to the SEC's adopted requirements; for example, Staff Accounting Bulletins (SABs), Staff Legal Bulletins, and speeches. Although such guidance may provide additional information with respect to the adopted requirements for MD&A, the practitioner should not be expected to attest to assertions on compliance with such guidance. The practitioner may find it helpful to also familiarize himself or herself with material contained on the SEC's website www.sec.gov that provides further information with respect to the SEC's views concerning MD&A disclosures.

the SEC that meet the definition of suitable criteria in section 101.23–.32. The practitioner should consider whether the SEC has adopted additional rules and regulations with respect to MD&A subsequent to the issuance of this section.

Conditions for Engagement Performance

Examination

.05 The practitioner's objective in an engagement to examine MD&A is to express an opinion on the MD&A presentation taken as a whole by reporting whether—

a. The presentation includes, in all material respects, the required elements of the rules and regulations adopted by the SEC.[10]

b. The historical financial amounts have been accurately derived, in all material respects, from the entity's financial statements.[11]

c. The underlying information, determinations, estimates, and assumptions of the entity provide a reasonable basis for the disclosures contained therein.[12]

.06 A practitioner may accept an engagement to examine MD&A of a public or nonpublic entity, provided the practitioner audits, in accordance with GAAS,[13] the financial statements for at least the latest period to which the MD&A presentation relates and the financial statements for the other periods covered by the MD&A presentation have been audited by the practitioner or a predecessor auditor. A base knowledge of the entity and its operations gained through an audit of the historical financial statements and knowledge about the industry and the environment is necessary to provide the practitioner with sufficient knowledge to properly evaluate the results of the procedures performed in connection with the examination.

.07 If a predecessor auditor has audited the financial statements for a prior period covered by the MD&A presentation, the practitioner (the successor auditor) should also consider whether, under the particular circumstances, he or she can acquire sufficient knowledge of the business and of the entity's accounting and financial reporting practices for such period so that he or she would be able to—

a. Identify types of potential material misstatements in MD&A and consider the likelihood of their occurrence.

---

10 The required elements as of the date of issuance of this SSAE include a discussion of the entity's financial condition, changes in financial condition, and results of operations, including a discussion of liquidity and capital resources.

11 Whether historical financial amounts are accurately derived from the financial statements includes both amounts that are derived from the face of the financial statements (which includes the notes to the financial statements) and financial statement schedules and those that are derived from underlying records supporting elements, accounts, or items included in the financial statements.

12 Whether the underlying information, determinations, estimates, and assumptions of the entity provide a reasonable basis for the disclosures contained therein requires consideration of management's interpretation of the disclosure criteria for MD&A, management's determinations as to the relevancy of information to be included, and estimates and assumptions made by management that affect reported information.

13 Restrictions on the scope of the audit of the financial statements will not necessarily preclude the practitioner from accepting an engagement to examine MD&A. Note that the SEC will generally not accept an auditor's report that is modified for a scope limitation. The practitioner should consider the nature and magnitude of the scope limitation and the form of the auditor's report in assessing whether an examination of MD&A could be performed.

b. Perform the procedures that will provide the practitioner with a basis for expressing an opinion as to whether the MD&A presentation includes, in all material respects, the required elements of the rules and regulations adopted by the SEC.

c. Perform the procedures that will provide the practitioner with a basis for expressing an opinion on the MD&A presentation with respect to whether the historical financial amounts have been accurately derived, in all material respects, from the entity's financial statements for such period.

d. Perform the procedures that will provide the practitioner with a basis for expressing an opinion as to whether the underlying information, determinations, estimates, and assumptions of the entity provide a reasonable basis for the disclosures contained therein.

Refer to paragraphs .99 through .101 for guidance regarding the review of the predecessor auditor's working papers.

Review

.08 The objective of a review of MD&A is to report whether any information came to the practitioner's attention to cause him or her to believe that—

a. The MD&A presentation does not include, in all material respects, the required elements of the rules and regulations adopted by the SEC.

b. The historical financial amounts included therein have not been accurately derived, in all material respects, from the entity's financial statements.

c. The underlying information, determinations, estimates, and assumptions of the entity do not provide a reasonable basis for the disclosures contained therein.

A review consists principally of applying analytical procedures and making inquiries of persons responsible for financial, accounting, and operational matters. A review ordinarily does not contemplate (*a*) tests of accounting records through inspection, observation, or confirmation, (*b*) obtaining corroborating evidential matter in response to inquiries, or (*c*) the application of certain other procedures ordinarily performed during an examination of MD&A. A review may bring to the practitioner's attention significant matters affecting the MD&A, but it does not provide assurance that the practitioner will become aware of all significant matters that would be disclosed in an examination.

.09 A practitioner may accept an engagement to review the MD&A presentation of a public entity for an annual period provided the practitioner has audited, in accordance with GAAS, the financial statements for at least the latest annual period to which the MD&A presentation relates and the financial statements for the other periods covered by the MD&A presentation have been audited by the practitioner or a predecessor auditor.[14] A base knowledge of the entity and its operations gained through an audit of the historical financial

---

[14] As discussed in paragraph .85*k*, a review report is not intended to be filed with the SEC as a report under the 1933 Act or the 1934 Act and, accordingly, the review report should contain a statement of restrictions on the use of the report to specified parties if the entity is (*a*) a public entity or (*b*) a nonpublic entity that is making or has made an offering of securities and it appears that the securities may subsequently be registered or subject to a filing with the SEC or other regulatory agency.

statements and knowledge about the industry and the environment is necessary to provide the practitioner with sufficient knowledge to properly evaluate the results of the procedures performed in connection with the review.

.10 If a predecessor auditor has audited the financial statements for a prior period covered by the MD&A presentation, the practitioner should also consider whether, under the particular circumstances, he or she can acquire sufficient knowledge of the business and of the entity's accounting and financial reporting practices for such period so he or she would be able to—

a. Identify types of potential material misstatements in the MD&A and consider the likelihood of their occurrence.

b. Perform the procedures that will provide the practitioner with a basis for reporting whether any information has come to the practitioner's attention to cause him or her to believe any of the following.

   (1) The MD&A presentation does not include, in all material respects, the required elements of the rules and regulations adopted by the SEC.

   (2) The historical financial amounts included therein have not been accurately derived, in all material respects, from the entity's financial statements for such period.

   (3) The underlying information, determinations, estimates, and assumptions of the entity do not provide a reasonable basis for the disclosures contained therein.

.11 A practitioner may accept an engagement to review the MD&A presentation of a public entity for an interim period provided that both of the following conditions are met.

a. The practitioner performs either (*1*) a review of the historical financial statements for the related comparative interim periods and issues a review report thereon in accordance with AU section 722, *Interim Financial Information*, or (*2*) an audit of the interim financial statements.

b. The MD&A presentation for the most recent fiscal year has been or will be examined or reviewed by either the practitioner or a predecessor auditor.

.12 If a predecessor auditor examined or reviewed the MD&A presentation of a public entity for the most recent fiscal year, the practitioner should not accept an engagement to review the MD&A presentation for an interim period unless he or she can acquire sufficient knowledge of the business and of the entity's accounting and financial reporting practices for the interim period to perform the procedures described in paragraph .10.

.13 If a nonpublic entity chooses to prepare MD&A, the practitioner should not accept an engagement to perform a review of such MD&A for an annual period under this section unless both of the following conditions are met.

a. The annual financial statements for the periods covered by the MD&A presentation have been or will be audited and the practitioner has audited or will audit the most recent year (refer to paragraph .07 if the financial statements for prior years were audited by a predecessor auditor).

b. Management will provide a written assertion that the presentation has been prepared using the rules and regulations adopted by the SEC as the criteria. (See paragraph .02.)

.14 A practitioner may accept an engagement to review the MD&A presentation of a nonpublic entity for an interim period provided that all of the following conditions are met.

a. The practitioner performs one of the following:

   (1) A review of the historical financial statements for the related interim periods under the Statements on Standards for Accounting and Review Services (SSARSs) and issues a review report thereon

   (2) A review of the condensed interim financial information for the related interim periods under AU section 722 and issues a review report thereon, and such interim financial information is accompanied by complete annual financial statements for the most recent fiscal year that have been audited

   (3) An audit of the interim financial statements

b. The MD&A presentation for the most recent fiscal year has been or will be examined or reviewed.

c. Management will provide a written assertion stating that the presentation has been prepared using the rules and regulations adopted by the SEC as the criteria. (See paragraph .02.)

Engagement Acceptance Considerations

.15 In determining whether to accept an engagement, the practitioner should consider whether management (and others engaged by management to assist them, such as legal counsel) has the appropriate knowledge of the rules and regulations adopted by the SEC to prepare MD&A.

Responsibilities of Management

.16 Management is responsible for the preparation of the entity's MD&A pursuant to the rules and regulations adopted by the SEC. The preparation of MD&A in conformity with the rules and regulations adopted by the SEC requires management to interpret the criteria, accurately derive the historical amounts from the entity's books and records, make determinations as to the relevancy of information to be included, and make estimates and assumptions that affect reported information.

.17 An entity should not name the practitioner in a client-prepared document as having examined or reviewed MD&A unless the MD&A presentation and related practitioner's report and the related financial statements and auditor's (or accountant's review) report are included in the document (or, in the case of a public entity, incorporated by reference to such information filed with a regulatory agency). If such a statement is made in a document that does not include (or incorporate by reference) such information, the practitioner should request that neither his or her name nor reference to the practitioner be made with respect to the MD&A information, or that such document be revised to include the required presentations and reports. If the client does not comply, the practitioner should advise the client that he or she does not consent to either the use of his or her name or the reference to the practitioner, and he or she should consider what other actions might be appropriate.[15]

Obtaining an Understanding of the SEC Rules and Regulations and Management's Methodology for the Preparation of MD&A

.18 The practitioner should obtain an understanding of the rules and regulations adopted by the SEC for MD&A. (Refer to paragraph .04.)

.19 The practitioner should inquire of management regarding the method of preparing MD&A, including matters such as the sources of the information, how the information is gathered, how management evaluates the types of factors having a material effect on financial condition (including liquidity and capital resources), results of operations, and cash flows, and whether there have been any changes in the procedures from the prior year.

Timing of Procedures

.20 Proper planning by the practitioner contributes to the effectiveness of the attest procedures in an examination or a review of MD&A. Performing some of the work in conjunction with the audit of the historical financial statements or the review of interim financial statements may permit the work to be carried out in a more efficient manner and to be completed at an earlier date. When performing an examination or a review of MD&A, the practitioner may consider the results of tests of controls, analytical procedures,[16] and substantive tests performed in a financial statement audit or analytical procedures and inquiries made in a review of financial statements or interim financial information.

Materiality

.21 The practitioner should consider the concept of materiality in planning and performing the engagement. The objective of an examination or a review is to report on the MD&A presentation taken as a whole and not on the individual amounts and disclosures contained therein. In the context of an MD&A presentation, the concept of materiality encompasses both material omissions (for example, the omission of trends, events, and uncertainties that are currently known to management that are reasonably likely to have material effects on the entity's financial condition, results of operations, liquidity, or capital resources) and material misstatements in MD&A, both of which are referred to herein as a misstatement. Assessing the significance of a misstatement of some items in MD&A may be more dependent upon qualitative than

---

[15] In considering what other actions, if any, may be appropriate in these circumstances, the practitioner may wish to consult his or her legal counsel.

[16] AU section 329, *Analytical Procedures*, defines analytical procedures as "evaluations of financial information made by a study of plausible relationships among both financial and nonfinancial data. Analytical procedures range from simple comparisons to the use of complex models involving many relationships and elements of data." In applying analytical procedures to MD&A, the practitioner develops expectations of matters that would be discussed in MD&A by identifying and using plausible relationships that are reasonably expected to exist based on the practitioner's understanding of the client and of the industry in which the client operates, and the knowledge of relationships among the various financial elements gained through the audit of financial statements or review of interim financial information. Refer to AU section 329 for further discussion of analytical procedures.

quantitative considerations. Qualitative aspects of materiality relate to the relevance and reliability of the information presented (for example, qualitative aspects of materiality are considered in assessing whether the underlying information, determinations, estimates, and assumptions of the entity provide a reasonable basis for the disclosures in the MD&A). Furthermore, quantitative information is often more meaningful when accompanied by qualitative disclosures. For example, quantitative information about market risk-sensitive instruments is more meaningful when accompanied by qualitative information about an entity's market risk exposures and how those exposures are managed. Materiality is also a concept that is judged in light of the expected range of reasonableness of the information; therefore, users should not expect prospective information (information about events that have not yet occurred) to be as precise as historical information.

.22 In expressing an opinion, or providing the limited assurance of a review engagement, on the presentation, the practitioner should consider the omission or misstatement of an individual assertion (see paragraph .34) to be material if the magnitude of the omission or misstatement—individually or when aggregated with other omissions or misstatements—is such that a reasonable person using the MD&A presentation would be influenced by the inclusion or correction of the individual assertion. The relative rather than absolute size of an omission or misstatement may determine whether it is material in a given situation.

Inclusion of Pro Forma Financial Information

.23 Management may include pro forma financial information with respect to a business combination or other transactions in MD&A. The practitioner should consider the guidance in section 401, *Reporting on Pro Forma Financial Information*, paragraph .10, when performing procedures with respect to such information, even if management indicates in MD&A that certain information has been derived from unaudited financial statements. For example, in an examination of MD&A, the practitioner's procedures would ordinarily include obtaining an understanding of the underlying transaction or event, discussing with management their assumptions, obtaining sufficient evidence in support of the adjustments, and other procedures for the purpose of expressing an opinion on the MD&A presentation taken as a whole and not for expressing an opinion on (or providing the limited assurance of a review of) the pro forma financial information included therein under section 401.

Inclusion of External Information

.24 An entity may also include in its MD&A information external to the entity, such as the rating of its debt by certain rating agencies or comparisons with statistics from a trade association. Such external information should also be subjected to the practitioner's examination or review procedures. For example, in an examination, the practitioner might compare information concerning the statistics of a trade organization to a published source; however, the practitioner would not be expected to test the underlying support for the trade association's calculation of such statistics.

Inclusion of Forward-Looking Information

.25 An entity may include certain forward-looking disclosures in the MD&A presentation, including cautionary language concerning the achievability of the matters disclosed. Although any forward-looking disclosures that are included in the MD&A presentation should be subjected to the practitioner's examination or review, such information is subjected to testing only for the purpose of expressing an opinion that the underlying information, determinations, estimates, and assumptions provide a reasonable basis for the disclosures contained therein or providing the limited assurance of a review on the MD&A presentation taken as a whole. The practitioner may consider the guidance in section 301, *Financial Forecasts and Projections*, when performing procedures with respect to forward-looking information. The practitioner may also consider whether meaningful cautionary language has been included with the forward-looking information.

.26 Section 27A of the Securities Act of 1933 (the 1933 Act) and Section 21E of the Securities Exchange Act of 1934 (the 1934 Act) provide a safe harbor from liability in private litigation with respect to forward-looking statements that include or make reference to meaningful cautionary language. However, such sections also include exclusions from safe harbor protection in certain situations. Whether an entity's forward-looking statements and the practitioner's report thereon qualify for safe harbor protection is a legal matter.

Inclusion of Voluntary Information

.27 An entity may voluntarily include other information in the MD&A presentation that is not required by the rules and regulations adopted by the SEC for MD&A. When the entity includes in MD&A additional information required by other rules and regulations of the SEC (for example, Item 305 of Regulation S-K, *Quantitative and Qualitative Disclosures About Market Risk*), the practitioner should also consider such other rules and regulations in subjecting such information to his or her examination or review procedures.[17]

Examination Engagement

.28 To express an opinion about whether (*a*) the presentation includes, in all material respects, the required elements of the rules and regulations adopted by the SEC, (*b*) the historical financial amounts have been accurately derived, in all material respects, from the entity's financial statements, and (*c*) the underlying information, determinations, estimates, and assumptions of the entity provide a reasonable basis for the disclosures contained therein, the practitioner seeks to obtain reasonable assurance by accumulating sufficient evidence in support of the disclosures and assumptions, thereby restricting attestation risk to an appropriately low level.

Attestation Risk

.29 In an engagement to examine MD&A, the practitioner plans and performs the examination to obtain reasonable assurance of detecting both intentional and unintentional misstatements that are material to the MD&A presentation taken as a whole. Absolute assurance is not attainable because of factors such as the need for judgment regarding the areas to be tested and the nature, timing, and extent of tests to be performed; the concept of selective testing of the data; and the inherent limitations of the controls applicable to the preparation of MD&A. The practitioner exercises professional judgment in

---

[17] To the extent that the voluntary information includes forward-looking information, refer to paragraphs .25 and .26.

assessing the significant determinations made by management as to the relevancy of information to be included, and the estimates and assumptions that affect reported information. As a result of these factors, in the great majority of cases, the practitioner has to rely on evidence that is persuasive rather than convincing. Also, procedures may be ineffective for detecting an intentional misstatement that is concealed through collusion among client personnel and third parties or among management or employees of the client. Therefore, the subsequent discovery that a material misstatement exists in the MD&A does not, in and of itself, evidence (*a*) failure to obtain reasonable assurance; (*b*) inadequate planning, performance, or judgment on the part of the practitioner; (*c*) the absence of due professional care; or (*d*) a failure to comply with this section.

.30 Factors to be considered by the practitioner in planning an examination of MD&A include (*a*) the anticipated level of attestation risk related to assertions embodied in the MD&A presentation, (*b*) preliminary judgments about materiality for attest purposes, (*c*) the items within the MD&A presentation that are likely to require revision or adjustment, and (*d*) conditions that may require extension or modification of attest procedures. For purposes of an engagement to examine MD&A, the components of attestation risk are defined as follows.

a. *Inherent risk* is the susceptibility of an assertion within MD&A to a material misstatement, assuming that there are no related controls. (See paragraphs .34 through .38.)

b. *Control risk* is the risk that a material misstatement that could occur in an assertion within MD&A will not be prevented or detected on a timely basis by the entity's controls; some control risk will always exist because of the inherent limitations of any internal control.

c. *Detection risk* is the risk that the practitioner will not detect a material misstatement that exists in an assertion within MD&A.

Inherent Risk

.31 The level of inherent risk varies with the nature of the assertion. For example, the inherent risk concerning financial information included in the MD&A presentation may be low, whereas the inherent risk concerning the completeness of the disclosure of the entity's risks or liquidity may be high.

Control Risk

.32 The practitioner should assess control risk as discussed in paragraphs .53 through .57. Assessing control risk contributes to the practitioner's evaluation of the risk that material misstatement in the MD&A exists. In the process of assessing control risk (together with assessing inherent risk), the practitioner may obtain evidential matter about the risk that such misstatement may exist. The practitioner uses this evidential matter as part of the reasonable basis for his or her opinion on the MD&A presentation taken as a whole.

Detection Risk

.33 In determining an acceptable level of detection risk, the practitioner assesses inherent risk and control risk, and considers the extent to which he or she seeks to restrict attestation risk. As assessed inherent risk or control risk decreases, the acceptable level of detection risk increases. Accordingly, the practitioner may alter the nature, timing, and extent of tests performed based on the assessments of inherent risk and control risk.

Nature of Assertions

.34 Assertions are representations by management that are embodied in the MD&A presentation. They can be either explicit or implicit and can be classified according to the following broad categories:

a. Occurrence

b. Consistency with the financial statements

c. Completeness

d. Presentation and disclosure

.35 Assertions about occurrence address whether reported transactions or events have occurred during a given period. Assertions about consistency with the financial statements address whether—

a. Reported transactions, events, and explanations are consistent with the financial statements.

b. Historical financial amounts have been accurately derived from the financial statements and related records.

c. Nonfinancial data have been accurately derived from related records.

.36 Assertions about completeness address whether descriptions of transactions and events necessary to obtain an understanding of the entity's financial condition (including liquidity and capital resources), changes in financial condition, results of operations, and material commitments for capital resources are included in MD&A; and whether known events, transactions, conditions, trends, demands, commitments, or uncertainties that will result in or are reasonably likely to result in material changes to these items are appropriately described in the MD&A presentation.

.37 For example, if management asserts that the reason for an increase in revenues is a price increase in the current year, they are explicitly asserting that both an increase in revenues and a price increase have occurred in the current year, and implicitly asserting that any historical financial amounts included are consistent with the financial statements for such period. They are also implicitly asserting that the explanation for the increase in revenues is complete; that there are no other significant reasons for the increase in revenues.

.38 Assertions about presentation and disclosure address whether information included in the MD&A presentation is properly classified, described, and disclosed. For example, management asserts that any forward-looking information included in MD&A is properly classified as being based on management's present assessment and includes an appropriate description of the expected results. To further disclose the nature of such information, management may also include a statement that actual results in the future may differ materially from management's present assessment. (See paragraphs .25 and .26.)

.39 The auditor of the underlying financial statements is responsible for obtaining and evaluating evidential matter concerning the assertions embodied in the account balance or transaction class of the financial statements as discussed in AU section 326, *Audit Evidence*. Although procedures designed to achieve the practitioner's objective of forming an opinion on the MD&A presentation taken as a whole may test certain assertions embodied in the underlying financial statements, the practitioner is not expected to test the underlying financial statement assertions in an examination of MD&A. For example, the practitioner is not expected to test the completeness of revenues or the existence of inventory when testing the assertions in MD&A concerning an increase in revenues or an increase in inventory levels; assurance related to completeness of revenues or for existence of inventory would be obtained as part of the audit. The practitioner is, however, responsible for testing the completeness of the explanation for the increase in revenues or the increase in inventory levels.

Performing an Examination Engagement

.40 The practitioner should exercise (*a*) due professional care in planning, performing, and evaluating the results of his or her examination procedures and (*b*) the proper degree of professional skepticism to obtain reasonable assurance that material misstatements will be detected.

.41 In an examination of MD&A, the practitioner should perform the following.

a. Obtain an understanding of the rules and regulations adopted by the SEC for MD&A and management's method of preparing MD&A. (See paragraphs .18 and .19.)

b. Plan the engagement. (See paragraphs .42 through .48.)

c. Consider relevant portions of the entity's internal control applicable to the preparation of MD&A. (See paragraphs .49 through .58.)

d. Obtain sufficient evidence, including testing completeness. (See paragraphs .59 through .64.)

e. Consider the effect of events subsequent to the balance-sheet date. (See paragraphs .65 and .66.)

f. Obtain written representations from management concerning its responsibility for MD&A, completeness of minutes, events subsequent to the balance-sheet date, and other matters about which the practitioner believes written representations are appropriate. (See paragraphs .110 through .112.)

g. Form an opinion about whether the MD&A presentation includes, in all material respects, the required elements of the rules and regulations adopted by the SEC, whether the historical financial amounts included therein have been accurately derived, in all material respects, from the entity's financial statements, and whether the underlying information, determinations, estimates, and assumptions of the entity provide a reasonable basis for the disclosures contained in the MD&A. (See paragraph .67.)

Planning the Engagement

General Considerations

.42 Planning an engagement to examine MD&A involves developing an overall strategy for the expected scope and performance of the engagement. When developing an overall strategy for the engagement, the practitioner should consider factors such as the following:

- Matters affecting the industry in which the entity operates, such as financial reporting practices, economic conditions, laws and regulations, and technological changes
- Knowledge of the entity's internal control applicable to the preparation of MD&A obtained during the audit of the financial statements and the extent of recent changes, if any
- Matters relating to the entity's business, including its organization, operating characteristics, capital structure, and distribution methods
- The types of relevant information that management reports to external analysts (for example, press releases and presentations to lenders and rating agencies, if any, concerning past and future performance)
- How the entity analyzes actual performance compared to budgets and the types of information provided in documents submitted to the board of directors for purposes of the entity's day-to-day operations and long-range planning
- The extent of management's knowledge of and experience with the rules and regulations adopted by the SEC for MD&A
- If the entity is a nonpublic entity, the intended use of the MD&A presentation
- Preliminary judgments about (*a*) materiality, (*b*) inherent risk at the individual assertion level, and (*c*) factors (for example, matters identified during the audit or review of the historical financial statements) relating to significant deficiencies in internal control applicable to the preparation of MD&A (See paragraph .58.)
- The fraud risk factors or other conditions identified during the audit of the most recent annual financial statements and the practitioner's response to such risk factors
- The type and extent of evidential matter supporting management's assertions and disclosures in the MD&A presentation
- The nature of complex or subjective matters potentially material to the MD&A presentation that may require special skill or knowledge and whether such matters may require using the work of a specialist to obtain sufficient evidential matter (See paragraph .47.)
- The presence of an internal audit function (See paragraph .48.)

.43 In planning an engagement when MD&A has not previously been examined, the practitioner should consider the degree to which the entity has information available for such prior periods and the continuity of the entity's personnel and their ability to respond to inquiries with respect to such periods. In addition, the practitioner should obtain an understanding of the entity's internal control in prior years applicable to the preparation of MD&A.

Consideration of Audit Results

.44 The practitioner should also consider the results of the audits of the financial statements for the periods covered by the MD&A presentation on the examination engagement, such as matters relating to the following:

- The availability and condition of the entity's records
- The nature and magnitude of audit adjustments

- Likely misstatements[18] that were not corrected in the financial statements that may affect MD&A disclosures (for example, misclassifications between financial statement line items)

.45 The practitioner should also consider the possible impact on the scope of the examination engagement of any modification or contemplated modification of the auditor's report, including matters addressed in explanatory language. For example, if the auditor has modified the auditor's report to include a going-concern uncertainty explanatory paragraph, the practitioner would consider such a matter in assessing attestation risk.

Multiple Components

.46 In an engagement to examine MD&A, if the entity has operations in several components (for example, locations, branches, subsidiaries, or programs), the practitioner should determine the components to which procedures should be applied. In making such a determination and in selecting the components to be tested, the practitioner should consider factors such as the following:

- The relative importance of each component to the applicable MD&A disclosure
- The degree of centralization of records
- The effectiveness of controls, particularly those that affect management's direct control over the exercise of authority delegated to others and its ability to supervise activities at various locations effectively
- The nature and extent of operations conducted at the various components
- The similarity of operations and internal control for different components

The practitioner should consider whether the audit base of the components is consistent with the components that are disclosed in MD&A. Accordingly, it may be desirable for the practitioner to coordinate the audit work with the components that will be disclosed.

Using the Work of a Specialist

.47 In some engagements to examine MD&A, the nature of complex or subjective matters potentially material to the MD&A presentation may require specialized skill or knowledge in a particular field other than accounting or auditing. For example, the entity may include information concerning plant production capacity, which would ordinarily be determined by an engineer. In such cases, the practitioner may use the work of a specialist and should consider the relevant guidance in AU section 336, *Using the Work of a Specialist*. AU section 311, *Planning and Supervision*, provides relevant guidance for situations in which a specialist employed by the practitioner's firm participates in the examination.

Internal Audit Function

.48 Another factor the practitioner should consider when planning the engagement is whether the entity has an internal audit function and the extent to which internal auditors are involved in directly testing the MD&A presentation, in monitoring the entity's internal control applicable to the preparation

---

[18] Refer to AU section 312, *Audit Risk and Materiality in Conducting on Audit*, paragraphs .34 through .40.

of MD&A, or in testing the underlying records supporting disclosures in the MD&A. A practitioner should consider the guidance in AU section 322, *The Auditor's Consideration of the Internal Audit Function in an Audit of Financial Statements*, when addressing the competence and objectivity of internal auditors; the nature, timing, and extent of work to be performed; and other related matters.

Consideration of Internal Control Applicable to the Preparation of MD&A

.49 The practitioner should obtain an understanding of the entity's internal control applicable to the preparation of MD&A sufficient to plan the engagement and to assess control risk. Generally, controls that are relevant to an examination pertain to the entity's objective of preparing MD&A in conformity with the rules and regulations adopted by the SEC, and may include controls within the control environment, risk assessment, control activities, information and communication, and monitoring components.

.50 The controls relating to operations and compliance objectives may be relevant to an examination if they pertain to data the practitioner evaluates or uses in applying examination procedures. For example, controls over the gathering of information, which are different from financial statement controls, and controls relating to nonfinancial data that are included in the MD&A presentation, may be relevant to an examination engagement.

.51 In planning the examination, knowledge of such controls should be used to identify types of potential misstatement (including types of potential material omissions), to consider factors that affect the risk of material misstatement and to design appropriate tests.

.52 A practitioner generally obtains an understanding of the design of the entity's internal control applicable to the preparation of MD&A by making inquiries of appropriate management, supervisory, and staff personnel; by inspection of the entity's documents; and by observation of the entity's relevant activities, including controls over matters discussed, nonfinancial data included, and management evaluation of the reasonableness of information included. The nature and extent of procedures a practitioner performs vary from entity to entity and are influenced by factors such as the entity's complexity, the length of time that the entity has prepared MD&A pursuant to the rules and regulations adopted by the SEC, the practitioner's knowledge of the entity's controls obtained in audits and previous professional engagements, and judgments about materiality.

.53 After obtaining an understanding of the entity's internal control applicable to the preparation of MD&A, the practitioner assesses control risk for the assertions embodied in the MD&A presentation. (Refer to paragraphs .34 through .39.) The practitioner may assess control risk at the maximum level (the greatest probability that a material misstatement that could occur in an assertion will not be prevented or detected on a timely basis by an entity's controls) because the practitioner believes controls are unlikely to pertain to an assertion, are unlikely to be effective, or because evaluating their effectiveness would be inefficient. Alternatively, the practitioner may obtain evidential matter about the effectiveness of both the design and operation of a control that supports a lower assessed level of control risk. Such evidential matter may be obtained from tests of controls planned and performed concurrently with obtaining the understanding of the internal control or from procedures performed to obtain the understanding that were not specifically planned as tests of controls.

.54 After obtaining the understanding and assessing control risk, the practitioner may desire to seek a further reduction in the assessed level of control risk for certain assertions. In such cases, the practitioner considers whether evidential matter sufficient to support a further reduction is likely to be available and whether performing additional tests of controls to obtain such evidential matter would be efficient.

.55 When seeking to assess control risk below the maximum for controls over financial and nonfinancial data, the practitioner should perform tests of controls to obtain evidence to support the assessed level of control risk. For example, the practitioner may perform tests of controls directed toward the effectiveness of the design or operation of internal control over the accumulation of the number of units sold for a manufacturing company, average interest rates earned and paid for a financial institution, or average net sales per square foot for a retail entity.

.56 The practitioner uses the knowledge provided by the understanding of internal control applicable to the preparation of MD&A and the assessed level of control risk in determining the nature, timing, and extent of substantive tests for the MD&A assertions.

.57 The practitioner should document the understanding of the internal control components obtained to plan the examination and the assessment of control risk. The form and extent of this documentation is influenced by the size and complexity of the entity, as well as the nature of the entity's controls applicable to the preparation of MD&A.

.58 During the course of an engagement to examine MD&A, the practitioner may become aware of control deficiencies in the design or operation of controls applicable to the preparation of MD&A that could adversely affect the entity's ability to prepare MD&A in accordance with the rules and regulations adopted by the SEC. The practitioner should consider the implications of such control deficiencies on his or her ability to rely on management's explanations and on comparisons to summary accounting records. A practitioner's responsibility to communicate these control deficiencies in an examination of MD&A is similar to the auditor's responsibility described in AU section 325, *Communicating Internal Control Related Matters Identified in an Audit*, and AU section 380, *The Auditor's Communication With Those Charged With Governance*. [Revised, March 2006, to reflect conforming changes necessary due to the issuance of Statement on Auditing Standards No. 112. Revised, January 2010, to reflect conforming changes necessary due to the issuance of SAS No. 115.]

Obtaining Sufficient Evidence

.59 The practitioner should apply procedures to obtain reasonable assurance of detecting material misstatements. In an audit of historical financial statements, the practitioner will have applied audit procedures to some of the information included in the MD&A. However, because the objective of those audit procedures is to have a reasonable basis for expressing an opinion on the financial statements taken as a whole rather than on the MD&A, certain additional examination procedures should be performed as discussed in paragraphs .60 through .64. Determining these procedures and evaluating the sufficiency of the evidence obtained are matters of professional judgment.

.60 The practitioner ordinarily should apply the following procedures.

a. Read the MD&A and compare the content for consistency with the audited financial statements; compare financial amounts to the audited financial statements or related accounting records and analyses; recompute the increases, decreases, and percentages disclosed.

b. Compare nonfinancial amounts to the audited financial statements, if applicable, or to other records. (Refer to paragraphs .62 through .64.)

c. Consider whether the explanations in MD&A are consistent with the information obtained during the audit; investigate further those explanations that cannot be substantiated by information in the audit working papers through inquiry (including inquiry of officers and other executives having responsibility for operational areas) and inspection of client records.

d. Examine internally generated documents (for example, variance analyses, sales analyses, wage cost analyses, sales or service pricing sheets, and business plans or programs) and externally generated documents (for example, correspondence, contracts, or loan agreements) in support of the existence, occurrence, or expected occurrence of events, transactions, conditions, trends, demands, commitments, and uncertainties disclosed in the MD&A.

e. Obtain available prospective financial information (for example, budgets; sales forecasts; forecasts of labor, overhead, and materials costs; capital expenditure requests; and financial forecasts and projections) and compare such information to forward-looking MD&A disclosures. Inquire of management as to the procedures used to prepare the prospective financial information. Evaluate whether the underlying information, determinations, estimates, and assumptions of the entity provide a reasonable basis for the MD&A disclosures of events, transactions, conditions, trends, demands, commitments, or uncertainties.[19]

f. Consider obtaining available prospective financial information relating to prior periods and comparing actual results with forecasted and projected amounts.

g. Make inquiries of officers and other executives having responsibility for operational areas (such as sales, marketing, and production) and financial and accounting matters, as to their plans and expectations for the future that could affect the entity's liquidity and capital resources.

h. Consider obtaining external information concerning industry trends, inflation, and changing prices and comparing the related MD&A disclosures to such information.

i. Compare the information in MD&A with the rules and regulations adopted by the SEC and consider whether the presentation includes the required elements of such rules and regulations.

---

[19] Refer to paragraph .26 for a discussion concerning the safe harbor rules for forward-looking statements.

j. Read the minutes of meetings to date of the board of directors and other significant committees to identify matters that may affect MD&A; consider whether such matters are appropriately addressed in MD&A.

k. Inquire of officers as to the entity's prior experience with the SEC and the extent of comments received upon review of documents by the SEC; read correspondence between the entity and the SEC with respect to such review, if any.

l. Obtain public communications (for example, press releases and quarterly reports) and the related supporting documentation dealing with historical and future results; consider whether MD&A is consistent with such communications.

m. Consider obtaining other types of publicly available information (for example, analyst reports and news articles); compare the MD&A presentation with such information.

Testing Completeness

.61 The practitioner should design procedures to test the presentation for completeness, including tests of the completeness of explanations that relate to historical disclosures as discussed in paragraphs .36 and .37. The practitioner should also consider whether the MD&A discloses matters that could significantly impact future financial condition and results of operations of the entity by considering information that he or she obtained through the following:

a. Audit of the financial statements

b. Inquiries of the entity's officers and other executives directed to current events, conditions, economic changes, commitments and uncertainties, within both the entity and its industry

c. Other information obtained through procedures such as those listed in paragraphs .60, .65, and .66

As discussed in paragraph .31, the inherent risk concerning the completeness of disclosures may be high; if it is, the practitioner may extend the procedures (for example, by making additional inquiries of management or by examining additional internally generated documents).

Nonfinancial Data

.62 Management may include nonfinancial data (such as units produced; the number of units sold, locations, or customers; plant utilization; or square footage) in the MD&A. The practitioner should consider whether the definitions used by management for such nonfinancial data are reasonable for the particular disclosure in the MD&A and whether there are suitable criteria (for example, industry standards with respect to square footage for retail operations), as discussed in section 101.23–.32.

.63 In some situations, the nonfinancial data or the controls over the nonfinancial data may have been tested by the practitioner in conjunction with the financial statement audit; however, the practitioner's consideration of the nature of the procedures to apply to nonfinancial data in an examination of MD&A is based on the concept of materiality with respect to the MD&A presentation. The practitioner should consider whether industry standards exist for the nonfinancial data or whether there are different methods of measurement that may be used, and, if such methods could result in significantly different results, whether the method of measurement selected by management is reasonable and consistent between periods covered by the MD&A presentation. For example, the number of customers reported by management could vary depending on whether management defines a customer as a subsidiary or "ship to" location of a company rather than the company itself.

.64 In testing nonfinancial data included in the MD&A, the practitioner may seek to assess control risk below the maximum for controls over such nonfinancial data, as discussed in paragraph .55. The practitioner weighs the increase in effort of the examination associated with the additional tests of controls that is necessary to obtain evidential matter against the resulting decrease in examination effort associated with the reduced substantive tests. For those nonfinancial assertions for which the practitioner performs additional tests of controls, the practitioner determines the assessed level of control risk that the results of those tests will support. This assessed level of control risk is used in determining the appropriate detection risk to accept for those nonfinancial assertions and, accordingly, in determining the nature, timing, and extent of substantive tests for such assertions.

Consideration of the Effect of Events Subsequent to the Balance-Sheet Date

.65 As there is an expectation by the SEC that MD&A considers events through a date at or near the filing date,[20] the practitioner should consider information about events[21] that comes to his or her attention after the end of the period addressed by MD&A and prior to the issuance of his or her report that may have a material effect on the entity's financial condition (including liquidity and capital resources), changes in financial condition, results of operations, and material commitments for capital resources. Events or matters that should be disclosed in MD&A include those that—[22]

- Are reasonably expected to have a material favorable or unfavorable impact on net sales or revenues or income from continuing operations.
- Are reasonably likely to result in the entity's liquidity increasing or decreasing in any material way.
- Will have a material effect on the entity's capital resources.
- Would cause reported financial information not to be necessarily indicative of future operating results or of future financial condition.

The practitioner should consider whether events identified during the examination of the MD&A presentation or the audit of the related financial statements require adjustment to or disclosure in the MD&A presentation. When MD&A will be included or incorporated by reference in a 1933 Act document that is filed with the SEC, the practitioner's procedures should extend up to the

---

20 A registration statement under the 1933 Act speaks as of its effective date.

21 Such events are only referred to as *subsequent events* in relation to an MD&A presentation if they occur after the MD&A presentation has been issued. The annual MD&A presentation ordinarily would not be updated for subsequent events if an MD&A presentation for a subsequent interim period has been issued or the event has been reported through a filing on Form 8-K.

22 The practitioner should refer to the rules and regulations adopted by the SEC for other examples of events that should be disclosed.

filing date or as close to it as is reasonable and practicable in the circumstances.[23] If a public entity's MD&A presentation is to be included only in a filing under the 1934 Act (for example, Forms 10-K or 10-KSB), the practitioner's responsibility to consider subsequent events does not extend beyond the date of the report on MD&A. Paragraphs .94 through .98 provide guidance when the practitioner is engaged subsequent to the filing of the MD&A presentation.

.66 In an examination of MD&A, the practitioner's fieldwork ordinarily extends beyond the date of the auditor's report on the related financial statements.[24] Accordingly, the practitioner generally should—

a. Read available minutes of meetings of stockholders, the board of directors, and other appropriate committees; as to meetings for which minutes are not available, inquire about matters dealt with at such meetings.

b. Read the latest available interim financial statements for periods subsequent to the date of the auditor's report, compare them with the financial statements for the periods covered by the MD&A, and inquire of and discuss with officers and other executives having responsibility for operational, financial, and accounting matters (limited where appropriate to major locations) matters such as the following:

- Whether interim financial statements have been prepared on the same basis as the audited financial statements
- Whether there were any significant changes in the entity's operations, liquidity, or capital resources in the subsequent period
- The current status of items in the financial statements for which the MD&A has been prepared that were accounted for on the basis of tentative, preliminary, or inconclusive data
- Whether any unusual adjustments were made during the period from the balance-sheet date to the date of inquiry

c. Make inquiries of members of senior management as to the current status of matters concerning litigation, claims, and assessments identified during the audit of the financial statements and of any new matters or unfavorable developments. Consider obtaining updated legal letters from legal counsel.[25]

d. Consider whether there have been any changes in economic conditions or in the industry that could have a significant effect on the entity.

---

[23] Additionally, if the practitioner's report on MD&A is included or incorporated by reference in a 1933 Act document, the practitioner should extend his or her procedures with respect to subsequent events from the date of his or her report on MD&A up to the effective date or as close thereto as is reasonable and practicable in the circumstances.

[24] Undertaking an engagement to examine MD&A does not extend the auditor's responsibility to update the subsequent events review procedures for the financial statements beyond the date of the auditor's report. However, see AU section 561, *Subsequent Discovery of Facts Existing at the Date of the Auditor's Report*. Also, see AU section 711, *Filings Under Federal Securities Statutes*, as to an auditor's responsibility when his or her report is included in a registration statement filed under the 1933 Act.

[25] See AU section 337, *Inquiry of a Client's Lawyer Concerning Litigation, Claims, and Assessments*, for guidance concerning obtaining legal letters.

e. Obtain written representations from appropriate officials as to whether any events occurred subsequent to the latest balance-sheet date that would require disclosure in the MD&A. (See paragraphs .110 through .112.)

f. Make such additional inquiries or perform such other procedures as considered necessary and appropriate to address questions that arise in carrying out the foregoing procedures, inquiries, and discussions.

Forming an Opinion

.67 The practitioner should consider the concept of materiality discussed in paragraphs .21 and .22, and the impact of any modification of the auditor's report on the historical financial statements in forming an opinion on the examination of MD&A, including the practitioner's ability to evaluate the results of inquiries and other procedures.

Reporting

.68 In order for the practitioner to issue a report on an examination of MD&A, the financial statements for the periods covered by the MD&A presentation and the related auditor's report(s) should accompany the MD&A presentation (or, with respect to a public entity, be incorporated in the document containing the MD&A by reference to information filed with a regulatory agency). In addition, if the entity is a nonpublic entity, one of the following conditions should be met.

a. A statement should be included in the body of the MD&A presentation that it has been prepared using the rules and regulations adopted by the SEC.

b. A separate written assertion should accompany the MD&A presentation or such assertion should be included in a representation letter obtained from the entity.

.69 The practitioner's report on an examination of MD&A should include the following:

a. A title that includes the word *independent*

b. An identification of the MD&A presentation, including the period covered

c. A statement that management is responsible for the preparation of the MD&A pursuant to the rules and regulations adopted by the SEC, and a statement that the practitioner's responsibility is to express an opinion on the presentation based on his or her examination

d. A reference to the auditor's report on the related financial statements, and if the report was other than a standard report, the substantive reasons therefor

e. A statement that the examination was conducted in accordance with attestation standards established by the AICPA and a description of the scope of an examination of MD&A

f. A statement that the practitioner believes the examination provides a reasonable basis for his or her opinion *g.* A paragraph stating that—

(1) The preparation of MD&A requires management to interpret the criteria, make determinations as to the relevancy of information to be included, and make estimates and assumptions that affect reported information

(2) Actual results in the future may differ materially from management's present assessment of information regarding the estimated future impact of transactions and events that have occurred or are expected to occur, expected sources of liquidity and capital resources, operating trends, commitments, and uncertainties

h. If the entity is a nonpublic entity, a statement that, although the entity is not subject to the rules and regulations of the SEC, the MD&A presentation is intended to be a presentation in accordance with the rules and regulations adopted by the SEC

i. The practitioner's opinion on whether—

(1) The presentation includes, in all material respects, the required elements of the rules and regulations adopted by the SEC

(2) The historical financial amounts have been accurately derived, in all material respects, from the entity's financial statements

(3) The underlying information, determinations, estimates, and assumptions of the entity provide a reasonable basis for the disclosures contained therein

j. The manual or printed signature of the practitioner's firm

k. The date of the examination report

Appendix A [paragraph .114], "Examination Reports," includes a standard examination report. (See Example 1.)

Dating

.70 The practitioner's report on the examination of MD&A should be dated as of the completion of the practitioner's examination procedures. That date should not precede the date of the auditor's report on the latest historical financial statements covered by the MD&A.

Report Modifications

.71 The practitioner should modify the standard report described in paragraph .69, if any of the following conditions exist.

- The presentation excludes a material required element under the rules and regulations adopted by the SEC. (See paragraph .72.)
- The historical financial amounts have not been accurately derived, in all material respects, from the entity's financial statements. (See paragraph .72.)
- The underlying information, determinations, estimates, and assumptions used by management do not provide the entity with a reasonable basis for the disclosure in the MD&A. (See paragraph .72.)
- There is a restriction on the scope of the engagement. (See paragraph .73.)

- The practitioner decides to refer to the report of another practitioner as the basis in part for his or her report. (See paragraph .74.)
- The practitioner is engaged to examine the MD&A presentation after it has been filed with the SEC or other regulatory agency. (See paragraphs .94 through .98.)

.72 The practitioner should express a qualified or an adverse opinion if (*a*) the MD&A presentation excludes a material required element, (*b*) historical financial amounts have not been accurately derived in all material respects, or (*c*) the underlying information, determinations, estimates, and assumptions of the entity do not provide a reasonable basis for the disclosures; for example, if there is a lack of consistency between management's method of measuring nonfinancial data between periods covered by the MD&A presentation. The basis for such opinion should be stated in the practitioner's report. Appendix A [paragraph .114] includes several examples of such modifications. (See Example 2.) Also refer to paragraph .107 for required communications with the audit committee.

.73 If the practitioner is unable to perform the procedures he or she considers necessary in the circumstances, the practitioner should modify the report or withdraw from the engagement. If the practitioner modifies the report, he or she should describe the limitation on the scope of the examination in an explanatory paragraph and qualify his or her opinion, or disclaim an opinion. However, limitations on the ability of the practitioner to perform necessary procedures could also arise because of the lack of adequate support for a significant representation in the MD&A. That circumstance may result in a conclusion that the unsupported representation constitutes a material misstatement of fact and, accordingly, the practitioner may qualify his or her opinion or express an adverse opinion, as described in paragraph .72.

Reference to Report of Another Practitioner

.74 If another practitioner examined the MD&A presentation of a component (refer to paragraph .46), the practitioner may decide to make reference to such report of the other practitioner as a basis for his or her opinion on the consolidated MD&A presentation. The practitioner should disclose this fact in the introductory paragraph of the report and should refer to the report of the other practitioner in expressing an opinion on the consolidated MD&A presentation. These references indicate a division of responsibility for performance of the examination. Appendix A [paragraph .114] provides an example of a report for such a situation. (See Example 3.) Refer to paragraph .105 for guidance when the other practitioner does not issue a report.

Emphasis of a Matter

.75 In a number of circumstances, the practitioner may wish to emphasize a matter regarding the MD&A presentation. For example, he or she may wish to emphasize that the entity has included information beyond the required elements of the rules and regulations adopted by the SEC. Such explanatory comments should be presented in a separate paragraph of the practitioner's report.

Review Engagement

.76 The objective of a review engagement, including a review of MD&A for an interim period, is to accumulate sufficient evidence to provide the practitioner with a basis for reporting whether any information came to the practitioner's attention to cause him or her to believe that (*a*) the MD&A presentation does not include, in all material respects, the required elements of the rules and regulations adopted by the SEC, (*b*) the historical financial amounts included therein have not been accurately derived, in all material respects, from the entity's financial statements, or (*c*) the underlying information, determinations, estimates, and assumptions of the entity do not provide a reasonable basis for the disclosures contained therein. MD&A for an interim period may be a freestanding presentation or it may be combined with the MD&A presentation for the most recent fiscal year. Procedures for conducting a review of MD&A generally are limited to inquiries and analytical procedures, rather than also including search and verification procedures, concerning factors that have a material effect on financial condition, including liquidity and capital resources, results of operations, and cash flows. In a review engagement, the practitioner should—

a. Obtain an understanding of the rules and regulations adopted by the SEC for MD&A and management's method of preparing MD&A. (See paragraphs .18 and .19.)

b. Plan the engagement. (See paragraph .77.)

c. Consider relevant portions of the entity's internal control applicable to the preparation of the MD&A. (See paragraph .78.)

d. Apply analytical procedures and make inquiries of management and others. (See paragraphs .79 and .80.)

e. Consider the effect of events subsequent to the balance-sheet date. The practitioner's consideration of such events in a review of MD&A is similar to the practitioner's consideration in an examination. (See paragraphs .65 and .66.)

f. Obtain written representations from management concerning its responsibility for MD&A, completeness of minutes, events subsequent to the balance-sheet date, and other matters about which the practitioner believes written representations are appropriate. (See paragraph .110.)

g. Form a conclusion as to whether any information came to the practitioner's attention that causes him or her to believe any of the following.

   (1) The MD&A presentation does not include, in all material respects, the required elements of the rules and regulations adopted by the SEC.

   (2) The historical financial amounts included therein have not been accurately derived, in all material respects, from the entity's financial statements.

   (3) The underlying information, determinations, estimates, and assumptions of the entity do not provide a reasonable basis for the disclosures contained therein.

Planning the Engagement

.77 Planning an engagement to review MD&A involves developing an overall strategy for the analytical procedures and inquiries to be performed. When developing an overall strategy for the review engagement, the practitioner should consider factors such as the following:

- Matters affecting the industry in which the entity operates, such as financial reporting practices, economic conditions, laws and regulations, and technological changes
- Matters relating to the entity's business, including its organization, operating characteristics, capital structure, and distribution methods
- The types of relevant information that management reports to external analysts (for example, press releases or presentations to lenders and rating agencies concerning past and future performance)
- The extent of management's knowledge of and experience with the rules and regulations adopted by the SEC for MD&A
- If the entity is a nonpublic entity, the intended use of the MD&A presentation
- Matters identified during the audit or review of the historical financial statements relating to MD&A reporting, including knowledge of the entity's internal control applicable to the preparation of MD&A and the extent of recent changes, if any
- Matters identified during prior engagements to examine or review MD&A
- Preliminary judgments about materiality
- The nature of complex or subjective matters potentially material to the MD&A that may require special skill or knowledge
- The presence of an internal audit function and the extent to which internal auditors are involved in directly testing the MD&A presentation or underlying records

Consideration of Internal Control Applicable to the Preparation of MD&A

.78 To perform a review of MD&A, the practitioner needs to have sufficient knowledge of the entity's internal control applicable to the preparation of MD&A to—

- Identify types of potential misstatements in MD&A, including types of material omissions, and consider the likelihood of their occurrence.
- Select the inquiries and analytical procedures that will provide a basis for reporting whether any information causes the practitioner to believe the following.
  - — The MD&A presentation does not include, in all material respects, the required elements of the rules and regulations adopted by the SEC, or the historical financial amounts included therein have not been accurately derived, in all material respects, from the entity's financial statements.
  - — The underlying information, determinations, estimates, and assumptions of the entity do not provide a reasonable basis for the disclosures contained therein.

Application of Analytical Procedures and Inquiries

.79 The practitioner ordinarily would not obtain corroborating evidential matter of management's responses to the practitioner's inquiries in performing a review of MD&A. The practitioner should, however, consider the consistency of management's responses in light of the results of other inquiries and the application of analytical procedures. The practitioner ordinarily should apply the following analytical procedures and inquiries.

a. Read the MD&A presentation and compare the content for consistency with the audited financial statements (or reviewed interim financial information if MD&A includes interim information); compare financial amounts to the audited or reviewed financial statements or related accounting records and analyses; recompute the increases, decreases, and percentages disclosed.

b. Compare nonfinancial amounts to the audited (or reviewed) financial statements, if applicable, or to other records. (Refer to paragraph .80.)

c. Consider whether the explanations in MD&A are consistent with the information obtained during the audit or the review of interim financial information; make further inquiries of officers and other executives having responsibility for operational areas as necessary.

d. Obtain available prospective financial information (for example, budgets; sales forecasts; forecasts of labor, overhead, and materials costs; capital expenditure requests; and financial forecasts and projections) and compare such information to forward-looking MD&A disclosures. Inquire of management as to the procedures used to prepare the prospective financial information. Consider whether information came to the practitioner's attention that causes him or her to believe that the underlying information, determinations, estimates, and assumptions of the entity do not provide a reasonable basis for the disclosures of trends, demands, commitments, events, or uncertainties.[26]

e. Make inquiries of officers and other executives having responsibility for operational areas (such as sales, marketing, and production) and financial and accounting matters, as to any plans and expectations for the future that could affect the entity's liquidity and capital resources.

f. Compare the information in MD&A with the rules and regulations adopted by the SEC and consider whether the presentation includes the required elements of such rules and regulations.

g. Read the minutes of meetings to date of the board of directors and other significant committees to identify actions that may affect MD&A; consider whether such matters are appropriately addressed in the MD&A presentation.

h. Inquire of officers as to the entity's prior experience with the SEC and the extent of comments received upon review of documents by the SEC; read correspondence between the entity and the SEC with respect to such review, if any.

i. Inquire of management regarding the nature of public communications (for example, press releases and quarterly reports) dealing with historical and future results and consider whether the MD&A presentation is consistent with such communications.

---

[26] Refer to paragraph .26 for a discussion concerning the safe harbor rules for forward-looking statements.

.80 If nonfinancial data are included in the MD&A presentation, the practitioner should inquire as to the nature of the records from which such information was derived and observe the existence of such records, but need not perform other tests of such records beyond analytical procedures and inquiries of individuals responsible for maintaining them. The practitioner should consider whether such nonfinancial data are relevant to users of the MD&A presentation and whether such data are clearly defined in the MD&A presentation. The practitioner should make inquiries regarding whether the definition of the nonfinancial data was consistently applied during the periods reported.

.81 However, if the practitioner becomes aware that the presentation may be incomplete or contain inaccuracies, or is otherwise unsatisfactory, the practitioner should perform the additional procedures he or she deems necessary to achieve the limited assurance contemplated by a review engagement.

Reporting

.82 In order for the practitioner to issue a report on a review of MD&A for an annual period, the financial statements for the periods covered by the MD&A presentation and the related auditor's report(s) should accompany the MD&A presentation (or with respect to a public entity be incorporated in the document containing the MD&A by reference to information filed with a regulatory agency).

.83 If the MD&A presentation relates to an interim period and the entity is a public entity, the financial statements for the interim periods covered by the MD&A presentation and the related accountant's review report(s) should accompany the MD&A presentation, or be incorporated in the document containing the MD&A by reference to information filed with a regulatory agency. The comparative financial statements for the most recent annual period and the related MD&A should accompany the MD&A presentation for the interim period, or be incorporated by reference to information filed with a regulatory agency. Generally, the requirement for inclusion of the annual financial statements and related MD&A is satisfied by a public entity that has met its reporting responsibility for filing its annual financial statements and MD&A in its annual report on Form 10-K.

.84 If the MD&A presentation relates to an interim period and the entity is a nonpublic entity, the following documents should accompany the interim MD&A presentation in order for the practitioner to issue a review report:

a. The MD&A presentation for the most recent fiscal year and related accountant's examination or review report(s)

b. The financial statements for the periods covered by the respective MD&A presentations (most recent fiscal year and interim periods and the related auditor's report(s) and accountant's review report(s))

In addition, one of the following conditions should be met.

- A statement should be included in the body of the MD&A presentation that it has been prepared using the rules and regulations adopted by the SEC.
- A separate written assertion should accompany the MD&A presentation or such assertion should be included in a representation letter obtained from the entity.

.85 The practitioner's report on a review of MD&A should include the following:

a. A title that includes the word *independent*

b. An identification of the MD&A presentation, including the period covered

c. A statement that management is responsible for the preparation of the MD&A pursuant to the rules and regulations adopted by the SEC

d. A reference to the auditor's report on the related financial statements, and, if the report was other than a standard report, the substantive reasons therefor

e. A statement that the review was conducted in accordance with attestation standards established by the AICPA

f. A description of the procedures for a review of MD&A

g. A statement that a review of MD&A is substantially less in scope than an examination, the objective of which is an expression of opinion regarding the MD&A presentation, and accordingly, no such opinion is expressed

h. A paragraph stating that—

(1) The preparation of MD&A requires management to interpret the criteria, make determinations as to the relevancy of information to be included, and make estimates and assumptions that affect reported information

(2) Actual results in the future may differ materially from management's present assessment of information regarding the estimated future impact of transactions and events that have occurred or are expected to occur, expected sources of liquidity and capital resources, operating trends, commitments, and uncertainties

i. If the entity is a nonpublic entity, a statement that although the entity is not subject to the rules and regulations of the SEC, the MD&A presentation is intended to be a presentation in accordance with the rules and regulations adopted by the SEC

j. A statement about whether any information came to the practitioner's attention that caused him or her to believe that—

(1) The MD&A presentation does not include, in all material respects, the required elements of the rules and regulations adopted by the SEC

(2) The historical financial amounts included therein have not been accurately derived, in all material respects, from the entity's financial statements

(3) The underlying information, determinations, estimates, and assumptions of the entity do not provide a reasonable basis for the disclosures contained therein

k. If the entity is a public entity as defined in paragraph .02, or a nonpublic entity that is making or has made an offering of securities and it appears that the securities may subsequently be registered or subject to a filing with the SEC or other regulatory agency (for example, certain offerings of securities under Rule 144A of the 1933 Act that purport to conform to Regulation S-K), a statement of restrictions on the use of the report to specified parties, because it is not intended to be filed with the SEC as a report under the 1933 Act or the 1934 Act.

l. The manual or printed signature of the practitioner's firm

m. The date of the review report

Appendix B [paragraph .115], "Review Reports," provides examples of a standard review report for an annual and interim period.

Dating

.86 The practitioner's report on the review of MD&A should be dated as of the completion of the practitioner's review procedures. That date should not precede the date of the accountant's report on the latest historical financial statements covered by the MD&A.

Report Modifications

.87 The practitioner should modify the standard review report described in paragraph .86 if any of the following conditions exist.

- The presentation excludes a material required element of the rules and regulations adopted by the SEC. (See paragraph .89.)
- The historical financial amounts have not been accurately derived, in all material respects, from the entity's financial statements. (See paragraph .89.)
- The underlying information, determinations, estimates, and assumptions used by management do not provide the entity with a reasonable basis for the disclosures in the MD&A. (See paragraph .89.)
- The practitioner decides to refer to the report of another practitioner as the basis, in part, for his or her report. (See paragraph .90.)
- The practitioner is engaged to review the MD&A presentation after it has been filed with the SEC or other regulatory agency. (See paragraphs .94 through .98.)

.88 When the practitioner is unable to perform the inquiry and analytical procedures he or she considers necessary to achieve the limited assurance provided by a review, or the client does not provide the practitioner with a representation letter, the review will be incomplete. A review that is incomplete is not an adequate basis for issuing a review report. If the practitioner is unable to complete a review because of a scope limitation, the practitioner should consider the implications of that limitation with respect to possible misstatements of the MD&A presentation. In those circumstances, the practitioner should also refer to paragraphs .107 through .109 for guidance concerning communications with the audit committee.

.89 If the practitioner becomes aware that the MD&A is materially misstated, the practitioner should modify the review report to describe the nature of the misstatement. Appendix B [paragraph .115] contains an example of such a modification of the accountant's report. (See Example 3.)

.90 If another practitioner reviewed or examined the MD&A for a material component, the practitioner may decide to make reference to such report of the other practitioner in reporting on the consolidated MD&A presentation. Such reference indicates a division of responsibility for performance of the review.

Emphasis of a Matter

.91 In some circumstances, the practitioner may wish to emphasize a matter regarding the MD&A presentation. For example, he or she may wish to emphasize that the entity has included information beyond the required elements of the rules and regulations adopted by the SEC. Such explanatory comments should be presented in a separate paragraph of the practitioner's report.

Combined Examination and Review Report on MD&A

.92 A practitioner may be engaged both to examine an MD&A presentation as of the most recent fiscal year-end and to review a separate MD&A presentation for a subsequent interim period. If the examination and review are completed at the same time, a combined report may be issued. Appendix C [paragraph .116], "Combined Reports," contains an example of a combined report on an examination of an annual MD&A presentation and the review of a separate MD&A presentation for an interim period. (See Example 1.)

.93 If an entity prepares a combined MD&A presentation for annual and interim periods in which there is a discussion of liquidity and capital resources only as of the most recent interim period but not as of the most recent annual period, the practitioner is limited to performing the highest level of service that is provided with respect to the historical financial statements for any of the periods covered by the MD&A presentation. For example, if the annual financial statements have been audited and the interim financial statements have been reviewed, the practitioner may be engaged to perform a review of the combined MD&A presentation. Appendix C [paragraph .116] contains an example of a review report on a combined MD&A presentation for annual and interim periods. (See Example 2.)

When Practitioner Is Engaged Subsequent to the Filing of MD&A

.94 Management's responsibility for updating an MD&A presentation for events occurring subsequent to the issuance of MD&A depends on whether the entity is a public or nonpublic entity. A public entity is required to report significant subsequent events in a Form 8-K or Form 10-Q, or in a registration statement; therefore, a public company would ordinarily not modify its MD&A presentation once it is filed with the SEC (or other regulatory agency).

.95 Therefore, if the practitioner is engaged to examine (or review) an MD&A presentation of a public entity that has already been filed with the SEC (or other regulatory agency), the practitioner should consider whether material subsequent events are appropriately disclosed in a Form 8-K or 10-Q, or a registration statement that includes or incorporates by reference such MD&A presentation. Refer to paragraphs .65 and .66 for guidance concerning consideration of events up to the filing date when the practitioner's report on MD&A will be included (or incorporated by reference) in a 1933 Act document filed with the SEC that will require a consent.

.96 If subsequent events of a public entity are appropriately disclosed in a Form 8-K or 10-Q, or in a registration statement, or if there have been no material subsequent events, the practitioner should add the following paragraph to his or her examination or review report following the opinion or concluding paragraph, respectively.

> The accompanying Management's Discussion and Analysis does not consider events that have occurred subsequent to Month XX, 20X6, the date as of which it was filed with the Securities and Exchange Commission.

.97 If there has been a material subsequent event that has not been disclosed in a manner described in paragraph .95 and if the practitioner determines that it is appropriate to issue a report even though the MD&A presentation has not been updated for such material subsequent event (for example, because the filing of the Form 10-Q that will disclose such events has not yet occurred), the practitioner should express a qualified or an adverse opinion (or appropriately modify the review report) on the MD&A presentation. As discussed in paragraph .107, if such material subsequent event is not appropriately disclosed, the practitioner should evaluate (*a*) whether to resign from the engagement related to the MD&A presentation and (*b*) whether to remain as the entity's auditor or stand for re-election to audit the entity's financial statements.

.98 Because a nonpublic entity is not subject to the filing requirements of the SEC, an MD&A presentation of a nonpublic entity should be updated for material subsequent events through the date of the practitioner's report.

When a Predecessor Auditor Has Audited Prior Period Financial Statements

.99 If a predecessor auditor has audited the financial statements for a prior period covered by the MD&A, the need by the practitioner reporting on the MD&A for an understanding of the business and the entity's accounting and financial reporting practices for such prior period, as discussed in paragraph .07, is not diminished and the practitioner should apply the appropriate procedures. In applying the appropriate procedures, the practitioner may consider reviewing the predecessor auditor's working papers with respect to audits of financial statements and examinations or reviews of MD&A presentations for such prior periods.

.100 Information that may be obtained from the audit or attest working papers of the predecessor auditor will not provide a sufficient basis in itself for the practitioner to express an opinion with respect to the MD&A disclosures for such prior periods. If the practitioner has audited the current year, the results of such audit may be considered in planning and performing the examination of MD&A and may provide evidential matter that is useful in performing the examination, including with respect to matters disclosed for prior periods. For example, an increase in salaries expense may be the result of an acquisition in the last half of the prior year. Auditing procedures applied to payroll expense in the current year that validate the increase as a result of the acquisition may provide evidential matter with respect to the increase in salaries expense in the prior year attributed to the acquisition.

.101 In addition to the procedures described in paragraphs .49 through .66, the practitioner will need to make inquiries of the predecessor auditor and management as to audit adjustments proposed by the predecessor auditor that were not recorded in the financial statements.

Communications Between Predecessor and Successor Auditors

.102 If the practitioner is appointed as the successor auditor, he or she follows the guidance AU section 315, *Communications Between Predecessor and Successor Auditors*, in considering whether or not to accept the engagement. If, at the time of the appointment as auditor, the practitioner is also being engaged to examine or review MD&A, the practitioner should also make specific inquiries of the predecessor auditor regarding MD&A.

.103 The practitioner's examination may be facilitated by (*a*) making specific inquiries of the predecessor regarding matters that the successor believes may affect the conduct of the examination (or review), such as areas that required an inordinate amount of time or problems that arose from the condition of the records, and (*b*) if the predecessor previously examined or reviewed MD&A, reviewing the predecessor's working papers for the predecessor's examination or review engagement.

.104 If, subsequent to his or her engagement to audit the financial statements, the practitioner is requested to examine MD&A, the practitioner should request the client to authorize the predecessor auditor to allow a review of the predecessor's audit working papers related to the financial statement periods included in the MD&A presentation. Although the practitioner may previously have had access to the predecessor auditor's working papers in connection with the successor's audit of the financial statements, ordinarily the predecessor auditor should permit the practitioner to review those audit working papers relating to matters that are disclosed or that would likely be disclosed in MD&A.

Another Auditor Audits a Significant Part of the Financial Statements

.105 When another auditor or auditors audit a significant part of the financial statements, the practitioner[27] may request that such other auditor or auditors perform procedures with respect to the MD&A or the practitioner may perform the procedures directly with respect to such component(s).[28] Unless the other auditor issues an examination or review report on a separate MD&A presentation of such component(s) (see paragraph .74), the principal practitioner should not make reference to the work of the other practitioner on MD&A in his or her report on MD&A.[29] Accordingly, if the practitioner has requested such other auditor to perform procedures, the principal practitioner should perform those procedures that he or she considers necessary to take responsibility for the work of the other auditor. Such procedures may include one or more of the following:

a. Visiting the other auditor and discussing the procedures followed and the results thereof.

b. Reviewing the working papers of the other auditor with respect to the component.

---

[27] The practitioner serving as principal auditor is presumed to have an audit base for purposes of examining or reviewing the consolidated MD&A presentation.

[28] The practitioner should consider whether he or she has sufficient industry expertise with respect to a subsidiary audited by another auditor to take sole responsibility for the consolidated MD&A presentation.

[29] This does not preclude the practitioner from referring to the other auditor's report on the financial statements in his or her report on MD&A.

c. Participating in discussions with the component's management regarding matters that may affect the preparation of MD&A.

d. Making supplemental tests with respect to such component.

The determination of the extent of the procedures to be applied by the principal practitioner rests with the principal practitioner alone in the exercise of his or her professional judgment and in no way constitutes a reflection on the adequacy of the other auditor's work. Because the principal practitioner in this case assumes responsibility for his or her opinion on the MD&A presentation without making reference to the procedures performed by the other auditor, the practitioner's judgment should govern as to the extent of procedures to be undertaken.

Responsibility for Other Information in Documents Containing MD&A

.106 A client may publish annual reports containing MD&A and other documents to which the practitioner, at the client's request, devotes attention. See section 101.91–.94 for pertinent guidance in these circumstances. See Appendix D [paragraph .117], "Comparison of Activities Performed Under SAS No. 8, *Other Information in Documents Containing Audited Financial Statements*, Versus a Review or an Examination Attest Engagement." The guidance in AU section 711, *Filings Under Federal Securities Statutes*, is pertinent when the practitioner's report on MD&A is included in a registration statement, proxy statement, or periodic report filed under the federal securities statutes.

Communications With the Audit Committee

.107 If the practitioner concludes that the MD&A presentation contains material inconsistencies with other information included in the document containing the MD&A presentation or with the historical financial statements,[30] material omissions, or material misstatements of fact, and management refuses to take corrective action, the practitioner should inform the audit committee or others with equivalent authority and responsibility. If the MD&A is not revised, the practitioner should evaluate (*a*) whether to resign from the engagement related to the MD&A, and (*b*) whether to remain as the entity's auditor or stand for re-election to audit the entity's financial statements. The practitioner may wish to consult with his or her attorney when making these evaluations.

.108 If the practitioner is engaged after the MD&A presentation has been filed with the SEC (or other regulatory agency), and becomes aware that such MD&A presentation on file with the SEC (or other regulatory agency) has not been revised for a matter for which the practitioner has or would qualify his or her opinion, the practitioner should discuss such matter with the audit committee and request that the MD&A presentation be revised. If the audit committee fails to take appropriate action, the practitioner should consider whether to resign as the independent auditor of the company. The practitioner may consider the guidance concerning communication with the audit committee and other considerations in AU section 317, *Illegal Acts by Clients*, paragraphs .17, .22, and .23).

---

30 See AU section 550A, *Information in Documents Containing Audited Financial Statements*, for guidance on the impact of material inconsistencies or material misstatements of fact on the auditor's report on the related historical financial statements.

.109 If, as a result of performing an examination or a review of MD&A, the practitioner has determined that there is evidence that fraud may exist, that matter should be brought to the attention of an appropriate level of management. This is generally appropriate even if the matter might be considered clearly inconsequential. If the matter relates to the audited financial statements, the practitioner should consider the guidance in AU section 316, *Consideration of Fraud in a Financial Statement Audit*, concerning communication responsibilities, and the effect on the auditor's report on the financial statements.

Obtaining Written Representations

.110 In an examination or a review engagement, the practitioner should obtain written representations from management.[31] The specific written representations obtained by the practitioner will depend on the circumstances of the engagement and the nature of the MD&A presentation. Specific representations should relate to the following matters:

a. Management's acknowledgment of its responsibility for the preparation of MD&A and management's assertion that the MD&A presentation has been prepared in accordance with the rules and regulations adopted by the SEC for MD&A[32]

b. A statement that the historical financial amounts included in MD&A have been accurately derived from the entity's financial statements

c. Management's belief that the underlying information, determinations, estimates, and assumptions of the entity provide a reasonable basis for the disclosures contained in the MD&A

d. A statement that management has made available all significant documentation related to compliance with SEC rules and regulations for MD&A

e. Completeness and availability of all minutes of meetings of stockholders, directors, and committees of directors

f. For a public entity, whether any communications from the SEC were received concerning noncompliance with or deficiencies in MD&A reporting practices

g. Whether any events occurred subsequent to the latest balance-sheet date that would require disclosure in the MD&A

h. If forward-looking information is included, a statement that—

- The forward-looking information is based on management's best estimate of expected events and operations, and is consistent with budgets, forecasts, or operating plans prepared for such periods

---

[31] AU section 333, *Management Representations*, paragraph .09, provides guidance on the date as of which management should sign such a representation letter and on which member(s) of management should sign it. AU section 711.10 provides guidance concerning obtaining updated representations from management in connection with accountant's reports included or incorporated by reference in filings under the 1933 Act. (See paragraph .65.)

[32] Management should specify the SEC rules (for example, Item 303 of Regulation S-K, Item 303 of Regulation S-B, or Item 9 of Form 20-F). For nonpublic entities, the practitioner also obtains a written assertion that the presentation has been prepared using the rules and regulations adopted by the SEC. (See paragraph .02.)

- The accounting principles expected to be used for the forward-looking information are consistent with the principles used in preparing the historical financial statements

- Management has provided the latest version of such budgets, forecasts, or operating plans, and has informed the practitioner of any anticipated changes or modifications to such information that could affect the disclosures contained in the MD&A presentation

i. If voluntary information is included that is subject to the rules and regulations adopted by the SEC (for example, information required by Item 305, *Quantitative and Qualitative Disclosures About Market Risk*), a statement that such voluntary information has been prepared in accordance with the related rules and regulations adopted by the SEC for such information

j. If pro forma information is included, a statement that—

- Management is responsible for the assumptions used in determining the pro forma adjustments

- Management believes that the assumptions provide a reasonable basis for presenting all the significant effects directly attributable to the transaction or event, that the related pro forma adjustments give appropriate effect to those assumptions, and that the pro forma column reflects the proper application of those adjustments to the historical financial statements

- Management believes that the significant effects directly attributable to the transaction or event are appropriately disclosed in the pro forma financial information

.111 In an examination, management's refusal to furnish written representations constitutes a limitation on the scope of the engagement sufficient to preclude an unqualified opinion and is ordinarily sufficient to cause a practitioner to disclaim an opinion or withdraw from the examination engagement. However, based on the nature of the representations not obtained or the circumstances of the refusal, the practitioner may conclude that a qualified opinion is appropriate in an examination engagement. In a review engagement, management's refusal to furnish written representations constitutes a limitation of the scope of the engagement sufficient to require withdrawal from the review engagement. Further, the practitioner should consider the effects of the refusal on his or her ability to rely on other management representations.

.112 If the practitioner is precluded from performing procedures he or she considers necessary in the circumstances with respect to a matter that is material to the MD&A presentation, even though management has given representations concerning the matter, there is a limitation on the scope of the engagement, and the practitioner should qualify his or her opinion or disclaim an opinion in an examination engagement, or withdraw from a review engagement.

Effective Date

.113 This section is effective when management's discussion and analysis is for a period ending on or after June 1, 2001. Early application is permitted.

.114

Appendix A

Examination Reports

Example 1: Standard Examination Report

1. The following is an illustration of a standard examination report.

Independent Accountant's Report

[*Introductory paragraph*]

We have examined XYZ Company's Management's Discussion and Analysis taken as a whole, included [*incorporated by reference*] in the Company's [*insert description of registration statement or document*]. Management is responsible for the preparation of the Company's Management's Discussion and Analysis pursuant to the rules and regulations adopted by the Securities and Exchange Commission. Our responsibility is to express an opinion on the presentation based on our examination. We have audited, in accordance with auditing standards generally accepted in the United States of America, the financial statements of XYZ Company as of December 31, 20X5 and 20X4, and for each of the years in the three-year period ended December 31, 20X5, and in our report dated [*Month*] XX, 20X6, we expressed an unqualified opinion on those financial statements.[33]

[*Scope paragraph*]

Our examination of Management's Discussion and Analysis was conducted in accordance with attestation standards established by the American Institute of Certified Public Accountants and, accordingly, included examining, on a test basis, evidence supporting the historical amounts and disclosures in the presentation. An examination also includes assessing the significant determinations made by management as to the relevancy of information to be included and the estimates and assumptions that affect reported information. We believe that our examination provides a reasonable basis for our opinion.

[*Explanatory paragraph*][34]

---

[33] If prior financial statements were audited by other auditors, this sentence would be replaced by the following.

> We have audited, in accordance with auditing standards generally accepted in the United States of America, the financial statements of XYZ Company as of and for the year ended December 31, 20X5, and in our report dated [*Month*] XX, 20X6, we expressed an unqualified opinion on those financial statements. The financial statements of XYZ Company as of December 31, 20X4, and for each of the years in the two-year period then ended were audited by other auditors, whose report dated [*Month*] XX, 20X5, expressed an unqualified opinion on those financial statements.

If the practitioner's opinion on the financial statements is based on the report of other auditors, this sentence would be replaced by the following:

> We have audited, in accordance with auditing standards generally accepted in the United States of America, the financial statements of XYZ Company as of December 31, 20X5 and 20X4, and for each of the years in the three-year period ended December 31, 20X5, and in our report dated [*Month*] XX, 20X6, we expressed an unqualified opinion on those financial statements based on our audits and the report of other auditors.

Refer to Example 3 if the practitioner's opinion on MD&A is based on the report of another practitioner on a component of the entity.

[34] The following sentence should be added to the beginning of the explanatory paragraph if the entity is a nonpublic entity, as discussed in paragraph .69*h*:

> Although XYZ Company is not subject to the rules and regulations of the Securities and Exchange Commission, the accompanying Management's Discussion and Analysis is intended to be a presentation in accordance with the rules and regulations adopted by the Securities and Exchange Commission.

The preparation of Management's Discussion and Analysis requires management to interpret the criteria, make determinations as to the relevancy of information to be included, and make estimates and assumptions that affect reported information. Management's Discussion and Analysis includes information regarding the estimated future impact of transactions and events that have occurred or are expected to occur, expected sources of liquidity and capital resources, operating trends, commitments, and uncertainties. Actual results in the future may differ materially from management's present assessment of this information because events and circumstances frequently do not occur as expected.

[*Opinion paragraph*]

In our opinion, the Company's presentation of Management's Discussion and Analysis includes, in all material respects, the required elements of the rules and regulations adopted by the Securities and Exchange Commission; the historical financial amounts included therein have been accurately derived, in all material respects, from the Company's financial statements; and the underlying information, determinations, estimates, and assumptions of the Company provide a reasonable basis for the disclosures contained therein.

[*Signature*]

[*Date*]

Example 2: Modifications to Examination Report for a Qualified Opinion

2. An example of a modification of an examination report for a qualified opinion due to a material omission described in paragraph .72 follows.

[*Additional explanatory paragraph preceding the opinion paragraph*]

Based on information furnished to us by management, we believe that the Company has excluded a discussion of the significant capital outlay required for its plans to expand into the telecommunications industry and the possible effects on the Company's financial condition, liquidity, and capital resources.

[*Opinion paragraph*]

In our opinion, except for the omission of the matter described in the preceding paragraph, the Company's presentation of Management's Discussion and Analysis includes, in all material respects, the required elements of the rules and regulations adopted by the Securities and Exchange Commission; the historical financial amounts included therein have been accurately derived, in all material respects, from the Company's financial statements; and the underlying information, determinations, estimates, and assumptions of the Company provide a reasonable basis for the disclosures contained therein.

3. An example of a modification of an examination report for a qualified opinion when overly subjective assertions are included in MD&A follows.

[*Additional explanatory paragraph preceding the opinion paragraph*]

Based on information furnished to us by management, we believe that the underlying information, determinations, estimates, and assumptions used by management do not provide the Company with a reasonable basis for the disclosure concerning [*describe*] in the Company's Management's Discussion and Analysis.

[*Opinion paragraph*]

In our opinion, except for the disclosure regarding [*describe*] discussed in the preceding paragraph, the Company's presentation of Management's Discussion and Analysis includes, in all material respects, the required elements of the rules and regulations adopted by the Securities and Exchange Commission; the historical financial amounts included therein have been accurately derived, in all material respects, from the Company's financial statements; and the underlying information, determinations, estimates, and assumptions of the Company provide a reasonable basis for the disclosures contained therein.

Example 3: Examination Report With Reference to the Report of Another Practitioner

4. The following is an illustration of an examination report indicating a division of responsibility with another practitioner, who has examined a separate MD&A presentation of a wholly-owned subsidiary, when the practitioner reporting is serving as the principal auditor of the related consolidated financial statements.

Independent Accountant's Report

[*Introductory paragraphs*]

We have examined XYZ Company's Management's Discussion and Analysis taken as a whole, included [*incorporated by reference*] in the Company's [*insert description of registration statement or document*]. Management is responsible for the preparation of the Company's Management's Discussion and Analysis pursuant to the rules and regulations adopted by the Securities and Exchange Commission. Our responsibility is to express an opinion on the presentation based on our examination. We did not examine Management's Discussion and Analysis of ABC Corporation, a wholly-owned subsidiary, included in ABC Corporation's [*insert description of registration statement or document*]. Such Management's Discussion and Analysis was examined by other accountants, whose report has been furnished to us, and our opinion, insofar as it relates to information included for ABC Corporation, is based solely on the report of the other accountants.

We have audited, in accordance with auditing standards generally accepted in the United States of America, the consolidated financial statements of XYZ Company as of December 31, 20X5 and 20X4, and for each of the years in the three-year period ended December 31, 20X5, and in our report dated [*Month*] XX, 20X6, we expressed an unqualified opinion on those financial statements based on our audits and the report of other auditors.

[*Scope paragraph*]

Our examination of Management's Discussion and Analysis was conducted in accordance with attestation standards established by the American Institute of Certified Public Accountants and, accordingly, included examining, on a test basis, evidence supporting the historical amounts and disclosures in the presentation. An examination also includes assessing the significant determinations made by management as to the relevancy of information to be included and the estimates and assumptions that affect reported information. We believe that our examination and the report of other accountants provide a reasonable basis for our opinion.

[*Explanatory paragraph*][35]

---

[35] The following sentence should be added to the beginning of the explanatory paragraph if the entity is a nonpublic entity, as discussed in paragraph .69*h*.

Although XYZ Company is not subject to the rules and regulations of the Securities and Exchange Commission, the accompanying Management's Discussion and Analysis is intended to be a presentation in accordance with the rules and regulations adopted by the Securities and Exchange Commission.

The preparation of Management's Discussion and Analysis requires management to interpret the criteria, make determinations as to the relevancy of information to be included, and make estimates and assumptions that affect reported information. Management's Discussion and Analysis includes information regarding the estimated future impact of transactions and events that have occurred or are expected to occur, expected sources of liquidity and capital resources, operating trends, commitments, and uncertainties. Actual results in the future may differ materially from management's present assessment of this information because events and circumstances frequently do not occur as expected.

[*Opinion paragraph*]

In our opinion, based on our examination and the report of other accountants, the Company's presentation of Management's Discussion and Analysis included [*incorporated by reference*] in the Company's [*insert description of registration statement or document*] includes, in all material respects, the required elements of the rules and regulations adopted by the Securities and Exchange Commission; the historical financial amounts included therein have been accurately derived, in all material respects, from the Company's financial statements; and the underlying information, determinations, estimates, and assumptions of the Company provide a reasonable basis for the disclosures contained therein.

[*Signature*]

[*Date*]

.115

Appendix B

Review Reports

Example 1: Standard Review Report on an Annual MD&A Presentation

1. The following is an illustration of a standard review report on an annual MD&A presentation.

Independent Accountant's Report

[Introductory paragraph]

We have reviewed XYZ Company's Management's Discussion and Analysis taken as a whole, included [*incorporated by reference*] in the Company's [*insert description of registration statement or document*]. Management is responsible for the preparation of the Company's Management's Discussion and Analysis pursuant to the rules and regulations adopted by the Securities and Exchange Commission. We have audited, in accordance with auditing standards generally accepted in the United States of America, the financial statements of XYZ Company as of December 31, 20X5 and 20X4, and for each of the years in the three-year period ended December 31, 20X5, and in our report dated [*Month*] XX, 20X6, we expressed an unqualified opinion on those financial statements.

[Scope paragraph]

We conducted our review of Management's Discussion and Analysis in accordance with attestation standards established by the American Institute of Certified Public Accountants. A review of Management's Discussion and Analysis consists principally of applying analytical procedures and making inquiries of persons responsible for financial, accounting, and operational matters. It is substantially less in scope than an examination, the objective of which is the expression of an opinion on the presentation. Accordingly, we do not express such an opinion.

[Explanatory paragraph][36]

The preparation of Management's Discussion and Analysis requires management to interpret the criteria, make determinations as to the relevancy of information to be included, and make estimates and assumptions that affect reported information. Management's Discussion and Analysis includes information regarding the estimated future impact of transactions and events that have occurred or are expected to occur, expected sources of liquidity and capital resources, operating trends, commitments, and uncertainties. Actual results in the future may differ materially from management's present assessment of this information because events and circumstances frequently do not occur as expected.

[Concluding paragraph]

---

[36] The following sentence should be added to the beginning of the explanatory paragraph if the entity is a nonpublic entity, as discussed in paragraph .85*i*.

Although XYZ Company is not subject to the rules and regulations of the Securities and Exchange Commission, the accompanying Management's Discussion and Analysis is intended to be a presentation in accordance with the rules and regulations adopted by the Securities and Exchange Commission.

Based on our review, nothing came to our attention that caused us to believe that the Company's presentation of Management's Discussion and Analysis does not include, in all material respects, the required elements of the rules and regulations adopted by the Securities and Exchange Commission, that the historical financial amounts included therein have not been accurately derived, in all material respects, from the Company's financial statements, or that the underlying information, determinations, estimates and assumptions of the Company do not provide a reasonable basis for the disclosures contained therein.

[*Restricted use paragraph*][37]

This report is intended solely for the information and use of [*list or refer to specified parties*] and is not intended to be and should not be used by anyone other than the specified parties.

[*Signature*]

[*Date*]

Example 2: Standard Review Report on an Interim MD&A Presentation

2. The following is an illustration of a standard review report on an MD&A presentation for an interim period.

Independent Accountant's Report

[*Introductory paragraph*]

We have reviewed XYZ Company's Management's Discussion and Analysis taken as a whole included in the Company's [*insert description of registration statement or document*]. Management is responsible for the preparation of the Company's Management's Discussion and Analysis pursuant to the rules and regulations adopted by the Securities and Exchange Commission. We have reviewed, in accordance with standards established by the American Institute of Certified Public Accountants, the interim financial information of XYZ Company as of June 30, 20X6 and 20X5, and for the three-month and six-month periods then ended, and have issued our report thereon dated July XX, 20X6.

[*Scope paragraph*]

We conducted our review of Management's Discussion and Analysis in accordance with attestation standards established by the American Institute of Certified Public Accountants. A review of Management's Discussion and Analysis consists principally of applying analytical procedures and making inquiries of persons responsible for financial, accounting, and operational matters. It is substantially less in scope than an examination, the objective of which is the expression of an opinion on the presentation. Accordingly, we do not express such an opinion.

[*Explanatory paragraph*][38]

---

[37] This paragraph may be omitted for certain nonpublic entities. (Refer to paragraph .85*k*.)

[38] The following sentence should be added to the beginning of the explanatory paragraph if the entity is a nonpublic entity, as discussed in paragraph .85*i*.

Although XYZ Company is not subject to the rules and regulations of the Securities and Exchange Commission, the accompanying Management's Discussion and Analysis is intended to be a presentation in accordance with the rules and regulations adopted by the Securities and Exchange Commission.

The preparation of Management's Discussion and Analysis requires management to interpret the criteria, make determinations as to the relevancy of information to be included, and make estimates and assumptions that affect reported information. Management's Discussion and Analysis includes information regarding the estimated future impact of transactions and events that have occurred or are expected to occur, expected sources of liquidity and capital resources, operating trends, commitments, and uncertainties. Actual results in the future may differ materially from management's present assessment of this information because events and circumstances frequently do not occur as expected.

[*Concluding paragraph*]

Based on our review, nothing came to our attention that caused us to believe that the Company's presentation of Management's Discussion and Analysis does not include, in all material respects, the required elements of the rules and regulations adopted by the Securities and Exchange Commission, that the historical financial amounts included therein have not been accurately derived, in all material respects, from the Company's financial statements, or that the underlying information, determinations, estimates, and assumptions of the Company do not provide a reasonable basis for the disclosures contained therein.

[*Restricted use paragraph*][39]

This report is intended solely for the information and use of [*list or refer to specified parties*] and is not intended to be and should not be used by anyone other than the specified parties.

[*Signature*]

[*Date*]

Example 3: Modification to Review Report for a Material Misstatement

3. An example of a modification of the accountant's report when MD&A is materially misstated, as discussed in paragraph .89, follows.

[*Additional explanatory paragraph preceding the concluding paragraph*]

Based on information furnished to us by management, we believe that the Company has excluded a discussion of the significant capital outlay required for its plans to expand into the telecommunications industry and the possible effects on the Company's financial condition, liquidity, and capital resources.

[*Concluding paragraph*]

Based on our review, with the exception of the matter described in the preceding paragraph, nothing came to our attention that caused us to believe that the Company's presentation of Management's Discussion and Analysis does not include, in all material respects, the required elements of the rules and regulations adopted by the Securities and Exchange Commission, that the historical financial amounts included therein have not been accurately derived, in all material respects, from the Company's financial statements, or that the underlying information, determinations, estimates and assumptions of the Company do not provide a reasonable basis for the disclosures contained therein.

---

[39] This paragraph may be omitted for certain nonpublic entities. (Refer to paragraph .85*k*.)

.116

Appendix C

Combined Reports

Example 1: Combined Examination and Review Report on MD&A

1. An example of a combined report on an examination of an annual MD&A presentation and the review of MD&A for an interim period discussed in paragraph .92 follows.

Independent Accountant's Report

[*Introductory paragraph*]

We have examined XYZ Company's Management's Discussion and Analysis taken as a whole for the three-year period ended December 31, 20X5, included [*incorporated by reference*] in the Company's [*insert description of registration statement or document*]. Management is responsible for the preparation of the Company's Management's Discussion and Analysis pursuant to the rules and regulations adopted by the Securities and Exchange Commission. Our responsibility is to express an opinion on the annual presentation based on our examination. We have audited, in accordance with auditing standards generally accepted in the United States of America, the financial statements of XYZ Company as of December 31, 20X5 and 20X4, and for each of the years in the three-year period ended December 31, 19X5, and in our report dated [*Month*] XX, 20X6, we expressed an unqualified opinion on those financial statements.

[*Scope paragraph*]

Our examination of Management's Discussion and Analysis was conducted in accordance with attestation standards established by the American Institute of Certified Public Accountants and, accordingly, included examining, on a test basis, evidence supporting the historical amounts and disclosures in the presentation. An examination also includes assessing the significant determinations made by management as to the relevancy of information to be included and the estimates and assumptions that affect reported information. We believe that our examination provides a reasonable basis for our opinion.

[*Explanatory paragraph*][40]

The preparation of Management's Discussion and Analysis requires management to interpret the criteria, make determinations as to the relevancy of information to be included, and make estimates and assumptions that affect reported information. Management's Discussion and Analysis includes information regarding the estimated future impact of transactions and events that have occurred or are expected to occur, expected sources of liquidity and capital resources, operating trends, commitments, and uncertainties. Actual results in

---

[40] The following sentence should be added to the beginning of the explanatory paragraph if the entity is a nonpublic entity, as discussed in paragraph .69*h*.

Although XYZ Company is not subject to the rules and regulations of the Securities and Exchange Commission, the accompanying Management's Discussion and Analysis is intended to be a presentation in accordance with the rules and regulations adopted by the Securities and Exchange Commission.

the future may differ materially from management's present assessment of this information because events and circumstances frequently do not occur as expected.

[Opinion paragraph]

In our opinion, the Company's presentation of Management's Discussion and Analysis for the three-year period ended December 31, 20X5, includes, in all material respects, the required elements of the rules and regulations adopted by the Securities and Exchange Commission; the historical financial amounts included therein have been accurately derived, in all material respects, from the Company's financial statements; and the underlying information, determinations, estimates, and assumptions of the Company provide a reasonable basis for the disclosures contained therein.

[Paragraphs on interims]

We have also reviewed XYZ Company's Management's Discussion and Analysis taken as a whole for the six-month period ended June 30, 20X6 included [*incorporated by reference*] in the Company's [*insert description of registration statement or document*]. We have reviewed, in accordance with standards established by the American Institute of Certified Public Accountants, the interim financial information of XYZ Company as of June 30, 20X6 and 20X5, and for the six-month periods then ended, and have issued our report thereon dated July XX, 20X6.

We conducted our review of Management's Discussion and Analysis in accordance with attestation standards established by the American Institute of Certified Public Accountants. A review of Management's Discussion and Analysis consists principally of applying analytical procedures and making inquiries of persons responsible for financial, accounting, and operational matters. It is substantially less in scope than an examination, the objective of which is the expression of an opinion on the presentation. Accordingly, we do not express such an opinion.

Based on our review, nothing came to our attention that caused us to believe that the Company's presentation of Management's Discussion and Analysis for the six-month period ended June 30, 20X6, does not include, in all material respects, the required elements of the rules and regulations adopted by the Securities and Exchange Commission, that the historical financial amounts included therein have not been accurately derived, in all material respects, from the Company's unaudited interim financial statements, or that the underlying information, determinations, estimates, and assumptions of the Company do not provide a reasonable basis for the disclosures contained therein.

[Restricted use paragraph][41]

This report is intended solely for the information and use of [*list or refer to specified parties*] and is not intended to be and should not be used by anyone other than the specified parties.

[*Signature*]

[*Date*]

Example 2: Review Report on a Combined Annual and Interim MD&A Presentation

2. An example of a review report on a combined MD&A presentation for annual and interim periods follows.

---

41 This paragraph may be omitted for certain nonpublic entities. (Refer to paragraph .85*k*.)

Independent Accountant's Report

[*Introductory paragraph*]

We have reviewed XYZ Company's Management's Discussion and Analysis taken as a whole included [*incorporated by reference*] in the Company's [*insert description of registration statement or document*]. Management is responsible for the preparation of the Company's Management's Discussion and Analysis pursuant to the rules and regulations adopted by the Securities and Exchange Commission. We have audited, in accordance with auditing standards generally accepted in the United States of America, the financial statements of XYZ Company as of December 31, 20X5 and 20X4, and for each of the years in the three-year period ended December 31, 20X5, and in our report dated [*Month*] XX, 20X6, we expressed an unqualified opinion on those financial statements. We have reviewed, in accordance with standards established by the American Institute of Certified Public Accountants, the interim financial information of XYZ Company as of June 30, 20X6 and 20X5, and for the six-month periods then ended, and have issued our report thereon dated July XX, 20X6.

[*Scope paragraph*]

We conducted our review of Management's Discussion and Analysis in accordance with attestation standards established by the American Institute of Certified Public Accountants. A review of Management's Discussion and Analysis consists principally of applying analytical procedures and making inquiries of persons responsible for financial, accounting, and operational matters. It is substantially less in scope than an examination, the objective of which is the expression of an opinion on the presentation. Accordingly, we do not express such an opinion.

[*Explanatory paragraph*][42]

The preparation of Management's Discussion and Analysis requires management to interpret the criteria, make determinations as to the relevancy of information to be included, and make estimates and assumptions that affect reported information. Management's Discussion and Analysis includes information regarding the estimated future impact of transactions and events that have occurred or are expected to occur, expected sources of liquidity and capital resources, operating trends, commitments, and uncertainties. Actual results in the future may differ materially from management's present assessment of this information because events and circumstances frequently do not occur as expected.

[*Concluding paragraph*]

Based on our review, nothing came to our attention that caused us to believe that the Company's presentation of Management's Discussion and Analysis does not include, in all material respects, the required elements of the rules and regulations adopted by the Securities and Exchange Commission, that the historical financial amounts included therein have not been accurately derived, in all material respects, from the Company's financial statements, or that the underlying information, determinations, estimates, and assumptions of the Company do not provide a reasonable basis for the disclosures contained therein.

[*Restricted use paragraph*][43]

---

[42] The following sentence should be added to the beginning of the explanatory paragraph if the entity is a nonpublic entity, as discussed in paragraph .69*h*.

Although XYZ Company is not subject to the rules and regulations of the Securities and Exchange Commission, the accompanying Management's Discussion and Analysis is intended to be a presentation in accordance with the rules and regulations adopted by the Securities and Exchange Commission.

[43] This paragraph may be omitted for certain nonpublic entities. (Refer to paragraph .85*k*.)

This report is intended solely for the information and use of [*list or refer to specified parties*] and is not intended to be and should not be used by anyone other than the specified parties.

[*Signature*]

[*Date*]

.117

Appendix D

Comparison of Activities Performed Under SAS No. 118, *Other Information in Documents Containing Audited Financial Statements* [AU Section 550], Versus a Review or an Examination Attest Engagement[´]

Activities	*SAS No. 118*	*Review*	*Examination*
Obtain an understanding of SEC rules and regulations and management's methodology for the preparation of Management's Discussion and Analysis (MD&A).	Not applicable (N/A)—Auditor is only required to read the information in the MD&A in order to identify material inconsistencies, if any, with the audited financial statements.	Obtain an understanding of the rules and regulations adopted by the SEC for MD&A. Inquire of management regarding the method of preparing MD&A.	Same as for a review.
Plan the engagement.	N/A	Develop an overall strategy for the analytical procedures and inquiries to be performed to provide negative assurance.	Develop an overall strategy for the expected scope and performance of the engagement to obtain reasonable assurance to express an opinion.
Consider internal control.	N/A	Consider relevant portions of the entity's internal control applicable to the preparation of MD&A to identify the types of potential misstatements and to select the inquiries and analytical procedures; no testing of controls would be performed.	Obtain an understanding of internal control applicable to the preparation of MD&A sufficient to plan the engagement and to assess control risk; controls may be tested by performing inquiries of client personnel, inspection of documents, and observation of relevant activities.

[´] Refer to AU section 550, *Other Information in Documents Containing Audited Financial Statements.*

(continued)

Activities	*SAS No. 118*	*Review*	*Examination*
Test assertions.	N/A	Apply the following analytical procedures and make inquiries of management and others; no corroborating evidential matter is obtained: † Read the MD&A and compare the content for consistency with the financial statements; compare financial amounts to the financial statements or related accounting records and analyses; recompute increases, decreases and percentages disclosed. † Compare nonfinancial amounts to the financial statements or other records. † Consider whether MD&A explanations are consistent with information obtained during the audit or review of financial statements; make further inquiries, as necessary. (Note: Such additional inquiries may result in a decision to perform other procedures or detail tests.) † Compare information in MD&A with the rules and regulations adopted by the SEC. † Obtain and read available prospective financial information; inquire of management as to the procedures used to prepare such information; consider whether information came to the practitioner's attention that causes him or her to believe that the underlying information, determinations, estimates, and assumptions do not provide a reasonable basis for the MD&A disclosures.	Apply the following analytical and corroborative procedures to obtain reasonable assurance of detecting material misstatements: † Read the MD&A and compare the content for consistency with the financial statements; compare financial amounts to the financial statements or related accounting records and analyses; recompute increases, decreases and percentages disclosed. † Compare nonfinancial amounts to the financial statements or other records; perform tests on other records based on the concept of materiality. † Consider whether explanations are consistent with the information obtained during the audit of financial statements; investigate further explanations that cannot be substantiated by information in the audit working papers through inquiry and inspection of client records. † Examine internally and externally generated documents in support of the existence, occurrence, or expected occurrence of events, transactions, conditions, trends, demands, commitments, and uncertainties disclosed in MD&A. † Compare information in MD&A with the rules and regulations adopted by the SEC.

Activities	*SAS No. 118*	*Review*	*Examination*
Test assertions. (*continued*)		† Obtain public communications and minutes of meetings for comparison with disclosures in MD&A. † Make inquiries of the officers or executives with responsibility for operational areas and financial and accounting matters as to their plans and expectations for the future. † Inquire as to prior experience with the SEC and the extent of comments received; read correspondence. † Consider whether there are any additional matters that should be disclosed in the MD&A based on the results of the preceding procedures and knowledge obtained during the audit or review of the financial statements.	† Obtain and read available prospective financial information; inquire of management as to the procedures used to prepare such information; evaluate whether the underlying information, determinations, estimates, and assumptions provide a reasonable basis for the MD&A disclosures. † Obtain public communications and minutes of meetings; consider obtaining other types of publicly available information for comparison with the disclosures in MD&A. † Make inquiries of the officers or executives with responsibility for operational areas and financial and accounting matters as to their plans and expectations for the future. † Inquire as to prior experience with the SEC and the extent of comments received; read correspondence. † Test completeness by considering the results of the preceding procedures and knowledge obtained during the audit of the financial statements, and whether such matters are appropriately disclosed in the MD&A; extend procedures if the inherent risk relating to completeness of disclosures is high.

(continued)

Activities	*SAS No. 118*	*Review*	*Examination*
Consider the effect of events subsequent to the balance-sheet date.	Yes	Yes	Yes
Obtain written representations from management.	Yes	Yes	Yes
Form a conclusion and report.	The auditor has no reporting responsibility with respect to MD&A unless the auditor concludes that there is a material inconsistency in the MD&A that has not been eliminated. In such a situation, the auditor may add an other matter paragraph to the auditor's report on the audited financial statements describing the material inconsistency or withhold the auditor's report. If, while reading the MD&A, the auditor becomes aware of an apparent material misstatement of fact, the auditor should discuss such matter with management and take other actions based on management's response.	Form a conclusion based on the results of the preceding procedures and report in the form of negative assurance.	Form an opinion based on the results of the preceding procedures and report conclusion by expressing an opinion.

[Revised, December 2010, to reflect conforming changes necessary due to the issuance of SAS Nos. 118–120.]

AT Section 801

Reporting on Controls at a Service Organization

(Supersedes the guidance for service auditors in AU section 324, *Service Organizations.*)

Source: SSAE No. 16.

Effective for service auditors' reports for periods ending on or after June 15, 2011. Earlier implementation is permitted.

Introduction

Scope of This Section

.01 This section addresses examination engagements undertaken by a service auditor to report on controls at organizations that provide services to user entities when those controls are likely to be relevant to user entities' internal control over financial reporting. It complements AU section 324, *Service Organizations*, in that reports prepared in accordance with this section may provide appropriate evidence under AU section 324. (Ref: par. .A1)

.02 The focus of this section is on controls at service organizations likely to be relevant to user entities' internal control over financial reporting. The guidance herein also may be helpful to a practitioner performing an engagement under section 101, *Attest Engagements*, to report on controls at a service organization

a. other than those that are likely to be relevant to user entities' internal control over financial reporting (for example, controls that affect user entities' compliance with specified requirements of laws, regulations, rules, contracts, or grants, or controls that affect user entities' production or quality control). Section 601, *Compliance Attestation*, is applicable if a practitioner is reporting on an entity's own compliance with specified requirements or on its controls over compliance with specified requirements. (Ref: par. .A2–.A3)

b. when management of the service organization is not responsible for the design of the system (for example, when the system has been designed by the user entity or the design is stipulated in a contract between the user entity and the service organization). (Ref: par. .A4)

.03 In addition to performing an examination of a service organization's controls, a service auditor may be engaged to (*a*) examine and report on a user entity's transactions or balances maintained by a service organization, or (*b*) perform and report the results of agreed upon procedures related to the controls of a service organization or to transactions or balances of a user entity maintained by a service organization. However, these engagements are not addressed in this section.

.04 The requirements and application material in this section are based on the premise that management of the service organization (also referred to as management) will provide the service auditor with a written assertion that is included in or attached to management's description of the service organization's system. Paragraph .10 of this section addresses the circumstance in which management refuses to provide such a written assertion. Section 101 indicates that when performing an attestation engagement, a practitioner may report directly on the subject matter or on management's assertion. For engagements conducted under this section, the service auditor is required to report directly on the subject matter.

Effective Date

.05 This section is effective for service auditors' reports for periods ending on or after June 15, 2011. Earlier implementation is permitted.

Objectives

.06 The objectives of the service auditor are to

a. obtain reasonable assurance about whether, in all material respects, based on suitable criteria,

   i. management's description of the service organization's system fairly presents the system that was designed and implemented throughout the specified period (or in the case of a type 1 report, as of a specified date).

   ii. the controls related to the control objectives stated in management's description of the service organization's system were suitably designed throughout the specified period (or in the case of a type 1 report, as of a specified date).

   iii. when included in the scope of the engagement, the controls operated effectively to provide reasonable assurance that the control objectives stated in management's description of the service organization's system were achieved throughout the specified period.

b. report on the matters in 6(a) in accordance with the service auditor's findings.

Definitions

.07 For purposes of this section, the following terms have the meanings attributed in the subsequent text:

Carve-out method. Method of addressing the services provided by a subservice organization whereby management's description of the service organization's system identifies the nature of the services performed by the subservice organization and excludes from the description and from the scope of the service auditor's engagement, the subservice organization's relevant control objectives and related controls. Management's description of the service organization's system and the scope of the service auditor's engagement include controls at the service organization that monitor the effectiveness of controls at the subservice organization, which may include management of the service organization's review of a service auditor's report on controls at the subservice organization.

Complementary user entity controls. Controls that management of the service organization assumes, in the design of the service provided by the service organization, will be implemented by user entities, and which, if necessary to achieve the control objectives stated in management's description of the service organization's system, are identified as such in that description.

Control objectives. The aim or purpose of specified controls at the service organization. Control objectives address the risks that controls are intended to mitigate.

Controls at a service organization. The policies and procedures at a service organization likely to be relevant to user entities' internal control over financial reporting. These policies and procedures are designed, implemented, and documented by the service organization to provide reasonable assurance about the achievement of the control objectives relevant to the services covered by the service auditor's report. (Ref: par. .A5)

Controls at a subservice organization. The policies and procedures at a subservice organization likely to be relevant to internal control over financial reporting of user entities of the service organization. These policies and procedures are designed, implemented, and documented by a subservice organization to provide reasonable assurance about the achievement of control objectives that are relevant to the services covered by the service auditor's report.

Criteria. The standards or benchmarks used to measure and present the subject matter and against which the service auditor evaluates the subject matter. (Ref: par. .A6)

Inclusive method. Method of addressing the services provided by a subservice organization whereby management's description of the service organization's system includes a description of the nature of the services provided by the subservice organization as well as the subservice organization's relevant control objectives and related controls. (Ref: par. .A7–.A9)

Internal audit function. The service organization's internal auditors and others, for example, members of a compliance or risk department, who perform activities similar to those performed by internal auditors. (Ref: par. .A10)

Report on management's description of a service organization's system and the suitability of the design of controls (referred to in this section as a *type 1 report*). A report that comprises the following:

a. Management's description of the service organization's system.

b. A written assertion by management of the service organization about whether, in all material respects, and based on suitable criteria,

  i. management's description of the service organization's system fairly presents the service organization's system that was designed and implemented as of a specified date.

  ii. the controls related to the control objectives stated in management's description of the service organization's system were suitably designed to achieve those control objectives as of the specified date.

c. A service auditor's report that expresses an opinion on the matters in (b)(i)–(b)(ii).

Report on management's description of a service organization's system and the suitability of the design and operating effectiveness of controls (referred to in this section as a *type 2 report*). A report that comprises the following:

a. Management's description of the service organization's system.

b. A written assertion by management of the service organization about whether in all material respects, and based on suitable criteria,

i. management's description of the service organization's system fairly presents the service organization's system that was designed and implemented throughout the specified period.

ii. the controls related to the control objectives stated in management's description of the service organization's system were suitably designed throughout the specified period to achieve those control objectives.

iii. the controls related to the control objectives stated in management's description of the service organization's system operated effectively throughout the specified period to achieve those control objectives.

c. A service auditor's report that

i. expresses an opinion on the matters in (b)(i)–(b)(iii).

ii. includes a description of the tests of controls and the results thereof.

Service auditor. A practitioner who reports on controls at a service organization.

Service organization. An organization or segment of an organization that provides services to user entities, which are likely to be relevant to those user entities' internal control over financial reporting.

Service organization's assertion. A written assertion about the matters referred to in part (b) of the definition of *Report on management's description of a service organization's system and the suitability of the design and operating effectiveness of controls*, for a type 2 report; and, for a type 1 report, the matters referred to in part (b) of the definition of *Report on management's description of a service organization's system and the suitability of the design of controls*.

Service organization's system. The policies and procedures designed, implemented, and documented, by management of the service organization to provide user entities with the services covered by the service auditor's report. Management's description of the service organization's system identifies the services covered, the period to which the description relates (or in the case of a type 1 report, the date to which the description relates), the control objectives specified by management or an outside party, the party specifying the control objectives (if not specified by management), and the related controls. (Ref: par. .A11)

Subservice organization. A service organization used by another service organization to perform some of the services provided to user entities that are likely to be relevant to those user entities' internal control over financial reporting.

Test of controls. A procedure designed to evaluate the operating effectiveness of controls in achieving the control objectives stated in management's description of the service organization's system.

User auditor. An auditor who audits and reports on the financial statements of a user entity.

User entity. An entity that uses a service organization.

Requirements

Management and Those Charged With Governance

.08 When this section requires the service auditor to inquire of, request representations from, communicate with, or otherwise interact with management of the service organization, the service auditor should determine the appropriate person(s) within the service organization's management or governance structure with whom to interact. This should include consideration of which person(s) have the appropriate responsibilities for and knowledge of the matters concerned. (Ref: par. .A12)

Acceptance and Continuance

.09 A service auditor should accept or continue an engagement to report on controls at a service organization only if (Ref: par. .A13)

a. the service auditor has the capabilities and competence to perform the engagement. (Ref: par. .A14–.A15)

b. the service auditor's preliminary knowledge of the engagement circumstances indicates that

  i. the criteria to be used will be suitable and available to the intended user entities and their auditors;

  ii. the service auditor will have access to sufficient appropriate evidence to the extent necessary; and

  iii. the scope of the engagement and management's description of the service organization's system will not be so limited that they are unlikely to be useful to user entities and their auditors.

c. management agrees to the terms of the engagement by acknowledging and accepting its responsibility for the following:

  i. Preparing its description of the service organization's system and its assertion, including the completeness, accuracy, and method of presentation of the description and assertion. (Ref: par. .A16)

  ii. Having a reasonable basis for its assertion. (Ref: par. .A17)

  iii. Selecting the criteria to be used and stating them in the assertion.

  iv. Specifying the control objectives, stating them in the description of the service organization's system, and, if the control objectives are specified by law, regulation, or another party (for example, a user group or a professional body), identifying in the description the party specifying the control objectives.

v. Identifying the risks that threaten the achievement of the control objectives stated in the description and designing, implementing, and documenting controls that are suitably designed and operating effectively to provide reasonable assurance that the control objectives stated in the description of the service organization's system will be achieved. (Ref: par. .A18)

vi. Providing the service auditor with

(1) access to all information, such as records and documentation, including service level agreements, of which management is aware that is relevant to the description of the service organization's system and the assertion;

(2) additional information that the service auditor may request from management for the purpose of the examination engagement;

(3) unrestricted access to personnel within the service organization from whom the service auditor determines it is necessary to obtain evidence relevant to the service auditor's engagement; and

(4) written representations at the conclusion of the engagement.

vii. Providing a written assertion that will be included in, or attached to management's description of the service organization's system, and provided to user entities.

.10 If management will not provide the service auditor with a written assertion, the service auditor should not circumvent the requirement to obtain an assertion by performing a service auditor's engagement under section 101. (Ref: par. .A19)

.11 Management's subsequent refusal to provide a written assertion represents a scope limitation and consequently, the service auditor should withdraw from the engagement. If law or regulation does not allow the service auditor to withdraw from the engagement, the service auditor should disclaim an opinion.

Request to Change the Scope of the Engagement

.12 If management requests a change in the scope of the engagement before the completion of the engagement, the service auditor should be satisfied, before agreeing to the change, that a reasonable justification for the change exists. (Ref: par. .A20–.A21)

Assessing the Suitability of the Criteria (Ref: par. .A6 and .A22–.A23)

.13 As required by paragraph .23 of section 101, the service auditor should assess whether management has used suitable criteria

a. in preparing its description of the service organization's system;

b. in evaluating whether controls were suitably designed to achieve the control objectives stated in the description; and

c. in the case of a type 2 report, in evaluating whether controls operated effectively throughout the specified period to achieve the control objectives stated in the description of the service organization's system.

.14 In assessing the suitability of the criteria to evaluate whether management's description of the service organization's system is fairly presented, the service auditor should determine if the criteria include, at a minimum,

a. whether management's description of the service organization's system presents how the service organization's system was designed and implemented, including the following information about the service organization's system, if applicable:

   i. The types of services provided including, as appropriate, the classes of transactions processed.

   ii. The procedures, within both automated and manual systems, by which services are provided, including, as appropriate, procedures by which transactions are initiated, authorized, recorded, processed, corrected as necessary, and transferred to the reports and other information prepared for user entities.

   iii. The related accounting records, whether electronic or manual, and supporting information involved in initiating, authorizing, recording, processing, and reporting transactions; this includes the correction of incorrect information and how information is transferred to the reports and other information prepared for user entities.

   iv. How the service organization's system captures and addresses significant events and conditions other than transactions.

   v. The process used to prepare reports and other information for user entities.

   vi. The specified control objectives and controls designed to achieve those objectives, including as applicable, complementary user entity controls contemplated in the design of the service organization's controls.

   vii. Other aspects of the service organization's control environment, risk assessment process, information and communication systems (including the related business processes), control activities, and monitoring controls that are relevant to the services provided. (Ref: par. A17 and .A24)

b. in the case of a type 2 report, whether management's description of the service organization's system includes relevant details of changes to the service organization's system during the period covered by the description. (Ref: par. .A44)

c. whether management's description of the service organization's system does not omit or distort information relevant to the service organization's system, while acknowledging that management's description of the service organization's system is prepared to meet the common needs of a broad range of user entities and their user auditors, and may not, therefore, include every aspect of the service organization's system that each individual user entity and its user auditor may consider important in its own particular environment.

.15 In assessing the suitability of the criteria to evaluate whether the controls are suitably designed, the service auditor should determine if the criteria include, at a minimum, whether *a.* the risks that threaten the achievement of the control objectives stated in management's description of the service organization's system have been identified by management.

b. the controls identified in management's description of the service organization's system would, if operating as described, provide reasonable assurance that those risks would not prevent the control objectives stated in the description from being achieved.

.16 In assessing the suitability of the criteria to evaluate whether controls operated effectively to provide reasonable assurance that the control objectives stated in management's description of the service organization's system were achieved, the service auditor should determine if the criteria include, at a minimum, whether the controls were consistently applied as designed throughout the specified period, including whether manual controls were applied by individuals who have the appropriate competence and authority.

Materiality

.17 When planning and performing the engagement, the service auditor should evaluate materiality with respect to the fair presentation of management's description of the service organization's system, the suitability of the design of controls to achieve the related control objectives stated in the description and, in the case of a type 2 report, the operating effectiveness of the controls to achieve the related control objectives stated in the description. (Ref: par. .A25–.A27)

Obtaining an Understanding of the Service Organization's System (Ref: par. .A28–.A30)

.18 The service auditor should obtain an understanding of the service organization's system, including controls that are included in the scope of the engagement.

Obtaining Evidence Regarding Management's Description of the Service Organization's System (Ref: par. .A26 and .A31–.A35)

.19 The service auditor should obtain and read management's description of the service organization's system and should evaluate whether those aspects of the description that are included in the scope of the engagement are presented fairly, including whether

a. the control objectives stated in management's description of the service organization's system are reasonable in the circumstances. (Ref: par. .A34)

b. controls identified in management's description of the service organization's system were implemented. (Ref: par. .A35)

c. complementary user entity controls, if any, are adequately described. (Ref: par. .A32)

d. services performed by a subservice organization, if any, are adequately described, including whether the inclusive method or the carve-out method has been used in relation to them.

.20 The service auditor should determine through inquiries made in combination with other procedures whether the service organization's system has been implemented. Such other procedures should include observation and inspection of records and other documentation of the manner in which the service organization's system operates and controls are applied. (Ref: par. .A35)

Obtaining Evidence Regarding the Design of Controls (Ref: par .A26 and .A36–.A39)

.21 The service auditor should determine which of the controls at the service organization are necessary to achieve the control objectives stated in management's description of the service organization's system and should assess whether those controls were suitably designed to achieve the control objectives by

a. identifying the risks that threaten the achievement of the control objectives stated in management's description of the service organization's system, and (Ref: par. .A36)

b. evaluating the linkage of the controls identified in management's description of the service organization's system with those risks.

Obtaining Evidence Regarding the Operating Effectiveness of Controls (Ref: par. .A26 and .A40–.A45)

Assessing Operating Effectiveness

.22 When performing a type 2 engagement, the service auditor should test those controls that the service auditor has determined are necessary to achieve the control objectives stated in management's description of the service organization's system and should assess their operating effectiveness throughout the period. Evidence obtained in prior engagements about the satisfactory operation of controls in prior periods does not provide a basis for a reduction in testing, even if it is supplemented with evidence obtained during the current period. (Ref: par. .A40–.A44)

.23 When performing a type 2 engagement, the service auditor should inquire about changes in the service organization's controls that were implemented during the period covered by the service auditor's report. If the service auditor believes the changes would be considered significant by user entities and their auditors, the service auditor should determine whether those changes are included in management's description of the service organization's system. If such changes are not included in the description, the service auditor should describe the changes in the service auditor's report and determine the effect on the service auditor's report. If the superseded controls are relevant to the achievement of the control objectives stated in the description, the service auditor should, if possible, test the superseded controls before the change. If the service auditor cannot test superseded controls relevant to the achievement of the control objectives stated in the description, the service auditor should determine the effect on the service auditor's report. (Ref: par. .A42(c) and .A45)

.24 When designing and performing tests of controls, the service auditor should

a. perform other procedures in combination with inquiry to obtain evidence about the following:

i. How the control was applied.

ii. The consistency with which the control was applied.

iii. By whom or by what means the control was applied.

b. determine whether the controls to be tested depend on other controls, and if so, whether it is necessary to obtain evidence supporting the operating effectiveness of those other controls.

c. determine an effective method for selecting the items to be tested to meet the objectives of the procedure.

.25 When determining the extent of tests of controls and whether sampling is appropriate, the service auditor should consider the characteristics of the population of the controls to be tested, including the nature of the controls, the frequency of their application (for example, monthly, daily, many times per day), and the expected rate of deviation. AU section 350, *Audit Sampling*, addresses planning, performing, and evaluating audit samples. If the service auditor determines that sampling is appropriate, the service auditor should apply the requirements in paragraphs .31–.43 of AU section 350, which address sampling in tests of controls. Paragraphs .01–.14 and .45–.46 of AU section 350 provide additional guidance regarding the principles underlying those paragraphs.

Nature and Cause of Deviations

.26 The service auditor should investigate the nature and cause of any deviations identified, and should determine whether

a. identified deviations are within the expected rate of deviation and are acceptable. If so, the testing that has been performed provides an appropriate basis for concluding that the control operated effectively throughout the specified period.

b. additional testing of the control or of other controls is necessary to reach a conclusion about whether the controls related to the control objectives stated in management's description of the service organization's system operated effectively throughout the specified period.

c. the testing that has been performed provides an appropriate basis for concluding that the control did not operate effectively throughout the specified period.

.27 If, as a result of performing the procedures in paragraph .26, the service auditor becomes aware that any identified deviations have resulted from intentional acts by service organization personnel, the service auditor should assess the risk that management's description of the service organization's system is not fairly presented, the controls are not suitably designed, and in a type 2 engagement, the controls are not operating effectively. (Ref: par. .A31)

Using the Work of the Internal Audit Function

Obtaining an Understanding of the Internal Audit Function (Ref: par. .A46–.A47)

.28 If the service organization has an internal audit function, the service auditor should obtain an understanding of the nature of the responsibilities of the internal audit function and of the activities performed in order to determine whether the internal audit function is likely to be relevant to the engagement.

Planning to Use the Work of the Internal Audit Function

.29 When the service auditor intends to use the work of the internal audit function, the service auditor should determine whether the work of the internal audit function is likely to be adequate for the purposes of the engagement by evaluating the following:

a. The objectivity and technical competence of the members of the internal audit function

b. Whether the work of the internal audit function is likely to be carried out with due professional care

c. Whether it is likely that effective communication will occur between the internal audit function and the service auditor, including consideration of the effect of any constraints or restrictions placed on the internal audit function by the service organization

.30 If the service auditor determines that the work of the internal audit function is likely to be adequate for the purposes of the engagement, in determining the planned effect of the work of the internal audit function on the nature, timing, or extent of the service auditor's procedures, the service auditor should evaluate the following:

a. The nature and scope of specific work performed, or to be performed, by the internal audit function

b. The significance of that work to the service auditor's conclusions

c. The degree of subjectivity involved in the evaluation of the evidence gathered in support of those conclusions

Using the Work of the Internal Audit Function (Ref: par. .A48)

.31 In order for the service auditor to use specific work of the internal audit function, the service auditor should evaluate and perform procedures on that work to determine its adequacy for the service auditor's purposes.

.32 To determine the adequacy of specific work performed by the internal audit function for the service auditor's purposes, the service auditor should evaluate whether

a. the work was performed by members of the internal audit function having adequate technical training and proficiency;

b. the work was properly supervised, reviewed, and documented;

c. sufficient appropriate evidence was obtained to enable the internal audit function to draw reasonable conclusions;

d. conclusions reached are appropriate in the circumstances and any reports prepared by the internal audit function are consistent with the results of the work performed; and

e. exceptions relevant to the engagement or unusual matters disclosed by the internal audit function are properly resolved.

Effect on the Service Auditor's Report

.33 If the work of the internal audit function has been used, the service auditor should not make reference to that work in the service auditor's opinion. Notwithstanding its degree of autonomy and objectivity, the internal audit function is not independent of the service organization. The service auditor has sole responsibility for the opinion expressed in the service auditor's report and, accordingly, that responsibility is not reduced by the service auditor's use of the work of the internal audit function. (Ref: par. .A49)

.34 In the case of a type 2 report, if the work of the internal audit function has been used in performing tests of controls, that part of the service auditor's report that describes the service auditor's tests of controls and results thereof should include a description of the internal auditor's work and of the service auditor's procedures with respect to that work. (Ref: par. .A50)

Direct Assistance

.35 When the service auditor uses members of the service organization's internal audit function to provide direct assistance, the service auditor should adapt and apply the requirements in paragraph .27 of AU section 322, *The Auditor's Consideration of the Internal Audit Function in an Audit of Financial Statements*.

Written Representations (Ref: par. .A51–.A55)

.36 The service auditor should request management to provide written representations that

a. reaffirm its assertion included in or attached to the description of the service organization's system;

b. it has provided the service auditor with all relevant information and access agreed to; and [1]

c. it has disclosed to the service auditor any of the following of which it is aware:

  i. Instances of noncompliance with laws and regulations or uncorrected errors attributable to the service organization that may affect one or more user entities.

  ii. Knowledge of any actual, suspected, or alleged intentional acts by management or the service organization's employees, that could adversely affect the fairness of the presentation of management's description of the service organization's system or the completeness or achievement of the control objectives stated in the description.

  iii. Design deficiencies in controls.

  iv. Instances when controls have not operated as described.

  v. Any events subsequent to the period covered by management's description of the service organization's system up to the date of the service auditor's report that could have a significant effect on management's assertion.

.37 If a service organization uses a subservice organization and management's description of the service organization's system uses the inclusive method, the service auditor also should obtain the written representations identified in paragraph .36 from management of the subservice organization.

.38 The written representations should be in the form of a representation letter addressed to the service auditor and should be as of the same date as the date of the service auditor's report.

.39 If management does not provide one or more of the written representations requested by the service auditor, the service auditor should do the following:

a. Discuss the matter with management

b. Evaluate the effect of such refusal on the service auditor's assessment of the integrity of management and evaluate the effect that

---

[1] See paragraph .09(c)(vi)(1).

this may have on the reliability of management's representations and evidence in general

c. Take appropriate actions, which may include disclaiming an opinion or withdrawing from the engagement

If management refuses to provide the representations in paragraphs .36(a)–.36(b) of this section, the service auditor should disclaim an opinion or withdraw from the engagement.

Other Information (Ref: par. .A56–.A57)

.40 The service auditor should read other information, if any, included in a document containing management's description of the service organization's system and the service auditor's report to identify material inconsistencies, if any, with that description. While reading the other information for the purpose of identifying material inconsistencies, the service auditor may become aware of an apparent misstatement of fact in the other information.

.41 If the service auditor becomes aware of a material inconsistency or an apparent misstatement of fact in the other information, the service auditor should discuss the matter with management. If the service auditor concludes that there is a material inconsistency or a misstatement of fact in the other information that management refuses to correct, the service auditor should take further appropriate action.[2]

Subsequent Events

.42 The service auditor should inquire whether management is aware of any events subsequent to the period covered by management's description of the service organization's system up to the date of the service auditor's report that could have a significant effect on management's assertion. If the service auditor becomes aware, through inquiry or otherwise, of such an event, or any other event that is of such a nature and significance that its disclosure is necessary to prevent users of a type 1 or type 2 report from being misled, and information about that event is not disclosed by management in its description, the service auditor should disclose such event in the service auditor's report.

.43 The service auditor has no responsibility to keep informed of events subsequent to the date of the service auditor's report; however, after the release of the service auditor's report, the service auditor may become aware of conditions that existed at the report date that might have affected management's assertion and the service auditor's report had the service auditor been aware of them. The evaluation of such subsequent information is similar to the evaluation of information discovered subsequent to the date of the report on an audit of financial statements, as described in AU section 561, *Subsequent Discovery of Facts Existing at the Date of the Auditor's Report*, and therefore, the service auditor should adapt and apply the guidance in AU section 561.

Documentation (Ref: par. .A58)

.44 The service auditor should prepare documentation that is sufficient to enable an experienced service auditor, having no previous connection with the engagement, to understand the following:

---

[2] See paragraphs .91–.94 of section 101, *Attest Engagements*.

a. The nature, timing, and extent of the procedures performed to comply with this section and with applicable legal and regulatory requirements

b. The results of the procedures performed and the evidence obtained

c. Significant findings or issues arising during the engagement, the conclusions reached thereon, and significant professional judgments made in reaching those conclusions

.45 In documenting the nature, timing, and extent of procedures performed, the service auditor should record the following:

a. Identifying characteristics of the specific items or matters being tested

b. Who performed the work and the date such work was completed

c. Who reviewed the work performed and the date and extent of such review

.46 If the service auditor uses specific work of the internal audit function, the service auditor should document the conclusions reached regarding the evaluation of the adequacy of the work of the internal audit function and the procedures performed by the service auditor on that work.

.47 The service auditor should document discussions of significant findings or issues with management and others, including the nature of the significant findings or issues, when the discussions took place, and with whom.

.48 If the service auditor has identified information that is inconsistent with the service auditor's final conclusion regarding a significant finding or issue, the service auditor should document how the service auditor addressed the inconsistency.

.49 The service auditor should assemble the engagement documentation in an engagement file and complete the administrative process of assembling the final engagement file on a timely basis, no later than 60 days following the service auditor's report release date.

.50 After the assembly of the final engagement file has been completed, the service auditor should not delete or discard documentation before the end of its retention period.

.51 If the service auditor finds it necessary to modify existing engagement documentation or add new documentation after the assembly of the final engagement file has been completed, the service auditor should, regardless of the nature of the modifications or additions, document the following:

a. The specific reasons for making them

b. When and by whom they were made and reviewed

Preparing the Service Auditor's Report

Content of the Service Auditor's Report (Ref: par. .A59)

.52 A service auditor's type 2 report should include the following elements:

a. A title that includes the word *independent*.

b. An addressee.

c. Identification of

i. management's description of the service organization's system and the function performed by the system.

ii. any parts of management's description of the service organization's system that are not covered by the service auditor's report. (Ref: par. .A56)

iii. any information included in a document containing the service auditor's report that is not covered by the service auditor's report. (Ref: par. .A56)

iv. the criteria.

v. any services performed by a subservice organization and whether the carve-out method or the inclusive method was used in relation to them. Depending on which method is used, the following should be included:

(1) If the carve-out method was used, a statement that management's description of the service organization's system excludes the control objectives and related controls at relevant subservice organizations, and that the service auditor's procedures do not extend to the subservice organization.

(2) If the inclusive method was used, a statement that management's description of the service organization's system includes the subservice organization's specified control objectives and related controls, and that the service auditor's procedures included procedures related to the subservice organization.

d. If management's description of the service organization's system refers to the need for complementary user entity controls, a statement that the service auditor has not evaluated the suitability of the design or operating effectiveness of complementary user entity controls, and that the control objectives stated in the description can be achieved only if complementary user entity controls are suitably designed and operating effectively, along with the controls at the service organization.

e. A reference to management's assertion and a statement that management is responsible for (Ref: par. .A60)

i. preparing the description of the service organization's system and the assertion, including the completeness, accuracy, and method of presentation of the description and assertion;

ii. providing the services covered by the description of the service organization's system;

iii. specifying the control objectives unless the control objectives are specified by law, regulation, or another party, and stating them in the description of the service organization's system;

iv. identifying the risks that threaten the achievement of the control objectives;

v. selecting the criteria; and

vi. designing, implementing, and documenting controls that are suitably designed and operating effectively to achieve the related control objectives stated in the description of the service organization's system.

f. A statement that the service auditor's responsibility is to express an opinion on the fairness of the presentation of management's description of the service organization's system and on the suitability of the design and operating effectiveness of the controls to achieve the related control objectives stated in the description, based on the service auditor's examination.

g. A statement that the examination was conducted in accordance with attestation standards established by the American Institute of Certified Public Accountants and that those standards require the service auditor to plan and perform the examination to obtain reasonable assurance about whether management's description of the service organization's system is fairly presented and the controls are suitably designed and operating effectively throughout the specified period to achieve the related control objectives.

h. A statement that an examination of management's description of a service organization's system and the suitability of the design and operating effectiveness of the service organization's controls to achieve the related control objectives stated in the description involves performing procedures to obtain evidence about the fairness of the presentation of the description and the suitability of the design and operating effectiveness of those controls to achieve the related control objectives stated in the description.

i. A statement that the examination included assessing the risks that management's description of the service organization's system is not fairly presented and that the controls were not suitably designed or operating effectively to achieve the related control objectives.

j. A statement that the examination also included testing the operating effectiveness of those controls that the service auditor considers necessary to provide reasonable assurance that the related control objectives stated in management's description of the service organization's system were achieved.

k. A statement that an examination engagement of this type also includes evaluating the overall presentation of management's description of the service organization's system and suitability of the control objectives stated in the description.

l. A statement that the service auditor believes the examination provides a reasonable basis for his or her opinion.

m. A statement about the inherent limitations of controls, including the risk of projecting to future periods any evaluation of the fairness of the presentation of management's description of the service organization's system or conclusions about the suitability of the design or operating effectiveness of controls.

n. The service auditor's opinion on whether, in all material respects, based on the criteria described in management's assertion,

i. management's description of the service organization's system fairly presents the service organization's system that was designed and implemented throughout the specified period.

ii. the controls related to the control objectives stated in management's description of the service organization's system were suitably designed to provide reasonable assurance that those control objectives would be achieved if the controls operated effectively throughout the specified period.

iii. the controls the service auditor tested, which were those necessary to provide reasonable assurance that the control objectives stated in management's description of the service organization's system were achieved, operated effectively throughout the specified period.

iv. if the application of complementary user entity controls is necessary to achieve the related control objectives stated in management's description of the service organization's system, a reference to this condition.

o. A reference to a description of the service auditor's tests of controls and the results thereof, that includes

i. identification of the controls that were tested, whether the items tested represent all or a selection of the items in the population, and the nature of the tests in sufficient detail to enable user auditors to determine the effect of such tests on their risk assessments. (Ref: par. .A50)

ii. if deviations have been identified in the operation of controls included in the description, the extent of testing performed by the service auditor that led to the identification of the deviations (including the number of items tested), and the number and nature of the deviations noted (even if, on the basis of tests performed, the service auditor concludes that the related control objective was achieved). (Ref: par. .A65)

p. A statement restricting the use of the service auditor's report to management of the service organization, user entities of the service organization's system during some or all of the period covered by the service auditor's report, and the independent auditors of such user entities. (Ref: par. .A61–.A64)

q. The date of the service auditor's report.

r. The name of the service auditor and the city and state where the service auditor maintains the office that has responsibility for the engagement.

.53 A service auditor's type 1 report should include the following elements:

a. A title that includes the word *independent*.

b. An addressee.

c. Identification of

i. management's description of the service organization's system and the function performed by the system.

ii. any parts of management's description of the service organization's system that are not covered by the service auditor's report. (Ref: par. .A56)

iii. any information included in a document containing the service auditor report that is not covered by the service auditor's report. (Ref: par. .A56)

iv. the criteria.

v. any services performed by a subservice organization and whether the carve-out method or the inclusive method was used in relation to them. Depending on which method is used, the following should be included:

(1) If the carve-out method was used, a statement that management's description of the service organization's system excludes the control objectives and related controls at relevant subservice organizations, and that the service auditor's procedures do not extend to the subservice organization.

(2) If the inclusive method was used, a statement that management's description of the service organization's system includes the subservice organization's specified control objectives and related controls, and that the service auditor's procedures included procedures related to the subservice organization.

d. If management's description of the service organization's system refers to the need for complementary user entity controls, a statement that the service auditor has not evaluated the suitability of the design or operating effectiveness of complementary user entity controls, and that the control objectives stated in the description can be achieved only if complementary user entity controls are suitably designed and operating effectively, along with the controls at the service organization.

e. A reference to management's assertion and a statement that management is responsible for (Ref: par. .A60)

i. preparing the description of the service organization's system and assertion, including the completeness, accuracy, and method of presentation of the description and assertion;

ii. providing the services covered by the description of the service organization's system;

iii. specifying the control objectives, unless the control objectives are specified by law, regulation, or another party, and stating them in the description of the service organization's system;

iv. identifying the risks that threaten the achievement of the control objectives,

v. selecting the criteria; and

vi. designing, implementing, and documenting controls that are suitably designed and operating effectively to achieve the related control objectives stated in the description of the service organization's system.

f. A statement that the service auditor's responsibility is to express an opinion on the fairness of the presentation of management's description of the service organization's system and on the suitability of the design of the controls to achieve the related control objectives stated in the description, based on the service auditor's examination.

g. A statement that the examination was conducted in accordance with attestation standards established by the American Institute of Certified Public Accountants, and that those standards require the service auditor to plan and perform the examination to obtain reasonable assurance about whether management's description of the service organization's system is fairly presented and the controls are suitably designed as of the specified date to achieve the related control objectives.

h. A statement that the service auditor has not performed any procedures regarding the operating effectiveness of controls and, therefore, expresses no opinion thereon.

i A statement that an examination of management's description of a service organization's system and the suitability of the design of the service organization's controls to achieve the related control objectives stated in the description involves performing procedures to obtain evidence about the fairness of the presentation of the description and the suitability of the design of those controls to achieve the related control objectives stated in the description.

j. A statement that the examination included assessing the risks that management's description of the service organization's system is not fairly presented and that the controls were not suitably designed to achieve the related control objectives.

k. A statement that an examination engagement of this type also includes evaluating the overall presentation of management's description of the service organization's system and suitability of the control objectives stated in the description.

l. A statement that the service auditor believes the examination provides a reasonable basis for his or her opinion.

m. A statement about the inherent limitations of controls, including the risk of projecting to future periods any evaluation of the fairness of the presentation of management's description of the service organization's system or conclusions about the suitability of the design of the controls to achieve the related control objectives.

n. The service auditor's opinion on whether, in all material respects, based on the criteria described in management's assertion,

   i. management's description of the service organization's system fairly presents the service organization's system that was designed and implemented as of the specified date.

   ii. the controls related to the control objectives stated in management's description of the service organization's system were suitably designed to provide reasonable assurance that those control objectives would be achieved if the controls operated effectively as of the specified date.

   ii. if the application of complementary user entity controls is necessary to achieve the related control objectives stated in management's description of the service organization's system, a reference to this condition.

o. A statement restricting the use of the service auditor's report to management of the service organization, user entities of the service organization's system as of the end of the period covered by the service auditor's report, and the independent auditors of such user entities. (Ref: par. .A61–.A64)

p. The date of the service auditor's report.

q. The name of the service auditor and the city and state where the service auditor maintains the office that has responsibility for the engagement.

Report Date

.54 The service auditor should date the service auditor's report no earlier than the date on which the service auditor has obtained sufficient appropriate evidence to support the service auditor's opinion.

Modified Opinions (Ref: par. .A66)

.55 The service auditor's opinion should be modified and the service auditor's report should contain a clear description of all the reasons for the modification, if the service auditor concludes that

a. management's description of the service organization's system is not fairly presented, in all material respects;

b. the controls are not suitably designed to provide reasonable assurance that the control objectives stated in management's description of the service organization's system would be achieved if the controls operated as described;

c. in the case of a type 2 report, the controls did not operate effectively throughout the specified period to achieve the related control objectives stated in management's description of the service organization's system; or

d. the service auditor is unable to obtain sufficient appropriate evidence

.56 If the service auditor plans to disclaim an opinion because of the inability to obtain sufficient appropriate evidence, and, based on the limited procedures performed, has concluded that,

a. certain aspects of management's description of the service organization's system are not fairly presented, in all material respects;

b. certain controls were not suitably designed to provide reasonable assurance that the control objectives stated in management's description of the service organization's system would be achieved if the controls operated as described; or

c. in the case of a type 2 report, certain controls did not operate effectively throughout the specified period to achieve the related control objectives stated in management's description of the service organization's system,

the service auditor should identify these findings in his or her report.

.57 If the service auditor plans to disclaim an opinion, the service auditor should not identify the procedures that were performed nor include statements describing the characteristics of a service auditor's engagement in the service auditor's report; to do so might overshadow the disclaimer.

Other Communication Responsibilities

.58 If the service auditor becomes aware of incidents of noncompliance with laws and regulations, fraud, or uncorrected errors attributable to management or other service organization personnel that are not clearly trivial and that may affect one or more user entities, the service auditor should determine the effect of such incidents on management's description of the service organization's system, the achievement of the control objectives, and the service auditor's report.

Additionally, the service auditor should determine whether this information has been communicated appropriately to affected user entities. If the information has not been so communicated, and management of the service organization is unwilling to do so, the service auditor should take appropriate action. (Ref: par. .A67)

Application and Other Explanatory Material

Scope of This Section

.A1 *Internal control* is a process designed to provide reasonable assurance regarding the achievement of objectives related to the reliability of financial reporting, effectiveness and efficiency of operations, and compliance with applicable laws and regulations. Controls related to a service organization's operations and compliance objectives may be relevant to a user entity's internal control over financial reporting. Such controls may pertain to assertions about presentation and disclosure relating to account balances, classes of transactions or disclosures, or may pertain to evidence that the user auditor evaluates or uses in applying auditing procedures. For example, a payroll processing service organization's controls related to the timely remittance of payroll deductions to government authorities may be relevant to a user entity because late remittances could incur interest and penalties that would result in a liability for the user entity. Similarly, a service organization's controls over the acceptability of investment transactions from a regulatory perspective may be considered relevant to a user entity's presentation and disclosure of transactions and account balances in its financial statements. (Ref: par. .01)

.A2 Paragraph .02 of this section refers to other engagements that the practitioner may perform and report on under section 101 to report on controls at a service organization. Paragraph .02 is not, however, intended to

- provide for the alteration of the definitions of *service organization* and *service organization's system* in paragraph .07 to permit reports issued under this section to include in the description of the service organization's system aspects of their services (including relevant control objectives and related controls) not likely to be relevant to user entities' internal control over financial reporting, or
- permit a report to be issued that combines reporting under this section on a service organization's controls that are likely to be relevant to user entities' internal control over financial reporting, with reporting under section 101 on controls that are not likely to be relevant to user entities' internal control over financial reporting. (Ref: par. .02(a))

.A3 When a service auditor conducts an engagement under section 101 to report on controls at a service organization other than those controls likely to be relevant to user entities' internal control over financial reporting, and the service auditor intends to use the guidance in this section in planning and performing that engagement, the service auditor may encounter issues that differ significantly from those associated with engagements to report on a service organization's controls likely to be relevant to user entities' internal control over financial reporting. For example,

- identification of suitable and available criteria, as prescribed in paragraphs .23–.34 of section 101, for evaluating the fairness of presentation of management's description of the service organization's system and the suitability of the design and the operating effectiveness of the controls.
- identification of appropriate control objectives, and the basis for evaluating the reasonableness of the control objectives in the circumstances of the particular engagement.

- identification of the intended users of the report and the manner in which they intend to use the report.
- relevance and appropriateness of the definitions in paragraph .07 of this section, many of which specifically relate to internal control over financial reporting.
- application of references to auditing standards (AU sections) that are intended to provide the service auditor with guidance relevant to internal control over financial reporting.
- application of the concept of materiality in the circumstances of the particular engagement.
- developing the language to be used in the practitioner's report, including addressing paragraphs .84–.87 of section 101, which identify the elements to be included in an examination report. (Ref: par. .02(a))

.A4 When management of the service organization is not responsible for the design of the system, it is unlikely that management of the service organization will be in a position to assert that the system is suitably designed. Controls cannot operate effectively unless they are suitably designed. Because of the inextricable link between the suitability of the design of controls and their operating effectiveness, the absence of an assertion with respect to the suitability of design will likely preclude the service auditor from opining on the operating effectiveness of controls. As an alternative, the practitioner may perform tests of controls in either an agreed-upon procedures engagement under section 201, *Agreed Upon Procedures Engagements*, or an examination of the operating effectiveness of the controls under section 101. (Ref: par. .02(b))

Definitions

Controls at a Service Organization (Ref: par. .07)

.A5 The policies and procedures referred to in the definition of *controls at a service organization* in paragraph .07 include aspects of user entities' information systems maintained by the service organization and may also include aspects of one or more of the other components of internal control at a service organization. For example, the definition of *controls at a service organization* may include aspects of the service organization's control environment, monitoring, and control activities when they relate to the services provided. Such definition does not, however, include controls at a service organization that are not related to the achievement of the control objectives stated in management's description of the service organization's system; for example, controls related to the preparation of the service organization's own financial statements.

Criteria (Ref: par. .07 and .14–.16)

.A6 For the purposes of engagements performed in accordance with this section, criteria need to be available to user entities and their auditors to enable them to understand the basis for the service organization's assertion about the fair presentation of management's description of the service organization's system, the suitability of the design of controls that address control objectives stated in the description of the system and, in the case of a type 2 report, the operating effectiveness of such controls. Information about suitable criteria is provided in paragraphs .23–.34 of section 101. Paragraphs .14–.16 of this section discuss the criteria for evaluating the fairness of the presentation of management's description of the service organization's system and the suitability of the design and operating effectiveness of the controls.

Inclusive Method (Ref: par. .07)

.A7 As indicated in the definition of *inclusive method* in paragraph .07, a service organization that uses a subservice organization presents management's description of the service organization's system to include a description of the services provided by the subservice organization as well as the subservice organization's relevant control objectives and related controls. When the inclusive method is used, the requirements of this section also apply to the services provided by the subservice organization, including the requirement to obtain management's acknowledgement and acceptance of responsibility for the matters in paragraph .09(c)(i)–(vii) as they relate to the subservice organization.

.A8 Performing procedures at the subservice organization entails coordination and communication between the service organization, the subservice organization, and the service auditor. The inclusive method generally is feasible if, for example, the service organization and the subservice organization are related, or if the contract between the service organization and the subservice organization provides for issuance of a service auditor's report. If the service auditor is unable to obtain an assertion from the subservice organization regarding management's description of the service organization's system provided, including the relevant control objectives and related controls at the subservice organization, the service auditor is unable to use the inclusive method but may instead use the carve-out method.

.A9 There may be instances when the service organization's controls, such as monitoring controls, permit the service organization to include in its assertion the relevant aspects of the subservice organization's system, including the relevant control objectives and related controls of the subservice organization. In such instances, the service auditor is basing his or her opinion solely on the controls at the service organization, and hence, the inclusive method is not applicable.

Internal Audit Function (Ref: par. .07)

.A10 The "others" referenced in the definition of *internal audit function* may be individuals who perform activities similar to those performed by internal auditors and include service organization personnel (in addition to internal auditors), and third parties working under the direction of management or those charged with governance.

Service Organization's System (Ref: par. .07)

.A11 The policies and procedures referred to in the definition of *service organization's system* refer to the guidelines and activities for providing transaction processing and other services to user entities and include the infrastructure, software, people, and data that support the policies and procedures.

Management and Those Charged With Governance (Ref: par. .08)

.A12 Management and governance structures vary by entity, reflecting influences such as size and ownership characteristics. Such diversity means that it is not possible for this section to specify for all engagements the person(s) with whom the service auditor is to interact regarding particular matters. For example, the service organization may be a segment of an organization and not a separate legal entity. In such cases, identifying the appropriate management personnel or those charged with governance from whom to request written representations may require the exercise of professional judgment.

Acceptance and Continuance

.A13 If one or more of the conditions in paragraph .09 are not met and the service auditor is nevertheless required by law or regulation to accept or continue an engagement to report on controls at a service organization, the service auditor is required, in accordance with the requirements in paragraphs .55–.56, to determine the effect on the service auditor's report of one or more of such conditions not being met. (Ref: par. .09)

Capabilities and Competence to Perform the Engagement (Ref: par. .09a)

.A14 Relevant capabilities and competence to perform the engagement include matters such as the following:

- Knowledge of the relevant industry
- An understanding of information technology and systems
- Experience in evaluating risks as they relate to the suitable design of controls
- Experience in the design and execution of tests of controls and the evaluation of the results

.A15 In performing a service auditor's engagement, the service auditor need not be independent of each user entity. (Ref: par. .09a)

Management's Responsibility for Documenting the Service Organization's System (Ref: par. .09(c)(i))

.A16 Management of the service organization is responsible for documenting the service organization's system. No one particular form of documentation is prescribed and the extent of documentation may vary depending on the size and complexity of the service organization and its monitoring activities.

Reasonable Basis for Management's Assertion (Ref: par. .07, definition of service organization's system; par. .09(c)(ii) and .14(a)(vii))

.A17 Management's monitoring activities may provide evidence of the design and operating effectiveness of controls in support of management's assertion. *Monitoring of controls* is a process to assess the effectiveness of internal control performance over time. It involves assessing the effectiveness of controls on a timely basis, identifying and reporting deficiencies to appropriate individuals within the service organization, and taking necessary corrective actions. Management accomplishes monitoring of controls through ongoing activities, separate evaluations, or a combination of the two. Ongoing monitoring activities are often built into the normal recurring activities of an entity and include regular management and supervisory activities. Internal auditors or personnel performing similar functions may contribute to the monitoring of a service organization's activities. Monitoring activities may also include using information communicated by external parties, such as customer complaints and regulator comments, which may indicate problems or highlight areas in need of improvement. The greater the degree and effectiveness of ongoing monitoring, the less need for separate evaluations. Usually, some combination of ongoing monitoring and separate evaluations will ensure that internal control maintains its effectiveness over time. The service auditor's report on controls is not a substitute for the service organization's own processes to provide a reasonable basis for its assertion.

Identification of Risks (Ref: par. .09(c)(v))

.A18 Control objectives relate to risks that controls seek to mitigate. For example, the risk that a transaction is recorded at the wrong amount or in the wrong period can be expressed as a control objective that transactions are recorded at the correct amount and in the correct period. Management is responsible for identifying the risks that threaten achievement of the control objectives stated in management's description of the service organization's system. Management may have a formal or informal process for identifying relevant risks. A formal process may include estimating the significance of identified risks, assessing the likelihood of their occurrence, and deciding about actions to address them. However, because control objectives relate to risks that controls seek to mitigate, thoughtful identification by management of control objectives when designing, implementing, and documenting the service organization's system may itself comprise an informal process for identifying relevant risks.

Management's Refusal to Provide a Written Assertion

.A19 A recent change in service organization management or the appointment of the service auditor by a party other than management are examples of situations that may cause management to be unwilling to provide the service auditor with a written assertion. However, other members of management may be in a position to, and will agree to, sign the assertion so that the service auditor can meet the requirement of paragraph .09(c)(vii). (Ref: par. .10)

Request to Change the Scope of the Engagement (Ref: par. .12)

.A20 A request to change the scope of the engagement may not have a reasonable justification if, for example, the request is made

- to exclude certain control objectives at the service organization from the scope of the engagement because of the likelihood that the service auditor's opinion would be modified with respect to those control objectives.
- to prevent the disclosure of deviations identified at a subservice organization by requesting a change from the inclusive method to the carve-out method.

.A21 A request to change the scope of the engagement may have a reasonable justification when, for example, the request is made to exclude from the engagement a subservice organization because the service organization cannot arrange for access by the service auditor, and the method used for addressing the services provided by that subservice organization is changed from the inclusive method to the carve-out method.

Assessing the Suitability of the Criteria (Ref: par. .13–.16)

.A22 Section 101 requires a practitioner, among other things, to determine whether the subject matter is capable of evaluation against criteria that are suitable and available to users. As indicated in paragraph .27 of section 101, regardless of who establishes or develops the criteria, management is responsible for selecting the criteria and for determining whether the criteria are appropriate. The subject matter is the underlying condition of interest to intended users of an attestation report. The following table identifies the subject matter and minimum criteria for each of the opinions in type 2 and type 1 reports.

	Subject Matter	*Criteria*	*Comment*
Opinion on the fair presentation of management's description of the service organization's system (type 1 and type 2 reports).	Management's description of the service organization's system that is likely to be relevant to user entities' internal control over financial reporting and is covered by the service auditor's report, and management's assertion about whether the description is fairly presented.	Management's description of the service organization's system is fairly presented if it *a.* presents how the service organization's system was designed and implemented including, as appropriate, the matters identified in paragraph .14(a) and, in the case of a type 2 report, includes relevant details of changes to the service organization's system during the period covered by the description. *b.* does not omit or distort information relevant to the service organization's system, while acknowledging that management's description of the service organization's system is prepared to meet the common needs of a broad range of user entities and may not, therefore, include every aspect of the service organization's system that each individual user entity may consider important in its own particular environment.	The specific wording of the criteria for this opinion may need to be tailored to be consistent with criteria established by, for example, law, regulation, user groups, or a professional body. Criteria for evaluating management's description of the service organization's system are provided in paragraph .14. Paragraphs .19–.20 and .A31–.A33 offer further guidance on determining whether these criteria are met.

(continued)

	Subject Matter	*Criteria*	*Comment*	
Opinion on suitability of design and operating effectiveness (type 2 reports).	The design and operating effectiveness of the controls that are necessary to achieve the control objectives stated in management's description of the service organization's system.	The controls are suitably designed and operating effectively to achieve the control objectives stated in management's description of the service organization's system if *a.* management has identified the risks that threaten the achievement of the control objectives stated in management's description of the service organization's system. *b.* the controls identified in management's description of the service organization's system would, if operating as described, provide reasonable assurance that those risks would not prevent the control objectives stated in the description from being achieved. *c.* the controls were consistently applied as designed throughout the specified period. This includes whether manual controls were applied by individuals who have the appropriate competence and authority.	When the criteria for this opinion are met, controls will have provided reasonable assurance that the related control objectives stated in management's description of the service organization's system were achieved throughout the specified period.	The control objectives stated in management's description of the service organization's system are part of the criteria for these opinions. The control objectives stated in the description will differ from engagement to engagement. If the service auditor concludes that the control objectives stated in the description are not fairly presented, then those control objectives would not be suitable as part of the criteria for forming an opinion on the design and operating effectiveness of the controls.

	Subject Matter	Criteria	Comment
Opinion on suitability of design (type 1 reports).	The suitability of the design of the controls necessary to achieve the control objectives stated in management's description of the service organization's system and relevant to the services covered by the service auditor's report.	The controls are suitably designed to achieve the control objectives stated in management's description of the service organization's system if *a.* management has identified the risks that threaten the achievement of the control objectives stated in its description of the service organization's system. *b.* the controls identified in management's description of the service organization's system would, if operating as described, provide reasonable assurance that those risks would not prevent the control objectives stated in the description from being achieved.	Meeting these criteria does not, of itself, provide any assurance that the control objectives stated in management's description of the service organization's system were achieved because no evidence has been obtained about the operating effectiveness of the controls.

.A23 Paragraph .14(a) identifies a number of elements that are included in management's description of the service organization's system as appropriate. These elements may not be appropriate if the system being described is not a system that processes transactions; for example, if the system relates to general controls over the hosting of an IT application but not the controls embedded in the application itself. (Ref: par. .14)

.A24 The requirement to include in management's description of the service organization's system "other aspects of the service organization's control environment, risk assessment process, information and communication systems (including the related business processes), control activities, and monitoring controls, that are relevant to the services provided" is also applicable to the internal control components of subservice organizations used by the service organization when the inclusive method is used. See AU section 314, *Understanding the Entity and Its Environment and Assessing the Risks of Material Misstatement*, for a discussion of these components. (Ref: par. .14(a)(vii))

Materiality (Ref: par. .17)

.A25 In an engagement to report on controls at a service organization, the concept of materiality relates to the information being reported on, not the financial statements of user entities. The service auditor plans and performs procedures to determine whether management's description of the service organization's system is fairly presented, in all material respects; whether controls at the service organization are suitably designed in all material respects to achieve the control objectives stated in the description; and in the case of a type 2 report, whether controls at the service organization operated effectively throughout the specified period in all material respects to achieve the control objectives stated in the description. The concept of materiality takes into account that the service auditor's report provides information about the service organization's system to meet the common information needs of a broad range of user entities and their auditors who have an understanding of the manner in which the system is being used by a particular user entity for financial reporting.

.A26 Materiality with respect to the fair presentation of management's description of the service organization's system and with respect to the design of controls primarily includes the consideration of qualitative factors; for example, whether

- management's description of the service organization's system includes the significant aspects of the processing of significant transactions.
- management's description of the service organization's system omits or distorts relevant information.
- the controls have the ability, as designed, to provide reasonable assurance that the control objectives stated in management's description of the service organization's system would be achieved.

Materiality with respect to the operating effectiveness of controls includes the consideration of both quantitative and qualitative factors; for example, the tolerable rate and observed rate of deviation (a quantitative matter) and the nature and cause of any observed deviations (a qualitative matter).

.A27 The concept of materiality is not applied when disclosing, in the description of the tests of controls, the results of those tests when deviations have been identified. This is because, in the particular circumstances of a specific user entity or user auditor, a deviation may have significance beyond whether or not, in the opinion of the service auditor, it prevents a control from operating effectively. For example, the control to which the deviation relates may be particularly significant in preventing a certain type of error that may be material in the particular circumstances of a user entity's financial statements.

Obtaining an Understanding of the Service Organization's System (Ref: par. .18)

.A28 Obtaining an understanding of the service organization's system, including related controls, assists the service auditor in the following:

- Identifying the boundaries of the system and how it interfaces with other systems
- Assessing whether management's description of the service organization's system fairly presents the service organization's system that has been designed and implemented
- Determining which controls are necessary to achieve the control objectives stated in management's description of the service organization's system, whether controls were suitably designed to achieve those control objectives, and, in the case of a type 2 report, whether controls were operating effectively throughout the period to achieve those control objectives

.A29 Management's description of the service organization's system includes "aspects of the service organization's control environment, risk assessment process, information and communication systems (including relevant business processes), control activities and monitoring activities that are relevant to the services provided." Although aspects of the service organization's control environment, risk assessment process, and monitoring activities may not be presented in the description in the context of control objectives, they may nevertheless be necessary to achieve the specified control objectives stated in the description. Likewise, deficiencies in these controls may have an effect on the service auditor's assessment of whether the controls, taken as a whole, were suitably designed or operating effectively to achieve the specified control objectives. See AU section 314 for a discussion of these components of internal control.

.A30 The service auditor's procedures to obtain the understanding referred to in paragraph .A28 may include the following:

- Inquiring of management and others within the service organization who, in the service auditor's judgment, may have relevant information
- Observing operations and inspecting documents, reports, and printed and electronic records of transaction processing
- Inspecting a selection of agreements between the service organization and user entities to identify their common terms
- Reperforming the application of a control

One or more of the preceding procedures may be accomplished through the performance of a walkthrough.

Obtaining Evidence Regarding Management's Description of the Service Organization's System (Ref: par. .19–.20)

.A31 In a service auditor's examination engagement, the service auditor plans and performs the engagement to obtain reasonable assurance of detecting errors or omissions in management's description of the service organization's system and instances in which control objectives were not achieved. Absolute assurance is not attainable because of factors such as the need for judgment, the use of sampling, and the inherent limitations of controls at the service organization that affect whether the description is fairly presented and the controls are suitably designed and operating effectively to achieve the control objectives, and because much of the evidence available to the service auditor is persuasive rather than conclusive in nature. Also, procedures that are effective for detecting unintentional errors or omissions in the description, and instances in which control objectives were not achieved, may be ineffective for detecting intentional errors or omissions in the description and instances in which the control objectives were not achieved that are concealed through collusion between service organization personnel and a third party or among management or employees of the service organization. Therefore, the subsequent discovery of the existence of material omissions or errors in the description or instances in which control objectives were not achieved does not, in and of itself, evidence inadequate planning, performance, or judgment on the part of the service auditor. (Ref: par. .27)

.A32 Considering the following questions may assist the service auditor in determining whether management's description of the service organization's system is fairly presented, in all material respects:

- Does management's description address the major aspects of the service provided and included in the scope of the engagement that could reasonably be expected to be relevant to the common needs of a broad range of user auditors in planning their audits of user entities' financial statements?

- Is the description prepared at a level of detail that could reasonably be expected to provide a broad range of user auditors with sufficient information to obtain an understanding of internal control in accordance with AU section 314? The description need not address every aspect of the service organization's processing or the services provided to user entities and need not be so detailed that it would potentially enable a reader to compromise security or other controls at the service organization.
- Is the description prepared in a manner that does not omit or distort information that might affect the decisions of a broad range of user auditors; for example, does the description contain any significant omissions or inaccuracies regarding processing of which the service auditor is aware?
- Does the description include relevant details of changes to the service organization's system during the period covered by the description when the description covers a period of time?
- Have the controls identified in the description actually been implemented?
- Are complementary user entity controls, if any, adequately described? In most cases, the control objectives stated in the description are worded so that they are capable of being achieved through the effective operation of controls implemented by the service organization alone. In some cases, however, the control objectives stated in the description cannot be achieved by the service organization alone because their achievement requires particular controls to be implemented by user entities. This may be the case when, for example, the control objectives are specified by a regulatory authority. When the description does include complementary user entity controls, the description separately identifies those controls along with the specific control objectives that cannot be achieved by the service organization alone. (Ref: par. .19(c))
- If the inclusive method has been used, does the description separately identify controls at the service organization and controls at the subservice organization? If the carve-out method is used, does the description identify the functions that are performed by the subservice organization? When the carve-out method is used, the description need not describe the detailed processing or controls at the subservice organization.

.A33 The service auditor's procedures to evaluate the fair presentation of management's description of the service organization's system may include the following:

- Considering the nature of the user entities and how the services provided by the service organization are likely to affect them; for example, the predominant types of user entities, and whether the user entities are regulated by government agencies
- Reading contracts with user entities to gain an understanding of the service organization's contractual obligations
- Observing procedures performed by service organization personnel

- Reviewing the service organization's policy and procedure manuals and other documentation of the system; for example, flowcharts and narratives

- Performing walkthroughs of transactions through the service organization's system

.A34 Paragraph .19(a) requires the service auditor to evaluate whether the control objectives stated in management's description of the service organization's system are reasonable in the circumstances. Considering the following questions may assist the service auditor in this evaluation:

- Have the control objectives stated in the description been specified by the service organization or by outside parties, such as regulatory authorities, a user group, a professional body, or others?

- Do the control objectives stated in the description and specified by the service organization relate to the types of assertions commonly embodied in the broad range of user entities' financial statements to which controls at the service organization could reasonably be expected to relate (for example, assertions about existence and accuracy that are affected by access controls that prevent or detect unauthorized access to the system)? Although the service auditor ordinarily will not be able to determine how controls at a service organization specifically relate to the assertions embodied in individual user entities' financial statements, the service auditor's understanding of the nature of the service organization's system, including controls, and the services being provided is used to identify the types of assertions to which those controls are likely to relate.

- Are the control objectives stated in the description and specified by the service organization complete? Although a complete set of control objectives can provide a broad range of user auditors with a framework to assess the effect of controls at the service organization on assertions commonly embodied in user entities' financial statements, the service auditor ordinarily will not be able to determine how controls at a service organization specifically relate to the assertions embodied in individual user entities' financial statements and cannot, therefore, determine whether control objectives are complete from the viewpoint of individual user entities or user auditors. It is the responsibility of individual user entities or user auditors to assess whether the service organization's description addresses the particular control objectives that are relevant to their needs. If the control objectives are specified by an outside party, including control objectives specified by law or regulation, the outside party is responsible for their completeness and reasonableness. (Ref: par. .19(a))

.A35 The service auditor's procedures to determine whether the system described by the service organization has been implemented may be similar to, and performed in conjunction with, procedures to obtain an understanding of that system. Other procedures that the service auditor may use in combination with inquiry of management and other service organization personnel include observation, inspection of records and other documentation, as well as reperformance of the manner in which transactions are processed through the system and controls are applied. (Ref: par. .19(b) and .20)

Obtaining Evidence Regarding the Design of Controls (Ref: par. .21)

.A36 The risks and control objectives identified in paragraph .21(a) encompass intentional and unintentional acts that threaten the achievement of the control objectives. (Ref: par. .21(a))

.A37 From the viewpoint of a user auditor, a control is suitably designed to achieve the control objectives stated in management's description of the service organization's system if individually or in combination with other controls, it would, when complied with satisfactorily, provide reasonable assurance that material misstatements are prevented, or detected and corrected. A service auditor, however, is not aware of the circumstances at individual user entities that would affect whether or not a misstatement resulting from a control deficiency is material to those user entities. Therefore, from the viewpoint of a service auditor, a control is suitably designed if individually or in combination with other controls, it would, when complied with satisfactorily, provide reasonable assurance that the control objective(s) stated in the description of the service organization's system are achieved.

.A38 A service auditor may consider using flowcharts, questionnaires, or decision tables to facilitate understanding the design of the controls.

.A39 Controls may consist of a number of activities directed at the achievement of various control objectives. Consequently, if the service auditor evaluates certain activities as being ineffective in achieving a particular control objective, the existence of other activities may allow the service auditor to conclude that controls related to the control objective are suitably designed to achieve the control objective.

Obtaining Evidence Regarding the Operating Effectiveness of Controls (Ref: par. .22–.27)

.A40 From the viewpoint of a user auditor, a control is operating effectively if individually or in combination with other controls, it provides reasonable assurance that material misstatements whether due to fraud or error are prevented, or detected and corrected. A service auditor, however, is not aware of the circumstances at individual user entities that would affect whether or not a misstatement resulting from a control deviation is material to those user entities. Therefore, from the viewpoint of a service auditor, a control is operating effectively if individually or in combination with other controls, it provides reasonable assurance that the control objectives stated in management's description of the service organization's system are achieved. Similarly, a service auditor is not in a position to determine whether any observed control deviation would result in a material misstatement from the viewpoint of an individual user entity. (Ref: par. .22)

.A41 Obtaining an understanding of controls sufficient to opine on the suitability of their design is not sufficient evidence regarding their operating effectiveness unless some automation provides for the consistent operation of the controls as they were designed and implemented. For example, obtaining information about the implementation of a manual control at a point in time does not provide evidence about operation of the control at other times. However, because of the inherent consistency of IT processing, performing procedures to determine the design of an automated control and whether it has been implemented may serve as evidence of that control's operating effectiveness, depending on the service auditor's assessment and testing of controls such as those over program changes. (Ref: par. .22)

.A42 A type 2 report that covers a period that is less than six months is unlikely to be useful to user entities and their auditors. If management's description of the service organization's system covers a period that is less than six months, the description may describe the reasons for the shorter period and the service auditor's report may include that information as well. Circumstances that may result in a report covering a period of less than six months include the following:

- The service auditor was engaged close to the date by which the report on controls is to be issued, and controls cannot be tested for operating effectiveness for a six month period.
- The service organization or a particular system or application has been in operation for less than six months.
- Significant changes have been made to the controls, and it is not practicable either to wait six months before issuing a report or to issue a report covering the system both before and after the changes. (Ref: par. .23)

.A43 Evidence about the satisfactory operation of controls in prior periods does not provide evidence of the operating effectiveness of controls during the current period. The service auditor expresses an opinion on the effectiveness of controls throughout each period; therefore, sufficient appropriate evidence about the operating effectiveness of controls throughout the current period is required for the service auditor to express that opinion for the current period. Knowledge of deviations observed in prior engagements may, however, lead the service auditor to increase the extent of testing during the current period. (Ref: par. .22)

.A44 Determining the effect of changes in the service organization's controls that were implemented during the period covered by the service auditor's report involves gathering information about the nature and extent of such changes, how they affect processing at the service organization, and how they might affect assertions in the user entities' financial statements. (Ref: par. .14(b) and .23)

.A45 Certain controls may not leave evidence of their operation that can be tested at a later date and, accordingly, the service auditor may find it appropriate to test the operating effectiveness of such controls at various times throughout the reporting period. (Ref: par. .22)

Using the Work of an Internal Audit Function

Obtaining an Understanding of the Internal Audit Function (Ref: par. .28)

.A46 An internal audit function may be responsible for providing analyses, evaluations, assurances, recommendations, and other information to management and those charged with governance. An internal audit function at a service organization may perform activities related to the service organization's internal control or activities related to the services and systems, including controls that the service organization provides to user entities.

.A47 The scope and objectives of an internal audit function vary widely and depend on the size and structure of the service organization and the requirements of management and those charged with governance. Internal audit function activities may include one or more of the following:

- Monitoring the service organization's internal control or the application processing systems. This may include controls relevant to the services provided to user entities. The internal audit function may be assigned specific responsibility for reviewing controls, monitoring their operation, and recommending improvements thereto.
- Examination of financial and operating information. The internal audit function may be assigned to review the means by which the service organization identifies, measures, classifies, and reports financial and operating information; to make inquiries about specific matters; and to perform other procedures including detailed testing of transactions, balances, and procedures.
- Evaluation of the economy, efficiency, and effectiveness of operating activities including nonfinancial activities of the service organization.
- Evaluation of compliance with laws, regulations, and other external requirements and with management policies, directives, and other internal requirements.

Using the Work of the Internal Audit Function (Ref: par .31–.32)

.A48 The nature, timing, and extent of the service auditor's procedures on specific work of the internal auditors will depend on the service auditor's assessment of the significance of that work to the service auditor's conclusions (for example, the significance of the risks that the controls tend to mitigate), the evaluation of the internal audit function, and the evaluation of the specific work of the internal auditors. Such procedures may include the following:

- Examination of items already examined by the internal auditors
- Examination of other similar items
- Observation of procedures performed by the internal auditors

Effect on the Service Auditor's Report (Ref: par. .33–.34)

.A49 The responsibility to report on management's description of the service organization's system and the suitability of the design and operating effectiveness of controls rests solely with the service auditor and cannot be shared with the internal audit function. Therefore, the judgments about the significance of deviations in the design or operating effectiveness of controls, the sufficiency of tests performed, the evaluation of identified deficiencies, and other matters affecting the service auditor's report are those of the service auditor. In making judgments about the extent of the effect of the work of the internal audit function on the service auditor's procedures, the service auditor may determine, based on risk associated with the controls and the significance of the judgments relating to them, that the service auditor will perform the work relating to some or all of the controls rather than using the work performed by the internal audit function.

.A50 In the case of a type 2 report, when the work of the internal audit function has been used in performing tests of controls, the service auditor's description of that work and of the service auditor's procedures with respect to that work may be presented in a number of ways, for example, (Ref: par. .34 and .52(o)(i))

- by including introductory material to the description of tests of controls indicating that certain work of the internal audit function was used in performing tests of controls.

- attribution of individual tests to internal audit.

Written Representations (Ref: par. .36–.39)

.A51 Written representations reaffirming the service organization's assertion about the effective operation of controls may be based on ongoing monitoring activities, separate evaluations, or a combination of the two. (Ref: par. .A12)

.A52 In certain circumstances, a service auditor may obtain written representations from parties in addition to management of the service organization, such as those charged with governance.

.A53 The written representations required by paragraph .36 are separate from and in addition to the assertion included in or attached to management's description of the service organization's system required by paragraph .09(c)(vii).

.A54 If the service auditor is unable to obtain written representations regarding relevant control objectives and related controls at the subservice organization, management of the service organization would be unable to use the inclusive method but could use the carve-out method.

.A55 In addition to the written representations required by paragraph .36, the service auditor may consider it necessary to request other written representations.

Other Information

.A56 The "other information" referred to in paragraphs .40–.41 may be the following:

- Information provided by the service organization and included in a section of the service auditor's type 1 or type 2 report, or
- Information outside the service auditor's type 1 or type 2 report included in a document that contains the service auditor's report. This other information may be provided by the service organization or by another party. (Ref: par. .40, .52(c)(ii)–(iii), and .53(c)(ii)–(iii))

.A57 If other information included in a document containing management's description of the service organization's system and the service auditor's report contains future-oriented information that cannot be reasonably substantiated, the service auditor may request that the information be removed or revised. (Ref: par. .41)

Documentation

.A58 Paragraph 57 of Statement on Quality Control Standards No. 7, *A Firm's System of Quality Control* (QC sec. 10B), requires the firm to establish policies and procedures that address engagement performance, supervision responsibilities, and review responsibilities. The requirement to document who reviewed the work performed and the extent of the review, in accordance with the firm's policies and procedures addressing review responsibilities, does not imply a need for each specific working paper to include evidence of review. The requirement, however, means documenting what work was reviewed, who reviewed such work, and when it was reviewed. (Ref: par. .44)

Preparing the Service Auditor's Report

Content of the Service Auditor's Report (Ref: par. .52–.53)

.A59 Examples of service auditors' reports are presented in appendixes A–C and illustrative assertions by management of the service organization are presented in exhibit A.

.A60 The service organization's assertion may be presented in management's description of the service organization's system or may be attached to the description. (Ref: par. .52(e) and .53(e))

Use of the Service Auditor's Report (Ref: par. .52(p) and .53(o))

.A61 Paragraph .79 of section 101 requires that the use of a practitioner's report be restricted to specified parties when the criteria used to evaluate or measure the subject matter are available only to specified parties or appropriate only for a limited number of parties who either participated in their establishment or can be presumed to have an adequate understanding of the criteria. The criteria used for engagements to report on controls at a service organization are relevant only for the purpose of providing information about the service organization's system, including controls, to those who have an understanding of how the system is used for financial reporting by user entities and, accordingly, the service auditor's report states that the report and the description of tests of controls are intended only for use by management of the service organization, user entities of the service organization ("during some or all of the period covered by the report" for a type 2 report, and "as of the ending date of the period covered by the report" for a type 1 report), and their user auditors. (The illustrative service auditor's reports in appendix A illustrate language for a paragraph restricting the use of a service auditor's report.)

.A62 Paragraph .79 of section 101 indicates that the need for restriction on the use of a report may result from a number of circumstances, including the potential for the report to be misunderstood when taken out of the context in which it was intended to be used, and the extent to which the procedures performed are known or understood.

.A63 Although a service auditor is not responsible for controlling a service organization's distribution of a service auditor's report, a service auditor may inform the service organization of the following:

- A service auditor's type 1 report is not intended for distribution to parties other than the service organization, user entities of the service organization's system as of the end of the period covered by the service auditor's report, and their user auditors.
- A service auditor's type 2 report is not intended for distribution to parties other than the service organization, user entities of the service organization's system during some or all of the period covered by the service auditor's report, and their user auditors.

.A64 A user entity is also considered a user entity of the service organization's subservice organizations if controls at subservice organizations are relevant to internal control over financial reporting of the user entity. In such case, the user entity is referred to as an indirect or downstream user entity of the subservice organization. Consequently, an indirect or downstream user entity may be included in the group to whom use of the service auditor's report is restricted if controls at the service organization are relevant to internal control over financial reporting of such indirect or downstream user entity.

Description of the Service Auditor's Tests of Controls and the Results Thereof (Ref: par. .52(o)(ii))

.A65 In describing the service auditor's tests of controls for a type 2 report, it assists readers if the service auditor's report includes information about causative factors for identified deviations, to the extent the service auditor has identified such factors.

Modified Opinions (Ref: par. .55–.57)

.A66 Examples of elements of modified service auditor's reports are presented in appendix B.

Other Communication Responsibilities (Ref: par. .58)

.A67 Actions that a service auditor may take when he or she becomes aware of noncompliance with laws and regulations, fraud, or uncorrected errors at the service organization (after giving additional consideration to instances in which the service organization has not appropriately communicated this information to affected user entities, and the service organization is unwilling to do so) include the following:

- Obtaining legal advice about the consequences of different courses of action
- Communicating with those charged with governance of the service organization
- Disclaiming an opinion, modifying the service auditor's opinion, or adding an emphasis paragraph
- Communicating with third parties, for example, a regulator, when required to do so
- Withdrawing from the engagement

.A68

Appendix A: Illustrative Service Auditor's Reports

The following illustrative reports are for guidance only and are not intended to be exhaustive or applicable to all situations.

Example 1: Type 2 Service Auditor's Report

Independent Service Auditor's Report on a Description of a Service Organization's System and the Suitability of the Design and Operating Effectiveness of Controls

To: XYZ Service Organization

Scope

We have examined XYZ Service Organization's description of its [*type or name of*] system for processing user entities' transactions [*or identification of the function performed by the system*] throughout the period [*date*] to [*date*] (description) and the suitability of the design and operating effectiveness of controls to achieve the related control objectives stated in the description.

Service organization's responsibilities

On page XX of the description, XYZ Service Organization has provided an assertion about the fairness of the presentation of the description and suitability of the design and operating effectiveness of the controls to achieve the related control objectives stated in the description. XYZ Service Organization is responsible for preparing the description and for the assertion, including the completeness, accuracy, and method of presentation of the description and the assertion, providing the services covered by the description, specifying the control objectives and stating them in the description, identifying the risks that threaten the achievement of the control objectives, selecting the criteria, and designing, implementing, and documenting controls to achieve the related control objectives stated in the description.

Service auditor's responsibilities

Our responsibility is to express an opinion on the fairness of the presentation of the description and on the suitability of the design and operating effectiveness of the controls to achieve the related control objectives stated in the description, based on our examination. We conducted our examination in accordance with attestation standards established by the American Institute of Certified Public Accountants. Those standards require that we plan and perform our examination to obtain reasonable assurance about whether, in all material respects, the description is fairly presented and the controls were suitably designed and operating effectively to achieve the related control objectives stated in the description throughout the period [*date*] to [*date*].

An examination of a description of a service organization's system and the suitability of the design and operating effectiveness of the service organization's controls to achieve the related control objectives stated in the description involves performing procedures to obtain evidence about the fairness of the presentation of the description and the suitability of the design and operating effectiveness of those controls to achieve the related control objectives stated in the description. Our procedures included assessing the risks that the description is not fairly presented and that the controls were not suitably designed or operating effectively to achieve the related control objectives stated in the description. Our procedures also included testing the operating effectiveness of those controls that we consider necessary to provide reasonable assurance that the related control objectives stated in the description were achieved. An examination engagement of this type also includes evaluating the overall presentation of the description and the suitability of the control objectives stated therein, and the suitability of the criteria specified by the service organization and described at page *[aa]*. We believe that the evidence we obtained is sufficient and appropriate to provide a reasonable basis for our opinion.

Inherent limitations

Because of their nature, controls at a service organization may not prevent, or detect and correct, all errors or omissions in processing or reporting transactions [*or identification of the function performed by the system*]. Also, the projection to the future of any evaluation of the fairness of the presentation of the description, or conclusions about the suitability of the design or operating effectiveness of the controls to achieve the related control objectives is subject to the risk that controls at a service organization may become inadequate or fail.

Opinion

In our opinion, in all material respects, based on the criteria described in XYZ Service Organization's assertion on page [*aa*],

a. the description fairly presents the [*type or name of*] system that was designed and implemented throughout the period [*date*] to [*date*].

b. the controls related to the control objectives stated in the description were suitably designed to provide reasonable assurance that the control objectives would be achieved if the controls operated effectively throughout the period [*date*] to [*date*].

c. the controls tested, which were those necessary to provide reasonable assurance that the control objectives stated in the description were achieved, operated effectively throughout the period [*date*] to [*date*].

Description of tests of controls

The specific controls tested and the nature, timing, and results of those tests are listed on pages [*yy–zz*].

Restricted use

This report, including the description of tests of controls and results thereof on pages [*yy–zz*], is intended solely for the information and use of XYZ Service Organization, user entities of XYZ Service Organization's [*type or name of*] system during some or all of the period [*date*] to [*date*], and the independent auditors of such user entities, who have a sufficient understanding to consider it, along with other information including information about controls implemented by user entities themselves, when assessing the risks of material misstatements of user entities' financial statements. This report is not intended to be and should not be used by anyone other than these specified parties.

[*Service auditor's signature*]

[*Date of the service auditor's report*]

[*Service auditor's city and state*]

Following is a modification of the scope paragraph in a type 2 service auditor's report if the description refers to the need for complementary user entity controls. (New language is shown in boldface italics):

> We have examined XYZ Service Organization's description of its [*type or name of*] system for processing user entities' transactions [*or identification of the function performed by the system*] throughout the period [*date*] to [*date*] (description) and the suitability of the design and operating effectiveness of controls to achieve the related control objectives stated in the description. ***The description indicates that certain control objectives specified in the description can be achieved only if complementary user entity controls contemplated in the design of XYZ Service Organization's controls are suitably designed and operating effectively, along with related controls at the service organization. We have not evaluated the suitability of the design or operating effectiveness of such complementary user entity controls.***

Following is a modification of the applicable subparagraphs of the opinion paragraph of a type 2 service auditor's report if the application of complementary user entity controls is necessary to achieve the related control objectives stated in the description of the service organization's system (New language is shown in boldface italics):

> *b.* The controls related to the control objectives stated in the description were suitably designed to provide reasonable assurance that those control objectives would be achieved if the controls operated effectively throughout the period [*date*] to [*date*] ***and user entities applied the complementary user entity controls contemplated in the design of XYZ Service Organization's controls throughout the period [date] to [date]***.
>
> *c.* The controls tested, which ***together with the complementary user entity controls referred to in the scope paragraph of this report, if operating effectively,*** were those necessary to provide reasonable assurance that the control objectives stated in the description were achieved, operated effectively throughout the period [*date*] to [*date*].

Following is a modification of the paragraph that describes the responsibilities of management of the service organization for use in a type 2 service auditor's report when the control objectives have been specified by an outside party. (New language is shown in boldface italics):

> On page XX of the description, XYZ Service Organization has provided an assertion about the fairness of the presentation of the description and suitability of the design and operating effectiveness of the controls to achieve the related control objectives stated in the description. XYZ Service Organization is responsible for preparing the description and for its assertion], including the completeness, accuracy, and method of presentation of the description and assertion, providing the services covered by the description, selecting the criteria, and designing, implementing, and documenting controls to achieve the related control objectives stated in the description. ***The control objectives have been specified by [name of party specifying the control objectives] and are stated on page [aa] of the description***.

Example 2: Type 1 Service Auditor's Report

Independent Service Auditor's Report on a Description of a Service Organization's System and the Suitability of the Design of Controls

To: XYZ Service Organization

Scope

We have examined XYZ Service Organization's description of its [*type or name of*] system for processing user entities' transactions [*or identification of the function performed by the system*] as of [*date*], and the suitability of the design of controls to achieve the related control objectives stated in the description.

Service organization's responsibilities

On page XX of the description, XYZ Service Organization has provided an assertion about the fairness of the presentation of the description and suitability of the design of the controls to achieve the related controls objectives stated in the description. XYZ Service Organization is responsible for preparing the description and for its assertion, including the completeness, accuracy, and method of presentation of the description and the assertion, providing the services covered by the description, specifying the control objectives and stating them in the description, identifying the risks that threaten the achievement of the control objectives, selecting the criteria, and designing, implementing, and documenting controls to achieve the related control objectives stated in the description.

Service auditor's responsibilities

Our responsibility is to express an opinion on the fairness of the presentation of the description and on the suitability of the design of the controls to achieve the related control objectives stated in the description, based on our examination. We conducted our examination in accordance with attestation standards established by the American Institute of Certified Public Accountants. Those standards require that we plan and perform our examination to obtain reasonable assurance, in all material respects, about whether the description is fairly presented and the controls were suitably designed to achieve the related control objectives stated in the description as of [*date*].

An examination of a description of a service organization's system and the suitability of the design of the service organization's controls to achieve the related control objectives stated in the description involves performing procedures to obtain evidence about the fairness of the presentation of the description of the system and the suitability of the design of the controls to achieve the related control objectives stated in the description. Our procedures included assessing the risks that the description is not fairly presented and that the controls were not suitably designed to achieve the related control objectives stated in the description. An examination engagement of this type also includes evaluating the overall presentation of the description and the suitability of the control objectives stated therein, and the suitability of the criteria specified by the service organization and described at page *[aa]*.

We did not perform any procedures regarding the operating effectiveness of the controls stated in the description and, accordingly, do not express an opinion thereon.

We believe that the evidence we obtained is sufficient and appropriate to provide a reasonable basis for our opinion.

Inherent limitations

Because of their nature, controls at a service organization may not prevent, or detect and correct, all errors or omissions in processing or reporting transactions [*or identification of the function performed by the system*]. The projection to the future of any evaluation of the fairness of the presentation of the description, or any conclusions about the suitability of the design of the controls to achieve the related control objectives is subject to the risk that controls at a service organization may become ineffective or fail.

Opinion

In our opinion, in all material respects, based on the criteria described in XYZ Service Organization's assertion,

a. the description fairly presents the [*type or name of*] system that was designed and implemented as of [*date*], and

b. the controls related to the control objectives stated in the description were suitably designed to provide reasonable assurance that the control objectives would be achieved if the controls operated effectively as of [*date*].

Restricted use

This report is intended solely for the information and use of XYZ Service Organization, user entities of XYZ Service Organization's [*type or name of*] system as of [*date*], and the independent auditors of such user entities, who have a sufficient understanding to consider it, along with other information including information about controls implemented by user entities themselves, when obtaining an understanding of user entities information and communication systems relevant to financial reporting. This report is not intended to be and should not be used by anyone other than these specified parties.

[*Service auditor's signature*]

[*Date of the service auditor's report*]

[*Service auditor's city and state*]

Following is a modification of the scope paragraph in a type 1 report if the description of the service organization's system refers to the need for complementary user entity controls. (New language is shown in boldface italics)

> We have examined XYZ Service Organization's description of its [type or name of] system (description) made available to user entities of the system for processing their transactions [or identification of the function performed by the system] as of [date], and the suitability of the design of controls to achieve the related control objectives stated in the description. ***The description indicates that certain complementary user entity controls must be suitably designed and implemented at user entities for related controls at the service organization to be considered suitably designed to achieve the related control objectives. We have not evaluated the suitability of the design or operating effectiveness of such complementary user entity controls.***

Following is a modification of the applicable subparagraph in the opinion paragraph of a type 1 report if the application of complementary user entity controls is necessary to achieve the related control objectives stated in management's description of the service organization's system (New language is shown in boldface italics):

> *b.* The controls related to the control objectives stated in the description were suitably designed to provide reasonable assurance that those control objectives would be achieved if the controls operated effectively as of [*date*] ***and user entities applied the complementary user entity controls contemplated in the design of XYZ Service Organization's controls as of [date].***

Following is a modification of the paragraph that describes management of XYZ Service Organization's responsibilities to be used in a type 1 report when the control objectives have been specified by an outside party. (New language is shown in boldface italics):

> On page XX of the description, XYZ Service Organization has provided an assertion about the fairness of the presentation of the description and suitability of the design of the controls to achieve the related control objectives stated in the description. XYZ Service Organization is responsible for preparing the description and assertion, including the completeness, accuracy, and method of presentation of the description and assertion, providing the services covered by the description, selecting the criteria, and designing, implementing, and documenting controls to achieve the related control objectives stated in the description. ***The control objectives have been specified by [name of party specifying the control objectives] and are stated on page [aa] of the description.***

.A69

Appendix B: Illustrative Modified Service Auditor's Reports

The following examples of modified service auditor's reports are for guidance only and are not intended to be exhaustive or applicable to all situations. They are based on the illustrative reports in appendix A.

Example 1: Qualified Opinion for a Type 2 Report—The Description of the Service Organization's System is Not Fairly Presented in All Material Respects

The following is an illustrative paragraph describing the basis for the qualified opinion. The paragraph would be inserted before the modified opinion paragraph. All other report paragraphs are unchanged.

Basis for qualified opinion

The accompanying description states on page [*mn*] that XYZ Service Organization uses operator identification numbers and passwords to prevent unauthorized access to the system. Based on inquiries of staff personnel and observation of activities, we have determined that operator identification numbers and passwords are employed in applications A and B but are not required to access the system in applications C and D.

Opinion

In our opinion, except for the matter described in the preceding paragraph, and based on the criteria described in XYZ Service Organization's assertion on page *[aa]*, in all material respects. . .

Example 2: Qualified Opinion—The Controls are Not Suitably Designed to Provide Reasonable Assurance That the Control Objectives Stated in the Description of the Service Organization's System Would be Achieved if the Controls Operated Effectively

The following is an illustrative paragraph describing the basis for the qualified opinion. The paragraph would be inserted before the modified opinion paragraph. All other report paragraphs are unchanged.

Basis for qualified opinion

As discussed on page [*mn*] of the accompanying description, from time to time, XYZ Service Organization makes changes in application programs to correct deficiencies or to enhance capabilities. The procedures followed in determining whether to make changes, in designing the changes, and in implementing them do not include review and approval by authorized individuals who are independent from those involved in making the changes. There also are no specified requirements to test such changes or provide test results to an authorized reviewer prior to implementing the changes. As a result the controls are not suitably designed to achieve the control objective, "Controls provide reasonable assurance that changes to existing applications are authorized, tested, approved, properly implemented, and documented."

Opinion

In our opinion, except for the matter described in the preceding paragraph, and based on the criteria described in XYZ Service Organization's assertion on page *[aa]*, in all material respects. . .

Example 3: Qualified Opinion for a Type 2 Report—The Controls Did Not Operate Effectively Throughout the Specified Period to Achieve the Control Objectives Stated in the Description of the Service Organization's System

The following is an illustrative paragraph describing the basis for the qualified opinion. The paragraph would be inserted before the modified opinion paragraph. All other report paragraphs are unchanged.

Basis for qualified opinion

XYZ Service Organization states in its description that it has automated controls in place to reconcile loan payments received with the various output reports. However, as noted on page [*mn*] of the description of tests of controls and results thereof, this control was not operating effectively throughout the period [*date*] to [*date*] due to a programming error. This resulted in the nonachievement of the control objective, "Controls provide reasonable assurance that loan payments received are properly recorded" throughout the period January 1, 20X1, to April 30, 20X1. XYZ Service Organization implemented a change to the program performing the calculation as of May 1, 20X1, and our tests indicate that it was operating effectively throughout the period May 1, 20X1, to December 31, 20X1.

Opinion

In our opinion, except for the matter described in the preceding paragraph, and based on the criteria described in XYZ Service Organization's assertion on page [*aa*], in all material respects. . . .

Example 4: Qualified Opinion—The Service Auditor is Unable to Obtain Sufficient Appropriate Evidence

The following is an illustrative paragraph describing the basis for the qualified opinion. The paragraph would be inserted before the modified opinion paragraph. All other report paragraphs are unchanged.

Basis for qualified opinion

XYZ Service Organization states in its description that it has automated controls in place to reconcile loan payments received with the output generated. However, electronic records of the performance of this reconciliation for the period from [*date*] to [*date*] were deleted as a result of a computer processing error and, therefore, we were unable to test the operation of this control for that period. Consequently, we were unable to determine whether the control objective, "Controls provide reasonable assurance that loan payments received are properly recorded" was achieved throughout the period [*date*] to [*date*].

Opinion

In our opinion, except for the matter described in the preceding paragraph, and based on the criteria described in XYZ Service Organization's assertion on page [*aa*], in all material respects. . .

.A70

Appendix C: Illustrative Report Paragraphs for Service Organizations That Use a Subservice Organization

Following are modifications of the illustrative type 2 report in example 1 of appendix A for use in engagements in which the service organization uses a subservice organization. (New language is shown in boldface italics; deleted language is shown by strikethrough.)

Example 1: Carve-Out Method

Scope

We have examined XYZ Service Organization's description of its system for processing user entities' transactions [*or identification of the function performed by the system*] throughout the period [*date*] to [*date*] (description) and the suitability of the design and operating effectiveness of controls to achieve the related control objectives stated in the description.

XYZ Service Organization uses a computer processing service organization for all of its computerized application processing. The description on pages [bb–cc] includes only the controls and related control objectives of XYZ Service Organization and excludes the control objectives and related controls of the computer processing service organization. Our examination did not extend to controls of the computer processing service organization.

All other report paragraphs are unchanged.

Example 2: Inclusive Method

Scope

We have examined XYZ Service Organization's ***and ABC Subservice Organization's*** description of ~~its~~ ***their*** [*type or name of*] system for processing user entities' transactions [*or identification of the function performed by the system*] throughout the period [*date*] to [*date*] (description) and the suitability of the design and operating effectiveness of ***XYZ Service Organization's and ABC Subservice Organization's*** controls to achieve the related control objectives stated in the description. ***ABC Subservice Organization is an independent service organization that provides computer processing services to XYZ Service Organization. XYZ Service Organization's description includes a description of ABC Subservice Organization's*** **[type or name of]** ***system used by XYZ Service Organization to process transactions for its user entities, as well as relevant control objectives and controls of ABC Subservice Organization.***

XYZ Service Organization's responsibilities

On page XX of the description, XYZ Service Organization ***and ABC Subservice Organization*** ~~has~~ ***have*** provided ~~an~~ ***their*** assertion***s*** about the fairness of the presentation of the description and suitability of the design and operating effectiveness of the controls to achieve the related control objectives stated in the description. XYZ Service Organization ***and ABC Subservice Organization are*** ~~is~~ responsible for preparing the description and assertion***s***, including the completeness, accuracy, and method of presentation of the description and assertion***s***, providing the services covered by the description, specifying the control objectives and stating them in the description, identifying the risks that threaten the achievement of the control objectives, selecting the criteria, and designing, implementing, and documenting controls to achieve the related control objectives stated in the description.

Inherent limitations

Because of their nature, controls at a service organization ***or subservice organization*** may not prevent, or detect and correct, all errors or omissions in processing or reporting transactions. Also, the projection to the future of any evaluation of the fairness of the presentation of the description or any conclusions about the suitability of the design or operating effectiveness of the controls to achieve the related control objectives is subject to the risk that controls at a service organization ***or subservice organization*** may become ineffective or fail.

Opinion

In our opinion, in all material respects, based on the criteria specified in XYZ Service Organization**'s and ABC Subservice Organization's** assertions on page [*aa*],

a. the description fairly presents ***XYZ Service Organization's*** ~~the~~ [*type or name of*] system ***and ABC Subservice Organization's [type or name of] system used by XYZ Service Organization to process transactions for its user entities [or identification of the function performed by the service organization's system]*** that ***were*** ~~was~~ designed and implemented throughout the period [*date*] to [*date*].

b. the controls related to the control objectives ***of XYZ Service Organization and ABC Subservice Organization*** stated in the description were suitably designed to provide reasonable assurance that the control objectives would be achieved if the controls operated effectively throughout the period [*date*] to [*date*].

c. the controls ***of XYZ Service Organization and ABC Subservice Organization that*** we tested, which were those necessary to provide reasonable assurance that the control objectives stated in the description were achieved, operated effectively throughout the period [*date*] to [*date*].

All other report paragraphs are unchanged.

.A71

Exhibit A: Illustrative Assertions by Management of a Service Organization

The assertion by management of the service organization may be included in management's description of the service organization's system or may be attached to the description. The following illustrative assertions are intended for assertions that are included in the description.

The following illustrative management assertions are for guidance only and are not intended to be exhaustive or applicable to all situations.

Example 1: Assertion by Management of a Service Organization for a Type 2 Report

XYZ Service Organization's Assertion

We have prepared the description of XYZ Service Organization's [*type or name of*] system (description) for user entities of the system during some or all of the period [*date*] to [*date*], and their user auditors who have a sufficient understanding to consider it, along with other information, including information about controls implemented by user entities of the system themselves, when assessing the risks of material misstatements of user entities' financial statements. We confirm, to the best of our knowledge and belief, that

a. the description fairly presents the [*type or name of*] system made available to user entities of the system during some or all of the period [*date*] to [*date*] for processing their transactions [*or identification of the function performed by the system*]. The criteria we used in making this assertion were that the description

i. presents how the system made available to user entities of the system was designed and implemented to process relevant transactions, including

(1) the classes of transactions processed.

(2) the procedures, within both automated and manual systems, by which those transactions are initiated, authorized, recorded, processed, corrected as necessary, and transferred to the reports presented to user entities of the system.

(3) the related accounting records, supporting information, and specific accounts that are used to initiate, authorize, record, process, and report transactions; this includes the correction of incorrect information and how information is transferred to the reports presented to user entities of the system.

(4) how the system captures and addresses significant events and conditions, other than transactions.

(5) the process used to prepare reports or other information provided to user entities' of the system.

(6) specified control objectives and controls designed to achieve those objectives.

(7) other aspects of our control environment, risk assessment process, information and communication systems (including the related business processes), control activities, and monitoring controls that are relevant to processing and reporting transactions of user entities of the system.

ii. does not omit or distort information relevant to the scope of the [*type or name of*] system, while acknowledging that the description is prepared to meet the common needs of a broad range of user entities of the system and the independent auditors of those user entities, and may not, therefore, include every aspect of the [*type or name of*] system that each individual user entity of the system and its auditor may consider important in its own particular environment.

b. the description includes relevant details of changes to the service organization's system during the period covered by the description when the description covers a period of time.

c. the controls related to the control objectives stated in the description were suitably designed and operated effectively throughout the period [*date*] to [*date*] to achieve those control objectives. The criteria we used in making this assertion were that

i. the risks that threaten the achievement of the control objectives stated in the description have been identified by the service organization;

ii. the controls identified in the description would, if operating as described, provide reasonable assurance that those risks would not prevent the control objectives stated in the description from being achieved; and

iii. the controls were consistently applied as designed, including whether manual controls were applied by individuals who have the appropriate competence and authority.

Example 2: Assertion by Management of a Service Organization for a Type 1 Report

XYZ Service Organization's Assertion

We have prepared the description of XYZ Service Organization's [*type or name of*] system (description) for user entities of the system as of [*date*], and their user auditors who have a sufficient understanding to consider it, along with other information including information about controls implemented by user entities themselves, when obtaining an understanding of user entities' information and communication systems relevant to financial reporting. We confirm, to the best of our knowledge and belief, that

a. the description fairly presents the [*type or name of*] system made available to user entities of the system as of [*date*] for processing their transactions [*or identification of the function performed by the system*]. The criteria we used in making this assertion were that the description

i. presents how the system made available to user entities of the system was designed and implemented to process relevant transactions, including

(1) the classes of transactions processed.

(2) the procedures, within both automated and manual systems, by which those transactions are initiated, authorized, recorded, processed, corrected as necessary, and transferred to the reports presented to user entities of the system.

(3) the related accounting records, supporting information, and specific accounts that are used to initiate, authorize, record, process, and report transactions; this includes the correction of incorrect information and how information is transferred to the reports provided to user entities of the system.

(4) how the system captures and addresses significant events and conditions, other than transactions.

(5) the process used to prepare reports or other information provided to user entities of the system.

(6) specified control objectives and controls designed to achieve those objectives.

(7) other aspects of our control environment, risk assessment process, information and communication systems (including the related business processes), control activities, and monitoring controls that are relevant to processing and reporting transactions of user entities of the system.

ii. does not omit or distort information relevant to the scope of the [*type or name of*] system, while acknowledging that the description is prepared to meet the common needs of a broad range of user entities of the system and the independent auditors of those user entities, and may not, therefore, include every aspect of the [*type or name of*] system that each individual user entity of the system and its auditor may consider important in its own particular environment.

b. the controls related to the control objectives stated in the description were suitably designed as of [*date*] to achieve those control objectives. The criteria we used in making this assertion were that

i. the risks that threaten the achievement of the control objectives stated in the description have been identified by the service organization.

ii. the controls identified in the description would, if operating as described, provide reasonable assurance that those risks would not prevent the control objectives stated in the description from being achieved.

.A72

Exhibit B: Comparison of Requirements of Section 801, *Reporting On Controls at a Service Organization*, With Requirements of International Standard on Assurance Engagements 3402, *Assurance Reports on Controls at a Service Organization*

This analysis was prepared by the AICPA Audit and Attest Standards staff to highlight substantive differences between section 801, *Reporting on Controls at a Service Organization*, and International Standard on Assurance Engagements (ISAE) 3402, *Assurance Reports on Controls at a Service Organization*, and to explain the rationale for those differences. This analysis is not authoritative and is prepared for informational purposes only.

1. Intentional Acts by Service Organization Personnel

Paragraph .26 of this section requires the service auditor to investigate the nature and cause of any deviations identified, as does paragraph 28 of ISAE 3402. Paragraph .27 of this section indicates that if the service auditor becomes aware that the deviations resulted from intentional acts by service organization personnel, the service auditor should assess the risk that the description of the service organization's system is not fairly presented and that the controls are not suitably designed or operating effectively. The ISAE does not contain the requirement included in paragraph .27 of this section. The Auditing Standards Board (ASB) believes that information about intentional acts affects the nature, timing, and extent of the service auditor's procedures. Therefore, paragraph .27 provides follow-up action for the service auditor when he or she obtains information about intentional acts as a result of performing the procedures in paragraph .26 of this section.

Paragraph .36(c)(ii) of this section, which is not included in ISAE 3402, also requires the service auditor to request written representations from management that it has disclosed to the service auditor knowledge of any actual, suspected, or alleged intentional acts by management or the service organization's employees, of which it is aware, that could adversely affect the fairness of the presentation of management's description of the service organization's system or the completeness or achievement of the control objectives stated in the description.

2. Anomalies

Paragraph 29 of ISAE 3402 contains a requirement that enables a service auditor to conclude that a deviation identified in tests of controls involving sampling is not representative of the population from which the sample was drawn. This section does not include this requirement because of concerns about use of terms such as, "in the extremely rare circumstances" and "a high degree of certainty." These terms are not used in U.S professional standards and the ASB believes their introduction in this section could have unintended consequences. The ASB also believes that the deletion of this requirement will enhance examination quality because deviations identified by the service auditor in tests of controls involving sampling will be treated in the same manner as any other deviation identified by the practitioner, rather than as an anomaly.

3. Direct Assistance

Paragraph .35 of this section requires the service auditor to adapt and apply the requirements in paragraph .27 of AU section 322, *The Auditor's Consideration of the Internal Audit Function in an Audit of Financial Statements*, when the service auditor uses members of the service organization's internal audit function to provide direct assistance. Because AU section 322 provides for an auditor to use the work of the internal audit function in a direct assistance capacity, paragraph .35 of this section also provides for this. The International Standards on Auditing and the ISAEs do not provide for use of the internal audit function for direct assistance.

4. Subsequent Events

With respect to events that occur subsequent to the period covered by the description of the service organization's system up to the date of the service auditor's report, paragraph .42 of this section requires the service auditor to disclose in the service auditor's report, if not disclosed by management in its description, any event that is of such a nature and significance that its disclosure is necessary to prevent users of a type 1 or type 2 report from being misled. The ASB believes that information about such events could be important to user entities and their auditors. ISAE 3402 limits the types of subsequent events that would need to be disclosed in the service auditor's report to those that could have a significant effect on the service auditor's report.

Paragraph .43 of this section requires the service auditor to adapt and apply the guidance in AU section 561, *Subsequent Discovery of Facts Existing at the Date of the Auditor's Report*, if, after the release of the service auditor's report, the service auditor becomes aware of conditions that existed at the report date that might have affected management's assertion and the service auditor's report had the service auditor been aware of them. The ISAE does not include a similar requirement. The ASB believes that, by analogy, AU section 561 provides needed guidance to a service auditor by presenting the various circumstances that could occur during the subsequent events period and the actions a service auditor should take.

5. Statement Restricting Use of the Service Auditor's Report

This section requires the service auditor's report to include a statement restricting the use of the report to management of the service organization, user entities of the service organization's system, and user auditors. The ASB believes that the unambiguous language in the restricted use statement prevents misunderstanding regarding who the report is intended for. Paragraphs .A61–.A62 of this section explain the reasons for restricting the use of the report. ISAE 3402 requires the service auditor's report to include a statement indicating that the report is intended only for user entities and their auditors, However, the ISAE does not require the inclusion of a statement restricting the use of the report to specified parties, although it does not prohibit the inclusion of restricted use language in the report.

6. Documentation Completion

Paragraph 50 of the ISAE requires the service auditor to assemble the documentation in an engagement file and complete the administrative process of assembling the final engagement file on a timely basis after the date of the service auditor's assurance report. Paragraph .49 of this section also requires the service auditor to assemble the engagement documentation in an engagement file and complete the administrative process of assembling the final engagement file on a timely basis, but also indicates that a timely basis is no later than 60 days following the service auditor's report release date. The ASB made this change to parallel the definition of *documentation completion date* in paragraph .27 of AU section 339, *Audit Documentation*.

7. Engagement Acceptance and Continuance

Paragraph .09 of this section establishes conditions for the acceptance and continuance of an engagement to report on controls at a service organization. One of the conditions is that management acknowledge and accept responsibility for providing the service auditor with written representations at the conclusion of the engagement. ISAE 3402 does not include this requirement as a condition of engagement acceptance and continuance.

8. Disclaimer of Opinion

If management does not provide the service auditor with certain written representations, paragraph 40 of ISAE 3402 requires the service auditor, after discussing the matter with management, to disclaim an opinion. In the same circumstances, paragraph .39 of this section requires the service auditor to take appropriate action, which may include disclaiming an opinion or withdrawing from the engagement.

Paragraphs .56–.57 of this section contain certain incremental requirements when the service auditor plans to disclaim an opinion.

9. Elements of the Section 801 Report That Are Not Required in the ISAE 3402 Report

Paragraphs .52–.53 of this section contain certain requirements regarding the content of the service auditor's report, which are incremental to those in ISAE 3402. These incremental requirements are included in paragraphs .52(c)(iii); .52(e)(iv); .52(i); and .52(k) for type 2 reports, and in paragraphs .53(c)(iii); .53(e)(iv); .53(j); and .53(k) for type 1 reports.

---

tion and complete the management representation process [illegible] engagement [illegible] on a timely basis [illegible] than 90 days [illegible] (paragraph [illegible] section [illegible]).

AT TOPICAL INDEX

References are to AT section and paragraph numbers.

A

References are to AT section and paragraph numbers.

References are to AT section and paragraph numbers.

References are to AT section and paragraph numbers.

L

M

References are to AT section and paragraph numbers.

S

U

References are to AT section and paragraph numbers.